Account Title	Classification	Financial Statement	Normal Balance
		L	
Land	Plant Asset	Balance Sheet	Debit
Loss on Disposal of Plant Assets	Other Expense	Income Statement	Debit
		M	
Maintenance and Repairs Expense	Operating Expense	Income Statement	Debit
Mortgage Payable	Long-Term Liability	Balance Sheet	Credit
		N	
Notes Payable	Current Liability/ Long-Term Liability	Balance Sheet	Credit
		P	
Patents	Intangible Asset	Balance Sheet	Debit
Paid-in Capital in Excess of Par Value—Common Stock	Stockholders' Equity	Balance Sheet	Credit
Paid-in Capital in Excess of Par Value—Preferred Stock	Stockholders' Equity	Balance Sheet	Credit
Preferred Stock	Stockholders' Equity	Balance Sheet	Credit
Premium on Bonds Payable	Long-Term Liability—Contra	Balance Sheet	Credit
Prepaid Insurance	Current Asset	Balance Sheet	Debit
Prepaid Rent	Current Asset	Balance Sheet	Debit
		R	
Rent Expense	Operating Expense	Income Statement	Debit
Retained Earnings	Stockholders' Equity	Balance Sheet and Retained Earnings Statement	Credit
		S	
Salaries and Wages Expense	Operating Expense	Income Statement	Debit
Salaries and Wages Payable	Current Liability	Balance Sheet	Credit
Sales Discounts	Revenue—Contra	Income Statement	Debit
Sales Returns and Allowances	Revenue—Contra	Income Statement	Debit
Sales Revenue	Revenue	Income Statement	Credit
Selling Expenses	Operating Expense	Income Statement	Debit
Service Revenue	Revenue	Income Statement	Credit
Stock Investments	Current Asset/Long-Term Investment	Balance Sheet	Debit
Supplies	Current Asset	Balance Sheet	Debit
Supplies Expense	Operating Expense	Income Statement	Debit
		T	
Treasury Stock	Stockholders' Equity	Balance Sheet	Debit
		U	
Unearned Service Revenue	Current Liability	Balance Sheet	Credit
Utilities Expense	Operating Expense	Income Statement	Debit

(1) The normal balance for Income Summary will be credit when there is a net income, debit when there is a net loss. The Income Summary account does not appear on any financial statement.

(2) If a periodic system is used, Inventory also appears on the income statement in the calculation of cost of goods sold.

The following is a sample chart of accounts. It does not represent a comprehensive chart of all the accounts used in this textbook but rather those accounts that are commonly used. This sample chart of accounts is for a company that generates both service revenue as well as sales revenue. It uses the perpetual approach to inventory. If a periodic system was used, the following temporary accounts would be needed to record inventory purchases: Purchases, Freight-In, Purchase Returns and Allowances, and Purchase Discounts.

CHART OF ACCOUNTS

Assets	Liabilities	Stockholders' Equity	Revenues	Expenses
Cash	Notes Payable	Common Stock	Service Revenue	Administrative Expenses
Accounts Receivable	Accounts Payable	Paid-in Capital in Excess of Par Value—Common Stock	Sales Revenue	Amortization Expense
Allowance for Doubtful Accounts	Unearned Service Revenue	Preferred Stock	Sales Discounts	Bad Debt Expense
Interest Receivable	Salaries and Wages Payable	Paid-in Capital in Excess of Par Value—Preferred Stock	Sales Returns and Allowances	Cost of Goods Sold
Inventory	Interest Payable	Treasury Stock	Interest Revenue	Depreciation Expense
Supplies	Dividends Payable	Retained Earnings	Gain on Disposal of Plant Assets	Freight-Out
Prepaid Insurance	Income Taxes Payable	Dividends		Income Tax Expense
Prepaid Rent	Bonds Payable	Income Summary		Insurance Expense
Land	Discount on Bonds Payable			Interest Expense
Equipment	Premium on Bonds Payable			Loss on Disposal of Plant Assets
Accumulated Depreciation—Equipment	Mortgage Payable			Maintenance and Repairs Expense
Buildings				Rent Expense
Accumulated Depreciation—Buildings				Salaries and Wages Expense
Copyrights				Selling Expenses
Goodwill				Supplies Expense
Patents				Utilities Expense

Paul D. Kimmel PhD, CPA
University of Wisconsin—Milwaukee
Milwaukee, Wisconsin

Jerry J. Weygandt PhD, CPA
University of Wisconsin—Madison
Madison, Wisconsin

Donald E. Kieso PhD, CPA
Northern Illinois University
DeKalb, Illinois

WILEY

DEDICATED TO

the Wiley sales representatives
who sell our books and service
our adopters in a professional
and ethical manner, and to
Merlynn, Enid, and Donna

Vice President and Director	George Hoffman
Executive Editor	Michael McDonald
Development Editor	Ed Brislin
Editorial Supervisor	Terry Ann Tatro
Editorial Associate	Margaret Thompson
Senior Content Manager	Dorothy Sinclair
Senior Production Editor	Suzie Pfister
Executive Marketing Manager	Karolina Zarychta Hons
Product Design Manager	Allison Morris
Product Designer	Matt Origoni
Media Specialist	Elena Santa Maria
Design Director	Harry Nolan
Cover Design	Maureen Eide
Interior Design	Maureen Eide
Senior Photo Editor	Mary Ann Price
Market Solutions Assistant	Elizabeth Kearns
Cover Credit	Susanna Price/Getty Images, Inc.

This book was set in New Aster LT Std by Aptara®, Inc. and printed and bound by RR Donnelley.
The cover was printed by RR Donnelley.

Founded in 1807, John Wiley & Sons, Inc. has been a valued source of knowledge and understanding for more than 200 years, helping people around the world meet their needs and fulfill their aspirations. Our company is built on a foundation of principles that include responsibility to the communities we serve and where we live and work. In 2008, we launched a Corporate Citizenship Initiative, a global effort to address the environmental, social, economic, and ethical challenges we face in our business. Among the issues we are addressing are carbon impact, paper specifications and procurement, ethical conduct within our business and among our vendors, and community and charitable support. For more information, please visit our website: www.wiley.com/go/citizenship.

ISBN-13 978-1-118-55255-1

Binder-Ready Version ISBN 978-1-118-95390-7

Printed in the United States of America

10 9 8 7 6 5 4 3

Brief Contents

From the Authors

Dear Student,

Why This Course? *Remember your biology course in high school? Did you have one of those "invisible man" models (or maybe something more high-tech than that) that gave you the opportunity to look "inside" the human body? This accounting course offers something similar. To understand a business, you have to understand the financial insides of a business organization. A financial accounting course will help you understand the essential financial components of businesses. Whether you are looking at a large multinational company like Apple or Starbucks or a single-owner software consulting business or coffee shop, knowing the fundamentals of financial accounting will help you understand what is happening. As an employee, a manager, an investor,a business owner, or a director of your own personal finances—any of which roles you will have at some point in your life—you will make better decisions for having taken this course.*

"Whether you are looking at a large multinational company like Apple or Starbucks or a single-owner software consulting business or coffee shop, knowing the fundamentals of financial accounting will help you understand what is happening."

Why This Book? *Hundreds of thousands of students have used this textbook. Your instructor has chosen it for you because of its trusted reputation. The authors have worked hard to keep the book fresh, timely, and accurate.*

How to Succeed? *We've asked many students and many instructors whether there is a secret for success in this course. The nearly unanimous answer turns out to be not much of a secret: "Do the homework." This is one course where doing is learning. The more time you spend on the homework assignments—using the various tools that this textbook provides—the more likely you are to learn the essential concepts, techniques, and methods of accounting. Besides the textbook itself, WileyPLUS and the book's companion website also offer various support resources.*

Good luck in this course. We hope you enjoy the experience and that you put to good use throughout a lifetime of success the knowledge you obtain in this course. We are sure you will not be disappointed.

Paul D. Kimmel
Jerry J. Weygandt
Donald E. Kieso

Author Commitment

Jerry Weygandt

JERRY J. WEYGANDT, PhD, CPA, is Arthur Andersen Alumni Emeritus Professor of Accounting at the University of Wisconsin—Madison. He holds a Ph.D. in accounting from the University of Illinois. Articles by Professor Weygandt have appeared in the Accounting Review, Journal of Accounting Research, Accounting Horizons, Journal of Accountancy, and other academic and professional journals. These articles have examined such financial reporting issues as accounting for price-level adjustments, pensions, convertible securities, stock option contracts, and interim reports. Professor Weygandt is author of other accounting and financial reporting books and is a member of the American Accounting Association, the American Institute of Certified Public Accountants, and the Wisconsin Society of Certified Public Accountants. He has served on numerous committees of the American Accounting Association and as a member of the editorial board of the Accounting Review; he also has served as President and Secretary-Treasurer of the American Accounting Association. In addition, he has been actively involved with the American Institute of Certified Public Accountants and has been a member of the Accounting Standards Executive Committee (AcSEC) of that organization. He has served on the FASB task force that examined the reporting issues related to accounting for income taxes and served as a trustee of the Financial Accounting Foundation. Professor Weygandt has received the Chancellor's Award for Excellence in Teaching and the Beta Gamma Sigma Dean's Teaching Award. He is on the board of directors of M & I Bank of Southern Wisconsin. He is the recipient of the Wisconsin Institute of CPA's Outstanding Educator's Award and the Lifetime Achievement Award. In 2001 he received the American Accounting Association's Outstanding Educator Award.

Paul Kimmel

PAUL D. KIMMEL, PhD, CPA, received his bachelor's degree from the University of Minnesota and his doctorate in accounting from the University of Wisconsin. He is an Associate Professor at the University of Wisconsin—Milwaukee, and has public accounting experience with Deloitte & Touche (Minneapolis). He was the recipient of the UWM School of Business Advisory Council Teaching Award, the Reggie Taite Excellence in Teaching Award and a three-time winner of the Outstanding Teaching Assistant Award at the University of Wisconsin. He is also a recipient of the Elijah Watts Sells Award for Honorary Distinction for his results on the CPA exam. He is a member of the American Accounting Association and the Institute of Management Accountants and has published articles in *Accounting Review, Accounting Horizons, Advances in Management Accounting, Managerial Finance, Issues in Accounting Education, Journal of Accounting Education,* as well as other journals. His research interests include accounting for financial instruments and innovation in accounting education. He has published papers and given numerous talks on incorporating critical thinking into accounting education, and helped prepare a catalog of critical thinking resources for the Federated Schools of Accountancy.

Don Kieso

DONALD E. KIESO, PhD, CPA, received his bachelor's degree from Aurora University and his doctorate in accounting from the University of Illinois. He has served as chairman of the Department of Accountancy and is currently the KPMG Emeritus Professor of Accountancy at Northern Illinois University. He has public accounting experience with Price Waterhouse & Co. (San Francisco and Chicago) and Arthur Andersen & Co. (Chicago) and research experience with the Research Division of the American Institute of Certified Public Accountants (New York). He has done postdoctoral work as a Visiting Scholar at the University of California at Berkeley and is a recipient of NIU's Teaching Excellence Award and four Golden Apple Teaching Awards. Professor Kieso is the author of other accounting and business books and is a member of the American Accounting Association, the American Institute of Certified Public Accountants, and the Illinois CPA Society. He has served as a member of the Board of Directors of the Illinois CPA Society, then AACSB's Accounting Accreditation Committees, the State of Illinois Comptroller's Commission, as Secretary-Treasurer of the Federation of Schools of Accountancy, and as Secretary-Treasurer of the American Accounting Association. Professor Kieso is currently serving on the Board of Trustees and Executive Committee of Aurora University, as a member of the Board of Directors of Kishwaukee Community Hospital, and as Treasurer and Director of Valley West Community Hospital. From 1989 to 1993 he served as a charter member of the national Accounting Education Change Commission. He is the recipient of the Outstanding Accounting Educator Award from the Illinois CPA Society, the FSA's Joseph A. Silvoso Award of Merit, the NIU Foundation's Humanitarian Award for Service to Higher Education, a Distinguished Service Award from the Illinois CPA Society, and in 2003 an honorary doctorate from Aurora University.

WileyPLUS with ORION

Quickly identify areas of strength and weakness before the first exam, and use the information to build a learning path to success.

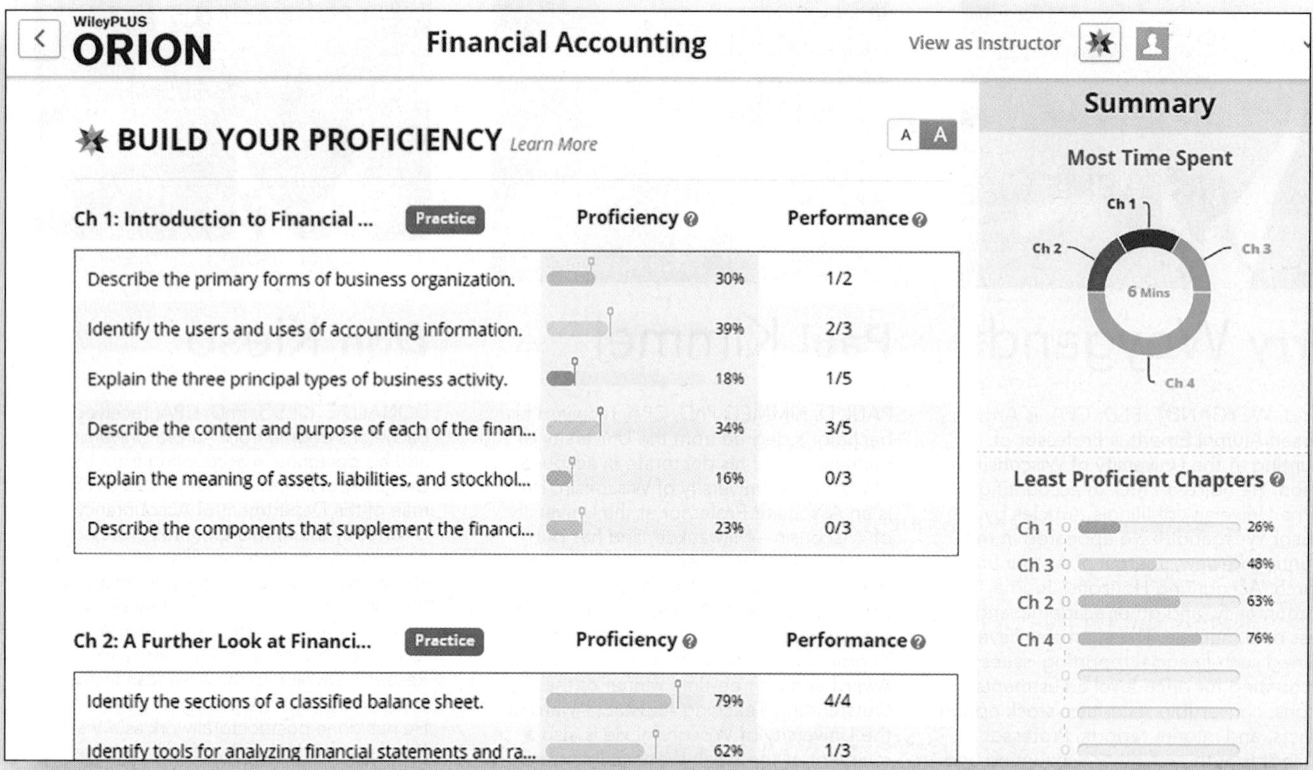

A little time with ORION goes a long way.

Based on usage data, students who engage in ORION adaptive practice—just a few minutes per week—get better outcomes. In fact, students who used ORION five or more times over the course of a semester reported the following results:

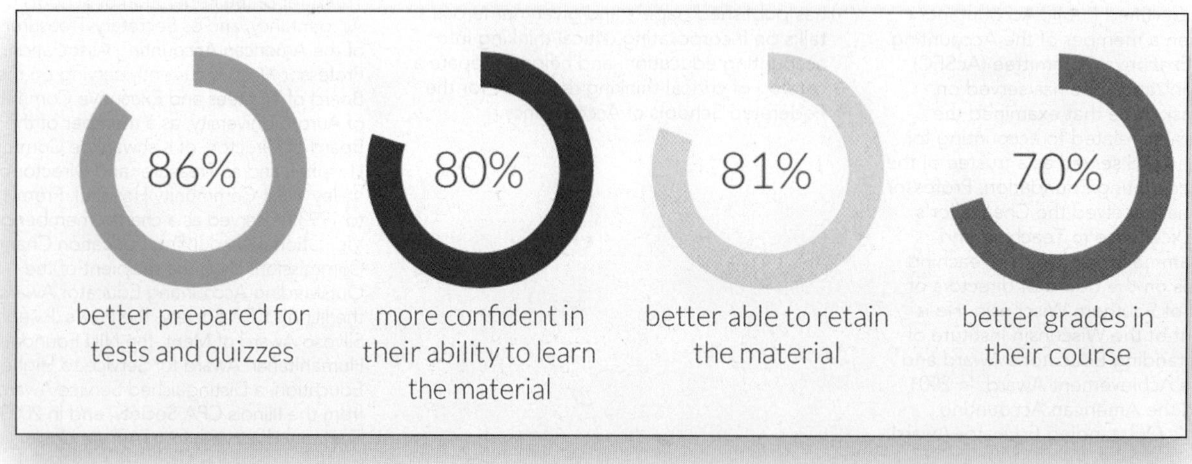

Developing effective problem solving skills requires practice, relevant feedback, and insightful examples.

New PRACTICE QUESTIONS WITH SOLUTIONS include:

- **BRIEF EXERCISES**
- **EXERCISES**
- **DO IT! Exercises**
- **PROBLEMS**

All new practice questions provide **assessment,** helping students see what they understand and where they can improve.

Algorithmic versions of the questions allow students to revisit practice questions until they understand a topic completely.

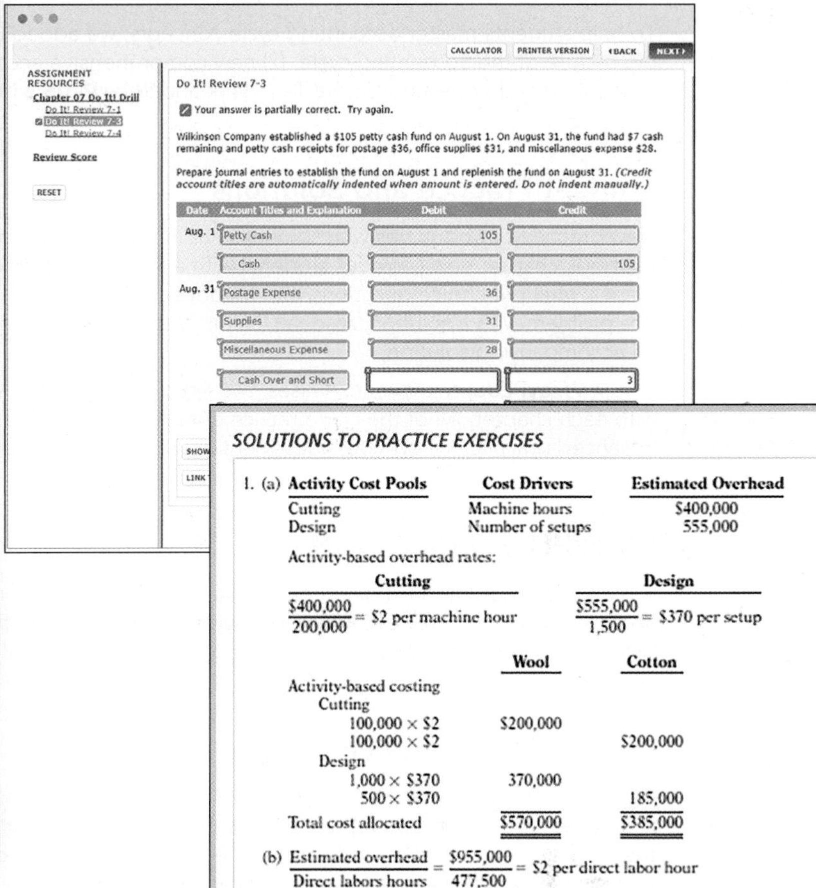

CALCULATOR PRINTER VERSION ‹BACK NEXT›

ASSIGNMENT RESOURCES
Chapter 07 Do It! Drill
Do It! Review 7-1
Do It! Review 7-3
Do It! Review 7-4
Review Score
RESET

Do It! Review 7-3

Your answer is partially correct. Try again.

Wilkinson Company established a $105 petty cash fund on August 1. On August 31, the fund had $7 cash remaining and petty cash receipts for postage $36, office supplies $31, and miscellaneous expense $28.

Prepare journal entries to establish the fund on August 1 and replenish the fund on August 31. *(Credit account titles are automatically indented when amount is entered. Do not indent manually.)*

Date	Account Titles and Explanation	Debit	Credit
Aug. 1	Petty Cash	105	
	Cash		105
Aug. 31	Postage Expense	36	
	Supplies	31	
	Miscellaneous Expense	28	
	Cash Over and Short		3

SOLUTIONS TO PRACTICE EXERCISES

1. (a)

Activity Cost Pools	Cost Drivers	Estimated Overhead
Cutting	Machine hours	$400,000
Design	Number of setups	555,000

Activity-based overhead rates:

Cutting: $\frac{\$400,000}{200,000} = \$2$ per machine hour

Design: $\frac{\$555,000}{1,500} = \$370$ per setup

	Wool	Cotton
Activity-based costing		
Cutting		
100,000 × $2	$200,000	
100,000 × $2		$200,000
Design		
1,000 × $370	370,000	
500 × $370		185,000
Total cost allocated	$570,000	$385,000

(b) $\frac{\text{Estimated overhead}}{\text{Direct labors hours}} = \frac{\$955,000}{477,500} = \$2$ per direct labor hour

Solutions to practice multiple-choice questions, exercises, and problems are now available at the end of each chapter.

REVIEW AND PRACTICE

LEARNING OBJECTIVES REVIEW

1 Discuss how to classify and determine inventory. Merchandisers need only one inventory classification, merchandise inventory, to describe the different items that make up total inventory. Manufacturers, on the other hand, usually classify inventory into three categories: finished goods, work in process, and raw materials. To determine inventory quantities, manufacturers (1) take a physical inventory of goods on hand and (2) determine the ownership of goods in transit or on consignment.

2 Apply inventory cost flow methods and discuss their financial effects. The primary basis of accounting for inventories is cost. Cost includes all expenditures necessary to acquire goods and place them in a condition ready for sale. Cost of goods available for sale includes (a) cost of beginning inventory and (b) cost of goods purchased. The inventory cost flow methods are specific identification and three assumed cost flow methods—FIFO, LIFO, and average-cost.

The cost of goods available for sale may be allocated to cost of goods sold and ending inventory by specific identification or by a method based on an assumed cost flow. When prices are rising, the first-in, first-out (FIFO) method results in lower cost of goods sold and higher net income than the average-cost and the last-in, first-out (LIFO) methods. The reverse is true when prices are falling. In the balance sheet, FIFO results in an ending inventory that is closest to current value, whereas the inventory under LIFO is the farthest from current value. LIFO

Inventory turnover is calculated as cost of goods sold divided by average inventory. It can be converted to average days in inventory by dividing 365 days by the inventory turnover. A higher inventory turnover or lower average days in inventory suggests that management is trying to keep inventory levels low relative to its sales level.

The LIFO reserve represents the difference between ending inventory using LIFO and ending inventory if FIFO were employed instead. For some companies this difference can be significant, and ignoring it can lead to inappropriate conclusions when using the current ratio or inventory turnover.

***4** Apply inventory cost flow methods to perpetual inventory records. Under FIFO, ... on hand prior to each sa... Under LIFO, the cost of... sale is charged to cost ... cost method, a new av... purchase.

***5** Indicate the effects ... cial statements. *In the year:* (1) An error in ... reverse effect on net ... inventory results in un... vice versa). (2) An err... a similar effect on ne... inventory results in o... ending inventory error...

INSTRUCTIONS

Prepare a schedule to determine the correct inventory amount. Provide explanations for each item above, saying why you did or did not make an adjustment for each item.

SOLUTION

1. Ending inventory—as reported	$650,000
1. Subtract from inventory: The goods belong to Bosnia Corporation. Sergei is merely holding them for Bosnia.	(200,000)
2. Add to inventory: The goods belong to Sergei when they were shipped.	40,000
3. Subtract from inventory: Office supplies should be carried in a separate account. They are not considered inventory held for resale.	(15,000)
4. Add to inventory: The goods belong to Sergei until they are shipped (Jan. 1).	30,000

SOLUTIONS

1. **(d)** A physical inventory is usually taken when a limited number of goods are being sold or received, and at the end of the company's fiscal year. Choice (a) is incorrect because a physical inventory count is usually taken when the company has the least, not greatest, amount of inventory. Choices (b) and (c) are correct, but (d) is the better answer.
2. **(a)** Goods held on consignment should not be included because another company has title (ownership) to the goods. The other choices are incorrect because (b) goods shipped on consignment to another company and (c) goods in transit from another company shipped FOB shipping point should be included in a company's ending inventory. Choice (d) is incorrect because (a) is not included in the physical inventory.
3. **(b)** The inventory held on consignment by Rogers should be included in Railway's inventory balance at cost ($35,000). The purchased goods of $13,000 should not be included in inventory until January 3 because the goods are shipped FOB destination. Therefore, the correct amount of inventory is $215,000 ($180,000 + $35,000), not (a) $230,000, (c) $228,000, or (d) $193,000.
4. **(c)** Under FIFO, ending inventory will consist of 5,000 units from the Nov. 8 purchase and 4,000 units from the June 19 purchase. Therefore, ending inventory is (5,000 × $13) + (4,000 × $12) = $113,000, not (a) $99,000, (b) $108,000, or (d) $117,000.
5. **(d)** Under LIFO, ending inventory will consist of 8,000 units from the inventory at Jan. 1 and 1,000 units from the June 19 purchase. Therefore, ending inventory is (8,000 × $11) + (1,000 × $12) = $100,000, not (a) $113,000, (b) $108,000, or (c) $99,000.

What's New?

Focus on the Accounting Cycle

To help students master accounting cycle concepts, we added (1) new, recurring illustrations that show students the big picture of the accounting cycle, (2) new comprehensive accounting cycle exercises and problems, and (3) new accounting cycle questions in the Test Bank and **WileyPLUS with ORION**.

Student Practice and Solutions

New practice opportunities with solutions are integrated throughout the textbook and WileyPLUS course. Each textbook chapter now provides students with a **Review and Practice** section that includes learning objective summaries, multiple-choice questions with feedback for each answer choice, practice exercises with solutions, and a practice problem with a solution. Also, all learning objective modules in the textbook are followed by a **DO IT!** exercise with an accompanying solution.

In **WileyPLUS**, two brief exercises, two **DO IT!** exercises, two exercises, and a new problem are available for practice with each chapter. All of the new practice questions are algorithmic, providing students with multiple opportunities for advanced practice. WileyPLUS assessment now includes new narrative student feedback.

WileyPLUS with ORION

Over 3,500 questions, including new medium-level, computational, and accounting-cycle-based questions, are available for practice and review. **WileyPLUS with ORION** is an adaptive study and practice tool that helps students build proficiency in course topics.

Updated Content and Design

We scrutinized all content to find new ways to engage students and help them learn accounting concepts.
A new learning objective structure helps students practice their understanding of concepts with **DO IT!** exercises before they move on to different topics in other learning objectives. Coupled with a new interior design, revised infographics, and the newly designed interactive chapter tutorials, the new outcomes-oriented approach motivates students and helps them make the best use of their time.

WileyPLUS Videos

Over 150 videos are available in WileyPLUS. More than 80 of the videos are new to the Eighth Edition. The videos walk students through relevant homework problems and solutions, review important concepts, provide overviews of Excel skills, and explore topics in a real-world context.

Real World Context: Feature Stories and Comprehensive Problems

New feature stories frame chapter topics in a real-world company example. Also, the feature stories now closely correlate with the Using Decision Tools problem at the end of each chapter. In WileyPLUS, real-world Insight boxes now have questions that can be assigned as homework.

More information about the Eighth Edition is available on the book's website at **www.wiley.com/college/kimmel**.

Table of Contents

Acknowledgments

Financial Accounting has benefitted greatly from the input of focus group participants, manuscript reviewers, those who have sent comments by letter or e-mail, ancillary authors, and proofers. We greatly appreciate the constructive suggestions and innovative ideas of reviewers and the creativity and accuracy of the ancillary authors and checkers.

Eighth Edition

Dennis Avola
Northeastern University

Thomas Bednarcik
Robert Morris University Illinois

Martin Blaine
Columbus State Community College

Bradley Blaylock
Oklahoma State University

Gary Bower
Community College of Rhode Island

Robert Braun
Southeastern Louisiana University

Lou Bravo
North Lake College

Myra Bruegger
Southeastern Community College

Barry Buchoff
Towson University

Matthew Calderisi
Fairleigh Dickinson University

Julia Camp
Providence College

Marian Canada
Ivy Tech Community College at Franklin

Bea Chiang
The College of New Jersey

Colleen Chung
Miami Dade College

Shifei Chung
Rowan University

Tony Cioffi
Lorain County Community College

Leslie Cohen
University of Arizona

Jim Coughlin
Robert Morris University

Patricia Crenny
Villanova University

Dori Danko
Grand Valley State University

Mingcherng Deng
Baruch College

Kathy Dunne
Rider University

Barbara Durham
University of Central Florida

David Emerson
Salisbury University

Caroline Falconetti
Nassau Community College

Nancy Fan
California State Polytechnic University, Pomona

Magdy Farag
California State Polytechnic University, Pomona

Linda Flaming
Monmouth University

Joseph Fournier
University of Rhode Island

Amy Geile
University of Arizona

Alan Glaser
Franklin & Marshall College

J. D. Golub
Northeastern University

Rita Grant
Grand Valley State University

Steve Groves
Ivy Tech Community College

Konrad Gunderson
Missouri Western State University

Marcye Hampton
University of Central Florida

Qian Hao
Wilkes University

Huong Higgins
Worcester Polytechnic Institute

Yongtao Hong
North Dakota State University

Robert Hurst
Franklin University

Wayne Ingalls
University of Maine

Jennifer Joe
University of Delaware

James B. Johnson
Community College of Philadelphia

Patricia Johnson
Canisius College

Jordan Kanter
University of Rhode Island

Ann Galligan Kelley
Providence College

Robert Kenny
The College of New Jersey

Emil Koren
Saint Leo University

Faith Lamprey
Providence College

Gary Laycock
Ivy Tech Community College

Charles Leflar
University of Arkansas

Jennifer LeSure
Ivy Tech Community College

Claudia Lubaski
Lorain County Community College

Yuanyuan Ma
University of Minnesota

Don McFall
Hiram College

Allison McLeod
University of North Texas

Maha Mitrelis
Providence College

Louella Moore
Washburn University

Sia Nassiripour
William Paterson University

Joseph Nesi
Monmouth University

Glenn Pate
Palm Beach State College

Suzy Pearse
Clemson University

Rachel Pernia
Essex County College

George Psaras
Aurora University

Patrick Reihing
Nassau Community College

John Ribezzo
Community College of Rhode Island

Vernon Richardson
University of Arkansas

Patrick Rogan
Consumnes River College

Juan Roman
Saint Leo University

John Rude
Bloomsburg University

Martin Rudnick
William Paterson University

August Saibeni
Consumnes River College

Barbara Sandler
Queens College

Barbara Scofield
Washburn University

Chris Severson
Franklin University

Suzanne Seymoure
Saint Leo University

Abdus Shahid
The College of New Jersey

Mike Shapeero
Bloomsburg University

Todd Shawver
Bloomsburg University

Eileen Shifflett
James Madison University

Ladd Simms
Mississippi Valley State University

Doug Stives
Monmouth University

Karen Tower
Ivy Tech Community College

Daniel Tschopp
Saint Leo University

Mark Ulrich
St. John's University

Nancy Wilburn
Northern Arizona University

Wayne W. Williams
Community College of Philadelphia

Hannah Wong
William Paterson University

Kenneth Zheng
University at Buffalo

Prior Editions

Thanks to the following reviewers and focus group participants of prior editions of Financial Accounting:

Dawn Addington, *Central New Mexico Community College;* Gilda Agacer, *Monmouth University;* Solochidi Ahiarah, *Buffalo State College;* C. Richard Aldridge, *Western Kentucky University;* Sylvia Allen, *Los Angeles Valley College;* Sheila Ammons, *Austin Community College;* Thomas G. Amyot, *College of Santa Rose;* Juanita Ardavany, *Los Angeles Valley College;* Brian Baick, *Montgomery College;* Timothy Baker, *California State University—Fresno;* Cheryl Bartlett, *Central New Mexico Community College;* Benjamin Bean, *Utah Valley State College.*

Victoria Beard, *University of North Dakota;* Angela H. Bell, *Jacksonville State University;* Charles Bokemeier, *Michigan State University;* John A. Booker, *Tennessee Technological University;* Duane Brandon, *Auburn University;* Gary Braun, *University of Texas—El Paso;* Jerold K. Braun, *Daytona State College;* Robert L. Braun, *Southeastern Louisiana University;* Daniel Brickner, *Eastern Michigan University;* Evangelie Brodie, *North Carolina State University;* Sarah Ruth Brown, *University of North Alabama;* Charles Bunn, *Wake Technical Community College;* Thane Butt, *Champlain College;* Sandra Byrd, *Missouri State University;* James Byrne, *Oregon State University.*

Judy Cadle, *Tarleton State University;* Julia Camp, *University of Massachusetts—Boston;* David Carr, *Austin Community College;* Jack Cathey, *University of North Carolina—Charlotte;* Andy Chen, *Northeast Illinois University;* Jim Christianson, *Austin Community College;* Siu Chung, *Los Angeles Valley College;* Laura Claus, *Louisiana State University;* Leslie A. Cohen, *University of Arizona;* Teresa L. Conover, *University of North Texas;* Rita Kingery Cook, *University of Delaware;* Cheryl Corke, *Genesee Community College;* Sue Counte, *St. Louis Community College—Meramec;* Janet Courts, *San Bernardino Valley College;* Samantha Cox, *Wake Technical Community College;* Cheryl Crespi, *Central Connecticut State University;* Dori Danko, *Grand Valley State University;* Brent W. Darwin, *Allan Hancock College;* Helen Davis, *Johnson and Wales University;* Paquita Davis-Friday, *Baruch College;* Michael Deschamps, *Mira Costa College;* Cheryl Dickerson, *Western Washington University;* Gadis Dillon, *Oakland University;* George M. Dow, *Valencia Community College—West;* Kathy J. Dow, *Salem State College;* Lola Dudley, *Eastern Illinois University.*

Mary Emery, *St. Olaf College;* Martin L. Epstein, *Central New Mexico Community College;* Ann Escaro, *McHenry County College;* Larry R. Falcetto, *Emporia State University;* Alan Falcon, *Loyola Marymount University;* Scott Fargason, *Louisiana State University;* Janet Farler, *Pima Community College;* Lance Fisher, *Oklahoma State University;* Sheila D. Foster, *The Citadel;* Jessica J. Frazier, *Eastern Kentucky University;* Roger Gee, *San Diego Mesa College;* Lisa Gillespie, *Loyola University—Chicago;* Hubert Glover, *Drexel University;* Norman H. Godwin, *Auburn University;* David Gotlob, *Indiana University—Purdue University—Fort Wayne;* Lisa Gray, *Seminole State College and Valencia Community College;* Emmett Griner, *Georgia State University;* Leon J. Hanouille, *Syracuse University;* Hassan Hefzi, *California State PolyTech University—Pomona;* Kenneth M. Hiltebeitel, *Villanova University;* Harry Hooper, *Santa Fe Community College;* Judith A. Hora, *University of San Diego;* Carol Olson Houston, *San Diego State University;* Ryan Huldah, *Iona College;* Sam Isley, *Wake Technical Community College.*

Norma Jacobs, *Austin Community College;* Marianne L. James, *California State University—Los Angeles;* Stanley Jenne, *University of Montana;* Christopher Jones, *George Washington University;* Siriyama Kanthi Herath, *Georgia Institute of Technology;* Jane Kaplan, *Drexel University;* John E. Karayan, *California State University—Pomona;* Susan Kattelus, *Eastern Michigan University;* Ann Kelly, *Providence College;* Dawn Kelly, *Texas Tech University;* Robert Kenny, *The College of New Jersey;* Cindi Khanlarian, *University of North Carolina—Greensboro;* Robert Kiddoo, *California State University—Northridge;* Marinilka Kimbro, *Gonzaga University;* Robert J. Kirsch, *Southern Connecticut State University;* Frank Korman, *Mountain View College;* Jerry G. Kreuze, *Western Michigan University.*

John Lacey, *California State University—Long Beach;* Joseph Larkin, *Saint Joseph's University;* Doulas Larson, *Salem State College;* Doug Laufer, *Metropolitan State College of Denver;* Keith Leeseberg, *Manatee Community College;* Glenda Levendowski, *Arizona State University;* Seth Levine, *DeVry University;* Lihon Liang, *Syracuse University;* James Lukawitz, *University of Memphis;* Nancy Lynch, *West Virginia University;* P. Merle Maddocks, *University of Alabama—Huntsville;* Janice Mardon, *Green River Community College;* Sal Marino, *Westchester Community College;* John Marts, *University of North Carolina—Wilmington;* Alan Mayer-Sommer, *Georgetown University;* Florence McGovern, *Bergen Community College;* Noel McKeon, *Florida Community College at Jacksonville;* Sara Melendy, *Gonzaga University;* Barbara Merino, *University of North Texas;* Paul Mihalek, *Central Connecticut State University;* Jeanne Miller, *Cypress College;* Robert Miller, *California State University—Fullerton;* Elizabeth Minbiole, *Northwood University;* Sherry Mirbod, *Montgomery College;* Andrew Morgret, *University of Memphis;* Michelle Moshier, *SUNY Albany;* Marguerite Muise, *Santa Ana College;* Kathy Munter, *Pima Community College;* William J. Nealon, *Schenectady County Community College;* James Neurath, *Central Michigan University;* Gale E. Newell, *Western Michigan University;* Garth Novack, *Utah State University;* Rosemary Nurre, *San Mateo Community College.*

Suzanne Ogilby, *Sacramento State University;* Sarah N. Palmer, *University of North Carolina—Charlotte;* Patricia Parker, *Columbus State Community College;* Terry Patton, *Midwestern State University;* Charles Pier, *Appalachian State University;* Ronald Pierno, *Florida State University;* Janice Pitera, *Broome Community College;* Franklin J. Plewa, *Idaho State University;* Meg Pollard, *American River College;* John Purisky, *Salem State College;* Donald J. Raux, *Siena College;* Ray Reisig, *Pace University, Pleasantville;* Judith Resnick, *Borough of Manhattan Community College;* Mary Ann Reynolds, *Western Washington University;* Ruthie G. Reynolds, *Howard University;* Carla Rich, *Pensacola Junior College;* Rod Ridenour, *Montana State University—Bozeman;* Ray Rigoli, *Ramapo College of New Jersey;* Larry Rittenberg, *University of Wisconsin;* Jeff Ritter, *St. Norbert College;* Cecile M. Roberti, *Community College of Rhode Island;* Brandi Roberts, *Southeastern Louisiana University;* Patricia A. Robinson, *Johnson and Wales University;* Nancy Rochman, *University of Arizona;* Lawrence Roman, *Cuyahoga Community College;* Marc A. Rubin, *Miami University;* John A. Rude, *Bloomsburg University;* Robert Russ, *Northern Kentucky University.*

Alfredo Salas, *El Paso Community College;* Christine Schalow, *California State University—San Bernardino;* Michael Schoderbek, *Rutgers University;* Richard Schroeder, *University of North Carolina—Charlotte;* Bill N. Schwartz, *Stevens Institute of Technology;* Jerry Searfoss, *University of Utah;* Cindy Seipel, *New Mexico State University;* Anne E. Selk, *University of Wisconsin—Green Bay;* William Seltz, *University of Massachusetts;* Suzanne Sevalstad, *University of Nevada;* Mary Alice Seville, *Oregon State University;* Donald Smillie, *Southwest Missouri State University;* Aileen Smith, *Stephen F. Austin State University;* Gerald Smith, *University of Northern Iowa;* Pam Smith, *Northern Illinois University;* Talitha Smith, *Auburn University;* William E. Smith, *Xavier University;* Will Snyder, *San Diego State University;* Naomi Soderstrom, *University of Colorado—Boulder;* Chris Solomon, *Trident Technical College;* Teresa A. Speck, *St. Mary's University of Minnesota;* Charles Stanley, *Baylor University;* Vic Stanton, *University of California, Berkeley;* Ron Stone, *California State University—Northridge;* Gary Stout, *California State University—Northridge;* Gracelyn Stuart, *Palm Beach Community College;* Paul Swanson, *Illinois Central College;* Ellen L. Sweatt, *Georgia Perimeter College.*

William Talbot, *Montgomery College;* Diane Tanner, *University of North Florida;* Pamadda Tantral, *Fairleigh Dickinson University;* Steve Teeter, *Utah Valley State College;* Michael Tydlaska, *Mountain View College;* Michael F. van Breda, *Texas Christian University;* Joan Van Hise, *Fairfield University;* Richard Van Ness, *Schenectady County Community College;* Christopher Wallace, *California State University—Sacramento;* Barbara Warschawski, *Schenectady County Community College;* Andrea B. Weickgenannt, *Northern Kentucky University;* David P. Weiner, *University of San Francisco;* Frederick Weis, *Claremont McKenna College;* T. Sterling Wetzel, *Oklahoma State University;* Wendy Wilson, *Southern Methodist University;* Allan Young, *DeVry University;* Linda G. Wade, *Tarleton State University;* Stuart K. Webster, *University of Wyoming;* Kathryn Yarbrough, *University of North Carolina—Charlotte;* V. Joyce Yearley, *New Mexico State University;* Judith Zander, *Grossmont College*

Ancillary Authors, Contributors, Proofers, and Accuracy Checkers

We sincerely thank the following individuals for their hard work in preparing the content that accompanies this textbook:

Ellen Bartley
St. Joseph's College

LuAnn Bean
Florida Institute of Technology

Jack Borke
University of Wisconsin—Platteville

Melanie Bunting
Edgewood College

Sandra Cohen
Columbia College—Chicago

James M. Emig
Villanova University

Larry R. Falcetto
Emporia State University

Heidi Hansel
Kirkwood Community College

Coby Harmon
University of California, Santa Barbara

DeAnna Kirchen
Golden West College

Laura McNally
Black Hills State University

Jill Mitchell
Northern Virginia Community College

Barb Muller
Arizona State University

George Psarsas
Aurora University

Laura Prosser
Black Hills State University

Alice Sineath
Forsyth Technical Community College

Teresa Speck
Saint Mary's University of Minnesota

Mark Ulrich
St. John's University

Sheila Viel
University of Wisconsin—Milwaukee

Dick D. Wasson
Southwestern College

Andrea Weickgenannt
Xavier University

Melanie Yon

Advisory Board

Robert Braun
Southeastern Louisiana University

Rita Grant
Grand Valley State University

Marcye Hampton
University of Central Florida

Michelle Moshier
State University of New York—Albany

Courtney Naismith
Collin College

Michael Newman
University of Houston

Pamela Rouse
Butler University

Chris Solomon
Trident Technical College

We appreciate the exemplary support and commitment given to us by executive editor Michael McDonald, executive marketing manager Karolina Zarychta Honsa, development editor Ed Brislin, market solutions assistant Elizabeth Kearns, development editors Terry Ann Tatro and Margaret Thompson, product design manager Allie Morris, product designer Matt Origoni, designer Maureen Eide, photo editor Mary Ann Price, and Jackie Henry at Aptara. All of these professionals provided innumerable services that helped the textbook take shape.

Finally, our thanks to George Hoffman, Tim Stookesberry, Douglas Reiner, Joe Heider, Brent Gordon, and Mark Allin for their support and leadership at Wiley. We will appreciate suggestions and comments from users—instructors and students alike. You can send your thoughts and ideas about the textbook to us via email at: *AccountingAuthors@yahoo.com*.

Paul D. Kimmel
Milwaukee, Wisconsin

Jerry J. Weygandt
Madison, Wisconsin

Donald E. Kieso
DeKalb, Illinois

1

Introduction to Financial Statements

CHAPTER PREVIEW

*The **Chapter Preview** describes the purpose of the chapter and highlights major topics.*

How do you start a business? How do you determine whether your business is making or losing money? How should you finance expansion—should you borrow, should you issue stock, should you use your own funds? How do you convince banks to lend you money or investors to buy your stock? Success in business requires making countless decisions, and decisions require financial information.

The purpose of this chapter is to show you what role accounting plays in providing financial information.

*The **Chapter Outline** presents the chapter's topics and subtopics, as well as practice opportunities.*

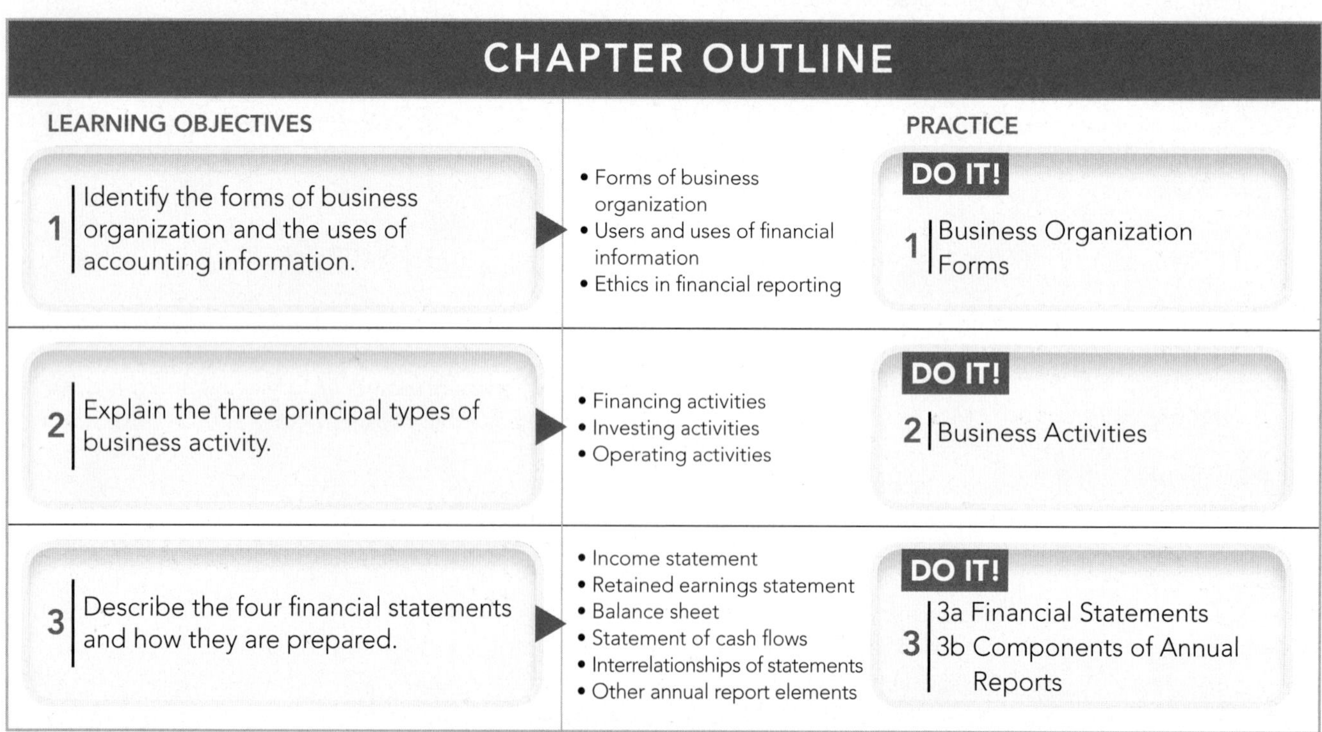

CHAPTER OUTLINE

LEARNING OBJECTIVES		PRACTICE
1 Identify the forms of business organization and the uses of accounting information.	• Forms of business organization • Users and uses of financial information • Ethics in financial reporting	DO IT! 1 Business Organization Forms
2 Explain the three principal types of business activity.	• Financing activities • Investing activities • Operating activities	DO IT! 2 Business Activities
3 Describe the four financial statements and how they are prepared.	• Income statement • Retained earnings statement • Balance sheet • Statement of cash flows • Interrelationships of statements • Other annual report elements	DO IT! 3 3a Financial Statements 3b Components of Annual Reports

Go to the ***REVIEW AND PRACTICE*** section at the end of the chapter for a targeted summary and exercises with solutions.

Visit **WileyPLUS** for additional tutorials and practice opportunities.

© My Good Images/Shutterstock

FEATURE STORY

*The **Feature Story** helps you picture how the chapter topic relates to the real world of accounting and business.*

Knowing the Numbers

Many students who take this course do not plan to be accountants. If you are in that group, you might be thinking, "If I'm not going to be an accountant, why do I need to know accounting?" Well, consider this quote from Harold Geneen, the former chairman of IT&T: "To be good at your business, you have to know the numbers—cold." In business, accounting and financial statements are the means for communicating the numbers. If you don't know how to read financial statements, you can't really know your business.

Knowing the numbers is sometimes even a matter of corporate survival. Consider the story of Columbia Sportswear Company, headquartered in Portland, Oregon. Gert Boyle's family fled Nazi Germany when she was 13 years old and then purchased a small hat company in Oregon, Columbia Hat Company. In 1971, Gert's husband, who was then running the company, died suddenly of a heart attack. The company was in the midst of an aggressive expansion, which had taken its sales above $1 million for the first time but which had also left the company financially stressed. Gert took over the small, struggling company with help from her son Tim, who was then a senior at the University of Oregon. Somehow, they kept the company afloat. Today, Columbia has more than 4,000 employees and annual sales in excess of $1 billion. Its brands include Columbia, Mountain Hardwear, Sorel, and Montrail. Gert still heads up the Board of Directors, and Tim is the company's President and CEO.

Columbia doesn't just focus on financial success. The company is very committed to corporate, social, and environmental responsibility. For example, several of its factories have participated in a project to increase health awareness of female factory workers in developing countries. Columbia was also a founding member of the Sustainable Apparel Coalition, which is a group that strives to reduce the environmental and social impact of the apparel industry. In addition, it monitors all of the independent factories that produce its products to ensure that they comply with the company's Standards of Manufacturing Practices. These standards address issues including forced labor, child labor, harassment, wages and benefits, health and safety, and the environment.

Employers such as Columbia Sportswear generally assume that managers in all areas of the company are "financially literate." To help prepare you for that, in this textbook you will learn how to read and prepare financial statements, and how to use basic tools to evaluate financial results.

LEARNING OBJECTIVE ▶1

Identify the forms of business organization and the uses of accounting information.

Suppose you graduate with a business degree and decide you want to start your own business. But what kind of business? You enjoy working with people, especially teaching them new skills. You also spend most of your free time outdoors, kayaking, backpacking, skiing, rock climbing, and mountain biking. You think you might be successful in opening an outdoor guide service where you grew up, in the Sierra Nevada mountains.

FORMS OF BUSINESS ORGANIZATION

Your next decision is to determine the organizational form of your business. You have three choices—sole proprietorship, partnership, or corporation.

Sole Proprietorship
-Simple to establish
-Owner controlled
-Tax advantages

SOLE PROPRIETORSHIP You might choose the sole proprietorship form for your outdoor guide service. A business owned by one person is a **sole proprietorship**. It is **simple to set up** and **gives you control** over the business. Small owner-operated businesses such as barber shops, law offices, and auto repair shops are often sole proprietorships, as are farms and small retail stores.

Partnership
-Simple to establish
-Shared control
-Broader skills and resources
-Tax advantages

PARTNERSHIP Another possibility is for you to join forces with other individuals to form a partnership. A business owned by two or more persons associated as partners is a **partnership**. Partnerships often are formed because one individual does not have **enough economic resources** to initiate or expand the business. Sometimes **partners bring unique skills or resources** to the partnership. You and your partners should formalize your duties and contributions in a written partnership agreement. Retail and service-type businesses, including professional practices (lawyers, doctors, architects, and certified public accountants), often organize as partnerships.

Corporation
-Easier to transfer ownership
-Easier to raise funds
-No personal liability

CORPORATION As a third alternative, you might organize as a corporation. A business organized as a separate legal entity owned by stockholders is a **corporation**. Investors in a corporation receive shares of stock to indicate their ownership claim. Buying stock in a corporation is often more attractive than investing in a partnership because shares of stock are **easy to sell** (transfer ownership). Selling a proprietorship or partnership interest is much more involved. Also, individuals can become **stockholders** by investing relatively small amounts of money. Therefore, it is **easier for corporations to raise funds**. Successful corporations often have thousands of stockholders, and their stock is traded on organized stock exchanges like the New York Stock Exchange. Many businesses start as sole proprietorships or partnerships and eventually incorporate.

ALTERNATIVE TERMINOLOGY
Stockholders are sometimes called *shareholders*.

Alternative Terminology notes present synonymous terms that you may come across in practice.

Other factors to consider in deciding which organizational form to choose are **taxes and legal liability**. If you choose a sole proprietorship or partnership, you generally receive more favorable tax treatment than a corporation. However, proprietors and partners are personally liable for all debts and legal obligations of the business; corporate stockholders are not. In other words, corporate stockholders generally pay higher taxes but have no personal legal liability. We will discuss these issues in more depth in a later chapter.

Finally, while sole proprietorships, partnerships, and corporations represent the main types of business organizations, hybrid forms are now allowed in all states. These hybrid business forms combine the tax advantages of partnerships with the limited liability of corporations. Probably the most common among these hybrids types are limited liability companies (LLCs) and subchapter S corporations. These forms are discussed extensively in business law classes.

The combined number of proprietorships and partnerships in the United States is more than five times the number of corporations. However, the revenue produced by corporations is eight times greater. Most of the largest businesses in the United States—for example, Coca-Cola, ExxonMobil, General Motors, Citigroup, and Microsoft—are corporations. Because the majority of U.S. business is done by corporations, the emphasis in this textbook is on the corporate form of organization.

USERS AND USES OF FINANCIAL INFORMATION

The purpose of financial information is to provide inputs for decision-making. **Accounting** is the information system that identifies, records, and communicates the economic events of an organization to interested users. **Users** of accounting information can be divided broadly into two groups: internal users and external users.

Internal Users

Internal users of accounting information are managers who plan, organize, and run a business. These include **marketing managers**, **production supervisors**, **finance directors**, and **company officers**. In running a business, managers must answer many important questions, as shown in Illustration 1-1.

ILLUSTRATION 1-1
Questions that internal users ask

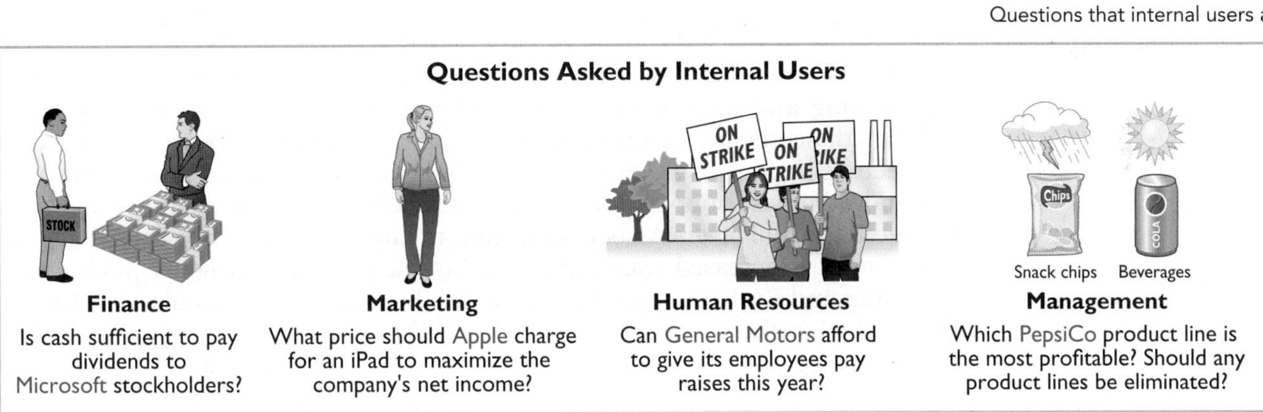

To answer these and other questions, you need detailed information on a timely basis. For internal users, accounting provides internal reports, such as financial comparisons of operating alternatives, projections of income from new sales campaigns, and forecasts of cash needs for the next year. In addition, companies present summarized financial information in the form of financial statements.

Accounting Across the Organization boxes show applications of accounting information in various business functions.

ACCOUNTING ACROSS THE ORGANIZATION Clif Bar & Company

© Dan Moore/iStockphoto

Owning a Piece of the Bar

The original Clif Bar® energy bar was created in 1990 after six months of experimentation by Gary Erickson and his mother in her kitchen. Today, the company has almost 300 employees and is considered one of the leading Landor's Breakaway Brands®. One of Clif Bar & Company's proudest moments was the creation of an employee stock ownership plan (ESOP) in 2010. This plan gives its employees 20% ownership of the company. The ESOP also resulted in Clif Bar enacting an open-book management program, including the commitment to educate all employee-owners about its finances. Armed with basic accounting knowledge, employees are more aware of the financial impact of their actions, which leads to better decisions.

What are the benefits to the company and to the employees of making the financial statements available to all employees? (Go to **WileyPLUS** for this answer and additional questions.)

External Users

There are several types of **external users** of accounting information. **Investors** (owners) use accounting information to make decisions to buy, hold, or sell stock. **Creditors** such as suppliers and bankers use accounting information to evaluate the risks of selling on credit or lending money. Some questions that investors and creditors may ask about a company are shown in Illustration 1-2.

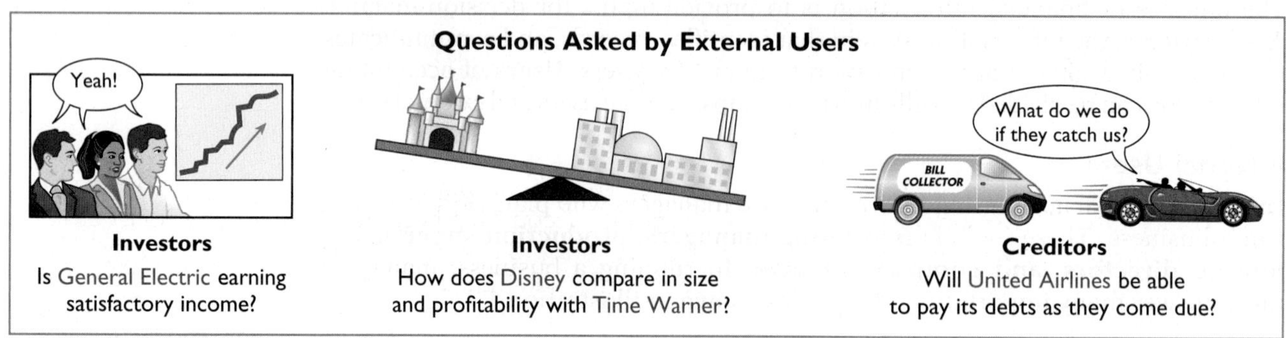

ILLUSTRATION 1-2
Questions that external users ask

The information needs and questions of other external users vary considerably. **Taxing authorities**, such as the Internal Revenue Service, want to know whether the company complies with the tax laws. **Customers** are interested in whether a company like General Motors will continue to honor product warranties and otherwise support its product lines. **Labor unions**, such as the Major League Baseball Players Association, want to know whether the owners have the ability to pay increased wages and benefits. **Regulatory agencies**, such as the Securities and Exchange Commission or the Federal Trade Commission, want to know whether the company is operating within prescribed rules. For example, Enron, Dynegy, Duke Energy, and other big energy-trading companies reported record profits at the same time as California was paying extremely high prices for energy and suffering from blackouts. This disparity caused regulators to investigate the energy traders to make sure that the profits were earned by legitimate and fair practices.

ACCOUNTING ACROSS THE ORGANIZATION

© Josef Volavka/iStockphoto

Spinning the Career Wheel

How will the study of accounting help you? A working knowledge of accounting is desirable for virtually every field of business. Some examples of how accounting is used in business careers include the following.

General management: Managers of Ford Motors, Massachusetts General Hospital, California State University–Fullerton, a McDonald's franchise, and a Trek bike shop all need to understand accounting data in order to make wise business decisions.

Marketing: Marketing specialists at Procter & Gamble must be sensitive to costs and benefits, which accounting helps them quantify and understand. Making a sale is meaningless unless it is a profitable sale.

Finance: Do you want to be a banker for Citicorp, an investment analyst for Goldman Sachs, or a stock broker for Merrill Lynch? These fields rely heavily on accounting knowledge to analyze financial statements. In fact, it is difficult to get a good job in a finance function without two or three courses in accounting.

Real estate: Are you interested in being a real estate broker for Prudential Real Estate? Because a third party—the bank—is almost always involved in financing a real estate transaction, brokers must understand the numbers involved: Can the buyer afford to make the payments to the bank? Does the cash flow from an industrial property justify the purchase price? What are the tax benefits of the purchase?

How might accounting help you? (Go to WileyPLUS for this answer and additional questions.)

ETHICS IN FINANCIAL REPORTING

People won't gamble in a casino if they think it is "rigged." Similarly, people won't "play" the stock market if they think stock prices are rigged. At one time, the financial press was full of articles about financial scandals at Enron, WorldCom, HealthSouth, and AIG. As more scandals came to light, a mistrust of financial reporting in general seemed to be developing. One article in the *Wall Street Journal* noted that "repeated disclosures about questionable accounting practices have bruised investors' faith in the reliability of earnings reports, which in turn has sent stock prices tumbling." Imagine trying to carry on a business or invest money if you could not depend on the financial statements to be honestly prepared. Information would have no credibility. There is no doubt that a sound, well-functioning economy depends on accurate and dependable financial reporting.

United States regulators and lawmakers were very concerned that the economy would suffer if investors lost confidence in corporate accounting because of unethical financial reporting. Congress passed the **Sarbanes-Oxley Act (SOX)** to reduce unethical corporate behavior and decrease the likelihood of future corporate scandals. As a result of SOX, top management must now certify the accuracy of financial information. In addition, penalties for fraudulent financial activity are much more severe. Also, SOX increased both the independence of the outside auditors who review the accuracy of corporate financial statements and the oversight role of boards of directors.

ETHICS NOTE

Circus-founder P.T. Barnum is alleged to have said, "Trust everyone, but cut the deck." What Sarbanes-Oxley does is to provide measures that (like cutting the deck of playing cards) help ensure that fraud will not occur.

Ethics Notes help sensitize you to some of the ethical issues in accounting.

Effective financial reporting depends on sound ethical behavior. To sensitize you to ethical situations and to give you practice at solving ethical dilemmas, we address ethics in a number of ways in this textbook. (1) A number of the *Feature Stories* and other parts of the text discuss the central importance of ethical behavior to financial reporting. (2) *Ethics Insight boxes* and marginal *Ethics Notes* highlight ethics situations and issues in actual business settings. (3) Many of the *People, Planet, and Profit Insight boxes* focus on ethical issues that companies face in measuring and reporting social and environmental issues. (4) At the end of each chapter, an *Ethics Case* simulates a business situation and asks you to put yourself in the position of a decision-maker in that case.

When analyzing these various ethics cases and your own ethical experiences, you should apply the three steps outlined in Illustration 1-3.

ILLUSTRATION 1-3
Steps in analyzing ethics cases

Solving an Ethical Dilemma

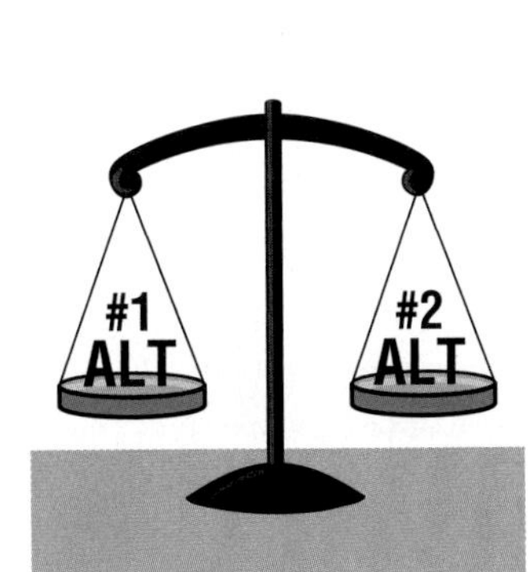

1. Recognize an ethical situation and the ethical issues involved.
Use your personal ethics to identify ethical situations and issues. Some businesses and professional organizations provide written codes of ethics for guidance in some business situations.

2. Identify and analyze the principal elements in the situation.
Identify the **stakeholders**—persons or groups who may be harmed or benefited. Ask the question: What are the responsibilities and obligations of the parties involved?

3. Identify the alternatives, and weigh the impact of each alternative on various stakeholders.
Select the most ethical alternative, considering all the consequences. Sometimes there will be one right answer. Other situations involve more than one right solution; these situations require you to evaluate each alternative and select the best one.

ETHICS INSIGHT Dewey & LeBoeuf LLP

Alliance/Shutterstock

I Felt the Pressure—Would You?

"I felt the pressure." That's what some of the employees of the now-defunct law firm of Dewey & LeBoeuf LLP indicated when they helped to overstate revenue and use accounting tricks to hide losses and cover up cash shortages. These employees worked for the former finance director and former chief financial officer (CFO) of the firm. Here are some of their comments:

- "I was instructed by the CFO to create invoices, knowing they would not be sent to clients. When I created these invoices, I knew that it was inappropriate."
- "I intentionally gave the auditors incorrect information in the course of the audit."

What happened here is that a small group of lower-level employees over a period of years carried out the instructions of their bosses. Their bosses, however, seemed to have no concern as evidenced by various e-mails with one another in which they referred to their financial manipulations as accounting tricks, cooking the books, and fake income.

Source: Ashby Jones, "Guilty Pleas of Dewey Staff Detail the Alleged Fraud," *Wall Street Journal* (March 28, 2014).

Why did these employees lie, and what do you believe should be their penalty for these lies? (Go to WileyPLUS for this answer and additional questions.)

***Insight** boxes provide examples of business situations from various perspectives—ethics, investor, international, and corporate social responsibility. Guideline answers to the critical thinking questions are available in **WileyPLUS** and at **www.wiley.com/college/weygandt**. Additional questions are offered in **WileyPLUS**.*

DO IT! 1 Business Organization Forms

*DO IT! exercises prompt you to stop and review the key points you have just studied. The **Action Plan** offers you tips about how to approach the problem.*

In choosing the organizational form for your outdoor guide service, you should consider the pros and cons of each. Identify each of the following organizational characteristics with the organizational form or forms with which it is associated.

1. Easier to raise funds.
2. Simple to establish.
3. No personal legal liability.
4. Tax advantages.
5. Easier to transfer ownership.

Action Plan

✔ **Know which organizational form best matches the business type, size, and preferences of the owner(s).**

SOLUTION

1. Easier to raise funds: Corporation.
2. Simple to establish: Sole proprietorship and partnership.
3. No personal legal liability: Corporation.
4. Tax advantages: Sole proprietorship and partnership.
5. Easier to transfer ownership: Corporation.

Related exercise material: **BE1-1** and  **1-1.**

LEARNING OBJECTIVE 2 Explain the three principal types of business activity.

All businesses are involved in three types of activity—financing, investing, and operating. For example, Gert Boyle's parents, the founders of Columbia Sportswear, obtained cash through financing to start and grow their business. Some of this **financing** came from personal savings, and some likely came from outside sources like banks. The family then **invested** the cash in equipment to run the business, such as sewing equipment and delivery vehicles. Once this equipment was in place, they could begin the **operating** activities of making and selling clothing.

The **accounting information system** keeps track of the results of each of the various business activities—financing, investing, and operating. Let's look at each type of business activity in more detail.

FINANCING ACTIVITIES

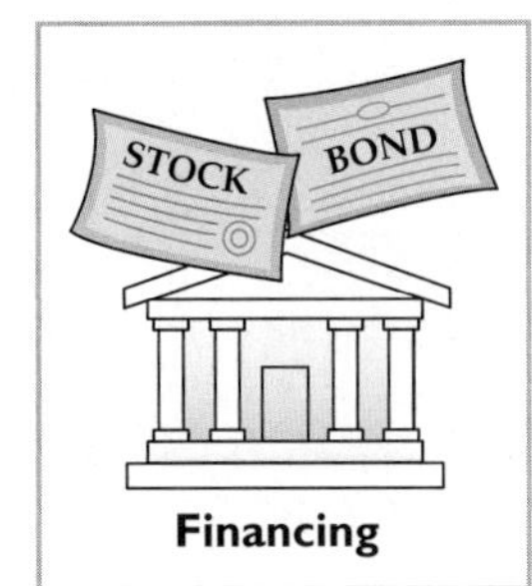

Financing

It takes money to make money. The two primary sources of outside funds for corporations are borrowing money (debt financing) and issuing (selling) shares of stock in exchange for cash (equity financing).

Columbia Sportswear may borrow money in a variety of ways. For example, it can take out a loan at a bank or borrow directly from investors by issuing debt securities called bonds. Persons or entities to whom Columbia owes money are its **creditors**. Amounts owed to creditors—in the form of debt and other obligations—are called **liabilities**. Specific names are given to different types of liabilities, depending on their source. Columbia may have a **note payable** to a bank for the money borrowed to purchase delivery trucks. Debt securities sold to investors that must be repaid at a particular date some years in the future are **bonds payable**.

Corporations also obtain funds by selling shares of stock to investors. **Common stock** is the term used to describe the total amount paid in by stockholders for the shares they purchase.

The claims of creditors differ from those of stockholders. If you loan money to a company, you are one of its creditors. In lending money, you specify a payment schedule (e.g., payment at the end of three months). As a creditor, you have a legal right to be paid at the agreed time. In the event of nonpayment, you may legally force the company to sell property to pay its debts. In the case of financial difficulty, creditor claims must be paid before stockholders' claims.

Stockholders, on the other hand, have no claim to corporate cash until the claims of creditors are satisfied. Suppose you buy a company's stock instead of loaning it money. You have no legal right to expect any payments from your stock ownership until all of the company's creditors are paid amounts currently due. However, many corporations make payments to stockholders on a regular basis as long as there is sufficient cash to cover required payments to creditors. These cash payments to stockholders are called **dividends**.

INVESTING ACTIVITIES

Investing

Once the company has raised cash through financing activities, it uses that cash in investing activities. Investing activities involve the purchase of the resources a company needs in order to operate. A growing company purchases many resources, such as computers, delivery trucks, furniture, and buildings. Resources owned by a business are called **assets**. Different types of assets are given different names. For example, Columbia Sportswear's sewing equipment is a type of asset referred to as **property, plant, and equipment**.

ALTERNATIVE TERMINOLOGY
Property, plant, and equipment is sometimes called *fixed assets*.

Cash is one of the more important assets owned by Columbia or any other business. If a company has excess cash that it does not need for a while, it might choose to invest in securities (stocks or bonds) of other corporations. **Investments** are another example of an investing activity.

OPERATING ACTIVITIES

Operating

Once a business has the assets it needs to get started, it begins operations. Columbia Sportswear is in the business of selling outdoor clothing and footwear. It sells TurboDown jackets, Millenium snowboard pants, Sorel® snow boots,

Bugaboots™, rainwear, and anything else you might need to protect you from the elements. We call amounts earned on the sale of these products **revenues**. **Revenue** is the increase in assets or decrease in liabilities resulting from the sale of goods or the performance of services in the normal course of business. For example, Columbia records revenue when it sells a footwear product.

Revenues arise from different sources and are identified by various names depending on the nature of the business. For instance, Columbia's primary source of revenue is the sale of sportswear. However, it also generates interest revenue on debt securities held as investments. Sources of revenue common to many businesses are **sales revenue**, **service revenue**, and **interest revenue**.

The company purchases its longer-lived assets through investing activities as described earlier. Other assets with shorter lives, however, result from operating activities. For example, **supplies** are assets used in day-to-day operations. Goods available for future sales to customers are assets called **inventory**. Also, if Columbia sells goods to a customer and does not receive cash immediately, then the company has a right to expect payment from that customer in the near future. This right to receive money in the future is called an **account receivable**.

Before Columbia can sell a single Sorel® boot, it must purchase wool, rubber, leather, metal lace loops, laces, and other materials. It then must process, wrap, and ship the finished product. It also incurs costs like salaries, rents, and utilities. All of these costs, referred to as **expenses**, are necessary to produce and sell the product. In accounting language, **expenses** are the cost of assets consumed or services used in the process of generating revenues.

Expenses take many forms and are identified by various names depending on the type of asset consumed or service used. For example, Columbia keeps track of these types of expenses: **cost of goods sold** (such as the cost of materials), **selling expenses** (such as the cost of salespersons' salaries), **marketing expenses** (such as the cost of advertising), **administrative expenses** (such as the salaries of administrative staff, and telephone and heating costs incurred at the corporate office), **interest expense** (amounts of interest paid on various debts), and **income taxes** (corporate taxes paid to the government).

Columbia may also have liabilities arising from these expenses. For example, it may purchase goods on credit from suppliers. The obligations to pay for these goods are called **accounts payable**. Additionally, Columbia may have **interest payable** on the outstanding amounts owed to the bank. It may also have **wages payable** to its employees and **sales taxes payable**, **property taxes payable**, and **income taxes payable** to the government.

Columbia compares the revenues of a period with the expenses of that period to determine whether it earned a profit. When revenues exceed expenses, **net income** results. When expenses exceed revenues, a **net loss** results.

DO IT! 2 Business Activities

Classify each item as an asset, liability, common stock, revenue, or expense.

1. Cost of renting property.
2. Truck purchased.
3. Notes payable.
4. Issuance of ownership shares.
5. Amount earned from performing service.
6. Amounts owed to suppliers.

Action Plan

✔ Classify each item based on its economic characteristics. Proper classification of items is critical if accounting is to provide useful information.

SOLUTION

1. Cost of renting property: Expense.
2. Truck purchased: Asset.

3. Notes payable: Liabilities.
4. Issuance of ownership shares: Common stock.
5. Amount earned from performing service: Revenue.
6. Amounts owed to suppliers: Liabilities.

Related exercise material: **BE1-3,**  **1-2,** and **E1-3.**

LEARNING OBJECTIVE 3

Describe the four financial statements and how they are prepared.

Assets, liabilities, expenses, and revenues are of interest to users of accounting information. This information is arranged in the format of four different **financial statements**, which form the backbone of financial accounting:

- To show how successfully your business performed during a period of time, you report its revenues and expenses in an **income statement**.
- To indicate how much of previous income was distributed to you and the other owners of your business in the form of dividends, and how much was retained in the business to allow for future growth, you present a **retained earnings statement**.
- To present a picture at a point in time of what your business owns (its assets) and what it owes (its liabilities), you prepare a **balance sheet**.
- To show where your business obtained cash during a period of time and how that cash was used, you present a **statement of cash flows**.

To introduce you to these statements, we have prepared the financial statements for your outdoor guide service, Sierra Corporation, after your first month of operations. To summarize, you officially started your business in Truckee, California, on October 1, 2017. Sierra provides guide services in the Lake Tahoe area of the Sierra Nevada mountains. Its promotional materials describe outdoor day trips, such as rafting, snowshoeing, and hiking, as well as multi-day backcountry experiences. To minimize your initial investment, at this point the company has limited outdoor equipment for customer use. Instead, your customers either bring their own equipment or rent equipment through local outfitters. The financial statements for Sierra's first month of business are provided in the following pages.

INTERNATIONAL NOTE
The primary types of financial statements required by International Financial Reporting Standards (IFRS) and U.S. generally accepted accounting principles (GAAP) are the same. Neither IFRS nor GAAP is very specific regarding format requirements for the primary financial statements. However, in practice, some format differences do exist in presentations commonly employed by IFRS companies as compared to GAAP companies.

International Notes highlight differences between U.S. and international accounting standards.

INCOME STATEMENT

The **income statement** reports a company's revenues and expenses and resulting net income or loss for a period of time. To indicate that its income statement reports the results of operations for a **specific period of time**, Sierra dates the income statement "For the Month Ended October 31, 2017." The income statement lists the company's revenues followed by its expenses. Finally, Sierra determines the net income (or net loss) by deducting expenses from revenues. Sierra Corporation's income statement is shown in Illustration 1-4 (page 12). Congratulations, you are already showing a profit!

Why are financial statement users interested in net income? **Investors are interested in a company's past net income because it provides useful information for predicting future net income.** Investors buy and sell stock based on their beliefs about a company's future performance. If investors believe that Sierra will be successful in the future and that this will result in a higher stock price, they will

Decision Tools that are useful for business decision-making are highlighted throughout the textbook. A summary of the Decision Tools, such as the one on page 21, is provided in each chapter.

DECISION TOOLS 
The income statement helps users determine if the company's operations are profitable.

ILLUSTRATION 1-4
Sierra Corporation's income statement

SIERRA CORPORATION
Income Statement
For the Month Ended October 31, 2017

Revenues		
Service revenue		$10,600
Expenses		
Salaries and wages expense	$5,200	
Rent expense	900	
Supplies expense	1,500	
Depreciation expense	40	
Interest expense	50	
Insurance expense	50	
Total expenses		7,740
Net income		$ 2,860

▼ **HELPFUL HINT**
The financial statement heading identifies the company, the type of statement, and the time period covered. Sometimes, another line indicates the unit of measure, e.g., "in thousands" or "in millions."

ETHICS NOTE
When companies find errors in previously released income statements, they restate those numbers. Perhaps because of the increased scrutiny shortly after Sarbanes-Oxley was implemented, companies filed a record 1,195 restatements.

buy its stock. Creditors also use the income statement to predict future earnings. When a bank loans money to a company, it believes that it will be repaid in the future. If it didn't think it would be repaid, it wouldn't loan the money. Therefore, prior to making the loan the bank loan officer uses the income statement as a source of information to predict whether the company will be profitable enough to repay its loan. Thus, reporting a strong profit will make it easier for Sierra to raise additional cash either by issuing shares of stock or borrowing.

Amounts received from issuing stock are not revenues, and amounts paid out as dividends are not expenses. As a result, they are not reported on the income statement. For example, Sierra Corporation does not treat as revenue the $10,000 of cash received from issuing new stock (see Illustration 1-7), nor does it regard as a business expense the $500 of dividends paid (see Illustration 1-5).

RETAINED EARNINGS STATEMENT

If Sierra is profitable, at the end of each period it must decide what portion of profits to pay to shareholders in dividends. In theory, it could pay all of its current-period profits, but few companies do this. Why? Because they want to retain part of the profits to allow for further expansion. High-growth companies, such as Google and Facebook, often pay no dividends. **Retained earnings** is the net income retained in the corporation.

DECISION TOOLS
The retained earnings statement helps users determine the company's policy toward dividends and growth.

The **retained earnings statement** shows the amounts and causes of changes in retained earnings for a specific time period. The time period is the same as that covered by the income statement. The beginning retained earnings amount appears on the first line of the statement. Then, the company adds net income and deducts dividends to determine the retained earnings at the end of the period. If a company has a net loss, it deducts (rather than adds) that amount in the retained earnings statement. Illustration 1-5 presents Sierra Corporation's retained earnings statement.

ILLUSTRATION 1-5
Sierra Corporation's retained earnings statement

SIERRA CORPORATION
Retained Earnings Statement
For the Month Ended October 31, 2017

Retained earnings, October 1	$ 0
Add: Net income	2,860
	2,860
Less: Dividends	500
Retained earnings, October 31	$2,360

▼ **HELPFUL HINT**
The heading of this statement identifies the company, the type of statement, and the time period covered by the statement.

By monitoring the retained earnings statement, financial statement users can evaluate dividend payment practices. Some investors seek companies, such as Dow Chemical, that have a history of paying high dividends. Other investors seek companies, such as Amazon.com, that reinvest earnings to increase the company's growth instead of paying dividends. Lenders monitor their corporate customers' dividend payments because any money paid in dividends reduces a company's ability to repay its debts.

BALANCE SHEET

The **balance sheet** reports assets and claims to assets at a specific **point** in time. Claims to assets are subdivided into two categories: claims of creditors and claims of owners. As noted earlier, claims of creditors are called **liabilities**. The owners' claim to assets is called **stockholders' equity**.

Illustration 1-6 shows the relationship among the categories on the balance sheet in equation form. This equation is referred to as the **basic accounting equation**.

DECISION TOOLS 

The balance sheet helps users determine if the company relies on debt or stockholders' equity to finance its assets.

Assets = Liabilities + Stockholders' Equity

ILLUSTRATION 1-6
Basic accounting equation

This relationship is where the name "balance sheet" comes from. Assets must balance with the claims to assets.

As you can see from looking at Sierra's balance sheet in Illustration 1-7, the balance sheet presents the company's financial position as of a specific date—in this case, October 31, 2017. It lists assets first, followed by liabilities and stockholders' equity. Stockholders' equity is comprised of two parts: (1) common stock and (2) retained earnings. As noted earlier, common stock results when the company

ALTERNATIVE TERMINOLOGY
Liabilities are also referred to as *debt*.

ILLUSTRATION 1-7
Sierra Corporation's balance sheet

▼ HELPFUL HINT
The heading of a balance sheet must identify the company, the statement, and the date.

SIERRA CORPORATION
Balance Sheet
October 31, 2017

Assets		
Cash		$15,200
Accounts receivable		200
Supplies		1,000
Prepaid insurance		550
Equipment, net		4,960
Total assets		$21,910
Liabilities and Stockholders' Equity		
Liabilities		
Notes payable	$ 5,000	
Accounts payable	2,500	
Unearned service revenue	800	
Salaries and wages payable	1,200	
Interest payable	50	
Total liabilities		$ 9,550
Stockholders' equity		
Common stock	10,000	
Retained earnings	2,360	
Total stockholders' equity		12,360
Total liabilities and stockholders' equity		$21,910

sells new shares of stock; retained earnings is the net income retained in the corporation. Sierra has common stock of $10,000 and retained earnings of $2,360, for total stockholders' equity of $12,360.

Creditors analyze a company's balance sheet to determine the likelihood that they will be repaid. They carefully evaluate the nature of the company's assets and liabilities. In operating the Sierra Corporation guide service, the balance sheet will be used to determine whether cash on hand is sufficient for immediate cash needs. The balance sheet will also be used to evaluate the relationship between debt and stockholders' equity to determine whether the company has a satisfactory proportion of debt and common stock financing.

STATEMENT OF CASH FLOWS

The primary purpose of a **statement of cash flows** is to provide financial information about the cash receipts and cash payments of a business for a specific period of time. To help investors, creditors, and others in their analysis of a company's cash position, the statement of cash flows reports the cash effects of a company's **operating**, **investing**, and **financing** activities. In addition, the statement shows the net increase or decrease in cash during the period, and the amount of cash at the end of the period.

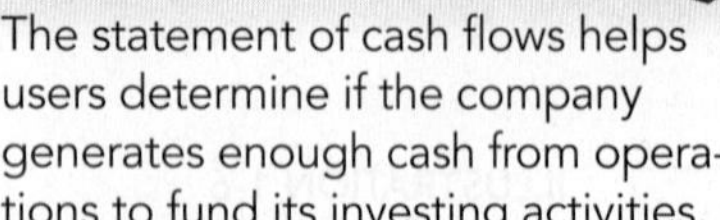

The statement of cash flows helps users determine if the company generates enough cash from operations to fund its investing activities.

Users are interested in the statement of cash flows because they want to know what is happening to a company's most important resource. The statement of cash flows provides answers to these simple but important questions:

- Where did cash come from during the period?
- How was cash used during the period?
- What was the change in the cash balance during the period?

The statement of cash flows for Sierra, in Illustration 1-8, shows that cash increased $15,200 during the month. This increase resulted because operating activities (services to clients) increased cash $5,700, and financing activities increased cash $14,500. Investing activities used $5,000 of cash for the purchase of equipment.

ILLUSTRATION 1-8
Sierra Corporation's statement of cash flows

SIERRA CORPORATION
Statement of Cash Flows
For the Month Ended October 31, 2017

Cash flows from operating activities		
Cash receipts from operating activities	$11,200	
Cash payments for operating activities	(5,500)	
Net cash provided by operating activities		$ 5,700
Cash flows from investing activities		
Purchased office equipment	(5,000)	
Net cash used by investing activities		(5,000)
Cash flows from financing activities		
Issuance of common stock	10,000	
Issuance of note payable	5,000	
Payment of dividend	(500)	
Net cash provided by financing activities		14,500
Net increase in cash		15,200
Cash at beginning of period		0
Cash at end of period		$15,200

▼ **HELPFUL HINT**
The heading of this statement identifies the company, the type of statement, and the time period covered by the statement. Negative numbers are shown in parentheses.

PEOPLE, PLANET, AND PROFIT INSIGHT

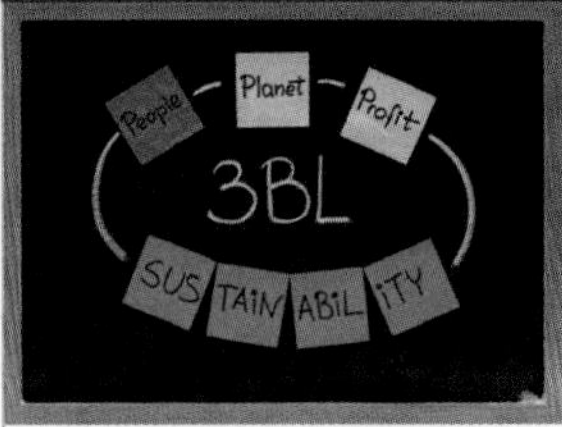

© Marek Uliasz/iStockphoto

Beyond Financial Statements

Should we expand our corporate reports beyond the income statement, retained earnings statement, balance sheet, and statement of cash flows? Some believe we should take into account ecological and social performance, in addition to financial results, in evaluating a company. The argument is that a company's responsibility lies with anyone who is influenced by its actions. In other words, a company should be interested in benefiting many different parties, instead of only maximizing stockholders' interests.

A socially responsible business does not exploit or endanger any group of individuals. It follows fair trade practices, provides safe environments for workers, and bears responsibility for environmental damage. Granted, measurement of these factors is difficult. How to report this information is also controversial. But many interesting and useful efforts are underway. Throughout this textbook, we provide additional insights into how companies are attempting to meet the challenge of measuring and reporting their contributions to society, as well as their financial results, to stockholders.

Why might a company's stockholders be interested in its environmental and social performance? (Go to WileyPLUS for this answer and additional questions.)

INTERRELATIONSHIPS OF STATEMENTS

Illustration 1-9 (page 16) shows the financial statements of Sierra Corporation. Because the results on some financial statements become inputs to other statements, the statements are interrelated. These interrelationships can be seen in Sierra's financial statements, as follows.

1. The retained earnings statement uses the results of the income statement. Sierra reported net income of $2,860 for the period. Net income is added to the beginning amount of retained earnings to determine ending retained earnings.
2. The balance sheet and retained earnings statement are also interrelated. Sierra reports the ending amount of $2,360 on the retained earnings statement as the retained earnings amount on the balance sheet.
3. Finally, the statement of cash flows relates to information on the balance sheet. The statement of cash flows shows how the Cash account changed during the period. It shows the amount of cash at the beginning of the period, the sources and uses of cash during the period, and the $15,200 of cash at the end of the period. The ending amount of cash shown on the statement of cash flows must agree with the amount of cash on the balance sheet.

Study these interrelationships carefully. **To prepare financial statements, you must understand the sequence in which these amounts are determined and how each statement impacts the next.**

ILLUSTRATION 1-9
Sierra Corporation's financial statements

▼ HELPFUL HINT
Note that final sums are double-underlined.

▼ HELPFUL HINT
The arrows in this illustration show interrelationships of the four financial statements.

▼ HELPFUL HINT
Negative amounts are presented in parentheses.

SIERRA CORPORATION
Income Statement
For the Month Ended October 31, 2017

Revenues		
Service revenue		$10,600
Expenses		
Salaries expense	$5,200	
Rent expense	900	
Supplies expense	1,500	
Depreciation expense	40	
Interest expense	50	
Insurance expense	50	
Total expenses		7,740
Net income		$ 2,860

SIERRA CORPORATION
Retained Earnings Statement
For the Month Ended October 31, 2017

Retained earnings, October 1	$ 0
Add: Net income	2,860
	2,860
Less: Dividends	500
Retained earnings, October 31	$ 2,360

SIERRA CORPORATION
Balance Sheet
October 31, 2017

Assets		
Cash		$15,200
Accounts receivable		200
Advertising supplies		1,000
Prepaid insurance		550
Equipment, net		4,960
Total assets		$21,910
Liabilities and Stockholders' Equity		
Liabilities		
Notes payable	$ 5,000	
Accounts payable	2,500	
Unearned service revenue	800	
Salaries and wages payable	1,200	
Interest payable	50	
Total liabilities		$ 9,550
Stockholders' equity		
Common stock	10,000	
Retained earnings	2,360	
Total stockholders' equity		12,360
Total liabilities and stockholders' equity		$21,910

SIERRA CORPORATION
Statement of Cash Flows
For the Month Ended October 31, 2017

Cash flows from operating activities		
Cash receipts from operating activities	$11,200	
Cash payments for operating activities	(5,500)	
Net cash provided by operating activities		$ 5,700
Cash flows from investing activities		
Purchased office equipment	(5,000)	
Net cash used by investing activities		(5,000)
Cash flows from financing activities		
Issuance of common stock	10,000	
Issued note payable	5,000	
Payment of dividend	(500)	
Net cash provided by financing activities		14,500
Net increase in cash		15,200
Cash at beginning of period		0
Cash at end of period		$15,200

DO IT! 3a Financial Statements

CSU Corporation began operations on January 1, 2017. The following information is available for CSU on December 31, 2017:

Accounts receivable	1,800	Retained earnings	?	Supplies expense	200
Accounts payable	2,000	Equipment	16,000	Cash	1,400
Rent expense	9,000	Insurance expense	1,000	Dividends	600
Notes payable	5,000	Service revenue	17,000		
Common stock	10,000	Supplies	4,000		

Prepare an income statement, a retained earnings statement, and a balance sheet.

Action Plan

✔ Report the revenues and expenses for a period of time in an income statement.

✔ Show the amounts and causes (net income and dividends) of changes in retained earnings during the period in the retained earnings statement.

✔ Present the assets and claims to those assets (liabilities and equity) at a specific point in time in the balance sheet.

SOLUTION

CSU CORPORATION
Income Statement
For the Year Ended December 31, 2017

Revenues		
Service revenue		$17,000
Expenses		
Rent expense	$9,000	
Insurance expense	1,000	
Supplies expense	200	
Total expenses		10,200
Net income		$ 6,800

CSU CORPORATION
Retained Earnings Statement
For the Year Ended December 31, 2017

Retained earnings, January 1	$ 0
Add: Net income	6,800
	6,800
Less: Dividends	600
Retained earnings, December 31	$6,200

CSU CORPORATION
Balance Sheet
December 31, 2017

Assets		
Cash		$ 1,400
Accounts receivable		1,800
Supplies		4,000
Equipment		16,000
Total assets		$23,200
Liabilities and Stockholders' Equity		
Liabilities		
Notes payable	$ 5,000	
Accounts payable	2,000	
Total liabilities		$ 7,000
Stockholders' equity		
Common stock	10,000	
Retained earnings	6,200	
Total stockholders' equity		16,200
Total liabilities and stockholders' equity		$23,200

Related exercise material: **BE1-5, BE1-6, BE1-7, BE1-8, BE1-9, BE1-10, DO IT! 1-3a, E1-4, E1-5, E1-6, E1-7, E1-8, E1-9, E1-10, E1-11, and E1-14.**

OTHER ELEMENTS OF AN ANNUAL REPORT

Publicly traded U.S. companies must provide shareholders with an **annual report**. The annual report always includes the financial statements introduced in this chapter. The annual report also includes other important information such as a management discussion and analysis section, notes to the financial statements, and an independent auditor's report. No analysis of a company's financial situation and performance is complete without a review of these items.

Management Discussion and Analysis

The **management discussion and analysis (MD&A)** section presents management's views on the company's **ability to pay near-term obligations, its ability to fund operations and expansion, and its results of operations**. Management must highlight favorable or unfavorable trends and identify significant events and uncertainties that affect these three factors. This discussion obviously involves a number of subjective estimates and opinions. A brief excerpt from the MD&A section of Columbia Sportswear's annual report, which addresses its liquidity requirements, is presented in Illustration 1-10.

ILLUSTRATION 1-10
Columbia Sportswear's management discussion and analysis

COLUMBIA SPORTSWEAR COMPANY
Management's Discussion and Analysis of
Seasonality and Variability of Business

Our operations are affected by seasonal trends typical in the outdoor apparel and footwear industry and have historically resulted in higher sales and profits in the third and fourth calendar quarters. This pattern has resulted primarily from the timing of shipments of fall season products to wholesale customers in the third and fourth quarters and proportionally higher sales in our direct-to-consumer operations in the fourth quarter, combined with an expense base that is spread more evenly throughout the year. We believe that our liquidity requirements for at least the next 12 months will be adequately covered by existing cash, cash provided by operations and existing short-term borrowing arrangements.

Notes to the Financial Statements

Explanatory notes and supporting schedules accompany every set of financial statements and are an integral part of the statements. The **notes to the financial statements** clarify the financial statements and provide additional detail. Information in the notes does not have to be quantifiable (numeric). Examples of notes are descriptions of the significant accounting policies and methods used in preparing the statements, explanations of uncertainties and contingencies, and various statistics and details too voluminous to be included in the statements. The notes are essential to understanding a company's operating performance and financial position.

Illustration 1-11 is an excerpt from the notes to Columbia Sportswear's financial statements. It describes the methods that the company uses to account for revenues.

ILLUSTRATION 1-11
Notes to Columbia Sportswear's financial statements

COLUMBIA SPORTSWEAR COMPANY
Notes to Financial Statements
Revenue Recognition

We record wholesale, distributor, e-commerce and licensed product revenues when title passes and the risks and rewards of ownership have passed to the customer. Title generally passes upon shipment to, or upon receipt by, the customer depending on the terms of sale with the customer. Retail store revenues are recorded at the time of sale.

Auditor's Report

An **auditor's report** is prepared by an independent outside auditor. It states the auditor's opinion as to the fairness of the presentation of the financial position and results of operations and their conformance with generally accepted accounting principles.

An **auditor** is an accounting professional who conducts an independent examination of a company's financial statements. Only accountants who meet certain criteria and thereby attain the designation **certified public accountant (CPA)** may perform audits. If the auditor is satisfied that the financial statements provide a fair representation of the company's financial position and results of operations in accordance with generally accepted accounting principles, then the auditor expresses an **unqualified opinion**. If the auditor expresses anything other than an unqualified opinion, then readers should only use the financial statements with caution. That is, without an unqualified opinion, we cannot have complete confidence that the financial statements give an accurate picture of the company's financial health. For example, recently Blockbuster, Inc.'s auditor stated that its financial situation raised "substantial doubt about the Company's ability to continue as a going concern."

Illustration 1-12 is an excerpt from the auditor's report from Columbia Sportswear's 2014 annual report. Columbia received an unqualified opinion from its auditor, Deloitte & Touche.

Real World

COLUMBIA SPORTSWEAR COMPANY

Excerpt from Auditor's Report

In our opinion, such consolidated financial statements present fairly, in all material respects, the financial position of Columbia Sportswear Company and subsidiaries as of December 31, 2014 and 2013, and the results of their operations and their cash flows for each of the three years in the period ended December 31, 2014, in conformity with accounting principles generally accepted in the United States of America. Also, in our opinion, such financial statement schedules, when considered in relation to the basic consolidated financial statements taken as a whole, presents fairly, in all material respects, the information set forth therein.

ILLUSTRATION 1-12
Excerpt from auditor's report on Columbia Sportswear's financial statements

DO IT! 3b Components of Annual Reports

State whether each of the following items is most closely associated with the management discussion and analysis (MD&A), the notes to the financial statements, or the auditor's report.

1. Descriptions of significant accounting policies.
2. Unqualified opinion.
3. Explanations of uncertainties and contingencies.
4. Description of ability to fund operations and expansion.
5. Description of results of operations.
6. Certified public accountant (CPA).

SOLUTION

1. Descriptions of significant accounting policies: Notes.
2. Unqualified opinion: Auditor's report.
3. Explanations of uncertainties and contingencies: Notes.
4. Description of ability to fund operations and expansion: MD&A.
5. Description of results of operations: MD&A.
6. Certified public accountant (CPA): Auditor's report.

Related exercise material: **BE1-11, DO IT! 1-3b,** and **E1-17.**

Action Plan

✔ Realize that financial statements provide information about a company's performance and financial position.

✔ Be familiar with the other elements of the annual report in order to gain a fuller understanding of a company.

USING DECISION TOOLS—VF CORPORATION

There is a good chance that you may have never heard of VF Corporation. There is also a very good chance that you are wearing one of VF's products right now. VF owns North Face, Lee, Vans, Nautica, Wrangler, Timberland, and numerous other brands. VF is a direct competitor to Columbia Sportswear. Suppose that you are considering investing in shares of VF's common stock.

INSTRUCTIONS

Answer these questions related to your decision whether to invest.

(a) What financial statements should you evaluate?

(b) What should these financial statements tell you?

(c) Do you care if the financial statements have been audited? Explain.

(d) Appendix B at the end of this textbook contains financial statements for Columbia, and Appendix C contains those for VF. You can make many comparisons between Columbia and VF in terms of their respective results from operations and financial position. Compare their respective total assets, total revenues, and net cash provided by operating activities.

SOLUTION

(a) Before you invest, you should evaluate the income statement, retained earnings statement, balance sheet, and statement of cash flows.

(b) You would probably be most interested in the income statement because it tells about past performance and thus gives an indication of future performance. The retained earnings statement provides a record of the company's dividend history. The balance sheet reveals the relationship between assets and liabilities. The statement of cash flows reveals where the company is getting and spending its cash. This is especially important for a company that wants to grow.

(c) You would want audited financial statements. These statements indicate that a CPA (certified public accountant) has examined and expressed an opinion that the statements present fairly the financial position and results of operations of the company. Investors and creditors should not make decisions without studying audited financial statements.

(d) Many interesting comparisons can be made between the two companies (all numbers are in thousands). Columbia is smaller, with total assets of $1,792,209 versus $9,980,140 for VF, and it has lower revenue—$2,100,590 versus $12,282,161 for VF. In addition, Columbia's net cash provided by operating activities of $185,783 is less than VF's $1,697,629. However, while useful, these basic measures are not enough to determine whether one company is a better investment than the other. In later chapters, you will learn tools that will allow you to compare the relative profitability and financial health of these and other companies.

__Using Decision Tools__ comprehensive exercises ask you to apply business information and the decision tools presented in the chapter. Most of these exercises are based on the companies highlighted in the Feature Story.

The __Review and Practice__ section provides opportunities for students to review key concepts and terms as well as complete multiple-choice questions, exercises, and a comprehensive problem. Detailed solutions are also included.

REVIEW AND PRACTICE

▶ LEARNING OBJECTIVES REVIEW

1 Identify the forms of business organization and the uses of accounting information. A sole proprietorship is a business owned by one person. A partnership is a business owned by two or more people associated as partners. A corporation is a separate legal entity for which evidence of ownership is provided by shares of stock.

Internal users are managers who need accounting information to plan, organize, and run business operations. The primary external users are investors and creditors. Investors (stockholders) use accounting information to decide whether to buy, hold, or sell shares of a company's stock. Creditors (suppliers and bankers) use accounting information to assess the risk of granting credit or loaning money to a business. Other groups who have an indirect interest in a business are taxing authorities, customers, labor unions, and regulatory agencies.

2 Explain the three principal types of business activity. Financing activities involve collecting the necessary funds to support the business. Investing activities involve acquiring the resources necessary to run the business. Operating activities involve putting the resources of the business into action to generate a profit.

3 Describe the four financial statements and how they are prepared. An income statement presents the revenues and expenses of a company for a specific period of time. A retained earnings statement summarizes the changes in retained earnings that have occurred for a specific period of time. A balance sheet reports the assets, liabilities, and stockholders' equity of a business at a specific date. A statement of cash flows summarizes information concerning the cash inflows (receipts) and outflows (payments) for a specific period of time.

Assets are resources owned by a business. Liabilities are the debts and obligations of the business. Liabilities represent claims of creditors on the assets of the business. Stockholders' equity represents the claims of owners on the assets of the business. Stockholders' equity is subdivided into two parts: common stock and retained earnings. The basic accounting equation is Assets = Liabilities + Stockholders' Equity.

Within the annual report, the management discussion and analysis provides management's interpretation of the company's results and financial position as well as a discussion of plans for the future. Notes to the financial statements provide additional explanation or detail to make the financial statements more informative. The auditor's report expresses an opinion as to whether the financial statements present fairly the company's results of operations and financial position.

DECISION TOOLS REVIEW

DECISION CHECKPOINTS	INFO NEEDED FOR DECISION	TOOL TO USE FOR DECISION	HOW TO EVALUATE RESULTS
Are the company's operations profitable?	Income statement	The income statement reports a company's revenues and expenses and resulting net income or loss for a period of time.	If the company's revenues exceed its expenses, it will report net income; otherwise, it will report a net loss.
What is the company's policy toward dividends and growth?	Retained earnings statement	The retained earnings statement reports how much of this year's income the company paid out in dividends to shareholders.	A company striving for rapid growth will pay a low (or no) dividend.
Does the company rely primarily on debt or stockholders' equity to finance its assets?	Balance sheet	The balance sheet reports the company's resources and claims to those resources. There are two types of claims: liabilities and stockholders' equity.	Compare the amount of debt versus the amount of stockholders' equity to determine whether the company relies more on creditors or owners for its financing.
Does the company generate sufficient cash from operations to fund its investing activities?	Statement of cash flows	The statement of cash flows shows the amount of net cash provided or used by operating activities, investing activities, and financing activities.	Compare the amount of net cash provided by operating activities with the amount of net cash used by investing activities. Any deficiency in cash from operating activities must be made up with cash from financing activities.

GLOSSARY REVIEW

Accounting The information system that identifies, records, and communicates the economic events of an organization to interested users. (p. 5).

Annual report A report prepared by corporate management that presents financial information including financial statements, a management discussion and analysis section, notes, and an independent auditor's report. (p. 18).

Assets Resources owned by a business. (p. 9).

Auditor's report A report prepared by an independent outside auditor stating the auditor's opinion as to the fairness of the presentation of the financial position and results of operations and their conformance with generally accepted accounting principles. (p. 19).

Balance sheet A financial statement that reports the assets and claims to those assets at a specific point in time. (p. 13).

Basic accounting equation Assets = Liabilities + Stockholders' Equity. (p. 13).

Certified public accountant (CPA) An individual who has met certain criteria and is thus allowed to perform audits of corporations. (p. 19).

Common stock Term used to describe the total amount paid in by stockholders for the shares they purchase. (p. 9).

Corporation A business organized as a separate legal entity owned by stockholders. (p. 4).

Dividends Payments of cash from a corporation to its stockholders. (p. 9).

Expenses The cost of assets consumed or services used in the process of generating revenues. (p. 10).

Income statement A financial statement that reports a company's revenues and expenses and resulting net income or net loss for a specific period of time. (p. 11).

Liabilities Amounts owed to creditors in the form of debts and other obligations. (p. 9).

Management discussion and analysis (MD&A) A section of the annual report that presents management's views on the company's ability to pay near-term obligations, its ability to fund operations and expansion, and its results of operations. (p. 18).

Net income The amount by which revenues exceed expenses. (p. 10).

Net loss The amount by which expenses exceed revenues. (p. 10).

Notes to the financial statements Notes clarify information presented in the financial statements and provide additional detail. (p. 18).

Partnership A business owned by two or more persons associated as partners. (p. 4).

Retained earnings The amount of net income retained in the corporation. (p. 12).

Retained earnings statement A financial statement that summarizes the amounts and causes of changes in retained earnings for a specific time period. (p. 12).

Revenue The increase in assets or decrease in liabilities resulting from the sale of goods or the performance of services in the normal course of business. (p. 10).

Sarbanes-Oxley Act (SOX) Regulations passed by Congress to reduce unethical corporate behavior. (p. 7).

Sole proprietorship A business owned by one person. (p. 4).

Statement of cash flows A financial statement that provides financial information about the cash receipts and cash payments of a business for a specific period of time. (p. 14).

Stockholders' equity The owners' claim to assets. (p. 13).

PRACTICE MULTIPLE-CHOICE QUESTIONS

(LO 1) **1.** Which is **not** one of the three forms of business organization?
(a) Sole proprietorship. (c) Partnership.
(b) Creditorship. (d) Corporation.

(LO 1) **2.** Which is an advantage of corporations relative to partnerships and sole proprietorships?
(a) Lower taxes.
(b) Harder to transfer ownership.
(c) Reduced legal liability for investors.
(d) Most common form of organization.

(LO 1) **3.** Which statement about users of accounting information is **incorrect**?
(a) Management is considered an internal user.
(b) Taxing authorities are considered external users.
(c) Present creditors are considered external users.
(d) Regulatory authorities are considered internal users.

(LO 1) **4.** Which of the following did **not** result from the Sarbanes-Oxley Act?
(a) Top management must now certify the accuracy of financial information.
(b) Penalties for fraudulent activity increased.
(c) Independence of auditors increased.
(d) Tax rates on corporations increased.

(LO 2) **5.** Which is **not** one of the three primary business activities?
(a) Financing. (c) Advertising.
(b) Operating. (d) Investing.

(LO 2) **6.** Which of the following is an example of a financing activity?
(a) Issuing shares of common stock.
(b) Selling goods on account.
(c) Buying delivery equipment.
(d) Buying inventory.

7. Net income will result during a time period when: (LO 2)
(a) assets exceed liabilities.
(b) assets exceed revenues.
(c) expenses exceed revenues.
(d) revenues exceed expenses.

8. The financial statements for Macias Corporation contained the following information. (LO 3)

Accounts receivable	$ 5,000
Sales revenue	75,000
Cash	15,000
Salaries and wages expense	20,000
Rent expense	10,000

What was Macias Corporation's net income?
(a) $60,000. (c) $65,000.
(b) $15,000. (d) $45,000.

9. What section of a statement of cash flows indicates the cash spent on new equipment during the past accounting period? (LO 3)
(a) The investing activities section.
(b) The operating activities section.
(c) The financing activities section.
(d) The statement of cash flows does not give this information.

10. Which statement presents information as of a specific point in time? (LO 3)
(a) Income statement.
(b) Balance sheet.
(c) Statement of cash flows.
(d) Retained earnings statement.

11. Which financial statement reports assets, liabilities, and stockholders' equity? (LO 3)
(a) Income statement.
(b) Retained earnings statement.

(c) Balance sheet.
(d) Statement of cash flows.

(LO 3) **12.** Stockholders' equity represents:
(a) claims of creditors.
(b) claims of employees.
(c) the difference between revenues and expenses.
(d) claims of owners.

(LO 3) **13.** As of December 31, 2017, Rockford Corporation has assets of $3,500 and stockholders' equity of $1,500. What are the liabilities for Rockford Corporation as of December 31, 2017?
(a) $1,500. (c) $2,500.
(b) $1,000. (d) $2,000.

14. The element of a corporation's annual report that describes the corporation's accounting methods is/are the: (LO 3)
(a) notes to the financial statements.
(b) management discussion and analysis.
(c) auditor's report.
(d) income statement.

15. The element of the annual report that presents an opinion regarding the fairness of the presentation of the financial position and results of operations is/are the: (LO 3)
(a) income statement.
(b) auditor's opinion.
(c) balance sheet.
(d) comparative statements.

SOLUTIONS

1. **(b)** Creditorship is not a form of business organization. The other choices are incorrect because (a) sole proprietorship, (c) partnership, and (d) corporation are all forms of business organization.
2. **(c)** An advantage of corporations is that investors are not personally liable for debts of the business. The other choices are incorrect because (a) lower taxes, (b) harder to transfer ownership, and (d) most common form of organization are not true of corporations.
3. **(d)** Regulatory authorities are considered external, not internal, users. The other choices are true statements.
4. **(d)** The Sarbanes-Oxley Act (SOX) was created to reduce unethical corporate behavior and decrease the likelihood of future corporate scandals, not to address tax rates. The other choices are incorrect because (a) top management must now certify the accuracy of financial information, (b) penalties for fraudulent activity increased, and (c) increased independence of auditors all resulted from SOX.
5. **(c)** Advertising is a type of operating activity. The other choices are incorrect because (a) financing, (b) operating, and (d) investing are the three primary business activities.
6. **(a)** Issuing shares of common stock is a financing activity. The other choices are incorrect because (b) selling goods on account is an operating activity, (c) buying delivery equipment is an investing activity, and (d) buying inventory is an operating activity.
7. **(d)** When a company earns more revenues than expenses, it will report net income during a time period. The other choices are incorrect because (a) assets and liabilities are on the balance sheet, not the income statement; (b) assets are on the balance sheet, not the income statement; and (c) net income results when revenues exceed expenses, not when expenses exceed revenues.
8. **(d)** Net income = Sales revenue ($75,000) − Salaries and wages expense ($20,000) − Rent expense ($10,000) = $45,000. The other choices are therefore incorrect.
9. **(a)** The investing activities section of the statement of cash flows provides information about property, plant, and equipment accounts, not (b) the operating activities section or (c) the financing activities section. Choice (d) is incorrect as the statement of cash flows does provide this information.
10. **(b)** The balance sheet presents information as of a specific point in time. The other choices are incorrect because the (a) income statement, (c) statement of cash flows, and (d) retained earnings statement all cover a period of time.
11. **(c)** The balance sheet is a formal presentation of the accounting equation, such that Assets = Liabilities + Stockholders' Equity, not the (a) income statement, (b) retained earnings statement, or (d) statement of cash flows.
12. **(d)** Stockholders' equity represents claims of owners. The other choices are incorrect because (a) claims of creditors and (b) claims of employees are liabilities. Choice (c) is incorrect because the difference between revenues and expenses is net income.
13. **(d)** Using the accounting equation, liabilities can be computed by subtracting stockholders' equity from assets, or $3,500 − $1,500 = $2,000, not (a) $1,500, (b) $1,000, or (c) $2,500.
14. **(a)** The corporation's accounting methods are described in the notes to the financial statements, not in the (b) management discussion and analysis, (c) auditor's report, or (d) income statement.
15. **(b)** The element of the annual report that presents an opinion regarding the fairness of the presentation of the financial position and results of operations is the auditor's opinion, not the (a) income statement, (c) balance sheet, or (d) comparative statements.

PRACTICE EXERCISES

Prepare an income statement.
(LO 3)

1. The following items and amounts were taken from Ricardo Inc.'s 2017 income statement and balance sheet.

Cash	$ 84,700	Inventory	$ 64,618
Retained earnings	123,192	Accounts receivable	88,419
Cost of goods sold	483,854	Sales revenue	693,485
Salaries and wages expense	125,000	Income taxes payable	6,499
Prepaid insurance	7,818	Accounts payable	49,384
Interest expense	994	Service revenue	8,998

INSTRUCTIONS

Prepare an income statement for Ricardo Inc. for the year ended December 31, 2017.

SOLUTION

1.

RICARDO INC. Income Statement For the Year Ended December 31, 2017		
Revenues		
Sales revenue	$693,485	
Service revenue	8,998	
Total revenues		$702,483
Expenses		
Cost of goods sold	483,854	
Salaries and wages expense	125,000	
Interest expense	994	
Total expenses		609,848
Net income		$ 92,635

Compute net income and prepare a balance sheet.
(LO 3)

2. Cozy Bear is a private camping ground near the Mountain Home Recreation Area. It has compiled the following financial information as of December 31, 2017.

Service revenue (from camping fees)	$148,000	Dividends	$ 9,000
Sales revenue (from general store)	35,000	Notes payable	50,000
Accounts payable	16,000	Expenses during 2017	135,000
Cash	18,500	Supplies	12,500
Equipment	129,000	Common stock	40,000
		Retained earnings (1/1/2017)	15,000

INSTRUCTIONS

(a) Determine net income from Cozy Bear for 2017.

(b) Prepare a retained earnings statement and a balance sheet for Cozy Bear as of December 31, 2017.

SOLUTION

2. (a)

Service revenue	$148,000
Sales revenue	35,000
Total revenue	183,000
Expenses	135,000
Net income	$ 48,000

(b)

COZY BEAR Retained Earnings Statement For the Year Ended December 31, 2017	
Retained earnings, January 1	$15,000
Add: Net income	48,000
	63,000
Less: Dividends	9,000
Retained earnings, December 31	$54,000

COZY BEAR Balance Sheet December 31, 2017		
Assets		
Cash		$ 18,500
Supplies		12,500
Equipment		129,000
Total assets		$160,000
Liabilities and Stockholders' Equity		
Liabilities		
Notes payable	$50,000	
Accounts payable	16,000	
Total liabilities		$ 66,000
Stockholders' equity		
Common stock	40,000	
Retained earnings	54,000	
Total stockholders' equity		94,000
Total liabilities and stockholders' equity		$160,000

▶ PRACTICE PROBLEM

Prepare financial statements.
(LO 3)

Jeff Andringa, a former college hockey player, quit his job and started Ice Camp, a hockey camp for kids ages 8 to 18. Eventually, he would like to open hockey camps nationwide. Jeff has asked you to help him prepare financial statements at the end of his first year of operations. He relates the following facts about his business activities.

In order to get the business off the ground, Jeff decided to incorporate. He sold shares of common stock to a few close friends, as well as bought some of the shares himself. He initially raised $25,000 through the sale of these shares. In addition, the company took out a $10,000 loan at a local bank.

Ice Camp purchased, for $12,000 cash, a bus for transporting kids. The company also bought hockey goals and other miscellaneous equipment with $1,500 cash. The company earned camp tuition during the year of $100,000 but had collected only $80,000 of this amount. Thus, at the end of the year, its customers still owed $20,000. The company rents time at a local rink for $50 per hour. Total rink rental costs during the year were $8,000, insurance was $10,000, salary expense was $20,000, and supplies used totaled $9,000, all of which were paid in cash. The company incurred $800 in interest expense on the bank loan, which it still owed at the end of the year.

The company paid dividends during the year of $5,000 cash. The balance in the corporate bank account at December 31, 2017, was $49,500.

INSTRUCTIONS

Using the format of the Sierra Corporation statements in this chapter, prepare an income statement, retained earnings statement, balance sheet, and statement of cash flows. (*Hint:* Prepare the statements in the order stated to take advantage of the flow of information from one statement to the next, as shown in Illustration 1-9 on page 16.)

SOLUTION

ICE CAMP
Income Statement
For the Year Ended December 31, 2017

Revenues		
Service revenue		$100,000
Expenses		
Salaries and wages expense	$20,000	
Insurance expense	10,000	
Supplies expense	9,000	
Rent expense	8,000	
Interest expense	800	
Total expenses		47,800
Net income		$ 52,200

ICE CAMP
Retained Earnings Statement
For the Year Ended December 31, 2017

Retained earnings, January 1, 2017	$ 0
Add: Net income	52,200
	52,200
Less: Dividends	5,000
Retained earnings, December 31, 2017	$ 47,200

ICE CAMP
Balance Sheet
December 31, 2017

Assets		
Cash		$ 49,500
Accounts receivable		20,000
Equipment ($12,000 + $1,500)		13,500
Total assets		$ 83,000
Liabilities and Stockholders' Equity		
Liabilities		
Notes payable	$10,000	
Interest payable	800	
Total liabilities		$ 10,800
Stockholders' equity		
Common stock	25,000	
Retained earnings	47,200	
Total stockholders' equity		72,200
Total liabilities and stockholders' equity		$ 83,000

ICE CAMP Statement of Cash Flows For the Year Ended December 31, 2017		
Cash flows from operating activities		
Cash receipts from operating activities	$80,000	
Cash payments for operating activities	(47,000)	
Net cash provided by operating activities		$33,000
Cash flows from investing activities		
Purchase of equipment	(13,500)	
Net cash used by investing activities		(13,500)
Cash flows from financing activities		
Issuance of common stock	25,000	
Issuance of notes payable	10,000	
Dividends paid	(5,000)	
Net cash provided by financing activities		30,000
Net increase in cash		49,500
Cash at beginning of period		0
Cash at end of period		$49,500

WileyPLUS Brief Exercises, DO IT! Exercises, Exercises, Problems, and many additional resources are available for practice in WileyPLUS.

The tool icon indicates that an activity employs one of the decision tools presented in the chapter. The indicates that an activity relates to a business function beyond accounting. The pencil icon indicates that an activity requires written communication.

QUESTIONS

1. What are the three basic forms of business organizations?
2. What are the advantages to a business of being formed as a corporation? What are the disadvantages?
3. What are the advantages to a business of being formed as a partnership or sole proprietorship? What are the disadvantages?
4. "Accounting is ingrained in our society and is vital to our economic system." Do you agree? Explain.
5. Who are the internal users of accounting data? How does accounting provide relevant data to the internal users?
6. Who are the external users of accounting data? Give examples.
7. What are the three main types of business activity? Give examples of each activity.
8. Listed here are some items found in the financial statements of Finzelberg. Indicate in which financial statement(s) each item would appear.
   (a) Service revenue.
   (b) Equipment.
   (c) Advertising expense.
   (d) Accounts receivable.
   (e) Common stock.
   (f) Interest payable.
9. Why would a bank want to monitor the dividend payment practices of the corporations to which it lends money?
10. "A company's net income appears directly on the income statement and the retained earnings statement, and it is included indirectly in the company's balance sheet." Do you agree? Explain.
11. What is the primary purpose of the statement of cash flows?
12. What are the three main categories of the statement of cash flows? Why do you think these categories were chosen?
13. What is retained earnings? What items increase the balance in retained earnings? What items decrease the balance in retained earnings?
14. What is the basic accounting equation?
15. (a) Define the terms assets, liabilities, and stockholders' equity.
   (b) What items affect stockholders' equity?

16. Which of these items are liabilities of White Glove Cleaning Service?
    (a) Cash.
    (b) Accounts payable.
    (c) Dividends.
    (d) Accounts receivable.
    (e) Supplies.
    (f) Equipment.
    (g) Salaries and wages payable.
    (h) Service revenue.
    (i) Rent expense.
17. How are each of the following financial statements interrelated? (a) Retained earnings statement and income statement. (b) Retained earnings statement and balance sheet. (c) Balance sheet and statement of cash flows.
18. What is the purpose of the management discussion and analysis section (MD&A)?
19. Why is it important for financial statements to receive an unqualified auditor's opinion?
20. What types of information are presented in the notes to the financial statements?
21. The accounting equation is Assets = Liabilities + Stockholders' Equity. Appendix A, at the end of this textbook, reproduces Apple's financial statements. Replacing words in the equation with dollar amounts, what is Apple's accounting equation at September 27, 2014?

BRIEF EXERCISES

Describe forms of business organization.
(LO 1), K

BE1-1 Match each of the following forms of business organization with a set of characteristics: sole proprietorship (SP), partnership (P), corporation (C).
(a) _____ Shared control, tax advantages, increased skills and resources.
(b) _____ Simple to set up and maintains control with owner.
(c) _____ Easier to transfer ownership and raise funds, no personal liability.

Identify users of accounting information.
(LO 1), K

BE1-2 Match each of the following types of evaluation with one of the listed users of accounting information.
1. Trying to determine whether the company complied with tax laws.
2. Trying to determine whether the company can pay its obligations.
3. Trying to determine whether an advertising proposal will be cost-effective.
4. Trying to determine whether the company's net income will result in a stock price increase.
5. Trying to determine whether the company should employ debt or equity financing.

(a) _____ Investors in common stock.
(b) _____ Marketing managers.
(c) _____ Creditors.
(d) _____ Chief Financial Officer.
(e) _____ Internal Revenue Service.

Classify items by activity.
(LO 2), K

BE1-3 Indicate in which part of the statement of cash flows each item would appear: operating activities (O), investing activities (I), or financing activities (F).
(a) _____ Cash received from customers.
(b) _____ Cash paid to stockholders (dividends).
(c) _____ Cash received from issuing new common stock.
(d) _____ Cash paid to suppliers.
(e) _____ Cash paid to purchase a new office building.

Determine effect of transactions on stockholders' equity.
(LO 3), C

BE1-4 Presented below are a number of transactions. Determine whether each transaction affects common stock (C), dividends (D), revenues (R), expenses (E), or does not affect stockholders' equity (NSE). Provide titles for the revenues and expenses.
(a) Costs incurred for advertising.
(b) Cash received for services performed.
(c) Costs incurred for insurance.
(d) Amounts paid to employees.
(e) Cash distributed to stockholders.
(f) Cash received in exchange for allowing the use of the company's building.
(g) Costs incurred for utilities used.
(h) Cash purchase of equipment.
(i) Cash received from investors.

Prepare a balance sheet.
(LO 3), AP

BE1-5 In alphabetical order below are balance sheet items for Karol Company at December 31, 2017. Prepare a balance sheet following the format of Illustration 1-7 (page 13).

Accounts payable	$65,000
Accounts receivable	71,000
Cash	22,000
Common stock	18,000
Retained earnings	10,000

BE1-6 Eskimo Pie Corporation markets a broad range of frozen treats, including its famous Eskimo Pie ice cream bars. The following items were taken from a recent income statement and balance sheet. In each case, identify whether the item would appear on the balance sheet (BS) or income statement (IS).

Determine where items appear on financial statements.

(LO 3), K

(a) _____ Income tax expense.
(b) _____ Inventory.
(c) _____ Accounts payable.
(d) _____ Retained earnings.
(e) _____ Equipment.
(f) _____ Sales revenue.
(g) _____ Cost of goods sold.
(h) _____ Common stock.
(i) _____ Accounts receivable.
(j) _____ Interest expense.

BE1-7 Indicate which statement you would examine to find each of the following items: income statement (IS), balance sheet (BS), retained earnings statement (RES), or statement of cash flows (SCF).

Determine proper financial statement.

(LO 3), K

(a) Revenue during the period.
(b) Supplies on hand at the end of the year.
(c) Cash received from issuing new bonds during the period.
(d) Total debts outstanding at the end of the period.

BE1-8 Use the basic accounting equation to answer these questions.

Use basic accounting equation.

(LO 3), AP

(a) The liabilities of Lantz Company are $90,000 and the stockholders' equity is $230,000. What is the amount of Lantz Company's total assets?
(b) The total assets of Salley Company are $170,000 and its stockholders' equity is $80,000. What is the amount of its total liabilities?
(c) The total assets of Brandon Co. are $800,000 and its liabilities are equal to one-fourth of its total assets. What is the amount of Brandon Co.'s stockholders' equity?

BE1-9 At the beginning of the year, Morales Company had total assets of $800,000 and total liabilities of $500,000. (Treat each item independently.)

Use basic accounting equation.

(LO 3), AP

(a) If total assets increased $150,000 during the year and total liabilities decreased $80,000, what is the amount of stockholders' equity at the end of the year?
(b) During the year, total liabilities increased $100,000 and stockholders' equity decreased $70,000. What is the amount of total assets at the end of the year?
(c) If total assets decreased $80,000 and stockholders' equity increased $110,000 during the year, what is the amount of total liabilities at the end of the year?

BE1-10 Indicate whether each of these items is an asset (A), a liability (L), or part of stockholders' equity (SE).

Identify assets, liabilities, and stockholders' equity.

(LO 3), K

(a) Accounts reçeivable.
(b) Salaries and wages payable.
(c) Equipment.
(d) Supplies.
(e) Common stock.
(f) Notes payable.

BE1-11 Which is **not** a required part of an annual report of a publicly traded company?

Determine required parts of annual report.

(LO 3), K

(a) Statement of cash flows.
(b) Notes to the financial statements.
(c) Management discussion and analysis.
(d) All of these are required.

DO IT! EXERCISES

DO IT! 1-1 Identify each of the following organizational characteristics with the business organizational form or forms with which it is associated.

Identify benefits of business organization forms.

(LO 1), C

(a) Easier to transfer ownership.
(b) Easier to raise funds.
(c) More owner control.
(d) Tax advantages.
(e) No personal legal liability.

DO IT! 1-2 Classify each item as an asset, liability, common stock, revenue, or expense.

Classify financial statement elements.

(LO 2), K

(a) Issuance of ownership shares.
(b) Land purchased.
(c) Amounts owed to suppliers.
(d) Bonds payable.
(e) Amount earned from selling a product.
(f) Cost of advertising.

Prepare financial statements.

(LO 3), AP

DO IT! 1-3a Gray Corporation began operations on January 1, 2017. The following information is available for Gray Corporation on December 31, 2017.

Accounts payable	$ 5,000	Notes payable	$ 7,000
Accounts receivable	2,000	Rent expense	10,000
Advertising expense	4,000	Retained earnings	?
Cash	3,100	Service revenue	25,000
Common stock	15,000	Supplies	1,900
Dividends	2,500	Supplies expense	1,700
Equipment	26,800		

Prepare an income statement, a retained earnings statement, and a balance sheet for Gray Corporation.

Identify components of annual reports.

(LO 3), K

DO IT! 1-3b Indicate whether each of the following items is most closely associated with the management discussion and analysis (MD&A), the notes to the financial statements, or the auditor's report.

(a) Description of ability to pay near-term obligations.
(b) Unqualified opinion.
(c) Details concerning liabilities, too voluminous to be included in the statements.
(d) Description of favorable and unfavorable trends.
(e) Certified public accountant (CPA).
(f) Descriptions of significant accounting policies.

▶ EXERCISES

Match items with descriptions.

(LO 1, 2, 3), K

E1-1 Here is a list of words or phrases discussed in this chapter:

1. Corporation	4. Partnership	7. Accounts payable
2. Creditor	5. Stockholder	8. Auditor's opinion
3. Accounts receivable	6. Common stock	

Instructions

Match each word or phrase with the best description of it.

______ (a) An expression about whether financial statements conform with generally accepted accounting principles.
______ (b) A business that raises money by issuing shares of stock.
______ (c) The portion of stockholders' equity that results from receiving cash from investors.
______ (d) Obligations to suppliers of goods.
______ (e) Amounts due from customers.
______ (f) A party to whom a business owes money.
______ (g) A party that invests in common stock.
______ (h) A business that is owned jointly by two or more individuals but does not issue stock.

Identify business activities.

(LO 2), C

E1-2 All businesses are involved in three types of activities—financing, investing, and operating. Listed below are the names and descriptions of companies in several different industries.

Abitibi Consolidated Inc.—manufacturer and marketer of newsprint
Cal State–Northridge Stdt Union—university student union
Oracle Corporation—computer software developer and retailer
Sportsco Investments—owner of the Vancouver Canucks hockey club
Grant Thornton LLP—professional accounting and business advisory firm
Southwest Airlines—low-cost airline

Instructions

(a) For each of the above companies, provide examples of (1) a financing activity, (2) an investing activity, and (3) an operating activity that the company likely engages in.
(b) Which of the activities that you identified in (a) are common to most businesses? Which activities are not?

E1-3 The Bonita Vista Golf & Country Club details the following accounts in its financial statements.

Classify accounts.

(LO 2, 3), C

Accounts payable	____
Accounts receivable	____
Equipment	____
Sales revenue	____
Service revenue	____
Inventory	____
Mortgage payable	____
Supplies expense	____
Rent expense	____
Salaries and wages expense	____

Instructions

Classify each of the above accounts as an asset (A), liability (L), stockholders' equity (SE), revenue (R), or expense (E) item.

E1-4 This information relates to Benser Co. for the year 2017.

Prepare income statement and retained earnings statement.

(LO 3), AP

Retained earnings, January 1, 2017	$67,000
Advertising expense	1,800
Dividends	6,000
Rent expense	10,400
Service revenue	58,000
Utilities expense	2,400
Salaries and wages expense	30,000

Instructions

After analyzing the data, prepare an income statement and a retained earnings statement for the year ending December 31, 2017.

E1-5 Suppose the following information was taken from the 2017 financial statements of pharmaceutical giant Merck and Co. (All dollar amounts are in millions.)

Prepare income statement and retained earnings statement.

(LO 3), AP

Retained earnings, January 1, 2017	$43,698.8
Cost of goods sold	9,018.9
Selling and administrative expenses	8,543.2
Dividends	3,597.7
Sales revenue	38,576.0
Research and development expense	5,845.0
Income tax expense	2,267.6

Instructions

(a) After analyzing the data, prepare an income statement and a retained earnings statement for the year ending December 31, 2017.

(b) Suppose that Merck decided to reduce its research and development expense by 50%. What would be the short-term implications? What would be the long-term implications? How do you think the stock market would react?

E1-6 Presented here is information for Zheng Inc. for 2017.

Prepare a retained earnings statement.

(LO 3), AP

Retained earnings, January 1	$130,000
Service revenue	400,000
Total expenses	175,000
Dividends	65,000

Instructions

Prepare the 2017 retained earnings statement for Zheng Inc.

E1-7 Consider each of the following independent situations.

Interpret financial facts.

(LO 3), AP

(a) The retained earnings statement of Lee Corporation shows dividends of $68,000, while net income for the year was $75,000.

(b) The statement of cash flows for Steele Corporation shows that cash provided by operating activities was $10,000, cash used in investing activities was $110,000, and cash provided by financing activities was $130,000.

Instructions

For each company, provide a brief discussion interpreting these financial facts. For example, you might discuss the company's financial health or its apparent growth philosophy.

Identify financial statement components and prepare income statement.

(LO 3), C

E1-8 The following items and amounts were taken from Lonyear Inc.'s 2017 income statement and balance sheet.

______	Cash	$ 84,700	______	Accounts receivable	$ 88,419
______	Retained earnings	123,192	______	Sales revenue	584,951
______	Cost of goods sold	438,458	______	Notes payable	6,499
______	Salaries and wages expense	115,131	______	Accounts payable	49,384
______	Prepaid insurance	7,818	______	Service revenue	4,806
______	Inventory	64,618	______	Interest expense	1,882

Instructions

(a) In each, case, identify on the blank line whether the item is an asset (A), liability (L), stockholders' equity (SE), revenue (R), or expense (E) item.

(b) Prepare an income statement for Lonyear Inc. for the year ended December 31, 2017.

Calculate missing amounts.

(LO 3), AN

E1-9 Here are incomplete financial statements for Donavan, Inc.

DONAVAN, INC.
Balance Sheet

Assets		**Liabilities and Stockholders' Equity**	
Cash	$ 7,000	Liabilities	
Inventory	10,000	Accounts payable	$ 5,000
Buildings	45,000	Stockholders' equity	
Total assets	$62,000	Common stock	(a)
		Retained earnings	(b)
		Total liabilities and stockholders' equity	$62,000

Income Statement

Revenues	$85,000
Cost of goods sold	(c)
Salaries and wages expense	10,000
Net income	$ (d)

Retained Earnings Statement

Beginning retained earnings	$12,000
Add: Net income	(e)
Less: Dividends	5,000
Ending retained earnings	$27,000

Instructions

Calculate the missing amounts.

Compute net income and prepare a balance sheet.

(LO 3), AP

E1-10 Otay Lakes Park is a private camping ground near the Mount Miguel Recreation Area. It has compiled the following financial information as of December 31, 2017.

Service revenue (from camping fees)	$132,000	Dividends	$ 9,000
Sales revenue (from general store)	25,000	Notes payable	50,000
Accounts payable	11,000	Expenses during 2017	126,000
Cash	8,500	Supplies	5,500
Equipment	114,000	Common stock	40,000
		Retained earnings (1/1/2017)	5,000

Instructions

(a) Determine Otay Lakes Park's net income for 2017.

(b) Prepare a retained earnings statement and a balance sheet for Otay Lakes Park as of December 31, 2017.

(c) Upon seeing this income statement, Walt Jones, the campground manager, immediately concluded, "The general store is more trouble than it is worth—let's get rid of it." The marketing director isn't so sure this is a good idea. What do you think?

Identify financial statement components and prepare an income statement.

(LO 3), AP

E1-11 Kellogg Company is the world's leading producer of ready-to-eat cereal and a leading producer of grain-based convenience foods such as frozen waffles and cereal bars. Suppose the following items were taken from its 2017 income statement and balance sheet. (All dollars are in millions.)

____	Retained earnings	$5,481	____	Bonds payable	$ 4,835
____	Cost of goods sold	7,184	____	Inventory	910
____	Selling and administrative expenses	3,390	____	Sales revenue	12,575
____	Cash	334	____	Accounts payable	1,077
____	Notes payable	44	____	Common stock	105
____	Interest expense	295	____	Income tax expense	498

Instructions

(a) In each case, identify whether the item is an asset (A), liability (L), stockholders' equity (SE), revenue (R), or expense (E).

(b) Prepare an income statement for Kellogg Company for the year ended December 31, 2017.

Prepare a statement of cash flows.

(LO 3), AP

E1-12 This information is for Williams Corporation for the year ended December 31, 2017.

Cash received from lenders	$20,000
Cash received from customers	50,000
Cash paid for new equipment	28,000
Cash dividends paid	8,000
Cash paid to suppliers	16,000
Cash balance 1/1/17	12,000

Instructions

(a) Prepare the 2017 statement of cash flows for Williams Corporation.

(b) Suppose you are one of Williams' creditors. Referring to the statement of cash flows, evaluate Williams' ability to repay its creditors.

Prepare a statement of cash flows.

(LO 3), AP

E1-13 Suppose the following data are derived from the 2017 financial statements of Southwest Airlines. (All dollars are in millions.) Southwest has a December 31 year-end.

Cash balance, January 1, 2017	$1,390
Cash paid for repayment of debt	122
Cash received from issuance of common stock	144
Cash received from issuance of long-term debt	500
Cash received from customers	9,823
Cash paid for property and equipment	1,529
Cash paid for dividends	14
Cash paid for repurchase of common stock	1,001
Cash paid for goods and services	6,978

Instructions

(a) After analyzing the data, prepare a statement of cash flows for Southwest Airlines for the year ended December 31, 2017.

(b) Discuss whether the company's net cash provided by operating activities was sufficient to finance its investing activities. If it was not, how did the company finance its investing activities?

Correct an incorrectly prepared balance sheet.

(LO 3), AP

E1-14 Wayne Holtz is the bookkeeper for Beeson Company. Wayne has been trying to get the balance sheet of Beeson Company to balance. It finally balanced, but now he's not sure it is correct.

BEESON COMPANY
Balance Sheet
December 31, 2017

Assets		Liabilities and Stockholders' Equity	
Cash	$18,000	Accounts payable	$16,000
Supplies	9,500	Accounts receivable	(12,000)
Equipment	40,000	Common stock	40,000
Dividends	8,000	Retained earnings	31,500
Total assets	$75,500	Total liabilities and stockholders' equity	$75,500

Instructions
Prepare a correct balance sheet.

Classify items as assets, liabilities, and stockholders' equity and prepare accounting equation.

(LO 3), AP

E1-15 Suppose the following items were taken from the balance sheet of Nike, Inc. (All dollars are in millions.)

1. Cash	$2,291.1	7. Inventory	$2,357.0
2. Accounts receivable	2,883.9	8. Income taxes payable	86.3
3. Common stock	2,874.2	9. Equipment	1,957.7
4. Notes payable	342.9	10. Retained earnings	5,818.9
5. Buildings	3,759.9	11. Accounts payable	2,815.8
6. Mortgage payable	1,311.5		

Instructions
Perform each of the following.

(a) Classify each of these items as an asset, liability, or stockholders' equity, and determine the total dollar amount for each classification.
(b) Determine Nike's accounting equation by calculating the value of total assets, total liabilities, and total stockholders' equity.
(c) To what extent does Nike rely on debt versus equity financing?

Use financial statement relationships to determine missing amounts.

(LO 3), AN

E1-16 The summaries of data from the balance sheet, income statement, and retained earnings statement for two corporations, Walco Corporation and Gunther Enterprises, are presented as follows for 2017.

	Walco Corporation	Gunther Enterprises
Beginning of year		
Total assets	$110,000	$150,000
Total liabilities	70,000	(d)
Total stockholders' equity	(a)	70,000
End of year		
Total assets	(b)	180,000
Total liabilities	120,000	55,000
Total stockholders' equity	60,000	(e)
Changes during year in retained earnings		
Dividends	(c)	5,000
Total revenues	215,000	(f)
Total expenses	165,000	80,000

Instructions
Determine the missing amounts. Assume all changes in stockholders' equity are due to changes in retained earnings.

Classify various items in an annual report.

(LO 3), K

E1-17 The annual report provides financial information in a variety of formats, including the following.

Management discussion and analysis (MD&A)
Financial statements
Notes to the financial statements
Auditor's opinion

Instructions

For each of the following, state in what area of the annual report the item would be presented. If the item would probably not be found in an annual report, state "Not disclosed."

(a) The total cumulative amount received from stockholders in exchange for common stock.
(b) An independent assessment concerning whether the financial statements present a fair depiction of the company's results and financial position.
(c) The interest rate that the company is being charged on all outstanding debts.
(d) Total revenue from operating activities.
(e) Management's assessment of the company's results.
(f) The names and positions of all employees hired in the last year.

EXERCISES: SET B AND CHALLENGE EXERCISES

Visit the book's companion website, at **www.wiley.com/college/kimmel**, and choose the Student Companion site to access Exercises: Set B and Challenge Exercises.

PROBLEMS: SET A

P1-1A Presented below are five independent situations.

Determine forms of business organization.

(LO 1), C

(a) Three physics professors at MIT have formed a business to improve the speed of information transfer over the Internet for stock exchange transactions. Each has contributed an equal amount of cash and knowledge to the venture. Although their approach looks promising, they are concerned about the legal liabilities that their business might confront.
(b) Bob Colt, a college student looking for summer employment, opened a bait shop in a small shed at a local marina.
(c) Alma Ortiz and Jaime Falco each owned separate shoe manufacturing businesses. They have decided to combine their businesses. They expect that within the coming year they will need significant funds to expand their operations.
(d) Alice, Donna, and Sam recently graduated with marketing degrees. They have been friends since childhood. They have decided to start a consulting business focused on marketing sporting goods over the Internet.
(e) Don Rolls has developed a low-cost GPS device that can be implanted into pets so that they can be easily located when lost. He would like to build a small manufacturing facility to make the devices and then sell them to veterinarians across the country. Don has no savings or personal assets. He wants to maintain control over the business.

Instructions

In each case, explain what form of organization the business is likely to take—sole proprietorship, partnership, or corporation. Give reasons for your choice.

P1-2A Financial decisions often place heavier emphasis on one type of financial statement over the others. Consider each of the following hypothetical situations independently.

Identify users and uses of financial statements.

(LO 3), C

(a) The North Face is considering extending credit to a new customer. The terms of the credit would require the customer to pay within 30 days of receipt of goods.
(b) An investor is considering purchasing common stock of Amazon.com. The investor plans to hold the investment for at least 5 years.
(c) JPMorgan Chase Bank is considering extending a loan to a small company. The company would be required to make interest payments at the end of each year for 5 years, and to repay the loan at the end of the fifth year.
(d) The president of Campbell Soup is trying to determine whether the company is generating enough cash to increase the amount of dividends paid to investors in this and future years, and still have enough cash to buy equipment as it is needed.

Instructions

In each situation, state whether the decision-maker would be most likely to place primary emphasis on information provided by the income statement, balance sheet, or statement of cash flows. In each case provide a brief justification for your choice. Choose only one financial statement in each case.

Prepare an income statement, retained earnings statement, and balance sheet; discuss results.

(LO 3), AP

P1-3A On June 1, 2017, Elite Service Co. was started with an initial investment in the company of $22,100 cash. Here are the assets, liabilities, and common stock of the company at June 30, 2017, and the revenues and expenses for the month of June, its first month of operations:

Cash	$ 4,600	Notes payable	$12,000
Accounts receivable	4,000	Accounts payable	500
Service revenue	7,500	Supplies expense	1,000
Supplies	2,400	Maintenance and repairs expense	600
Advertising expense	400	Utilities expense	300
Equipment	26,000	Salaries and wages expense	1,400
Common stock	22,100		

Check figures provide a key number to let you know you are on the right track.

In June, the company issued no additional stock but paid dividends of $1,400.

Instructions

(a) Net income $ 3,800
Ret. earnings $ 2,400
Tot. assets $37,000

(a) Prepare an income statement and a retained earnings statement for the month of June and a balance sheet at June 30, 2017.
(b) Briefly discuss whether the company's first month of operations was a success.
(c) Discuss the company's decision to distribute a dividend.

Determine items included in a statement of cash flows, prepare the statement, and comment.

(LO 3), AP

P1-4A Presented below is selected financial information for Rojo Corporation for December 31, 2017.

Inventory	$ 25,000	Cash paid to purchase equipment	$ 12,000
Cash paid to suppliers	104,000	Equipment	40,000
Buildings	200,000	Service revenue	100,000
Common stock	50,000	Cash received from customers	132,000
Cash dividends paid	7,000	Cash received from issuing	
Cash at beginning of period	9,000	common stock	22,000

Instructions

(a) Net increase $31,000

(a) Determine which items should be included in a statement of cash flows and then prepare the statement for Rojo Corporation.
(b) Comment on the adequacy of net cash provided by operating activities to fund the company's investing activities and dividend payments.

Comment on proper accounting treatment and prepare a corrected balance sheet.

(LO 3), AN

P1-5A Micado Corporation was formed on January 1, 2017. At December 31, 2017, Miko Liu, the president and sole stockholder, decided to prepare a balance sheet, which appeared as follows.

MICADO CORPORATION
Balance Sheet
December 31, 2017

Assets		**Liabilities and Stockholders' Equity**	
Cash	$20,000	Accounts payable	$30,000
Accounts receivable	50,000	Notes payable	15,000
Inventory	36,000	Boat loan	22,000
Boat	24,000	Stockholders' equity	63,000

Miko willingly admits that she is not an accountant by training. She is concerned that her balance sheet might not be correct. She has provided you with the following additional information.

1. The boat actually belongs to Miko, not to Micado Corporation. However, because she thinks she might take customers out on the boat occasionally, she decided to list it as an asset of the company. To be consistent, she also listed as a liability of the corporation her personal loan that she took out at the bank to buy the boat.
2. The inventory was originally purchased for $25,000, but due to a surge in demand Miko now thinks she could sell it for $36,000. She thought it would be best to record it at $36,000.

3. Included in the accounts receivable balance is $10,000 that Miko loaned to her brother 5 years ago. Miko included this in the receivables of Micado Corporation so she wouldn't forget that her brother owes her money.

Instructions

(a) Comment on the proper accounting treatment of the three items above.
(b) Provide a corrected balance sheet for Micado Corporation. (*Hint:* To get the balance sheet to balance, adjust stockholders' equity.)

(b) Tot. assets $85,000

PROBLEMS: SET B AND SET C

Visit the book's companion website, at **www.wiley.com/college/kimmel**, and choose the Student Companion site to access Problems: Set B and Set C.

CONTINUING PROBLEM Cookie Creations

CC1 Natalie Koebel spent much of her childhood learning the art of cookie-making from her grandmother. They spent many happy hours mastering every type of cookie imaginable and later devised new recipes that were both healthy and delicious. Now at the start of her second year in college, Natalie is investigating possibilities for starting her own business as part of the entrepreneurship program in which she is enrolled.

A long-time friend insists that Natalie has to include cookies in her business plan. After a series of brainstorming sessions, Natalie settles on the idea of operating a cookie-making school. She will start on a part-time basis and offer her services in people's homes. Now that she has started thinking about it, the possibilities seem endless. During the fall, she will concentrate on holiday cookies. She will offer group sessions (which will probably be more entertainment than education) and individual lessons. Natalie also decides to include children in her target market. The first difficult decision is coming up with the perfect name for her business. She settles on "Cookie Creations," and then moves on to more important issues.

© leungchopan/ Shutterstock

*The **Cookie Creations** problem starts in Chapter 1 and continues in every chapter. You can also find this problem at the book's companion website.*

Instructions

(a) What form of business organization—proprietorship, partnership, or corporation—do you recommend that Natalie use for her business? Discuss the benefits and weaknesses of each form that Natalie might consider.
(b) Will Natalie need accounting information? If yes, what information will she need and why? How often will she need this information?
(c) Identify specific asset, liability, revenue, and expense accounts that Cookie Creations will likely use to record its business transactions.
(d) Should Natalie open a separate bank account for the business? Why or why not?
(e) Natalie expects she will have to use her car to drive to people's homes and to pick up supplies, but she also needs to use her car for personal reasons. She recalls from her first-year accounting course something about keeping business and personal assets separate. She wonders what she should do for accounting purposes. What do you recommend?

EXPAND YOUR CRITICAL THINKING

FINANCIAL REPORTING PROBLEM: Apple Inc.

Financial Reporting

E

CT1-1 The financial statements of Apple Inc. for 2014 are presented in Appendix A.

Instructions

Refer to Apple's financial statements and answer the following questions.

(a) What were Apple's total assets at September 27, 2014? At September 28, 2013?
(b) How much cash (and cash equivalents) did Apple have on September 27, 2014?
(c) What amount of accounts payable did Apple report on September 27, 2014? On September 28, 2013?
(d) What were Apple's net sales in 2012? In 2013? In 2014?
(e) What is the amount of the change in Apple's net income from 2013 to 2014?

Financial Analysis

COMPARATIVE ANALYSIS PROBLEM: Columbia Sportswear Company vs. VF Corporation

E **CT1-2** Columbia Sportswear Company's financial statements are presented in Appendix B. Financial statements of VF Corporation are presented in Appendix C.

Instructions

(a) Based on the information in these financial statements, determine the following for each company.
   (1) Total liabilities at December 31, 2014.
   (2) Net property, plant, and equipment at December 31, 2014.
   (3) Net cash provided or (used) in investing activities for 2014.
   (4) Net income for 2014.

(b) What conclusions concerning the two companies can you draw from these data?

Financial Analysis

COMPARATIVE ANALYSIS PROBLEM: Amazon.com, Inc. vs. Wal-Mart Stores, Inc.

E **CT1-3** Amazon.com, Inc.'s financial statements are presented in Appendix D. Financial statements of Wal-Mart Stores, Inc. are presented in Appendix E.

Instructions

(a) Based on the information contained in these financial statements, determine the following for each company.
   (1) Total assets at December 31, 2014, for Amazon and for Wal-Mart at January 31, 2015.
   (2) Receivables (net) at December 31, 2014, for Amazon and for Wal-Mart at January 31, 2015.
   (3) Net sales (product only) for the year ended in 2014 (2015 for Wal-Mart).
   (4) Net income for year ended in 2014 (2015 for Wal-Mart).

(b) What conclusions concerning these two companies can be drawn from these data?

Financial Analysis

INTERPRETING FINANCIAL STATEMENTS

E **CT1-4** Xerox was not having a particularly pleasant year. The company's stock price had already fallen in the previous year from $60 per share to $30. Just when it seemed things couldn't get worse, Xerox's stock fell to $4 per share. The data below were taken from the statement of cash flows of Xerox. (All dollars are in millions.)

Cash used in operating activities		$ (663)
Cash used in investing activities		(644)
Financing activities		
Dividends paid	$ (587)	
Net cash received from issuing debt	3,498	
Cash provided by financing activities		2,911

Instructions

Analyze the information, and then answer the following questions.

(a) If you were a creditor of Xerox, what reaction might you have to the above information?

(b) If you were an investor in Xerox, what reaction might you have to the above information?

(c) If you were evaluating the company as either a creditor or a stockholder, what other information would you be interested in seeing?

(d) Xerox decided to pay a cash dividend. This dividend was approximately equal to the amount paid in the previous year. Discuss the issues that were probably considered in making this decision.

REAL-WORLD FOCUS

E **CT1-5** ***Purpose:*** Identify summary information about companies. This information includes basic descriptions of the company's location, activities, industry, financial health, and financial performance.

Address: **http://biz.yahoo.com/i**

Steps

1. Type in a company name, or use the index to find company name.
2. Under **Financials**, choose **Income Statement**. Perform instructions (a) and (b) below.
3. Under **Company**, choose **Industry** to identify others in this industry. Perform instructions (c)–(e) below.

Instructions

Answer the following questions.

(a) What is the company's net income? Over what period was this measured?
(b) What is the company's total sales? Over what period was this measured?
(c) What is the company's industry?
(d) What are the names of four companies in this industry?
(e) Choose one of the competitors. What is this competitor's name? What is its total sales? What is its net income?

CT1-6 The June 22, 2011, issue of the *Wall Street Journal Online* includes an article by Michael Rapoport entitled "Auditors Urged to Tell More." It provides an interesting discussion of the possible expanding role of CPAs. S

Instructions

Read the article and answer the following questions.

(a) What are some of the ideas that the Public Company Accounting Oversight Board proposed for expanding the role of auditors in "passing judgment on more of what a company does and says?"
(b) How might the financial crisis influence the public's opinion regarding the need for more information from auditors?
(c) Describe the proposed "Auditor's Discussion and Analysis."
(d) Discuss whether you think that auditors will view these proposals positively or negatively.

DECISION-MAKING ACROSS THE ORGANIZATION

Financial Analysis

Writing

Group Project

CT1-7 Sylvia Ayala recently accepted a job in the production department at Apple. Before she starts work, she decides to review the company's annual report to better understand its operations.

The content and organization of corporate annual reports have become fairly standardized. Excluding the public relations part of the report (pictures, products, etc.), the following are the traditional financial portions of the annual report: E

- Financial Highlights
- Letter to the Stockholders
- Management's Discussion and Analysis
- Financial Statements
- Notes to the Financial Statements
- Management's Responsibility for Financial Reporting
- Management's Report on Internal Control over Financial Reporting
- Report of Independent Registered Public Accounting Firm
- Selected Financial Data

The official SEC filing of the annual report is called a **Form 10-K**, which often omits the public relations pieces found in most standard annual reports. To access Apple's Form 10-K, including notes to the financial statements, follow these steps:

1. Go to **http://investor.apple.com**.
2. Select the Financial Information tab.
3. Select the 10-K annual report dated September 2014.
4. The financial portions of the annual report begin on page 21.

Instructions

Use Apple's annual report to answer the following questions.

(a) What CPA firm performed the audit of Apple's financial statements?
(b) What was the amount of Apple's basic earnings per share in 2014?

(c) What are the company's net sales in foreign countries in 2014?
(d) What were net sales in 2012?
(e) How many shares of common stock have been authorized?
(f) How much cash was spent on capital expenditures in 2014?
(g) Over what life does the company depreciate its buildings?
(h) What was the value of inventory in 2013?

COMMUNICATION ACTIVITY

S **CT1-8** Marci Ling is the bookkeeper for Samco Company, Inc. Marci has been trying to get the company's balance sheet to balance. She finally got it to balance, but she still isn't sure that it is correct.

SAMCO COMPANY, INC.
Balance Sheet
For the Month Ended December 31, 2017

Assets		**Liabilities and Stockholders' Equity**	
Equipment	$18,000	Common stock	$12,000
Cash	9,000	Accounts receivable	(6,000)
Supplies	1,000	Dividends	(2,000)
Accounts payable	(4,000)	Notes payable	10,000
Total assets	$24,000	Retained earnings	10,000
		Total liabilities and stockholders' equity	$24,000

Instructions
Explain to Marci Ling in a memo (a) the purpose of a balance sheet, and (b) why this balance sheet is incorrect and what she should do to correct it.

ETHICS CASE

E **CT1-9** Rules governing the investment practices of individual certified public accountants prohibit them from investing in the stock of a company that their firm audits. The Securities and Exchange Commission (SEC) became concerned that some accountants were violating this rule. In response to an SEC investigation, PricewaterhouseCoopers fired 10 people and spent $25 million educating employees about the investment rules and installing an investment tracking system.

Instructions
Answer the following questions.

(a) Why do you think rules exist that restrict auditors from investing in companies that are audited by their firms?
(b) Some accountants argue that they should be allowed to invest in a company's stock as long as they themselves aren't involved in working on the company's audit or consulting. What do you think of this idea?
(c) Today, a very high percentage of publicly traded companies are audited by only four very large public accounting firms. These firms also do a high percentage of the consulting work that is done for publicly traded companies. How does this fact complicate the decision regarding whether CPAs should be allowed to invest in companies audited by their firm?
(d) Suppose you were a CPA and you had invested in IBM when IBM was not one of your firm's clients. Two years later, after IBM's stock price had fallen considerably, your firm won the IBM audit contract. You will be involved in working with the IBM audit. You know that your firm's rules require that you sell your shares immediately. If you do sell immediately, you will sustain a large loss. Do you think this is fair? What would you do?
(e) Why do you think PricewaterhouseCoopers took such extreme steps in response to the SEC investigation?

ALL ABOUT YOU

CT1-10 Some people are tempted to make their finances look worse to get financial aid. Companies sometimes also manage their financial numbers in order to accomplish certain goals. Earnings management is the planned timing of revenues, expenses, gains, and losses to smooth out bumps in net income. In managing earnings, companies' actions vary from being within the range of ethical activity, to being both unethical and illegal attempts to mislead investors and creditors. E

Instructions

Provide responses for each of the following questions.

(a) Discuss whether you think each of the following actions (adapted from **www.finaid.org/fafsa/maximize.phtml**) to increase the chances of receiving financial aid is ethical.
  (i) Spend down the student's assets and income first, before spending parents' assets and income.
  (ii) Accelerate necessary expenses to reduce available cash. For example, if you need a new car, buy it before applying for financial aid.
  (iii) State that a truly financially dependent child is independent.
  (iv) Have a parent take an unpaid leave of absence for long enough to get below the "threshold" level of income.

(b) What are some reasons why a **company** might want to overstate its earnings?

(c) What are some reasons why a **company** might want to understate its earnings?

(d) Under what circumstances might an otherwise ethical person decide to illegally overstate or understate earnings?

FASB CODIFICATION ACTIVITY

CT1-11 The FASB has developed the Financial Accounting Standards Board Accounting Standards Codification (or more simply "the Codification"). The FASB's primary goal in developing the Codification is to provide in one place all the authoritative literature related to a particular topic. To provide easy access to the Codification, the FASB also developed the Financial Accounting Standards Board Codification Research System (CRS). CRS is an online, real-time database that provides easy access to the Codification. The Codification and the related CRS provide a topically organized structure, subdivided into topic, subtopics, sections, and paragraphs, using a numerical index system. C

You may find this system useful in your present and future studies, and so we have provided an opportunity to use this online system as part of the *Expand Your Critical Thinking* section.

Instructions

Academic access to the FASB Codification is available through university subscriptions, obtained from the American Accounting Association (at **http://aaahq.org/FASB/Access.cfm**), for an annual fee of $150. This subscription covers an unlimited number of students within a single institution. Once this access has been obtained by your school, you should log in (at **http://aaahq.org/ascLogin.cfm**) and familiarize yourself with the resources that are accessible at the FASB Codification site.

CONSIDERING PEOPLE, PLANET, AND PROFIT

CT1-12 Although Clif Bar & Company is not a public company, it does share its financial information with its employees as part of its open-book management approach. Further, although it does not publicly share its financial information, it does provide a different form of an annual report to external users. In this report, the company provides information regarding its sustainability efforts. E

***Address:* www.clifbar.com/article/our-five-aspirations**

Instructions

Access the article at the site shown above and then answer the following questions.

(a) What are the Five Aspirations?

(b) Click on the "All Aspirations Annual Report" link at the bottom of the page. How does this annual report differ from the annual report discussed in the chapter? Are there any similarities?

A Look at IFRS

LEARNING OBJECTIVE 4

Describe the impact of international accounting standards on U.S. financial reporting.

Most agree that there is a need for one set of international accounting standards. Here is why:

Multinational corporations. Today's companies view the entire world as their market. For example, Coca-Cola, Intel, and McDonald's generate more than 50% of their sales outside the United States. Many foreign companies, such as Toyota, Nestlé, and Sony, find their largest market to be the United States.

Mergers and acquisitions. The mergers between Fiat/Chrysler and Vodafone/Mannesmann suggest that we will see even more such business combinations of companies from different countries in the future.

Information technology. As communication barriers continue to topple through advances in technology, companies and individuals in different countries and markets are becoming more comfortable buying and selling goods and services from one another.

Financial markets. Financial markets are of international significance today. Whether it is currency, equity securities (stocks), bonds, or derivatives, there are active markets throughout the world trading these types of instruments.

KEY POINTS

Following are the key similarities and differences between GAAP and IFRS as related to accounting fundamentals.

Similarities

- The basic techniques for recording business transactions are the same for U.S. and international companies.
- Both international and U.S. accounting standards emphasize transparency in financial reporting. Both sets of standards are primarily driven by meeting the needs of investors and creditors.
- The three most common forms of business organizations, proprietorships, partnerships, and corporations, are also found in countries that use international accounting standards.

Differences

- International standards are referred to as International Financial Reporting Standards (IFRS), developed by the International Accounting Standards Board. Accounting standards in the United States are referred to as generally accepted accounting principles (GAAP) and are developed by the Financial Accounting Standards Board.
- IFRS tends to be simpler in its accounting and disclosure requirements; some people say it is more "principles-based." GAAP is more detailed; some people say it is more "rules-based."
- The internal control standards applicable to Sarbanes-Oxley (SOX) apply only to large public companies listed on U.S. exchanges. There is continuing debate as to whether non-U.S. companies should have to comply with this extra layer of regulation.

LOOKING TO THE FUTURE

Both the IASB and the FASB are hard at work developing standards that will lead to the elimination of major differences in the way certain transactions are accounted for and reported.

IFRS Practice

IFRS SELF-TEST QUESTIONS

1. Which of the following is **not** a reason why a single set of high-quality international accounting standards would be beneficial?
(a) Mergers and acquisition activity.
(b) Financial markets.
(c) Multinational corporations.
(d) GAAP is widely considered to be a superior reporting system.

2. The Sarbanes-Oxley Act determines:
(a) international tax regulations.
(b) internal control standards as enforced by the IASB.
(c) internal control standards of U.S. publicly traded companies.
(d) U.S. tax regulations.

3. IFRS is considered to be more:
(a) principles-based and less rules-based than GAAP.
(b) rules-based and less principles-based than GAAP.
(c) detailed than GAAP.
(d) None of the above.

IFRS EXERCISES

IFRS1-1 Who are the two key international players in the development of international accounting standards? Explain their role.

IFRS1-2 What is the benefit of a single set of high-quality accounting standards?

INTERNATIONAL FINANCIAL REPORTING PROBLEM: Louis Vuitton

IFRS1-3 The financial statements of Louis Vuitton are presented in Appendix F. Instructions for accessing and using the company's complete annual report, including the notes to its financial statements, are also provided in Appendix F.

Instructions
Visit Louis Vuitton's corporate website and answer the following questions from the company's 2014 annual report.

(a) What accounting firm performed the audit of Louis Vuitton's financial statements?
(b) What is the address of the company's corporate headquarters?
(c) What is the company's reporting currency?

Answers to IFRS Self-Test Questions
1. d **2.** c **3.** a

2

A Further Look at Financial Statements

CHAPTER PREVIEW

If you are thinking of purchasing Best Buy stock, or any stock, how can you decide what the shares are worth? If you manage Columbia Sportswear's credit department, how should you determine whether to extend credit to a new customer? If you are a financial executive at Google, how do you decide whether your company is generating adequate cash to expand operations without borrowing? Your decision in each of these situations will be influenced by a variety of considerations. One of them should be your careful analysis of a company's financial statements. The reason: Financial statements offer relevant and reliable information, which will help you in your decision-making.

In this chapter, we take a closer look at the balance sheet and introduce some useful ways for evaluating the information provided by the financial statements. We also examine the financial reporting concepts underlying the financial statements. We begin by introducing the classified balance sheet.

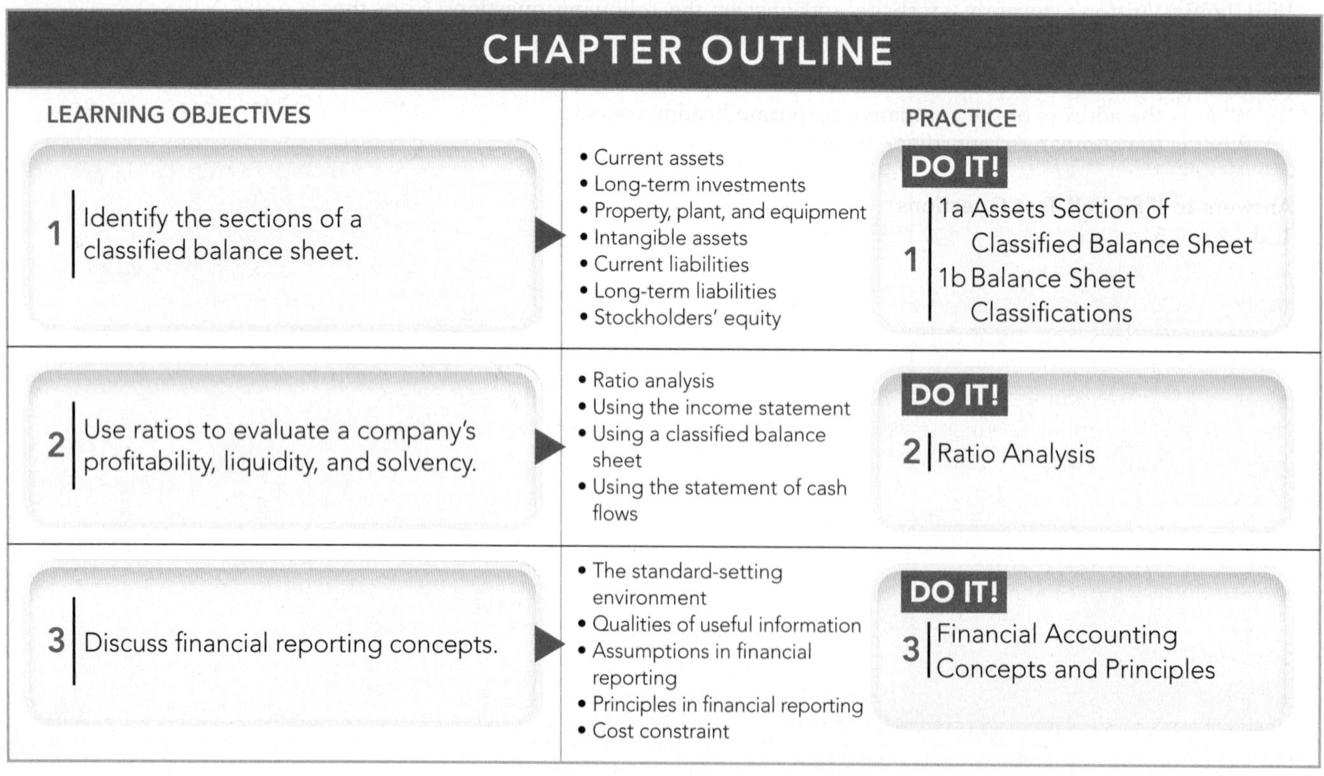

CHAPTER OUTLINE

LEARNING OBJECTIVES		PRACTICE
1 Identify the sections of a classified balance sheet.	• Current assets • Long-term investments • Property, plant, and equipment • Intangible assets • Current liabilities • Long-term liabilities • Stockholders' equity	DO IT! 1 1a Assets Section of Classified Balance Sheet 1b Balance Sheet Classifications
2 Use ratios to evaluate a company's profitability, liquidity, and solvency.	• Ratio analysis • Using the income statement • Using a classified balance sheet • Using the statement of cash flows	DO IT! 2 Ratio Analysis
3 Discuss financial reporting concepts.	• The standard-setting environment • Qualities of useful information • Assumptions in financial reporting • Principles in financial reporting • Cost constraint	DO IT! 3 Financial Accounting Concepts and Principles

Go to the ***REVIEW AND PRACTICE*** section at the end of the chapter for a targeted summary and exercises with solutions.

Visit **WileyPLUS** for additional tutorials and practice opportunities.

FEATURE STORY

Just Fooling Around?

Few people could have predicted how dramatically the Internet would change the investment world. One of the most interesting results is how it has changed the way ordinary people invest their savings. More and more people are striking out on their own, making their own investment decisions.

Two early pioneers in providing investment information to the masses were Tom and David Gardner, brothers who created an online investor website called The Motley Fool. The name comes from Shakespeare's *As You Like It*. The fool in Shakespeare's play was the only one who could speak unpleasant truths to kings and queens without being killed. Tom and David view themselves as 21st-century "fools," revealing the "truths" of the stock market to the small investor, who they feel has been taken advantage of by Wall Street insiders. The Motley Fool's online bulletin board enables investors to exchange information and insights about companies.

Critics of these bulletin boards contend that they are simply high-tech rumor mills that cause investors to bid up stock prices to unreasonable levels. For example, the stock of PairGain Technologies jumped 32% in a single day as a result of a bogus takeover rumor on an investment bulletin board. Some observers are concerned that small investors—ironically, the very people the Gardner brothers are trying to help—will be hurt the most by misinformation and intentional scams.

To show how these bulletin boards work, suppose that you had $10,000 to invest. You were considering Best Buy Company, the largest seller of electronics equipment in the United States. You scanned the Internet investment bulletin boards and found messages posted by two different investors. Here are excerpts from actual postings:

> *TMPVenus:* "Where are the prospects for positive movement for this company? Poor margins, poor management, astronomical P/E!"
>
> *broachman:* "I believe that this is a LONG TERM winner, and presently at a good price."

One says sell, and one says buy. Whom should you believe? If you had taken "broachman's" advice and purchased the stock, the $10,000 you invested would have been worth over $300,000 five years later. Best Buy was one of America's best-performing stocks during that period of time.

Rather than getting swept away by rumors, investors must sort out the good information from the bad. One thing is certain—as information services such as The Motley Fool increase in number, gathering information will become even easier. Evaluating it will be the harder task.

LEARNING OBJECTIVE 1

Identify the sections of a classified balance sheet.

In Chapter 1, you learned that a balance sheet presents a snapshot of a company's financial position at a point in time. It lists individual asset, liability, and stockholders' equity items. However, to improve users' understanding of a company's financial position, companies often use a **classified** balance sheet instead. A **classified balance sheet** groups together similar assets and similar liabilities, using a number of standard classifications and sections. This is useful because items within a group have similar economic characteristics. A classified balance sheet generally contains the standard classifications listed in Illustration 2-1.

ILLUSTRATION 2-1
Standard balance sheet classifications

Assets	Liabilities and Stockholders' Equity
Current assets	Current liabilities
Long-term investments	Long-term liabilities
Property, plant, and equipment	Stockholders' equity
Intangible assets	

These groupings help financial statement readers determine such things as (1) whether the company has enough assets to pay its debts as they come due, and (2) the claims of short- and long-term creditors on the company's total assets. Many of these groupings can be seen in the balance sheet of Franklin Corporation shown in Illustration 2-2 on the next page. In the sections that follow, we explain each of these groupings.

CURRENT ASSETS

Current assets are assets that a company expects to convert to cash or use up within one year or its operating cycle, whichever is longer. In Illustration 2-2, Franklin Corporation had current assets of $22,100. For most businesses, the cutoff for classification as current assets is one year from the balance sheet date. For example, accounts receivable are current assets because the company will collect them and convert them to cash within one year. Supplies is a current asset because the company expects to use the supplies in operations within one year.

Some companies use a period longer than one year to classify assets and liabilities as current because they have an operating cycle longer than one year. The **operating cycle** of a company is the average time required to go from cash to cash in producing revenue—to purchase inventory, sell it on account, and then collect cash from customers. For most businesses, this cycle takes less than a year, so they use a one-year cutoff. But for some businesses, such as vineyards or airplane manufacturers, this period may be longer than a year. **Except where noted, we will assume that companies use one year to determine whether an asset or liability is current or long-term.**

Common types of current assets are (1) cash, (2) investments (such as short-term U.S. government securities), (3) receivables (accounts receivable, notes receivable, and interest receivable), (4) inventories, and (5) prepaid expenses (insurance and supplies). **Companies list current assets in the order in which they expect to convert them into cash.** *Follow this rule when doing your homework.*

ILLUSTRATION 2-2
Classified balance sheet

FRANKLIN CORPORATION
Balance Sheet
October 31, 2017

Assets			
Current assets			
Cash		$ 6,600	
Debt investments		2,000	
Accounts receivable		7,000	
Notes receivable		1,000	
Inventory		3,000	
Supplies		2,100	
Prepaid insurance		400	
Total current assets			$22,100
Long-term investments			
Stock investments		5,200	
Investment in real estate		2,000	7,200
Property, plant, and equipment			
Land		10,000	
Equipment	$24,000		
Less: Accumulated depreciation—equipment	5,000	19,000	29,000
Intangible assets			
Patents			3,100
Total assets			$61,400
Liabilities and Stockholders' Equity			
Current liabilities			
Notes payable		$11,000	
Accounts payable		2,100	
Unearned sales revenue		900	
Salaries and wages payable		1,600	
Interest payable		450	
Total current liabilities			$16,050
Long-term liabilities			
Mortgage payable		10,000	
Notes payable		1,300	
Total long-term liabilities			11,300
Total liabilities			27,350
Stockholders' equity			
Common stock		14,000	
Retained earnings		20,050	
Total stockholders' equity			34,050
Total liabilities and stockholders' equity			$61,400

▼ **HELPFUL HINT**
Recall that the accounting equation is Assets = Liabilities + Stockholders' Equity.

Illustration 2-3 presents the current assets of Southwest Airlines Co. in a recent year.

ILLUSTRATION 2-3
Current assets section

Real World

SOUTHWEST AIRLINES CO.
Balance Sheet (partial)
(in millions)

Current assets	
Cash and cash equivalents	$1,355
Short-term investments	1,797
Accounts receivable	419
Inventories	467
Prepaid expenses and other current assets	418
Total current assets	$4,456

As explained later in the chapter, a company's current assets are important in assessing its short-term debt-paying ability.

LONG-TERM INVESTMENTS

ALTERNATIVE TERMINOLOGY
Long-term investments are often referred to simply as *investments.*

Long-term investments are generally (1) investments in stocks and bonds of other corporations that are held for more than one year, (2) long-term assets such as land or buildings that a company is not currently using in its operating activities, and (3) long-term notes receivable. In Illustration 2-2, Franklin Corporation reported total long-term investments of $7,200 on its balance sheet.

Google Inc. reported long-term investments on its balance sheet in a recent year as shown in Illustration 2-4.

ILLUSTRATION 2-4
Long-term investments section

Real World

GOOGLE INC. Balance Sheet (partial) (in millions)	
Long-term investments	
Non-marketable equity investments	$1,469

PROPERTY, PLANT, AND EQUIPMENT

ALTERNATIVE TERMINOLOGY
Property, plant, and equipment is sometimes called *fixed assets* or *plant assets.*

Property, plant, and equipment are assets with relatively long useful lives that are currently used in operating the business. This category includes land, buildings, equipment, delivery vehicles, and furniture. In Illustration 2-2, Franklin Corporation reported property, plant, and equipment of $29,000.

Depreciation is the allocation of the cost of an asset to a number of years. Companies do this by systematically assigning a portion of an asset's cost as an expense each year (rather than expensing the full purchase price in the year of purchase). The assets that the company depreciates are reported on the balance sheet at cost less accumulated depreciation. The **accumulated depreciation** account shows the total amount of depreciation that the company has expensed thus far in the asset's life. In Illustration 2-2, Franklin Corporation reported accumulated depreciation of $5,000.

Illustration 2-5 presents the property, plant, and equipment of Tesla Motors, Inc. in a recent year.

ILLUSTRATION 2-5
Property, plant, and equipment section

Real World

TESLA MOTORS, INC. Balance Sheet (partial) (in thousands)	
Property, plant, and equipment	
Machinery, equipment and office furniture	$ 322,394
Tooling	230,385
Leasehold improvements	94,763
Building and building improvements	67,707
Land	45,020
Computer equipment and software	42,073
Construction in progress	76,294
	878,636
Less: Accumulated depreciation and amortization	(140,142)
Total	$ 738,494

▼ HELPFUL HINT
Sometimes intangible assets are reported under a broader heading called "*Other assets.*"

INTANGIBLE ASSETS

Many companies have assets that do not have physical substance and yet often are very valuable. We call these assets **intangible assets**. One common intangible is goodwill. Others include patents, copyrights, and trademarks or trade names that give the company **exclusive right** of use for a specified period of time. In Illustration 2-2, Franklin Corporation reported intangible assets of $3,100.

Illustration 2-6 shows the intangible assets of media and theme park giant The Walt Disney Company in a recent year.

ILLUSTRATION 2-6
Intangible assets section

Real World

THE WALT DISNEY COMPANY
Balance Sheet (partial)
(in millions)

Intangible assets and goodwill	
Character/franchise intangibles and copyrights	$ 5,830
Other amortizable intangible assets	903
Accumulated amortization	(1,204)
Net amortizable intangible assets	5,529
FCC licenses	667
Trademarks	1,218
Other indefinite lived intangible assets	20
	7,434
Goodwill	27,881
	$35,315

DO IT! 1a Assets Section of Classified Balance Sheet

Baxter Hoffman recently received the following information related to Hoffman Corporation's December 31, 2017, balance sheet.

Prepaid insurance	$ 2,300	Inventory	$3,400
Cash	800	Accumulated depreciation—equipment	2,700
Equipment	10,700	Accounts receivable	1,100

Prepare the assets section of Hoffman Corporation's classified balance sheet.

SOLUTION

HOFFMAN CORPORATION
Balance Sheet (partial)
December 31, 2017

Assets

Current assets		
Cash	$ 800	
Accounts receivable	1,100	
Inventory	3,400	
Prepaid insurance	2,300	
Total current assets		$ 7,600
Property, plant, and equipment		
Equipment	10,700	
Less: Accumulated depreciation—equipment	2,700	8,000
Total assets		$15,600

Action Plan

- ✔ Present current assets first. Current assets are cash and other resources that the company expects to convert to cash or use up within one year.
- ✔ Present current assets in the order in which the company expects to convert them into cash.
- ✔ Subtract accumulated depreciation—equipment from equipment to determine net equipment.

Related exercise material: **BE2-2, DO IT! 2-1a, E2-3,** and **E2-4.**

CURRENT LIABILITIES

In the liabilities and stockholders' equity section of the balance sheet, the first grouping is current liabilities. **Current liabilities** are obligations that the company is to pay within the next year or operating cycle, whichever is longer. Common examples are accounts payable, salaries and wages payable, notes payable, interest payable, and income taxes payable. Also included as current liabilities are current maturities of long-term obligations—payments to be made within the next year on long-term obligations. In Illustration 2-2, Franklin Corporation reported five different types of current liabilities, for a total of $16,050.

Illustration 2-7 shows the current liabilities section adapted from the balance sheet of Google Inc. in a recent year.

ILLUSTRATION 2-7
Current liabilities section

Real World

GOOGLE INC.
Balance Sheet (partial)
(in millions)

Current liabilities	
Accounts payable	$ 2,012
Short-term debt	2,549
Accrued compensation and benefits	2,239
Accrued expenses and other current liabilities	7,297
Income taxes payable, net	240
Total current liabilities	$14,337

LONG-TERM LIABILITIES

Long-term liabilities (long-term debt) are obligations that a company expects to pay **after** one year. Liabilities in this category include bonds payable, mortgages payable, long-term notes payable, lease liabilities, and pension liabilities. Many companies report long-term debt maturing after one year as a single amount in the balance sheet and show the details of the debt in notes that accompany the financial statements. Others list the various types of long-term liabilities. In Illustration 2-2, Franklin Corporation reported long-term liabilities of $11,300.

Illustration 2-8 shows the long-term liabilities that Nike, Inc. reported in its balance sheet in a recent year.

ILLUSTRATION 2-8
Long-term liabilities section

Real World

NIKE, INC.
Balance Sheet (partial)
(in millions)

Long-term liabilities	
Bonds payable	$1,106
Notes payable	51
Deferred income taxes and other	1,544
Total long-term liabilities	$2,701

STOCKHOLDERS' EQUITY

ALTERNATIVE TERMINOLOGY
Common stock is sometimes called *capital stock*.

Stockholders' equity consists of two parts: common stock and retained earnings. Companies record as **common stock** the investments of assets into the business by the stockholders. They record as **retained earnings** the income retained for use in the business. These two parts, combined, make up **stockholders' equity** on the balance sheet. In Illustration 2-2, Franklin Corporation reported common stock of $14,000 and retained earnings of $20,050.

DO IT! 1b Balance Sheet Classifications

The following financial statement items were taken from the financial statements of Callahan Corp.

_______ Salaries and wages payable
_______ Service revenue
_______ Interest payable
_______ Goodwill
_______ Debt investments (short-term)
_______ Mortgage payable (due in 3 years)
_______ Investment in real estate
_______ Equipment
_______ Accumulated depreciation—equipment
_______ Depreciation expense
_______ Retained earnings
_______ Unearned service revenue

Match each of the items to its proper balance sheet classification, shown below. If the item would not appear on a balance sheet, use "NA."

Current assets (CA)
Long-term investments (LTI)
Property, plant, and equipment (PPE)
Intangible assets (IA)
Current liabilities (CL)
Long-term liabilities (LTL)
Stockholders' equity (SE)

SOLUTION

CL Salaries and wages payable
NA Service revenue
CL Interest payable
IA Goodwill
CA Debt investments (short-term)
LTL Mortgage payable (due in 3 years)
LTI Investment in real estate
PPE Equipment
PPE Accumulated depreciation—equipment
NA Depreciation expense
SE Retained earnings
CL Unearned service revenue

Action Plan

✔ Analyze whether each financial statement item is an asset, liability, or stockholders' equity item.

✔ Determine if asset and liability items are current or long-term.

Related exercise material: **BE2-1, DO IT! 2-1b, E2-1, E2-2, E2-3, E2-5,** and **E2-6.**

LEARNING OBJECTIVE 2 Use ratios to evaluate a company's profitability, liquidity, and solvency.

In Chapter 1, we introduced the four financial statements. We discussed how these statements provide information about a company's performance and financial position. In this chapter, we extend this discussion by showing you specific tools that you can use to analyze financial statements in order to make a more meaningful evaluation of a company.

RATIO ANALYSIS

Ratio analysis expresses the relationship among selected items of financial statement data. A **ratio** expresses the mathematical relationship between one quantity and another. For analysis of the primary financial statements, we classify ratios as shown in Illustration 2-9 (page 52).

A single ratio by itself is not very meaningful. Accordingly, in this and the following chapters, we will use various comparisons to shed light on company performance:

1. **Intracompany comparisons** covering two years for the same company.
2. **Industry-average comparisons** based on average ratios for particular industries.
3. **Intercompany comparisons** based on comparisons with a competitor in the same industry.

ILLUSTRATION 2-9
Financial ratio classifications

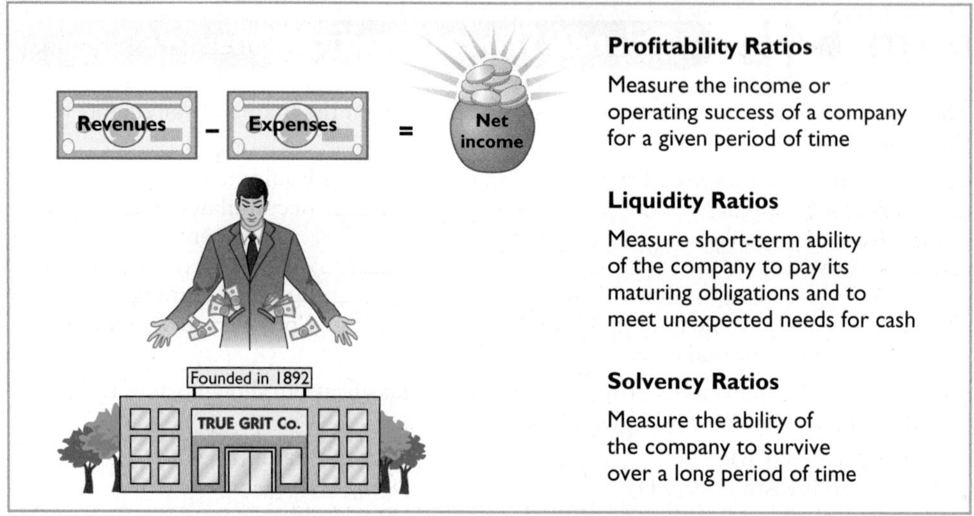

Next, we use some ratios and comparisons to analyze the financial statements of Best Buy.

USING THE INCOME STATEMENT

Best Buy generates profits for its stockholders by selling electronics. The income statement reveals how successful the company is at generating a profit from its sales. The income statement reports the amount earned during the period (revenues) and the costs incurred during the period (expenses). Illustration 2-10 shows a simplified income statement for Best Buy.

ILLUSTRATION 2-10
Best Buy's income statement

Real World

BEST BUY CO., INC.
Income Statements
For the 12 Months Ended February 1, 2014,
and 11 Months Ended February 2, 2013 (in millions)

	2014	2013
Revenues		
Net sales and other revenue	$42,410	$39,827
Expenses		
Cost of goods sold	32,720	30,528
Selling, general, and administrative expenses and other	8,760	9,471
Income tax expense	398	269
Total expenses	41,878	40,268
Net income/(loss)	$ 532	$ (441)

From this income statement, we can see that Best Buy's sales and net income increased during the period. Net income increased from a $441 million loss to a positive $532 million. One extremely unusual aspect of Best Buy's income statement is that the 2013 comparative column only covers 11 months. This occurred because Best Buy changed its year-end from "the Saturday nearest the end of February to the Saturday nearest the end of January." Such a change is very uncommon and complicates efforts to compare performance across years.

A much smaller competitor of Best Buy is hhgregg. hhgregg operates 228 stores in 20 states and is headquartered in Indianapolis, Indiana. It reported net income of $228,000 for the year ended March 31, 2014.

To evaluate the profitability of Best Buy, we will use ratio analysis. **Profitability ratios**, such as earnings per share, measure the operating success of a company for a given period of time.

Earnings per Share

Earnings per share (EPS) measures the net income earned on each share of common stock. Stockholders usually think in terms of the number of shares they own or plan to buy or sell, so stating net income earned as a per share amount provides a useful perspective for determining the investment return. Advanced accounting courses present more refined techniques for calculating earnings per share.

DECISION TOOLS

Earnings per share helps users compare a company's performance with that of previous years.

For now, a basic approach for calculating earnings per share is to divide earnings available to common stockholders by weighted-average common shares outstanding during the year. What is "earnings available to common stockholders"? It is an earnings amount calculated as net income less dividends paid on another type of stock, called preferred stock (Net income − Preferred dividends).

By comparing earnings per share of **a single company over time**, we can evaluate its relative earnings performance from the perspective of a stockholder—that is, on a per share basis. It is very important to note that comparisons of earnings per share across companies are **not meaningful** because of the wide variations in the numbers of shares of outstanding stock among companies.

Illustration 2-11 shows the earnings per share calculation for Best Buy in 2014 and 2013, based on the information presented below. Recall that Best Buy's 2013 income is based on 11 months of results. Further, to simplify our calculations, we assumed that any change in the number of shares for Best Buy occurred in the middle of the year.

(in millions)	2014	2013
Net income (loss)	$532	$(441)
Preferred dividends	–0–	–0–
Shares outstanding at beginning of year	338	341
Shares outstanding at end of year	347	338

ILLUSTRATION 2-11
Best Buy's earnings per share

$$\text{Earnings per Share} = \frac{\text{Net Income} - \text{Preferred Dividends}}{\text{Weighted-Average Common Shares Outstanding}}$$

($ and shares in millions)	2014	2013
Earnings per share	$\frac{\$532 - \$0}{(347 + 338)/2} = \$1.55$	$\frac{-\$441 - \$0}{(338 + 341)/2} = -\$1.30$

USING A CLASSIFIED BALANCE SHEET

You can learn a lot about a company's financial health by also evaluating the relationship between its various assets and liabilities. Illustration 2-12 (page 54) provides a simplified balance sheet for Best Buy.

Liquidity

Suppose you are a banker at CitiGroup considering lending money to Best Buy, or you are a sales manager at Hewlett-Packard interested in selling computers to Best Buy on credit. You would be concerned about Best Buy's **liquidity**—its ability to pay obligations expected to become due within the next year or operating cycle. You would look closely at the relationship of its current assets to current liabilities.

ILLUSTRATION 2-12
Best Buy's balance sheet

Real World

BEST BUY CO., INC.
Balance Sheets
(in millions)

Assets	February 1, 2014	February 2, 2013
Current assets		
Cash and cash equivalents	$ 2,678	$ 1,826
Short-term investments	223	0
Receivables	1,308	2,704
Merchandise inventories	5,376	6,571
Other current assets	900	946
Total current assets	10,485	12,047
Property and equipment	7,575	8,375
Less: Accumulated depreciation	4,977	5,105
Net property and equipment	2,598	3,270
Other assets	930	1,470
Total assets	$14,013	$16,787
Liabilities and Stockholders' Equity		
Current liabilities		
Accounts payable	$ 5,122	$ 6,951
Accrued liabilities	873	1,188
Accrued income taxes	147	129
Accrued compensation payable	444	520
Other current liabilities	850	2,022
Total current liabilities	7,436	10,810
Long-term liabilities		
Long-term debt	976	1,109
Other long-term liabilities	1,612	1,153
Total long-term liabilities	2,588	2,262
Total liabilities	10,024	13,072
Stockholders' equity		
Common stock	335	88
Retained earnings and other	3,654	3,627
Total stockholders' equity	3,989	3,715
Total liabilities and stockholders' equity	$14,013	$16,787

WORKING CAPITAL One measure of liquidity is **working capital**, which is the difference between the amounts of current assets and current liabilities:

ILLUSTRATION 2-13
Working capital

Working Capital = Current Assets − Current Liabilities

When current assets exceed current liabilities, working capital is positive. When this occurs, there is a greater likelihood that the company will pay its liabilities. When working capital is negative, a company might not be able to pay short-term creditors, and the company might ultimately be forced into bankruptcy. Best Buy had working capital in 2014 of $3,049 million ($10,485 million − $7,436 million).

DECISION TOOLS 

The current ratio helps users determine if a company can meet its near-term obligations.

CURRENT RATIO **Liquidity ratios** measure the short-term ability of the company to pay its maturing obligations and to meet unexpected needs for cash. One liquidity ratio is the **current ratio**, computed as current assets divided by current liabilities.

The current ratio is a more dependable indicator of liquidity than working capital. Two companies with the same amount of working capital may have significantly different current ratios. Illustration 2-14 shows the 2014 and 2013 current ratios for Best Buy and for hhgregg, along with the 2014 industry average.

ILLUSTRATION 2-14
Current ratio

$$\text{Current Ratio} = \frac{\text{Current Assets}}{\text{Current Liabilities}}$$

Best Buy ($ in millions)		hhgregg	Industry Average
2014	2013	2014	2014
$\frac{\$10,485}{\$7,436} = 1.41:1$	1.11:1	1.68:1	.88:1

What does the ratio actually mean? Best Buy's 2014 current ratio of 1.41:1 means that for every dollar of current liabilities, Best Buy has $1.41 of current assets. Best Buy's current ratio increased in 2014. When compared to the industry average of .88:1, Best Buy's liquidity seems strong. It is lower than hhgregg's but not significantly so.

One potential weakness of the current ratio is that it does not take into account the **composition** of the current assets. For example, a satisfactory current ratio does not disclose whether a portion of the current assets is tied up in slow-moving inventory. The composition of the current assets matters because a dollar of cash is more readily available to pay the bills than is a dollar of inventory. For example, suppose a company's cash balance declined while its merchandise inventory increased substantially. If inventory increased because the company is having difficulty selling its products, then the current ratio might not fully reflect the reduction in the company's liquidity.

ETHICS NOTE

A company that has more current assets than current liabilities can increase the ratio of current assets to current liabilities by using cash to pay off some current liabilities. This gives the appearance of being more liquid. Do you think this move is ethical?

ACCOUNTING ACROSS THE ORGANIZATION — REL Consultancy Group

Jorge Salcedo/iStockphoto

Can a Company Be Too Liquid?

There actually is a point where a company can be too liquid—that is, it can have too much working capital. While it is important to be liquid enough to be able to pay short-term bills as they come due, a company does not want to tie up its cash in extra inventory or receivables that are not earning the company money.

By one estimate from the REL Consultancy Group, the thousand largest U.S. companies had cumulative excess working capital of $1.017 trillion in a recent year. This was an 18% increase, which REL said represented a "deterioration in the management of operations." Given that managers throughout a company are interested in improving profitability, it is clear that they should have an eye toward managing working capital. They need to aim for a "Goldilocks solution"—not too much, not too little, but just right.

Source: Maxwell Murphy, "The Big Number," *Wall Street Journal* (November 9, 2011).

What can various company managers do to ensure that working capital is managed efficiently to maximize net income? (Go to **WileyPLUS** for this answer and additional questions.)

Solvency

Now suppose that instead of being a short-term creditor, you are interested in either buying Best Buy's stock or extending the company a long-term loan. Long-term creditors and stockholders are interested in a company's **solvency**—its ability to pay interest as it comes due and to repay the balance of a debt due at its maturity. **Solvency ratios** measure the ability of the company to survive over a long period of time.

▼ HELPFUL HINT
Some users evaluate solvency using a ratio of liabilities divided by stockholders' equity. The higher this "debt to equity" ratio, the lower is a company's solvency.

DEBT TO ASSETS RATIO The **debt to assets ratio** is one measure of solvency. It is calculated by dividing total liabilities (both current and long-term) by total assets. It measures the percentage of total financing provided by creditors rather than stockholders. Debt financing is more risky than equity financing because debt must be repaid at specific points in time, whether the company is performing well or not. Thus, the higher the percentage of debt financing, the riskier the company.

The higher the percentage of total liabilities (debt) to total assets, the greater the risk that the company may be unable to pay its debts as they come due. Illustration 2-15 shows the debt to assets ratios for Best Buy and hhgregg, along with the industry average.

ILLUSTRATION 2-15
Debt to assets ratio

$$\text{Debt to Assets Ratio} = \frac{\text{Total Liabilities}}{\text{Total Assets}}$$

Best Buy ($ in millions)		hhgregg	Industry Average
2014	2013	2014	2014
$\frac{\$10,024}{\$14,013} = 72\%$	78%	51%	88%

The 2014 ratio of 72% means that every dollar of assets was financed by 72 cents of debt. Best Buy's ratio is less than the industry average of 88% and is significantly higher than hhgregg's ratio of 51%. The higher the ratio, the more reliant the company is on debt financing. This means that Best Buy has a lower equity "buffer" available to creditors if the company becomes insolvent when compared to hhgregg. Thus, from the creditors' point of view, a high ratio of debt to assets is undesirable. Best Buy's solvency appears lower than hhgregg's and higher than the average company in the industry.

The adequacy of this ratio is often judged in light of the company's earnings. Generally, companies with relatively stable earnings, such as public utilities, can support higher debt to assets ratios than can cyclical companies with widely fluctuating earnings, such as many high-tech companies. In later chapters, you will learn additional ways to evaluate solvency.

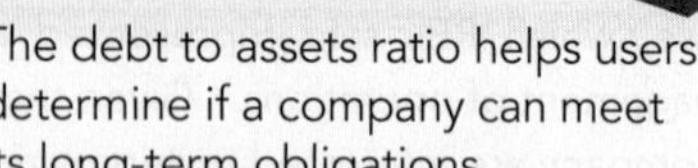

The debt to assets ratio helps users determine if a company can meet its long-term obligations.

INVESTOR INSIGHT

© David Crockett/iStockphoto

When Debt Is Good

Debt financing differs greatly across industries and companies. Here are some debt to assets ratios for selected companies in a recent year:

	Debt to Assets Ratio
Google	23%
Nike	41%
Microsoft	48%
ExxonMobil	48%
General Motors	74%

Discuss the difference in the debt to assets ratio of Microsoft and General Motors. (Go to WileyPLUS for this answer and additional questions.)

USING THE STATEMENT OF CASH FLOWS

In the statement of cash flows, net cash provided by operating activities is intended to indicate the cash-generating capability of the company. Analysts have noted, however, that **net cash provided by operating activities fails to take into account that a company must invest in new property, plant, and equipment** (capital expenditures) just to maintain its current level of operations. Companies also must at least **maintain dividends at current levels** to satisfy investors. A measurement to provide additional insight regarding a company's cash-generating ability is free cash flow. **Free cash flow** describes the net cash provided by operating activities after adjusting for capital expenditures and dividends paid.

Consider the following example. Suppose that MPC produced and sold 10,000 personal computers this year. It reported $100,000 net cash provided by operating activities. In order to maintain production at 10,000 computers, MPC invested $15,000 in equipment. It chose to pay $5,000 in dividends. Its free cash flow was $80,000 ($100,000 − $15,000 − $5,000). The company could use this $80,000 to purchase new assets to expand the business, pay off debts, or increase its dividend distribution. In practice, analysts often calculate free cash flow with the formula shown in Illustration 2-16. (Alternative definitions also exist.)

DECISION TOOLS

Free cash flow helps users determine the amount of cash a company generated to expand operations, pay off debts, or increase dividends.

ILLUSTRATION 2-16
Free cash flow

Free Cash Flow	=	Net Cash Provided by Operating Activities	−	Capital Expenditures	−	Cash Dividends

We can calculate Best Buy's 2014 free cash flow as shown in Illustration 2-17 (dollars in millions).

ILLUSTRATION 2-17
Best Buy's free cash flow

Net cash provided by operating activities	$1,094
Less: Expenditures on property, plant, and equipment	547
Dividends paid	233
Free cash flow	$ 314

Best Buy generated free cash flow of $314 million, which is available for the acquisition of new assets, the retirement of stock or debt, or the payment of additional dividends. Long-term creditors consider a high free cash flow amount an indication of solvency. hhgregg's free cash flow for 2014 is $60 million. Given that hhgregg is considerably smaller than Best Buy, we would expect its free cash flow to be much lower.

DO IT!  2 Ratio Analysis

The following information is available for Ozone Inc.

	2017	2016
Current assets	$ 88,000	$ 60,800
Total assets	400,000	341,000
Current liabilities	40,000	38,000
Total liabilities	120,000	150,000
Net income	100,000	50,000
Net cash provided by operating activities	110,000	70,000
Preferred dividends	10,000	10,000
Common dividends	5,000	2,500
Expenditures on property, plant, and equipment	45,000	20,000
Shares outstanding at beginning of year	60,000	40,000
Shares outstanding at end of year	120,000	60,000

(a) Compute earnings per share for 2017 and 2016 for Ozone, and comment on the change. Ozone's primary competitor, Frost Corporation, had earnings per share of $2 in 2017. Comment on the difference in the ratios of the two companies.

(b) Compute the current ratio and debt to assets ratio for each year, and comment on the changes.

(c) Compute free cash flow for each year, and comment on the changes.

Action Plan

✔ Use the formula for earnings per share (EPS): (Net income − Preferred dividends) ÷ Weighted-average common shares outstanding.

✔ Use the formula for the current ratio: Current assets ÷ Current liabilities.

✔ Use the formula for the debt to assets ratio: Total liabilities ÷ Total assets.

✔ Use the formula for free cash flow: Net cash provided by operating activities − Capital expenditures − Cash dividends.

SOLUTION

(a) Earnings per share

2017	2016
$\frac{(\$100{,}000 - \$10{,}000)}{(120{,}000 + 60{,}000)/2} = \$1.00$	$\frac{(\$50{,}000 - \$10{,}000)}{(60{,}000 + 40{,}000)/2} = \$0.80$

Ozone's profitability, as measured by the amount of income available to each share of common stock, increased by 25% [($1.00 − $0.80) ÷ $0.80] during 2017. Earnings per share should not be compared across companies because the number of shares issued by companies varies widely. Thus, we cannot conclude that Frost Corporation is more profitable than Ozone based on its higher EPS.

(b)

	2017	2016
Current ratio	$\frac{\$88{,}000}{\$40{,}000} = 2.20{:}1$	$\frac{\$60{,}800}{\$38{,}000} = 1.60{:}1$
Debt to assets ratio	$\frac{\$120{,}000}{\$400{,}000} = 30\%$	$\frac{\$150{,}000}{\$341{,}000} = 44\%$

The company's liquidity, as measured by the current ratio, improved from 1.60:1 to 2.20:1. Its solvency also improved, as measured by the debt to assets ratio, which declined from 44% to 30%.

(c) Free cash flow

2017: $110,000 − $45,000 − ($10,000 + $5,000) = $50,000
2016: $70,000 − $20,000 − ($10,000 + $2,500) = $37,500

The amount of cash generated by the company above its needs for dividends and capital expenditures increased from $37,500 to $50,000.

Related exercise material: **BE2-3, BE2-4, BE2-5, DO IT! 2-2, E2-7, E2-9, E2-10,** and **E2-11.**

LEARNING OBJECTIVE 3

Discuss financial reporting concepts.

You have now learned about the four financial statements and some basic ways to interpret those statements. In this last section, we will discuss concepts that underlie these financial statements. It would be unwise to make business decisions based on financial statements without understanding the implications of these concepts.

THE STANDARD-SETTING ENVIRONMENT

How does Best Buy decide on the type of financial information to disclose? What format should it use? How should it measure assets, liabilities, revenues, and expenses? Accounting professionals at Best Buy and all other U.S. companies get guidance from a set of accounting standards that have authoritative support, referred to as **generally accepted accounting principles (GAAP)**. Standard-setting bodies, in consultation with the accounting profession and the business community, determine these accounting standards.

The **Securities and Exchange Commission (SEC)** is the agency of the U.S. government that oversees U.S. financial markets and accounting standard-setting bodies. The **Financial Accounting Standards Board (FASB)** is the primary accounting standard-setting body in the United States. The **International Accounting Standards Board (IASB)** issues standards called **International Financial Reporting Standards (IFRS)**, which have been adopted by many countries outside of the United States. Today, the FASB and IASB are working closely together to minimize the differences in their standards. Recently, the SEC announced that foreign companies that wish to have their shares traded on U.S stock exchanges no longer have to prepare reports that conform with GAAP, as long as their reports conform with IFRS. The SEC is currently evaluating whether the United States should eventually adopt IFRS as the required set of standards for U.S. publicly traded companies. Another relatively recent change to the financial reporting environment was that, as a result of the Sarbanes-Oxley Act, the **Public Company Accounting Oversight Board (PCAOB)** was created. Its job is to determine auditing standards and review the performance of auditing firms. If the United States adopts IFRS for its accounting standards, it will also have to coordinate its auditing regulations with those of other countries.

INTERNATIONAL NOTE
Over 115 countries use international standards (called IFRS). For example, all companies in the European Union follow IFRS. In this textbook, we highlight any significant differences using International Notes like this one, as well as a more in-depth discussion in the *A Look at IFRS* section at the end of each chapter.

INTERNATIONAL INSIGHT

SeongJoon Cho/Bloomberg/Getty Images, Inc.

The Korean Discount

If you think that accounting standards don't matter, consider recent events in South Korea. For many years, international investors complained that the financial reports of South Korean companies were inadequate and inaccurate. Accounting practices there often resulted in huge differences between stated revenues and actual revenues. Because investors did not have faith in the accuracy of the numbers, they were unwilling to pay as much for the shares of these companies relative to shares of comparable companies in different countries. This difference in share price was often referred to as the "Korean discount."

In response, Korean regulators decided that companies would have to comply with international accounting standards. This change was motivated by a desire to "make the country's businesses more transparent" in order to build investor confidence and spur economic growth. Many other Asian countries, including China, India, Japan, and Hong Kong, have also decided either to adopt international standards or to create standards that are based on the international standards.

Source: Evan Ramstad, "End to 'Korea Discount'?" *Wall Street Journal* (March 16, 2007).

What is meant by the phrase "make the country's businesses more transparent"? Why would increasing transparency spur economic growth? (Go to **WileyPLUS** for this answer and additional questions.)

QUALITIES OF USEFUL INFORMATION

Recently, the FASB and IASB completed the first phase of a joint project in which they developed a conceptual framework to serve as the basis for future accounting standards. The framework begins by stating that the primary objective of financial reporting is to provide financial information that is **useful** to investors and creditors for making decisions about providing capital. According to the FASB, useful information should possess two fundamental qualities, relevance and faithful representation, as shown in Illustration 2-18 (page 60).

Enhancing Qualities

In addition to the two fundamental qualities, the FASB and IASB also describe a number of enhancing qualities of useful information. These include **comparability**, **verifiability**, **timeliness**, and **understandability**. In accounting,

ILLUSTRATION 2-18
Fundamental qualities of useful information

Relevance Accounting information has **relevance** if it would make a difference in a business decision. Information is considered relevant if it provides information that has **predictive value**, that is, helps provide accurate expectations about the future, and has **confirmatory value**, that is, confirms or corrects prior expectations. **Materiality** is a company-specific aspect of relevance. An item is material when its **size** makes it likely to influence the decision of an investor or creditor.

Faithful Representation **Faithful representation** means that information accurately depicts what really happened. To provide a faithful representation, information must be **complete** (nothing important has been omitted), **neutral** (is not biased toward one position or another), and **free from error**.

comparability results when different companies use the same accounting principles. Another type of comparability is consistency. **Consistency** means that a company uses the same accounting principles and methods from year to year. Information is **verifiable** if independent observers, using the same methods, obtain similar results. As noted in Chapter 1, certified public accountants (CPAs) perform audits of financial statements to verify their accuracy. For accounting information to have relevance, it must be **timely**. That is, it must be available to decision-makers before it loses its capacity to influence decisions. The SEC requires that large public companies provide their annual reports to investors within 60 days of their year-end. Information has the quality of **understandability** if it is presented in a clear and concise fashion, so that reasonably informed users of that information can interpret it and comprehend its meaning.

ACCOUNTING ACROSS THE ORGANIZATION

© Skip O'Donnell/iStockphoto

What Do These Companies Have in Common?

Another issue related to comparability is the accounting time period. An accounting period that is one-year long is called a **fiscal year**. But a fiscal year need not match the calendar year. For example, a company could end its fiscal year on April 30 rather than on December 31.

Why do companies choose the particular year-ends that they do? For example, why doesn't every company use December 31 as its accounting year-end? Many companies choose to end their accounting year when inventory or operations are at a low point. This is advantageous because compiling accounting information requires much time and effort by managers, so they would rather do it when they aren't as busy operating the business. Also, inventory is easier and less costly to count when its volume is low.

Some companies whose year-ends differ from December 31 are Delta Air Lines, June 30; The Walt Disney Company, September 30; and Dunkin' Donuts, Inc., October 31. In the notes to its financial statements, Best Buy states that its accounting year-end is the Saturday nearest the end of January.

What problems might Best Buy's year-end create for analysts? (Go to **WileyPLUS** for this answer and additional questions.)

ASSUMPTIONS IN FINANCIAL REPORTING

To develop accounting standards, the FASB relies on some key assumptions, as shown in Illustration 2-19. These include assumptions about the monetary unit, economic entity, periodicity, and going concern.

ILLUSTRATION 2-19
Key assumptions in financial reporting

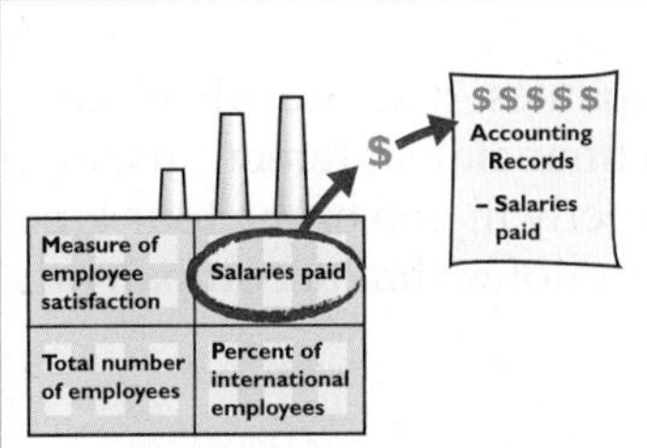

Monetary Unit Assumption The **monetary unit assumption** requires that only those things that can be expressed in money are included in the accounting records. This means that certain important information needed by investors, creditors, and managers, such as customer satisfaction, is not reported in the financial statements. This assumption relies on the monetary unit remaining relatively stable in value.

Economic Entity Assumption The **economic entity assumption** states that every economic entity can be separately identified and accounted for. In order to assess a company's performance and financial position accurately, it is important to not blur company transactions with personal transactions (especially those of its managers) or transactions of other companies.

ETHICS NOTE

The importance of the economic entity assumption is illustrated by scandals involving Adelphia. In this case, senior company employees entered into transactions that blurred the line between the employees' financial interests and those of the company. For example, Adelphia guaranteed over $2 billion of loans to the founding family.

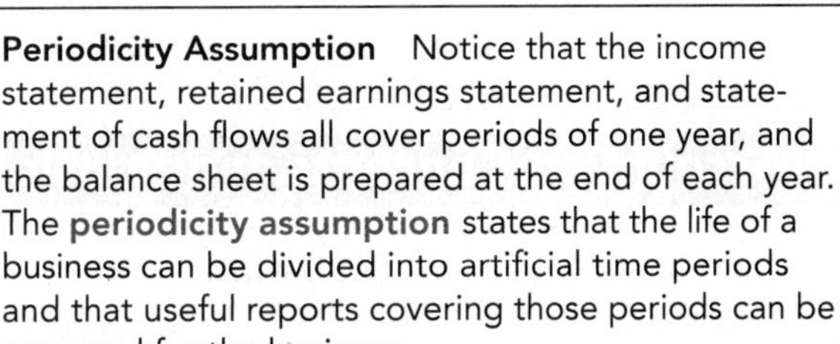

Periodicity Assumption Notice that the income statement, retained earnings statement, and statement of cash flows all cover periods of one year, and the balance sheet is prepared at the end of each year. The **periodicity assumption** states that the life of a business can be divided into artificial time periods and that useful reports covering those periods can be prepared for the business.

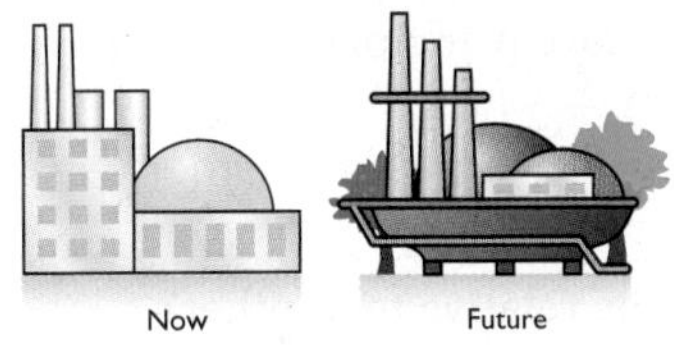

Going Concern Assumption The **going concern assumption** states that the business will remain in operation for the foreseeable future. Of course, many businesses do fail, but in general it is reasonable to assume that the business will continue operating.

PRINCIPLES IN FINANCIAL REPORTING

Measurement Principles

GAAP generally uses one of two measurement principles, the historical cost principle or the fair value principle. Selection of which principle to follow generally relates to trade-offs between relevance and faithful representation.

HISTORICAL COST PRINCIPLE The **historical cost principle** (or cost principle) dictates that companies record assets at their cost. This is true not only at the time the asset is purchased but also over the time the asset is held. For example, if land that was purchased for $30,000 increases in value to $40,000, it continues to be reported at $30,000.

FAIR VALUE PRINCIPLE The **fair value principle** indicates that assets and liabilities should be reported at fair value (the price received to sell an asset or settle a liability). Fair value information may be more useful than historical cost for certain types of assets and liabilities. For example, certain investment securities are reported at fair value because market price information is often readily available for these types of assets. In choosing between cost and fair value, the FASB uses two qualities that make accounting information useful for decision-making—relevance and faithful representation. In determining which measurement principle to use, the FASB weighs the factual nature of cost figures versus the relevance of fair value. In general, the FASB indicates that most assets must follow the historical cost principle because market values may not be representationally faithful. Only in situations where assets are actively traded, such as investment securities, is the fair value principle applied.

Full Disclosure Principle

The **full disclosure principle** requires that companies disclose all circumstances and events that would make a difference to financial statement users. If an important item cannot reasonably be reported directly in one of the four types of financial statements, then it should be discussed in notes that accompany the statements.

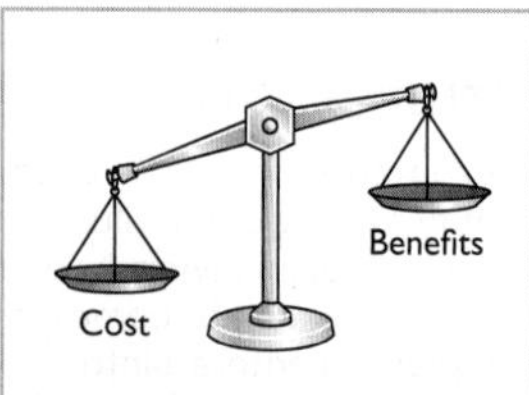

COST CONSTRAINT

Providing information is costly. In deciding whether companies should be required to provide a certain type of information, accounting standard-setters consider the **cost constraint**. It weighs the cost that companies will incur to provide the information against the benefit that financial statement users will gain from having the information available.

DO IT! 3 Financial Accounting Concepts and Principles

The following items guide the FASB when it creates accounting standards.

Relevance	Periodicity assumption
Faithful representation	Going concern assumption
Comparability	Historical cost principle
Consistency	Full disclosure principle
Monetary unit assumption	Materiality
Economic entity assumption	

Match each item above with a description below.

1. _______ Ability to easily evaluate one company's results relative to another's.
2. _______ Belief that a company will continue to operate for the foreseeable future.
3. _______ The judgment concerning whether an item is large enough to matter to decision-makers.
4. _______ The reporting of all information that would make a difference to financial statement users.
5. _______ The practice of preparing financial statements at regular intervals.
6. _______ The quality of information that indicates the information makes a difference in a decision.
7. _______ A belief that items should be reported on the balance sheet at the price that was paid to acquire the item.
8. _______ A company's use of the same accounting principles and methods from year to year.
9. _______ Tracing accounting events to particular companies.
10. _______ The desire to minimize errors and bias in financial statements.
11. _______ Reporting only those things that can be measured in dollars.

Action Plan

✔ Understand the need for conceptual guidelines in accounting.

✔ List the characteristics of useful financial information.

✔ Review the assumptions, principles, and constraint that comprise the guidelines in accounting.

SOLUTION

1. Comparability
2. Going concern assumption
3. Materiality
4. Full disclosure principle
5. Periodicity assumption
6. Relevance
7. Historical cost principle
8. Consistency
9. Economic entity assumption
10. Faithful representation
11. Monetary unit assumption

Related exercise material: **BE2-8, BE2-9, BE2-10, DO IT! 2-3, E2-12,** and **E2-13.**

USING DECISION TOOLS—TWEETER HOME ENTERTAINMENT

In this chapter, we evaluated a home electronics giant, Best Buy. Tweeter Home Entertainment sold consumer electronics products from 154 stores on the East Coast under various names. It specialized in products with high-end features. Tweeter filed for bankruptcy in June 2007 and was acquired by another company in July 2007. Financial data for Tweeter, prior to its bankruptcy, are provided below.

	September 30	
(amounts in millions)	**2006**	**2005**
Current assets	$146.4	$158.2
Total assets	258.6	284.0
Current liabilities	107.1	119.0
Total liabilities	190.4	201.1
Total common stockholders' equity	68.2	82.9
Net income (loss)	(16.5)	(74.4)
Net cash provided (used) by operating activities	15.6	(26.7)
Capital expenditures (net)	17.4	22.2
Dividends paid	0	0
Weighted-average shares of common stock (millions)	25.2	24.6

INSTRUCTIONS

Using the data provided, answer the following questions and discuss how these results might have provided an indication of Tweeter's financial troubles.

1. Calculate the current ratio for Tweeter for 2006 and 2005 and discuss its liquidity position.
2. Calculate the debt to assets ratio and free cash flow for Tweeter for 2006 and 2005 and discuss its solvency.
3. Calculate the earnings per share for Tweeter for 2006 and 2005, and discuss its change in profitability.
4. Best Buy's accounting year-end was February 28, 2006; Tweeter's was September 30, 2006. How does this difference affect your ability to compare their profitability?

SOLUTION

1. Current ratio:

   2006: $146.4 ÷ $107.1 = 1.37:1   *2005:* $158.2 ÷ $119.0 = 1.33:1

   Tweeter's liquidity improved slightly from 2005 to 2006, but in both years it would most likely have been considered inadequate. In 2006, Tweeter had only $1.37 in current assets for every dollar of current liabilities. Sometimes larger companies, such as Best Buy, can function with lower current ratios because they have alternative sources of working capital. But a company of Tweeter's size would normally want a higher ratio.

2. Debt to assets ratio:

   2006: $190.4 ÷ $258.6 = 73.6%   *2005:* $201.1 ÷ $284.0 = 70.8%

   Tweeter's solvency, as measured by its debt to assets ratio, declined from 2005 to 2006. Its ratio of 73.6% meant that every dollar of assets was financed by 73.6 cents of debt. For a retailer, this is extremely high reliance on debt. This low solvency suggests Tweeter's ability to meet its debt payments was questionable.

   Free cash flow:

   2006: $15.6 − $17.4 − $0 = −$1.8 million

   2005: −$26.7 − $22.2 − $0 = −$48.9 million

   Tweeter's free cash flow was negative in both years. The company did not generate enough net cash provided by operating activities even to cover its capital expenditures, and it was not paying a dividend. While this is not unusual for new companies in their early years, it is also not sustainable for very long. Part of the reason that its debt to assets ratio, discussed above, was so high was that it had to borrow money to make up for its deficient free cash flow.

3. Loss per share:

   2006: −$16.5 ÷ 25.2 = −$0.65 per share

   2005: −$74.4 ÷ 24.6 = −$3.02 per share

   Tweeter's loss per share declined substantially. However, this was little consolation for its shareholders, who experienced losses in previous years as well. The company's lack of profitability, combined with its poor liquidity and solvency, increased the likelihood that it would eventually file for bankruptcy.

4. Tweeter's income statement covers 7 months not covered by Best Buy's. Suppose that the economy changed dramatically during this 7-month period, either improving or declining. This change in the economy would be reflected in Tweeter's income statement but would not be reflected in Best Buy's income statement until the following March, thus reducing the usefulness of a comparison of the income statements of the two companies.

REVIEW AND PRACTICE

LEARNING OBJECTIVES REVIEW

1 Identify the sections of a classified balance sheet. In a classified balance sheet, companies classify assets as current assets; long-term investments; property, plant, and equipment; and intangibles. They classify liabilities as either current or long-term. A stockholders' equity section shows common stock and retained earnings.

2 Use ratios to evaluate a company's profitability, liquidity, and solvency. Ratio analysis expresses the relationship among selected items of financial statement data. Profitability ratios, such as earnings per share (EPS), measure aspects of the operating success of a company for a given period of time.

Liquidity ratios, such as the current ratio, measure the short-term ability of a company to pay its maturing obligations and to meet unexpected needs for cash. Solvency ratios, such as the debt to assets ratio, measure the ability of a company to survive over a long period. Free cash flow indicates a company's ability to generate net cash provided by operating activities that is sufficient to pay debts, acquire assets, and distribute dividends.

3 Discuss financial reporting concepts. Generally accepted accounting principles are a set of rules and practices recognized as a general guide for financial reporting purposes. The basic objective of financial reporting is to provide information that is useful for decision-making.

To be judged useful, information should have the primary characteristics of relevance and faithful representation. In addition, useful information is comparable, consistent, verifiable, timely, and understandable.

The **monetary unit assumption** requires that companies include in the accounting records only transaction data that can be expressed in terms of money. The **economic entity assumption** states that economic events can be identified with a particular unit of accountability. The **periodicity assumption** states that the economic life of a business can be divided into artificial time periods and that meaningful accounting reports can be prepared for each period. The **going concern assumption** states that the company will continue in operation long enough to carry out its existing objectives and commitments.

The **historical cost principle** states that companies should record assets at their cost. The **fair value principle** indicates that assets and liabilities should be reported at fair value. The **full disclosure principle** requires that companies disclose circumstances and events that matter to financial statement users.

The **cost constraint** weighs the cost that companies incur to provide a type of information against its benefit to financial statement users.

DECISION TOOLS REVIEW

DECISION CHECKPOINTS	INFO NEEDED FOR DECISION	TOOL TO USE FOR DECISION	HOW TO EVALUATE RESULTS
How does the company's earnings performance compare with that of previous years?	Net income available to common stockholders and weighted-average common shares outstanding	$\text{Earnings per share} = \frac{\text{Net income} - \text{Preferred dividends}}{\text{Weighted-average common shares outstanding}}$	A higher measure suggests improved performance, although the number is subject to manipulation. Values should not be compared across companies.
Can the company meet its near-term obligations?	Current assets and current liabilities	$\text{Current ratio} = \frac{\text{Current assets}}{\text{Current liabilities}}$	Higher ratio suggests favorable liquidity.
Can the company meet its long-term obligations?	Total liabilities and total assets	$\text{Debt to assets ratio} = \frac{\text{Total liabilities}}{\text{Total assets}}$	Lower value suggests favorable solvency.
How much cash did the company generate to expand operations, pay off debts, or distribute dividends?	Net cash provided by operating activities, cash spent on fixed assets, and cash dividends	$\text{Free cash flow} = \text{Net cash provided by operating activities} - \text{Capital expenditures} - \text{Cash dividends}$	Significant free cash flow indicates greater potential to finance new investments and pay additional dividends.

GLOSSARY REVIEW

Classified balance sheet A balance sheet that groups together similar assets and similar liabilities, using a number of standard classifications and sections. (p. 46).

Comparability Ability to compare the accounting information of different companies because they use the same accounting principles. (p. 60).

Consistency Use of the same accounting principles and methods from year to year within a company. (p. 60).

Cost constraint Constraint that weighs the cost that companies will incur to provide the information against the benefit that financial statement users will gain from having the information available. (p. 62).

Current assets Assets that companies expect to convert to cash or use up within one year or the operating cycle, whichever is longer. (p. 46).

Current liabilities Obligations that a company expects to pay within the next year or operating cycle, whichever is longer. (p. 50).

Current ratio A measure of liquidity computed as current assets divided by current liabilities. (p. 54).

Debt to assets ratio A measure of solvency calculated as total liabilities divided by total assets. It measures the percentage of total financing provided by creditors. (p. 56).

Earnings per share (EPS) A measure of the net income earned on each share of common stock; computed as net income minus preferred dividends divided by the weighted-average number of common shares outstanding during the year. (p. 53).

Economic entity assumption An assumption that every economic entity can be separately identified and accounted for. (p. 61).

Fair value principle Assets and liabilities should be reported at fair value (the price received to sell an asset or settle a liability). (p. 61).

Faithful representation Information that is complete, neutral, and free from error. (p. 60).

Financial Accounting Standards Board (FASB) The primary accounting standard-setting body in the United States. (p. 59).

Free cash flow Net cash provided by operating activities after adjusting for capital expenditures and cash dividends paid. (p. 57).

Full disclosure principle Accounting principle that dictates that companies disclose circumstances and events that make a difference to financial statement users. (p. 62).

Generally accepted accounting principles (GAAP) A set of accounting standards that have substantial authoritative support and which guide accounting professionals. (p. 58).

Going concern assumption The assumption that the company will continue in operation for the foreseeable future. (p. 61).

Historical cost principle An accounting principle that states that companies should record assets at their cost. (p. 61).

Intangible assets Assets that do not have physical substance. (p. 48).

International Accounting Standards Board (IASB) An accounting standard-setting body that issues standards adopted by many countries outside of the United States. (p. 59).

International Financial Reporting Standards (IFRS) Accounting standards, issued by the IASB, that have been adopted by many countries outside of the United States. (p. 59).

Liquidity The ability of a company to pay obligations that are expected to become due within the next year or operating cycle. (p. 53).

Liquidity ratios Measures of the short-term ability of the company to pay its maturing obligations and to meet unexpected needs for cash. (p. 54).

Long-term investments Generally, (1) investments in stocks and bonds of other corporations that companies hold for more than one year; (2) long-term assets, such as land and buildings, not currently being used in the company's operations; and (3) long-term notes receivable. (p. 48).

Long-term liabilities (long-term debt) Obligations that a company expects to pay after one year. (p. 50).

Materiality Whether an item is large enough to likely influence the decision of an investor or creditor. (p. 60).

Monetary unit assumption An assumption that requires that only those things that can be expressed in money are included in the accounting records. (p. 61).

Operating cycle The average time required to purchase inventory, sell it on account, and then collect cash from customers—that is, go from cash to cash. (p. 46).

Periodicity assumption An assumption that the life of a business can be divided into artificial time periods and that useful reports covering those periods can be prepared for the business. (p. 61).

Profitability ratios Measures of the operating success of a company for a given period of time. (p. 53).

Property, plant, and equipment Assets with relatively long useful lives that are currently used in operating the business. (p. 48).

Public Company Accounting Oversight Board (PCAOB) The group charged with determining auditing standards and reviewing the performance of auditing firms. (p. 59).

Ratio An expression of the mathematical relationship between one quantity and another. (p. 51).

Ratio analysis A technique that expresses the relationship among selected items of financial statement data. (p. 51).

Relevance The quality of information that indicates the information makes a difference in a decision. (p. 60).

Securities and Exchange Commission (SEC) The agency of the U.S. government that oversees U.S. financial markets and accounting standard-setting bodies. (p. 59).

Solvency The ability of a company to pay interest as it comes due and to repay the balance of debt due at its maturity. (p. 55).

Solvency ratios Measures of the ability of the company to survive over a long period of time. (p. 56).

Timely Information that is available to decision-makers before it loses its capacity to influence decisions. (p. 60).

Understandability Information presented in a clear and concise fashion so that users can interpret it and comprehend its meaning. (p. 60).

Verifiable The quality of information that occurs when independent observers, using the same methods, obtain similar results. (p. 60).

Working capital The difference between the amounts of current assets and current liabilities. (p. 54).

PRACTICE MULTIPLE-CHOICE QUESTIONS

(LO 1) 1. In a classified balance sheet, assets are usually classified as:
(a) current assets; long-term assets; property, plant, and equipment; and intangible assets.
(b) current assets; long-term investments; property, plant, and equipment; and common stock.
(c) current assets; long-term investments; tangible assets; and intangible assets.
(d) current assets; long-term investments; property, plant, and equipment; and intangible assets.

(LO 1) 2. Current assets are listed:
(a) by order of expected conversion to cash.
(b) by importance.
(c) by longevity.
(d) alphabetically.

(LO 1) 3. The correct order of presentation in a classified balance sheet for the following current assets is:
(a) accounts receivable, cash, prepaid insurance, inventory.
(b) cash, inventory, accounts receivable, prepaid insurance.
(c) cash, accounts receivable, inventory, prepaid insurance.
(d) inventory, cash, accounts receivable, prepaid insurance.

(LO 1) 4. A company has purchased a tract of land. It expects to build a production plant on the land in approximately 5 years. During the 5 years before construction, the land will be idle. The land should be reported as:
(a) property, plant, and equipment.
(b) land expense.
(c) a long-term investment.
(d) an intangible asset.

(LO 1) 5. The balance in retained earnings is **not** affected by:
(a) net income.
(b) net loss.
(c) issuance of common stock.
(d) dividends.

(LO 2) 6. Which is an indicator of profitability?
(a) Current ratio.
(b) Earnings per share.
(c) Debt to assets ratio.
(d) Free cash flow.

(LO 2) 7. For 2017, Spanos Corporation reported net income $26,000, net sales $400,000, and weighted-average shares outstanding 4,000. There were preferred dividends of $2,000. What was the 2017 earnings per share?
(a) $6.00. (c) $99.50.
(b) $6.50. (d) $100.00.

(LO 2) 8. Which of these measures is an evaluation of a company's ability to pay current liabilities?
(a) Earnings per share.
(b) Current ratio.
(c) Both (a) and (b).
(d) None of the above.

9. The following ratios are available for Reilly Inc. and O'Hare Inc. (LO 2)

	Current Ratio	Debt to Assets Ratio	Earnings per Share
Reilly Inc.	2:1	75%	$3.50
O'Hare Inc.	1.5:1	40%	$2.75

Compared to O'Hare Inc., Reilly Inc. has:
(a) higher liquidity, higher solvency, and higher profitability.
(b) lower liquidity, higher solvency, and higher profitability.
(c) higher liquidity, lower solvency, and higher profitability.
(d) higher liquidity and lower solvency, but profitability cannot be compared based on information provided.

10. Companies can use free cash flow to: (LO 2)
(a) pay additional dividends.
(b) acquire more property, plant, and equipment.
(c) pay off debts.
(d) All of the above.

11. Generally accepted accounting principles are: (LO 3)
(a) a set of standards and rules that are recognized as a general guide for financial reporting.
(b) usually established by the Internal Revenue Service.
(c) the guidelines used to resolve ethical dilemmas.
(d) fundamental truths that can be derived from the laws of nature.

12. What organization issues U.S. accounting standards? (LO 3)
(a) Financial Accounting Standards Board.
(b) International Accounting Standards Committee.
(c) International Auditing Standards Committee.
(d) None of the above.

13. What is the primary criterion by which accounting information can be judged? (LO 3)
(a) Consistency.
(b) Predictive value.
(c) Usefulness for decision-making.
(d) Comparability.

14. Neutrality is an ingredient of: (LO 3)

	Faithful Representation	Relevance
(a)	Yes	Yes
(b)	No	No
(c)	Yes	No
(d)	No	Yes

15. The characteristic of information that evaluates whether it is large enough to impact a decision. (LO 3)
(a) Comparability. (c) Cost.
(b) Materiality. (d) Consistency.

SOLUTIONS

1. **(d)** Assets are classified as current assets; long-term investments; property, plant and equipment; and intangible assets. The other choices are incorrect because (a) long-term assets includes long-term investments; property, plant, and equipment; and intangible assets; (b) common stock refers to the equity of the firm and is not an asset; and

(c) while tangible assets describes property, plant, and equipment, it is better to use the more common terminology of property, plant, and equipment.

2. **(a)** Current assets should be listed by order of expected conversion to cash (liquidity), not (b) by importance, (c) by longevity, or (d) alphabetically.
3. **(c)** The correct order of presentation for current assets is cash, accounts receivable, inventory, and then prepaid insurance. The other choices are therefore incorrect.
4. **(c)** Land or buildings that are currently not used in operations are considered to be long-term investments. The other choices are incorrect because (a) this classification is for property, plant, and equipment used in operations; (b) land is never expensed; and (d) intangible assets have no physical existence and are used in the production of income.
5. **(c)** Issuance of common stock has no impact on retained earnings. The other choices are incorrect because (a) net income increases retained earnings, (b) net loss decreases retained earnings, and (d) dividends decrease retained earnings.
6. **(b)** Earnings per share is a measure of profitability. The other choices are incorrect because (a) the current ratio is a measure of liquidity, (c) the debt to assets ratio is a measure of solvency, and (d) free cash flow is a measure of solvency.
7. **(a)** Earnings per share = Net income ($26,000) less Preferred dividends ($2,000) divided by Weighted-average shares outstanding (4,000) = $6.00/share, not (b) $6.50, (c) $99.50, or (d) $100.00.
8. **(b)** The current ratio measures liquidity. Higher current ratios indicate higher liquidity. The other choices are incorrect because (a) earnings per share is a measure of a firm's profitability, not its ability to pay its current liabilities; (c) one of these answers is incorrect; and (d) there is a correct answer.
9. **(d)** Reilly Inc. has higher liquidity as it has a higher current ratio, and lower solvency due to its higher debt to assets ratio. However, profitability cannot be compared across companies using earnings per share because of the wide variations in the number of shares of common stock of different companies. The other choices are therefore incorrect.
10. **(d)** Free cash flow can be used to pay dividends; acquire more property, plant, and equipment; and pay off debts. Although choices (a), (b), and (c) are correct, choice (d) is the better answer.
11. **(a)** All U.S. companies get guidance from a set of rules and practices that have authoritative support, referred to as generally accepted accounting principles (GAAP). Standard-setting bodies, in consultation with the accounting profession and the business community, determine these accounting standards. The other choices are incorrect because GAAP is (b) not established by the Internal Revenue Service, (c) not intended to provide guidance in resolving ethical dilemmas, or (d) created by people and can evolve over time, unlike laws of nature, such as those in physics and chemistry.
12. **(a)** The Financial Accounting Standards Board (FASB) is the organization that issues U.S. accounting standards, not the (b) International Accounting Standards Committee or (c) International Auditing Standards Committee. Choice (d) is wrong as there is a correct answer.
13. **(c)** Usefulness for decision-making is the primary criterion by which accounting information can be judged. The other choices are incorrect because (a) consistency, (b) predictive value, and (d) comparability all help to make accounting information more useful but are not the primary criterion by which accounting information is judged.
14. **(c)** Neutrality is an ingredient of faithful representation but not relevance. The other choices are therefore incorrect.
15. **(b)** Materiality evaluates whether information is large enough to impact a decision, not (a) comparability, (c) cost, or (d) consistency.

▶ PRACTICE EXERCISES

Prepare assets section of a classified balance sheet.

(LO 1)

1. Suppose the following information (in thousands of dollars) is available for H. J. Heinz Company—famous for ketchup and other fine food products—for the year ended April 30, 2017.

Prepaid insurance	$ 168,182	Buildings	$4,344,269
Land	56,007	Cash	617,687
Goodwill	4,411,521	Accounts receivable	1,161,481
Trademarks	723,243	Accumulated depreciation—buildings	2,295,563
Inventory	1,378,216		

INSTRUCTIONS

Prepare the assets section of a classified balance sheet, listing the items in proper sequence and including a statement heading.

SOLUTION

1.

H. J. HEINZ COMPANY Partial Balance Sheet April 30, 2017 (in thousands)			
Assets			
Current assets			
Cash		$ 617,687	
Accounts receivable		1,161,481	
Inventory		1,378,216	
Prepaid insurance		168,182	
Total current assets			$ 3,325,566
Property, plant, and equipment			
Land		56,007	
Buildings	$4,344,269		
Less: Accumulated depr.—buildings	2,295,563	2,048,706	2,104,713
Intangible assets			
Goodwill		4,411,521	
Trademarks		723,243	5,134,764
Total assets			$10,565,043

Compute and interpret various ratios.

(LO 2)

2. Suppose the following data were taken from the 2017 and 2016 financial statements of American Eagle Outfitters. (All dollars are in thousands.)

	2017	2016
Current assets	$1,020,834	$1,189,108
Total assets	1,867,680	1,979,558
Current liabilities	376,178	464,618
Total liabilities	527,216	562,246
Net income	400,019	387,359
Net cash provided by operating activities	464,270	749,268
Capital expenditures	250,407	225,939
Dividends paid on common stock	80,796	61,521
Weighted-average shares outstanding	216,119	222,662

INSTRUCTIONS

Perform each of the following.

(a) Calculate the current ratio for each year.

(b) Calculate earnings per share for each year.

(c) Calculate the debt to assets ratio for each year.

(d) Calculate the free cash flow for each year.

(e) Discuss American Eagle's solvency in 2017 versus 2016.

SOLUTION

2.

	2017	2016
(a) Current ratio	$\frac{\$1,020,834}{\$376,178} = 2.71:1$	$\frac{\$1,189,108}{\$464,618} = 2.56:1$

	2017	2016
(b) Earning per share	$\frac{\$400,019}{216,119} = \$1.85$	$\frac{\$387,359}{222,662} = \$1.74$
(c) Debt to assets ratio	$\frac{\$527,216}{\$1,867,680} = 28.2\%$	$\frac{\$562,246}{\$1,979,558} = 28.4\%$
(d) Free cash flow	\$464,270 − \$250,407 − \$80,796 = \$133,067	\$749,268 − \$225,939 − \$61,521 = \$461,808

(e) Using the debt to assets ratio and free cash flow as measures of solvency produces negative results for American Eagle Outfitters. Its debt to assets ratio decreased slightly from 28.4% for 2016 to 28.2% for 2017, indicating a very small increase in solvency for 2017. Its free cash flow decreased by 71%, indicating a significant decline in solvency.

▶ PRACTICE PROBLEM

Prepare financial statements. (LO 1)

Listed here are items taken from the income statement and balance sheet of Bargain Electronics, Inc. for the year ended December 31, 2017. Certain items have been combined for simplification. (Amounts are given in thousands.)

Notes payable (due in 3 years)	$ 50.5
Cash	141.1
Salaries and wages expense	2,933.6
Common stock	454.9
Accounts payable	922.2
Accounts receivable	723.3
Equipment, net	921.0
Cost of goods sold	9,501.4
Income taxes payable	7.2
Interest expense	1.5
Mortgage payable	451.5
Retained earnings	1,336.3
Inventory	1,636.5
Sales revenue	12,456.9
Debt investments (short-term)	382.6
Income tax expense	30.5
Goodwill	202.7
Notes payable (due in 6 months)	784.6

INSTRUCTIONS

Prepare an income statement and a classified balance sheet using the items listed. Do not use any item more than once.

SOLUTION

BARGAIN ELECTRONICS, INC.
Income Statement
For the Year Ended December 31, 2017
(in thousands)

Revenues		
Sales revenue		$12,456.9
Expenses		
Cost of goods sold	$9,501.4	
Salaries and wages expense	2,933.6	
Interest expense	1.5	
Income tax expense	30.5	
Total expenses		12,467.0
Net loss		$ (10.1)

BARGAIN ELECTRONICS, INC. Balance Sheet December 31, 2017 (in thousands)		
Assets		
Current assets		
Cash	$ 141.1	
Debt investments	382.6	
Accounts receivable	723.3	
Inventory	1,636.6	
Total current assets		$2,883.5
Equipment, net		921.0
Goodwill		202.7
Total assets		$4,007.2
Liabilities and Stockholders' Equity		
Current liabilities		
Notes payable	$ 784.6	
Accounts payable	922.2	
Income taxes payable	7.2	
Total current liabilities		$1,714.0
Long-term liabilities		
Mortgage payable	451.5	
Notes payable	50.5	502.0
Total liabilities		2,216.0
Stockholders' equity		
Common stock	454.9	
Retained earnings	1,336.3	
Total stockholders' equity		1,791.2
Total liabilities and stockholders' equity		$4,007.2

WileyPLUS Brief Exercises, DO IT! Exercises, Exercises, Problems, and many additional resources are available for practice in WileyPLUS.

QUESTIONS

1. What is meant by the term operating cycle?
2. Define current assets. What basis is used for ordering individual items within the current assets section?
3. Distinguish between long-term investments and property, plant, and equipment.
4. How do current liabilities differ from long-term liabilities?
5. Identify the two parts of stockholders' equity in a corporation and indicate the purpose of each.
6. (a) Geena Lowe believes that the analysis of financial statements is directed at two characteristics of a company: liquidity and profitability. Is Geena correct? Explain.
   (b) Are short-term creditors, long-term creditors, and stockholders primarily interested in the same characteristics of a company? Explain.
7. Name ratios useful in assessing (a) liquidity, (b) solvency, and (c) profitability.
8. Tom Dawes, the founder of Footwear Inc., needs to raise $500,000 to expand his company's

operations. He has been told that raising the money through debt will increase the riskiness of his company much more than issuing stock. He doesn't understand why this is true. Explain it to him.

9. What do these classes of ratios measure?
   (a) Liquidity ratios.
   (b) Profitability ratios.
   (c) Solvency ratios.

10. Holding all other factors constant, indicate whether each of the following signals generally good or bad news about a company.
    (a) Increase in earnings per share.
    (b) Increase in the current ratio.
    (c) Increase in the debt to assets ratio.
    (d) Decrease in free cash flow.

11. Which ratio or ratios from this chapter do you think should be of greatest interest to:
    (a) a pension fund considering investing in a corporation's 20-year bonds?
    (b) a bank contemplating a short-term loan?
    (c) an investor in common stock?

12. (a) What are generally accepted accounting principles (GAAP)?
    (b) What body provides authoritative support for GAAP?

13. (a) What is the primary objective of financial reporting?
    (b) Identify the characteristics of useful accounting information.

14. Merle Hawkins, the president of Pathway Company, is pleased. Pathway substantially increased its net income in 2017 while keeping its unit inventory relatively the same. Jon Dietz, chief accountant, cautions Merle, however. Dietz says that since Pathway changed its method of inventory valuation, there is a consistency problem and it is difficult to determine whether Pathway is better off. Is Dietz correct? Why or why not?

15. What is the distinction between comparability and consistency?

16. Describe the constraint inherent in the presentation of accounting information.

17. Your roommate believes that accounting standards are uniform throughout the world. Is your roommate correct? Explain.

18. Wanda Roberts is president of Best Texts. She has no accounting background. Wanda cannot understand why fair value is not used as the basis for all accounting measurement and reporting. Discuss.

19. What is the economic entity assumption? Give an example of its violation.

20. What was Apple's largest current asset, largest current liability, and largest item under "Assets" at September 27, 2014?

BRIEF EXERCISES

Classify accounts on balance sheet.
(LO 1), K

BE2-1 The following are the major balance sheet classifications:

Current assets (CA)	Current liabilities (CL)
Long-term investments (LTI)	Long-term liabilities (LTL)
Property, plant, and equipment (PPE)	Common stock (CS)
Intangible assets (IA)	Retained earnings (RE)

Match each of the following accounts to its proper balance sheet classification.

_____ Accounts payable	_____ Income taxes payable
_____ Accounts receivable	_____ Investment in long-term bonds
_____ Accumulated depreciation	_____ Land
_____ Buildings	_____ Inventory
_____ Cash	_____ Patent
_____ Goodwill	_____ Supplies

Prepare the current assets section of a balance sheet.
(LO 1), AP

BE2-2 A list of financial statement items for Chin Company includes the following: accounts receivable $14,000, prepaid insurance $2,600, cash $10,400, supplies $3,800, and debt investments (short-term) $8,200. Prepare the current assets section of the balance sheet listing the items in the proper sequence.

Compute earnings per share.
(LO 2), AP

BE2-3 The following information (in millions of dollars) is available for Limited Brands for a recent year: sales revenue $9,043, net income $220, preferred dividend $0, and weighted-average shares outstanding 333 million. Compute the earnings per share for Limited Brands.

Calculate liquidity ratios.
(LO 2), AP

BE2-4 These selected condensed data are taken from a recent balance sheet of Bob Evans Farms (in millions of dollars).

Cash	$ 29.3
Accounts receivable	20.5
Inventory	28.7
Other current assets	24.0
Total current assets	$102.5
Total current liabilities	$201.2

Compute working capital and the current ratio.

Calculate liquidity and solvency ratios.

(LO 2), AP

BE2-5 Ross Music Inc. reported the following selected information at March 31.

	2017
Total current assets	$262,787
Total assets	439,832
Total current liabilities	293,625
Total liabilities	376,002
Net cash provided by operating activities	62,300

Calculate (a) the current ratio, (b) the debt to assets ratio, and (c) free cash flow for March 31, 2017. The company paid dividends of $12,000 and spent $24,787 on capital expenditures.

Recognize generally accepted accounting principles.

(LO 3), K

BE2-6 Indicate whether each statement is true or false.

(a) GAAP is a set of rules and practices established by accounting standard-setting bodies to serve as a general guide for financial reporting purposes.

(b) Substantial authoritative support for GAAP usually comes from two standards-setting bodies: the FASB and the IRS.

Identify characteristics of useful information.

(LO 3), K

BE2-7 The accompanying chart shows the qualitative characteristics of useful accounting information. Fill in the blanks.

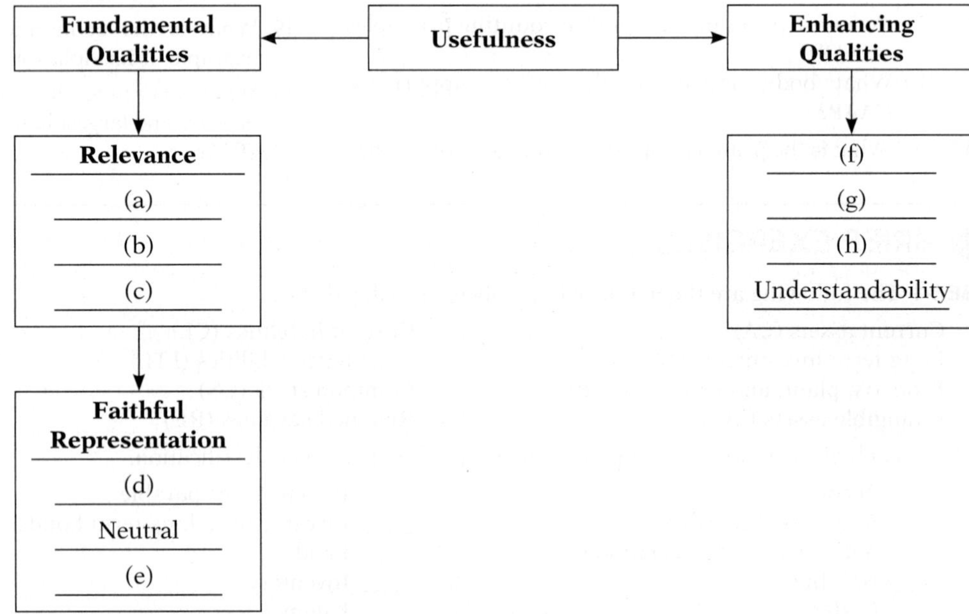

Identify characteristics of useful information.

(LO 3), K

BE2-8 Given the characteristics of useful accounting information, complete each of the following statements.

(a) For information to be _____, it should have predictive and confirmatory value.

(b) _____ means that information accurately depicts what really happened.

(c) _____ means using the same accounting principles and methods from year to year within a company.

Identify characteristics of useful information.

(LO 3), K

BE2-9 Here are some qualitative characteristics of useful accounting information:

1. Predictive value
2. Neutral
3. Verifiable
4. Timely

Match each qualitative characteristic to one of the following statements.

______ (a) Accounting information should help provide accurate expectations about future events.

______ (b) Accounting information cannot be selected, prepared, or presented to favor one set of interested users over another.

______ (c) The quality of information that occurs when independent observers, using the same methods, obtain similar results.

______ (d) Accounting information must be available to decision-makers before it loses its capacity to influence their decisions.

BE2-10 The full disclosure principle dictates that:

Define full disclosure principle.

(LO 3), K

(a) financial statements should disclose all assets at their cost.
(b) financial statements should disclose only those events that can be measured in dollars.
(c) financial statements should disclose all events and circumstances that would matter to users of financial statements.
(d) financial statements should not be relied on unless an auditor has expressed an unqualified opinion on them.

DO IT! EXERCISES

DO IT! 2-1a Mylar Corporation has collected the following information related to its December 31, 2017, balance sheet.

Prepare assets section of balance sheet.

(LO 1), AP

Accounts receivable	$22,000	Equipment	$180,000
Accumulated depreciation—equipment	50,000	Inventory	58,000
Cash	13,000	Supplies	7,000

Prepare the assets section of Mylar Corporation's balance sheet.

DO IT! 2-1b The following financial statement items were taken from the financial statements of Gomez Corp.

Classify financial statement items by balance sheet classification.

(LO 1), AP

____ Trademarks	____ Inventory
____ Notes payable (current)	____ Accumulated depreciation
____ Interest revenue	____ Land
____ Income taxes payable	____ Common stock
____ Debt investments (long-term)	____ Advertising expense
____ Unearned sales revenue	____ Mortgage payable (due in 3 years)

Match each of the financial statement items to its proper balance sheet classification. (See E2-1, on page 74, for a list of the balance sheet classifications.) If the item would not appear on a balance sheet, use "NA."

DO IT! 2-2 The following information is available for Nguoi Corporation.

Compute ratios and analyze.

(LO 2), AP

	2017	2016
Current assets	$ 54,000	$ 36,000
Total assets	240,000	205,000
Current liabilities	22,000	30,000
Total liabilities	72,000	100,000
Net income	80,000	40,000
Net cash provided by operating activities	90,000	56,000
Preferred dividends	6,000	6,000
Common dividends	3,000	1,500
Expenditures on property, plant, and equipment	27,000	12,000
Shares outstanding at beginning of year	40,000	30,000
Shares outstanding at end of year	75,000	40,000

(a) Compute earnings per share for 2017 and 2016 for Nguoi, and comment on the change. Nguoi's primary competitor, Matisse Corporation, had earnings per share of $1 per share in 2017. Comment on the difference in the ratios of the two companies.
(b) Compute the current ratio and debt to assets ratio for each year, and comment on the changes.
(c) Compute free cash flow for each year, and comment on the changes.

DO IT! 2-3 The following characteristics, assumptions, principles, and constraint guide the FASB when it creates accounting standards.

Identify financial accounting concepts and principles.

(LO 3), K

Relevance	Periodicity assumption
Faithful representation	Going concern assumption
Comparability	Historical cost principle
Consistency	Full disclosure principle
Monetary unit assumption	Materiality
Economic entity assumption	Cost constraint

Match each item above with a description below.

1. ________ Items not easily quantified in dollar terms are not reported in the financial statements.
2. ________ Accounting information must be complete, neutral, and free from error.
3. ________ Personal transactions are not mixed with the company's transactions.
4. ________ The cost to provide information should be weighed against the benefit that users will gain from having the information available.
5. ________ A company's use of the same accounting principles from year to year.
6. ________ Assets are recorded and reported at original purchase price.
7. ________ Accounting information should help users predict future events, and should confirm or correct prior expectations.
8. ________ The life of a business can be divided into artificial segments of time.
9. ________ The reporting of all information that would make a difference to financial statement users.
10. ________ The judgment concerning whether an item's size makes it likely to influence a decision-maker.
11. ________ Assumes a business will remain in operation for the foreseeable future.
12. ________ Different companies use the same accounting principles.

EXERCISES

Classify accounts on balance sheet.

(LO 1), AP

E2-1 The following are the major balance sheet classifications.

Current assets (CA)	Current liabilities (CL)
Long-term investments (LTI)	Long-term liabilities (LTL)
Property, plant, and equipment (PPE)	Stockholders' equity (SE)
Intangible assets (IA)	

Instructions

Classify each of the following financial statement items taken from Ming Corporation's balance sheet.

____ Accounts payable	____ Income taxes payable
____ Accounts receivable	____ Inventory
____ Accumulated depreciation—equipment	____ Stock investments (to be sold in 7 months)
	____ Land (in use)
____ Buildings	____ Mortgage payable
____ Cash	____ Supplies
____ Interest payable	____ Equipment
____ Goodwill	____ Prepaid rent

Classify financial statement items by balance sheet classification.

(LO 1), AP

E2-2 The major balance sheet classifications are listed in E2-1.

Instructions

Classify each of the following financial statement items based upon the major balance sheet classifications listed in E2-1.

____ Prepaid advertising	____ Patents
____ Equipment	____ Bonds payable
____ Trademarks	____ Common stock
____ Salaries and wages payable	____ Accumulated depreciation—equipment
____ Income taxes payable	
____ Retained earnings	____ Unearned sales revenue
____ Accounts receivable	____ Inventory
____ Land (held for future use)	

Classify items as current or noncurrent, and prepare assets section of balance sheet.

(LO 1), AP

E2-3 Suppose the following items were taken from the December 31, 2017, assets section of the Boeing Company balance sheet. (All dollars are in millions.)

Inventory	$16,933	Patents	$12,528
Notes receivable—due after December 31, 2018	5,466	Buildings	21,579
		Cash	9,215
Notes receivable—due before December 31, 2018	368	Accounts receivable	5,785
		Debt investments (short-term)	2,008
Accumulated depreciation—buildings	12,795		

Instructions

Prepare the assets section of a classified balance sheet, listing the current assets in order of their liquidity.

E2-4 Suppose the following information (in thousands of dollars) is available for H. J. Heinz Company—famous for ketchup and other fine food products—for the year ended April 30, 2017.

Prepare assets section of a classified balance sheet.

(LO 1), AP

Prepaid insurance	$ 125,765	Buildings	$4,033,369
Land	76,193	Cash	373,145
Goodwill	3,982,954	Accounts receivable	1,171,797
Trademarks	757,907	Accumulated depreciation—buildings	2,131,260
Inventory	1,237,613		

Instructions

Prepare the assets section of a classified balance sheet, listing the items in proper sequence and including a statement heading.

E2-5 These items are taken from the financial statements of Longhorn Co. at December 31, 2017.

Prepare a classified balance sheet.

(LO 1), AP

Buildings	$105,800
Accounts receivable	12,600
Prepaid insurance	3,200
Cash	11,840
Equipment	82,400
Land	61,200
Insurance expense	780
Depreciation expense	5,300
Interest expense	2,600
Common stock	60,000
Retained earnings (January 1, 2017)	40,000
Accumulated depreciation—buildings	45,600
Accounts payable	9,500
Notes payable	93,600
Accumulated depreciation—equipment	18,720
Interest payable	3,600
Service revenue	14,700

Instructions

Prepare a classified balance sheet. Assume that $13,600 of the note payable will be paid in 2018.

E2-6 Suppose the following items were taken from the 2017 financial statements of Texas Instruments, Inc. (All dollars are in millions.)

Prepare a classified balance sheet.

(LO 1), AP

Common stock	$2,826	Accumulated depreciation—equipment	$3,547
Prepaid rent	164	Accounts payable	1,459
Equipment	6,705	Patents	2,210
Stock investments (long-term)	637	Notes payable (long-term)	810
Debt investments (short-term)	1,743	Retained earnings	6,896
Income taxes payable	128	Accounts receivable	1,823
Cash	1,182	Inventory	1,202

Instructions

Prepare a classified balance sheet in good form as of December 31, 2017.

E2-7 Suppose the following information is available for Callaway Golf Company for the years 2017 and 2016. (Dollars are in thousands, except share information.)

Compute and interpret profitability ratio.

(LO 2), AP

	2017	**2016**
Net sales	$1,117,204	$1,124,591
Net income (loss)	66,176	54,587
Total assets	855,338	838,078

Share information	2017	2016
Shares outstanding at year-end	64,507,000	66,282,000
Preferred dividends	–0–	–0–

There were 73,139,000 shares outstanding at the end of 2015.

Instructions

(a) What was the company's earnings per share for each year?

(b) Based on your findings above, how did the company's profitability change from 2016 to 2017?

(c) Suppose the company had paid dividends on preferred stock and on common stock during the year. How would this affect your calculation in part (a)?

Prepare financial statements.

(LO 1, 2), AP

E2-8 These financial statement items are for Fairview Corporation at year-end, July 31, 2017.

Salaries and wages payable	$ 2,080
Salaries and wages expense	57,500
Supplies expense	15,600
Equipment	18,500
Accounts payable	4,100
Service revenue	66,100
Rent revenue	8,500
Notes payable (due in 2020)	1,800
Common stock	16,000
Cash	29,200
Accounts receivable	9,780
Accumulated depreciation—equipment	6,000
Dividends	4,000
Depreciation expense	4,000
Retained earnings (beginning of the year)	34,000

Instructions

(a) Prepare an income statement and a retained earnings statement for the year. Fairview Corporation did not issue any new stock during the year.

(b) Prepare a classified balance sheet at July 31.

(c) Compute the current ratio and debt to assets ratio.

(d) Suppose that you are the president of Lunar Equipment. Your sales manager has approached you with a proposal to sell $20,000 of equipment to Fairview. He would like to provide a loan to Fairview in the form of a 10%, 5-year note payable. Evaluate how this loan would change Fairview's current ratio and debt to assets ratio, and discuss whether you would make the sale.

Compute liquidity ratios and compare results.

(LO 2), AP

E2-9 Nordstrom, Inc. operates department stores in numerous states. Selected financial statement data (in millions of dollars) for a recent year follow.

	End of Year	Beginning of Year
Cash and cash equivalents	$ 72	$ 358
Receivables (net)	1,942	1,788
Merchandise inventory	900	956
Other current assets	303	259
Total current assets	$3,217	$3,361
Total current liabilities	$1,601	$1,635

Instructions

(a) Compute working capital and the current ratio at the beginning of the year and at the end of the year.

(b) Did Nordstrom's liquidity improve or worsen during the year?

(c) Using the data in the chapter, compare Nordstrom's liquidity with Best Buy's (see page 55).

Compute liquidity measures and discuss findings.

(LO 2), AP  

E2-10 The chief financial officer (CFO) of Myeneke Corporation requested that the accounting department prepare a preliminary balance sheet on December 30, 2017, so that the CFO could get an idea of how the company stood. He knows that certain debt agreements with its creditors require the company to maintain a current ratio of at least 2:1. The preliminary balance sheet is as follows.

MYENEKE CORP.
Balance Sheet
December 30, 2017

Current assets			Current liabilities		
Cash	$25,000		Accounts payable	$ 20,000	
Accounts receivable	30,000		Salaries and wages payable	10,000	$ 30,000
Prepaid insurance	5,000	$ 60,000	Long-term liabilities		
Equipment (net)		200,000	Notes payable		80,000
Total assets		$260,000	Total liabilities		110,000
			Stockholders' equity		
			Common stock	100,000	
			Retained earnings	50,000	150,000
			Total liabilities and stockholders' equity		$260,000

Instructions

(a) Calculate the current ratio and working capital based on the preliminary balance sheet.
(b) Based on the results in (a), the CFO requested that $20,000 of cash be used to pay off the balance of the Accounts Payable account on December 31, 2017. Calculate the new current ratio and working capital after the company takes these actions.
(c) Discuss the pros and cons of the current ratio and working capital as measures of liquidity.
(d) Was it unethical for the CFO to take these steps?

E2-11 Suppose the following data were taken from the 2017 and 2016 financial statements of American Eagle Outfitters. (All numbers, including share data, are in thousands.)

Compute and interpret solvency ratios.

(LO 2), AP

	2017	2016
Current assets	$ 925,359	$1,020,834
Total assets	1,963,676	1,867,680
Current liabilities	401,763	376,178
Total liabilities	554,645	527,216
Net income	179,061	400,019
Net cash provided by operating activities	302,193	464,270
Capital expenditures	265,335	250,407
Dividends paid on common stock	82,394	80,796
Weighted-average shares outstanding	205,169	216,119

Instructions

Perform each of the following.
(a) Calculate the current ratio for each year.
(b) Calculate earnings per share for each year.
(c) Calculate the debt to assets ratio for each year.
(d) Calculate the free cash flow for each year.
(e) Discuss American Eagle's solvency in 2017 versus 2016.
(f) Discuss American Eagle's ability to finance its investment activities with net cash provided by operating activities, and how any deficiency would be met.

E2-12 Presented below are the assumptions and principles discussed in this chapter.

Identify accounting assumptions and principles.

(LO 3), K

1. Full disclosure principle
2. Going concern assumption
3. Monetary unit assumption
4. Periodicity assumption
5. Historical cost principle
6. Economic entity assumption

Instructions

Identify by number the accounting assumption or principle that is described below. Do not use a number more than once.

_____ (a) Is the rationale for why plant assets are not reported at liquidation value. (*Note:* Do not use the historical cost principle.)

______ (b) Indicates that personal and business recordkeeping should be separately maintained.
______ (c) Assumes that the dollar is the "measuring stick" used to report on financial performance.
______ (d) Separates financial information into time periods for reporting purposes.
______ (e) Measurement basis used when a reliable estimate of fair value is not available.
______ (f) Dictates that companies should disclose all circumstances and events that make a difference to financial statement users.

Identify the assumption or principle that has been violated.

(LO 3), C

E2-13 Lopez Co. had three major business transactions during 2017.

(a) Reported at its fair value of $260,000 merchandise inventory with a cost of $208,000.
(b) The president of Lopez Co., Victor Lopez, purchased a truck for personal use and charged it to his expense account.
(c) Lopez Co. wanted to make its 2017 income look better, so it added 2 more weeks to its income statement reporting period (a 54-week year). Previous years were 52 weeks.

Instructions

In each situation, identify the assumption or principle that has been violated, if any, and discuss what the company should have done.

EXERCISES: SET B AND CHALLENGE EXERCISES

Visit the book's companion website, at **www.wiley.com/college/kimmel**, and choose the Student Companion site to access Exercises: Set B and Challenge Exercises.

PROBLEMS: SET A

Prepare a classified balance sheet.

(LO 1), AP

P2-1A Suppose the following items are taken from the 2017 balance sheet of Yahoo! Inc. (All dollars are in millions.)

Goodwill	$3,927
Common stock	6,283
Equipment	1,737
Accounts payable	152
Patents	234
Stock investments (long-term)	3,247
Accounts receivable	1,061
Prepaid rent	233
Debt investments (short-term)	1,160
Retained earnings	6,108
Cash	2,292
Notes payable (long-term)	734
Unearned sales revenue	413
Accumulated depreciation—equipment	201

Tot. current assets $4,746
Tot. assets $13,690

Instructions

Prepare a classified balance sheet for Yahoo! Inc. as of December 31, 2017.

Prepare financial statements.

(LO 1), AP

P2-2A These items are taken from the financial statements of Martin Corporation for 2017.

Retained earnings (beginning of year)	$31,000
Utilities expense	2,000
Equipment	66,000
Accounts payable	18,300
Cash	10,100
Salaries and wages payable	3,000
Common stock	12,000
Dividends	12,000

Service revenue	68,000
Prepaid insurance	3,500
Maintenance and repairs expense	1,800
Depreciation expense	3,600
Accounts receivable	11,700
Insurance expense	2,200
Salaries and wages expense	37,000
Accumulated depreciation—equipment	17,600

Instructions

Prepare an income statement, a retained earnings statement, and a classified balance sheet as of December 31, 2017.

Net income	$21,400
Tot. assets	$73,700

P2-3A You are provided with the following information for Lazuris Enterprises, effective as of its April 30, 2017, year-end.

Prepare financial statements.

(LO 1), AP

Accounts payable	$ 834
Accounts receivable	810
Accumulated depreciation—equipment	670
Cash	1,270
Common stock	900
Cost of goods sold	1,060
Depreciation expense	335
Dividends	325
Equipment	2,420
Income tax expense	165
Income taxes payable	135
Insurance expense	210
Interest expense	400
Inventory	967
Land	3,100
Mortgage payable	3,500
Notes payable	61
Prepaid insurance	60
Retained earnings (beginning)	1,600
Salaries and wages expense	700
Salaries and wages payable	222
Sales revenue	5,100
Stock investments (short-term)	1,200

Instructions

(a) Prepare an income statement and a retained earnings statement for Lazuris Enterprises for the year ended April 30, 2017.

(b) Prepare a classified balance sheet for Lazuris Enterprises as of April 30, 2017.

(a) Net income	$2,230
(b) Tot. current assets	$4,307
Tot. assets	$9,157

P2-4A Comparative financial statement data for Loeb Corporation and Bowsh Corporation, two competitors, appear below. All balance sheet data are as of December 31, 2017.

Compute ratios; comment on relative profitability, liquidity, and solvency.

(LO 2), AN

	Loeb Corporation	Bowsh Corporation
	2017	2017
Net sales	$1,800,000	$620,000
Cost of goods sold	1,175,000	340,000
Operating expenses	283,000	98,000
Interest expense	9,000	3,800
Income tax expense	85,000	36,000
Current assets	407,200	190,336
Plant assets (net)	532,000	139,728
Current liabilities	66,325	33,716
Long-term liabilities	108,500	40,684
Net cash provided by operating activities	138,000	36,000
Capital expenditures	90,000	20,000
Dividends paid on common stock	36,000	15,000
Weighted-average number of shares outstanding	80,000	50,000

Instructions

(a) Comment on the relative profitability of the companies by computing the net income and earnings per share for each company for 2017.

(b) Comment on the relative liquidity of the companies by computing working capital and the current ratio for each company for 2017.

(c) Comment on the relative solvency of the companies by computing the debt to assets ratio and the free cash flow for each company for 2017.

Compute and interpret liquidity, solvency, and profitability ratios.

(LO 2), AP

P2-5A The following are financial statements of Ohara Company.

OHARA COMPANY
Income Statement
For the Year Ended December 31, 2017

Net sales	$2,218,500
Cost of goods sold	1,012,400
Selling and administrative expenses	906,000
Interest expense	78,000
Income tax expense	69,000
Net income	$ 153,100

OHARA COMPANY
Balance Sheet
December 31, 2017

Assets	
Current assets	
Cash	$ 60,100
Debt investments	84,000
Accounts receivable (net)	169,800
Inventory	145,000
Total current assets	458,900
Plant assets (net)	575,300
Total assets	$1,034,200
Liabilities and Stockholders' Equity	
Current liabilities	
Accounts payable	$ 160,000
Income taxes payable	35,500
Total current liabilities	195,500
Bonds payable	200,000
Total liabilities	395,500
Stockholders' equity	
Common stock	350,000
Retained earnings	288,700
Total stockholders' equity	638,700
Total liabilities and stockholders' equity	$1,034,200

Additional information: The net cash provided by operating activities for 2017 was $190,800. The cash used for capital expenditures was $92,000. The cash used for dividends was $31,000. The weighted-average number of shares outstanding during the year was 50,000.

Instructions

(a) Compute the following values and ratios for 2017. (We provide the results from 2016 for comparative purposes.)

(i) Working capital. (2016: $160,500)

(ii) Current ratio. (2016: 1.65:1)

(iii) Free cash flow. (2016: $48,700)

(iv) Debt to assets ratio. (2016: 31%)

(v) Earnings per share. (2016: $3.15)

(b) Using your calculations from part (a), discuss changes from 2016 in liquidity, solvency, and profitability.

P2-6A Condensed balance sheet and income statement data for Danke Corporation are presented as follows.

Compute and interpret liquidity, solvency, and profitability ratios.

(LO 2), AP

DANKE CORPORATION
Balance Sheets
December 31

	2017	2016
Assets		
Cash	$ 28,000	$ 20,000
Receivables (net)	70,000	62,000
Other current assets	90,000	73,000
Long-term investments	62,000	60,000
Property, plant, and equipment (net)	510,000	470,000
Total assets	$760,000	$685,000
Liabilities and Stockholders' Equity		
Current liabilities	$ 75,000	$ 70,000
Long-term liabilities	80,000	90,000
Common stock	330,000	300,000
Retained earnings	275,000	225,000
Total liabilities and stockholders' equity	$760,000	$685,000

DANKE CORPORATION
Income Statements
For the Years Ended December 31

	2017	2016
Sales revenue	$750,000	$680,000
Cost of goods sold	440,000	400,000
Operating expenses (including income taxes)	240,000	220,000
Net income	$ 70,000	$ 60,000

Additional information:

Net cash provided by operating activities	$82,000	$56,000
Cash used for capital expenditures	$45,000	$38,000
Dividends paid	$20,000	$15,000
Weighted-average number of shares outstanding	33,000	30,000

Instructions
Compute these values and ratios for 2016 and 2017.

(a) Earnings per share.
(b) Working capital.
(c) Current ratio.
(d) Debt to assets ratio.
(e) Free cash flow.
(f) Based on the ratios calculated, discuss briefly the improvement or lack thereof in financial position and operating results from 2016 to 2017 of Danke Corporation.

P2-7A Selected financial data of two competitors, Target and Wal-Mart, are presented here. (All dollars are in millions.) Suppose the data were taken from the 2017 financial statements of each company.

Compute ratios and compare liquidity, solvency, and profitability for two companies.

(LO 2), AP

	Target (1/31/17)	Wal-Mart (1/31/17)
	Income Statement Data for Year	
Net sales	$64,948	$401,244
Cost of goods sold	44,157	306,158
Selling and administrative expenses	16,389	76,651
Interest expense	894	2,103
Other income	28	4,213
Income taxes	1,322	7,145
Net income	$ 2,214	$ 13,400

	Target	Wal-Mart
	Balance Sheet Data (End of Year)	
Current assets	$17,488	$ 48,949
Noncurrent assets	26,618	114,480
Total assets	$44,106	$163,429
Current liabilities	$10,512	$ 55,390
Long-term liabilities	19,882	42,754
Total stockholders' equity	13,712	65,285
Total liabilities and stockholders' equity	$44,106	$163,429
Net cash provided by operating activities	$4,430	$23,147
Cash paid for capital expenditures	$3,547	$11,499
Dividends declared and paid on common stock	$465	$3,746
Weighted-average shares outstanding (millions)	774	3,951

Instructions

For each company, compute these values and ratios.

(a) Working capital.
(b) Current ratio.
(c) Debt to assets ratio.
(d) Free cash flow.
(e) Earnings per share.
(f) Compare the liquidity and solvency of the two companies.

Comment on the objectives and qualitative characteristics of financial reporting.

(LO 3), E

P2-8A A friend of yours, Saira Ortiz, recently completed an undergraduate degree in science and has just started working with a biotechnology company. Saira tells you that the owners of the business are trying to secure new sources of financing which are needed in order for the company to proceed with development of a new healthcare product. Saira said that her boss told her that the company must put together a report to present to potential investors.

Saira thought that the company should include in this package the detailed scientific findings related to the Phase I clinical trials for this product. She said, "I know that the biotech industry sometimes has only a 10% success rate with new products, but if we report all the scientific findings, everyone will see what a sure success this is going to be! The president was talking about the importance of following some set of accounting principles. Why do we need to look at some accounting rules? What they need to realize is that we have scientific results that are quite encouraging, some of the most talented employees around, and the start of some really great customer relationships. We haven't made any sales yet, but we will. We just need the funds to get through all the clinical testing and get government approval for our product. Then these investors will be quite happy that they bought in to our company early!"

Instructions

(a) What is accounting information? Explain to Saira what is meant by generally accepted accounting principles.
(b) Comment on how Saira's suggestions for what should be reported to prospective investors conforms to the qualitative characteristics of accounting information. Do you think that the things that Saira wants to include in the information for investors will conform to financial reporting guidelines?

▶ PROBLEMS: SET B AND SET C

Visit the book's companion website, at **www.wiley.com/college/kimmel**, and choose the Student Companion site to access Problems: Set B and Set C.

▶ CONTINUING PROBLEM Cookie Creations

(*Note:* This is a continuation of the Cookie Creations problem from Chapter 1.)

CC2 After investigating the different forms of business organization, Natalie Koebel decides to operate her business as a corporation, Cookie Creations Inc. She then begins the process of getting her business running.

Go to the book's companion website, **www.wiley.com/college/kimmel**, *to see the completion of this problem.*

© leungchopan/ Shutterstock

EXPAND YOUR CRITICAL THINKING

FINANCIAL REPORTING PROBLEM: Apple Inc.

Financial Reporting

E

CT2-1 The financial statements of Apple Inc. are presented in Appendix A at the end of this textbook.

Instructions

Answer the following questions using the financial statements and the notes to the financial statements.

(a) What were Apple's total current assets at September 27, 2014, and September 28, 2013?
(b) Are the assets included in current assets listed in the proper order? Explain.
(c) How are Apple's assets classified?
(d) What were Apple's current liabilities at September 27, 2014, and September 28, 2013?

COMPARATIVE ANALYSIS PROBLEM: Columbia Sportswear Company vs. VF Corporation

Financial Analysis

E

CT2-2 The financial statements of Columbia Sportswear Company are presented in Appendix B. Financial statements of VF Corporation are presented in Appendix C. Assume Columbia's weighted-average number of shares outstanding was 227,514,000, and VF's was 56,997,000.

Instructions

(a) For each company, calculate the following values for 2014.
    (1) Working capital.
    (2) Current ratio.
    (3) Debt to assets ratio.
    (4) Free cash flow.
    (*Hint:* When calculating free cash flow, **do not** consider business acquisitions to be part of capital expenditures.)
(b) Based on your findings above, discuss the relative liquidity and solvency of the two companies.

COMPARATIVE ANALYSIS PROBLEM: Amazon.com, Inc. vs. Wal-Mart Stores, Inc.

Financial Analysis

E

CT2-3 Amazon.com, Inc.'s financial statements are presented in Appendix D. Financial statements of Wal-Mart Stores, Inc. are presented in Appendix E.

Instructions

(a) For each company, calculate the following values for 2014.
    (1) Working capital.
    (2) Current ratio.
    (3) Debt to assets ratio.
    (4) Free cash flow.
(b) Based on your findings above, discuss the relative liquidity and solvency of the two companies.

INTERPRETING FINANCIAL STATEMENTS

Financial Analysis

CT2-4 Suppose the following information was reported by Gap, Inc.

E

	2017	2016	2015	2014	2013
Total assets (millions)	$7,065	$7,985	$7,564	$7,838	$8,544
Working capital	$1,831	$2,533	$1,847	$1,653	$2,757
Current ratio	1.87:1	2.19:1	1.86:1	1.68:1	2.21:1
Debt to assets ratio	.42:1	.39:1	.42:1	.45:1	.39:1
Earnings per share	$1.89	$1.59	$1.35	$1.05	$0.94

(a) Determine the overall percentage decrease in Gap's total assets from 2013 to 2017. What was the average decrease per year?
(b) Comment on the change in Gap's liquidity. Does working capital or the current ratio appear to provide a better indication of Gap's liquidity? What might explain the change in Gap's liquidity during this period?
(c) Comment on the change in Gap's solvency during this period.
(d) Comment on the change in Gap's profitability during this period. How might this affect your prediction about Gap's future profitability?

REAL-WORLD FOCUS

E **CT2-5** ***Purpose:*** Identify summary liquidity, solvency, and profitability information about companies, and compare this information across companies in the same industry.

Address: **http://biz.yahoo.com/i**

Steps

1. Type in a company name, or use the index to find a company name. Choose **Profile**. Choose **Key Statistics**. Perform instruction (a) below.
2. Go back to **Profile**. Click on the company's particular industry behind the heading "Industry." Perform instructions (b), (c), and (d).

Instructions

Answer the following questions.

(a) What is the company's name? What was the company's current ratio and debt to equity ratio (a variation of the debt to assets ratio)?
(b) What is the company's industry?
(c) What is the name of a competitor? What is the competitor's current ratio and its debt to equity ratio?
(d) Based on these measures, which company is more liquid? Which company is more solvent?

E **CT2-6** The Feature Story described the dramatic effect that investment bulletin boards are having on the investment world. This exercise will allow you to evaluate a bulletin board discussing a company of your choice.

Address: **http://biz.yahoo.com/i**

Steps

1. Type in a company name, or use the index to find a company name.
2. Choose **Msgs** or **Message Board**. (for messages).
3. Read the 10 most recent messages.

Instructions

Answer the following questions.

(a) State the nature of each of these messages (e.g., offering advice, criticizing company, predicting future results, ridiculing other people who have posted messages).
(b) For those messages that expressed an opinion about the company, was evidence provided to support the opinion?
(c) What effect do you think it would have on bulletin board discussions if the participants provided their actual names? Do you think this would be a good policy?

S **CT2-7** The July 6, 2011, edition of the *Wall Street Journal Online* includes an article by Michael Rapoport entitled "U.S. Firms Clash Over Accounting Rules." The article discusses why some U.S. companies favored adoption of International Financial Reporting Standards (IFRS) while other companies opposed it.

Instructions
Read the article and answer the following questions.

(a) The articles says that the switch to IFRS tends to be favored by "larger companies, big accounting firms, and rule makers." What reasons are given for favoring the switch?
(b) What two reasons are given by many smaller companies that oppose the switch?
(c) What criticism of IFRS is raised with regard to regulated companies?
(d) Explain what is meant by "condorsement."

DECISION-MAKING ACROSS THE ORGANIZATION

Financial Analysis

Writing

Group Project

CT2-8 As a financial analyst in the planning department for Erin Industries, Inc., you must develop ratios from the comparative financial statements. This information is to be used to convince creditors that, despite a slight decline in sales, Erin Industries, Inc. is liquid, solvent, and profitable, and that it deserves their continued support. Lenders are particularly concerned about the company's ability to continue as a going concern. E

Here are the data requested and the computations developed from the financial statements:

	2017	2016
Current ratio	3.1	2.1
Working capital	Up 22%	Down 7%
Free cash flow	Up 25%	Up 18%
Debt to assets ratio	0.60	0.70
Net income	Up 32%	Down 8%
Earnings per share	$2.40	$1.15

Instructions
Erin Industries, Inc. asks you to prepare brief comments stating how each of these items supports the argument that its financial health is improving. The company wishes to use these comments to support presentation of data to its creditors. With the class divided into groups, prepare the comments as requested, giving the implications and the limitations of each item regarding Erin's financial well-being.

COMMUNICATION ACTIVITY

CT2-9 B. P. Palmer is the chief executive officer of Future Products. Palmer is an expert engineer but a novice in accounting. S

Instructions
Write a letter to B. P. Palmer that explains (a) the three main types of ratios; (b) examples of each, how they are calculated, and what they measure; and (c) the bases for comparison in analyzing Future Products' financial statements.

ETHICS CASE

CT2-10 At one time, Boeing closed a giant deal to acquire another manufacturer, McDonnell Douglas. Boeing paid for the acquisition by issuing shares of its own stock to the stockholders of McDonnell Douglas. In order for the deal not to be revoked, the value of Boeing's stock could not decline below a certain level for a number of months after the deal. E

During the first half of the year, Boeing suffered significant cost overruns because of inefficiencies in its production methods. Had these problems been disclosed in the quarterly financial statements during the first and second quarters of the year, the company's stock most likely would have plummeted, and the deal would have been revoked. Company managers spent considerable time debating when the bad news should be disclosed. One public relations manager suggested that the company's problems be revealed on the date of either Princess Diana's or Mother Teresa's funeral, in the hope that it would be lost among those big stories that day. Instead, the company waited until October 22 of that year to announce a $2.6 billion write-off due to cost overruns. Within one week, the company's stock price had fallen 20%, but by this time the McDonnell Douglas deal could not be reversed.

Instructions

Answer the following questions.

(a) Who are the stakeholders in this situation?
(b) What are the ethical issues?
(c) What assumptions or principles of accounting are relevant to this case?
(d) Do you think it is ethical to try to "time" the release of a story so as to diminish its effect?
(e) What would you have done if you were the chief executive officer of Boeing?
(f) Boeing's top management maintains that it did not have an obligation to reveal its problems during the first half of the year. What implications does this have for investors and analysts who follow Boeing's stock?

ALL ABOUT YOU

CT2-11 Every company needs to plan in order to move forward. Its top management must consider where it wants the company to be in three to five years. Like a company, you need to think about where you want to be three to five years from now, and you need to start taking steps now in order to get there.

Instructions

Provide responses to each of the following items.

(a) Where would you like to be working in three to five years? Describe your plan for getting there by identifying between five and 10 specific steps that you need to take in order to get there.
(b) In order to get the job you want, you will need a résumé. Your résumé is the equivalent of a company's annual report. It needs to provide relevant and reliable information about your past accomplishments so that employers can decide whether to "invest" in you. Do a search on the Internet to find a good résumé format. What are the basic elements of a résumé?
(c) A company's annual report provides information about a company's accomplishments. In order for investors to use the annual report, the information must be reliable; that is, users must have faith that the information is accurate and believable. How can you provide assurance that the information on your résumé is reliable?
(d) Prepare a résumé assuming that you have accomplished the five to 10 specific steps you identified in part (a). Also, provide evidence that would give assurance that the information is reliable.

FASB CODIFICATION ACTIVITY

CT2-12 If your school has a subscription to the FASB Codification, go to **http://aaahq.org/ascLogin.cfm** to log in and prepare responses to the following.

Instructions

(a) Access the glossary ("Master Glossary") at the FASB Codification website to answer the following.
   (1) What is the definition of current assets?
   (2) What is the definition of current liabilities?
(b) A company wants to offset its accounts payable against its cash account and show a cash amount net of accounts payable on its balance sheet. Identify the criteria (found in the FASB Codification) under which a company has the right of set off. Does the company have the right to offset accounts payable against the cash account?

CONSIDERING PEOPLE, PLANET, AND PROFIT

CT2-13 Auditors provide a type of certification of corporate financial statements. Certification is used in many other aspects of business as well. For example, it plays a critical role in the sustainability movement. The February 7, 2012, issue of the *New York Times* contained an article by S. Amanda Caudill entitled "Better Lives in Better Coffee," which discusses the role of certification in the coffee business.

Address: **http://scientistatwork.blogs.nytimes.com/2012/02/07/better-lives-in-better-coffee/**

Instructions

Read the article and answer the following questions.

(a) The article mentions three different certification types that coffee growers can obtain from three different certification bodies. Using financial reporting as an example, what potential problems might the existence of multiple certification types present to coffee purchasers?

(b) According to the author, which certification is most common among coffee growers? What are the possible reasons for this?

(c) What social and environmental benefits are coffee certifications trying to achieve? Are there also potential financial benefits to the parties involved?

A Look at IFRS

LEARNING OBJECTIVE ▶4 **Compare the classified balance sheet format under GAAP and IFRS.**

The classified balance sheet, although generally required internationally, contains certain variations in format when reporting under IFRS.

KEY POINTS

Following are the key similarities and differences between GAAP and IFRS related to the financial statements.

Similarities

- IFRS generally requires a classified statement of financial position similar to the classified balance sheet under GAAP.
- IFRS follows the same guidelines as this textbook for distinguishing between current and noncurrent assets and liabilities.

Differences

- IFRS recommends but does not require the use of the title "statement of financial position" rather than balance sheet.
- The format of statement of financial position information is often presented differently under IFRS. Although no specific format is required, many companies that follow IFRS present statement of financial position information in this order:
  - Non-current assets
  - Current assets
  - Equity
  - Non-current liabilities
  - Current liabilities
- Under IFRS, current assets are usually listed in the reverse order of liquidity. For example, under GAAP cash is listed first, but under IFRS it is listed last.
- IFRS has many differences in terminology from what are shown in your textbook. For example, in the sample statement of financial position illustrated on the next page, notice in the investment category that stock is called shares.

FRANKLIN CORPORATION Statement of Financial Position October 31, 2017			
Assets			
Intangible assets			
Patents			$ 3,100
Property, plant, and equipment			
Land		$10,000	
Equipment	$24,000		
Less: Accumulated depreciation	5,000	19,000	29,000
Long-term investments			
Share investments		5,200	
Investment in real estate		2,000	7,200
Current assets			
Prepaid insurance		400	
Supplies		2,100	
Inventory		3,000	
Notes receivable		1,000	
Accounts receivable		7,000	
Debt investments		2,000	
Cash		6,600	22,100
Total assets			$61,400
Equity and Liabilities			
Equity			
Share capital			$20,050
Retained earnings			14,000
Non-current liabilities			
Mortgage payable		$10,000	
Notes payable		1,300	11,300
Current liabilities			
Notes payable		11,000	
Accounts payable		2,100	
Salaries and wages payable		1,600	
Unearned service revenue		900	
Interest payable		450	16,050
Total equity and liabilities			$61,400

- Both GAAP and IFRS are increasing the use of fair value to report assets. However, at this point IFRS has adopted it more broadly. As examples, under IFRS companies can apply fair value to property, plant, and equipment, and in some cases intangible assets.

LOOKING TO THE FUTURE

The IASB and the FASB are working on a project to converge their standards related to financial statement presentation. A key feature of the proposed framework is that each of the statements will be organized in the same format, to separate an entity's financing activities from its operating and investing activities and, further, to separate financing activities into transactions with owners and creditors. Thus, the same classifications used in the statement of financial position would also be used in the income statement and the statement of cash flows. The project has three phases. You can follow the joint financial presentation project at the following link: **http://www.fasb.org/project/-financial_statement_presentation.shtml**.

IFRS Practice

IFRS SELF-TEST QUESTIONS

1. A company has purchased a tract of land and expects to build a production plant on the land in approximately 5 years. During the 5 years before construction, the land will be idle. Under IFRS, the land should be reported as:
   (a) land expense.
   (b) property, plant, and equipment.

(c) an intangible asset.
(d) a long-term investment.

2. Current assets under IFRS are listed generally:
(a) by importance.
(b) in the reverse order of their expected conversion to cash.
(c) by longevity.
(d) alphabetically.

3. Companies that use IFRS:
(a) may report all their assets on the statement of financial position at fair value.
(b) may offset assets against liabilities and show net assets and net liabilities on their statements of financial position, rather than the underlying detailed line items.
(c) may report non-current assets before current assets on the statement of financial position.
(d) do not have any guidelines as to what should be reported on the statement of financial position.

4. Companies that follow IFRS to prepare a statement of financial position generally use the following order of classification:
(a) current assets, current liabilities, non-current assets, non-current liabilities, equity.
(b) non-current assets, non-current liabilities, current assets, current liabilities, equity.
(c) non-current assets, current assets, equity, non-current liabilities, current liabilities.
(d) equity, non-current assets, current assets, non-current liabilities, current liabilities.

IFRS EXERCISES

IFRS2-1 In what ways does the format of a statement of financial of position under IFRS often differ from a balance sheet presented under GAAP?

IFRS2-2 What term is commonly used under IFRS in reference to the balance sheet?

IFRS2-3 The statement of financial position for Sundell Company includes the following accounts (in British pounds): Accounts Receivable £12,500, Prepaid Insurance £3,600, Cash £15,400, Supplies £5,200, and Debt Investments (short-term) £6,700. Prepare the current assets section of the statement of financial position, listing the accounts in proper sequence.

IFRS2-4 The following information is available for Lessila Bowling Alley at December 31, 2017.

Buildings	$128,800	Share Capital	$100,000
Accounts Receivable	14,520	Retained Earnings (beginning)	15,000
Prepaid Insurance	4,680	Accumulated Depreciation—Buildings	42,600
Cash	18,040	Accounts Payable	12,300
Equipment	62,400	Notes Payable	97,780
Land	64,000	Accumulated Depreciation—Equipment	18,720
Insurance Expense	780	Interest Payable	2,600
Depreciation Expense	7,360	Bowling Revenues	14,180
Interest Expense	2,600		

Prepare a classified statement of financial position. Assume that $13,900 of the notes payable will be paid in 2018.

INTERNATIONAL COMPARATIVE ANALYSIS PROBLEM: Apple vs. Louis Vuitton

IFRS2-5 The financial statements of Louis Vuitton are presented in Appendix F. Instructions for accessing and using the company's complete annual report, including the notes to its financial statements, are also provided in Appendix F.

Instructions
Identify five differences in the format of the statement of financial position used by Louis Vuitton compared to a company, such as Apple, that follows GAAP. (Apple's financial statements are available in Appendix A.)

Answers to IFRS Self-Test Questions
1. d **2.** b **3.** c **4.** c

3

The Accounting Information System

CHAPTER PREVIEW

As indicated in the Feature Story, a reliable information system is a necessity for any company. The purpose of this chapter is to explain and illustrate the features of an accounting information system.

CHAPTER OUTLINE

LEARNING OBJECTIVES		PRACTICE
1 Analyze the effect of business transactions on the basic accounting equation.	• Accounting transactions • Analyzing transactions • Summary of transactions	DO IT! 1 Transaction Analysis
2 Explain how accounts, debits, and credits are used to record business transactions.	• Debits and credits • Debit and credit procedures • Stockholders' equity relationships • Summary of debit/credit rules	DO IT! 2 Debits and Credits for Balance Sheet Accounts
3 Indicate how a journal is used in the recording process.	• The recording process • The journal	DO IT! 3 Journal Entries
4 Explain how a ledger and posting help in the recording process.	• The ledger • Chart of accounts • Posting • The recording process illustrated • Summary illustration	DO IT! 4 Posting
5 Prepare a trial balance.	• Limitations of a trial balance	DO IT! 5 Trial Balance

Go to the ***REVIEW AND PRACTICE*** section at the end of the chapter for a targeted summary and exercises with solutions.

Visit **WileyPLUS** for additional tutorials and practice opportunities.

© Nick Laham/Getty Images, Inc.

FEATURE STORY

Accidents Happen

How organized are you financially? Take a short quiz. Answer yes or no to each question:

- Does your wallet contain so many cash machine receipts that you've been declared a walking fire hazard?
- Do you wait until your debit card is denied before checking the status of your funds?
- Was Aaron Rodgers (the quarterback for the **Green Bay Packers**) playing high school football the last time you verified the accuracy of your bank account?

If you think it is hard to keep track of the many transactions that make up *your* life, imagine how difficult it is for a big corporation to do so. Not only that, but now consider how important it is for a big company to have good accounting records, especially if it has control of *your* life savings. **MF Global Holdings Ltd** was such a company. As a large investment broker, it held billions of dollars of investments for clients. If you had your life savings invested at MF Global, you might be slightly displeased if you heard this from one of its representatives: "You know, I kind of remember an account for someone with a name like yours—now what did we do with that?"

Unfortunately, that is almost exactly what happened to MF Global's clients shortly before it filed for bankruptcy. During the days immediately following the bankruptcy filing, regulators and auditors struggled to piece things together. In the words of one regulator, "Their books are a disaster . . . we're trying to figure out what numbers are real numbers." One company that considered buying an interest in MF Global walked away from the deal because it "couldn't get a sense of what was on the balance sheet." That company said the information that should have been instantly available instead took days to produce.

It now appears that MF Global did not properly segregate customer accounts from company accounts. And, because of its sloppy recordkeeping, customers were not protected when the company had financial troubles. Total customer losses were approximately $1 billion. As you can see, accounting matters!

Source: S. Patterson and A. Lucchetti, "Inside the Hunt for MF Global Cash," *Wall Street Journal Online* (November 11, 2011).

LEARNING OBJECTIVE ▶1

Analyze the effect of business transactions on the basic accounting equation.

Analyze business transactions | JOURNALIZE | POST | TRIAL BALANCE | ADJUSTING ENTRIES | ADJUSTED TRIAL BALANCE | FINANCIAL STATEMENTS | CLOSING ENTRIES | POST-CLOSING TRIAL BALANCE

*The **accounting cycle graphic** above illustrates the steps companies follow each period to record transactions and eventually prepare financial statements.*

The system of collecting and processing transaction data and communicating financial information to decision-makers is known as the **accounting information system**. Factors that shape an accounting information system include the nature of the company's business, the types of transactions, the size of the company, the volume of data, and the information demands of management and others.

Most businesses use computerized accounting systems—sometimes referred to as electronic data processing (EDP) systems. These systems handle all the steps involved in the recording process, from initial data entry to preparation of the financial statements. In order to remain competitive, companies continually improve their accounting systems to provide accurate and timely data for decision-making. For example, in a recent annual report, Tootsie Roll stated, "We also invested in additional processing and data storage hardware during the year. We view information technology as a key strategic tool, and are committed to deploying leading edge technology in this area." In addition, many companies have upgraded their accounting information systems in response to the requirements of Sarbanes-Oxley.

Accounting information systems rely on a process referred to as **the accounting cycle**. As you can see from the graphic above, the accounting cycle begins with the analysis of business transactions and ends with the preparation of a post-closing trial balance. We explain each of the steps in this chapter as well as in Chapter 4.

In this chapter, in order to emphasize the underlying concepts and principles, we focus on a manual accounting system. The accounting concepts and principles do not change whether a system is computerized or manual.

ACCOUNTING TRANSACTIONS

To use an accounting information system, you need to know which economic events to recognize (record). Not all events are recorded and reported in the financial statements. For example, suppose General Motors hired a new employee and purchased a new computer. Are these events entered in its accounting records? The first event would not be recorded, but the second event would. We call economic events that require recording in the financial statements **accounting transactions**.

An accounting transaction occurs when assets, liabilities, or stockholders' equity items change as a result of some economic event. The purchase of a computer by General Motors, the payment of rent by Microsoft, and the sale of a multi-day guided trip by Sierra Corporation are examples of events that change a company's assets, liabilities, or stockholders' equity. Illustration 3-1 summarizes the decision process companies use to decide whether or not to record economic events.

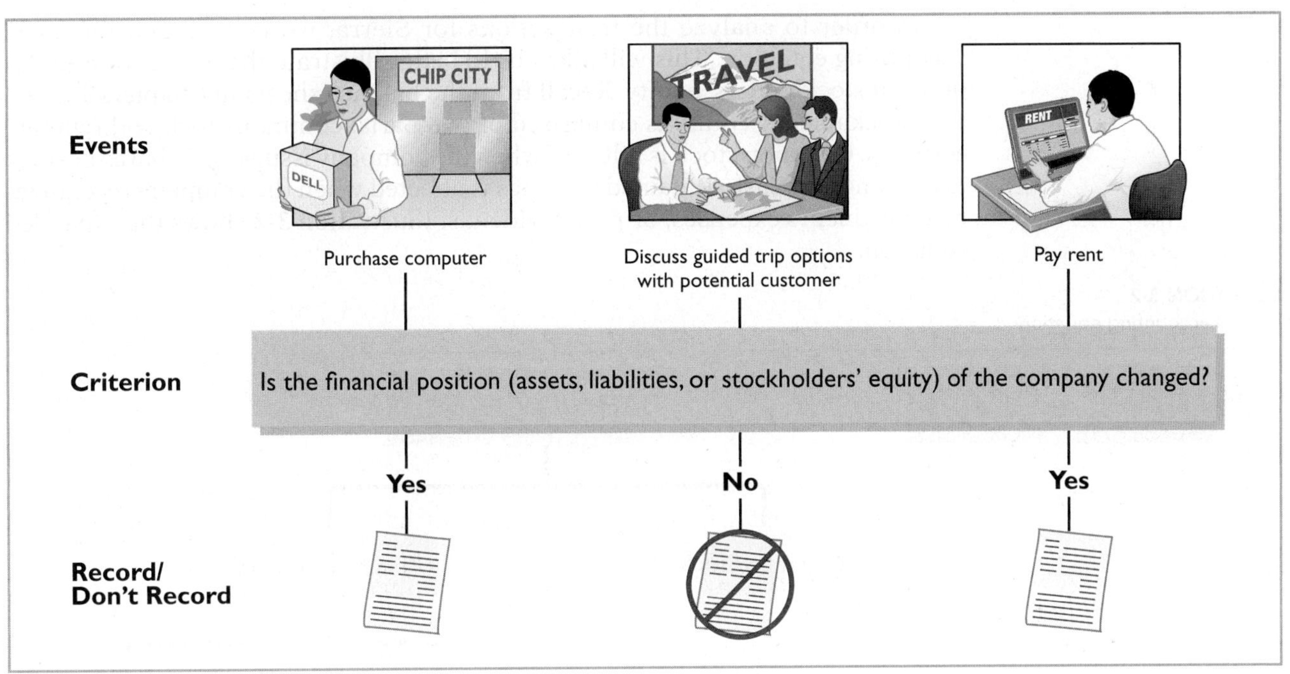

ILLUSTRATION 3-1
Transaction identification process

ANALYZING TRANSACTIONS

In Chapter 1, you learned the basic accounting equation:

Assets = Liabilities + Stockholders' Equity

In this chapter, you will learn how to analyze transactions in terms of their effect on assets, liabilities, and stockholders' equity. **Transaction analysis** is the process of identifying the specific effects of economic events on the accounting equation.

DECISION TOOLS 

The accounting equation is used to determine if an accounting transaction has occurred.

The accounting equation must always balance. Each transaction has a dual (double-sided) effect on the equation. For example, if an individual asset is increased, there must be a corresponding:

- Decrease in another asset, *or*
- Increase in a specific liability, *or*
- Increase in stockholders' equity.

Two or more items could be affected when an asset is increased. For example, if a company purchases a computer for $10,000 by paying $6,000 in cash and signing a note for $4,000, one asset (equipment) increases $10,000, another asset (cash) decreases $6,000, and a liability (notes payable) increases $4,000. The result is that the accounting equation remains in balance—assets increased by a net $4,000 and liabilities increased by $4,000, as shown below.

Assets	=	Liabilities	+	Stockholders' Equity
+$10,000		+$4,000		
− 6,000				
$ 4,000	=	$4,000		

Chapter 1 presented the financial statements for Sierra Corporation for its first month. You should review those financial statements (on page 16) at this time. To illustrate how economic events affect the accounting equation, we will examine events affecting Sierra during its first month.

In order to analyze the transactions for Sierra, we will expand the basic accounting equation. This will allow us to better illustrate the impact of transactions on stockholders' equity. Recall from the balance sheets in Chapters 1 and 2 that stockholders' equity is comprised of two parts: common stock and retained earnings. Common stock is affected when the company issues new shares of stock in exchange for cash. Retained earnings is affected when the company recognizes revenue, incurs expenses, or pays dividends. Illustration 3-2 shows the expanded equation.

ILLUSTRATION 3-2
Expanded accounting equation

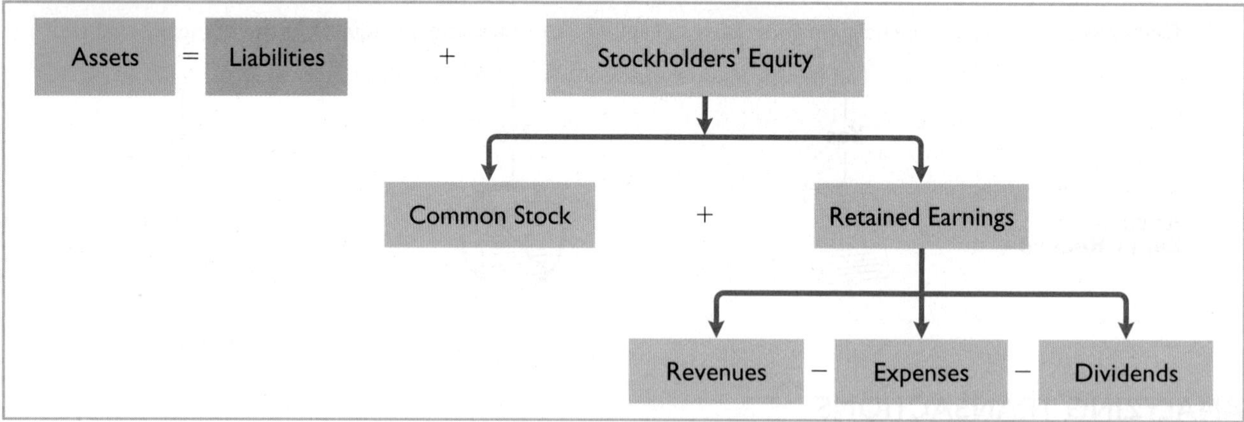

If you are tempted to skip ahead after you've read a few of the following transaction analyses, don't do it. Each has something unique to teach, something you'll need later. (We assure you that we've kept them to the minimum needed!)

EVENT (1). INVESTMENT OF CASH BY STOCKHOLDERS. On October 1, cash of $10,000 is invested in the business by investors in exchange for $10,000 of common stock. This event is an accounting transaction that results in an increase in both assets and stockholders' equity.

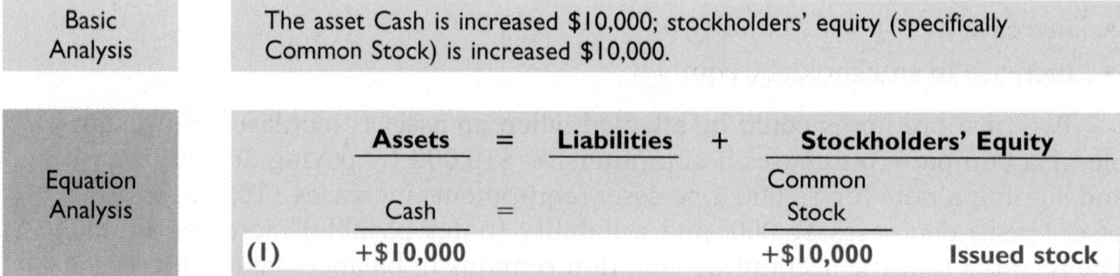

Basic Analysis	The asset Cash is increased $10,000; stockholders' equity (specifically Common Stock) is increased $10,000.			
Equation Analysis		**Assets** = **Liabilities** +	**Stockholders' Equity**	
		Cash =	Common Stock	
	(1)	+$10,000	+$10,000	**Issued stock**

The equation is in balance after the issuance of common stock. Keeping track of the source of each change in stockholders' equity is essential for later accounting activities. In particular, items recorded in the revenue and expense columns are used for the calculation of net income.

EVENT (2). NOTE ISSUED IN EXCHANGE FOR CASH. On October 1, Sierra borrowed $5,000 from Castle Bank by signing a 3-month, 12%, $5,000 note payable. This transaction results in an equal increase in assets and liabilities. The specific effect of this transaction and the cumulative effect of the first two transactions are as follows.

Basic Analysis: The asset Cash is increased $5,000; the liability Notes Payable is increased $5,000.

Equation Analysis

	Assets	=	Liabilities	+	Stockholders' Equity
	Cash	=	Notes Payable	+	Common Stock
	$10,000				$10,000
(2)	+5,000		+$5,000		
	$15,000	=	$5,000	+	$10,000
			$15,000		

Total assets are now $15,000, and liabilities plus stockholders' equity also total $15,000.

EVENT (3). PURCHASE OF EQUIPMENT FOR CASH. On October 2, Sierra purchased equipment by paying $5,000 cash to Superior Equipment Sales Co. This transaction results in an equal increase and decrease in Sierra's assets.

Basic Analysis: The asset Equipment is increased $5,000; the asset Cash is decreased $5,000.

Equation Analysis

	Assets			=	Liabilities	+	Stockholders' Equity
	Cash	+	Equipment	=	Notes Payable	+	Common Stock
	$15,000				$5,000		$10,000
(3)	−5,000		+$5,000				
	$10,000	+	$5,000	=	$5,000	+	$10,000
	$15,000				$15,000		

The total assets are now $15,000, and liabilities plus stockholders' equity also total $15,000.

EVENT (4). RECEIPT OF CASH IN ADVANCE FROM CUSTOMER. On October 2, Sierra received a $1,200 cash advance from R. Knox, a client. Sierra received cash (an asset) for guide services for multi-day trips that it expects to complete in the future. Although Sierra received cash, **it does not record revenue until it has performed the work**. In some industries, such as the magazine and airline industries, customers are expected to prepay. These companies have a liability to the customer until they deliver the magazines or provide the flight. When the company eventually provides the product or service, it records the revenue.

Since Sierra received cash prior to performance of the service, Sierra has a liability for the work due.

Basic Analysis: The asset Cash is increased $1,200; the liability Unearned Service Revenue is increased $1,200 because the service has not been performed yet. That is, when an advance payment is received, unearned revenue (a liability) should be recorded in order to recognize the obligation that exists.

Equation Analysis

	Assets			=	Liabilities			+	Stockholders' Equity
	Cash	+	Equipment	=	Notes Payable	+	Unearned Service Revenue	+	Common Stock
	$10,000		$5,000		$5,000				$10,000
(4)	+1,200						+$1,200		
	$11,200	+	$5,000	=	$5,000	+	$1,200	+	$10,000
	$16,200				$16,200				

EVENT (5). SERVICES PERFORMED FOR CASH. On October 3, Sierra received $10,000 in cash (an asset) from Copa Company for guide services performed for a corporate event. Guide service is the principal revenue-producing activity of Sierra. **Revenue increases stockholders' equity.** This transaction, then, increases both assets and stockholders' equity.

Basic Analysis	The asset Cash is increased $10,000; the revenue Service Revenue is increased $10,000.

Equation Analysis

	Assets			=	Liabilities			+	Stockholders' Equity						
			Equip-		Notes		Unearned		Common		Retained Earnings				
	Cash	+	ment	=	Pay.	+	Serv. Rev.	+	Stock	+	Rev.	−	Exp.	−	Div.
	$11,200		$5,000		$5,000		$1,200		$10,000						
(5)	+10,000										+$10,000				Service Revenue
	$21,200	+	$5,000	=	$5,000	+	$1,200	+	$10,000	+	$10,000				
	$26,200				$26,200										

Often companies perform services "on account." That is, they perform services for which they are paid at a later date. Revenue, however, is recorded when services are performed. Therefore, revenues would increase when services are performed, even though cash has not been received. Instead of receiving cash, the company receives a different type of asset, an **account receivable**. Accounts receivable represent the right to receive payment at a later date. Suppose that Sierra had performed these services on account rather than for cash. This event would be reported using the accounting equation as:

Assets	=	Liabilities	+	Stockholders' Equity	
Accounts Receivable	=			Revenues	
+$10,000				+$10,000	Service Revenue

Later, when Sierra collects the $10,000 from the customer, Accounts Receivable decreases by $10,000, and Cash increases by $10,000.

Assets		=	Liabilities	+	Stockholders' Equity
Cash	Accounts Receivable				
+$10,000	−$10,000				

Note that in this case, revenues are not affected by the collection of cash. Instead Sierra records an exchange of one asset (Accounts Receivable) for a different asset (Cash).

EVENT (6). PAYMENT OF RENT. On October 3, Sierra paid its office rent for the month of October in cash, $900. This rent payment is a transaction that results in a decrease in an asset, cash.

Rent is a cost incurred by Sierra in its effort to generate revenues. It is treated as an expense because it pertains only to the current month. **Expenses decrease stockholders' equity.** Sierra records the rent payment by decreasing cash and increasing expenses to maintain the balance of the accounting equation.

Basic Analysis	The expense account Rent Expense is increased $900 because the payment pertains only to the current month; the asset Cash is decreased $900.

Equation Analysis

	Assets			=	Liabilities			+	Stockholders' Equity							
											Retained Earnings					
	Cash	+	Equipment	=	Notes Pay.	+	Unearned Serv. Rev.	+	Common Stock	+	Rev.	–	Exp.	–	Div.	
	$21,200		$5,000		$5,000		$1,200		$10,000		$10,000					
(6)	−900												−$900			Rent Expense
	$20,300	+	$5,000	=	$5,000	+	$1,200	+	$10,000	+	$10,000	–	$900			
	$25,300				$25,300											

EVENT (7). PURCHASE OF INSURANCE POLICY FOR CASH. On October 4, Sierra paid $600 for a one-year insurance policy that will expire next year on September 30. Payments of expenses that will benefit more than one accounting period are identified as assets called prepaid expenses or prepayments.

Basic Analysis	The asset Cash is decreased $600; the asset Prepaid Insurance is increased $600.

Equation Analysis

	Assets					=	Liabilities			+	Stockholders' Equity					
													Retained Earnings			
	Cash	+	Prepaid Insurance	+	Equipment	=	Notes Pay.	+	Unearned Serv. Rev.	+	Common Stock	+	Rev.	–	Exp.	– Div.
	$20,300				$5,000		$5,000		$1,200		$10,000		$10,000		$900	
(7)	−600		+$600													
	$19,700	+	$600	+	$5,000	=	$5,000	+	$1,200	+	$10,000	+	$10,000	–	$900	
	$25,300						$25,300									

The balance in total assets did not change; one asset account decreased by the same amount that another increased.

EVENT (8). PURCHASE OF SUPPLIES ON ACCOUNT. On October 5, Sierra purchased an estimated three months of supplies on account from Aero Supply for $2,500. In this case, "on account" means that the company receives goods or services that it will pay for at a later date. This transaction increases both an asset (supplies) and a liability (accounts payable).

Basic Analysis	The asset Supplies is increased $2,500; the liability Accounts Payable is increased $2,500.

Equation Analysis

	Assets							=	Liabilities					+	Stockholders' Equity					
																	Retained Earnings			
	Cash	+	Supplies	+	Prepd. Insur.	+	Equipment	=	Notes Pay.	+	Accounts Payable	+	Unearned Serv. Rev.	+	Common Stock	+	Rev.	–	Exp.	– Div.
	$19,700				$600		$5,000		$5,000				$1,200		$10,000		$10,000		$900	
(8)			+$2,500								+$2,500									
	$19,700	+	$2,500	+	$600	+	$5,000	=	$5,000	+	$2,500	+	$1,200	+	$10,000	+	$10,000	–	$900	
	$27,800								$27,800											

EVENT (9). HIRING OF NEW EMPLOYEES. On October 9, Sierra hired four new employees to begin work on October 15. Each employee will receive a weekly salary of $500 for a five-day work week, payable every two weeks. Employees will receive their first paychecks on October 26. On the date Sierra hires the employees, there is no effect on the accounting equation because the assets, liabilities, and stockholders' equity of the company have not changed.

Basic Analysis

An accounting transaction has not occurred. There is only an agreement that the employees will begin work on October 15. (See Event (11) for the first payment.)

EVENT (10). PAYMENT OF DIVIDEND. On October 20, Sierra paid a $500 cash dividend. **Dividends** are a reduction of stockholders' equity but not an expense. Dividends are not included in the calculation of net income. Instead, a dividend is a distribution of the company's assets to its stockholders.

Basic Analysis

The Dividends account is increased $500; the asset Cash is decreased $500.

Equation Analysis

	Assets				=	Liabilities			+	Stockholders' Equity			
											Retained Earnings		
	Cash	+ Supplies	+ Prepd. Insur.	+ Equipment	=	Notes Pay.	+ Accts. Pay.	+ Unearned Serv. Rev.	+	Common Stock	+ Rev.	− Exp.	− Div.
	$19,700	$2,500	$600	$5,000		$5,000	$2,500	$1,200		$10,000	$10,000	$900	
(10)	−500												− $500
	$19,200	+ $2,500	+ $600	+ $5,000	=	$5,000	+ $2,500	+ $1,200	+	$10,000	+ $10,000	− $900	− $500
	$27,300					$27,300							

EVENT (11). PAYMENT OF CASH FOR EMPLOYEE SALARIES. Employees have worked two weeks, earning $4,000 in salaries, which were paid on October 26. Salaries and Wages Expense is an expense that reduces stockholders' equity. In this transaction, both assets and stockholders' equity are reduced.

Basic Analysis

The asset Cash is decreased $4,000; the expense account Salaries and Wages Expense is increased $4,000.

Equation Analysis

	Assets				=	Liabilities			+	Stockholders' Equity				
											Retained Earnings			
	Cash	+ Supplies	+ Prepd. Insur.	+ Equipment	=	Notes Pay.	+ Accts. Pay.	+ Unearned Serv. Rev.	+	Common Stock	+ Rev.	− Exp.	− Div.	
	$19,200	$2,500	$600	$5,000		$5,000	$2,500	$1,200		$10,000	$10,000	$ 900	$500	
(11)	−4,000											− 4,000		Sal./Wages Expense
	$15,200	+ $2,500	+ $600	+ $5,000	=	$5,000	+ $2,500	+ $1,200	+	$10,000	+ $10,000	− $4,900	− $500	
	$23,300					$23,300								

INVESTOR INSIGHT

© Enviromatic/iStockphoto

Why Accuracy Matters

While most companies record transactions very carefully, the reality is that mistakes still happen. For example, bank regulators fined Bank One Corporation (now JPMorgan Chase) $1.8 million because they felt that the unreliability of the bank's accounting system caused it to violate regulatory requirements.

Also, in recent years Fannie Mae, the government-chartered mortgage association, announced a series of large accounting errors. These announcements caused alarm among investors, regulators, and politicians because they feared that the errors might suggest larger, undetected problems. This was important because the home-mortgage market depends on Fannie Mae to buy hundreds of billions of dollars of mortgages each year from banks, thus enabling the banks to issue new mortgages.

Finally, before a major overhaul of its accounting system, the financial records of Waste Management Company were in such disarray that of the company's 57,000 employees, 10,000 were receiving pay slips that were in error.

The Sarbanes-Oxley Act was created to minimize the occurrence of errors like these by increasing every employee's responsibility for accurate financial reporting.

In order for these companies to prepare and issue financial statements, their accounting equations (debits and credits) must have been in balance at year-end. How could these errors or misstatements have occurred? (Go to WileyPLUS for this answer and additional questions.)

SUMMARY OF TRANSACTIONS

Illustration 3-3 summarizes the transactions of Sierra Corporation to show their cumulative effect on the basic accounting equation. It includes the transaction number in the first column on the left. The right-most column shows the specific effect of any transaction that affects stockholders' equity. Remember that Event (9) did not result in a transaction, so no entry is included for that event. The illustration demonstrates three important points:

1. Each transaction is analyzed in terms of its effect on assets, liabilities, and stockholders' equity.
2. The two sides of the equation must always be equal.
3. The cause of each change in stockholders' equity must be indicated.

ILLUSTRATION 3-3
Summary of transactions

	Assets				=	Liabilities			+	Stockholders' Equity				
											Retained Earnings			
	Cash +	Supplies +	Prepd. Insur. +	Equipment	=	Notes Pay. +	Accts. Pay. +	Unearned Serv. Rev.	+	Common Stock +	Rev. −	Exp. −	Div.	
(1)	+$10,000				=					+$10,000				Issued stock
(2)	+5,000					+$5,000								
(3)	−5,000			+$5,000										
(4)	+1,200							+$1,200						
(5)	+10,000										+$10,000			Service Revenue
(6)	−900											−$ 900		Rent Expense
(7)	−600		+$600											
(8)		+$2,500					+$2,500							
(10)	−500												−$500	Dividends
(11)	−4,000											−4,000		Sal./Wages Expense
	$15,200 +	$2,500 +	$600 +	$5,000	=	$5,000 +	$2,500 +	$1,200	+	$10,000 +	$10,000 −	$4,900 −	$500	
	$23,300					$23,300								

DO IT! 1 Transaction Analysis

A tabular analysis of the transactions made by Roberta Mendez & Co., a certified public accounting firm, for the month of August is shown below. Each increase and decrease in stockholders' equity is explained.

	Assets		=	Liabilities	+	Stockholders' Equity					
				Accounts		Common		Retained Earnings			
	Cash	+ Equipment	=	Payable	+	Stock	+	Revenue	−	Expenses	
1.	+$25,000					+$25,000					Issued stock
2.		+$7,000	=	+$7,000							
3.	+8,000							+$8,000			Service Revenue
4.	−850									−$850	Rent Expense
	$32,150	+ $7,000	=	$7,000	+	$25,000	+	$8,000	−	$850	
	$39,150					$39,150					

Action Plan

✔ Analyze the tabular analysis to determine the nature and effect of each transaction.

✔ Keep the accounting equation in balance.

✔ Remember that a change in an asset will require a change in another asset, a liability, or in stockholders' equity.

Describe each transaction that occurred for the month.

SOLUTION

1. The company issued shares of stock to stockholders for $25,000 cash.
2. The company purchased $7,000 of equipment on account.
3. The company received $8,000 of cash in exchange for services performed.
4. The company paid $850 for this month's rent.

Related exercise material: **BE3-1, BE3-2, BE3-3,**  **3-1, E3-1, E3-2, E3-3,** and **E3-4.**

LEARNING OBJECTIVE 2 Explain how accounts, debits, and credits are used to record business transactions.

Rather than using a tabular summary like the one in Illustration 3-3 for Sierra Corporation, an accounting information system uses accounts. An **account** is an individual accounting record of increases and decreases in a specific asset, liability, stockholders' equity, revenue, or expense item. For example, Sierra Corporation has separate accounts for Cash, Accounts Receivable, Accounts Payable, Service Revenue, Salaries and Wages Expense, and so on. (Note that whenever we are referring to a specific account, we capitalize the name.)

In its simplest form, an account consists of three parts: (1) the title of the account, (2) a left or debit side, and (3) a right or credit side. Because the alignment of these parts of an account resembles the letter T, it is referred to as a **T-account**. The basic form of an account is shown in Illustration 3-4.

ILLUSTRATION 3-4
Basic form of account

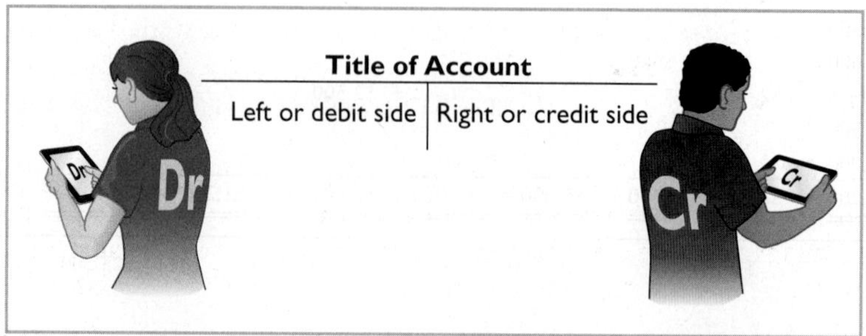

We use this form of account often throughout this textbook to explain basic accounting relationships.

DEBITS AND CREDITS

The term **debit** indicates the left side of an account, and **credit** indicates the right side. They are commonly abbreviated as **Dr.** for debit and **Cr.** for credit. They **do not** mean increase or decrease, as is commonly thought. We use the terms debit and credit repeatedly in the recording process to describe **where** entries are made in accounts. For example, the act of entering an amount on the left side of an account is called **debiting** the account. Making an entry on the right side is **crediting** the account.

When comparing the totals of the two sides, an account shows a **debit balance** if the total of the debit amounts exceeds the credits. An account shows a **credit balance** if the credit amounts exceed the debits. Note the position of the debit side and credit side in Illustration 3-4.

The procedure of recording debits and credits in an account is shown in Illustration 3-5 for the transactions affecting the Cash account of Sierra Corporation. The data are taken from the Cash column of the tabular summary in Illustration 3-3.

ILLUSTRATION 3-5
Tabular summary and account form for Sierra Corporation's Cash account

Tabular Summary

Cash
$10,000
5,000
–5,000
1,200
10,000
–900
–600
–500
–4,000
$15,200

Account Form

	Cash		
(Debits)	10,000	(Credits)	5,000
	5,000		900
	1,200		600
	10,000		500
			4,000
Balance (Debit)	15,200		

Every positive item in the tabular summary represents a receipt of cash; every negative amount represents a payment of cash. **Notice that in the account form, we record the increases in cash as debits and the decreases in cash as credits.** For example, the $10,000 receipt of cash (in blue) is debited to Cash, and the −$5,000 payment of cash (in red) is credited to Cash.

Having increases on one side and decreases on the other reduces recording errors and helps in determining the totals of each side of the account as well as the account balance. The balance is determined by netting the two sides (subtracting one amount from the other). The account balance, a debit of $15,200, indicates that Sierra had $15,200 more increases than decreases in cash. That is, since it started with a balance of zero, it has $15,200 in its Cash account.

DEBIT AND CREDIT PROCEDURES

Each transaction must affect two or more accounts to keep the basic accounting equation in balance. In other words, **for each transaction, debits must equal credits**. The equality of debits and credits provides the basis for the double-entry accounting system.

Under the **double-entry system**, the two-sided effect of each transaction is recorded in appropriate accounts. This system provides a logical method for recording transactions. The double-entry system also helps to ensure the accuracy of the recorded amounts and helps to detect errors such as those at MF Global as discussed in the Feature Story. If every transaction is recorded with equal debits

INTERNATIONAL NOTE
Rules for accounting for specific events sometimes differ across countries. For example, European companies rely less on historical cost and more on fair value than U.S. companies. Despite the differences, the double-entry accounting system is the basis of accounting systems worldwide.

and credits, then the sum of all the debits to the accounts must equal the sum of all the credits. The double-entry system for determining the equality of the accounting equation is much more efficient than the plus/minus procedure used earlier.

Dr./Cr. Procedures for Assets and Liabilities

In Illustration 3-5 for Sierra Corporation, increases in Cash—an asset—are entered on the left side, and decreases in Cash are entered on the right side. We know that both sides of the basic equation (Assets = Liabilities + Stockholders' Equity) must be equal. It therefore follows that increases and decreases in liabilities have to be recorded **opposite from** increases and decreases in assets. Thus, increases in liabilities are entered on the right or credit side, and decreases in liabilities are entered on the left or debit side. The effects that debits and credits have on assets and liabilities are summarized in Illustration 3-6.

ILLUSTRATION 3-6
Debit and credit effects–assets and liabilities

Debits	Credits
Increase assets	Decrease assets
Decrease liabilities	Increase liabilities

Asset accounts normally show debit balances. That is, debits to a specific asset account should exceed credits to that account. Likewise, **liability accounts normally show credit balances**. That is, credits to a liability account should exceed debits to that account. The **normal balances** may be diagrammed as in Illustration 3-7.

ILLUSTRATION 3-7
Normal balances–assets and liabilities

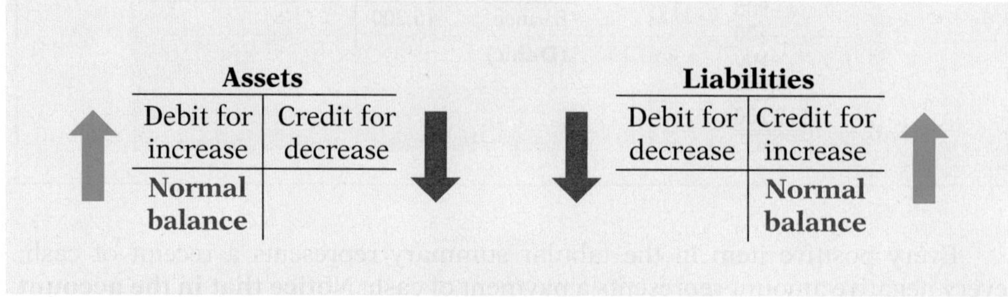

▼ HELPFUL HINT
The normal balance is the side where increases in the account are recorded.

Knowing which is the normal balance in an account may help when you are trying to identify errors. For example, a credit balance in an asset account, such as Land, or a debit balance in a liability account, such as Salaries and Wages Payable, usually indicates errors in recording. Occasionally, however, an abnormal balance may be correct. The Cash account, for example, will have a credit balance when a company has overdrawn its bank balance by spending more than it has in its account. In automated accounting systems, the computer is programmed to flag violations of the normal balance and to print out error or exception reports. In manual systems, careful visual inspection of the accounts is required to detect normal balance problems.

Dr./Cr. Procedures for Stockholders' Equity

In Chapter 1, we indicated that stockholders' equity is comprised of two parts: common stock and retained earnings. In the transaction events earlier in this chapter, you saw that revenues, expenses, and the payment of dividends affect retained earnings. Therefore, the subdivisions of stockholders' equity are common stock, retained earnings, dividends, revenues, and expenses.

COMMON STOCK Common stock is issued to investors in exchange for the stockholders' investment. The Common Stock account is increased by credits and decreased by debits. For example, when cash is invested in the business, Cash is debited and Common Stock is credited. The effects of debits and credits on the Common Stock account are shown in Illustration 3-8.

ILLUSTRATION 3-8
Debit and credit effects–common stock

Debits	Credits
Decrease Common Stock	Increase Common Stock

The normal balance in the Common Stock account may be diagrammed as in Illustration 3-9.

ILLUSTRATION 3-9
Normal balance–common stock

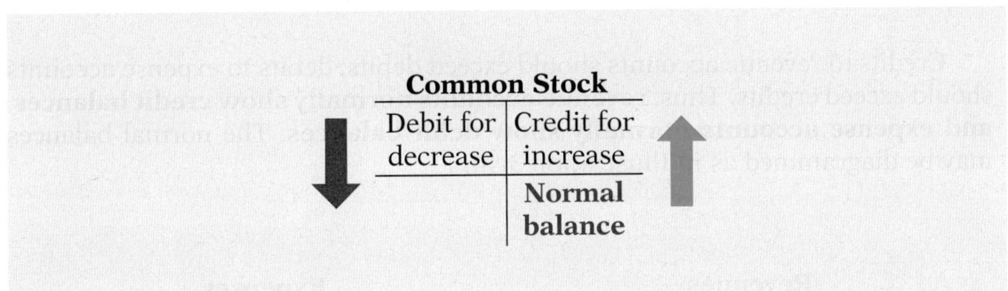

RETAINED EARNINGS Retained earnings is net income that is retained in the business. It represents the portion of stockholders' equity that has been accumulated through the profitable operation of the company. Retained Earnings is increased by credits (for example, by net income) and decreased by debits (for example, by a net loss), as shown in Illustration 3-10.

ILLUSTRATION 3-10
Debit and credit effects–retained earnings

Debits	Credits
Decrease Retained Earnings	Increase Retained Earnings

The normal balance for the Retained Earnings account may be diagrammed as in Illustration 3-11.

ILLUSTRATION 3-11
Normal balance–retained earnings

Retained Earnings	
Debit for decrease	Credit for increase
	Normal balance

DIVIDENDS A dividend is a distribution by a corporation to its stockholders. The most common form of distribution is a cash dividend. Dividends result in a reduction of the stockholders' claims on retained earnings. Because dividends reduce stockholders' equity, increases in the Dividends account are recorded with debits. As shown in Illustration 3-12, the Dividends account normally has a debit balance.

ILLUSTRATION 3-12
Normal balance–dividends

Dividends	
Debit for increase	Credit for decrease
Normal balance	

REVENUES AND EXPENSES When a company recognizes revenues, stockholders' equity is increased. Revenue accounts are increased by credits and decreased by debits.

Expenses decrease stockholders' equity. Thus, expense accounts are increased by debits and decreased by credits. The effects of debits and credits on revenues and expenses are shown in Illustration 3-13.

ILLUSTRATION 3-13
Debit and credit effects–revenues and expenses

Debits	Credits
Decrease revenue	Increase revenue
Increase expenses	Decrease expenses

Credits to revenue accounts should exceed debits; debits to expense accounts should exceed credits. Thus, **revenue accounts normally show credit balances, and expense accounts normally show debit balances**. The normal balances may be diagrammed as in Illustration 3-14.

ILLUSTRATION 3-14
Normal balances–revenues and expenses

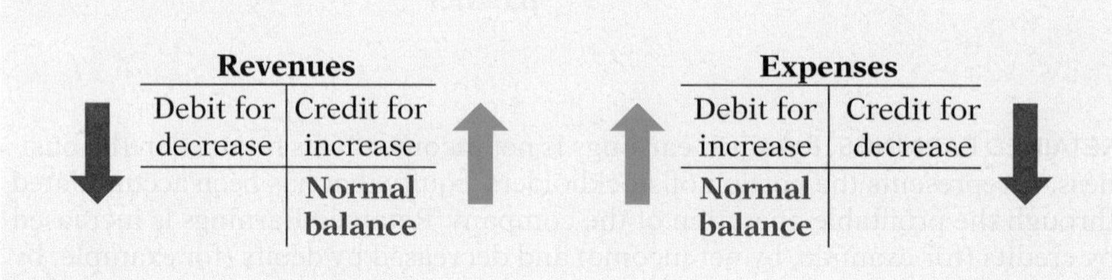

INVESTOR INSIGHT Chicago Cubs

© Jonathan Daniel/Getty Images, Inc.

Keeping Score

The Chicago Cubs baseball team has these major revenue and expense accounts:

Revenues	Expenses
Admissions (ticket sales)	Players' salaries
Concessions	Administrative salaries
Television and radio	Travel
Advertising	Ballpark maintenance

Do you think that the Chicago Bears football team would be likely to have the same major revenue and expense accounts as the Cubs? (Go to WileyPLUS for this answer and additional questions.)

STOCKHOLDERS' EQUITY RELATIONSHIPS

Companies report the subdivisions of stockholders' equity in various places in the financial statements:

- Common stock and retained earnings: in the stockholders' equity section of the balance sheet.
- Dividends: on the retained earnings statement.
- Revenues and expenses: on the income statement.

Dividends, revenues, and expenses are eventually transferred to retained earnings at the end of the period. As a result, a change in any one of these three items affects stockholders' equity. Illustration 3-15 shows the relationships of the accounts affecting stockholders' equity.

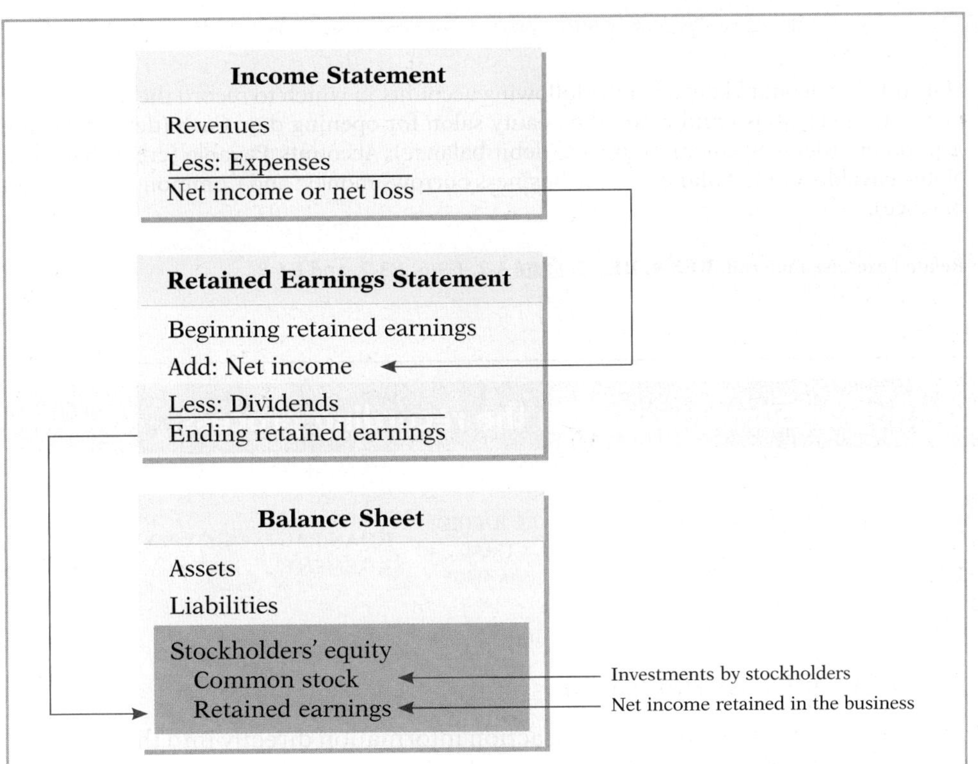

ILLUSTRATION 3-15
Stockholders' equity relationships

SUMMARY OF DEBIT/CREDIT RULES

Illustration 3-16 summarizes the debit/credit rules and effects on each type of account. **Study this diagram carefully.** It will help you understand the fundamentals of the double-entry system. No matter what the transaction, total debits must equal total credits in order to keep the accounting equation in balance.

ILLUSTRATION 3-16
Summary of debit/credit rules

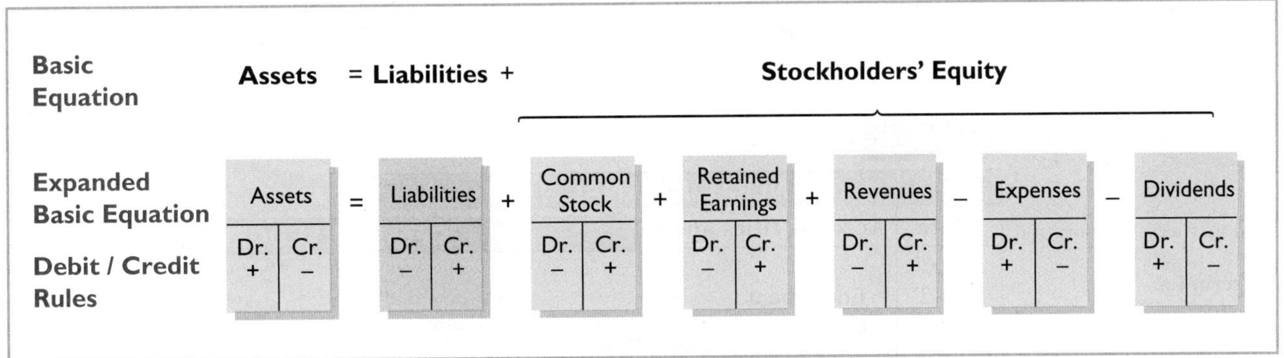

DO IT! ▶2 Debits and Credits for Balance Sheet Accounts

Kate Browne, president of Hair It Is Inc., has just rented space in a shopping mall for the purpose of opening and operating a beauty salon. Long before opening day and before purchasing equipment, hiring assistants, and remodeling the space, Kate was strongly advised to set up a double-entry set of accounting records in which to record all of her business transactions.

Identify the balance sheet accounts that Hair It Is Inc. will likely need to record the transactions necessary to establish and open for business. Also, indicate whether the normal balance of each account is a debit or a credit.

Action Plan

✔ **First identify asset accounts for each different type of asset invested in the business.**

✔ **Then identify liability accounts for debts incurred by the business.**

Action Plan (cont.)

✔ Hair It Is Inc. needs only one stockholders' equity account, Common Stock, when it begins the business. The other stockholders' equity account, Retained Earnings, will be needed after the business is operating.

SOLUTION

Hair It Is Inc. would likely need the following accounts in which to record the transactions necessary to establish and ready the beauty salon for opening day: Cash (debit balance); Equipment (debit balance); Supplies (debit balance); Accounts Payable (credit balance); Notes Payable (credit balance), if the business borrows money; and Common Stock (credit balance).

Related exercise material: **BE3-4, BE3-5, DO IT! 3-2, E3-6, E3-7,** and **E3-8.**

LEARNING OBJECTIVE 3

Indicate how a journal is used in the recording process.

ANALYZE | **Journalize the transactions** | POST | TRIAL BALANCE | ADJUSTING ENTRIES | ADJUSTED TRIAL BALANCE | FINANCIAL STATEMENTS | CLOSING ENTRIES | POST-CLOSING TRIAL BALANCE

THE RECORDING PROCESS

Although it is possible to enter transaction information directly into the accounts, few businesses do so. Practically every business uses these basic steps in the recording process (an integral part of the accounting cycle):

1. Analyze each transaction in terms of its effect on the accounts.
2. Enter the transaction information in a journal.
3. Transfer the journal information to the appropriate accounts in the ledger.

The actual sequence of events begins with the transaction. Evidence of the transaction comes in the form of a **source document**, such as a sales slip, a check, a bill, or a cash register document. This evidence is analyzed to determine the effect of the transaction on specific accounts. The transaction is then entered in the **journal**. Finally, the journal entry is transferred to the designated accounts in the **ledger**. The sequence of events in the recording process is shown in Illustration 3-17.

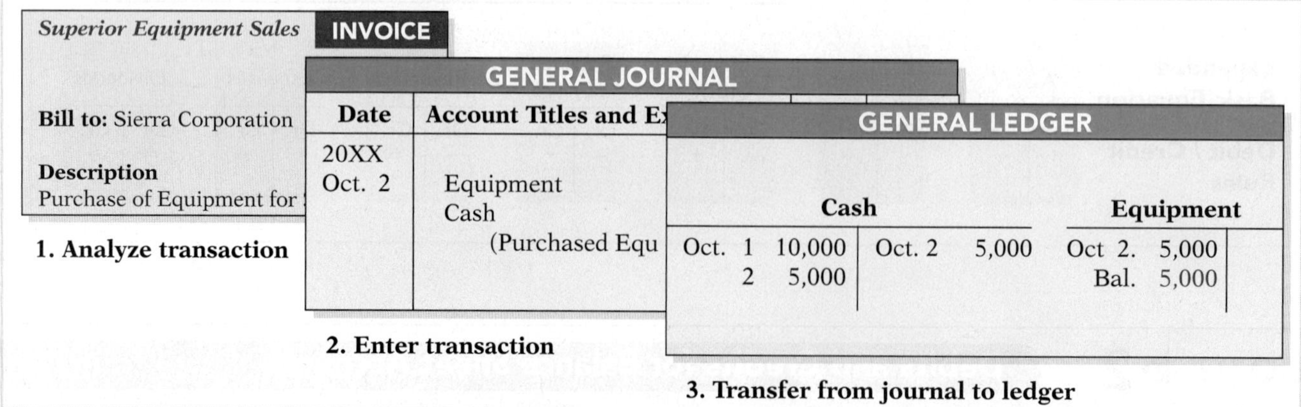

ILLUSTRATION 3-17
The recording process

THE JOURNAL

Transactions are initially recorded in chronological order in a **journal** before they are transferred to the accounts. For each transaction, the journal shows the debit and credit effects on specific accounts. (In a computerized system, journals are kept as files, and accounts are recorded in computer databases.)

Companies may use various kinds of journals, but every company has at least the most basic form of journal, a **general journal. The journal makes three significant contributions to the recording process:**

1. It discloses in one place the **complete effect of a transaction.**
2. It provides a **chronological record** of transactions.
3. It **helps to prevent or locate errors** because the debit and credit amounts for each entry can be readily compared.

Entering transaction data in the journal is known as **journalizing.** To illustrate the technique of journalizing, let's look at the first three transactions of Sierra Corporation in equation form.

ETHICS NOTE

Business documents provide evidence that transactions actually occurred. International Outsourcing Services, LLC was accused of submitting fraudulent documents (store coupons) to companies such as Kraft Foods and PepsiCo for reimbursement of as much as $250 million. Use of proper business documents reduces the likelihood of fraudulent activity.

On October 1, Sierra issued common stock in exchange for $10,000 cash:

Assets	=	Liabilities	+	Stockholders' Equity	
Cash	=			Common Stock	
+$10,000				+$10,000	Issued stock

On October 1, Sierra borrowed $5,000 by signing a note:

Assets	=	Liabilities	+	Stockholders' Equity
Cash	=	Notes Payable		
+$5,000		+$5,000		

On October 2, Sierra purchased equipment for $5,000:

Assets		=	Liabilities	+	Stockholders' Equity
Cash	Equipment				
−$5,000	+$5,000				

Sierra makes separate journal entries for each transaction. A complete entry consists of (1) the date of the transaction, (2) the accounts and amounts to be debited and credited, and (3) a brief explanation of the transaction. These transactions are journalized in Illustration 3-18.

ILLUSTRATION 3-18
Recording transactions in journal form

GENERAL JOURNAL

Date		Account Titles and Explanation	Debit	Credit
2017				
Oct.	1	Cash	10,000	
		Common Stock		10,000
		(Issued stock for cash)		
	1	Cash	5,000	
		Notes Payable		5,000
		(Issued 3-month, 12% note payable for cash)		
	2	Equipment	5,000	
		Cash		5,000
		(Purchased equipment for cash)		

Note the following features of the journal entries.

1. The date of the transaction is entered in the Date column.
2. The account to be debited is entered first at the left. The account to be credited is then entered on the next line, indented under the line above. The indentation differentiates debits from credits and decreases the possibility of switching the debit and credit amounts.
3. The amounts for the debits are recorded in the Debit (left) column, and the amounts for the credits are recorded in the Credit (right) column.
4. A brief explanation of the transaction is given.

It is important to use correct and specific account titles in journalizing. Erroneous account titles lead to incorrect financial statements. Some flexibility exists initially in selecting account titles. The main criterion is that each title must appropriately describe the content of the account. For example, a company could use any of these account titles for recording the cost of delivery trucks: Equipment, Delivery Equipment, Delivery Trucks, or Trucks. Once the company chooses the specific title to use, however, it should record under that account title all subsequent transactions involving the account.

ACCOUNTING ACROSS THE ORGANIZATION Microsoft

© flyfloor/iStockphoto

Boosting Profits

Microsoft originally designed the Xbox 360 to have 256 megabytes of memory. But the design department said that amount of memory wouldn't support the best special effects. The purchasing department said that adding more memory would cost $30—which was 10% of the estimated selling price of $300. The marketing department, however, "determined that adding the memory would let Microsoft reduce marketing costs and attract more game developers, boosting royalty revenue. It would also extend the life of the console, generating more sales."

As a result of these changes, Xbox enjoyed great success. But, it does have competitors. Its newest video game console, Xbox One, is now in a battle with Sony's Playstation4 for market share. How to compete? First, Microsoft bundled the critically acclaimed *Titanfall* with its Xbox One. By including the game most Xbox One buyers were going to purchase anyway, Microsoft was making its console more attractive. In addition, retailers are also discounting the Xbox, which should get the momentum going for increased sales. What Microsoft is doing is making sure that Xbox One is the center of the home entertainment system in the long run.

Sources: Robert A. Guth, "New Xbox Aim for Microsoft: Profitability," *Wall Street Journal* (May 24, 2005), p. C1; and David Thier, "Will Microsoft Give the Xbox One a $50 Price Cut? *www.Forbes.com* (March 26, 2014).

In what ways is this Microsoft division using accounting to assist in its effort to become more profitable? (Go to WileyPLUS for this answer and additional questions.)

DO IT! 3 Journal Entries

The following events occurred during the first month of business of Hair It Is Inc., Kate Browne's beauty salon:

1. Issued common stock to shareholders in exchange for $20,000 cash.
2. Purchased $4,800 of equipment on account (to be paid in 30 days).
3. Interviewed three people for the position of stylist.

Prepare the entries to record the transactions.

SOLUTION

The three activities are recorded as follows.

1. Cash	20,000	
Common Stock		20,000
(Issued stock for cash)		
2. Equipment	4,800	
Accounts Payable		4,800
(Purchased equipment on account)		

3. No entry because no transaction occurred.

Action Plan

✔ **Make sure to provide a complete and accurate representation of the transactions' effects on the assets, liabilities, and stockholders' equity of the business.**

Related exercise material: **BE3-6, BE3-9, DO IT! 3-3, E3-7, E3-9, E3-10, E3-11,** and **E3-12.**

LEARNING OBJECTIVE ▶4

Explain how a ledger and posting help in the recording process.

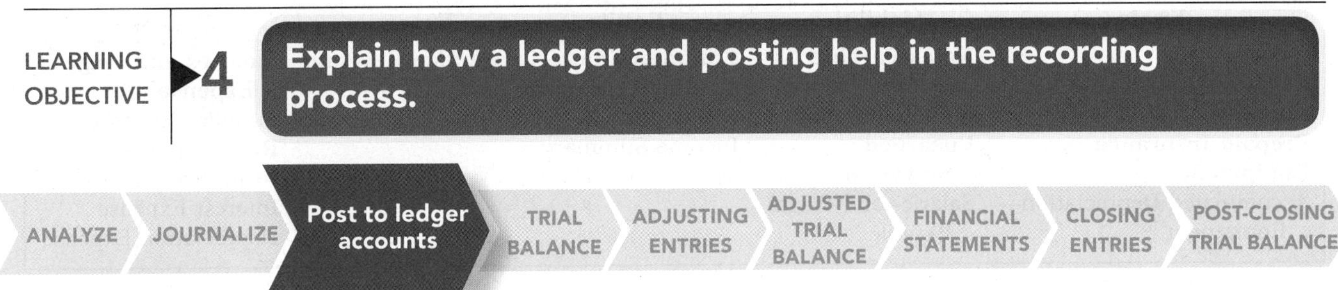

THE LEDGER

The entire group of accounts maintained by a company is referred to collectively as the **ledger**. The ledger provides the balance in each of the accounts as well as keeps track of changes in these balances.

Companies may use various kinds of ledgers, but every company has a general ledger. A **general ledger** contains all the asset, liability, stockholders' equity, revenue, and expense accounts, as shown in Illustration 3-19. Whenever we use the term **ledger** in this textbook without additional specification, it will mean the general ledger.

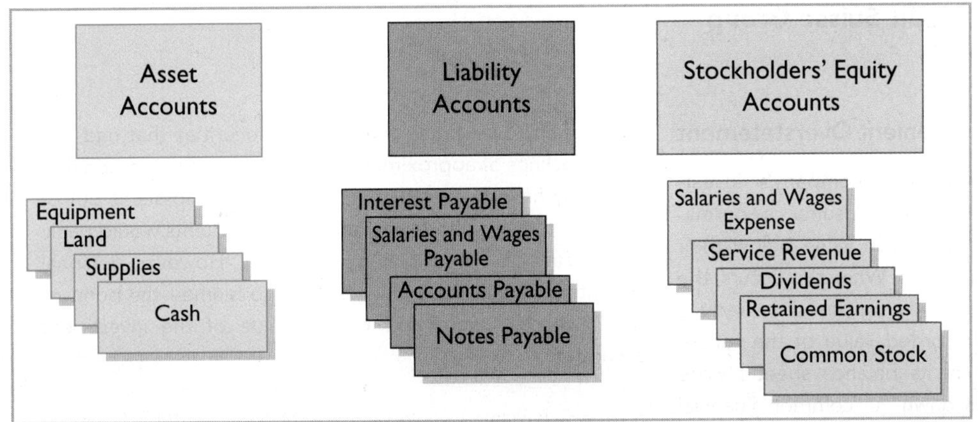

ILLUSTRATION 3-19
The general ledger

CHART OF ACCOUNTS

The number and type of accounts used differ for each company, depending on the size, complexity, and type of business. For example, the number of accounts depends on the amount of detail desired by management. The management of one company may want one single account for all types of utility expense. Another may keep separate expense accounts for each type of utility expenditure, such as gas, electricity, and water. A small corporation like Sierra Corporation will not have many accounts compared with a corporate giant like Ford Motor Company. Sierra may be able to manage and report its activities in 20 to 30 accounts, whereas Ford requires thousands of accounts to keep track of its worldwide activities.

Most companies list the accounts in a **chart of accounts**. They may create new accounts as needed during the life of the business. Illustration 3-20 shows the chart of accounts for Sierra in the order that they are typically listed (assets, liabilities, stockholders' equity, revenues, and expenses). **Accounts shown in red are used in this chapter**; accounts shown in black are explained in later chapters.

ILLUSTRATION 3-20
Chart of accounts for Sierra Corporation

SIERRA CORPORATION
Chart of Accounts

Assets	Liabilities	Stockholders' Equity	Revenues	Expenses
Cash	**Notes Payable**	**Common Stock**	**Service Revenue**	**Salaries and Wages Expense**
Accounts Receivable	**Accounts Payable**	**Retained Earnings**		Supplies Expense
Supplies	Interest Payable	**Dividends**		**Rent Expense**
Prepaid Insurance	**Unearned Service Revenue**	Income Summary		Insurance Expense
Equipment	Salaries and Wages Payable			Interest Expense
Accumulated Depreciation—Equipment				Depreciation Expense

POSTING

The procedure of transferring journal entry amounts to ledger accounts is called **posting**. **This phase of the recording process accumulates the effects of journalized transactions in the individual accounts.** Posting involves these steps:

1. In the ledger, enter in the appropriate columns of the debited account(s) the date and debit amount shown in the journal.
2. In the ledger, enter in the appropriate columns of the credited account(s) the date and credit amount shown in the journal.

ETHICS INSIGHT **Credit Suisse Group**

© Nuno Silva/iStockphoto

A Convenient Overstatement

Sometimes a company's investment securities suffer a permanent decline in value below their original cost. When this occurs, the company is supposed to reduce the recorded value of the securities on its balance sheet ("write them down" in common financial lingo) and record a loss. It appears, however, that during the financial crisis of 2008, employees at some financial institutions chose to look the other way as the value of their investments skidded.

A number of Wall Street traders that worked for the investment bank Credit Suisse Group were charged with intentionally overstating the value of securities that had suffered declines of approximately $2.85 billion. One reason that they may have been reluctant to record the losses is out of fear that the company's shareholders and clients would panic if they saw the magnitude of the losses. However, personal self-interest might have been equally to blame—the bonuses of the traders were tied to the value of the investment securities.

Source: S. Pulliam, J. Eaglesham, and M. Siconolfi, "U.S. Plans Changes on Bond Fraud," *Wall Street Journal Online* (February 1, 2012).

What incentives might employees have had to overstate the value of these investment securities on the company's financial statements? (Go to WileyPLUS for this answer and additional questions.)

THE RECORDING PROCESS ILLUSTRATED

Illustrations 3-21 through 3-31 on the following pages show the basic steps in the recording process using the October transactions of Sierra Corporation. Sierra's accounting period is a month. A basic analysis and a debit–credit analysis precede the journalizing and posting of each transaction. Study these transaction analyses carefully. **The purpose of transaction analysis is first to identify the type of account involved and then to determine whether a debit or a credit to the account is required.** You should always perform this type of analysis before preparing a journal entry. Doing so will help you understand the journal entries discussed in this chapter as well as more complex journal entries to be described in later chapters.

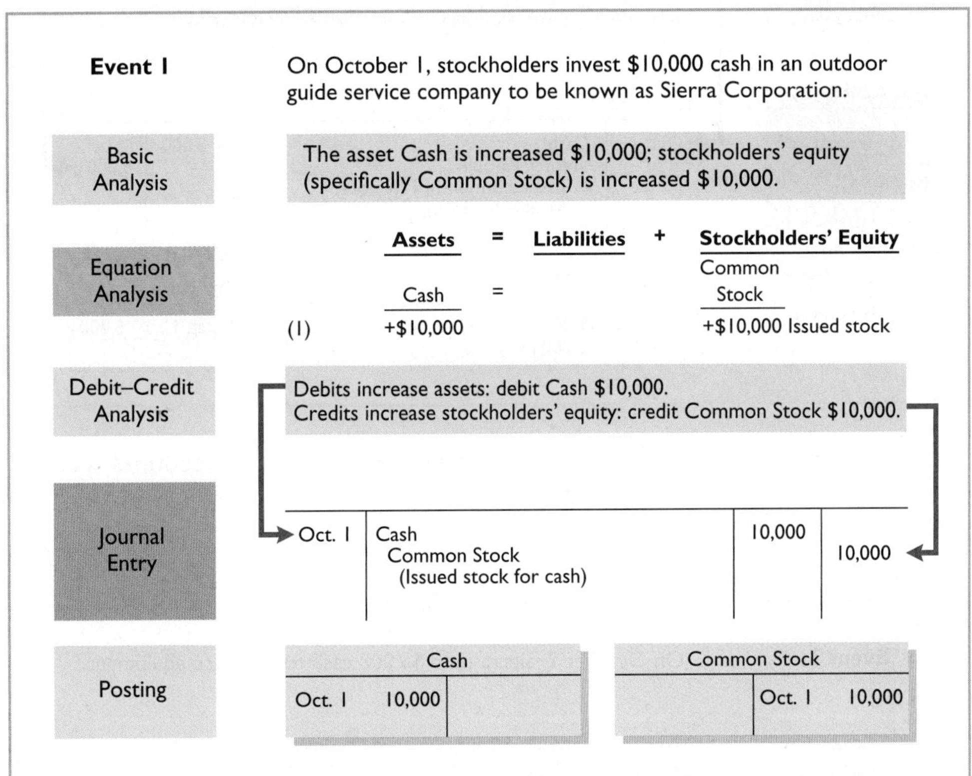

ILLUSTRATION 3-21
Investment of cash by stockholders

Cash flow analyses show the impact of each transaction on cash.

Cash Flows
+10,000

ILLUSTRATION 3-22
Issue of note payable

Cash Flows
+5,000

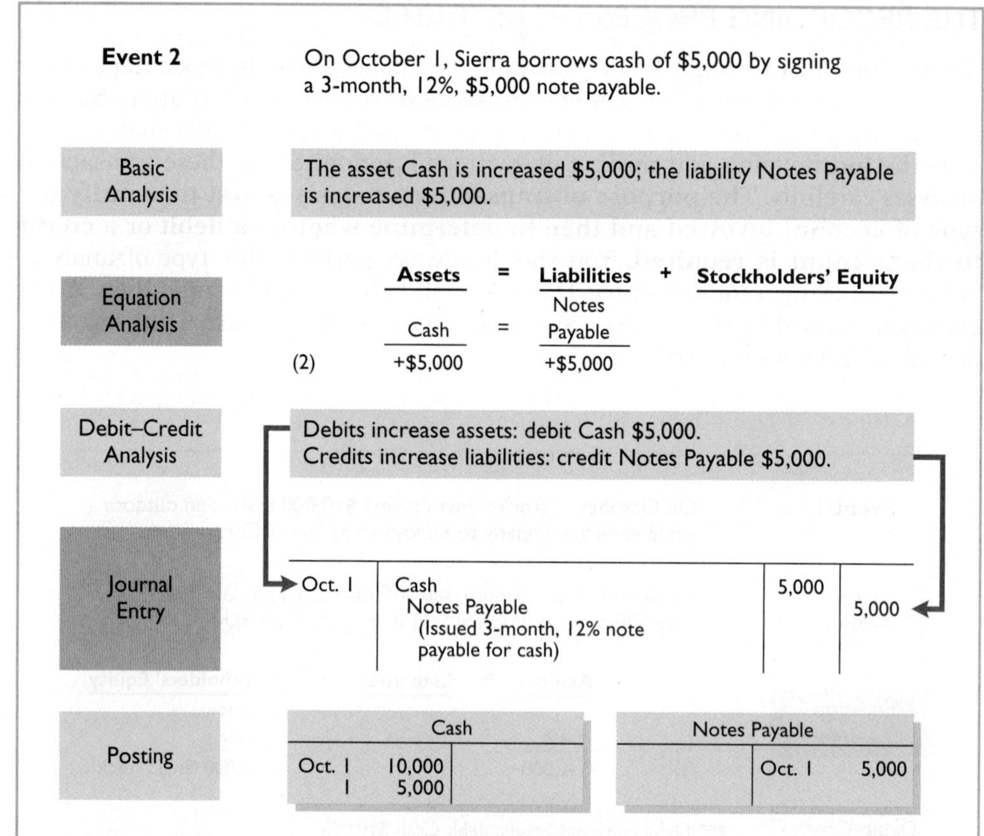

ILLUSTRATION 3-23
Purchase of equipment

Cash Flows
–5,000

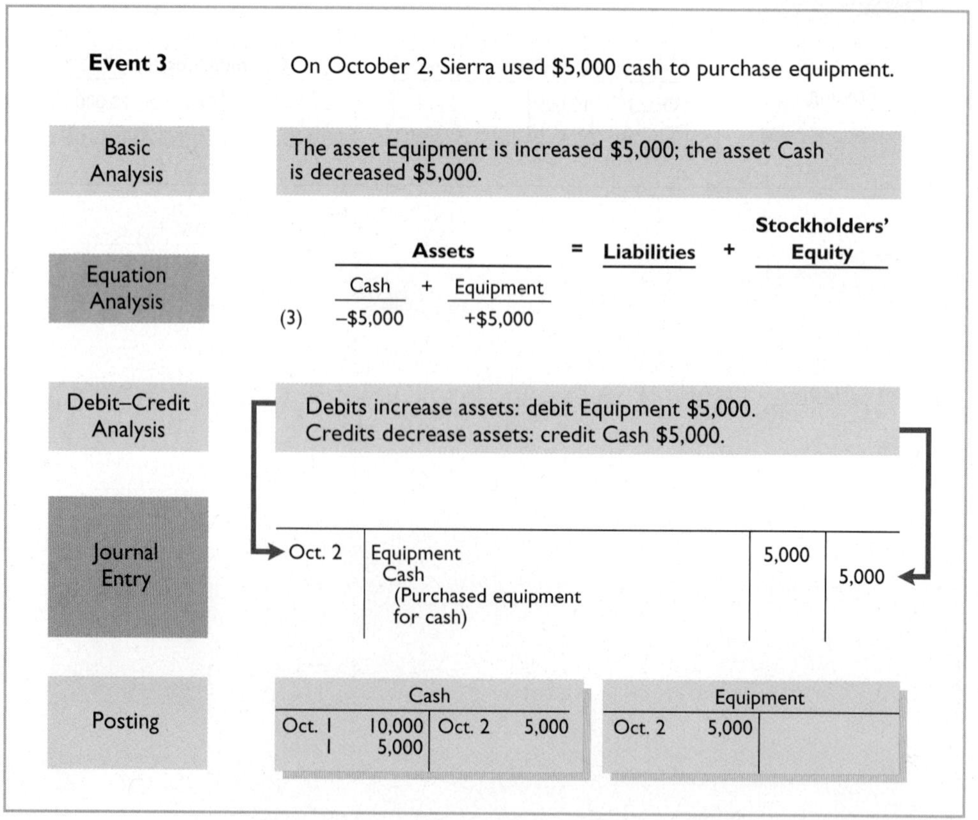

ILLUSTRATION 3-24
Receipt of cash in advance from customer

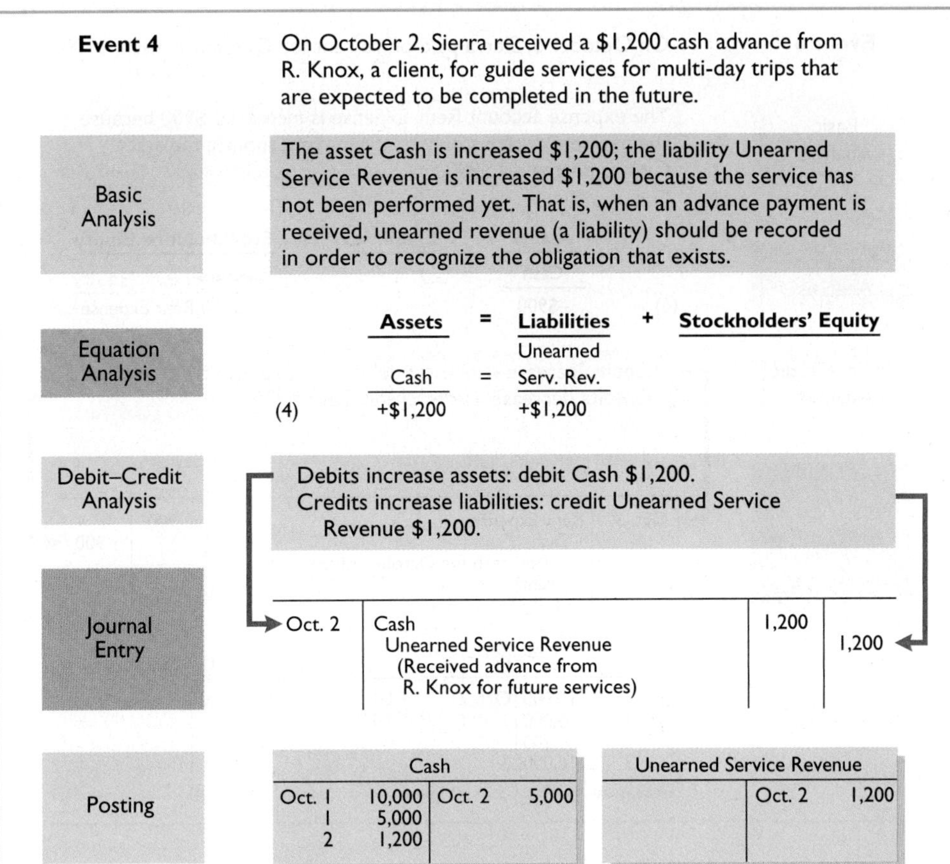

▼ **HELPFUL HINT**
Many liabilities have the word "payable" in their title. But, note that Unearned Service Revenue is considered a liability even though the word *payable* is not used.

Cash Flows
+1,200

ILLUSTRATION 3-25
Services performed for cash

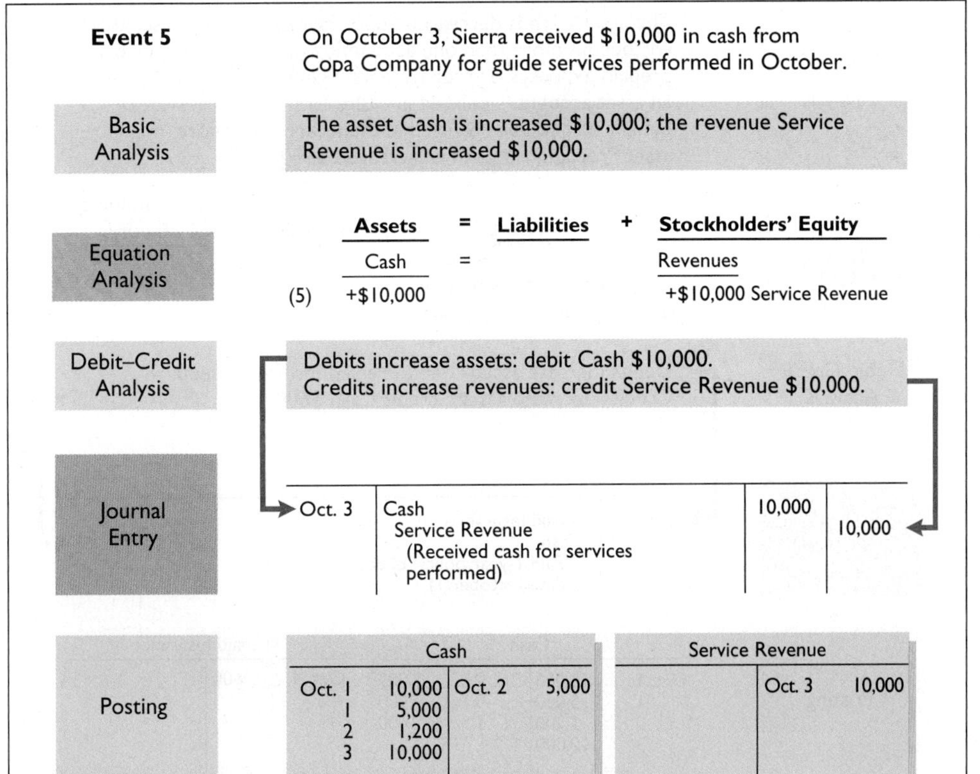

Cash Flows
+10,000

ILLUSTRATION 3-26
Payment of rent with cash

Cash Flows
−900

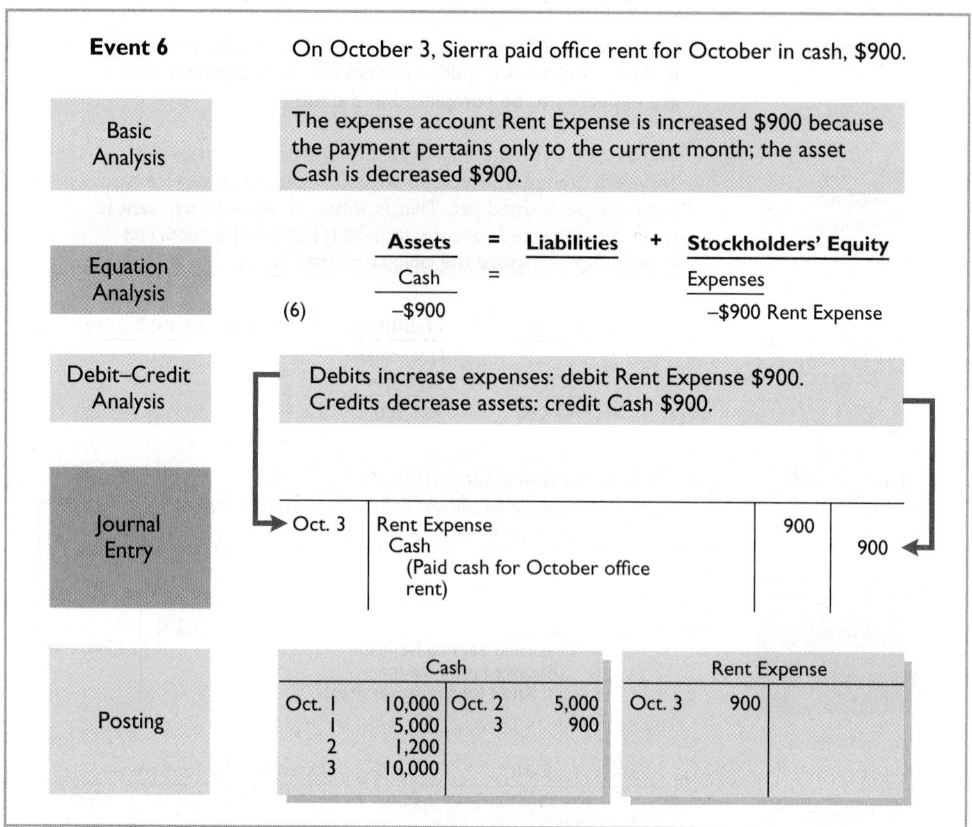

ILLUSTRATION 3-27
Purchase of insurance policy with cash

Cash Flows
−600

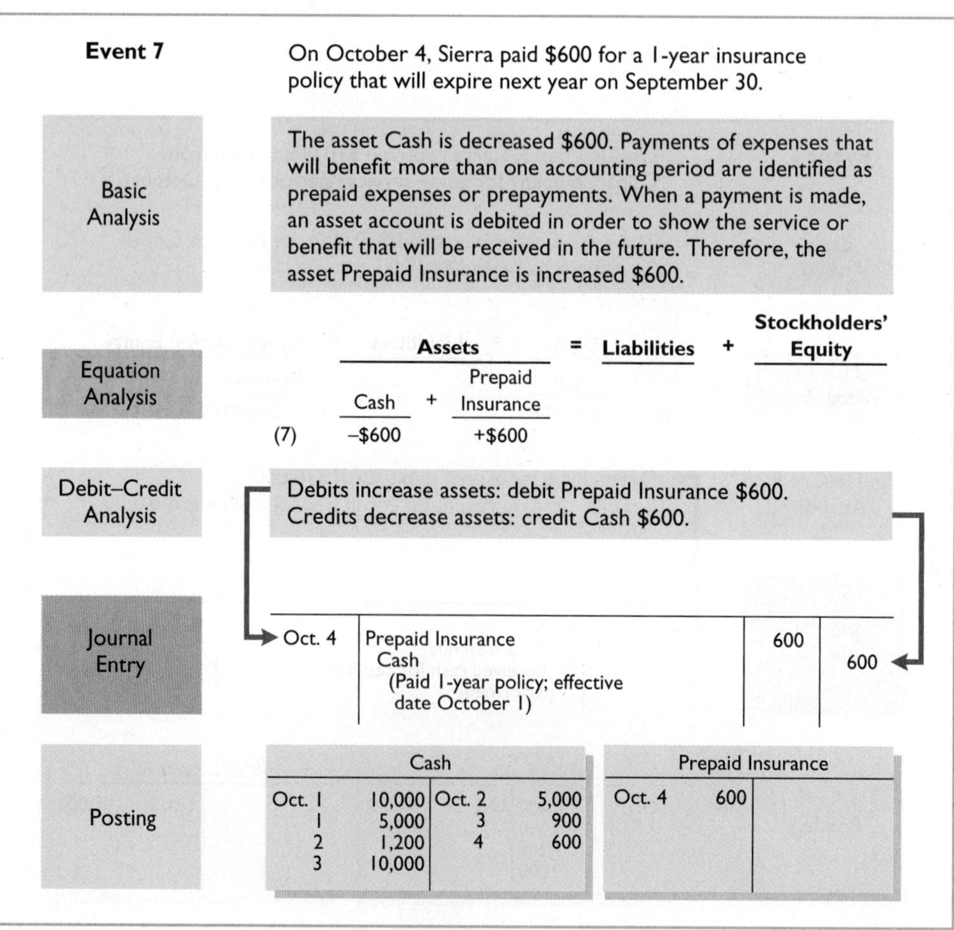

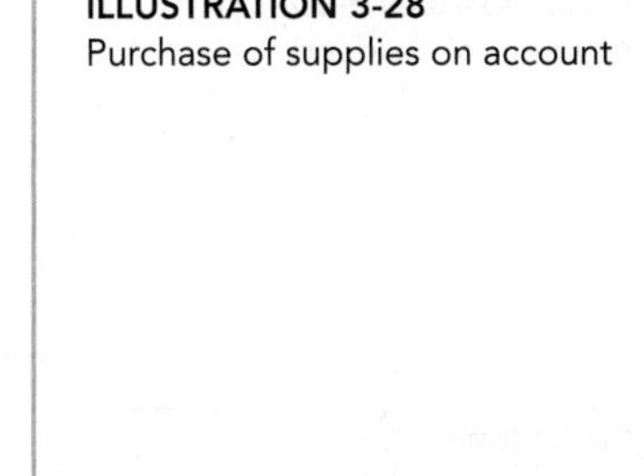

ILLUSTRATION 3-28
Purchase of supplies on account

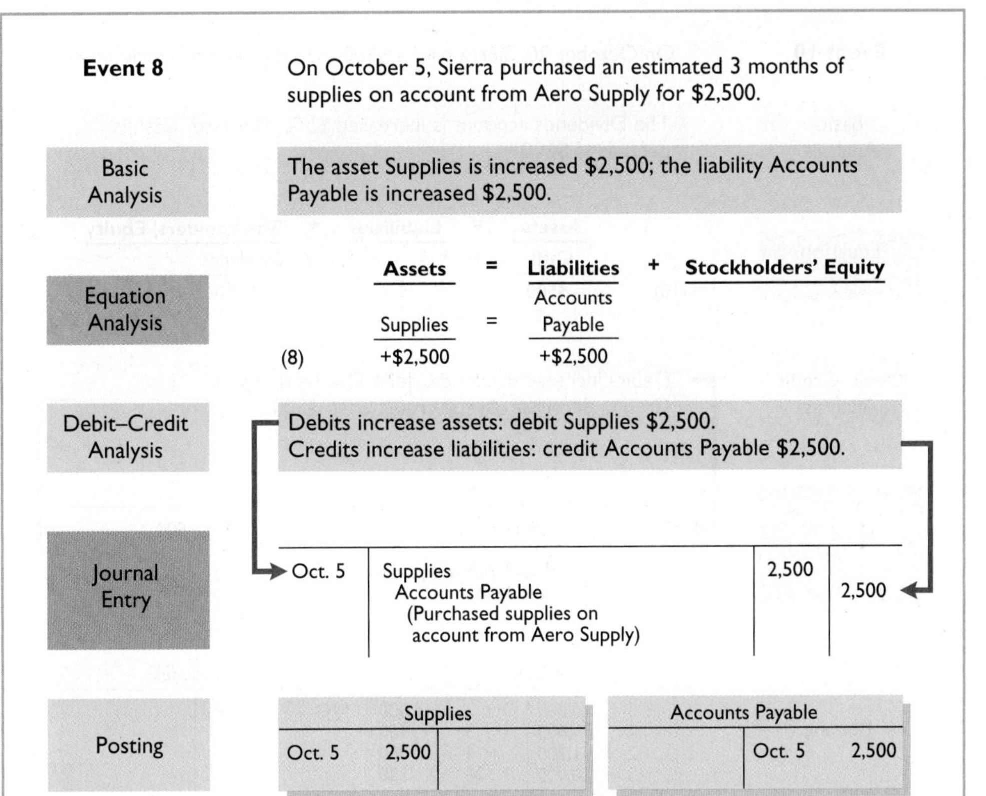

Cash Flows
no effect

ILLUSTRATION 3-29
Hiring of new employees

Event 9

On October 9, Sierra hired four employees to begin work on October 15. Each employee will receive a weekly salary of $500 for a 5-day work week, payable every 2 weeks—first payment made on October 26.

Basic Analysis

An accounting transaction has not occurred. There is only an agreement that the employees will begin work on October 15. Thus, a debit–credit analysis is not needed because there is no accounting entry. (See transaction of October 26 (Event II) for first payment.)

ILLUSTRATION 3-30
Payment of dividend

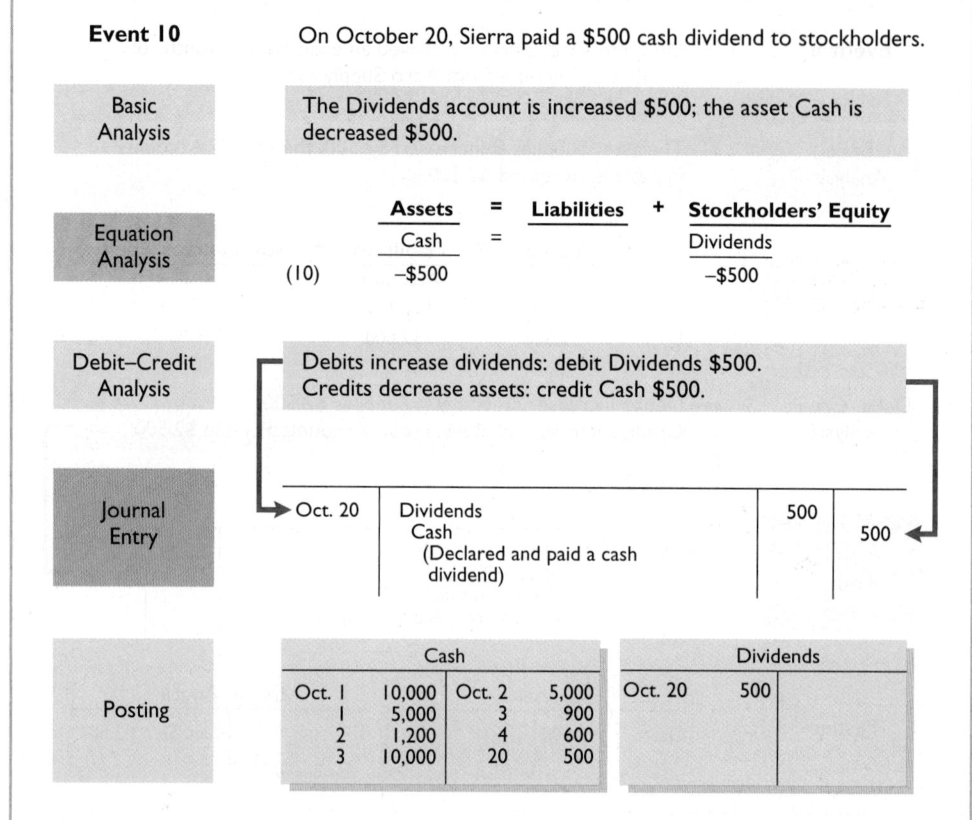

ILLUSTRATION 3-31
Payment of cash for employee salaries

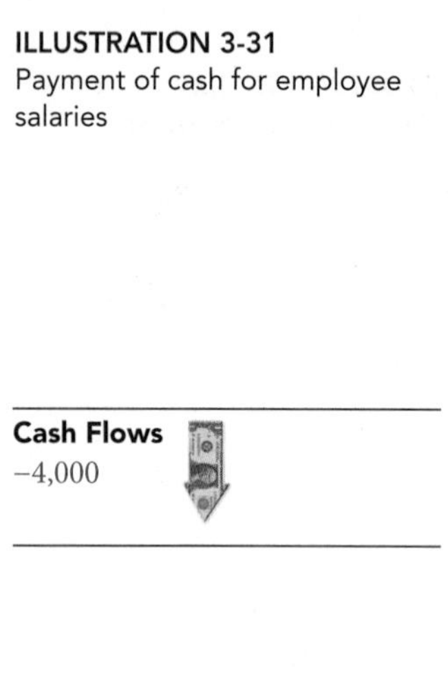

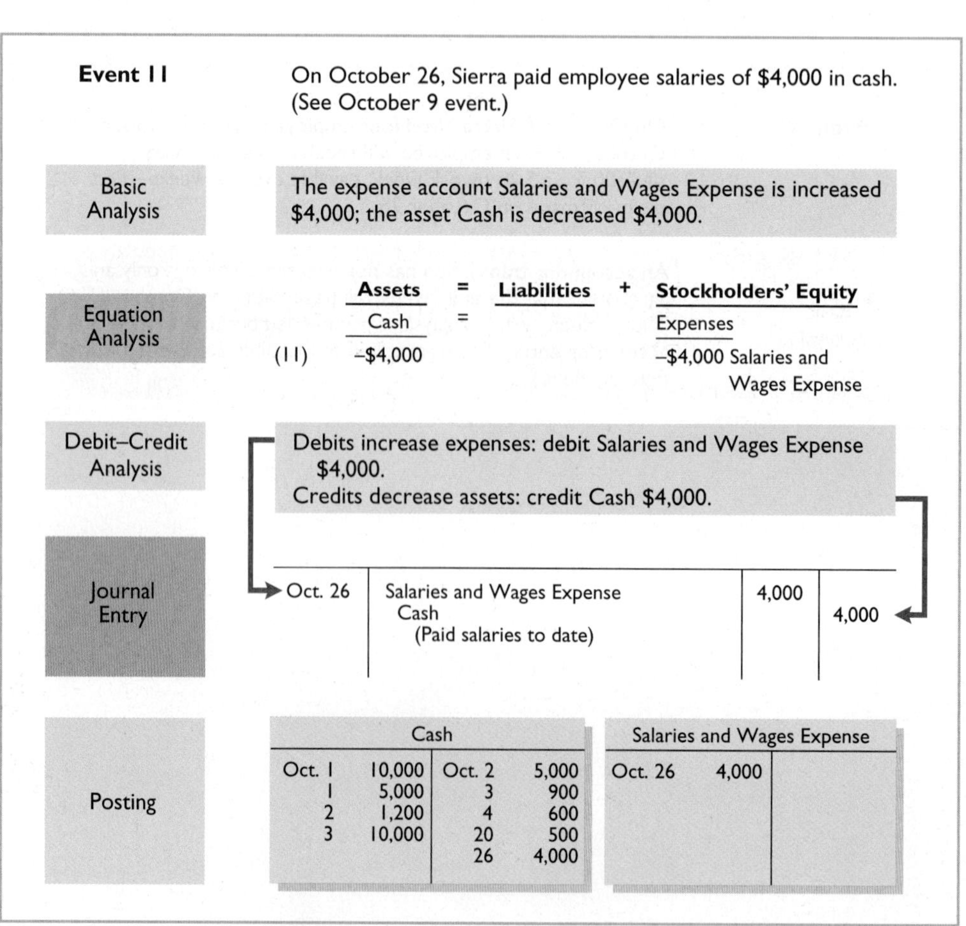

SUMMARY ILLUSTRATION OF JOURNALIZING AND POSTING

The journal for Sierra Corporation for the month of October is summarized in Illustration 3-32. The ledger is shown in Illustration 3-33 (on page 118) with all balances highlighted in red.

ILLUSTRATION 3-32
General journal for Sierra Corporation

GENERAL JOURNAL

Date		Account Titles and Explanation	Debit	Credit
2017				
Oct.	1	Cash	10,000	
		Common Stock		10,000
		(Issued stock for cash)		
	1	Cash	5,000	
		Notes Payable		5,000
		(Issued 3-month, 12% note payable for cash)		
	2	Equipment	5,000	
		Cash		5,000
		(Purchased equipment for cash)		
	2	Cash	1,200	
		Unearned Service Revenue		1,200
		(Received advance from R. Knox for future service)		
	3	Cash	10,000	
		Service Revenue		10,000
		(Received cash for services performed)		
	3	Rent Expense	900	
		Cash		900
		(Paid cash for October office rent)		
	4	Prepaid Insurance	600	
		Cash		600
		(Paid 1-year policy; effective date October 1)		
	5	Supplies	2,500	
		Accounts Payable		2,500
		(Purchased supplies on account from Aero Supply)		
	20	Dividends	500	
		Cash		500
		(Declared and paid a cash dividend)		
	26	Salaries and Wages Expense	4,000	
		Cash		4,000
		(Paid salaries to date)		

ILLUSTRATION 3-33
General ledger for Sierra Corporation

GENERAL LEDGER

Cash

Date	Debit	Date	Credit
Oct. 1	10,000	Oct. 2	5,000
1	5,000	3	900
2	1,200	4	600
3	10,000	20	500
		26	4,000
Bal.	**15,200**		

Unearned Service Revenue

Date	Debit	Date	Credit
		Oct. 2	1,200
		Bal.	**1,200**

Supplies

Date	Debit	Date	Credit
Oct. 5	2,500		
Bal.	**2,500**		

Common Stock

Date	Debit	Date	Credit
		Oct. 1	10,000
		Bal.	**10,000**

Prepaid Insurance

Date	Debit	Date	Credit
Oct. 4	600		
Bal.	**600**		

Dividends

Date	Debit	Date	Credit
Oct. 20	500		
Bal.	**500**		

Equipment

Date	Debit	Date	Credit
Oct. 2	5,000		
Bal.	**5,000**		

Service Revenue

Date	Debit	Date	Credit
		Oct. 3	10,000
		Bal.	**10,000**

Notes Payable

Date	Debit	Date	Credit
		Oct. 1	5,000
		Bal.	**5,000**

Salaries and Wages Expense

Date	Debit	Date	Credit
Oct. 26	4,000		
Bal.	**4,000**		

Accounts Payable

Date	Debit	Date	Credit
		Oct. 5	2,500
		Bal.	**2,500**

Rent Expense

Date	Debit	Date	Credit
Oct. 3	900		
Bal.	**900**		

DO IT! 4 Posting

Selected transactions from the journal of Faital Inc. during its first month of operations are presented below. Post these transactions to T-accounts.

Date	Account Titles	Debit	Credit
July 1	Cash	30,000	
	Common Stock		30,000
9	Accounts Receivable	6,000	
	Service Revenue		6,000
24	Cash	4,000	
	Accounts Receivable		4,000

Action Plan

- ✔ Journalize transactions to keep track of financial activities (receipts, payments, receivables, payables, etc.).
- ✔ To make entries useful, classify and summarize them by posting the entries to specific ledger accounts.

SOLUTION

Cash

Date	Debit	Date	Credit
July 1	30,000		
24	4,000		

Accounts Receivable

Date	Debit	Date	Credit
July 9	6,000	July 24	4,000

Common Stock

Date	Debit	Date	Credit
		July 1	30,000

Service Revenue

Date	Debit	Date	Credit
		July 9	6,000

Related exercise material: **BE3-10, DO IT! 3-4, and E3-14.**

LEARNING OBJECTIVE 5

Prepare a trial balance.

ANALYZE | JOURNALIZE | POST | **Prepare a trial balance** | ADJUSTING ENTRIES | ADJUSTED TRIAL BALANCE | FINANCIAL STATEMENTS | CLOSING ENTRIES | POST-CLOSING TRIAL BALANCE

A **trial balance** lists accounts and their balances at a given time. A company usually prepares a trial balance at the end of an accounting period. The accounts are listed in the order in which they appear in the ledger. Debit balances are listed in the left column and credit balances in the right column. The totals of the two columns must be equal.

DECISION TOOLS

A trial balance proves that debits equal credits.

The trial balance proves the mathematical equality of debits and credits after posting. Under the double-entry system, this equality occurs when the sum of the debit account balances equals the sum of the credit account balances. **A trial balance may also uncover errors in journalizing and posting.** For example, a trial balance may well have detected the error at MF Global discussed in the Feature Story. **In addition, a trial balance is useful in the preparation of financial statements.**

These are the procedures for preparing a trial balance:

1. List the account titles and their balances.
2. Total the debit column and total the credit column.
3. Verify the equality of the two columns.

Illustration 3-34 presents the trial balance prepared from the ledger of Sierra Corporation. Note that the total debits, \$28,700, equal the total credits, \$28,700.

ILLUSTRATION 3-34
Sierra Corporation trial balance

SIERRA CORPORATION
Trial Balance
October 31, 2017

	Debit	Credit
Cash	$ 15,200	
Supplies	2,500	
Prepaid Insurance	600	
Equipment	5,000	
Notes Payable		$ 5,000
Accounts Payable		2,500
Unearned Service Revenue		1,200
Common Stock		10,000
Dividends	500	
Service Revenue		10,000
Salaries and Wages Expense	4,000	
Rent Expense	900	
	$28,700	$28,700

▼ **HELPFUL HINT**
Note that the order of presentation in the trial balance is:
- Assets
- Liabilities
- Stockholders' equity
- Revenues
- Expenses

LIMITATIONS OF A TRIAL BALANCE

A trial balance does not prove that all transactions have been recorded or that the ledger is correct. Numerous errors may exist even though the trial balance column totals agree. For example, the trial balance may balance even when any of the following occurs: (1) a transaction is not journalized, (2) a correct journal entry is not posted, (3) a journal entry is posted twice, (4) incorrect accounts are

ETHICS NOTE
An **error** is the result of an unintentional mistake. It is neither ethical nor unethical. An **irregularity** is an intentional misstatement, which is viewed as unethical.

used in journalizing or posting, or (5) offsetting errors are made in recording the amount of a transaction. In other words, as long as equal debits and credits are posted, even to the wrong account or in the wrong amount, the total debits will equal the total credits. Nevertheless, despite these limitations, the trial balance is a useful screen for finding errors and is frequently used in practice.

KEEPING AN EYE ON CASH

The Cash account shown below reflects all of the inflows and outflows of cash that occurred during October for Sierra Corporation (see Illustrations 3-21 to 3-31). We have also provided a description of each transaction that affected the Cash account.

1. Oct. 1 Issued stock for $10,000 cash.
2. Oct. 1 Issued note payable for $5,000 cash.
3. Oct. 2 Purchased equipment for $5,000 cash.
4. Oct. 2 Received $1,200 cash in advance from customer.
5. Oct. 3 Received $10,000 cash for services performed.
6. Oct. 3 Paid $900 cash for October rent.
7. Oct. 4 Paid $600 cash for one-year insurance policy.
8. Oct. 20 Paid $500 cash dividend to stockholders.
9. Oct. 26 Paid $4,000 cash salaries.

The Cash account and the related cash transactions indicate why cash changed during October. However, to make this information useful for analysis, it is summarized in a statement of cash flows. The statement of cash flows classifies each transaction as an operating activity, an investing activity, or a financing activity. A user of this statement can then determine the amount of net cash provided by operating activities, the amount of cash used for investing purposes, and the amount of cash provided by financing activities.

Cash			
Oct. 1	10,000	Oct. 2	5,000
1	5,000	3	900
2	1,200	4	600
3	10,000	20	500
		26	4,000
Bal.	15,200		

Operating activities are the types of activities the company performs to generate profits. Sierra is an outdoor guide business, so its operating activities involve providing guide services. Activities 4, 5, 6, 7, and 9 relate to cash received or spent to directly support its guide services.

Investing activities include the purchase or sale of long-lived assets used in operating the business, or the purchase or sale of investment securities (stocks and bonds of companies other than Sierra). Activity 3, the purchase of equipment, is an investing activity.

The primary types of **financing activities** are borrowing money, issuing shares of stock, and paying dividends. The financing activities of Sierra are Activities 1, 2, and 8.

DO IT! 5 Trial Balance

The following accounts come from the ledger of SnowGo Corporation at December 31, 2017.

Equipment	$88,000	Common Stock	$20,000
Dividends	8,000	Salaries and Wages Payable	2,000
Accounts Payable	22,000	Notes Payable (due in 3 months)	19,000
Salaries and Wages Expense	42,000	Utilities Expense	3,000
Accounts Receivable	4,000	Prepaid Insurance	6,000
Service Revenue	95,000	Cash	7,000

Prepare a trial balance in good form.

SOLUTION

SNOWGO CORPORATION
Trial Balance
December 31, 2017

	Debit	Credit
Cash	$ 7,000	
Accounts Receivable	4,000	
Prepaid Insurance	6,000	
Equipment	88,000	
Notes Payable		$ 19,000
Accounts Payable		22,000
Salaries and Wages Payable		2,000
Common Stock		20,000
Dividends	8,000	
Service Revenue		95,000
Utilities Expense	3,000	
Salaries and Wages Expense	42,000	
	$158,000	$158,000

Action Plan

✔ Determine normal balances and list accounts in the order they appear in the ledger.

✔ Accounts with debit balances appear in the left column, and those with credit balances in the right column.

✔ Total the debit and credit columns to prove equality.

Related exercise material: **BE3-11, BE3-12, DO IT! 3-5, E3-13, E3-15, E3-16, E3-17, E3-18, E3-19, E3-20, E3-21, and E3-22.**

USING DECISION TOOLS—KANSAS FARMERS' VERTICALLY INTEGRATED COOPERATIVE, INC.

The Kansas Farmers' Vertically Integrated Cooperative, Inc. (K-VIC) was formed by over 200 northeast Kansas farmers in the late 1980s. Its purpose is to process raw materials, primarily grain and meat products grown by K-VIC's members, into end-user food products and then to distribute the products nationally. Profits not needed for expansion or investment are returned to the members annually, on a pro rata basis, according to the fair value of the grain and meat products received from each farmer.

Assume that the following trial balance was prepared for K-VIC.

KANSAS FARMERS' VERTICALLY INTEGRATED COOPERATIVE, INC.
Trial Balance
December 31, 2017
(in thousands)

	Debit	Credit
Accounts Receivable	$ 712,000	
Accounts Payable		$ 673,000
Buildings	365,000	
Cash	32,000	
Cost of Goods Sold	2,384,000	
Notes Payable (due in 2018)		12,000
Inventory	1,291,000	
Land	110,000	
Mortgage Payable		873,000
Equipment	63,000	
Retained Earnings		822,000
Sales Revenue		3,741,000
Salaries and Wages Payable		62,000
Salaries and Wages Expense	651,000	
Maintenance and Repairs Expense	500,000	
	$6,108,000	$6,183,000

Because the trial balance is not in balance, you have checked with various people responsible for entering accounting data and have discovered the following.

1. The purchase of 35 new trucks, costing $7 million and paid for with cash, was not recorded.
2. A data entry clerk accidentally deleted the account name for an account with a credit balance of $472 million, so the amount was added to the Mortgage Payable account in the trial balance.
3. December cash sales revenue of $75 million was credited to the Sales Revenue account, but the other half of the entry was not made.
4. $50 million of salaries expense were mistakenly charged to Maintenance and Repairs Expense.

INSTRUCTIONS

Answer these questions.

(a) Which mistake(s) have caused the trial balance to be out of balance?

(b) Should all of the items be corrected? Explain.

(c) What is the name of the account the data entry clerk deleted?

(d) Make the necessary corrections and prepare a correct trial balance with accounts listed in proper order.

(e) On your trial balance, write BAL beside the accounts that go on the balance sheet and INC beside those that go on the income statement.

SOLUTION

(a) Only mistake #3 has caused the trial balance to be out of balance.

(b) All of the items should be corrected. The misclassification error (mistake #4) on the salaries expense would not affect bottom-line net income, but it does affect the amounts reported in the two expense accounts.

(c) There is no Common Stock account, so that must be the account that was deleted by the data entry clerk.

(d) and **(e)**

KANSAS FARMERS' VERTICALLY INTEGRATED COOPERATIVE, INC.
Trial Balance
December 31, 2017
(in thousands)

	Debit	Credit	
Cash ($32,000 − $7,000 + $75,000)	$ 100,000		BAL
Accounts Receivable	712,000		BAL
Inventory	1,291,000		BAL
Land	110,000		BAL
Buildings	365,000		BAL
Equipment ($63,000 + $7,000)	70,000		BAL
Accounts Payable		$ 673,000	BAL
Salaries and Wages Payable		62,000	BAL
Notes Payable (due in 2018)		12,000	BAL
Mortgage Payable ($873,000 − $472,000)		401,000	BAL
Common Stock		472,000	BAL
Retained Earnings		822,000	BAL
Sales Revenue		3,741,000	INC
Cost of Goods Sold	2,384,000		INC
Salaries and Wages Expense ($651,000 + $50,000)	701,000		INC
Maintenance and Repairs Expense ($500,000 − $50,000)	450,000		INC
	$6,183,000	$6,183,000	

REVIEW AND PRACTICE

LEARNING OBJECTIVE REVIEW

1 Analyze the effect of business transactions on the basic accounting equation. Each business transaction must have a dual effect on the accounting equation. For example, if an individual asset is increased, there must be a corresponding (a) decrease in another asset, or (b) increase in a specific liability, or (c) increase in stockholders' equity.

2 Explain how accounts, debits, and credits are used to record business transactions. An account is an individual accounting record of increases and decreases in specific asset, liability, and stockholders' equity items.

The terms debit and credit are synonymous with left and right. Assets, dividends, and expenses are increased by debits and decreased by credits. Liabilities, common stock, retained earnings, and revenues are increased by credits and decreased by debits.

3 Indicate how a journal is used in the recording process. The basic steps in the recording process are (a) analyze each transaction in terms of its effect on the accounts, (b) enter the transaction information in a journal, and (c) transfer the journal information to the appropriate accounts in the ledger.

The initial accounting record of a transaction is entered in a journal before the data are entered in the accounts. A journal (a) discloses in one place the complete effect of a transaction, (b) provides a chronological record of transactions, and (c) prevents or locates errors because the debit and credit amounts for each entry can be readily compared.

4 Explain how a ledger and posting help in the recording process. The entire group of accounts maintained by a company is referred to collectively as a ledger. The ledger provides the balance in each of the accounts as well as keeps track of changes in these balances.

Posting is the procedure of transferring journal entries to the ledger accounts. This phase of the recording process accumulates the effects of journalized transactions in the individual accounts.

5 Prepare a trial balance. A trial balance is a list of accounts and their balances at a given time. The primary purpose of the trial balance is to prove the mathematical equality of debits and credits after posting. A trial balance also uncovers errors in journalizing and posting and is useful in preparing financial statements.

DECISION TOOLS REVIEW

DECISION CHECKPOINTS	INFO NEEDED FOR DECISION	TOOL TO USE FOR DECISION	HOW TO EVALUATE RESULTS
Has an accounting transaction occurred?	Details of the event	Accounting equation	If the event affected assets, liabilities, or stockholders' equity, then record as a transaction.
How do you determine that debits equal credits?	All account balances	Trial balance	List the account titles and their balances; total the debit and credit columns; verify equality.

GLOSSARY REVIEW

Account An individual accounting record of increases and decreases in specific asset, liability, stockholders' equity, revenue, or expense items. (p. 100).

Accounting information system The system of collecting and processing transaction data and communicating financial information to decision-makers. (p. 92).

Accounting transactions Events that require recording in the financial statements because they affect assets, liabilities, or stockholders' equity. (p. 92).

Chart of accounts A list of a company's accounts. (p. 110).

Credit The right side of an account. (p. 101).

Debit The left side of an account. (p. 101).

Double-entry system A system that records the two-sided effect of each transaction in appropriate accounts. (p. 101).

General journal The most basic form of journal. (p. 107).

General ledger A ledger that contains all asset, liability, stockholders' equity, revenue, and expense accounts. (p. 109).

Journal An accounting record in which transactions are initially recorded in chronological order. (p. 106).

Journalizing The procedure of entering transaction data in the journal. (p. 107).

Ledger The group of accounts maintained by a company. (p. 109).

Posting The procedure of transferring journal entry amounts to the ledger accounts. (p. 110).

T-account The basic form of an account. (p. 100).

Trial balance A list of accounts and their balances at a given time. (p. 119).

PRACTICE MULTIPLE-CHOICE QUESTIONS

(LO 1) 1. The effects on the basic accounting equation of performing services for cash are to:
(a) increase assets and decrease stockholders' equity.
(b) increase assets and increase stockholders' equity.
(c) increase assets and increase liabilities.
(d) increase liabilities and increase stockholders' equity.

(LO 1) 2. Genesis Company buys a $900 machine on credit. This transaction will affect the:
(a) income statement only.
(b) balance sheet only.
(c) income statement and retained earnings statement only.
(d) income statement, retained earnings statement, and balance sheet.

(LO 1) 3. Which of the following events is **not** recorded in the accounting records?
(a) Equipment is purchased on account.
(b) An employee is terminated.
(c) A cash investment is made into the business.
(d) Company pays dividend to stockholders.

(LO 1) 4. During 2017, Gibson Company assets decreased $50,000 and its liabilities decreased $90,000. Its stockholders' equity therefore:
(a) increased $40,000.
(b) decreased $140,000.
(c) decreased $40,000.
(d) increased $140,000.

(LO 2) 5. Which statement about an account is **true**?
(a) In its simplest form, an account consists of two parts.
(b) An account is an individual accounting record of increases and decreases in specific asset, liability, and stockholders' equity items.
(c) There are separate accounts for specific assets and liabilities but only one account for stockholders' equity items.
(d) The left side of an account is the credit, or decrease, side.

(LO 2) 6. Debits:
(a) increase both assets and liabilities.
(b) decrease both assets and liabilities.
(c) increase assets and decrease liabilities.
(d) decrease assets and increase liabilities.

(LO 2) 7. A revenue account:
(a) is increased by debits.
(b) is decreased by credits.
(c) has a normal balance of a debit.
(d) is increased by credits.

(LO 2) 8. Which accounts normally have debit balances?
(a) Assets, expenses, and revenues.
(b) Assets, expenses, and retained earnings.
(c) Assets, liabilities, and dividends.
(d) Assets, dividends, and expenses.

9. Paying an account payable with cash affects the components of the accounting equation in the following way: (LO 2)
(a) Decreases stockholders' equity and decreases liabilities.
(b) Increases assets and decreases liabilities.
(c) Decreases assets and increases stockholders' equity.
(d) Decreases assets and decreases liabilities.

10. Which is **not** part of the recording process? (LO 3)
(a) Analyzing transactions.
(b) Preparing an income statement.
(c) Entering transactions in a journal.
(d) Posting journal entries.

11. Which of these statements about a journal is **false**? (LO 3)
(a) It contains only revenue and expense accounts.
(b) It provides a chronological record of transactions.
(c) It helps to locate errors because the debit and credit amounts for each entry can be readily compared.
(d) It discloses in one place the complete effect of a transaction.

12. A ledger: (LO 4)
(a) contains only asset and liability accounts.
(b) should show accounts in alphabetical order.
(c) is a collection of the entire group of accounts maintained by a company.
(d) provides a chronological record of transactions.

13. Posting: (LO 4)
(a) normally occurs before journalizing.
(b) transfers ledger transaction data to the journal.
(c) is an optional step in the recording process.
(d) transfers journal entries to ledger accounts.

14. A trial balance: (LO 5)
(a) is a list of accounts with their balances at a given time.
(b) proves that proper account titles were used.
(c) will not balance if a correct journal entry is posted twice.
(d) proves that all transactions have been recorded.

15. A trial balance will **not** balance if: (LO 5)
(a) a correct journal entry is posted twice.
(b) the purchase of supplies on account is debited to Supplies and credited to Cash.
(c) a $100 cash dividend is debited to Dividends for $1,000 and credited to Cash for $100.
(d) a $450 payment on account is debited to Accounts Payable for $45 and credited to Cash for $45.

SOLUTIONS

1. **(b)** When services are performed for cash, assets are increased and stockholders' equity is increased. The other choices are therefore incorrect.
2. **(b)** When equipment is purchased on credit, assets are increased and liabilities are increased. These are both balance sheet accounts. The other choices are incorrect because neither the income statement nor the retained earnings statement is affected.

3. **(b)** Termination of an employee is not a recordable event in the accounting records. The other choices all represent events that are recorded.
4. **(a)** Since assets decreased by $50,000 and liabilities decreased by $90,000, stockholders' equity has to increase by $40,000 to keep the accounting equation balanced. The other choices are therefore incorrect.
5. **(b)** An account is an individual accounting record of increases and decreases in specific asset, liability, and stockholders' equity items. The other choices are incorrect because (a) in its simplest form, an account consists of three parts: a title and debit and credit side; (c) there are specific accounts for different types of stockholders' equity, such as Common Stock, Retained Earnings, and Dividends; and (d) the left side of an account is the debit side.
6. **(c)** Debits increase assets and decrease liabilities. The other choices are therefore incorrect.
7. **(d)** Revenues are increased by credits. Revenues have a normal credit balance. The other choices are therefore incorrect.
8. **(d)** Assets, dividends, and expenses have normal debit balances. The other choices are incorrect because (a) revenues have a normal credit balance, (b) retained earnings has a normal credit balance, and (c) liabilities have a normal credit balance.
9. **(d)** When paying an account payable with cash, the asset cash decreases. Accounts payable, a liability, decreases as well. The other choices are therefore incorrect.
10. **(b)** Preparing an income statement is not part of the recording process. Choices (a) analyzing transactions, (c) entering transactions in a journal, and (d) posting transactions are all steps in the recording process.
11. **(a)** A journal contains entries affecting all accounts, not just revenue and expense accounts. The other choices are true statements.
12. **(c)** A ledger is a collection of the entire group of accounts maintained by a company. The other choices are therefore incorrect.
13. **(d)** Posting transfers journal entries to ledger accounts. The other choices are incorrect because posting (a) occurs after journalizing, (b) transfers the information contained in journal entries to the ledger, and (c) is a required step in the recording process. If posting is not done, the ledger accounts will not reflect changes in the accounts resulting from transactions.
14. **(a)** A trial balance is a list of accounts with their balances at a given time. The other choices are incorrect because (b) it does not confirm that proper account titles were used; (c) if a journal entry is posted twice, the trial balance will still balance; and (d) a trial balance does not prove that all transactions have been recorded.
15. **(c)** The entry will cause the trial balance to be out of balance. The other choices are incorrect because although these entries are incorrect, they will still allow the trial balance to balance.

PRACTICE EXERCISES

Prepare a tabular presentation.

(LO 1)

1. Legal Services Inc. was incorporated on July 1, 2017. During the first month of operations, the following transactions occurred.

1. Stockholders invested $10,000 in cash in exchange for common stock of Legal Services Inc.
2. Paid $800 for July rent on office space.
3. Purchased office equipment on account $3,000.
4. Performed legal services for clients for cash $1,500.
5. Borrowed $700 cash from a bank on a note payable.
6. Performed legal services for client on account $2,000.
7. Paid monthly expenses: salaries $500, utilities $300, and advertising $100.

INSTRUCTIONS

Prepare a tabular summary of the transactions.

SOLUTION

1.

Transaction	Assets			=	Liabilities		+	Stockholders' Equity				
									Retained Earnings			
	Cash	+ Accounts Receivable	+ Equipment	=	Notes Payable	+ Accounts Payable	+	Common Stock	+ Rev.	− Exp.	− Div.	
(1)	+$10,000			=				+$10,000				Issued Stock
(2)	−800									−$800		Rent Expense
(3)			+$3,000	=		+$3,000						
(4)	+1,500								+$1,500			Service Revenue
(5)	+700				+$700							
(6)		+$2,000							+2,000			Service Revenue
(7)	−500									−500		Sal./Wages Exp.
	−300									−300		Utilities Expense
	−100									−100		Advertising Expense
	$10,500	+ $2,000	+ $3,000	=	$700	+ $3,000	+	$10,000	+ $3,500	− $1,700		
	$15,500				$15,500							

Journalize transactions.

(LO 3)

2. Presented below is information related to Conan Real Estate Agency.

Oct. 1 Arnold Conan begins business as a real estate agent with a cash investment of $18,000 in exchange for common stock.

2 Hires an administrative assistant.

3 Purchases office equipment for $1,700, on account.

6 Sells a house and lot for B. Clinton; bills B. Clinton $4,200 for realty services performed.

27 Pays $900 on the balance related to the transaction of October 3.

30 Pays the administrative assistant $2,800 in salary for October.

INSTRUCTIONS

Journalize the transactions. (You may omit explanations.)

SOLUTION

2. **GENERAL JOURNAL**

Date	Account Titles and Explanation	Debit	Credit
Oct. 1	Cash	18,000	
	Common Stock		18,000
2	No entry required		
3	Equipment	1,700	
	Accounts Payable		1,700
6	Accounts Receivable	4,200	
	Service Revenue		4,200
27	Accounts Payable	900	
	Cash		900
30	Salaries and Wages Expense	2,800	
	Cash		2,800

▶ PRACTICE PROBLEM

Journalize transactions, post, and prepare a trial balance.

(LO 3, 4, 5)

Bob Sample and other student investors opened Campus Carpet Cleaning, Inc. on September 1, 2017. During the first month of operations, the following transactions occurred.

Sept.	1	Stockholders invested $20,000 cash in the business.
	2	Paid $1,000 cash for store rent for the month of September.
	3	Purchased industrial carpet-cleaning equipment for $25,000, paying $10,000 in cash and signing a $15,000 6-month, 12% note payable.
	4	Paid $1,200 for 1-year accident insurance policy.
	10	Received bill from the *Daily News* for advertising the opening of the cleaning service, $200.
	15	Performed services on account for $6,200.
	20	Paid a $700 cash dividend to stockholders.
	30	Received $5,000 from customers billed on September 15.

The chart of accounts for the company is the same as for Sierra Corporation except for the following additional account: Advertising Expense.

INSTRUCTIONS

(a) Journalize the September transactions.
(b) Open ledger accounts and post the September transactions.
(c) Prepare a trial balance at September 30, 2017.

SOLUTION

(a) **GENERAL JOURNAL**

Date	Account Titles and Explanation	Debit	Credit
2017			
Sept. 1	Cash	20,000	
	Common Stock		20,000
	(Issued stock for cash)		
2	Rent Expense	1,000	
	Cash		1,000
	(Paid September rent)		
3	Equipment	25,000	
	Cash		10,000
	Notes Payable		15,000
	(Purchased cleaning equipment for cash and 6-month, 12% note payable)		
4	Prepaid Insurance	1,200	
	Cash		1,200
	(Paid 1-year insurance policy)		
10	Advertising Expense	200	
	Accounts Payable		200
	(Received bill from *Daily News* for advertising)		
15	Accounts Receivable	6,200	
	Service Revenue		6,200
	(Services performed on account)		
20	Dividends	700	
	Cash		700
	(Declared and paid a cash dividend)		
30	Cash	5,000	
	Accounts Receivable		5,000
	(Collection of accounts receivable)		

(b)

GENERAL LEDGER

Cash

Debit		Credit	
Sept. 1	20,000	Sept. 2	1,000
30	5,000	3	10,000
		4	1,200
		20	700
Bal.	12,100		

Common Stock

Debit		Credit	
		Sept. 1	20,000
		Bal.	20,000

Accounts Receivable

Debit		Credit	
Sept. 15	6,200	Sept. 30	5,000
Bal.	1,200		

Dividends

Debit		Credit	
Sept. 20	700		
Bal.	700		

Prepaid Insurance

Debit		Credit	
Sept. 4	1,200		
Bal.	1,200		

Service Revenue

Debit		Credit	
		Sept. 15	6,200
		Bal.	6,200

Equipment

Debit		Credit	
Sept. 3	25,000		
Bal.	25,000		

Advertising Expense

Debit		Credit	
Sept. 10	200		
Bal.	200		

Notes Payable

Debit		Credit	
		Sept. 3	15,000
		Bal.	15,000

Rent Expense

Debit		Credit	
Sept. 2	1,000		
Bal.	1,000		

Accounts Payable

Debit		Credit	
		Sept. 10	200
		Bal.	200

(c)

CAMPUS CARPET CLEANING, INC.

Trial Balance

September 30, 2017

	Debit	Credit
Cash	$12,100	
Accounts Receivable	1,200	
Prepaid Insurance	1,200	
Equipment	25,000	
Notes Payable		$15,000
Accounts Payable		200
Common Stock		20,000
Dividends	700	
Service Revenue		6,200
Advertising Expense	200	
Rent Expense	1,000	
	$41,400	$41,400

WileyPLUS Brief Exercises, DO IT! Exercises, Exercises, Problems, and many additional resources are available for practice in WileyPLUS.

QUESTIONS

1. Describe the accounting information system.
2. Can a business enter into a transaction that affects only the left side of the basic accounting equation? If so, give an example.
3. Are the following events recorded in the accounting records? Explain your answer in each case.
   (a) A major stockholder of the company dies.
   (b) Supplies are purchased on account.
   (c) An employee is fired.
   (d) The company pays a cash dividend to its stockholders.
4. Indicate how each business transaction affects the basic accounting equation.
   (a) Paid cash for janitorial services.
   (b) Purchased equipment for cash.
   (c) Issued common stock to investors in exchange for cash.
   (d) Paid an account payable in full.
5. Why is an account referred to as a T-account?
6. The terms debit and credit mean "increase" and "decrease," respectively. Do you agree? Explain.
7. Barry Barack, a fellow student, contends that the double-entry system means each transaction must be recorded twice. Is Barry correct? Explain.
8. Misty Reno, a beginning accounting student, believes debit balances are favorable and credit balances are unfavorable. Is Misty correct? Discuss.
9. State the rules of debit and credit as applied to (a) asset accounts, (b) liability accounts, and (c) the Common Stock account.
10. What is the normal balance for each of these accounts?
    (a) Accounts Receivable.
    (b) Cash.
    (c) Dividends.
    (d) Accounts Payable.
    (e) Service Revenue.
    (f) Salaries and Wages Expense.
    (g) Common Stock.
11. Indicate whether each account is an asset, a liability, or a stockholders' equity account, and whether it would have a normal debit or credit balance.
    (a) Accounts Receivable. (d) Dividends.
    (b) Accounts Payable. (e) Supplies.
    (c) Equipment.
12. For the following transactions, indicate the account debited and the account credited.
    (a) Supplies are purchased on account.
    (b) Cash is received on signing a note payable.
    (c) Employees are paid salaries in cash.
13. For each account listed here, indicate whether it generally will have debit entries only, credit entries only, or both debit and credit entries.
    (a) Cash.
    (b) Accounts Receivable.
    (c) Dividends.
    (d) Accounts Payable.
    (e) Salaries and Wages Expense.
    (f) Service Revenue.
14. What are the normal balances for the following accounts of Apple? (a) Accounts Receivable, (b) Accounts Payable, (c) Sales, and (d) Selling, General, and Administrative Expenses.
15. What are the basic steps in the recording process?
16. (a) When entering a transaction in the journal, should the debit or credit be written first?
    (b) Which should be indented, the debit or the credit?
17. (a) Should accounting transaction debits and credits be recorded directly in the ledger accounts?
    (b) What are the advantages of first recording transactions in the journal and then posting to the ledger?
18. Journalize these accounting transactions.
    (a) Stockholders invested $12,000 in the business in exchange for common stock.
    (b) Insurance of $800 is paid for the year.
    (c) Supplies of $1,800 are purchased on account.
    (d) Cash of $7,500 is received for services rendered.
19. (a) What is a ledger?
    (b) Why is a chart of accounts important?
20. What is a trial balance and what are its purposes?
21. Brad Tyler is confused about how accounting information flows through the accounting system. He believes information flows in this order:
    (a) Debits and credits are posted to the ledger.
    (b) Accounting transaction occurs.
    (c) Information is entered in the journal.
    (d) Financial statements are prepared.
    (e) Trial balance is prepared.

    Indicate to Brad the proper flow of the information.
22. Two students are discussing the use of a trial balance. They wonder whether the following errors, each considered separately, would prevent the trial balance from balancing. What would you tell them?
    (a) The bookkeeper debited Cash for $600 and credited Salaries and Wages Expense for $600 for payment of wages.
    (b) Cash collected on account was debited to Cash for $800, and Service Revenue was credited for $80.

BRIEF EXERCISES

Determine effect of transactions on basic accounting equation.
(LO 1), C

BE3-1 Presented below are three economic events. On a sheet of paper, list the letters (a), (b), and (c) with columns for assets, liabilities, and stockholders' equity. In each column, indicate whether the event increased (+), decreased (−), or had no effect (NE) on assets, liabilities, and stockholders' equity.
(a) Purchased supplies on account.
(b) Received cash for performing a service.
(c) Expenses paid in cash.

Determine effect of transactions on basic accounting equation.
(LO 1), AP

BE3-2 During 2017, Manion Corp. entered into the following transactions.
1. Borrowed $60,000 by issuing bonds.
2. Paid $9,000 cash dividend to stockholders.
3. Received $13,000 cash from a previously billed customer for services performed.
4. Purchased supplies on account for $3,100.

Using the following tabular analysis, show the effect of each transaction on the accounting equation. Put explanations for changes to Stockholders' Equity in the right-hand margin. For Retained Earnings, use separate columns for Revenues, Expenses, and Dividends if necessary. Use Illustration 3-3 (page 99) as a model.

Assets					=	Liabilities			+	Stockholders' Equity		
Cash	+	Accounts Receivable	+	Supplies	=	Accounts Payable	+	Bonds Payable	+	Common Stock	+	Retained Earnings

Determine effect of transactions on basic accounting equation.
(LO 1), AP

BE3-3 During 2017, Rostock Company entered into the following transactions.
1. Purchased equipment for $286,176 cash.
2. Issued common stock to investors for $137,590 cash.
3. Purchased inventory of $68,480 on account.

Using the following tabular analysis, show the effect of each transaction on the accounting equation. Put explanations for changes to Stockholders' Equity in the right-hand margin. For Retained Earnings, use separate columns for Revenues, Expenses, and Dividends if necessary. Use Illustration 3-3 (page 99) as a model.

Assets					=	Liabilities	+	Stockholders' Equity		
Cash	+	Inventory	+	Equipment	=	Accounts Payable	+	Common Stock	+	Retained Earnings

Indicate debit and credit effects.
(LO 2), K

BE3-4 For each of the following accounts, indicate the effect of a debit or a credit on the account and the normal balance.
(a) Accounts Payable.
(b) Advertising Expense.
(c) Service Revenue.
(d) Accounts Receivable.
(e) Retained Earnings.
(f) Dividends.

Identify accounts to be debited and credited.
(LO 2), C

BE3-5 Transactions for Jayne Company for the month of June are presented below. Identify the accounts to be debited and credited for each transaction.

June 1 Issues common stock to investors in exchange for $5,000 cash.
2 Buys equipment on account for $1,100.
3 Pays $740 to landlord for June rent.
12 Sends Wil Wheaton a bill for $700 after completing welding work.

Journalize transactions.
(LO 3), AP

BE3-6 Use the data in BE3-5 and journalize the transactions. (You may omit explanations.)

Identify steps in the recording process.
(LO 3), C

BE3-7 Rae Mohlee, a fellow student, is unclear about the basic steps in the recording process. Identify and briefly explain the steps in the order in which they occur.

Indicate basic debit–credit analysis.
(LO 3), C

BE3-8 Tilton Corporation has the following transactions during August of the current year. Indicate (a) the basic analysis and (b) the debit–credit analysis illustrated on pages 111–116.

Aug. 1 Issues shares of common stock to investors in exchange for $10,000.
4 Pays insurance in advance for 3 months, $1,500.
16 Receives $900 from clients for services rendered.
27 Pays the secretary $620 salary.

BE3-9 Use the data in BE3-8 and journalize the transactions. (You may omit explanations.)

Journalize transactions.

(LO 3), AP

BE3-10 Selected transactions for Montes Company are presented below in journal form (without explanations). Post the transactions to T-accounts.

Post journal entries to T-accounts.

(LO 4), AP

Date		Account Title	Debit	Credit
May	5	Accounts Receivable	3,800	
		Service Revenue		3,800
	12	Cash	1,600	
		Accounts Receivable		1,600
	15	Cash	2,000	
		Service Revenue		2,000

BE3-11 From the ledger balances below, prepare a trial balance for Peete Company at June 30, 2017. All account balances are normal.

Prepare a trial balance.

(LO 5), AP

Accounts Payable	$ 1,000	Service Revenue	$8,600
Cash	5,400	Accounts Receivable	3,000
Common Stock	18,000	Salaries and Wages Expense	4,000
Dividends	1,200	Rent Expense	1,000
Equipment	13,000		

BE3-12 An inexperienced bookkeeper prepared the following trial balance that does not balance. Prepare a correct trial balance, assuming all account balances are normal.

Prepare a corrected trial balance.

(LO 5), AN

BIRELLIE COMPANY
Trial Balance
December 31, 2017

	Debit	Credit
Cash	$20,800	
Prepaid Insurance		$ 3,500
Accounts Payable		2,500
Unearned Service Revenue	1,800	
Common Stock		10,000
Retained Earnings		6,600
Dividends		5,000
Service Revenue		25,600
Salaries and Wages Expense	14,600	
Rent Expense		2,600
	$37,200	$55,800

DO IT! EXERCISES

DO IT! 3-1 Transactions made by Mickelson Co. for the month of March are shown below. Prepare a tabular analysis that shows the effects of these transactions on the expanded accounting equation, similar to that shown in Illustration 3-3 (page 99).

Prepare tabular analysis.

(LO 1), AP

1. The company performed $20,000 of services for customers on account.
2. The company received $20,000 in cash from customers who had been billed for services [in transaction (1)].
3. The company received a bill for $1,800 of advertising but will not pay it until a later date.
4. Mickelson Co. paid a cash dividend of $3,000.

Identify normal balances.
(LO 2), C

DO IT! 3-2 Boyd Docker has just rented space in a strip mall. In this space, he will open a photography studio, to be called SnapShot! A friend has advised Boyd to set up a double-entry set of accounting records in which to record all of his business transactions.

Identify the balance sheet accounts that Boyd will likely need to record the transactions needed to open his business (a corporation). Indicate whether the normal balance of each account is a debit or credit.

Record business activities.
(LO 3), AP

DO IT! 3-3 Boyd Docker engaged in the following activities in establishing his photography studio, SnapShot!:

1. Opened a bank account in the name of SnapShot! and deposited $8,000 of his own money into this account in exchange for common stock.
2. Purchased photography supplies at a total cost of $950. The business paid $400 in cash, and the balance is on account.
3. Obtained estimates on the cost of photography equipment from three different manufacturers.

Prepare the journal entries to record the transactions.

Post transactions.
(LO 4), AP

DO IT! 3-4 Boyd Docker recorded the following transactions during the month of April.

Apr. 3	Cash	3,400	
	Service Revenue		3,400
16	Rent Expense	500	
	Cash		500
20	Salaries and Wages Expense	300	
	Cash		300

Post these entries to the Cash account of the general ledger to determine the ending balance in cash. The beginning balance in cash on April 1 was $1,900.

Prepare a trial balance.
(LO 5), AP

DO IT! 3-5 The following accounts are taken from the ledger of Chillin' Company at December 31, 2017.

Notes Payable	$20,000	Cash	$6,000
Common Stock	25,000	Supplies	5,000
Equipment	76,000	Rent Expense	2,000
Dividends	8,000	Salaries and Wages Payable	3,000
Salaries and Wages Expense	38,000	Accounts Payable	9,000
Service Revenue	86,000	Accounts Receivable	8,000

Prepare a trial balance in good form.

▶ EXERCISES

Analyze the effect of transactions.
(LO 1), C

E3-1 Selected transactions for Thyme Advertising Company, Inc. are listed here.

1. Issued common stock to investors in exchange for cash received from investors.
2. Paid monthly rent.
3. Received cash from customers when service was performed.
4. Billed customers for services performed.
5. Paid dividend to stockholders.
6. Incurred advertising expense on account.
7. Received cash from customers billed in (4).
8. Purchased additional equipment for cash.
9. Purchased equipment on account.

Instructions

Describe the effect of each transaction on assets, liabilities, and stockholders' equity. For example, the first answer is (1) Increase in assets and increase in stockholders' equity.

Analyze the effect of transactions on assets, liabilities, and stockholders' equity.
(LO 1), AP

E3-2 Brady Company entered into these transactions during May 2017, its first month of operations.

1. Stockholders invested $40,000 in the business in exchange for common stock of the company.

2. Purchased computers for office use for $30,000 from Ladd on account.
3. Paid $4,000 cash for May rent on storage space.
4. Performed computer services worth $19,000 on account.
5. Performed computer services for Wharton Construction Company for $5,000 cash.
6. Paid Western States Power Co. $8,000 cash for energy usage in May.
7. Paid Ladd for the computers purchased in (2).
8. Incurred advertising expense for May of $1,300 on account.
9. Received $12,000 cash from customers for contracts billed in (4).

Instructions

Using the following tabular analysis, show the effect of each transaction on the accounting equation. Put explanations for changes to Stockholders' Equity in the right-hand margin. Use Illustration 3-3 (page 99) as a model.

Assets							=	**Liabilities**	+	**Stockholders' Equity**						
		Accounts						Accounts		Common		Retained Earnings				
Cash	+	Receivable	+	Equipment			=	Payable	+	Stock	+	Revenues	−	Expenses	−	Dividends

E3-3 During 2017, its first year of operations as a delivery service, Persimmon Corp. entered into the following transactions.

Determine effect of transactions on basic accounting equation.

(LO 1), AP

1. Issued shares of common stock to investors in exchange for $100,000 in cash.
2. Borrowed $45,000 by issuing bonds.
3. Purchased delivery trucks for $60,000 cash.
4. Received $16,000 from customers for services performed.
5. Purchased supplies for $4,700 on account.
6. Paid rent of $5,200.
7. Performed services on account for $10,000.
8. Paid salaries of $28,000.
9. Paid a dividend of $11,000 to shareholders.

Instructions

Using the following tabular analysis, show the effect of each transaction on the accounting equation. Put explanations for changes to Stockholders' Equity in the right-hand margin. Use Illustration 3-3 (page 99) as a model.

Assets							=	**Liabilities**			+	**Stockholders' Equity**						
		Accounts				Equip-		Accounts		Bonds		Common		Retained Earnings				
Cash	+	Receivable	+	Supplies	+	ment	=	Payable	+	Payable	+	Stock	+	Revenues	−	Expenses	−	Dividends

E3-4 A tabular analysis of the transactions made during August 2017 by Wolfe Company during its first month of operations is shown below. Each increase and decrease in stockholders' equity is explained.

Analyze transactions and compute net income.

(LO 1), AP

	Assets				=	**Liabilities**	+	**Stockholders' Equity**				
						Accounts		Common	Retained Earnings			
	Cash	+ A/R	+ Supp.	+ Equip.	=	Payable	+	Stock	+ Rev.	− Exp.	− Div.	
1.	+$20,000							+$20,000				Com. Stock
2.	−1,000			+$5,000		+$4,000						
3.	−750		+$750									
4.	+4,100	+$5,400							+$9,500			Serv. Rev.
5.	−1,500					−1,500						
6.	−2,000										−$2,000	Div.
7.	−800									−$ 800		Rent Exp.
8.	+450	−450										
9.	−3,000									−3,000		Salar. Exp.
10.						+300				−300		Util. Exp.

Instructions

(a) Describe each transaction.
(b) Determine how much stockholders' equity increased for the month.
(c) Compute the net income for the month.

Prepare an income statement, retained earnings statement, and balance sheet.

(LO 2), AP

E3-5 The tabular analysis of transactions for Wolfe Company is presented in E3-4.

Instructions

Prepare an income statement and a retained earnings statement for August and a classified balance sheet at August 31, 2017.

Identify normal account balance and corresponding financial statement.

(LO 2), K

E3-6 The following accounts, in alphabetical order, were selected from recent financial statements of Krispy Kreme Doughnuts, Inc.

Accounts Payable	Interest Income
Accounts Receivable	Inventories
Common Stock	Prepaid Expenses
Depreciation Expense	Property and Equipment
Interest Expense	Revenues

Instructions

For each account, indicate (a) whether the normal balance is a debit or a credit, and (b) the financial statement—balance sheet or income statement—where the account should be presented.

Identify debits, credits, and normal balances and journalize transactions.

(LO 2, 3), AP

E3-7 Selected transactions for Front Room, an interior decorator corporation, in its first month of business, are as follows.

1. Issued stock to investors for $15,000 in cash.
2. Purchased used car for $10,000 cash for use in business.
3. Purchased supplies on account for $300.
4. Billed customers $3,700 for services performed.
5. Paid $200 cash for advertising at the start of the business.
6. Received $1,100 cash from customers billed in transaction (4).
7. Paid creditor $300 cash on account.
8. Paid dividends of $400 cash to stockholders.

Instructions

(a) For each transaction indicate (a) the basic type of account debited and credited (asset, liability, stockholders' equity); (b) the specific account debited and credited (Cash, Rent Expense, Service Revenue, etc.); (c) whether the specific account is increased or decreased; and (d) the normal balance of the specific account. Use the following format, in which transaction (1) is given as an example.

	Account Debited				Account Credited			
Transaction	**(a) Basic Type**	**(b) Specific Account**	**(c) Effect**	**(d) Normal Balance**	**(a) Basic Type**	**(b) Specific Account**	**(c) Effect**	**(d) Normal Balance**
1	Asset	Cash	Increase	Debit	Stockholders' equity	Common Stock	Increase	Credit

(b) Journalize the transactions. Do not provide explanations.

Analyze transactions and determine their effect on accounts.

(LO 2), C

E3-8 This information relates to McCall Real Estate Agency.

Oct.	1	Stockholders invest $30,000 in exchange for common stock of the corporation.
	2	Hires an administrative assistant at an annual salary of $36,000.
	3	Buys office furniture for $3,800, on account.
	6	Sells a house and lot for E. C. Roads; commissions due from Roads, $10,800 (not paid by Roads at this time).
	10	Receives cash of $140 as commission for acting as rental agent renting an apartment.
	27	Pays $700 on account for the office furniture purchased on October 3.
	30	Pays the administrative assistant $3,000 in salary for October.

Instructions

Prepare the debit–credit analysis for each transaction, as illustrated on pages 111–116.

E3-9 Transaction data for McCall Real Estate Agency are presented in E3-8.

Journalize transactions.

(LO 3), AP

Instructions

Journalize the transactions. Do not provide explanations.

E3-10 The May transactions of Chulak Corporation were as follows.

Journalize a series of transactions.

(LO 3), AP

May	4	Paid $700 due for supplies previously purchased on account.
	7	Performed advisory services on account for $6,800.
	8	Purchased supplies for $850 on account.
	9	Purchased equipment for $1,000 in cash.
	17	Paid employees $530 in cash.
	22	Received bill for equipment repairs of $900.
	29	Paid $1,200 for 12 months of insurance policy. Coverage begins June 1.

Instructions

Journalize the transactions. Do not provide explanations.

E3-11 Selected transactions for Sophie's Dog Care are as follows during the month of March.

Journalize a series of transactions.

(LO 3), AP

March	1	Paid monthly rent of $1,200.
	3	Performed services for $140 on account.
	5	Performed services for cash of $75.
	8	Purchased equipment for $600. The company paid cash of $80 and the balance was on account.
	12	Received cash from customers billed on March 3.
	14	Paid wages to employees of $525.
	22	Paid utilities of $72.
	24	Borrowed $1,500 from Grafton State Bank by signing a note.
	27	Paid $220 to repair service for plumbing repairs.
	28	Paid balance amount owed from equipment purchase on March 8.
	30	Paid $1,800 for six months of insurance.

Instructions

Journalize the transactions. Do not provide explanations.

E3-12 On April 1, Adventures Travel Agency, Inc. began operations. The following transactions were completed during the month.

Record journal entries.

(LO 3), AP

1. Issued common stock for $24,000 cash.
2. Obtained a bank loan for $7,000 by issuing a note payable.
3. Paid $11,000 cash to buy equipment.
4. Paid $1,200 cash for April office rent.
5. Paid $1,450 for supplies.
6. Purchased $600 of advertising in the *Daily Herald,* on account.
7. Performed services for $18,000: cash of $2,000 was received from customers, and the balance of $16,000 was billed to customers on account.
8. Paid $400 cash dividend to stockholders.
9. Paid the utility bill for the month, $2,000.
10. Paid *Daily Herald* the amount due in transaction (6).
11. Paid $40 of interest on the bank loan obtained in transaction (2).
12. Paid employees' salaries, $6,400.
13. Received $12,000 cash from customers billed in transaction (7).
14. Paid income tax, $1,500.

Instructions

Journalize the transactions. Do not provide explanations.

E3-13 Transaction data and journal entries for McCall Real Estate Agency are presented in E3-8 and E3-9.

Post journal entries and prepare a trial balance.

(LO 4, 5), AP

Instructions

(a) Post the transactions to T-accounts.
(b) Prepare a trial balance at October 31, 2017.

Analyze transactions, prepare journal entries, and post transactions to T-accounts.

(LO 1, 3, 4), AP

E3-14 Selected transactions for Therow Corporation during its first month in business are presented below.

Sept.	1	Issued common stock in exchange for $20,000 cash received from investors.
	5	Purchased equipment for $9,000, paying $3,000 in cash and the balance on account.
	8	Performed services on account for $18,000.
	14	Paid salaries of $1,200.
	25	Paid $4,000 cash on balance owed for equipment.
	30	Paid $500 cash dividend.

Therow's chart of accounts shows Cash, Accounts Receivable, Equipment, Accounts Payable, Common Stock, Dividends, Service Revenue, and Salaries and Wages Expense.

Instructions

(a) Prepare a tabular analysis of the September transactions. The column headings should be Cash + Accounts Receivable + Equipment = Accounts Payable + Common Stock + Revenues − Expenses − Dividends. For transactions affecting stockholders' equity, provide explanations in the right margin, as shown on Illustration 3-3 on page 99.

(b) Journalize the transactions. Do not provide explanations.

(c) Post the transactions to T-accounts.

Journalize transactions from T-accounts and prepare a trial balance.

(LO 3, 5), AN

E3-15 The T-accounts below summarize the ledger of Salvador's Gardening Company, Inc. at the end of the first month of operations.

Cash

Date	Debit	Date	Credit
Apr. 1	15,000	Apr. 15	800
12	700	25	3,500
29	800		
30	900		

Unearned Service Revenue

Date	Debit	Date	Credit
		Apr. 30	900

Accounts Receivable

Date	Debit	Date	Credit
Apr. 7	3,400	Apr. 29	800

Common Stock

Date	Debit	Date	Credit
		Apr. 1	15,000

Supplies

Date	Debit	Date	Credit
Apr. 4	5,200		

Service Revenue

Date	Debit	Date	Credit
		Apr. 7	3,400
		12	700

Accounts Payable

Date	Debit	Date	Credit
Apr. 25	3,500	Apr. 4	5,200

Salaries and Wages Expense

Date	Debit	Date	Credit
Apr. 15	800		

Instructions

(a) Prepare the journal entries (including explanations) that resulted in the amounts posted to the accounts. Present them in the order they occurred.

(b) Prepare a trial balance at April 30, 2017. (*Hint:* Compute ending balances of T-accounts first.)

Post journal entries and prepare a trial balance.

(LO 4, 5), AP

E3-16 Selected transactions from the journal of Baylee Inc. during its first month of operations are presented here.

Date		Account Titles	Debit	Credit
Aug.	1	Cash	8,000	
		Common Stock		8,000
	10	Cash	1,700	
		Service Revenue		1,700
	12	Equipment	6,200	
		Cash		1,200
		Notes Payable		5,000
	25	Accounts Receivable	3,400	
		Service Revenue		3,400
	31	Cash	600	
		Accounts Receivable		600

Instructions

(a) Post the transactions to T-accounts.

(b) Prepare a trial balance at August 31, 2017.

E3-17 Here is the ledger for Kriscoe Co.

Journalize transactions from T-accounts and prepare a trial balance.

(LO 3, 5), AN

Cash

Oct.	1	7,000	Oct.	4	400
	10	980		12	1,500
	10	8,000		15	250
	20	700		30	300
	25	2,000		31	500

Common Stock

			Oct.	1	7,000
				25	2,000

Accounts Receivable

Oct.	6	800	Oct.	20	700
	20	920			

Dividends

Oct.	30	300			

Supplies

Oct.	4	400	Oct.	31	180

Service Revenue

			Oct.	6	800
				10	980
				20	920

Equipment

Oct.	3	3,000			

Salaries and Wages Expense

Oct.	31	500			

Notes Payable

			Oct.	10	8,000

Supplies Expense

Oct.	31	180			

Accounts Payable

Oct.	12	1,500	Oct.	3	3,000

Rent Expense

Oct.	15	250			

Instructions

(a) Reproduce the journal entries for only the transactions that **occurred on October 1, 10, and 20,** and provide explanations for each.

(b) Prepare a trial balance at October 31, 2017. (*Hint:* Compute ending balances of T-accounts first.)

E3-18 Beyers Corporation provides security services. Selected transactions for Beyers are presented below.

Journalize transactions, post transactions to T-accounts, and prepare trial balance.

(LO 3, 4, 5), AP

Oct.	1	Issued common stock in exchange for $66,000 cash from investors.
	2	Hired part-time security consultant. Salary will be $2,000 per month. First day of work will be October 15.
	4	Paid 1 month of rent for building for $2,000.
	7	Purchased equipment for $18,000, paying $4,000 cash and the balance on account.
	8	Paid $500 for advertising.
	10	Received bill for equipment repair cost of $390.
	12	Provided security services for event for $3,200 on account.
	16	Purchased supplies for $410 on account.
	21	Paid balance due from October 7 purchase of equipment.
	24	Received and paid utility bill for $148.
	27	Received payment from customer for October 12 services performed.
	31	Paid employee salaries and wages of $5,100.

Instructions

(a) Journalize the transactions. Do not provide explanations.

(b) Post the transactions to T-accounts.

(c) Prepare a trial balance at October 31, 2017. (*Hint:* Compute ending balances of T-accounts first.)

E3-19 The bookkeeper for Birmingham Corporation made these errors in journalizing and posting.

Analyze errors and their effects on trial balance.

(LO 5), AN

1. A credit posting of $400 to Accounts Receivable was omitted.
2. A debit posting of $750 for Prepaid Insurance was debited to Insurance Expense.

3. A collection on account of $100 was journalized and posted as a debit to Cash $100 and a credit to Accounts Payable $100.
4. A credit posting of $300 to Income Taxes Payable was made twice.
5. A cash purchase of supplies for $250 was journalized and posted as a debit to Supplies $25 and a credit to Cash $25.
6. A debit of $395 to Advertising Expense was posted as $359.

Instructions

For each error, indicate (a) whether the trial balance will balance; if the trial balance will not balance, indicate (b) the amount of the difference and (c) the trial balance column that will have the larger total. Consider each error separately. Use the following form, in which error 1 is given as an example.

Error	(a) In Balance	(b) Difference	(c) Larger Column
1	No	$400	Debit

Prepare a trial balance and financial statements.

(LO 5), AP

E3-20 The accounts in the ledger of Rapid Delivery Service contain the following balances on July 31, 2017.

Accounts Receivable	$13,400	Prepaid Insurance	$ 2,200
Accounts Payable	8,400	Service Revenue	15,500
Cash	?	Dividends	700
Equipment	59,360	Common Stock	40,000
Maintenance and Repairs Expense	1,958	Salaries and Wages Expense	7,428
Insurance Expense	900	Salaries and Wages Payable	820
Notes Payable (due 2020)	28,450	Retained Earnings (July 1, 2017)	5,200

Instructions

(a) Prepare a trial balance with the accounts arranged as illustrated in the chapter, and fill in the missing amount for Cash.

(b) Prepare an income statement, a retained earnings statement, and a classified balance sheet for the month of July 2017.

Classify transactions as cash-flow activities.

(LO 5), AP

E3-21 Review the transactions listed in E3-1 for Thyme Advertising Company. Classify each transaction as either an operating activity, investing activity, or financing activity, or if no cash is exchanged, as a noncash event.

Classify transactions as cash-flow activities.

(LO 5), AP

E3-22 Review the transactions listed in E3-3 for Persimmon Corp. Classify each transaction as either an operating activity, investing activity, or financing activity, or if no cash is exchanged, as a noncash event.

EXERCISES: SET B AND CHALLENGE EXERCISES

Visit the book's companion website, at **www.wiley.com/college/kimmel**, and choose the Student Companion site to access Exercises: Set B and Challenge Exercises.

PROBLEMS: SET A

Analyze transactions and compute net income.

(LO 1), AP

P3-1A On April 1, Wonder Travel Agency Inc. was established. These transactions were completed during the month.

1. Stockholders invested $30,000 cash in the company in exchange for common stock.
2. Paid $900 cash for April office rent.
3. Purchased office equipment for $3,400 cash.
4. Purchased $200 of advertising in the *Chicago Tribune*, on account.
5. Paid $500 cash for office supplies.
6. Performed services worth $12,000. Cash of $3,000 is received from customers, and the balance of $9,000 is billed to customers on account.
7. Paid $400 cash dividend.

8. Paid *Chicago Tribune* amount due in transaction (4).
9. Paid employees' salaries $1,800.
10. Received $9,000 in cash from customers billed previously in transaction (6).

Instructions

(a) Prepare a tabular analysis of the transactions using these column headings: Cash, Accounts Receivable, Supplies, Equipment, Accounts Payable, Common Stock, and Retained Earnings (with separate columns for Revenues, Expenses, and Dividends). Include margin explanations for any changes in Retained Earnings.

(b) From an analysis of the Retained Earnings columns, compute the net income or net loss for April.

(a) Cash $34,800
Total assets $38,700

P3-2A Nona Curry started her own consulting firm, Curry Consulting Inc., on May 1, 2017. The following transactions occurred during the month of May.

Analyze transactions and prepare financial statements.

(LO 1, 2), AP

GLS

May	1	Stockholders invested $15,000 cash in the business in exchange for common stock.
	2	Paid $600 for office rent for the month.
	3	Purchased $500 of supplies on account.
	5	Paid $150 to advertise in the *County News*.
	9	Received $1,400 cash for services performed.
	12	Paid $200 cash dividend.
	15	Performed $4,200 of services on account.
	17	Paid $2,500 for employee salaries.
	20	Paid for the supplies purchased on account on May 3.
	23	Received a cash payment of $1,200 for services performed on account on May 15.
	26	Borrowed $5,000 from the bank on a note payable.
	29	Purchased office equipment for $2,000 paying $200 in cash and the balance on account.
	30	Paid $180 for utilities.

Instructions

(a) Show the effects of the previous transactions on the accounting equation using the following format. Assume the note payable is to be repaid within the year.

(a) Cash $18,270
Total assets $23,770

	Assets				=	Liabilities		+	Stockholders' Equity			
										Retained Earnings		
Date	Cash	+ Accounts Receivable	+ Supplies	+ Equipment	=	Notes Payable	+ Accounts Payable	+	Common Stock	+ Revenues	− Expenses	− Dividends

Include margin explanations for any changes in Retained Earnings.

(b) Prepare an income statement for the month of May 2017.

(c) Prepare a classified balance sheet at May 31, 2017.

(b) Net income $2,170

P3-3A Bindy Crawford created a corporation providing legal services, Bindy Crawford Inc., on July 1, 2017. On July 31 the balance sheet showed Cash $4,000, Accounts Receivable $2,500, Supplies $500, Equipment $5,000, Accounts Payable $4,200, Common Stock $6,200, and Retained Earnings $1,600. During August, the following transactions occurred.

Analyze transactions and prepare an income statement, retained earnings statement, and balance sheet.

(LO 1, 2), AP

Aug.	1	Collected $1,100 of accounts receivable due from customers.
	4	Paid $2,700 cash for accounts payable due.
	9	Performed services worth $5,400, of which $3,600 is collected in cash and the balance is due in September.
	15	Purchased additional office equipment for $4,000, paying $700 in cash and the balance on account.
	19	Paid salaries $1,400, rent for August $700, and advertising expenses $350.
	23	Paid a cash dividend of $700.
	26	Borrowed $5,000 from American Federal Bank; the money was borrowed on a 4-month note payable.
	31	Incurred utility expenses for the month on account $380.

(a) Cash $7,150

(b) Net income $2,570
Ret. earnings $3,470

Instructions

(a) Prepare a tabular analysis of the August transactions beginning with July 31 balances. The column heading should be Cash + Accounts Receivable + Supplies + Equipment = Notes Payable + Accounts Payable + Common Stock + Retained Earnings + Revenues − Expenses − Dividends. Include margin explanations for any changes in Retained Earnings.

(b) Prepare an income statement for August, a retained earnings statement for August, and a classified balance sheet at August 31.

Journalize a series of transactions.

(LO 3), AP

P3-4A Bradley's Miniature Golf and Driving Range Inc. was opened on March 1 by Bob Dean. These selected events and transactions occurred during March.

Mar. 1 Stockholders invested $50,000 cash in the business in exchange for common stock of the corporation.
3 Purchased Snead's Golf Land for $38,000 cash. The price consists of land $23,000, building $9,000, and equipment $6,000. (Record this in a single entry.)
5 Advertised the opening of the driving range and miniature golf course, paying advertising expenses of $1,200 cash.
6 Paid cash $2,400 for a 1-year insurance policy.
10 Purchased golf clubs and other equipment for $5,500 from Tahoe Company, payable in 30 days.
18 Received golf fees of $1,600 in cash from customers for golf services performed.
19 Sold 100 coupon books for $25 each in cash. Each book contains 10 coupons that enable the holder to play one round of miniature golf or to hit one bucket of golf balls. (*Hint:* The revenue should not be recognized until the customers use the coupons.)
25 Paid a $500 cash dividend.
30 Paid salaries of $800.
30 Paid Tahoe Company in full for equipment purchased on March 10.
31 Received $900 in cash from customers for golf services performed.

The company uses these accounts: Cash, Prepaid Insurance, Land, Buildings, Equipment, Accounts Payable, Unearned Service Revenue, Common Stock, Retained Earnings, Dividends, Service Revenue, Advertising Expense, and Salaries and Wages Expense.

Instructions

Journalize the March transactions, including explanations. Bradley's records golf fees as service revenue.

Journalize transactions, post, and prepare a trial balance.

(LO 3, 4, 5), AP

P3-5A Ayala Architects incorporated as licensed architects on April 1, 2017. During the first month of the operation of the business, these events and transactions occurred:

Apr. 1 Stockholders invested $18,000 cash in exchange for common stock of the corporation.
1 Hired a secretary-receptionist at a salary of $375 per week, payable monthly.
2 Paid office rent for the month $900.
3 Purchased architectural supplies on account from Burmingham Company $1,300.
10 Completed blueprints on a carport and billed client $1,900 for services.
11 Received $700 cash advance from M. Jason to design a new home.
20 Received $2,800 cash for services completed and delivered to S. Melvin.
30 Paid secretary-receptionist for the month $1,500.
30 Paid $300 to Burmingham Company for accounts payable due.

The company uses these accounts: Cash, Accounts Receivable, Supplies, Accounts Payable, Unearned Service Revenue, Common Stock, Service Revenue, Salaries and Wages Expense, and Rent Expense.

Instructions

(a) Journalize the transactions, including explanations.

(b) Post to the ledger T-accounts.

(c) Prepare a trial balance on April 30, 2017.

(c) Cash $18,800
Tot. trial balance $24,400

P3-6A This is the trial balance of Lacey Company on September 30.

Journalize transactions, post, and prepare a trial balance.

(LO 3, 4, 5), AP

LACEY COMPANY
Trial Balance
September 30, 2017

	Debit	Credit
Cash	$19,200	
Accounts Receivable	2,600	
Supplies	2,100	
Equipment	8,000	
Accounts Payable		$ 4,800
Unearned Service Revenue		1,100
Common Stock		15,000
Retained Earnings		11,000
	$31,900	$31,900

The October transactions were as follows.

Oct. 5 Received $1,300 in cash from customers for accounts receivable due.
10 Billed customers for services performed $5,100.
15 Paid employee salaries $1,200.
17 Performed $600 of services in exchange for cash.
20 Paid $1,900 to creditors for accounts payable due.
29 Paid a $300 cash dividend.
31 Paid utilities $400.

Instructions

(a) Prepare a general ledger using T-accounts. Enter the opening balances in the ledger accounts as of October 1. (*Hint:* The October 1 beginning amounts are the September 30 balances in the trial balance above.) Provision should be made for these additional accounts: Dividends, Service Revenue, Salaries and Wages Expense, and Utilities Expense.
(b) Journalize the transactions, including explanations.
(c) Post to the ledger accounts.
(d) Prepare a trial balance on October 31, 2017.

(d) Cash $17,300
Tot. trial balance $35,700

P3-7A This trial balance of Washburn Co. does not balance.

Prepare a correct trial balance.

(LO 5), AN

WASHBURN CO.
Trial Balance
June 30, 2017

	Debit	Credit
Cash		$ 3,090
Accounts Receivable	$ 3,190	
Supplies	800	
Equipment	3,000	
Accounts Payable		3,686
Unearned Service Revenue	1,200	
Common Stock		9,000
Dividends	800	
Service Revenue		3,480
Salaries and Wages Expense	3,600	
Utilities Expense	910	
	$13,500	$19,256

Each of the listed accounts has a normal balance per the general ledger. An examination of the ledger and journal reveals the following errors:

1. Cash received from a customer on account was debited for $780, and Accounts Receivable was credited for the same amount. The actual collection was for $870.
2. The purchase of a printer on account for $340 was recorded as a debit to Supplies for $340 and a credit to Accounts Payable for $340.
3. Services were performed on account for a client for $900. Accounts Receivable was debited for $90 and Service Revenue was credited for $900.
4. A debit posting to Salaries and Wages Expense of $700 was omitted.

5. A payment on account for $206 was credited to Cash for $206 and credited to Accounts Payable for $260.
6. Payment of a $600 cash dividend to Washburn's stockholders was debited to Salaries and Wages Expense for $600 and credited to Cash for $600.

Tot. trial balance $16,900

Instructions

Prepare the correct trial balance. (*Hint:* All accounts have normal balances.)

Journalize transactions, post, and prepare a trial balance.

(LO 3, 4, 5), AP

P3-8A The Triquel Theater Inc. was recently formed. It began operations in March 2017. The Triquel is unique in that it will show only triple features of sequential theme movies. On March 1, the ledger of The Triquel showed Cash $16,000, Land $38,000, Buildings (concession stand, projection room, ticket booth, and screen) $22,000, Equipment $16,000, Accounts Payable $12,000, and Common Stock $80,000. During the month of March, the following events and transactions occurred.

Mar.	2	Rented the first three *Star Wars* movies (*Star Wars®*, *The Empire Strikes Back*, and *The Return of the Jedi*) to be shown for the first three weeks of March. The film rental was $10,000; $2,000 was paid in cash and $8,000 will be paid on March 10.
	3	Ordered the first three *Star Trek* movies to be shown the last 10 days of March. It will cost $500 per night.
	9	Received $9,900 cash from admissions.
	10	Paid balance due on *Star Wars* movies' rental and $2,900 on March 1 accounts payable.
	11	The Triquel Theater contracted with R. Lazlo to operate the concession stand. Lazlo agrees to pay The Triquel 15% of gross receipts, payable monthly, for the rental of the concession stand.
	12	Paid advertising expenses $500.
	20	Received $8,300 cash from customers for admissions.
	20	Received the *Star Trek* movies and paid rental fee of $5,000.
	31	Paid salaries of $3,800.
	31	Received statement from R. Lazlo showing gross receipts from concessions of $10,000 and the balance due to The Triquel of $1,500 ($10,000 × .15) for March. Lazlo paid half the balance due and will remit the remainder on April 5.
	31	Received $20,000 cash from customers for admissions.

In addition to the accounts identified above, the chart of accounts includes Accounts Receivable, Service Revenue, Rent Revenue, Advertising Expense, Rent Expense, and Salaries and Wages Expense.

Instructions

(a) Using T-accounts, enter the beginning balances to the ledger.

(b) Journalize the March transactions, including explanations. The Triquel records admission revenue as service revenue, concession revenue as sales revenue, and film rental expense as rent expense.

(d) Cash $32,750
Tot. trial balance $128,800

(c) Post the March journal entries to the ledger.

(d) Prepare a trial balance on March 31, 2017.

Journalize transactions, post, and prepare a trial balance.

(LO 3, 4, 5), AP

P3-9A On July 31, 2017, the general ledger of Hills Legal Services Inc. showed the following balances: Cash $4,000, Accounts Receivable $1,500, Supplies $500, Equipment $5,000, Accounts Payable $4,100, Common Stock $3,500, and Retained Earnings $3,400. During August, the following transactions occurred.

Aug.	3	Collected $1,200 of accounts receivable due from customers.
	5	Received $1,300 cash for issuing common stock to new investors.
	6	Paid $2,700 cash on accounts payable.
	7	Performed legal services of $6,500, of which $3,000 was collected in cash and the remainder was due on account.
	12	Purchased additional equipment for $1,200, paying $400 in cash and the balance on account.
	14	Paid salaries $3,500, rent $900, and advertising expenses $275 for the month of August.
	18	Collected the balance for the services performed on August 7.
	20	Paid cash dividend of $500 to stockholders.

24 Billed a client $1,000 for legal services performed.
26 Received $2,000 from Laurentian Bank; the money was borrowed on a bank note payable that is due in 6 months.
27 Agreed to perform legal services for a client in September for $4,500. The client will pay the amount owing after the services have been performed.
28 Received the utility bill for the month of August in the amount of $275; it is not due until September 15.
31 Paid income tax for the month $500.

Instructions

(a) Using T-accounts, enter the beginning balances to the ledger.
(b) Journalize the August transactions.
(c) Post the August journal entries to the ledger.
(d) Prepare a trial balance on August 31, 2017.

(d) Cash $6,225
Tot. trial balance $20,175

P3-10A Pamper Me Salon Inc.'s general ledger at April 30, 2017, included the following: Cash $5,000, Supplies $500, Equipment $24,000, Accounts Payable $2,100, Notes Payable $10,000, Unearned Service Revenue (from gift certificates) $1,000, Common Stock $5,000, and Retained Earnings $11,400. The following events and transactions occurred during May.

Journalize transactions, post, and prepare trial balance.
(LO 3, 4, 5), AP

May 1 Paid rent for the month of May $1,000.
4 Paid $1,100 of the account payable at April 30.
7 Issued gift certificates for future services for $1,500 cash.
8 Received $1,200 cash from customers for services performed.
14 Paid $1,200 in salaries to employees.
15 Received $800 in cash from customers for services performed.
15 Customers receiving services worth $700 used gift certificates in payment.
21 Paid the remaining accounts payable from April 30.
22 Received $1,000 in cash from customers for services performed.
22 Purchased supplies of $700 on account. All of these were used during the month.
25 Received a bill for advertising for $500. This bill is due on June 13.
25 Received and paid a utilities bill for $400.
29 Received $1,700 in cash from customers for services performed.
29 Customers receiving services worth $600 used gift certificates in payment.
31 Interest of $50 was paid on the note payable.
31 Paid $1,200 in salaries to employees.
31 Paid income tax payment for the month $150.

Instructions

(a) Using T-accounts, enter the beginning balances in the general ledger as of April 30, 2017.
(b) Journalize the May transactions.
(c) Post the May journal entries to the general ledger.
(d) Prepare a trial balance on May 31, 2017.

(d) Cash $5,100
Tot. trial balance $34,800

P3-11A The bookkeeper for Roger's Dance Studio made the following errors in journalizing and posting.

Analyze errors and their effects on the trial balance.
(LO 5), AN

1. A credit to Supplies of $600 was omitted.
2. A debit posting of $300 to Accounts Payable was inadvertently debited to Accounts Receivable.
3. A purchase of supplies on account of $450 was debited to Supplies for $540 and credited to Accounts Payable for $540.
4. A credit posting of $680 to Interest Payable was posted twice.
5. A debit posting to Income Taxes Payable for $250 and a credit posting to Cash for $250 were made twice.
6. A debit posting for $1,200 of Dividends was inadvertently posted to Salaries and Wages Expense instead.
7. A credit to Service Revenue for $450 was inadvertently posted as a debit to Service Revenue.
8. A credit to Accounts Receivable of $250 was credited to Accounts Payable.

Instructions

For each error, indicate (a) whether the trial balance will balance, (b) the amount of the difference if the trial balance will not balance, and (c) the trial balance column that will have the larger total. Consider each error separately. Use the following form, in which error 1 is given as an example.

Error	(a) In Balance	(b) Difference	(c) Larger Column
1	No	$600	Debit

PROBLEMS: SET B AND SET C

Visit the book's companion website, at **www.wiley.com/college/kimmel**, and choose the Student Companion site to access Problems: Set B and Set C.

CONTINUING PROBLEM Cookie Creations

© leungchopan/ Shutterstock

(*Note*: This is a continuation of the Cookie Creations problem from Chapters 1 and 2.)

CC3 In November 2017, after having incorporated Cookie Creations Inc., Natalie begins operations. She has decided not to pursue the offer to supply cookies to Biscuits. Instead, the company will focus on offering cooking classes.

Go to the book's companion website, **www.wiley.com/college/kimmel**, *to see the completion of this problem.*

EXPAND YOUR CRITICAL THINKING

Financial Reporting

FINANCIAL REPORTING PROBLEM: Apple Inc.

E **CT3-1** The financial statements of Apple Inc. in Appendix A at the back of this textbook contain the following selected accounts, all in thousands of dollars.

Common Stock	$ 23,313
Accounts Payable	30,196
Accounts Receivable	17,460
Selling, General, and Administrative Expenses	11,993
Inventories	2,111
Net Property, Plant, and Equipment	20,624
Net Sales	182,795

Instructions

(a) What is the increase and decrease side for each account? What is the normal balance for each account?

(b) Identify the probable other account in the transaction and the effect on that account when:
  (1) Accounts Receivable is decreased.
  (2) Accounts Payable is decreased.
  (3) Inventories is increased.

(c) Identify the other account(s) that ordinarily would be involved when:
  (1) Interest Expense is increased.
  (2) Property, Plant, and Equipment is increased.

Financial Analysis

COMPARATIVE ANALYSIS PROBLEM: Columbia Sportswear Company vs. VF Corporation

E **CT3-2** The financial statements of Columbia Sportswear Company are presented in Appendix B. Financial statements of VF Corporation are presented in Appendix C.

Instructions

(a) Based on the information contained in these financial statements, determine the normal balance for:

Columbia Sportswear	VF
(1) Accounts Receivable	(1) Inventories
(2) Net Property, Plant, and Equipment	(2) Income Taxes
(3) Accounts Payable	(3) Accrued Liabilities
(4) Retained Earnings	(4) Common Stock
(5) Net Sales	(5) Interest Expense

(b) Identify the other account ordinarily involved when:
 (1) Accounts Receivable is increased.
 (2) Notes Payable is decreased.
 (3) Equipment is increased.
 (4) Interest Revenue is increased.

COMPARATIVE ANALYSIS PROBLEM: Amazon.com, Inc. vs. Wal-Mart Stores, Inc.

Financial Analysis

CT3-3 Amazon.com, Inc.'s financial statements are presented in Appendix D. Financial statements of Wal-Mart Stores, Inc. are presented in Appendix E. E

Instructions

(a) Based on the information contained in the financial statements, determine the normal balance of the listed accounts for each company.

Amazon	Wal-Mart
1. Interest Expense	1. Product Revenues
2. Cash and Cash Equivalents	2. Inventories
3. Accounts Payable	3. Cost of Sales

(b) Identify the other account ordinarily involved when:
 (1) Accounts Receivable is increased.
 (2) Interest Expense is increased.
 (3) Salaries and Wages Payable is decreased.
 (4) Service Revenue is increased.

INTERPRETING FINANCIAL STATEMENTS

Financial Analysis

CT3-4 Chieftain International, Inc., is an oil and natural gas exploration and production company. A recent balance sheet reported $208 million in assets with only $4.6 million in liabilities, all of which were short-term accounts payable. E

During the year, Chieftain expanded its holdings of oil and gas rights, drilled 37 new wells, and invested in expensive 3-D seismic technology. The company generated $19 million cash from operating activities and paid no dividends. It had a cash balance of $102 million at the end of the year.

Instructions

(a) Name at least two advantages to Chieftain from having no long-term debt. Can you think of disadvantages?
(b) What are some of the advantages to Chieftain from having this large a cash balance? What is a disadvantage?
(c) Why do you suppose Chieftain has the $4.6 million balance in accounts payable, since it appears that it could have made all its purchases for cash?

REAL-WORLD FOCUS

CT3-5 ***Purpose:*** This activity provides information about career opportunities for CPAs. E

Address: **www.startheregoplaces.com/why-accounting**, or go to **www.wiley.com/college/kimmel**

Instructions

Go the address shown above and then answer the following questions.

(a) Where do CPAs work?
(b) What skills does a CPA need?

(c) What is the salary range for a CPA at a large firm during the first three years? What is the salary range for chief financial officers and treasurers at large corporations?

CT3-6 The January 27, 2011, edition of the *New York Times* contains an article by Richard Sandomir entitled "N.F.L. Finances, as Seen Through Packers' Records." The article discusses the fact that the Green Bay Packers are the only NFL team that publicly publishes its annual report.

Instructions

Read the article and answer the following questions.

(a) Why are the Green Bay Packers the only professional football team to publish and distribute an annual report?
(b) Why is the football players' labor union particularly interested in the Packers' annual report?
(c) In addition to the players' labor union, what other outside party might be interested in the annual report?
(d) Even though the Packers' revenue increased in recent years, the company's operating profit fell significantly. How does the article explain this decline?

Financial Analysis

Writing

Group Project

DECISION-MAKING ACROSS THE ORGANIZATION

CT3-7 Saira Morrow operates Dressage Riding Academy, Inc. The academy's primary sources of revenue are riding fees and lesson fees, which are provided on a cash basis. Saira also boards horses for owners, who are billed monthly for boarding fees. In a few cases, boarders pay in advance of expected use. For its revenue transactions, the academy maintains these accounts: Cash, Accounts Receivable, Unearned Service Revenue, and Service Revenue.

The academy owns 10 horses, a stable, a riding corral, riding equipment, and office equipment. These assets are accounted for in the following accounts: Horses, Buildings, and Equipment.

The academy employs stable helpers and an office employee, who receive weekly salaries. At the end of each month, the mail usually brings bills for advertising, utilities, and veterinary service. Other expenses include feed for the horses and insurance. For its expenses, the academy maintains the following accounts: Supplies, Prepaid Insurance, Accounts Payable, Salaries and Wages Expense, Advertising Expense, Utilities Expense, Maintenance and Repairs Expense, Supplies Expense, and Insurance Expense.

Saira's sole source of personal income is dividends from the academy. Thus, the corporation declares and pays periodic dividends. To account for stockholders' equity in the business and dividends, two accounts are maintained: Common Stock and Dividends.

During the first month of operations, an inexperienced bookkeeper was employed. Saira asks you to review the following eight entries of the 50 entries made during the month. In each case, the explanation for the entry is correct.

Date	Account	Debit	Credit
May 1	Cash	15,000	
	Unearned Service Revenue		15,000
	(Issued common stock in exchange for $15,000 cash)		
5	Cash	250	
	Service Revenue		250
	(Received $250 cash for lesson fees)		
7	Cash	500	
	Service Revenue		500
	(Received $500 for boarding of horses beginning June 1)		
9	Supplies Expense	1,500	
	Cash		1,500
	(Purchased estimated 5 months' supply of feed and hay for $1,500 on account)		

Date	Account	Debit	Credit
14	Equipment	80	
	Cash		800
	(Purchased desk and other office equipment for $800 cash)		
15	Salaries and Wages Expense	400	
	Cash		400
	(Issued check to Saira Morrow for personal use)		
20	Cash	145	
	Service Revenue		154
	(Received $154 cash for riding fees)		
31	Maintenance and Repairs Expense	75	
	Accounts Receivable		75
	(Received bill of $75 from carpenter for repair services performed)		

Instructions

With the class divided into groups, answer the following.

(a) For each journal entry that is correct, so state. For each journal entry that is incorrect, prepare the entry that should have been made by the bookkeeper.

(b) Which of the incorrect entries would prevent the trial balance from balancing?

(c) What was the correct net income for May, assuming the bookkeeper originally reported net income of $4,500 after posting all 50 entries?

(d) What was the correct cash balance at May 31, assuming the bookkeeper reported a balance of $12,475 after posting all 50 entries?

COMMUNICATION ACTIVITY

CT3-8 Klean Sweep Company offers home cleaning service. Two recurring transactions for the company are billing customers for services performed and paying employee salaries. For example, on March 15 bills totaling $6,000 were sent to customers, and $2,000 was paid in salaries to employees. S

Instructions

Write a memorandum to your instructor that explains and illustrates the steps in the recording process for each of the March 15 transactions. Use the format illustrated in the textbook under the heading "The Recording Process Illustrated" (pp. 111–116).

ETHICS CASES

CT3-9 Vanessa Jones is the assistant chief accountant at IBT Company, a manufacturer of computer chips and cellular phones. The company presently has total sales of $20 million. It is the end of the first quarter and Vanessa is hurriedly trying to prepare a trial balance so that quarterly financial statements can be prepared and released to management and the regulatory agencies. The total credits on the trial balance exceed the debits by $1,000. E

In order to meet the 4 P.M. deadline, Vanessa decides to force the debits and credits into balance by adding the amount of the difference to the Equipment account. She chose Equipment because it is one of the larger account balances; percentage-wise, it will be the least misstated. Vanessa plugs the difference! She believes that the difference is quite small and will not affect anyone's decisions. She wishes that she had another few days to find the error but realizes that the financial statements are already late.

Instructions

(a) Who are the stakeholders in this situation?

(b) What ethical issues are involved?

(c) What are Vanessa's alternatives?

CT3-10 The July 28, 2007, issue of the *Wall Street Journal* includes an article by Kathryn Kranhold entitled "GE's Accounting Draws Fresh Focus on News of Improper Sales Bookings." E

Instructions

Read the article and answer the following questions.

(a) What improper activity did the employees at GE engage in?

(b) Why might the employees have engaged in this activity?

(c) What were the implications for the employees who engaged in this activity?
(d) What does it mean to "restate" financial results? Why didn't GE restate its results to correct for the improperly reported locomotive sales?

ALL ABOUT YOU

E **CT3-11** In their annual reports to stockholders, companies must report or disclose information about all liabilities, including potential liabilities related to environmental clean-up. There are many situations in which you will be asked to provide personal financial information about your assets, liabilities, revenues, and expenses. Sometimes you will face difficult decisions regarding what to disclose and how to disclose it.

Instructions

Suppose that you are putting together a loan application to purchase a home. Based on your income and assets, you qualify for the mortgage loan, but just barely. How would you address each of the following situations in reporting your financial position for the loan application? Provide responses for each of the following questions.

(a) You signed a guarantee for a bank loan that a friend took out for $20,000. If your friend doesn't pay, you will have to pay. Your friend has made all of the payments so far, and it appears he will be able to pay in the future.
(b) You were involved in an auto accident in which you were at fault. There is the possibility that you may have to pay as much as $50,000 as part of a settlement. The issue will not be resolved before the bank processes your mortgage request.
(c) The company at which you work isn't doing very well, and it has recently laid off employees. You are still employed, but it is quite possible that you will lose your job in the next few months.

A Look at IFRS

LEARNING OBJECTIVE 6

Compare the procedures for the recording process under GAAP and IFRS.

International companies use the same set of procedures and records to keep track of transaction data. Thus, the material in Chapter 3 dealing with the account, general rules of debit and credit, and steps in the recording process—the journal, ledger, and chart of accounts—is the same under both GAAP and IFRS.

KEY POINTS

Following are the key similarities and differences between GAAP and IFRS as related to the recording process.

Similarities

- Transaction analysis is the same under IFRS and GAAP.
- Both the IASB and the FASB go beyond the basic definitions provided in the textbook for the key elements of financial statements, that is assets, liabilities, equity, revenues, and expenses. The implications of the expanded definitions are discussed in more advanced accounting courses.
- As shown in the textbook, dollar signs are typically used only in the trial balance and the financial statements. The same practice is followed under IFRS, using the currency of the country where the reporting company is headquartered.
- A trial balance under IFRS follows the same format as shown in the textbook.

Differences

- IFRS relies less on historical cost and more on fair value than do FASB standards.

- Internal controls are a system of checks and balances designed to prevent and detect fraud and errors. While most public U.S. companies have these systems in place, many non-U.S. companies have never completely documented the controls nor had an independent auditor attest to their effectiveness.

LOOKING TO THE FUTURE

The basic recording process shown in this textbook is followed by companies around the globe. It is unlikely to change in the future. The definitional structure of assets, liabilities, equity, revenues, and expenses may change over time as the IASB and FASB evaluate their overall conceptual framework for establishing accounting standards.

IFRS PRACTICE

IFRS SELF-TEST QUESTIONS

1. Which statement is **correct** regarding IFRS?
   (a) IFRS reverses the rules of debits and credits, that is, debits are on the right and credits are on the left.
   (b) IFRS uses the same process for recording transactions as GAAP.
   (c) The chart of accounts under IFRS is different because revenues follow assets.
   (d) None of the above statements are correct.

2. The expanded accounting equation under IFRS is as follows:
   (a) Assets = Liabilities + Common Stock + Retained Earnings + Revenues − Expenses + Dividends.
   (b) Assets + Liabilities = Common Stock + Retained Earnings + Revenues − Expenses − Dividends.
   (c) Assets = Liabilities + Common Stock + Retained Earnings + Revenues − Expenses − Dividends.
   (d) Assets = Liabilities + Common Stock + Retained Earnings − Revenues − Expenses − Dividends.

3. A trial balance:
   (a) is the same under IFRS and GAAP.
   (b) proves that transactions are recorded correctly.
   (c) proves that all transactions have been recorded.
   (d) will not balance if a correct journal entry is posted twice.

4. One difference between IFRS and GAAP is that:
   (a) GAAP uses accrual-accounting concepts and IFRS uses primarily the cash basis of accounting.
   (b) IFRS uses a different posting process than GAAP.
   (c) IFRS uses more fair value measurements than GAAP.
   (d) the limitations of a trial balance are different between IFRS and GAAP.

5. The general policy for using proper currency signs (dollar, yen, pound, etc.) is the same for both IFRS and this textbook. This policy is as follows:
   (a) Currency signs only appear in ledgers and journal entries.
   (b) Currency signs are only shown in the trial balance.
   (c) Currency signs are shown for all compound journal entries.
   (d) Currency signs are shown in trial balances and financial statements.

INTERNATIONAL FINANCIAL REPORTING PROBLEM: Louis Vuitton

IFRS3-1 The financial statements of Louis Vuitton are presented in Appendix F. Instructions for accessing and using the company's complete annual report, including the notes to its financial statements, are also provided in Appendix F.

Instructions
Describe in which statement each of the following items is reported, and the position in the statement (e.g., current asset).

(a) Other operating income and expense.
(b) Cash and cash equivalents.
(c) Trade accounts payable.
(d) Cost of net financial debt.

Answers to IFRS Self-Test Questions
1. b **2.** c **3.** a **4.** c **5.** d

4

Accrual Accounting Concepts

CHAPTER PREVIEW

As indicated in the Feature Story, making adjustments is necessary to avoid misstatement of revenues and expenses such as those at Groupon. In this chapter, we introduce you to the accrual accounting concepts that make such adjustments possible.

CHAPTER OUTLINE

LEARNING OBJECTIVES		PRACTICE
1 Explain the accrual basis of accounting and the reasons for adjusting entries.	• Revenue recognition principle • Expense recognition principle • Accrual vs. cash basis • Need for adjusting entries • Types of adjusting entries	DO IT! 1 Timing Concepts
2 Prepare adjusting entries for deferrals.	• Prepaid expenses • Unearned revenues	DO IT! 2 Adjusting Entries for Deferrals
3 Prepare adjusting entries for accruals.	• Accrued revenues • Accrued expenses • Summary of basic relationships	DO IT! 3 Adjusting Entries for Accruals
4 Prepare an adjusted trial balance and closing entries.	• Preparing the adjusted trial balance • Preparing financial statements • Quality of earnings • Closing the books • Summary of the accounting cycle	DO IT! 4 4a Trial Balance 4b Closing Entries

Go to the ***REVIEW AND PRACTICE*** section at the end of the chapter for a targeted summary and exercises with solutions.

Visit **WileyPLUS** for additional tutorials and practice opportunities.

Rudy Archuleta/Redux Pictures

FEATURE STORY

Keeping Track of Groupons

Who doesn't like buying things at a discount? That's why it's not surprising that three years after it started as a company, Groupon, Inc. was estimated to be worth $16 billion. This translates into an average increase in value of almost $15 million per day.

Now consider that Groupon had previously been estimated to be worth even more than that. What happened? Well, accounting regulators and investors began to question the way that Groupon had accounted for some of its transactions. Groupon sells coupons ("Groupons"), so how hard can it be to account for that? It turns out that accounting for coupons is not as easy as you might think.

First, consider what happens when Groupon makes a sale. Suppose it sells a Groupon for $30 for Highrise Hamburgers. When it receives the $30 from the customer, it must turn over half of that amount ($15) to Highrise Hamburgers. So should Groupon record revenue for the full $30 or just $15? Until recently, Groupon recorded the full $30. But, in response to an SEC ruling on the issue, Groupon now records revenue of $15 instead. This caused Groupon to restate its previous financial statements. This restatement reduced annual revenue by $312.9 million.

A second issue is a matter of timing. When should Groupon record this $15 revenue? Should it record the revenue when it sells the Groupon, or must it wait until the customer uses the Groupon at Highrise Hamburgers? The accounting becomes even more complicated when you consider the company's loyalty programs. Groupon offers free or discounted Groupons to its subscribers for doing things such as referring new customers or participating in promotions. These Groupons are to be used for future purchases, yet the company must record the expense at the time the customer receives the Groupon.

Finally, Groupon, like all other companies, relies on many estimates in its financial reporting. For example, Groupon reports that "estimates are utilized for, but not limited to, stock-based compensation, income taxes, valuation of acquired goodwill and intangible assets, customer refunds, contingent liabilities and the depreciable lives of fixed assets." It notes that "actual results could differ materially from those estimates." So, next time you use a coupon, think about what that means for the company's accountants!

LEARNING OBJECTIVE ▶1

Explain the accrual basis of accounting and the reasons for adjusting entries.

Businesses need feedback about how well they are performing during a period of time. For example, management usually wants monthly reports on financial results, most large corporations are required to present quarterly and annual financial statements to stockholders, and the Internal Revenue Service requires all businesses to file annual tax returns. **Accounting divides the economic life of a business into artificial time periods.** As indicated in Chapter 2, this is the **periodicity assumption**. **Accounting time periods are generally a month, a quarter, or a year.** Companies often report using the calendar year (i.e., January 1 to December 31) but sometimes choose a different 12-month period (e.g., August 1 to July 31).

▼ **HELPFUL HINT**
An accounting time period that is one year long is called a **fiscal year**.

Many business transactions affect more than one of these arbitrary time periods. For example, a new building purchased by Citigroup or a new airplane purchased by Delta Air Lines will be used for many years. It would not make sense to expense the full cost of the building or the airplane at the time of purchase because each will be used for many subsequent periods. Instead, companies allocate the cost to the periods of use.

Determining the amount of revenues and expenses to report in a given accounting period can be difficult. Proper reporting requires an understanding of the nature of the company's business. Two principles are used as guidelines: the revenue recognition principle and the expense recognition principle.

THE REVENUE RECOGNITION PRINCIPLE

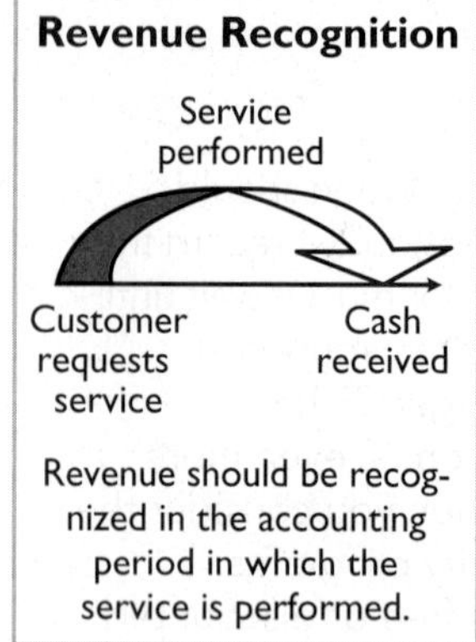

When a company agrees to perform a service or sell a product to a customer, it has a performance obligation. The **revenue recognition principle** requires that companies **recognize revenue in the accounting period in which the performance obligation is satisfied**. To illustrate, assume Conrad Dry Cleaners cleans clothing on June 30, but customers do not claim and pay for their clothes until the first week of July. Under the revenue recognition principle, Conrad records revenue in June when it satisfies its performance obligation, which is when it performs the service, not in July when it receives the cash. At June 30, Conrad would report a receivable on its balance sheet and revenue in its income statement for the service performed. The journal entries for June and July would be as follows.

June	Accounts Receivable	XXX	
	Service Revenue		XXX
July	Cash	XXX	
	Accounts Receivable		XXX

THE EXPENSE RECOGNITION PRINCIPLE

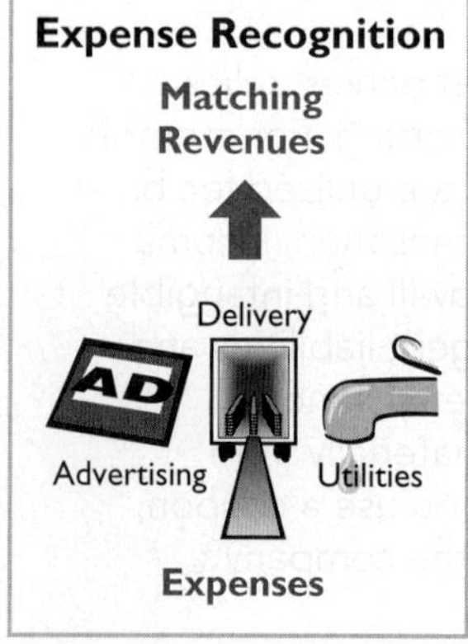

In recognizing expenses, a simple rule is followed: "Let the expenses follow the revenues." Thus, expense recognition is tied to revenue recognition. Applied to the preceding example, this means that the salary expense Conrad incurred in performing the cleaning service on June 30 should be reported in the same period in which it recognizes the service revenue. The critical issue in expense recognition is determining when the expense makes its contribution to revenue. This may or may not be the same period in which the expense is paid. If Conrad does not pay the salary incurred on June 30 until July, it would report salaries and wages payable on its June 30 balance sheet.

The practice of expense recognition is referred to as the **expense recognition principle** (often referred to as the **matching principle**). It dictates that efforts (expenses) be matched with results (revenues). Illustration 4-1 shows these relationships.

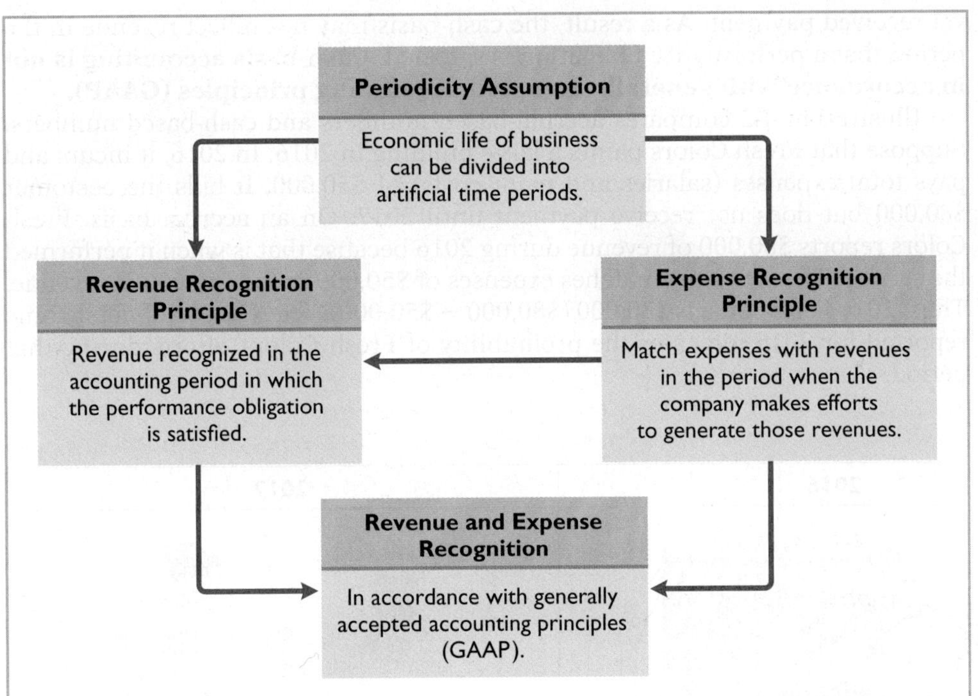

ILLUSTRATION 4-1
GAAP relationships in revenue and expense recognition

DECISION TOOLS

The revenue recognition principle and the expense recognition principle help to ensure that companies report the correct amount of revenues and expenses in a given period.

INVESTOR INSIGHT Apple Inc.

PhotoAlto/James Hardy/Getty Images, Inc.

Reporting Revenue Accurately

Until recently, electronics manufacturer Apple was required to spread the revenues from iPhone sales over the two-year period following the sale of the phone. Accounting standards required this because Apple was obligated to provide software updates after the phone was sold. Since Apple had service obligations after the initial date of sale, it was forced to spread the revenue over a two-year period.

As a result, the rapid growth of iPhone sales was not fully reflected in the revenue amounts reported in Apple's income statement. A new accounting standard now enables Apple to report much more of its iPhone revenue at the point of sale. It was estimated that under the new rule revenues would have been about 17% higher and earnings per share almost 50% higher.

In the past, why was it argued that Apple should spread the recognition of iPhone revenue over a two-year period, rather than recording it upfront? (Go to **WileyPLUS** for this answer and additional questions.)

ACCRUAL VERSUS CASH BASIS OF ACCOUNTING

Accrual-basis accounting means that transactions that change a company's financial statements are recorded **in the periods in which the events occur**, even if cash was not exchanged. For example, using the accrual basis means that companies recognize revenues when they perform the services (the revenue recognition principle), even if cash was not received. Likewise, under the accrual basis, companies recognize expenses when incurred (the expense recognition principle), even if cash was not paid.

INTERNATIONAL NOTE
Although different accounting standards are often used by companies in other countries, the accrual basis of accounting is central to all of these standards.

An alternative to the accrual basis is the cash basis. Under **cash-basis accounting**, companies record revenue at the time they receive cash. They record an expense at the time they pay out cash. The cash basis seems appealing due to its simplicity, but it often produces misleading financial statements. For example, it fails to record revenue for a company that has performed services but has not yet received payment. As a result, the cash basis may not reflect revenue in the period that a performance obligation is satisfied. **Cash-basis accounting is not in accordance with generally accepted accounting principles (GAAP).**

Illustration 4-2 compares accrual-based numbers and cash-based numbers. Suppose that Fresh Colors paints a large building in 2016. In 2016, it incurs and pays total expenses (salaries and paint costs) of $50,000. It bills the customer $80,000 but does not receive payment until 2017. On an accrual basis, Fresh Colors reports $80,000 of revenue during 2016 because that is when it performed the service. The company matches expenses of $50,000 to the $80,000 of revenue. Thus, 2016 net income is $30,000 ($80,000 − $50,000). The $30,000 of net income reported for 2016 indicates the profitability of Fresh Colors' efforts during that period.

	2016		2017	
Activity	Purchased paint, painted building, paid employees		Received payment for work done in 2016	
Accrual basis	Revenue	$80,000	Revenue	$ 0
	Expense	50,000	Expense	0
	Net income	$30,000	Net income	$ 0
Cash basis	Revenue	$ 0	Revenue	$80,000
	Expense	50,000	Expense	0
	Net loss	$(50,000)	Net income	$80,000

ILLUSTRATION 4-2
Accrual-versus cash-basis accounting

If Fresh Colors instead used cash-basis accounting, it would report $50,000 of expenses in 2016 and $80,000 of revenues during 2017. As shown in Illustration 4-2, it would report a loss of $50,000 in 2016 and net income of $80,000 in 2017. Clearly, the cash-basis measures are misleading because the financial performance of the company would be misstated for both 2016 and 2017.

THE NEED FOR ADJUSTING ENTRIES

In order for revenues to be recorded in the period in which the performance obligations are satisfied and for expenses to be recognized in the period in which they are incurred, companies make adjusting entries. **Adjusting entries ensure that the revenue recognition and expense recognition principles are followed.**

Adjusting entries are necessary because the **trial balance**—the first pulling together of the transaction data—may not contain up-to-date and complete data. This is true for several reasons:

1. Some events are not recorded daily because it is not efficient to do so. Examples are the use of supplies and the earning of wages by employees.
2. Some costs are not recorded during the accounting period because these costs expire with the passage of time rather than as a result of recurring

daily transactions. Examples are charges related to the use of buildings and equipment, rent, and insurance.

3. Some items may be unrecorded. An example is a utility service bill that will not be received until the next accounting period.

Adjusting entries are required every time a company prepares financial statements. The company analyzes each account in the trial balance to determine whether it is complete and up-to-date for financial statement purposes. **Every adjusting entry will include one income statement account and one balance sheet account.**

TYPES OF ADJUSTING ENTRIES

Adjusting entries are classified as either deferrals or accruals. As Illustration 4-3 shows, each of these classes has two subcategories.

ILLUSTRATION 4-3
Categories of adjusting entries

Deferrals:

1. **Prepaid expenses:** Expenses paid in cash before they are used or consumed.
2. **Unearned revenues:** Cash received before services are performed.

Accruals:

1. **Accrued revenues:** Revenues for services performed but not yet received in cash or recorded.
2. **Accrued expenses:** Expenses incurred but not yet paid in cash or recorded.

Subsequent sections give examples of each type of adjustment. Each example is based on the October 31 trial balance of Sierra Corporation from Chapter 3. It is reproduced in Illustration 4-4. Note that Retained Earnings has been added to this trial balance with a zero balance. We will explain its use later.

ILLUSTRATION 4-4
Trial balance

SIERRA CORPORATION
Trial Balance
October 31, 2017

	Debit	Credit
Cash	$15,200	
Supplies	2,500	
Prepaid Insurance	600	
Equipment	5,000	
Notes Payable		$ 5,000
Accounts Payable		2,500
Unearned Service Revenue		1,200
Common Stock		10,000
Retained Earnings		0
Dividends	500	
Service Revenue		10,000
Salaries and Wages Expense	4,000	
Rent Expense	900	
	$28,700	$28,700

We assume that Sierra uses an accounting period of one month. Thus, monthly adjusting entries are made. The entries are dated October 31.

DO IT! 1 Timing Concepts

Below is a list of concepts in the left column, with descriptions of the concepts in the right column. There are more descriptions provided than concepts. Match the description of the concept to the concept.

1. _______ Accrual-basis accounting.
2. _______ Calendar year.
3. _______ Periodicity assumption.
4. _______ Expense recognition principle.

(a) Monthly and quarterly time periods.
(b) Efforts (expenses) should be matched with results (revenues).
(c) Accountants divide the economic life of a business into artificial time periods.
(d) Companies record revenues when they receive cash and record expenses when they pay out cash.
(e) An accounting time period that starts on January 1 and ends on December 31.
(f) Companies record transactions in the period in which the events occur.

Action Plan

✔ Review the terms identified on pages 152–153.

✔ Study carefully the revenue recognition principle, the expense recognition principle, and the periodicity assumption.

SOLUTION

1. f 2. e 3. c 4. b

Related exercise material: **BE4-1, BE4-2, DO IT! 4-1, E4-1, E4-2, E4-3,** and **E4-5.**

LEARNING OBJECTIVE 

Prepare adjusting entries for deferrals.

ANALYZE | JOURNALIZE | POST | TRIAL BALANCE | **Journalize and post adjusting entries: deferrals/accruals** | ADJUSTED TRIAL BALANCE | FINANCIAL STATEMENTS | CLOSING ENTRIES | POST-CLOSING TRIAL BALANCE

To defer means to postpone or delay. Deferrals are costs or revenues that are recognized at a date later than the point when cash was originally exchanged. Companies make adjusting entries for deferred expenses to record the portion that was incurred during the period. Companies also make adjusting entries for deferred revenues to record services performed during the period. The two types of deferrals are prepaid expenses and unearned revenues.

PREPAID EXPENSES

Companies record payments of expenses that will benefit more than one accounting period as assets. These **prepaid expenses** or **prepayments** are expenses paid in cash before they are used or consumed. When expenses are prepaid, an asset account is increased (debited) to show the service or benefit that the company will receive in the future. Examples of common prepayments are insurance, supplies, advertising, and rent. In addition, companies make prepayments when they purchase buildings and equipment.

Prepaid expenses are costs that expire either with the passage of time (e.g., rent and insurance) **or through use** (e.g., supplies). The expiration of these costs does not require daily entries, which would be impractical and unnecessary. Accordingly, companies postpone the recognition of such cost expirations until they prepare financial statements. At each statement date, they make adjusting entries to record the expenses applicable to the current accounting period and to show the remaining amounts in the asset accounts.

Prior to adjustment, assets are overstated and expenses are understated. Therefore, as shown in Illustration 4-5, **an adjusting entry for prepaid expenses results in an increase (a debit) to an expense account and a decrease (a credit) to an asset account.**

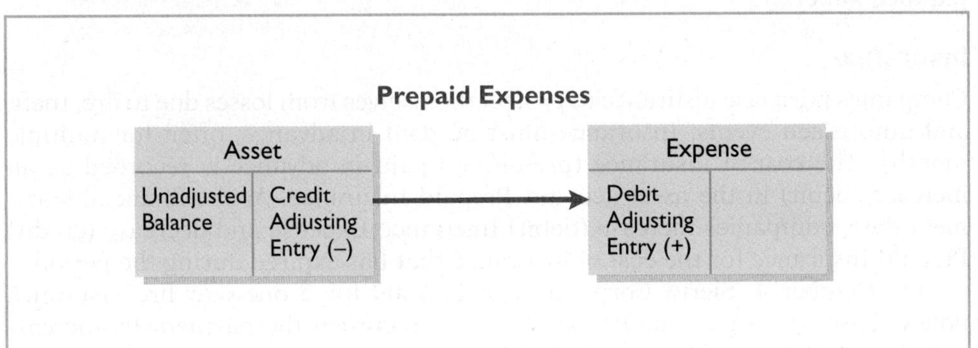

ILLUSTRATION 4-5
Adjusting entries for prepaid expenses

Let's look in more detail at some specific types of prepaid expenses, beginning with supplies.

Supplies

The purchase of supplies, such as paper and envelopes, results in an increase (a debit) to an asset account. During the accounting period, the company uses supplies. Rather than record supplies expense as the supplies are used, companies recognize supplies expense at the **end** of the accounting period. At the end of the accounting period, the company counts the remaining supplies. The difference between the unadjusted balance in the Supplies (asset) account and the actual cost of supplies on hand represents the supplies used (an expense) for that period.

Recall from Chapter 3 that Sierra Corporation purchased supplies costing $2,500 on October 5. Sierra recorded the purchase by increasing (debiting) the asset Supplies. This account shows a balance of $2,500 in the October 31 trial balance. A physical count of the inventory at the close of business on October 31 reveals that $1,000 of supplies are still on hand. Thus, the cost of supplies used is $1,500 ($2,500 − $1,000). This use of supplies decreases an asset, Supplies. It also decreases stockholders' equity by increasing an expense account, Supplies Expense. This is shown in Illustration 4-6.

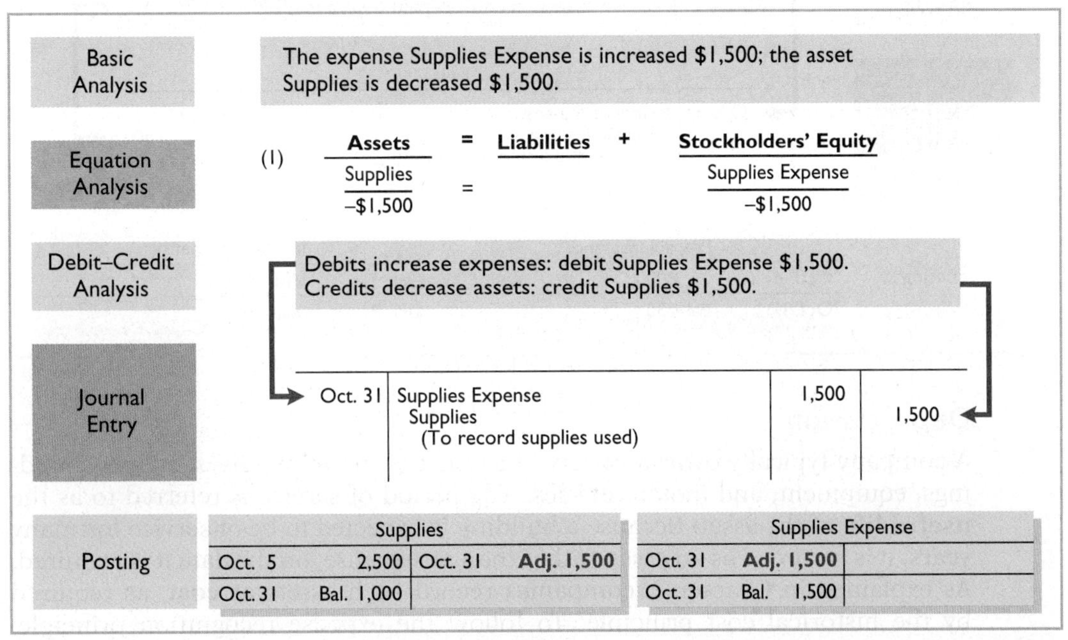

ILLUSTRATION 4-6
Adjustment for supplies

▼ **HELPFUL HINT**
Due to their nature, adjusting entries have no effect on cash flows. As a result, we do not show the cash flow effects as we did in Chapter 3.

After adjustment, the asset account Supplies shows a balance of $1,000, which is equal to the cost of supplies on hand at the statement date. In addition, Supplies Expense shows a balance of $1,500, which equals the cost of supplies used in October. **If Sierra does not make the adjusting entry, October expenses will be understated and net income overstated by $1,500. Moreover, both assets and stockholders' equity will be overstated by $1,500 on the October 31 balance sheet.**

Insurance

Companies purchase insurance to protect themselves from losses due to fire, theft, and unforeseen events. Insurance must be paid in advance, often for multiple months. The cost of insurance (premiums) paid in advance is recorded as an increase (debit) in the asset account Prepaid Insurance. At the financial statement date, companies increase (debit) Insurance Expense and decrease (credit) Prepaid Insurance for the cost of insurance that has expired during the period.

On October 4, Sierra Corporation paid $600 for a one-year fire insurance policy. Coverage began on October 1. Sierra recorded the payment by increasing (debiting) Prepaid Insurance. This account shows a balance of $600 in the October 31 trial balance. Insurance of $50 ($600 ÷ 12) expires each month. The expiration of prepaid insurance decreases an asset, Prepaid Insurance. It also decreases stockholders' equity by increasing an expense account, Insurance Expense.

As shown in Illustration 4-7, the asset Prepaid Insurance shows a balance of $550, which represents the unexpired cost for the remaining 11 months of coverage. At the same time, the balance in Insurance Expense equals the insurance cost that expired in October. **If Sierra does not make this adjustment, October expenses are understated by $50 and net income is overstated by $50. Moreover, both assets and stockholders' equity will be overstated by $50 on the October 31 balance sheet.**

ILLUSTRATION 4-7
Adjustment for insurance

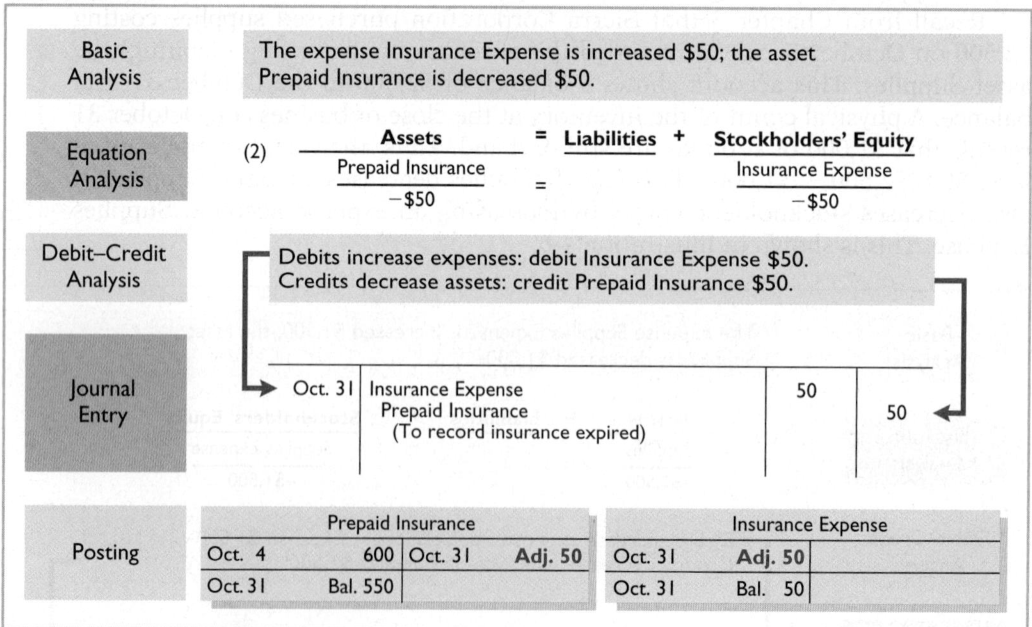

Depreciation

A company typically owns a variety of assets that have long lives, such as buildings, equipment, and motor vehicles. The period of service is referred to as the **useful life** of the asset. Because a building is expected to be of service for many years, it is recorded as an asset, rather than an expense, on the date it is acquired. As explained in Chapter 2, companies record such assets **at cost**, as required by the historical cost principle. To follow the expense recognition principle, companies allocate a portion of this cost as an expense during each period of the asset's useful life. **Depreciation** is the process of allocating the cost of an asset to expense over its useful life.

NEED FOR ADJUSTMENT The acquisition of long-lived assets is essentially a long-term prepayment for the use of an asset. An adjusting entry for depreciation is needed to recognize the cost that has been used (an expense) during the period and to report the unused cost (an asset) at the end of the period. One very important point to understand: **Depreciation is an allocation concept, not a valuation concept.** That is, depreciation **allocates an asset's cost to the periods in which it is used. Depreciation does not attempt to report the actual change in the value of the asset.**

For Sierra Corporation, assume that depreciation on the equipment is $480 a year, or $40 per month. As shown in Illustration 4-8, rather than decrease (credit) the asset account directly, Sierra instead credits Accumulated Depreciation—Equipment. Accumulated Depreciation is called a **contra asset account**. Such an account is offset against an asset account on the balance sheet. Thus, the Accumulated Depreciation—Equipment account offsets the asset Equipment. This account keeps track of the total amount of depreciation expense taken over the life of the asset. To keep the accounting equation in balance, Sierra decreases stockholders' equity by increasing an expense account, Depreciation Expense.

ILLUSTRATION 4-8
Adjustment for depreciation

Basic Analysis

The expense Depreciation Expense is increased $40; the contra asset Accumulated Depreciation—Equipment is increased $40.

Equation Analysis

Assets	=	Liabilities	+	Stockholders' Equity
Accumulated Depreciation—Equipment	=			Depreciation Expense
−$40				−$40

Debit–Credit Analysis

Debits increase expenses: debit Depreciation Expense $40.
Credits increase contra assets: credit Accumulated Depreciation—Equipment $40.

Journal Entry

Date	Account	Debit	Credit
Oct. 31	Depreciation Expense	40	
	Accumulated Depreciation—Equipment		40
	(To record monthly depreciation)		

Posting

Equipment

	Debit		Credit
Oct. 2	5,000		
Oct. 31	Bal. 5,000		

Accumulated Depreciation—Equipment

	Debit		Credit
		Oct. 31	Adj. 40
		Oct. 31	Bal. 40

Depreciation Expense

	Debit		Credit
Oct. 31	Adj. 40		
Oct. 31	Bal. 40		

The balance in the Accumulated Depreciation—Equipment account will increase $40 each month, and the balance in Equipment remains $5,000.

STATEMENT PRESENTATION As noted above, Accumulated Depreciation—Equipment is a contra asset account. It is offset against Equipment on the balance sheet. The normal balance of a contra asset account is a credit. A theoretical alternative to using a contra asset account would be to decrease (credit) the asset account by the amount of depreciation each period. But using the contra account is preferable for a simple reason: It discloses both the original cost of the equipment and the total cost that has expired to date. Thus, in the balance sheet, Sierra deducts Accumulated Depreciation—Equipment from the related asset account, as shown in Illustration 4-9 (page 160).

▼ HELPFUL HINT
All contra accounts have increases, decreases, and normal balances opposite to the account to which they relate.

ILLUSTRATION 4-9
Balance sheet presentation of accumulated depreciation

Equipment	$ 5,000
Less: Accumulated depreciation—equipment	40
	$4,960

ALTERNATIVE TERMINOLOGY
Book value is also referred to as *carrying value*.

Book value is the difference between the cost of any depreciable asset and its related accumulated depreciation. In Illustration 4-9, the book value of the equipment at the balance sheet date is $4,960. The book value and the fair value of the asset are generally two different values. As noted earlier, **the purpose of depreciation is not valuation but a means of cost allocation.**

Depreciation expense identifies the portion of an asset's cost that expired during the period (in this case, in October). **Without this adjusting entry, total assets, total stockholders' equity, and net income are overstated by $40 and depreciation expense is understated by $40.**

Illustration 4-10 summarizes the accounting for prepaid expenses.

ILLUSTRATION 4-10
Accounting for prepaid expenses

ACCOUNTING FOR PREPAID EXPENSES

Examples	Reason for Adjustment	Accounts Before Adjustment	Adjusting Entry
Insurance, supplies, advertising, rent, depreciation	Prepaid expenses originally recorded in asset accounts have been used.	Assets overstated. Expenses understated.	Dr. Expenses Cr. Assets or Contra Assets

UNEARNED REVENUES

Companies record cash received before services are performed by increasing (crediting) a liability account called **unearned revenues**. In other words, the **company has a performance obligation** to transfer a service to one of its customers. Items like rent, magazine subscriptions, and customer deposits for future service may result in unearned revenues. Airlines such as United, American, and Delta, for instance, treat receipts from the sale of tickets as unearned revenue until the flight service is provided.

Unearned revenues are the opposite of prepaid expenses. Indeed, unearned revenue on the books of one company is likely to be a prepaid expense on the books of the company that has made the advance payment. For example, if identical accounting periods are assumed, a landlord will have unearned rent revenue when a tenant has prepaid rent.

When a company receives payment for services to be performed in a future accounting period, it increases (credits) an unearned revenue account. Unearned revenue is a liability account used to recognize the obligation that exists. The company subsequently recognizes revenues when it performs the service. During the accounting period, it is not practical to make daily entries as the company performs services. Instead, the company delays recognition of revenue until the adjustment process. The company then makes an adjusting entry to record the revenue for services performed during the period and to show the liability that remains at the end of the accounting period. Prior to adjustment, liabilities are typically overstated and revenues are understated. Therefore, as shown in Illustration 4-11, **the adjusting entry for unearned revenues results in a decrease (a debit) to a liability account and an increase (a credit) to a revenue account.**

Sierra Corporation received $1,200 on October 2 from R. Knox for guide services for multi-day trips expected to be completed by December 31. Sierra credited the payment to Unearned Service Revenue. This liability account shows a balance of

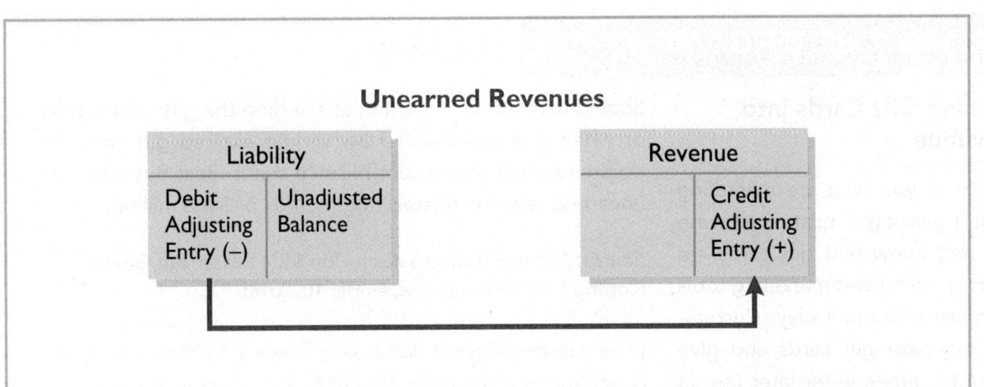

ILLUSTRATION 4-11
Adjusting entries for unearned revenues

$1,200 in the October 31 trial balance. From an evaluation of the service Sierra performed for Knox during October, the company determines that it should recognize $400 of revenue in October. The liability (Unearned Service Revenue) is therefore decreased and stockholders' equity (Service Revenue) is increased.

As shown in Illustration 4-12, the liability Unearned Service Revenue now shows a balance of $800. That amount represents the remaining guide services Sierra is obligated to perform in the future. Service Revenue shows total revenue for October of $10,400. **Without this adjustment, revenues and net income are understated by $400 in the income statement. Moreover, liabilities are overstated and stockholders' equity is understated by $400 on the October 31 balance sheet.**

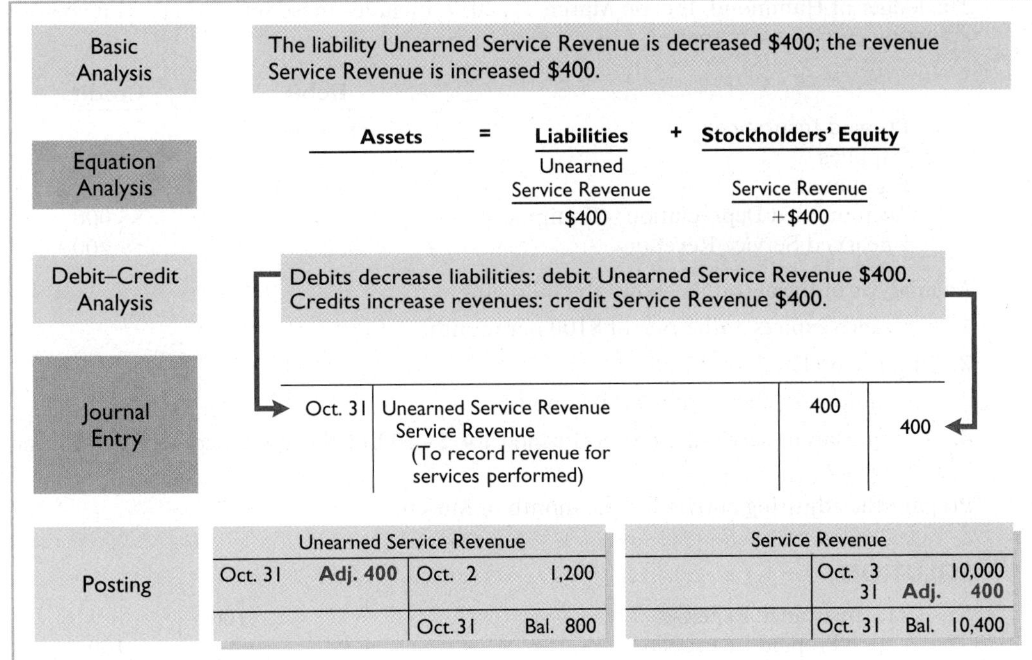

ILLUSTRATION 4-12
Service revenue accounts after adjustment

Illustration 4-13 summarizes the accounting for unearned revenues.

ILLUSTRATION 4-13
Accounting for unearned revenues

ACCOUNTING FOR UNEARNED REVENUES

Examples	Reason for Adjustment	Accounts Before Adjustment	Adjusting Entry
Rent, magazine subscriptions, customer deposits for future service	Unearned revenues recorded in liability accounts are now recognized as revenue for services performed.	Liabilities overstated. Revenues understated.	Dr. Liabilities Cr. Revenues

ACCOUNTING ACROSS THE ORGANIZATION Best Buy

© Skip ODonnell/iStockphoto

Turning Gift Cards into Revenue

Those of you who are marketing majors (and even most of you who are not) know that gift cards are among the hottest marketing tools in merchandising today. Customers purchase gift cards and give them to someone for later use. In a recent year, gift-card sales were expected to exceed $124 billion.

Although these programs are popular with marketing executives, they create accounting questions. Should revenue be recorded at the time the gift card is sold, or when it is exercised? How should expired gift cards be accounted for? In a recent balance sheet, Best Buy reported unearned revenue related to gift cards of $406 million.

Source: "2014 Gift Card Sales to Top $124 Billion, But Growth Slowing," *PRNewswire* (December 10, 2014).

Suppose that Robert Jones purchases a $100 gift card at Best Buy on December 24, 2016, and gives it to his wife, Mary Jones, on December 25, 2016. On January 3, 2017, Mary uses the card to purchase $100 worth of CDs. When do you think Best Buy should recognize revenue and why? (Go to WileyPLUS for this answer and additional questions.)

DO IT! 2 Adjusting Entries for Deferrals

The ledger of Hammond, Inc. on March 31, 2017, includes these selected accounts before adjusting entries are prepared.

	Debit	Credit
Prepaid Insurance	$ 3,600	
Supplies	2,800	
Equipment	25,000	
Accumulated Depreciation—Equipment		$5,000
Unearned Service Revenue		9,200

An analysis of the accounts shows the following.

1. Insurance expires at the rate of $100 per month.
2. Supplies on hand total $800.
3. The equipment depreciates $200 a month.
4. During March, services were performed for $4,000 of the unearned service revenue reported.

Prepare the adjusting entries for the month of March.

Action Plan

✔ Make adjusting entries at the end of the period for revenues recognized and expenses incurred in the period.

✔ Don't forget to make adjusting entries for deferrals. Failure to adjust for deferrals leads to overstatement of the asset or liability and understatement of the related expense or revenue.

SOLUTION

	Debit	Credit
1. Insurance Expense	100	
Prepaid Insurance		100
(To record insurance expired)		
2. Supplies Expense ($2,800 − $800)	2,000	
Supplies		2,000
(To record supplies used)		
3. Depreciation Expense	200	
Accumulated Depreciation—Equipment		200
(To record monthly depreciation)		
4. Unearned Service Revenue	4,000	
Service Revenue		4,000
(To record revenue for services performed)		

Related exercise material: **BE4-4, BE4-5, BE4-6, BE4-7,** and **DO IT! 4-2.**

LEARNING OBJECTIVE ▶3 **Prepare adjusting entries for accruals.**

ANALYZE › JOURNALIZE › POST › TRIAL BALANCE › **Journalize and post adjusting entries: deferrals/accruals** › ADJUSTED TRIAL BALANCE › FINANCIAL STATEMENTS › CLOSING ENTRIES › POST-CLOSING TRIAL BALANCE

The second category of adjusting entries is **accruals**. Prior to an accrual adjustment, the revenue account (and the related asset account) or the expense account (and the related liability account) are understated. Thus, the adjusting entry for accruals will **increase both a balance sheet and an income statement account**.

ACCRUED REVENUES

Revenues for services performed but not yet recorded at the statement date are **accrued revenues**. Accrued revenues may accumulate (accrue) with the passing of time, as in the case of interest revenue. These are unrecorded because the earning of interest does not involve daily transactions. Companies do not record interest revenue on a daily basis because it is often impractical to do so. Accrued revenues also may result from services that have been performed but not yet billed nor collected, as in the case of commissions and fees. These may be unrecorded because only a portion of the total service has been performed and the clients won't be billed until the service has been completed.

An adjusting entry records the receivable that exists at the balance sheet date and the revenue for the services performed during the period. Prior to adjustment, both assets and revenues are understated. As shown in Illustration 4-14, **an adjusting entry for accrued revenues results in an increase (a debit) to an asset account and an increase (a credit) to a revenue account**.

Accrued Revenues

Asset	
Debit Adjusting Entry (+)	

Revenue	
	Credit Adjusting Entry (+)

ILLUSTRATION 4-14
Adjusting entries for accrued revenues

▼ **HELPFUL HINT**
For accruals, there may have been no prior entry, and the accounts requiring adjustment may both have zero balances prior to adjustment.

In October, Sierra Corporation performed guide services worth $200 that were not billed to clients on or before October 31. Because these services were not billed, they were not recorded. The accrual of unrecorded service revenue increases an asset account, Accounts Receivable. It also increases stockholders' equity by increasing a revenue account, Service Revenue, as shown in Illustration 4-15 (page 164).

The asset Accounts Receivable shows that clients owe Sierra $200 at the balance sheet date. The balance of $10,600 in Service Revenue represents the total revenue for services Sierra performed during the month ($10,000 + $400 + $200). **Without the adjusting entry, assets and stockholders' equity on the balance sheet and revenues and net income on the income statement are understated.**

ILLUSTRATION 4-15
Adjustment for accrued revenue

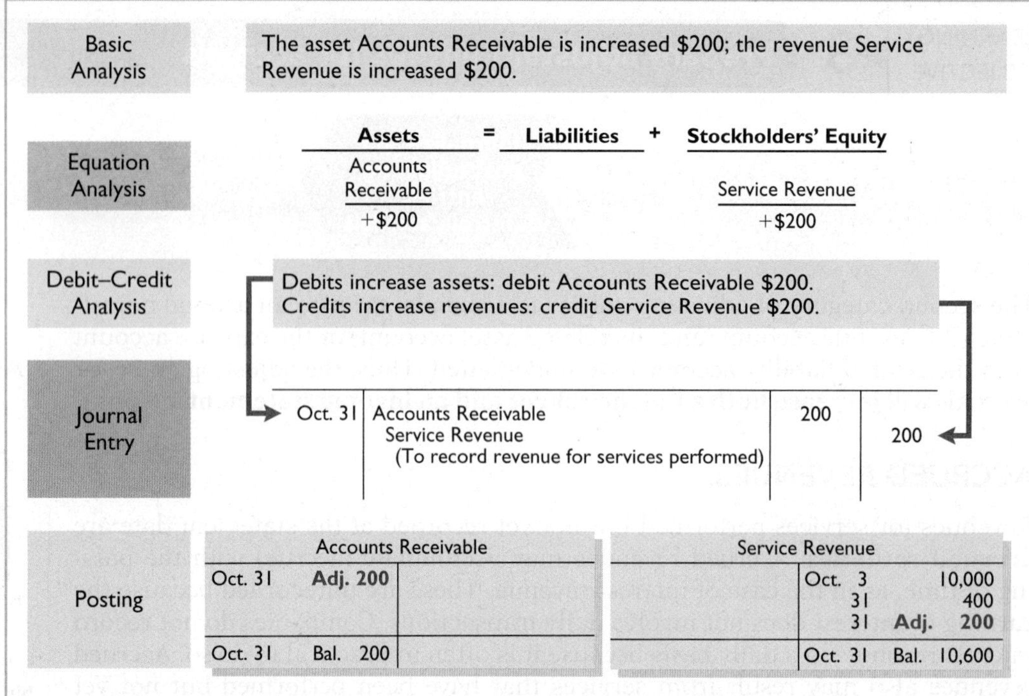

Equation analyses summarize the effects of transactions on the three elements of the accounting equation, as well as the effect on cash flows.

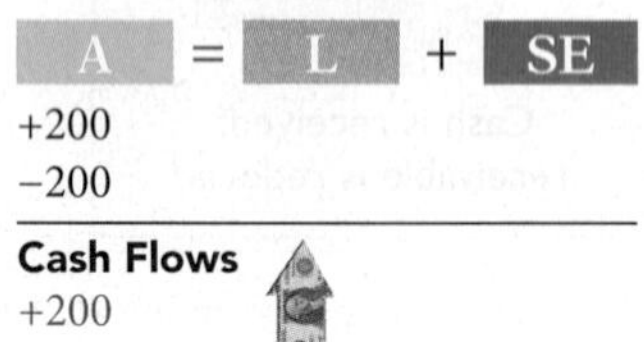

On November 10, Sierra receives cash of $200 for the services performed in October and makes the following entry.

Nov. 10	Cash	200	
	Accounts Receivable		200
	(To record cash collected on account)		

The company records the collection of the receivables by a debit (increase) to Cash and a credit (decrease) to Accounts Receivable.

Illustration 4-16 summarizes the accounting for accrued revenues.

ILLUSTRATION 4-16
Accounting for accrued revenues

ACCOUNTING FOR ACCRUED REVENUES

Examples	Reason for Adjustment	Accounts Before Adjustment	Adjusting Entry
Interest, rent, services	Services performed but not yet received in cash or recorded.	Assets understated. Revenues understated.	Dr. Assets Cr. Revenues

ACCRUED EXPENSES

ETHICS NOTE

A report released by Fannie Mae's board of directors stated that improper adjusting entries at the mortgage-finance company resulted in delayed recognition of expenses caused by interest-rate changes. The motivation for this improper accounting apparently was the desire to meet earnings targets.

Expenses incurred but not yet paid or recorded at the statement date are called **accrued expenses**. Interest, taxes, utilities, and salaries are common examples of accrued expenses.

Companies make adjustments for accrued expenses to record the obligations that exist at the balance sheet date and to recognize the expenses that apply to the current accounting period. Prior to adjustment, both liabilities and expenses are understated. Therefore, as shown in Illustration 4-17, **an adjusting entry for accrued expenses results in an increase (a debit) to an expense account and an increase (a credit) to a liability account.**

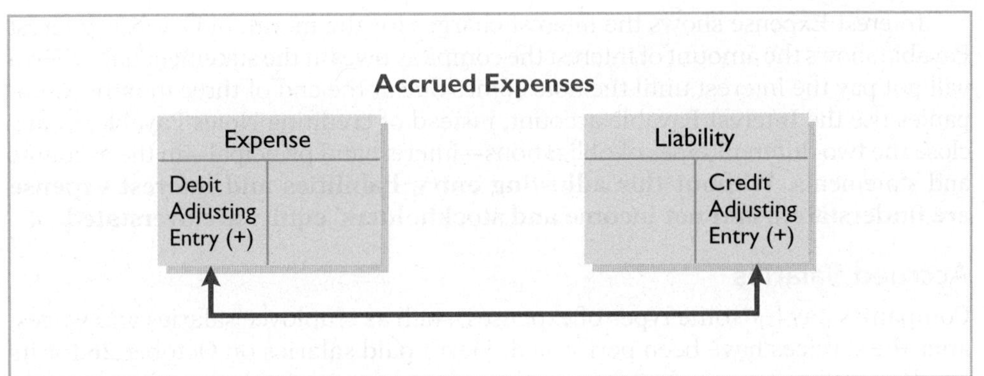

ILLUSTRATION 4-17
Adjusting entries for accrued expenses

Let's look in more detail at some specific types of accrued expenses, beginning with accrued interest.

Accrued Interest

Sierra Corporation signed a three-month note payable in the amount of $5,000 on October 1. The note requires Sierra to pay interest at an annual rate of 12%.

The amount of the interest recorded is determined by three factors: (1) the face value of the note; (2) the interest rate, which is always expressed as an annual rate; and (3) the length of time the note is outstanding. For Sierra, the total interest due on the $5,000 note at its maturity date three months in the future is $150 ($5,000 × 12% × $\frac{3}{12}$), or $50 for one month. Illustration 4-18 shows the formula for computing interest and its application to Sierra for the month of October.

Face Value of Note	×	Annual Interest Rate	×	Time in Terms of One Year	=	Interest
$5,000	×	12%	×	$\frac{1}{12}$	=	$50

ILLUSTRATION 4-18
Formula for computing interest

▼ **HELPFUL HINT**
In computing interest, we express the time period as a fraction of a year.

As Illustration 4-19 shows, the accrual of interest at October 31 increases a liability account, Interest Payable. It also decreases stockholders' equity by increasing an expense account, Interest Expense.

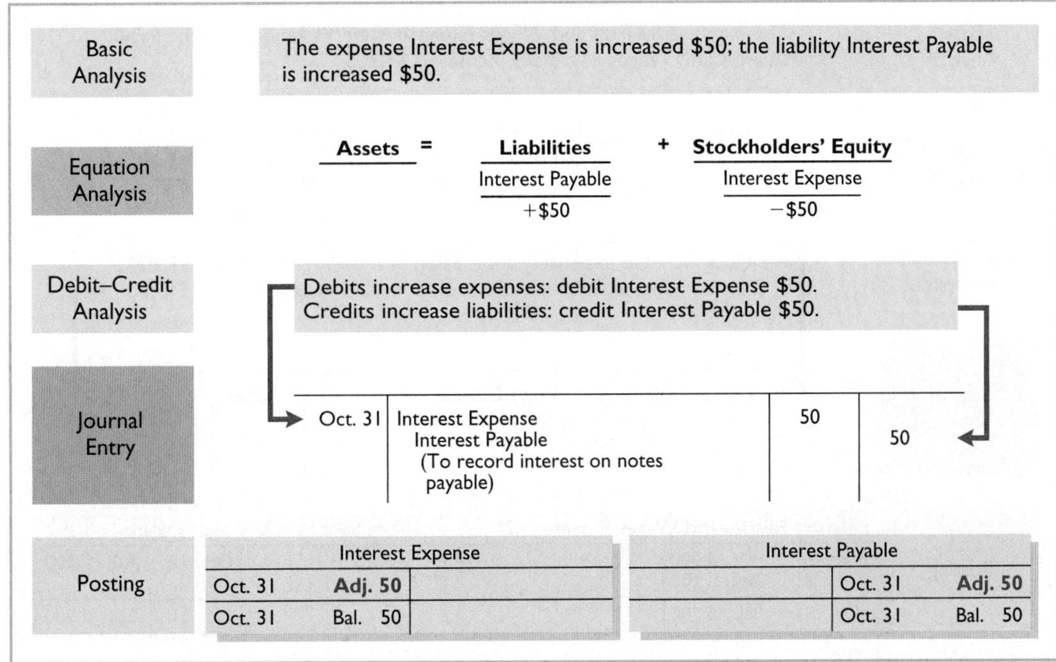

ILLUSTRATION 4-19
Adjustment for accrued interest

Interest Expense shows the interest charges for the month of October. Interest Payable shows the amount of interest the company owes at the statement date. Sierra will not pay the interest until the note comes due at the end of three months. Companies use the Interest Payable account, instead of crediting Notes Payable, to disclose the two different types of obligations—interest and principal—in the accounts and statements. **Without this adjusting entry, liabilities and interest expense are understated, and net income and stockholders' equity are overstated.**

Accrued Salaries

Companies pay for some types of expenses, such as employee salaries and wages, after the services have been performed. Sierra paid salaries on October 26 for its employees' first two weeks of work; the next payment of salaries will not occur until November 9. As Illustration 4-20 shows, three working days remain in October (October 29–31).

ILLUSTRATION 4-20
Calendar showing Sierra Corporation's pay periods

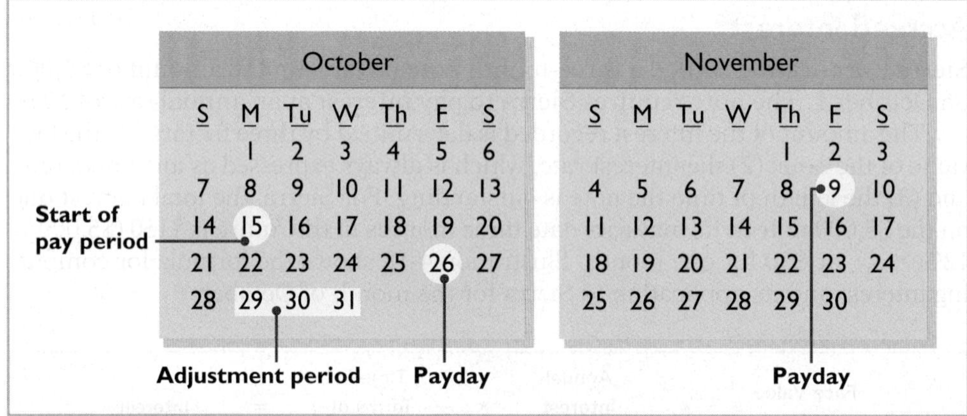

At October 31, the salaries for these three days represent an accrued expense and a related liability to Sierra. The employees receive total salaries of $2,000 for a five-day work week, or $400 per day. Thus, accrued salaries at October 31 are $1,200 ($400 × 3). This accrual increases a liability, Salaries and Wages Payable. It also decreases stockholders' equity by increasing an expense account, Salaries and Wages Expense, as shown in Illustration 4-21.

ILLUSTRATION 4-21
Adjustment for accrued salaries

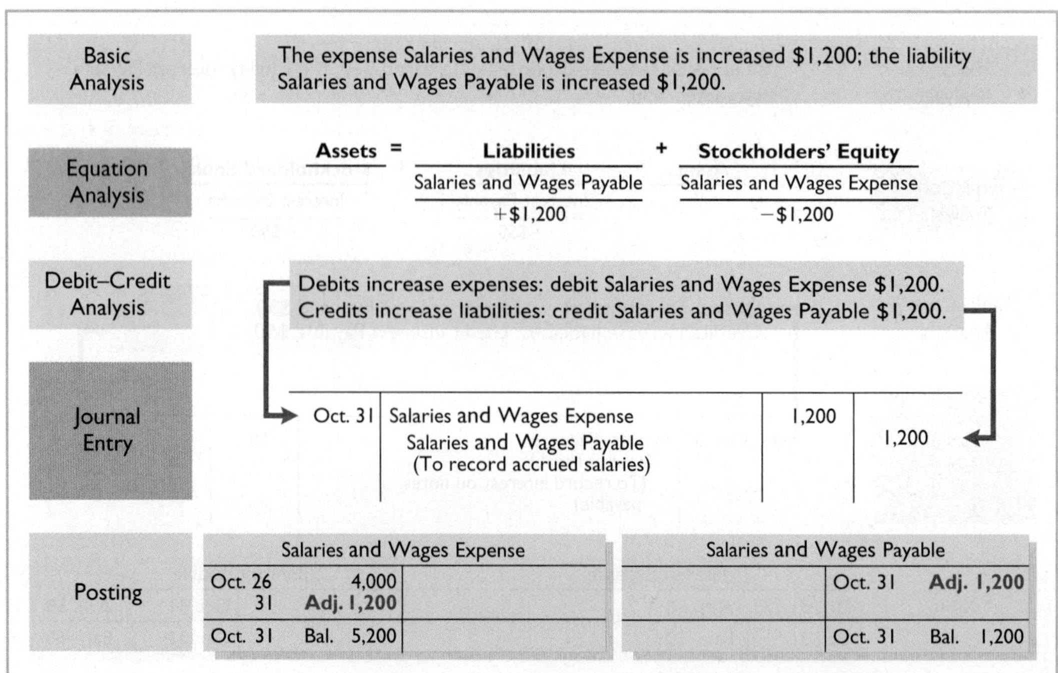

After this adjustment, the balance in Salaries and Wages Expense of $5,200 (13 days × $400) is the actual salary expense for October. (The employees worked 13 days in October after beginning work on October 15.) The balance in Salaries and Wages Payable of $1,200 is the amount of the liability for salaries Sierra owes as of October 31. **Without the $1,200 adjustment for salaries, Sierra's expenses are understated $1,200 and its liabilities are understated $1,200.**

Sierra pays salaries every two weeks. Consequently, the next payday is November 9, when the company will again pay total salaries of $4,000. The payment consists of $1,200 of salaries and wages payable at October 31 plus $2,800 of salaries and wages expense for November (7 working days as shown in the November calendar × $400). Therefore, Sierra makes the following entry on November 9.

Nov. 9	Salaries and Wages Payable	1,200	
	Salaries and Wages Expense	2,800	
	Cash		4,000
	(To record November 9 payroll)		

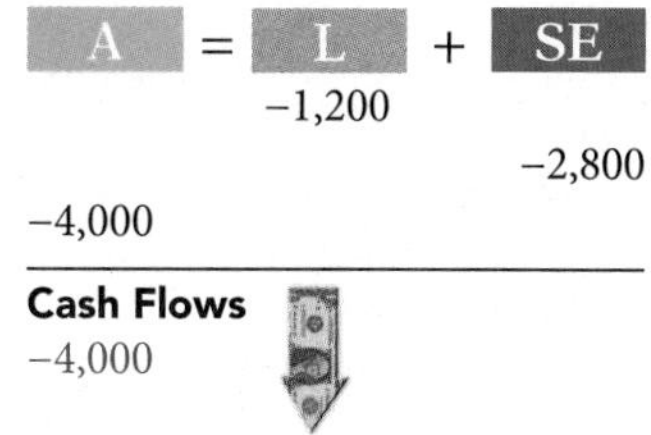

This entry eliminates the liability for Salaries and Wages Payable that Sierra recorded in the October 31 adjusting entry, and it records the proper amount of Salaries and Wages Expense for the period between November 1 and November 9.

Illustration 4-22 summarizes the accounting for accrued expenses.

ILLUSTRATION 4-22
Accounting for accrued expenses

ACCOUNTING FOR ACCRUED EXPENSES

Examples	Reason for Adjustment	Accounts Before Adjustment	Adjusting Entry
Interest, rent, salaries	Expenses have been incurred but not yet paid in cash or recorded.	Expenses understated. Liabilities understated.	Dr. Expenses Cr. Liabilities

PEOPLE, PLANET, AND PROFIT INSIGHT

© Nathan Gleave/iStockphoto

Got Junk?

Do you have an old computer or two in your garage? How about an old TV that needs replacing? Many people do. Approximately 163,000 computers and televisions become obsolete **each day**. Yet, in a recent year, only 11% of computers were recycled. It is estimated that 75% of all computers ever sold are sitting in storage somewhere, waiting to be disposed of. Each of these old TVs and computers is loaded with lead, cadmium, mercury, and other toxic chemicals. If you have one of these electronic gadgets, you have a responsibility, and a probable cost, for disposing of it. Companies have the same problem, but their discarded materials may include lead paint, asbestos, and other toxic chemicals.

What accounting issue might this cause for companies? (Go to WileyPLUS for this answer and additional questions.)

SUMMARY OF BASIC RELATIONSHIPS

Illustration 4-23 (page 168) summarizes the four basic types of adjusting entries. Take some time to study and analyze the adjusting entries. Be sure to note that **each adjusting entry affects one balance sheet account and one income statement account.**

ILLUSTRATION 4-23
Summary of adjusting entries

Type of Adjustment	Accounts Before Adjustment	Adjusting Entry
Prepaid expenses	Assets overstated. Expenses understated.	Dr. Expenses Cr. Assets or Contra Assets
Unearned revenues	Liabilities overstated. Revenues understated.	Dr. Liabilities Cr. Revenues
Accrued revenues	Assets understated. Revenues understated.	Dr. Assets Cr. Revenues
Accrued expenses	Expenses understated. Liabilities understated.	Dr. Expenses Cr. Liabilities

Illustrations 4-24 and 4-25 show the journalizing and posting of adjusting entries for Sierra Corporation on October 31. When reviewing the general ledger in Illustration 4-25, note that for learning purposes we have highlighted the adjustments in red.

ILLUSTRATION 4-24
General journal showing adjusting entries

GENERAL JOURNAL

Date	Account Titles and Explanation	Debit	Credit
2017	Adjusting Entries		
Oct. 31	Supplies Expense	1,500	
	Supplies		1,500
	(To record supplies used)		
31	Insurance Expense	50	
	Prepaid Insurance		50
	(To record insurance expired)		
31	Depreciation Expense	40	
	Accumulated Depreciation—Equipment		40
	(To record monthly depreciation)		
31	Unearned Service Revenue	400	
	Service Revenue		400
	(To record revenue for services performed)		
31	Accounts Receivable	200	
	Service Revenue		200
	(To record revenue for services performed)		
31	Interest Expense	50	
	Interest Payable		50
	(To record interest on notes payable)		
31	Salaries and Wages Expense	1,200	
	Salaries and Wages Payable		1,200
	(To record accrued salaries)		

ILLUSTRATION 4-25
General ledger after adjustments

GENERAL LEDGER

Cash			
Oct. 1	10,000	Oct. 2	5,000
1	5,000	3	900
2	1,200	4	600
3	10,000	20	500
		26	4,000
Oct. 31 Bal.	15,200		

Accounts Receivable			
Oct. 31	**200**		
Oct. 31 Bal.	200		

Supplies			
Oct. 5	2,500	Oct. 31	**1,500**
Oct. 31 Bal.	1,000		

Prepaid Insurance			
Oct. 4	600	Oct. 31	**50**
Oct. 31 Bal.	550		

Equipment			
Oct. 2	5,000		
Oct. 31 Bal.	5,000		

Accumulated Depreciation—Equipment			
		Oct. 31	**40**
		Oct. 31 Bal.	40

Notes Payable			
		Oct. 1	5,000
		Oct. 31 Bal.	5,000

Accounts Payable			
		Oct. 5	2,500
		Oct. 31 Bal.	2,500

Interest Payable			
		Oct. 31	**50**
		Oct. 31 Bal.	50

Unearned Service Revenue			
Oct. 31	**400**	Oct. 2	1,200
		Oct. 31 Bal.	800

Salaries and Wages Payable			
		Oct. 31	**1,200**
		Oct. 31 Bal.	1,200

Common Stock			
		Oct. 1	10,000
		Oct. 31 Bal.	10,000

Retained Earnings			
		Oct. 31 Bal.	0

Dividends			
Oct. 20	500		
Oct. 31 Bal.	500		

Service Revenue			
		Oct. 3	10,000
		31	**400**
		31	**200**
		Oct. 31 Bal.	10,600

Salaries and Wages Expense			
Oct. 26	4,000		
31	**1,200**		
Oct. 31 Bal.	5,200		

Supplies Expense			
Oct. 31	**1,500**		
Oct. 31 Bal.	1,500		

Rent Expense			
Oct. 3	900		
Oct. 31 Bal.	900		

Insurance Expense			
Oct. 31	**50**		
Oct. 31 Bal.	50		

Interest Expense			
Oct. 31	**50**		
Oct. 31 Bal.	50		

Depreciation Expense			
Oct. 31	**40**		
Oct. 31 Bal.	40		

DO IT! 3 Adjusting Entries for Accruals

Micro Computer Services Inc. began operations on August 1, 2017. At the end of August 2017, management attempted to prepare monthly financial statements. The following information relates to August.

1. At August 31, the company owed its employees $800 in salaries that will be paid on September 1.
2. On August 1, the company borrowed $30,000 from a local bank on a 15-year mortgage. The annual interest rate is 10%.
3. Revenue for services performed but unrecorded for August totaled $1,100.

Prepare the adjusting entries needed at August 31, 2017.

Action Plan

✔ Make adjusting entries at the end of the period to recognize revenue for services performed and for expenses incurred.

✔ Don't forget to make adjusting entries for accruals. Adjusting entries for accruals will increase both a balance sheet and an income statement account.

SOLUTION

	Debit	Credit
1. Salaries and Wages Expense	800	
Salaries and Wages Payable		800
(To record accrued salaries)		
2. Interest Expense	250	
Interest Payable		250
(To record accrued interest: $\$30,000 \times 10\% \times \frac{1}{12} = \$250$)		
3. Accounts Receivable	1,100	
Service Revenue		1,100
(To record revenue for services performed)		

Related exercise material: **BE4-8, DO IT! 4-3, E4-8, E4-9, E4-10, E4-11, E4-12, E4-13, E4-14, E4-15, E4-16, E4-17,** and **E4-18.**

LEARNING OBJECTIVE 4 Prepare an adjusted trial balance and closing entries.

ANALYZE → JOURNALIZE → POST → TRIAL BALANCE → ADJUSTING ENTRIES → **Adjusted trial balance** → **Prepare financial statements** → **Journalize and post closing entries** → **Prepare a post-closing trial balance**

After a company has journalized and posted all adjusting entries, it prepares another trial balance from the ledger accounts. This trial balance is called an **adjusted trial balance.** It shows the balances of all accounts, including those adjusted, at the end of the accounting period. The purpose of an adjusted trial balance is to **prove the equality** of the total debit balances and the total credit balances in the ledger after all adjustments. Because the accounts contain all data needed for financial statements, the adjusted trial balance is the **primary basis for the preparation of financial statements**.

PREPARING THE ADJUSTED TRIAL BALANCE

Illustration 4-26 presents the adjusted trial balance for Sierra Corporation prepared from the ledger accounts in Illustration 4-25. The amounts affected by the adjusting entries are highlighted in red.

ILLUSTRATION 4-26
Adjusted trial balance

SIERRA CORPORATION
Adjusted Trial Balance
October 31, 2017

	Debit	Credit
Cash	$ 15,200	
Accounts Receivable	**200**	
Supplies	**1,000**	
Prepaid Insurance	**550**	
Equipment	5,000	
Accumulated Depreciation—Equipment		$ **40**
Notes Payable		5,000
Accounts Payable		2,500
Interest Payable		**50**
Unearned Service Revenue		**800**
Salaries and Wages Payable		**1,200**
Common Stock		10,000
Retained Earnings		0
Dividends	500	
Service Revenue		**10,600**
Salaries and Wages Expense	**5,200**	
Supplies Expense	**1,500**	
Rent Expense	900	
Insurance Expense	**50**	
Interest Expense	**50**	
Depreciation Expense	**40**	
	$30,190	**$30,190**

PREPARING FINANCIAL STATEMENTS

Companies can prepare financial statements directly from an adjusted trial balance. Illustrations 4-27 (page 172) and 4-28 (page 173) present the relationships between the data in the adjusted trial balance of Sierra Corporation and the corresponding financial statements. As Illustration 4-27 shows, companies prepare the income statement from the revenue and expense accounts. Similarly, they derive the retained earnings statement from the Retained Earnings account, Dividends account, and the net income (or net loss) shown in the income statement. As Illustration 4-28 shows, companies then prepare the balance sheet from the asset, liability, and stockholders' equity accounts. They obtain the amount reported for retained earnings on the balance sheet from the ending balance in the retained earnings statement.

ILLUSTRATION 4-27
Preparation of the income statement and retained earnings statement from the adjusted trial balance

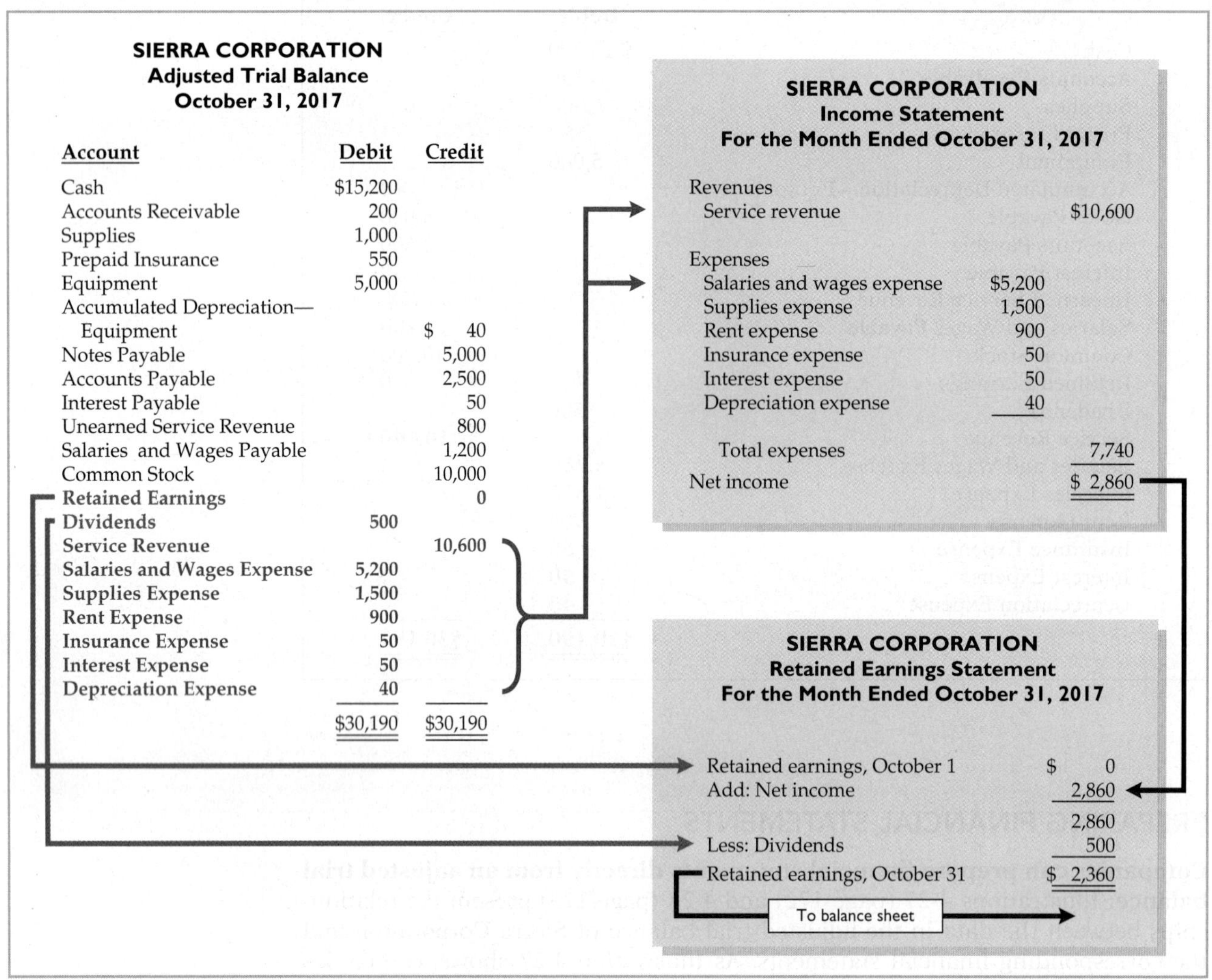

SIERRA CORPORATION
Adjusted Trial Balance
October 31, 2017

Account	Debit	Credit
Cash	$15,200	
Accounts Receivable	200	
Supplies	1,000	
Prepaid Insurance	550	
Equipment	5,000	
Accumulated Depreciation—Equipment		$ 40
Notes Payable		5,000
Accounts Payable		2,500
Interest Payable		50
Unearned Service Revenue		800
Salaries and Wages Payable		1,200
Common Stock		10,000
Retained Earnings		0
Dividends	500	
Service Revenue		10,600
Salaries and Wages Expense	5,200	
Supplies Expense	1,500	
Rent Expense	900	
Insurance Expense	50	
Interest Expense	50	
Depreciation Expense	40	
	$30,190	$30,190

SIERRA CORPORATION
Income Statement
For the Month Ended October 31, 2017

Revenues		
Service revenue		$10,600
Expenses		
Salaries and wages expense	$5,200	
Supplies expense	1,500	
Rent expense	900	
Insurance expense	50	
Interest expense	50	
Depreciation expense	40	
Total expenses		7,740
Net income		$ 2,860

SIERRA CORPORATION
Retained Earnings Statement
For the Month Ended October 31, 2017

Retained earnings, October 1	$ 0
Add: Net income	2,860
	2,860
Less: Dividends	500
Retained earnings, October 31	$ 2,360

QUALITY OF EARNINGS

Companies and employees are continually under pressure to "make the numbers"—that is, to have earnings that are in line with expectations. Therefore, it is not surprising that many companies practice earnings management. **Earnings management** is the planned timing of revenues, expenses, gains, and losses to smooth out bumps in net income. The quality of earnings is greatly affected when a company manages earnings up or down to meet some targeted earnings number. A company that has a high **quality of earnings** provides full and transparent information that will not confuse or mislead financial statement users. A company with questionable quality of earnings may mislead investors and creditors, who believe they are relying on relevant information that provides a faithful representation of the company. As a result, investors and creditors lose confidence in financial reporting, and it becomes difficult for our capital markets to work efficiently.

Companies manage earnings in a variety of ways. One way is through the use of **one-time items** to prop up earnings numbers. For example, ConAgra Foods

ILLUSTRATION 4-28
Preparation of the balance sheet from the adjusted trial balance

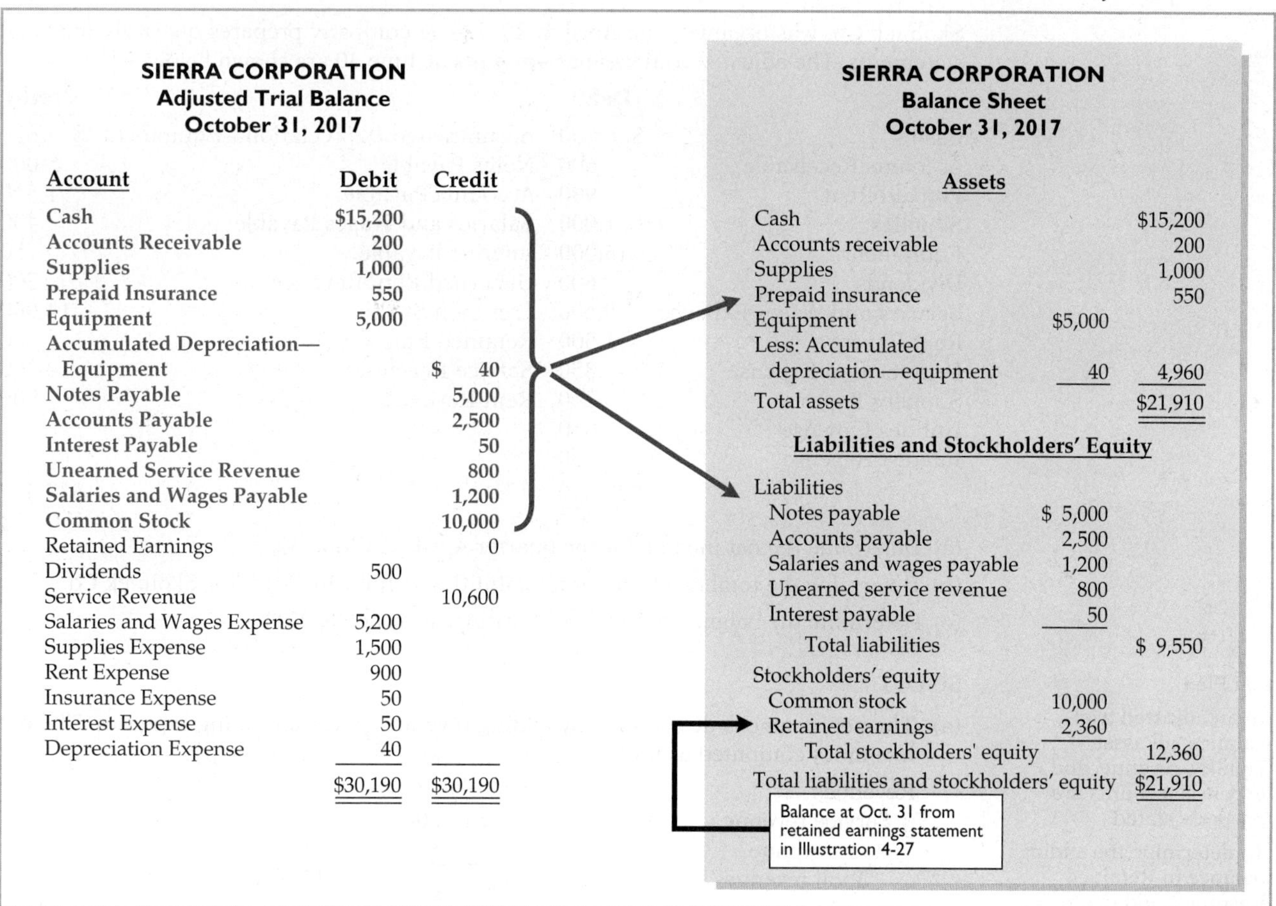

SIERRA CORPORATION
Adjusted Trial Balance
October 31, 2017

Account	Debit	Credit
Cash	$15,200	
Accounts Receivable	200	
Supplies	1,000	
Prepaid Insurance	550	
Equipment	5,000	
Accumulated Depreciation—Equipment		$ 40
Notes Payable		5,000
Accounts Payable		2,500
Interest Payable		50
Unearned Service Revenue		800
Salaries and Wages Payable		1,200
Common Stock		10,000
Retained Earnings		0
Dividends	500	
Service Revenue		10,600
Salaries and Wages Expense	5,200	
Supplies Expense	1,500	
Rent Expense	900	
Insurance Expense	50	
Interest Expense	50	
Depreciation Expense	40	
	$30,190	$30,190

SIERRA CORPORATION
Balance Sheet
October 31, 2017

Assets		
Cash		$15,200
Accounts receivable		200
Supplies		1,000
Prepaid insurance		550
Equipment	$5,000	
Less: Accumulated depreciation—equipment	40	4,960
Total assets		$21,910
Liabilities and Stockholders' Equity		
Liabilities		
Notes payable	$ 5,000	
Accounts payable	2,500	
Salaries and wages payable	1,200	
Unearned service revenue	800	
Interest payable	50	
Total liabilities		$ 9,550
Stockholders' equity		
Common stock	10,000	
Retained earnings	2,360	
Total stockholders' equity		12,360
Total liabilities and stockholders' equity		$21,910

recorded a non-recurring gain from the sale of Pilgrim's Pride stock for $186 million to help meet an earnings projection for the quarter.

Another way is to **inflate revenue** numbers in the short-run to the detriment of the long-run. For example, Bristol-Myers Squibb provided sales incentives to its wholesalers to encourage them to buy products at the end of the quarter (often referred to as channel-stuffing). This practice allowed Bristol-Myers to meet its sales projections. The problem was that the wholesalers could not sell that amount of merchandise and ended up returning it to Bristol-Myers. The result was that Bristol-Myers had to restate its income numbers.

Companies also manage earnings through **improper adjusting entries**. Regulators investigated Xerox for accusations that it was booking too much revenue upfront on multi-year contract sales. Financial executives at Office Max resigned amid accusations that the company was recognizing rebates from its vendors too early and therefore overstating revenue. Finally, WorldCom's abuse of adjusting entries to meet its net income targets is unsurpassed. It used adjusting entries to increase net income by reclassifying liabilities as revenue and reclassifying expenses as assets. Investigations of the company's books after it went bankrupt revealed adjusting entries of more than a billion dollars that had no supporting documentation.

DO IT! 4a Trial Balance

Skolnick Co. was organized on April 1, 2017. The company prepares quarterly financial statements. The adjusted trial balance amounts at June 30 are shown below.

	Debit		Credit
Cash	$ 6,700	Accumulated Depreciation—Equipment	$ 850
Accounts Receivable	600	Notes Payable	5,000
Prepaid Rent	900	Accounts Payable	1,510
Supplies	1,000	Salaries and Wages Payable	400
Equipment	15,000	Interest Payable	50
Dividends	600	Unearned Rent Revenue	500
Salaries and Wages Expense	9,400	Common Stock	14,000
Rent Expense	1,500	Retained Earning	0
Depreciation Expense	850	Service Revenue	14,200
Supplies Expense	200	Rent Revenue	800
Utilities Expense	510		
Interest Expense	50		
	$37,310		$37,310

(a) Determine the net income for the quarter April 1 to June 30.

(b) Determine the total assets and total liabilities at June 30, 2017, for Skolnick Co.

(c) Determine the balance in Retained Earnings at June 30, 2017.

Action Plan

✔ **In an adjusted trial balance, all asset, liability, revenue, and expense accounts are properly stated.**

✔ **To determine the ending balance in Retained Earnings, add net income and subtract dividends.**

SOLUTION

(a) The net income is determined by adding revenues and subtracting expenses. The net income is computed as follows.

Revenues		
Service revenue	$14,200	
Rent revenue	800	
Total revenues		$15,000
Expenses		
Salaries and wages expense	9,400	
Rent expense	1,500	
Depreciation expense	850	
Utilities expense	510	
Supplies expense	200	
Interest expense	50	
Total expenses		12,510
Net income		$ 2,490

(b) Total assets and liabilities are computed as follows.

Assets			Liabilities	
Cash		$ 6,700	Notes payable	$5,000
Accounts receivable		600	Accounts payable	1,510
Supplies		1,000	Unearned rent revenue	500
Prepaid rent		900	Salaries and wages payable	400
Equipment	$15,000		Interest payable	50
Less: Accumulated depreciation—equipment	850	14,150		
Total assets		$23,350	Total liabilities	$7,460

(c)

Retained earnings, April 1	$ 0
Add: Net income	2,490
Less: Dividends	600
Retained earnings, June 30	$1,890

Related exercise material: **BE4-9, BE4-10, BE4-11, BE4-12, DO IT! 4-4a, E4-21,** and **E4-22.**

CLOSING THE BOOKS

In previous chapters, you learned that revenue and expense accounts and the Dividends account are subdivisions of retained earnings, which is reported in the stockholders' equity section of the balance sheet. Because revenues, expenses, and dividends relate only to a given accounting period, they are considered **temporary accounts**. In contrast, all balance sheet accounts are considered **permanent accounts** because their balances are carried forward into future accounting periods. Illustration 4-29 identifies the accounts in each category.

ALTERNATIVE TERMINOLOGY
Temporary accounts are sometimes called *nominal accounts*, and permanent accounts are sometimes called *real accounts*.

ILLUSTRATION 4-29
Temporary versus permanent accounts

Temporary	Permanent
All revenue accounts All expense accounts Dividends	All asset accounts All liability accounts Stockholders' equity accounts

Preparing Closing Entries

At the end of the accounting period, companies transfer the temporary account balances to the permanent stockholders' equity account—Retained Earnings—through the preparation of closing entries. **Closing entries** transfer net income (or net loss) and dividends to Retained Earnings, so the balance in Retained Earnings agrees with the retained earnings statement. For example, in the adjusted trial balance in Illustration 4-26 (page 171), Retained Earnings has a balance of zero. Prior to the closing entries, the balance in Retained Earnings is its beginning-of-the-period balance. (For Sierra Corporation, this is zero because it is the company's first month of operations.)

In addition to updating Retained Earnings to its correct ending balance, closing entries produce a **zero balance in each temporary account**. As a result, these accounts are ready to accumulate data about revenues, expenses, and dividends that occur in the next accounting period. **Permanent accounts are not closed.**

When companies prepare closing entries, they could close each income statement account directly to Retained Earnings. However, to do so would result in excessive detail in the Retained Earnings account. Instead, companies close the revenue and expense accounts to another temporary account, **Income Summary**. The balance in Income Summary is the net income or loss for the accounting period. Income Summary is then closed, which transfers the net income or net loss from this account to Retained Earnings. Illustration 4-30 (page 176) depicts the closing process. While it still takes the average large company seven days to close, some companies such as Cisco employ technology that allows them to do a so-called "virtual close" almost instantaneously any time during the year. Besides dramatically reducing the cost of closing, the virtual close provides companies with accurate data for decision-making whenever they desire it.

ILLUSTRATION 4-30
The closing process

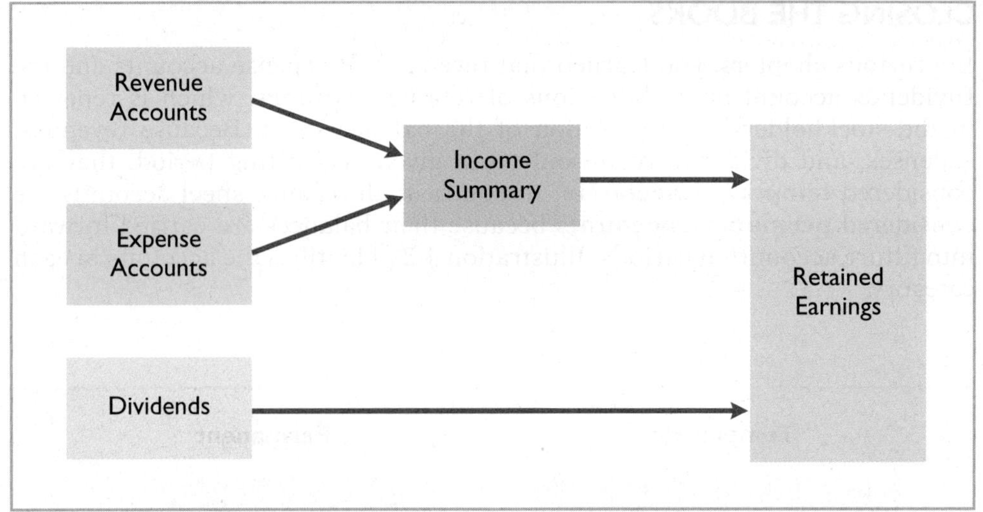

Illustration 4-31 shows the closing entries for Sierra Corporation. Illustration 4-32 (page 177) diagrams the posting process for Sierra's closing entries.

ILLUSTRATION 4-31
Closing entries journalized

GENERAL JOURNAL

Date	Account Titles and Explanation	Debit	Credit
	Closing Entries		
	(1)		
2017 Oct. 31	Service Revenue	10,600	
	Income Summary		10,600
	(To close revenue account)		
	(2)		
31	Income Summary	7,740	
	Salaries and Wages Expense		5,200
	Supplies Expense		1,500
	Rent Expense		900
	Insurance Expense		50
	Interest Expense		50
	Depreciation Expense		40
	(To close expense accounts)		
	(3)		
31	Income Summary	2,860	
	Retained Earnings		2,860
	(To close net income to retained earnings)		
	(4)		
31	Retained Earnings	500	
	Dividends		500
	(To close dividends to retained earnings)		

▼ HELPFUL HINT
Income Summary is a very descriptive title: Companies close total revenues to Income Summary and total expenses to Income Summary. The balance in Income Summary in this case is net income of $2,860.

Preparing a Post-Closing Trial Balance

After a company journalizes and posts all closing entries, it prepares another trial balance, called a **post-closing trial balance**, from the ledger. A post-closing trial balance is a list of all permanent accounts and their balances after closing entries are journalized and posted. **The purpose of this trial balance is to prove the equality of the total debit balances and total credit balances of the permanent account balances that the company carries forward into the next accounting period.** Since all temporary accounts will have zero balances, **the post-closing trial balance will contain only permanent—balance sheet—accounts.**

ILLUSTRATION 4-32
Posting of closing entries

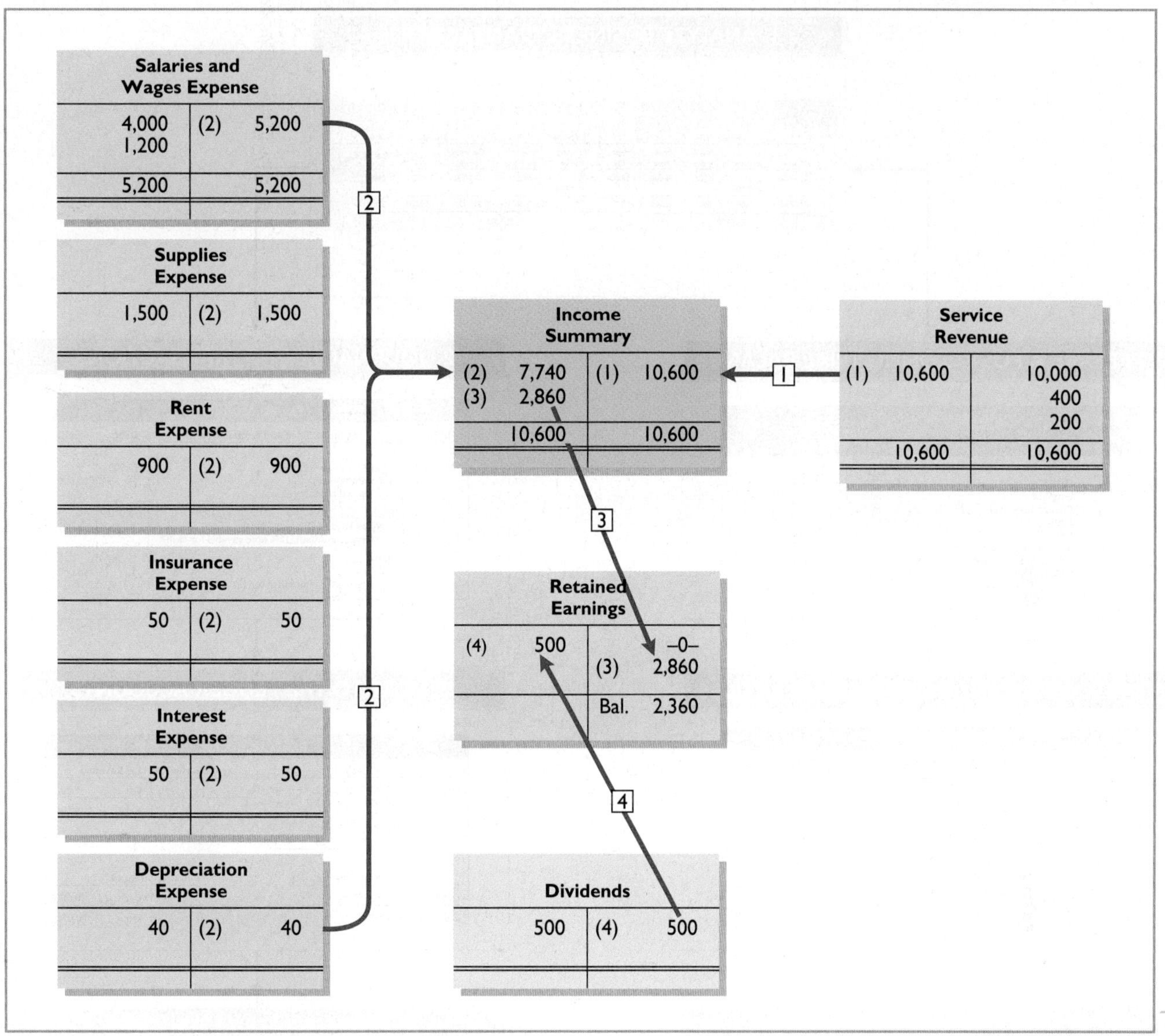

SUMMARY OF THE ACCOUNTING CYCLE

Illustration 4-33 (page 178) shows the required steps in the accounting cycle. You can see that the cycle begins with the analysis of business transactions and ends with the preparation of a post-closing trial balance. Companies perform the steps in the cycle in sequence and repeat them in each accounting period.

Steps 1–3 may occur daily during the accounting period, as explained in Chapter 3. Companies perform Steps 4–7 on a periodic basis, such as monthly, quarterly, or annually. Steps 8 and 9, closing entries and a post-closing trial balance, usually take place only at the end of a company's **annual** accounting period.

▼ **HELPFUL HINT**
Some companies reverse certain adjusting entries at the beginning of a new accounting period. The company makes a **reversing entry** at the beginning of the next accounting period. This entry is the exact opposite of the adjusting entry made in the previous period.

ILLUSTRATION 4-33
Required steps in the accounting cycle

THE ACCOUNTING CYCLE

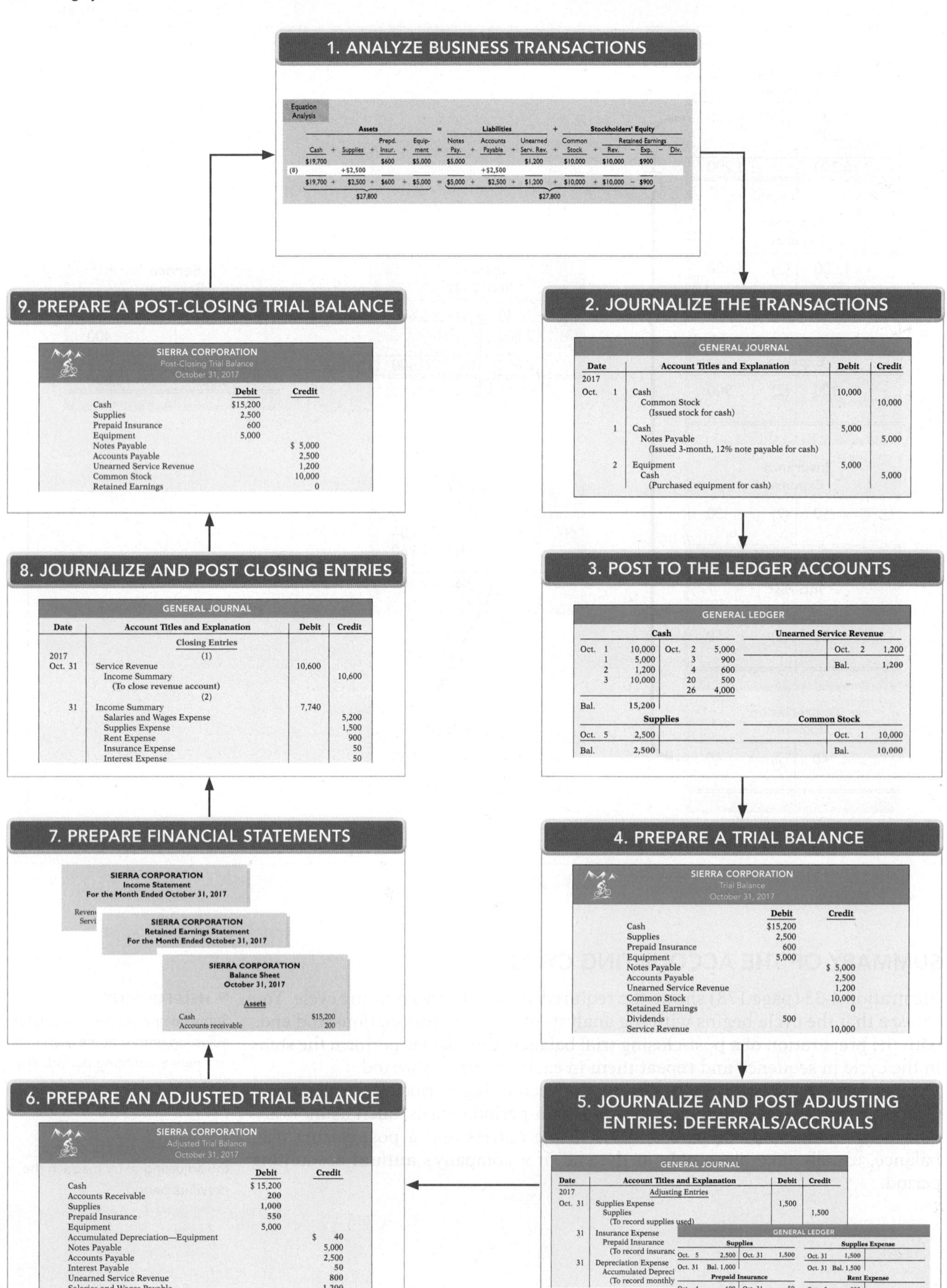

KEEPING AN EYE ON CASH

In this chapter, you learned that adjusting entries are used to adjust numbers that would otherwise be stated on a cash basis. Sierra Corporation's income statement (Illustration 4-27, page 172) shows net income of $2,860. The statement of cash flows reports a form of cash-basis income referred to as "Net cash provided by operating activities." For example, Illustration 1-8 (page 14), which shows a statement of cash flows, reports net cash provided by operating activities of $5,700 for Sierra. Net income and net cash provided by operating activities often differ. The difference for Sierra is $2,840 ($5,700 − $2,860). The following summary shows the causes of this difference of $2,840.

	Computation of Net Cash Provided by Operating Activities	Computation of Net Income
(1) Cash received in advance from customer	$ 1,200	$ 0
(2) Cash received from customers for services performed	10,000	10,000
(3) Services performed for cash received previously in (1)	0	400
(4) Services performed on account	0	200
(5) Payment of rent	(900)	(900)
(6) Purchase of insurance	(600)	0
(7) Payment of employee salaries	(4,000)	(4,000)
(8) Use of supplies	0	(1,500)
(9) Use of insurance	0	(50)
(10) Depreciation	0	(40)
(11) Interest cost incurred, but not paid	0	(50)
(12) Salaries incurred, but not paid	0	(1,200)
	$ 5,700	$ 2,860

For each item included in the computation of net cash provided by operating activities, confirm that cash was either received or paid. For each item in the income statement, confirm that revenue should be recorded because a performance obligation has been satisfied (even when cash was not received) or that an expense was incurred (even when cash was not paid).

DO IT! 4b Closing Entries

Hancock Company has the following balances in selected accounts of its adjusted trial balance.

Accounts Payable	$27,000	Dividends	$15,000
Service Revenue	98,000	Retained Earnings	42,000
Rent Expense	22,000	Accounts Receivable	38,000
Salaries and Wages Expense	51,000	Supplies Expense	7,000

Prepare the closing entries at December 31.

SOLUTION

Date	Account	Debit	Credit
Dec. 31	Service Revenue	98,000	
	Income Summary		98,000
	(To close revenue account to Income Summary)		
31	Income Summary	80,000	
	Salaries and Wages Expense		51,000
	Rent Expense		22,000
	Supplies Expense		7,000
	(To close expense accounts to Income Summary)		

Action Plan

- ✔ Close revenue and expense accounts to Income Summary.
- ✔ Close Income Summary to Retained Earnings.
- ✔ Close Dividends to Retained Earnings.

Dec. 31	Income Summary ($98,000 − $80,000)	18,000	
	Retained Earnings		18,000
	(To close net income to retained earnings)		
31	Retained Earnings	15,000	
	Dividends		15,000
	(To close dividends to retained earnings)		

Related exercise material: **BE4-13, BE4-14, DO IT! 4-4b, E4-19, E4-20, and E4-23.**

USING DECISION TOOLS—GROUPON, INC.

Groupon, Inc. operates online marketplaces that provide goods and services at discounted prices worldwide. Headquartered in Chicago, Illinois, it has over 11,843 employees. Suppose that the information shown in the trial balance below was taken from Groupon's 2017 financial records.

GROUPON, INC.
Adjusted Trial Balance
December 31, 2017
(in millions)

Account	Dr.	Cr.
Cash	$1,072	
Accounts Receivable	105	
Other Current Assets	224	
Equipment	377	
Accumulated Depreciation—Equipment		$ 195
Stock Investments (noncurrent)	24	
Goodwill	558	
Other Long-Term Assets	61	
Accounts and Other Payables		932
Accrued Expenses Payable		230
Other Current Liabilities		163
Notes Payable (noncurrent)		137
Common Stock		1,687
Dividends	0	
Accumulated Deficit	849	
Revenues		3,181
Cost of Goods Sold	1,643	
Selling and Administrative Expenses	1,294	
Marketing Expense	269	
Other Expense	33	
Income Tax Expense	16	
	$6,525	$6,525

INSTRUCTIONS

From the trial balance, prepare an income statement, retained earnings statement, and classified balance sheet. **Be sure to prepare them in that order since each statement depends on information determined in the preceding statement.** (*Hint:* Note that because Groupon has experienced losses, it reports an Accumulated Deficit rather than Retained Earnings. Remember that the amount of the Accumulated Deficit reported in the trial balance represents the balance at the beginning of the year.)

SOLUTION

GROUPON, INC. Income Statement For the Year Ended December 31, 2017 (in millions)		
Revenues		$3,181
Cost of goods sold	$1,643	
Selling and administrative expenses	1,294	
Marketing expense	269	
Other expense	33	
Income tax expense	16	3,255
Net loss		$ (74)

GROUPON, INC. Retained Earnings Statement For the Year Ended December 31, 2017 (in millions)	
Beginning accumulated deficit	$(849)
Less: Net loss	74
Less: Dividends	0
Ending accumulated deficit	$(923)

GROUPON, INC. Balance Sheet December 31, 2017 (in millions)		
Assets		
Current assets		
Cash	$1,072	
Accounts receivable	105	
Other current assets	224	
Total current assets		$1,401
Long-term investments		
Stock investments		24
Property, plant, and equipment		
Equipment	377	
Accumulated depreciation—equipment	195	182
Intangible assets		
Goodwill		558
Other long-term assets		61
Total assets		$2,226
Liabilities and Stockholders' Equity		
Liabilities		
Current liabilities		
Accounts and other payables	$ 932	
Accrued expenses payable	230	
Other current liabilities	163	
Total current liabilities		$1,325
Long-term liabilities		
Notes payable		137
Total liabilities		1,462
Stockholders' equity		
Common stock	1,687	
Accumulated deficit	(923)	
Total stockholders' equity		764
Total liabilities and stockholders' equity		$2,226

LEARNING OBJECTIVE *5

APPENDIX 4A: Describe the purpose and the basic form of a worksheet.

In Chapter 4, we used T-accounts and trial balances to arrive at the amounts used to prepare financial statements. Accountants frequently use a device known as a worksheet to determine these amounts. A **worksheet** is a multiple-column form that may be used in the adjustment process and in preparing financial statements. Accountants can prepare worksheets manually, but today most use computer spreadsheets.

As its name suggests, the worksheet is a working tool for the accountant. **A worksheet is not a permanent accounting record**; it is neither a journal nor a part of the general ledger. The worksheet is merely a supplemental device used to make it easier to prepare adjusting entries and the financial statements. Small companies with relatively few accounts and adjustments may not need a worksheet. In large companies with numerous accounts and many adjustments, a worksheet is almost indispensable.

Illustration 4A-1 shows the basic form and procedures for preparing a worksheet. Note the headings. The worksheet starts with two columns for the Trial Balance. The next two columns record all Adjustments. Next is the Adjusted Trial Balance. The last two sets of columns correspond to the Income Statement and the Balance Sheet. All items listed in the Adjusted Trial Balance columns are included in either the Income Statement or the Balance Sheet columns.

ILLUSTRATION 4A-1
Form and procedure for a worksheet

Sierra Corporation.xls

Home | Insert | Page Layout | Formulas | Data | Review | View

P18 | fx

SIERRA CORPORATION
Worksheet
For the Month Ended October 31, 2017

	A	B	C	D	E	F	G	H	I	J	K
5–6		Trial Balance		Adjustments		Adjusted Trial Balance		Income Statement		Balance Sheet	
7	Account Titles	Dr.	Cr.	Dr.	Cr.	Dr.	Cr.	Dr.	Cr.	Dr.	Cr.
8	Cash	15,200				15,200				15,200	
9	Supplies	2,500			(a) 1,500	1,000				1,000	
10	Prepaid Insurance	600			(b) 50	550				550	
11	Equipment	5,000				5,000				5,000	
12	Notes Payable		5,000				5,000				5,000
13	Accounts Payable		2,500				2,500				2,500
14	Unearned Service Revenue		1,200	(d) 400			800				800
15	Common Stock		10,000				10,000				10,000
16	Retained Earnings		–0–				–0–				–0–
17	Dividends	500				500				500	
18	Service Revenue		10,000		(d) 400		10,600		10,600		
19					(e) 200						
20	Salaries and Wages Expense	4,000		(g) 1,200		5,200		5,200			
21	Rent Expense	900				900		900			
22	Totals	28,700	28,700								
23											
24	Supplies Expense			(a) 1,500		1,500		1,500			
25	Insurance Expense			(b) 50		50		50			
26	Accum. Depreciation—										
27	Equipment				(c) 40		40				40
28	Depreciation Expense			(c) 40		40		40			
29	Interest Expense			(f) 50		50		50			
30	Accounts Receivable			(e) 200		200				200	
31	Interest Payable				(f) 50		50				50
32	Salaries and Wages Payable				(g) 1,200		1,200				1,200
33	Totals			3,440	3,440	30,190	30,190	7,740	10,600	22,450	19,590
34											
35	Net Income							2,860			2,860
36	Totals							10,600	10,600	22,450	22,450

1 Prepare a trial balance on the worksheet

2 Enter adjustment data

3 Enter adjusted balances

4 Extend adjusted balances to appropriate statement columns

5 Total the statement columns, compute net income (or net loss), and complete worksheet

REVIEW AND PRACTICE

LEARNING OBJECTIVES REVIEW

1 Explain the accrual basis of accounting and the reasons for adjusting entries. The revenue recognition principle dictates that companies recognize revenue when a performance obligation has been satisfied. The expense recognition principle dictates that companies recognize expenses in the period when the company makes efforts to generate those revenues.

Under the cash basis, companies record events only in the periods in which the company receives or pays cash. Accrual-based accounting means that companies record, in the periods in which the events occur, events that change a company's financial statements even if cash has not been exchanged.

Companies make adjusting entries at the end of an accounting period. These entries ensure that companies record revenues in the period in which the performance obligation is satisfied and that companies recognize expenses in the period in which they are incurred. The major types of adjusting entries are prepaid expenses, unearned revenues, accrued revenues, and accrued expenses.

2 Prepare adjusting entries for deferrals. Deferrals are either prepaid expenses or unearned revenues. Companies make adjusting entries for deferrals at the statement date to record the portion of the deferred item that represents the expense incurred or the revenue for services performed in the current accounting period.

3 Prepare adjusting entries for accruals. Accruals are either accrued revenues or accrued expenses. Adjusting entries for accruals record revenues for services performed and expenses incurred in the current accounting period that have not been recognized through daily entries.

4 Prepare an adjusted trial balance and closing entries. An adjusted trial balance is a trial balance that shows the balances of all accounts, including those that have been adjusted, at the end of an accounting period. The purpose of an adjusted trial balance is to show the effects of all financial events that have occurred during the accounting period.

One purpose of closing entries is to transfer net income or net loss for the period to Retained Earnings. A second purpose is to "zero-out" all temporary accounts (revenue accounts, expense accounts, and Dividends) so that they start each new period with a zero balance. To accomplish this, companies "close" all temporary accounts at the end of an accounting period. They make separate entries to close revenues and expenses to Income Summary, Income Summary to Retained Earnings, and Dividends to Retained Earnings. Only temporary accounts are closed.

The required steps in the accounting cycle are (a) analyze business transactions, (b) journalize the transactions, (c) post to ledger accounts, (d) prepare a trial balance, (e) journalize and post adjusting entries, (f) prepare an adjusted trial balance, (g) prepare financial statements, (h) journalize and post closing entries, and (i) prepare a post-closing trial balance.

***5 Describe the purpose and the basic form of a worksheet.** The worksheet is a device to make it easier to prepare adjusting entries and the financial statements. Companies often prepare a worksheet using a computer spreadsheet. The sets of columns of the worksheet are, from left to right, the unadjusted trial balance, adjustments, adjusted trial balance, income statement, and balance sheet.

DECISION TOOLS REVIEW

DECISION CHECKPOINTS	INFO NEEDED FOR DECISION	TOOL TO USE FOR DECISION	HOW TO EVALUATE RESULTS
At what point should the company record revenue?	Need to understand the nature of the company's business	Record revenue in the period in which the performance obligation is satisfied.	Recognizing revenue too early overstates current period revenue; recognizing it too late understates current period revenue.
At what point should the company record expenses?	Need to understand the nature of the company's business	Expenses should "follow" revenues—that is, match the effort (expense) with the result (revenue).	Recognizing expenses too early overstates current period expense; recognizing them too late understates current period expense.

GLOSSARY REVIEW

Accrual-basis accounting Accounting basis in which companies record, in the periods in which the events occur, transactions that change a company's financial statements, even if cash was not exchanged. (p. 153).

Accrued expenses Expenses incurred but not yet paid in cash or recorded. (p. 164).

Accrued revenues Revenues for services performed but not yet received in cash or recorded. (p. 163).

Adjusted trial balance A list of accounts and their balances after all adjustments have been made. (p. 170).

Adjusting entries Entries made at the end of an accounting period to ensure that the revenue recognition and expense recognition principles are followed. (p. 154).

Book value The difference between the cost of a depreciable asset and its related accumulated depreciation. (p. 160).

Cash-basis accounting Accounting basis in which a company records revenue only when it receives cash and an expense only when it pays cash. (p. 153).

Closing entries Entries at the end of an accounting period to transfer the balances of temporary accounts to a permanent stockholders' equity account, Retained Earnings. (p. 175).

Contra asset account An account that is offset against an asset account on the balance sheet. (p. 159).

Depreciation The process of allocating the cost of an asset to expense over its useful life. (p. 159).

Earnings management The planned timing of revenues, expenses, gains, and losses to smooth out bumps in net income. (p. 172).

Expense recognition principle (matching principle) The principle that matches expenses with revenues in the period when the company makes efforts to generate those revenues. (p. 152).

Fiscal year An accounting period that is one year long. (p. 152, in margin).

Income Summary A temporary account used in closing revenue and expense accounts. (p. 175).

Periodicity assumption An assumption that the economic life of a business can be divided into artificial time periods. (p. 152).

Permanent accounts Balance sheet accounts whose balances are carried forward to the next accounting period. (p. 175).

Post-closing trial balance A list of permanent accounts and their balances after a company has journalized and posted closing entries. (p. 176).

Prepaid expenses (prepayments) Expenses paid in cash before they are used or consumed. (p. 156).

Quality of earnings Indicates the level of full and transparent information that a company provides to users of its financial statements. (p. 172).

Revenue recognition principle The principle that companies recognize revenue in the accounting period in which the performance obligation is satisfied. (p. 152).

Reversing entry An entry made at the beginning of the next accounting period; the exact opposite of the adjusting entry made in the previous period. (p. 177, in margin).

Temporary accounts Revenue, expense, and dividend accounts whose balances a company transfers to Retained Earnings at the end of an accounting period. (p. 175).

Unearned revenues Cash received and a liability recorded before services are performed. (p. 160).

Useful life The length of service of a productive asset. (p. 158).

***Worksheet** A multiple-column form that companies may use in the adjustment process and in preparing financial statements. (p. 182).

PRACTICE MULTIPLE-CHOICE QUESTIONS

(LO 1) 1. What is the periodicity assumption?
   (a) Companies should recognize revenue in the accounting period in which services are performed.
   (b) Companies should match expenses with revenues.
   (c) The economic life of a business can be divided into artificial time periods.
   (d) The fiscal year should correspond with the calendar year.

(LO 1) 2. Which principle dictates that efforts (expenses) be recorded with accomplishments (revenues)?
   (a) Expense recognition principle.
   (b) Historical cost principle.
   (c) Periodicity principle.
   (d) Revenue recognition principle.

(LO 1) 3. Which one of these statements about the accrual basis of accounting is **false**?
   (a) Companies record events that change their financial statements in the period in which events occur, even if cash was not exchanged.
   (b) Companies recognize revenue in the period in which the performance obligation is satisfied.
   (c) This basis is in accordance with generally accepted accounting principles.
   (d) Companies record revenue only when they receive cash and record expense only when they pay out cash.

4. Adjusting entries are made to ensure that: (LO 1)
   (a) expenses are recognized in the period in which they are incurred.
   (b) revenues are recorded in the period in which the performance obligation is satisfied.
   (c) balance sheet and income statement accounts have correct balances at the end of an accounting period.
   (d) All of the above.

5. Each of the following is a major type (or category) of adjusting entry **except**: (LO 2, 3)
   (a) prepaid expenses. (c) accrued expenses.
   (b) accrued revenues. (d) unearned expenses.

6. The trial balance shows Supplies $1,350 and Supplies Expense $0. If $600 of supplies are on hand at the end of the period, the adjusting entry is: (LO 2)

(a) Supplies	600	
Supplies Expense		600
(b) Supplies	750	
Supplies Expense		750
(c) Supplies Expense	750	
Supplies		750
(d) Supplies Expense	600	
Supplies		600

7. Adjustments for unearned revenues: (LO 2)
   (a) decrease liabilities and increase revenues.
   (b) increase liabilities and increase revenues.

(c) increase assets and increase revenues.
(d) decrease revenues and decrease assets.

(LO 2) 8. Adjustments for prepaid expenses:
(a) decrease assets and increase revenues.
(b) decrease expenses and increase assets.
(c) decrease assets and increase expenses.
(d) decrease revenues and increase assets.

(LO 2) 9. Queenan Company computes depreciation on delivery equipment at $1,000 for the month of June. The adjusting entry to record this depreciation is as follows:

(a) Depreciation Expense | 1,000 |
Accumulated Depreciation—Queenan Company | | 1,000

(b) Depreciation Expense | 1,000 |
Equipment | | 1,000

(c) Depreciation Expense | 1,000 |
Accumulated Depreciation—Equipment | | 1,000

(d) Equipment Expense | 1,000 |
Accumulated Depreciation—Equipment | | 1,000

(LO 3) 10. Adjustments for accrued revenues:
(a) increase assets and increase liabilities.
(b) increase assets and increase revenues.
(c) decrease assets and decrease revenues.
(d) decrease liabilities and increase revenues.

(LO 3) 11. Colleen Mooney earned a salary of $400 for the last week of September. She will be paid on October 1. The adjusting entry for Colleen's employer at September 30 is:
(a) No entry is required.

(b) Salaries and Wages Expense | 400 |
Salaries and Wages Payable | | 400

(c) Salaries and Wages Expense | 400 |
Cash | | 400

(d) Salaries and Wages Payable | 400 |
Cash | | 400

12. Which statement is **incorrect** concerning the adjusted trial balance? (LO 4)
(a) An adjusted trial balance proves the equality of the total debit balances and the total credit balances in the ledger after all adjustments are made.
(b) The adjusted trial balance provides the primary basis for the preparation of financial statements.
(c) The adjusted trial balance does not list temporary accounts.
(d) The company prepares the adjusted trial balance after it has journalized and posted the adjusting entries.

13. Which account will have a zero balance after a company has journalized and posted closing entries? (LO 4)
(a) Service Revenue.
(b) Supplies.
(c) Prepaid Insurance.
(d) Accumulated Depreciation.

14. Which types of accounts will appear in the post-closing trial balance? (LO 4)
(a) Permanent accounts.
(b) Temporary accounts.
(c) Expense accounts.
(d) None of the above.

15. All of the following are required steps in the accounting cycle **except**: (LO 4)
(a) journalizing and posting closing entries.
(b) preparing an adjusted trial balance.
(c) preparing a post-closing trial balance.
(d) prepare financial statements from the unadjusted trial balance.

SOLUTIONS

1. **(c)** The periodicity assumption states that the economic life of a business can be divided into artificial time periods. The other choices are incorrect because (a) this statement describes the revenue recognition principle, (b) this statement describes the expense recognition principle, and (d) the periodicity assumption states that the life of a business can be divided into artificial time periods, not that the fiscal year and calendar year must coincide.
2. **(a)** The expense recognition principle dictates that efforts (expenses) be recorded with accomplishments (revenues). The other choices are incorrect because (b) the historical cost principle states that when assets are purchased, they should be recorded at cost; (c) the periodicity assumption states that the life of a business can be divided into artificial time periods; and (d) the revenue recognition principle states that revenue should be recorded in the period in which the performance obligation is satisfied.
3. **(d)** If companies record revenue only when they receive cash and record expense only when they pay out cash, they are using the cash basis of accounting. The other choices are true statements about accrual-basis accounting.
4. **(d)** Adjusting entries are made to ensure that expenses are recognized in the period in which they are incurred, that revenues are recorded in the period in which the performance obligation is satisfied, and that balance sheet and income statement accounts have correct balances at the end of an accounting period. Although choices (a), (b), and (c) are correct, choice (d) is the better answer.
5. **(d)** Unearned expenses are not a major type of adjusting entry. Choices (a) prepaid expenses, (b) accrued revenues, and (c) accrued expenses are all a major type of adjusting entry.
6. **(c)** The adjusting entry is to debit Supplies Expense for $750 ($1,350 − $600) and credit Supplies for $750. The other choices are therefore incorrect.
7. **(a)** Adjustments for unearned revenues decrease liabilities and increase revenues. The other choices are therefore incorrect.
8. **(c)** Adjustments for prepaid expenses decrease assets and increase expenses. The other choices are therefore incorrect.

9. **(c)** The adjusting entry is to debit Depreciation Expense and credit Accumulation Depreciation—Equipment. The other choices are incorrect because (a) the contra asset account title includes the asset being depreciated, not the company name; (b) the credit should be to the contra asset account, not the asset; and (d) the debit should be to Depreciation Expense, not Equipment Expense.
10. **(b)** When the adjustment is made for accrued revenues, an asset account (usually Accounts Receivable) is increased and a revenue account is increased. The other choices are therefore incorrect.
11. **(b)** The adjusting entry should be to debit Salaries and Wages Expense $400 and credit Salaries and Wages Payable for $400. Choice (a) is incorrect because if an adjusting entry is not made, the amount of money owed (liability) that is shown on the balance sheet will be understated and the amount of salaries and wages expense will also be understated. Choices (c) and (d) are incorrect because adjusting entries never affect cash.
12. **(c)** The adjusted trial balance does list temporary accounts. The other choices are true statements about the adjusted trial balance.
13. **(a)** Service Revenue will have a zero balance after a company has journalized and posted closing entries. The other choices are incorrect because (b) Supplies is an asset, or permanent account, and will not be closed at the end of the year; (c) Prepaid Insurance is an asset, or permanent account, and will not be closed at the end of the year; and (d) Accumulated Depreciation is a contra asset account. Contra asset accounts are permanent accounts and are not closed at the end of the year.
14. **(a)** Permanent accounts are the only type of accounts that appear in the post-closing trial balance because they are not closed at the end of the accounting period. Choices (b) and (c) are temporary accounts. Choice (d) is wrong because there is a correct answer.
15. **(d)** Financial statements are prepared from the **adjusted** trial balance, not the **un**adjusted trial balance. The other choices are incorrect because (a) journalizing and posting closing entries, (b) preparing an adjusted trial balance, and (c) preparing a post-closing trial balance are all required steps in the accounting cycle.

PRACTICE EXERCISES

Prepare correct income statement.

(LO 2, 3)

1. The income statement of Bragg Co. for the month of July shows net income of $1,400 based on Service Revenue $5,500, Salaries and Wages Expense $2,300, Supplies Expense $1,200, and Utilities Expense $600. In reviewing the statement, you discover the following.

1. Insurance expired during July of $450 was omitted.
2. Supplies expense includes $300 of supplies that are still on hand at July 31.
3. Depreciation on equipment of $180 was omitted.
4. Accrued but unpaid salaries and wages at July 31 of $400 were not included.
5. Services performed but unrecorded totaled $600.

INSTRUCTIONS

Prepare a correct income statement for July 2017.

SOLUTION

1.

BRAGG CO.
Income Statement
For the Month Ended July 31, 2017

Revenues		
Service revenue ($5,500 + $600)		$6,100
Expenses		
Salaries and wages expense ($2,300 + $400)	$2,700	
Supplies expense ($1,200 − $300)	900	
Utilities expense	600	
Insurance expense	450	
Depreciation expense	180	
Total expenses		4,830
Net income		$1,270

Journalize and post closing entries, and prepare a post-closing trial balance.

(LO 4)

2. Arapaho Company ended its fiscal year on July 31, 2017. The company's adjusted trial balance as of the end of its fiscal year is as shown below.

ARAPAHO COMPANY
Adjusted Trial Balance
July 31, 2017

Account Titles	Debit	Credit
Cash	$ 15,940	
Accounts Receivable	8,580	
Equipment	16,900	
Accumulated Depreciation—Equipment		$ 7,500
Accounts Payable		4,420
Unearned Rent Revenue		1,600
Common Stock		20,500
Retained Earnings		25,000
Dividends	14,000	
Service Revenue		64,000
Rent Revenue		5,500
Depreciation Expense	4,500	
Salaries and Wages Expense	54,700	
Utilities Expense	13,900	
	$128,520	$128,520

INSTRUCTIONS

(a) Prepare the closing entries.

(b) Post to Retained Earnings and Income Summary T-accounts.

(c) Prepare a post-closing trial balance at July 31, 2017.

SOLUTION

2. (a)

GENERAL JOURNAL J15

Date	Account Titles	Debit	Credit
July 31	Service Revenue	64,000	
	Rent Revenue	5,500	
	Income Summary		69,500
	(To close revenue accounts)		
31	Income Summary	73,100	
	Depreciation Expense		4,500
	Salaries and Wages Expense		54,700
	Utilities Expense		13,900
	(To close expense accounts)		
31	Retained Earnings ($73,100 – $69,500)	3,600	
	Income Summary		3,600
	(To close net loss to retained earnings)		
31	Retained Earnings	14,000	
	Dividends		14,000
	(To close dividends to retained earnings)		

(b)

Retained Earnings

Debit	Credit
	Bal. 25,000
3,600	
14,000	
	Bal. 7,400

Income Summary

Debit	Credit
	69,500
73,100	
	3,600
	Bal. 0

(c)

ARAPAHO COMPANY Post-Closing Trial Balance July 31, 2017		
	Debit	**Credit**
Cash	$15,940	
Accounts Receivable	8,580	
Equipment	16,900	
Accumulated Depreciation—Equipment		$ 7,500
Accounts Payable		4,420
Unearned Rent Revenue		1,600
Common Stock		20,500
Retained Earnings		7,400
	$41,420	$41,420

PRACTICE PROBLEM

Prepare adjusting entries from selected data.

(LO 2, 3)

Terry Thomas and a group of investors incorporated the Green Thumb Lawn Care Corporation on April 1. At April 30, the trial balance shows the following balances for selected accounts.

Prepaid Insurance	$ 3,600
Equipment	28,000
Notes Payable	20,000
Unearned Service Revenue	4,200
Service Revenue	1,800

Analysis reveals the following additional data pertaining to these accounts.

1. Prepaid insurance is the cost of a 2-year insurance policy, effective April 1.
2. Depreciation on the equipment is $500 per month.
3. The note payable is dated April 1. It is a 6-month, 6% note.
4. Seven customers paid for the company's 6-month lawn service package of $600 beginning in April. These customers received the first month of services in April.
5. Lawn services performed for other customers but not billed at April 30 totaled $1,500.

INSTRUCTIONS

Prepare the adjusting entries for the month of April. Show computations.

SOLUTION

GENERAL JOURNAL			
Date	**Account Titles and Explanation**	**Debit**	**Credit**
	Adjusting Entries		
Apr. 30	Insurance Expense	150	
	Prepaid Insurance		150
	(To record insurance expired: $3,600 ÷ 24 = $150 per month)		
30	Depreciation Expense	500	
	Accumulated Depreciation—Equipment		500
	(To record monthly depreciation)		
30	Interest Expense	100	
	Interest Payable		100
	(To accrue interest on notes payable: $20,000 × 6% × $\frac{1}{12}$ = $100)		

30	Unearned Service Revenue	700	
	Service Revenue		700
	(To record revenue for services performed: $600 ÷ 6 = $100; $100 per month × 7 = $700)		
30	Accounts Receivable	1,500	
	Service Revenue		1,500
	(To accrue revenue for services performed)		

WileyPLUS Brief Exercises, DO IT! Exercises, Exercises, Problems, and many additional resources are available for practice in WileyPLUS.

NOTE: All asterisked Questions, Exercises, and Problems relate to material in the appendix to the chapter.

QUESTIONS

1. (a) How does the periodicity assumption affect an accountant's analysis of accounting transactions?
   (b) Explain the term fiscal year.
2. Identify and state two generally accepted accounting principles that relate to adjusting the accounts.
3. Max Wilson, a lawyer, accepts a legal engagement in March, performs the work in April, and is paid in May. If Wilson's law firm prepares monthly financial statements, when should it recognize revenue from this engagement? Why?
4. In completing the engagement in Question 3, Wilson pays no costs in March, $2,500 in April, and $2,200 in May (incurred in April). How much expense should the firm deduct from revenues in the month when it recognizes the revenue? Why?
5. "The historical cost principle of accounting requires adjusting entries." Do you agree? Explain.
6. Why may the financial information in an unadjusted trial balance not be up-to-date and complete?
7. Distinguish between the two categories of adjusting entries, and identify the types of adjustments applicable to each category.
8. What types of accounts does a company debit and credit in a prepaid expense adjusting entry?
9. "Depreciation is a process of valuation that results in the reporting of the fair value of the asset." Do you agree? Explain.
10. Explain the differences between depreciation expense and accumulated depreciation.
11. Steele Company purchased equipment for $15,000. By the current balance sheet date, the company had depreciated $7,000. Indicate the balance sheet presentation of the data.
12. What types of accounts are debited and credited in an unearned revenue adjusting entry?
13. Abe Technologies provides maintenance service for computers and office equipment for companies throughout the Northeast. The sales manager is elated because she closed a $300,000, 3-year maintenance contract on December 29, 2016, two days before the company's year-end. "Now we will hit this year's net income target for sure," she crowed. The customer is required to pay $100,000 on December 29 (the day the deal was closed). Two more payments of $100,000 each are also required on December 29, 2017 and 2018. Discuss the effect that this event will have on the company's financial statements.
14. BeneMart, a large national retail chain, is nearing its fiscal year-end. It appears that the company is not going to hit its revenue and net income targets. The company's marketing manager, Ed Mellon, suggests running a promotion selling $50 gift cards for $45. He believes that this would be very popular and would enable the company to meet its targets for revenue and net income. What do you think of this idea?
15. Whistler Corp. performed services for a customer but has not received payment, nor has it recorded any entry related to the work. Which of the following types of accounts are involved in the adjusting entry: (a) asset, (b) liability, (c) revenue, or (d) expense? For the accounts selected, indicate whether they would be debited or credited in the entry.
16. A company fails to recognize an expense incurred but not paid. Indicate which of the following types of accounts is debited and which is credited in the adjusting entry: (a) asset, (b) liability, (c) revenue, or (d) expense.
17. A company makes an accrued revenue adjusting entry for $780 and an accrued expense adjusting entry for $510. How much was net income understated or overstated prior to these entries? Explain.
18. On January 9, a company pays $6,200 for salaries, of which $1,100 was reported as Salaries and Wages Payable on December 31. Give the entry to record the payment.
19. For each of the following items before adjustment, indicate the type of adjusting entry—prepaid expense, unearned revenue, accrued revenue, and accrued expense—that is needed to correct the misstatement.

If an item could result in more than one type of adjusting entry, indicate each of the types.
(a) Assets are understated.
(b) Liabilities are overstated.
(c) Liabilities are understated.
(d) Expenses are understated.
(e) Assets are overstated.
(f) Revenue is understated.

20. One-half of the adjusting entry is given below. Indicate the account title for the other half of the entry.
(a) Salaries and Wages Expense is debited.
(b) Depreciation Expense is debited.
(c) Interest Payable is credited.
(d) Supplies is credited.
(e) Accounts Receivable is debited.
(f) Unearned Service Revenue is debited.

21. "An adjusting entry may affect more than one balance sheet or income statement account." Do you agree? Why or why not?

22. Which balance sheet account provides evidence that Apple records sales on an accrual basis rather than a cash basis? Explain.

23. Why is it possible to prepare financial statements directly from an adjusted trial balance?

24.
(a) What information do accrual-basis financial statements provide that cash-basis statements do not?
(b) What information do cash-basis financial statements provide that accrual-basis statements do not?

25. What is the relationship, if any, between the amount shown in the adjusted trial balance column for an account and that account's ledger balance?

26. Identify the account(s) debited and credited in each of the four closing entries, assuming the company has net income for the year.

27. Some companies employ technologies that allow them to do a so-called "virtual close." This enables them to close their books nearly instantaneously any time during the year. What advantages does a "virtual close" provide?

28. Describe the nature of the Income Summary account, and identify the types of summary data that may be posted to this account.

29. What items are disclosed on a post-closing trial balance. What is its purpose?

30. Which of these accounts would not appear in the post-closing trial balance? Interest Payable, Equipment, Depreciation Expense, Dividends, Unearned Service Revenue, Accumulated Depreciation—Equipment, and Service Revenue.

31. Indicate, in the sequence in which they are made, the three required steps in the accounting cycle that involve journalizing.

32. Identify, in the sequence in which they are prepared, the three trial balances that are required in the accounting cycle.

33. Explain the terms earnings management and quality of earnings.

34. Give examples of how companies manage earnings.

***35.** What is the purpose of a worksheet?

***36.** What is the basic form of a worksheet?

BRIEF EXERCISES

Identify impact of transactions on cash and net income.
(LO 1), C

BE4-1 Transactions that affect earnings do not necessarily affect cash. Identify the effect, if any, that each of the following transactions would have upon cash and net income. The first transaction has been completed as an example.

	Cash	Net Income
(a) Purchased $100 of supplies for cash.	−$100	$ 0
(b) Recorded an adjusting entry to record use of $20 of the above supplies.		
(c) Made sales of $1,300, all on account.		
(d) Received $800 from customers in payment of their accounts.		
(e) Purchased equipment for cash, $2,500.		
(f) Recorded depreciation of building for period used, $600.		

Indicate why adjusting entries are needed.
(LO 1), C

BE4-2 The ledger of Melmann Company includes the following accounts. Explain why each account may require adjustment.
(a) Prepaid Insurance.
(b) Depreciation Expense.
(c) Unearned Service Revenue.
(d) Interest Payable.

Identify the major types of adjusting entries.
(LO 1), AN

BE4-3 Cortina Company accumulates the following adjustment data at December 31. Indicate (1) the type of adjustment (prepaid expense, accrued revenue, and so on) and (2) the status of the accounts before adjustment (for example, "assets understated and revenues understated").
(a) Supplies of $400 are on hand. Supplies account shows $1,600 balance.
(b) Services performed but unbilled total $700.
(c) Interest of $300 has accumulated on a note payable.
(d) Rent collected in advance totaling $1,100 has been earned.

Prepare adjusting entry for supplies.

(LO 2), AP

BE4-4 Lahey Advertising Company's trial balance at December 31 shows Supplies $8,800 and Supplies Expense $0. On December 31, there are $1,100 of supplies on hand. Prepare the adjusting entry at December 31 and, using T-accounts, enter the balances in the accounts, post the adjusting entry, and indicate the adjusted balance in each account.

Prepare adjusting entry for depreciation.

(LO 2), AP

BE4-5 At the end of its first year, the trial balance of Rayburn Company shows Equipment $22,000 and zero balances in Accumulated Depreciation—Equipment and Depreciation Expense. Depreciation for the year is estimated to be $2,750. Prepare the annual adjusting entry for depreciation at December 31, post the adjustments to T-accounts, and indicate the balance sheet presentation of the equipment at December 31.

Prepare adjusting entry for prepaid expense.

(LO 2), AP

BE4-6 On July 1, 2017, Ling Co. pays $12,400 to Marsh Insurance Co. for a 2-year insurance contract. Both companies have fiscal years ending December 31. For Ling Co., journalize and post the entry on July 1 and the annual adjusting entry on December 31.

Prepare adjusting entry for unearned revenue.

(LO 2), AP

BE4-7 Using the data in BE4-6, journalize and post the entry on July 1 and the adjusting entry on December 31 for Marsh Insurance Co. Marsh uses the accounts Unearned Service Revenue and Service Revenue.

Prepare adjusting entries for accruals.

(LO 3), AP

BE4-8 The bookkeeper for Tran Company asks you to prepare the following accrual adjusting entries at December 31. Use these account titles: Service Revenue, Accounts Receivable, Interest Expense, Interest Payable, Salaries and Wages Expense, and Salaries and Wages Payable.

(a) Interest on notes payable of $300 is accrued.
(b) Services performed but unbilled totals $1,700.
(c) Salaries of $780 earned by employees have not been recorded.

Analyze accounts in an adjusted trial balance.

(LO 4), AN

BE4-9 The trial balance of Woods Company includes the following balance sheet accounts. Identify the accounts that might require adjustment. For each account that requires adjustment, indicate (1) the type of adjusting entry (prepaid expense, unearned revenue, accrued revenue, or accrued expense) and (2) the related account in the adjusting entry.

(a) Accounts Receivable.
(b) Prepaid Insurance.
(c) Equipment.
(d) Accumulated Depreciation—Equipment.
(e) Notes Payable.
(f) Interest Payable.
(g) Unearned Service Revenue.

Prepare an income statement from an adjusted trial balance.

(LO 4), AP

BE4-10 The adjusted trial balance of Levin Corporation at December 31, 2017, includes the following accounts: Retained Earnings $17,200, Dividends $6,000, Service Revenue $32,000, Salaries and Wages Expense $14,000, Insurance Expense $1,800, Rent Expense $3,900, Supplies Expense $1,500, and Depreciation Expense $1,000. Prepare an income statement for the year.

Prepare a retained earnings statement from an adjusted trial balance.

(LO 4), AP

BE4-11 Partial adjusted trial balance data for Levin Corporation are presented in BE4-10. The balance in Retained Earnings is the balance as of January 1. Prepare a retained earnings statement for the year assuming net income is $10,400.

Identify financial statement for selected accounts.

(LO 4), K

BE4-12 The following selected accounts appear in the adjusted trial balance for Deane Company. Indicate the financial statement on which each account would be reported.

(a) Accumulated Depreciation.
(b) Depreciation Expense.
(c) Retained Earnings (beginning).
(d) Dividends.
(e) Service Revenue.
(f) Supplies.
(g) Accounts Payable.

Identify post-closing trial balance accounts.

(LO 4), K

BE4-13 Using the data in BE4-12, identify the accounts that would be included in a post-closing trial balance.

Prepare and post closing entries.

(LO 4), AP

BE4-14 The income statement for the Bonita Pines Golf Club Inc. for the month ended July 31 shows Service Revenue $16,000, Salaries and Wages Expense $8,400, Maintenance and Repairs Expense $2,500, and Income Tax Expense $1,000. The statement of retained earnings shows an opening balance for Retained Earnings of $20,000 and Dividends $1,300.

(a) Prepare closing journal entries.
(b) What is the ending balance in Retained Earnings?

BE4-15 The required steps in the accounting cycle are listed in random order below. List the steps in proper sequence.

List required steps in the accounting cycle sequence.

(LO 4), K

(a) Prepare a post-closing trial balance.
(b) Prepare an adjusted trial balance.
(c) Analyze business transactions.
(d) Prepare a trial balance.
(e) Journalize the transactions.
(f) Journalize and post closing entries.
(g) Prepare financial statements.
(h) Journalize and post adjusting entries.
(i) Post to ledger accounts.

DO IT! EXERCISES

DO IT! 4-1 A list of concepts is provided below in the left column, with descriptions of the concepts in the right column. There are more descriptions provided than concepts. Match the description to the concept.

Identify timing concepts.

(LO 1), C

1. _____ Cash-basis accounting.
2. _____ Fiscal year.
3. _____ Revenue recognition principle.
4. _____ Expense recognition principle.

(a) Monthly and quarterly time periods.
(b) Accountants divide the economic life of a business into artificial time periods.
(c) Efforts (expenses) should be matched with accomplishments (revenues).
(d) Companies record revenues when they receive cash and record expenses when they pay out cash.
(e) An accounting time period that is one year in length.
(f) An accounting time period that starts on January 1 and ends on December 31.
(g) Companies record transactions in the period in which the events occur.
(h) Recognize revenue in the accounting period in which a performance obligation is satisfied.

DO IT! 4-2 The ledger of Umatilla, Inc. on March 31, 2017, includes the following selected accounts before adjusting entries.

Prepare adjusting entries for deferrals.

(LO 2), AP

	Debit	Credit
Supplies	2,500	
Prepaid Insurance	2,400	
Equipment	30,000	
Unearned Service Revenue		10,000

An analysis of the accounts shows the following.

1. Insurance expires at the rate of $300 per month.
2. Supplies on hand total $900.
3. The equipment depreciates $200 per month.
4. During March, services were performed for two-fifths of the unearned service revenue.

Prepare the adjusting entries for the month of March.

DO IT! 4-3 Jean Karns is the new owner of Jean's Computer Services. At the end of July 2017, her first month of ownership, Jean is trying to prepare monthly financial statements. She has the following information for the month.

Prepare adjusting entries for accruals.

(LO 3), AP

1. At July 31, Jean owed employees $1,100 in salaries that the company will pay in August.
2. On July 1, Jean borrowed $20,000 from a local bank on a 10-year note. The annual interest rate is 9%.
3. Service revenue unrecorded in July totaled $1,600.

Prepare the adjusting entries needed at July 31, 2017.

DO IT! 4-4a Indicate in which financial statement each of the following adjusted trial balance accounts would be presented.

Prepare financial statements from adjusted trial balance.

(LO 4), C

Service Revenue	Accounts Receivable
Notes Payable	Accumulated Depreciation
Common Stock	Utilities Expense

Prepare closing entries.

(LO 4), AP

DO IT! 4-4b Paloma Company shows the following balances in selected accounts of its adjusted trial balance.

Supplies	$32,000	Service Revenue	$108,000
Supplies Expense	6,000	Salaries and Wages Expense	40,000
Accounts Receivable	12,000	Utilities Expense	8,000
Dividends	22,000	Rent Expense	18,000
Retained Earnings	70,000		

Prepare the remaining closing entries at December 31.

EXERCISES

Identify point of revenue recognition.

(LO 1), C

E4-1 The following independent situations require professional judgment for determining when to recognize revenue from the transactions.

(a) Southwest Airlines sells you an advance-purchase airline ticket in September for your flight home in December.

(b) Ultimate Electronics sells you a home theater on a "no money down and full payment in three months" promotional deal.

(c) The Toronto Blue Jays sell season tickets online to games in the Skydome. Fans can purchase the tickets at any time, although the season doesn't officially begin until April. The major league baseball season runs from April through October.

(d) RBC Financial Group loans money on August 1. The loan and the interest are repayable in full in November.

(e) In August, you order a sweater from Sears using its online catalog. The sweater arrives in September, which you charged to your Sears credit card. You receive and pay the Sears bill in October.

Instructions

Identify when revenue should be recognized in each of the above situations.

Identify accounting assumptions, principles, and constraint.

(LO 1), K

E4-2 These accounting concepts were discussed in this and previous chapters.

1. Economic entity assumption.
2. Expense recognition principle.
3. Monetary unit assumption.
4. Periodicity assumption.
5. Historical cost principle.
6. Materiality.
7. Full disclosure principle.
8. Going concern assumption.
9. Revenue recognition principle.
10. Cost constraint.

Instructions

Identify by number the accounting concept that describes each situation below. Do not use a number more than once.

_____ (a) Is the rationale for why plant assets are not reported at liquidation value. (Do not use the historical cost principle.)

_____ (b) Indicates that personal and business recordkeeping should be separately maintained.

_____ (c) Ensures that all relevant financial information is reported.

_____ (d) Assumes that the dollar is the "measuring stick" used to report on financial performance.

_____ (e) Requires that accounting standards be followed for all items of **significant** size.

_____ (f) Separates financial information into time periods for reporting purposes.

_____ (g) Requires recognition of expenses in the same period as related revenues.

_____ (h) Indicates that fair value changes subsequent to purchase are not recorded in the accounts.

Identify the violated assumption, principle, or constraint.

(LO 1), C

E4-3 Here are some accounting reporting situations.

(a) East Lake Company recognizes revenue at the end of the production cycle but before sale. The price of the product, as well as the amount that can be sold, is not certain.

(b) Hilo Company is in its fifth year of operation and has yet to issue financial statements. (Do not use the full disclosure principle.)

(c) Gomez, Inc. is carrying inventory at its original cost of $100,000. Inventory has a fair value of $110,000.

(d) Bly Hospital Supply Corporation reports only current assets and current liabilities on its balance sheet. Equipment and bonds payable are reported as current assets and current liabilities, respectively. Liquidation of the company is unlikely.
(e) Chieu Company has inventory on hand that cost $400,000. Chieu reports inventory on its balance sheet at its current fair value of $425,000.
(f) Toxy Syles, president of Classic Music Company, bought a computer for her personal use. She paid for the computer by using company funds and debited the "Computers" account.

Instructions
For each situation, list the assumption, principle, or constraint that has been violated, if any. (Some were presented in earlier chapters.) List only one answer for each situation.

Convert earnings from cash to accrual basis.
(LO 1, 2, 3), AP

E4-4 Your examination of the records of a company that follows the cash basis of accounting tells you that the company's reported cash-basis earnings in 2017 are $33,640. If this firm had followed accrual-basis accounting practices, it would have reported the following year-end balances.

	2017	2016
Accounts receivable	$3,400	$2,800
Supplies on hand	1,300	1,460
Unpaid wages owed	2,000	2,400
Other unpaid expenses	1,400	1,100

Instructions
Determine the company's net earnings on an accrual basis for 2017. Show all your calculations in an orderly fashion.

Determine cash-basis and accrual-basis earnings.
(LO 1), AP

E4-5 In its first year of operations, Gomes Company recognized $28,000 in service revenue, $6,000 of which was on account and still outstanding at year-end. The remaining $22,000 was received in cash from customers.

The company incurred operating expenses of $15,800. Of these expenses, $12,000 were paid in cash; $3,800 was still owed on account at year-end. In addition, Gomes prepaid $2,400 for insurance coverage that would not be used until the second year of operations.

Instructions
(a) Calculate the first year's net earnings under the cash basis of accounting, and calculate the first year's net earnings under the accrual basis of accounting.
(b) Which basis of accounting (cash or accrual) provides more useful information for decision-makers?

Convert earnings from cash to accrual basis; prepare accrual-based financial statements.
(LO 1, 2, 3), AP

E4-6 Franken Company, a ski tuning and repair shop, opened on November 1, 2016. The company carefully kept track of all its cash receipts and cash payments. The following information is available at the end of the ski season, April 30, 2017.

	Cash Receipts	Cash Payments
Issuance of common shares	$20,000	
Payment to purchase repair shop equipment		$ 9,200
Payments to landlord		1,225
Newspaper advertising payment		375
Utility bill payments		970
Part-time helper's wage payments		2,600
Income tax payment		10,000
Cash receipts from ski and snowboard repair services	32,150	
Subtotals	52,150	24,370
Cash balance		27,780
Totals	$52,150	$52,150

The repair shop equipment was purchased on November 1 and has an estimated useful life of 4 years. Lease payments to the landlord are made at the beginning of each month. The amount of the payments to the landlord shown above includes a one-time security deposit of $175. The part-time helper is owed $420 at April 30, 2017, for unpaid wages. At April 30, 2017, customers owe Franken Company $540 for services they have received but have not yet paid for.

Instructions

(a) Prepare an accrual-basis income statement for the 6 months ended April 30, 2017.
(b) Prepare the April 30, 2017, classified balance sheet.

Identify differences between cash and accrual accounting.
(LO 1, 2, 3), C

E4-7 BizCon, a consulting firm, has just completed its first year of operations. The company's sales growth was explosive. To encourage clients to hire its services, BizCon offered 180-day financing—meaning its largest customers do not pay for nearly 6 months. Because BizCon is a new company, its equipment suppliers insist on being paid cash on delivery. Also, it had to pay up front for 2 years of insurance. At the end of the year, BizCon owed employees for one full month of salaries, but due to a cash shortfall, it promised to pay them the first week of next year.

Instructions

(a) Explain how cash and accrual accounting would differ for each of the events listed above and describe the proper accrual accounting.
(b) Assume that at the end of the year, BizCon reported a favorable net income, yet the company's management is concerned because the company is very short of cash. Explain how BizCon could have positive net income and yet run out of cash.

Identify types of adjustments and accounts before adjustment.
(LO 1, 2, 3), AN

E4-8 Wang Company accumulates the following adjustment data at December 31.

(a) Services performed but unbilled total $600.
(b) Store supplies of $160 are on hand. The supplies account shows a $1,900 balance.
(c) Utility expenses of $275 are unpaid.
(d) Services performed of $490 collected in advance.
(e) Salaries of $620 are unpaid.
(f) Prepaid insurance totaling $400 has expired.

Instructions

For each item, indicate (1) the type of adjustment (prepaid expense, unearned revenue, accrued revenue, or accrued expense) and (2) the status of the accounts before adjustment (overstated or understated).

Prepare adjusting entries from selected account data.
(LO 2, 3), AP

E4-9 The ledger of Howard Rental Agency on March 31 of the current year includes the selected accounts below before adjusting entries have been prepared.

	Debit	Credit
Supplies	$ 3,000	
Prepaid Insurance	3,600	
Equipment	25,000	
Accumulated Depreciation—Equipment		$ 8,400
Notes Payable		20,000
Unearned Rent Revenue		12,400
Rent Revenue		60,000
Interest Expense	0	
Salaries and Wages Expense	14,000	

An analysis of the accounts shows the following.

1. The equipment depreciates $280 per month.
2. Half of the unearned rent revenue was earned during the quarter.
3. Interest of $400 is accrued on the notes payable.
4. Supplies on hand total $850.
5. Insurance expires at the rate of $400 per month.

Instructions

Prepare the adjusting entries at March 31, assuming that adjusting entries are made quarterly. Additional accounts are Depreciation Expense, Insurance Expense, Interest Payable, and Supplies Expense.

Prepare adjusting entries.
(LO 2, 3), AP

E4-10 Al Medina, D.D.S., opened an incorporated dental practice on January 1, 2017. During the first month of operations, the following transactions occurred.

1. Performed services for patients who had dental plan insurance. At January 31, $760 of such services was completed but not yet billed to the insurance companies.
2. Utility expenses incurred but not paid prior to January 31 totaled $450.
3. Purchased dental equipment on January 1 for $80,000, paying $20,000 in cash and signing a $60,000, 3-year note payable (interest is paid each December 31). The equipment depreciates $400 per month. Interest is $500 per month.

4. Purchased a 1-year malpractice insurance policy on January 1 for $24,000.
5. Purchased $1,750 of dental supplies (recorded as increase to Supplies). On January 31, determined that $550 of supplies were on hand.

Instructions
Prepare the adjusting entries on January 31. Account titles are Accumulated Depreciation—Equipment, Depreciation Expense, Service Revenue, Accounts Receivable, Insurance Expense, Interest Expense, Interest Payable, Prepaid Insurance, Supplies, Supplies Expense, Utilities Expense, and Accounts Payable.

Prepare adjusting entries.

(LO 2, 3), AP

E4-11 The unadjusted trial balance for Sierra Corp. is shown in Illustration 4-4 (page 155). Instead of the adjusting entries shown in the text at October 31, assume the following adjustment data.

1. Supplies on hand at October 31 total $500.
2. Expired insurance for the month is $100.
3. Depreciation for the month is $75.
4. As of October 31, services worth $800 related to the previously recorded unearned revenue had been performed.
5. Services performed but unbilled (and no receivable has been recorded) at October 31 are $280.
6. Interest expense accrued at October 31 is $70.
7. Accrued salaries at October 31 are $1,400.

Instructions
Prepare the adjusting entries for the items above.

Prepare adjusting entries from selected account data.

(LO 2, 3), AP

E4-12 The ledger of Armour Lake Lumber Supply on July 31, 2017, includes the selected accounts below before adjusting entries have been prepared.

	Debit	Credit
Investment in Note Receivable	$ 20,000	
Supplies	24,000	
Prepaid Rent	3,600	
Buildings	250,000	
Accumulated Depreciation—Buildings		$140,000
Unearned Service Revenue		11,500

An analysis of the company's accounts shows the following.

1. The investment in the notes receivable earns interest at a rate of 6% per year.
2. Supplies on hand at the end of the month totaled $18,600.
3. The balance in Prepaid Rent represents 4 months of rent costs.
4. Employees were owed $3,100 related to unpaid salaries and wages.
5. Depreciation on buildings is $6,000 per year.
6. During the month, the company satisfied obligations worth $4,700 related to the Unearned Services Revenue.
7. Unpaid maintenance and repairs costs were $2,300.

Instructions
Prepare the adjusting entries at July 31 assuming that adjusting entries are made monthly. Use additional accounts as needed.

Prepare a correct income statement.

(LO 1, 2, 3), AN

E4-13 The income statement of Norski Co. for the month of July shows net income of $2,000 based on Service Revenue $5,500, Salaries and Wages Expense $2,100, Supplies Expense $900, and Utilities Expense $500. In reviewing the statement, you discover the following:

1. Insurance expired during July of $350 was omitted.
2. Supplies expense includes $200 of supplies that are still on hand at July 31.
3. Depreciation on equipment of $150 was omitted.
4. Accrued but unpaid wages at July 31 of $360 were not included.
5. Services performed but unrecorded totaled $700.

Instructions
Prepare a correct income statement for July 2017.

Journalize basic transactions and adjusting entries.

(LO 2, 3), AN

E4-14 Selected accounts of Villa Company are shown here.

Supplies Expense

July 31	750		

Salaries and Wages Payable

		July 31	1,000

Salaries and Wages Expense

July 15	1,000		
31	1,000		

Accounts Receivable

July 31	500		

Service Revenue

		July 14	3,800
		31	900
		31	500

Unearned Service Revenue

July 31	900	July 1 Bal.	1,500
		20	600

Supplies

July 1 Bal.	1,100	July 31	750
10	200		

Instructions

After analyzing the accounts, journalize (a) the July transactions and (b) the adjusting entries that were made on July 31. (*Hint:* July transactions were for cash.)

Analyze adjusted data.

(LO 1, 2, 3), AN

E4-15 This is a partial adjusted trial balance of Ramon Company.

RAMON COMPANY
Adjusted Trial Balance
January 31, 2017

	Debit	Credit
Supplies	$ 700	
Prepaid Insurance	1,560	
Salaries and Wages Payable		$1,060
Unearned Service Revenue		750
Supplies Expense	950	
Insurance Expense	520	
Salaries and Wages Expense	1,800	
Service Revenue		4,000

Instructions

Answer these questions, assuming the year begins January 1.

(a) If the amount in Supplies Expense is the January 31 adjusting entry and $300 of supplies was purchased in January, what was the balance in Supplies on January 1?

(b) If the amount in Insurance Expense is the January 31 adjusting entry and the original insurance premium was for 1 year, what was the total premium and when was the policy purchased?

(c) If $2,500 of salaries was paid in January, what was the balance in Salaries and Wages Payable at December 31, 2016?

(d) If $1,800 was received in January for services performed in January, what was the balance in Unearned Service Revenue at December 31, 2016?

Determine effect of adjusting entries.

(LO 2, 3), AN

E4-16 On December 31, 2017, Waters Company prepared an income statement and balance sheet, but failed to take into account three adjusting entries. The balance sheet showed total assets $150,000, total liabilities $70,000, and stockholders' equity $80,000. The incorrect income statement showed net income of $70,000.

The data for the three adjusting entries were:

1. Salaries and wages amounting to $10,000 for the last 2 days in December were not paid and not recorded. The next payroll will be in January.
2. Rent payments of $8,000 was received for two months in advance on December 1. The entire amount was credited to Unearned Rent Revenue when paid.
3. Depreciation expense for 2017 is $9,000.

Instructions

Complete the following table to correct the financial statement amounts shown (indicate deductions with parentheses).

Item	Net Income	Total Assets	Total Liabilities	Stockholders' Equity
Incorrect balances	$70,000	$150,000	$70,000	$80,000
Effects of:				
Salaries and Wages				
Rent Revenue				
Depreciation				
Correct balances				

E4-17 Action Quest Games Inc. adjusts its accounts annually. The following information is available for the year ended December 31, 2017.

Prepare and post transaction and adjusting entries for prepayments.

(LO 2, 3), AP

1. Purchased a 1-year insurance policy on June 1 for $1,800 cash.
2. Paid $6,500 on August 31 for 5 months' rent in advance.
3. On September 4, received $3,600 cash in advance from a corporation to sponsor a game each month for a total of 9 months for the most improved students at a local school.
4. Signed a contract for cleaning services starting December 1 for $1,000 per month. Paid for the first 2 months on November 30. (*Hint:* Use the account Prepaid Cleaning to record prepayments.)
5. On December 5, received $1,500 in advance from a gaming club. Determined that on December 31, $475 of these games had not yet been played.

Instructions

(a) For each of the above transactions, prepare the journal entry to record the initial transaction.

(b) For each of the above transactions, prepare the adjusting journal entry that is required on December 31. (*Hint:* Use the account Service Revenue for item 3 and Repairs and Maintenance Expense for item 4.)

(c) Post the journal entries in parts (a) and (b) to T-accounts and determine the final balance in each account balance. (*Note:* Posting to the Cash account is not required.)

E4-18 Greenock Limited has the following information available for accruals for the year ended December 31, 2017. The company adjusts its accounts annually.

Prepare adjusting and subsequent entries for accruals.

(LO 2, 3), AP

1. The December utility bill for $425 was unrecorded on December 31. Greenock paid the bill on January 11.
2. Greenock is open 7 days a week and employees are paid a total of $3,500 every Monday for a 7-day (Monday–Sunday) workweek. December 31 is a Thursday, so employees will have worked 4 days (Monday, December 28–Thursday, December 31) that they have not been paid for by year-end. Employees will be paid next on January 4.
3. Greenock signed a $45,000, 5% bank loan on November 1, 2016, due in 2 years. Interest is payable on the first day of each following month.
4. Greenock receives a fee from Pizza Shop next door for all pizzas sold to customers using Greenock's facility. The amount owed for December is $300, which Pizza Shop will pay on January 4. (*Hint:* Use the Service Revenue account.)
5. Greenock rented some of its unused warehouse space to a client for $6,000 a month, payable the first day of the following month. It received the rent for the month of December on January 2.

Instructions

(a) For each situation, prepare the adjusting entry required at December 31. (Round all calculations to the nearest dollar.)

(b) For each situation, prepare the journal entry to record the subsequent cash transaction in 2018.

E4-19 A partial adjusted trial balance for Ramon Company is given in E4-15.

Prepare closing entries.

(LO 4), AP

Instructions

Prepare the closing entries at January 31, 2017.

Prepare closing entries.

(LO 4), AP

E4-20 Selected year-end account balances from the adjusted trial balance as of December 31, 2017, for Tippy Corporation is provided below.

	Debit	Credit
Accounts Receivable	$ 72,600	
Dividends	26,300	
Depreciation Expense	13,200	
Equipment	212,800	
Salaries and Wages Expense	91,100	
Accounts Payable		$ 53,000
Accumulated Depreciation—Equipment		114,800
Unearned Rent Revenue		22,900
Service Revenue		183,800
Rent Revenue		6,200
Rent Expense	3,600	
Retained Earnings		61,800
Supplies Expense	1,400	

Instructions

(a) Prepare closing entries

(b) Determine the post-closing balance in Retained Earnings.

Prepare adjusting entries from analysis of trial balance.

(LO 2, 3, 4), AN

E4-21 The trial balances shown below are before and after adjustment for Ryan Company at the end of its fiscal year.

RYAN COMPANY
Trial Balance
August 31, 2017

	Before Adjustment		After Adjustment	
	Dr.	**Cr.**	**Dr.**	**Cr.**
Cash	$10,900		$10,900	
Accounts Receivable	8,800		9,400	
Supplies	2,500		500	
Prepaid Insurance	4,000		2,500	
Equipment	16,000		16,000	
Accumulated Depreciation—Equipment		$ 3,600		$ 4,800
Accounts Payable		5,800		5,800
Salaries and Wages Payable		0		1,100
Unearned Rent Revenue		1,800		800
Common Stock		10,000		10,000
Retained Earnings		5,500		5,500
Dividends	2,800		2,800	
Service Revenue		34,000		34,600
Rent Revenue		12,100		13,100
Salaries and Wages Expense	17,000		18,100	
Supplies Expense	0		2,000	
Rent Expense	10,800		10,800	
Insurance Expense	0		1,500	
Depreciation Expense	0		1,200	
	$72,800	$72,800	$75,700	$75,700

Instructions

Prepare the adjusting entries that were made.

Prepare financial statements from adjusted trial balance.

(LO 4), AP

E4-22 The adjusted trial balance for Ryan Company is given in E4-21.

Instructions

Prepare the income and retained earnings statements for the year and the classified balance sheet at August 31.

Prepare closing entries.

(LO 4), AP

E4-23 The adjusted trial balance for Ryan Company is given in E4-21.

Instructions

Prepare the closing entries for the temporary accounts at August 31.

▶ EXERCISES: SET B AND CHALLENGE EXERCISES

Visit the book's companion website, at **www.wiley.com/college/kimmel**, and choose the Student Companion site to access Exercises: Set B and Challenge Exercises.

▶ PROBLEMS: SET A

Record transactions on accrual basis; convert revenue to cash receipts.

(LO 1, 2, 3), AP

P4-1A The following selected data are taken from the comparative financial statements of Yankee Curling Club. The club prepares its financial statements using the accrual basis of accounting.

September 30	2017	2016
Accounts receivable for member dues	$ 15,000	$ 19,000
Unearned sales revenue	20,000	23,000
Service revenue (from member dues)	151,000	135,000

Dues are billed to members based upon their use of the club's facilities. Unearned sales revenues arise from the sale of tickets to events, such as the Skins Game.

Instructions

(*Hint:* You will find it helpful to use T-accounts to analyze the following data. You must analyze these data sequentially, as missing information must first be deduced before moving on. Post your journal entries as you progress, rather than waiting until the end.)

(a) Prepare journal entries for each of the following events that took place during 2017.
1. Dues receivable from members from 2016 were all collected during 2017.
2. During 2017, goods were provided for all of the unearned sales revenue at the end of 2016.
3. Additional tickets were sold for $44,000 cash during 2017; a portion of these were used by the purchasers during the year. The entire balance remaining in Unearned Sales Revenue relates to the upcoming Skins Game in 2017.
4. Dues for the 2016–2017 fiscal year were billed to members.
5. Dues receivable for 2017 (i.e., those billed in item 4 above) were partially collected.

(b) Determine the amount of cash received by Yankee from the above transactions during the year ended September 30, 2017.

(b) Cash received $199,000

Prepare adjusting entries, post to ledger accounts, and prepare adjusted trial balance.

(LO 2, 3, 4), AP

P4-2A Len Kumar started his own consulting firm, Kumar Consulting, on June 1, 2017. The trial balance at June 30 is as follows.

KUMAR CONSULTING
Trial Balance
June 30, 2017

	Debit	Credit
Cash	$ 6,850	
Accounts Receivable	7,000	
Supplies	2,000	
Prepaid Insurance	2,880	
Equipment	15,000	
Accounts Payable		$ 4,230
Unearned Service Revenue		5,200
Common Stock		22,000
Service Revenue		8,300
Salaries and Wages Expense	4,000	
Rent Expense	2,000	
	$39,730	$39,730

In addition to those accounts listed on the trial balance, the chart of accounts for Kumar also contains the following accounts: Accumulated Depreciation—Equipment, Salaries and Wages Payable, Depreciation Expense, Insurance Expense, Utilities Expense, and Supplies Expense.

Other data:

1. Supplies on hand at June 30 total $720.
2. A utility bill for $180 has not been recorded and will not be paid until next month.
3. The insurance policy is for a year.
4. Services were performed for $4,100 of unearned service revenue by the end of the month.
5. Salaries of $1,250 are accrued at June 30.
6. The equipment has a 5-year life with no salvage value and is being depreciated at $250 per month for 60 months.
7. Invoices representing $3,900 of services performed during the month have not been recorded as of June 30.

Instructions

(b) Service rev. $16,300

(c) Tot. trial balance $45,310

(a) Prepare the adjusting entries for the month of June.
(b) Post the adjusting entries to the ledger accounts. Enter the totals from the trial balance as beginning account balances. (Use T-accounts.)
(c) Prepare an adjusted trial balance at June 30, 2017.

Prepare adjusting entries, adjusted trial balance, and financial statements.

(LO 2, 3, 4), AP

P4-3A The Moto Hotel opened for business on May 1, 2017. Here is its trial balance before adjustment on May 31.

MOTO HOTEL
Trial Balance
May 31, 2017

	Debit	**Credit**
Cash	$ 2,500	
Supplies	2,600	
Prepaid Insurance	1,800	
Land	15,000	
Buildings	70,000	
Equipment	16,800	
Accounts Payable		$ 4,700
Unearned Rent Revenue		3,300
Mortgage Payable		36,000
Common Stock		60,000
Rent Revenue		9,000
Salaries and Wages Expense	3,000	
Utilities Expense	800	
Advertising Expense	500	
	$113,000	$113,000

Other data:

1. Insurance expires at the rate of $450 per month.
2. A count of supplies shows $1,050 of unused supplies on May 31.
3. Annual depreciation is $3,600 on the building and $3,000 on equipment.
4. The mortgage interest rate is 6%. (The mortgage was taken out on May 1.)
5. Unearned rent of $2,500 has been earned.
6. Salaries of $900 are accrued and unpaid at May 31.

Instructions

(c) Rent revenue $11,500
Tot. adj. trial balance $114,630
(d) Net income $3,570

(a) Journalize the adjusting entries on May 31.
(b) Prepare a ledger using T-accounts. Enter the trial balance amounts and post the adjusting entries.
(c) Prepare an adjusted trial balance on May 31.
(d) Prepare an income statement and a retained earnings statement for the month of May and a classified balance sheet at May 31.
(e) Identify which accounts should be closed on May 31.

Prepare adjusting entries and financial statements; identify accounts to be closed.

(LO 2, 3, 4), AP

GLS

P4-4A Salt Creek Golf Inc. was organized on July 1, 2017. Quarterly financial statements are prepared. The trial balance and adjusted trial balance on September 30 are shown on page 203.

SALT CREEK GOLF INC.
Trial Balance
September 30, 2017

	Unadjusted Dr.	Unadjusted Cr.	Adjusted Dr.	Adjusted Cr.
Cash	$ 6,700		$ 6,700	
Accounts Receivable	400		1,000	
Supplies	1,200		180	
Prepaid Rent	1,800		900	
Equipment	15,000		15,000	
Accumulated Depreciation—Equipment				$ 350
Notes Payable		$ 5,000		5,000
Accounts Payable		1,070		1,070
Salaries and Wages Payable				600
Interest Payable				50
Unearned Rent Revenue		1,000		800
Common Stock		14,000		14,000
Retained Earnings		0		0
Dividends	600		600	
Service Revenue		14,100		14,700
Rent Revenue		700		900
Salaries and Wages Expense	8,800		9,400	
Rent Expense	900		1,800	
Depreciation Expense			350	
Supplies Expense			1,020	
Utilities Expense	470		470	
Interest Expense			50	
	$35,870	$35,870	$37,470	$37,470

Instructions

(a) Journalize the adjusting entries that were made.

(b) Prepare an income statement and a retained earnings statement for the 3 months ending September 30 and a classified balance sheet at September 30.

(b) Net income $2,510
Tot. assets $23,430

(c) Identify which accounts should be closed on September 30.

(d) If the note bears interest at 12%, how many months has it been outstanding?

P4-5A A review of the ledger of Lewis Company at December 31, 2017, produces these data pertaining to the preparation of annual adjusting entries.

Prepare adjusting entries.
(LO 2, 3), AP

1. Prepaid Insurance $15,200. The company has separate insurance policies on its buildings and its motor vehicles. Policy B4564 on the building was purchased on July 1, 2016, for $9,600. The policy has a term of 3 years. Policy A2958 on the vehicles was purchased on January 1, 2017, for $7,200. This policy has a term of 18 months.
2. Unearned Rent Revenue $429,000. The company began subleasing office space in its new building on November 1. At December 31, the company had the following rental contracts that are paid in full for the entire term of the lease.

2. Rent revenue $84,000

Date	Term (in months)	Monthly Rent	Number of Leases
Nov. 1	9	$5,000	5
Dec. 1	6	$8,500	4

3. Notes Payable $40,000. This balance consists of a note for 6 months at an annual interest rate of 7%, dated October 1.
4. Salaries and Wages Payable $0. There are eight salaried employees. Salaries are paid every Friday for the current week. Five employees receive a salary of $600 each per week, and three employees earn $700 each per week. Assume December 31 is a Wednesday. Employees do not work weekends. All employees worked the last 3 days of December.

Instructions

Prepare the adjusting entries at December 31, 2017.

Prepare adjusting entries and a corrected income statement.

(LO 2, 3), AN

P4-6A Roadside Travel Court was organized on July 1, 2016, by Betty Johnson. Betty is a good manager but a poor accountant. From the trial balance prepared by a part-time bookkeeper, Betty prepared the following income statement for her fourth quarter, which ended June 30, 2017.

ROADSIDE TRAVEL COURT
Income Statement
For the Quarter Ended June 30, 2017

Revenues		
Rent revenue		$212,000
Operating expenses		
Advertising expense	$ 3,800	
Salaries and wages expense	80,500	
Utilities expense	900	
Depreciation expense	2,700	
Maintenance and repairs expense	4,300	
Total operating expenses		92,200
Net income		$119,800

Betty suspected that something was wrong with the statement because net income had never exceeded $30,000 in any one quarter. Knowing that you are an experienced accountant, she asks you to review the income statement and other data.

You first look at the trial balance. In addition to the account balances reported above in the income statement, the trial balance contains the following additional selected balances at June 30, 2017.

Supplies	$ 8,200
Prepaid Insurance	14,400
Notes Payable	14,000

You then make inquiries and discover the following.

1. Roadside rental revenues include advanced rental payments received for summer occupancy, in the amount of $57,000.
2. There were $1,800 of supplies on hand at June 30.
3. Prepaid insurance resulted from the payment of a 1-year policy on April 1, 2017.
4. The mail in July 2017 brought the following bills: advertising for the week of June 24, $110; repairs made June 18, $4,450; and utilities for the month of June, $215.
5. Wage expense is $300 per day. At June 30, 4 days' wages have been incurred but not paid.
6. The note payable is a 6% note dated May 1, 2017, and due on July 31, 2017.
7. Income tax of $13,400 for the quarter is due in July but has not yet been recorded.

Instructions

(a) Prepare any adjusting journal entries required at June 30, 2017.

(b) Net income $33,285

(b) Prepare a correct income statement for the quarter ended June 30, 2017.

(c) Explain to Betty the generally accepted accounting principles that she did not recognize in preparing her income statement and their effect on her results.

Journalize transactions and follow through accounting cycle to preparation of financial statements.

(LO 2, 3, 4), AP

P4-7A On November 1, 2017, the following were the account balances of Soho Equipment Repair.

	Debit		Credit
Cash	$ 2,790	Accumulated Depreciation—Equipment	$ 500
Accounts Receivable	2,910	Accounts Payable	2,300
Supplies	1,120	Unearned Service Revenue	400
Equipment	10,000	Salaries and Wages Payable	620
		Common Stock	10,000
		Retained Earnings	3,000
	$16,820		$16,820

During November, the following summary transactions were completed.

Nov.	8	Paid $1,220 for salaries due employees, of which $600 is for November and $620 is for October salaries payable.
	10	Received $1,800 cash from customers in payment of account.
	12	Received $3,700 cash for services performed in November.
	15	Purchased store equipment on account $3,600.
	17	Purchased supplies on account $1,300.
	20	Paid creditors $2,500 of accounts payable due.
	22	Paid November rent $480.
	25	Paid salaries $1,000.
	27	Performed services on account worth $900 and billed customers.
	29	Received $750 from customers for services to be performed in the future.

Adjustment data:

1. Supplies on hand are valued at $1,100.
2. Accrued salaries payable are $480.
3. Depreciation for the month is $250.
4. Services were performed to satisfy $500 of unearned service revenue.

Instructions

(a) Enter the November 1 balances in the ledger accounts. (Use T-accounts.)
(b) Journalize the November transactions.
(c) Post to the ledger accounts. Use Service Revenue, Depreciation Expense, Supplies Expense, Salaries and Wages Expense, and Rent Expense.
(d) Prepare a trial balance at November 30.
(e) Journalize and post adjusting entries.
(f) Prepare an adjusted trial balance.
(g) Prepare an income statement and a retained earnings statement for November and a classified balance sheet at November 30.

(f) Cash	$3,840
Tot. adj. trial balance	$24,680
(g) Net income	$970

PROBLEMS: SET B AND SET C

Visit the book's companion website, at **www.wiley.com/college/kimmel**, and choose the Student Companion site to access Problems: Set B and Set C.

CONTINUING PROBLEM Cookie Creations

(*Note:* This is a continuation of the Cookie Creations problem from Chapters 1 through 3.)

CC4 It is the end of November and Natalie has been in touch with her grandmother. Her grandmother asked Natalie how well things went in her first month of business. Natalie, too, would like to know if her business has been profitable or not during November. Natalie realizes that in order to determine Cookie Creations' income, she must first make adjustments.

© leungchopan/ Shutterstock

Go to the book's companion website, **www.wiley.com/college/kimmel**, *to see the completion of this problem.*

COMPREHENSIVE ACCOUNTING CYCLE REVIEW

ACR4-1 Mike Greenberg opened Kleene Window Washing Inc. on July 1, 2017. During July, the following transactions were completed.

Complete all steps in accounting cycle.

(LO 2, 3, 4), AP

July	1	Issued 12,000 shares of common stock for $12,000 cash.
	1	Purchased used truck for $8,000, paying $2,000 cash and the balance on account.
	3	Purchased cleaning supplies for $900 on account.
	5	Paid $1,800 cash on a 1-year insurance policy effective July 1.
	12	Billed customers $3,700 for cleaning services performed.
	18	Paid $1,000 cash on amount owed on truck and $500 on amount owed on cleaning supplies.

July 20 Paid $2,000 cash for employee salaries.
21 Collected $1,600 cash from customers billed on July 12.
25 Billed customers $2,500 for cleaning services performed.
31 Paid $290 for maintenance of the truck during month.
31 Declared and paid $600 cash dividend.

The chart of accounts for Kleene Window Washing contains the following accounts: Cash, Accounts Receivable, Supplies, Prepaid Insurance, Equipment, Accumulated Depreciation—Equipment, Accounts Payable, Salaries and Wages Payable, Common Stock, Retained Earnings, Dividends, Income Summary, Service Revenue, Maintenance and Repairs Expense, Supplies Expense, Depreciation Expense, Insurance Expense, and Salaries and Wages Expense.

Instructions

(a) Journalize the July transactions.
(b) Post to the ledger accounts. (Use T-accounts.)
(c) Prepare a trial balance at July 31.
(d) Journalize the following adjustments.
  (1) Services performed but unbilled and uncollected at July 31 were $1,700.
  (2) Depreciation on equipment for the month was $180.
  (3) One-twelfth of the insurance expired.
  (4) A count shows $320 of cleaning supplies on hand at July 31.
  (5) Accrued but unpaid employee salaries were $400.
(e) Post adjusting entries to the T-accounts.
(f) Prepare an adjusted trial balance.
(g) Prepare the income statement and a retained earnings statement for July and a classified balance sheet at July 31.
(h) Journalize and post closing entries and complete the closing process.
(i) Prepare a post-closing trial balance at July 31.

(f) Cash $5,410
(g) Tot. assets $21,500

Complete all steps in accounting cycle.

(LO 2, 3, 4), AP

ACR4-2 Lars Linken opened Lars Cleaners on March 1, 2017. During March, the following transactions were completed.

Mar. 1 Issued 10,000 shares of common stock for $15,000 cash.
1 Borrowed $6,000 cash by signing a 6-month, 6%, $6,000 note payable. Interest will be paid the first day of each subsequent month.
1 Purchased used truck for $8,000 cash.
2 Paid $1,500 cash to cover rent from March 1 through May 31.
3 Paid $2,400 cash on a 6-month insurance policy effective March 1.
6 Purchased cleaning supplies for $2,000 on account.
14 Billed customers $3,700 for cleaning services performed.
18 Paid $500 on amount owed on cleaning supplies.
20 Paid $1,750 cash for employee salaries.
21 Collected $1,600 cash from customers billed on March 14.
28 Billed customers $4,200 for cleaning services performed.
31 Paid $350 for gas and oil used in truck during month (use Maintenance and Repairs Expense).
31 Declared and paid a $900 cash dividend.

The chart of accounts for Lars Cleaners contains the following accounts: Cash, Accounts Receivable, Supplies, Prepaid Insurance, Prepaid Rent, Equipment, Accumulated Depreciation—Equipment, Accounts Payable, Salaries and Wages Payable, Notes Payable, Interest Payable, Common Stock, Retained Earnings, Dividends, Income Summary, Service Revenue, Maintenance and Repairs Expense, Supplies Expense, Depreciation Expense, Insurance Expense, Salaries and Wages Expense, Rent Expense, and Interest Expense.

Instructions

(a) Journalize the March transactions.
(b) Post to the ledger accounts. (Use T-accounts.)
(c) Prepare a trial balance at March 31.
(d) Journalize the following adjustments.
  1. Services performed but unbilled and uncollected at March 31 was $200.
  2. Depreciation on equipment for the month was $250.
  3. One-sixth of the insurance expired.
  4. An inventory count shows $280 of cleaning supplies on hand at March 31.

5. Accrued but unpaid employee salaries were $1,080.
6. One month of the prepaid rent has expired.
7. One month of interest expense related to the note payable has accrued and will be paid April 1. (*Hint:* Use the formula from Illustration 4-18 to compute interest.)

(e) Post adjusting entries to the T-accounts.
(f) Prepare an adjusted trial balance.
(g) Prepare the income statement and a retained earnings statement for March and a classified balance sheet at March 31.
(h) Journalize and post closing entries and complete the closing process.
(i) Prepare a post-closing trial balance at March 31.

(f) Tot. adj. trial balance $31,960
(g) Tot. assets $24,730

ACR4-3 On August 1, 2017, the following were the account balances of B&B Repair Services.

Journalize transactions and follow through accounting cycle to preparation of financial statements.

(LO 2, 3, 4), AP

	Debit		Credit
Cash	$ 6,040	Accumulated Depreciation—Equipment	$ 600
Accounts Receivable	2,910	Accounts Payable	2,300
Notes Receivable	4,000	Unearned Service Revenue	1,260
Supplies	1,030	Salaries and Wages Payable	1,420
Equipment	10,000	Common Stock	12,000
		Retained Earnings	6,400
	$23,980		$23,980

During August, the following summary transactions were completed.

Aug.	1	Paid $400 cash for advertising in local newspapers. Advertising flyers will be included with newspapers delivered during August and September.
	3	Paid August rent $380.
	5	Received $1,200 cash from customers in payment of account.
	10	Paid $3,120 for salaries due employees, of which $1,700 is for August and $1,420 is for July salaries payable.
	12	Received $2,800 cash for services performed in August.
	15	Purchased store equipment on account $2,000.
	20	Paid creditors $2,000 of accounts payable due.
	22	Purchased supplies on account $800.
	25	Paid $2,900 cash for employees' salaries.
	27	Billed customers $3,760 for services performed.
	29	Received $780 from customers for services to be performed in the future.

Adjustment data:

1. A count shows supplies on hand of $960.
2. Accrued but unpaid employees' salaries are $1,540.
3. Depreciation on equipment for the month is $320.
4. Services were performed to satisfy $800 of unearned service revenue.
5. One month's worth of advertising services has been received.
6. One month of interest revenue related to the $4,000 note receivable has accrued. The 4-month note has a 6% annual interest rate. (*Hint:* Use the formula from Illustration 4-18 to compute interest.)

Instructions

(a) Enter the August 1 balances in the ledger accounts. (Use T-accounts.)
(b) Journalize the August transactions.
(c) Post to the ledger accounts. B&B's chart of accounts includes Prepaid Advertising, Interest Receivable, Service Revenue, Interest Revenue, Advertising Expense, Depreciation Expense, Supplies Expense, Salaries and Wages Expense, and Rent Expense.
(d) Prepare a trial balance at August 31.
(e) Journalize and post adjusting entries.
(f) Prepare an adjusted trial balance.
(g) Prepare an income statement and a retained earnings statement for August and a classified balance sheet at August 31.
(h) Journalize and post closing entries and complete the closing process.
(i) Prepare a post-closing trial balance at August 31.

(f) Cash $2,020
Tot. Adj. trial balance $32,580
(g) Net loss $530

Record and post transaction, adjusting, and closing journal entries; prepare adjusted trial balance and financial statements.

(LO 2, 3, 4), AP

ACR4-4 At June 30, 2017, the end of its most recent fiscal year, Green River Computer Consultants' post-closing trial balance was as follows:

	Debit	Credit
Cash	$5,230	
Accounts receivable	1,200	
Supplies	690	
Accounts payable		$ 400
Unearned service revenue		1,120
Common stock		3,600
Retained earnings		2,000
	$7,120	$7,120

The company underwent a major expansion in July. New staff was hired and more financing was obtained. Green River conducted the following transactions during July 2017, and adjusts its accounts monthly.

July 1 Purchased equipment, paying $4,000 cash and signing a 2-year note payable for $20,000. The equipment has a 4-year useful life. The note has a 6% interest rate which is payable on the first day of each following month.

2 Issued 20,000 shares of common stock for $50,000 cash.

3 Paid $3,600 cash for a 12-month insurance policy effective July 1.

3 Paid the first 2 (July and August 2017) months' rent for an annual lease of office space for $4,000 per month.

6 Paid $3,800 for supplies.

9 Visited client offices and agreed on the terms of a consulting project. Green River will bill the client, Connor Productions, on the 20th of each month for services performed.

10 Collected $1,200 cash on account from Milani Brothers. This client was billed in June when Green River performed the service.

13 Performed services for Fitzgerald Enterprises. This client paid $1,120 in advance last month. All services relating to this payment are now completed.

14 Paid $400 cash for a utility bill. This related to June utilities that were accrued at the end of June.

16 Met with a new client, Thunder Bay Technologies. Received $12,000 cash in advance for future services to be performed.

18 Paid semi-monthly salaries for $11,000.

20 Performed services worth $28,000 on account and billed customers.

20 Received a bill for $2,200 for advertising services received during July. The amount is not due until August 15.

23 Performed the first phase of the project for Thunder Bay Technologies. Recognized $10,000 of revenue from the cash advance received July 16.

27 Received $15,000 cash from customers billed on July 20.

Adjustment data:

1. Adjustment of prepaid insurance.
2. Adjustment of prepaid rent.
3. Supplies used, $1,250.
4. Equipment depreciation, $500 per month.
5. Accrual of interest on note payable. (*Hint:* Use the formula from Illustration 4-18 to compute interest.)
6. Salaries for the second half of July, $11,000, to be paid on August 1.
7. Estimated utilities expense for July, $800 (invoice will be received in August).
8. Income tax for July, $1,200, will be paid in August.

The chart of accounts for Green River Computer Consultants contains the following accounts: Cash, Accounts Receivable, Supplies, Prepaid Insurance. Prepaid Rent, Equipment, Accumulated Depreciation—Equipment, Accounts Payable, Notes Payable, Interest Payable, Income Taxes Payable, Salaries and Wages Payable, Unearned Service Revenue, Common Stock, Retained Earnings, Dividends, Income Summary, Service Revenue, Supplies Expense, Depreciation Expense, Insurance Expense, Salaries and Wages Expense, Advertising Expense, Income Tax Expense, Interest Expense, Rent Expense, Supplies Expense, and Utilities Expense.

Instructions

(a) Enter the July 1 balances in the ledger accounts. (Use T-accounts.)
(b) Journalize the July transactions.
(c) Post to the ledger accounts.
(d) Prepare a trial balance at July 31.
(e) Journalize and post adjusting entries for the month ending July 31.
(f) Prepare an adjusted trial balance.
(g) Prepare an income statement and a retained earning statement for July and a classified balance sheet at July 31.
(h) Journalize and post closing entries and complete the closing process.
(i) Prepare a post-closing trial balance at July 31.

(g) Net income $6,770
Tot. assets $99,670

EXPAND YOUR CRITICAL THINKING

FINANCIAL REPORTING PROBLEM: Apple Inc.

Financial Reporting

CT4-1 The financial statements of Apple Inc. are presented in Appendix A at the end of this textbook.

E

Instructions

(a) Using the consolidated income statement and balance sheet, identify items that may result in adjusting entries for deferrals.
(b) Using the consolidated income statement, identify two items that may result in adjusting entries for accruals.
(c) What was the amount of depreciation and amortization expense for 2014 and 2013? (You will need to examine the notes to the financial statements or the statement of cash flows.) Where was accumulated depreciation and amortization reported?
(d) What was the cash paid for income taxes during 2014, reported at the bottom of the consolidated statement of cash flows? What was income tax expense (provision for income taxes) for 2014?

COMPARATIVE ANALYSIS PROBLEM: Columbia Sportswear Company vs. VF Corporation

Financial Analysis

CT4-2 The financial statements of Columbia Sportswear Company are presented in Appendix B. Financial statements of VF Corporation are presented in Appendix C.

E

Instructions

(a) Identify two accounts on Columbia's balance sheet that provide evidence that Columbia uses accrual accounting. In each case, identify the income statement account that would be affected by the adjustment process.
(b) Identify two accounts on VF's balance sheet that provide evidence that VF uses accrual accounting (different from the two you listed for Columbia). In each case, identify the income statement account that would be affected by the adjustment process.

COMPARATIVE ANALYSIS PROBLEM: Amazon.com, Inc. vs. Wal-Mart Stores, Inc.

Financial Analysis

CT4-3 The financial statements of Amazon.com, Inc. are presented in Appendix D. Financial statements of Wal-Mart Stores, Inc. are presented in Appendix E.

E

Instructions

(a) Identify two accounts on Amazon's balance sheet that provide evidence that Amazon uses accrual accounting. In each case, identify the income statement account that would be affected by the adjustment process.
(b) Identify two accounts on Wal-Mart's balance sheet that provide evidence that Wal-Mart uses accrual accounting (different from the two you listed for Amazon). In each case, identify the income statement account that would be affected by the adjustment process.

INTERPRETING FINANCIAL STATEMENTS

Financial Analysis

CT4-4 Laser Recording Systems, founded in 1981, produces disks for use in the home market. The following is an excerpt from Laser Recording Systems' financial statements (all dollars in thousands).

E

LASER RECORDING SYSTEMS
Management Discussion

Accrued liabilities increased to $1,642 at January 31, from $138 at the end of the previous fiscal year. Compensation and related accruals increased $195 due primarily to increases in accruals for severance, vacation, commissions, and relocation expenses. Accrued professional services increased by $137 primarily as a result of legal expenses related to several outstanding contractual disputes. Other expenses increased $35, of which $18 was for interest payable.

Instructions

(a) Can you tell from the discussion whether Laser Recording Systems has prepaid its legal expenses and is now making an adjustment to the asset account Prepaid Legal Expenses, or whether the company is handling the legal expense via an accrued expense adjustment?

(b) Identify each of the adjustments Laser Recording Systems is discussing as one of the four types of possible adjustments discussed in the chapter. How is net income ultimately affected by each of the adjustments?

(c) What journal entry did Laser Recording make to record the accrued interest?

REAL-WORLD FOCUS

CT4-5 ***Purpose:*** To learn about the functions of the Securities and Exchange Commission (SEC).

Address: **www.sec.gov/about/whatwedo.shtml**, or go to **www.wiley.com/college/kimmel**

Instructions

Use the information in this site to answer the following questions.

(a) What event spurred the creation of the SEC? Why was the SEC created?

(b) What are the five divisions of the SEC? Briefly describe the purpose of each.

(c) What are the responsibilities of the chief accountant?

DECISION-MAKING ACROSS THE ORGANIZATION

Financial Analysis

Writing

Group Project

CT4-6 Abbey Park was organized on April 1, 2016, by Trudy Crawford. Trudy is a good manager but a poor accountant. From the trial balance prepared by a part-time bookkeeper, Trudy prepared the following income statement for the quarter that ended March 31, 2017.

ABBEY PARK
Income Statement
For the Quarter Ended March 31, 2017

Revenues		
Rent revenue		$83,000
Operating expenses		
Advertising expense	$ 4,200	
Salaries and wages expense	27,600	
Utilities expense	1,500	
Depreciation expense	800	
Maintenance and repairs expense	2,800	
Total operating expenses		36,900
Net income		$46,100

Trudy knew that something was wrong with the statement because net income had never exceeded $20,000 in any one quarter. Knowing that you are an experienced accountant, she asks you to review the income statement and other data.

You first look at the trial balance. In addition to the account balances reported in the income statement, the ledger contains these selected balances at March 31, 2017.

Supplies	$ 4,500
Prepaid Insurance	7,200
Notes Payable	20,000

You then make inquiries and discover the following.

1. Rent revenue includes advanced rentals for summer-month occupancy, $21,000.
2. There were $600 of supplies on hand at March 31.

3. Prepaid insurance resulted from the payment of a 1-year policy on January 1, 2017.
4. The mail on April 1, 2017, brought the following bills: advertising for week of March 24, $110; repairs made March 10, $1,040; and utilities $240.
5. Wage expense totals $290 per day. At March 31, 3 days' wages have been incurred but not paid.
6. The note payable is a 3-month, 7% note dated January 1, 2017.

Instructions

With the class divided into groups, answer the following.

(a) Prepare a correct income statement for the quarter ended March 31, 2017.
(b) Explain to Trudy the generally accepted accounting principles that she did not follow in preparing her income statement and their effect on her results.

COMMUNICATION ACTIVITY

CT4-7 On numerous occasions, proposals have surfaced to put the federal government on the accrual basis of accounting. This is no small issue because if this basis were used, it would mean that billions in unrecorded liabilities would have to be booked and the federal deficit would increase substantially. S

Instructions

(a) What is the difference between accrual-basis accounting and cash-basis accounting?
(b) Comment on why politicians prefer a cash-basis accounting system over an accrual-basis system.
(c) Write a letter to your senators explaining why you think the federal government should adopt the accrual basis of accounting.

ETHICS CASE

CT4-8 Wells Company is a pesticide manufacturer. Its sales declined greatly this year due to the passage of legislation outlawing the sale of several of Wells' chemical pesticides. During the coming year, Wells will have environmentally safe and competitive replacement chemicals to replace these discontinued products. Sales in the next year are expected to greatly exceed those of any prior year. Therefore, the decline in this year's sales and profits appears to be a one-year aberration. E

Even so, the company president believes that a large dip in the current year's profits could cause a significant drop in the market price of Wells' stock and make it a takeover target. To avoid this possibility, he urges Tim Allen, controller, to accrue every possible revenue and to defer as many expenses as possible in making this period's year-end adjusting entries. The president says to Tim, "We need the revenues this year, and next year we can easily absorb expenses deferred from this year. We can't let our stock price be hammered down!" Tim didn't get around to recording the adjusting entries until January 17, but he dated the entries December 31 as if they were recorded then. Tim also made every effort to comply with the president's request.

Instructions

(a) Who are the stakeholders in this situation?
(b) What are the ethical considerations of the president's request and Tim's dating the adjusting entries December 31?
(c) Can Tim accrue revenues and defer expenses and still be ethical?

ALL ABOUT YOU

CT4-9 Companies prepare balance sheets in order to know their financial position at a specific point in time. This enables them to make a comparison to their position at previous points in time and gives them a basis for planning for the future. In order to evaluate *your* financial position, you can prepare a personal balance sheet. Assume that you have compiled the following information regarding your finances. (*Hint:* Some of the items might not be used in your personal balance sheet.) AP

Amount owed on student loan balance (long-term)	$ 5,000
Balance in checking account	1,200
Certificate of deposit (6-month)	3,000
Annual earnings from part-time job	11,300
Automobile	7,000
Balance on automobile loan (current portion)	1,500
Balance on automobile loan (long-term portion)	4,000

Home computer	800
Amount owed to you by younger brother	300
Balance in money market account	1,800
Annual tuition	6,400
Video and stereo equipment	1,250
Balance owed on credit card (current portion)	150
Balance owed on credit card (long-term portion)	1,650

Instructions

Prepare a personal balance sheet using the format you have learned for a classified balance sheet for a company. For the equity account, use M. Y. Own, Capital.

FASB CODIFICATION ACTIVITY

C **CT4-10** If your school has a subscription to the FASB Codification, go to **http://aaahq.org/ascLogin.cfm** to log in and prepare responses to the following.

Instructions

Access the glossary ("Master Glossary") to answer the following.

(a) What is the definition of revenue?
(b) What is the definition of compensation?

A Look at IFRS

LEARNING OBJECTIVE 6 **Compare the procedures for adjusting entries under GAAP and IFRS.**

It is often difficult for companies to determine in what time period they should report particular revenues and expenses. Both the IASB and FASB are working on a joint project to develop a common conceptual framework that will enable companies to better use the same principles to record transactions consistently over time.

KEY POINTS

Following are the key similarities and differences between GAAP and IFRS as related to accrual accounting.

Similarities

- In this chapter, you learned accrual-basis accounting applied under GAAP. Companies applying IFRS also use accrual-basis accounting to ensure that they record transactions that change a company's financial statements in the period in which events occur.
- Similar to GAAP, cash-basis accounting is not in accordance with IFRS.
- IFRS also divides the economic life of companies into artificial time periods. Under both GAAP and IFRS, this is referred to as the **periodicity assumption**.
- The **general** revenue recognition principle required by GAAP that is used in this textbook is similar to that used under IFRS.
- Revenue recognition fraud is a major issue in U.S. financial reporting. The same situation occurs in other countries, as evidenced by revenue recognition breakdowns at Dutch software company Baan NV, Japanese electronics giant NEC, and Dutch grocer Ahold NV.

Differences

- Under IFRS, revaluation (using fair value) of items such as land and buildings is permitted. IFRS allows depreciation based on revaluation of assets, which is not permitted under GAAP.
- The terminology used for revenues and gains, and expenses and losses, differs somewhat between IFRS and GAAP. For example, income under IFRS includes both revenues, which arise during the normal course of operating activities, and gains, which arise from activities outside of the normal sales of goods and services. The term income

is not used this way under GAAP. Instead, under GAAP income refers to the net difference between revenues and expenses.
- Under IFRS, expenses include both those costs incurred in the normal course of operations as well as losses that are not part of normal operations. This is in contrast to GAAP, which defines each separately.

LOOKING TO THE FUTURE

The IASB and FASB are completing a joint project on revenue recognition. The purpose of this project is to develop comprehensive guidance on when to recognize revenue. It is hoped that this approach will lead to more consistent accounting in this area. For more on this topic, see **www.fasb.org/project/revenue_recognition.shtml**.

IFRS Practice

IFRS SELF-TEST QUESTIONS

1. IFRS:
   (a) uses accrual accounting.
   (b) uses cash-basis accounting.
   (c) allows revenue to be recognized when a customer makes an order.
   (d) requires that revenue not be recognized until cash is received.

2. Which of the following statements is **false**?
   (a) IFRS employs the periodicity assumption.
   (b) IFRS employs accrual accounting.
   (c) IFRS requires that revenues and costs must be capable of being measured reliably.
   (d) IFRS uses the cash basis of accounting.

3. As a result of the revenue recognition project by the FASB and IASB:
   (a) revenue recognition places more emphasis on when the performance obligation is satisfied.
   (b) revenue recognition places more emphasis on when revenue is realized.
   (c) revenue recognition places more emphasis on when expenses are incurred.
   (d) revenue is no longer recorded unless cash has been received.

4. Which of the following is **false**?
   (a) Under IFRS, the term income describes both revenues and gains.
   (b) Under IFRS, the term expenses includes losses.
   (c) Under IFRS, companies do not engage in the adjusting process.
   (d) Under IFRS, revenue recognition fraud is a major issue.

5. Accrual-basis accounting:
   (a) is optional under IFRS.
   (b) results in companies recording transactions that change a company's financial statements in the period in which events occur.
   (c) has been eliminated as a result of the IASB/FASB joint project on revenue recognition.
   (d) is not consistent with the IASB conceptual framework.

INTERNATIONAL FINANCIAL REPORTING PROBLEM: Louis Vuitton

IFRS4-1 The financial statements of Louis Vuitton are presented in Appendix F. Instructions for accessing and using the company's complete annual report, including the notes to its financial statements, are also provided in Appendix F.

Instructions

Visit Louis Vuitton's corporate website and answer the following questions from Louis Vuitton's 2014 annual report.

(a) From the notes to the financial statements, how does the company determine the amount of revenue to record at the time of a sale?
(b) From the notes to the financial statements, how does the company determine the provision for product returns?
(c) Using the consolidated income statement and consolidated statement of financial position, identify items that may result in adjusting entries for deferrals.
(d) Using the consolidated income statement, identify two items that may result in adjusting entries for accruals.

Answers to IFRS Self-Test Questions

1. a **2.** d **3.** a **4.** c **5.** b

5

Merchandising Operations and the Multiple-Step Income Statement

CHAPTER PREVIEW

Merchandising is one of the largest and most influential industries in the United States. It is likely that a number of you will work for a merchandiser. Therefore, understanding the financial statements of merchandising companies is important. In this chapter, you will learn the basics about reporting merchandising transactions. In addition, you will learn how to prepare and analyze a commonly used form of the income statement—the multiple-step income statement.

CHAPTER OUTLINE

LEARNING OBJECTIVES		PRACTICE
1 Describe merchandising operations and inventory systems.	• Operating cycles • Flow of costs	DO IT! 1 Merchandising Operations and Inventory Systems
2 Record purchases under a perpetual inventory system.	• Freight costs • Purchase returns and allowances • Purchase discounts	DO IT! 2 Purchase Transactions
3 Record sales under a perpetual inventory system.	• Sales returns and allowances • Sales discounts	DO IT! 3 Sales Transactions
4 Prepare a multiple-step income statement and a comprehensive income statement.	• Single-step income statement • Multiple-step income statement • Comprehensive income statement	DO IT! 4 Multiple-Step Income Statement
5 Determine cost of goods sold under a periodic inventory system.	• Cost of goods purchased • Cost of goods sold	DO IT! 5 Cost of Goods Sold—Periodic System
6 Compute and analyze gross profit rate and profit margin.	• Gross profit rate • Profit margin	DO IT! 6 Gross Profit Rate and Profit Margin

Go to the ***REVIEW AND PRACTICE*** section at the end of the chapter for a targeted summary and exercises with solutions.

Visit **WileyPLUS** for additional tutorials and practice opportunities.

© omgimages/iStockphoto

Buy Now, Vote Later

Have you ever shopped for outdoor gear at an REI (Recreational Equipment Incorporated) store? If so, you might have been surprised if a salesclerk asked if you were a member. A member? What do you mean a member? REI is a consumer cooperative, or "co-op" for short. To figure out what that means, consider this quote from the company's annual report:

> As a cooperative, the Company is owned by its members. Each member is entitled to one vote in the election of the Company's Board of Directors. Since January 1, 2008, the nonrefundable, nontransferable, one-time membership fee has been $20 dollars. As of December 31, 2010, there were approximately 10.8 million members.

Voting rights? Now that's something you don't get from shopping at Wal-Mart. REI members get other benefits as well, including sharing in the company's profits through a dividend at the end of the year. The more you spend, the bigger your dividend.

Since REI is a co-op, you might wonder whether management's incentives might be a little different. Management is still concerned about making a profit, as it ensures the long-term viability of the company. REI's members also want the company to be run efficiently, so that prices remain low. In order for its members to evaluate just how well management is doing, REI publishes an audited annual report, just like publicly traded companies do.

How well is this business model working for REI? Well, it has consistently been rated as one of the best places to work in the United States by *Fortune* magazine. Also, REI had sustainable business practices long before social responsibility became popular at other companies. The CEO's Stewardship Report states "we reduced the absolute amount of energy we use despite opening four new stores and growing our business; we grew the amount of FSC-certified paper we use to 58.4 percent of our total paper footprint—including our cash register receipt paper; we facilitated 2.2 million volunteer hours and we provided $3.7 million to more than 330 conservation and recreation nonprofits."

So, while REI, like other retailers, closely monitors its financial results, it also strives to succeed in other areas. And, with over 10 million votes at stake, REI's management knows that it has to deliver.

LEARNING OBJECTIVE 1

Describe merchandising operations and inventory systems.

REI, Wal-Mart, and Amazon.com are called merchandising companies because they buy and sell merchandise rather than perform services as their primary source of revenue. Merchandising companies that purchase and sell directly to consumers are called **retailers**. Merchandising companies that sell to retailers are known as **wholesalers**. For example, retailer Walgreens might buy goods from wholesaler McKesson; retailer Office Depot might buy office supplies from wholesaler United Stationers. The primary source of revenue for merchandising companies is the sale of merchandise, often referred to simply as **sales revenue** or **sales**. A merchandising company has two categories of expenses: cost of goods sold and operating expenses.

Cost of goods sold is the total cost of merchandise sold during the period. This expense is directly related to the revenue recognized from the sale of goods. Illustration 5-1 shows the income measurement process for a merchandising company. The items in the two blue boxes are unique to a merchandising company; they are not used by a service company.

ILLUSTRATION 5-1
Income measurement process for a merchandising company

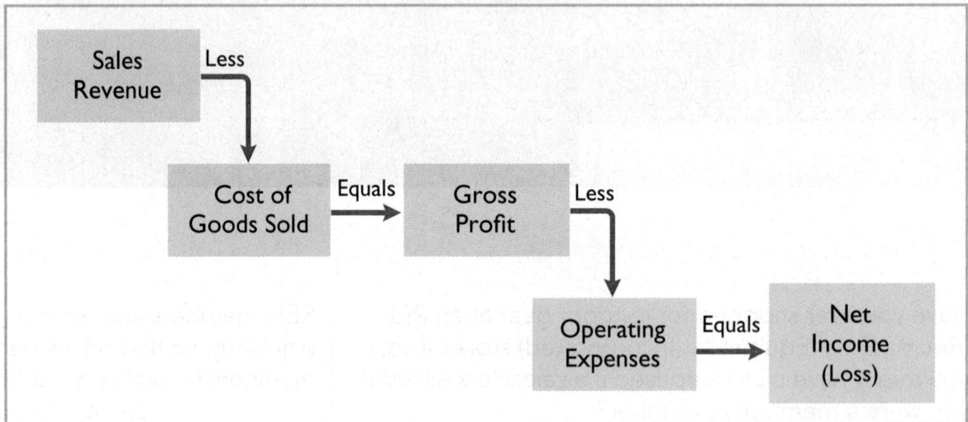

OPERATING CYCLES

The operating cycle of a merchandising company ordinarily is longer than that of a service company. The purchase of inventory and its eventual sale lengthen the cycle. Illustration 5-2 contrasts the operating cycles of service and merchandising companies. Note that the added asset account for a merchandising company is the Inventory account.

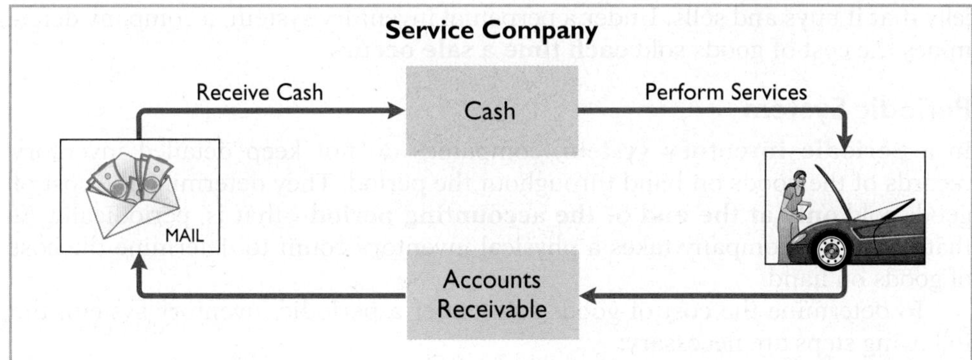

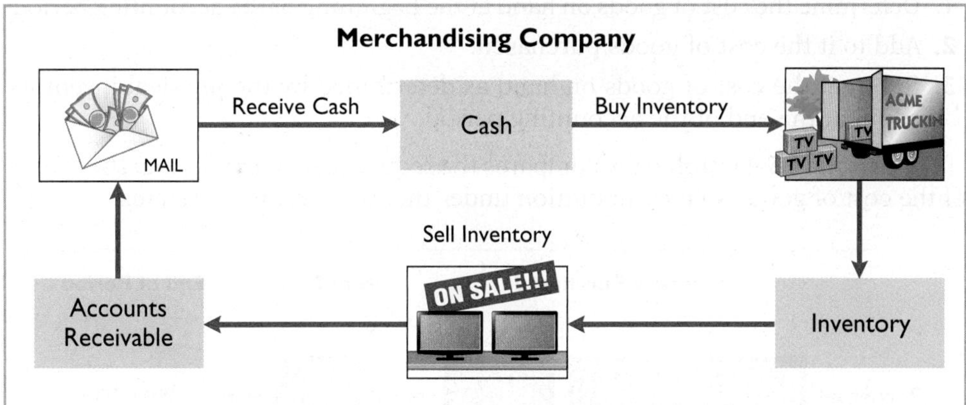

ILLUSTRATION 5-2
Operating cycles for a service company and a merchandising company

FLOW OF COSTS

The flow of costs for a merchandising company is as follows. Beginning inventory plus the cost of goods purchased is the cost of goods available for sale. As goods are sold, they are assigned to cost of goods sold. Those goods that are not sold by the end of the accounting period represent ending inventory. Illustration 5-3 describes these relationships. Companies use one of two systems to account for inventory: a **perpetual inventory system** or a **periodic inventory system**.

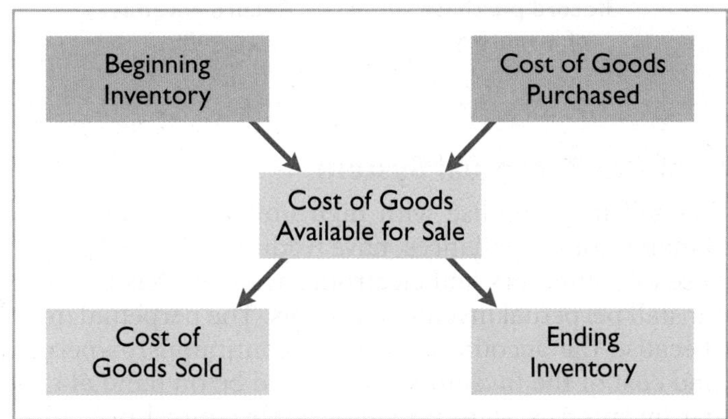

ILLUSTRATION 5-3
Flow of costs

Perpetual System

In a **perpetual inventory system**, companies maintain detailed records of the cost of each inventory purchase and sale. These records continuously—perpetually—show the inventory that should be on hand for every item. For example, a Ford dealership has separate inventory records for each automobile, truck, and van on its lot and showroom floor. Similarly, a grocery store uses bar codes and optical scanners to keep a daily running record of every box of cereal and every jar of

▼ HELPFUL HINT
Even under perpetual inventory systems, companies perform physical inventory counts. This is done as a control procedure to verify inventory levels, in order to detect theft or "shrinkage."

jelly that it buys and sells. Under a perpetual inventory system, a company determines the cost of goods sold **each time a sale occurs.**

Periodic System

In a **periodic inventory system**, companies do not keep detailed inventory records of the goods on hand throughout the period. They determine the cost of goods sold **only at the end of the accounting period**—that is, periodically. At that point, the company takes a physical inventory count to determine the cost of goods on hand.

To determine the cost of goods sold under a periodic inventory system, the following steps are necessary:

1. Determine the cost of goods on hand at the beginning of the accounting period.
2. Add to it the cost of goods purchased.
3. Subtract the cost of goods on hand as determined by the physical inventory count at the end of the accounting period.

Illustration 5-4 graphically compares the sequence of activities and the timing of the cost of goods sold computation under the two inventory systems.

ILLUSTRATION 5-4
Comparing perpetual and periodic inventory systems

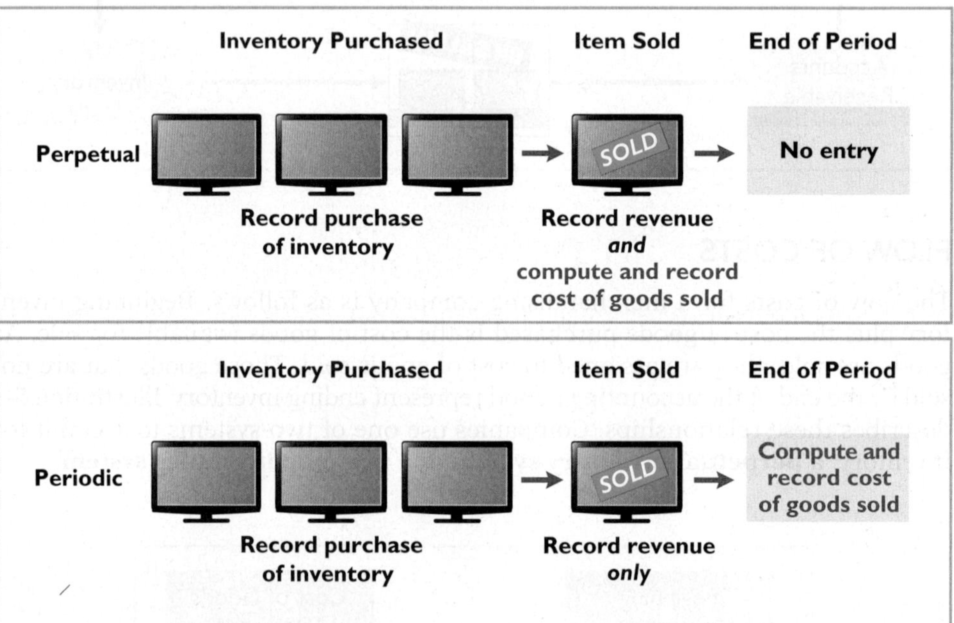

Advantages of the Perpetual System

Companies that sell merchandise with high unit values, such as automobiles, furniture, and major home appliances, have traditionally used perpetual systems. The growing use of computers and electronic scanners has enabled many more companies to install perpetual inventory systems. The perpetual inventory system is so named because the accounting records continuously—perpetually—show the quantity and cost of the inventory that should be on hand at any time.

A perpetual inventory system provides better control over inventories than a periodic system. Since the inventory records show the quantities that should be on hand, the company can count the goods at any time to see whether the amount of goods actually on hand agrees with the inventory records. If shortages are uncovered, the company can investigate immediately. Although a perpetual inventory system requires additional clerical work and additional cost to maintain inventory records, a computerized system can minimize this cost. Much of Amazon.com's success is attributed to its sophisticated inventory system.

Some businesses find it either unnecessary or uneconomical to invest in a sophisticated, computerized perpetual inventory system such as Amazon's.

However, many small merchandising businesses now use basic accounting software, which provides some of the essential benefits of a perpetual inventory system. Yet, managers of some small businesses still find that they can control their merchandise and manage day-to-day operations using a periodic inventory system.

Because of the widespread use of the perpetual inventory system, we illustrate it in this chapter. An appendix to this chapter describes the journal entries for the periodic system.

INVESTOR INSIGHT **Morrow Snowboards, Inc.**

© Ben Blankenburg/iStockphoto

Improving Stock Appeal

Investors are often eager to invest in a company that has a hot new product. However, when snowboard maker Morrow Snowboards, Inc. issued shares of stock to the public for the first time, some investors expressed reluctance to invest in Morrow because of a number of accounting control problems. To reduce investor concerns, Morrow implemented a perpetual inventory system to improve its control over inventory. In addition, it stated that it would perform a physical inventory count every quarter until it felt that its perpetual inventory system was reliable.

If a perpetual system keeps track of inventory on a daily basis, why do companies ever need to do a physical count? (Go to **WileyPLUS** for this answer and additional questions.)

DO IT! ▶1 Merchandising Operations and Inventory Systems

Indicate whether the following statements are true or false. If false, indicate how to correct the statement.

1. The primary source of revenue for a merchandising company results from performing services for customers.
2. The operating cycle of a service company is usually shorter than that of a merchandising company.
3. Sales revenue less cost of goods sold equals gross profit.
4. Ending inventory plus the cost of goods purchased equals cost of goods available for sale.

SOLUTION

1. False. The primary source of revenue for a service company results from performing services for customers. 2. True. 3. True. 4. False. Beginning inventory plus the cost of goods purchased equals cost of goods available for sale.

Related exercise material: **BE1-1** and  **5-1.**

Action Plan

✔ Review merchandising concepts.

✔ Understand the flow of costs in a merchandising company.

LEARNING OBJECTIVE ▶2 Record purchases under a perpetual inventory system.

Companies may purchase inventory for cash or on account (credit). They normally record purchases when they receive the goods from the seller. Every purchase should be supported by business documents that provide written evidence of the transaction. Each cash purchase should be supported by a canceled check or a cash register receipt indicating the items purchased and amounts paid. Companies record cash purchases by an increase (debit) in Inventory and a decrease (credit) in Cash.

Each purchase should be supported by a **purchase invoice**, which indicates the total purchase price and other relevant information. However, the purchaser does not prepare a separate purchase invoice. Instead, the purchaser uses as a purchase invoice the copy of the sales invoice sent by the seller. In Illustration 5-5, for example, Sauk Stereo (the buyer) uses as a purchase invoice the sales invoice prepared by PW Audio Supply, Inc. (the seller).

ILLUSTRATION 5-5
Sales invoice used as purchase invoice by Sauk Stereo

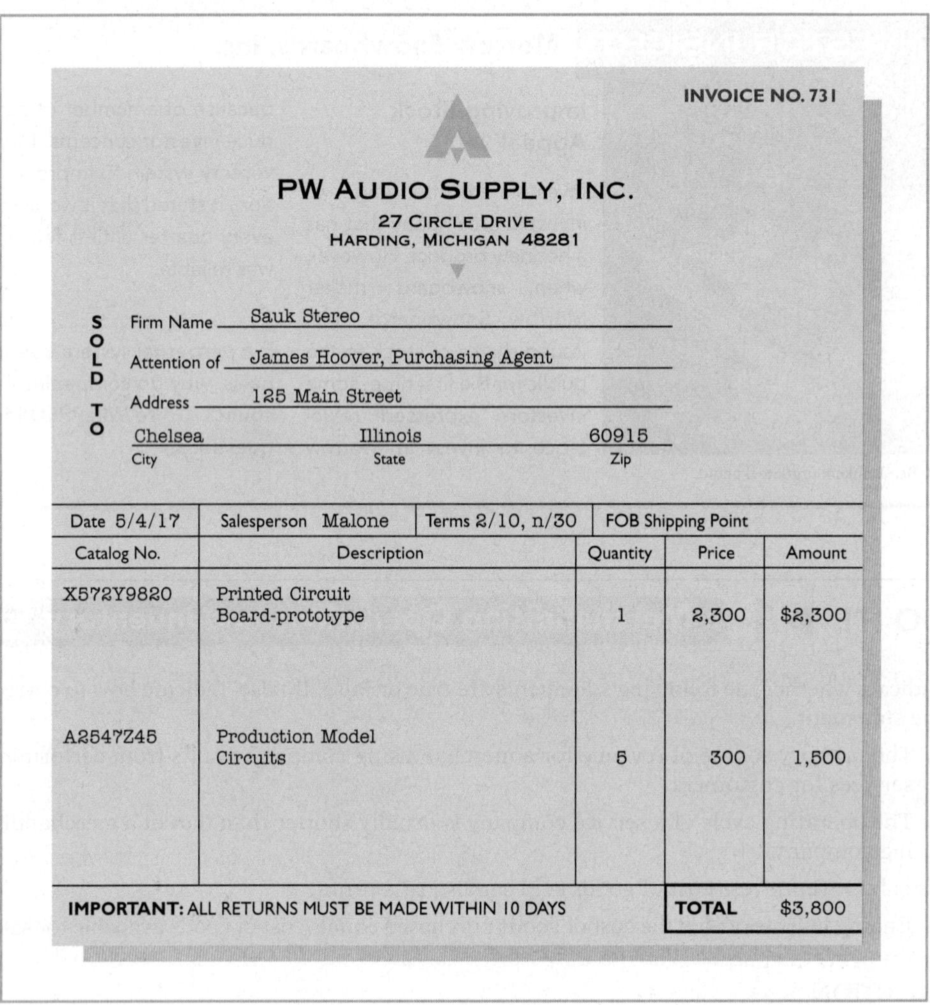

INVOICE NO. 731

PW AUDIO SUPPLY, INC.
27 CIRCLE DRIVE
HARDING, MICHIGAN 48281

SOLD TO
Firm Name: Sauk Stereo
Attention of: James Hoover, Purchasing Agent
Address: 125 Main Street
City: Chelsea State: Illinois Zip: 60915

Date 5/4/17 | Salesperson Malone | Terms 2/10, n/30 | FOB Shipping Point

Catalog No.	Description	Quantity	Price	Amount
X572Y9820	Printed Circuit Board-prototype	1	2,300	$2,300
A2547Z45	Production Model Circuits	5	300	1,500

IMPORTANT: ALL RETURNS MUST BE MADE WITHIN 10 DAYS — TOTAL $3,800

▼ HELPFUL HINT
To better understand the contents of this invoice, identify these items:
1. Seller
2. Invoice date
3. Purchaser
4. Salesperson
5. Credit terms
6. Freight terms
7. Goods sold: catalog number, description, quantity, price per unit
8. Total invoice amount

The associated entry for Sauk Stereo for the invoice from PW Audio Supply increases (debits) Inventory and increases (credits) Accounts Payable.

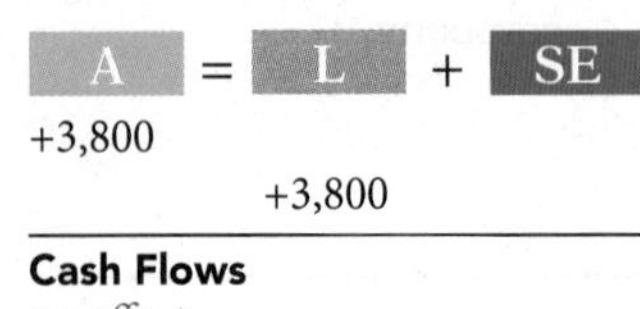

Cash Flows
no effect

May 4	Inventory	3,800	
	Accounts Payable		3,800
	(To record goods purchased on account from PW Audio Supply)		

Under the perpetual inventory system, companies record purchases of merchandise for sale in the Inventory account. Thus, REI would increase (debit) Inventory for clothing, sporting goods, and anything else purchased for resale to customers.

Not all purchases are debited to Inventory, however. Companies record purchases of assets acquired for use and not for resale, such as supplies, equipment, and similar items, as increases to specific asset accounts rather than to Inventory. For example, to record the purchase of materials used to make shelf signs or for cash register receipt paper, REI would increase (debit) Supplies.

FREIGHT COSTS

The sales agreement should indicate who—the seller or the buyer—is to pay for transporting the goods to the buyer's place of business. When a common carrier such as a railroad, trucking company, or airline transports the goods, the carrier prepares a freight bill in accord with the sales agreement.

Freight terms are expressed as either FOB shipping point or FOB destination. The letters FOB mean **free on board**. Thus, **FOB shipping point** means that the seller places the goods free on board the carrier, and the buyer pays the freight costs. Conversely, **FOB destination** means that the seller places the goods free on board to the buyer's place of business, and the seller pays the freight. For example, the sales invoice in Illustration 5-5 indicates FOB shipping point. Thus, the buyer (Sauk Stereo) pays the freight charges. Illustration 5-6 illustrates these shipping terms.

ILLUSTRATION 5-6
Shipping terms

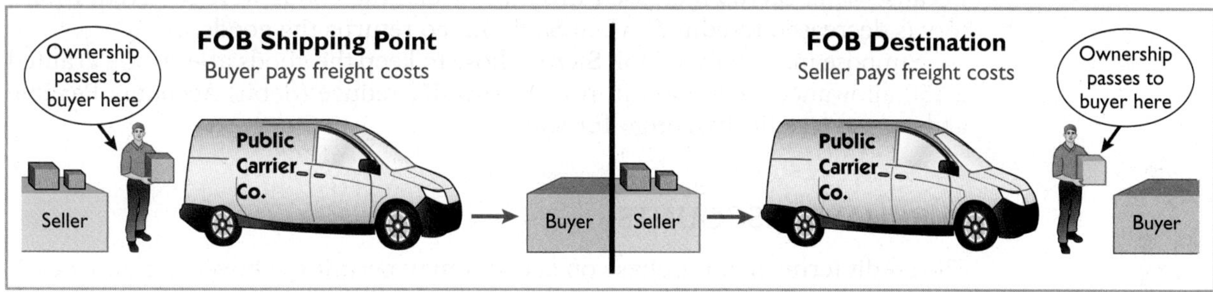

Freight Costs Incurred by Buyer

When the buyer pays the transportation costs, these costs are considered part of the cost of purchasing inventory. As a result, the account **Inventory is increased (debited)**. For example, if Sauk Stereo (the buyer) pays Public Freight Company $150 for freight charges on May 6, the entry on Sauk Stereo's books is:

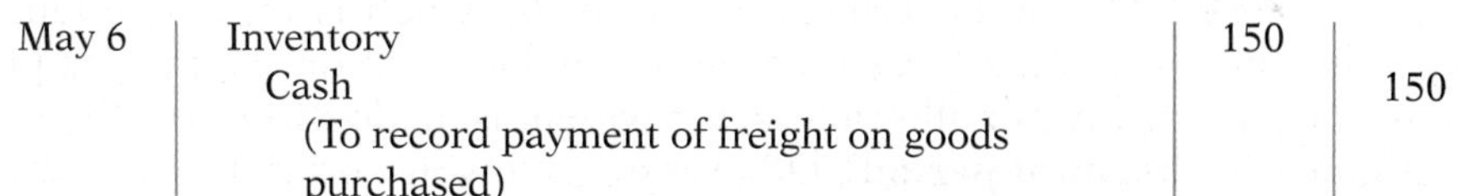

May 6	Inventory	150	
	Cash		150
	(To record payment of freight on goods purchased)		

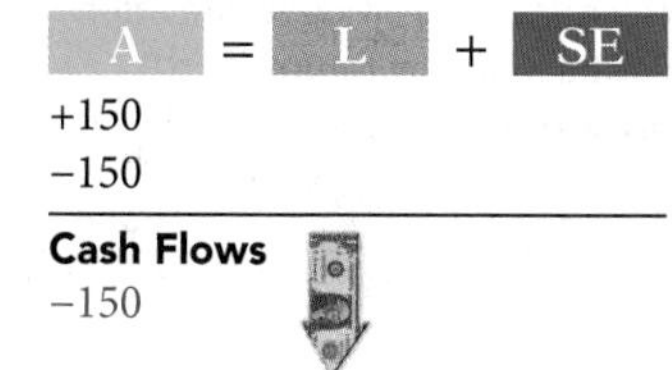

Thus, any freight costs incurred by the buyer are part of the cost of merchandise purchased. The reason: Inventory cost should include all costs to acquire the inventory, including freight necessary to deliver the goods to the buyer. Companies recognize these costs as cost of goods sold when inventory is sold.

Freight Costs Incurred by Seller

In contrast, **freight costs incurred by the seller on outgoing merchandise are an operating expense to the seller**. These costs increase an expense account titled Freight-Out (sometimes called Delivery Expense). For example, if the freight terms on the invoice in Illustration 5-5 had required that PW Audio Supply (the seller) pay the $150 freight charges, the entry by PW Audio Supply would be:

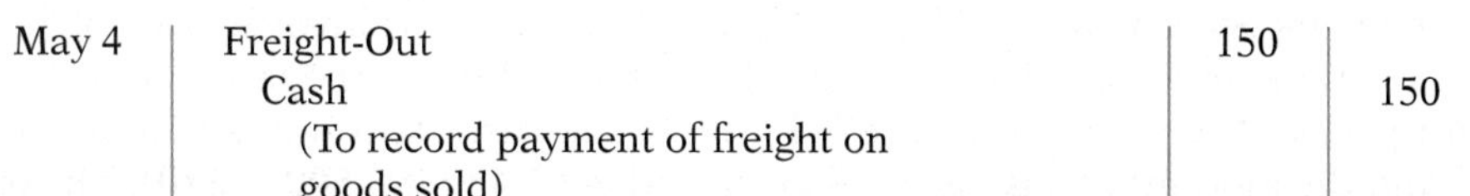

May 4	Freight-Out	150	
	Cash		150
	(To record payment of freight on goods sold)		

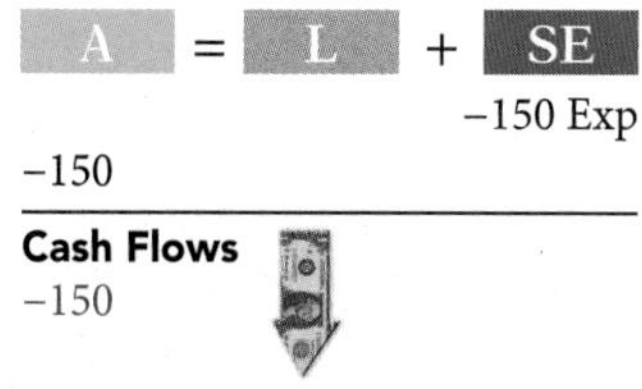

When the seller pays the freight charges, the seller will usually establish a higher invoice price for the goods, to cover the expense of shipping.

PURCHASE RETURNS AND ALLOWANCES

A purchaser may be dissatisfied with the merchandise received because the goods are damaged or defective, of inferior quality, or do not meet the purchaser's specifications. In such cases, the purchaser may return the goods to the seller for credit if the sale was made on credit, or for a cash refund if the purchase was for cash. This transaction is known as a **purchase return**. Alternatively, the purchaser may choose to keep the merchandise if the seller is willing to grant a reduction of the purchase price. This transaction is known as a **purchase allowance**.

Assume that Sauk Stereo returned goods costing $300 to PW Audio Supply on May 8. The following entry by Sauk Stereo for the returned merchandise decreases (debits) Accounts Payable and decreases (credits) Inventory.

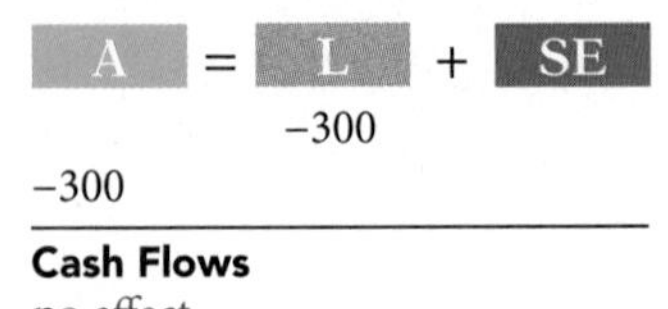

Cash Flows
no effect

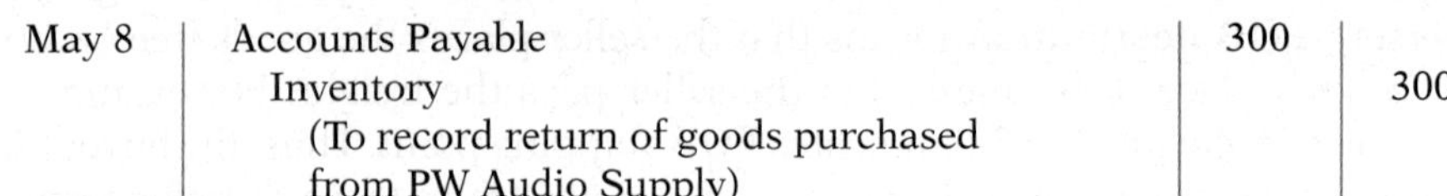

May 8	Accounts Payable	300	
	Inventory		300
	(To record return of goods purchased from PW Audio Supply)		

Because Sauk Stereo increased Inventory when the goods were received, Inventory is decreased (credited) when Sauk Stereo returns the goods.

Suppose instead that Sauk Stereo chose to keep the goods after being granted a $50 allowance (reduction in price). It would reduce (debit) Accounts Payable and reduce (credit) Inventory for $50.

PURCHASE DISCOUNTS

The credit terms of a purchase on account may permit the buyer to claim a cash discount for prompt payment. The buyer calls this cash discount a **purchase discount**. This incentive offers advantages to both parties. The purchaser saves money, and the seller is able to shorten the operating cycle by converting the accounts receivable into cash earlier.

▼ **HELPFUL HINT**
The term *net* in "net 30" means the remaining amount due after subtracting any returns and allowances and partial payments.

The credit terms specify the amount of the cash discount and time period during which it is offered. They also indicate the length of time in which the purchaser is expected to pay the full invoice price. In the sales invoice in Illustration 5-5 (page 220), credit terms are 2/10, n/30, which is read "two-ten, net thirty." This means that a 2% cash discount may be taken on the invoice price, less ("net of") any returns or allowances, if payment is made within 10 days of the invoice date (the **discount period**). Otherwise, the invoice price, less any returns or allowances, is due 30 days from the invoice date. Alternatively, the discount period may extend to a specified number of days following the month in which the sale occurs. For example, 1/10 EOM (end of month) means that a 1% discount is available if the invoice is paid within the first 10 days of the next month.

When the seller elects not to offer a cash discount for prompt payment, credit terms will specify only the maximum time period for paying the balance due. For example, the credit terms may state the time period as n/30, n/60, or n/10 EOM. This means, respectively, that the buyer must pay the net amount in 30 days, 60 days, or within the first 10 days of the next month.

When an invoice is paid within the discount period, the amount of the discount decreases Inventory. Why? Because the merchandiser records inventory at its cost and, by paying within the discount period, it has reduced that cost. To illustrate, assume Sauk Stereo pays the balance due of $3,500 (gross invoice price of $3,800 less purchase returns and allowances of $300) on May 14, the last day of the discount period. Since the terms are 2/10, n/30, the cash discount is $70 ($3,500 × 2%) and the amount of cash Sauk Stereo paid is $3,430 ($3,500 − $70). The entry Sauk Stereo makes to record its May 14 payment decreases (debits) Accounts Payable by the amount of the gross invoice price, reduces (credits) Inventory by the $70 discount, and reduces (credits) Cash by the net amount owed.

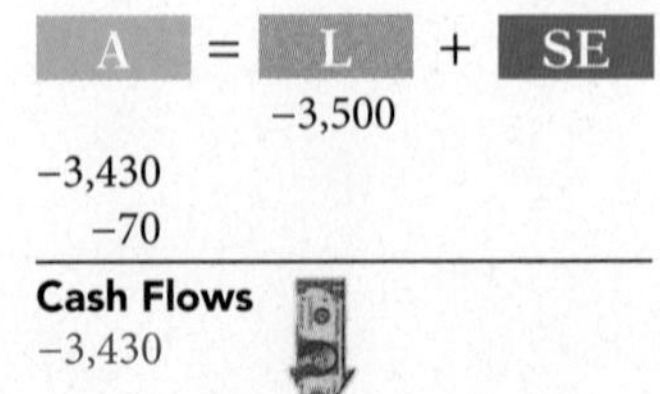

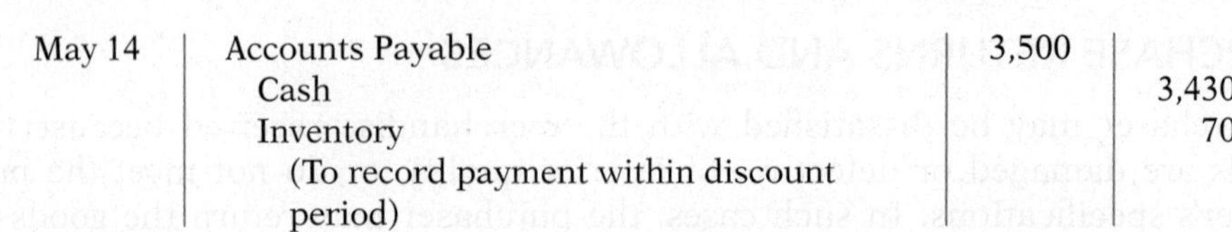

May 14	Accounts Payable	3,500	
	Cash		3,430
	Inventory		70
	(To record payment within discount period)		

If Sauk Stereo failed to take the discount and instead made full payment of $3,500 on June 3, Sauk Stereo would reduce (debit) Accounts Payable and reduce (credit) Cash for $3,500 each.

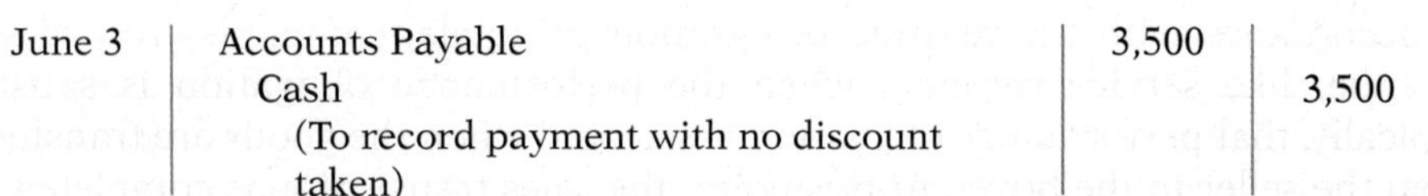

June 3	Accounts Payable	3,500	
	Cash		3,500
	(To record payment with no discount taken)		

A	=	L	+	SE
		−3,500		
−3,500				

Cash Flows
−3,500

A merchandising company usually should take all available discounts. Passing up the discount may be viewed as **paying interest** for use of the money. For example, passing up the discount offered by PW Audio Supply would be like Sauk Stereo paying an interest rate of 2% for the use of $3,500 for 20 days. This is the equivalent of an annual interest rate of approximately 36.5% (2% × 365/20). Obviously, it would be better for Sauk Stereo to borrow at prevailing bank interest rates of 6% to 10% than to lose the discount.

SUMMARY OF PURCHASING TRANSACTIONS

The following T-account (with transaction descriptions in red) provides a summary of the effect of the previous transactions on Inventory. Sauk Stereo originally purchased $3,800 worth of inventory for resale. It then returned $300 of goods. It paid $150 in freight charges, and finally, it received a $70 discount off the balance owed because it paid within the discount period. This results in a balance in Inventory of $3,580.

	Inventory				
Purchase	May 4	3,800	May 8	300	**Purchase return**
Freight-in	6	150	14	70	**Purchase discount**
Balance		3,580			

DO IT! ▶2 Purchase Transactions

On September 5, De La Hoya Company buys merchandise on account from Junot Diaz Company. The purchase price of the goods paid by De La Hoya is $1,500. On September 8, De La Hoya returns defective goods with a selling price of $200. Record the transactions on the books of De La Hoya Company.

SOLUTION

Sept. 5	Inventory	1,500	
	Accounts Payable		1,500
	(To record goods purchased on account)		
8	Accounts Payable	200	
	Inventory		200
	(To record return of defective goods)		

Action Plan

✔ Purchaser records goods at cost.

✔ When goods are returned, purchaser reduces Inventory.

Related exercise material: **BE5-2, BE5-4, DO IT! 5-2, E5-1, E5-2,** and **E5-4.**

LEARNING OBJECTIVE **3**

Record sales under a perpetual inventory system.

In accordance with the revenue recognition principle, companies record sales revenue, like service revenue, when the performance obligation is satisfied. Typically, that performance obligation is satisfied when the goods are transferred from the seller to the buyer. At this point, the sales transaction is completed and the sales price is established.

Sales may be made on credit or for cash. Every sales transaction should be supported by a **business document** that provides written evidence of the sale. **Cash register documents** provide evidence of cash sales. A **sales invoice**, like the one that was shown in Illustration 5-5 (page 220), provides support for each sale. The original copy of the invoice goes to the customer, and the seller keeps a copy for use in recording the sale. The invoice shows the date of sale, customer name, total sales price, and other relevant information.

▼ HELPFUL HINT
The merchandiser credits the Sales Revenue account only for sales of goods held for resale. Sales of assets not held for resale, such as equipment or land, are credited directly to the asset account.

The seller makes two entries for each sale. (1) It increases (debits) Accounts Receivable or Cash, as well as increases (credits) Sales Revenue. (2) It increases (debits) Cost of Goods Sold and decreases (credits) Inventory. As a result, the Inventory account will show at all times the amount of inventory that should be on hand.

To illustrate a credit sales transaction, PW Audio Supply records the sale of $3,800 on May 4 to Sauk Stereo (see Illustration 5-5) as follows (assume the merchandise cost PW Audio Supply $2,400).

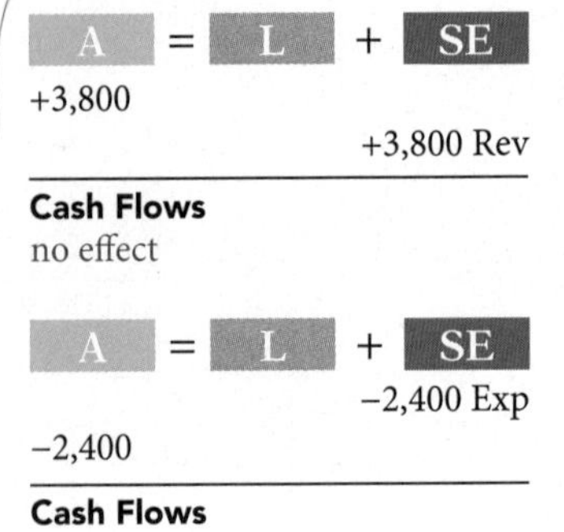

Date	Account	Debit	Credit
May 4	Accounts Receivable	3,800	
	Sales Revenue		3,800
	(To record credit sale to Sauk Stereo per invoice #731)		
4	Cost of Goods Sold	2,400	
	Inventory		2,400
	(To record cost of merchandise sold on invoice #731 to Sauk Stereo)		

For internal decision-making purposes, merchandising companies may use more than one sales account. For example, PW Audio Supply may decide to keep separate sales accounts for its sales of TVs, Blu-ray players, and headsets. REI might use separate accounts for camping gear, children's clothing, and ski equipment—or it might have even more narrowly defined accounts. By using separate sales accounts for major product lines, rather than a single combined sales account, company management can monitor sales trends more closely and respond to changes in sales patterns more strategically. For example, if TV sales are increasing while Blu-ray player sales are decreasing, the company might reevaluate both its advertising and pricing policies on each of these items to ensure they are optimal.

ETHICS NOTE
Many companies are trying to improve the quality of their financial reporting. For example, General Electric now provides more detail on its revenues and operating profits.

On its income statement presented to outside investors, a merchandising company would normally provide only a single sales figure—the sum of all of its individual sales accounts. This is done for two reasons. First, providing detail on all of its individual sales accounts would add considerable length to its income statement. Second, companies do not want their competitors to know the details of their operating results. However, at one time Microsoft expanded its disclosure of revenue from three to five types. The reason: The additional categories enabled financial statement users to better evaluate the growth of the company's consumer and Internet businesses.

At the end of "Anatomy of a Fraud" stories, which describe real-world frauds, we discuss the missing control activity that would likely have presented or uncovered the fraud.

ANATOMY OF A FRAUD[1]

Holly Harmon was a cashier at a national superstore for only a short time when she began stealing merchandise using three methods. Under the first method, her husband or friends took UPC labels from cheaper items and put them on more expensive items. Holly then scanned the goods at the register. Using the second method, Holly scanned an item at the register but then voided the sale and left the merchandise in the shopping cart. A third approach was to put goods into large plastic containers. She scanned the plastic containers but not the goods within them. After Holly quit, a review of past surveillance tapes enabled the store to observe the thefts and to identify the participants.

Total take: $12,000

THE MISSING CONTROLS

Human resource controls. A background check would have revealed Holly's previous criminal record. She would not have been hired as a cashier.

Physical controls. Software can flag high numbers of voided transactions or a high number of sales of low-priced goods. Random comparisons of video records with cash register records can ensure that the goods reported as sold on the register are the same goods that are shown being purchased on the video recording. Finally, employees should be aware that they are being monitored.

Source: Adapted from Wells, *Fraud Casebook* (2007), pp. 251–259.

SALES RETURNS AND ALLOWANCES

We now look at the "flip side" of purchase returns and allowances, which the seller records as **sales returns and allowances**. These are transactions where the seller either accepts goods back from a purchaser (a return) or grants a reduction in the purchase price (an allowance) so that the buyer will keep the goods. PW Audio Supply's entries to record credit for returned goods involve (1) an increase (debit) in Sales Returns and Allowances (a contra account to Sales Revenue) and a decrease (credit) in Accounts Receivable at the $300 selling price, and (2) an increase (debit) in Inventory (assume a $140 cost) and a decrease (credit) in Cost of Goods Sold, as shown below. (We assumed that the goods were not defective. If they were defective, PW Audio Supply would make an entry to the Inventory account to reflect their decline in value.)

May 8	Sales Returns and Allowances	300	
	Accounts Receivable		300
	(To record credit granted to Sauk Stereo for returned goods)		
8	Inventory	140	
	Cost of Goods Sold		140
	(To record cost of goods returned)		

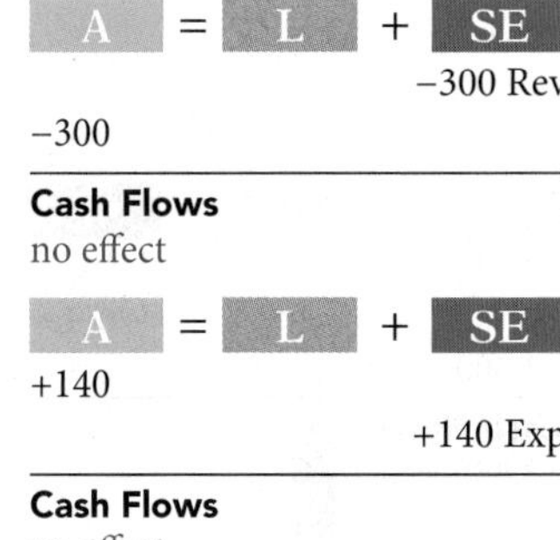

Suppose instead that the goods were not returned but the seller granted the buyer an allowance by reducing the purchase price. In this case, the seller would debit Sales Returns and Allowances and credit Accounts Receivable for the amount of the allowance. An allowance has no impact on Inventory or Cost of Goods Sold.

[1]The "Anatomy of a Fraud" stories in this textbook are adapted from *Fraud Casebook: Lessons from the Bad Side of Business,* edited by Joseph T. Wells (Hoboken, NJ: John Wiley & Sons, Inc., 2007). Used by permission. The names of some of the people and organizations in the stories are fictitious, but the facts in the stories are true.

Sales Returns and Allowances is a **contra revenue account** to Sales Revenue, which means it is offset against a revenue account on the income statement. The normal balance of Sales Returns and Allowances is a debit. Companies use a contra account, instead of debiting Sales Revenue, to disclose in the accounts and in the income statement the amount of sales returns and allowances. Disclosure of this information is important to management. Excessive returns and allowances suggest problems—inferior merchandise, inefficiencies in filling orders, errors in billing customers, or mistakes in delivery or shipment of goods. Moreover, a decrease (debit) recorded directly to Sales Revenue would obscure the relative importance of sales returns and allowances as a percentage of sales. It also could distort comparisons between total sales in different accounting periods.

At the end of the accounting period, if the company anticipates that sales returns and allowances will be material, the company should make an adjusting entry to estimate the amount of returns. In some industries, such as those relating to the sale of books and periodicals, returns are often material. The accounting for situations where returns must be estimated is addressed in advanced accounting courses.

ACCOUNTING ACROSS THE ORGANIZATION **Costco Wholesale Corp.**

© Jacob Wackerhausen/iStockphoto

The Point of No Returns?

In most industries, sales returns are relatively minor. But returns of consumer electronics can really take a bite out of profits. Recently, the marketing executives at Costco Wholesale Corp. faced a difficult decision. Costco has always prided itself on its generous return policy. Most goods have had an unlimited grace period for returns. A new policy will require that certain electronics must be returned within 90 days of their purchase. The reason? The cost of returned products such as high-definition TVs, computers, and iPods cut an estimated 8¢ per share off Costco's earnings per share, which was $2.30.

Source: Kris Hudson, "Costco Tightens Policy on Returning Electronics," *Wall Street Journal* (February 27, 2007), p. B4.

If a company expects significant returns, what are the implications for revenue recognition? (Go to WileyPLUS for this answer and additional questions.)

SALES DISCOUNTS

As mentioned in our discussion of purchase transactions, the seller may offer the customer a cash discount—called by the seller a **sales discount**—for the prompt payment of the balance due. Like a purchase discount, a sales discount is based on the invoice price less returns and allowances, if any. The seller increases (debits) the Sales Discounts account for discounts that are taken. The entry by PW Audio Supply to record the cash receipt on May 14 from Sauk Stereo within the discount period is:

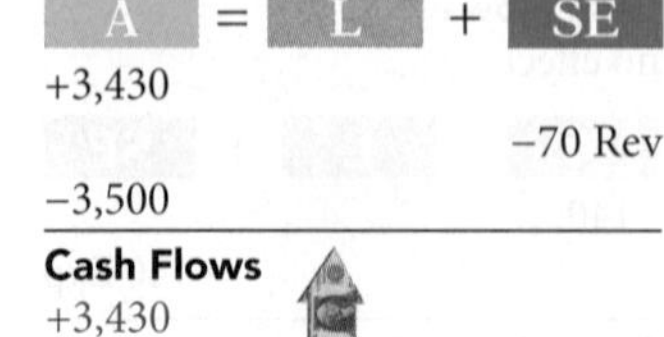

A	=	L	+	SE
+3,430				
				−70 Rev
−3,500				

Cash Flows
+3,430

May 14	Cash	3,430	
	Sales Discounts	70	
	Accounts Receivable		3,500
	(To record collection within 2/10, n/30 discount period from Sauk Stereo)		

Like Sales Returns and Allowances, Sales Discounts is a **contra revenue account** to Sales Revenue. Its normal balance is a debit. Sellers use this account, instead of debiting Sales Revenue, to disclose the amount of cash discounts taken by customers. If the customer does not take the discount, PW Audio Supply increases (debits) Cash for $3,500 and decreases (credits) Accounts Receivable for the same amount at the date of collection.

At the end of the accounting period, if the amount of potential discounts is material, the company should make an adjusting entry to estimate the discounts. This would not usually be the case for sales discounts but might be necessary for other types of discounts such as volume discounts, which are addressed in more advanced accounting courses. The following T-accounts summarize the three sales-related transactions and show their combined effect on net sales.

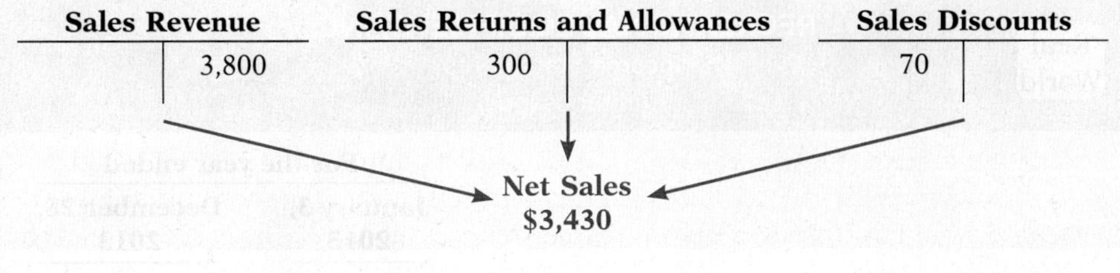

DO IT! 3 Sales Transactions

On September 5, De La Hoya Company buys merchandise on account from Junot Diaz Company. The selling price of the goods is $1,500, and the cost to Diaz Company was $800. On September 8, De La Hoya returns goods with a selling price of $200 and a cost of $105. Record the transactions on the books of Junot Diaz Company.

SOLUTION

Date	Account	Debit	Credit
Sept. 5	Accounts Receivable	1,500	
	Sales Revenue		1,500
	(To record credit sale)		
5	Cost of Goods Sold	800	
	Inventory		800
	(To record cost of goods sold)		
Sept. 8	Sales Returns and Allowances	200	
	Accounts Receivable		200
	(To record credit granted for receipt of returned goods)		
8	Inventory	105	
	Cost of Goods Sold		105
	(To record cost of goods returned)		

Action Plan

✔ Seller records both the sale and the cost of goods sold at the time of the sale.

✔ When goods are returned, the seller records the return in a contra account, Sales Returns and Allowances, and reduces Accounts Receivable.

✔ Any goods returned increase Inventory and reduce Cost of Goods Sold. The inventory should be recorded at the lower of its cost or its fair value (scrap value).

Related exercise material: **BE5-2, BE5-3,**  **5-3, E5-2, E5-3,** and **E5-4.**

LEARNING OBJECTIVE 4 Prepare a multiple-step income statement and a comprehensive income statement.

SINGLE-STEP INCOME STATEMENT

Companies widely use two forms of the income statement. One is the **single-step income statement**. The statement is so named because only one step, subtracting total expenses from total revenues, is required in determining net income (or net loss).

In a single-step statement, all data are classified into two categories: (1) **revenues**, which include both operating revenues and nonoperating revenues and gains (for example, interest revenue and gain on sale of equipment); and (2) **expenses**, which include cost of goods sold, operating expenses, and nonoperating expenses and losses (for example, interest expense, loss on sale of equipment, or income tax expense). The single-step income statement is the form we have used thus far in the text. Illustration 5-7 (page 228) shows a single-step statement for REI.

There are two primary reasons for using the single-step form. (1) A company does not realize any type of profit or income until total revenues exceed total expenses, so it makes sense to divide the statement into these two categories. (2) The form is simple and easy to read.

ILLUSTRATION 5-7
Single-step income statements

Real World

RECREATIONAL EQUIPMENT, INC.
Income Statements
(in thousands)

	For the year ended	
	January 3, 2015	**December 28, 2013**
Revenues		
Net sales	$2,217,131	$2,017,476
Expenses		
Cost of goods sold	1,257,002	1,148,668
Payroll-related expenses	423,061	393,505
Occupancy, general and administrative	355,190	345,643
Patronage refunds and other	110,611	100,802
Income taxes	27,149	10,017
	2,173,013	1,998,635
Net income	$ 44,118	$ 18,841

MULTIPLE-STEP INCOME STATEMENT

INTERNATIONAL NOTE
The IASB and FASB are involved in a joint project to evaluate the format of financial statements. The first phase of that project involves a focus on how to best present revenues and expenses. One longer-term result of the project may be an income statement format that better reflects how businesses are run.

A second form of the income statement is the **multiple-step income statement**. The multiple-step income statement is often considered more useful because it highlights the components of net income. The REI income statement in Illustration 5-8 is an example.

The multiple-step income statement has three important line items: gross profit, income from operations, and net income. They are determined as follows.

1. Subtract cost of goods sold from net sales to determine **gross profit**.
2. Deduct operating expenses from gross profit to determine **income from operations**.
3. Add or subtract the results of activities not related to operations to determine **net income**.

ILLUSTRATION 5-8
Multiple-step income statements

Real World

RECREATIONAL EQUIPMENT, INC.
Income Statements
(in thousands)

	For the year ended	
	January 3, 2015	**December 28, 2013**
Net sales	$2,217,131	$2,017,476
Cost of goods sold	1,257,002	1,148,668
Gross profit	960,129	868,808
Operating expenses		
Payroll-related expenses	423,061	393,505
Occupancy, general and administrative	355,190	345,643
Total operating expenses	778,251	739,148
Income from operations	181,878	129,660
Other revenues and gains		
Other revenues	-0-	-0-
Other expenses and losses		
Patronage refunds and other	110,611	100,802
Income before income taxes	71,267	28,858
Income tax expense	27,149	10,017
Net income	$ 44,118	$ 18,841

Note that companies report income tax expense in a separate section of the income statement before net income. The net incomes in Illustrations 5-7 and 5-8 are the same. The two income statements differ in the amount of detail displayed and the order presented. The following discussion provides additional information about the components of a multiple-step income statement.

Sales

The income statement for a merchandising company typically presents gross sales for the period. The company deducts sales returns and allowances and sales discounts (both contra accounts) from sales revenue in the income statement to arrive at **net sales**. Illustration 5-9 shows the sales section of the income statement for PW Audio Supply.

ILLUSTRATION 5-9
Statement presentation of sales section

PW AUDIO SUPPLY, INC. Income Statement (partial)		
Sales		
Sales revenue		$ 480,000
Less: Sales returns and allowances	$12,000	
Sales discounts	8,000	20,000
Net sales		**$460,000**

Gross Profit

The excess of net sales over cost of goods sold is **gross profit**. It is determined by deducting **cost of goods sold** from net sales. As shown in Illustration 5-8, REI had a gross profit of $960 million for the year ended January 3, 2015. This computation uses **net sales**, which takes into account sales returns and allowances and sales discounts.

ALTERNATIVE TERMINOLOGY
Gross profit is sometimes referred to as *gross margin*.

On the basis of the PW Audio Supply sales data presented in Illustration 5-9 (net sales of $460,000) and the cost of goods sold (assume a balance of $316,000), PW Audio Supply's gross profit is $144,000, computed as follows.

Net sales	$ 460,000
Cost of goods sold	316,000
Gross profit	**$144,000**

It is important to understand what gross profit is—and what it is not. Gross profit represents the **merchandising profit** of a company. Because operating expenses have not been deducted, it is **not a measure of the overall profit** of a company. Nevertheless, management and other interested parties closely watch the amount and trend of gross profit. Comparisons of current gross profit with past amounts and rates and with those in the industry indicate the effectiveness of a company's purchasing and pricing policies.

Operating Expenses

Operating expenses are the next component in measuring net income for a merchandising company. At REI, for example, operating expenses were $778 million for the year ended January 3, 2015.

At PW Audio Supply, operating expenses were $114,000. The firm determines its income from operations by subtracting operating expenses from gross profit. Thus, income from operations is $30,000, as shown below.

Gross profit	$144,000
Operating expenses	**114,000**
Income from operations	$ 30,000

Nonoperating Activities

Nonoperating activities consist of various revenues and expenses and gains and losses that are unrelated to the company's main line of operations. When nonoperating items are included, the label "**Income from operations**" (or "Operating income") precedes them. This label clearly identifies the results of the company's normal operations, an amount determined by subtracting cost of goods sold and operating expenses from net sales. The results of nonoperating activities are shown in the categories "**Other revenues and gains**" and "**Other expenses and losses.**" Illustration 5-10 lists examples of each.

ILLUSTRATION 5-10
Examples of nonoperating activities

Other Revenues and Gains
Interest revenue from notes receivable and marketable securities.
Dividend revenue from investments in capital stock.
Rent revenue from subleasing a portion of the store.
Gain from the sale of property, plant, and equipment.

Other Expenses and Losses
Interest expense on notes and loans payable.
Casualty losses from such causes as vandalism and accidents.
Loss from the sale or abandonment of property, plant, and equipment.
Loss from strikes by employees and suppliers.

ETHICS NOTE
Companies manage earnings in various ways. ConAgra Foods recorded a non-recurring gain for $186 million from the sale of Pilgrim's Pride stock to help meet an earnings projection for the quarter.

Nonoperating income is sometimes very significant. For example, in one quarter, Sears Holdings earned more than half of its net income from investments in derivative securities.

The distinction between operating and nonoperating activities is crucial to external users of financial data. These users view operating income as sustainable and many nonoperating activities as non-recurring. When forecasting next year's income, analysts put the most weight on this year's operating income and less weight on this year's nonoperating activities.

ETHICS INSIGHT IBM

ImageRite/Getty Images, Inc.

Disclosing More Details

After Enron, increased investor criticism and regulator scrutiny forced many companies to improve the clarity of their financial disclosures. For example, IBM began providing more detail regarding its "Other gains and losses." It had previously included these items in its selling, general, and administrative expenses, with little disclosure. For example, previously if IBM sold off one of its buildings at a gain, it included this gain in the selling, general, and administrative expense line item, thus reducing that expense. This made it appear that the company had done a better job of controlling operating expenses than it actually had.

As another example, when eBay recently sold the remainder of its investment in Skype to Microsoft, it reported a gain in "Other revenues and gains" of $1.7 billion. Since eBay's total income from operations was $2.4 billion, it was very important that the gain from the Skype sale not be buried in operating income.

Why have investors and analysts demanded more accuracy in isolating "Other gains and losses" from operating items? (Go to WileyPLUS for this answer and additional questions.)

Nonoperating activities are reported in the income statement immediately after operating activities. Included among "Other revenues and gains" in Illustration 5-11 (page 231) are Interest Revenue and Gain on Disposal of Plant Assets. Included in "Other expenses and losses" are Interest Expense and Casualty Loss from Vandalism.

In Illustration 5-11, we have provided the multiple-step income statement of PW Audio Supply. This statement provides more detail than that of REI and thus is useful as a guide for homework. *For homework problems, use the multiple-step form of the income statement unless the requirements state otherwise.*

ILLUSTRATION 5-11
Multiple-step income statement

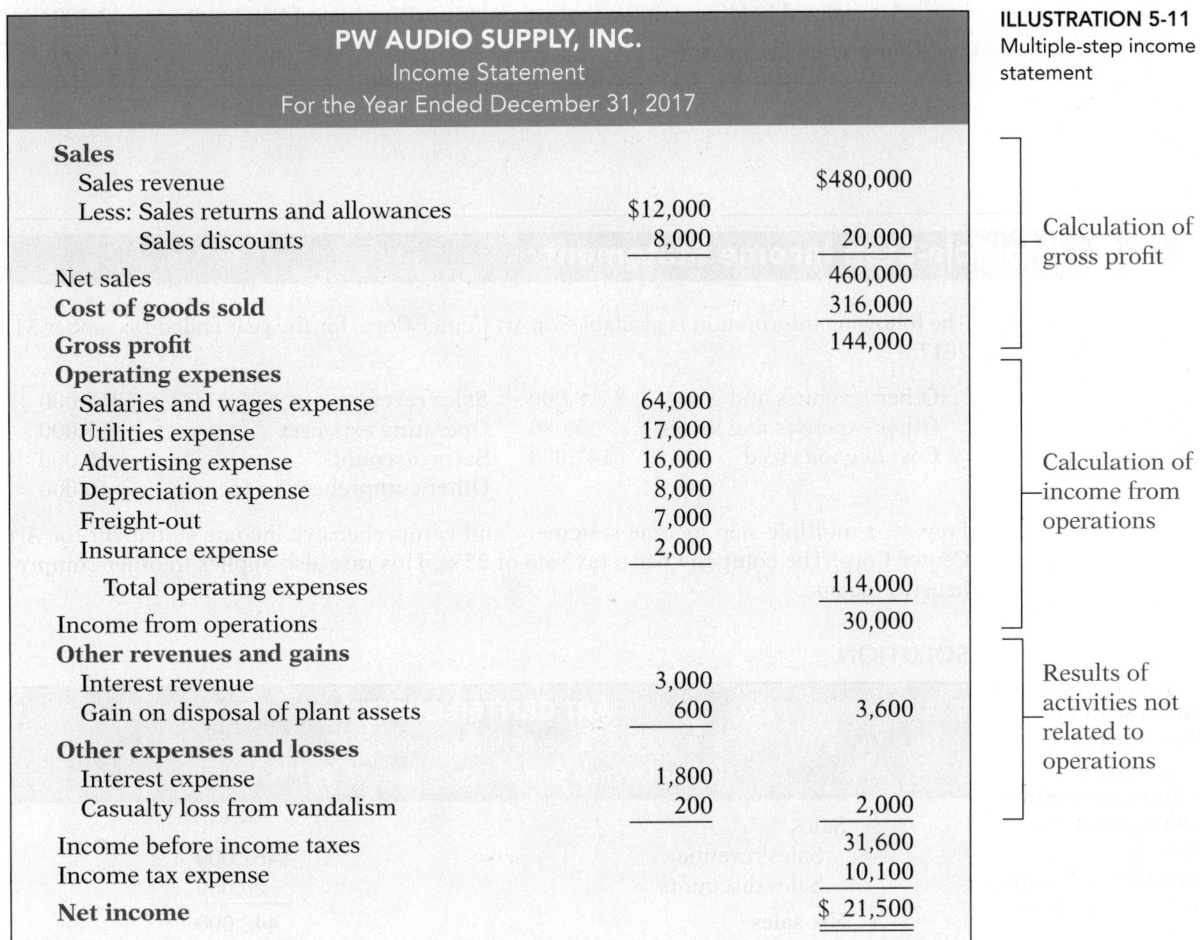

PW AUDIO SUPPLY, INC. Income Statement For the Year Ended December 31, 2017			
Sales			
Sales revenue		$480,000	
Less: Sales returns and allowances	$12,000		
Sales discounts	8,000	20,000	Calculation of gross profit
Net sales		460,000	
Cost of goods sold		316,000	
Gross profit		144,000	
Operating expenses			
Salaries and wages expense	64,000		
Utilities expense	17,000		
Advertising expense	16,000		
Depreciation expense	8,000		Calculation of income from operations
Freight-out	7,000		
Insurance expense	2,000		
Total operating expenses		114,000	
Income from operations		30,000	
Other revenues and gains			
Interest revenue	3,000		
Gain on disposal of plant assets	600	3,600	Results of activities not related to operations
Other expenses and losses			
Interest expense	1,800		
Casualty loss from vandalism	200	2,000	
Income before income taxes		31,600	
Income tax expense		10,100	
Net income		$ 21,500	

COMPREHENSIVE INCOME STATEMENT

Chapter 2 discussed the fair value principle. Accounting standards require companies to mark the recorded values of certain types of assets and liabilities to their fair values at the end of each reporting period. In some instances, the unrealized gains or losses that result from adjusting recorded amounts to fair value are included in net income. However, in other cases, these unrealized gains and losses are not included in net income. Instead, these excluded items are reported as part of a more inclusive earnings measure, called **comprehensive income**. Examples of such items include certain adjustments to pension plan assets, gains and losses on foreign currency translation, and unrealized gains and losses on certain types of investments. Items that are excluded from net income but included in comprehensive income are either reported in a combined statement of net income and comprehensive income, or in a separate comprehensive income statement. The **comprehensive income statement** presents items that are not included in the determination of net income, referred to as other comprehensive income. Illustration 5-12 (page 232) shows how comprehensive income is presented in a separate comprehensive income statement. It assumes that PW Audio Supply had an unrealized gain of $2,700 with $400 of related tax expense. *Use this format when preparing your homework.*

ILLUSTRATION 5-12
Combined statement of net income and comprehensive income

PW AUDIO SUPPLY, INC.
Comprehensive Income Statement
For the Year Ended December 31, 2017

Net income	$21,500
Other comprehensive income	
Unrealized holding gain on investment securities (net of $400 tax)	2,300
Comprehensive income	$23,800

DO IT! 4 Multiple-Step Income Statement

The following information is available for Art Center Corp. for the year ended December 31, 2017.

Other revenues and gains	$ 8,000	Sales revenue	$462,000
Other expenses and losses	3,000	Operating expenses	187,000
Cost of goods sold	147,000	Sales discounts	20,000
		Other comprehensive income	10,000

Prepare a multiple-step income statement and comprehensive income statement for Art Center Corp. The company has a tax rate of 25%. This rate also applies to other comprehensive income.

Action Plan

- ✔ Subtract cost of goods sold from net sales to determine gross profit.
- ✔ Subtract operating expenses from gross profit to determine income from operations.
- ✔ Add/subtract nonoperating items to determine income before tax.
- ✔ Multiply the tax rate by income before tax to determine tax expense.

SOLUTION

ART CENTER CORP.
Income Statement
For the Year Ended December 31, 2017

Sales		
Sales revenue		$462,000
Sales discounts		20,000
Net sales		442,000
Cost of goods sold		147,000
Gross profit		295,000
Operating expenses		187,000
Income from operations		108,000
Other revenues and gains	$8,000	
Other expenses and losses	3,000	5,000
Income before income taxes		113,000
Income tax expense		28,250
Net income		$ 84,750

ART CENTER CORP.
Comprehensive Income Statement
For the Year Ended December 31, 2017

Net income	$84,750
Other comprehensive income (net of $2,500 tax)	7,500
Comprehensive income	$92,250

Related exercise material: **BE5-5, BE5-6, BE5-7, DO IT! 5-4, E5-5, E5-6, E5-7, E5-8, E5-9, E5-10,** and **E5-11.**

LEARNING OBJECTIVE 5 Determine cost of goods sold under a periodic inventory system.

Determining cost of goods sold is different when a periodic inventory system is used rather than a perpetual system. As you have seen, a company using a **perpetual system** makes an entry to record cost of goods sold and to reduce inventory **each time a sale is made**. A company using a **periodic system** does not determine cost of goods sold **until the end of the period**. At the end of the period, the company performs a count to determine the ending balance of inventory. It then **calculates cost of goods sold by subtracting ending inventory from the goods available for sale**. Cost of goods available for sale is the sum of beginning inventory plus purchases, as shown in Illustration 5-13.

ILLUSTRATION 5-13
Basic formula for cost of goods sold using the periodic system

	Beginning Inventory
+	Cost of Goods Purchased
	Cost of Goods Available for Sale
−	Ending Inventory
	Cost of Goods Sold

Another difference between the two approaches is that the perpetual system directly adjusts the Inventory account for any transaction that affects inventory (such as freight costs, purchase returns, and purchase discounts). The periodic system does not do this. Instead, it creates different accounts for purchases, freight costs, purchase returns, and purchase discounts. These various accounts are shown in Illustration 5-14, which presents the calculation of cost of goods sold for PW Audio Supply using the periodic approach. Note that the basic elements from Illustration 5-13 are highlighted in Illustration 5-14. You will learn more in Chapter 6 about how to determine cost of goods sold using the periodic system.

ILLUSTRATION 5-14
Cost of goods sold for a merchandiser using a periodic inventory system

PW AUDIO SUPPLY, INC.
Cost of Goods Sold
For the Year Ended December 31, 2017

Cost of goods sold			
Inventory, January 1			$ 36,000
Purchases		$325,000	
Less: Purchase returns and allowances	$10,400		
Purchase discounts	6,800	17,200	
Net purchases		307,800	
Add: Freight-in		12,200	
Cost of goods purchased			**320,000**
Cost of goods available for sale			356,000
Inventory, December 31			**40,000**
Cost of goods sold			**$316,000**

▼ **HELPFUL HINT**
The far right column identifies the primary items that make up cost of goods sold of $316,000. The middle column explains cost of goods purchased of $320,000. The left column reports contra purchase items of $17,200.

The use of the periodic inventory system does not affect the form of presentation in the balance sheet. As under the perpetual system, a company reports inventory in the current assets section.

Appendix 5A provides further detail on the use of the periodic system.

DO IT! 5 Cost of Goods Sold—Periodic System

Aerosmith Company's accounting records show the following at the year-end December 31, 2017.

Purchase Discounts	$ 3,400
Freight-In	6,100
Purchases	162,500
Beginning Inventory	18,000
Ending Inventory	20,000
Purchase Returns and Allowances	5,200

Assuming that Aerosmith Company uses the periodic system, compute (a) cost of goods purchased and (b) cost of goods sold.

Action Plan

✔ To determine cost of goods purchased, adjust purchases for returns, discounts, and freight-in.

✔ To determine cost of goods sold, add cost of goods purchased to beginning inventory, and subtract ending inventory.

SOLUTION

(a) Cost of goods purchased = $160,000:

Purchases	−	Purchase returns and allowances	−	Purchase discounts	+	Freight-in	
$162,500	−	$5,200	−	$3,400	+	$6,100	= $160,000

(b) Cost of goods sold = $158,000:

Beginning inventory	+	Cost of goods purchased	−	Ending inventory	
$18,000	+	$160,000	−	$20,000	= $158,000

Related exercise material: **BE5-8, BE5-9, BE5-10, DO IT! 5-5, E5-12,** and **E5-13.**

LEARNING OBJECTIVE 6 Compute and analyze gross profit rate and profit margin.

GROSS PROFIT RATE

A company's gross profit may be expressed as a percentage by dividing the amount of gross profit by net sales. This is referred to as the **gross profit rate**. For PW Audio Supply, the gross profit rate is 31.3% ($144,000 ÷ $460,000).

DECISION TOOLS 

The gross profit rate helps companies decide if the prices of their goods are in line with changes in the cost of inventory.

Analysts generally consider the gross profit **rate** to be more informative than the gross profit **amount** because it expresses a more meaningful (qualitative) relationship between gross profit and net sales. For example, a gross profit amount of $1,000,000 may sound impressive. But if it was the result of sales of $100,000,000, the company's gross profit rate was only 1%. Illustration 5-15 demonstrates that gross profit rates differ greatly across industries.

ILLUSTRATION 5-15
Gross profit rate by industry

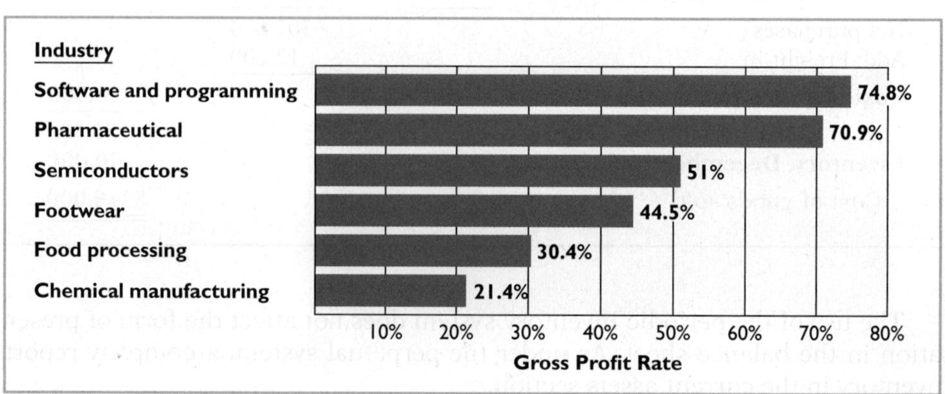

A decline in a company's gross profit rate might have several causes. The company may have begun to sell products with a lower "markup"—for example, budget blue jeans versus designer blue jeans. Increased competition may have resulted in a lower selling price. Or, maybe the company was forced to pay higher prices to its suppliers and was not able to pass these costs on to its customers. The gross profit rates for REI and Dick's Sporting Goods, and the industry average, are presented in Illustration 5-16.

ILLUSTRATION 5-16
Gross profit rate

$$\text{Gross Profit Rate} = \frac{\text{Gross Profit}}{\text{Net Sales}}$$

REI ($ in thousands)		Dick's Sporting Goods	Industry Average
2014	2013	2014	2014
$\frac{\$960,129}{\$2,217,131} = 43.3\%$	43.1%	31.3%	34.0%

REI's gross profit rate increased from 43.1% in 2013 to 43.3% in 2014. What might cause changes in REI's gross profit rate? When the economy changes, retailers also often adjust their selling prices. Changes in national weather patterns can also affect the amount of time people spend outdoors—and therefore impact their purchases of REI merchandise.

Why does REI's gross profit rate differ so much from that of Dick's Sporting Goods and the industry average? The gross profit rate often differs across retailers because of differences in the nature of their goods. First, REI focuses on outdoor equipment, while Dick's also sells sporting goods and hunting gear. The markup may differ significantly in these different product sectors. Also, although REI and Dick's both sell outdoor equipment, the quality of the equipment they sell differs. REI tends to sell more "high-end" goods, while Dick's tends to sell goods in a more "affordable" range. Higher-quality goods often receive a higher markup, but the retailer also sells fewer of them. In general, retailers adopt either a high-volume–low-margin approach (e.g., Wal-Mart) or a low-volume–high-margin approach (e.g., Saks Fifth Avenue). The strategic choice is often revealed in differences in the companies' gross profit rates.

PROFIT MARGIN

DECISION TOOLS 

The profit margin helps companies decide if they are maintaining an adequate margin between sales and expenses.

The **profit margin** measures the percentage of each dollar of sales that results in net income. We compute this ratio by dividing net income by net sales (revenue) for the period.

How do the gross profit rate and profit margin differ? The gross profit rate measures the margin by which selling price exceeds cost of goods sold. **The profit margin measures the extent by which selling price covers all expenses** (including cost of goods sold). A company can improve its profit margin by either increasing its gross profit rate and/or by controlling its operating expenses and other costs. For example, at one time Radio Shack reported increased profit margins which it accomplished by closing stores and slashing costs. Eventually, however, it was forced to file for bankruptcy as sales continued to decline.

Profit margins vary across industries. Businesses with high turnovers, such as grocery stores (Safeway and Kroger) and discount stores (Target and Wal-Mart), generally experience low profit margins. Low-turnover businesses, such as high-end jewelry stores (Tiffany and Co.) or major drug manufacturers (Merck), have high profit margins. Illustration 5-17 shows profit margins from a variety of industries.

ILLUSTRATION 5-17
Profit margins by industry

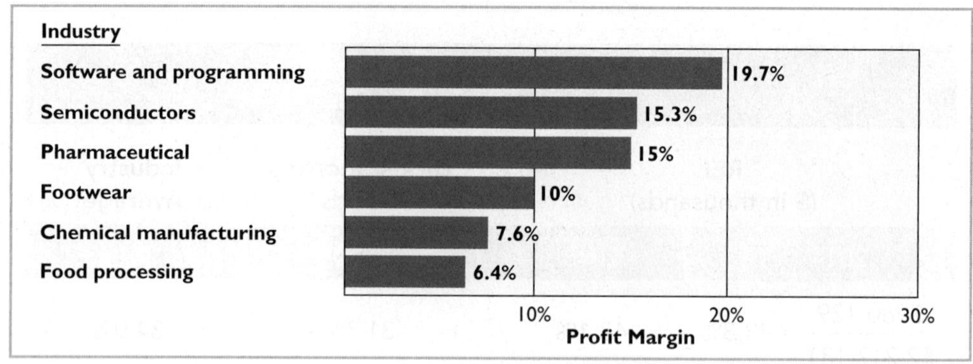

Profit margins for REI and Dick's Sporting Goods and the industry average are presented in Illustration 5-18.

ILLUSTRATION 5-18
Profit margin

$$\text{Profit Margin} = \frac{\text{Net Income}}{\text{Net Sales}}$$

REI ($ in thousands) 2014	REI 2013	Dick's Sporting Goods 2014	Industry Average 2014
$\frac{\$44,118}{\$2,217,131} = 2.0\%$	0.9%	5.4%	5.1%

REI's profit margin increased from 0.9% to 2.0% between 2013 and 2014. This means that the company generated 2.0¢ of profit on each dollar of sales. This increase occurred partly because the gross profit rate increased.

A change in the profit margin can be caused by a change in the gross profit rate, a change in the amount of operating expenses relative to sales, or a change in the amount of other items (other revenues and gains, or other expenses and losses) relative to sales. From Illustration 5-16, we know that REI's gross profit rate increased slightly. From analyzing the information in Illustration 5-8, we see that operating expenses as a percentage of sales decreased from 36.6% ($739,148 ÷ $2,017,476) in 2013 to 35.1% ($778,251 ÷ $2,217,131) in 2014. Therefore, in 2014, most of the increase in REI's profit margin occurred because of the decline in operating expenses as a percentage of sales.

How does REI compare to its competitors? Its profit margin was lower than Dick's in 2014 and was less than the industry average. Thus, its profit margin does not suggest exceptional profitability.

PEOPLE, PLANET, AND PROFIT INSIGHT PepsiCo Inc.

Helen Sessions/Alamy

Selling Green

Here is a question an executive of PepsiCo Inc. was asked: Should PepsiCo market green? The executive indicated that the company should, as he believes it's the No. 1 thing consumers all over the world care about. Here are some of his thoughts on this issue:

"Sun Chips are part of the food business I run. It's a 'healthy snack.' We decided that Sun Chips, if it's a healthy snack, should be made in facilities that have a net-zero footprint. In other words, I want off the electric grid everywhere we make Sun Chips. We did that. Sun Chips should be made in a facility that puts back more water than it uses. It does that. And we partnered with our suppliers and came out with the world's first compostable chip package.

Now, there was an issue with this package: It was louder than the New York subway, louder than jet engines taking off. What would a company that's committed to green do: walk away or stay committed? If your people are passionate, they're going to fix it for you as long as you stay committed. Six months later, the compostable bag has half the noise of our current package.

So the view today is: we should market green, we should be proud to do it . . . it has to be a 360 process, both internal and external. And if you do that, you can monetize environmental sustainability for the shareholders."

Source: "Four Problems—and Solutions," *Wall Street Journal* (March 7, 2011), p. R2.

What is meant by "monetize environmental sustainability" for shareholders? (Go to WileyPLUS for this answer and additional questions.)

KEEPING AN EYE ON CASH

In Chapter 4, you learned that **earnings have high quality if they provide a full and transparent depiction of how a company performed**. In order to quickly assess earnings quality, analysts sometimes employ the **quality of earnings ratio**. It is calculated as net cash provided by operating activities divided by net income.

$$\text{Quality of Earnings Ratio} = \frac{\text{Net Cash Provided by Operating Activities}}{\text{Net Income}}$$

In general, a measure significantly less than 1 suggests that a company may be using more aggressive accounting techniques in order to accelerate income recognition (record income in earlier periods). A measure significantly greater than 1 suggests that a company is using conservative accounting techniques, which cause it to delay the recognition of income.

Measures that are significantly less than 1 do not provide definitive evidence of low-quality earnings. Low measures do, however, indicate that analysts should investigate the causes of the difference between net income and net cash provided by operating activities. Examples of factors that would cause differences are presented in Chapter 4 (page 179).

Here are recent quality of earnings ratios for a number of well-known companies, all of which have measures in excess of 1.

Company Name ($ in millions)	Net Cash Provided by Operating Activities	÷	Net Income	=	Quality of Earnings Ratio
DuPont	$4,741		$1,769		2.7
Intel	$11,170		$4,369		2.6
Nike	$1,736		$1,487		1.2
Microsoft	$19,037		$14,569		1.3
Wal-Mart	$26,249		$14,335		1.8

DO IT! 6 Gross Profit Rate and Profit Margin

Rachel Rose, Inc. reported the following in its 2017 and 2016 income statements.

	2017	2016
Net sales	$80,000	$120,000
Cost of goods sold	40,000	60,000
Operating expenses	14,000	28,000
Income tax expense	8,000	12,000
Net income	$18,000	$ 20,000

Determine the company's gross profit rate and profit margin. Discuss the cause for changes in the ratios.

Action Plan

✔ **To determine gross profit rate, divide gross profit by net sales.**

✔ **To find profit margin, divide net income by net sales.**

SOLUTION

	2017	2016
Gross profit rate	$\frac{(\$80,000 - \$40,000)}{\$80,000} = 50\%$	$\frac{(\$120,000 - \$60,000)}{\$120,000} = 50\%$
Profit margin	$18,000 ÷ $80,000 = 22.5%	$20,000 ÷ $120,000 = 16.7%

The company's gross profit rate remained constant. However, its profit margin increased significantly due to a sharp decline in its operating costs as a percentage of sales, which declined from 23% ($28,000 ÷ $120,000) in 2016 to 17.5% ($14,000 ÷ $80,000) in 2017.

Related exercise material: **BE5-11, BE5-12, BE5-13, DO IT! 5-6, E5-7, E5-8, E5-9,** and **E5-14.**

USING DECISION TOOLS—MOUNTAIN EQUIPMENT COOPERATIVE

Like REI, Mountain Equipment Cooperative (MEC) is a retailer of outdoor equipment organized as a cooperative (though MEC *only* sells to its members, who pay a one-time fee of $5). Also like REI, MEC has a significant commitment to sustainability. Many of its stores employ state-of-the-art building techniques to minimize energy use, and it pledges 1% of annual sales revenue to environmental causes. Since MEC is a Canadian company, it follows International Financial Reporting Standards (IFRS) rather than U.S. GAAP. The *A Look at IFRS* section at the end of each chapter of this textbook discusses some of the main accounting differences that you would need to be aware of to make a thorough comparison of REI and MEC. Here is recent data for MEC.

	Year ended	
($ in thousands)	**12/28/14**	**12/29/13**
Net income	$ 60	$ 361
Sales revenue	336,071	320,871
Cost of goods sold	226,099	215,614

INSTRUCTIONS

Using the basic facts in the table, evaluate the following components of MEC's profitability for the years ended December 28, 2014, and December 29, 2013.

Profit margin
Gross profit rate

How do MEC's profit margin and gross profit rate compare to those of REI and Dick's Sporting Goods for 2014?

SOLUTION

($ in thousands)	Year ended 12/28/14	Year ended 12/29/13
Profit margin	$\frac{\$60}{\$336,071} = 0.0\%$	$\frac{\$361}{\$320,871} = 0.1\%$
Gross profit rate	$\frac{\$109,972^*}{\$336,071} = 32.7\%$	$\frac{\$105,257^{**}}{\$320,871} = 32.8\%$

*$336,071 − $226,099 **$320,871 − $215,614

MEC's profit margin (income per dollar of sales) remained constant at 0.0%. This is well below both REI's (2.0%) and Dick's (5.4%). Thus, MEC is not as effective at turning its sales into net income as these two competitors.

MEC's gross profit rate declined slightly from 32.8% to 32.7%. This suggests that its ability to maintain its markup above its cost of goods sold declined slightly during this period. MEC's gross profit rate of 32.7% is lower than REI's (43.3%) but higher than Dick's (31.3%). Dick's gross profit is depressed by the fact that it sells many low-margin products. REI is superior to MEC both in its ability to maintain its markup above its costs of goods sold (its gross profit rate) and in its ability to control operating costs (its profit margin).

LEARNING OBJECTIVE 

APPENDIX 5A: Record purchases and sales of inventory under a periodic inventory system.

As described in this chapter, companies may use one of two basic systems of accounting for inventories: (1) the perpetual inventory system or (2) the periodic inventory system. In the chapter, we focused on the characteristics of the perpetual inventory system. In this appendix, we discuss and illustrate the **periodic inventory system**. One key difference between the two systems is the point at which the company computes cost of goods sold. For a visual reminder of this difference, you may want to refer back to Illustration 5-4 on page 218.

RECORDING MERCHANDISE TRANSACTIONS

In a **periodic inventory system**, companies record revenues from the sale of merchandise when sales are made, just as in a perpetual system. Unlike the perpetual system, however, companies **do not attempt on the date of sale to record the cost of the merchandise sold**. Instead, they take a physical inventory count at the **end of the period** to determine (1) the cost of the merchandise then on hand and (2) the cost of the goods sold during the period. And, **under a periodic system, companies record purchases of merchandise in the Purchases account rather than the Inventory account**. Purchase returns and allowances, purchase discounts, and freight costs on purchases are recorded in separate accounts.

To illustrate the recording of merchandise transactions under a periodic inventory system, we will use purchase/sale transactions between PW Audio Supply, Inc. and Sauk Stereo, as illustrated for the perpetual inventory system in this chapter.

RECORDING PURCHASES OF MERCHANDISE

On the basis of the sales invoice (Illustration 5-5, shown on page 220) and receipt of the merchandise ordered from PW Audio Supply, Sauk Stereo records the $3,800 purchase as follows.

May 4	Purchases	3,800	
	Accounts Payable		3,800
	(To record goods purchased on account from PW Audio Supply)		

Purchases is a temporary account whose normal balance is a debit.

FREIGHT COSTS

When the purchaser directly incurs the freight costs, it debits the account Freight-In (or Transportation-In). For example, if Sauk Stereo pays Public Freight Company $150 for freight charges on its purchase from PW Audio Supply on May 6, the entry on Sauk Stereo's books is as follows.

May 6	Freight-In (Transportation-In)	150	
	Cash		150
	(To record payment of freight on goods purchased)		

Like Purchases, Freight-In is a temporary account whose normal balance is a debit. **Freight-In is part of cost of goods purchased.** The reason is that cost of goods purchased should include any freight charges necessary to bring the goods to the purchaser. Freight costs are not subject to a purchase discount. Purchase discounts apply on the invoice cost of the merchandise.

Purchase Returns and Allowances

Sauk Stereo returns goods costing $300 to PW Audio Supply and prepares the following entry to recognize the return.

May 8	Accounts Payable	300	
	Purchase Returns and Allowances		300
	(To record return of goods purchased from PW Audio Supply)		

Purchase Returns and Allowances is a temporary account whose normal balance is a credit.

Purchase Discounts

On May 14, Sauk Stereo pays the balance due on account to PW Audio Supply, taking the 2% cash discount allowed by PW Audio Supply for payment within 10 days. Sauk Stereo records the payment and discount as follows.

May 14	Accounts Payable ($3,800 − $300)	3,500	
	Purchase Discounts ($3,500 × .02)		70
	Cash		3,430
	(To record payment within the discount period)		

Purchase Discounts is a temporary account whose normal balance is a credit.

RECORDING SALES OF MERCHANDISE

The seller, PW Audio Supply, records the sale of $3,800 of merchandise to Sauk Stereo on May 4 (sales invoice No. 731, Illustration 5-5, page 220) as follows.

May 4	Accounts Receivable	3,800	
	Sales Revenue		3,800
	(To record credit sale to Sauk Stereo per invoice #731)		

Sales Returns and Allowances

To record the returned goods received from Sauk Stereo on May 8, PW Audio Supply records the $300 sales return as follows.

May 8	Sales Returns and Allowances	300	
	Accounts Receivable		300
	(To record credit granted to Sauk Stereo for returned goods)		

Sales Discounts

On May 14, PW Audio Supply receives payment of $3,430 on account from Sauk Stereo. PW Audio Supply honors the 2% cash discount and records the payment of Sauk Stereo's account receivable in full as follows.

May 14	Cash	3,430	
	Sales Discounts ($3,500 × .02)	70	
	Accounts Receivable ($3,800 − $300)		3,500
	(To record collection within 2/10, n/30 discount period from Sauk Stereo)		

COMPARISON OF ENTRIES—PERPETUAL VS. PERIODIC

ENTRIES ON SAUK STEREO'S BOOKS

Transaction		Perpetual Inventory System			Periodic Inventory System		
May 4	Purchase of merchandise on credit.	Inventory	3,800		Purchases	3,800	
		Accounts Payable		3,800	Accounts Payable		3,800
May 6	Freight costs on purchases.	Inventory	150		Freight-In	150	
		Cash		150	Cash		150
May 8	Purchase returns and allowances.	Accounts Payable	300		Accounts Payable	300	
		Inventory		300	Purchase Returns and Allowances		300
May 14	Payment on account with a discount.	Accounts Payable	3,500		Accounts Payable	3,500	
		Cash		3,430	Cash		3,430
		Inventory		70	Purchase Discounts		70

ENTRIES ON PW AUDIO SUPPLY'S BOOKS

Transaction		Perpetual Inventory System			Periodic Inventory System		
May 4	Sale of merchandise on credit.	Accounts Receivable	3,800		Accounts Receivable	3,800	
		Sales Revenue		3,800	Sales Revenue		3,800
		Cost of Goods Sold	2,400		No entry for cost of goods sold		
		Inventory		2,400			
May 8	Return of merchandise sold.	Sales Returns and Allowances	300		Sales Returns and Allowances	300	
		Accounts Receivable		300	Accounts Receivable		300
		Inventory	140		No entry		
		Cost of Goods Sold		140			
May 14	Cash received on account with a discount.	Cash	3,430		Cash	3,430	
		Sales Discounts	70		Sales Discounts	70	
		Accounts Receivable		3,500	Accounts Receivable		3,500

REVIEW AND PRACTICE

▶ LEARNING OBJECTIVES REVIEW

1 Describe merchandising operations and inventory systems. Because of the presence of inventory, a merchandising company has sales revenue, cost of goods sold, and gross profit. To account for inventory, a merchandising company must choose between a perpetual inventory system and a periodic inventory system.

2 Record purchases under a perpetual inventory system. The Inventory account is debited for all purchases of merchandise and for freight costs, and it is credited for purchase discounts and purchase returns and allowances.

3 Record sales under a perpetual inventory system. When inventory is sold, Accounts Receivable (or Cash) is debited and Sales Revenue is credited for the selling price of the merchandise. At the same time, Cost of Goods Sold is debited and Inventory is credited for the cost of inventory items sold. Separate contra revenue accounts are maintained for Sales Returns and Allowances and Sales Discounts. These accounts are debited as needed to record returns, allowances, or discounts related to the sale.

4 Prepare a multiple-step income statement and a comprehensive income statement. In a single-step income statement, companies classify all data under two categories, revenues or expenses, and net income is determined in one step. A multiple-step income statement shows numerous steps in determining net income, including results of nonoperating activities. A comprehensive income statement adds or subtracts any items of other comprehensive income to net income to arrive at comprehensive income.

5 Determine cost of goods sold under a periodic inventory system. The periodic system uses multiple accounts to keep track of transactions that affect inventory. To determine cost of goods sold, first calculate cost of goods purchased by adjusting purchases for returns, allowances, discounts, and freight-in. Then calculate cost of goods sold by adding cost of goods purchased to beginning inventory and subtracting ending inventory.

6 Compute and analyze gross profit rate and profit margin. Profitability is affected by gross profit, as measured by the gross profit rate, and by management's ability to control costs, as measured by the profit margin.

***7 Record purchases and sales of inventory under a periodic inventory system.** To record purchases, entries are required for (a) cash and credit purchases, (b) purchase returns and allowances, (c) purchase discounts, and (d) freight costs. To record sales, entries are required for (a) cash and credit sales, (b) sales returns and allowances, and (c) sales discounts.

DECISION TOOLS REVIEW

DECISION CHECKPOINTS	INFO NEEDED FOR DECISION	TOOL TO USE FOR DECISION	HOW TO EVALUATE RESULTS
Is the price of goods keeping pace with changes in the cost of inventory?	Gross profit and net sales	$\text{Gross profit rate} = \dfrac{\text{Gross profit}}{\text{Net sales}}$	Higher ratio suggests the average margin between selling price and inventory cost is increasing. Too high a margin may result in lost sales.
Is the company maintaining an adequate margin between sales and expenses?	Net income and net sales	$\text{Profit margin} = \dfrac{\text{Net income}}{\text{Net sales}}$	Higher value suggests favorable return on each dollar of sales.

GLOSSARY REVIEW

Comprehensive income An income measure that includes gains and losses that are excluded from the determination of net income. (p. 231).

Comprehensive income statement A statement that presents items that are not included in the determination of net income, referred to as other comprehensive income. (p. 231).

Contra revenue account An account that is offset against a revenue account on the income statement. (p. 226).

Cost of goods sold The total cost of merchandise sold during the period. (p. 216).

Gross profit The excess of net sales over the cost of goods sold. (p. 229).

Gross profit rate Gross profit expressed as a percentage by dividing the amount of gross profit by net sales. (p. 234).

Net sales Sales less sales returns and allowances and sales discounts. (p. 229).

Periodic inventory system An inventory system in which a company does not maintain detailed records of goods on hand throughout the period and determines the cost of goods sold only at the end of an accounting period. (p. 218).

Perpetual inventory system A detailed inventory system in which a company maintains the cost of each inventory item, and the records continuously show the inventory that should be on hand. (p. 217).

Profit margin Measures the percentage of each dollar of sales that results in net income, computed by dividing net income by net sales. (p. 235).

Purchase allowance A deduction made to the selling price of merchandise, granted by the seller, so that the buyer will keep the merchandise. (p. 222).

Purchase discount A cash discount claimed by a buyer for prompt payment of a balance due. (p. 222).

Purchase invoice A document that provides support for each purchase. (p. 220).

Purchase return A return of goods from the buyer to the seller for cash or credit. (p. 222).

Quality of earnings ratio A measure used to indicate the extent to which a company's earnings provide a full and transparent depiction of its performance; computed as net cash provided by operating activities divided by net income. (p. 237).

Sales discount A reduction given by a seller for prompt payment of a credit sale. (p. 226).

Sales invoice A document that provides support for each sale. (p. 224).

Sales returns and allowances Transactions in which the seller either accepts goods back from the purchaser (a return) or grants a reduction in the purchase price (an allowance) so that the buyer will keep the goods. (p. 225).

Sales revenue Primary source of revenue for a merchandising company. (p. 216).

PRACTICE MULTIPLE-CHOICE QUESTIONS

(LO 1) 1. Which of the following statements about a periodic inventory system is **true**?
(a) Companies determine cost of goods sold only at the end of the accounting period.
(b) Companies continuously maintain detailed records of the cost of each inventory purchase and sale.
(c) The periodic system provides better control over inventories than a perpetual system.
(d) The increased use of computerized systems has increased the use of the periodic system.

(LO 2) 2. Under a perpetual inventory system, when goods are purchased for resale by a company:
(a) purchases on account are debited to Inventory.
(b) purchases on account are debited to Purchases.
(c) purchase returns are debited to Purchase Returns and Allowances.
(d) freight costs are debited to Freight-Out.

(LO 3) 3. Which sales accounts normally have a debit balance?
(a) Sales Discounts.
(b) Sales Returns and Allowances.
(c) Both (a) and (b).
(d) Neither (a) nor (b).

(LO 3) 4. A company makes a credit sale of $750 on June 13, terms 2/10, n/30, on which it grants a return of $50 on June 16. What amount is received as payment in full on June 23?
(a) $700. (c) $685.
(b) $686. (d) $650.

(LO 3) 5. To record the sale of goods for cash in a perpetual inventory system:
(a) only one journal entry is necessary to record cost of goods sold and reduction of inventory.
(b) only one journal entry is necessary to record the receipt of cash and the sales revenue.
(c) two journal entries are necessary: one to record the receipt of cash and sales revenue, and one to record the cost of goods sold and reduction of inventory.
(d) two journal entries are necessary: one to record the receipt of cash and reduction of inventory, and one to record the cost of goods sold and sales revenue.

(LO 4) 6. Gross profit will result if:
(a) operating expenses are less than net income.
(b) net sales are greater than operating expenses.
(c) net sales are greater than cost of goods sold.
(d) operating expenses are greater than cost of goods sold.

(LO 4) 7. If net sales are $400,000, cost of goods sold is $310,000, and operating expenses are $60,000, what is the gross profit?
(a) $30,000. (c) $340,000.
(b) $90,000. (d) $400,000.

(LO 4) 8. The multiple-step income statement for a merchandising company shows each of these features **except**:
(a) gross profit.
(b) cost of goods sold.
(c) a sales section.
(d) an investing activities section.

9. If beginning inventory is $60,000, cost of goods purchased is $380,000, and ending inventory is $50,000, what is cost of goods sold under a periodic system? (LO 5)
(a) $390,000. (c) $330,000.
(b) $370,000. (d) $420,000.

10. Bufford Corporation had reported the following amounts at December 31, 2017: sales revenue $184,000, ending inventory $11,600, beginning inventory $17,200, purchases $60,400, purchase discounts $3,000, purchase returns and allowances $1,100, freight-in $600, and freight-out $900. Calculate the cost of goods available for sale. (LO 5)
(a) $69,400. (c) $56,900.
(b) $74,100. (d) $197,700.

11. Which of the following would affect the gross profit rate? (Assume sales remains constant.) (LO 6)
(a) An increase in advertising expense.
(b) A decrease in depreciation expense.
(c) An increase in cost of goods sold.
(d) A decrease in insurance expense.

12. The gross profit rate is equal to: (LO 6)
(a) net income divided by sales.
(b) cost of goods sold divided by sales.
(c) net sales minus cost of goods sold, divided by net sales.
(d) sales minus cost of goods sold, divided by cost of goods sold.

13. During the year ended December 31, 2017, Bjornstad Corporation had the following results: net sales $267,000, cost of goods sold $107,000, net income $92,400, operating expenses $55,400, and net cash provided by operating activities $108,950. What was the company's profit margin? (LO 6)
(a) 40%. (c) 20.5%.
(b) 60%. (d) 34.6%.

14. A quality of earnings ratio:
(a) is computed as net income divided by net cash provided by operating activities. (LO 6)
(b) that is less than 1 indicates that a company might be using aggressive accounting tactics.
(c) that is greater than 1 indicates that a company might be using aggressive accounting tactics.
(d) is computed as net cash provided by operating activities divided by total assets.

*15. When goods are purchased for resale by a company using a periodic inventory system: (LO 7)
(a) purchases on account are debited to Inventory.
(b) purchases on account are debited to Purchases.
(c) purchase returns are debited to Purchase Returns and Allowances.
(d) freight costs are debited to Purchases.

SOLUTIONS

1. **(a)** Under the periodic inventory system, cost of goods sold is determined only at the end of the accounting period. The other choices are incorrect because (b) detailed records of the cost of each inventory purchase and sale are maintained continuously when a perpetual, not periodic, system is used; (c) the perpetual system provides better control over inventories than a periodic system; and (d) the increased use of computerized systems has increased the use of the perpetual, not periodic, system.
2. **(a)** Under a perpetual inventory system, when a company purchases goods for resale, purchases on account are debited to the Inventory account, not (b) Purchases or (c) Purchase Returns and Allowances. Choice (d) is incorrect because freight costs are also debited to the Inventory account, not the Freight-Out account.
3. **(c)** Both Sales Discounts and Sales Returns and Allowances normally have a debit balance. Choices (a) and (b) are both correct, but (c) is the better answer. Choice (d) is incorrect as both (a) and (b) are correct.
4. **(b)** The full amount of $686 is paid within 10 days of the purchase ($750 − $50) − [($750 − $50) × 2%]. The other choices are incorrect because (a) does not consider the discount of $14; (c) the amount of the discount is based upon the amount after the return is granted ($700 × 2%), not the amount before the return of merchandise ($750 × 2%); and (d) does not constitute payment in full on June 23.
5. **(c)** Two journal entries are necessary: one to record the receipt of cash and sales revenue, and one to record the cost of goods sold and reduction of inventory. The other choices are incorrect because (a) only considers the recognition of the expense and ignores the revenue, (b) only considers the recognition of revenue and leaves out the expense or cost of merchandise sold, and (d) the receipt of cash and sales revenue, not reduction of inventory, are paired together, and the cost of goods sold and reduction of inventory, not sales revenue, are paired together.
6. **(c)** Gross profit will result if net sales are greater than cost of goods sold. The other choices are incorrect because (a) operating expenses and net income are not used in the computation of gross profit; (b) gross profit results when net sales are greater than cost of goods sold, not operating expenses; and (d) gross profit results when net sales, not operating expenses, are greater than cost of goods sold.
7. **(b)** Gross profit = Net sales ($400,000) − Cost of goods sold ($310,000) = $90,000, not (a) $30,000, (c) $340,000, or (d) $400,000.
8. **(d)** An investing activities section appears on the statement of cash flows, not on a multiple-step income statement. Choices (a) gross profit, (b) cost of goods sold, and (c) a sales section are all features of a multiple-step income statement.
9. **(a)** Beginning inventory ($60,000) + Cost of goods purchased ($380,000) − Ending inventory ($50,000) = Cost of goods sold ($390,000), not (b) $370,000, (c) $330,000, or (d) $420,000.
10. **(b)** Beginning inventory ($17,200) + Purchases ($60,400) − Purchases discounts ($3,000) − Purchase returns and allowances ($1,100) + Freight-in ($600) = Cost of goods available for sale ($74,100). The other choices are therefore incorrect.
11. **(c)** Gross profit rate = Gross profit ÷ Net sales. Therefore, any changes in sale revenue, sales returns and allowances, sales discounts, or cost of goods sold will affect the ratio. Changes in (a) advertising expense, (b) depreciation expense, or (d) insurance expense will not affect the computation of the gross profit rate.
12. **(c)** Gross profit rate = Gross profit (Net sales − Cost of goods sold) ÷ Net sales. The other choices are therefore incorrect.
13. **(d)** Net income ($92,400) ÷ Net sales ($267,000) = Profit margin of 34.6%, not (a) 40%, (b) 60%, or (c) 20.5%.
14. **(b)** A quality of earnings ratio that is less than 1 indicates that a company might be using aggressive accounting tactics. The other choices are incorrect because (a) Quality of earnings = Net cash provided by operating activities ÷ Net income, not vice versa; (c) a ratio that is significantly greater than 1 suggests that a company is using conservative accounting techniques, and (d) Quality of earnings = Net cash provided by operating activities ÷ Net income (not Total assets).

*15. **(b)** Purchases for resale are debited to the Purchases account. The other choices are incorrect because (a) purchases on account are debited to Purchases, not Inventory; (c) Purchase Returns and Allowances are always credited; and (d) freight costs are debited to Freight-In, not Purchases.

PRACTICE EXERCISES

Prepare purchase and sales entries.

(LO 2, 3)

1. On June 10, Vareen Company purchased $8,000 of merchandise from Harrah Company, FOB shipping point, terms 3/10, n/30. Vareen pays the freight costs of $400 on June 11. Damaged goods totaling $300 are returned to Harrah for credit on June 12. The fair value of these goods in $70. On June 19, Vareen pays Harrah Company in full, less the purchase discount. Both companies use a perpetual inventory system.

INSTRUCTIONS

(a) Prepare separate entries for each transaction on the books of Vareen Company.

(b) Prepare separate entries for each transaction for Harrah Company. The merchandise purchased by Vareen on June 10 had cost Harrah $4,800.

SOLUTION

1. (a)

		Debit	Credit
June 10	Inventory	8,000	
	Accounts Payable		8,000
11	Inventory	400	
	Cash		400
12	Accounts Payable	300	
	Inventory		300
19	Accounts Payable ($8,000 – $300)	7,700	
	Inventory ($7,700 × 3%)		231
	Cash ($7,700 – $231)		7,469

(b)

		Debit	Credit
June 10	Accounts Receivable	8,000	
	Sales Revenue		8,000
	Cost of Goods Sold	4,800	
	Inventory		4,800
12	Sales Returns and Allowances	300	
	Accounts Receivable		300
	Inventory	70	
	Cost of Goods Sold		70
19	Cash ($7,700 – $231)	7,469	
	Sales Discounts ($7,700 × 3%)	231	
	Accounts Receivable ($8,000 – $300)		7,700

2. In its income statement for the year ended December 31, 2017, Marten Company reported the following condensed data.

Prepare multiple-step and single-step income statements.

(LO 4)

Interest expense	$ 70,000	Net sales	$2,200,000
Operating expenses	725,000	Interest revenue	25,000
Cost of goods sold	1,300,000	Loss on disposal of plant assets	17,000
		Income tax expense	10,000

INSTRUCTIONS

(a) Prepare a multiple-step income statement.

(b) Prepare a single-step income statement.

SOLUTION

2. (a)

MARTEN COMPANY
Income Statement
For the Year Ended December 31, 2017

Net sales			$2,200,000
Cost of goods sold			1,300,000
Gross profit			900,000
Operating expenses			725,000
Income from operations			175,000
Other revenues and gains			
Interest revenue		$25,000	
Other expenses and losses			
Interest expense	$70,000		
Loss on disposal of plant assets	17,000	87,000	(62,000)
Income before income taxes			113,000
Income tax expense			10,000
Net income			$ 103,000

(b)

MARTEN COMPANY Income Statement For the Year Ended December 31, 2017		
Revenues		
Net sales		$2,200,000
Interest revenue		25,000
Total revenues		2,225,000
Expenses		
Cost of goods sold	$1,300,000	
Operating expenses	725,000	
Interest expense	70,000	
Loss on disposal of plant assets	17,000	
Income tax expense	10,000	
Total expenses		2,122,000
Net income		$ 103,000

PRACTICE PROBLEM

Prepare a multiple-step income statement.

(LO 4)

The adjusted trial balance for the year ended December 31, 2017, for Dykstra Company is shown below.

DYKSTRA COMPANY Adjusted Trial Balance For the Year Ended December 31, 2017	Debit	Credit
Cash	$ 14,500	
Accounts Receivable	11,100	
Inventory	29,000	
Prepaid Insurance	2,500	
Equipment	95,000	
Accumulated Depreciation—Equipment		$ 18,000
Notes Payable		25,000
Accounts Payable		10,600
Common Stock		70,000
Retained Earnings		11,000
Dividends	12,000	
Sales Revenue		536,800
Sales Returns and Allowances	6,700	
Sales Discounts	5,000	
Cost of Goods Sold	363,400	
Freight-Out	7,600	
Advertising Expense	12,000	
Salaries and Wages Expense	56,000	
Utilities Expense	18,000	
Rent Expense	24,000	
Depreciation Expense	9,000	
Insurance Expense	4,500	
Interest Expense	3,600	
Interest Revenue		2,500
	$673,900	$673,900

INSTRUCTIONS

Prepare a multiple-step income statement for Dykstra Company. Assume a tax rate of 30%.

SOLUTION

DYKSTRA COMPANY		
Income Statement		
For the Year Ended December 31, 2017		
Sales		
Sales revenue		$536,800
Less: Sales returns and allowances	$ 6,700	
Sales discounts	5,000	11,700
Net sales		525,100
Cost of goods sold		363,400
Gross profit		161,700
Operating expenses		
Salaries and wages expense	56,000	
Rent expense	24,000	
Utilities expense	18,000	
Advertising expense	12,000	
Depreciation expense	9,000	
Freight-out	7,600	
Insurance expense	4,500	
Total operating expenses		131,100
Income from operations		30,600
Other revenues and gains		
Interest revenue		2,500
Other expenses and losses		
Interest expense		3,600
Income before income taxes		29,500
Income tax expense		8,850
Net income		$ 20,650

NOTE: All asterisked Questions, Exercises, and Problems relate to material in the appendix to the chapter.

QUESTIONS

1. (a) "The steps in the accounting cycle for a merchandising company differ from the steps in the accounting cycle for a service company." Do you agree or disagree?
   (b) Is the measurement of net income in a merchandising company conceptually the same as in a service company? Explain.
2. How do the components of revenues and expenses differ between a merchandising company and a service company?
3. Maria Lopez, CEO of Sales Bin Stores, is considering a recommendation made by both the company's purchasing manager and director of finance that the company should invest in a sophisticated new perpetual inventory system to replace its periodic system. Explain the primary difference between the two systems, and discuss the potential benefits of a perpetual inventory system.
4. (a) Explain the income measurement process in a merchandising company.
   (b) How does income measurement differ between a merchandising company and a service company?
5. Waymon Co. has net sales of $100,000, cost of goods sold of $70,000, and operating expenses of $18,000. What is its gross profit?
6. Masie Ascot believes revenues from credit sales may be recorded before they are collected in cash. Do you agree? Explain.

7. (a) What is the primary source document for recording (1) cash sales and (2) credit sales?
   (b) Using XXs for amounts, give the journal entry for each of the transactions in part (a), assuming perpetual inventory.
8. A credit sale is made on July 10 for $900, terms 1/15, n/30. On July 12, the purchaser returns $100 of goods for credit. Give the journal entry on July 19 to record the receipt of the balance due within the discount period.
9. As the end of Smyle Company's fiscal year approached, it became clear that the company had considerable excess inventory. Marvin Ross, the head of marketing and sales, ordered salespeople to "add 20% more units to each order that you ship. The customers can always ship the extra back next period if they decide they don't want it. We've got to do it to meet this year's sales goal." Discuss the accounting implications of Marvin's action.
10. To encourage bookstores to buy a broader range of book titles and to discourage price discounting, the publishing industry allows bookstores to return unsold books to the publisher. This results in very significant returns each year. To ensure proper recognition of revenues, how should publishing companies account for these returns?
11. Goods costing $1,900 are purchased on account on July 15 with credit terms of 2/10, n/30. On July 18, the purchaser receives a $300 credit from the supplier for damaged goods. Give the journal entry on July 24 to record payment of the balance due within the discount period.
12. Scribe Company reports net sales of $800,000, gross profit of $560,000, and net income of $230,000. What are its operating expenses?
13. Mai Company has always provided its customers with payment terms of 1/10, n/30. Members of its sale force have commented that competitors are offering customers 2/10, n/45. Explain what these terms mean, and discuss the implications to Mai of switching its payment terms to those of its competitors.
14. In its year-end earnings announcement press release, Ransome Corp. announced that its earnings increased by $15 million relative to the previous year. This represented a 20% increase. Inspection of its income statement reveals that the company reported a $20 million gain under "Other revenues and gains" from the sale of one of its factories. Discuss the implications of this gain from the perspective of a potential investor.
15. Identify the distinguishing features of an income statement for a merchandising company.
16. Why is the normal operating cycle for a merchandising company likely to be longer than for a service company?
17. What title does Apple use for gross profit? By how much did its total gross profit change, and in what direction, in 2014?
18. What merchandising account(s) will appear in the post-closing trial balance?
19. What types of businesses are most likely to use a perpetual inventory system?
20. Identify the accounts that are added to or deducted from purchases to determine the cost of goods purchased under a periodic system. For each account, indicate (a) whether it is added or deducted, and (b) its normal balance.
21. In the following cases, use a periodic inventory system to identify the item(s) designated by the letters *X* and *Y*.
   (a) Purchases − *X* − *Y* = Net purchases.
   (b) Cost of goods purchased − Net purchases = *X*.
   (c) Beginning inventory + *X* = Cost of goods available for sale.
   (d) Cost of goods available for sale − Cost of goods sold = *X*.
22. What two ratios measure factors that affect profitability?
23. What factors affect a company's gross profit rate—that is, what can cause the gross profit rate to increase and what can cause it to decrease?
24. Earl Massey, director of marketing, wants to reduce the selling price of his company's products by 15% to increase market share. He says, "I know this will reduce our gross profit rate, but the increased number of units sold will make up for the lost margin." Before this action is taken, what other factors does the company need to consider?
25. Mark Coney is considering investing in Wiggles Pet Food Company. Wiggles' net income increased considerably during the most recent year even though many other companies in the same industry reported disappointing earnings. Mark wants to know whether the company's earnings provide a reasonable depiction of its results. What initial step can Mark take to help determine whether he needs to investigate further?

*26. On July 15, a company purchases on account goods costing $1,900, with credit terms of 2/10, n/30. On July 18, the company receives a $400 credit memo from the supplier for damaged goods. Give the journal entry on July 24 to record payment of the balance due within the discount period assuming a periodic inventory system.

▶ BRIEF EXERCISES

Compute missing amounts in determining net income.

(LO 1, 4), AP

BE5-1 Presented here are the components in Salas Company's income statement. Determine the missing amounts.

Sales Revenue	Cost of Goods Sold	Gross Profit	Operating Expenses	Net Income
$ 71,200	(b)	$ 30,000	(d)	$12,100
$108,000	$70,000	(c)	(e)	$29,500
(a)	$71,900	$109,600	$46,200	(f)

BE5-2 Rita Company buys merchandise on account from Linus Company. The selling price of the goods is $900 and the cost of the goods sold is $590. Both companies use perpetual inventory systems. Journalize the transactions on the books of both companies.

Journalize perpetual inventory entries.

(LO 2, 3), AP

BE5-3 Prepare the journal entries to record the following transactions on Borst Company's books using a perpetual inventory system.

Journalize sales transactions.

(LO 3), AP

(a) On March 2, Borst Company sold $800,000 of merchandise to McLeena Company, terms 2/10, n/30. The cost of the merchandise sold was $540,000.
(b) On March 6, McLeena Company returned $140,000 of the merchandise purchased on March 2. The cost of the merchandise returned was $94,000.
(c) On March 12, Borst Company received the balance due from McLeena Company.

BE5-4 From the information in BE5-3, prepare the journal entries to record these transactions on McLeena Company's books under a perpetual inventory system.

Journalize purchase transactions.

(LO 2), AP

BE5-5 Barto Company provides this information for the month ended October 31, 2017: sales on credit $300,000, cash sales $150,000, sales discounts $5,000, and sales returns and allowances $19,000. Prepare the sales section of the income statement based on this information.

Prepare sales section of income statement.

(LO 4), AP

BE5-6 Explain where each of these items would appear on a multiple-step income statement: gain on disposal of plant assets, cost of goods sold, depreciation expense, and sales returns and allowances.

Identify placement of items on a multiple-step income statement.

(LO 4), AP

BE5-7 The following information relates to Karen Weigel Inc. for the year 2017.

Prepare a comprehensive income statement.

(LO 4), AP

Retained earnings, January 1, 2017	$48,000	Advertising expense	$ 1,800
Dividends during 2017	5,000	Rent expense	10,400
Service revenue	62,500	Utilities expense	3,100
Salaries and wages expense	28,000	Other comprehensive income (net of tax)	400

After analyzing the data, (a) compute net income and (b) prepare a comprehensive income statement for the year ending December 31, 2017.

BE5-8 Silas Company sold goods with a total selling price of $800,000 during the year. It purchased goods for $380,000 and had beginning inventory of $67,000. A count of its ending inventory determined that goods on hand was $50,000. What was its cost of goods sold?

Determine cost of goods sold using basic periodic formula.

(LO 5), AP

BE5-9 Assume that Spacey Company uses a periodic inventory system and has these account balances: Purchases $404,000, Purchase Returns and Allowances $13,000, Purchase Discounts $9,000, and Freight-In $16,000. Determine net purchases and cost of goods purchased.

Compute net purchases and cost of goods purchased.

(LO 5), AP

BE5-10 Assume the same information as in BE5-9 and also that Spacey Company has beginning inventory of $60,000, ending inventory of $90,000, and net sales of $612,000. Determine the amounts to be reported for cost of goods sold and gross profit.

Compute cost of goods sold and gross profit.

(LO 5), AP

BE5-11 Dublin Corporation reported net sales of $250,000, cost of goods sold of $150,000, operating expenses of $50,000, net income of $32,500, beginning total assets of $520,000, and ending total assets of $600,000. Calculate each of the following values and explain what they mean: (a) profit margin and (b) gross profit rate.

Calculate profitability ratios.

(LO 6), AP

BE5-12 Garten Corporation reported net sales $800,000, cost of goods sold $520,000, operating expenses $210,000, and net income $68,000. Calculate the following values and explain what they mean: (a) profit margin and (b) gross profit rate.

Calculate profitability ratios.

(LO 6), AP

BE5-13 Cabo Corporation reported net income of $346,000, cash of $67,800, and net cash provided by operating activities of $221,200. What does this suggest about the quality of the company's earnings? What further steps should be taken?

Evaluate quality of earnings.

(LO 6), C

***BE5-14** Prepare the journal entries to record these transactions on Kimble Company's books using a periodic inventory system.

Journalize purchase transactions.

(LO 7), AP

(a) On March 2, Kimble Company purchased $800,000 of merchandise from Poe Company, terms 2/10, n/30.
(b) On March 6, Kimble Company returned $95,000 of the merchandise purchased on March 2.
(c) On March 12, Kimble Company paid the balance due to Poe Company.

DO IT! EXERCISES

Answer general questions about merchandisers.

(LO 1), C

DO IT! 5-1 Indicate whether the following statements are true or false.

1. A merchandising company reports gross profit but a service company does not.
2. Under a periodic inventory system, a company determines the cost of goods sold each time a sale occurs.
3. A service company is likely to use accounts receivable but a merchandising company is not likely to do so.
4. Under a periodic inventory system, the cost of goods on hand at the beginning of the accounting period plus the cost of goods purchased less the cost of goods on hand at the end of the accounting period equals cost of goods sold.

Record transactions of purchasing company.

(LO 2), AP

DO IT! 5-2 On October 5, Iverson Company buys merchandise on account from Lasse Company. The selling price of the goods is $5,000, and the cost to Lasse Company is $3,000. On October 8, Iverson returns defective goods with a selling price of $640 and a scrap value of $240. Record the transactions of Iverson Company, assuming a perpetual approach.

Record transactions of selling company.

(LO 3), AP

DO IT! 5-3 Assume information similar to that in DO IT! 5-2. That is: On October 5, Iverson Company buys merchandise on account from Lasse Company. The selling price of the goods is $5,000, and the cost to Lasse Company is $3,000. On October 8, Iverson returns defective goods with a selling price of $640 and a scrap value of $240. Record the transactions on the books of Lasse Company, assuming a perpetual approach.

Prepare multiple-step income statement and comprehensive income statement.

(LO 4), AP

DO IT! 5-4 The following information is available for Berlin Corp. for the year ended December 31, 2017:

Other revenues and gains	$ 12,700	Sales revenue	$592,000
Other expenses and losses	13,300	Operating expenses	186,000
Cost of goods sold	156,000	Sales returns and allowances	40,000
Other comprehensive income	5,400		

Prepare a multiple-step income statement for Berlin Corp. and comprehensive income statement. The company has a tax rate of 30%. This rate also applies to the other comprehensive income.

Determine cost of goods sold using periodic system.

(LO 5), AP

DO IT! 5-5 Clean Lake Corporation's accounting records show the following at year-end December 31, 2017:

Purchase Discounts	$ 5,900	Beginning Inventory	$31,720
Freight-In	8,400	Ending Inventory	27,950
Freight-Out	11,100	Purchase Returns and Allowances	3,600
Purchases	162,500		

Assuming that Clean Lake Corporation uses the periodic system, compute (a) cost of goods purchased and (b) cost of goods sold.

Compute and analyze profitability ratios.

(LO 6), AN

DO IT! 5-6 Owen Wise, Inc. reported the following in its 2017 and 2016 income statements.

	2017	2016
Net sales	$150,000	$120,000
Cost of goods sold	90,000	72,000
Operating expenses	32,000	16,000
Income tax expense	18,000	10,000
Net income	$ 10,000	$ 22,000

Determine the company's gross profit rate and profit margin for both years. Discuss the cause for changes in the ratios.

EXERCISES

Journalize purchase transactions.

(LO 2), AP

E5-1 This information relates to Rice Co.

1. On April 5, purchased merchandise from Jax Company for $28,000, terms 2/10, n/30.
2. On April 6, paid freight costs of $700 on merchandise purchased from Jax.
3. On April 7, purchased equipment on account for $30,000.

4. On April 8, returned $3,600 of April 5 merchandise to Jax Company.
5. On April 15, paid the amount due to Jax Company in full.

Instructions

(a) Prepare the journal entries to record the transactions listed above on Rice Co.'s books. Rice Co. uses a perpetual inventory system.

(b) Assume that Rice Co. paid the balance due to Jax Company on May 4 instead of April 15. Prepare the journal entry to record this payment.

E5-2 Assume that on September 1, Office Depot had an inventory that included a variety of calculators. The company uses a perpetual inventory system. During September, these transactions occurred.

Journalize perpetual inventory entries.

(LO 2, 3), AP

Sept.	6	Purchased calculators from Dragoo Co. at a total cost of $1,650, terms n/30.
	9	Paid freight of $50 on calculators purchased from Dragoo Co.
	10	Returned calculators to Dragoo Co. for $66 credit because they did not meet specifications.
	12	Sold calculators costing $520 for $690 to Fryer Book Store, terms n/30.
	14	Granted credit of $45 to Fryer Book Store for the return of one calculator that was not ordered. The calculator cost $34.
	20	Sold calculators costing $570 for $760 to Heasley Card Shop, terms n/30.

Instructions

Journalize the September transactions.

E5-3 The following transactions are for Alonzo Company.

Journalize sales transactions.

(LO 3), AP

1. On December 3, Alonzo Company sold $500,000 of merchandise to Arte Co., terms 1/10, n/30. The cost of the merchandise sold was $330,000.
2. On December 8, Arte Co. was granted an allowance of $25,000 for merchandise purchased on December 3.
3. On December 13, Alonzo Company received the balance due from Arte Co.

Instructions

(a) Prepare the journal entries to record these transactions on the books of Alonzo Company. Alonzo uses a perpetual inventory system.

(b) Assume that Alonzo Company received the balance due from Arte Co. on January 2 of the following year instead of December 13. Prepare the journal entry to record the receipt of payment on January 2.

E5-4 On June 10, Pais Company purchased $9,000 of merchandise from McGiver Company, terms 3/10, n/30. Pais pays the freight costs of $400 on June 11. Goods totaling $600 are returned to McGiver for credit on June 12. On June 19, Pais Company pays McGiver Company in full, less the purchase discount. Both companies use a perpetual inventory system.

Journalize perpetual inventory entries.

(LO 2, 3), AP

Instructions

(a) Prepare separate entries for each transaction on the books of Pais Company.

(b) Prepare separate entries for each transaction for McGiver Company. The merchandise purchased by Pais on June 10 cost McGiver $5,000, and the goods returned cost McGiver $310.

E5-5 The adjusted trial balance of Doqe Company shows these data pertaining to sales at the end of its fiscal year, October 31, 2017: Sales Revenue $900,000, Freight-Out $14,000, Sales Returns and Allowances $22,000, and Sales Discounts $13,500.

Prepare sales section of income statement.

(LO 4), AP

Instructions

Prepare the sales section of the income statement.

E5-6 Presented below is information for Lieu Co. for the month of January 2017.

Prepare an income statement, a comprehensive income statement, and calculate profitability ratios.

(LO 4, 6), AP

Cost of goods sold	$212,000	Rent expense	$ 32,000
Freight-out	7,000	Sales discounts	8,000
Insurance expense	12,000	Sales returns and allowances	20,000
Salaries and wages expense	60,000	Sales revenue	370,000
Income tax expense	5,000	Other comprehensive income (net of $400 tax)	2,000

Instructions

(a) Prepare an income statement using the format presented in Illustration 5-11.
(b) Prepare a comprehensive income statement.
(c) Calculate the profit margin and the gross profit rate.

Compute missing amounts and calculate profitability ratios.

(LO 4, 6), AP

E5-7 Financial information is presented here for two companies.

	Yoste Company	Noone Company
Sales revenue	$90,000	?
Sales returns and allowances	?	$ 5,000
Net sales	84,000	100,000
Cost of goods sold	58,000	?
Gross profit	?	40,000
Operating expenses	14,380	?
Net income	?	17,000

Instructions

(a) Fill in the missing amounts. Show all computations.
(b) Calculate the profit margin and the gross profit rate for each company.
(c) Discuss your findings in part (b).

Prepare multiple-step income statement and calculate profitability ratios.

(LO 4, 6), AP

XLS

E5-8 In its income statement for the year ended December 31, 2017, Darren Company reported the following condensed data.

Salaries and wages expense	$465,000	Loss on disposal of plant assets	$ 83,500
Cost of goods sold	987,000	Sales revenue	2,210,000
Interest expense	71,000	Income tax expense	25,000
Interest revenue	65,000	Sales discounts	160,000
Depreciation expense	310,000	Utilities expense	110,000

Instructions

(a) Prepare a multiple-step income statement.
(b) Calculate the profit margin and gross profit rate.
(c) In 2016, Darren had a profit margin of 5%. Is the decline in 2017 a cause for concern? (Ignore income tax effects.)

Prepare multiple-step income statement and calculate profitability ratios.

(LO 4, 6), AP

E5-9 Suppose in its income statement for the year ended June 30, 2017, The Clorox Company reported the following condensed data (dollars in millions).

Salaries and wages expense	$ 460	Research and development expense	$ 114
Depreciation expense	90	Income tax expense	276
Sales revenue	5,730	Loss on disposal of plant assets	46
Interest expense	161	Cost of goods sold	3,104
Advertising expense	499	Rent expense	105
Sales returns and allowances	280	Utilities expense	60

Instructions

(a) Prepare a multiple-step income statement.
(b) Calculate the gross profit rate and the profit margin and explain what each means.
(c) Assume the marketing department has presented a plan to increase advertising expenses by $340 million. It expects this plan to result in an increase in both net sales and cost of goods sold of 25%. (*Hint:* Increase both sales revenue and sales returns and allowances by 25%.) Redo parts (a) and (b) and discuss whether this plan has merit. (Assume a tax rate of 34%, and round all amounts to whole dollars.)

Prepare an income statement and comprehensive income statement.

(LO 4), AP

E5-10 In its income statement for the year ended December 31, 2017, Laine Inc. reported the following condensed data.

Operating expenses	$ 725,000	Interest revenue	$ 33,000
Cost of goods sold	1,256,000	Loss on disposal of plant assets	17,000
Interest expense	70,000	Net sales	2,200,000
Income tax expense	47,000	Other comprehensive income (net of $1,200 tax)	8,300

Instructions

(a) Prepare an income statement.
(b) Prepare a comprehensive income statement.

Prepare a multiple-step income statement.

(LO 4), AP

E5-11 The following selected accounts from the Blue Door Corporation's general ledger are presented below for the year ended December 31, 2017:

Advertising expense	$ 55,000	Interest revenue	$ 30,000
Common stock	250,000	Inventory	67,000
Cost of goods sold	1,085,000	Rent revenue	24,000
Depreciation expense	125,000	Retained earnings	535,000
Dividends	150,000	Salaries and wages expense	675,000
Freight-out	25,000	Sales discounts	8,500
Income tax expense	70,000	Sales returns and allowances	41,000
Insurance expense	15,000		
Interest expense	70,000	Sales revenue	2,400,000

Instructions

Prepare a multiple-step income statement.

Prepare cost of goods sold section using periodic system.

(LO 5), AP

E5-12 The trial balance of Mendez Company at the end of its fiscal year, August 31, 2017, includes these accounts: Beginning Inventory $18,700, Purchases $154,000, Sales Revenue $190,000, Freight-In $8,000, Sales Returns and Allowances $3,000, Freight-Out $1,000, and Purchase Returns and Allowances $5,000. The ending inventory is $21,000.

Instructions

Prepare a cost of goods sold section (periodic system) for the year ending August 31, 2017.

Prepare cost of goods sold section using periodic system.

(LO 5), AP

E5-13 Below is a series of cost of goods sold sections for companies B, M, O, and S.

	B	M	O	S
Beginning inventory	$ 250	$ 120	$ 700	$ (j)
Purchases	1,500	1,080	(g)	43,590
Purchase returns and allowances	80	(d)	290	(k)
Net purchases	(a)	1,040	7,410	42,290
Freight-in	130	(e)	(h)	2,240
Cost of goods purchased	(b)	1,230	8,050	(l)
Cost of goods available for sale	1,800	1,350	(i)	49,530
Ending inventory	310	(f)	1,150	6,230
Cost of goods sold	(c)	1,230	7,600	43,300

Instructions

Fill in the lettered blanks to complete the cost of goods sold sections.

Evaluate quality of earnings.

(LO 6), C

E5-14 Dorsett Corporation reported sales revenue of $257,000, net income of $45,300, cash of $9,300, and net cash provided by operating activities of $23,200. Accounts receivable have increased at three times the rate of sales during the last 3 years.

Instructions

(a) Explain what is meant by high quality of earnings.
(b) Evaluate the quality of the company's earnings. Discuss your findings.
(c) What factors might have contributed to the company's quality of earnings?

Journalize purchase transactions.

(LO 7), AP

***E5-15** This information relates to Alfie Co.

1. On April 5, purchased merchandise from Bach Company for $27,000, terms 2/10, n/30.
2. On April 6, paid freight costs of $1,200 on merchandise purchased from Bach Company.
3. On April 7, purchased equipment on account for $30,000.
4. On April 8, returned some of the April 5 merchandise to Bach Company, which cost $3,600.
5. On April 15, paid the amount due to Bach Company in full.

Instructions

(a) Prepare the journal entries to record these transactions on the books of Alfie Co. using a periodic inventory system.

(b) Assume that Alfie Co. paid the balance due to Bach Company on May 4 instead of April 15. Prepare the journal entry to record this payment.

EXERCISES: SET B AND CHALLENGE EXERCISES

Visit the book's companion website, at **www.wiley.com/college/kimmel**, and choose the Student Companion site to access Exercises: Set B and Challenge Exercises.

PROBLEMS: SET A

Journalize, post, and prepare partial income statement, and calculate ratios.

(LO 2, 3, 4, 6), AP

P5-1A Winters Hardware Store completed the following merchandising transactions in the month of May. At the beginning of May, Winters' ledger showed Cash of $8,000 and Common Stock of $8,000.

May	1	Purchased merchandise on account from Black Wholesale Supply for $8,000, terms 1/10, n/30.
	2	Sold merchandise on account for $4,400, terms 2/10, n/30. The cost of the merchandise sold was $3,300.
	5	Received credit from Black Wholesale Supply for merchandise returned $200.
	9	Received collections in full, less discounts, from customers billed on May 2.
	10	Paid Black Wholesale Supply in full, less discount.
	11	Purchased supplies for cash $900.
	12	Purchased merchandise for cash $3,100.
	15	Received $230 refund for return of poor-quality merchandise from supplier on cash purchase.
	17	Purchased merchandise from Wilhelm Distributors for $2,500, terms 2/10, n/30.
	19	Paid freight on May 17 purchase $250.
	24	Sold merchandise for cash $5,500. The cost of the merchandise sold was $4,100.
	25	Purchased merchandise from Clasps Inc. for $800, terms 3/10, n/30.
	27	Paid Wilhelm Distributors in full, less discount.
	29	Made refunds to cash customers for returned merchandise $124. The returned merchandise had cost $90.
	31	Sold merchandise on account for $1,280, terms n/30. The cost of the merchandise sold was $830.

Winters Hardware's chart of accounts includes Cash, Accounts Receivable, Inventory, Supplies, Accounts Payable, Common Stock, Sales Revenue, Sales Returns and Allowances, Sales Discounts, and Cost of Goods Sold.

Instructions

(a) Journalize the transactions using a perpetual inventory system.

(b) Post the transactions to T-accounts. Be sure to enter the beginning cash and common stock balances.

(c) Gross profit $2,828

(c) Prepare an income statement through gross profit for the month of May 2017.

(d) Calculate the profit margin and the gross profit rate. (Assume operating expenses were $1,400.)

Journalize purchase and sale transactions under a perpetual system.

(LO 2, 3), AP

P5-2A Powell Warehouse distributes hardback books to retail stores and extends credit terms of 2/10, n/30 to all of its customers. During the month of June, the following merchandising transactions occurred.

June	1	Purchased books on account for $1,040 (including freight) from Catlin Publishers, terms 2/10, n/30.
	3	Sold books on account to Garfunkel Bookstore for $1,200. The cost of the merchandise sold was $720.
	6	Received $40 credit for books returned to Catlin Publishers.
	9	Paid Catlin Publishers in full.
	15	Received payment in full from Garfunkel Bookstore.
	17	Sold books on account to Bell Tower for $1,200. The cost of the merchandise sold was $730.

20	Purchased books on account for $720 from Priceless Book Publishers, terms 1/15, n/30.
24	Received payment in full from Bell Tower.
26	Paid Priceless Book Publishers in full.
28	Sold books on account to General Bookstore for $1,300. The cost of the merchandise sold was $780.
30	Granted General Bookstore $130 credit for books returned costing $80.

Instructions

Journalize the transactions for the month of June for Powell Warehouse, using a perpetual inventory system.

P5-3A At the beginning of the current season on April 1, the ledger of Granite Hills Pro Shop showed Cash $2,500, Inventory $3,500, and Common Stock $6,000. The following transactions were completed during April 2017.

Journalize, post, and prepare trial balance and partial income statement.

(LO 2, 3, 4), AP

Apr.	5	Purchased golf bags, clubs, and balls on account from Arnie Co. $1,500, terms 3/10, n/60.
	7	Paid freight on Arnie purchase $80.
	9	Received credit from Arnie Co. for merchandise returned $200.
	10	Sold merchandise on account to members $1,340, terms n/30. The merchandise sold had a cost of $820.
	12	Purchased golf shoes, sweaters, and other accessories on account from Woods Sportswear $830, terms 1/10, n/30.
	14	Paid Arnie Co. in full.
	17	Received credit from Woods Sportswear for merchandise returned $30.
	20	Made sales on account to members $810, terms n/30. The cost of the merchandise sold was $550.
	21	Paid Woods Sportswear in full.
	27	Granted an allowance to members for clothing that did not fit properly $80.
	30	Received payments on account from members $1,220.

The chart of accounts for the pro shop includes Cash, Accounts Receivable, Inventory, Accounts Payable, Common Stock, Sales Revenue, Sales Returns and Allowances, and Cost of Goods Sold.

Instructions

(a) Journalize the April transactions using a perpetual inventory system.
(b) Using T-accounts, enter the beginning balances in the ledger accounts and post the April transactions.
(c) Prepare a trial balance on April 30, 2017.
(d) Prepare an income statement through gross profit for the month of April 2017.

(c) Tot. trial balance $8,150
(d) Gross profit $ 700

P5-4A Wolford Department Store is located in midtown Metropolis. During the past several years, net income has been declining because suburban shopping centers have been attracting business away from city areas. At the end of the company's fiscal year on November 30, 2017, these accounts appeared in its adjusted trial balance.

Prepare financial statements and calculate profitability ratios.

(LO 4, 6), AP

Accounts Payable	$ 26,800
Accounts Receivable	17,200
Accumulated Depreciation—Equipment	68,000
Cash	8,000
Common Stock	35,000
Cost of Goods Sold	614,300
Freight-Out	6,200
Equipment	157,000
Depreciation Expense	13,500
Dividends	12,000
Gain on Disposal of Plant Assets	2,000
Income Tax Expense	10,000
Insurance Expense	9,000
Interest Expense	5,000
Inventory	26,200
Notes Payable	43,500
Prepaid Insurance	6,000

Advertising Expense	$ 33,500
Rent Expense	34,000
Retained Earnings	14,200
Salaries and Wages Expense	117,000
Salaries and Wages Payable	6,000
Sales Returns and Allowances	20,000
Sales Revenue	904,000
Utilities Expense	10,600

Additional data: Notes payable are due in 2021.

(a) Net income $ 32,900
Tot. assets $146,400

Instructions

(a) Prepare a multiple-step income statement, a retained earnings statement, and a classified balance sheet.
(b) Calculate the profit margin and the gross profit rate.
(c) The vice president of marketing and the director of human resources have developed a proposal whereby the company would compensate the sales force on a strictly commission basis. Given the increased incentive, they expect net sales to increase by 15%. As a result, they estimate that gross profit will increase by $40,443 and expenses by $58,600. Compute the expected new net income. (*Hint:* You do not need to prepare an income statement.) Then, compute the revised profit margin and gross profit rate. Comment on the effect that this plan would have on net income and on the ratios, and evaluate the merit of this proposal. (Ignore income tax effects.)

Prepare a correct multiple-step income statement.

(LO 4), AP

P5-5A An inexperienced accountant prepared this condensed income statement for Simon Company, a retail firm that has been in business for a number of years.

SIMON COMPANY
Income Statement
For the Year Ended December 31, 2017

Revenues	
Net sales	$850,000
Other revenues	22,000
	872,000
Cost of goods sold	555,000
Gross profit	317,000
Operating expenses	
Selling expenses	109,000
Administrative expenses	103,000
	212,000
Net earnings	$105,000

As an experienced, knowledgeable accountant, you review the statement and determine the following facts.

1. Net sales consist of sales $911,000, less freight-out on merchandise sold $33,000, and sales returns and allowances $28,000.
2. Other revenues consist of sales discounts $18,000 and rent revenue $4,000.
3. Selling expenses consist of salespersons' salaries $80,000, depreciation on equipment $10,000, advertising $13,000, and sales commissions $6,000. The commissions represent commissions paid. At December 31, $3,000 of commissions have been earned by salespersons but have not been paid. All compensation should be recorded as Salaries and Wages Expense.
4. Administrative expenses consist of office salaries $47,000, dividends $18,000, utilities $12,000, interest expense $2,000, and rent expense $24,000, which includes prepayments totaling $6,000 for the first quarter of 2018.

Net income $67,500

Instructions

Prepare a correct detailed multiple-step income statement. Assume a 25% tax rate.

Journalize, post, and prepare adjusted trial balance and financial statements.

(LO 4), AP

P5-6A The trial balance of People's Choice Wholesale Company contained the following accounts shown at December 31, the end of the company's fiscal year.

PEOPLE'S CHOICE WHOLESALE COMPANY
Trial Balance
December 31, 2017

	Debit	Credit
Cash	$ 31,400	
Accounts Receivable	37,600	
Inventory	70,000	
Land	92,000	
Buildings	200,000	
Accumulated Depreciation—Buildings		$ 60,000
Equipment	83,500	
Accumulated Depreciation—Equipment		40,500
Notes Payable		54,700
Accounts Payable		17,500
Common Stock		160,000
Retained Earnings		67,200
Dividends	10,000	
Sales Revenue		922,100
Sales Discounts	6,000	
Cost of Goods Sold	709,900	
Salaries and Wages Expense	51,300	
Utilities Expense	11,400	
Maintenance and Repairs Expense	8,900	
Advertising Expense	5,200	
Insurance Expense	4,800	
	$1,322,000	$1,322,000

Adjustment data:

1. Depreciation is $8,000 on buildings and $7,000 on equipment. (Both are operating expenses.)
2. Interest of $4,500 is due and unpaid on notes payable at December 31.
3. Income tax due and unpaid at December 31 is $24,000.

Other data: $15,000 of the notes payable are payable next year.

Instructions

(a) Journalize the adjusting entries.
(b) Create T-accounts for all accounts used in part (a). Enter the trial balance amounts into the T-accounts and post the adjusting entries.
(c) Prepare an adjusted trial balance.
(d) Prepare a multiple-step income statement and a retained earnings statement for the year, and a classified balance sheet at December 31, 2017.

(c) Tot. trial balance $1,365,500
(d) Net income $ 81,100
Tot. assets $ 399,000

P5-7A At the end of Oates Department Store's fiscal year on November 30, 2017, these accounts appeared in its adjusted trial balance.

Determine cost of goods sold and gross profit under a periodic system.

(LO 4, 5), AP

Freight-In	$ 5,060
Inventory (beginning)	41,300
Purchases	613,000
Purchase Discounts	7,000
Purchase Returns and Allowances	6,760
Sales Revenue	902,000
Sales Returns and Allowances	20,000

Additional facts:

1. Inventory on November 30, 2017, is $36,200.
2. Note that Oates Department Store uses a periodic system.

Instructions

Prepare an income statement through gross profit for the year ended November 30, 2017.

Gross profit $272,600

P5-8A Zhou Inc. operates a retail operation that purchases and sells snowmobiles, among other outdoor products. The company purchases all inventory on credit and uses a periodic inventory system. The Accounts Payable account is used for recording inventory purchases only; all other current liabilities are accrued in separate accounts. You are provided with the following selected information for the fiscal years 2015 through 2018, inclusive.

Calculate missing amounts and assess profitability.

(LO 4, 5, 6), AN

	2015	2016	2017	2018
Income Statement Data				
Sales revenue		$96,890	$ (e)	$82,220
Cost of goods sold		(a)	28,060	26,490
Gross profit		67,800	59,620	(i)
Operating expenses		63,640	(f)	52,870
Net income		$ (b)	$ 3,510	$ (j)
Balance Sheet Data				
Inventory	$13,000	$ (c)	$14,700	$ (k)
Accounts payable	5,800	6,500	4,600	(l)
Additional Information				
Purchases of inventory on account		$25,890	$ (g)	$24,050
Cash payments to suppliers		(d)	(h)	24,650

Instructions

(a) Calculate the missing amounts.

(b) The vice presidents of sales, marketing, production, and finance are discussing the company's results with the CEO. They note that sales declined over the 3-year fiscal period, 2016–2018. Does that mean that profitability necessarily also declined? Explain, computing the gross profit rate and the profit margin for each fiscal year to help support your answer.

Journalize, post, and prepare trial balance and partial income statement under a periodic system.

(LO 5, 7), AP

***P5-9A** At the beginning of the current season on April 1, the ledger of Granite Hills Pro Shop showed Cash $2,500, Inventory $3,500, and Common Stock $6,000. The following transactions occurred during April 2017.

Apr.	5	Purchased golf bags, clubs, and balls on account from Arnie Co. $1,500, terms 3/10, n/60.
	7	Paid freight on Arnie Co. purchases $80.
	9	Received credit from Arnie Co. for merchandise returned $200.
	10	Sold merchandise on account to members $1,340, terms n/30.
	12	Purchased golf shoes, sweaters, and other accessories on account from Woods Sportswear $830, terms 1/10, n/30.
	14	Paid Arnie Co. in full.
	17	Received credit from Woods Sportswear for merchandise returned $30.
	20	Made sales on account to members $810, terms n/30.
	21	Paid Woods Sportswear in full.
	27	Granted credit to members for clothing that did not fit properly $80.
	30	Received payments on account from members $1,220.

The chart of accounts for the pro shop includes Cash, Accounts Receivable, Inventory, Accounts Payable, Common Stock, Sales Revenue, Sales Returns and Allowances, Purchases, Purchase Returns and Allowances, Purchase Discounts, and Freight-In.

Instructions

(a) Journalize the April transactions using a periodic inventory system.

(b) Using T-accounts, enter the beginning balances in the ledger accounts and post the April transactions.

(c) Prepare a trial balance on April 30, 2017.

(d) Prepare an income statement through gross profit, assuming inventory on hand at April 30 is $4,263.

(c) Tot. trial balance $8,427
(d) Gross profit $ 700

▶ PROBLEMS: SET B AND SET C

Visit the book's companion website, at **www.wiley.com/college/kimmel**, and choose the Student Companion site to access Problems: Set B and Set C.

▶ CONTINUING PROBLEM Cookie Creations

(*Note:* This is a continuation of the Cookie Creations problem from Chapters 1 through 4.)

© leungchopan/ Shutterstock

CC5 Because Natalie has had such a successful first few months, she is considering other opportunities to develop her business. One opportunity is to become the exclusive distributor of a line of fine European mixers. Natalie comes to you for advice on how to account for these mixers.

Go to the book's companion website, at **www.wiley.com/college/kimmel**, *to see the completion of this problem.*

COMPREHENSIVE ACCOUNTING CYCLE REVIEW

ACR5-1 On December 1, 2017, Devine Distributing Company had the following account balances.

	Debit		Credit
Cash	$ 7,200	Accumulated Depreciation—Equipment	$ 2,200
Accounts Receivable	4,600	Accounts Payable	4,500
Inventory	12,000	Salaries and Wages Payable	1,000
Supplies	1,200	Common Stock	15,000
Equipment	22,000	Retained Earnings	24,300
	$47,000		$47,000

During December, the company completed the following summary transactions.

Dec. 6 Paid $1,600 for salaries due employees, of which $600 is for December and $1,000 is for November salaries payable.
8 Received $1,900 cash from customers in payment of account (no discount allowed).
10 Sold merchandise for cash $6,300. The cost of the merchandise sold was $4,100.
13 Purchased merchandise on account from Hecht Co. $9,000, terms 2/10, n/30.
15 Purchased supplies for cash $2,000.
18 Sold merchandise on account $12,000, terms 3/10, n/30. The cost of the merchandise sold was $8,000.
20 Paid salaries $1,800.
23 Paid Hecht Co. in full, less discount.
27 Received collections in full, less discounts, from customers billed on December 18.

Adjustment data:

1. Accrued salaries payable $800.
2. Depreciation $200 per month.
3. Supplies on hand $1,500.
4. Income tax due and unpaid at December 31 is $200.

Instructions

(a) Journalize the December transactions using a perpetual inventory system.

(b) Enter the December 1 balances in the ledger T-accounts and post the December transactions. Use Cost of Goods Sold, Depreciation Expense, Salaries and Wages Expense, Sales Revenue, Sales Discounts, Supplies Expense, Income Tax Expense, and Income Taxes Payable.

(c) Journalize and post adjusting entries.

(d) Prepare an adjusted trial balance.

(e) Prepare an income statement and a retained earnings statement for December and a classified balance sheet at December 31.

(d) Totals $65,500
(e) Net income $540

ACR5-2 On November 1, 2017, IKonk, Inc. had the following account balances. The company uses the perpetual inventory method.

	Debit		Credit
Cash	$ 9,000	Accumulated Depreciation—	
Accounts Receivable	2,240	Equipment	$ 1,000
Supplies	860	Accounts Payable	3,400
Equipment	25,000	Unearned Service Revenue	4,000
	$37,100	Salaries and Wages Payable	1,700
		Common Stock	20,000
		Retained Earnings	7,000
			$37,100

During November, the following summary transactions were completed.

Nov. 8 Paid $3,550 for salaries due employees, of which $1,850 is for November and $1,700 is for October.
10 Received $1,900 cash from customers in payment of account.
11 Purchased merchandise on account from Dimas Discount Supply for $8,000, terms 2/10, n/30.
12 Sold merchandise on account for $5,500, terms 2/10, n/30. The cost of the merchandise sold was $4,000.
15 Received credit from Dimas Discount Supply for merchandise returned $300.
19 Received collections in full, less discounts, from customers billed on sales of $5,500 on November 12.
20 Paid Dimas Discount Supply in full, less discount.
22 Received $2,300 cash for services performed in November.
25 Purchased equipment on account $5,000.
27 Purchased supplies on account $1,700.
28 Paid creditors $3,000 of accounts payable due.
29 Paid November rent $375.
29 Paid salaries $1,300.
29 Performed services on account and billed customers $700 for those services.
29 Received $675 from customers for services to be performed in the future.

Adjustment data:

1. Supplies on hand are valued at $1,600.
2. Accrued salaries payable are $500.
3. Depreciation for the month is $250.
4. $650 of services related to the unearned service revenue has not been performed by month-end.

Instructions

(a) Enter the November 1 balances in ledger T-accounts.
(b) Journalize the November transactions.
(c) Post to the ledger accounts. You will need to add some accounts.
(d) Journalize and post adjusting entries.
(e) Prepare an adjusted trial balance at November 30.
(f) Prepare a multiple-step income statement and a retained earnings statement for November and a classified balance sheet at November 30.
(g) Journalize and post closing entries.

EXPAND YOUR CRITICAL THINKING

Financial Reporting

FINANCIAL REPORTING PROBLEM: Apple Inc.

E **CT5-1** The financial statements for Apple Inc. appear in Appendix A at the end of this textbook.

Instructions

Answer these questions using the Consolidated Income Statement.

(a) What was the percentage change in total revenue and in net income from 2013 to 2014?
(b) What was the profit margin in each of the 3 years? (Use "Total Revenue.") Comment on the trend.
(c) What was Apple's gross profit rate in each of the 3 years? (Use "Net Sales" amounts.) Comment on the trend.

COMPARATIVE ANALYSIS PROBLEM: Columbia Sportswear Company vs. VF Corporation

Financial Analysis

CT5-2 The financial statements of Columbia Sportswear Company are presented in Appendix B. Financial statements of VF Corporation are presented in Appendix C. E

Instructions

(a) Based on the information contained in these financial statements, determine the following values for each company.
   (1) Profit margin for 2014. (For VF, use "Total Revenues.")
   (2) Gross profit for 2014.
   (3) Gross profit rate for 2014.
   (4) Operating income for 2014.
   (5) Percentage change in operating Income from 2014 to 2013. (For Columbia, use Income from operations.)

(b) What conclusions concerning the relative profitability of the two companies can be drawn from these data?

COMPARATIVE ANALYSIS PROBLEM: Amazon.com, Inc. vs. Wal-Mart Stores, Inc.

Financial Analysis

CT5-3 The financial statements of Amazon.com, Inc. are presented in Appendix D. Financial statements of Wal-Mart Stores, Inc. are presented in Appendix E. E

Instructions

(a) Based on the information contained in these financial statements, determine the following values for each company.
   (1) Profit margin for 2014. (For Amazon, use "Total net sales.")
   (2) Gross profit for 2014.
   (3) Gross profit rate for 2014.
   (4) Operating income for 2014.
   (5) Percentage change in operating income from 2014 to 2013.

(b) What conclusions concerning the relative profitability of the two companies can be drawn from these data?

INTERPRETING FINANCIAL STATEMENTS

CT5-4 Recently, it was announced that two giant French retailers, Carrefour SA and Promodes SA, would merge. A headline in the *Wall Street Journal* blared, "French Retailers Create New Wal-Mart Rival." While Wal-Mart's total sales would still exceed those of the combined company, Wal-Mart's international sales are far less than those of the combined company. This is a serious concern for Wal-Mart, since its primary opportunity for future growth lies outside of the United States. E

Below are basic financial data for the combined corporation (in euros) and Wal-Mart (in U.S. dollars). Even though their results are presented in different currencies, by employing ratios we can make some basic comparisons.

	Carrefour (in millions)	Wal-Mart (in millions)
Sales revenue	€70,486	$256,329
Cost of goods sold	54,630	198,747
Net income	1,738	9,054
Total assets	39,063	104,912
Current assets	14,521	34,421
Current liabilities	13,660	37,418
Total liabilities	29,434	61,289

Instructions

Compare the two companies by answering the following.

(a) Calculate the gross profit rate for each of the companies, and discuss their relative abilities to control cost of goods sold.

(b) Calculate the profit margin, and discuss the companies' relative profitability.

(c) Calculate the current ratio and debt to assets ratio for each of the two companies, and discuss their relative liquidity and solvency.

(d) What concerns might you have in relying on this comparison?

REAL-WORLD FOCUS

E **CT5-5** ***Purpose:*** No financial decision-maker should ever rely solely on the financial information reported in the annual report to make decisions. It is important to keep abreast of financial news. This activity demonstrates how to search for financial news on the Internet.

Address: **http://biz.yahoo.com/i**, or go to **www.wiley.com/college/kimmel**

Steps

1. Type in either Wal-Mart, Target Corp., or Kmart.
2. Choose **News.**
3. Select an article that sounds interesting to you and that would be relevant to an investor in these companies.

Instructions

(a) What was the source of the article (e.g., Reuters, Businesswire, Prnewswire)?

(b) Assume that you are a personal financial planner and that one of your clients owns stock in the company. Write a brief memo to your client summarizing the article and explaining the implications of the article for their investment.

Financial Analysis

Writing

Group Project

DECISION-MAKING ACROSS THE ORGANIZATION

E **CT5-6** Three years ago, Karen Suez and her brother-in-law Reece Jones opened Gigasales Department Store. For the first 2 years, business was good, but the following condensed income statement results for 2017 were disappointing.

GIGASALES DEPARTMENT STORE
Income Statement
For the Year Ended December 31, 2017

Net sales		$700,000
Cost of goods sold		560,000
Gross profit		140,000
Operating expenses		
Selling expenses	$100,000	
Administrative expenses	20,000	
		120,000
Net income		$ 20,000

Karen believes the problem lies in the relatively low gross profit rate of 20%. Reece believes the problem is that operating expenses are too high. Karen thinks the gross profit rate can be improved by making two changes. (1) Increase average selling prices by 15%; this increase is expected to lower sales volume so that total sales dollars will increase only 4%. (2) Buy merchandise in larger quantities and take all purchase discounts. These changes to purchasing practices are expected to increase the gross profit rate from its current rate of 20% to a new rate of 25%. Karen does not anticipate that these changes will have any effect on operating expenses.

Reece thinks expenses can be cut by making these two changes. (1) Cut 2018 sales salaries of $60,000 in half and give sales personnel a commission of 2% of net sales. (2) Reduce store deliveries to one day per week rather than twice a week; this change will reduce 2018 delivery expenses of $40,000 by 40%. Reece feels that these changes will not have any effect on net sales.

Karen and Reece come to you for help in deciding the best way to improve net income.

Instructions

With the class divided into groups, answer the following.

(a) Prepare a condensed income statement for 2018 assuming (1) Karen's changes are implemented and (2) Reece's ideas are adopted.

(b) What is your recommendation to Karen and Reece?

(c) Prepare a condensed income statement for 2018 assuming both sets of proposed changes are made.

(d) Discuss the impact that other factors might have. For example, would increasing the quantity of inventory increase costs? Would a salary cut affect employee morale? Would decreased morale affect sales? Would decreased store deliveries decrease customer satisfaction? What other suggestions might be considered?

COMMUNICATION ACTIVITY

CT5-7 The following situation is presented in chronological order. E

1. Aikan decides to buy a surfboard.
2. He calls Surfing Hawaii Co. to inquire about their surfboards.
3. Two days later, he requests Surfing Hawaii Co. to make him a surfboard.
4. Three days later, Surfing Hawaii Co. sends him a purchase order to fill out.
5. He sends back the purchase order.
6. Surfing Hawaii Co. receives the completed purchase order.
7. Surfing Hawaii Co. completes the surfboard.
8. Aikan picks up the surfboard.
9. Surfing Hawaii Co. bills Aikan.
10. Surfing Hawaii Co. receives payment from Aikan.

Instructions

In a memo to the president of Surfing Hawaii Co., answer the following questions.

(a) When should Surfing Hawaii Co. record the sale?

(b) Suppose that with his purchase order, Aikan is required to make a down payment. Would that change your answer to part (a)?

ETHICS CASE

CT5-8 Tabitha Andes was just hired as the assistant treasurer of Southside Stores, a specialty chain store company that has nine retail stores concentrated in one metropolitan area. Among other things, the payment of all invoices is centralized in one of the departments Tabitha will manage. Her primary responsibility is to maintain the company's high credit rating by paying all bills when due and to take advantage of all cash discounts. E

Pete Wilson, the former assistant treasurer who has been promoted to treasurer, is training Tabitha in her new duties. He instructs Tabitha that she is to continue the practice of preparing all checks "net of discount" and dating the checks the last day of the discount period. "But," Pete continues, "we always hold the checks at least 4 days beyond the discount period before mailing them. That way we get another 4 days of interest on our money. Most of our creditors need our business and don't complain. And, if they scream about our missing the discount period, we blame it on the mailroom or the post office. We've only lost one discount out of every hundred we take that way. I think everybody does it. By the way, welcome to our team!"

Instructions

(a) What are the ethical considerations in this case?

(b) What stakeholders are harmed or benefited?

(c) Should Tabitha continue the practice started by Pete? Does she have any choice?

ALL ABOUT YOU

CT5-9 There are many situations in business where it is difficult to determine the proper period in which to record revenue. Suppose that after graduation with a degree in finance, you take a job as a manager at a consumer electronics store called FarWest Electronics. The company has expanded rapidly in order to compete with Best Buy. E

FarWest has also begun selling gift cards. The cards are available in any dollar amount and allow the holder of the card to purchase an item for up to 2 years from the time the card is purchased. If the card is not used during those 2 years, it expires.

Instructions

Answer the following questions.

At what point should the revenue from the gift cards be recognized? Should the revenue be recognized at the time the card is sold, or should it be recorded when the card is redeemed? Explain the reasoning to support your answers.

FASB CODIFICATION ACTIVITY

CT5-10 If your school has a subscription to the FASB Codification, go to **http://aaahg.org/ascLogin.cfm** to log in and prepare responses to the following. E

(a) Access the glossary ("Master Glossary") to answer the following.
(1) What is the definition provided for inventory?
(2) What is a customer?
(b) What guidance does the Codification provide concerning reporting inventories above cost?

A Look at IFRS

LEARNING OBJECTIVE 8

Compare the accounting for merchandising under GAAP and IFRS.

The basic accounting entries for merchandising are the same under both GAAP and IFRS. The income statement is a required statement under both sets of standards. The basic format is similar although some differences do exist.

KEY POINTS

Following are the key similarities and differences between GAAP and IFRS related to inventories.

Similarities

- Under both GAAP and IFRS, a company can choose to use either a perpetual or a periodic inventory system.
- The definition of inventories is basically the same under GAAP and IFRS.
- As indicated above, the basic accounting entries for merchandising are the same under both GAAP and IFRS.
- Both GAAP and IFRS require that income statement information be presented for multiple years. For example, IFRS requires that 2 years of income statement information be presented, whereas GAAP requires 3 years.

Differences

- Under GAAP, companies generally classify income statement items by function. Classification by function leads to descriptions like administration, distribution, and manufacturing. Under IFRS, companies must classify expenses either by nature or by function. Classification by nature leads to descriptions such as the following: salaries, depreciation expense, and utilities expense. If a company uses the functional-expense method on the income statement, disclosure by nature is required in the notes to the financial statements.
- Presentation of the income statement under GAAP follows either a single-step or multiple-step format. IFRS does not mention a single-step or multiple-step approach.
- Under IFRS, revaluation of land, buildings, and intangible assets is permitted. The initial gains and losses resulting from this revaluation are reported as adjustments to equity, often referred to as **other comprehensive income**. The effect of this difference is that the use of IFRS result in more transactions affecting equity (other comprehensive income) but not net income.

LOOKING TO THE FUTURE

The IASB and FASB are working on a project that would rework the structure of financial statements. Specifically, this project will address the issue of how to classify various items in the income statement. A main goal of this new approach is to provide information that better represents how businesses are run. In addition, this approach draws attention away from just one number—net income. It will adopt major groupings similar to those currently used by the statement of cash flows (operating, investing, and financing), so that numbers can be more readily traced across statements. For example, the amount of income that is generated by operations would be traceable to the assets and liabilities used to generate the income. Finally, this approach would also provide detail, beyond that currently seen in most statements (either GAAP or IFRS), by requiring that line items be presented both by function and by nature. The new financial statement format was heavily influenced by suggestions from financial statement analysts.

IFRS Practice

IFRS SELF-TEST QUESTIONS

1. Which of the following would **not** be included in the definition of inventory under IFRS?
   (a) Photocopy paper held for sale by an office-supply store.
   (b) Stereo equipment held for sale by an electronics store.
   (c) Used office equipment held for sale by the human relations department of a plastics company.
   (d) All of the above would meet the definition.
2. Which of the following would **not** be a line item of a company reporting costs by nature?
   (a) Depreciation expense.
   (b) Salaries expense.
   (c) Interest expense.
   (d) Manufacturing expense.
3. Which of the following would **not** be a line item of a company reporting costs by function?
   (a) Administration.
   (b) Manufacturing.
   (c) Utilities expense.
   (d) Distribution.
4. Which of the following statements is **false**?
   (a) IFRS specifically requires use of a multiple-step income statement.
   (b) Under IFRS, companies can use either a perpetual or periodic system.
   (c) The proposed new format for financial statements was heavily influenced by the suggestions of financial statement analysts.
   (d) The new income statement format will try to de-emphasize the focus on the "net income" line item.

IFRS EXERCISES

IFRS5-1 Explain the difference between the "nature-of-expense" and "function-of-expense" classifications.

IFRS5-2 For each of the following income statement line items, state whether the item is a "by nature" expense item or a "by function" expense item.

________ Cost of goods sold.
________ Depreciation expense.
________ Salaries and wages expense.
________ Selling expenses.
________ Utilities expense.
________ Delivery expense.
________ General and administrative expenses.

IFRS5-3 Matilda Company reported the following amounts (in euros) in 2017: Net income, €150,000; Unrealized gain related to revaluation of buildings, €10,000; and Unrealized loss on non-trading securities, €(35,000). Determine Matilda's total comprehensive income for 2017.

INTERNATIONAL FINANCIAL REPORTING PROBLEM: Louis Vuitton

IFRS5-4 The financial statements of Louis Vuitton are presented in Appendix F. Instructions for accessing and using the company's complete annual report, including the notes to its financial statements, are also provided in Appendix F.

Instructions
Use Louis Vuitton's annual report to answer the following questions.

(a) Does Louis Vuitton use a multiple-step or a single-step income statement format? Explain how you made your determination.
(b) Instead of "interest expense," what label does Louis Vuitton use for interest costs that it incurs?
(c) Using the notes to the company's financial statements, determine the following:
   (1) Composition of the inventory.
   (2) Amount of inventory (gross) before impairment.

Answers to IFRS Self-Test Questions
1. c **2.** d **3.** c **4.** a

6

Reporting and Analyzing Inventory

CHAPTER PREVIEW

In the previous chapter, we discussed the accounting for merchandise inventory using a perpetual inventory system. In this chapter, we explain the methods used to calculate the cost of inventory on hand at the balance sheet date and the cost of goods sold. We conclude by illustrating methods for analyzing inventory.

CHAPTER OUTLINE

LEARNING OBJECTIVES		PRACTICE
1 Discuss how to classify and determine inventory.	• Classifying inventory • Determining inventory quantities	DO IT! 1 Rules of Ownership
2 Apply inventory cost flow methods and discuss their financial effects.	• Specific identification • Cost flow assumptions • Financial statement and tax effects • Using inventory cost flow methods consistently	DO IT! 2 Cost Flow Methods
3 Explain the statement presentation and analysis of inventory.	• Presentation • Lower-of-cost-or-market • Analysis • Adjustments for LIFO reserve	DO IT! 3 3a LCM Basis 3b Inventory Turnover

Go to the ***REVIEW AND PRACTICE*** section at the end of the chapter for a targeted summary and exercises with solutions.

Visit **WileyPLUS** for additional tutorials and practice opportunities.

James Porter/Workbook Stock/Getty Images, Inc.

FEATURE STORY

"Where Is That Spare Bulldozer Blade?"

Let's talk inventory—big, bulldozer-size inventory. Caterpillar Inc. is the world's largest manufacturer of construction and mining equipment, diesel and natural gas engines, and industrial gas turbines. It sells its products in over 200 countries, making it one of the most successful U.S. exporters.

In the past, Caterpillar's profitability suffered, but today it is very successful. A big part of this turnaround can be attributed to effective management of its inventory. Imagine what it costs Caterpillar to have too many bulldozers sitting around in inventory—a situation the company definitely wants to avoid. Yet, Caterpillar must also make sure it has enough inventory to meet demand.

At one time during a 7-year period, Caterpillar's sales increased by 100%, while its inventory increased by only 50%. To achieve this dramatic reduction in the amount of resources tied up in inventory, while continuing to meet customers' needs, Caterpillar used a two-pronged approach. First, it completed a factory modernization program, which dramatically increased its production efficiency. The program reduced by 60% the amount of inventory the company processed at any one time. It also reduced by an incredible 75% the time it takes to manufacture a part.

Second, Caterpillar dramatically improved its parts distribution system. It ships more than 100,000 items daily from its 23 distribution centers strategically located around the world (10 million square feet of warehouse space—remember, we're talking bulldozers). The company can virtually guarantee that it can get any part to anywhere in the world within 24 hours.

These changes led to record exports, profits, and revenues for Caterpillar. It would have seemed that things couldn't have been better. But industry analysts, as well as the company's managers, thought otherwise. In order to maintain Caterpillar's position as the industry leader, management began another major overhaul of inventory production and inventory management processes. The goal: to cut the number of repairs in half, increase productivity by 20%, and increase inventory turnover by 40%.

In short, Caterpillar's ability to manage its inventory has been a key reason for its past success and will very likely play a huge part in its future profitability as well.

LEARNING OBJECTIVE 1

Discuss how to classify and determine inventory.

Two important steps in the reporting of inventory at the end of the accounting period are the classification of inventory based on its degree of completeness and the determination of inventory amounts.

CLASSIFYING INVENTORY

How a company classifies its inventory depends on whether the firm is a merchandiser or a manufacturer. In a **merchandising** company, such as those described in Chapter 5, inventory consists of many different items. For example, in a grocery store, canned goods, dairy products, meats, and produce are just a few of the inventory items on hand. These items have two common characteristics: (1) they are owned by the company, and (2) they are in a form ready for sale to customers in the ordinary course of business. Thus, merchandisers need only one inventory classification, **merchandise inventory**, to describe the many different items that make up the total inventory.

▼ **HELPFUL HINT**
Regardless of the classification, companies report all inventories under Current Assets on the balance sheet.

In a **manufacturing** company, some inventory may not yet be ready for sale. As a result, manufacturers usually classify inventory into three categories: finished goods, work in process, and raw materials. **Finished goods inventory** is manufactured items that are completed and ready for sale. **Work in process** is that portion of manufactured inventory that has begun the production process but is not yet complete. **Raw materials** are the basic goods that will be used in production but have not yet been placed into production.

For example, Caterpillar classifies earth-moving tractors completed and ready for sale as **finished goods**. It classifies the tractors on the assembly line in various stages of production as **work in process**. The steel, glass, tires, and other components that are on hand waiting to be used in the production of tractors are identified as **raw materials**. Illustration 6-1 shows an excerpt from Note 7 of Caterpillar's annual report.

ILLUSTRATION 6-1
Composition of Caterpillar's inventory

	December 31		
(millions of dollars)	**2014**	**2013**	**2012**
Raw materials	$ 2,986	$ 2,966	$ 3,573
Work-in-process	2,455	2,589	2,920
Finished goods	6,504	6,785	8,767
Other	260	285	287
Total inventories	**$12,205**	**$12,625**	**$15,547**

By observing the levels and changes in the levels of these three inventory types, financial statement users can gain insight into management's production plans. For example, low levels of raw materials and high levels of finished goods suggest that management believes it has enough inventory on hand, and production will be slowing down—perhaps in anticipation of a recession. Conversely, high levels of raw materials and low levels of finished goods probably signal that management is planning to step up production.

Many companies have significantly lowered inventory levels and costs using **just-in-time (JIT) inventory** methods. Under a just-in-time method, companies manufacture or purchase goods only when needed. Dell is famous for having developed a system for making computers in response to individual customer requests. Even though it makes computers to meet a customer's particular specifications, Dell is able to assemble the computer and put it on a truck in less than 48 hours. The success of a JIT system depends on reliable suppliers. By integrating its information systems with those of its suppliers, Dell reduced its inventories to nearly zero. This is a huge advantage in an industry where products become obsolete nearly overnight.

The accounting concepts discussed in this chapter apply to the inventory classifications of both merchandising and manufacturing companies. Our focus throughout most of this chapter is on merchandise inventory. Additional issues specific to manufacturing companies are discussed in managerial accounting courses.

ACCOUNTING ACROSS THE ORGANIZATION **Ford**

© PeskyMonkey/iStockphoto

A Big Hiccup

JIT can save a company a lot of money, but it isn't without risk. An unexpected disruption in the supply chain can cost a company a lot of money. Japanese automakers experienced just such a disruption when a 6.8-magnitude earthquake caused major damage to the company that produces 50% of their piston rings. The rings themselves cost only $1.50, but you cannot make a car without them. As a result, the automakers were forced to shut down production for a few days—a loss of tens of thousands of cars.

Similarly, a major snowstorm halted production at the Canadian plants of Ford. A Ford spokesperson said, "Because the plants run with just-in-time inventory, we don't have large stockpiles of parts sitting around. When you have a somewhat significant disruption, you can pretty quickly run out of parts."

Sources: Amy Chozick, "A Key Strategy of Japan's Car Makers Backfires," *Wall Street Journal* (July 20, 2007); and Kate Linebaugh, "Canada Military Evacuates Motorists Stranded by Snow," *Wall Street Journal* (December 15, 2010).

What steps might the companies take to avoid such a serious disruption in the future? (Go to WileyPLUS for this answer and additional questions.)

DETERMINING INVENTORY QUANTITIES

No matter whether they are using a periodic or perpetual inventory system, all companies need to determine inventory quantities at the end of the accounting period. If using a perpetual system, companies take a physical inventory for the following reasons. The first is to check the accuracy of their perpetual inventory records. The second is to determine the amount of inventory lost due to wasted raw materials, shoplifting, or employee theft.

Companies using a periodic inventory system must take a physical inventory for two different purposes: to determine the inventory on hand at the balance sheet date, and to determine the cost of goods sold for the period.

Determining inventory quantities involves two steps: (1) taking a physical inventory of goods on hand and (2) determining the ownership of goods.

Taking a Physical Inventory

Companies take the physical inventory at the end of the accounting period. Taking a physical inventory involves actually counting, weighing, or measuring each kind of inventory on hand. In many companies, taking an inventory is a formidable task. Retailers such as Target, True Value Hardware, or Home Depot have thousands of different inventory items. An inventory count is generally more accurate when a limited number of goods are being sold or received during the counting. Consequently, companies often "take inventory" when the business is closed or when business is slow. Many retailers close early on a chosen day in January—after the holiday sales and returns, when inventories are at their lowest level—to count inventory. Wal-Mart, for example, has a year-end of January 31.

ETHICS NOTE

In a famous fraud, a salad oil company filled its storage tanks mostly with water. The oil rose to the top, so auditors thought the tanks were full of oil. The company also said it had more tanks than it really did: it repainted numbers on the tanks to confuse auditors.

ETHICS INSIGHT **Leslie Fay**

© Greg Brookes/iStockphoto

Falsifying Inventory to Boost Income

Managers at women's apparel maker Leslie Fay were convicted of falsifying inventory records to boost net income in an attempt to increase management bonuses. In another case, executives at Craig Consumer Electronics were accused of defrauding lenders by manipulating inventory records. The indictment said the company classified "defective goods as new or refurbished" and claimed that it owned certain shipments "from overseas suppliers" when, in fact, Craig either did not own the shipments or the shipments did not exist.

What effect does an overstatement of inventory have on a company's financial statements? (Go to WileyPLUS for this answer and additional questions.)

Determining Ownership of Goods

One challenge in determining inventory quantities is making sure a company owns the inventory. To determine ownership of goods, two questions must be answered: Do all of the goods included in the count belong to the company? Does the company own any goods that were not included in the count?

GOODS IN TRANSIT A complication in determining ownership is **goods in transit** (on board a truck, train, ship, or plane) at the end of the period. The company may have purchased goods that have not yet been received, or it may have sold goods that have not yet been delivered. To arrive at an accurate count, the company must determine ownership of these goods.

Goods in transit should be included in the inventory of the company that has legal title to the goods. Legal title is determined by the terms of the sale, as shown in Illustration 6-2 and described below.

ILLUSTRATION 6-2
Terms of sale

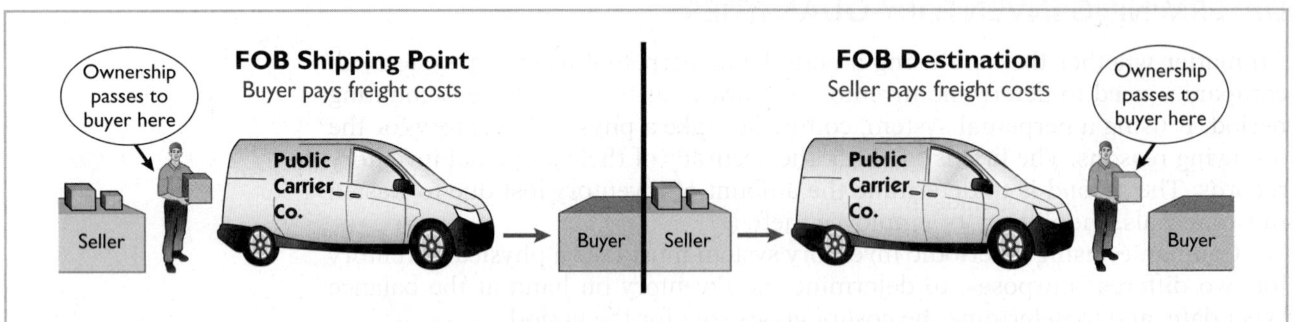

1. When the terms are **FOB (free on board) shipping point**, ownership of the goods passes to the buyer when the public carrier accepts the goods from the seller.
2. When the terms are **FOB destination**, ownership of the goods remains with the seller until the goods reach the buyer.

CONSIGNED GOODS In some lines of business, it is common to hold the goods of other parties and try to sell the goods for them for a fee, but without taking ownership of the goods. These are called **consigned goods**.

For example, you might have a used car that you would like to sell. If you take the item to a dealer, the dealer might be willing to put the car on its lot and charge you a commission if it is sold. Under this agreement, the dealer **would not take ownership** of the car, which would still belong to you. If an inventory count were taken, the car would not be included in the dealer's inventory because the dealer does not own it.

Many car, boat, and antique dealers sell goods on consignment to keep their inventory costs down and to avoid the risk of purchasing an item that they will not be able to sell. Today, even some manufacturers are making consignment agreements with their suppliers in order to keep their inventory levels low.

ANATOMY OF A FRAUD

Ted Nickerson, CEO of clock manufacturer Dally Industries, had expensive tastes. To support this habit, Ted took out large loans, which he collateralized with his shares of Dally Industries stock. If the price of Dally's stock fell, he was required to provide the bank with more shares of stock. To achieve target net income figures and thus maintain the stock price, Ted coerced employees in the company to alter inventory figures. Inventory quantities were manipulated by changing the amounts on inventory control tags after the year-end physical inventory count. For example, if a tag said there were 20 units of a particular item, the tag was changed to 220. Similarly, the unit costs that were used to determine the value of ending inventory were increased from, for example, $125 per unit to $1,250. Both of these fraudulent changes had the effect of increasing the amount of reported ending inventory. This reduced cost of goods sold and increased net income.

Total take: $245,000

THE MISSING CONTROL

Independent internal verification. The company should have spot-checked its inventory records periodically, verifying that the number of units in the records agreed with the amount on hand and that the unit costs agreed with vendor price sheets.

Source: Adapted from Wells, *Fraud Casebook* (2007), pp. 502–509.

DO IT!  1 Rules of Ownership

Hasbeen Company completed its inventory count. It arrived at a total inventory value of $200,000. You have been given the information listed below. Discuss how this information affects the reported cost of inventory.

1. Hasbeen included in the inventory goods held on consignment for Falls Co., costing $15,000.
2. The company did not include in the count purchased goods of $10,000, which were in transit (terms: FOB shipping point).
3. The company did not include in the count inventory that had been sold with a cost of $12,000, which was in transit (terms: FOB shipping point).

SOLUTION

The goods of $15,000 held on consignment should be deducted from the inventory count. The goods of $10,000 purchased FOB shipping point should be added to the inventory count. Item 3 was treated correctly. Sold goods of $12,000 which were in transit FOB shipping point should not be included in the ending inventory. Inventory should be $195,000 ($200,000 − $15,000 + $10,000).

Action Plan

✔ Apply the rules of ownership to goods held on consignment.

✔ Apply the rules of ownership to goods in transit.

Related exercise material: **BE6-1, DO IT! 6-1, E6-1, E6-2,** and **E6-3.**

LEARNING OBJECTIVE  2 Apply inventory cost flow methods and discuss their financial effects.

Inventory is accounted for at cost. Cost includes all expenditures necessary to acquire goods and place them in a condition ready for sale. For example, freight costs incurred to acquire inventory are added to the cost of inventory, but the cost of shipping goods to a customer is a selling expense. After a company has determined the quantity of units of inventory, it applies unit costs to the quantities to determine the total cost of the inventory and the cost of goods sold. This process can be complicated if a company has purchased inventory items at different times and at different prices.

For example, assume that Crivitz TV Company purchases three identical 50-inch TVs on different dates at costs of $700, $750, and $800. During the year, Crivitz sold two TVs at $1,200 each. These facts are summarized in Illustration 6-3.

ILLUSTRATION 6-3
Data for inventory costing example

Purchases	
February 3	1 TV at $700
March 5	1 TV at $750
May 22	1 TV at $800
Sales	
June 1	2 TVs for $2,400 ($1,200 × 2)

Cost of goods sold will differ depending on which two TVs the company sold. For example, it might be $1,450 ($700 + $750), or $1,500 ($700 + $800), or $1,550 ($750 + $800). In this section, we discuss alternative costing methods available to Crivitz.

SPECIFIC IDENTIFICATION

If Crivitz can positively identify which particular units it sold and which are still in ending inventory, it can use the **specific identification method** of inventory costing. For example, if Crivitz sold the TVs it purchased on February 3 and May 22, then its cost of goods sold is $1,500 ($700 + $800), and its ending inventory is $750 (see Illustration 6-4). Using this method, companies can accurately determine ending inventory and cost of goods sold.

ILLUSTRATION 6-4
Specific identification method

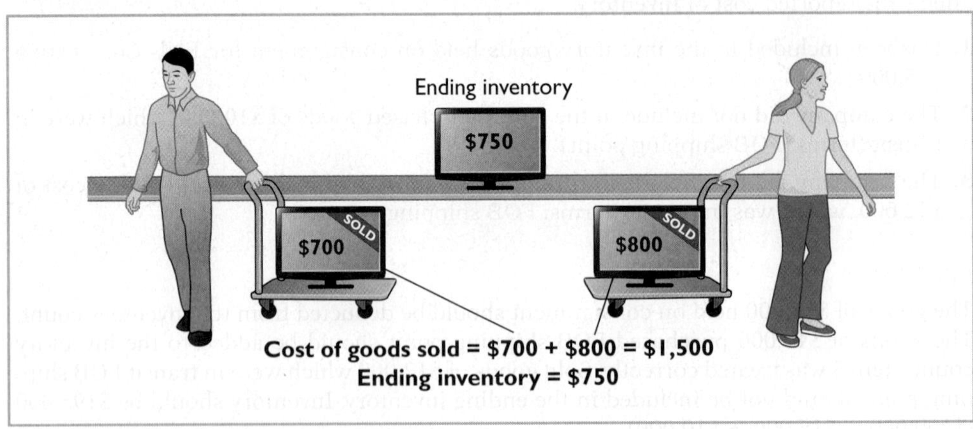

ETHICS NOTE
A major disadvantage of the specific identification method is that management may be able to manipulate net income. For example, it can boost net income by selling units purchased at a low cost, or reduce net income by selling units purchased at a high cost.

Specific identification requires that companies keep records of the original cost of each individual inventory item. Historically, specific identification was possible only when a company sold a limited variety of high-unit-cost items that could be identified clearly from the time of purchase through the time of sale. Examples of such products are cars, pianos, or expensive antiques.

Today, with bar coding, electronic product codes, and radio frequency identification, it is theoretically possible to do specific identification with nearly any type of product. The reality is, however, that this practice is still relatively rare. Instead, rather than keep track of the cost of each particular item sold, most companies make assumptions, called **cost flow assumptions**, about which units were sold.

COST FLOW ASSUMPTIONS

Because specific identification is often impractical, other cost flow methods are permitted. These differ from specific identification in that they **assume** flows of costs that may be unrelated to the actual physical flow of goods. There are three assumed cost flow methods:

1. First-in, first-out (FIFO)
2. Last-in, first-out (LIFO)
3. Average-cost

There is no accounting requirement that the cost flow assumption be consistent with the physical movement of the goods. Company management selects the appropriate cost flow method.

To demonstrate the three cost flow methods, we will use a **periodic** inventory system. We assume a periodic system because very few companies use **perpetual** LIFO, FIFO, or average-cost to cost their inventory and related cost of goods sold. Instead, companies that use perpetual systems, as shown in Chapter 5, often use an assumed cost (called a standard cost) to record cost of goods sold at the time of sale. Then, at the end of the period when they count their inventory, they **recalculate** cost of goods sold using **periodic** FIFO, LIFO, or average-cost as shown in this chapter and adjust cost of goods sold to this recalculated number.[1]

To illustrate the three inventory cost flow methods, we will use the data for Houston Electronics' Astro condensers, shown in Illustration 6-5.

ILLUSTRATION 6-5
Data for Houston Electronics

HOUSTON ELECTRONICS
Astro Condensers

Date	Explanation	Units	Unit Cost	Total Cost
Jan. 1	Beginning inventory	100	$10	$ 1,000
Apr. 15	Purchase	200	11	2,200
Aug. 24	Purchase	300	12	3,600
Nov. 27	Purchase	400	13	5,200
	Total units available for sale	1,000		$12,000
	Units in ending inventory	450		
	Units sold	550		

From Chapter 5, the cost of goods sold formula in a periodic system is:

(Beginning Inventory + Purchases) − Ending Inventory = Cost of Goods Sold

Houston Electronics had a total of 1,000 units available to sell during the period (beginning inventory plus purchases). The total cost of these 1,000 units is $12,000, referred to as **cost of goods available for sale**. A physical inventory taken at December 31 determined that there were 450 units in ending inventory. Therefore, Houston sold 550 units (1,000 − 450) during the period. To determine the cost of the 550 units that were sold (the cost of goods sold), we assign a cost

[1]Also, some companies use a perpetual system to keep track of units, but they do not make an entry for perpetual cost of goods sold. In addition, firms that employ LIFO tend to use **dollar-value LIFO**, a method discussed in upper-level courses. FIFO periodic and FIFO perpetual give the same result. Therefore, firms should not incur the additional cost to use FIFO perpetual. Few firms use perpetual average-cost because of the added cost of recordkeeping. Finally, for instructional purposes, we believe it is easier to demonstrate the cost flow assumptions under the periodic system, which makes it more pedagogically appropriate.

to the ending inventory and subtract that value from the cost of goods available for sale. The value assigned to the ending inventory **depends on which cost flow method we use**. No matter which cost flow assumption we use, though, the sum of cost of goods sold plus the cost of the ending inventory must equal the cost of goods available for sale—in this case, $12,000.

First-In, First-Out (FIFO)

The **first-in, first-out (FIFO) method** assumes that the **earliest goods** purchased are the first to be sold. FIFO often parallels the actual physical flow of merchandise because it generally is good business practice to sell the oldest units first. Under the FIFO method, therefore, the **costs** of the earliest goods purchased are the first to be recognized in determining cost of goods sold, regardless of which units were actually sold. (Note that this does not mean that the oldest units **are** sold first, but that the costs of the oldest units are **recognized** first. In a bin of picture hangers at the hardware store, for example, no one really knows, nor would it matter, which hangers are sold first.) Illustration 6-6 shows the allocation of the cost of goods available for sale at Houston Electronics under FIFO.

ILLUSTRATION 6-6
Allocation of costs—FIFO method

▼ HELPFUL HINT
Note the sequencing of the allocation: (1) compute ending inventory, and (2) determine cost of goods sold.

▼ HELPFUL HINT
Another way of thinking about the calculation of FIFO ending inventory is the **LISH assumption**—last in still here.

COST OF GOODS AVAILABLE FOR SALE

Date	Explanation	Units	Unit Cost	Total Cost
Jan. 1	Beginning inventory	100	$10	$ 1,000
Apr. 15	Purchase	200	11	2,200
Aug. 24	Purchase	300	12	3,600
Nov. 27	Purchase	400	13	5,200
	Total	1,000		**$12,000**

STEP 1: ENDING INVENTORY

Date	Units	Units Cost	Total Cost
Nov. 27	400	$13	$ 5,200
Aug. 24	50	12	600
Total	450		**$5,800**

STEP 2: COST OF GOODS SOLD

Cost of goods available for sale	$12,000
Less: Ending inventory	**5,800**
Cost of goods sold	**$ 6,200**

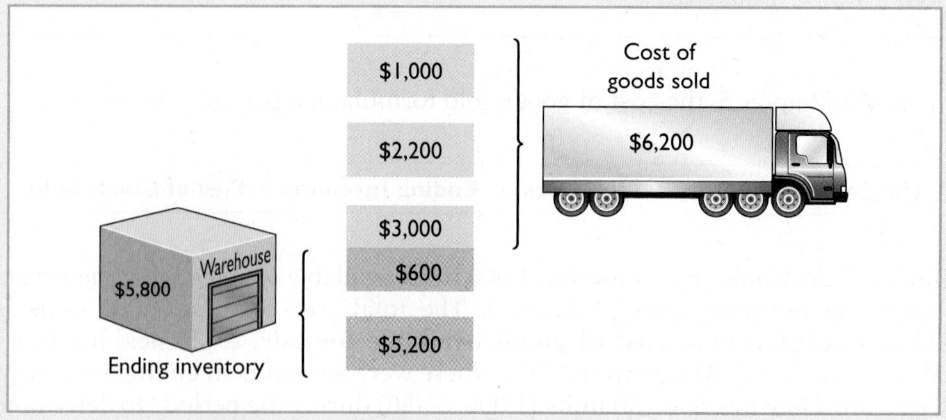

Under FIFO, since it is assumed that the first goods purchased were the first goods sold, ending inventory is based on the prices of the most recent units purchased. That is, **under FIFO, companies determine the cost of the ending inventory by taking the unit cost of the most recent purchase and working backward until all units of inventory have been costed**. In this example, Houston Electronics prices the 450 units of ending inventory using the **most recent** prices.

The last purchase was 400 units at $13 on November 27. The remaining 50 units are priced using the unit cost of the second most recent purchase, $12, on August 24. Next, Houston Electronics calculates cost of goods sold by subtracting the cost of the units **not sold** (ending inventory) from the cost of all goods available for sale.

Illustration 6-7 demonstrates that companies also can calculate cost of goods sold by pricing the 550 units sold using the prices of the first 550 units acquired. Note that of the 300 units purchased on August 24, only 250 units are assumed sold. This agrees with our calculation of the cost of ending inventory, where 50 of these units were assumed unsold and thus included in ending inventory.

ILLUSTRATION 6-7
Proof of cost of goods sold

Date	Units	Unit Cost	Total Cost
Jan. 1	100	$10	$ 1,000
Apr. 15	200	11	2,200
Aug. 24	250	12	3,000
Total	550		$6,200

Last-In, First-Out (LIFO)

The **last-in, first-out (LIFO) method** assumes that the **latest goods** purchased are the first to be sold. LIFO seldom coincides with the actual physical flow of inventory. (Exceptions include goods stored in piles, such as coal or hay, where goods are removed from the top of the pile as they are sold.) Under the LIFO method, the **costs** of the latest goods purchased are the first to be recognized in determining cost of goods sold. Illustration 6-8 shows the allocation of the cost of goods available for sale at Houston Electronics under LIFO.

ILLUSTRATION 6-8
Allocation of costs—LIFO method

COST OF GOODS AVAILABLE FOR SALE

Date	Explanation	Units	Unit Cost	Total Cost
Jan. 1	Beginning inventory	100	$10	$ 1,000
Apr. 15	Purchase	200	11	2,200
Aug. 24	Purchase	300	12	3,600
Nov. 27	Purchase	400	13	5,200
	Total	1,000		$12,000

STEP 1: ENDING INVENTORY

Date	Units	Unit Cost	Total Cost
Jan. 1	100	$10	$ 1,000
Apr. 15	200	11	2,200
Aug. 24	150	12	1,800
Total	450		$5,000

STEP 2: COST OF GOODS SOLD

Cost of goods available for sale	$12,000
Less: Ending inventory	5,000
Cost of goods sold	$ 7,000

▼ HELPFUL HINT
Another way of thinking about the calculation of LIFO ending inventory is the **FISH assumption**—first in still here.

Under LIFO, since it is assumed that the first goods sold were those that were most recently purchased, ending inventory is based on the prices of the oldest units purchased. That is, **under LIFO, companies obtain the cost of the ending inventory by taking the unit cost of the earliest goods available for sale and working forward until all units of inventory have been costed**. In this example, Houston Electronics prices the 450 units of ending inventory using the **earliest** prices. The first purchase was 100 units at $10 in the January 1 beginning inventory. Then, 200 units were purchased at $11. The remaining 150 units needed are priced at $12 per unit (August 24 purchase). Next, Houston Electronics calculates cost of goods sold by subtracting the cost of the units **not sold** (ending inventory) from the cost of all goods available for sale.

Illustration 6-9 demonstrates that we can also calculate cost of goods sold by pricing the 550 units sold using the prices of the last 550 units acquired. Note that of the 300 units purchased on August 24, only 150 units are assumed sold. This agrees with our calculation of the cost of ending inventory, where 150 of these units were assumed unsold and thus included in ending inventory.

ILLUSTRATION 6-9
Proof of cost of goods sold

Date	Units	Unit Cost	Total Cost
Nov. 27	400	$13	$ 5,200
Aug. 24	150	12	1,800
Total	550		$7,000

Under a periodic inventory system, which we are using here, **all goods purchased during the period are assumed to be available for the first sale, regardless of the date of purchase.**

Average-Cost

The **average-cost method** allocates the cost of goods available for sale on the basis of the **weighted-average unit cost** incurred. Illustration 6-10 presents the formula and a sample computation of the weighted-average unit cost.

ILLUSTRATION 6-10
Formula for weighted-average unit cost

Cost of Goods Available for Sale	÷	Total Units Available for Sale	=	Weighted-Average Unit Cost
$12,000	÷	1,000	=	$12.00

The company then applies the weighted-average unit cost to the units on hand to determine the cost of the ending inventory. Illustration 6-11 shows the allocation of the cost of goods available for sale at Houston Electronics using average-cost.

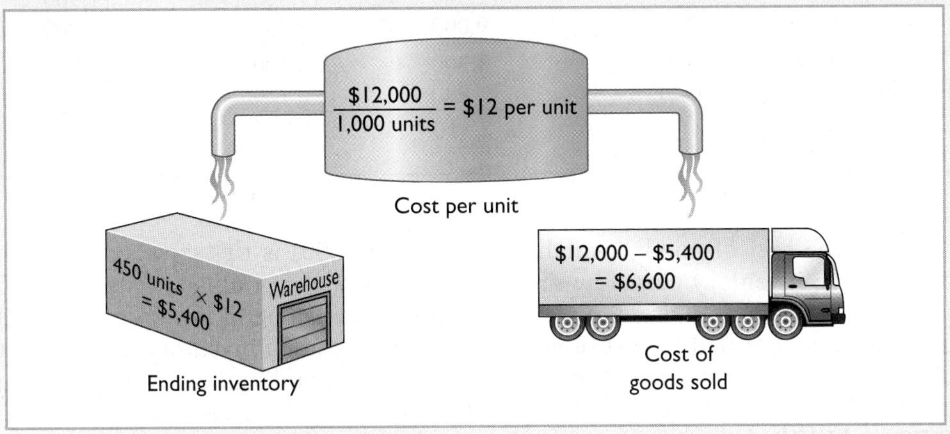

ILLUSTRATION 6-11
Allocation of costs—average-cost method

COST OF GOODS AVAILABLE FOR SALE

Date	Explanation	Units	Unit Cost	Total Cost
Jan. 1	Beginning inventory	100	$10	$ 1,000
Apr. 15	Purchase	200	11	2,200
Aug. 24	Purchase	300	12	3,600
Nov. 27	Purchase	400	13	5,200
	Total	1,000		$12,000

STEP 1: ENDING INVENTORY

$12,000	÷	1,000	=	$ 12.00
Units	×	**Unit Cost**	=	**Total Cost**
450		$12.00		$5,400

STEP 2: COST OF GOODS SOLD

Cost of goods available for sale	$12,000
Less: Ending inventory	5,400
Cost of goods sold	$ 6,600

$12,000 / 1,000 units = $12 per unit

Cost per unit

450 units × $12 = $5,400

Warehouse

Ending inventory

$12,000 – $5,400 = $6,600

Cost of goods sold

We can verify the cost of goods sold under this method by multiplying the units sold times the weighted-average unit cost (550 × $12 = $6,600). Note that this method does **not** use the simple average of the unit costs. The simple average is $11.50 ($10 + $11 + $12 + $13 = $46; $46 ÷ 4). The average-cost method instead uses the average **weighted by** the quantities purchased at each unit cost.

FINANCIAL STATEMENT AND TAX EFFECTS OF COST FLOW METHODS

DECISION TOOLS 

Analyzing financial statement and tax effects helps users determine which inventory costing method best meets the company's objectives.

Each of the three assumed cost flow methods is acceptable for use under GAAP. For example, Reebok International Ltd. and Wendy's International currently use the FIFO method of inventory costing. Campbell Soup Company, Krogers, and Walgreens use LIFO for part or all of their inventory. Bristol-Myers Squibb, Starbucks, and Motorola use the average-cost method. In fact, a company may also use more than one cost flow method at the same time. Stanley Black & Decker Manufacturing Company, for example, uses LIFO for domestic inventories and FIFO for foreign inventories. Illustration 6-12 (in the margin) shows the use of the three cost flow methods in 500 large U.S. companies.

The reasons companies adopt different inventory cost flow methods are varied, but they usually involve at least one of the following three factors: (1) income statement effects, (2) balance sheet effects, or (3) tax effects.

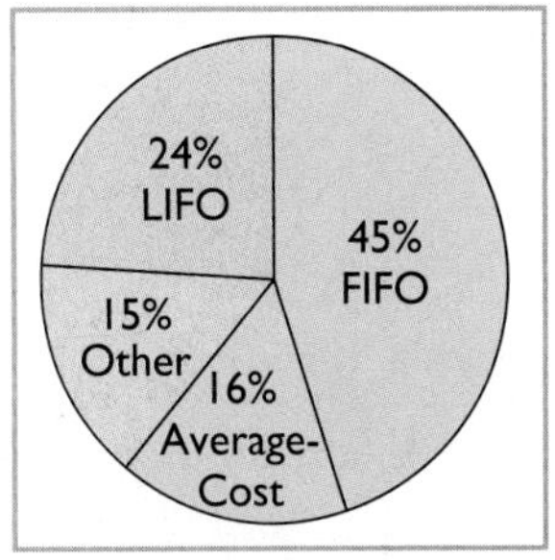

ILLUSTRATION 6-12
Use of cost flow methods in major U.S. companies

Income Statement Effects

To understand why companies might choose a particular cost flow method, let's examine the effects of the different cost flow assumptions on the financial statements of Houston Electronics. The condensed income statements in Illustration 6-13 assume that Houston sold its 550 units for $18,500, had operating expenses of $9,000, and is subject to an income tax rate of 30%.

ILLUSTRATION 6-13
Comparative effects of cost flow methods

HOUSTON ELECTRONICS
Condensed Income Statements

	FIFO	LIFO	Average-Cost
Sales revenue	$18,500	$18,500	$18,500
Beginning inventory	1,000	1,000	1,000
Purchases	11,000	11,000	11,000
Cost of goods available for sale	12,000	12,000	12,000
Less: Ending inventory	**5,800**	**5,000**	**5,400**
Cost of goods sold	6,200	7,000	6,600
Gross profit	12,300	11,500	11,900
Operating expenses	9,000	9,000	9,000
Income before income taxes	3,300	2,500	2,900
Income tax expense (30%)	990	750	870
Net income	**$ 2,310**	**$ 1,750**	**$ 2,030**

Note the cost of goods available for sale ($12,000) is the same under each of the three inventory cost flow methods. However, the ending inventories and the costs of goods sold are different. This difference is due to the unit costs that the company allocated to cost of goods sold and to ending inventory. Each dollar of difference in ending inventory results in a corresponding dollar difference in income before income taxes. For Houston, an $800 difference exists between FIFO and LIFO cost of goods sold.

In periods of changing prices, the cost flow assumption can have significant impacts both on income and on evaluations of income, such as the following.

1. In a period of inflation, FIFO produces a higher net income because lower unit costs of the first units purchased are matched against revenue.
2. In a period of inflation, LIFO produces a lower net income because higher unit costs of the last goods purchased are matched against revenue.
3. If prices are falling, the results from the use of FIFO and LIFO are reversed. FIFO will report the lowest net income and LIFO the highest.
4. Regardless of whether prices are rising or falling, average-cost produces net income between FIFO and LIFO.

To management, higher net income is an advantage. It causes external users to view the company more favorably. In addition, management bonuses, if based on net income, will be higher. Therefore, when prices are rising (which is usually the case), companies tend to prefer FIFO because it results in higher net income.

Others believe that LIFO presents a more realistic net income number. That is, LIFO matches the more recent costs against current revenues to provide a better measure of net income. During periods of inflation, many challenge the quality of non-LIFO earnings, noting that failing to match current costs against current revenues leads to an understatement of cost of goods sold and an overstatement of net income. As some indicate, net income computed using FIFO creates **"paper or phantom profits"**—that is, earnings that do not really exist.

Balance Sheet Effects

A major advantage of the FIFO method is that in a period of inflation, the costs allocated to ending inventory will approximate their current cost. For example, for Houston Electronics, 400 of the 450 units in the ending inventory are costed under FIFO at the higher November 27 unit cost of $13.

Conversely, a major shortcoming of the LIFO method is that in a period of inflation, the costs allocated to ending inventory may be significantly understated in terms of current cost. The understatement becomes greater over prolonged periods of inflation if the inventory includes goods purchased in one or more prior accounting periods. For example, Caterpillar has used LIFO for 50 years. Its balance sheet shows ending inventory of $14.5 billion. But the inventory's actual current cost if FIFO had been used is $17.0 billion.

Tax Effects

We have seen that both inventory on the balance sheet and net income on the income statement are higher when companies use FIFO in a period of inflation. Yet, many companies use LIFO. Why? The reason is that LIFO results in the lowest income taxes (because of lower net income) during times of rising prices. For example, in Illustration 6-13 income taxes are $750 under LIFO, compared to $990 under FIFO. The tax savings of $240 makes more cash available for use in the business.

▼ HELPFUL HINT

A tax rule, often referred to as the **LIFO conformity rule**, requires that if companies use LIFO for tax purposes, they must also use it for financial reporting purposes. This means that if a company chooses the LIFO method to reduce its tax bills, it will also have to report lower net income in its financial statements.

INTERNATIONAL INSIGHT ExxonMobil Corporation

Bloomberg/Getty Images

Is LIFO Fair?

ExxonMobil Corporation, like many U.S. companies, uses LIFO to value its inventory for financial reporting and tax purposes. In one recent year, this resulted in a cost of goods sold figure that was $5.6 billion higher than under FIFO. By increasing cost of goods sold, ExxonMobil reduces net income, which reduces taxes. Critics say that LIFO provides an unfair "tax dodge." As Congress looks for more sources of tax revenue, some lawmakers favor the elimination of LIFO. Supporters of LIFO argue that the method is conceptually sound because it matches current costs with current revenues. In addition, they point out that this matching provides protection against inflation.

International accounting standards do not allow the use of LIFO. Because of this, the net income of foreign oil companies such as BP and Royal Dutch Shell are not directly comparable to U.S. companies, which can make analysis difficult.

Source: David Reilly, "Big Oil's Accounting Methods Fuel Criticism," *Wall Street Journal* (August 8, 2006), p. C1.

What are the arguments for and against the use of LIFO? (Go to **WileyPLUS** for this answer and additional questions.)

KEEPING AN EYE ON CASH

You have just seen that when prices are rising the use of LIFO can have a big effect on taxes. The lower taxes paid using LIFO can significantly increase cash flows. To demonstrate the effect of the cost flow assumptions on cash flow, we will calculate net cash provided by operating activities using the data for Houston Electronics from Illustration 6-13. To simplify our example, we assume that Houston's sales and purchases are all cash transactions. We also assume that operating expenses, other than $4,600 of depreciation, are cash transactions.

	FIFO	LIFO	Average-Cost
Cash received from customers	$18,500	$18,500	$18,500
Cash purchases of goods	11,000	11,000	11,000
Cash paid for operating expenses ($9,000 − $4,600)	4,400	4,400	4,400
Cash paid for taxes	990	750	870
Net cash provided by operating activities	$ 2,110	$ 2,350	$ 2,230

LIFO has the highest net cash provided by operating activities because it results in the lowest tax payments. Since cash flow is the lifeblood of any organization, the choice of inventory method is very important.

LIFO also impacts the quality of earnings ratio. Recall that the quality of earnings ratio is net cash provided by operating activities divided by net income. Here, we calculate the quality of earnings ratio under each cost flow assumption.

	FIFO	LIFO	Average-Cost
Net income (from Illustration 6-13)	$2,310	$1,750	$2,030
Quality of earnings ratio	0.91	1.34	1.1

LIFO has the highest quality of earnings ratio for two reasons. (1) It has the highest net cash provided by operating activities, which increases the ratio's numerator. (2) It reports a conservative measure of net income, which decreases the ratio's denominator. As discussed earlier, LIFO provides a conservative measure of net income because it does not include the phantom profits reported under FIFO.

USING INVENTORY COST FLOW METHODS CONSISTENTLY

▼ HELPFUL HINT
As you learned in Chapter 2, consistency and comparability are important characteristics of accounting information.

Whatever cost flow method a company chooses, it should use that method consistently from one accounting period to another. Consistent application enhances the ability to analyze a company's financial statements over successive time periods. In contrast, using the FIFO method one year and the LIFO method the next year would make it difficult to compare the net incomes of the two years.

Although consistent application is preferred, it does not mean that a company may never change its method of inventory costing. When a company adopts a different method, it should disclose in the financial statements the change and its effects on net income. A typical disclosure is shown in Illustration 6-14, using information from recent financial statements of Quaker Oats (now a unit of PepsiCo).

ILLUSTRATION 6-14
Disclosure of change in cost flow method

QUAKER OATS
Notes to the Financial Statements

Note 1: Effective July 1, the Company adopted the LIFO cost flow assumption for valuing the majority of U.S. Grocery Products inventories. The Company believes that the use of the LIFO method better matches current costs with current revenues. The effect of this change on the current year was to decrease net income by $16.0 million.

DO IT! ▶ 2 Cost Flow Methods

The accounting records of Shumway Ag Implement show the following data.

Beginning inventory	4,000 units at $3
Purchases	6,000 units at $4
Sales	7,000 units at $12

Determine (a) the cost of goods available for sale and (b) the cost of goods sold during the period under a periodic system using (i) FIFO, (ii) LIFO, and (iii) average-cost.

SOLUTION

(a) Cost of goods available for sale: (4,000 × $3) + (6,000 × $4) = $36,000

(b) Cost of goods sold using:

(i) FIFO: $36,000 − (3,000* × $4) = $24,000

(ii) LIFO: $36,000 − (3,000 × $3) = $27,000

(iii) Average-cost: Weighted-average price = ($36,000 ÷ 10,000) = $3.60
$36,000 − (3,000 × $3.60) = $25,200

*(4,000 + 6,000 − 7,000)

Action Plan

✔ Understand the periodic inventory system.

✔ Allocate costs between goods sold and goods on hand (ending inventory) for each cost flow method.

✔ Compute cost of goods sold for each cost flow method.

Related exercise material: **BE6-2, BE6-3, BE6-5, DO IT! 6-2, E6-4, E6-5, E6-6, E6-7,** and **E6-8.**

LEARNING OBJECTIVE 3 **Explain the statement presentation and analysis of inventory.**

PRESENTATION

As indicated in Chapter 5, inventory is classified in the balance sheet as a current asset immediately below receivables. In a multiple-step income statement, cost of goods sold is subtracted from net sales. There also should be disclosure of (1) the major inventory classifications, (2) the basis of accounting (cost, or lower-of-cost-or-market), and (3) the cost method (FIFO, LIFO, or average-cost).

Wal-Mart Stores, Inc., for example, in its January 31, 2014, balance sheet reported inventories of $44,858 million under current assets. The accompanying notes to the financial statements, as shown in Illustration 6-15, disclosed the following information.

ILLUSTRATION 6-15
Inventory disclosures by Wal-Mart

Real World

WAL-MART STORES, INC.
Notes to the Financial Statements

Note 1. Summary of Significant Accounting Policies
Inventories

The Company values inventories at the lower of cost or market as determined primarily by the retail method of accounting, using the last-in, first-out ("LIFO") method for substantially all of the WalMart U.S. segment's inventories. The WalMart International segment's inventories are primarily valued by the retail method of accounting, using the first-in, first-out ("FIFO") method. The retail method of accounting results in inventory being valued at the lower of cost or market since permanent markdowns are currently taken as a reduction of the retail value of inventory. The Sam's Club segment's inventories are valued based on the weighted-average cost using the LIFO method. At January 31, 2014 and 2013, the Company's inventories valued at LIFO approximate those inventories as if they were valued at FIFO.

As indicated in this note, Wal-Mart values its inventories at the lower-of-cost-or-market using LIFO and FIFO.

LOWER-OF-COST-OR-MARKET

The value of inventory for companies selling high-technology or fashion goods can drop very quickly due to changes in technology or changes in fashions. These circumstances sometimes call for inventory valuation methods other than those presented so far. For example, at one time, purchasing managers at Ford decided to make a large purchase of palladium, a precious metal used in vehicle emission devices. They made this large purchase because they feared a future shortage.

The shortage did not materialize, and by the end of the year the price of palladium had plummeted. Ford's inventory was then worth $1 billion less than its original cost. Do you think Ford's inventory should have been stated at cost, in accordance with the historical cost principle, or at its lower replacement cost?

INTERNATIONAL NOTE
Under U.S. GAAP, companies cannot reverse inventory write-downs if inventory increases in value in subsequent periods. IFRS permits companies to reverse write-downs in some circumstances.

As you probably reasoned, this situation requires a departure from the cost basis of accounting. This is done by valuing the inventory at the **lower-of-cost-or-market (LCM)** in the period in which the price decline occurs. LCM is a basis whereby inventory is stated at the lower of either its cost or market value as determined by current replacement cost. LCM is an example of the accounting convention of **conservatism**. Conservatism means that the approach adopted among accounting alternatives is the method that is least likely to overstate assets and net income.

Companies apply LCM to the items in inventory after they have used one of the cost flow methods (specific identification, FIFO, LIFO, or average-cost) to determine cost. Under the LCM basis, market is defined as **current replacement cost**, not selling price. For a merchandising company, current replacement cost is the cost of purchasing the same goods at the present time from the usual suppliers in the usual quantities. Current replacement cost is used because a decline in the replacement cost of an item usually leads to a decline in the selling price of the item.

To illustrate the application of LCM, assume that Ken Tuckie TV has the following lines of merchandise with costs and market values as indicated. LCM produces the results shown in Illustration 6-16. Note that the amounts shown in the final column are the lower-of-cost-or-market amounts for each item.

ILLUSTRATION 6-16
Computation of lower-of-cost-or-market

	Units	Cost per Unit	Market per Unit	Lower-of-Cost-or-Market	
Flat-screen TVs	100	$600	**$550**	$ 55,000	($550 × 100)
Satellite radios	500	**90**	104	45,000	($90 × 500)
Blu-ray players	850	50	**48**	40,800	($48 × 850)
CDs	3,000	**5**	6	15,000	($5 × 3,000)
Total inventory				$155,800	

Adherence to LCM is important. Acer Inc. recently took a charge of $150 million on personal computers, which declined in value before they could be sold. A Chinese manufacturer of silicon wafers for solar energy panels, LDK Solar Co., was accused of violating LCM. When the financial press reported accusations that two-thirds of its inventory of silicon was unsuitable for processing, the company's stock price fell by 40%.

DO IT! 3a LCM Basis

Tracy Company sells three different types of home heating stoves (gas, wood, and pellet). The cost and market value of its inventory of stoves are as follows.

	Cost	Market
Gas	$ 84,000	$ 79,000
Wood	250,000	280,000
Pellet	112,000	101,000

Determine the value of the company's inventory under the lower-of-cost-or-market approach.

Action Plan
✔ Determine whether cost or market value is lower for each inventory type.
✔ Sum the lower value of each inventory type to determine the total value of inventory.

SOLUTION

The lower value for each inventory type is gas $79,000, wood $250,000, and pellet $101,000. The total inventory value is the sum of these figures, $430,000.

Related exercise material: **BE6-7, DO IT! 6-3a, E6-9, and E6-10.**

ANALYSIS

For companies that sell goods, managing inventory levels can be one of the most critical tasks. Having too much inventory on hand costs the company money in storage costs, interest cost (on funds tied up in inventory), and costs associated with the obsolescence of technical goods (e.g., computer chips) or shifts in fashion (e.g., clothes). But having too little inventory on hand results in lost sales. In this section, we discuss some issues related to evaluating inventory levels.

Inventory Turnover

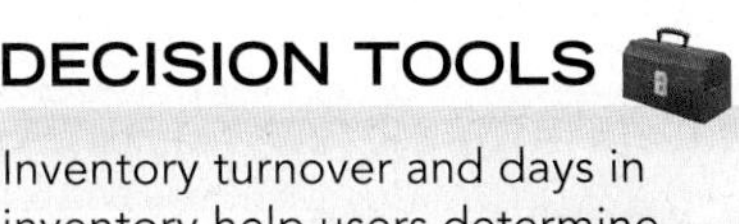

DECISION TOOLS

Inventory turnover and days in inventory help users determine how long an item is in inventory.

The **inventory turnover** is calculated as cost of goods sold divided by average inventory. It indicates the liquidity of inventory by measuring the number of times the average inventory "turns over" (is sold) during the year. Inventory turnover can be divided into 365 days to compute **days in inventory**, which indicates the average number of days inventory is held.

High inventory turnover (low days in inventory) indicates the company has minimal funds tied up in inventory—that it has a minimal amount of inventory on hand at any one time. Although minimizing the funds tied up in inventory is efficient, too high an inventory turnover may indicate that the company is losing sales opportunities because of inventory shortages. For example, investment analysts at one time suggested that Office Depot had gone too far in reducing its inventory—they said they were seeing too many empty shelves. Thus, management should closely monitor this ratio to achieve the best balance between too much and too little inventory.

In Chapter 5, we discussed the increasingly competitive environment of retailers, such as Wal-Mart and Target. Wal-Mart has implemented **just-in-time inventory procedures** as well as many technological innovations to improve the efficiency of its inventory management. The following data are available for Wal-Mart.

(in millions)	2014	2013
Ending inventory	$ 44,858	$43,803
Cost of goods sold	358,069	

Illustration 6-17 presents the inventory turnovers and days in inventory for Wal-Mart and Target, using data from the financial statements of those corporations for 2014 and 2013.

ILLUSTRATION 6-17
Inventory turnovers and days in inventory

$$\text{Inventory Turnover} = \frac{\text{Cost of Goods Sold}}{\text{Average Inventory}}$$

$$\text{Days in Inventory} = \frac{365}{\text{Inventory Turnover}}$$

Ratio	Wal-Mart ($ in millions) 2014	Wal-Mart 2013	Target 2014	Industry Average 2014
Inventory turnover	$\frac{\$358{,}069}{(\$44{,}858 + \$43{,}803)/2}$ = 8.1 times	8.3 times	6.1 times	8.4 times
Days in inventory	$\frac{365 \text{ days}}{8.1}$ = 45.1 days	44.0 days	59.8 days	43.5 days

The calculations in Illustration 6-17 show that Wal-Mart turns its inventory more frequently than Target (8.1 times for Wal-Mart versus 6.1 times for Target). Consequently, the average time an item spends on a Wal-Mart shelf is shorter (45.1 days for Wal-Mart versus 59.8 days for Target).

This analysis suggests that Wal-Mart is more efficient than Target in its inventory management. Wal-Mart's sophisticated inventory tracking and distribution system allows it to keep minimum amounts of inventory on hand, while still keeping the shelves full of what customers are looking for.

ACCOUNTING ACROSS THE ORGANIZATION Sony

© Dmitry Kutlayev/iStockphoto

Too Many TVs or Too Few?

Financial analysts closely monitor the inventory management practices of companies. For example, some analysts following Sony expressed concern because the company built up its inventory of televisions in an attempt to sell 25 million liquid crystal display (LCD) TVs—a 60% increase over the prior year. A year earlier, Sony had cut its inventory levels so that its quarterly days in inventory was down to 38 days, compared to 61 days for the same quarter a year before that. But in the next year, as a result of its inventory build-up, days in inventory rose to 59 days. Management said that it didn't think that Sony's inventory levels were too high. However, analysts were concerned that the company would have to engage in very heavy discounting in order to sell off its inventory. Analysts noted that the losses from discounting can be "punishing."

Source: Daisuke Wakabayashi, "Sony Pledges to Corral Inventory," *Wall Street Journal Online* (November 2, 2010).

For Sony, what are the advantages and disadvantages of having a low days in inventory measure? (Go to WileyPLUS for this answer and additional questions.)

ADJUSTMENTS FOR LIFO RESERVE

Earlier, we noted that using LIFO rather than FIFO can result in significant differences in the results reported in the balance sheet and the income statement. With increasing prices, FIFO will result in higher income than LIFO. On the balance sheet, FIFO will result in higher reported inventory. The financial statement differences from using LIFO normally increase the longer a company uses LIFO.

DECISION TOOLS 

Adjusting inventory from LIFO to FIFO helps users analyze the impact of LIFO on the company's reported income.

Use of different inventory cost flow assumptions complicates analysts' attempts to compare companies' results. Fortunately, companies using LIFO are required to report the difference between inventory reported using LIFO and inventory using FIFO. This amount is referred to as the **LIFO reserve**. Reporting the LIFO reserve enables analysts to make adjustments to compare companies that use different cost flow methods.

Illustration 6-18 presents an excerpt from the notes to Caterpillar's 2014 financial statements that discloses and discusses Caterpillar's LIFO reserve.

ILLUSTRATION 6-18
Caterpillar's LIFO reserve

Real World

CATERPILLAR INC.
Notes to the Financial Statements

Inventories: Inventories are stated at the lower of cost or market. Cost is principally determined using the last-in, first-out (LIFO) method . . . . If the FIFO (first-in, first-out) method had been in use, inventories would have been $2,430, $2,504, and $2,750 million higher than reported at December 31, 2014, 2013, and 2012, respectively.

Caterpillar has used LIFO for over 50 years. Thus, the cumulative difference between LIFO and FIFO reflected in the Inventory account is very large. In fact, the 2014 LIFO reserve of $2,430 million is 20% of the 2014 LIFO inventory of $12,205 million. Such a huge difference would clearly distort any comparisons you might try to make with one of Caterpillar's competitors that used FIFO.

To adjust Caterpillar's inventory balance, we add the LIFO reserve to reported inventory, as shown in Illustration 6-19. That is, if Caterpillar had used FIFO all along, its inventory would be $14,635 million, rather than $12,205 million.

ILLUSTRATION 6-19
Conversion of inventory from LIFO to FIFO

	(in millions)
2014 inventory using LIFO	$ 12,205
2014 LIFO reserve	2,430
2014 inventory assuming FIFO	**$14,635**

The LIFO reserve can have a significant effect on ratios that analysts commonly use. Using the LIFO reserve adjustment, Illustration 6-20 calculates the value of the current ratio (current assets ÷ current liabilities) for Caterpillar under both the LIFO and FIFO cost flow assumptions.

ILLUSTRATION 6-20
Impact of LIFO reserve on ratios

($ in millions)	LIFO	FIFO
Current ratio	$\frac{\$38,867}{\$27,877} = 1.39:1$	$\frac{\$38,867 + \$2,430}{\$27,877} = 1.48:1$

As Illustration 6-20 shows, if Caterpillar used FIFO, its current ratio would be 1.48:1 rather than 1.39:1 under LIFO. Thus, Caterpillar's liquidity appears stronger if a FIFO assumption were used in valuing inventories.

CNH Global, a competitor of Caterpillar, uses FIFO to account for its inventory. Comparing Caterpillar to CNH without converting Caterpillar's inventory to FIFO would lead to distortions and potentially erroneous decisions.

DO IT! 3b Inventory Turnover

Early in 2017, Westmoreland Company switched to a just-in-time inventory system. Its sales, cost of goods sold, and inventory amounts for 2016 and 2017 are shown below.

	2016	**2017**
Sales revenue	$2,000,000	$1,800,000
Cost of goods sold	1,000,000	910,000
Beginning inventory	290,000	210,000
Ending inventory	210,000	50,000

Determine the inventory turnover and days in inventory for 2016 and 2017. Discuss the changes in the amount of inventory, the inventory turnover and days in inventory, and the amount of sales across the two years.

Action Plan

✔ To find the inventory turnover, divide cost of goods sold by average inventory.

✔ To determine days in inventory, divide 365 days by the inventory turnover.

✔ Just-in-time inventory reduces the amount of inventory on hand, which reduces carrying costs. Reducing inventory levels by too much has potential negative implications for sales.

SOLUTION

	2016	**2017**
Inventory turnover	$\frac{\$1,000,000}{(\$290,000 + \$210,000)/2} = 4$	$\frac{\$910,000}{(\$210,000 + \$50,000)/2} = 7$
Days in inventory	365 ÷ 4 = 91.3 days	365 ÷ 7 = 52.1 days

The company experienced a very significant decline in its ending inventory as a result of the just-in-time inventory. This decline improved its inventory turnover and its days in inventory. However, its sales declined by 10%. It is possible that this decline was caused by the dramatic reduction in the amount of inventory that was on hand, which increased the likelihood of "stockouts." To determine the optimal inventory level, management must weigh the benefits of reduced inventory against the potential lost sales caused by stockouts.

Related exercise material: **BE6-8, DO IT! 6-3b, E6-11, E6-12, and E6-13.**

USING DECISION TOOLS—MANITOWOC COMPANY

The Manitowoc Company is located in Manitowoc, Wisconsin. In recent years, it has made a series of strategic acquisitions to grow and enhance its market-leading positions in each of its three business segments: (1) cranes and related products (crawler cranes, tower cranes, and boom trucks), (2) food service equipment (commercial ice-cube machines, ice-beverage dispensers, and commercial refrigeration equipment), and (3) marine operations (shipbuilding and ship-repair services). The company reported inventory of $644.5 million for 2014 and of $720.8 million for 2013. Here is the inventory note taken from the 2014 financial statements.

THE MANITOWOC COMPANY
Notes to the Financial Statements

Inventories: The components of inventories at December 31, 2014 and December 31, 2013 are summarized as follows:

(in millions)	2014	2013
Inventories—gross:		
Raw materials	$226.2	$259.0
Work-in-process	103.7	130.2
Finished goods	414.8	436.8
Total inventories—gross	744.7	826.0
Excess and obsolete inventory reserve	(64.0)	(69.0)
Net inventories at FIFO cost	680.7	757.0
Excess of FIFO costs over LIFO value	(36.2)	(36.2)
Inventories—net (as reported on balance sheet)	$644.5	$720.8

Manitowoc carries inventory at the lower-of-cost-or-market using the first-in, first-out (FIFO) method for approximately 84% and 87% of total inventory for 2014 and 2013, respectively. The remainder of the inventory is costed using the last-in, first-out (LIFO) method.

Additional facts (amounts in millions):

2014 Current liabilities	$1,011.3
2014 Current assets (as reported)	1,186.1
2014 Cost of goods sold	2,900.4

INSTRUCTIONS

Answer the following questions.

1. Why does the company report its inventory in three components?
2. Why might the company use two methods (LIFO and FIFO) to account for its inventory?
3. Perform each of the following.
   (a) Calculate the inventory turnover and days in inventory using the LIFO inventory.
   (b) Calculate the 2014 current ratio using LIFO and the current ratio using FIFO. Discuss the difference.

SOLUTION

1. The Manitowoc Company is a manufacturer, so it purchases raw materials and makes them into finished products. At the end of each period, it has some goods that have been started but are not yet complete (work in process).

   By reporting all three components of inventory, a company reveals important information about its inventory position. For example, if amounts of raw materials have increased significantly compared to the previous year, we might assume the company is planning to step up production. On the other hand, if levels of finished goods have increased relative to last year and raw materials have declined, we might conclude that sales are slowing down—that the company has too much inventory on hand and is cutting back production.

2. Companies are free to choose different cost flow assumptions for different types of inventory. A company might choose to use FIFO for a product that is expected to decrease in price over time. One common reason for choosing a method other than LIFO is that many foreign countries do not allow LIFO; thus, the company cannot use LIFO for its foreign operations.

3. (a) $\text{Inventory turnover} = \frac{\text{Cost of goods sold}}{\text{Average inventory}} = \frac{\$2{,}900.4}{(\$644.5 + \$720.8)/2} = 4.2$

   $\text{Days in inventory} = \frac{365}{\text{Inventory turnover}} = \frac{365}{4.2} = 86.9 \text{ days}$

   (b) Current ratio

   LIFO: $\frac{\text{Current assets}}{\text{Current liabilities}} = \frac{\$1{,}186.1}{\$1{,}011.3} = 1.17{:}1$

   FIFO: $\frac{\$1{,}186.1 + \$36.2}{\$1{,}011.3} = 1.21{:}1$

   This represents a 3.4% increase in the current ratio [(1.21 − 1.17)/1.17].

LEARNING OBJECTIVE *4

APPENDIX 6A: Apply inventory cost flow methods to perpetual inventory records.

Each of the inventory cost flow methods described in the chapter for a periodic inventory system may be used in a perpetual inventory system. To illustrate the application of the three assumed cost flow methods (FIFO, LIFO, and average-cost), we will use the data shown in Illustration 6A-1 and in this chapter for Houston Electronics' Astro condensers.

ILLUSTRATION 6A-1
Inventoriable units and costs

HOUSTON ELECTRONICS
Astro Condensers

Date	Explanation	Units	Unit Cost	Total Cost	Balance in Units
1/1	Beginning inventory	100	$10	$ 1,000	100
4/15	Purchase	200	11	2,200	300
8/24	Purchase	300	12	3,600	600
9/10	Sale	550			50
11/27	Purchase	400	13	5,200	450
				$12,000	

FIRST-IN, FIRST-OUT (FIFO)

Under FIFO, the cost of the earliest goods on hand **prior to each sale** is charged to cost of goods sold. Therefore, the cost of goods sold on September 10 consists of the units on hand January 1 and the units purchased April 15 and August 24. Illustration 6A-2 (page 288) shows the inventory under a FIFO method perpetual system.

ILLUSTRATION 6A-2
Perpetual system—FIFO

Date	Purchases	Cost of Goods Sold	Balance
Jan. 1			(100 @ $10) $1,000
Apr. 15	(200 @ $11) $2,200		(100 @ $10) (200 @ $11) } $3,200
Aug. 24	(300 @ $12) $3,600		(100 @ $10) (200 @ $11) (300 @ $12) } $6,800
Sept. 10		(100 @ $10) (200 @ $11) (250 @ $12) **$6,200**	(50 @ $12) $ 600
Nov. 27	(400 @ $13) $5,200		(50 @ $12) (400 @ $13) } **$5,800**

The ending inventory in this situation is $5,800, and the cost of goods sold is $6,200 [(100 @ $10) + (200 @ $11) + (250 @ $12)].

The results under FIFO in a perpetual system are the **same as in a periodic system**. (See Illustration 6-6 on page 274 where, similarly, the ending inventory is $5,800 and cost of goods sold is $6,200.) Regardless of the system, the first costs in are the costs assigned to cost of goods sold.

LAST-IN, FIRST-OUT (LIFO)

Under the LIFO method using a perpetual system, the cost of the most recent purchase prior to sale is allocated to the units sold. Therefore, the cost of the goods sold on September 10 consists of all the units from the August 24 and April 15 purchases plus 50 of the units in beginning inventory. The ending inventory under the LIFO method is computed in Illustration 6A-3.

ILLUSTRATION 6A-3
Perpetual system—LIFO

Date	Purchases	Cost of Goods Sold	Balance
Jan. 1			(100 @ $10) $1,000
Apr. 15	(200 @ $11) $2,200		(100 @ $10) (200 @ $11) } $3,200
Aug. 24	(300 @ $12) $3,600		(100 @ $10) (200 @ $11) (300 @ $12) } $6,800
Sept. 10		(300 @ $12) (200 @ $11) (50 @ $10) **$6,300**	(50 @ $10) $ 500
Nov. 27	(400 @ $13) $5,200		(50 @ $10) (400 @ $13) } **$5,700**

The use of LIFO in a perpetual system will usually produce cost allocations that differ from use of LIFO in a periodic system. In a perpetual system, the latest units purchased **prior to each sale** are allocated to cost of goods sold. In contrast, in a periodic system, the latest units purchased **during the period** are allocated to cost of goods sold. Thus, when a purchase is made after the last sale, the LIFO periodic system will apply this purchase to the previous sale. See Illustration 6-9 (on page 276) where the proof shows the 400 units at $13 purchased on November 27 applied to the sale of 550 units on September 10.

As shown above, under the LIFO perpetual system the 400 units at $13 purchased on November 27 are all applied to the ending inventory.

The ending inventory in this LIFO perpetual illustration is $5,700 and cost of goods sold is $6,300. Compare this to the LIFO periodic illustration (Illustration 6-8 on page 275) where the ending inventory is $5,000 and cost of goods sold is $7,000.

AVERAGE-COST

The average-cost method in a perpetual inventory system is called the **moving-average method**. Under this method, the company computes a new average **after each purchase**. The average cost is computed by dividing the cost of goods available for sale by the units on hand. The average cost is then applied to (1) the units sold, to determine the cost of goods sold, and (2) the remaining units on hand, to determine the ending inventory amount. Illustration 6A-4 shows the application of the average-cost method by Houston Electronics.

ILLUSTRATION 6A-4
Perpetual system—average-cost method

Date	Purchases		Cost of Goods Sold	Balance	
Jan. 1				(100 @ $10)	$1,000
Apr. 15	(200 @ $11)	$2,200		(300 @ $10.667)	$3,200
Aug. 24	(300 @ $12)	$3,600		(600 @ $11.333)	$6,800
Sept. 10			(550 @ $11.333) **$6,233**	(50 @ $11.333)	$ 567
Nov. 27	(400 @ $13)	$5,200		(450 @ $12.816)	**$5,767**

As indicated above, the company computes **a new average each time it makes a purchase**. On April 15, after 200 units are purchased for $2,200, a total of 300 units costing $3,200 ($1,000 + $2,200) are on hand. The average unit cost is $10.667 ($3,200 ÷ 300). On August 24, after 300 units are purchased for $3,600, a total of 600 units costing $6,800 ($1,000 + $2,200 + $3,600) are on hand at an average cost per unit of $11.333 ($6,800 ÷ 600). Houston Electronics uses this unit cost of $11.333 in costing sales until another purchase is made, when the company computes a new unit cost. Accordingly, the unit cost of the 550 units sold on September 10 is $11.333, and the total cost of goods sold is $6,233. On November 27, following the purchase of 400 units for $5,200, there are 450 units on hand costing $5,767 ($567 + $5,200) with a new average cost of $12.816 ($5,767 ÷ 450).

Compare this moving-average cost under the perpetual inventory system to Illustration 6-11 (on page 277) showing the weighted-average method under a periodic inventory system.

LEARNING OBJECTIVE  *5

APPENDIX 6B: Indicate the effects of inventory errors on the financial statements.

Unfortunately, errors occasionally occur in accounting for inventory. In some cases, errors are caused by failure to count or price the inventory correctly. In other cases, errors occur because companies do not properly recognize the transfer of legal title to goods that are in transit. When inventory errors occur, they affect both the income statement and the balance sheet.

INCOME STATEMENT EFFECTS

The ending inventory of one period automatically becomes the beginning inventory of the next period. Thus, inventory errors affect the computation of cost of goods sold and net income in two periods.

The effects on cost of goods sold can be computed by entering incorrect data in the formula in Illustration 6B-1 and then substituting the correct data.

ILLUSTRATION 6B-1
Formula for cost of goods sold

Beginning Inventory	+	Cost of Goods Purchased	−	Ending Inventory	=	Cost of Goods Sold

If **beginning** inventory is understated, cost of goods sold will be understated. If **ending** inventory is understated, cost of goods sold will be overstated. Illustration 6B-2 shows the effects of inventory errors on the current year's income statement.

ILLUSTRATION 6B-2
Effects of inventory errors on current year's income statement

Inventory Error	Cost of Goods Sold	Net Income
Beginning inventory understated	Understated	Overstated
Beginning inventory overstated	Overstated	Understated
Ending inventory understated	Overstated	Understated
Ending inventory overstated	Understated	Overstated

ETHICS NOTE
Inventory fraud increases during recessions. Such fraud includes pricing inventory at amounts in excess of its actual value, or claiming to have inventory when no inventory exists. Inventory fraud is usually done to overstate ending inventory, thereby understating cost of goods sold and creating higher income.

An error in the ending inventory of the current period will have a **reverse effect on net income of the next accounting period**. This is shown in Illustration 6B-3. Note that the understatement of ending inventory in 2016 results in an understatement of beginning inventory in 2017 and an overstatement of net income in 2017.

Over the two years, total net income is correct because the errors offset each other. Notice that total two-year income using incorrect data is $35,000 ($22,000 + $13,000), which is the same as the total two-year income of $35,000 ($25,000 + $10,000) using correct data. Also note in this example that an error in the beginning inventory does not result in a corresponding error in the ending inventory for that period. The correctness of the ending inventory depends entirely on the accuracy of taking and costing the inventory at the balance sheet date under the periodic inventory system.

ILLUSTRATION 6B-3
Effects of inventory errors on two years' income statements

SAMPLE COMPANY
Condensed Income Statements

	2016				2017			
	Incorrect		Correct		Incorrect		Correct	
Sales revenue		$80,000		$80,000		$90,000		$90,000
Beginning inventory	$20,000		$20,000		**$12,000**		**$15,000**	
Cost of goods purchased	40,000		40,000		68,000		68,000	
Cost of goods available for sale	60,000		60,000		80,000		83,000	
Ending inventory	**12,000**		**15,000**		23,000		23,000	
Cost of goods sold		48,000		45,000		57,000		60,000
Gross profit		32,000		35,000		33,000		30,000
Operating expenses		10,000		10,000		20,000		20,000
Net income		$22,000		$25,000		$13,000		$10,000
	$(3,000) Net income understated				$3,000 Net income overstated			

The errors cancel. Thus, the combined total income for the 2-year period is correct.

BALANCE SHEET EFFECTS

The effect of ending inventory errors on the balance sheet can be determined by using the basic accounting equation: Assets = Liabilities + Stockholders' Equity. Errors in the ending inventory have the effects shown in Illustration 6B-4.

Ending Inventory Error	Assets	Liabilities	Stockholders' Equity
Overstated	Overstated	No effect	Overstated
Understated	Understated	No effect	Understated

ILLUSTRATION 6B-4
Effects of ending inventory errors on balance sheet

The effect of an error in ending inventory on the subsequent period was shown in Illustration 6B-3. Recall that if the error is not corrected, the combined total net income for the two periods would be correct. Thus, total stockholders' equity reported on the balance sheet at the end of 2017 will also be correct.

REVIEW AND PRACTICE

▶ LEARNING OBJECTIVES REVIEW

1 Discuss how to classify and determine inventory. Merchandisers need only one inventory classification, merchandise inventory, to describe the different items that make up total inventory. Manufacturers, on the other hand, usually classify inventory into three categories: finished goods, work in process, and raw materials. To determine inventory quantities, manufacturers (1) take a physical inventory of goods on hand and (2) determine the ownership of goods in transit or on consignment.

2 Apply inventory cost flow methods and discuss their financial effects. The primary basis of accounting for inventories is cost. Cost includes all expenditures necessary to acquire goods and place them in a condition ready for sale. Cost of goods available for sale includes (a) cost of beginning inventory and (b) cost of goods purchased. The inventory cost flow methods are specific identification and three assumed cost flow methods—FIFO, LIFO, and average-cost.

The cost of goods available for sale may be allocated to cost of goods sold and ending inventory by specific identification or by a method based on an assumed cost flow. When prices are rising, the first-in, first-out (FIFO) method results in lower cost of goods sold and higher net income than the average-cost and the last-in, first-out (LIFO) methods. The reverse is true when prices are falling. In the balance sheet, FIFO results in an ending inventory that is closest to current value, whereas the inventory under LIFO is the farthest from current value. LIFO results in the lowest income taxes (because of lower taxable income).

3 Explain the statement presentation and analysis of inventory. Companies use the lower-of-cost-or-market (LCM) basis when the current replacement cost (market) is less than cost. Under LCM, companies recognize the loss in the period in which the price decline occurs.

Inventory turnover is calculated as cost of goods sold divided by average inventory. It can be converted to average days in inventory by dividing 365 days by the inventory turnover. A higher inventory turnover or lower average days in inventory suggests that management is trying to keep inventory levels low relative to its sales level.

The LIFO reserve represents the difference between ending inventory using LIFO and ending inventory if FIFO were employed instead. For some companies this difference can be significant, and ignoring it can lead to inappropriate conclusions when using the current ratio or inventory turnover.

***4 Apply inventory cost flow methods to perpetual inventory records.** Under FIFO, the cost of the earliest goods on hand prior to each sale is charged to cost of goods sold. Under LIFO, the cost of the most recent purchase prior to sale is charged to cost of goods sold. Under the average-cost method, a new average cost is computed after each purchase.

***5 Indicate the effects of inventory errors on the financial statements.** *In the income statement of the current year:* (1) An error in beginning inventory will have a reverse effect on net income (e.g., overstatement of inventory results in understatement of net income, and vice versa). (2) An error in ending inventory will have a similar effect on net income (e.g., overstatement of inventory results in overstatement of net income). If ending inventory errors are not corrected in the following period, their effect on net income for that period is reversed, and total net income for the two years will be correct.

In the balance sheet: Ending inventory errors will have the same effect on total assets and total stockholders' equity and no effect on liabilities.

DECISION TOOLS REVIEW

DECISION CHECKPOINTS	INFO NEEDED FOR DECISION	TOOL TO USE FOR DECISION	HOW TO EVALUATE RESULTS
Which inventory costing method should be used?	Are prices increasing, or are they decreasing?	Income statement, balance sheet, and tax effects	Depends on objective. In a period of rising prices, income and inventory are higher and cash flow is lower under FIFO. LIFO provides opposite results. Average-cost can moderate the impact of changing prices.
How long is an item in inventory?	Cost of goods sold; beginning and ending inventory	$\text{Inventory turnover} = \frac{\text{Cost of goods sold}}{\text{Average inventory}}$ $\text{Days in inventory} = \frac{\text{365 days}}{\text{Inventory turnover}}$	A higher inventory turnover or lower average days in inventory suggests that management is reducing the amount of inventory on hand, relative to cost of goods sold.
What is the impact of LIFO on the company's reported inventory?	LIFO reserve, cost of goods sold, ending inventory, current assets, current liabilities	LIFO inventory + LIFO reserve = FIFO inventory	If these adjustments are material, they can significantly affect such measures as the current ratio and the inventory turnover.

GLOSSARY REVIEW

Average-cost method An inventory costing method that uses the weighted-average unit cost to allocate the cost of goods available for sale to ending inventory and cost of goods sold. (p. 276).

Consigned goods Goods held for sale by one party although ownership of the goods is retained by another party. (p. 270).

Current replacement cost The cost of purchasing the same goods at the present time from the usual suppliers in the usual quantities. (p. 282).

Days in inventory Measure of the average number of days inventory is held; calculated as 365 divided by inventory turnover. (p. 283).

Finished goods inventory Manufactured items that are completed and ready for sale. (p. 268).

First-in, first-out (FIFO) method An inventory costing method that assumes that the earliest goods purchased are the first to be sold. (p. 274).

FOB destination Freight terms indicating that ownership of goods remains with the seller until the goods reach the buyer. (p. 270).

FOB shipping point Freight terms indicating that ownership of goods passes to the buyer when the public carrier accepts the goods from the seller. (p. 270).

Inventory turnover A ratio that indicates the liquidity of inventory by measuring the number of times average inventory is sold during the period; computed by dividing cost of goods sold by the average inventory during the period. (p. 283).

Just-in-time (JIT) inventory Inventory system in which companies manufacture or purchase goods only when needed. (p. 268).

Last-in, first-out (LIFO) method An inventory costing method that assumes that the latest units purchased are the first to be sold. (p. 275).

LIFO reserve For a company using LIFO, the difference between inventory reported using LIFO and inventory using FIFO. (p. 284).

Lower-of-cost-or-market (LCM) A basis whereby inventory is stated at the lower of either its cost or its market value as determined by current replacement cost. (p. 282).

Raw materials Basic goods that will be used in production but have not yet been placed in production. (p. 268).

Specific identification method An actual physical-flow costing method in which particular items sold and items still in inventory are specifically costed to arrive at cost of goods sold and ending inventory. (p. 272).

Weighted-average unit cost Average cost that is weighted by the number of units purchased at each unit cost. (p. 276).

Work in process That portion of manufactured inventory that has begun the production process but is not yet complete. (p. 268).

▶ PRACTICE MULTIPLE CHOICE QUESTIONS

(LO 1) **1.** When is a physical inventory usually taken?
(a) When the company has its greatest amount of inventory.
(b) When a limited number of goods are being sold or received.
(c) At the end of the company's fiscal year.
(d) Both (b) and (c).

(LO 1) **2.** Which of the following should **not** be included in the physical inventory of a company?
(a) Goods held on consignment from another company.
(b) Goods shipped on consignment to another company.
(c) Goods in transit from another company shipped FOB shipping point.
(d) All of the above should be included.

(LO 1) **3.** As a result of a thorough physical inventory, Railway Company determined that it had inventory worth $180,000 at December 31, 2017. This count did not take into consideration the following facts. Rogers Consignment Store currently has goods worth $35,000 on its sales floor that belong to Railway but are being sold on consignment by Rogers. The selling price of these goods is $50,000. Railway purchased $13,000 of goods that were shipped on December 27, FOB destination, that will be received by Railway on January 3. Determine the correct amount of inventory that Railway should report.
(a) $230,000. (c) $228,000.
(b) $215,000. (d) $193,000.

(LO 2) **4.** Kam Company has the following units and costs.

	Units	Unit Cost
Inventory, Jan. 1	8,000	$11
Purchase, June 19	13,000	12
Purchase, Nov. 8	5,000	13

If 9,000 units are on hand at December 31, what is the cost of the ending inventory under FIFO?
(a) $99,000. (c) $113,000.
(b) $108,000. (d) $117,000.

(LO 2) **5.** From the data in Question 4, what is the cost of the ending inventory under LIFO?
(a) $113,000. (c) $99,000.
(b) $108,000. (d) $100,000.

(LO 2) **6.** Davidson Electronics has the following:

	Units	Unit Cost
Inventory, Jan. 1	5,000	$ 8
Purchase, April 2	15,000	10
Purchase, Aug. 28	20,000	12

If Davidson has 7,000 units on hand at December 31, the cost of ending inventory under the average-cost method is:
(a) $84,000. (c) $56,000.
(b) $70,000. (d) $75,250.

(LO 2) **7.** In periods of rising prices, LIFO will produce:
(a) higher net income than FIFO.
(b) the same net income as FIFO.
(c) lower net income than FIFO.
(d) higher net income than average-cost.

8. Cost of goods available for sale consists of two elements: beginning inventory and: (LO 2)
(a) ending inventory.
(b) cost of goods purchased.
(c) cost of goods sold.
(d) All of the answer choices are correct.

9. Considerations that affect the selection of an inventory costing method do **not** include: (LO 2)
(a) tax effects.
(b) balance sheet effects.
(c) income statement effects.
(d) perpetual versus periodic inventory system.

10. The lower-of-cost-or-market rule for inventory is an example of the application of: (LO 3)
(a) the conservatism convention.
(b) the historical cost principle.
(c) the materiality concept.
(d) the economic entity assumption.

11. Which of these would cause inventory turnover to increase the most? (LO 3)
(a) Increasing the amount of inventory on hand.
(b) Keeping the amount of inventory on hand constant but increasing sales.
(c) Keeping the amount of inventory on hand constant but decreasing sales.
(d) Decreasing the amount of inventory on hand and increasing sales.

12. Carlos Company had beginning inventory of $80,000, ending inventory of $110,000, cost of goods sold of $285,000, and sales of $475,000. Carlos's days in inventory is: (LO 3)
(a) 73 days. (c) 102.5 days.
(b) 121.7 days. (d) 84.5 days.

13. Norton Company purchased 1,000 widgets and has 200 widgets in its ending inventory at a cost of $91 each and a current replacement cost of $80 each. The ending inventory under lower-of-cost-or-market is: (LO 3)
(a) $91,000. (c) $18,200.
(b) $80,000. (d) $16,000.

14. The LIFO reserve is: (LO 3)
(a) the difference between the value of the inventory under LIFO and the value under FIFO.
(b) an amount used to adjust inventory to the lower-of-cost-or-market.
(c) the difference between the value of the inventory under LIFO and the value under average-cost.
(d) an amount used to adjust inventory to historical cost.

***15.** In a perpetual inventory system: (LO 4)
(a) LIFO cost of goods sold will be the same as in a periodic inventory system.
(b) average costs are based entirely on unit-cost simple averages.
(c) a new average is computed under the average-cost method after each sale.
(d) FIFO cost of goods sold will be the same as in a periodic inventory system.

***16.** Fran Company's ending inventory is understated by $4,000. The effects of this error on the current year's cost of goods sold and net income, respectively, are: (LO 5)
(a) understated and overstated.

(b) overstated and understated.
(c) overstated and overstated.
(d) understated and understated.

(LO 5) *17. Harold Company overstated its inventory by $15,000 at December 31, 2016. It did not correct the error in 2016 or 2017. As a result, Harold's stockholders' equity was:
(a) overstated at December 31, 2016, and understated at December 31, 2017.
(b) overstated at December 31, 2016, and properly stated at December 31, 2017.
(c) understated at December 31, 2016, and understated at December 31, 2017.
(d) overstated at December 31, 2016, and overstated at December 31, 2017.

SOLUTIONS

1. **(d)** A physical inventory is usually taken when a limited number of goods are being sold or received, and at the end of the company's fiscal year. Choice (a) is incorrect because a physical inventory count is usually taken when the company has the least, not greatest, amount of inventory. Choices (b) and (c) are correct, but (d) is the better answer.
2. **(a)** Goods held on consignment should not be included because another company has title (ownership) to the goods. The other choices are incorrect because (b) goods shipped on consignment to another company and (c) goods in transit from another company shipped FOB shipping point should be included in a company's ending inventory. Choice (d) is incorrect because (a) is not included in the physical inventory.
3. **(b)** The inventory held on consignment by Rogers should be included in Railway's inventory balance at cost ($35,000). The purchased goods of $13,000 should not be included in inventory until January 3 because the goods are shipped FOB destination. Therefore, the correct amount of inventory is $215,000 ($180,000 + $35,000), not (a) $230,000, (c) $228,000, or (d) $193,000.
4. **(c)** Under FIFO, ending inventory will consist of 5,000 units from the Nov. 8 purchase and 4,000 units from the June 19 purchase. Therefore, ending inventory is (5,000 × $13) + (4,000 × $12) = $113,000, not (a) $99,000, (b) $108,000, or (d) $117,000.
5. **(d)** Under LIFO, ending inventory will consist of 8,000 units from the inventory at Jan. 1 and 1,000 units from the June 19 purchase. Therefore, ending inventory is (8,000 × $11) + (1,000 × $12) = $100,000, not (a) $113,000, (b) $108,000, or (c) $99,000.
6. **(d)** Under the average-cost method, total cost of goods available for sale needs to be calculated in order to determine average cost per unit. The total cost of goods available is $430,000 = (5,000 × $8) + (15,000 × $10) + (20,000 × $12). The average cost per unit = ($430,000/40,000 total units available for sale) = $10.75. Therefore, ending inventory is ($10.75 × 7,000) = $75,250, not (a) $84,000, (b) $70,000, or (c) $56,000.
7. **(c)** In periods of rising prices, LIFO will produce lower net income than FIFO, not (a) higher than FIFO or (b) the same as FIFO. Choice (d) is incorrect because in periods of rising prices, LIFO will produce lower net income than average-cost. LIFO therefore charges the highest inventory cost against revenues in a period of rising prices.
8. **(b)** Cost of goods available for sale consists of beginning inventory and cost of goods purchased, not (a) ending inventory or (c) cost of goods sold. Therefore, choice (d) is also incorrect.
9. **(d)** Perpetual vs. periodic inventory system is not one of the factors that affect the selection of an inventory costing method. The other choices are incorrect because (a) tax effects, (b) balance sheet effects, and (c) income statement effects all affect the selection of an inventory costing method.
10. **(a)** Conservatism means to use the lowest value for assets and revenues when in doubt. The other choices are incorrect because (b) historical cost means that companies value assets at the original cost, (c) materiality means that an amount is large enough to affect a decision-maker, and (d) economic entity means to keep the company's transactions separate from the transactions of other entities.
11. **(d)** Decreasing the amount of inventory on hand will cause the denominator to decrease, causing inventory turnover to increase. Increasing sales will cause the numerator of the ratio to increase (higher sales means higher COGS), thus causing inventory turnover to increase even more. The other choices are incorrect because (a) increasing the amount of inventory on hand causes the denominator of the ratio to increase while the numerator stays the same, causing inventory turnover to decrease; (b) keeping the amount of inventory on hand constant but increasing sales will cause inventory turnover to increase because the numerator of the ratio will increase (higher sales means higher COGS) while the denominator stays the same, which will result in a lesser inventory increase than decreasing amount of inventory on hand and increasing sales; and (c) keeping the amount of inventory on hand constant but decreasing sales will cause inventory turnover to decrease because the numerator of the ratio will decrease (lower sales means lower COGS) while the denominator stays the same.
12. **(b)** Carlos's days in inventory = 365/Inventory turnover = 365/[$285,000/($80,000 + $110,000)/2)] = 121.7 days, not (a) 73 days, (c) 102.5 days, or (d) 84.5 days.
13. **(d)** Under the LCM basis, "market" is defined as the current replacement cost. Therefore, ending inventory would be valued at 200 widgets × $80 each = $16,000, not (a) $91,000, (b) $80,000, or (c) $18,200.
14. **(a)** The LIFO reserve is the difference in ending inventory value under LIFO and FIFO. The other choices are therefore incorrect.

*15. **(d)** FIFO cost of goods sold is the same under both a periodic and a perpetual inventory system. The other choices are incorrect because (a) LIFO cost of goods sold is not the same under a periodic and a perpetual inventory system; (b) average costs are based on a moving average of unit costs, not an average of unit costs; and (c) a new average is computed under the average-cost method after each purchase, not sale.

*16. **(b)** Because ending inventory is too low, cost of goods sold will be too high (overstated) and since cost of goods sold (an expense) is too high, net income will be too low (understated). Therefore, the other choices are incorrect.

*17. **(b)** Stockholders' equity is overstated by $15,000 at December 31, 2016, and is properly stated at December 31, 2017. An ending inventory error in one period will have an equal and opposite effect on cost of goods sold and net income in the next period; after two years, the errors have offset each other. The other choices are incorrect because stockholders' equity (a) is properly stated, not understated, at December 31, 2017; (c) is overstated, not understated, by $15,000 at December 31, 2016, and is properly stated, not understated, at December 31, 2017; and (d) is properly stated at December 31, 2017, not overstated.

PRACTICE EXERCISES

Determine the correct inventory amount.

(LO 1)

1. Mika Sorbino, an auditor with Martinez CPAs, is performing a review of Sergei Company's inventory account. Sergei's did not have a good year and top management is under pressure to boost reported income. According to its records, the inventory balance at year-end was $650,000. However, the following information was not considered when determining that amount.

1. Included in the company's count were goods with a cost of $200,000 that the company is holding on consignment. The goods belong to Bosnia Corporation.
2. The physical count did not include goods purchased by Sergei with a cost of $40,000 that were shipped FOB shipping point on December 28 and did not arrive at Sergei's warehouse until January 3.
3. Included in the inventory account was $15,000 of office supplies that were stored in the warehouse and were to be used by the company's supervisors and managers during the coming year.
4. The company received an order on December 28 that was boxed and was sitting on the loading dock awaiting pick-up on December 31. The shipper picked up the goods on January 1 and delivered them on January 6. The shipping terms were FOB shipping point. The goods had a selling price of $40,000 and a cost of $30,000. The goods were not included in the count because they were sitting on the dock.
5. On December 29, Sergei shipped goods with a selling price of $80,000 and a cost of $60,000 to Oman Sales Corporation FOB shipping point. The goods arrived on January 3. Oman Sales had only ordered goods with a selling price of $10,000 and a cost of $8,000. However, a Sergei's sales manager had authorized the shipment and said that if Oman wanted to ship the goods back next week, it could.
6. Included in the count was $30,000 of goods that were parts for a machine that the company no longer made. Given the high-tech nature of Sergei's products, it was unlikely that these obsolete parts had any other use. However, management would prefer to keep them on the books at cost, "since that is what we paid for them, after all."

INSTRUCTIONS

Prepare a schedule to determine the correct inventory amount. Provide explanations for each item above, saying why you did or did not make an adjustment for each item.

SOLUTION

1. Ending inventory—as reported	$650,000
1. Subtract from inventory: The goods belong to Bosnia Corporation. Sergei is merely holding them for Bosnia.	(200,000)
2. Add to inventory: The goods belong to Sergei when they were shipped.	40,000
3. Subtract from inventory: Office supplies should be carried in a separate account. They are not considered inventory held for resale.	(15,000)
4. Add to inventory: The goods belong to Sergei until they are shipped (Jan. 1).	30,000

5. Add to inventory: Oman Sales ordered goods with a cost of $8,000. Sergei should record the corresponding sales revenue of $10,000. Sergei's decision to ship extra "unordered" goods does not constitute a sale. The manager's statement that Oman could ship the goods back indicates that Sergei knows this overshipment is not a legitimate sale. The manager acted unethically in an attempt to improve Sergei's reported income by overshipping. 52,000
6. Subtract from inventory: GAAP require that inventory be valued at the lower-of-cost-or-market. Obsolete parts should be adjusted from cost to zero if they have no other use. (30,000)

Correct inventory $527,000

Determine LCM valuation.

(LO 3)

2. Creve Couer Camera Inc. uses the lower-of-cost-or-market basis for its inventory. The following data are available at December 31.

	Units	Cost per Unit	Market per Unit
Cameras:			
Minolta	5	$160	$156
Canon	7	145	153
Light Meters:			
Vivitar	12	120	114
Kodak	10	130	142

INSTRUCTIONS

What amount should be reported on Creve Couer Camera's financial statements, assuming the lower-of-cost-or-market rule is applied?

SOLUTION

2.

	Cost per Unit	Market per Unit	Lower-of-Cost-or-Market	Units	Inventory at Lower-of-Cost-or-Market
Cameras:					
Minolta	$160	$156	$156	5	$ 780
Canon	145	153	145	7	1,015
Light Meters:					
Vivitar	120	114	114	12	1,368
Kodak	130	142	130	10	1,300
Total					$4,463

PRACTICE PROBLEMS

Compute inventory and cost of goods sold using three cost flow methods in a periodic inventory system.

(LO 2)

1. Englehart Company has the following inventory, purchases, and sales data for the month of March.

Inventory: March 1	200 units @ $4.00	$ 800
Purchases:		
March 10	500 units @ $4.50	2,250
March 20	400 units @ $4.75	1,900
March 30	300 units @ $5.00	1,500
Sales:		
March 15	500 units	
March 25	400 units	

The physical inventory count on March 31 shows 500 units on hand.

INSTRUCTIONS

Under a **periodic inventory system**, determine the cost of inventory on hand at March 31 and the cost of goods sold for March under (a) the first-in, first-out (FIFO) method; (b) the last-in, first-out (LIFO) method; and (c) the average-cost method. (For average-cost, carry cost per unit to three decimal places.)

SOLUTION

1. The cost of goods available for sale is $6,450:

Inventory: March 1	200 units @ $4.00	$ 800
Purchases:		
March 10	500 units @ $4.50	2,250
March 20	400 units @ $4.75	1,900
March 30	300 units @ $5.00	1,500
Total cost of goods available for sale		$6,450

(a) **FIFO Method**

Ending inventory:

Date	Units	Unit Cost	Total Cost	
Mar. 30	300	$5.00	$1,500	
Mar. 20	200	4.75	950	$2,450
Cost of goods sold: $6,450 − $2,450 =				$4,000

(b) **LIFO Method**

Ending inventory:

Date	Units	Unit Cost	Total Cost	
Mar. 1	200	$4.00	$ 800	
Mar. 10	300	4.50	1,350	$2,150
Cost of goods sold: $6,450 − $2,150 =				$4,300

(c) **Average-Cost Method**

Weighted-average unit cost: $6,450 ÷ 1,400 = $4.607

Ending inventory: 500 × $4.607 = $2,303.50

Cost of goods sold: $6,450 − $2,303.50 = $4,146.50

Compute inventory and cost of goods sold using three cost flow methods in a perpetual inventory system.

(LO 4)

***2. Practice Problem 1** showed cost of goods sold computations under a periodic inventory system. Now let's assume that Englehart Company uses a perpetual inventory system. The company has the same inventory, purchases, and sales data for the month of March as shown earlier:

Inventory: March 1		200 units @ $4.00	$ 800
Purchases:			
	March 10	500 units @ $4.50	2,250
	March 20	400 units @ $4.75	1,900
	March 30	300 units @ $5.00	1,500
Sales:			
	March 15	500 units	
	March 25	400 units	

The physical inventory count on March 31 shows 500 units on hand.

INSTRUCTIONS

Under a **perpetual inventory system**, determine the cost of inventory on hand at March 31 and the cost of goods sold for March under (a) FIFO, (b) LIFO, and (c) moving-average cost.

SOLUTION

2. The cost of goods available for sale is $6,450, as follows.

Inventory:		200 units @ $4.00	$ 800
Purchases:	March 10	500 units @ $4.50	2,250
	March 20	400 units @ $4.75	1,900
	March 30	300 units @ $5.00	1,500
Total:		1,400	$6,450

Under a **perpetual inventory system**, the cost of goods sold under each cost flow method is as follows.

(a) **FIFO Method**

Date	Purchases	Cost of Goods Sold	Balance	
March 1			(200 @ $4.00)	$ 800
March 10	(500 @ $4.50) $2,250		(200 @ $4.00) (500 @ $4.50)	$3,050
March 15		(200 @ $4.00) (300 @ $4.50) $2,150	(200 @ $4.50)	$ 900
March 20	(400 @ $4.75) $1,900		(200 @ $4.50) (400 @ $4.75)	$2,800
March 25		(200 @ $4.50) (200 @ $4.75) $1,850	(200 @ $4.75)	$ 950
March 30	(300 @ $5.00) $1,500		(200 @ $4.75) (300 @ $5.00)	$2,450
	Ending inventory $2,450	Cost of goods sold: $2,150 + $1,850 = $4,000		

(b) **LIFO Method**

Date	Purchases	Cost of Goods Sold	Balance	
March 1			(200 @ $4.00)	$ 800
March 10	(500 @ $4.50) $2,250		(200 @ $4.00) (500 @ $4.50)	$3,050
March 15		(500 @ $4.50) $2,250	(200 @ $4.00)	$ 800
March 20	(400 @ $4.75) $1,900		(200 @ $4.00) (400 @ $4.75)	$2,700
March 25		(400 @ $4.75) $1,900	(200 @ $4.00)	$ 800
March 30	(300 @ $5.00) $1,500		(200 @ $4.00) (300 @ $5.00)	$2,300
	Ending inventory $2,300	Cost of goods sold: $2,250 + $1,900 = $4,150		

(c) **Moving-Average Cost Method**

Date	Purchases	Cost of Goods Sold	Balance	
March 1			(200 @ $ 4.00)	$ 800
March 10	(500 @ $4.50) $2,250		(700 @ $4.357)	$3,050
March 15		(500 @ $4.357) $2,179	(200 @ $4.357)	$ 871
March 20	(400 @ $4.75) $1,900		(600 @ $4.618)	$2,771
March 25		(400 @ $4.618) $1,847	(200 @ $4.618)	$ 924
March 30	(300 @ $5.00) $1,500		(500 @ $4.848)	$2,424
	Ending inventory $2,424	Cost of goods sold: $2,179 + $1,847 = $4,026		

WileyPLUS Brief Exercises, DO IT! Exercises, Exercises, Problems, and many additional resources are available for practice in WileyPLUS.

NOTE: All asterisked Questions, Exercises, and Problems relate to material in the appendices to the chapter.

▶ QUESTIONS

1. "The key to successful business operations is effective inventory management." Do you agree? Explain.
2. An item must possess two characteristics to be classified as inventory. What are these two characteristics?
3. What is just-in-time inventory management? What are its potential advantages?
4. Your friend Will Juritz has been hired to help take the physical inventory in Byrd's Hardware Store. Explain to Will what this job will entail.
5. (a) Bonita Company ships merchandise to Myan Corporation on December 30. The merchandise reaches the buyer on January 5. Indicate the

terms of sale that will result in the goods being included in (1) Bonita's December 31 inventory and (2) Myan's December 31 inventory.
(b) Under what circumstances should Bonita Company include consigned goods in its inventory?

6. Nona Hat Shop received a shipment of hats for which it paid the wholesaler $2,940. The price of the hats was $3,000, but Nona was given a $60 cash discount and required to pay freight charges of $75. What amount should Nona include in inventory? Why?
7. What is the primary basis of accounting for inventories?
8. Ken McCall believes that the allocation of cost of goods available for sale should be based on the actual physical flow of the goods. Explain to Ken why this may be both impractical and inappropriate.
9. What is the major advantage and major disadvantage of the specific identification method of inventory costing?
10. "The selection of an inventory cost flow method is a decision made by accountants." Do you agree? Explain. Once a method has been selected, what accounting requirement applies?
11. Which assumed inventory cost flow method:
    (a) usually parallels the actual physical flow of merchandise?
    (b) divides cost of goods available for sale by total units available for sale to determine a unit cost?
    (c) assumes that the latest units purchased are the first to be sold?
12. In a period of rising prices, the inventory reported in Short Company's balance sheet is close to the current cost of the inventory, whereas King Company's inventory is considerably below its current cost. Identify the inventory cost flow method used by each company. Which company probably has been reporting the higher gross profit?
13. Mamosa Corporation has been using the FIFO cost flow method during a prolonged period of inflation. During the same time period, Mamosa has been paying out all of its net income as dividends. What adverse effects may result from this policy?
14. Oscar Geer, a mid-level product manager for Theresa's Shoes, thinks his company should switch from LIFO to FIFO. He says, "My bonus is based on net income. If we switch it will increase net income and increase my bonus. The company would be better off and so would I." Is he correct? Explain.
15. Discuss the impact the use of LIFO has on taxes paid, cash flows, and the quality of earnings ratio relative to the impact of FIFO when prices are increasing.
16. Hank Artisan is studying for the next accounting midterm examination. What should Hank know about (a) departing from the cost basis of accounting for inventories and (b) the meaning of "market" in the lower-of-cost-or-market method?
17. Jackson Music Center has five TVs on hand at the balance sheet date that cost $400 each. The current replacement cost is $350 per unit. Under the lower-of-cost-or-market basis of accounting for inventories, what value should Jackson report for the TVs on the balance sheet? Why?
18. What cost flow assumption may be used under the lower-of-cost-or-market basis of accounting for inventories?
19. Why is it inappropriate for a company to include freight-out expense in the Cost of Goods Sold account?
20. Tilton Company's balance sheet shows Inventory $162,800. What additional disclosures should be made?
21. Under what circumstances might inventory turnover be too high—that is, what possible negative consequences might occur?
22. What is the LIFO reserve? What are the consequences of ignoring a large LIFO reserve when analyzing a company?

*23. "When perpetual inventory records are kept, the results under the FIFO and LIFO methods are the same as they would be in a periodic inventory system." Do you agree? Explain.

*24. How does the average-cost method of inventory costing differ between a perpetual inventory system and a periodic inventory system?

*25. Albert Company discovers in 2017 that its ending inventory at December 31, 2016, was $5,000 understated. What effect will this error have on (a) 2016 net income, (b) 2017 net income, and (c) the combined net income for the 2 years?

BRIEF EXERCISES

Identify items to be included in taking a physical inventory.

(LO 1), C

BE6-1 Peete Company identifies the following items for possible inclusion in the physical inventory. Indicate whether each item should be included or excluded from the inventory taking.
(a) 900 units of inventory shipped on consignment by Peete to another company.
(b) 3,000 units of inventory in transit from a supplier shipped FOB destination.
(c) 1,200 units of inventory sold but being held for customer pickup.
(d) 500 units of inventory held on consignment from another company.

Compute ending inventory using FIFO and LIFO.

(LO 2), AP

BE6-2 In its first month of operations, McLanie Company made three purchases of merchandise in the following sequence: (1) 300 units at $6, (2) 400 units at $8, and (3) 500 units at $9. Assuming there are 200 units on hand at the end of the period, compute the cost of the ending inventory under (a) the FIFO method and (b) the LIFO method. McLanie uses a periodic inventory system.

Compute the ending inventory using average-cost.
(LO 2), AP

BE6-3 Data for McLanie Company are presented in BE6-2. Compute the cost of the ending inventory under the average-cost method. (Round the cost per unit to three decimal places.)

Explain the financial statement effect of inventory cost flow assumptions.
(LO 2), C

BE6-4 The management of Milque Corp. is considering the effects of various inventory-costing methods on its financial statements and its income tax expense. Assuming that the price the company pays for inventory is increasing, which method will:
(a) provide the highest net income?
(b) provide the highest ending inventory?
(c) result in the lowest income tax expense?
(d) result in the most stable earnings over a number of years?

Explain the financial statement effect of inventory cost flow assumptions.
(LO 2), AP

BE6-5 In its first month of operation, Hoffman Company purchased 100 units of inventory for $6, then 200 units for $7, and finally 140 units for $8. At the end of the month, 180 units remained. Compute the amount of phantom profit that would result if the company used FIFO rather than LIFO. Explain why this amount is referred to as phantom profit. The company uses the periodic method.

Identify the impact of LIFO versus FIFO.
(LO 2), C

BE6-6 For each of the following cases, state whether the statement is true for LIFO or for FIFO. Assume that prices are rising.
(a) Results in a higher quality of earnings ratio.
(b) Results in higher phantom profits.
(c) Results in higher net income.
(d) Results in lower taxes.
(e) Results in lower net cash provided by operating activities.

Determine the LCM valuation.
(LO 3), AP

BE6-7 Wahlowitz Video Center accumulates the following cost and market data at December 31.

Inventory Categories	Cost Data	Market Data
Cameras	$12,500	$13,400
Camcorders	9,000	9,500
DVDs	13,000	12,200

Compute the lower-of-cost-or-market valuation for the company's inventory.

Compute inventory turnover and days in inventory.
(LO 3), AP

BE6-8 Suppose at December 31 of a recent year, the following information (in thousands) was available for sunglasses manufacturer Oakley, Inc.: ending inventory $155,377, beginning inventory $119,035, cost of goods sold $349,114, and sales revenue $761,865. Calculate the inventory turnover and days in inventory for Oakley, Inc. (Round inventory turnover to two decimal places.)

Determine ending inventory using LIFO reserve.
(LO 3), AP

BE6-9 Winnebago Industries, Inc. is a leading manufacturer of motor homes. Suppose Winnebago reported ending inventory at August 29, 2017, of $46,850,000 under the LIFO inventory method. In the notes to its financial statements, assume Winnebago reported a LIFO reserve of $30,346,000 at August 29, 2017. What would Winnebago Industries' ending inventory have been if it had used FIFO?

Apply cost flow methods to perpetual inventory records.
(LO 4), AP

***BE6-10** Loggins Department Store uses a perpetual inventory system. Data for product E2-D2 include the following purchases.

Date	Number of Units	Unit Price
May 7	50	$10
July 28	30	15

On June 1, Loggins sold 25 units, and on August 27, 30 more units. Compute the cost of goods sold using (a) FIFO, (b) LIFO, and (c) average-cost. (Round the cost per unit to three decimal places.)

Determine correct financial statement amount.
(LO 5), AN

***BE6-11** Fennick Company reports net income of $92,000 in 2017. However, ending inventory was understated by $7,000. What is the correct net income for 2017? What effect, if any, will this error have on total assets as reported in the balance sheet at December 31, 2017?

DO IT! EXERCISES

DO IT! 6-1 Sheldon Company just took its physical inventory on December 31. The count of inventory items on hand at the company's business locations resulted in a total inventory cost of $300,000. In reviewing the details of the count and related inventory transactions, you have discovered the following items that had not been considered.

Apply rules of ownership to determine inventory cost.

(LO 1), AN

1. Sheldon has sent inventory costing $28,000 on consignment to Richfield Company. All of this inventory was at Richfield's showrooms on December 31.
2. The company did not include in the count inventory (cost, $20,000) that was sold on December 28, terms FOB shipping point. The goods were in transit on December 31.
3. The company did not include in the count inventory (cost, $13,000) that was purchased with terms of FOB shipping point. The goods were in transit on December 31.

Compute the correct December 31 inventory.

DO IT! 6-2 The accounting records of Ohm Electronics show the following data.

Compute cost of goods sold under different cost flow methods.

(LO 2), AP

Beginning inventory	3,000 units at $5
Purchases	8,000 units at $7
Sales	9,400 units at $10

Determine cost of goods sold during the period under a periodic inventory system using (a) the FIFO method, (b) the LIFO method, and (c) the average-cost method. (Round unit cost to three decimal places.)

DO IT! 6-3a Jeri Company sells three different categories of tools (small, medium and large). The cost and market value of its inventory of tools are as follows.

Compute inventory value under LCM.

(LO 3), AP

	Cost	Market
Small	$ 64,000	$ 61,000
Medium	290,000	260,000
Large	152,000	167,000

Determine the value of the company's inventory under the lower-of-cost-or-market approach.

DO IT! 6-3b Early in 2017, Fedor Company switched to a just-in-time inventory system. Its sales and inventory amounts for 2016 and 2017 are shown below.

Compute inventory turnover and assess inventory level.

(LO 3), AN

	2016	2017
Sales revenue	$3,120,000	$3,713,000
Cost of goods sold	1,200,000	1,425,000
Beginning inventory	170,000	210,000
Ending inventory	210,000	90,000

Determine the inventory turnover and days in inventory for 2016 and 2017. Discuss the changes in the amount of inventory, the inventory turnover and days in inventory, and the amount of sales across the 2 years.

EXERCISES

E6-1 Umatilla Bank and Trust is considering giving Pohl Company a loan. Before doing so, it decides that further discussions with Pohl's accountant may be desirable. One area of particular concern is the Inventory account, which has a year-end balance of $275,000. Discussions with the accountant reveal the following.

Determine the correct inventory amount.

(LO 1), AN

1. Pohl sold goods costing $55,000 to Hemlock Company FOB shipping point on December 28. The goods are not expected to reach Hemlock until January 12. The goods were not included in the physical inventory because they were not in the warehouse.
2. The physical count of the inventory did not include goods costing $95,000 that were shipped to Pohl FOB destination on December 27 and were still in transit at year-end.
3. Pohl received goods costing $25,000 on January 2. The goods were shipped FOB shipping point on December 26 by Yanice Co. The goods were not included in the physical count.

4. Pohl sold goods costing $51,000 to Ehler of Canada FOB destination on December 30. The goods were received in Canada on January 8. They were not included in Pohl's physical inventory.
5. Pohl received goods costing $42,000 on January 2 that were shipped FOB destination on December 29. The shipment was a rush order that was supposed to arrive December 31. This purchase was included in the ending inventory of $275,000.

Instructions

Determine the correct inventory amount on December 31.

Determine the correct inventory amount.

(LO 1), AN

E6-2 Farley Bains, an auditor with Nolls CPAs, is performing a review of Ryder Company's Inventory account. Ryder did not have a good year, and top management is under pressure to boost reported income. According to its records, the inventory balance at year-end was $740,000. However, the following information was not considered when determining that amount.

1. Included in the company's count were goods with a cost of $228,000 that the company is holding on consignment. The goods belong to Nader Corporation.
2. The physical count did not include goods purchased by Ryder with a cost of $40,000 that were shipped FOB shipping point on December 28 and did not arrive at Ryder's warehouse until January 3.
3. Included in the Inventory account was $17,000 of office supplies that were stored in the warehouse and were to be used by the company's supervisors and managers during the coming year.
4. The company received an order on December 29 that was boxed and was sitting on the loading dock awaiting pick-up on December 31. The shipper picked up the goods on January 1 and delivered them on January 6. The shipping terms were FOB shipping point. The goods had a selling price of $40,000 and a cost of $29,000. The goods were not included in the count because they were sitting on the dock.
5. Included in the count was $50,000 of goods that were parts for a machine that the company no longer made. Given the high-tech nature of Ryder's products, it was unlikely that these obsolete parts had any other use. However, management would prefer to keep them on the books at cost, "since that is what we paid for them, after all."

Instructions

Prepare a schedule to determine the correct inventory amount. Provide explanations for each item above, stating why you did or did not make an adjustment for each item.

Identify items in inventory.

(LO 1), K

E6-3 Gato Inc. had the following inventory situations to consider at January 31, its year-end.

(a) Goods held on consignment for Steele Corp. since December 12.
(b) Goods shipped on consignment to Logan Holdings Inc. on January 5.
(c) Goods shipped to a customer, FOB destination, on January 29 that are still in transit.
(d) Goods shipped to a customer, FOB shipping point, on January 29 that are still in transit.
(e) Goods purchased FOB destination from a supplier on January 25 that are still in transit.
(f) Goods purchased FOB shipping point from a supplier on January 25 that are still in transit.
(g) Office supplies on hand at January 31.

Instructions

Identify which of the preceding items should be included in inventory. If the item should not be included in inventory, state in what account, if any, it should have been recorded.

Compute inventory and cost of goods sold using periodic FIFO, LIFO, and average-cost.

(LO 2), AP

E6-4 Mather sells a snowboard, EZslide, that is popular with snowboard enthusiasts. Below is information relating to Mather's purchases of EZslide snowboards during September. During the same month, 102 EZslide snowboards were sold. Mather uses a periodic inventory system.

Date	Explanation	Units	Unit Cost	Total Cost
Sept. 1	Inventory	12	$100	$ 1,200
Sept. 12	Purchases	45	103	4,635
Sept. 19	Purchases	50	104	5,200
Sept. 26	Purchases	20	105	2,100
	Totals	127		$13,135

Instructions
Compute the ending inventory at September 30 and the cost of goods sold using the FIFO, LIFO, and average-cost methods. (For average-cost, round the average unit cost to three decimal places.) Prove the amount allocated to cost of goods sold under each method.

Calculate inventory and cost of goods sold using FIFO, average-cost, and LIFO in a periodic inventory system.

(LO 2), AP

E6-5 Rusthe Inc. uses a periodic inventory system. Its records show the following for the month of May, in which 74 units were sold.

Date	Explanation	Units	Unit Cost	Total Cost
May 1	Inventory	30	$ 9	$270
15	Purchase	25	10	250
24	Purchase	38	11	418
	Total	93		$938

Instructions
Calculate the ending inventory at May 31 using the (a) FIFO, (b) LIFO, and (c) average-cost methods. (For average-cost, round the average unit cost to three decimal places.) Prove the amount allocated to cost of goods sold under each method.

Calculate cost of goods sold using specific identification and FIFO periodic.

(LO 2), AN

E6-6 On December 1, Premium Electronics has three DVD players left in stock. All are identical, all are priced to sell at $85. One of the three DVD players left in stock, with serial #1012, was purchased on June 1 at a cost of $52. Another, with serial #1045, was purchased on November 1 for $48. The last player, serial #1056, was purchased on November 30 for $40.

Instructions
(a) Calculate the cost of goods sold using the FIFO periodic inventory method, assuming that two of the three players were sold by the end of December, Premium Electronics' year-end.
(b) If Premium Electronics used the specific identification method instead of the FIFO method, how might it alter its earnings by "selectively choosing" which particular players to sell to the two customers? What would Premium's cost of goods sold be if the company wished to minimize earnings? Maximize earnings?
(c) Which inventory method, FIFO or specific identification, do you recommend that Premium use? Explain why.

Compute inventory and cost of goods sold using periodic FIFO, LIFO, and average-cost.

(LO 2), AP

E6-7 Jeters Company reports the following for the month of June.

Date	Explanation	Units	Unit Cost	Total Cost
June 1	Inventory	120	$5	$ 600
12	Purchase	370	6	2,220
23	Purchase	200	7	1,400
30	Inventory	230		

Instructions
(a) Compute the cost of the ending inventory and the cost of goods sold under (1) FIFO, (2) LIFO, and (3) average-cost. (Round average unit cost to three decimal places.)
(b) Which costing method gives the highest ending inventory? The highest cost of goods sold? Why?
(c) How do the average-cost values for ending inventory and cost of goods sold relate to ending inventory and cost of goods sold for FIFO and LIFO?
(d) Explain why the average cost is not $6.

Evaluate impact of LIFO and FIFO on cash flows and earnings quality.

(LO 2), AP

E6-8 The following comparative information is available for Rose Company for 2017.

	LIFO	FIFO
Sales revenue	$86,000	$86,000
Cost of goods sold	38,000	29,000
Operating expenses		
(including depreciation)	27,000	27,000
Depreciation	10,000	10,000
Cash paid for inventory purchases	32,000	32,000

Instructions

(a) Determine net income under each approach. Assume a 30% tax rate.

(b) Determine net cash provided by operating activities under each approach. Assume that all sales were on a cash basis and that income taxes and operating expenses, other than depreciation, were on a cash basis.

(c) Calculate the quality of earnings ratio under each approach and explain your findings. (Round answer to two decimal places.)

Determine LCM valuation.

(LO 3), AP

E6-9 Digital Camera Shop Inc. uses the lower-of-cost-or-market basis for its inventory. The following data are available at December 31.

	Units	Cost per Unit	Market per Unit
Cameras			
Minolta	5	$170	$158
Canon	7	145	152
Light Meters			
Vivitar	12	125	114
Kodak	10	120	135

Instructions

What amount should be reported on Digital Camera Shop's financial statements, assuming the lower-of-cost-or-market rule is applied?

Determine LCM valuation.

(LO 3), AP

E6-10 Tascon Corporation sells coffee beans, which are sensitive to price fluctuations. The following inventory information is available for this product at December 31, 2017.

Coffee Bean	Units	Unit Cost	Market
Coffea arabica	13,000 bags	$5.60	$5.55
Coffea robusta	5,000 bags	3.40	3.50

Instructions

Calculate Tascon's inventory by applying the lower-of-cost-or-market basis.

Compute inventory turnover, days in inventory, and gross profit rate.

(LO 3), AP

E6-11 Suppose this information is available for PepsiCo, Inc. for 2015, 2016, and 2017.

(in millions)	2015	2016	2017
Beginning inventory	$ 1,926	$ 2,290	$ 2,522
Ending inventory	2,290	2,522	2,618
Cost of goods sold	18,038	20,351	20,099
Sales revenue	39,474	43,251	43,232

Instructions

(a) Calculate the inventory turnover for 2015, 2016, and 2017. (Round to one decimal place.)

(b) Calculate the days in inventory for 2015, 2016, and 2017.

(c) Calculate the gross profit rate for 2015, 2016, and 2017.

(d) Comment on any trends observed in your answers to parts (a), (b), and (c).

Calculate inventory turnover, days in inventory, and gross profit rate.

(LO 3), AP

E6-12 The following information is available for Zoe's Activewear Inc. for three recent fiscal years.

	2017	2016	2015
Inventory	$ 553,000	$ 568,000	$ 332,000
Net sales	1,948,000	1,725,000	1,311,000
Cost of goods sold	1,552,000	1,288,000	947,000

Instructions

(a) Calculate the inventory turnover, days in inventory, and gross profit rate for 2017 and 2016.

(b) Based on the ratios calculated in part (a), did Zoe's liquidity and profitability improve or deteriorate in 2017?

Compute inventory turnover and determine the effect of the LIFO reserve on current ratio.

(LO 3), AP

E6-13 Deere & Company is a global manufacturer and distributor of agricultural, construction, and forestry equipment. Suppose it reported the following information in its 2017 annual report.

(in millions)	2017	2016
Inventories (LIFO)	$ 2,397	$3,042
Current assets	30,857	
Current liabilities	12,753	
LIFO reserve	1,367	
Cost of goods sold	16,255	

Instructions

(a) Compute Deere's inventory turnover and days in inventory for 2017. (Round inventory turnover to 2 decimal places.)

(b) Compute Deere's current ratio using the 2017 data as presented, and then again after adjusting for the LIFO reserve.

(c) Comment on how ignoring the LIFO reserve might affect your evaluation of Deere's liquidity.

***E6-14** Inventory data for Jeters Company are presented in E6-7.

Calculate inventory and cost of goods sold using three cost flow methods in a perpetual inventory system.

(LO 4), AP

Instructions

(a) Calculate the cost of the ending inventory and the cost of goods sold for each cost flow assumption, using a perpetual inventory system. Assume a sale of 410 units occurred on June 15 for a selling price of $8 and a sale of 50 units on June 27 for $9. (*Note:* For the moving-average method, round unit cost to three decimal places.)

(b) How do the results differ from E6-7?

(c) Why is the average unit cost not $6 [($5 + $6 + $7) ÷ 3 = $6]?

***E6-15** Information about Mather is presented in E6-4. Additional data regarding the company's sales of EZslide snowboards are provided below. Assume that Mather uses a perpetual inventory system.

Apply cost flow methods to perpetual records.

(LO 4), AP

Date		Units
Sept. 5	Sale	8
Sept. 16	Sale	48
Sept. 29	Sale	46
	Totals	102

Instructions

Compute ending inventory at September 30 using FIFO, LIFO, and moving-average. (*Note:* For moving-average, round unit cost to three decimal places.)

***E6-16** Dowell Hardware reported cost of goods sold as follows.

Determine effects of inventory errors.

(LO 5), AN

	2017	2016
Beginning inventory	$ 30,000	$ 20,000
Cost of goods purchased	175,000	164,000
Cost of goods available for sale	205,000	184,000
Less: Ending inventory	37,000	30,000
Cost of goods sold	$168,000	$154,000

Dowell made two errors:

1. 2016 ending inventory was overstated by $2,000.
2. 2017 ending inventory was understated by $5,000.

Instructions

Compute the correct cost of goods sold for each year.

***E6-17** Sheen Company reported these income statement data for a 2-year period.

Prepare correct income statements.

(LO 5), AN

	2017	2016
Sales revenue	$250,000	$210,000
Beginning inventory	40,000	32,000
Cost of goods purchased	202,000	173,000
Cost of goods available for sale	242,000	205,000
Less: Ending inventory	55,000	40,000
Cost of goods sold	187,000	165,000
Gross profit	$ 63,000	$ 45,000

Sheen Company uses a periodic inventory system. The inventories at January 1, 2016, and December 31, 2017, are correct. However, the ending inventory at December 31, 2016, is overstated by $8,000.

Instructions

(a) Prepare correct income statement data for the 2 years.

(b) What is the cumulative effect of the inventory error on total gross profit for the 2 years?

(c) Explain in a letter to the president of Sheen Company what has happened—that is, the nature of the error and its effect on the financial statements.

EXERCISES: SET B AND CHALLENGE EXERCISES

Visit the book's companion website, at **www.wiley.com/college/kimmel**, and choose the Student Companion site to access Exercises: Set B and Challenge Exercises.

PROBLEMS: SET A

Determine items and amounts to be recorded in inventory.

(LO 1), AN

P6-1A Pitt Limited is trying to determine the value of its ending inventory as of February 28, 2017, the company's year-end. The accountant counted everything that was in the warehouse as of February 28, which resulted in an ending inventory valuation of $48,000. However, she didn't know how to treat the following transactions so she didn't record them.

(a) On February 26, Pitt shipped to a customer goods costing $800. The goods were shipped FOB shipping point, and the receiving report indicates that the customer received the goods on March 2.

(b) On February 26, Martine Inc. shipped goods to Pitt FOB destination. The invoice price was $350 plus $25 for freight. The receiving report indicates that the goods were received by Pitt on March 2.

(c) Pitt had $500 of inventory at a customer's warehouse "on approval." The customer was going to let Pitt know whether it wanted the merchandise by the end of the week, March 4.

(d) Pitt also had $400 of inventory at a Belle craft shop, on consignment from Pitt.

(e) On February 26, Pitt ordered goods costing $750. The goods were shipped FOB shipping point on February 27. Pitt received the goods on March 1.

(f) On February 28, Pitt packaged goods and had them ready for shipping to a customer FOB destination. The invoice price was $350 plus $25 for freight; the cost of the items was $280. The receiving report indicates that the goods were received by the customer on March 2.

(g) Pitt had damaged goods set aside in the warehouse because they are no longer saleable. These goods originally cost $400 and, originally, Pitt expected to sell these items for $600.

Instructions

For each of the above transactions, specify whether the item in question should be included in ending inventory, and if so, at what amount. For each item that is not included in ending inventory, indicate who owns it and what account, if any, it should have been recorded in.

Determine cost of goods sold and ending inventory using FIFO, LIFO, and average-cost with analysis.

(LO 2), AP

XLS

P6-2A Mullins Distribution markets CDs of numerous performing artists. At the beginning of March, Mullins had in beginning inventory 2,500 CDs with a unit cost of $7. During March, Mullins made the following purchases of CDs.

March 5	2,000 @ $8	March 21	5,000 @ $10
March 13	3,500 @ $9	March 26	2,000 @ $11

During March 12,000 units were sold. Mullins uses a periodic inventory system.

(b) Cost of goods sold:

FIFO	$105,000
LIFO	$115,500
Average	$109,601

Instructions

(a) Determine the cost of goods available for sale.

(b) Determine (1) the ending inventory and (2) the cost of goods sold under each of the assumed cost flow methods (FIFO, LIFO, and average-cost). Prove the accuracy of the

cost of goods sold under the FIFO and LIFO methods. (*Note:* For average-cost, round cost per unit to three decimal places.)
(c) Which cost flow method results in (1) the highest inventory amount for the balance sheet and (2) the highest cost of goods sold for the income statement?

Determine cost of goods sold and ending inventory using FIFO, LIFO, and average-cost in a periodic inventory system and assess financial statement effects.

(LO 2), AP

P6-3A Vista Company Inc. had a beginning inventory of 100 units of Product RST at a cost of $8 per unit. During the year, purchases were:

Feb. 20	600 units at $ 9	Aug. 12	400 units at $11
May 5	500 units at $10	Dec. 8	100 units at $12

Vista Company uses a periodic inventory system. Sales totaled 1,500 units.

Instructions
(a) Determine the cost of goods available for sale.
(b) Determine the ending inventory and the cost of goods sold under each of the assumed cost flow methods (FIFO, LIFO, and average-cost). Prove the accuracy of the cost of goods sold under the FIFO and LIFO methods. (Round average unit cost to three decimal places.)
(c) Which cost flow method results in the lowest inventory amount for the balance sheet? The lowest cost of goods sold for the income statement?

(b) Cost of goods sold:

FIFO	$14,500
LIFO	$15,100
Average	$14,824

Compute ending inventory, prepare income statements, and answer questions using FIFO and LIFO.

(LO 2), AN

P6-4A The management of National Inc. asks your help in determining the comparative effects of the FIFO and LIFO inventory cost flow methods. For 2017, the accounting records show these data.

Inventory, January 1 (10,000 units)	$ 35,000
Cost of 120,000 units purchased	468,500
Selling price of 98,000 units sold	750,000
Operating expenses	124,000

Units purchased consisted of 35,000 units at $3.70 on May 10, 60,000 units at $3.90 on August 15, and 25,000 units at $4.20 on November 20. Income taxes are 28%.

Instructions
(a) Prepare comparative condensed income statements for 2017 under FIFO and LIFO. (Show computations of ending inventory.)
(b) Answer the following questions for management in the form of a business letter.
(1) Which inventory cost flow method produces the inventory amount that most closely approximates the amount that would have to be paid to replace the inventory? Why?
(2) Which inventory cost flow method produces the net income amount that is a more likely indicator of next period's net income? Why?
(3) Which inventory cost flow method is most likely to approximate the actual physical flow of the goods? Why?
(4) How much more cash will be available under LIFO than under FIFO? Why?
(5) How much of the gross profit under FIFO is illusionary in comparison with the gross profit under LIFO?

(a) Gross profit:

FIFO	$378,800
LIFO	$362,900

Calculate ending inventory, cost of goods sold, gross profit, and gross profit rate under periodic method; compare results.

(LO 2), AP

P6-5A You have the following information for Van Gogh Inc. for the month ended October 31, 2017. Van Gogh uses a periodic method for inventory.

Date	Description	Units	Unit Cost or Selling Price
Oct. 1	Beginning inventory	60	$24
Oct. 9	Purchase	120	26
Oct. 11	Sale	100	35
Oct. 17	Purchase	100	27
Oct. 22	Sale	60	40
Oct. 25	Purchase	70	29
Oct. 29	Sale	110	40

Instructions
(a) Calculate (i) ending inventory, (ii) cost of goods sold, (iii) gross profit, and (iv) gross profit rate under each of the following methods.
(1) LIFO.
(2) FIFO.
(3) Average-cost. (Round cost per unit to three decimal places.)
(b) Compare results for the three cost flow assumptions.

(a) Gross profit:

LIFO	$2,970
FIFO	$3,310
Average	$3,133

Compare specific identification, FIFO, and LIFO under periodic method; use cost flow assumption to influence earnings.

(LO 2), AP

P6-6A You have the following information for Jewels Gems. Jewels uses the periodic method of accounting for its inventory transactions. Jewels only carries one brand and size of diamonds—all are identical. Each batch of diamonds purchased is carefully coded and marked with its purchase cost.

March 1	Beginning inventory 150 diamonds at a cost of $310 per diamond.
March 3	Purchased 200 diamonds at a cost of $350 each.
March 5	Sold 180 diamonds for $600 each.
March 10	Purchased 330 diamonds at a cost of $375 each.
March 25	Sold 390 diamonds for $650 each.

(a) Gross profit:
Maximum $162,500
Minimum $155,350

Instructions

(a) Assume that Jewels Gems uses the specific identification cost flow method.
    (1) Demonstrate how Jewels could maximize its gross profit for the month by specifically selecting which diamonds to sell on March 5 and March 25.
    (2) Demonstrate how Jewels could minimize its gross profit for the month by selecting which diamonds to sell on March 5 and March 25.
(b) Assume that Jewels uses the FIFO cost flow assumption. Calculate cost of goods sold. How much gross profit would Jewels report under this cost flow assumption?
(c) Assume that Jewels uses the LIFO cost flow assumption. Calculate cost of goods sold. How much gross profit would the company report under this cost flow assumption?
(d) Which cost flow method should Jewels Gems select? Explain.

Compute inventory turnover and days in inventory; compute current ratio based on LIFO and after adjusting for LIFO reserve.

(LO 3), AP

P6-7A Suppose this information (in millions) is available for the Automotive and Other Operations Divisions of General Motors Corporation for a recent year. General Motors uses the LIFO inventory method.

Beginning inventory	$ 13,921
Ending inventory	14,939
LIFO reserve	1,423
Current assets	60,135
Current liabilities	70,308
Cost of goods sold	166,259
Sales revenue	178,199

Instructions

(a) Calculate the inventory turnover and days in inventory. (Round to one decimal place.)
(b) Calculate the current ratio based on inventory as reported using LIFO.
(c) Calculate the current ratio after adjusting for the LIFO reserve.
(d) Comment on any difference between parts (b) and (c).

Calculate cost of goods sold, ending inventory, and gross profit for LIFO, FIFO, and moving-average under the perpetual system; compare results.

(LO 4), AP

***P6-8A** Bieber Inc. is a retailer operating in Calgary, Alberta. Bieber uses the perpetual inventory method. Assume that there are no credit transactions; all amounts are settled in cash. You are provided with the following information for Bieber for the month of January 2017.

Date	Description	Quantity	Unit Cost or Selling Price
Dec. 31	Ending inventory	160	$20
Jan. 2	Purchase	100	22
Jan. 6	Sale	180	40
Jan. 9	Purchase	75	24
Jan. 10	Sale	50	45
Jan. 23	Purchase	100	25
Jan. 30	Sale	130	48

(a) Gross profit:
LIFO $7,490
FIFO $7,865
Average $7,763

Instructions

(a) For each of the following cost flow assumptions, calculate (i) cost of goods sold, (ii) ending inventory, and (iii) gross profit.
    (1) LIFO.
    (2) FIFO.
    (3) Moving-average. (Round cost per unit to three decimal places.)
(b) Compare results for the three cost flow assumptions.

***P6-9A** Lyon Center began operations on July 1. It uses a perpetual inventory system. During July, the company had the following purchases and sales.

Determine ending inventory under a perpetual inventory system.

(LO 4), AP

	Purchases		
Date	**Units**	**Unit Cost**	**Sales Units**
July 1	7	$62	
July 6			5
July 11	3	$66	
July 14			3
July 21	4	$71	
July 27			3

Instructions

(a) Determine the ending inventory under a perpetual inventory system using (1) FIFO, (2) moving-average (round unit cost to three decimal places), and (3) LIFO.

(b) Which costing method produces the highest ending inventory valuation?

(a) FIFO $213
Average $207
LIFO $195

PROBLEMS: SET B AND SET C

Visit the book's companion website, at **www.wiley.com/college/kimmel**, and choose the Student Companion site to access Problems: Set B and Set C.

CONTINUING PROBLEM Cookie Creations

(*Note:* This is a continuation of the Cookie Creations problem from Chapters 1 through 5.)

CC6 Natalie is busy establishing both divisions of her business (cookie classes and mixer sales) and completing her business degree. Her goals for the next 11 months are to sell one mixer per month and to give two to three classes per week. Natalie has decided to use a periodic inventory system and now must choose a cost flow assumption for her mixer inventory.

Go to the book's companion website, at **www.wiley.com/college/kimmel**, *to see the completion of this problem.*

© leungchopan/ Shutterstock

COMPREHENSIVE ACCOUNTING CYCLE REVIEW

ACR6 On December 1, 2017, Waylon Company had the account balances shown below.

	Debit		**Credit**
Cash	$ 4,800	Accumulated Depreciation—Equipment	$ 1,500
Accounts Receivable	3,900	Accounts Payable	3,000
Inventory	1,800*	Common Stock	10,000
Equipment	21,000	Retained Earnings	17,000
	$31,500		$31,500

*(3,000 × $0.60)

The following transactions occurred during December.

Dec. 3 Purchased 4,000 units of inventory on account at a cost of $0.72 per unit.
5 Sold 4,400 units of inventory on account for $0.90 per unit. (Waylon sold 3,000 of the $0.60 units and 1,400 of the $0.72.)
7 Granted the December 5 customer $180 credit for 200 units of inventory returned costing $144. These units were returned to inventory.
17 Purchased 2,200 units of inventory for cash at $0.80 each.
22 Sold 2,000 units of inventory on account for $0.95 per unit. (Waylon sold 2,000 of the $0.72 units.)

Adjustment data:

1. Accrued salaries and wages payable $400.
2. Depreciation on equipment $200 per month.
3. Income tax expense was $215, to be paid next year.

Instructions

(a) Journalize the December transactions and adjusting entries, assuming Waylon uses the perpetual inventory method.
(b) Enter the December 1 balances in the ledger T-accounts and post the December transactions. In addition to the accounts mentioned above, use the following additional accounts: Income Taxes Payable, Salaries and Wages Payable, Sales Revenue, Sales Returns and Allowances, Cost of Goods Sold, Depreciation Expense, Salaries and Wages Expense, and Income Tax Expense.
(c) Prepare an adjusted trial balance as of December 31, 2017.
(d) Prepare an income statement for December 2017 and a classified balance sheet at December 31, 2017.
(e) Compute ending inventory and cost of goods sold under FIFO, assuming Waylon Company uses the periodic inventory system.
(f) Compute ending inventory and cost of goods sold under LIFO, assuming Waylon Company uses the periodic inventory system.

EXPAND YOUR CRITICAL THINKING

Financial Reporting

FINANCIAL REPORTING PROBLEM: Apple Inc.

AN

CT6-1 The notes that accompany a company's financial statements provide informative details that would clutter the amounts and descriptions presented in the statements. Refer to the financial statements of Apple Inc. in Appendix A. Instructions for accessing and using the company's complete annual report, including the notes to the financial statements, are also provided in Appendix A.

Instructions

Answer the following questions. (Give the amounts in thousands of dollars, as shown in Apple's annual report.)

(a) What did Apple report for the amount of inventories in its Consolidated Balance Sheet at September 27, 2014? At September 28, 2013?
(b) Compute the dollar amount of change and the percentage change in inventories between 2013 and 2014. Compute inventory as a percentage of current assets for 2014.
(c) What are the cost of sales reported by Apple for 2014, 2013, and 2012? Compute the ratio of cost of sales to net sales in 2014.

Financial Analysis

COMPARATIVE ANALYSIS PROBLEM: Columbia Sportswear Company vs. VF Corporation

AN

CT6-2 The financial statements of Columbia Sportswear Company are presented in Appendix B. Financial statements for VF Corporation are presented in Appendix C.

Instructions

(a) Based on the information in the financial statements, compute these 2014 values for each company.
    (1) Inventory turnover. (Use cost of goods sold or cost of sales and inventories.)
    (2) Days in inventory.
(b) What conclusions concerning the management of the inventory can you draw from these data?

Financial Analysis

COMPARATIVE ANALYSIS PROBLEM: Amazon.com, Inc. vs. Wal-Mart Stores, Inc.

AN

CT6-3 The financial statements of Amazon.com, Inc. are presented in Appendix D. Financial statements for Wal-Mart Stores, Inc. are presented in Appendix E.

Instructions

(a) Based on the information in the financial statements, compute these 2014 values for each company.
   (1) Inventory turnover. (Use cost of sales and inventories.)
   (2) Days in inventory.
(b) What conclusions concerning the management of the inventory can you draw from these data?

INTERPRETING FINANCIAL STATEMENTS

CT6-4 Suppose the following information is from the 2017 annual report of American Greetings Corporation (all dollars in thousands). AN

	Feb. 28, 2017	**Feb. 28, 2016**
Inventories		
Finished goods	$232,893	$244,379
Work in process	7,068	10,516
Raw materials and supplies	49,937	43,861
	289,898	298,756
Less: LIFO reserve	86,025	82,085
Total (as reported)	$203,873	$216,671
Cost of goods sold	$809,956	$780,771
Current assets (as reported)	$561,395	$669,340
Current liabilities	$343,405	$432,321

The notes to the company's financial statements also include the following information.

> Finished products, work in process, and raw material inventories are carried at the lower-of-cost-or-market. The last-in, first-out (LIFO) cost method is used for approximately 75% of the domestic inventories in 2017 and approximately 70% in 2016. The foreign subsidiaries principally use the first-in, first-out (FIFO) method. Display material and factory supplies are carried at average-cost.

Instructions

(a) Define each of the following: finished goods, work in process, and raw materials.
(b) What might be a possible explanation for why the company uses FIFO for its nondomestic inventories?
(c) Calculate the company's inventory turnover and days in inventory for 2016 and 2017. (2015 inventory was $182,618.) Discuss the implications of any change in the ratios.
(d) What percentage of total inventory does the 2017 LIFO reserve represent? If the company used FIFO in 2017, what would be the value of its inventory? Do you consider this difference a "material" amount from the perspective of an analyst? Which value accurately represents the value of the company's inventory?
(e) Calculate the company's 2017 current ratio with the numbers as reported, then recalculate after adjusting for the LIFO reserve.

REAL-WORLD FOCUS

CT6-5 ***Purpose:*** Use SEC filings to learn about a company's inventory accounting practices. S

Address: **http://biz.yahoo.com/p/_capgds-bldmch.html**

Steps

1. Go to this site and click on the name of an equipment manufacturer other than those discussed in the chapter.
2. Click on **SEC filings.**
3. Under "Recent filings" choose **Form 10K** (annual report) and click on **Full Filing at Edgar Online.**
4. Choose option "3," **Online HTML Version.**

If the 10K is not listed among the recent filings, then click on **View All Filings on EDGAR Online.**

Instructions

Review the 10K to answer the following questions.

(a) What is the name of the company?
(b) How has its inventory changed from the previous year?
(c) What is the amount of raw materials, work in process, and finished goods inventory?
(d) What inventory method does the company use?
(e) Calculate the inventory turnover and days in inventory for the current year.
(f) If the company uses LIFO, what was the amount of its LIFO reserve?

CT6-6 The July 15, 2010, edition of *CFO.com* contains an article by Marie Leone entitled "Sucking the LIFO out of Inventory."

Instructions
Read the article, which can be found at **www.cfo.com/printable/article.cfm/14508745**, and answer the following questions.

(a) What type of company benefits most from the use of LIFO?
(b) What is the estimated boost in federal tax receipts over 10 years if the use of LIFO for taxes was not allowed?
(c) If the United States decides to adopt International Financial Reporting Standards (IFRS), what would be the implications for the use of LIFO?
(d) What conceptual justification for LIFO do its proponents provide?
(e) What types of companies prefer to use FIFO?

Financial Analysis

Writing

Group Project

DECISION-MAKING ACROSS THE ORGANIZATION

CT6-7 Solar Electronics has enjoyed tremendous sales growth during the last 10 years. However, even though sales have steadily increased, the company's CEO, Dana Byrnes, is concerned about certain aspects of its performance. She has called a meeting with the corporate controller and the vice presidents of finance, operations, sales, and marketing to discuss the company's performance. Dana begins the meeting by making the following observations:

> We have been forced to take significant write-downs on inventory during each of the last three years because of obsolescence. In addition, inventory storage costs have soared. We rent four additional warehouses to store our increasingly diverse inventory. Five years ago inventory represented only 20% of the value of our total assets. It now exceeds 35%. Yet, even with all of this inventory, "stockouts" (measured by complaints by customers that the desired product is not available) have increased by 40% during the last three years. And worse yet, it seems that we constantly must discount merchandise that we have too much of.

Dana asks the group to review the following data and make suggestions as to how the company's performance might be improved.

(in millions)	2017	2016	2015	2014
Inventory				
Raw materials	$242	$198	$155	$128
Work in process	116	77	49	33
Finished goods	567	482	398	257
Total inventory	$925	$757	$602	$418
Current assets	$1,800	$1,423	$1,183	$841
Total assets	$2,643	$2,523	$2,408	$2,090
Current liabilities	$600	$590	$525	$420
Sales revenue	$9,428	$8,674	$7,536	$6,840
Cost of goods sold	$6,328	$5,474	$4,445	$3,557
Net income	$754	$987	$979	$958

Instructions
Using the information provided, answer the following questions.

(a) Compute the current ratio, gross profit rate, profit margin, inventory turnover, and days in inventory for 2015, 2016, and 2017.
(b) Discuss the trends and potential causes of the changes in the ratios in part (a).
(c) Discuss potential remedies to any problems discussed in part (b).
(d) What concerns might be raised by some members of management with regard to your suggestions in part (c)?

COMMUNICATION ACTIVITIES

CT6-8 In a discussion of dramatic increases in coffee-bean prices, a *Wall Street Journal* article noted the following fact about Starbucks. E

> Before this year's bean-price hike, Starbucks added several defenses that analysts say could help it maintain earnings and revenue. The company last year began accounting for its coffee-bean purchases by taking the average price of all beans in inventory.

Prior to this change, the company was using FIFO.

Instructions

Your client, the CEO of Superior Coffee, Inc., read this article and sent you an e-mail message requesting that you explain why Starbucks might have taken this action. Your response should explain what impact this change in accounting method has on earnings, why the company might want to do this, and any possible disadvantages of such a change.

***CT6-9** You are the controller of Garton Inc. H. K. Logan, the president, recently mentioned to you that she found an error in the 2016 financial statements which she believes has corrected itself. She determined, in discussions with the purchasing department, that 2016 ending inventory was overstated by $1 million. H. K. says that the 2017 ending inventory is correct, and she assumes that 2017 income is correct. H. K. says to you, "What happened has happened—there's no point in worrying about it anymore." AN

Instructions

You conclude that H. K. is incorrect. Write a brief, tactful memo to her, clarifying the situation.

ETHICS CASE

CT6-10 Nixon Wholesale Corp. uses the LIFO cost flow method. In the current year, profit at Nixon is running unusually high. The corporate tax rate is also high this year, but it is scheduled to decline significantly next year. In an effort to lower the current year's net income and to take advantage of the changing income tax rate, the president of Nixon Wholesale instructs the plant accountant to recommend to the purchasing department a large purchase of inventory for delivery 3 days before the end of the year. The price of the inventory to be purchased has doubled during the year, and the purchase will represent a major portion of the ending inventory value. E

Instructions

(a) What is the effect of this transaction on this year's and next year's income statement and income tax expense? Why?
(b) If Nixon Wholesale had been using the FIFO method of inventory costing, would the president give the same directive?
(c) Should the plant accountant order the inventory purchase to lower income? What are the ethical implications of this order?

ALL ABOUT YOU

CT6-11 Some of the largest business frauds ever perpetrated have involved the misstatement of inventory. Two classics were at Leslie Fay and McKesson Corporation. E

Instructions

There is considerable information regarding inventory frauds available on the Internet. Search for information about one of the two cases mentioned above, or inventory fraud at any other company, and prepare a short explanation of the nature of the inventory fraud.

FASB CODIFICATION ACTIVITY

CT6-12 If your school has a subscription to the FASB Codification, go to **http://aaahq.org/ascLogin.cfm** to log in and prepare responses to the following. AP

(a) The primary basis for accounting for inventories is cost. How is cost defined in the Codification?
(b) What does the Codification state regarding the use of consistency in the selection or employment of a basis for inventory?
(c) What does the Codification indicate is a justification for the use of the lower-of-cost-or-market for inventory valuation?

CONSIDERING PEOPLE, PLANET, AND PROFIT

AP **CT6-13** Caterpillar publishes an annual Sustainability Report to explain its position on sustainability, describe its goals, and report on its achievements. The report can be found at **http://www.caterpillar.com/sustainability/sustainability-report**.

Instructions

Access the report and answer the following questions.

(a) Page 66 describes the company's goals for the year 2020. What are these goals?

(b) Page 67 describes the company's results relative to 2003 with regard to worker safety. Summarize the company's progress in this area.

(c) Page 68 describes the company's results regarding energy use. Explain how the company measures its progress, and comment on its results thus far.

A Look at IFRS

LEARNING OBJECTIVE  6 **Compare the accounting for inventories under GAAP and IFRS.**

The major IFRS requirements related to accounting and reporting for inventories are the same as GAAP. The major differences are that IFRS prohibits the use of the LIFO cost flow assumption and determines market in the lower-of-cost-or-market inventory valuation differently.

RELEVANT FACTS

Following are the key similarities and differences between GAAP and IFRS related inventories.

Similarities

- IFRS and GAAP account for inventory acquisitions at historical cost and value inventory at the lower-of-cost-or-market subsequent to acquisition.
- Who owns the goods—goods in transit or consigned goods—as well as the costs to include in inventory are essentially accounted for the same under IFRS and GAAP.

Differences

- The requirements for accounting for and reporting inventories are more principles-based under IFRS. That is, GAAP provides more detailed guidelines in inventory accounting.
- A major difference between IFRS and GAAP relates to the LIFO cost flow assumption. GAAP permits the use of LIFO for inventory valuation. IFRS prohibits its use. FIFO and average-cost are the only two acceptable cost flow assumptions permitted under IFRS. Both sets of standards permit specific identification where appropriate.
- In the lower-of-cost-or-market test for inventory valuation, IFRS defines market as net realizable value. GAAP, on the other hand, defines market as replacement cost.

LOOKING TO THE FUTURE

One convergence issue that will be difficult to resolve relates to the use of the LIFO cost flow assumption. As indicated, IFRS specifically prohibits its use. Conversely, the LIFO cost flow assumption is widely used in the United States because of its favorable tax advantages. In addition, many argue that LIFO from a financial reporting point of view provides a better matching of current costs against revenue and, therefore, enables companies to compute a more realistic income.

IFRS Practice

IFRS SELF-TEST QUESTIONS

1. Which of the following should **not** be included in the inventory of a company using IFRS?
(a) Goods held on consignment from another company.
(b) Goods shipped on consignment to another company.
(c) Goods in transit from another company shipped FOB shipping point.
(d) None of the above.

2. Which method of inventory costing is prohibited under IFRS?
(a) Specific identification.
(b) LIFO.
(c) FIFO.
(d) Average-cost.

IFRS EXERCISES

IFRS6-1 Briefly describe some of the similarities and differences between GAAP and IFRS with respect to the accounting for inventories.

IFRS6-2 LaTour Inc. is based in France and prepares its financial statements (in euros) in accordance with IFRS. In 2017, it reported cost of goods sold of €578 million and average inventory of €154 million. Briefly discuss how analysis of LaTour's inventory turnover (and comparisons to a company using GAAP) might be affected by differences in inventory accounting between IFRS and GAAP.

INTERNATIONAL FINANCIAL REPORTING PROBLEM: Louis Vuitton

IFRS6-3 The financial statements of Louis Vuitton are presented in Appendix F. Instructions for accessing and using the company's complete annual report, including the notes to its financial statements, are also provided in Appendix F.

Instructions

Using the notes to the company's financial statements, answer the following questions.

(a) What cost flow assumption does the company use to value inventory?
(b) What amount of goods purchased for retail and finished products did the company report at December 31, 2014?

Answers to IFRS Self-Test Questions

1. a **2.** b

7

Fraud, Internal Control, and Cash

CHAPTER PREVIEW

As the Feature Story about recording cash sales at Barriques indicates, control of cash is important to ensure that fraud does not occur. Companies also need controls to safeguard other types of assets. For example, Barriques undoubtedly has controls to prevent the theft of food and supplies, and controls to prevent the theft of tableware and dishes from its kitchen.

In this chapter, we explain the essential features of an internal control system and how it prevents fraud. We also describe how those controls apply to a specific asset—cash. The applications include some controls with which you may be already familiar, such as the use of a bank.

CHAPTER OUTLINE

LEARNING OBJECTIVES		PRACTICE
1 Define fraud and the principles of internal control.	• Fraud • The Sarbanes-Oxley Act • Internal control • Principles of internal control activities • Limitations of internal control	DO IT! 1 Control Activities
2 Apply internal control principles to cash.	• Cash receipts controls • Cash disbursements controls	DO IT! 2 Control over Cash Receipts
3 Identify the control features of a bank account.	• EFT system • Bank statements • Reconciling the bank account	DO IT! 3 Bank Reconciliation
4 Explain the reporting of cash and the basic principles of cash management.	• Reporting cash • Managing and monitoring cash • Cash budgeting	DO IT! 4 4a Reporting Cash 4b Cash Budget

Go to the ***REVIEW AND PRACTICE*** section at the end of the chapter for a targeted summary and exercises with solutions.

Visit **WileyPLUS** for additional tutorials and practice opportunities.

© James Pauls/iStockphoto

Minding the Money in Madison

For many years, Barriques in Madison, Wisconsin, has been named the city's favorite coffeehouse. Barriques not only does a booming business in coffee but also has wonderful baked goods, delicious sandwiches, and a fine selection of wines.

"Our customer base ranges from college students to neighborhood residents as well as visitors to our capital city," says bookkeeper Kerry Stoppleworth, who joined the company shortly after it was founded in 1998. "We are unique because we have customers who come in early on their way to work for a cup of coffee and then will stop back after work to pick up a bottle of wine for dinner. We stay very busy throughout all three parts of the day."

Like most businesses where purchases are low-cost and high-volume, cash control has to be simple. "We use a computerized point-of-sale (POS) system to keep track of our inventory and allow us to efficiently ring through an order for a customer," explains Stoppleworth. "You can either scan a barcode for an item or enter in a code for items that don't have a barcode such as cups of coffee or bakery items." The POS system also automatically tracks sales by department and maintains an electronic journal of all the sales transactions that occur during the day.

"There are two POS stations at each store, and throughout the day any of the staff may operate them," says Stoppleworth. At the end of the day, each POS station is reconciled separately. The staff counts the cash in the drawer and enters this amount into the closing totals in the POS system. The POS system then compares the cash and credit amounts, less the cash being carried forward to the next day (the float), to the shift total in the electronic journal. If there are discrepancies, a recount is done and the journal is reviewed transaction by transaction to identify the problem. The staff then creates a deposit ticket for the cash less the float and puts this in a drop safe with the electronic journal summary report for the manager to review and take to the bank the next day. Ultimately, the bookkeeper reviews all of these documents as well as the deposit receipt that the bank produces to make sure they are all in agreement.

As Stoppleworth concludes, "We keep the closing process and accounting simple so that our staff can concentrate on taking care of our customers and making great coffee and food."

LEARNING OBJECTIVE 1

Define fraud and the principles of internal control.

The Feature Story describes many of the internal control procedures used by Barriques. These procedures are necessary to discourage employees from fraudulent activities.

FRAUD

A **fraud** is a dishonest act by an employee that results in personal benefit to the employee at a cost to the employer. Examples of fraud reported in the financial press include the following.

- A bookkeeper in a small company diverted $750,000 of bill payments to a personal bank account over a three-year period.
- A shipping clerk with 28 years of service shipped $125,000 of merchandise to himself.
- A computer operator embezzled $21 million from Wells Fargo Bank over a two-year period.
- A church treasurer "borrowed" $150,000 of church funds to finance a friend's business dealings.

Why does fraud occur? The three main factors that contribute to fraudulent activity are depicted by the **fraud triangle** in Illustration 7-1.

The most important element of the fraud triangle is **opportunity**. For an employee to commit fraud, the workplace environment must provide opportunities that an employee can exploit. Opportunities occur when the workplace lacks sufficient controls to deter and detect fraud. For example, inadequate monitoring of employee actions can create opportunities for theft and can embolden employees because they believe they will not be caught.

ILLUSTRATION 7-1
Fraud triangle

A second factor that contributes to fraud is **financial pressure**. Employees sometimes commit fraud because of personal financial problems caused by too much debt. Or they might commit fraud because they want to lead a lifestyle that they cannot afford on their current salary.

The third factor that contributes to fraud is **rationalization**. In order to justify their fraud, employees rationalize their dishonest actions. For example, employees sometimes justify fraud because they believe they are underpaid while the employer is making lots of money. These employees feel justified in stealing because they believe they deserve to be paid more.

THE SARBANES-OXLEY ACT

What can be done to prevent or to detect fraud? After numerous corporate scandals came to light in the early 2000s, Congress addressed this issue by passing the **Sarbanes-Oxley Act (SOX)**. Under SOX, all publicly traded U.S. corporations are required to maintain an adequate system of internal control. Corporate executives and boards of directors must ensure that these controls are reliable and effective. In addition, independent outside auditors must attest to the adequacy of the internal control system. Companies that fail to comply are subject to fines, and company officers can be imprisoned. SOX also created the Public Company Accounting Oversight Board (PCAOB) to establish auditing standards and regulate auditor activity.

One poll found that 60% of investors believe that SOX helps safeguard their stock investments. Many say they would be unlikely to invest in a company that fails to follow SOX requirements. Although some corporate executives have criticized the time and expense involved in following SOX requirements, SOX appears to be working well. For example, the chief accounting officer of Eli Lily noted that SOX triggered a comprehensive review of how the company documents controls. This review uncovered redundancies and pointed out controls that needed to be added. In short, it added up to time and money well spent. And the finance chief at General Electric noted, "We have seen value in SOX. It helps build investors' trust and gives them more confidence."

INTERNAL CONTROL

Internal control is a process designed to provide reasonable assurance regarding the achievement of company objectives related to operations, reporting, and compliance. In more detail, the purposes of internal control are to safeguard assets, enhance the reliability of accounting records, increase efficiency of operations, and ensure compliance with laws and regulations. Internal control systems have five primary components as listed below.[1]

- **A control environment.** It is the responsibility of top management to make it clear that the organization values integrity and that unethical activity will not be tolerated. This component is often referred to as the "tone at the top."
- **Risk assessment.** Companies must identify and analyze the various factors that create risk for the business and must determine how to manage these risks.
- **Control activities.** To reduce the occurrence of fraud, management must design policies and procedures to address the specific risks faced by the company.
- **Information and communication.** The internal control system must capture and communicate all pertinent information both down and up the organization, as well as communicate information to appropriate external parties.
- **Monitoring.** Internal control systems must be monitored periodically for their adequacy. Significant deficiencies need to be reported to top management and/or the board of directors.

PEOPLE, PLANET, AND PROFIT INSIGHT

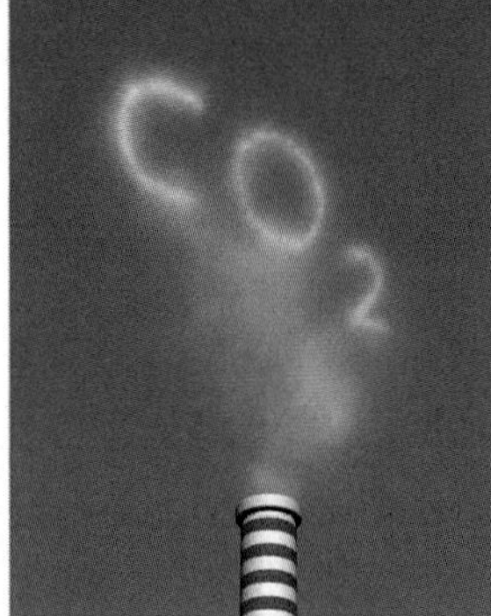

© Karl Dolenc/iStockphoto

And the Controls Are . . .

Internal controls are important for an effective financial reporting system. The same is true for sustainability reporting. An effective system of internal controls for sustainability reporting will help in the following ways: (1) prevent the unauthorized use of data; (2) provide reasonable assurance that the information is accurate, valid, and complete; and (3) report information that is consistent with overall sustainability accounting policies. With these types of controls, users will have the confidence that they can use the sustainability information effectively.

Some regulators are calling for even more assurance through audits of this information. Companies that potentially can cause environmental damage through greenhouse gases, as well as companies in the mining and extractive industries, are subject to reporting requirements. And, as demand for more information in the sustainability area expands, the need for audits of this information will grow.

Why is sustainability information important to investors? (Go to WileyPLUS for this answer and additional questions.)

[1]The Committee of Sponsoring Organizations of the Treadway Commission, "Internal Control—Integrated Framework," *www.coso.org/documents/990025p_Executive_Summary_final_may20_e.pdf*; and Stephen J. McNally, "The 2013 COSO Framework and SOX Compliance," *Strategic Finance* (June 2013).

PRINCIPLES OF INTERNAL CONTROL ACTIVITIES

DECISION TOOLS 

The six principles of internal control activities help to ensure that a company's financial statements are adequately supported by internal controls.

Each of the five components of an internal control system is important. Here, we will focus on one component, the control activities. The reason? These activities are the backbone of the company's efforts to address the risks it faces, such as fraud. The specific control activities used by a company will vary, depending on management's assessment of the risks faced. This assessment is heavily influenced by the size and nature of the company.

The six principles of control activities are as follows.

- Establishment of responsibility
- Segregation of duties
- Documentation procedures
- Physical controls
- Independent internal verification
- Human resource controls

We explain these principles in the following sections. You should recognize that they apply to most companies and are relevant to both manual and computerized accounting systems.

Establishment of Responsibility

An essential principle of internal control is to assign responsibility to specific employees. **Control is most effective when only one person is responsible for a given task.**

Transfer of cash drawers

To illustrate, assume that the cash on hand at the end of the day in a Safeway supermarket is $10 short of the cash entered in the cash register. If only one person has operated the register, the shift manager can quickly determine responsibility for the shortage. What happens, though, if two or more individuals work the register? Many retailers solve this problem by having registers with multiple drawers. This makes it possible for more than one person to operate a register but still allows identification of a particular employee with a specific drawer. Only the signed-in cashier has access to his or her drawer.

Establishing responsibility often requires limiting access only to authorized personnel, and then identifying those personnel. For example, the automated systems used by many companies have mechanisms such as identifying passcodes that keep track of who made a journal entry, who entered a sale, or who went into an inventory storeroom at a particular time. Use of identifying passcodes enables the company to establish responsibility by identifying the particular employee who carried out the activity.

ANATOMY OF A FRAUD

Maureen Frugali was a training supervisor for claims processing at Colossal Healthcare. As a standard part of the claims-processing training program, Maureen created fictitious claims for use by trainees. These fictitious claims were then sent to the accounts payable department. After the training claims had been processed, she was to notify accounts payable of all fictitious claims, so that they would not be paid. However, she did not inform accounts payable about every fictitious claim. She created some fictitious claims for entities that she controlled (that is, she would receive the payment), and she let accounts payable pay her.

Total take: $11 million

THE MISSING CONTROL

Establishment of responsibility. The healthcare company did not adequately restrict the responsibility for authorizing and approving claims transactions. The training supervisor should not have been authorized to create claims in the company's "live" system.

Source: Adapted from Wells, *Fraud Casebook* (2007), pp. 61–70.

Segregation of Duties

Segregation of duties is indispensable in an internal control system. There are two common applications of this principle:

1. Different individuals should be responsible for related activities.
2. The responsibility for recordkeeping for an asset should be separate from the physical custody of that asset.

The rationale for segregation of duties is this: **The work of one employee should, without a duplication of effort, provide a reliable basis for evaluating the work of another employee.** For example, the personnel that design and program computerized systems should not be assigned duties related to day-to-day use of the system. Otherwise, they could design the system to benefit them personally and conceal the fraud through day-to-day use.

SEGREGATION OF RELATED ACTIVITIES **Making one individual responsible for related activities increases the potential for errors and irregularities.**

Purchasing activities. Companies should, for example, assign related **purchasing activities** to different individuals. Related purchasing activities include ordering merchandise, approving orders, receiving goods, authorizing payment, and paying for goods or services. Various frauds are possible when one person handles related purchasing activities:

- If a purchasing agent is allowed to order goods without supervisory approval, the likelihood of the agent receiving kickbacks from suppliers increases.
- If an employee who orders goods also handles the invoice and receipt of the goods, as well as payment authorization, he or she might authorize payment for a fictitious invoice.

These abuses are less likely to occur when companies divide the purchasing tasks.

Sales activities. Similarly, companies should assign related **sales activities** to different individuals. Related selling activities include making a sale, shipping (or delivering) the goods to the customer, billing the customer, and receiving payment. Various frauds are possible when one person handles related sales activities. For example:

- If a salesperson can make a sale without obtaining supervisory approval, he or she might make sales at unauthorized prices to increase sales commissions.
- A shipping clerk who also has access to accounting records could ship goods to himself.
- A billing clerk who handles billing and cash receipts could understate the amount billed for sales made to friends and relatives.

These abuses are less likely to occur when companies divide the sales tasks. The salespeople make the sale, the shipping department ships the goods on the basis of the sales order, and the billing department prepares the sales invoice after comparing the sales order with the report of goods shipped.

ANATOMY OF A FRAUD

Lawrence Fairbanks, the assistant vice-chancellor of communications at Aesop University, was allowed to make purchases of under $2,500 for his department without external approval. Unfortunately, he also sometimes bought items for himself, such as expensive antiques and other collectibles. How did he do it? He replaced the vendor invoices he received with fake vendor invoices that he created. The fake invoices had descriptions that were more consistent with communications department purchases. He submitted these fake invoices to the accounting department as the basis for their journal entries and to the accounts payable department as the basis for payment.

Total take: $475,000

THE MISSING CONTROL

Segregation of duties. The university had not properly segregated related purchasing activities. Lawrence was ordering items, receiving the items, and receiving the invoice. By receiving the invoice, he had control over the documents that were used to account for the purchase and thus was able to substitute a fake invoice.

Source: Adapted from Wells, *Fraud Casebook* (2007), pp. 3–15.

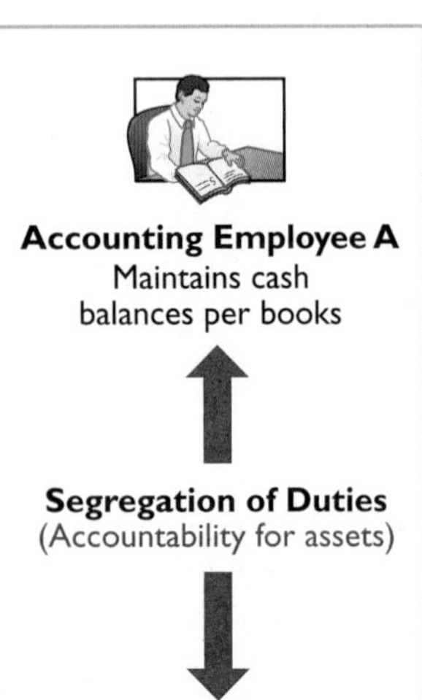

SEGREGATION OF RECORDKEEPING FROM PHYSICAL CUSTODY The accountant should have neither physical custody of the asset nor access to it. Likewise, the custodian of the asset should not maintain or have access to the accounting records. **The custodian of the asset is not likely to convert the asset to personal use when one employee maintains the record of the asset, and a different employee has physical custody of the asset.** The separation of accounting responsibility from the custody of assets is especially important for cash and inventories because these assets are very vulnerable to fraud.

ANATOMY OF A FRAUD

Angela Bauer was an accounts payable clerk for Aggasiz Construction Company. Angela prepared and issued checks to vendors and reconciled bank statements. She perpetrated a fraud in this way: She wrote checks for costs that the company had not actually incurred (e.g., fake taxes). A supervisor then approved and signed the checks. Before issuing the check, though, Angela would "white-out" the payee line on the check and change it to personal accounts that she controlled. She was able to conceal the theft because she also reconciled the bank account. That is, nobody else ever saw that the checks had been altered.

Total take: $570,000

THE MISSING CONTROL

Segregation of duties. Aggasiz Construction Company did not properly segregate recordkeeping from physical custody. Angela had physical custody of the blank checks, which essentially was control of the cash. She also had recordkeeping responsibility because she prepared the bank reconciliation.

Source: Adapted from Wells, *Fraud Casebook* (2007), pp. 100–107.

Documentation Procedures

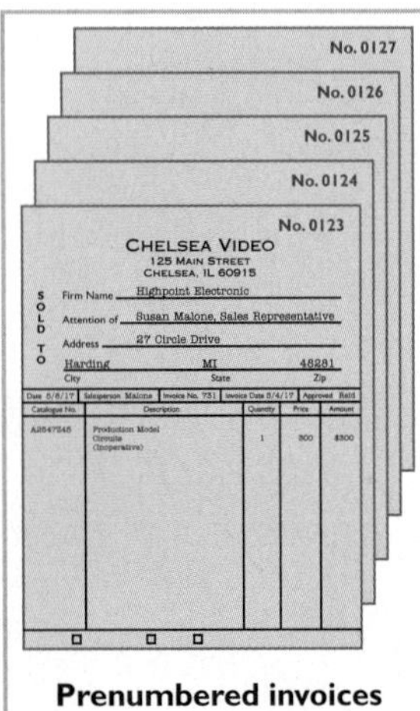

Prenumbered invoices

Documents provide evidence that transactions and events have occurred. For example, point-of-sale terminals are networked with a company's computing and accounting records, which results in direct documentation. Similarly, a shipping document indicates that the goods have been shipped, and a sales invoice indicates that the company has billed the customer for the goods. By requiring signatures (or initials) on the documents, the company can identify the individual(s) responsible for the transaction or event. Companies should document transactions when the transactions occur.

Companies should establish procedures for documents. First, whenever possible, companies should use **prenumbered documents, and all documents should be accounted for**. Prenumbering helps to prevent a transaction from being recorded more than once or, conversely, from not being recorded at all. Second, the control system should require that employees **promptly forward source documents for accounting entries to the accounting department. This control measure helps to ensure timely recording of the transaction** and contributes directly to the accuracy and reliability of the accounting records.

ANATOMY OF A FRAUD

To support their reimbursement requests for travel costs incurred, employees at Mod Fashions Corporation's design center were required to submit receipts. The receipts could include the detailed bill provided for a meal, the credit card receipt provided when the credit card payment is made, or a copy of the employee's monthly credit card bill that listed the item. A number of the designers who frequently traveled together came up with a fraud scheme: They submitted claims for the same expenses. For example, if they had a meal together that cost $200, one person submitted the detailed meal bill, another submitted the credit card receipt, and a third submitted a monthly credit card bill showing the meal as a line item. Thus, all three received a $200 reimbursement.

Total take: $75,000

THE MISSING CONTROL

Documentation procedures. Mod Fashions should require the original, detailed receipt. It should not accept photocopies, and it should not accept credit card statements. In addition, documentation procedures could be further improved by requiring the use of a corporate credit card (rather than personal credit card) for all business expenses.

Source: Adapted from Wells, *Fraud Casebook* (2007), pp. 79–90.

Physical Controls

Use of physical controls is essential. **Physical controls** relate to the safeguarding of assets and enhance the accuracy and reliability of the accounting records. Illustration 7-2 (page 324) shows examples of these controls.

ANATOMY OF A FRAUD

At Centerstone Health, a large insurance company, the mailroom each day received insurance applications from prospective customers. Mailroom employees scanned the applications into electronic documents before the applications were processed. Once the applications were scanned, they could be accessed online by authorized employees.

Insurance agents at Centerstone Health earn commissions based upon successful applications. The sales agent's name is listed on the application. However, roughly 15% of the applications are from customers who did not work with a sales agent. Two friends—Alex, an employee in recordkeeping, and Parviz, a sales agent—thought up a way to perpetrate a fraud. Alex identified scanned applications that did not list a sales agent. After business hours, he entered the mailroom and found the hardcopy applications that did not show a sales agent. He wrote in Parviz's name as the sales agent and then rescanned the application for processing. Parviz received the commission, which the friends then split.

Total take: $240,000

THE MISSING CONTROL

Physical controls. Centerstone Health lacked two basic physical controls that could have prevented this fraud. First, the mailroom should have been locked during nonbusiness hours, and access during business hours should have been tightly controlled. Second, the scanned applications supposedly could be accessed only by authorized employees using their password. However, the password for each employee was the same as the employee's user-ID. Since employee user-ID numbers were available to all other employees, all employees knew each other's passwords. Thus, Alex could enter the system using another employee's password and access the scanned applications.

Source: Adapted from Wells, *Fraud Casebook* (2007), pp. 316–326.

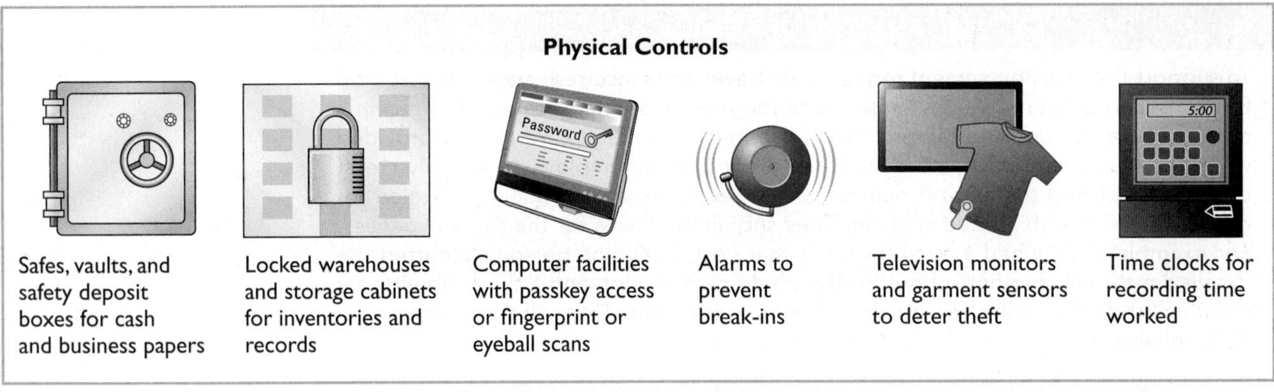

ILLUSTRATION 7-2
Physical controls

Independent Internal Verification

Most internal control systems provide for **independent internal verification**. This principle involves the review of data prepared by employees. To obtain maximum benefit from independent internal verification:

1. Companies should verify records periodically or on a surprise basis.
2. An employee who is independent of the personnel responsible for the information should make the verification.
3. Discrepancies and exceptions should be reported to a management level that can take appropriate corrective action.

Independent internal verification is especially useful in comparing recorded transactions with existing assets. The reconciliation of the electronic journal with the cash in the point-of-sale terminal at Barriques is an example of this internal control principle. Another common example is the reconciliation of a company's cash balance per books with the cash balance per bank and the verification of the perpetual inventory records through a count of physical inventory. Illustration 7-3 shows the relationship between this principle and the segregation of duties principle.

ILLUSTRATION 7-3
Comparison of segregation of duties principle with independent internal verification principle

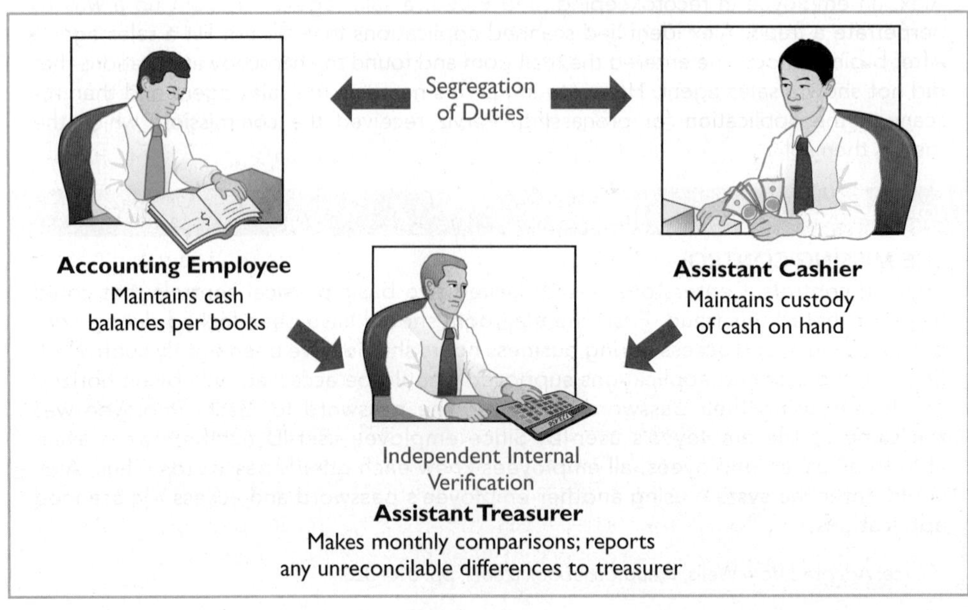

Large companies often assign independent internal verification to internal auditors. **Internal auditors** are company employees who continuously evaluate the effectiveness of the company's internal control systems. They review the activities of departments and individuals to determine whether prescribed internal controls are being followed. They also recommend improvements when needed. In fact, most fraud is discovered by the company through internal mechanisms such as existing internal controls and internal audits. For example, WorldCom was at one time the second largest U.S. telecommunications company. The fraud that caused its bankruptcy (the largest ever when it occurred) involved billions of dollars. It was uncovered by an internal auditor.

ANATOMY OF A FRAUD

Bobbi Jean Donnelly, the office manager for Mod Fashions Corporation's design center, was responsible for preparing the design center budget and reviewing expense reports submitted by design center employees. Her desire to upgrade her wardrobe got the better of her, and she enacted a fraud that involved filing expense-reimbursement requests for her own personal clothing purchases. She was able to conceal the fraud because she was responsible for reviewing all expense reports, including her own. In addition, she sometimes was given ultimate responsibility for signing off on the expense reports when her boss was "too busy." Also, because she controlled the budget, when she submitted her expenses, she coded them to budget items that she knew were running under budget, so that they would not catch anyone's attention.

Total take: $275,000

THE MISSING CONTROL

Independent internal verification. Bobbi Jean's boss should have verified her expense reports. When asked what he thought her expenses for a year were, the boss said about $10,000. At $115,000 per year, her actual expenses were more than 10 times what would have been expected. However, because he was "too busy" to verify her expense reports or to review the budget, he never noticed.

Source: Adapted from Wells, *Fraud Casebook* (2007), pp. 79–90.

Human Resource Controls

Human resource control activities include the following.

1. **Bond employees who handle cash. Bonding** involves obtaining insurance protection against theft by employees. It contributes to the safeguarding of cash in two ways. First, the insurance company carefully screens all individuals before adding them to the policy and may reject risky applicants. Second, bonded employees know that the insurance company will vigorously prosecute all offenders.
2. **Rotate employees' duties and require employees to take vacations.** These measures deter employees from attempting thefts since they will not be able to permanently conceal their improper actions. Many banks, for example, have discovered employee thefts when the employee was on vacation or assigned to a new position.
3. **Conduct thorough background checks.** Many believe that the most important and inexpensive measure any business can take to reduce employee theft and fraud is for the human resources department to conduct thorough background checks. Two tips: (1) Check to see whether job applicants actually graduated from the schools they list. (2) Never use telephone numbers for previous employers provided by the applicant; always look them up yourself.

ANATOMY OF A FRAUD

Ellen Lowry was the desk manager and Josephine Rodriquez was the head of housekeeping at the Excelsior Inn, a luxury hotel. The two best friends were so dedicated to their jobs that they never took vacations, and they frequently filled in for other employees. In fact, Ms. Rodriquez, whose job as head of housekeeping did not include cleaning rooms, often cleaned rooms herself, "just to help the staff keep up." These two "dedicated" employees, working as a team, found a way to earn a little more cash. Ellen, the desk manager, provided significant discounts to guests who paid with cash. She kept the cash and did not register the guests in the hotel's computerized system. Instead, she took the room out of circulation "due to routine maintenance." Because the room did not show up as being used, it did not receive a normal housekeeping assignment. Instead, Josephine, the head of housekeeping, cleaned the rooms during the guests' stay.

Total take: $95,000

THE MISSING CONTROL

Human resource controls. Ellen, the desk manager, had been fired by a previous employer after being accused of fraud. If the Excelsior Inn had conducted a thorough background check, it would not have hired her. The hotel fraud was detected when Ellen missed work for a few days due to illness. A system of mandatory vacations and rotating days off would have increased the chances of detecting the fraud before it became so large.

Source: Adapted from Wells, *Fraud Casebook* (2007), pp. 145–155.

ACCOUNTING ACROSS THE ORGANIZATION

Stockbyte/Getty Images, Inc.

SOX Boosts the Role of Human Resources

Under SOX, a company needs to keep track of employees' degrees and certifications to ensure that employees continue to meet the specified requirements of a job. Also, to ensure proper employee supervision and proper separation of duties, companies must develop and monitor an organizational chart. When one corporation went through this exercise it found that out of 17,000 employees, there were 400 people who did not report to anyone. The corporation had 35 people who reported to each other. In addition, SOX also mandates that, if an employee complains of an unfair firing and mentions financial issues at the company, the human resources department must refer the case to the company audit committee and possibly to its legal counsel.

Why would unsupervised employees or employees who report to each other represent potential internal control threats? (Go to WileyPLUS for this answer and additional questions.)

LIMITATIONS OF INTERNAL CONTROL

▼ HELPFUL HINT
Controls may vary with the risk level of the activity. For example, management may consider cash to be high risk and maintaining inventories in the stockroom as lower risk. Thus, management would have stricter controls for cash.

Companies generally design their systems of internal control to provide **reasonable assurance** of proper safeguarding of assets and reliability of the accounting records. The concept of reasonable assurance rests on the premise that the costs of establishing control procedures should not exceed their expected benefit.

To illustrate, consider shoplifting losses in retail stores. Stores could eliminate such losses by having a security guard stop and search customers as they leave the store. But store managers have concluded that the negative effects of such a procedure cannot be justified. Instead, they have attempted to control shoplifting losses by less costly procedures. They post signs saying, "We reserve the right to inspect all packages" and "All shoplifters will be prosecuted." They use hidden cameras and store detectives to monitor customer activity, and they install sensor equipment at exits.

The **human element** is an important factor in every system of internal control. A good system can become ineffective as a result of employee fatigue, carelessness, or indifference. For example, a receiving clerk may not bother to count goods received and may just "fudge" the counts. Occasionally, two or more individuals work together to get around prescribed controls. Such **collusion** can significantly reduce the effectiveness of a system, eliminating the protection offered by segregation of duties. No system of internal control is perfect.

The **size of the business** also may impose limitations on internal control. Small companies often find it difficult to segregate duties or to provide for independent internal verification. A study by the Association of Certified Fraud Examiners (*2014 Report to the Nation on Occupational Fraud and Abuse*) indicates that businesses with fewer than 100 employees are most at risk for employee theft. In fact, 29% of frauds occurred at companies with fewer than 100 employees. The median loss at small companies was $154,000, which was nearly as high as the median fraud at companies with more than 10,000 employees ($160,000). A $154,000 loss can threaten the very existence of a small company.

DO IT! 1 Control Activities

Identify which control activity is violated in each of the following situations, and explain how the situation creates an opportunity for a fraud.

1. The person with primary responsibility for reconciling the bank account and making all bank deposits is also the company's accountant.
2. Wellstone Company's treasurer received an award for distinguished service because he had not taken a vacation in 30 years.
3. In order to save money on order slips and to reduce time spent keeping track of order slips, a local bar/restaurant does not buy prenumbered order slips.

SOLUTION

1. Violates the control activity of segregation of duties. Recordkeeping should be separate from physical custody. As a consequence, the employee could embezzle cash and make journal entries to hide the theft.
2. Violates the control activity of human resource controls. Key employees, such as a treasurer, should be required to take vacations. The treasurer, who manages the company's cash, might embezzle cash and use his position to conceal the theft.
3. Violates the control activity of documentation procedures. If prenumbered documents are not used, then it is virtually impossible to account for the documents. As a consequence, an employee could write up a dinner sale, receive the cash from the customer, and then throw away the order slip and keep the cash.

Action Plan

✔ Familiarize yourself with each of the control activities listed on page 320.

✔ Understand the nature of the frauds that each control activity is intended to address.

Related exercise material: **BE7-1, BE7-2, BE7-3, DO IT! 7-1, E7-1,** and **E7-2.**

LEARNING OBJECTIVE 2 Apply internal control principles to cash.

Cash is the one asset that is readily convertible into any other type of asset. It also is easily concealed and transported, and is highly desired. Because of these characteristics, **cash is the asset most susceptible to fraudulent activities**. In addition, because of the large volume of cash transactions, numerous errors may occur in executing and recording them. To safeguard cash and to ensure the accuracy of the accounting records for cash, effective internal control over cash is critical.

CASH RECEIPTS CONTROLS

Illustration 7-4 shows how the internal control principles explained earlier apply to cash receipts transactions. As you might expect, companies vary considerably in how they apply these principles. To illustrate internal control over cash receipts, we will examine control activities for a retail store with both over-the-counter and mail receipts.

Establishment of Responsibility
Only designated personnel are authorized to handle cash receipts (cashiers)

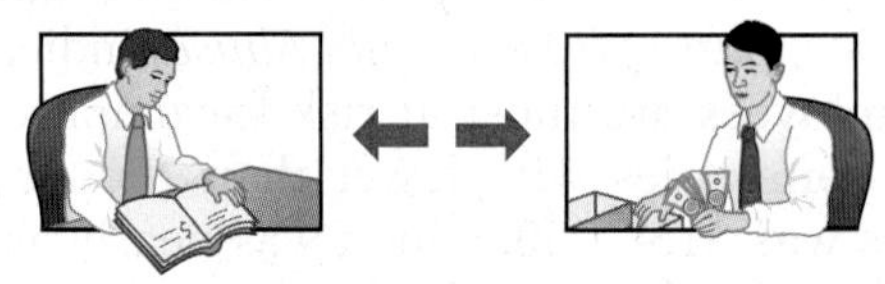

Segregation of Duties
Different individuals receive cash, record cash receipts, and hold the cash

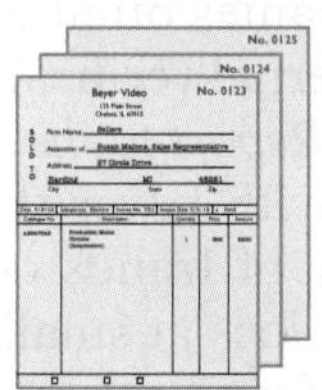

Documentation Procedures
Use remittance advice (mail receipts), cash register tapes or computer records, and deposit slips

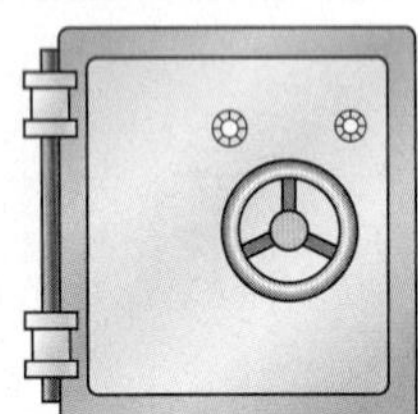

Physical Controls
Store cash in safes and bank vaults; limit access to storage areas; use cash registers or point-of-sale terminals

Independent Internal Verification
Supervisors count cash receipts daily; assistant treasurer compares total receipts to bank deposits daily

Human Resource Controls
Bond personnel who handle cash; require employees to take vacations; conduct background checks

ILLUSTRATION 7-4
Application of internal control principles to cash receipts

Over-the-Counter Receipts

In retail businesses, control of over-the-counter receipts centers on cash registers that are visible to customers. A cash sale is entered in a cash register with the amount clearly visible to the customer. This activity prevents the cashier from entering a lower amount and pocketing the difference. The customer receives an itemized cash register receipt and is expected to count the change received. (One weakness at Barriques in the Feature Story is that customers are only given a receipt if requested.) The cash register's tape is locked in the register until a supervisor removes it. This tape accumulates the daily transactions and totals. Alternatively, cash registers called point-of-sale terminals are often networked with the company's computers for direct recording in its records.

At the end of the clerk's shift, the clerk counts the cash and sends the cash and the count to the cashier. The cashier counts the cash, prepares a deposit slip, and deposits the cash at the bank. The cashier also sends a duplicate of the deposit slip to the accounting department to indicate cash received. The supervisor removes the cash register tape and sends it to the accounting department (in a non-point-of-sale system) as the basis for a journal entry to record the cash received. The tape is compared to the deposit slip for any discrepancies. Illustration 7-5 summarizes this process.

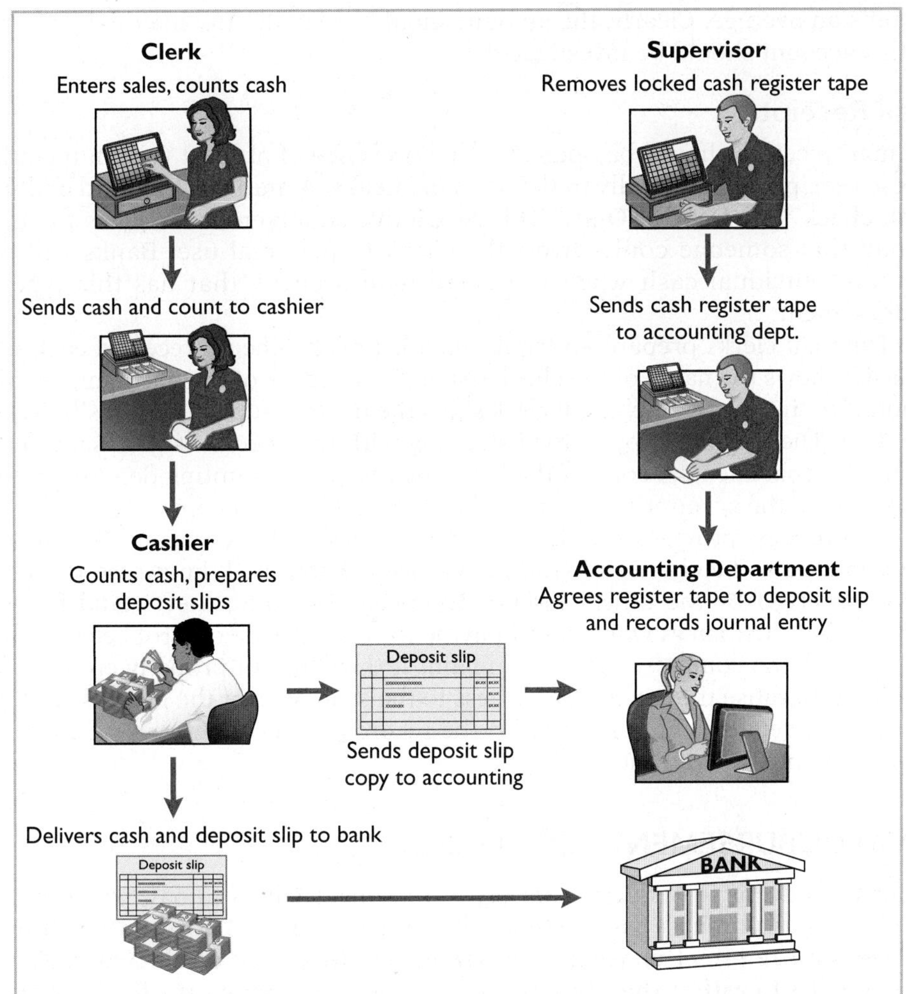

ILLUSTRATION 7-5
Control of over-the-counter receipts

▼ **HELPFUL HINT**
Flowcharts such as this one enhance the understanding of the flow of documents, the processing steps, and the internal control procedures.

This system for handling cash receipts uses an important internal control principle—segregation of recordkeeping from physical custody. The supervisor has access to the cash register tape, but **not** to the cash. The clerk and the cashier have access to the cash, but **not** to the register tape. In addition, the cash register tape provides documentation and enables independent internal verification with the deposit slip. Use of these three principles of internal control (segregation of recordkeeping from physical custody, documentation, and independent internal verification) provides an effective system of internal control. Any attempt at fraudulent activity should be detected unless there is collusion among the employees.

In some instances, the amount deposited at the bank will not agree with the cash recorded in the accounting records based on the cash register tape. These differences often result because the clerk hands incorrect change back to the retail customer. In this case, the difference between the actual cash and the amount reported on the cash register tape is reported in a Cash Over and Short account. For example, suppose that the cash register tape indicated sales of $6,956.20 but the amount of cash was only $6,946.10. A cash shortfall of $10.10 exists. To account for this cash shortfall and related cash, the company makes the following entry.

Cash	6,946.10	
Cash Over and Short	10.10	
Sales Revenue		6,956.20
(To record cash shortfall)		

A	=	L	+	SE
+6,946.10				
				−10.10
				+6,956.20

Cash Flows
+6,946.10

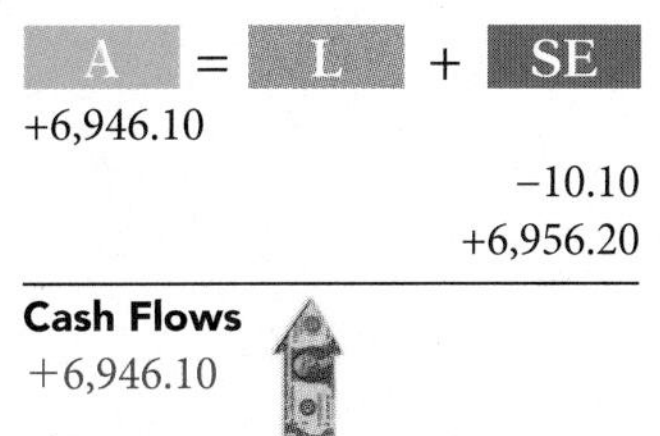

Cash Over and Short is an income statement item. It is reported as miscellaneous expense when there is a cash shortfall, and as miscellaneous revenue when there is an overage. Clearly, the amount should be small. Any material amounts in this account should be investigated.

Mail Receipts

All mail receipts should be opened in the presence of at least two mail clerks. These receipts are generally in the form of checks. A mail clerk should endorse each check "For Deposit Only." This restrictive endorsement reduces the likelihood that someone could divert the check to personal use. Banks will not give an individual cash when presented with a check that has this type of endorsement.

The mail clerks prepare, in triplicate, a list of the checks received each day. This list shows the name of the check issuer, the purpose of the payment, and the amount of the check. Each mail clerk signs the list to establish responsibility for the data. The original copy of the list, along with the checks, is then sent to the cashier's department. A copy of the list is sent to the accounting department for recording in the accounting records. The clerks also keep a copy.

This process provides excellent internal control for the company. By employing two clerks, the chance of fraud is reduced. Each clerk knows he or she is being observed by the other clerk(s). To engage in fraud, they would have to collude. The customers who submit payments also provide control because they will contact the company with a complaint if they are not properly credited for payment. Because the cashier has access to the cash but not the records, and the accounting department has access to the records but not the cash, neither can engage in undetected fraud.

CASH DISBURSEMENTS CONTROLS

Companies disburse cash for a variety of reasons, such as to pay expenses and liabilities or to purchase assets. **Generally, internal control over cash disbursements is more effective when companies pay by check or electronic funds transfer (EFT) rather than by cash.** One exception is **payments for incidental amounts that are paid out of petty cash**.[2]

Companies generally issue checks only after following specified control procedures. Illustration 7-6 shows how principles of internal control apply to cash disbursements.

Voucher System Controls

Most medium and large companies use vouchers as part of their internal control over cash disbursements. A **voucher system** is a network of approvals by authorized individuals, acting independently, to ensure that all disbursements by check are proper.

The system begins with the authorization to incur a cost or expense. It ends with the issuance of a check for the liability incurred. A **voucher** is an authorization form prepared for each expenditure in a voucher system. Companies require vouchers for all types of cash disbursements except those from petty cash.

The starting point in preparing a voucher is to fill in the appropriate information about the liability on the face of the voucher. The vendor's invoice provides most of the needed information. Then, an employee in accounts payable records the voucher (in a journal called a **voucher register**) and files it according to the date on which it is to be paid. The company issues and sends a check on that date, and stamps the voucher "paid." The paid voucher is sent to the accounting department for recording (in a journal called the **check register**). A voucher system involves two journal entries, one to record the liability when the voucher is issued and a second to pay the liability that relates to the voucher.

---

[2]We explain the operation of a petty cash fund in the appendix to this chapter on pages 347–348.

Cash Disbursements Controls

Establishment of Responsibility
Only designated personnel are authorized to sign checks (treasurer) and approve vendors

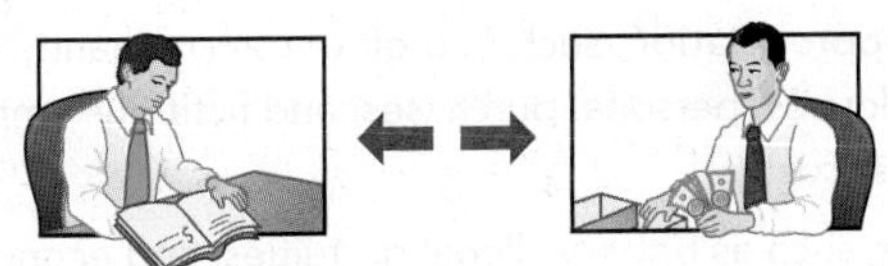

Segregation of Duties
Different individuals approve and make payments; check-signers do not record disbursements

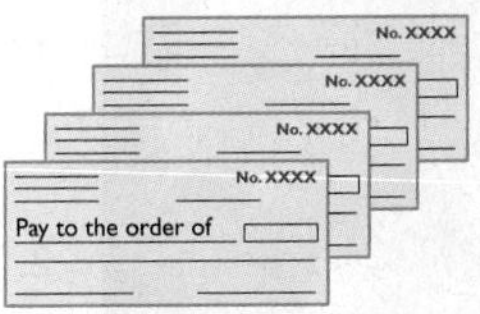

Documentation Procedures
Use prenumbered checks and account for them in sequence; each check must have an approved invoice; require employees to use corporate credit cards for reimbursable expenses; stamp invoices "paid"

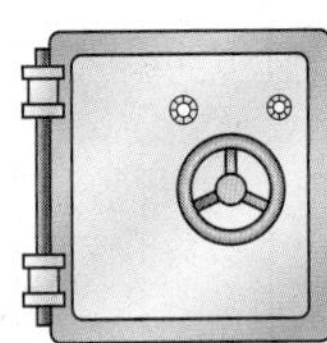

Physical Controls
Store blank checks in safes, with limited access; print check amounts by machine in indelible ink

Independent Internal Verification
Compare checks to invoices; reconcile bank statement monthly

Human Resource Controls
Bond personnel who handle cash; require employees to take vacations; conduct background checks

ILLUSTRATION 7-6
Application of internal control principles to cash disbursements

The use of a voucher system, whether done manually or electronically, improves internal control over cash disbursements. First, the authorization process inherent in a voucher system establishes responsibility. Each individual has responsibility to review the underlying documentation to ensure that it is correct. In addition, the voucher system keeps track of the documents that back up each transaction. By keeping these documents in one place, a supervisor can independently verify the authenticity of each transaction. Consider, for example, the case of Aesop University presented on pages 321–322. Aesop did not use a voucher system for transactions under $2,500. As a consequence, there was no independent verification of the documents, which enabled the employee to submit fake invoices to hide his unauthorized purchases.

ETHICS NOTE

Internal control over a petty cash fund is strengthened by (1) having a supervisor make surprise counts of the fund to confirm whether the paid petty cash receipts and fund cash equal the fund amount, and (2) canceling or mutilating the paid petty cash receipts so they cannot be resubmitted for reimbursement.

Petty Cash Fund

As you learned earlier in the chapter, better internal control over cash disbursements is possible when companies make payments by check. However, using checks to pay such small amounts as those for postage due, employee working lunches, and taxi fares is both impractical and a nuisance. A common way of handling such payments, while maintaining satisfactory control, is to use a petty cash fund. A **petty cash fund** is a cash fund used to pay relatively small amounts. We explain the operation of a petty cash fund in the appendix at the end of this chapter.

ETHICS INSIGHT

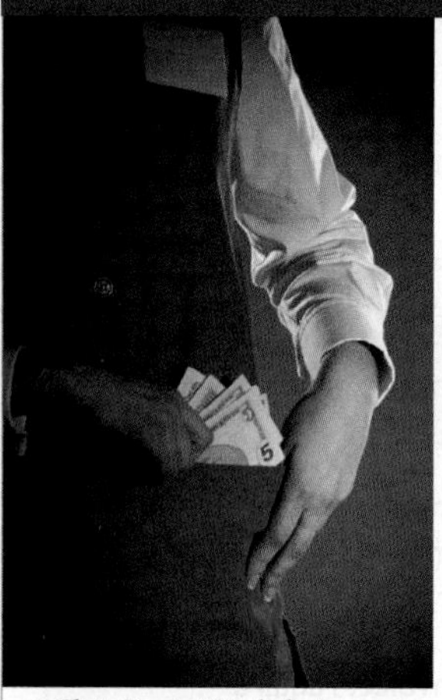
© Chris Fernig/iStockphoto

How Employees Steal

Occupational fraud is using your own occupation for personal gain through the misuse or misapplication of the company's resources or assets. This type of fraud is one of three types:

1. **Asset misappropriation**, such as theft of cash on hand, fraudulent disbursements, false refunds, ghost employees, personal purchases, and fictitious employees. This fraud is the most common but the least costly.
2. **Corruption**, such as bribery, illegal gratuities, and economic extortion. This fraud generally falls in the middle between asset misappropriation and financial statement fraud as regards frequency and cost.
3. **Financial statement fraud**, such as fictitious revenues, concealed liabilities and expenses, improper disclosures, and improper asset values. This fraud occurs less frequently than other types of fraud but it is the most costly.

The graph below shows the frequency and the median loss for each type of occupational fraud. (Note that the sum of percentages exceeds 100% because some cases of fraud involved more than one type.)

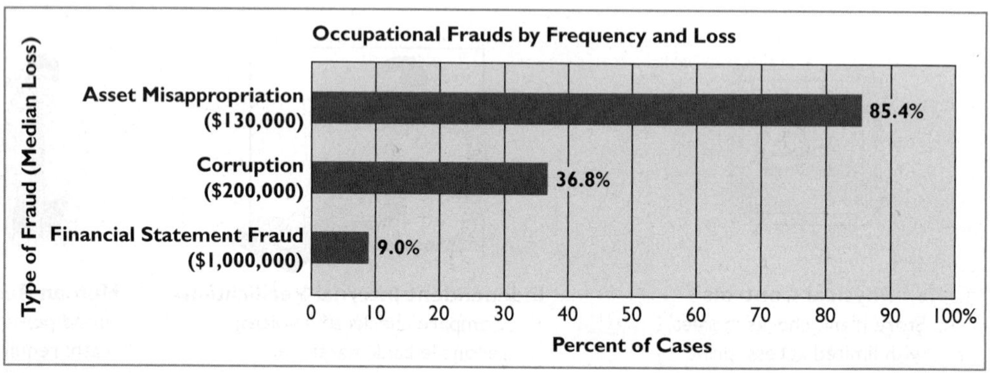

Source: 2014 Report to the Nations on Occupational Fraud and Abuse, Association of Certified Fraud Examiners, pp. 10–12.

How can companies reduce the likelihood of occupational fraud? (Go to WileyPLUS for this answer and additional questions.)

DO IT! 2 Control over Cash Receipts

L. R. Cortez is concerned about the control over cash receipts in his fast-food restaurant, Big Cheese. The restaurant has two cash registers. At no time do more than two employees take customer orders and enter sales. Work shifts for employees range from 4 to 8 hours. Cortez asks your help in installing a good system of internal control over cash receipts.

Action Plan

✔ Differentiate among the internal control principles of (1) establishing responsibility, (2) physical controls, and (3) independent internal verification.

✔ Design an effective system of internal control over cash receipts.

SOLUTION

Cortez should assign a separate cash register drawer to each employee at the start of each work shift, with register totals set at zero. Each employee should have access to only the assigned register drawer to enter all sales. Each customer should be given a receipt. At the end of the shift, the employee should do a cash count. A separate employee should compare the cash count with the register tape (or point-of-sale records) to be sure they agree. In addition, Cortez should install an automated point-of-sale system that would enable the company to compare orders entered in the register to orders processed by the kitchen.

Related exercise material: **BE7-4, BE7-5, DO IT! 7-2,** and **E7-3.**

LEARNING OBJECTIVE **3** Identify the control features of a bank account.

The use of a bank contributes significantly to good internal control over cash. A company safeguards its cash by using a bank as a depository and clearinghouse for checks received and checks written. The use of a bank checking account minimizes the amount of currency that must be kept on hand. It also facilitates control of cash because a double record is maintained of all bank transactions—one by the business and the other by the bank. The asset account Cash maintained by the company is the "flipside" of the bank's liability account for that company. A **bank reconciliation** is the process of comparing the bank's balance with the company's balance, and explaining the differences to make them agree.

Many companies have more than one bank account. For efficiency of operations and better control, national retailers like Wal-Mart and Target often have regional bank accounts. Similarly, a company such as ExxonMobil with more than 100,000 employees may have a payroll bank account as well as one or more general bank accounts. In addition, a company may maintain several bank accounts in order to have more than one source for short-term loans.

ELECTRONIC FUNDS TRANSFER (EFT) SYSTEM

It is not surprising that companies and banks have developed approaches to transfer funds among parties without the use of paper (deposit tickets, checks, etc.). Such procedures, called **electronic funds transfers (EFTs)**, are disbursement systems that use wire, telephone, or computers to transfer cash from one location to another. Use of EFT is quite common. For example, many employees receive no formal payroll checks from their employers. Instead, employers send electronic payroll data to the appropriate banks. Also, companies now frequently make regular payments such as those for utilities, rent, and insurance by EFT.

EFT transactions normally result in better internal control since no cash or checks are handled by company employees. This does not mean that opportunities for fraud are eliminated. In fact, the same basic principles related to internal control apply to EFT transactions. For example, without proper segregation of duties and authorizations, an employee might be able to redirect electronic payments into a personal bank account and conceal the theft with fraudulent accounting entries.

BANK STATEMENTS

Each month, the company receives from the bank a **bank statement** showing its bank transactions and balances.[3] For example, the statement for Laird Company in Illustration 7-7 (page 334) shows the following: (1) checks paid and other debits (such as debit card transactions or electronic funds transfers for bill payments) that reduce the balance in the depositor's account, (2) deposits (by direct deposit, automated teller machine, or electronic funds transfer) and other credits that increase the balance in the depositor's account, and (3) the account balance after each day's transactions.

Remember that **bank statements are prepared from the *bank's* perspective**. For example, **every deposit the bank receives is an increase in the bank's liabilities (an account payable to the depositor)**. Therefore, in Illustration 7-7, National Bank and Trust **credits** to Laird Company every deposit it received from

[3]Our presentation assumes that a company makes all adjustments at the end of the month. In practice, a company may also make journal entries during the month as it reviews information from the bank regarding its account.

ILLUSTRATION 7-7
Bank statement

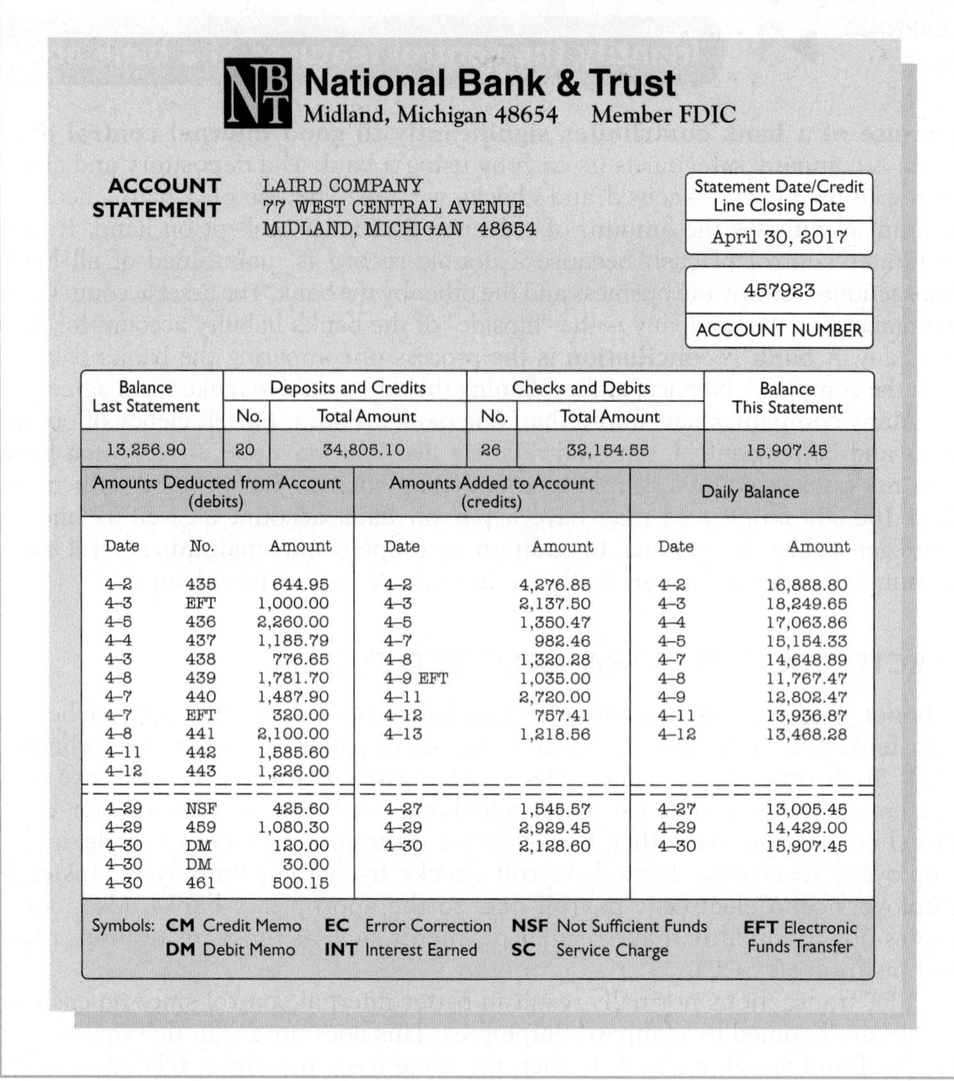

National Bank & Trust
Midland, Michigan 48654 Member FDIC

ACCOUNT STATEMENT

LAIRD COMPANY
77 WEST CENTRAL AVENUE
MIDLAND, MICHIGAN 48654

Statement Date/Credit Line Closing Date: April 30, 2017

ACCOUNT NUMBER: 457923

Balance Last Statement	Deposits and Credits		Checks and Debits		Balance This Statement
	No.	Total Amount	No.	Total Amount	
13,256.90	20	34,805.10	26	32,154.55	15,907.45

Amounts Deducted from Account (debits)			Amounts Added to Account (credits)		Daily Balance	
Date	No.	Amount	Date	Amount	Date	Amount
4–2	435	644.95	4–2	4,276.85	4–2	16,888.80
4–3	EFT	1,000.00	4–3	2,137.50	4–3	18,249.65
4–5	436	2,260.00	4–5	1,350.47	4–4	17,063.86
4–4	437	1,185.79	4–7	982.46	4–5	15,154.33
4–3	438	776.65	4–8	1,320.28	4–7	14,648.89
4–8	439	1,781.70	4–9 EFT	1,035.00	4–8	11,767.47
4–7	440	1,487.90	4–11	2,720.00	4–9	12,802.47
4–7	EFT	320.00	4–12	757.41	4–11	13,936.87
4–8	441	2,100.00	4–13	1,218.56	4–12	13,468.28
4–11	442	1,585.60				
4–12	443	1,226.00				
4–29	NSF	425.60	4–27	1,545.57	4–27	13,005.45
4–29	459	1,080.30	4–29	2,929.45	4–29	14,429.00
4–30	DM	120.00	4–30	2,128.60	4–30	15,907.45
4–30	DM	30.00				
4–30	461	500.15				

Symbols: **CM** Credit Memo **EC** Error Correction **NSF** Not Sufficient Funds **EFT** Electronic Funds Transfer
DM Debit Memo **INT** Interest Earned **SC** Service Charge

Laird. The reverse occurs when the bank "pays" a check issued by Laird Company on its checking account balance: Payment reduces the bank's liability and is therefore **debited** to Laird's account with the bank.

▼ **HELPFUL HINT**
Essentially, the bank statement is a copy of the bank's records sent to the customer or made available online for review.

The bank statement lists in numerical sequence all paid checks along with the date the check was paid and its amount. Upon paying a check, the bank stamps the check "paid"; a paid check is sometimes referred to as a **canceled** check. In addition, the bank includes with the bank statement memoranda explaining other debits and credits it made to the depositor's account.

A check that is not paid by a bank because of insufficient funds in a bank account is called an **NSF check** (not sufficient funds). The bank uses a debit memorandum when a previously deposited customer's check "bounces" because of insufficient funds. In such a case, the customer's bank marks the check NSF (not sufficient funds) and returns it to the depositor's bank. The bank then debits (decreases) the depositor's account, as shown by the symbol NSF in Illustration 7-7, and sends the NSF check and debit memorandum to the depositor as notification of the charge. The NSF check creates an account receivable for the depositor and reduces cash in the bank account.

RECONCILING THE BANK ACCOUNT

Because the bank and the company maintain independent records of the company's checking account, you might assume that the respective balances will always agree. In fact, the two balances are seldom the same at any given time, and both balances differ from the "correct or true" balance. Therefore, it is necessary to make the balance per books and the balance per bank agree with the correct or true amount—a process called **reconciling the bank account**. The need for reconciliation has two causes:

1. **Time lags** that prevent one of the parties from recording the transaction in the same period.
2. **Errors** by either party in recording transactions.

Time lags occur frequently. For example, several days may elapse between the time a company pays by check and the date the bank pays the check. Similarly, when a company uses the bank's night depository to make its deposits, there will be a difference of one day between the time the company records the receipts and the time the bank does so. A time lag also occurs whenever the bank mails a debit or credit memorandum to the company.

You might think that if a company never writes checks (for example, if a small company uses only a debit card or electronic bill funds transfers), it does not need to reconcile its account. However, **the possibility of errors or fraud still necessitates periodic reconciliation**. The incidence of errors or fraud depends on the effectiveness of the internal controls maintained by the company and the bank. Bank errors are infrequent. However, either party could accidentally record a $450 check as $45 or $540. In addition, the bank might mistakenly charge a check drawn by C. D. Berg to the account of C. D. Burg.

Reconciliation Procedure

In reconciling the bank account, it is customary to reconcile the balance per books and balance per bank to their adjusted (correct or true) cash balances. **To obtain maximum benefit from a bank reconciliation, an employee who has no other responsibilities related to cash should prepare the reconciliation.** When companies do not follow the internal control principle of independent internal verification in preparing the reconciliation, cash embezzlements may escape unnoticed. For example, in the Anatomy of a Fraud box on page 322, a bank reconciliation by someone other than Angela Bauer might have exposed her embezzlement.

Illustration 7-8 (page 336) shows the reconciliation process. The starting point in preparing the reconciliation is to enter the balance per bank statement and balance per books on a schedule. The following steps should reveal all the reconciling items that cause the difference between the two balances.

RECONCILING ITEMS PER BANK On the bank side of the reconciliation, the items to reconcile are deposits in transit (amounts added), outstanding checks (amounts deducted), and bank errors (if any). By adjusting the bank balance for these items, a company brings that balance up to date.

Step 1. Deposits in transit (+). Compare the individual deposits on the bank statement with the deposits in transit from the preceding bank reconciliation and with the deposits per company records or copies of duplicate deposit slips. Deposits recorded by the depositor that have not been recorded by the bank represent **deposits in transit**. Add these deposits to the balance per bank.

Step 2. Outstanding checks (−). Compare the paid checks shown on the bank statement or the paid checks returned with the bank statement with (a) checks outstanding from the preceding bank reconciliation, and (b) checks issued by the company as recorded in the cash payments journal. Issued checks recorded by the company that have not been paid by the bank represent **outstanding checks**. Deduct outstanding checks from the balance per bank.

ILLUSTRATION 7-8
Bank reconciliation adjustments

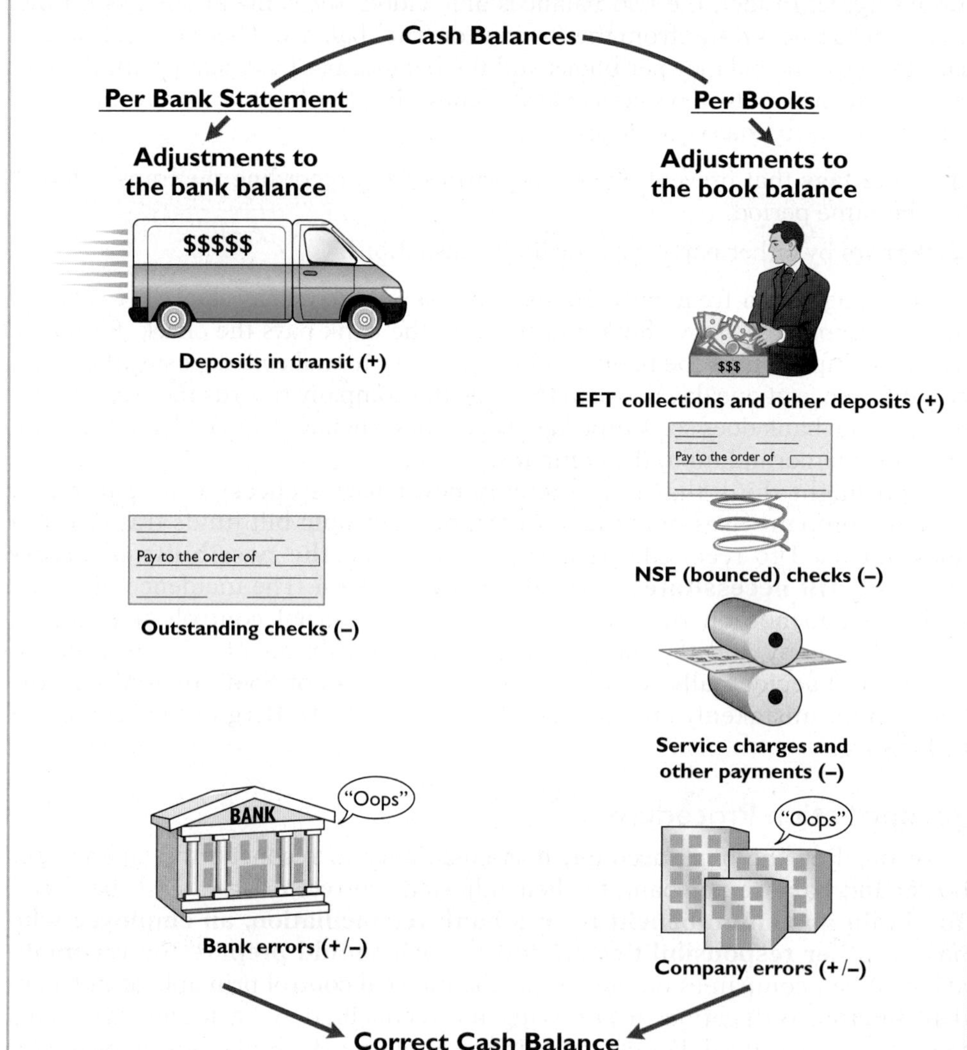

▼ HELPFUL HINT
Deposits in transit and outstanding checks are reconciling items because of time lags.

Step 3. Bank errors (+/−). Note any errors made by the bank that were discovered in the previous steps. For example, if the bank processed a deposit of $1,693 as $1,639 in error, the difference of $54 ($1,693 − $1,639) is added to the balance per bank on the bank reconciliation. All errors made by the bank are reconciling items in determining the adjusted cash balance per the bank.

RECONCILING ITEMS PER BOOKS Reconciling items on the book side relate to amounts not yet recorded on the company's books and include adjustments from deposits and other amounts added, payments and other amounts deducted, and company errors (if any).

Step 1. Other deposits (+). Compare the other deposits on the bank statement with the company records. Any unrecorded amounts should be added to the balance per books. For example, if the bank statement shows electronic funds transfers from customers paying their accounts online, these amounts should be added to the balance per books on the bank reconciliation to update the company's records unless they had previously been recorded by the company.

Step 2. Other payments (−). Similarly, any unrecorded other payments should be deducted from the balance per books. For example, if the bank statement shows service charges (such as debit and credit card fees and other bank service charges), this amount is deducted from the balance per books on the bank reconciliation to make the company's records agree with the bank's records. **Normally, the company will already have recorded electronic payments.** However, if this has not been the case then these payments must be deducted from the balance per books on the bank reconciliation to make the company's records agree with the bank's records.

Step 3. Book errors (+/−). Note any errors made by the depositor that have been discovered in the previous steps. For example, say a company wrote check No. 493 to a supplier in the amount of $1,226 on April 12, but the accounting clerk recorded the check amount as $1,262. The error of $36 ($1,262 − $1,226) is added to the balance per books because the company reduced the balance per books by $36 too much when it recorded the check as $1,262 instead of $1,226. Only errors made by the company, not the bank, are included as reconciling items in determining the adjusted cash balance per books.

Bank Reconciliation Illustrated

Illustration 7-7 (page 334) presented the bank statement for Laird Company which the company accessed online. It shows a balance per bank of $15,907.45 on April 30, 2017. On this date the balance of cash per books is $11,709.45.

From the foregoing steps, Laird determines the following reconciling items for the bank.

> ▼ **HELPFUL HINT**
> Note in the bank statement in Illustration 7-7 that the bank has paid checks No. 459 and 461, but check No. 460 is not listed. Thus, this check is outstanding. If a complete bank statement were provided, checks No. 453 and 457 also would not be listed. Laird obtains the amounts for these three checks from its cash payments records.

Step 1. Deposits in transit (+): April 30 deposit (received by bank on May 1).	$2,201.40
Step 2. Outstanding checks (−): No. 453, $3,000.00; No. 457, $1,401.30; No. 460, $1,502.70.	5,904.00
Step 3. Bank errors (+/−): None.	

Reconciling items per books are as follows:

Step 1. Other deposits (+): Unrecorded electronic receipt from customer on account on April 9 determined from the bank statement.	$1,035.00
Step 2. Other payments (−): The electronic payments on April 3 and 7 were previously recorded by the company when they were initiated. Unrecorded charges determined from the bank statement are as follows:	
Returned NSF check on April 29	425.60
Debit and credit card fees on April 30	120.00
Bank service charges on April 30	30.00
Step 3. Company errors (+): Check No. 443 was correctly written by Laird for $1,226 and was correctly paid by the bank on April 12. However, it was recorded as $1,262 on Laird's books.	36.00

Illustration 7-9 shows Laird's bank reconciliation.

ILLUSTRATION 7-9
Bank reconciliation

LAIRD COMPANY Bank Reconciliation April 30, 2017		
Cash balance per bank statement		$ 15,907.45
Add: Deposits in transit		2,201.40
		18,108.85
Less: Outstanding checks		
No. 453	$3,000.00	
No. 457	1,401.30	
No. 460	1,502.70	5,904.00
Adjusted cash balance per bank		**$12,204.85**
Cash balance per books		$ 11,709.45
Add: Electronic funds transfer received	$1,035.00	
Error in recording check No. 443	36.00	1,071.00
		12,780.45
Less: NSF check	425.60	
Debit and credit card fees	120.00	
Bank service charge	30.00	575.60
Adjusted cash balance per books		**$12,204.85**

ALTERNATIVE TERMINOLOGY
The terms *adjusted cash balance, true cash balance,* and *correct cash balance* are used interchangeably.

Entries from Bank Reconciliation

▼ HELPFUL HINT
These entries are adjusting entries. In prior chapters, we considered Cash an account that did not require adjustment because we had not yet explained a bank reconciliation.

The depositor (that is, the company) next must record each reconciling item used to determine the **adjusted cash balance per books**. If the company does not journalize and post these items, the Cash account will not show the correct balance. The adjusting entries for the Laird Company bank reconciliation on April 30 are as follows.

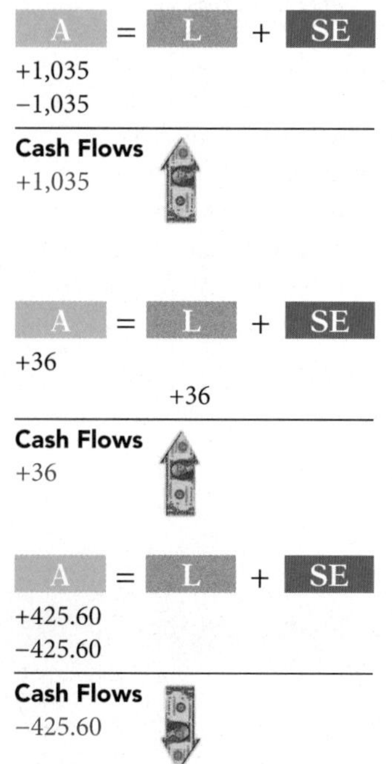

COLLECTION OF ELECTRONIC FUNDS TRANSFER A payment of an account by a customer is recorded in the same way, whether the cash is received through the mail or electronically. The entry is as follows.

Apr. 30	Cash	1,035	
	Accounts Receivable		1,035
	(To record receipt of electronic funds transfer)		

BOOK ERROR An examination of the cash disbursements journal shows that check No. 443 was a payment on account to Andrea Company, a supplier. The correcting entry is as follows.

Apr. 30	Cash	36	
	Accounts Payable—Andrea Company		36
	(To correct error in recording check No. 443)		

NSF CHECK As indicated earlier, an NSF check becomes an accounts receivable to the depositor. The entry is as follows.

Apr. 30	Accounts Receivable—J. R. Baron	425.60	
	Cash		425.60
	(To record NSF check)		

BANK CHARGES EXPENSE Fees for processing debit and credit card transactions are normally debited to the Bank Charges Expense account, as are bank service charges. We have chosen to combine and record these in one journal entry, as shown on the next page, although they also could be journalized separately.

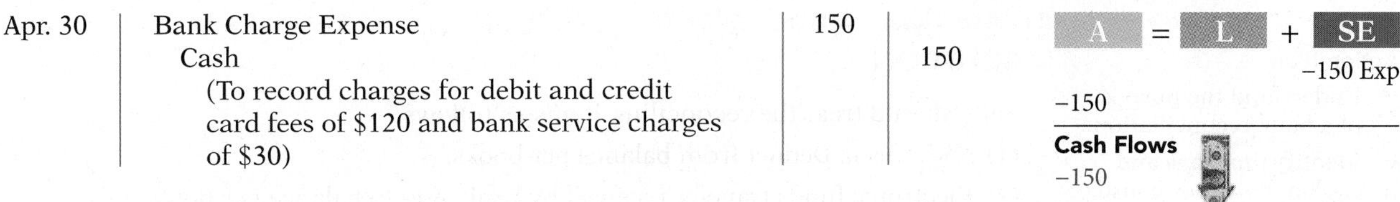

		Debit	Credit
Apr. 30	Bank Charge Expense	150	
	Cash		150
	(To record charges for debit and credit card fees of $120 and bank service charges of $30)		

After Laird posts the entries, the Cash account will appear as in Illustration 7-10. The adjusted cash balance in the ledger should agree with the adjusted cash balance per books in the bank reconciliation in Illustration 7-9 (page 338).

ILLUSTRATION 7-10
Adjusted balance in Cash account

Cash				
Apr. 30	Bal.	11,709.45	Apr. 30	425.60
30		1,035.00	30	150.00
30		36.00		
Apr. 30	Bal.	**12,204.85**		

What entries does the bank make? If the company discovers any bank errors in preparing the reconciliation, it should notify the bank so the bank can make the necessary corrections on its records. The bank does not make any entries for deposits in transit or outstanding checks. Only when these items reach the bank will the bank record these items.

INVESTOR INSIGHT

Mary Altaffer/©AP/Wide World Photos

Madoff's Ponzi Scheme

No recent fraud has generated more interest and rage than the one perpetrated by Bernard Madoff. Madoff was an elite New York investment fund manager who was highly regarded by securities regulators. Investors flocked to him because he delivered steady returns of between 10% and 15%, no matter whether the market was going up or going down. However, for many years, Madoff did not actually invest the cash that people gave to him. Instead, he was running a Ponzi scheme: He paid returns to existing investors using cash received from new investors. As long as the size of his investment fund continued to grow from new investments at a rate that exceeded the amounts that he needed to pay out in returns, Madoff was able to operate his fraud smoothly.

To conceal his misdeeds, Madoff fabricated false investment statements that were provided to investors. In addition, Madoff hired an auditor that never verified the accuracy of the investment records but automatically issued unqualified opinions each year. A competing fund manager warned the SEC a number of times over a nearly 10-year period that he thought Madoff was engaged in fraud. The SEC never aggressively investigated the allegations. Investors, many of which were charitable organizations, lost more than $18 billion. Madoff was sentenced to a jail term of 150 years.

How was Madoff able to conceal such a giant fraud? (Go to WileyPLUS for this answer and additional questions.)

DO IT!  3 Bank Reconciliation

Sally Kist owns Linen Kist Fabrics. Sally asks you to explain how she should treat the following reconciling items when reconciling the company's bank account: (1) a debit memorandum for an NSF check, (2) a credit memorandum for an electronic funds transfer from one of the company's customers received by the bank, (3) outstanding checks, and (4) a deposit in transit.

Action Plan

✔ Understand the purpose of a bank reconciliation.

✔ Identify time lags and explain how they cause reconciling items.

SOLUTION

Sally should treat the reconciling items as follows.

(1) NSF check: Deduct from balance per books.

(2) Electronic funds transfer received by bank: Add to balance per books.

(3) Outstanding checks: Deduct from balance per bank.

(4) Deposit in transit: Add to balance per bank.

Related exercise material: **BE7-8, BE7-9, BE7-10, BE7-11,**  **7-3, E7-6, E7-7, E7-8, E7-9, E7-10,** and **E7-11.**

LEARNING OBJECTIVE 4

Explain the reporting of cash and the basic principles of cash management.

REPORTING CASH

Cash consists of coins, currency (paper money), checks, money orders, and money on hand or on deposit in a bank or similar depository. Checks that are dated later than the current date (post-dated checks) are not included in cash. Companies report cash in two different statements: the balance sheet and the statement of cash flows. The balance sheet reports the amount of cash available at a given point in time. The statement of cash flows shows the sources and uses of cash during a period of time. The statement of cash flows was introduced in Chapters 1 and 2 and will be discussed in much detail in Chapter 12. In this section, we discuss some important points regarding the presentation of cash in the balance sheet.

When presented in a balance sheet, cash on hand, cash in banks, and petty cash are often combined and reported simply as **Cash**. Because it is the most liquid asset owned by the company, cash is listed first in the current assets section of the balance sheet.

Cash Equivalents

Many companies use the designation "Cash and cash equivalents" in reporting cash. (See Illustration 7-11 for an example.) **Cash equivalents** are short-term, highly liquid investments that are both:

1. Readily convertible to known amounts of cash, and
2. So near their maturity that their market value is relatively insensitive to changes in interest rates. (Generally only investments with maturities of three months or less qualify under this definition.)

ILLUSTRATION 7-11
Balance sheet presentation of cash

Real World

DELTA AIR LINES, INC.
Balance Sheet (partial)
December 31, 2013
(in millions)

Assets	
Current assets	
Cash and cash equivalents	**$2,844**
Short-term investments	959
Restricted cash	**122**

Examples of cash equivalents are Treasury bills, commercial paper (short-term corporate notes), and money market funds. All typically are purchased with cash that is in excess of immediate needs.

Occasionally a company will have a net negative balance in its bank account. In this case, the company should report the negative balance among current liabilities. For example, farm equipment manufacturer Ag-Chem at one time reported "Checks outstanding in excess of cash balances" of $2,145,000 among its current liabilities.

ETHICS NOTE

Recently, some companies were forced to restate their financial statements because they had too broadly interpreted which types of investments could be treated as cash equivalents. By reporting these items as cash equivalents, the companies made themselves look more liquid.

Restricted Cash

A company may have **restricted cash**, cash that is not available for general use but rather is restricted for a special purpose. For example, landfill companies are often required to maintain a fund of restricted cash to ensure they will have adequate resources to cover closing and clean-up costs at the end of a landfill site's useful life. McKesson Corp. recently reported restricted cash of $962 million to be paid out as the result of investor lawsuits.

DECISION TOOLS 

Reporting restricted cash helps users determine the amount of cash available for a company's general use.

Cash restricted in use should be reported separately on the balance sheet as restricted cash. If the company expects to use the restricted cash within the next year, it reports the amount as a current asset. When this is not the case, it reports the restricted funds as a noncurrent asset.

Illustration 7-11 shows restricted cash reported in the financial statements of Delta Air Lines. The company is required to maintain restricted cash as collateral to support insurance obligations related to workers' compensation claims. Delta does not have access to these funds for general use, and so it must report them separately, rather than as part of cash and cash equivalents.

DO IT! 4a Reporting Cash

Indicate whether each of the following statements is true or false. If false, indicate how to correct the statement.

1. Cash and cash equivalents are comprised of coins, currency (paper money), money orders, and NSF checks.
2. Restricted cash is classified as either a current asset or noncurrent asset, depending on the circumstances.
3. A company may have a negative balance in its bank account. In this case, it should offset this negative balance against cash and cash equivalents on the balance sheet.
4. Because cash and cash equivalents often includes short-term investments, accounts receivable should be reported as the first item on the balance sheet.

SOLUTION

1. False. NSF checks should be reported as receivables, not cash and cash equivalents. 2. True. 3. False. Companies that have a negative balance in their bank accounts should report the negative balance as a current liability. 4. False. Cash equivalents are readily convertible to known amounts of cash, and so near maturity (less than 3 months) that they are considered more liquid than accounts receivable and therefore are reported before accounts receivable on the balance sheet.

Action Plan

✔ Understand how companies present cash and restricted cash on the balance sheet.

✔ Review the designations of cash equivalents and restricted cash, and how companies typically handle them.

Related exercise material: **BE7-12, DO IT! 7-4a,** and **E7-12.**

MANAGING AND MONITORING CASH

Many companies struggle, not because they fail to generate sales, but because they cannot manage their cash. A real-life example of this is a clothing manufacturing company owned by Sharon McCollick. McCollick gave up a stable, high-paying marketing job with Intel Corporation to start her own company. Soon she had more orders from stores such as JC Penney and Dayton Hudson (now Target) than she could fill. Yet she found herself on the brink of financial disaster, owing three mortgage payments on her house and $2,000 to the IRS. Her company could generate sales, but it was not collecting cash fast enough to support its operations. The bottom line is that a business must have cash.[4]

A merchandising company's operating cycle is generally shorter than that of a manufacturing company. Illustration 7-12 shows the cash to cash operating cycle of a merchandising operation.

ILLUSTRATION 7-12
Operating cycle of a merchandising company

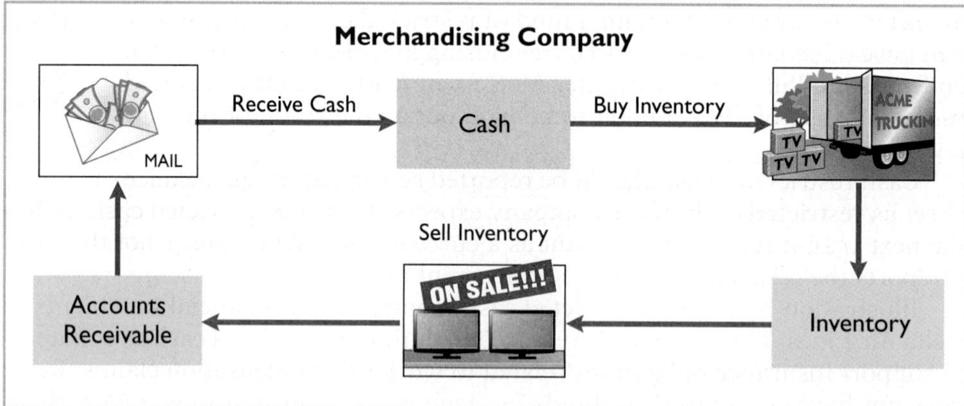

To understand cash management, consider the operating cycle of Sharon McCollick's clothing manufacturing company. First, it purchases cloth. Let's assume that it purchases the cloth on credit provided by the supplier, so the company owes its supplier money. Second, employees convert the cloth to clothing. Now the company also owes its employees money. Third, it sells the clothing to retailers, on credit. McCollick's company will have no money to repay suppliers or employees until it receives payments from customers. In a manufacturing operation, there may be a significant lag between the original purchase of raw materials and the ultimate receipt of cash from customers.

Managing the often-precarious balance created by the ebb and flow of cash during the operating cycle is one of a company's greatest challenges. The objective is to ensure that a company has sufficient cash to meet payments as they come due, yet minimize the amount of non-revenue-generating cash on hand.

Basic Principles of Cash Management

Management of cash is the responsibility of the company **treasurer**. Any company can improve its chances of having adequate cash by following five basic principles of cash management.

1. **Increase the speed of receivables collection.** Money owed Sharon McCollick by her customers is money that she cannot use. The more quickly customers pay her, the more quickly she can use those funds. Thus, rather than have an average collection period of 30 days, she may want an average collection period of 15 days. However, she must carefully weigh any attempt to force her customers to pay earlier against the possibility that she may anger or alienate them. Perhaps her competitors are willing to provide a 30-day grace period. As noted in Chapter 5, one common way to encourage customers to pay more quickly is to offer cash discounts for early payment under such terms as 2/10, n/30.

[4]Adapted from T. Petzinger, Jr., "The Front Lines—Sharon McCollick Got Mad and Tore Down a Bank's Barriers," *Wall Street Journal* (May 19, 1995), p. B1.

2. **Keep inventory levels low.** Maintaining a large inventory of cloth and finished clothing is costly. It ties up large amounts of cash, as well as warehouse space. Increasingly, companies are using techniques to reduce the inventory on hand, thus conserving their cash. Of course, if Sharon McCollick has inadequate inventory, she will lose sales. The proper level of inventory is an important decision.
3. **Monitor payment of liabilities.** Sharon McCollick should monitor when her bills are due, so she avoids paying them too early. Let's say her supplier allows 30 days for payment. If she pays in 10 days, she has lost the use of that cash for 20 days. Therefore, she should use the full payment period. But, she should not pay late. This could damage her credit rating (and future borrowing ability). Also, late payments to suppliers can damage important supplier relationships and may even threaten a supplier's viability. McCollick's company also should conserve cash by taking cash discounts offered by suppliers, when possible.
4. **Plan the timing of major expenditures.** To maintain operations or to grow, all companies must make major expenditures. These often require some form of outside financing. To increase the likelihood of obtaining outside financing, Sharon McCollick should carefully consider the timing of major expenditures in light of her company's operating cycle. If at all possible, she should make any major expenditure when the company normally has excess cash—usually during the off-season.
5. **Invest idle cash.** Cash on hand earns nothing. An important part of the treasurer's job is to ensure that the company invests any excess cash, even if it is only overnight. Many businesses, such as Sharon McCollick's clothing company, are seasonal. During her slow season, when she has excess cash, she should invest it.

   To avoid a cash crisis, it is very important that investments of idle cash be highly liquid and risk-free. A **liquid investment** is one with a market in which someone is always willing to buy or sell the investment. A **risk-free investment** means there is no concern that the party will default on its promise to pay its principal and interest. For example, using excess cash to purchase stock in a small company because you heard that it was probably going to increase in value in the near term is totally inappropriate. First, the stock of small companies is often illiquid. Second, if the stock suddenly decreases in value, you might be forced to sell the stock at a loss in order to pay your bills as they come due. The most common form of liquid investments is interest-paying U.S. government securities.

INTERNATIONAL NOTE
International sales complicate cash management. For example, if Nike must repay a Japanese supplier 30 days from today in Japanese yen, Nike will be concerned about how the exchange rate of U.S. dollars for yen might change during those 30 days. Often, corporate treasurers make investments known as *hedges* to lock in an exchange rate to reduce the company's exposure to exchange-rate fluctuation.

Illustration 7-13 summarizes these five principles of cash management.

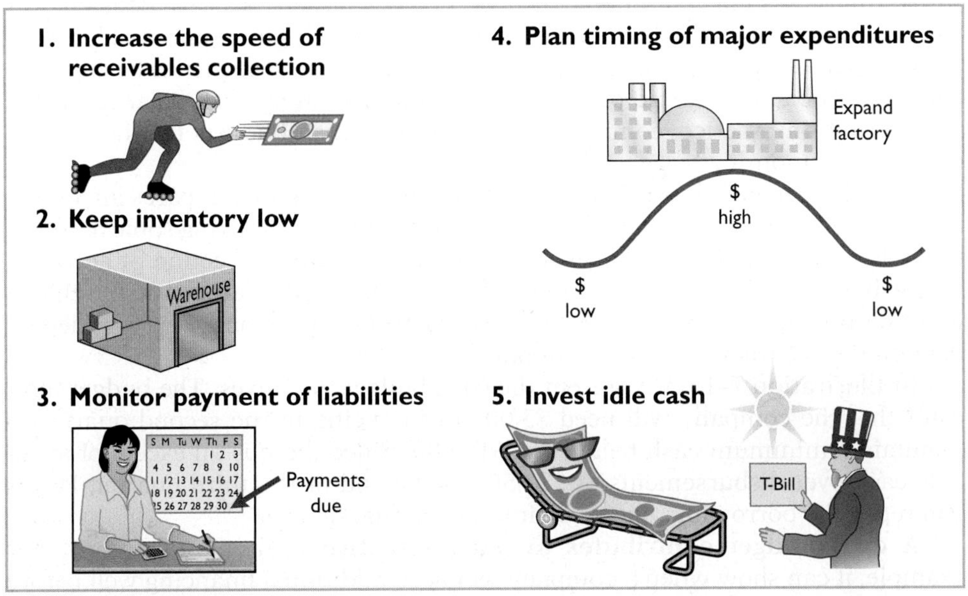

ILLUSTRATION 7-13
Five principles of sound cash management

1. Increase the speed of receivables collection

2. Keep inventory low

Warehouse

3. Monitor payment of liabilities

Payments due

4. Plan timing of major expenditures

Expand factory

$ high

$ low

$ low

5. Invest idle cash

T-Bill

CASH BUDGETING

DECISION TOOLS 

The cash budget helps users determine if the company will be able to meet its projected cash needs.

Because cash is so vital to a company, **planning the company's cash needs** is a key business activity. It enables the company to plan ahead to cover possible cash shortfalls and to make investments of idle funds. The **cash budget** shows anticipated cash flows, usually over a one- to two-year period. In this section, we introduce the basics of cash budgeting. More advanced discussion of cash budgets and budgets in general is provided in managerial accounting texts.

As shown in Illustration 7-14, the cash budget contains three sections—cash receipts, cash disbursements, and financing—and the beginning and ending cash balances.

ILLUSTRATION 7-14
Basic form of cash budget

ANY COMPANY Cash Budget	
Beginning cash balance	$X,XXX
Add: **Cash receipts** (itemized)	X,XXX
Total available cash	X,XXX
Less: **Cash disbursements** (itemized)	X,XXX
Excess (deficiency) of available cash over cash disbursements	X,XXX
Financing	
Add: Borrowings	X,XXX
Less: Repayments	X,XXX
Ending cash balance	$X,XXX

The **Cash receipts** section includes expected receipts from the company's principal source(s) of cash, such as cash sales and collections from customers on credit sales. This section also shows anticipated receipts of interest and dividends, and proceeds from planned sales of investments, plant assets, and the company's capital stock.

The **Cash disbursements** section shows expected payments for inventory, labor, overhead, and selling and administrative expenses. It also includes projected payments for income taxes, dividends, investments, and plant assets. Note that it does not include depreciation since depreciation expense does not use cash.

The **Financing** section shows expected borrowings and repayments of borrowed funds plus interest. Financing is needed when there is a cash deficiency or when the cash balance is less than management's minimum required balance.

Companies must prepare multi-period cash budgets in sequence because the ending cash balance of one period becomes the beginning cash balance for the next period. In practice, companies often prepare cash budgets for the next 12 months on a monthly basis.

To minimize detail, we will assume that Hayes Company prepares an annual cash budget by quarters. Preparing a cash budget requires making some assumptions. For example, Hayes makes assumptions regarding collection of accounts receivable, sales of securities, payments for materials and salaries, and purchases of property, plant, and equipment. The accuracy of the cash budget is very dependent on the accuracy of these assumptions.

In Illustration 7–15, we present the cash budget for Hayes. The budget indicates that the company will need $3,000 of financing in the second quarter to maintain a minimum cash balance of $15,000. Since there is an excess of available cash over disbursements of $22,500 at the end of the third quarter, Hayes will repay the borrowing, plus $100 interest, in that quarter.

A cash budget contributes to more effective cash management. For example, it can show when a company will need additional financing well before the actual need arises. Conversely, it can indicate when the company will have excess cash available for investments or other purposes.

ILLUSTRATION 7-15
Sample cash budget

HAYES COMPANY
Cash Budget
For the Year Ending December 31, 2017

	Quarter			
	1	2	3	4
Beginning cash balance	$ 38,000	$ 25,500	$ 15,000	$ 19,400
Add: **Cash receipts**				
Collections from customers	168,000	198,000	228,000	258,000
Sale of securities	2,000	0	0	0
Total receipts	170,000	198,000	228,000	258,000
Total available cash	208,000	223,500	243,000	277,400
Less: **Cash disbursements**				
Inventory	23,200	27,200	31,200	35,200
Salaries	62,000	72,000	82,000	92,000
Selling and administrative expenses (excluding depreciation)	94,300	99,300	104,300	109,300
Purchase of truck	0	10,000	0	0
Income tax expense	3,000	3,000	3,000	3,000
Total disbursements	182,500	211,500	220,500	239,500
Excess (deficiency) of available cash over disbursements	25,500	12,000	22,500	37,900
Financing				
Add: Borrowings	0	3,000	0	0
Less: Repayments—plus $100 interest	0	0	3,100	0
Ending cash balance	$ 25,500	$ 15,000	$ 19,400	$ 37,900

DO IT! 4b Cash Budget

Martian Company's management wants to maintain a minimum monthly cash balance of $15,000. At the beginning of March, the cash balance is $16,500, expected cash receipts for March are $210,000, and cash disbursements are expected to be $220,000. How much cash, if any, must Martian borrow to maintain the desired minimum monthly balance?

SOLUTION

Beginning cash balance	$ 16,500
Add: Cash receipts for March	210,000
Total available cash	226,500
Less: Cash disbursements for March	220,000
Excess of available cash over cash disbursements	6,500
Financing	
Add: **Borrowings**	**8,500**
Ending cash balance	$ 15,000

To maintain the desired minimum cash balance of $15,000, Martian Company must borrow $8,500 of cash.

Action Plan

- ✔ Add the beginning cash balance to receipts to determine total available cash.
- ✔ Subtract disbursements to determine excess or deficiency.
- ✔ Compare excess or deficiency with desired minimum cash to determine borrowing needs.

Related exercise material: **BE7-13, DO IT! 7-4b,** and **E7-14.**

USING DECISION TOOLS—MATTEL CORPORATION

Presented below is hypothetical financial information for Mattel Corporation from the year ended December 31, 2016. Mattel is a toy manufacturing company, at one time named by *Fortune* magazine as one of the top 100 companies for which to work.

Selected Financial Information
Year Ended December 31, 2016
(in millions)

Net cash provided by operating activities	$325
Capital expenditures	162
Dividends paid	80
Total expenses	680
Depreciation expense	40
Cash balance	206

Also provided below are estimates of the company's sources and uses of cash during the year ended December 31, 2017. This information should be used to prepare a cash budget for 2017.

Projected Sources and Uses of Cash
(in millions)

Beginning cash balance	$206
Cash receipts from sales of product	355
Cash receipts from sale of short-term investments	20
Cash payments for inventory	357
Cash payments for selling and administrative costs	201
Cash payments for property, plant, and equipment	45
Cash payments for taxes	17

Mattel's management believes it should maintain a balance of $200 million cash.

INSTRUCTIONS

(a) Using the hypothetical projected sources and uses of cash information presented above, prepare a cash budget for 2017 for Mattel Corporation.

(b) Comment on the company's cash adequacy, and discuss steps that might be taken to improve its cash position.

SOLUTION

(a)

MATTEL CORPORATION
Cash Budget
For the Year Ending December 31, 2017
(in millions)

Beginning cash balance		$206
Add: Cash receipts		
From sales of product	$355	
From sale of short-term investments	20	375
Total available cash		581
Less: Cash disbursements		
Payments for inventory	357	
Payments for selling and administrative costs	201	
Payments for property, plant, and equipment	45	
Payments for taxes	17	
Total disbursements		620
Excess (deficiency) of available cash over disbursements		(39)
Financing		
Add: **Borrowings**		**239**
Ending cash balance		$200

(b) Using these hypothetical data, Mattel's cash position appears adequate. For 2017, Mattel is projecting a cash shortfall. This is not necessarily of concern, but it should be investigated. Its primary line of business is toys. Most toys are sold during December. We would expect Mattel's cash position to vary significantly during the course of the year. After the holiday season, once its customers have paid Mattel, it probably has a lot of excess cash. However, when it is making and selling its product but has not yet been paid, it may need to borrow to meet any temporary cash shortfalls.

If Mattel's management is concerned with its cash position, it could take the following steps. (1) Offer its customers cash discounts for early payment, such as 2/10, n/30. (2) Implement inventory management techniques to reduce the need for large inventories of such things as the plastics used to make its toys. (3) Carefully time payments to suppliers by keeping track of when payments are due, so as not to pay too early. (4) If it has plans for major expenditures, time those expenditures to coincide with its seasonal period of excess cash.

LEARNING OBJECTIVE *5

APPENDIX 7A: Explain the operation of a petty cash fund.

The operation of a petty cash fund involves (1) establishing the fund, (2) making payments from the fund, and (3) replenishing the fund.

ESTABLISHING THE PETTY CASH FUND

ETHICS NOTE

Petty cash funds are authorized and legitimate. In contrast, "slush" funds are unauthorized and hidden (under the table).

Two essential steps in establishing a petty cash fund are (1) appointing a petty cash custodian who will be responsible for the fund, and (2) determining the size of the fund. Ordinarily, a company expects the amount in the fund to cover anticipated disbursements for a three- to four-week period.

When the company establishes the petty cash fund, it issues a check payable to the petty cash custodian for the stipulated amount. If Laird Company decides to establish a $100 fund on March 1, the entry in general journal form is as follows.

Mar. 1	Petty Cash	100	
	Cash		100
	(To establish a petty cash fund)		

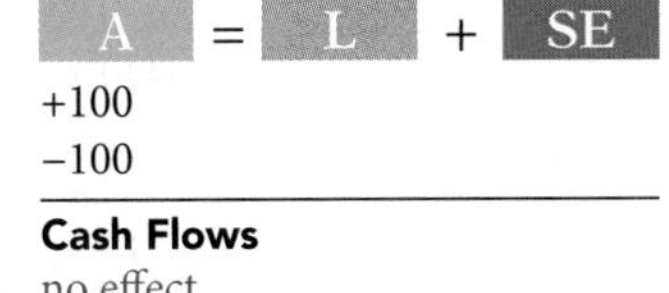

The fund custodian cashes the check and places the proceeds in a locked petty cash box or drawer. Most petty cash funds are established on a fixed-amount basis. Moreover, the company will make no additional entries to the Petty Cash account unless the stipulated amount of the fund is changed. For example, if Laird decides on July 1 to increase the size of the fund to $250, it would debit Petty Cash $150 and credit Cash $150.

MAKING PAYMENTS FROM PETTY CASH

The custodian of the petty cash fund has the authority to make payments from the fund that conform to prescribed management policies. Usually, management limits the size of expenditures that come from petty cash and does not permit use of the fund for certain types of transactions (such as making short-term loans to employees).

Each payment from the fund must be documented on a prenumbered petty cash receipt (or petty cash voucher). The signatures of both the custodian and the individual receiving payment are required on the receipt. If other supporting documents such as a freight bill or invoice are available, they should be attached to the petty cash receipt.

▼ HELPFUL HINT

From the standpoint of internal control, the petty cash receipt satisfies two principles: (1) establishment of responsibility (signature of custodian), and (2) documentation procedures.

The custodian keeps the receipts in the petty cash box until the fund is replenished. As a result, the sum of the petty cash receipts and money in the fund should equal the established total at all times. This means that management can make surprise counts at any time by an independent person, such as an internal auditor, to determine the correctness of the fund.

The company does not make an accounting entry to record a payment at the time it is taken from petty cash. It is considered both inexpedient and unnecessary to do so. Instead, the company recognizes the accounting effects of each payment when the fund is replenished.

REPLENISHING THE PETTY CASH FUND

▼ **HELPFUL HINT**
Replenishing involves three internal control procedures: segregation of duties, documentation procedures, and independent internal verification.

When the money in the petty cash fund reaches a minimum level, the company replenishes the fund. The petty cash custodian initiates a request for reimbursement. This individual prepares a schedule (or summary) of the payments that have been made and sends the schedule, supported by petty cash receipts and other documentation, to the treasurer's office. The receipts and supporting documents are examined in the treasurer's office to verify that they were proper payments from the fund. The treasurer then approves the request, and a check is prepared to restore the fund to its established amount. At the same time, all supporting documentation is stamped "paid" so that it cannot be submitted again for payment.

To illustrate, assume that on March 15 the petty cash custodian requests a check for $87. The fund contains $13 cash and petty cash receipts for postage $44, supplies $38, and miscellaneous expenses $5. The entry, in general journal form, to record the check is as follows.

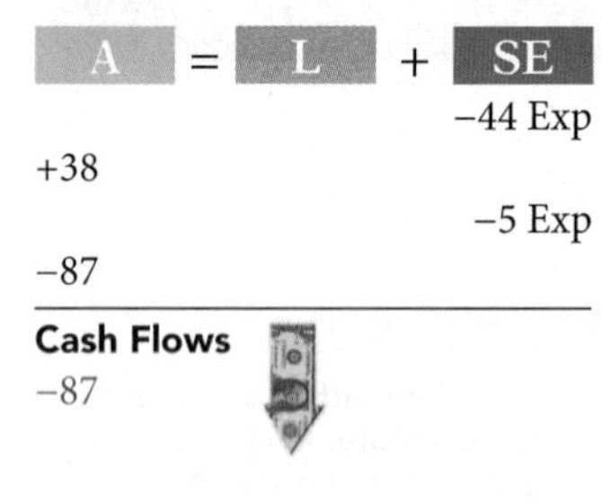

Date	Account	Debit	Credit
Mar. 15	Postage Expense	44	
	Supplies	38	
	Miscellaneous Expense	5	
	Cash		87
	(To replenish petty cash fund)		

Note that the reimbursement entry does not affect the Petty Cash account. Replenishment changes the composition of the fund by replacing the petty cash receipts with cash, but it does not change the balance in the fund.

Occasionally, in replenishing a petty cash fund the company may need to recognize a cash shortage or overage. To illustrate, assume in the preceding example that the custodian had only $12 in cash in the fund plus the receipts as listed. The request for reimbursement would therefore be for $88, and the following entry would be made.

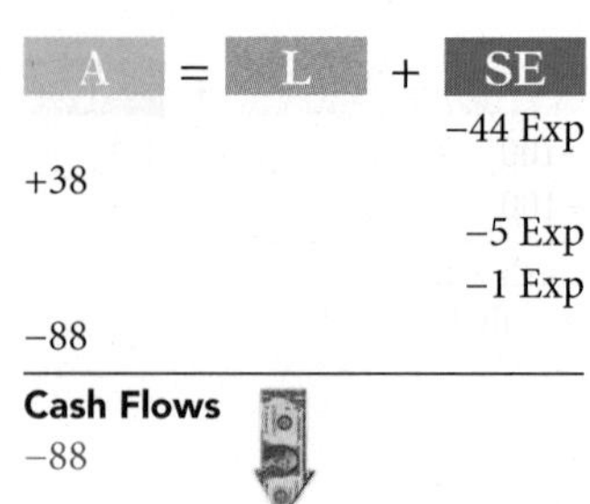

Date	Account	Debit	Credit
Mar. 15	Postage Expense	44	
	Supplies	38	
	Miscellaneous Expense	5	
	Cash Over and Short	1	
	Cash		88
	(To replenish petty cash fund)		

Conversely, if the custodian had $14 in cash, the reimbursement request would be for $86, and Cash Over and Short would be credited for $1. A debit balance in Cash Over and Short is reported in the income statement as miscellaneous expense; a credit balance is reported as miscellaneous revenue. The company closes Cash Over and Short to Income Summary at the end of the year.

Companies should replenish a petty cash fund **at the end of the accounting period, regardless of the cash in the fund**. Replenishment at this time is necessary in order to recognize the effects of the petty cash payments on the financial statements.

Internal control over a petty cash fund is strengthened by (1) having a supervisor make surprise counts of the fund to ascertain whether the paid petty cash receipts and fund cash equal the designated amount, and (2) canceling or mutilating the paid petty cash receipts so they cannot be resubmitted for reimbursement.

REVIEW AND PRACTICE

▶ LEARNING OBJECTIVES REVIEW

1 Define fraud and the principles of internal control. A fraud is a dishonest act by an employee that results in personal benefit to the employee at a cost to the employer. The fraud triangle refers to the three factors that contribute to fraudulent activity by employees: opportunity, financial pressure, and rationalization. Internal control consists of all the related methods and measures adopted within an organization to safeguard assets, enhance the reliability of accounting records, increase efficiency of operations, and ensure compliance with laws and regulations.

The principles of internal control are establishment of responsibility, segregation of duties, documentation procedures, physical controls, independent internal verification, and human resource controls.

2 Apply internal control principles to cash. Internal controls over cash receipts include (a) designating only personnel such as cashiers to handle cash; (b) assigning the duties of receiving cash, recording cash, and having custody of cash to different individuals; (c) obtaining remittance advices for mail receipts, cash register tapes or computer records for over-the-counter receipts, and deposit slips for bank deposits; (d) using company safes and bank vaults to store cash with access limited to authorized personnel, and using cash registers or point-of-sale terminals in executing over-the-counter receipts; (e) making independent daily counts of register receipts and daily comparisons of total receipts with total deposits; and (f) conducting background checks and bonding personnel who handle cash, as well as requiring them to take vacations.

Internal controls over cash disbursements include (a) having only specified individuals such as the treasurer authorized to sign checks and approve vendors; (b) assigning the duties of approving items for payment, paying the items, and recording the payment to different individuals; (c) using prenumbered checks and accounting for all checks, with each check supported by an approved invoice; after payment, stamping each approved invoice "paid"; (d) storing blank checks in a safe or vault with access restricted to authorized personnel, and using a machine with indelible ink to imprint amounts on checks; (e) comparing each check with the approved invoice before issuing the check, and making monthly reconciliations of bank and book balances; and (f) bonding personnel who handle cash, requiring employees to take vacations, and conducting background checks.

3 Identify the control features of a bank account. In reconciling the bank account, it is customary to reconcile the balance per books and the balance per bank to their adjusted balance. The steps reconciling the Cash account are to determine deposits in transit and electronic funds transfers received by bank, outstanding checks, errors by the depositor or the bank, and unrecorded bank memoranda.

4 Explain the reporting of cash and the basic principles of cash management. Cash is listed first in the current assets section of the balance sheet. Companies often report cash together with cash equivalents. Cash restricted for a special purpose is reported separately as a current asset or as a noncurrent asset, depending on when the company expects to use the cash.

The basic principles of cash management include (a) increase the speed of receivables collection, (b) keep inventory levels low, (c) monitor the timing of payment of liabilities, (d) plan timing of major expenditures, and (e) invest idle cash.

The three main elements of a cash budget are the cash receipts section, cash disbursements section, and financing section.

***5 Explain the operation of a petty cash fund.** In operating a petty cash fund, a company establishes the fund by appointing a custodian and determining the size of the fund. The custodian makes payments from the fund for documented expenditures. The company replenishes the fund as needed, and at the end of each accounting period. Accounting entries to record payments are made each time the fund is replenished.

DECISION TOOLS REVIEW

DECISION CHECKPOINTS	INFO NEEDED FOR DECISION	TOOL TO USE FOR DECISION	HOW TO EVALUATE RESULTS
Are the company's financial statements supported by adequate internal controls?	Auditor's report, management discussion and analysis, articles in financial press	The principles of internal control activities are (1) establishment of responsibility, (2) segregation of duties, (3) documentation procedures, (4) physical controls, (5) independent internal verification, and (6) human resource controls.	If any indication is given that these or other controls are lacking, use the financial statements with caution.
Is all of the company's cash available for general use?	Balance sheet and notes to financial statements	The company reports restricted cash in assets section of balance sheet.	A restriction on the use of cash limits management's ability to use those resources for general obligations. This might be considered when assessing liquidity.
Will the company be able to meet its projected cash needs?	Cash budget (typically available only to management)	The cash budget shows projected sources and uses of cash. If cash uses exceed internal cash sources, then the company must look for outside sources.	Two issues: (1) Are management's projections reasonable? (2) If outside sources are needed, are they available?

GLOSSARY REVIEW

Bank reconciliation The process of comparing the bank's account balance with the company's balance, and explaining the differences to make them agree. (p. 333).

Bank statement A statement received monthly from the bank that shows the depositor's bank transactions and balances. (p. 333).

Bonding Obtaining insurance protection against theft by employees. (p. 325).

Cash Resources that consist of coins, currency, checks, money orders, and money on hand or on deposit in a bank or similar depository. (p. 340).

Cash budget A projection of anticipated cash flows, usually over a one- to two-year period. (p. 344).

Cash equivalents Short-term, highly liquid investments that can be readily converted to a specific amount of cash and which are relatively insensitive to interest rate changes. (p. 340).

Deposits in transit Deposits recorded by the depositor that have not been recorded by the bank. (p. 335).

Electronic funds transfer (EFT) A disbursement system that uses wire, telephone, or computer to transfer cash from one location to another. (p. 333).

Fraud A dishonest act by an employee that results in personal benefit to the employee at a cost to the employer. (p. 318).

Fraud triangle The three factors that contribute to fraudulent activity by employees: opportunity, financial pressure, and rationalization. (p. 318).

Internal auditors Company employees who continuously evaluate the effectiveness of the company's internal control systems. (p. 325).

Internal control A process designed to provide reasonable assurance regarding the achievement of company objectives related to operations, reporting, and compliance. (p. 319).

NSF check A check that is not paid by a bank because of insufficient funds in a bank account. (p. 334).

Outstanding checks Checks issued and recorded by a company that have not been paid by the bank. (p. 335).

Petty cash fund A cash fund used to pay relatively small amounts. (p. 331).

Restricted cash Cash that is not available for general use but instead is restricted for a particular purpose. (p. 341).

Sarbanes-Oxley Act (SOX) Law that requires publicly traded companies to maintain adequate systems of internal control. (p. 318).

Treasurer Employee responsible for the management of a company's cash. (p. 342).

Voucher An authorization form prepared for each expenditure in a voucher system. (p. 330).

Voucher system A network of approvals by authorized individuals, acting independently, to ensure that all disbursements by check are proper. (p. 330).

PRACTICE MULTIPLE-CHOICE QUESTIONS

(LO 1) 1. Which of the following is **not** an element of the fraud triangle?
(a) Rationalization. (c) Segregation of duties.
(b) Financial pressure. (d) Opportunity.

(LO 1) 2. Internal control is used in a business to enhance the accuracy and reliability of its accounting records and to:
(a) safeguard its assets.
(b) prevent fraud.
(c) produce correct financial statements.
(d) deter employee dishonesty.

(LO 1) 3. The principles of internal control do **not** include:
(a) establishment of responsibility.
(b) documentation procedures.
(c) management responsibility.
(d) independent internal verification.

(LO 1) 4. Physical controls do **not** include:
(a) safes and vaults to store cash.
(b) independent bank reconciliations.
(c) locked warehouses for inventories.
(d) bank safety deposit boxes for important papers.

(LO 1) 5. Which of the following was **not** a result of the Sarbanes-Oxley Act?
(a) Companies must file financial statements with the Internal Revenue Service.
(b) All publicly traded companies must maintain adequate internal controls.
(c) The Public Company Accounting Oversight Board was created to establish auditing standards and regulate auditor activity.
(d) Corporate executives and boards of directors must ensure that controls are reliable and effective, and they can be fined or imprisoned for failure to do so.

6. Which of the following control activities is **not** relevant when a company uses a computerized (rather than manual) accounting system? (LO 1)
(a) Establishment of responsibility.
(b) Segregation of duties.
(c) Independent internal verification.
(d) All of these control activities are relevant to a computerized system.

7. Permitting only designated personnel such as cashiers to handle cash receipts is an application of the principle of: (LO 2)
(a) segregation of duties.
(b) establishment of responsibility.
(c) independent internal verification.
(d) human resource controls.

8. The use of prenumbered checks in disbursing cash is an application of the principle of: (LO 2)
(a) establishment of responsibility.
(b) segregation of duties.
(c) physical controls.
(d) documentation procedures.

(LO 3) 9. The control features of a bank account do **not** include:
(a) having bank auditors verify the correctness of the bank balance per books.
(b) minimizing the amount of cash that must be kept on hand.
(c) providing a double record of all bank transactions.
(d) safeguarding cash by using a bank as a depository.

(LO 3) 10. In a bank reconciliation, deposits in transit are:
(a) deducted from the book balance.
(b) added to the book balance.
(c) added to the bank balance.
(d) deducted from the bank balance.

(LO 3) 11. The reconciling item in a bank reconciliation that will result in an adjusting entry by the depositor is:
(a) outstanding checks. (c) a bank error.
(b) deposit in transit. (d) bank service charges.

(LO 4) 12. Which of the following items in a cash drawer at November 30 is **not** cash?
(a) Money orders.
(b) Coins and currency.
(c) An NSF check.
(d) A customer check dated November 28.

(LO 4) 13. Which statement correctly describes the reporting of cash?
(a) Cash cannot be combined with cash equivalents.
(b) Restricted cash funds may be combined with cash.
(c) Cash is listed first in the current assets section.
(d) Restricted cash funds cannot be reported as a current asset.

14. Which of the following would **not** be an example of good cash management? (LO 4)
(a) Provide discounts to customers to encourage early payment.
(b) Invest temporary excess cash in stock of a small company.
(c) Carefully monitor payments so that payments are not made early.
(d) Employ just-in-time inventory methods to keep inventory low.

15. Which of the following is **not** one of the sections of a cash budget? (LO 4)
(a) Cash receipts section.
(b) Cash disbursements section.
(c) Financing section.
(d) Cash from operations section.

*16. A check is written to replenish a $100 petty cash fund when the fund contains receipts of $94 and $4 in cash. In recording the check: (LO 5)
(a) debit Cash Over and Short for $2.
(b) debit Petty Cash for $94.
(c) credit Cash for $94.
(d) credit Petty Cash for $2.

SOLUTIONS

1. **(c)** Segregation of duties is not an element of the fraud triangle. The other choices are fraud triangle elements.
2. **(a)** Safeguarding assets is one of the purposes of using internal control. The other choices are incorrect because while internal control can help to (b) prevent fraud, (c) produce correct financial statements, and (d) deter employee dishonesty, these are not the main purposes of using it.
3. **(c)** Management responsibility is not one of the principles of internal control. The other choices are true statements.
4. **(b)** Independent bank reconciliations are not a physical control. The other choices are true statements.
5. **(a)** Filing financial statements with the IRS is not a result of the Sarbanes-Oxley Act (SOX); SOX focuses on the prevention or detection of fraud. The other choices are results of SOX.
6. **(d)** Establishment of responsibility, segregation of duties, and independent internal verification are all relevant to a computerized system. Although choices (a), (b), and (c) are correct, choice (d) is the better answer.
7. **(b)** Permitting only designated personnel to handle cash receipts is an application of the principle of establishment of responsibility, not (a) segregation of duties, (c) independent internal verification, or (d) human resource controls.
8. **(d)** The use of prenumbered checks in disbursing cash is an application of the principle of documentation procedures, not (a) establishment of responsibility, (b) segregation of duties, or (c) physical controls.
9. **(a)** Having bank auditors verify the correctness of the bank balance per books is not one of the control features of a bank account. The other choices are true statements.
10. **(c)** Deposits in transit are added to the bank balance on a bank reconciliation, not (a) deducted from the book balance, (b) added to the book balance, or (d) deducted from the bank balance.
11. **(d)** Because the depositor does not know the amount of the bank service charges until the bank statement is received, an adjusting entry must be made when the statement is received. The other choices are incorrect because (a) outstanding checks do not require an adjusting entry by the depositor because the checks have already been recorded in the depositor's books, (b) deposits in transit do not require an adjusting entry by the depositor because the deposits have already been recorded in the depositor's books, and (c) bank errors do not require an adjusting entry by the depositor, but the depositor does need to inform the bank of the error so it can be corrected.
12. **(c)** An NSF check should not be considered cash. The other choices are true statements.
13. **(c)** Cash is listed first in the current assets section. The other choices are incorrect because (a) cash and cash equivalents can be appropriately combined when reporting cash on the balance sheet, (b) restricted cash is not to be combined with cash when reporting cash on the balance sheet, and (d) restricted funds can be reported as current assets if they will be used within one year.

14. **(b)** Investing excess cash to purchase stock in a small company is inappropriate because the stock of small companies is often not easily converted to cash. Choices (a) providing discounts to customers to encourage early payment, (c) carefully monitoring payments so that cash is held until just before the payment date of liabilities, and (d) keeping inventory levels low are all good cash management practices.

15. **(d)** Cash from operations is not a section of a cash budget. Choices (a) cash receipts section, (b) cash disbursements section, and (c) financing section are all elements of a cash budget.

*16. **(a)** When this check is recorded, the company should debit Cash Over and Short for the shortage of $2 (total of the receipts plus cash in the drawer ($98) versus $100), not (b) debit Petty Cash for $94, (c) credit Cash for $94, or (d) credit Petty Cash for $2.

PRACTICE EXERCISES

Indicate whether procedure is good or weak internal control.

(LO 1, 2)

1. Listed below are five procedures followed by Shepherd Company.

1. Total cash receipts are compared to bank deposits daily by someone who has no other cash responsibilities.
2. Time clocks are used for recording time worked by employees.
3. Employees are required to take vacations.
4. Any member of the sales department can approve credit sales.
5. Sam Hill ships goods to customers, bills customers, and receives payment from customers.

INSTRUCTIONS

Indicate whether each procedure is an example of good internal control or of weak internal control. If it is an example of good internal control, indicate which internal control principle is being followed. If it is an example of weak internal control, indicate which internal control principle is violated. Use the table below.

Procedure	IC Good or Weak?	Related Internal Control Principle
1.		
2.		
3.		
4.		
5.		

SOLUTION

1.

Procedure	IC Good or Weak?	Related Internal Control Principle
1.	Good	Independent internal verification
2.	Good	Physical controls
3.	Good	Human resource controls
4.	Weak	Establishment of responsibility
5.	Weak	Segregation of duties

Prepare bank reconciliation and adjusting entries.

(LO 3)

2. The information below relates to the Cash account in the ledger of Ansel Company.

Balance June 1—$17,450; Cash deposited—$64,000.
Balance June 30—$17,704; Checks written—$63,746.

The June bank statement shows a balance of $16,422 on June 30 and the following memoranda.

Credits		Debits	
Collection of $1,530 through electronic funds transfer	$1,530	NSF check: Anne Adams	$425
Interest earned on checking account	$35	Safety deposit box rent	$55

At June 30, deposits in transit were $4,750, and outstanding checks totaled $2,383.

INSTRUCTIONS

(a) Prepare the bank reconciliation at June 30.

(b) Prepare the adjusting entries at June 30, assuming (1) the NSF check was from a customer on account, and (2) no interest had been accrued on the note.

SOLUTION

2. (a)

ANSEL COMPANY
Bank Reconciliation
June 30

Cash balance per bank statement		$16,422
Add: Deposits in transit		4,750
		21,172
Less: Outstanding checks		2,383
Adjusted cash balance per bank		$18,789
Cash balance per books		$17,704
Add: Electronic funds transfer received	$1,530	
Interest earned	35	1,565
		19,269
Less: NSF check	425	
Safety deposit box rent	55	480
Adjusted cash balance per books		$18,789

(b)

June 30	Cash	1,530	
	Accounts Receivable		1,530
30	Cash	35	
	Interest Revenue		35
30	Accounts Receivable (Anne Adams)	425	
	Cash		425
30	Bank Charges Expense	55	
	Cash		55

PRACTICE PROBLEM

Prepare bank reconciliation and journalize entries.

(LO 3)

Trillo Company's bank statement for May 2017 shows these data.

Balance May 1	$12,650	Balance May 31	$14,280
Debit memorandum:		Credit memorandum:	
NSF check	175	Collection of electronic funds transfer	505

The cash balance per books at May 31 is $13,319. Your review of the data reveals the following.

1. The NSF check was from Hup Co., a customer.
2. Outstanding checks at May 31 total $2,410.
3. Deposits in transit at May 31 total $1,752.
4. A Trillo Company check for $352 dated May 10 cleared the bank on May 25. This check, which was a payment on account, was journalized for $325.

INSTRUCTIONS

(a) Prepare a bank reconciliation at May 31.

(b) Journalize the entries required by the reconciliation.

SOLUTION

(a)

Cash balance per bank statement		$14,280
Add: Deposits in transit		1,752
		16,032
Less: Outstanding checks		2,410
Adjusted cash balance per bank		$13,622
Cash balance per books		$13,319
Add: Electronic funds transfer received		505
		13,824
Less: NSF check	$175	
Error in recording check ($352 − $325)	27	202
Adjusted cash balance per books		$13,622

(b)

Date	Account	Debit	Credit
May 31	Cash	505	
	Accounts Receivable		505
	(To record receipt of electronic funds transfer)		
31	Accounts Receivable (Hup Co.)	175	
	Cash		175
	(To record NSF check from Hup Co.)		
31	Accounts Payable	27	
	Cash		27
	(To correct error in recording check)		

WileyPLUS Brief Exercises, DO IT! Exercises, Exercises, Problems, and many additional resources are available for practice in WileyPLUS.

NOTE: All asterisked Questions, Exercises, and Problems relate to material in the appendix to the chapter.

QUESTIONS

1. A local bank reported that it lost $150,000 as the result of employee fraud. Ray Fairburn is not clear on what is meant by "employee fraud." Explain the meaning of fraud to Ray and give an example of fraud that might occur at a bank.
2. Fraud experts often say that there are three primary factors that contribute to employee fraud. Identify the three factors and explain what is meant by each.
3. Identify the five components of a good internal control system.
4. "Internal control is concerned only with enhancing the accuracy of the accounting records." Do you agree? Explain.
5. Discuss how the Sarbanes-Oxley Act has increased the importance of internal control to top managers of a company.
6. What principles of internal control apply to most businesses?
7. In the corner grocery store, all sales clerks make change out of one cash register drawer. Is this a violation of internal control? Why?
8. Branden Doyle is reviewing the principle of segregation of duties. What are the two common applications of this principle?
9. How do documentation procedures contribute to good internal control?
10. What internal control objectives are met by physical controls?
11. (a) Explain the control principle of independent internal verification.
    (b) What practices are important in applying this principle?
12. As the company accountant, explain the following ideas to the management of Ortiz Company.
    (a) The concept of reasonable assurance in internal control.
    (b) The importance of the human factor in internal control.
13. Discuss the human resources department's involvement in internal controls.
14. Robbins Inc. owns the following assets at the balance sheet date.

Cash in bank—savings account	$ 8,000
Cash on hand	1,100
Cash refund due from the IRS	1,000
Checking account balance	12,000
Postdated checks	500

What amount should be reported as Cash in the balance sheet?

15. What principle(s) of internal control is (are) involved in making daily cash counts of over-the-counter receipts?

16. Assume that Kohl's Department Stores installed new cash registers in its stores. How do cash registers improve internal control over cash receipts?

17. At Lazlo Wholesale Company, two mail clerks open all mail receipts. How does this strengthen internal control?

18. "To have maximum effective internal control over cash disbursements, all payments should be made by check." Is this true? Explain.

19. Pauli Company's internal controls over cash disbursements provide for the treasurer to sign checks imprinted by a checkwriter after comparing the check with the approved invoice. Identify the internal control principles that are present in these controls.

20. How do these principles apply to cash disbursements?
(a) Physical controls.
(b) Human resource controls.

21. What is the essential feature of an electronic funds transfer (EFT) procedure?

22. "The use of a bank contributes significantly to good internal control over cash." Is this true? Why?

23. Hank Cook is confused about the lack of agreement between the cash balance per books and the balance per bank. Explain the causes for the lack of agreement to Hank and give an example of each cause.

24. Identify the basic principles of cash management.

25. Trisha Massey asks for your help concerning an NSF check. Explain to Trisha (a) what an NSF check is, (b) how it is treated in a bank reconciliation, and (c) whether it will require an adjusting entry on the company's books.

26.
(a) Describe cash equivalents and explain how they are reported.
(b) How should restricted cash funds be reported on the balance sheet?

27. What was Apple's balance in cash and cash equivalents at December 31, 2014? Did it report any restricted cash? How did Apple define cash equivalents?

*28. (a) Identify the three activities that pertain to a petty cash fund, and indicate an internal control principle that is applicable to each activity.
(b) When are journal entries required in the operation of a petty cash fund?

BRIEF EXERCISES

BE7-1 Match each situation with the fraud triangle factor (opportunity, financial pressure, or rationalization) that best describes it.

Identify fraud triangle concepts.
(LO 1), C

(a) An employee's monthly credit card payments are nearly 75% of their monthly earnings.
(b) An employee earns minimum wage at a firm that has reported record earnings for each of the last five years.
(c) An employee has an expensive gambling habit.
(d) An employee has check-writing and -signing responsibilities for a small company, and is also responsible for reconciling the bank account.

BE7-2 Pat Buhn is the new owner of Young Co. She has heard about internal control but is not clear about its importance for her business. Explain to Pat the four purposes of internal control, and give her one application of each purpose for Young Co.

Explain the importance of internal control.
(LO 1), C

BE7-3 The internal control procedures in Dayton Company result in the following provisions. Identify the principles of internal control that are being followed in each case.

Identify internal control principles.
(LO 1), C

(a) Employees who have physical custody of assets do not have access to the accounting records.
(b) Each month, the assets on hand are compared to the accounting records by an internal auditor.
(c) A prenumbered shipping document is prepared for each shipment of goods to customers.

BE7-4 Jolson Company has the following internal control procedures over cash receipts. Identify the internal control principle that is applicable to each procedure.

Identify the internal control principles applicable to cash receipts.
(LO 2), C

(a) All over-the-counter receipts are entered in cash registers.
(b) All cashiers are bonded.
(c) Daily cash counts are made by cashier department supervisors.
(d) The duties of receiving cash, recording cash, and having custody of cash are assigned to different individuals.
(e) Only cashiers may operate cash registers.

Make journal entry using cash count sheet.

(LO 2), AP

BE7-5 While examining cash receipts information, the accounting department determined the following information: opening cash balance $150, cash on hand $1,125.74, and cash sales per register tape $988.62. Prepare the required journal entry based upon the cash count sheet.

Identify the internal control principles applicable to cash disbursements.

(LO 2), C

BE7-6 Tott Company has the following internal control procedures over cash disbursements. Identify the internal control principle that is applicable to each procedure.
(a) Company checks are prenumbered.
(b) The bank statement is reconciled monthly by an internal auditor.
(c) Blank checks are stored in a safe in the treasurer's office.
(d) Only the treasurer or assistant treasurer may sign checks.
(e) Check-signers are not allowed to record cash disbursement transactions.

Identify the control features of a bank account.

(LO 3), C

BE7-7 Luke Roye is uncertain about the control features of a bank account. Explain the control benefits of (a) a checking account and (b) a bank statement.

Indicate location of reconciling items in a bank reconciliation.

(LO 3), C

BE7-8 The following reconciling items are applicable to the bank reconciliation for Forde Co. Indicate how each item should be shown on a bank reconciliation.
(a) Outstanding checks.
(b) Bank debit memorandum for service charge.
(c) Bank credit memorandum for collecting an electronic funds transfer.
(d) Deposit in transit.

Identify reconciling items that require adjusting entries.

(LO 3), C

BE7-9 Using the data in BE7-8, indicate (a) the items that will result in an adjustment to the depositor's records and (b) why the other items do not require adjustment.

Prepare partial bank reconciliation.

(LO 3), AP

BE7-10 At July 31, Planter Company has this bank information: cash balance per bank $7,291, outstanding checks $762, deposits in transit $1,350, and a bank service charge $40. Determine the adjusted cash balance per bank at July 31.

Analyze outstanding checks.

(LO 3), AP

BE7-11 In the month of November, Fiesta Company Inc. wrote checks in the amount of $9,750. In December, checks in the amount of $11,762 were written. In November, $8,800 of these checks were presented to the bank for payment, and $10,889 in December. What is the amount of outstanding checks at the end of November? At the end of December?

Explain the statement presentation of cash balances.

(LO 4), C

BE7-12 Spahn Company has these cash balances: cash in bank $12,742, payroll bank account $6,000, and plant expansion fund cash $25,000. Explain how each balance should be reported on the balance sheet.

Prepare a cash budget.

(LO 4), AP

BE7-13 The following information is available for Bonkers Company for the month of January: expected cash receipts $59,000, expected cash disbursements $67,000, and cash balance on January 1, $12,000. Management wishes to maintain a minimum cash balance of $9,000. Prepare a basic cash budget for the month of January.

Prepare entry to replenish a petty cash fund.

(LO 5), AP

***BE7-14** On March 20, Harbor's petty cash fund of $100 is replenished when the fund contains $19 in cash and receipts for postage $40, supplies $26, and travel expense $15. Prepare the journal entry to record the replenishment of the petty cash fund.

DO IT! EXERCISES

Identify violations of control activities.

(LO 1), C

DO IT! 7-1 Identify which control activity is violated in each of the following situations, and explain how the situation creates an opportunity for fraud or inappropriate accounting practices.

1. Once a month, the sales department sends sales invoices to the accounting department to be recorded.
2. Steve Nicoles orders merchandise for Binn Company; he also receives merchandise and authorizes payment for merchandise.
3. Several clerks at Draper's Groceries use the same cash register drawer.

Design system of internal control over cash receipts.

(LO 2), C

DO IT! 7-2 Wes Unsel is concerned with control over mail receipts at Wooden Sporting Goods. All mail receipts are opened by Mel Blount. Mel sends the checks to the accounting department, where they are stamped "For Deposit Only." The accounting department records and deposits the mail receipts weekly. Wes asks your help in installing a good system of internal control over mail receipts.

Explain treatment of items in bank reconciliation.

(LO 3), K

DO IT! 7-3 Ned Douglas owns Ned's Blankets. Ned asks you to explain how he should treat the following reconciling items when reconciling the company's bank account.

1. Outstanding checks.
2. A deposit in transit.
3. The bank charged to our account a check written by another company.
4. A debit memorandum for a bank service charge.

Analyze statements about the reporting of cash.

(LO 4), AP

DO IT! 7-4a Indicate whether each of the following statements is true or false.

1. A company has the following assets at the end of the year: cash on hand $40,000, cash refund due from customer $30,000, and checking account balance $22,000. Cash and cash equivalents is therefore $62,000.
2. A company that has received NSF checks should report these checks as a current liability on the balance sheet.
3. Restricted cash that is a current asset is reported as part of cash and cash equivalents.
4. A company has cash in the bank of $50,000, petty cash of $400, and stock investments of $100,000. Total cash and cash equivalents is therefore $50,400.

Prepare a cash budget.

(LO 4), AP

DO IT! 7-4b Stern Corporation's management wants to maintain a minimum monthly cash balance of $8,000. At the beginning of September, the cash balance is $12,270, expected cash receipts for September are $97,200, and cash disbursements are expected to be $115,000. How much cash, if any, must Stern borrow to maintain the desired minimum monthly balance? Determine your answer by using the basic form of the cash budget.

EXERCISES

Identify the principles of internal control.

(LO 1), C

E7-1 Bank employees use a system known as the "maker-checker" system. An employee will record an entry in the appropriate journal, and then a supervisor will verify and approve the entry. These days, as all of a bank's accounts are computerized, the employee first enters a batch of entries into the computer, and then the entries are posted automatically to the general ledger account after the supervisor approves them on the system.

Access to the computer system is password-protected and task-specific, which means that the computer system will not allow the employee to approve a transaction or the supervisor to record a transaction.

Instructions
Identify the principles of internal control inherent in the "maker-checker" procedure used by banks.

Identify the principles of internal control.

(LO 1), C

E7-2 Ricci's Pizza operates strictly on a carryout basis. Customers pick up their orders at a counter where a clerk exchanges the pizza for cash. While at the counter, the customer can see other employees making the pizzas and the large ovens in which the pizzas are baked.

Instructions
Identify the six principles of internal control and give an example of each principle that you might observe when picking up your pizza. (*Note:* It may not be possible to observe all the principles.)

List internal control weaknesses over cash receipts and suggest improvements.

(LO 2), E

E7-3 The following control procedures are used in Keaton Company for over-the-counter cash receipts.

1. Each store manager is responsible for interviewing applicants for cashier jobs. They are hired if they seem honest and trustworthy.
2. All over-the-counter receipts are registered by three clerks who share a cash register with a single cash drawer.
3. To minimize the risk of robbery, cash in excess of $100 is stored in an unlocked briefcase in the stock room until it is deposited in the bank.
4. At the end of each day, the total receipts are counted by the cashier on duty and reconciled to the cash register total.
5. The company accountant makes the bank deposit and then records the day's receipts.

Instructions

(a) For each procedure, explain the weakness in internal control and identify the control principle that is violated.
(b) For each weakness, suggest a change in the procedure that will result in good internal control.

List internal control weaknesses for cash disbursements and suggest improvements.

(LO 2), E

E7-4 The following control procedures are used in Bunny's Boutique Shoppe for cash disbursements.

1. Each week, 100 company checks are left in an unmarked envelope on a shelf behind the cash register.
2. The store manager personally approves all payments before she signs and issues checks.
3. The store purchases used goods for resale from people that bring items to the store. Since that can occur anytime that the store is open, all employees are authorized to purchase goods for resale by disbursing cash from the register. The purchase is documented by having the store employee write on a piece of paper a description of the item that was purchased and the amount that was paid. The employee then signs the paper and puts it in the register.
4. After payment, bills are "filed" in a paid invoice folder.
5. The company accountant prepares the bank reconciliation and reports any discrepancies to the owner.

Instructions

(a) For each procedure, explain the weakness in internal control and identify the internal control principle that is violated.
(b) For each weakness, suggest a change in the procedure that will result in good internal control.

Identify internal control weaknesses for cash disbursements and suggest improvements.

(LO 2), E

E7-5 At Martinez Company, checks are not prenumbered because both the purchasing agent and the treasurer are authorized to issue checks. Each signer has access to unissued checks kept in an unlocked file cabinet. The purchasing agent pays all bills pertaining to goods purchased for resale. Prior to payment, the purchasing agent determines that the goods have been received and verifies the mathematical accuracy of the vendor's invoice. After payment, the invoice is filed by vendor name and the purchasing agent records the payment in the cash disbursements journal. The treasurer pays all other bills following approval by authorized employees. After payment, the treasurer stamps all bills "paid," files them by payment date, and records the checks in the cash disbursements journal. Martinez Company maintains one checking account that is reconciled by the treasurer.

Instructions

(a) List the weaknesses in internal control over cash disbursements.
(b) Identify improvements for correcting these weaknesses.

Prepare bank reconciliation and adjusting entries.

(LO 3), AP

E7-6 Rachel Sells is unable to reconcile the bank balance at January 31. Rachel's reconciliation is shown here.

Cash balance per bank	$3,677.20
Add: NSF check	450.00
Less: Bank service charge	28.00
Adjusted balance per bank	$4,099.20
Cash balance per books	$3,975.20
Less: Deposits in transit	590.00
Add: Outstanding checks	770.00
Adjusted balance per books	$4,155.20

Instructions

(a) What is the proper adjusted cash balance per bank?
(b) What is the proper adjusted cash balance per books?
(c) Prepare the adjusting journal entries necessary to determine the adjusted cash balance per books.

Determine outstanding checks.

(LO 3), AP

E7-7 At April 30, the bank reconciliation of Back 40 Company shows three outstanding checks: No. 254 $650, No. 255 $700, and No. 257 $410. The May bank statement and the May cash payments journal are given here.

Bank Statement Checks Paid		
Date	**Check No.**	**Amount**
5-4	254	$650
5-2	257	410
5-17	258	159
5-12	259	275
5-20	260	925
5-29	263	480
5-30	262	750

Cash Payments Journal Checks Issued		
Date	**Check No.**	**Amount**
5-2	258	$159
5-5	259	275
5-10	260	925
5-15	261	500
5-22	262	750
5-24	263	480
5-29	264	360

Instructions

Using step 2 in the reconciliation procedure (see page 335), list the outstanding checks at May 31.

Prepare bank reconciliation and adjusting entries.

(LO 3), AP

E7-8 The following information pertains to Lance Company.

1. Cash balance per bank, July 31, $7,328.
2. July bank service charge not recorded by the depositor $38.
3. Cash balance per books, July 31, $7,364.
4. Deposits in transit, July 31, $2,700.
5. $2,016 collected for Lance Company in July by the bank through electronic funds transfer. The collection has not been recorded by Lance Company.
6. Outstanding checks, July 31, $686.

Instructions

(a) Prepare a bank reconciliation at July 31, 2017.
(b) Journalize the adjusting entries at July 31 on the books of Lance Company.

Prepare bank reconciliation and adjusting entries.

(LO 3), AP

E7-9 This information relates to the Cash account in the ledger of Howard Company.

Balance September 1—$16,400; Cash deposited—$64,000
Balance September 30—$17,600; Checks written—$62,800

The September bank statement shows a balance of $16,500 at September 30 and the following memoranda.

Credits		Debits	
Collection of electronic funds transfer	$1,830	NSF check: H. Kane	$560
Interest earned on checking account	45	Safety deposit box rent	60

At September 30, deposits in transit were $4,738 and outstanding checks totaled $2,383.

Instructions

(a) Prepare the bank reconciliation at September 30, 2017.
(b) Prepare the adjusting entries at September 30, assuming the NSF check was from a customer on account.

Compute deposits in transit and outstanding checks for two bank reconciliations.

(LO 3), AP

E7-10 The cash records of Upton Company show the following.

For July:

1. The June 30 bank reconciliation indicated that deposits in transit total $580. During July, the general ledger account Cash shows deposits of $16,900, but the bank statement indicates that only $15,600 in deposits were received during the month.
2. The June 30 bank reconciliation also reported outstanding checks of $940. During the month of July, Upton Company books show that $17,500 of checks were issued, yet the bank statement showed that $16,400 of checks cleared the bank in July.

For September:

3. In September, deposits per bank statement totaled $25,900, deposits per books were $26,400, and deposits in transit at September 30 were $2,200.
4. In September, cash disbursements per books were $23,500, checks clearing the bank were $24,000, and outstanding checks at September 30 were $2,100.

There were no bank debit or credit memoranda, and no errors were made by either the bank or Upton Company.

Instructions

Answer the following questions.

(a) In situation 1, what were the deposits in transit at July 31?
(b) In situation 2, what were the outstanding checks at July 31?
(c) In situation 3, what were the deposits in transit at August 31?
(d) In situation 4, what were the outstanding checks at August 31?

Prepare bank reconciliation and adjusting entries.

(LO 3), AP

E7-11 Perth Inc.'s bank statement from Main Street Bank at August 31, 2017, gives the following information.

Balance, August 1	$18,400	Bank debit memorandum:	
August deposits	71,000	Safety deposit box fee	$ 25
Checks cleared in August	68,678	Service charge	50
Bank credit memorandum:		Balance, August 31	20,692
Interest earned	45		

A summary of the Cash account in the ledger for August shows the following: balance, August 1, $18,700; receipts $74,000; disbursements $73,570; and balance, August 31, $19,130. Analysis reveals that the only reconciling items on the July 31 bank reconciliation were a deposit in transit for $4,800 and outstanding checks of $4,500. In addition, you determine that there was an error involving a company check drawn in August: A check for $400 to a creditor on account that cleared the bank in August was journalized and posted for $40.

Instructions

(a) Determine deposits in transit.
(b) Determine outstanding checks. (*Hint:* You need to correct disbursements for the check error.)
(c) Prepare a bank reconciliation at August 31.
(d) Journalize the adjusting entry(ies) to be made by Perth Inc. at August 31.

Identify reporting of cash.

(LO 4), AP

E7-12 A new accountant at Wyne Inc. is trying to identify which of the amounts shown below should be reported as the current asset "Cash and cash equivalents" in the year-end balance sheet, as of April 30, 2017.

1. $60 of currency and coin in a locked box used for incidental cash transactions.
2. A $10,000 U.S. Treasury bill, due May 31, 2017.
3. $260 of April-dated checks that Wyne has received from customers but not yet deposited.
4. An $85 check received from a customer in payment of its April account, but postdated to May 1.
5. $2,500 in the company's checking account.
6. $4,800 in its savings account.
7. $75 of prepaid postage in its postage meter.
8. A $25 IOU from the company receptionist.

Instructions

(a) What balance should Wyne report as its "Cash and cash equivalents" balance at April 30, 2017?
(b) In what account(s) and in what financial statement(s) should the items not included in "Cash and cash equivalents" be reported?

Review cash management practices.

(LO 4), C

E7-13 Lance, Art, and Wayne have joined together to open a law practice but are struggling to manage their cash flow. They haven't yet built up sufficient clientele and revenues to support their legal practice's ongoing costs. Initial costs, such as advertising, renovations to their premises, and the like, all result in outgoing cash flow at a time when little is coming in. Lance, Art, and Wayne haven't had time to establish a billing system since most of their clients' cases haven't yet reached the courts, and the lawyers didn't think it would be right to bill them until "results were achieved."

Unfortunately, Lance, Art, and Wayne's suppliers don't feel the same way. Their suppliers expect them to pay their accounts payable within a few days of receiving their bills. So far, there hasn't even been enough money to pay the three lawyers, and they are not sure how long they can keep practicing law without getting some money into their pockets.

Instructions

Can you provide any suggestions for Lance, Art, and Wayne to improve their cash management practices?

E7-14 Rigley Company expects to have a cash balance of $46,000 on January 1, 2017. These are the relevant monthly budget data for the first two months of 2017.

Prepare a cash budget for two months.

(LO 4), AP

1. Collections from customers: January $71,000 and February $146,000.
2. Payments to suppliers: January $40,000 and February $75,000.
3. Wages: January $30,000 and February $40,000. Wages are paid in the month they are incurred.
4. Administrative expenses: January $21,000 and February $24,000. These costs include depreciation of $1,000 per month. All other costs are paid as incurred.
5. Selling expenses: January $15,000 and February $20,000. These costs are exclusive of depreciation. They are paid as incurred.
6. Sales of short-term investments in January are expected to realize $12,000 in cash. Rigley has a line of credit at a local bank that enables it to borrow up to $25,000. The company wants to maintain a minimum monthly cash balance of $20,000.

Instructions

Prepare a cash budget for January and February.

***E7-15** During October, Bismark Light Company experiences the following transactions in establishing a petty cash fund.

Prepare journal entries for a petty cash fund.

(LO 5), AP

Oct. 1 A petty cash fund is established with a check for $150 issued to the petty cash custodian.

31 A check was written to reimburse the fund and increase the fund to $200. A count of the petty cash fund disclosed the following items:

Currency		$59.00
Coins		0.70
Expenditure receipts (vouchers):		
Supplies	$26.10	
Telephone, Internet, and fax	16.40	
Postage	39.70	
Freight-out	6.80	

Instructions

Journalize the entries in October that pertain to the petty cash fund.

***E7-16** Kael Company maintains a petty cash fund for small expenditures. These transactions occurred during the month of August.

Journalize and post petty cash fund transactions.

(LO 5), AP

Aug. 1 Established the petty cash fund by writing a check payable to the petty cash custodian for $200.

15 Replenished the petty cash fund by writing a check for $175. On this date, the fund consisted of $25 in cash and these petty cash receipts: freight-out $74.40, entertainment expense $36, postage expense $33.70, and miscellaneous expense $27.50.

16 Increased the amount of the petty cash fund to $400 by writing a check for $200.

31 Replenished the petty cash fund by writing a check for $283. On this date, the fund consisted of $117 in cash and these petty cash receipts: postage expense $145, entertainment expense $90.60, and freight-out $46.40.

Instructions

(a) Journalize the petty cash transactions.
(b) Post to the Petty Cash account.
(c) What internal control features exist in a petty cash fund?

EXERCISES: SET B AND CHALLENGE EXERCISES

Visit the book's companion website, at **www.wiley.com/college/kimmel**, and choose the Student Companion site to access Exercises: Set B and Challenge Exercises.

PROBLEMS: SET A

P7-1A Gary Theater is in the Hoosier Mall. A cashier's booth is located near the entrance to the theater. Two cashiers are employed. One works from 1:00 to 5:00 P.M., the other from 5:00 to 9:00 P.M. Each cashier is bonded. The cashiers receive cash from customers and operate a machine that ejects serially numbered tickets. The rolls of tickets are inserted

Identify internal control weaknesses for cash receipts.

(LO 2), C

and locked into the machine by the theater manager at the beginning of each cashier's shift.

After purchasing a ticket, the customer takes the ticket to a doorperson stationed at the entrance of the theater lobby some 60 feet from the cashier's booth. The doorperson tears the ticket in half, admits the customer, and returns the ticket stub to the customer. The other half of the ticket is dropped into a locked box by the doorperson.

At the end of each cashier's shift, the theater manager removes the ticket rolls from the machine and makes a cash count. The cash count sheet is initialed by the cashier. At the end of the day, the manager deposits the receipts in total in a bank night deposit vault located in the mall. In addition, the manager sends copies of the deposit slip and the initialed cash count sheets to the theater company treasurer for verification and to the company's accounting department. Receipts from the first shift are stored in a safe located in the manager's office.

Instructions

(a) Identify the internal control principles and their application to the cash receipts transactions of Gary Theater.

(b) If the doorperson and cashier decided to collaborate to misappropriate cash, what actions might they take?

Identify internal control weaknesses in cash receipts and cash disbursements.

(LO 2), C

P7-2A Blue Bayou Middle School wants to raise money for a new sound system for its auditorium. The primary fund-raising event is a dance at which the famous disc jockey Kray Zee will play classic and not-so-classic dance tunes. Grant Hill, the music and theater instructor, has been given the responsibility for coordinating the fund-raising efforts. This is Grant's first experience with fund-raising. He decides to put the eighth-grade choir in charge of the event; he will be a relatively passive observer.

Grant had 500 unnumbered tickets printed for the dance. He left the tickets in a box on his desk and told the choir students to take as many tickets as they thought they could sell for $5 each. In order to ensure that no extra tickets would be floating around, he told them to dispose of any unsold tickets. When the students received payment for the tickets, they were to bring the cash back to Grant, and he would put it in a locked box in his desk drawer.

Some of the students were responsible for decorating the gymnasium for the dance. Grant gave each of them a key to the money box and told them that if they took money out to purchase materials, they should put a note in the box saying how much they took and what it was used for. After 2 weeks, the money box appeared to be getting full, so Grant asked Lynn Dandi to count the money, prepare a deposit slip, and deposit the money in a bank account that Grant had opened.

The day of the dance, Grant wrote a check from the account to pay Kray Zee. The DJ said, however, that he accepted only cash and did not give receipts. So Grant took $200 out of the cash box and gave it to Kray. At the dance, Grant had Dana Uhler working at the entrance to the gymnasium, collecting tickets from students and selling tickets to those who had not pre-purchased them. Grant estimated that 400 students attended the dance.

The following day, Grant closed out the bank account, which had $250 in it, and gave that amount plus the $180 in the cash box to Principal Sanchez. Principal Sanchez seemed surprised that, after generating roughly $2,000 in sales, the dance netted only $430 in cash. Grant did not know how to respond.

Instructions

Identify as many internal control weaknesses as you can in this scenario, and suggest how each could be addressed.

Prepare a bank reconciliation and adjusting entries.

(LO 3), AP

P7-3A On July 31, 2017, Keeds Company had a cash balance per books of $6,140. The statement from Dakota State Bank on that date showed a balance of $7,690.80. A comparison of the bank statement with the Cash account revealed the following facts.

1. The bank service charge for July was $25.
2. The bank collected $1,520 for Keeds Company through electronic funds transfer.
3. The July 31 receipts of $1,193.30 were not included in the bank deposits for July. These receipts were deposited by the company in a night deposit vault on July 31.
4. Company check No. 2480 issued to L. Taylor, a creditor, for $384 that cleared the bank in July was incorrectly entered in the cash payments journal on July 10 for $348.
5. Checks outstanding on July 31 totaled $1,860.10.
6. On July 31, the bank statement showed an NSF charge of $575 for a check received by the company from W. Krueger, a customer, on account.

Instructions

(a) Prepare the bank reconciliation as of July 31.
(b) Prepare the necessary adjusting entries at July 31.

(a) Adjusted cash bal. $7,024.00

P7-4A The bank portion of the bank reconciliation for Bogalusa Company at October 31, 2017, is shown below.

Prepare a bank reconciliation and adjusting entries from detailed data.

(LO 3), AP

BOGALUSA COMPANY
Bank Reconciliation
October 31, 2017

Cash balance per bank			$12,367.90
Add: Deposits in transit			1,530.20
			13,898.10
Less: Outstanding checks			
	Check Number	**Check Amount**	
	2451	$1,260.40	
	2470	684.20	
	2471	844.50	
	2472	426.80	
	2474	1,050.00	4,265.90
Adjusted cash balance per bank			$ 9,632.20

The adjusted cash balance per bank agreed with the cash balance per books at October 31. The November bank statement showed the following checks and deposits.

Bank Statement

Checks			**Deposits**	
Date	**Number**	**Amount**	**Date**	**Amount**
11-1	2470	$ 684.20	11-1	$ 1,530.20
11-2	2471	844.50	11-4	1,211.60
11-5	2474	1,050.00	11-8	990.10
11-4	2475	1,640.70	11-13	2,575.00
11-8	2476	2,830.00	11-18	1,472.70
11-10	2477	600.00	11-21	2,945.00
11-15	2479	1,750.00	11-25	2,567.30
11-18	2480	1,330.00	11-28	1,650.00
11-27	2481	695.40	11-30	1,186.00
11-30	2483	575.50	Total	$16,127.90
11-29	2486	940.00		
	Total	$12,940.30		

The cash records per books for November showed the following.

Cash Payments Journal

Date	**Number**	**Amount**	**Date**	**Number**	**Amount**
11-1	2475	$1,640.70	11-20	2483	$ 575.50
11-2	2476	2,830.00	11-22	2484	829.50
11-2	2477	600.00	11-23	2485	974.80
11-4	2478	538.20	11-24	2486	940.00
11-8	2479	1,705.00	11-29	2487	398.00
11-10	2480	1,330.00	11-30	2488	800.00
11-15	2481	695.40	Total		$14,469.10
11-18	2482	612.00			

Cash Receipts Journal

Date	**Amount**
11-3	$ 1,211.60
11-7	990.10
11-12	2,575.00
11-17	1,472.70
11-20	2,954.00
11-24	2,567.30
11-27	1,650.00
11-29	1,186.00
11-30	1,304.00
Total	$15,910.70

The bank statement contained two bank memoranda:

1. A credit of $2,242 for the collection for Bogalusa Company of an electronic funds transfer.
2. A debit for the printing of additional company checks $85.

At November 30, the cash balance per books was $11,073.80 and the cash balance per bank statement was $17,712.50. The bank did not make any errors, but **Bogalusa Company made two errors.**

Instructions

(a) Adjusted cash bal. $13,176.80

(a) Using the steps in the reconciliation procedure described on pages 355–356, prepare a bank reconciliation at November 30, 2017.
(b) Prepare the adjusting entries based on the reconciliation. (*Note:* The correction of any errors pertaining to recording checks should be made to Accounts Payable. The correction of any errors relating to recording cash receipts should be made to Accounts Receivable.)

Prepare a bank reconciliation and adjusting entries.
(LO 3), AP

P7-5A Timmins Company of Emporia, Kansas, spreads herbicides and applies liquid fertilizer for local farmers. On May 31, 2017, the company's Cash account per its general ledger showed a balance of $6,738.90.

The bank statement from Emporia State Bank on that date showed the following balance.

EMPORIA STATE BANK

Checks and Debits	Deposits and Credits	Daily Balance
XXX	XXX	5-31 6,968.00

A comparison of the details on the bank statement with the details in the Cash account revealed the following facts.

1. The statement included a debit memo of $40 for the printing of additional company checks.
2. Cash sales of $883.15 on May 12 were deposited in the bank. The cash receipts journal entry and the deposit slip were incorrectly made for $933.15. The bank credited Timmins Company for the correct amount.
3. Outstanding checks at May 31 totaled $276.25, and deposits in transit were $1,880.15.
4. On May 18, the company issued check No. 1181 for $685 to H. Moses, on account. The check, which cleared the bank in May, was incorrectly journalized and posted by Timmins Company for $658.
5. $2,690 was collected by the bank for Timmins Company on May 31 through electronic funds transfer.
6. Included with the canceled checks was a check issued by Tomins Company to C. Pernod for $360 that was incorrectly charged to Timmins Company by the bank.
7. On May 31, the bank statement showed an NSF charge of $380 for a check issued by Sara Ballard, a customer, to Timmins Company on account.

Instructions

(a) Adjusted cash bal. $8,931.90

(a) Prepare the bank reconciliation at May 31, 2017.
(b) Prepare the necessary adjusting entries for Timmins Company at May 31, 2017.

Prepare a comprehensive bank reconciliation with theft and internal control deficiencies.
(LO 1, 2, 3), E

P7-6A Daisey Company is a very profitable small business. It has not, however, given much consideration to internal control. For example, in an attempt to keep clerical and office expenses to a minimum, the company has combined the jobs of cashier and bookkeeper. As a result, Bret Turrin handles all cash receipts, keeps the accounting records, and prepares the monthly bank reconciliations.

The balance per the bank statement on October 31, 2017, was $18,380. Outstanding checks were No. 62 for $140.75, No. 183 for $180, No. 284 for $253.25, No. 862 for $190.71, No. 863 for $226.80, and No. 864 for $165.28. Included with the statement was a credit memorandum of $185 indicating the collection of a note receivable for Daisey Company by the bank on October 25. This memorandum has not been recorded by Daisey.

The company's ledger showed one Cash account with a balance of $21,877.72. The balance included undeposited cash on hand. Because of the lack of internal controls, Bret took for personal use all of the undeposited receipts in excess of $3,795.51. He then prepared the following bank reconciliation in an effort to conceal his theft of cash.

Cash balance per books, October 31		$21,877.72
Add: Outstanding checks		
No. 862	$190.71	
No. 863	226.80	
No. 864	165.28	482.79
		22,360.51
Less: Undeposited receipts		3,795.51
Unadjusted balance per bank, October 31		18,565.00
Less: Bank credit memorandum		185.00
Cash balance per bank statement, October 31		$18,380.00

Instructions

(a) Prepare a correct bank reconciliation. (*Hint:* Deduct the amount of the theft from the adjusted balance per books.)

(a) Adjusted cash bal. $21,018.72

(b) Indicate the three ways that Bret attempted to conceal the theft and the dollar amount involved in each method.

(c) What principles of internal control were violated in this case?

P7-7A You are provided with the following information taken from Moynahan Inc.'s March 31, 2017, balance sheet.

Prepare a cash budget.

(LO 4), AP

Cash	$ 11,000
Accounts receivable	20,000
Inventory	36,000
Property, plant, and equipment, net of depreciation	120,000
Accounts payable	22,400
Common stock	150,000
Retained earnings	11,600

Additional information concerning Moynahan Inc. is as follows.

1. Gross profit is 25% of sales.
2. Actual and budgeted sales data:

March (actual)	$46,000
April (budgeted)	70,000

3. Sales are both cash and credit. Cash collections expected in April are:

March	$18,400	(40% of $46,000)
April	42,000	(60% of $70,000)
	$60,400	

4. Half of a month's purchases are paid for in the month of purchase and half in the following month. Cash disbursements expected in April are:

Purchases March	$22,400
Purchases April	28,100
	$50,500

5. Cash operating costs are anticipated to be $11,200 for the month of April.
6. Equipment costing $2,500 will be purchased for cash in April.
7. The company wishes to maintain a minimum cash balance of $9,000. An open line of credit is available at the bank. All borrowing is done at the beginning of the month, and all repayments are made at the end of the month. The interest rate is 12% per year, and interest expense is accrued at the end of the month and paid in the following month.

Instructions

Prepare a cash budget for the month of April. Determine how much cash Moynahan Inc. must borrow, or can repay, in April.

Apr. borrowings $1,800

P7-8A Bastille Corporation prepares monthly cash budgets. Here are relevant data from operating budgets for 2017.

Prepare a cash budget.

(LO 4), AP

	January	**February**
Sales	$360,000	$400,000
Purchases	120,000	130,000
Salaries	84,000	81,000
Administrative expenses	72,000	75,000
Selling expenses	79,000	88,000

All sales and purchases are on account. Budgeted collections and disbursement data are given below. All other expenses are paid in the month incurred. Administrative expenses include $1,000 of depreciation per month.

Other data.

1. Collections from customers: January $326,000; February $378,000.
2. Payments for purchases: January $110,000; February $135,000.
3. Other receipts: January: collection of December 31, 2016, notes receivable $15,000; February: proceeds from sale of securities $4,000.
4. Other disbursements: February $10,000 cash dividend.

The company's cash balance on January 1, 2017, is expected to be $46,000. The company wants to maintain a minimum cash balance of $40,000.

Instructions

Jan. 31 cash bal. $43,000

Prepare a cash budget for January and February.

PROBLEMS: SET B AND SET C

Visit the book's companion website, at **www.wiley.com/college/kimmel**, and choose the Student Companion site to access Problems: Set B and Set C.

CONTINUING PROBLEM Cookie Creations

© leungchopan/ Shutterstock

(*Note:* This is a continuation of the Cookie Creations problem from Chapters 1 through 6.)

CC7 Part 1 Natalie is struggling to keep up with the recording of her accounting transactions. She is spending a lot of time marketing and selling mixers and giving her cookie classes. Her friend John is an accounting student who runs his own accounting service. He has asked Natalie if she would like to have him do her accounting. John and Natalie meet and discuss her business.

Part 2 Natalie decides that she cannot afford to hire John to do her accounting. One way that she can ensure that her Cash account does not have any errors and is accurate and up-to-date is to prepare a bank reconciliation at the end of each month. Natalie would like you to help her.

Go to the book's companion website, at **www.wiley.com/college/kimmel**, *to see the completion of this problem.*

COMPREHENSIVE ACCOUNTING CYCLE REVIEW

CP7 On December 1, 2017, Ravenwood Company had the following account balances.

	Debit		Credit
Cash	$18,200	Accumulated Depreciation—	
Notes Receivable	2,000	Equipment	$ 3,000
Accounts Receivable	7,500	Accounts Payable	6,100
Inventory	16,000	Common Stock	50,000
Prepaid Insurance	1,600	Retained Earnings	14,200
Equipment	28,000		$73,300
	$73,300		

During December, the company completed the following transactions.

Dec. 7 Received $3,600 cash from customers in payment of account (no discount allowed).
12 Purchased merchandise on account from Greene Co. $12,000, terms 1/10, n/30.
17 Sold merchandise on account $16,000, terms 2/10, n/30. The cost of the merchandise sold was $10,000.
19 Paid salaries $2,200.
22 Paid Greene Co. in full, less discount.
26 Received collections in full, less discounts, from customers billed on December 17.
31 Received $2,700 cash from customers in payment of account (no discount allowed).

Adjustment data:

1. Depreciation $200 per month.
2. Insurance expired $400.
3. Income tax expense was $425. It was unpaid at December 31.

Instructions

(a) Journalize the December transactions. (Assume a perpetual inventory system.)
(b) Enter the December 1 balances in the ledger T-accounts and post the December transactions. Use Cost of Goods Sold, Depreciation Expense, Insurance Expense, Salaries and Wages Expense, Sales Revenue, Sales Discounts, Income Taxes Payable, and Income Tax Expense.
(c) The statement from Lyon County Bank on December 31 showed a balance of $25,930. A comparison of the bank statement with the Cash account revealed the following facts.
  1. The bank collected the $2,000 note receivable for Ravenwood Company on December 15 through electronic funds transfer.
  2. The December 31 receipts were deposited in a night deposit vault on December 31. These deposits were recorded by the bank in January.
  3. Checks outstanding on December 31 totaled $1,210.
  4. On December 31, the bank statement showed a NSF charge of $680 for a check received by the company from M. Lawrence, a customer, on account.

  Prepare a bank reconciliation as of December 31 based on the available information. (*Hint:* The cash balance per books is $26,100. This can be proven by finding the balance in the Cash account from parts (a) and (b).)
(d) Journalize the adjusting entries resulting from the bank reconciliation and adjustment data.
(e) Post the adjusting entries to the ledger T-accounts.
(f) Prepare an adjusted trial balance.
(g) Prepare an income statement for December and a classified balance sheet at December 31.

(f) Totals $89,500
(g) Net income $ 2,455
Total assets $73,180

EXPAND YOUR CRITICAL THINKING

FINANCIAL REPORTING PROBLEM: Apple Inc.

Financial Reporting

AN

CT7-1 The financial statements of Apple Inc. are presented in Appendix A. Instructions for accessing and using the company's complete annual report, including the notes to its financial statements, are also provided in Appendix A.

Instructions

Using the financial statements and reports, answer these questions about Apple's internal controls and cash.

(a) What comments, if any, are made about cash in the "Report of Independent Registered Public Accounting Firm"?
(b) What data about cash and cash equivalents are shown in the consolidated balance sheet (statement of financial position)?
(c) What activities are identified in the consolidated statement of cash flows as being responsible for the changes in cash during 2014?
(d) How are cash equivalents defined in the Notes to Consolidated Financial Statements?
(e) Read the section of the report titled "Management's Report on Internal Control Over Financial Reporting." Summarize the statements made in that section of the report.

Financial Analysis

COMPARATIVE ANALYSIS PROBLEM: Columbia Sportswear Company vs. VF Corporation

AN **CT7-2** The financial statements of Columbia Sportswear Company are presented in Appendix B. Financial statements of VF Corporation are presented in Appendix C.

Instructions

Answer the following questions for each company.

(a) What is the balance in cash and cash equivalents at December 31, 2014?
(b) What percentage of total assets does cash represent for each company over the last 2 years? Has it changed significantly for either company?
(c) How much cash was provided by operating activities during 2014?
(d) Comment on your findings in parts (a) through (c).

Financial Analysis

COMPARATIVE ANALYSIS PROBLEM: Amazon.com, Inc. vs. Wal-Mart Stores, Inc.

AN **CT7-3** The financial statements of Amazon.com, Inc. are presented in Appendix D. Financial statements of Wal-Mart Stores, Inc. are presented in Appendix E.

Instructions

Answer the following questions for each company.

(a) What is the balance in cash and cash equivalents at December 31, 2014?
(b) What percentage of total assets does cash represent for each company over the last two years? Has it changed significantly for either company?
(c) How much cash was provided by operating activities during 2014?
(d) Comment on your findings in parts (a) through (c).

INTERPRETING FINANCIAL STATEMENTS

AN **CT7-4** The international accounting firm Ernst & Young performed a global survey on fraud. The results of that survey are summarized in a report titled "Driving Ethical Growth—New Markets, New Challenges" (Ernst & Young, *13th Global Fraud Survey*). You can find this report by doing an Internet search on the title, or go to **https://webforms.ey.com/Publication/vwLUAssets/EY-13th-Global-Fraud-Survey/$FILE/EY-13th-Global-Fraud-Survey.pdf**.

Instructions

Read the Executive Summary section, and then skim the remainder of the report to answer the following questions.

(a) What was the global percentage of companies that experienced fraud during the period covered by the survey, and what country had the highest rate?
(b) What percentage of survey respondents were asked to participate in an anti-bribery/anti-corruption (ABAC) risk assessment in the last two years prior to the survey?
(c) What percentage of C-suite executives have not attended ABAC training?
(d) According to Figure 3, what source of cybercrime concerns respondents the most?

REAL-WORLD FOCUS

AP **CT7-5** The Financial Accounting Standards Board (FASB) is a private organization established to improve accounting standards and financial reporting. The FASB conducts extensive research before issuing a "Statement of Financial Accounting Standards," which represents an authoritative expression of generally accepted accounting principles.

Address: **www.fasb.org**, or go to **www.wiley.com/college/kimmel**

Steps

Choose **About FASB**.

Instructions
Answer the following questions.

(a) What is the mission of the FASB?
(b) How are topics added to the FASB technical agenda? (*Hint:* See Project Plans in Our Rules of Procedure.)
(c) What characteristics make the FASB's procedures an "open" decision-making process? (*Hint:* See Due Process in Our Rules of Procedure.)

CT7-6 The Public Company Accounting Oversight Board (PCAOB) was created as a result of the Sarbanes-Oxley Act. It has oversight and enforcement responsibilities over accounting firms in the United States. AP

Address: **http://www.pcaobus.org/**, or go to **www.wiley.com/college/kimmel**

Instructions
Answer the following questions.

(a) What is the mission of the PCAOB?
(b) Briefly summarize its responsibilities related to inspections.
(c) Briefly summarize its responsibilities related to enforcement.

CT7-7 The website **www.cpa2biz.com** has an article dated February 4, 2010, by Mary Schaeffer entitled "Emerging Issues: Demise of Paper Checks." AP

Instructions
Go to the website and do a search on the article title. Read the article and answer the following questions.

(a) How many different forms of payment types does the article list? What are the payment types?
(b) What problems does the shift away from paper checks to alternative payment options present for companies?
(c) What five controls does the article suggest incorporating, to decrease problems associated with multiple payment options?

DECISION-MAKING ACROSS THE ORGANIZATION

Financial Analysis

Writing

Group Project

CT7-8 Alternative Distributor Corp., a distributor of groceries and related products, is headquartered in Medford, Massachusetts.

During a recent audit, Alternative Distributor Corp. was advised that existing internal controls necessary for the company to develop reliable financial statements were inadequate. The audit report stated that the current system of accounting for sales, receivables, and cash receipts constituted a material weakness. Among other items, the report focused on nontimely deposit of cash receipts, exposing Alternative Distributor to potential loss or misappropriation, excessive past due accounts receivable due to lack of collection efforts, E disregard of advantages offered by vendors for prompt payment of invoices, absence of appropriate segregation of duties by personnel consistent with appropriate control objectives, inadequate procedures for applying accounting principles, lack of qualified management personnel, lack of supervision by an outside board of directors, and overall poor recordkeeping.

Instructions
(a) Identify the principles of internal control violated by Alternative Distributor Corp.
(b) Explain why managers of various functional areas in the company should be concerned about internal controls.

COMMUNICATION ACTIVITY

CT7-9 As a new auditor for the CPA firm of Blacke and Whyte, you have been assigned to review the internal controls over mail cash receipts of Simon Company. Your review E reveals that checks are promptly endorsed "For Deposit Only," but no list of the checks is prepared by the person opening the mail. The mail is opened either by the cashier or by the employee who maintains the accounts receivable records. Mail receipts are deposited in the bank weekly by the cashier.

Instructions

Write a letter to Frank Simon, owner of Simon Company, explaining the weaknesses in internal control and your recommendations for improving the system.

ETHICS CASES

E **CT7-10** Banks charge fees for "bounced" checks—that is, checks that exceed the balance in the account. It has been estimated that processing bounced checks costs a bank roughly $1.50 per check. Thus, the profit margin on bounced checks is very high. Recognizing this, some banks have started to process checks from largest to smallest. By doing this, they maximize the number of checks that bounce if a customer overdraws an account. For example, NationsBank (now Bank of America) projected a $14 million increase in fee revenue as a result of processing largest checks first. In response to criticism, banks have responded that their customers prefer to have large checks processed first, because those tend to be the most important. At the other extreme, some banks will cover their customers' bounced checks, effectively extending them an interest-free loan while their account is overdrawn.

Instructions

Answer each of the following questions.

(a) Carl Roen had a balance of $1,500 in his checking account at First National Bank on a day when the bank received the following five checks for processing against his account.

Check Number	Amount	Check Number	Amount
3150	$ 35	3165	$ 550
3162	400	3166	1,510
		3169	180

Assuming a $30 fee assessed by the bank for each bounced check, how much fee revenue would the bank generate if it processed checks (1) from largest to smallest, (2) from smallest to largest, and (3) in order of check number?

(b) Do you think that processing checks from largest to smallest is an ethical business practice?

(c) In addition to ethical issues, what other issues must a bank consider in deciding whether to process checks from largest to smallest?

(d) If you were managing a bank, what policy would you adopt on bounced checks?

E **CT7-11** The National Fraud Information Center (NFIC) was originally established in 1992 by the National Consumers League, the oldest nonprofit consumer organization in the United States, to fight the growing menace of telemarketing fraud by improving prevention and enforcement. It maintains a website that provides many useful fraud-related resources.

Address: **www.fraud.org/scamsagainstbusinesses/bizscams.htm** or go to **www.wiley.com/college/kimmel**

Instructions

Go to the site and find an item of interest to you. Write a short summary of your findings.

ALL ABOUT YOU

AP **CT7-12** The print and electronic media are full of stories about potential security risks that can arise from your personal computer. It is important to keep in mind, however, that there are also many ways that your identity can be stolen other than from your computer. The federal government provides many resources to help protect you from identity thieves.

Instructions

Go to **http://onguardonline.gov/idtheft.html**, and click Games, then click ID Theft Faceoff. Complete the quiz provided there.

FASB CODIFICATION ACTIVITY

CT7-13 If your school has a subscription to the FASB Codification, go to **http://aaahq.org/ascLogin.cfm** to log in and prepare responses to the following. AP

(a) How is cash defined in the Codification?
(b) How are cash equivalents defined in the Codification?
(c) What are the disclosure requirements related to cash and cash equivalents?

A Look at IFRS

LEARNING OBJECTIVE 6 **Compare the accounting procedures for fraud, internal control, and cash under GAAP and IFRS.**

Fraud can occur anywhere. And because the three main factors that contribute to fraud are universal in nature, the principles of internal control activities are used globally by companies. While Sarbanes-Oxley (SOX) does not apply to international companies, most large international companies have internal controls similar to those indicated in the chapter. IFRS and GAAP are also very similar in accounting for cash. *IAS No. 1 (revised),* "Presentation of Financial Statements," is the only standard that discusses issues specifically related to cash.

RELEVANT FACTS

Following are the key similarities and differences between GAAP and IFRS related to fraud, internal control, and cash.

Similarities

- The fraud triangle discussed in this chapter is applicable to all international companies. Some of the major frauds on an international basis are Parmalat (Italy), Royal Ahold (the Netherlands), and Satyam Computer Services (India).
- Rising economic crime poses a growing threat to companies, with 34% of all organizations worldwide being victims of fraud in a recent 12-month period.
- Accounting scandals both in the United States and internationally have re-ignited the debate over the relative merits of GAAP, which takes a "rules-based" approach to accounting, versus IFRS, which takes a "principles-based" approach. The FASB announced that it intends to introduce more principles-based standards.
- On a lighter note, at one time the Ig Nobel Prize in Economics went to the CEOs of those companies involved in the corporate accounting scandals of that year for "adapting the mathematical concept of imaginary numbers for use in the business world." A parody of the Nobel Prizes, the Ig Nobel Prizes (read Ignoble, as not noble) are given each year in early October for 10 achievements that "first make people laugh, and then make them think." Organized by the scientific humor magazine *Annals of Improbable Research* (*AIR*), they are presented by a group that includes genuine Nobel laureates at a ceremony at Harvard University's Sanders Theater (see **en.wikipedia.org/wiki/Ig_Nobel_Prize**).
- Internal controls are a system of checks and balances designed to prevent and detect fraud and errors. While most companies have these systems in place, many have never completely documented them, nor had an independent auditor attest to their effectiveness. Both of these actions are required under SOX.

- Companies find that internal control review is a costly process but badly needed. One study estimates the cost of SOX compliance for U.S. companies at over $35 billion, with audit fees doubling in the first year of compliance. At the same time, examination of internal controls indicates lingering problems in the way companies operate. One study of first compliance with the internal-control testing provisions documented material weaknesses for about 13% of companies reporting in a two-year period (*PricewaterhouseCoopers' Global Economic Crime Survey*, 2005).
- The accounting and internal control procedures related to cash are essentially the same under both IFRS and this textbook. In addition, the definition used for cash equivalents is the same.
- Most companies report cash and cash equivalents together under IFRS, as shown in this textbook. In addition, IFRS follows the same accounting policies related to the reporting of restricted cash.

Differences

- The SOX internal control standards apply only to companies listed on U.S. exchanges. There is continuing debate over whether foreign issuers should have to comply with this extra layer of regulation.

LOOKING TO THE FUTURE

Ethics has become a very important aspect of reporting. Different cultures have different perspectives on bribery and other questionable activities, and consequently penalties for engaging in such activities vary considerably across countries.

High-quality international accounting requires both high-quality accounting standards and high-quality auditing. Similar to the convergence of GAAP and IFRS, there is movement to improve international auditing standards. The International Auditing and Assurance Standards Board (IAASB) functions as an independent standard-setting body. It works to establish high-quality auditing and assurance and quality-control standards throughout the world. Whether the IAASB adopts internal control provisions similar to those in SOX remains to be seen. You can follow developments in the international audit arena at **http://www.ifac.org/iaasb/**.

IFRS Practice

IFRS SELF-TEST QUESTIONS

1. Non-U.S companies that follow IFRS:
  (a) do not normally use the principles of internal control activities described in this textbook.
  (b) often offset cash with accounts payable on the balance sheet.
  (c) are not required to follow SOX.
  (d) None of the above.

2. The Sarbanes-Oxley Act applies to:
  (a) all U.S. companies listed on U.S. exchanges.
  (b) all companies that list stock on any stock exchange in any country.
  (c) all European companies listed on European exchanges.
  (d) Both (a) and (c).

3. High-quality international accounting requires both high-quality accounting standards and:
  (a) a reconsideration of SOX to make it less onerous.
  (b) high-quality auditing standards.
  (c) government intervention to ensure that the public interest is protected.
  (d) the development of new principles of internal control activities.

IFRS EXERCISE

IFRS7-1 Some people argue that the internal control requirements of the Sarbanes-Oxley Act (SOX) put U.S. companies at a competitive disadvantage to companies outside the United States. Discuss the competitive implications (both pros and cons) of SOX.

INTERNATIONAL FINANCIAL REPORTING PROBLEM: Louis Vuitton

IFRS7-2 The financial statements of Louis Vuitton are presented in Appendix F. Instructions for accessing and using the company's complete annual report, including the notes to its financial statements, are also provided in Appendix F.

Instructions
Using the notes to the company's financial statements, what are Louis Vuitton's accounting policies related to cash and cash equivalents?

Answers to IFRS Self-Test Questions
1. c **2.** a **3.** b

8

Reporting and Analyzing Receivables

CHAPTER PREVIEW

In this chapter, we discuss some of the decisions related to reporting and analyzing receivables. As indicated in the Feature Story, receivables are a significant asset on the books of Nike. Receivables are important to companies in other industries as well because a large portion of sales in the United States are credit sales. As a consequence, companies must pay close attention to their receivables balances and manage them carefully. In this chapter, we will look at the accounting and management of receivables at Nike and one of its competitors, Skechers USA.

CHAPTER OUTLINE

LEARNING OBJECTIVES		PRACTICE
1 Explain how companies recognize accounts receivable.	• Types of receivables • Recognizing accounts receivable	DO IT! 1 Recognizing Accounts Receivable
2 Describe how companies value accounts receivable and record their disposition.	• Valuing accounts receivable • Disposing of accounts receivable	DO IT! 2 2a Bad Debt Expense 2b Factoring
3 Explain how companies recognize, value, and dispose of notes receivable.	• Determining the maturity date • Computing interest • Recognizing notes receivable • Valuing notes receivable • Disposing of notes receivable	DO IT! 3 Notes Receivable
4 Describe the statement presentation of receivables and the principles of receivables management.	• Financial statement presentation of receivables • Managing receivables • Evaluating liquidity of receivables • Accelerating cash receipts	DO IT! 4 Analysis of Receivables

Go to the ***REVIEW AND PRACTICE*** section at the end of the chapter for a targeted summary and exercises with solutions.

Visit **WileyPLUS** for additional tutorials and practice opportunities.

FEATURE STORY

What's Cooking?

What major U.S corporation got its start 38 years ago with a waffle iron? *Hint:* It doesn't sell food. *Another hint:* Swoosh. *Another hint:* "Just do it." That's right, Nike. In 1971, Nike co-founder Bill Bowerman put a piece of rubber into a kitchen waffle iron, and the trademark waffle sole was born. It seems fair to say that at Nike, "They don't make 'em like they used to."

Nike was co-founded by Bowerman and Phil Knight, a member of Bowerman's University of Oregon track team. Each began in the shoe business independently during the early 1960s. Bowerman got his start by making hand-crafted running shoes for his University of Oregon track team. Knight, after completing graduate school, started a small business importing low-cost, high-quality shoes from Japan. In 1964, the two joined forces, each contributing $500, and formed Blue Ribbon Sports, a partnership that marketed Japanese shoes.

It wasn't until 1971 that the company began manufacturing its own line of shoes. With the new shoes came a new corporate name–Nike–the Greek goddess of victory. It is hard to imagine that the company that now boasts a stable full of world-class athletes as promoters at one time had part-time employees selling shoes out of car trunks at track meets on a cash-and-carry basis.

As the business grew, Nike sold its shoes to sporting good shops and department stores on a credit basis. This necessitated receivables management. Today, with sales of $20.8 billion and accounts receivable of $3.1 billion, managing accounts receivable is vitally important to Nike's success. If it makes a major mistake with its receivables, it will definitely affect the bottom line.

In recent years, Nike has expanded its product line to a diverse range of products, including performance equipment such as soccer balls and golf clubs. While this has increased sales revenue, it has also complicated Nike's receivables management efforts. Now, instead of selling shoes at a limited number of retail outlets, it sells its vast number of products to a diverse array of stores, large and small. For example, Nike golf clubs are sold at local country clubs and golf shops across the country, while soccer equipment can be sold directly to customers through Internet sales. This diversification of its customer list complicates matters because Nike has to approve each new store or customer for credit sales, monitor cash collections, and pursue slow-paying accounts. That's a lot of work. Maybe cash-and-carry wasn't so bad after all.

LEARNING OBJECTIVE 1

Explain how companies recognize accounts receivable.

The term **receivables** refers to amounts due from individuals and companies. Receivables are claims that are expected to be collected in cash. The management of receivables is a very important activity for any company that sells goods or services on credit.

Receivables are important because they represent one of a company's most liquid assets. For many companies, receivables are also one of the largest assets. For example, receivables represent 18.5% of the assets of Nike. Illustration 8-1 lists receivables as a percentage of total assets for five other well-known companies in a recent year.

ILLUSTRATION 8-1
Receivables as a percentage of assets

Company	Receivables as a Percentage of Total Assets
Ford Motor Company	43.2%
General Electric	41.5
Minnesota Mining and Manufacturing Company (3M)	12.7
DuPont Co.	11.7
Intel Corporation	3.9

TYPES OF RECEIVABLES

The relative significance of a company's receivables as a percentage of its assets depends on various factors: its industry, the time of year, whether it extends long-term financing, and its credit policies. To reflect important differences among receivables, they are frequently classified as (1) accounts receivable, (2) notes receivable, and (3) other receivables.

Accounts receivable are amounts customers owe on account. They result from the sale of goods and services. Companies generally expect to collect accounts receivable within 30 to 60 days. They are usually the most significant type of claim held by a company.

Notes receivable are a written promise (as evidenced by a formal instrument) for amounts to be received. The note normally requires the collection of interest and extends for time periods of 60–90 days or longer. Notes and accounts receivable that result from sales transactions are often called **trade receivables**.

ETHICS NOTE
Companies report receivables from employees separately in the financial statements. The reason: Sometimes these receivables are not the result of an "arm's-length" transaction.

Other receivables include nontrade receivables such as interest receivable, loans to company officers, advances to employees, and income taxes refundable. These do not generally result from the operations of the business. Therefore, they are generally classified and reported as separate items in the balance sheet.

RECOGNIZING ACCOUNTS RECEIVABLE

Recognizing accounts receivable is relatively straightforward. A service organization records a receivable when it performs a service on account. A merchandiser records accounts receivable at the point of sale of merchandise on account. When a merchandiser sells goods, it increases (debits) Accounts Receivable and increases (credits) Sales Revenue.

The seller may offer terms that encourage early payment by providing a discount. Sales returns also reduce receivables. The buyer might find some of the goods unacceptable and choose to return the unwanted goods.

To review, assume that Jordache Co. on July 1, 2017, sells merchandise on account to Polo Company for $1,000, terms 2/10, n/30. On July 5, Polo returns merchandise with a sales price of $100 to Jordache Co. On July 11, Jordache receives payment from Polo Company for the balance due. The journal entries to record these transactions on the books of Jordache Co. are as follows. **(Cost of goods sold entries are omitted.)**

July 1	Accounts Receivable—Polo Company	1,000	
	Sales Revenue		1,000
	(To record sales on account)		
July 5	Sales Returns and Allowances	100	
	Accounts Receivable—Polo Company		100
	(To record merchandise returned)		
July 11	Cash ($900 − $18)	882	
	Sales Discounts ($900 × .02)	18	
	Accounts Receivable—Polo Company		900
	(To record collection of accounts receivable)		

▼ **HELPFUL HINT**

These entries are the same as those described in Chapter 5. For simplicity, we have omitted inventory and cost of goods sold from this set of journal entries and from end-of-chapter material.

Some retailers issue their own credit cards. When you use a retailer's credit card (JCPenney, for example), the retailer charges interest on the balance due if not paid within a specified period (usually 25–30 days).

To illustrate, assume that you use your JCPenney credit card to purchase clothing with a sales price of $300 on June 1, 2017. JCPenney will increase (debit) Accounts Receivable for $300 and increase (credit) Sales Revenue for $300 (cost of goods sold entry omitted), as follows.

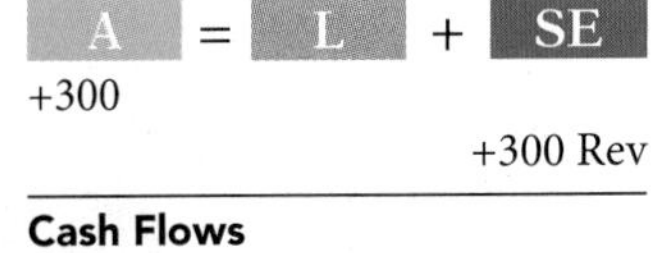

Cash Flows
no effect

June 1	Accounts Receivable	300	
	Sales Revenue		300
	(To record sales on account)		

Assuming that you owe $300 at the end of the month and JCPenney charges 1.5% per month on the balance due, the adjusting entry that JCPenney makes to record interest revenue of $4.50 ($300 × 1.5%) on June 30 is as follows.

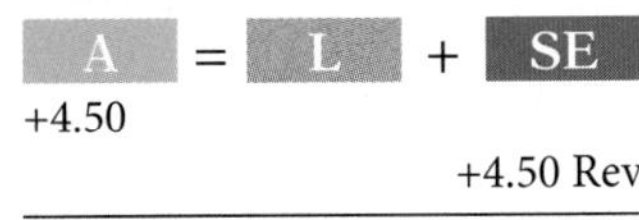

Cash Flows
no effect

June 30	Accounts Receivable	4.50	
	Interest Revenue		4.50
	(To record interest on amount due)		

Interest revenue is often substantial for many retailers.

ANATOMY OF A FRAUD

Tasanee was the accounts receivable clerk for a large non-profit foundation that provided performance and exhibition space for the performing and visual arts. Her responsibilities included activities normally assigned to an accounts receivable clerk, such as recording revenues from various sources (donations, facility rental fees, ticket revenue, and bar receipts). However, she was also responsible for handling all cash and checks from the time they were received until the time she deposited them, as well as preparing the bank reconciliation. Tasanee took advantage of her situation by falsifying bank deposits and bank reconciliations so that she could steal cash from the bar receipts. Since nobody else logged the donations or matched the donation receipts to pledges prior to Tasanee receiving them, she was able to offset the cash that was stolen against donations that she received but didn't record. Her crime was made easier by the fact that her boss, the company's controller, only did a very superficial review of the bank reconciliation and thus didn't notice that some numbers had been cut out from other documents and taped onto the bank reconciliation.

Total take: $1.5 million

THE MISSING CONTROLS

Segregation of duties. The foundation should not have allowed an accounts receivable clerk, whose job was to record receivables, to also handle cash, record cash, and make deposits, and especially prepare the bank reconciliation.

Independent internal verification. The controller was supposed to perform a thorough review of the bank reconciliation. Because he did not, he was terminated from his position.

Source: Adapted from Wells, *Fraud Casebook* (2007), pp. 183–194.

DO IT  1 Recognizing Accounts Receivable

On May 1, Wilton sold merchandise on account to Bates for $50,000 terms 3/15, net 45. On May 4, Bates returns merchandise with a sales price of $2,000. On May 16, Wilton receives payment from Bates for the balance due. Prepare journal entries to record the May transactions on Wilton's books. (You may ignore cost of goods sold entries and explanations.)

Action Plan

✔ Prepare entry to record the receivable and related return.

✔ Compute the sales discount and related entry.

SOLUTION

Date	Account	Debit	Credit
May 1	Accounts Receivable—Bates	50,000	
	Sales Revenue		50,000
4	Sales Returns and Allowances	2,000	
	Accounts Receivable—Bates		2,000
16	Cash ($48,000 − $1,440)	46,560	
	Sales Discounts ($48,000 × .03)	1,440	
	Accounts Receivable—Bates		48,000

Related exercise material: **BE8-1, BE8-2, DO IT! 8-1, E8-1,** and **E8-2.**

LEARNING OBJECTIVE 2 Describe how companies value accounts receivable and record their disposition.

VALUING ACCOUNTS RECEIVABLE

Once companies record receivables in the accounts, the next question is: How should they report receivables in the financial statements? Companies report accounts receivable on the balance sheet as an asset. Determining the **amount** to report is sometimes difficult because some receivables will become uncollectible.

Although each customer must satisfy the credit requirements of the seller before the credit sale is approved, inevitably some accounts receivable become uncollectible. For example, a corporate customer may not be able to pay because it experienced a sales decline due to an economic downturn. Similarly, individuals may be laid off from their jobs or be faced with unexpected hospital bills. The seller records these losses that result from extending credit as **Bad Debt Expense**. Such losses are a normal and necessary risk of doing business on a credit basis.

ALTERNATIVE TERMINOLOGY
You will sometimes see Bad Debt Expense called Uncollectible Accounts Expense.

When U.S. home prices fell, home foreclosures rose, and the economy in general slowed as a result of the financial crisis of 2008, lenders experienced huge increases in their bad debt expense. For example, during a recent quarter Wachovia, a large U.S. bank now owned by Wells Fargo, increased bad debt expense from $108 million to $408 million. Similarly, American Express increased its bad debt expense by 70%.

Two methods are used in accounting for uncollectible accounts: (1) the direct write-off method and (2) the allowance method. We explain both methods in the following sections.

Direct Write-Off Method for Uncollectible Accounts

Under the **direct write-off method**, when a company determines receivables from a particular company to be uncollectible, it charges the loss to Bad Debt Expense. Assume, for example, that Warden Co. writes off M. E. Doran's $200 balance as uncollectible on December 12. Warden's entry is as follows.

Dec. 12	Bad Debt Expense	200	
	Accounts Receivable—M. E. Doran		200
	(To record write-off of M. E. Doran account)		

A	=	L	+	SE
				−200 Exp
−200				

Cash Flows
no effect

Under this method, bad debt expense will show only **actual losses** from uncollectibles. The company reports accounts receivable at its gross amount without any adjustment for estimated losses for bad debts.

Use of the direct write-off method can reduce the usefulness of both the income statement and balance sheet. Consider the following example. In 2017, Quick Buck Computer Company decided it could increase its revenues by offering computers to college students without requiring any money down and with no credit-approval process. It went on campuses across the country and sold one million computers at a selling price of $800 each. This promotion increased Quick Buck's revenues and receivables by $800 million, a huge success! The 2017 balance sheet and income statement looked wonderful. Unfortunately, during 2018, nearly 40% of the college student customers defaulted on their loans. The 2018 income statement and balance sheet looked terrible. Illustration 8-2 shows the effect of these events on the financial statements using the direct write-off method.

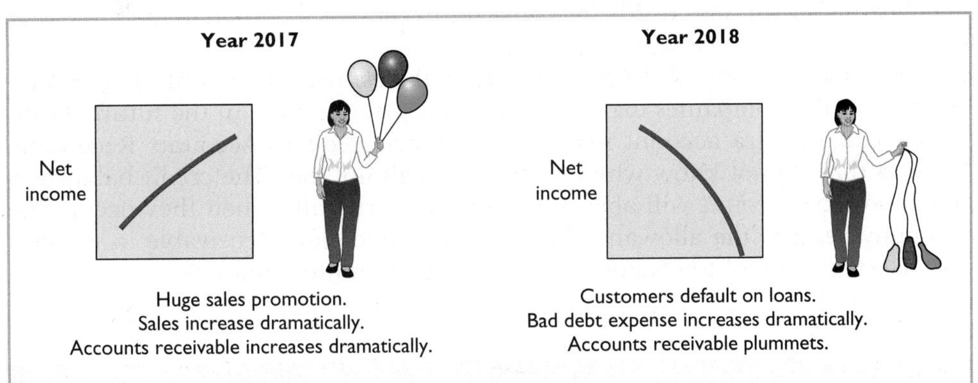

ILLUSTRATION 8-2
Effects of direct write-off method

Under the direct write-off method, companies often record bad debt expense in a period different from the period in which they recorded the revenue. Thus, no attempt is made to match bad debt expense to sales revenue in the income statement. Nor does the company try to show accounts receivable in the balance sheet at the amount actually expected to be received. Consequently, unless a company expects bad debt losses to be insignificant, **the direct write-off method is not acceptable for financial reporting purposes.**

Allowance Method for Uncollectible Accounts

The **allowance method** of accounting for bad debts involves estimating uncollectible accounts at the end of each period. This provides better matching of expenses with revenues on the income statement. It also ensures that receivables are stated at their cash (net) realizable value on the balance sheet. **Cash (net) realizable value** is the net amount a company expects to receive in cash from receivables. It excludes amounts that the company estimates it will not collect. Estimated uncollectible receivables therefore reduce receivables on the balance sheet through use of the allowance method.

Companies must use the allowance method for financial reporting purposes when bad debts are material in amount. It has three essential features:

▼ **HELPFUL HINT**
In this context, *material* means significant or important to financial statement users.

1. Companies **estimate** uncollectible accounts receivable and **match them against revenues** in the same accounting period in which the revenues are recorded.

2. Companies record estimated uncollectibles as an increase (a debit) to Bad Debt Expense and an increase (a credit) to Allowance for Doubtful Accounts through an adjusting entry at the end of each period. Allowance for Doubtful Accounts is a contra account to Accounts Receivable.
3. Companies debit actual uncollectibles to Allowance for Doubtful Accounts and credit them to Accounts Receivable at the time the specific account is written off as uncollectible.

RECORDING ESTIMATED UNCOLLECTIBLES To illustrate the allowance method, assume that Hampson Furniture has credit sales of $1,200,000 in 2017, of which $200,000 remains uncollected at December 31. The credit manager estimates that $12,000 of these sales will prove uncollectible. The adjusting entry to record the estimated uncollectibles increases (debits) Bad Debt Expense and increases (credits) Allowance for Doubtful Accounts, as follows.

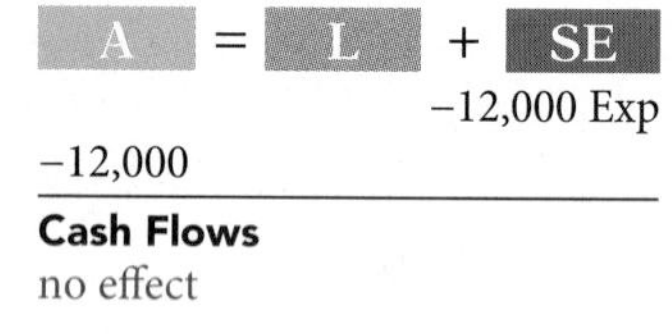

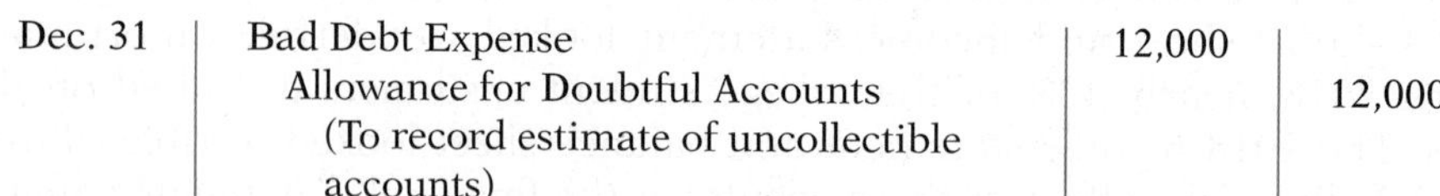

Dec. 31	Bad Debt Expense	12,000	
	Allowance for Doubtful Accounts		12,000
	(To record estimate of uncollectible accounts)		

Companies report Bad Debt Expense in the income statement as an operating expense (usually as a selling expense). Thus, Hampson matches the estimated uncollectibles with sales in 2017 because the expense is recorded in the same year the company makes the sales.

Allowance for Doubtful Accounts shows the estimated amount of claims on customers that companies expect will become uncollectible in the future. Companies use a contra account instead of a direct credit to Accounts Receivable because they do not know which customers will not pay. The credit balance in the allowance account will absorb the specific write-offs when they occur. The company deducts the allowance account from Accounts Receivable in the current assets section of the balance sheet, as shown in Illustration 8-3.

ILLUSTRATION 8-3
Presentation of allowance for doubtful accounts

HAMPSON FURNITURE Balance Sheet (partial)		
Current assets		
Cash		$ 14,800
Accounts receivable	**$200,000**	
Less: Allowance for doubtful accounts	**12,000**	**188,000**
Inventory		310,000
Supplies		25,000
Total current assets		$537,800

The amount of $188,000 in Illustration 8-3 represents the expected **cash realizable value** of the accounts receivable at the statement date. **Companies do not close Allowance for Doubtful Accounts at the end of the fiscal year.**

RECORDING THE WRITE-OFF OF AN UNCOLLECTIBLE ACCOUNT Various methods are used to collect past-due accounts. When a company exhausts all means of collecting a past-due account and collection appears unlikely, the company writes off the account. In the credit card industry, it is standard practice to write off accounts that are 210 days past due. To prevent premature or unauthorized write-offs, authorized management personnel should formally approve each write-off. **To maintain segregation of duties, the employee authorized to write off accounts should not have daily responsibilities related to cash or receivables.**

To illustrate a receivables write-off, assume that the vice president of finance of Hampson Furniture on March 1, 2018, authorizes a write-off of the $500 balance owed by R. A. Ware. The entry to record the write-off is as follows.

Mar. 1	Allowance for Doubtful Accounts	500	
	Accounts Receivable—R. A. Ware		500
	(Write-off of R. A. Ware account)		

A = L + SE
+500
−500
Cash Flows
no effect

The company does not increase Bad Debt Expense when the write-off occurs. **Under the allowance method, a company debits every bad debt write-off to the allowance account and not to Bad Debt Expense.** A debit to Bad Debt Expense would be incorrect because the company has already recognized the expense when it made the adjusting entry for estimated bad debts. Instead, the entry to record the write-off of an uncollectible account reduces both Accounts Receivable and Allowance for Doubtful Accounts. After posting, the general ledger accounts appear as shown in Illustration 8-4.

ILLUSTRATION 8-4
General ledger balances after write-off

Accounts Receivable		**Allowance for Doubtful Accounts**	
Jan. 1 Bal. 200,000	Mar. 1 **500**	Mar. 1 **500**	Jan. 1 Bal. 12,000
Mar. 1 Bal. 199,500			Mar. 1 Bal. 11,500

A write-off affects only balance sheet accounts. Cash realizable value in the balance sheet, therefore, remains the same before and after the write-off, as shown in Illustration 8-5.

ILLUSTRATION 8-5
Cash realizable value comparison

	Before Write-Off	**After Write-Off**
Accounts receivable	$ 200,000	$ 199,500
Allowance for doubtful accounts	12,000	11,500
Cash realizable value	**$188,000**	**$188,000**

RECOVERY OF AN UNCOLLECTIBLE ACCOUNT Occasionally, a company collects from a customer after the account has been written off as uncollectible. The company must make two entries to record the recovery of a bad debt: (1) It reverses the entry made in writing off the account. This reinstates the customer's account. (2) It journalizes the collection in the usual manner.

To illustrate, assume that on July 1, R. A. Ware pays the $500 amount that Hampson Furniture had written off on March 1. Hampson makes these entries:

	(1)		
July 1	Accounts Receivable—R. A. Ware	500	
	Allowance for Doubtful Accounts		500
	(To reverse write-off of R. A. Ware account)		

	(2)		
1	Cash	500	
	Accounts Receivable—R. A. Ware		500
	(To record collection from R. A. Ware)		

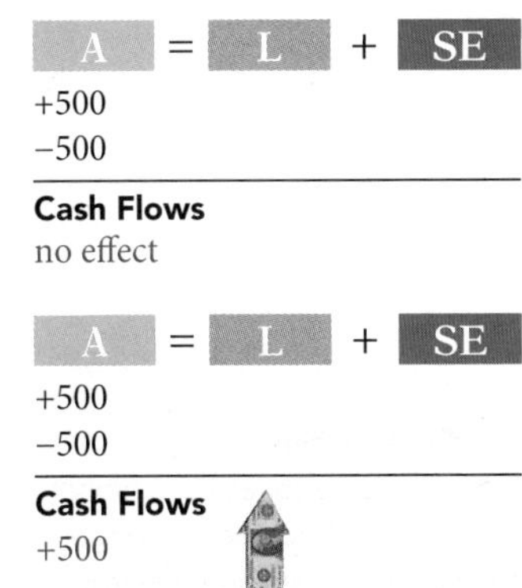

A = L + SE
+500
−500
Cash Flows
no effect

A = L + SE
+500
−500
Cash Flows
+500

Note that the recovery of a bad debt, like the write-off of a bad debt, affects only balance sheet accounts. The net effect of the two entries is an increase in Cash and an increase in Allowance for Doubtful Accounts for $500. Accounts Receivable and Allowance for Doubtful Accounts both increase in entry (1) for two reasons. First, the company made an error in judgment when it wrote off the account receivable. Second, R. A. Ware did pay, and therefore the Accounts Receivable account should show this reinstatement and collection for possible future credit purposes.

▼ **HELPFUL HINT**
Like the write-off, a recovery does not involve the income statement.

ESTIMATING THE ALLOWANCE For Hampson Furniture in Illustration 8-3, the amount of the expected uncollectibles was given. However, in "real life," companies must estimate the amount of expected uncollectible accounts if they use the allowance method. Illustration 8-6 shows an excerpt from the notes to Nike's financial statements discussing its use of the allowance method.

ILLUSTRATION 8-6
Nike's allowance method disclosure

Allowance for Uncollectible Accounts Receivable

We make ongoing estimates relating to the ability to collect our accounts receivable and maintain an allowance for estimated losses resulting from the inability of our customers to make required payments. In determining the amount of the allowance, we consider our historical level of credit losses and make judgments about the creditworthiness of significant customers based on ongoing credit evaluations. Since we cannot predict future changes in the financial stability of our customers, actual future losses from uncollectible accounts may differ from our estimates.

▼ HELPFUL HINT
Where appropriate, the percentage-of-receivables basis may use only a single percentage rate.

Allowance for Doubtful Accounts	
	Dec. 31 Unadj. Bal. 1,500
	Dec. 31 Adj. **8,500**
	Dec. 31 Bal. 10,000

Frequently, companies estimate the allowance as a percentage of the outstanding receivables. Under the **percentage-of-receivables basis**, management establishes a percentage relationship between the amount of receivables and expected losses from uncollectible accounts. For example, suppose Steffen Company has an ending balance in Accounts Receivable of $200,000 and an unadjusted credit balance in Allowance for Doubtful Accounts of $1,500. It estimates that 5% of its accounts receivable will eventually be uncollectible. It should report a balance in Allowance for Doubtful Accounts of $10,000 (.05 × $200,000). To increase the balance in Allowance for Doubtful Accounts from $1,500 to $10,000, the company debits (increases) Bad Debt Expense and credits (increases) Allowance for Doubtful Accounts by $8,500 ($10,000 − $1,500).

DECISION TOOLS

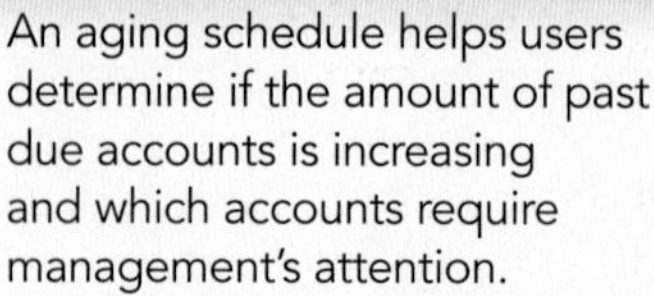

An aging schedule helps users determine if the amount of past due accounts is increasing and which accounts require management's attention.

To more accurately estimate the ending balance in the allowance account, a company often prepares a schedule, called **aging the accounts receivable**. This schedule classifies customer balances by the length of time they have been unpaid.

After the company arranges the accounts by age, it determines the expected bad debt losses by applying percentages, based on past experience, to the totals of each category. The longer a receivable is past due, the less likely it is to be collected. As a result, the estimated percentage of uncollectible debts increases as the number of days past due increases. Illustration 8-7

ILLUSTRATION 8-7
Aging schedule

▼ HELPFUL HINT
The older categories have higher percentages because the longer an account is past due, the less likely it is to be collected.

Worksheet.xls

	A	B	C	D	E	F	G
1				Number of Days Past Due			
2			Not				
3	Customer	Total	Yet Due	1–30	31–60	61–90	Over 90
4	T. E. Adert	$ 600		$ 300		$ 200	$ 100
5	R. C. Bortz	300	$ 300				
6	B. A. Carl	450		200	$ 250		
7	O. L. Diker	700	500			200	
8	T. O. Ebbet	600			300		300
9	Others	36,950	26,200	5,200	2,450	1,600	1,500
10		$39,600	$27,000	$5,700	$3,000	$2,000	$1,900
11	Estimated percentage uncollectible		2%	4%	10%	20%	40%
12	Total estimated uncollectible accounts	$ 2,228	$ 540	$ 228	$ 300	$ 400	$ 760
13							

shows an aging schedule for Dart Company. Note the increasing uncollectible percentages from 2% to 40%.

Total estimated uncollectible accounts for Dart Company ($2,228) represent the existing customer claims expected to become uncollectible in the future. Thus, this amount represents the **required balance** in Allowance for Doubtful Accounts at the balance sheet date. Accordingly, **the amount of bad debt expense that should be recorded in the adjusting entry is the difference between the required balance and the existing balance in the allowance account.** The existing, unadjusted balance in Allowance for Doubtful Accounts is the net result of the beginning balance (a normal credit balance) less the write-offs of specific accounts during the year (debits to the allowance account).

For example, if the unadjusted trial balance shows Allowance for Doubtful Accounts with a credit balance of $528, then an adjusting entry for $1,700 ($2,228 − $528) is necessary:

Date	Account	Debit	Credit
Dec. 31	Bad Debt Expense	1,700	
	Allowance for Doubtful Accounts		1,700
	(To adjust allowance account to total estimated uncollectibles)		

A	=	L	+	SE
				−1,700 Exp
−1,700				

Cash Flows
no effect

After Dart posts the adjusting entry, its accounts appear as shown in Illustration 8-8.

ILLUSTRATION 8-8
Bad debt accounts after posting

Bad Debt Expense		Allowance for Doubtful Accounts	
Dec. 31 Adj. **1,700**			Dec. 31 Unadj. Bal. 528
			Dec. 31 Adj. **1,700**
			Dec. 31 Bal. 2,228

An important aspect of accounts receivable management is simply maintaining a close watch on the accounts. Studies have shown that accounts more than 60 days past due lose approximately 50% of their value if no payment activity occurs within the next 30 days. For each additional 30 days that pass, the collectible value halves once again.

Occasionally, the allowance account will have a **debit balance** prior to adjustment. This occurs because the debits to the allowance account from write-offs during the year **exceeded** the beginning balance in the account which was based on previous estimates for bad debts. In such a case, the company **adds the debit balance to the required balance** when it makes the adjusting entry. Thus, if there was a $500 **debit** balance in the allowance account before adjustment, the adjusting entry would be for $2,728 ($2,228 + $500) to arrive at a credit balance of $2,228 as shown below.

Date	Account	Debit	Credit
Dec. 31	Bad Debt Expense	2,728	
	Allowance for Doubtful Accounts		2,728
	(To adjust allowance account to total estimated uncollectibles)		

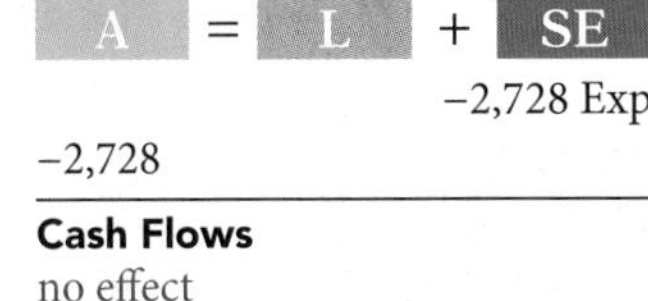

After Dart posts the adjusting entry, its accounts appear as shown in Illustration 8-9.

ILLUSTRATION 8-9
Bad debt accounts after posting

Bad Debt Expense		Allowance for Doubtful Accounts	
Dec. 31 Adj. **2,728**		Dec. 31 Unadj. Bal. 500	Dec. 31 Adj. **2,728**
			Dec. 31 Bal. 2,228

The percentage-of-receivables basis provides an estimate of the cash realizable value of the receivables. It also provides a reasonable matching of expenses to revenue.

The following note regarding accounts receivable comes from the annual report of the shoe company Skechers USA.

ILLUSTRATION 8-10
Skechers USA's note disclosure of accounts receivable

SKECHERS USA
Notes to the Financial Statements

The likelihood of a material loss on an uncollectible account would be mainly dependent on deterioration in the overall economic conditions in a particular country or region. Reserves are fully provided for all probable losses of this nature. For receivables that are not specifically identified as high risk, we provide a reserve based upon our historical loss rate as a percentage of sales. Gross trade accounts receivable were $293.1 million and $241.9 million, and the allowance for bad debts, returns, sales allowances and customer chargebacks were $21.0 million and $15.9 million, at December 31, 2014 and 2013, respectively. Our credit losses charged to expense for the years ended December 31, 2014, 2013 and 2012 were $11.8 million, $2.6 million and $1.5 million, respectively. In addition, we recorded sales return and allowance expense (recoveries) for the years ended December 31, 2014, 2013 and 2012 of $2.3 million, $0.2 million and $(0.4) million, respectively.

ETHICS INSIGHT

© Christy Thompson/Shutterstock

Cookie Jar Allowances

There are many pressures on companies to achieve earnings targets. For managers, poor earnings can lead to dismissal or lack of promotion. It is not surprising then that management may be tempted to look for ways to boost their earnings number.

One way a company can achieve greater earnings is to lower its estimate of what is needed in its Allowance for Doubtful Accounts (sometimes referred to as "tapping the cookie jar"). For example, suppose a company has an Allowance for Doubtful Accounts of $10 million and decides to reduce this balance to $9 million. As a result of this change, Bad Debt Expense decreases by $1 million and earnings increase by $1 million.

Large banks such as JP Morgan Chase, Wells Fargo, and Bank of America recently decreased their Allowance for Doubtful Accounts by over $4 billion. These reductions came at a time when these big banks were still suffering from lower mortgage lending and trading activity, both of which lead to lower earnings. They justified these reductions in the allowance balances by noting that credit quality and economic conditions had improved. This may be so, but it sure is great to have a cookie jar that might be tapped when a boost in earnings is needed.

How might investors determine that a company is managing its earnings? (Go to WileyPLUS for this answer and additional questions.)

DO IT! 2a Bad Debt Expense

Action Plan

- ✔ Estimate the amount the company does not expect to collect.
- ✔ Consider the existing balance in the allowance account when using the percentage-of-receivables basis.
- ✔ Report receivables at their cash (net) realizable value—that is, the amount the company expects to collect in cash.

Brule Corporation has been in business for 5 years. The unadjusted trial balance at the end of the current year shows Accounts Receivable $30,000, Sales Revenue $180,000, and Allowance for Doubtful Accounts with a debit balance of $2,000. Brule estimates bad debts to be 10% of accounts receivable. Prepare the entry necessary to adjust Allowance for Doubtful Accounts.

SOLUTION

Brule should make the following entry to bring the debit balance in Allowance for Doubtful Accounts up to a normal, credit balance of $3,000 (10% × $30,000):

Bad Debt Expense [(10% × $30,000) + $2,000]	5,000	
Allowance for Doubtful Accounts		5,000
(To record estimate of uncollectible accounts)		

Related exercise material: **BE8-3, BE8-4, BE8-5, DO IT! 8-2a, E8-3, E8-4, E8-5,** and **E8-6.**

DISPOSING OF ACCOUNTS RECEIVABLE

Sale of Receivables to a Factor

A common way to accelerate receivables collection is a sale to a factor. A **factor** is a finance company or bank that buys receivables from businesses for a fee and then collects the payments directly from the customers.

Factoring was traditionally associated with the textiles, apparel, footwear, furniture, and home furnishing industries. It has now spread to other types of businesses and is a multibillion dollar industry. For example, Sears, Roebuck & Co. (now Sears Holdings) once sold $14.8 billion of customer accounts receivable. McKesson at one time had a pre-arranged agreement allowing it to sell up to $700 million of its receivables.

INTERNATIONAL NOTE
GAAP has less stringent requirements regarding the sale of receivables. Thus, GAAP companies can more easily use factoring transactions as a form of financing without showing a related liability on their books. Some argue that this type of so-called "off-balance-sheet financing" would be more difficult to achieve under IFRS.

Factoring arrangements vary widely, but typically the factor charges a commission. It often ranges from 1% to 3% of the amount of receivables purchased. To illustrate, assume that Hendredon Furniture factors $600,000 of receivables to Federal Factors, Inc. Federal Factors assesses a service charge of 2% of the amount of receivables sold. The following journal entry records Hendredon's sale of receivables on April 2, 2017.

Apr. 2	Cash	588,000	
	Service Charge Expense (2% × $600,000)	12,000	
	Accounts Receivable		600,000
	(To record the sale of accounts receivable)		

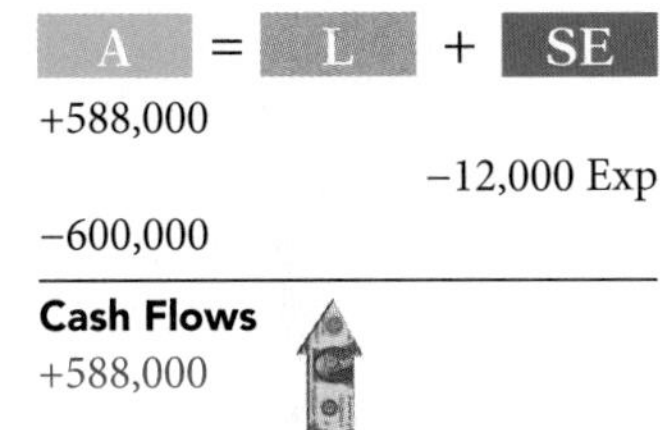

If Hendredon sells its receivables, it records the service charge expense as a selling expense. If the company sells receivables infrequently, it may report this amount under "Other expenses and losses" in the income statement.

National Credit Card Sales

Approximately one billion credit cards were in use recently—more than three credit cards for every man, woman, and child in this country. A common type of credit card is a national credit card such as Visa and MasterCard. Three parties are involved when national credit cards are used in making retail sales: (1) the credit card issuer, who is independent of the retailer; (2) the retailer; and (3) the customer. **A retailer's acceptance of a national credit card is another form of selling—factoring—the receivable by the retailer.**

ETHICS NOTE
In exchange for lower interest rates, some companies have eliminated the 25-day grace period before finance charges kick in. Be sure you read the fine print in any credit agreement you sign.

The use of national credit cards translates to more sales and zero bad debts for the retailer. Both are powerful reasons for a retailer to accept such cards. Illustration 8-11 (page 386) shows the major advantages of national credit cards to the retailer. In exchange for these advantages, the retailer pays the credit card issuer a fee of 2% to 4% of the invoice price for its services.

The retailer considers sales resulting from the use of Visa and MasterCard as **cash sales**. Upon notification of a credit card charge from a retailer, the bank that issued the card immediately adds the amount to the seller's bank balance. Companies therefore record these credit card charges in the same manner as checks deposited from a cash sale.

To illustrate, Morgan Marie purchases $1,000 of compact discs for her restaurant from Sondgeroth Music Co., and she charges this amount on her Visa First Bank Card. The service fee that First Bank charges Sondgeroth Music is 3%. Sondgeroth Music's entry to record this transaction on March 22, 2017, is as follows.

Mar. 22	Cash	970	
	Service Charge Expense	30	
	Sales Revenue		1,000
	(To record Visa credit card sales)		

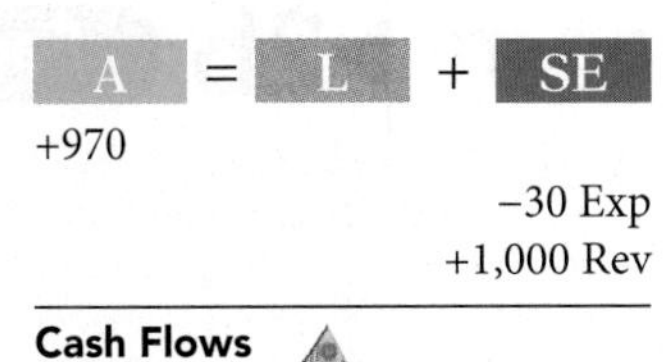

ILLUSTRATION 8-11
Advantages of credit cards to the retailer

ACCOUNTING ACROSS THE ORGANIZATION Nordstrom

Michael Braun/iStockphoto

How Does a Credit Card Work?

Most of you know how to use a credit card, but do you know what happens in the transaction and how the transaction is processed? Suppose that you use a Visa card to purchase some new ties at Nordstrom. The salesperson swipes your card, which allows the information on the magnetic strip on the back of the card to be read. The salesperson then enters in the amount of the purchase. The machine contacts the Visa computer, which routes the call back to the bank that issued your Visa card. The issuing bank verifies that the account exists, that the card is not stolen, and that you have not exceeded your credit limit. At this point, the slip is printed, which you sign.

Visa acts as the clearing agent for the transaction. It transfers funds from the issuing bank to Nordstrom's bank account. Generally this transfer of funds, from sale to the receipt of funds in the merchant's account, takes two to three days.

In the meantime, Visa puts a pending charge on your account for the amount of the tie purchase; that amount counts immediately against your available credit limit. At the end of the billing period, Visa sends you an invoice (your credit card bill) which shows the various charges you made, and the amounts that Visa expended on your behalf, for the month. You then must "pay the piper" for your stylish new ties.

Assume that Nordstrom prepares a bank reconciliation at the end of each month. If some credit card sales have not been processed by the bank, how should Nordstrom treat these transactions on its bank reconciliation? (Go to **WileyPLUS** for this answer and additional questions.)

DO IT! ▶2b Factoring

Peter M. Kell Wholesalers Co. needs to raise $120,000 in cash to safely cover next Friday's employee payroll. Kell has reached its debt ceiling. Kell's present balance of outstanding receivables totals $750,000. Kell decides to factor $125,000 of its receivables on September 7, 2017, to alleviate this cash crunch. Record the entry that Kell would make when it raises the needed cash. (Assume a 1% service charge.)

SOLUTION

Assuming that Kell Co. factors $125,000 of its accounts receivable at a 1% service charge, it would make this entry:

Sept. 7	Cash	123,750	
	Service Charge Expense (1% × $125,000)	1,250	
	Accounts Receivable		125,000
	(To record sale of receivables to factor)		

Action Plan

✔ Consider sale of receivables to a factor.

✔ Weigh cost of factoring against benefit of having cash in hand.

Related exercise material: **BE8-6, DO IT! 8-2b, E8-7, E8-8,** and **E8-9.**

LEARNING OBJECTIVE ▶3

Explain how companies recognize, value, and dispose of notes receivable.

Companies also may grant credit in exchange for a formal credit instrument known as a promissory note. A **promissory note** is a written promise to pay a specified amount of money on demand or at a definite time. Promissory notes may be used (1) when individuals and companies lend or borrow money, (2) when the amount of the transaction and the credit period exceed normal limits, and (3) in settlement of accounts receivable.

In a promissory note, the party making the promise to pay is called the **maker**. The party to whom payment is to be made is called the **payee**. The promissory note may specifically identify the payee by name or may designate the payee simply as the bearer of the note.

In the note shown in Illustration 8-12, Brent Company is the maker, and Wilma Company is the payee. To Wilma Company, the promissory note is a note receivable. To Brent Company, the note is a note payable.

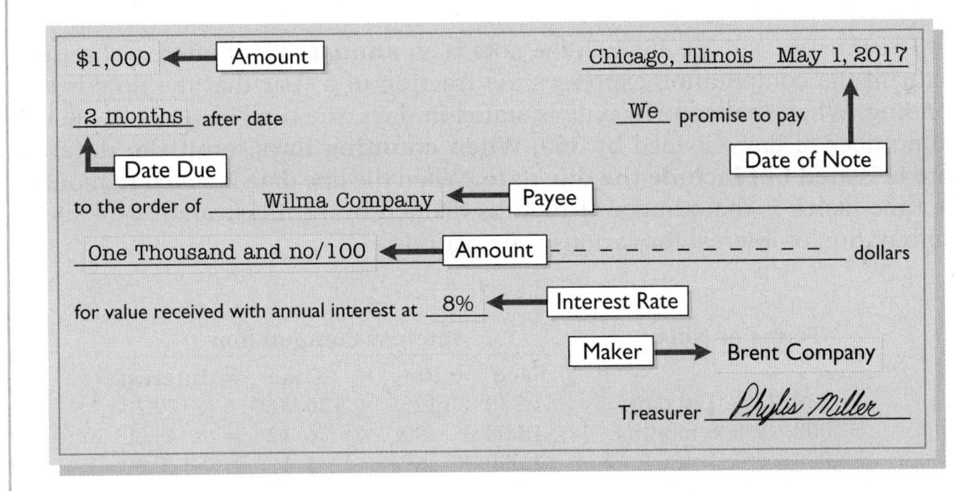

ILLUSTRATION 8-12
Promissory note

▼ **HELPFUL HINT**
For this note, the maker, Brent Company, credits Notes Payable. The payee, Wilma Company, debits Notes Receivable.

Notes receivable give the holder a stronger legal claim to assets than do accounts receivable. Like accounts receivable, notes receivable can be readily sold to another party. Promissory notes are negotiable instruments (as are checks), which means that, when sold, the seller can transfer them to another party by endorsement.

Companies frequently accept notes receivable from customers who need to extend the payment of an outstanding account receivable. Companies also often require notes from high-risk customers. In some industries (e.g., the pleasure and sport boat industry), all credit sales are supported by notes. The majority of notes, however, originate from lending transactions.

The basic issues in accounting for notes receivable are the same as those for accounts receivable. On the following pages, we look at these issues. Before we do, however, we need to consider two issues that do not apply to accounts receivable: determining the maturity date and computing interest.

DETERMINING THE MATURITY DATE

▼ **HELPFUL HINT**

The maturity date of a 60-day note dated July 17 is determined as follows.

Term of note		60 days
July (31 − 17)	14	
August	31	45
September		15
(Maturity date)		

The maturity date of a promissory note may be stated in one of three ways: (1) on demand, (2) on a stated date, and (3) at the end of a stated period of time. When it is stated to be at the end of a period of time, the parties to the note will need to determine the maturity date.

When the life of a note is expressed in terms of months, you find the date when it matures by counting the months from the date of issue. For example, the maturity date of a three-month note dated May 1 is August 1. A note drawn on the last day of a month matures on the last day of a subsequent month. That is, a July 31 note due in two months matures on September 30.

When the due date is stated in terms of days, you need to count the exact number of days to determine the maturity date. In counting, **omit the date the note is issued but include the due date.**

COMPUTING INTEREST

Illustration 8-13 gives the basic formula for computing interest on an interest-bearing note.

ILLUSTRATION 8-13
Formula for computing interest

Face Value of Note	×	Annual Interest Rate	×	Time in Terms of One Year	=	Interest

The interest rate specified on the note is an **annual** rate of interest. The time factor in the computation expresses the fraction of a year that the note is outstanding. When the maturity date is stated in days, the time factor is frequently the number of days divided by 360. **When counting days, omit the date the note is issued but include the due date.** When the due date is stated in months, the time factor is the number of months divided by 12. Illustration 8-14 shows computation of interest for various time periods.

ILLUSTRATION 8-14
Computation of interest

Terms of Note	Face	×	Rate	×	Time	=	Interest
$ 730, 12%, 120 days	$ 730	×	12%	×	120/360	=	$ 29.20
$1,000, 9%, 6 months	$1,000	×	9%	×	6/12	=	$ 45.00
$2,000, 6%, 1 year	$2,000	×	6%	×	1/1	=	$120.00

There are different ways to calculate interest. For example, the computation in Illustration 8-14 assumes 360 days for the year. Financial institutions use 365 days to compute interest. *For homework problems, assume 360 days to simplify computations*.

RECOGNIZING NOTES RECEIVABLE

To illustrate the basic entry for notes receivable, we will use Brent Company's $1,000, two-month, 8% promissory note dated May 1. Assuming that Brent

Company wrote the note to settle an open account, Wilma Company makes the following entry for the receipt of the note.

May 1	Notes Receivable	1,000	
	Accounts Receivable—Brent Company		1,000
	(To record acceptance of Brent Company note)		

A	=	L	+	SE
+1,000				
−1,000				

Cash Flows
no effect

The company records the note receivable at its **face value**, the value shown on the face of the note. No interest revenue is reported when the company accepts the note because the revenue recognition principle does not recognize revenue until the performance obligation is satisfied. Interest is earned (accrued) as time passes.

If a company issues cash in exchange for a note, the entry is a debit to Notes Receivable and a credit to Cash in the amount of the loan.

VALUING NOTES RECEIVABLE

Like accounts receivable, companies report short-term notes receivable at their **cash (net) realizable value**. The notes receivable allowance account is Allowance for Doubtful Accounts. Valuing short-term notes receivable is the same as valuing accounts receivable. The computations and estimations involved in determining cash realizable value and in recording the proper amount of bad debt expense and related allowance are similar.

Long-term notes receivable, however, pose additional estimation problems. As an example, we need only look at the problems large U.S. banks sometimes have in collecting their receivables. Loans to less-developed countries are particularly worrisome. Developing countries need loans for development but often find repayment difficult. In some cases, developed nations have intervened to provide financial assistance to the financially troubled borrowers so as to minimize the political and economic turmoil to the borrower and to ensure the survival of the lender.

INTERNATIONAL INSIGHT

© Andrzej Tokarski/iStockphoto

Can Fair Value Be Unfair?

The FASB and the International Accounting Standards Board (IASB) are considering proposals for how to account for financial instruments. The FASB has proposed that loans and receivables be accounted for at their fair value (the amount they could currently be sold for), as are most investments. The FASB believes that this would provide a more accurate view of a company's financial position. It might be especially useful as an early warning when a bank is in trouble because of poor-quality loans. But, banks argue that fair values are difficult to estimate accurately. They are also concerned that volatile fair values could cause large swings in a bank's reported net income.

Source: David Reilly, "Banks Face a Mark-to-Market Challenge," *Wall Street Journal Online* (March 15, 2010).

What are the arguments in favor of and against fair value accounting for loans and receivables? (Go to **WileyPLUS** for this answer and additional questions.)

DISPOSING OF NOTES RECEIVABLE

Notes may be held to their maturity date, at which time the face value plus accrued interest is due. In some situations, the maker of the note defaults, and the payee must make an appropriate adjustment. In other situations, similar to accounts receivable, the holder of the note speeds up the conversion to cash by selling the receivables (as described later in this chapter).

Honor of Notes Receivable

▼ **HELPFUL HINT**
The number of days of interest that should be accrued at September 30 for a 90-day note issued on August 16 is 45 days (15 days in August plus 30 days in September).

A note is **honored** when its maker pays in full at its maturity date. For each interest-bearing note, the **amount due at maturity** is the face value of the note plus interest for the length of time specified on the note.

To illustrate, assume that Wolder Co. lends Higley Inc. $10,000 on June 1, accepting a five-month, 9% interest note. In this situation, interest is $375 ($\$10,000 \times 9\% \times \frac{5}{12}$). The amount due, the **maturity value**, is $10,375 ($10,000 + $375). To obtain payment, Wolder (the payee) must present the note either to Higley Inc. (the maker) or to the maker's agent, such as a bank. If Wolder presents the note to Higley Inc. on November 1, the maturity date, Wolder's entry to record the collection is as follows.

A	=	L	+	SE
+10,375				
−10,000				
				+375 Rev

Cash Flows
+10,375

Nov. 1	Cash	10,375	
	Notes Receivable		10,000
	Interest Revenue ($\$10,000 \times 9\% \times \frac{5}{12}$)		375
	(To record collection of Higley Inc. note and interest)		

Accrual of Interest Receivable

Suppose instead that Wolder Co. prepares financial statements as of September 30. The timeline in Illustration 8-15 presents this situation.

ILLUSTRATION 8-15
Timeline of interest earned

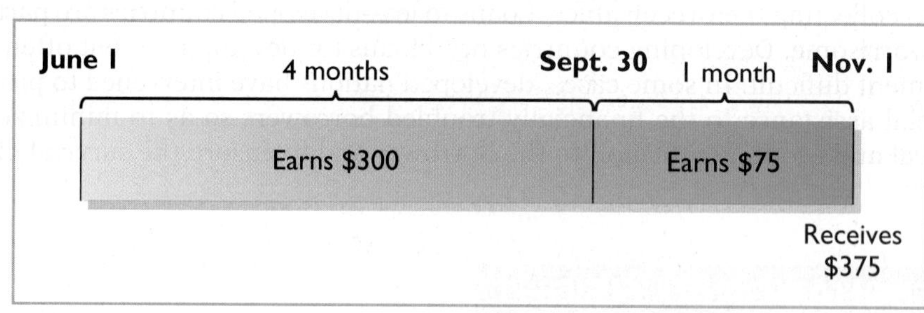

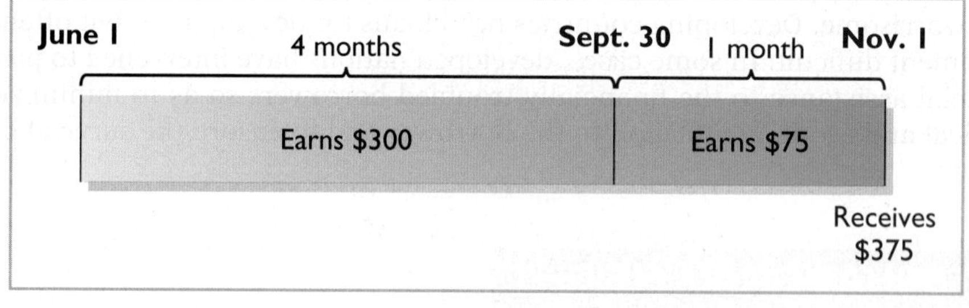

To reflect interest earned but not yet received, Wolder must accrue interest on September 30. In this case, the adjusting entry by Wolder is for four months of interest, or $300, as shown below.

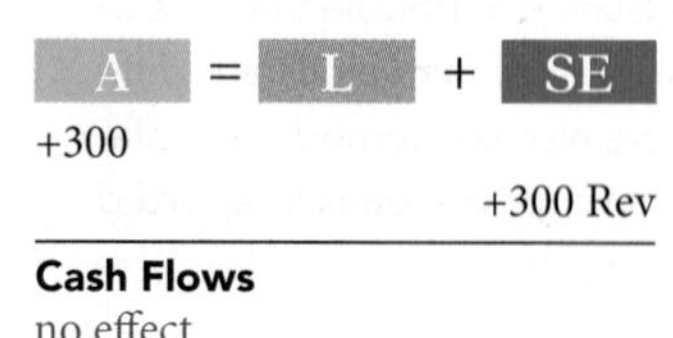

A	=	L	+	SE
+300				+300 Rev

Cash Flows
no effect

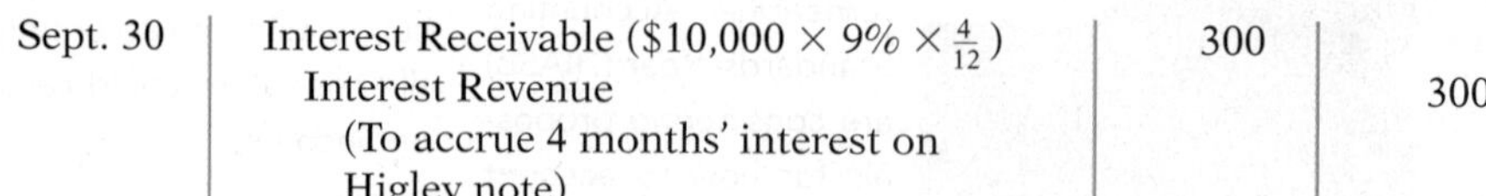

Sept. 30	Interest Receivable ($\$10,000 \times 9\% \times \frac{4}{12}$)	300	
	Interest Revenue		300
	(To accrue 4 months' interest on Higley note)		

At the note's maturity on November 1, Wolder receives $10,375. This amount represents repayment of the $10,000 note as well as five months of interest, or $375, as shown below. The $375 is comprised of the $300 Interest Receivable accrued on September 30 plus $75 earned during October. Wolder's entry to record the honoring of the Higley note on November 1 is as follows.

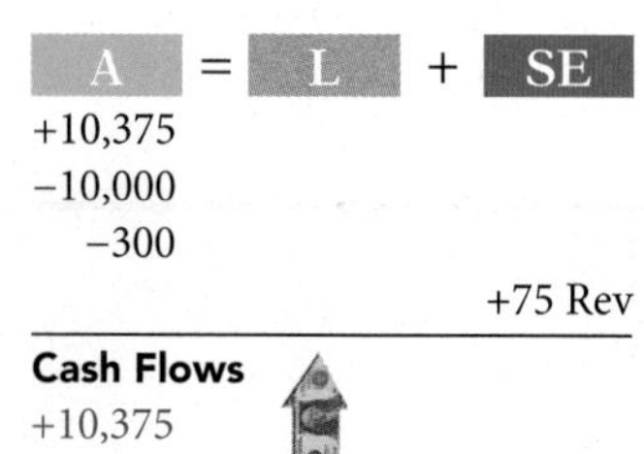

A	=	L	+	SE
+10,375				
−10,000				
−300				
				+75 Rev

Cash Flows
+10,375

Nov. 1	Cash [$\$10,000 + (\$10,000 \times 9\% \times \frac{5}{12})$]	10,375	
	Notes Receivable		10,000
	Interest Receivable		300
	Interest Revenue ($\$10,000 \times 9\% \times \frac{1}{12}$)		75
	(To record collection of Higley Inc. note and interest)		

In this case, Wolder credits Interest Receivable because the receivable was established in the adjusting entry on September 30.

Dishonor of Notes Receivable

A **dishonored (defaulted) note** is a note that is not paid in full at maturity. A dishonored note receivable is no longer negotiable. However, the payee still has a claim against the maker of the note for both the note and the interest. If the lender expects that it eventually will be able to collect, the two parties negotiate new terms to make it easier for the borrower to repay the debt. If there is no hope of collection, the payee should write off the face value of the note.

DO IT! ▶ 3 Notes Receivable

Gambit Stores accepts from Leonard Co. a $3,400, 90-day, 6% note dated May 10 in settlement of Leonard's overdue open account. The note matures on August 8. What entry does Gambit make at the maturity date, assuming Leonard pays the note and interest in full at that time?

SOLUTION

The interest payable at maturity date is $51, computed as follows.

$$\text{Face} \times \text{Rate} \times \text{Time} = \text{Interest}$$

$$\$3{,}400 \times 6\% \times \frac{90}{360} = \$51$$

Gambit Stores records this entry at the maturity date:

Cash	3,451	
Notes Receivable		3,400
Interest Revenue		51
(To record collection of Leonard note and interest)		

Action Plan

✔ Compute the accrued interest.

✔ Prepare the entry for payment of the note and the interest.

Related exercise material: **BE8-7, BE8-8, DO IT! 8-3, E8-10,** and **E8-11.**

LEARNING OBJECTIVE 

Describe the statement presentation of receivables and the principles of receivables management.

If a company has significant receivables, analysts carefully review the company's financial statement disclosures to evaluate how well the company is managing its receivables.

FINANCIAL STATEMENT PRESENTATION OF RECEIVABLES

Companies should identify in the balance sheet or in the notes to the financial statements each of the major types of receivables. Short-term receivables are reported in the current assets section of the balance sheet, below short-term investments. Short-term investments appear before short-term receivables because these investments are nearer to cash. Companies report both the gross amount of receivables and the allowance for doubtful accounts.

Receivables represent 60% of the total assets of heavy equipment manufacturer Deere & Company. Illustration 8-16 (page 392) shows a presentation of receivables for Deere & Company from its balance sheet and notes in a recent year.

In the income statement, companies report bad debt expense under "Selling expenses" in the operating expenses section. They show interest revenue under "Other revenues and gains" in the nonoperating section of the income statement.

ILLUSTRATION 8-16
Balance sheet presentation of receivables

Real World

DEERE & COMPANY Balance Sheet (partial) (in millions)	
Receivables	
Receivables from unconsolidated subsidiaries	$ 30
Trade accounts and notes receivable	3,278
Financing receivables	27,583
Restricted financing receivables	4,616
Other receivables	1,500
Total receivables	37,007
Less: Allowance for doubtful trade receivables	175
Net receivables	$36,832

If a company has significant risk of uncollectible accounts or other problems with its receivables, it is required to discuss this possibility in the notes to the financial statements.

MANAGING RECEIVABLES

Managing accounts receivable involves five steps:

1. Determine to whom to extend credit.
2. Establish a payment period.
3. Monitor collections.
4. Evaluate the liquidity of receivables.
5. Accelerate cash receipts from receivables when necessary.

Extending Credit

Every entrepreneur struggles with financing issues. For example, the very first order that Apple's founders received was 50 circuit boards for a computer hobby shop. To produce the $25,000 order, Steve Jobs and Steve Wozniak needed $15,000 of parts. To purchase the parts, they borrowed $5,000 from friends but then were turned down when they applied for a bank loan for the $10,000 balance. They approached two parts suppliers in an effort to negotiate a purchase on credit, but both suppliers said no. Finally, a third supplier agreed to sell them the parts on 30-day credit after he called the computer hobby shop to confirm that it had, in fact, placed a $25,000 order to purchase goods.

A critical part of managing receivables is determining who should be extended credit and who should not. Many companies increase sales by being generous with their credit policy. However, they sometimes extend credit to risky customers who do not pay. But if your credit policy is too tight, you will lose sales. If it is too loose, you may sell to "deadbeats" who will pay either very late or not at all. One CEO noted that prior to getting his credit and collection department in order, his salespeople had 300 square feet of office space **per person**, while the people in credit and collections had six people crammed into a single 300-square-foot space. Although this focus on sales boosted sales revenue, it had very expensive consequences in bad debt expense.

Companies can take certain steps to help minimize losses due to bad debts when they decide to relax credit standards for new customers. They might require risky customers to provide letters of credit or bank guarantees. Then, if the customer does not pay, the bank that provided the guarantee will do so. Particularly risky customers might be required to pay cash on delivery. For example, at one time retailer Linens'n Things, Inc. reported that its largest suppliers were requiring cash payment before delivery. The suppliers had cut off shipments because the company had been slow in paying. Kmart's suppliers also required it to pay cash in advance when it was financially troubled.

In addition, companies should ask potential customers for references from banks and suppliers, to determine their payment history. It is important to check references of potential new customers as well as periodically to check the financial health of continuing customers. Many resources are available for investigating customers. For example, *The Dun & Bradstreet Reference Book of American Business* (**www.dnb.com**) lists millions of companies and provides credit ratings for many of them.

ACCOUNTING ACROSS THE ORGANIZATION **Countrywide Financial Corporation**

© Andy Dean/iStockphoto

Bad Information Can Lead to Bad Loans

Many factors contributed to the recent credit crisis. One significant factor that resulted in many bad loans was a failure by lenders to investigate loan customers sufficiently. For example, Countrywide Financial Corporation wrote many loans under its "Fast and Easy" loan program. That program allowed borrowers to provide little or no documentation for their income or their assets. Other lenders had similar programs, which earned the nickname "liars' loans." One study found that in these situations, 60% of applicants overstated their incomes by more than 50% in order to qualify for a loan. Critics of the banking industry say that because loan officers were compensated for loan volume, and because banks were selling the loans to investors rather than holding them, the lenders had little incentive to investigate the borrowers' creditworthiness.

Sources: Glenn R. Simpson and James R. Hagerty, "Countrywide Loss Focuses Attention on Underwriting," *Wall Street Journal* (April 30, 2008), p. B1; and Michael Corkery, "Fraud Seen as Driver in Wave of Foreclosures," *Wall Street Journal* (December 21, 2007), p. A1.

What steps should the banks have taken to ensure the accuracy of financial information provided on loan applications? (Go to **WileyPLUS** for this answer and additional questions.)

Establishing a Payment Period

Companies that extend credit should determine a required payment period and communicate that policy to their customers. It is important that the payment period is consistent with that of competitors. For example, if you require payment within 15 days but your competitors allow payment within 45 days, you may lose sales to your competitors. To match your competitors' generous terms yet still encourage prompt payment of accounts, you might allow up to 45 days to pay but offer a sales discount for people paying within 15 days.

Monitoring Collections

DECISION TOOLS 

Monitoring the accounts receivable aging schedule helps users determine if the company's credit risk is increasing.

We discussed preparation of the accounts receivable aging schedule earlier in the chapter (pages 382–383). Companies should prepare an accounts receivable aging schedule at least monthly. In addition to estimating the allowance for doubtful accounts, the aging schedule has other uses. It helps managers estimate the timing of future cash inflows, which is very important to the treasurer's efforts to prepare a cash budget. It provides information about the overall collection experience of the company and identifies problem accounts. For example, management would compute and compare the percentage of receivables that are over 90 days past due. Illustration 8-17 (page 394) contains an excerpt from the notes to Skechers' financial statements discussing how it monitors receivables.

ILLUSTRATION 8-17
Note on monitoring Skechers' receivables

SKECHERS USA
Notes to the Financial Statements

To minimize the likelihood of uncollectibility, customers' credit-worthiness is reviewed periodically based on external credit reporting services, financial statements issued by the customer and our experience with the account, and it is adjusted accordingly. When a customer's account becomes significantly past due, we generally place a hold on the account and discontinue further shipments to that customer, minimizing further risk of loss.

The aging schedule identifies problem accounts that the company needs to pursue with phone calls, letters, and occasionally legal action. Sometimes, special arrangements must be made with problem accounts. For example, it was reported that Intel Corporation (a major manufacturer of computer chips) required that Packard Bell (at one time one of the largest U.S. sellers of personal computers) exchange its past-due account receivable for an interest-bearing note receivable. This caused concern within the investment community. The move suggested that Packard Bell was in trouble, which worried Intel investors concerned about Intel's accounts receivable.

If a company has significant concentrations of credit risk, it must discuss this risk in the notes to its financial statements. A **concentration of credit risk** is a threat of nonpayment from a single large customer or class of customers that could adversely affect the financial health of the company. Illustration 8-18 shows an excerpt from the credit risk note from the 2014 annual report of Skechers. Skechers reports that its five largest customers account for 15.7% of its net sales.

DECISION TOOLS

Identifying risky credit customers helps users determine if the company has significant concentrations of credit risk.

ILLUSTRATION 8-18
Excerpt from Skechers' note on concentration of credit risk

SKECHERS USA
Notes to the Financial Statements

We Depend Upon a Relatively Small Group of Customers for a Large Portion of Our Sales.

During 2014, 2013 and 2012, our net sales to our five largest customers accounted for approximately 15.7%, 18.1% and 18.1% of total net sales, respectively. No customer accounted for more than 10.0% of our net sales during 2014, 2013 and 2012. No customer accounted for more than 10.0% of net trade receivables at December 31, 2014 and 2013. Although we have long-term relationships with many of our customers, our customers do not have a contractual obligation to purchase our products and we cannot be certain that we will be able to retain our existing major customers. Furthermore, the retail industry regularly experiences consolidation, contractions and closings which may result in our loss of customers or our inability to collect accounts receivable of major customers. If we lose a major customer, experience a significant decrease in sales to a major customer or are unable to collect the accounts receivable of a major customer, our business could be harmed.

This note to Skechers' financial statements indicates it has a relatively high concentration of credit risk. A default by any of these large customers could have a significant negative impact on its financial performance.

EVALUATING LIQUIDITY OF RECEIVABLES

Investors and managers keep a watchful eye on the relationship among sales, accounts receivable, and cash collections. If sales increase, then accounts receivable are also expected to increase. But a disproportionate increase in accounts receivable might signal trouble. Perhaps the company increased its

sales by loosening its credit policy, and these receivables may be difficult or impossible to collect. Such receivables are considered less liquid. Recall that liquidity is measured by how quickly certain assets can be converted to cash.

DECISION TOOLS 

The accounts receivable turnover and the average collection period help users determine if a company's collections are being made in a timely fashion.

The ratio that analysts use to assess the liquidity of receivables is the **accounts receivable turnover**, computed by dividing net credit sales (net sales less cash sales) by the average net accounts receivable during the year. This ratio measures the number of times, on average, a company collects receivables during the period. Unless seasonal factors are significant, **average** accounts receivable outstanding can be computed from the beginning and ending balances of the net receivables.[1]

A popular variant of the accounts receivable turnover is the **average collection period**, which measures the average amount of time that a receivable is outstanding. This is done by dividing the accounts receivable turnover into 365 days. Companies use the average collection period to assess the effectiveness of a company's credit and collection policies. The average collection period should not greatly exceed the credit term period (i.e., the time allowed for payment).

The following data (in millions) are available for Nike.

	For the year ended March 31,	
	2014	**2013**
Sales	$27,799	$25,313
Accounts receivable (net)	3,434	3,117

Illustration 8-19 shows the accounts receivable turnover and average collection period for Nike and Skechers, along with comparative industry data. These calculations assume that all sales were credit sales.

$$\text{Accounts Receivable Turnover} = \frac{\text{Net Credit Sales}}{\text{Average Net Accounts Receivable}}$$

$$\text{Average Collection Period} = \frac{365}{\text{Accounts Receivable Turnover}}$$

Ratio	Nike ($ in millions) 2014	Nike 2013	Skechers USA 2014	Industry Average 2014
Accounts receivable turnover	$\frac{\$27{,}799}{(\$3{,}434 + \$3{,}117)/2} = 8.5$ times	8.1 times	9.6 times	12.2 times
Average collection period	$\frac{365 \text{ days}}{8.5} = 42.9$ days	45.1 days	38.0 days	29.9 days

ILLUSTRATION 8-19
Accounts receivable turnover and average collection period

Nike's accounts receivable turnover was 8.5 times in 2014, with a corresponding average collection period of 42.9 days. This was slightly faster than its 2013 collection period. It was slower than the industry average collection period of 29.9 days and higher than Skechers, which was 38 days. What this means is that Nike turned its receivables into cash more slowly than most other companies

[1]If seasonal factors are significant, determine the average accounts receivable balance by using monthly or quarterly amounts.

in its industry. Therefore, it was less likely to pay its current obligations than a company with a quicker accounts receivable turnover (all else equal) and is more likely to need outside financing to meet cash shortfalls.

In some cases, accounts receivable turnover may be misleading. Some large retail chains that issue their own credit cards encourage customers to use these cards for purchases. If customers pay slowly, the stores earn a healthy return on the outstanding receivables in the form of interest at rates of 18% to 22%. On the other hand, companies that sell (factor) their receivables on a consistent basis will have a faster turnover than those that do not. Thus, to interpret accounts receivable turnover, you must know how a company manages its receivables. In general, the faster the turnover, the greater the reliability of the current ratio for assessing liquidity.

ACCELERATING CASH RECEIPTS

In the normal course of events, companies collect accounts receivable in cash and remove them from the books. However, as credit sales and receivables have grown in size and significance, the "normal course of events" has changed. Two common expressions apply to the collection of receivables: (1) "Time is money"—that is, waiting for the normal collection process costs money. (2) "A bird in the hand is worth two in the bush"—that is, getting the cash now is better than getting it later or not at all. Therefore, in order to accelerate the receipt of cash from receivables, companies frequently sell their receivables to another company for cash, thereby shortening the cash-to-cash operating cycle.

There are three reasons for the sale of receivables. The first is their **size**. In recent years, for competitive reasons, sellers (retailers, wholesalers, and manufacturers) often have provided financing to purchasers of their goods. For example, many major companies in the automobile, truck, industrial and farm equipment, computer, and appliance industries have created companies that accept responsibility for accounts receivable financing. Caterpillar has Caterpillar Financial Services, General Electric has GE Capital, and Ford has Ford Motor Credit Corp. (FMCC). These companies are referred to as **captive finance companies** because they are owned by the company selling the product. The purpose of captive finance companies is to encourage the sale of the company's products by assuring financing to buyers. However, the parent companies involved do not necessarily want to hold large amounts of receivables, so they may sell them.

Second, **companies may sell receivables because they may be the only reasonable source of cash**. When credit is tight, companies may not be able to borrow money in the usual credit markets. Even if credit is available, the cost of borrowing may be prohibitive.

A final reason for selling receivables is that **billing and collection are often time-consuming and costly**. As a result, it is often easier for a retailer to sell the receivables to another party that has expertise in billing and collection matters. Credit card companies such as MasterCard, Visa, American Express, and Discover specialize in billing and collecting accounts receivable.

Illustration 8-20 summarizes the basic principles of managing accounts receivable.

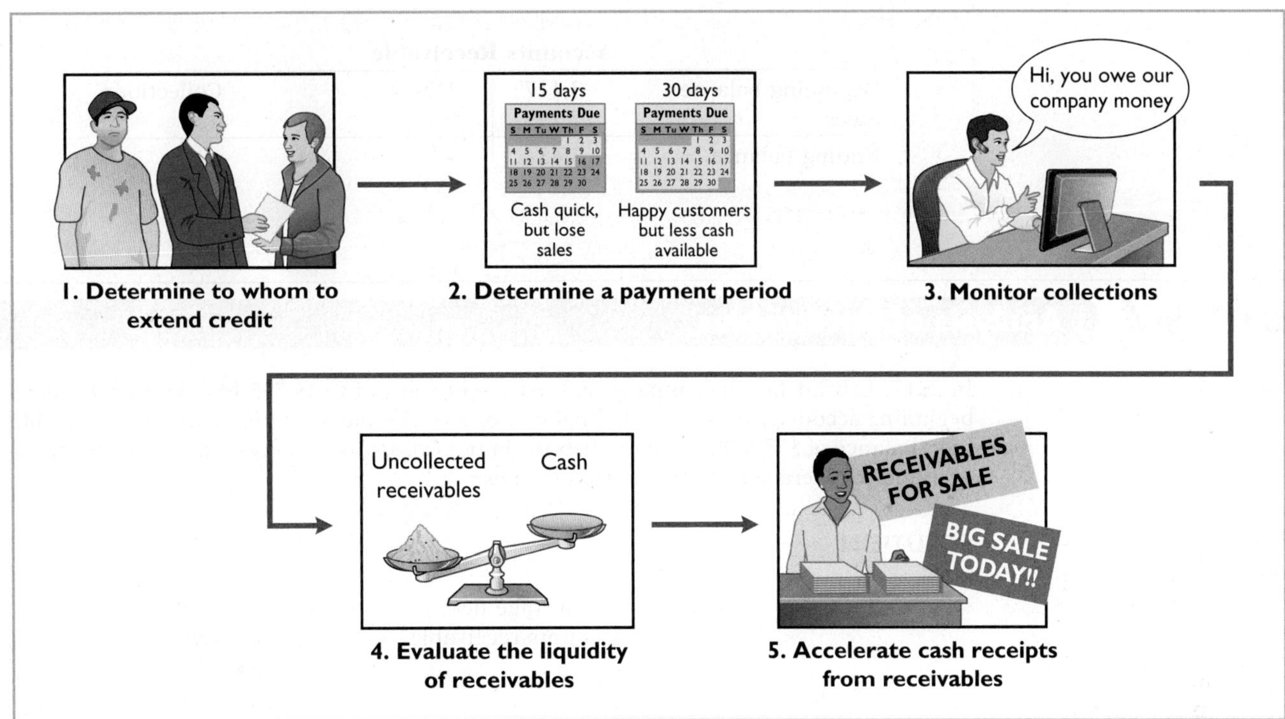

ILLUSTRATION 8-20
Managing receivables

KEEPING AN EYE ON CASH

A lot of companies report strong sales growth but have cash flow problems. How can this be? The reason for the difference is timing: Sales revenue is recorded when goods are delivered even if cash is not received until later. For example, Nike had sales of $27,799 million during 2014. Does that mean it received cash of $27,799 million from its customers? Most likely not. So how do we determine the amount of cash related to sales revenue that is actually received from customers? We analyze the changes that take place in Accounts Receivable.

To illustrate, suppose Bestor Corporation started the year with $10,000 in accounts receivable. During the year, it had credit sales of $100,000. At the end of the year, the balance in accounts receivable was $25,000. As a result, accounts receivable increased $15,000 during the year. How much cash did Bestor collect from customers during the year? Using the following T-account, we can determine that collections were $85,000.

Accounts Receivable

Beginning balance	10,000	85,000	Collections
Sales	100,000		
Ending balance	25,000		

As shown, the difference between sales and cash collections is explained by the change in Accounts Receivable. Accounts Receivable increased by $15,000. Therefore, since credit sales were $100,000, cash collections were only $85,000.

To illustrate another situation, let's use Nike (see data on page 395). Recall that it had net credit sales of $27,799 million. Its ending receivables balance was $3,434 million, and its beginning receivables balance was $3,117 million—an increase of $317 million. Given this change, we can determine that the cash collected from customers during the year was $27,482 million ($27,799 − $317). This is shown in the following T-account.

Accounts Receivable			
Beginning balance	3,117	27,482	Collections
Sales	27,799		
Ending balance	3,434		

DO IT! 4 Analysis of Receivables

In 2017, Lebron James Company had net credit sales of $923,795 for the year. It had a beginning accounts receivable (net) balance of $38,275 and an ending accounts receivable (net) balance of $35,988. Compute Lebron James Company's (a) accounts receivable turnover and (b) average collection period in days.

Action Plan

✔ Review the formula to compute the accounts receivable turnover.

✔ Make sure that both the beginning and ending accounts receivable are considered in the computation.

✔ Review the formula to compute the average collection period in days.

SOLUTION

(a)

Net credit sales	÷	Average net accounts receivable	=	Accounts receivable turnover
$923,795	÷	$\frac{\$38,275 + \$35,988}{2}$	=	24.9 times

(b)

Days in year	÷	Accounts receivable turnover	=	Average collection period in days
365	÷	24.9 times	=	14.7 days

Related exercise material: **BE8-10, BE8-11, DO IT! 8-4, E8-14,** and **E8-15.**

USING DECISION TOOLS—ADIDAS

The information below was taken from the 2014 financial statements of adidas. Similar to Nike and Skechers, adidas sells shoes as well as other products.

ADIDAS AG
Selected Financial Information
(in millions)

	2014	2013
Sales	$14,534	$14,203
Current assets		
Cash and cash equivalents	$ 1,683	$ 1,587
Short-term investment securities	5	41
Accounts receivable (net)	1,946	1,809
Merchandise inventories	2,526	2,634
Other	1,187	786
Total current assets	$ 7,347	$ 6,857
Total current liabilities	$ 4,378	$ 4,732

INSTRUCTIONS

Comment on adidas' accounts receivable management and liquidity relative to that of Nike, using (1) the current ratio and (2) the accounts receivable turnover and average collection period. Nike's current ratio was 2.72:1. The other ratio values for Nike were calculated earlier in the chapter (page 395).

SOLUTION

1. Here is the 2014 current ratio (Current assets ÷ Current liabilities) for each company.

Nike	adidas
2.72:1	$\frac{\$7,347}{\$4,378} = 1.68:1$

Nike's current ratio far exceeds that of adidas. In fact, Nike's might be excessive. A company of its size would not normally want to have so much capital tied up in current assets.

2. The accounts receivable turnover and average collection period for each company are:

	Nike	adidas
Accounts receivable turnover	8.5 times	$\frac{\$14,534}{(\$1,946 + \$1,809)/2} = 7.7$ times
Average collection period	42.9 days	$\frac{365}{7.7} = 47.4$ days

adidas' accounts receivable turnover of 7.7 compared to Nike's 8.5, and its average collection period of 47.4 days versus Nike's 42.9 days, suggest that adidas is able to collect from its customers slightly less quickly. It is important to note, however, that adidas is a German corporation. It reports under IFRS. A thorough comparison of adidas and Nike would require consideration of differences in the treatment of accounts receivable under IFRS and GAAP.

REVIEW AND PRACTICE

LEARNING OBJECTIVES REVIEW

1 Explain how companies recognize accounts receivable. Receivables are frequently classified as accounts, notes, and other. Accounts receivable are amounts customers owe on account. Notes receivable represent claims that are evidenced by formal instruments of credit. Other receivables include nontrade receivables such as interest receivable, loans to company officers, advances to employees, and income taxes refundable.

Companies record accounts receivable when they perform a service on account or at the point-of-sale of merchandise on account. Sales returns and allowances and cash discounts reduce the amount received on accounts receivable.

2 Describe how companies value accounts receivable and record their disposition. The two methods of accounting for uncollectible accounts are the allowance method and the direct write-off method. Under the allowance method, companies estimate uncollectible accounts as a percentage of receivables. It emphasizes the cash realizable value of the accounts receivable. An aging schedule is frequently used with this approach.

3 Explain how companies recognize, value, and dispose of notes receivable. The formula for computing interest is Face value of note × Annual interest rate × Time in terms of one year. Notes can be held to maturity, at which time the borrower (maker) pays the face value plus accrued interest and the payee removes the note from the accounts. In many cases, however, similar to accounts receivable, the holder of the note speeds up the conversion by selling the receivable to another party. In some situations, the maker of the note dishonors the note (defaults), and the note is written off.

4 Describe the statement presentation of receivables and the principles of receivables management. Companies should identify each major type of receivable in the balance sheet or in the notes to the financial statements. Short-term receivables are considered current assets. Companies report the gross amount of receivables and the allowance for doubtful accounts. They report bad debt and service charge expenses in the income statement as operating (selling) expenses, and interest revenue as other revenues and gains in the nonoperating section of the statement.

To properly manage receivables, management must (a) determine to whom to extend credit, (b) establish a payment period, (c) monitor collections, (d) evaluate the liquidity of receivables, and (e) accelerate cash receipts from receivables when necessary. The accounts receivable turnover and the average collection period both are useful in analyzing management's effectiveness in managing receivables. The accounts receivable aging schedule also provides useful information. If the company needs additional cash, management can accelerate the collection of cash from receivables by selling (factoring) its receivables or by allowing customers to pay with bank credit cards.

DECISION TOOLS REVIEW

DECISION CHECKPOINTS	INFO NEEDED FOR DECISION	TOOL TO USE FOR DECISION	HOW TO EVALUATE RESULTS
Is the amount of past due accounts increasing? Which accounts require management's attention?	List of outstanding receivables and their due dates	Prepare an aging schedule showing the receivables in various stages: outstanding 0–30 days, 31–60 days, 61–90 days, and over 90 days.	Accounts in the older categories require follow-up: letters, phone calls, and possible renegotiation of terms.
Is the company's credit risk increasing?	Customer account balances and due dates	Accounts receivable aging schedule	Compute and compare the percentage of receivables over 90 days old.
Does the company have significant concentrations of credit risk?	Note to the financial statements on concentrations of credit risk	If risky credit customers are identified, the financial health of those customers should be evaluated to gain an independent assessment of the potential for a material credit loss.	If a material loss appears likely, the potential negative impact of that loss on the company should be carefully evaluated, along with the adequacy of the allowance for doubtful accounts.
Are collections being made in a timely fashion?	Net credit sales and average net accounts receivable balance	$\text{Accounts receivable turnover} = \frac{\text{Net credit sales}}{\text{Average net accounts receivable}}$ $\text{Average collection period} = \frac{\text{365 days}}{\text{Accounts receivable turnover}}$	Average collection period should be consistent with corporate credit policy. An increase may suggest a decline in financial health of customers.

▶ GLOSSARY REVIEW

Accounts receivable Amounts customers owe on account. (p. 376).

Accounts receivable turnover A measure of the liquidity of accounts receivable, computed by dividing net credit sales by average net accounts receivable. (p. 395).

Aging the accounts receivable A schedule of customer balances classified by the length of time they have been unpaid. (p. 382).

Allowance method A method of accounting for bad debts that involves estimating uncollectible accounts at the end of each period. (p. 379).

Average collection period The average amount of time that a receivable is outstanding, calculated by dividing 365 days by the accounts receivable turnover. (p. 395).

Bad Debt Expense An expense account to record losses from extending credit. (p. 378).

Cash (net) realizable value The net amount a company expects to receive in cash from receivables. (p. 379).

Concentration of credit risk The threat of nonpayment from a single large customer or class of customers that could adversely affect the financial health of the company. (p. 394).

Direct write-off method A method of accounting for bad debts that involves charging receivable balances to Bad Debt Expense at the time receivables from a particular company are determined to be uncollectible. (p. 378).

Dishonored (defaulted) note A note that is not paid in full at maturity. (p. 391).

Factor A finance company or bank that buys receivables from businesses for a fee and then collects the payments directly from the customers. (p. 385).

Maker The party in a promissory note who is making the promise to pay. (p. 387).

Notes receivable Written promise (as evidenced by a formal instrument) for amounts to be received. (p. 376).

Payee The party to whom payment of a promissory note is to be made. (p. 387).

Percentage-of-receivables basis A method of estimating the amount of bad debt expense whereby management establishes a percentage relationship between the amount of receivables and the expected losses from uncollectible accounts. (p. 382).

Promissory note A written promise to pay a specified amount of money on demand or at a definite time. (p. 387).

Receivables Amounts due from individuals and companies that are expected to be collected in cash. (p. 376).

Trade receivables Notes and accounts receivable that result from sales transactions. (p. 376).

▶ PRACTICE MULTIPLE-CHOICE QUESTIONS

(LO 1) **1.** A receivable that is evidenced by a formal instrument and that normally requires the payment of interest is:
(a) an account receivable.
(b) a trade receivable.
(c) a note receivable.
(d) a classified receivable.

(LO 1) **2.** Receivables are frequently classified as:
(a) accounts receivable, company receivables, and other receivables.
(b) accounts receivable, notes receivable, and employee receivables.
(c) accounts receivable and general receivables.
(d) accounts receivable, notes receivable, and other receivables.

(LO 1) **3.** Kersee Company on June 15 sells merchandise on account to Eng Co. for $1,000, terms 2/10, n/30. On June 20, Eng Co. returns merchandise worth $300 to Kersee Company. On June 24, payment is received from Eng Co. for the balance due. What is the amount of cash received?
(a) $700. (c) $686.
(b) $680. (d) None of the above.

(LO 2, 4) **4.** Accounts and notes receivable are reported in the current assets section of the balance sheet at:
(a) cash (net) realizable value
(b) net book value.
(c) lower-of-cost-or-market value.
(d) invoice cost.

(LO 2) **5.** Net credit sales for the month are $800,000. The accounts receivable balance is $160,000. The allowance is calculated as 7.5% of the receivables balance using the percentage-of-receivables basis. If Allowance for Doubtful Accounts has a credit balance of $5,000 before adjustment, what is the balance after adjustment?
(a) $12,000. (c) $17,000.
(b) $7,000. (d) $31,000.

(LO 2) **6.** In 2017, Patterson Wholesale Company had net credit sales of $750,000. On January 1, 2017, Allowance for Doubtful Accounts had a credit balance of $18,000. During 2017, $30,000 of uncollectible accounts receivable were written off. Past experience indicates that the allowance should be 10% of the balance in receivables (percentage-of-receivables basis). If the accounts receivable balance at December 31 was $200,000, what is the required adjustment to Allowance for Doubtful Accounts at December 31, 2017?
(a) $20,000. (c) $32,000.
(b) $75,000. (d) $30,000.

(LO 2) **7.** An analysis and aging of the accounts receivable of Raja Company at December 31 reveal these data:

Accounts receivable	$800,000
Allowance for doubtful accounts per books before adjustment (credit)	50,000
Amounts expected to become uncollectible	65,000

What is the cash realizable value of the accounts receivable at December 31, after adjustment?
(a) $685,000. (c) $800,000.
(b) $750,000. (d) $735,000.

(LO 2) **8.** Which of these statements about Visa credit card sales is **incorrect?**
(a) The credit card issuer conducts the credit investigation of the customer.
(b) The retailer is not involved in the collection process.
(c) The retailer must wait to receive payment from the issuer.
(d) The retailer receives cash more quickly than it would from individual customers.

9. Good Stuff Retailers accepted $50,000 of Citibank Visa credit card charges for merchandise sold on July 1. Citibank charges 4% for its credit card use. The entry to record this transaction by Good Stuff Retailers will include a credit to Sales Revenue of $50,000 and a debit(s) to: (LO 2)
(a) Cash $48,000 and Service Charge Expense $2,000.
(b) Accounts Receivable $48,000 and Service Charge Expense $2,000.
(c) Cash $50,000.
(d) Accounts Receivable $50,000.

10. A company can accelerate its cash receipts by all of the following **except:** (LO 2)
(a) offering discounts for early payment.
(b) accepting national credit cards for customer purchases.
(c) selling receivables to a factor.
(d) writing off receivables.

11. Hughes Company has a credit balance of $5,000 in its Allowance for Doubtful Accounts before any adjustments are made at the end of the year. Based on review and aging of its accounts receivable at the end of the year, Hughes estimates that $60,000 of its receivables are uncollectible. The amount of bad debt expense which should be reported for the year is: (LO 2)
(a) $5,000. (c) $60,000.
(b) $55,000. (d) $65,000.

12. Use the same information as in Question 11, except that Hughes has a debit balance of $5,000 in its Allowance for Doubtful Accounts before any adjustments are made at the end of the year. In this situation, the amount of bad debt expense that should be reported for the year is: (LO 2)
(a) $5,000. (c) $60,000.
(b) $55,000. (d) $65,000.

13. Which of these statements about promissory notes is **incorrect?** (LO 3)
(a) The party making the promise to pay is called the maker.
(b) The party to whom payment is to be made is called the payee.
(c) A promissory note is not a negotiable instrument.
(d) A promissory note is more liquid than an account receivable.

14. Michael Co. accepts a $1,000, 3-month, 12% promissory note in settlement of an account with Tani Co. The entry to record this transaction is: (LO 3)

(a) Notes Receivable	1,030	
Accounts Receivable		1,030
(b) Notes Receivable	1,000	
Accounts Receivable		1,000
(c) Notes Receivable	1,000	
Sales Revenue		1,000
(d) Notes Receivable	1,020	
Accounts Receivable		1,020

(LO 3) **15.** Schleis Co. holds Murphy Inc.'s $10,000, 120-day, 9% note. The entry made by Schleis Co. when the note is collected, assuming no interest has previously been accrued, is:

(a) Cash	10,300	
Notes Receivable		10,300
(b) Cash	10,000	
Notes Receivable		10,000
(c) Accounts Receivable	10,300	
Notes Receivable		10,000
Interest Revenue		300
(d) Cash	10,300	
Notes Receivable		10,000
Interest Revenue		300

(LO 4) **16.** If a company is concerned about extending credit to a risky customer, it could do any of the following **except:**
(a) require the customer to pay cash in advance.
(b) require the customer to provide a letter of credit or a bank guarantee.
(c) contact references provided by the customer, such as banks and other suppliers.
(d) provide the customer a lengthy payment period to increase the chance of paying.

17. Eddy Corporation had net credit sales during the year of $800,000 and cost of goods sold of $500,000. The balance in receivables at the beginning of the year was $100,000 and at the end of the year was $150,000. What was the accounts receivable turnover and average collection period in days? (LO 4)
(a) 4.0 and 91.3 days. (c) 6.4 and 57 days.
(b) 5.3 and 68.9 days. (d) 8.0 and 45.6 days.

18. Prall Corporation sells its goods on terms of 2/10, n/30. It has an accounts receivable turnover of 7. What is its average collection period (days)? (LO 4)
(a) 2,555 (c) 52
(b) 30 (d) 210

SOLUTIONS

1. **(c)** A note receivable represent claims for which formal instruments of credit are issued as evidence of the debt. The note normally requires the payment of the principal and interest on a specific date. Choices (a) account receivable, (b) trade receivable, and (d) classified receivable rarely require the payment of interest if paid within a 30-day period.
2. **(d)** Receivables are frequently classified as accounts receivable, notes receivable, and other receivables. The other choices are incorrect because receivables are not frequently classified as (a) company receivables, (b) employee receivables, or (c) general receivables.
3. **(c)** Because payment is made within the discount period of 10 days, the amount received is $700 ($1,000 − $300 return) minus the discount of $14 ($700 × 2%), for a cash amount of $686, not (a) $700 or (b) $680. Choice (d) is wrong as there is a correct answer.
4. **(a)** Accounts and notes receivable are reported in the current assets section of the balance sheet at cash (net) realizable value, not (b) net book value, (c) lower-of-cost-or-market value, or (d) invoice cost.
5. **(a)** The ending balance required in the allowance account is 7.5% × $160,000, or $12,000. Since there is already a balance of $5,000 in Allowance for Doubtful Accounts, the difference of $7,000 should be added, resulting in a balance of $12,000, not (b) $7,000, (c) $17,000, or (d) $31,000.
6. **(c)** After the write-offs are recorded, Allowance for Doubtful Accounts will have a debit balance of $12,000 ($18,000 credit beginning balance combined with a $30,000 debit for the write-offs). The desired balance, using the percentage-of-receivables basis, is a credit balance of $20,000 ($200,000 × 10%). In order to have an ending balance of $20,000, the required adjustment to Allowance for Doubtful Accounts is $32,000, not (a) $20,000, (b) $75,000, or (d) $30,000.
7. **(d)** The cash realizable value of the accounts receivable is Accounts Receivable ($800,000) less the expected ending balance in Allowance for Doubtful Accounts after adjustments ($65,000) = $735,000, not (a) $685,000, (b) $750,000, or (c) $800,000.
8. **(c)** There is no wait for payment. The retailer receives payment at the time the credit card is accepted from the customer. The other choices are true statements.
9. **(a)** The entry includes a credit to Sales Revenue for $50,000, a $48,000 debit to Cash, and a debit to Service Charge Expense for $2,000. The other choices are therefore incorrect.
10. **(d)** Writing off receivables will result in a company failing to collect any money. Instead, choices (a) offering discounts for early payment, (b) accepting national credit cards for customer purchases, and (c) selling receivables to a factor will all allow a company to accelerate its cash receipts.
11. **(b)** By crediting Allowance for Doubtful Accounts for $55,000, the new balance will be the required balance of $60,000. This adjusting entry debits Bad Debt Expense for $55,000 and credits Allowance for Doubtful Accounts for $55,000, not (a) $5,000, (c) $60,000, or (d) $65,000.
12. **(d)** By crediting Allowance for Doubtful Accounts for $65,000, the new balance will be the required balance of $60,000. This adjusting entry debits Bad Debt Expense for $65,000 and credits Allowance for Doubtful Accounts for $65,000, not (a) $5,000, (b) $55,000, or (c) $60,000.
13. **(c)** Promissory notes are negotiable instruments, meaning if sold, the seller can transfer to another party by endorsement. The other choices are true statements.

14. **(b)** On the date Michael accepts the note, Notes Receivable is debited for $1,000 and Accounts Receivable is credited for $1,000. Interest is accrued only with the passage of time. The other choices are therefore incorrect.
15. **(d)** When Schleis receives payment, it will increase cash, reduce the notes receivable account, and recognize interest earned for the term of the note. Interest = $10,000 × 9% × 120/360 = $300. Total cash received = $10,000 + $300 = $10,300. The other choices are therefore incorrect.
16. **(d)** A longer payment period will increase the chances the customer will not pay. The other choices are incorrect as companies might require risky customers to (a) pay cash in advance, (b) provide letters of credit or bank guarantees, or (c) ask for references from banks and suppliers to determine their payment history.
17. **(c)** Accounts receivable turnover = Net credit sales ($800,000) ÷ Average net accounts receivable [($100,000 + $150,000)/2] = 6.4. The average collection period in days = (365 ÷ 6.4) = 57 days. The other choices are therefore incorrect.
18. **(c)** Average collection period = Number of days in the year (365) ÷ Accounts receivable turnover (7) = 52 days, not (a) 2.555, (b) 30, or (d) 210.

PRACTICE EXERCISES

1. The ledger of J.C. Cobb Company at the end of the current year shows Accounts Receivable $150,000, Sales Revenue $850,000, and Sales Returns and Allowances $30,000.

Journalize entries to record allowance for doubtful accounts using two different bases.

(LO 2)

INSTRUCTIONS

(a) If J.C. Cobb uses the direct write-off method to account for uncollectible accounts, journalize the adjusting entry at December 31, assuming J.C. Cobb determines that M. Jack's $1,500 balance is uncollectible.

(b) If Allowance for Doubtful Accounts has a credit balance of $2,400 in the trial balance, journalize the adjusting entry at December 31, assuming bad debts are expected to be 10% of accounts receivable.

(c) If Allowance for Doubtful Accounts has a debit balance of $200 in the trial balance, journalize the adjusting entry at December 31, assuming bad debts are expected to be 6% of accounts receivable.

SOLUTION

	Date	Account	Debit	Credit
1. (a)	Dec. 31	Bad Debt Expense	1,500	
		Accounts Receivable—M. Jack		1,500
(b)	Dec. 31	Bad Debt Expense	12,600	
		Allowance for Doubtful Accounts		
		[($150,000 × 10%) − $2,400]		12,600
(c)	Dec. 31	Bad Debt Expense	9,200	
		Allowance for Doubtful Accounts		
		[($150,000 × 6%) + $200]		9,200

2. Troope Supply Co. has the following transactions related to notes receivable during the last 3 months of 2017.

Journalize entries for notes receivable transactions.

(LO 3)

Oct. 1	Loaned $16,000 cash to Juan Vasquez on a 1-year, 10% note.
Dec. 11	Sold goods to A. Palmer, Inc., receiving a $6,750, 90-day, 8% note.
16	Received a $6,400, 6-month, 9% note in exchange for J. Nicholas's outstanding accounts receivable.
31	Accrued interest revenue on all notes receivable.

INSTRUCTIONS

(a) Journalize the transactions for Troope Supply Co.

(b) Record the collection of the Vasquez note at its maturity in 2018.

SOLUTION

2. (a)

Date	Account	Debit	Credit
	2017		
Oct. 1	Notes Receivable	16,000	
	Cash		16,000
Dec. 11	Notes Receivable	6,750	
	Sales Revenue		6,750

			Debit	Credit
Dec.	16	Notes Receivable	6,400	
		Accounts Receivable—Nicholas		6,400
	31	Interest Receivable	454	
		Interest Revenue*		454

*Calculation of interest revenue:

Vasquez's note:	$16,000 ×	10% ×	3/12	=	$400
Palmer's note:	6,750 ×	8% ×	20/360	=	30
Nicholas's note:	6,400 ×	9% ×	15/360	=	24
Total accrued interest					$454

(b)

2018

			Debit	Credit
Oct.	1	Cash	17,600	
		Interest Receivable		400
		Interest Revenue**		1,200
		Notes Receivable		16,000

**($16,000 × 10% × 9/12)

PRACTICE PROBLEM

Prepare entries for various receivables transactions.

(LO 1, 2, 3)

Presented here are selected transactions related to B. Dylan Corp.

Mar.	1	Sold $20,000 of merchandise to Potter Company, terms 2/10, n/30.
	11	Received payment in full from Potter Company for balance due on existing accounts receivable.
	12	Accepted Juno Company's $20,000, 6-month, 12% note for balance due on outstanding account receivable.
	13	Made B. Dylan Corp. credit card sales for $13,200.
	15	Made Visa credit sales totaling $6,700. A 5% service fee is charged by Visa.
Apr.	11	Sold accounts receivable of $8,000 to Harcot Factor. Harcot Factor assesses a service charge of 2% of the amount of receivables sold.
	13	Received collections of $8,200 on B. Dylan Corp. credit card sales.
May	10	Wrote off as uncollectible $16,000 of accounts receivable. (B. Dylan Corp. uses the percentage-of-receivables basis to estimate bad debts.)
June	30	The balance in accounts receivable at the end of the first 6 months is $200,000. The company estimates that 10% of accounts receivable will become uncollectible. At June 30, the credit balance in the allowance account prior to adjustment is $3,500. Recorded bad debt expense.
July	16	One of the accounts receivable written off in May pays the amount due, $4,000, in full.

INSTRUCTIONS

Prepare the journal entries for the transactions. (Omit cost of goods sold entries.)

SOLUTION*

			Debit	Credit
Mar.	1	Accounts Receivable—Potter Company	20,000	
		Sales Revenue		20,000
		(To record sales on account)		
	11	Cash	19,600	
		Sales Discounts (2% × $20,000)	400	
		Accounts Receivable—Potter Company		20,000
		(To record collection of accounts receivable)		
	12	Notes Receivable	20,000	
		Accounts Receivable—Juno Company		20,000
		(To record acceptance of Juno Company note)		
	13	Accounts Receivable	13,200	
		Sales Revenue		13,200
		(To record company credit card sales)		

Date	Account	Debit	Credit
15	Cash	6,365	
	Service Charge Expense (5% × $6,700)	335	
	Sales Revenue		6,700
	(To record credit card sales)		
Apr. 11	Cash	7,840	
	Service Charge Expense (2% × $8,000)	160	
	Accounts Receivable		8,000
	(To record sale of receivables to factor)		
13	Cash	8,200	
	Accounts Receivable		8,200
	(To record collection of accounts receivable)		
May 10	Allowance for Doubtful Accounts	16,000	
	Accounts Receivable		16,000
	(To record write-off of accounts receivable)		
June 30	Bad Debt Expense	16,500	
	Allowance for Doubtful Accounts [($200,000 × 10%) − $3,500]		16,500
	(To record estimate of uncollectible accounts)		
July 16	Accounts Receivable	4,000	
	Allowance for Doubtful Accounts		4,000
	(To reverse write-off of accounts receivable)		
	Cash	4,000	
	Accounts Receivable		4,000
	(To record collection of accounts receivable)		

*Cost of goods sold entries are omitted here as well as in homework material.

WileyPLUS Brief Exercises, DO IT! Exercises, Exercises, Problems, and many additional resources are available for practice in WileyPLUS.

QUESTIONS

1. What is the difference between an account receivable and a note receivable?
2. What are some common types of receivables other than accounts receivable or notes receivable?
3. What are the essential features of the allowance method of accounting for bad debts?
4. Lance Morrow cannot understand why the cash realizable value does not decrease when an uncollectible account is written off under the allowance method. Clarify this point for Lance.
5. Sarasota Company has a credit balance of $2,200 in Allowance for Doubtful Accounts before adjustment. The estimated uncollectibles under the percentage-of-receivables basis is $5,100. Prepare the adjusting entry.
6. What types of receivables does Apple report on its balance sheet? Does it use the allowance method or the direct write-off method to account for uncollectibles?
7. How are bad debts accounted for under the direct write-off method? What are the disadvantages of this method?
8. Tawnya Dobbs, the vice president of sales for Tropical Pools and Spas, wants the company's credit department to be less restrictive in granting credit. "How can we sell anything when you guys won't approve anybody?" she asks. Discuss the pros and cons of "easy credit." What are the accounting implications?
9. JCPenney Company accepts both its own credit cards and national credit cards. What are the advantages of accepting both types of cards?

10. An article in the *Wall Street Journal* indicated that companies are selling their receivables at a record rate. Why do companies sell their receivables?

11. Calico Corners decides to sell $400,000 of its accounts receivable to Fast Cash Factors Inc. Fast Cash Factors assesses a service charge of 3% of the amount of receivables sold. Prepare the journal entry that Calico Corners makes to record this sale.

12. Your roommate is uncertain about the advantages of a promissory note. Compare the advantages of a note receivable with those of an account receivable.

13. How may the maturity date of a promissory note be stated?

14. Compute the missing amounts for each of the following notes.

Principal	Annual Interest Rate	Time	Total Interest
(a)	6%	60 days	$ 270
$30,000	8%	3 years	(d)
$60,000	(b)	5 months	$2,500
$50,000	11%	(c)	$2,750

15. Mendosa Company dishonors a note at maturity. What are the options available to the lender?

16. General Motors Company has accounts receivable and notes receivable. How should the receivables be reported on the balance sheet?

17. What are the steps to good receivables management?

18. How might a company monitor the risk related to its accounts receivable?

19. What is meant by a concentration of credit risk?

20. The president of Ericson Inc. proudly announces her company's improved liquidity since its current ratio has increased substantially from one year to the next. Does an increase in the current ratio always indicate improved liquidity? What other ratio or ratios might you review to determine whether or not the increase in the current ratio is an improvement in financial health?

21. Since hiring a new sales director, Tilton Inc. has enjoyed a 50% increase in sales. The CEO has also noticed, however, that the company's average collection period has increased from 17 days to 38 days. What might be the cause of this increase? What are the implications to management of this increase?

22. The Coca-Cola Company's accounts receivable turnover was 9.05 in 2014, and its average amount of net receivables during the period was $3,424 million. What is the amount of its net credit sales for the period? What is the average collection period in days?

23. Douglas Corp. has experienced tremendous sales growth this year, but it is always short of cash. What is one explanation for this occurrence?

24. How can the amount of collections from customers be determined?

BRIEF EXERCISES

Identify different types of receivables.

(LO 1), C

BE8-1 Presented below are three receivables transactions. Indicate whether these receivables are reported as accounts receivable, notes receivable, or other receivables on a balance sheet.

(a) Advanced $10,000 to an employee.
(b) Received a promissory note of $34,000 for services performed.
(c) Sold merchandise on account for $60,000 to a customer.

Record basic accounts receivable transactions.

(LO 1), AP

BE8-2 Record the following transactions on the books of Jarvis Co. (Omit cost of goods sold entries.)

(a) On July 1, Jarvis Co. sold merchandise on account to Stacey Inc. for $23,000, terms 2/10, n/30.
(b) On July 8, Stacey Inc. returned merchandise worth $2,400 to Jarvis Co.
(c) On July 11, Stacey Inc. paid for the merchandise.

Prepare entry for write-off, and determine cash realizable value.

(LO 2), AP

BE8-3 At the end of 2016, Safer Co. has accounts receivable of $700,000 and an allowance for doubtful accounts of $25,000. On January 24, 2017, it is learned that the company's receivable from Madonna Inc. is not collectible and therefore management authorizes a write-off of $4,300.

(a) Prepare the journal entry to record the write-off.
(b) What is the cash realizable value of the accounts receivable (1) before the write-off and (2) after the write-off?

Prepare entries for collection of bad debt write-off.

(LO 2), AP

BE8-4 Assume the same information as BE8-3 and that on March 4, 2017, Safer Co. receives payment of $4,300 in full from Madonna Inc. Prepare the journal entries to record this transaction.

BE8-5 Byrd Co. uses the percentage-of-receivables basis to record bad debt expense and concludes that 2% of accounts receivable will become uncollectible. Accounts receivable are $400,000 at the end of the year, and the allowance for doubtful accounts has a credit balance of $2,800.

Prepare entry using percentage-of-receivables method.

(LO 2), AP

(a) Prepare the adjusting journal entry to record bad debt expense for the year.
(b) If the allowance for doubtful accounts had a debit balance of $900 instead of a credit balance of $2,800, prepare the adjusting journal entry for bad debt expense.

BE8-6 Consider these transactions:

Prepare entries for credit card sale and sale of accounts receivable.

(LO 2), AP

(a) Tastee Restaurant accepted a Visa card in payment of a $200 lunch bill. The bank charges a 3% fee. What entry should Tastee make?
(b) Martin Company sold its accounts receivable of $65,000. What entry should Martin make, given a service charge of 3% on the amount of receivables sold?

BE8-7 Compute interest and find the maturity date for the following notes.

Compute interest and determine maturity dates on notes.

(LO 3), AP

	Date of Note	Principal	Interest Rate (%)	Terms
(a)	June 10	$80,000	6%	60 days
(b)	July 14	$50,000	7%	90 days
(c)	April 27	$12,000	8%	75 days

BE8-8 Presented below are data on three promissory notes. Determine the missing amounts.

Determine maturity dates and compute interest and rates on notes.

(LO 3), AP

	Date of Note	Terms	Maturity Date	Principal	Annual Interest Rate	Total Interest
(a)	April 1	60 days	?	$600,000	9%	?
(b)	July 2	30 days	?	90,000	?	$600
(c)	March 7	6 months	?	120,000	10%	?

BE8-9 On January 10, 2017, Masterson Co. sold merchandise on account to Tompkins for $8,000, terms n/30. On February 9, Tompkins gave Masterson Co. a 7% promissory note in settlement of this account. Prepare the journal entry to record the sale and the settlement of the accounts receivable. (Omit cost of goods sold entries.)

Prepare entry for note receivable exchanged for accounts receivable.

(LO 3), AP

BE8-10 During its first year of operations, Fertig Company had credit sales of $3,000,000, of which $400,000 remained uncollected at year-end. The credit manager estimates that $18,000 of these receivables will become uncollectible.

Prepare entry for estimated uncollectibles and classifications, and compute ratios.

(LO 2, 4), AP

(a) Prepare the journal entry to record the estimated uncollectibles. (Assume an unadjusted balance of zero in Allowance for Doubtful Accounts.)
(b) Prepare the current assets section of the balance sheet for Fertig Company, assuming that in addition to the receivables it has cash of $90,000, merchandise inventory of $180,000, and supplies of $13,000.
(c) Calculate the accounts receivable turnover and average collection period. Assume that average net accounts receivable were $300,000. Explain what these measures tell us.

BE8-11 Suppose the 2017 financial statements of 3M Company report net sales of $23.1 billion. Accounts receivable (net) are $3.2 billion at the beginning of the year and $3.25 billion at the end of the year. Compute 3M's accounts receivable turnover. Compute 3M's average collection period for accounts receivable in days.

Analyze accounts receivable.

(LO 4), AP

BE8-12 Kennewick Corp. had a beginning balance in accounts receivable of $70,000 and an ending balance of $91,000. Credit sales during the period were $598,000. Determine cash collections.

Determine cash collections.

(LO 4), AP

DO IT! EXERCISES

DO IT! 8-1 On March 1, Lincoln sold merchandise on account to Amelia Company for $28,000, terms 1/10, net 45. On March 6, Amelia returns merchandise with a sales price of $1,000. On March 11, Lincoln receives payment from Amelia for the balance due. Prepare journal entries to record the March transactions on Lincoln's books. (You may ignore cost of goods sold entries and explanations.)

Prepare entries to recognize accounts receivable.

(LO 1), AP

Prepare entry for uncollectible accounts.

(LO 2), AP

DO IT! 8-2a Mantle Company has been in business several years. At the end of the current year, the unadjusted trial balance shows:

Accounts Receivable	$ 310,000 Dr.
Sales Revenue	2,200,000 Cr.
Allowance for Doubtful Accounts	5,700 Cr.

Bad debts are estimated to be 7% of receivables. Prepare the entry to adjust Allowance for Doubtful Accounts.

Prepare entry for factored accounts.

(LO 2), AP

DO IT! 8-2b Neumann Distributors is a growing company whose ability to raise capital has not been growing as quickly as its expanding assets and sales. Neumann's local banker has indicated that the company cannot increase its borrowing for the foreseeable future. Neumann's suppliers are demanding payment for goods acquired within 30 days of the invoice date, but Neumann's customers are slow in paying for their purchases (60–90 days). As a result, Neumann has a cash flow problem.

Neumann needs $160,000 to cover next Friday's payroll. Its balance of outstanding accounts receivable totals $800,000. To alleviate this cash crunch, the company sells $170,000 of its receivables. Record the entry that Neumann would make. (Assume a 2% service charge.)

Prepare entries for notes receivable.

(LO 3), AP

DO IT! 8-3 Buffet Wholesalers accepts from Gates Stores a $6,200, 4-month, 9% note dated May 31 in settlement of Gates' overdue account. The maturity date of the note is September 30. What entry does Buffet make at the maturity date, assuming Gates pays the note and interest in full at that time?

Compute ratios for receivables.

(LO 4), AP

DO IT! 8-4 In 2017, Bismark Company has net credit sales of $1,600,000 for the year. It had a beginning accounts receivable (net) balance of $108,000 and an ending accounts receivable (net) balance of $120,000. Compute Bismark Company's (a) accounts receivable turnover and (b) average collection period in days.

▶ EXERCISES

Prepare entries for recognizing accounts receivable.

(LO 1), AP

E8-1 On January 6, Jacob Co. sells merchandise on account to Harley Inc. for $9,200, terms 1/10, n/30. On January 16, Harley pays the amount due.

Instructions

Prepare the entries on Jacob Co.'s books to record the sale and related collection. (Omit cost of goods sold entries.)

Prepare entries for recognizing accounts receivable.

(LO 1), AP

E8-2 On January 10, Molly Amise uses her Lawton Co. credit card to purchase merchandise from Lawton Co. for $1,700. On February 10, Molly is billed for the amount due of $1,700. On February 12, Molly pays $1,100 on the balance due. On March 10, Molly is billed for the amount due, including interest at 1% per month on the unpaid balance as of February 12.

Instructions

Prepare the entries on Lawton Co.'s books related to the transactions that occurred on January 10, February 12, and March 10. (Omit cost of goods sold entries.)

Journalize receivables transactions.

(LO 1, 2), AP

E8-3 At the beginning of the current period, Rose Corp. had balances in Accounts Receivable of $200,000 and in Allowance for Doubtful Accounts of $9,000 (credit). During the period, it had net credit sales of $800,000 and collections of $763,000. It wrote off as uncollectible accounts receivable of $7,300. However, a $3,100 account previously written off as uncollectible was recovered before the end of the current period. Uncollectible accounts are estimated to total $25,000 at the end of the period. (Omit cost of goods sold entries.)

Instructions

(a) Prepare the entries to record sales and collections during the period.
(b) Prepare the entry to record the write-off of uncollectible accounts during the period.
(c) Prepare the entries to record the recovery of the uncollectible account during the period.
(d) Prepare the entry to record bad debt expense for the period.
(e) Determine the ending balances in Accounts Receivable and Allowance for Doubtful Accounts.
(f) What is the net realizable value of the receivables at the end of the period?

E8-4 The ledger of Macarty Company at the end of the current year shows Accounts Receivable $78,000, Credit Sales $810,000, and Sales Returns and Allowances $40,000.

Prepare entries to record allowance for doubtful accounts.

(LO 2), AP

Instructions

(a) If Macarty uses the direct write-off method to account for uncollectible accounts, journalize the adjusting entry at December 31, assuming Macarty determines that Matisse's $900 balance is uncollectible.

(b) If Allowance for Doubtful Accounts has a credit balance of $1,100 in the trial balance, journalize the adjusting entry at December 31, assuming bad debts are expected to be 10% of accounts receivable.

(c) If Allowance for Doubtful Accounts has a debit balance of $500 in the trial balance, journalize the adjusting entry at December 31, assuming bad debts are expected to be 8% of accounts receivable.

E8-5 Godfreid Company has accounts receivable of $95,400 at March 31, 2017. Credit terms are 2/10, n/30. At March 31, 2017, there is a $2,100 credit balance in Allowance for Doubtful Accounts prior to adjustment. The company uses the percentage-of-receivables basis for estimating uncollectible accounts. The company's estimates of bad debts are as shown below.

Determine bad debt expense, and prepare the adjusting entry.

(LO 2), AP

	Balance, March 31		
Age of Accounts	**2017**	**2016**	**Estimated Percentage Uncollectible**
Current	$65,000	$75,000	2%
1–30 days past due	12,900	8,000	5
31–90 days past due	10,100	2,400	30
Over 90 days past due	7,400	1,100	50
	$95,400	$86,500	

Instructions

(a) Determine the total estimated uncollectibles.

(b) Prepare the adjusting entry at March 31, 2017, to record bad debt expense.

(c) Discuss the implications of the changes in the aging schedule from 2016 to 2017.

E8-6 On December 31, 2016, when its Allowance for Doubtful Accounts had a debit balance of $1,400, Dallas Co. estimates that 9% of its accounts receivable balance of $90,000 will become uncollectible and records the necessary adjustment to Allowance for Doubtful Accounts. On May 11, 2017, Dallas Co. determined that B. Jared's account was uncollectible and wrote off $1,200. On June 12, 2017, Jared paid the amount previously written off.

Prepare entry for estimated uncollectibles, write-off, and recovery.

(LO 2), AP

Instructions

Prepare the journal entries on December 31, 2016, May 11, 2017, and June 12, 2017.

E8-7 On March 3, Plume Appliances sells $710,000 of its receivables to Western Factors Inc. Western Factors Inc. assesses a service charge of 4% of the amount of receivables sold.

Prepare entry for sale of accounts receivable.

(LO 2), AP

Instructions

Prepare the entry on Plume Appliances' books to record the sale of the receivables.

E8-8 On May 10, Keene Company sold merchandise for $4,000 and accepted the customer's Best Business Bank MasterCard. At the end of the day, the Best Business Bank MasterCard receipts were deposited in the company's bank account. Best Business Bank charges a 3.8% service charge for credit card sales.

Prepare entry for credit card sale.

(LO 2), AP

Instructions

Prepare the entry on Keene Company's books to record the sale of merchandise.

E8-9 On July 4, Mazie's Restaurant accepts a Visa card for a $250 dinner bill. Visa charges a 4% service fee.

Prepare entry for credit card sale.

(LO 2), AP

Instructions

Prepare the entry on Mazie's books related to the transaction.

Prepare entries for notes receivable transactions.

(LO 3), AP

E8-10 Moses Supply Co. has the following transactions related to notes receivable during the last 2 months of the year. The company does not make entries to accrue interest except at December 31.

Nov.	1	Loaned $60,000 cash to C. Bohr on a 12-month, 7% note.
Dec.	11	Sold goods to K. R. Pine, Inc., receiving a $3,600, 90-day, 8% note.
	16	Received a $12,000, 180-day, 9% note to settle an open account from A. Murdock.
	31	Accrued interest revenue on all notes receivable.

Instructions

Journalize the transactions for Moses Supply Co. (Omit cost of goods sold entries.)

Journalize notes receivable transactions.

(LO 3), AP

E8-11 These transactions took place for Bramson Co.

2016		
May	1	Received a $5,000, 12-month, 6% note in exchange for an outstanding account receivable from R. Stoney.
Dec.	31	Accrued interest revenue on the R. Stoney note.
2017		
May	1	Received principal plus interest on the R. Stoney note. (No interest has been accrued since December 31, 2016.)

Instructions

Record the transactions in the general journal. The company does not make entries to accrue interest except at December 31.

Prepare a balance sheet presentation of receivables.

(LO 4), AP

E8-12 Eileen Corp. had the following balances in receivable accounts at October 31, 2017 (in thousands): Allowance for Doubtful Accounts $52, Accounts Receivable $2,910, Other Receivables $189, and Notes Receivable $1,353.

Instructions

Prepare the balance sheet presentation of Eileen Corp.'s receivables in good form.

Identify the principles of receivables management.

(LO 4), K

E8-13 The following is a list of activities that companies perform in relation to their receivables.

1. Selling receivables to a factor.
2. Reviewing company ratings in *The Dun and Bradstreet Reference Book of American Business*.
3. Collecting information on competitors' payment period policies.
4. Preparing monthly accounts receivable aging schedule and investigating problem accounts.
5. Calculating the accounts receivable turnover and average collection period.

Instructions

Match each of the activities listed above with a purpose of the activity listed below.

(a) Determine to whom to extend credit.
(b) Establish a payment period.
(c) Monitor collections.
(d) Evaluate the liquidity of receivables.
(e) Accelerate cash receipts from receivable when necessary.

Compute ratios to evaluate a company's receivables balance.

(LO 4), AN

E8-14 Suppose the following information was taken from the 2017 financial statements of FedEx Corporation, a major global transportation/delivery company.

(in millions)	2017	2016
Accounts receivable (gross)	$ 3,587	$ 4,517
Accounts receivable (net)	3,391	4,359
Allowance for doubtful accounts	196	158
Sales revenue	35,497	37,953
Total current assets	7,116	7,244

Instructions

Answer each of the following questions.

(a) Calculate the accounts receivable turnover and the average collection period for 2017 for FedEx.

(b) Is accounts receivable a material component of the company's total current assets?
(c) Evaluate the balance in FedEx's allowance for doubtful accounts.

Evaluate liquidity.

(LO 4), AN

E8-15 The following ratios are available for Ming Inc.

	2017	2016
Current ratio	1.3:1	1.5:1
Accounts receivable turnover	12 times	10 times
Inventory turnover	11 times	9 times

Instructions

(a) Is Ming's short-term liquidity improving or deteriorating in 2017? Be specific in your answer, referring to relevant ratios.
(b) Do changes in turnover ratios affect profitability? Explain.
(c) Identify any steps Ming might have taken, or might wish to take, to improve its management of its accounts receivable and inventory turnovers.

Identify reason for sale of receivables.

(LO 4), C

E8-16 In a recent annual report, Office Depot, Inc. notes that the company entered into an agreement to sell all of its credit card program receivables to financial service companies.

Instructions

Explain why Office Depot, a financially stable company with positive cash flow, would choose to sell its receivables.

Determine cash flows and evaluate quality of earnings.

(LO 4), AN

E8-17 Bailey Corp. significantly reduced its requirements for credit sales. As a result, sales during the current year increased dramatically. It had receivables at the beginning of the year of $38,000 and ending receivables of $191,000. Credit sales were $380,000.

Instructions

(a) Determine cash collections during the period.
(b) Discuss how your findings in part (a) would affect Bailey Corp.'s quality of earnings ratio. (Do not compute.)
(c) What concerns might you have regarding Bailey's accounting?

EXERCISES: SET B AND CHALLENGE EXERCISES

Visit the book's companion website, at **www.wiley.com/college/kimmel**, and choose the Student Companion site to access Exercises: Set B and Challenge Exercises.

PROBLEMS: SET A

Journalize transactions related to bad debts.

(LO 2), AP

P8-1A Rianna.com uses the allowance method of accounting for bad debts. The company produced the following aging of the accounts receivable at year-end.

		Number of Days Outstanding				
	Total	0–30	31–60	61–90	91–120	Over 120
Accounts receivable	$377,000	$222,000	$90,000	$38,000	$15,000	$12,000
% uncollectible		1%	4%	5%	8%	10%
Estimated bad debts						

Instructions

(a) Calculate the total estimated bad debts based on the above information.
(b) Prepare the year-end adjusting journal entry to record the bad debts using the aged uncollectible accounts receivable determined in (a). Assume the unadjusted balance in Allowance for Doubtful Accounts is a $4,000 debit.
(c) Of the above accounts, $5,000 is determined to be specifically uncollectible. Prepare the journal entry to write off the uncollectible account.

(a) Tot. est. bad debts $10,120

(d) The company collects $5,000 subsequently on a specific account that had previously been determined to be uncollectible in (c). Prepare the journal entry(ies) necessary to restore the account and record the cash collection.

(e) Comment on how your answers to (a)–(d) would change if Rianna.com used 3% of total accounts receivable, rather than aging the accounts receivable. What are the advantages to the company of aging the accounts receivable rather than applying a percentage to total accounts receivable?

Prepare journal entries related to bad debt expense, and compute ratios.

(LO 2, 4), AP

P8-2A At December 31, 2016, Suisse Imports reported this information on its balance sheet.

Accounts receivable	$600,000
Less: Allowance for doubtful accounts	37,000

During 2017, the company had the following transactions related to receivables.

1. Sales on account	$2,500,000
2. Sales returns and allowances	50,000
3. Collections of accounts receivable	2,200,000
4. Write-offs of accounts receivable deemed uncollectible	41,000
5. Recovery of bad debts previously written off as uncollectible	15,000

Instructions

(a) Prepare the journal entries to record each of these five transactions. Assume that no cash discounts were taken on the collections of accounts receivable. (Omit cost of goods sold entries.)

(b) A/R bal. $809,000

(b) Enter the January 1, 2017, balances in Accounts Receivable and Allowance for Doubtful Accounts, post the entries to the two accounts (use T-accounts), and determine the balances.

(c) Prepare the journal entry to record bad debt expense for 2017, assuming that aging the accounts receivable indicates that estimated bad debts are $46,000.

(d) Compute the accounts receivable turnover and average collection period.

Journalize transactions related to bad debts.

(LO 2), AP

P8-3A Presented below is an aging schedule for Bryan Company.

			Number of Days Past Due			
Customer	**Total**	**Not Yet Due**	**1–30**	**31–60**	**61–90**	**Over 90**
Aneesh	$ 24,000		$ 9,000	$15,000		
Bird	30,000	$ 30,000				
Cope	50,000	5,000	5,000		$40,000	
DeSpears	38,000					$38,000
Others	120,000	72,000	35,000	13,000		
	$262,000	$107,000	$49,000	$28,000	$40,000	$38,000
Estimated percentage uncollectible		3%	7%	12%	24%	60%
Total estimated bad debts	$ 42,400	$ 3,210	$ 3,430	$ 3,360	$ 9,600	$22,800

At December 31, 2016, the unadjusted balance in Allowance for Doubtful Accounts is a credit of $8,000.

Instructions

(a) Journalize and post the adjusting entry for bad debts at December 31, 2016. (Use T-accounts.)

(b) Journalize and post to the allowance account these 2017 events and transactions:
1. March 1, a $600 customer balance originating in 2016 is judged uncollectible.
2. May 1, a check for $600 is received from the customer whose account was written off as uncollectible on March 1.

(c) Journalize the adjusting entry for bad debts at December 31, 2017, assuming that the unadjusted balance in Allowance for Doubtful Accounts is a debit of $1,400 and the aging schedule indicates that total estimated bad debts will be $36,700.

P8-4A Here is information related to Morgane Company for 2017.

Compute bad debt amounts.

(LO 2), AP

Total credit sales	$1,500,000
Accounts receivable at December 31	840,000
Bad debts written off	37,000

Instructions

(a) What amount of bad debt expense will Morgane Company report if it uses the direct write-off method of accounting for bad debts?

(b) Assume that Morgane Company decides to estimate its bad debt expense based on 4% of accounts receivable. What amount of bad debt expense will the company record if Allowance for Doubtful Accounts has a credit balance of $3,000?

(c) Assume the same facts as in part (b), except that there is a $1,000 debit balance in Allowance for Doubtful Accounts. What amount of bad debt expense will Morgane record?

(d) What is a weakness of the direct write-off method of reporting bad debt expense?

P8-5A At December 31, 2017, the trial balance of Malone Company contained the following amounts before adjustment.

Journalize entries to record transactions related to bad debts.

(LO 2), AP

	Debit	Credit
Accounts Receivable	$180,000	
Allowance for Doubtful Accounts		$ 1,500
Sales Revenue		875,000

Instructions

(a) Prepare the adjusting entry at December 31, 2017, to record bad debt expense, assuming that the aging schedule indicates that $10,200 of accounts receivable will be uncollectible.

(b) Repeat part (a), assuming that instead of a credit balance there is a $1,500 debit balance in Allowance for Doubtful Accounts.

(c) During the next month, January 2018, a $2,100 account receivable is written off as uncollectible. Prepare the journal entry to record the write-off.

(d) Repeat part (c), assuming that Malone Company uses the direct write-off method instead of the allowance method in accounting for uncollectible accounts receivable.

(e) What are the advantages of using the allowance method in accounting for uncollectible accounts as compared to the direct write-off method?

P8-6A On January 1, 2017, Harvee Company had Accounts Receivable of $54,200 and Allowance for Doubtful Accounts of $3,700. Harvee Company prepares financial statements annually. During the year, the following selected transactions occurred.

Journalize various receivables transactions.

(LO 1, 3), AP

Jan.	5	Sold $4,000 of merchandise to Rian Company, terms n/30.
Feb.	2	Accepted a $4,000, 4-month, 9% promissory note from Rian Company for balance due.
	12	Sold $12,000 of merchandise to Cato Company and accepted Cato's $12,000, 2-month, 10% note for the balance due.
	26	Sold $5,200 of merchandise to Malcolm Co., terms n/10.
Apr.	5	Accepted a $5,200, 3-month, 8% note from Malcolm Co. for balance due.
	12	Collected Cato Company note in full.
June	2	Collected Rian Company note in full.
	15	Sold $2,000 of merchandise to Gerri Inc. and accepted a $2,000, 6-month, 12% note for the amount due.

Instructions

Journalize the transactions. (Omit cost of goods sold entries.)

Explain the impact of transactions on ratios.

(LO 4), C

P8-7A The president of Mossy Enterprises asks if you could indicate the impact certain transactions have on the following ratios.

Transaction	Current Ratio (2:1)	Accounts Receivable Turnover (10×)	Average Collection Period (36.5 days)
1. Received $5,000 on cash sale. The cost of the goods sold was $2,600.			
2. Recorded bad debt expense of $500 using allowance method.			
3. Wrote off a $100 account receivable as uncollectible (Uses allowance method.)			
4. Recorded $2,500 sales on account. The cost of the goods sold was $1,500.			

Instructions

Complete the table, indicating whether each transaction will increase (I), decrease (D), or have no effect (NE) on the specific ratios provided for Mossy Enterprises.

Prepare entries for various credit card and notes receivable transactions.

(LO 2, 3, 4), AP

P8-8A Milton Company closes its books on its July 31 year-end. The company does not make entries to accrue for interest except at its year-end. On June 30, the Notes Receivable account balance is $23,800. Notes Receivable include the following.

Date	Maker	Face Value	Term	Maturity Date	Interest Rate
April 21	Coote Inc.	$ 6,000	90 days	July 20	8%
May 25	Brady Co.	7,800	60 days	July 24	10%
June 30	BMG Corp.	10,000	6 months	December 31	6%

During July, the following transactions were completed.

July 5 Made sales of $4,500 on Milton credit cards.
14 Made sales of $600 on Visa credit cards. The credit card service charge is 3%.
20 Received payment in full from Coote Inc. on the amount due.
24 Received payment in full from Brady Co. on the amount due.

Instructions

(a) Journalize the July transactions and the July 31 adjusting entry for accrued interest receivable. (Interest is computed using 360 days; omit cost of goods sold entries.)

(b) A/R bal. $ 4,500

(b) Enter the balances at July 1 in the receivable accounts and post the entries to all of the receivable accounts. (Use T-accounts.)

(c) Tot. receivables $14,550

(c) Show the balance sheet presentation of the receivable accounts at July 31.

Calculate and interpret various ratios.

(LO 4), AN

P8-9A Suppose the amounts presented here are basic financial information (in millions) from the 2017 annual reports of Nike and adidas.

	Nike	adidas
Sales revenue	$19,176.1	$10,381
Allowance for doubtful accounts, beginning	78.4	119
Allowance for doubtful accounts, ending	110.8	124
Accounts receivable balance (gross), beginning	2,873.7	1,743
Accounts receivable balance (gross), ending	2,994.7	1,553

Instructions

Calculate the accounts receivable turnover and average collection period for both companies. Comment on the difference in their collection experiences.

▶ PROBLEMS: SET B AND SET C

Visit the book's companion website, at **www.wiley.com/college/kimmel**, and choose the Student Companion site to access Problems: Set B and Set C.

▶ CONTINUING PROBLEM Cookie Creations

(*Note:* This is a continuation of the Cookie Creations problem from Chapters 1 through 7.)

© leungchopan/ Shutterstock

CC8 One of Natalie's friends, Curtis Lesperance, runs a coffee shop where he sells specialty coffees and prepares and sells muffins and cookies. He is eager to buy one of Natalie's fine European mixers, which would enable him to make larger batches of muffins and cookies. However, Curtis cannot afford to pay for the mixer for at least 30 days. He asks Natalie if she would be willing to sell him the mixer on credit. Natalie comes to you for advice.

Go to the book's companion website, at **www.wiley.com/college/kimmel**, *to see the completion of this problem.*

COMPREHENSIVE ACCOUNTING CYCLE REVIEW

ACR8 Hudson Corporation's balance sheet at December 31, 2016, is presented below.

HUDSON CORPORATION
Balance Sheet
December 31, 2016

Cash	$13,100	Accounts payable	$ 8,750
Accounts receivable	19,780	Common stock	20,000
Allowance for doubtful accounts	(800)	Retained earnings	12,730
Inventory	9,400		
	$41,480		$41,480

During January 2017, the following transactions occurred. Hudson uses the perpetual inventory method.

Jan.	1	Hudson accepted a 4-month, 8% note from Betheny Company in payment of Betheny's $1,200 account.
	3	Hudson wrote off as uncollectible the accounts of Walter Corporation ($450) and Drake Company ($280).
	8	Hudson purchased $17,200 of inventory on account.
	11	Hudson sold for $25,000 on account inventory that cost $17,500.
	15	Hudson sold inventory that cost $700 to Jack Rice for $1,000. Rice charged this amount on his Visa First Bank card. The service fee charged Hudson by First Bank is 3%.
	17	Hudson collected $22,900 from customers on account.
	21	Hudson paid $16,300 on accounts payable.
	24	Hudson received payment in full ($280) from Drake Company on the account written off on January 3.
	27	Hudson purchased advertising supplies for $1,400 cash.
	31	Hudson paid other operating expenses, $3,218.

Adjustment data:

1. Interest is recorded for the month on the note from January 1.
2. Bad debts are expected to be 6% of the January 31, 2017, accounts receivable.
3. A count of advertising supplies on January 31, 2017, reveals that $560 remains unused.
4. The income tax rate is 30%. (*Hint:* Prepare the income statement up to "Income before taxes" and multiply by 30% to compute the amount; round to whole dollars.)

Instructions

(You may want to set up T-accounts to determine ending balances.)

(a) Prepare journal entries for the transactions listed above and adjusting entries. (Include entries for cost of goods sold using the perpetual inventory system.)
(b) Prepare an adjusted trial balance at January 31, 2017.
(c) Prepare an income statement and a retained earnings statement for the month ending January 31, 2017, and a classified balance sheet as of January 31, 2017.

EXPAND YOUR CRITICAL THINKING

Financial Reporting

FINANCIAL REPORTING PROBLEM: Apple Inc.

CT8-1 Refer to the financial statements of Apple Inc. in Appendix A.

AN

Instructions

(a) Calculate the accounts receivable turnover and average collection period for 2014. (Assume all sales were credit sales.)
(b) Did Apple have any potentially significant credit risks in 2014?
(c) What conclusions can you draw from the information in parts (a) and (b)?

Financial Analysis

COMPARATIVE ANALYSIS PROBLEM: Columbia Sportswear Company vs. VF Corporation

AN **CT8-2** The financial statements of Columbia Sportswear Company are presented in Appendix B. Financial statements of VF Corporation are presented in Appendix C.

Instructions

(a) Based on the information contained in these financial statements, compute the following 2014 values for each company.
    (1) Accounts receivable turnover. (For VF, use "Net sales." Assume all sales were credit sales.)
    (2) Average collection period for accounts receivable.
(b) What conclusions concerning the management of accounts receivable can be drawn from these data?

Financial Analysis

COMPARATIVE ANALYSIS PROBLEM: Amazon.com, Inc. vs. Wal-Mart Stores, Inc.

AN **CT8-3** The financial statements of Amazon.com, Inc. are presented in Appendix D. Financial statements of Wal-Mart Stores, Inc. are presented in Appendix E.

Instructions

(a) Based on the information contained in these financial statements, compute the following values for each company for the most recent fiscal year.
    (1) Accounts receivable turnover. (For Amazon.com, use "Net product sales." Assume all sales were credit sales.)
    (2) Average collection period for accounts receivable.
(b) What conclusions concerning the management of accounts receivable can be drawn from these data?

Financial Analysis

INTERPRETING FINANCIAL STATEMENTS

CT8-4 Suppose the information below is from the 2017 financial statements and accompanying notes of The Scotts Company, a major manufacturer of lawn-care products.

AN

(in millions)	2017	2016
Accounts receivable	$ 270.4	$ 259.7
Allowance for uncollectible accounts	10.6	11.4
Sales revenue	2,981.8	2,871.8
Total current assets	1,044.9	999.3

THE SCOTTS COMPANY
Notes to the Financial Statements

Note 19. Concentrations of Credit Risk

Financial instruments which potentially subject the Company to concentration of credit risk consist principally of trade accounts receivable. The Company sells its consumer products to a wide variety of retailers, including mass merchandisers, home centers, independent hardware stores, nurseries, garden outlets, warehouse clubs, food and drug stores and local and regional chains. Professional products are sold to commercial nurseries, greenhouses, landscape services and growers of specialty agriculture crops. Concentrations of accounts receivable at September 30, net of accounts receivable pledged under the terms of the New MARP Agreement whereby the purchaser has assumed the risk associated with the debtor's financial inability to pay ($146.6 million and $149.5 million for 2017 and 2016, respectively), were as follows.

	2017	**2016**
Due from customers geographically located in North America	53%	52%
Applicable to the consumer business	61%	54%
Applicable to Scotts LawnService®, the professional businesses (primarily distributors), Smith & Hawken® and Morning Song®	39%	46%
Top 3 customers within consumer business as a percent of total consumer accounts receivable	0%	0%

The remainder of the Company's accounts receivable at September 30, 2017 and 2016, were generated from customers located outside of North America, primary retailers, distributors, nurseries and growers in Europe. No concentrations of customers of individual customers within this group account for more than 10% of the Company's accounts receivable at either balance sheet date.

The Company's three largest customers are reported within the Global Consumer segment, and are the only customers that individually represent more than 10% of reported consolidated net sales for each of the last three fiscal years. These three customers accounted for the following percentages of consolidated net sales for the fiscal years ended September 30:

	Largest Customer	**2nd Largest Customer**	**3rd Largest Customer**
2017	21.0%	13.5%	13.4%
2016	20.2%	10.9%	10.2%
2015	21.5%	11.2%	10.5%

Instructions
Answer each of the following questions.

(a) Calculate the accounts receivable turnover and average collection period for 2017 for the company.
(b) Is accounts receivable a material component of the company's total 2017 current assets?
(c) Scotts sells seasonal products. How might this affect the accuracy of your answer to part (a)?
(d) Evaluate the credit risk of Scotts' 2017 concentrated receivables.
(e) Comment on the informational value of Scotts' Note 19 on concentrations of credit risk.

REAL-WORLD FOCUS

CT8-5 ***Purpose:*** To learn more about factoring from websites that provide factoring services. E

Address: **www.ccapital.net**, or go to **www.wiley.com/college/kimmel**

Instructions
Go to the website, click on **Invoice Factoring**, and answer the following questions.

(a) What are some of the benefits of factoring?
(b) What is the range of the percentages of the typical discount rate?
(c) If a company factors its receivables, what percentage of the value of the receivables can it expect to receive from the factor in the form of cash, and how quickly will it receive the cash?

CT8-6 The August 31, 2009, issue of the *Wall Street Journal* includes an article by Serena Ng and Cari Tuna entitled "Big Firms Are Quick to Collect, Slow to Pay." S

Instructions
Read the article and answer the following questions.

(a) How many days did InBev tell its suppliers that it was going to take to pay? How many days did it take previously?
(b) What steps did General Electric take to free up cash? How much cash did it free up?
(c) On average, how many days did companies with more than $5 billion take to pay suppliers, and how many days did they take to collect from their customers? How did this compare to companies with less than $500 million in sales?
(d) Are there any risks involved with being too tough in negotiating delayed payment terms with suppliers?

Financial Analysis

Writing

Group Project

DECISION-MAKING ACROSS THE ORGANIZATION

CT8-7 Emilio and René Santos own Club Fandango. From its inception, Club Fandango has sold merchandise on either a cash or credit basis, but no credit cards have been accepted. During the past several months, the Santos have begun to question their credit-sales policies. First, they have lost some sales because of their refusal to accept credit cards. Second, representatives of two metropolitan banks have convinced them to accept their national credit cards. One bank, Business National Bank, has stated that (1) its credit card fee is 4% and (2) it pays the retailer 96 cents on each $1 of sales within 3 days of receiving the credit card billings.

E

The Santos decide that they should determine the cost of carrying their own credit sales. From the accounting records of the past 3 years, they accumulate these data:

	2017	2016	2015
Net credit sales	$500,000	$600,000	$400,000
Collection agency fees for slow-paying customers	2,900	2,600	1,600
Salary of part-time accounts receivable clerk	4,400	4,400	4,400

Credit and collection expenses as a percentage of net credit sales are as follows: uncollectible accounts 1.6%, billing and mailing costs .5%, and credit investigation fee on new customers .2%.

Emilio and René also determine that the average accounts receivable balance outstanding during the year is 5% of net credit sales. The Santos estimate that they could earn an average of 10% annually on cash invested in other business opportunities.

Instructions
With the class divided into groups, answer the following.

(a) Prepare a tabulation for each year showing total credit and collection expenses in dollars and as a percentage of net credit sales.
(b) Determine the net credit and collection expenses in dollars and as a percentage of sales after considering the revenue not earned from other investment opportunities. (*Note:* The income lost on the cash held by the bank for 3 days is considered to be immaterial.)
(c) Discuss both the financial and nonfinancial factors that are relevant to the decision.

COMMUNICATION ACTIVITY

E **CT8-8** Chien Corporation is a recently formed business selling the "World's Best Doormat." The corporation is selling doormats faster than Chien can make them. It has been selling the product on a credit basis, telling customers to "pay when they can." Oddly, even though sales are tremendous, the company is having trouble paying its bills.

Instructions
Write a memo to the president of Chien Corporation discussing these questions:

(a) What steps should be taken to improve the company's ability to pay its bills?
(b) What accounting steps should be taken to measure its success in improving collections and in recording its collection success?
(c) If the corporation is still unable to pay its bills, what additional steps can be taken with its receivables to ease its liquidity problems?

ETHICS CASE

E **CT8-9** As its year-end approaches, it appears that Mendez Corporation's net income will increase 10% this year. The president of Mendez Corporation, nervous that the stockholders might expect the company to sustain this 10% growth rate in net income in future years, suggests that the controller increase the allowance for doubtful accounts to 4% of receivables in order to lower this year's net income. The president thinks that the lower net income, which reflects a 6% growth rate, will be a more sustainable rate of growth for Mendez Corporation in future years. The controller of Mendez Corporation believes that the company's yearly allowance for doubtful accounts should be 2% of receivables.

Instructions

(a) Who are the stakeholders in this case?
(b) Does the president's request pose an ethical dilemma for the controller?
(c) Should the controller be concerned with Mendez Corporation's growth rate in estimating the allowance? Explain your answer.

ALL ABOUT YOU

CT8-10 Credit card usage in the United States is substantial. Many startup companies use credit cards as a way to help meet short-term financial needs. The most common forms of debt for startups are use of credit cards and loans from relatives. E

Suppose that you start up Fantastic Sandwich Shop. You invested your savings of $20,000 and borrowed $70,000 from your relatives. Although sales in the first few months are good, you see that you may not have sufficient cash to pay expenses and maintain your inventory at acceptable levels, at least in the short term. You decide you may need to use one or more credit cards to fund the possible cash shortfall.

Instructions

(a) Go to the Internet and find two sources that provide insight into how to compare credit card terms.
(b) Develop a list, in descending order of importance, as to what features are most important to you in selecting a credit card for your business.
(c) Examine the features of your present credit card. (If you do not have a credit card, select a likely one online for this exercise.) Given your analysis above, what are the three major disadvantages of your present credit card?

FASB CODIFICATION ACTIVITY

CT8-11 If your school has a subscription to the FASB Codification, go to **http://aaahq.org/ascLogin.cfm** to log in and prepare responses to the following. AP

(a) How are receivables defined in the Codification?
(b) What are the conditions under which losses from uncollectible receivables (Bad Debt Expense) should be reported?

A Look at IFRS

LEARNING OBJECTIVE ▶5 **Compare the accounting for receivables under GAAP and IFRS.**

The basic accounting and reporting issues related to the recognition, measurement, and disposition of receivables are essentially the same between IFRS and GAAP.

KEY POINTS

Following are the key similarities and differences between GAAP and IFRS related to the accounting for receivables.

Similarities

- The recording of receivables, recognition of sales returns and allowances and sales discounts, and the allowance method to record bad debts are the same between GAAP and IFRS.
- Both IFRS and GAAP often use the term impairment to indicate that a receivable or a percentage of receivables may not be collected.
- The FASB and IASB have worked to implement fair value measurement (the amount they currently could be sold for) for financial instruments, such as receivables. Both Boards have faced bitter opposition from various factions.

Differences

- Although IFRS implies that receivables with different characteristics should be reported separately, there is no standard that mandates this segregation.
- IFRS and GAAP differ in the criteria used to determine how to record a factoring transaction. IFRS uses a combination approach focused on risks and rewards and loss of control. GAAP uses loss of control as the primary criterion. In addition, IFRS permits partial derecognition of receivables; GAAP does not.

LOOKING TO THE FUTURE

The question of recording fair values for financial instruments will continue to be an important issue to resolve as the Boards work toward convergence. Both the IASB and the FASB have indicated that they believe that financial statements would be more transparent and understandable if companies recorded and reported all financial instruments at fair value. That said, in *IFRS 9*, which was issued in 2009, the IASB created a split model, where some financial instruments are recorded at fair value, but other financial assets, such as loans and receivables, can be accounted for at amortized cost if certain criteria are met. Critics say that this can result in two companies with identical securities accounting for those securities in different ways. A proposal by the FASB would require that practically all equity instruments be reported at fair value, and that debt instruments may or may not be reported at fair value depending on whether certain criteria are met.

IFRS Practice

IFRS SELF-TEST QUESTIONS

1. Which of the following statements is **false**?
   (a) Receivables include equity securities purchased by the company.
   (b) Receivables include credit card receivables.
   (c) Receivables include amounts owed by employees as a result of company loans to employees.
   (d) Receivables include amounts resulting from transactions with customers.
2. In recording a factoring transaction:
   (a) IFRS focuses on loss of control.
   (b) GAAP focuses on loss of control and risks and rewards.
   (c) IFRS and GAAP allow partial derecognition.
   (d) IFRS allows partial derecognition.
3. Under IFRS:
   (a) the entry to record estimated uncollected accounts is the same as GAAP.
   (b) it is always acceptable to use the direct write-off method.
   (c) all financial instruments are recorded at fair value.
   (d) None of the above.

INTERNATIONAL FINANCIAL REPORTING PROBLEM: Louis Vuitton

IFRS8-1 The financial statements of Louis Vuitton are presented in Appendix F. Instructions for accessing and using the company's complete annual report, including the notes to its financial statements, are also provided in Appendix F.

Instructions

Use the company's annual report to answer the following questions.

(a) What is the accounting policy related to accounting for trade accounts receivable?
(b) According to the notes to the financial statements, what accounted for the difference between gross trade accounts receivable and net accounts receivable?
(c) According to the notes to the financial statements, what was the major reason why the balance in receivables increased relative to the previous year?
(d) Using information in the notes to the financial statements, determine what percentage the provision for impairment of receivables was as a percentage of total trade receivables for 2014 and 2013. How did the ratio change from 2013 to 2014, and what does this suggest about the company's receivables?

Answers to IFRS Self-Test Questions

1. a **2.** d **3.** a

9

Reporting and Analyzing Long-Lived Assets

CHAPTER PREVIEW

For airlines and many other companies, making the right decisions regarding long-lived assets is critical because these assets represent huge investments. The discussion in this chapter is in two parts: plant assets and intangible assets. **Plant assets** are the property, plant, and equipment (physical assets) that commonly come to mind when we think of what a company owns. **Intangible assets**, such as copyrights and patents, lack physical substance but can be extremely valuable and vital to a company's success.

CHAPTER OUTLINE

LEARNING OBJECTIVES		PRACTICE
1 Explain the accounting for plant asset expenditures.	• Determining the cost of plant assets • Expenditures during useful life • To buy or lease?	DO IT! 1 Cost of Plant Assets
2 Apply depreciation methods to plant assets.	• Factors in computing depreciation • Depreciation methods • Revising depreciation • Impairments	DO IT! 2 2a Straight-Line Depreciation 2b Revised Depreciation
3 Explain how to account for the disposal of plant assets.	• Sale of plant assets • Retirement of plant assets	DO IT! 3 Plant Asset Disposals
4 Identify the basic issues related to reporting intangible assets.	• Accounting for intangible assets • Types of intangible assets	DO IT! 4 Classification Concepts
5 Discuss how long-lived assets are reported and analyzed.	• Presentation • Analysis	DO IT! 5 Asset Turnover

Go to the ***REVIEW AND PRACTICE*** section at the end of the chapter for a targeted summary and exercises with solutions.

Visit **WileyPLUS** for additional tutorials and practice opportunities.

© Linda & ColinMcKie/iStockphoto

FEATURE STORY

A Tale of Two Airlines

So, you're interested in starting a new business. Have you thought about the airline industry? Today, the most profitable airlines in the industry are not well-known majors like American Airlines and United. In fact, most giant, older airlines seem to be either bankrupt or on the verge of bankruptcy. In a recent year, five major airlines representing 24% of total U.S. capacity were operating under bankruptcy protection.

Not all airlines are hurting. The growth and profitability in the airline industry today is found at relative newcomers like Southwest Airlines and JetBlue Airways. These and other new airlines compete primarily on ticket prices. During a recent five-year period, the low-fare airline market share increased by 47%, reaching 22% of U.S. airline capacity.

Southwest was the first upstart to make it big. It did so by taking a different approach. It bought small, new, fuel-efficient planes. Also, instead of the "hub-and-spoke" approach used by the majors, it opted for direct, short hop, no frills flights. It was all about controlling costs—getting the most out of its efficient new planes.

JetBlue, founded by former employees of Southwest, was recently ranked as the number 1 airline in the United States by the airline rating company SkyTrax. Management initially attempted to differentiate JetBlue by offering amenities not found on other airlines, such as seatback entertainment systems, while adopting Southwest's low-fare model. This approach was successful during JetBlue's early years, as it enjoyed both profitability and rapid growth. However, more recently the company has had to take aggressive steps to rein in costs in order to return to profitability.

In the past, upstarts such as Valujet chose a different approach. The company bought planes that were 20 to 30 years old (known in the industry as *zombies*), which allowed it to quickly add planes to its fleet. Valujet started with a $3.4 million investment and grew to be worth $630 million in its first three years.

But with high fuel costs, airlines are no longer in the market for old planes which generally can't be operated efficiently. Today, success in the airline business comes from owning the newest and most efficient equipment, and knowing how to get the most out of it.

LEARNING OBJECTIVE ▶1

Explain the accounting for plant asset expenditures.

Plant assets are resources that have physical substance (a definite size and shape), are used in the operations of a business, and are not intended for sale to customers. They are called various names—property, plant, and equipment; plant and equipment; and fixed assets. By whatever name, these assets are expected to be of service to the company for a number of years. Except for land, plant assets decline in service potential (ability to produce revenue) over their useful lives.

Plant assets are critical to a company's success because they determine the company's capacity and therefore its ability to satisfy customers. With too few planes, for example, JetBlue Airways and Southwest Airlines would lose customers to their competitors. But with too many planes, they would be flying with empty seats. Management must constantly monitor its needs and acquire assets accordingly. Failure to do so results in lost business opportunities or inefficient use of existing assets and, eventually, poor financial results.

It is important for a company to (1) keep assets in good operating condition, (2) replace worn-out or outdated assets, and (3) expand its productive assets as needed. The decline of rail travel in the United States can be traced in part to the failure of railroad companies to maintain and update their assets. Conversely, the growth of air travel in this country can be attributed in part to the general willingness of airline companies to follow these essential guidelines.

For many companies, investments in plant assets are substantial. Illustration 9-1 shows the percentages of plant assets in relation to total assets in various companies in a recent year.

ILLUSTRATION 9-1
Percentages of plant assets in relation to total assets

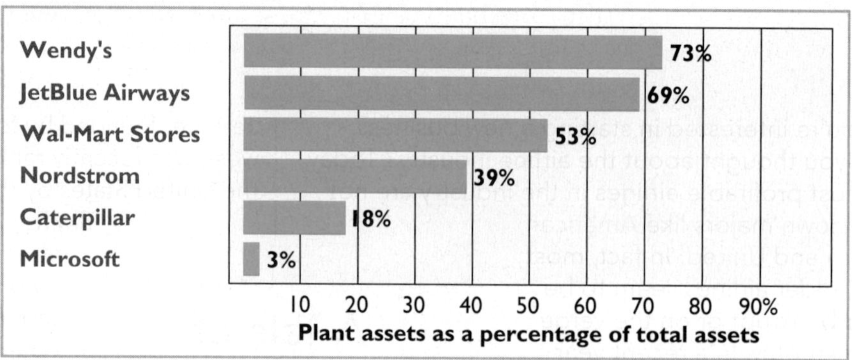

DETERMINING THE COST OF PLANT ASSETS

The **historical cost principle** requires that companies record plant assets at cost. Thus, JetBlue Airways and Southwest Airlines record their planes at cost. **Cost consists of all expenditures necessary to acquire an asset and make it ready for its intended use.** For example, when Boeing buys equipment, the purchase price, freight costs paid by Boeing, and installation costs are all part of the cost of the equipment.

Determining which costs to include in a plant asset account and which costs not to include is very important. If a cost is not included in a plant asset account, then it must be expensed immediately. Such costs are referred to as **revenue expenditures**. On the other hand, costs that are not expensed immediately but are instead included in a plant asset account are referred to as **capital expenditures**. JetBlue reported capital expenditures of $730 million during 2014.

This distinction is important; it has immediate, and often material, implications for the income statement. Some companies, in order to boost current income, have **improperly capitalized expenditures** that they should have expensed. For example, suppose that a company improperly capitalizes to a building account $1,000 of maintenance costs incurred at the end of the year. (That is, the costs are included in the asset account Buildings rather than being expensed immediately as Maintenance and Repairs Expense.) If the company is allocating the cost of the building as an expense (depreciating it) over a 40-year life, then the maintenance cost of $1,000 will be incorrectly spread across 40 years instead of being expensed in the current year. As a result, the company will understate current-year expenses by approximately $1,000 and will overstate current-year income by approximately $1,000. Thus, determining which costs to capitalize and which to expense is very important.

Cost is measured by the cash paid in a cash transaction or by the **cash equivalent price** paid when companies use noncash assets in payment. **The cash equivalent price is equal to the fair value of the asset given up or the fair value of the asset received, whichever is more clearly determinable.** Once cost is established, it becomes the basis of accounting for the plant asset over its useful life. Current fair value is not used to increase the recorded cost after acquisition. We explain the application of the historical cost principle to each of the major classes of plant assets in the following sections.

INTERNATIONAL NOTE
IFRS is more flexible regarding asset valuation. Companies revalue to fair value when they believe this information is more relevant.

Land

Companies often use land as a building site for a manufacturing plant or office site. The cost of land includes (1) the cash purchase price, (2) closing costs such as title and attorney's fees, (3) real estate brokers' commissions, and (4) accrued property taxes and other liens on the land assumed by the purchaser. For example, if the cash price is $50,000 and the purchaser agrees to pay accrued taxes of $5,000, the cost of the land is $55,000.

All necessary costs incurred in making land **ready for its intended use** increase (debit) the Land account. When a company acquires vacant land, its cost includes expenditures for clearing, draining, filling, and grading. If the land has a building on it that must be removed to make the site suitable for construction of a new building, the company includes all demolition and removal costs, less any proceeds from salvaged materials, in the Land account.

To illustrate, assume that Hayes Company acquires real estate at a cash cost of $100,000. The property contains an old warehouse that is removed at a net cost of $6,000 ($7,500 in costs less $1,500 proceeds from salvaged materials). Additional expenditures are for the attorney's fee $1,000 and the real estate broker's commission $8,000. Given these factors, the cost of the land is $115,000, computed as shown in Illustration 9-2.

ILLUSTRATION 9-2
Computation of cost of land

Land	
Cash price of property	$ 100,000
Net removal cost of warehouse	6,000
Attorney's fee	1,000
Real estate broker's commission	8,000
Cost of land	**$115,000**

When Hayes records the acquisition, it debits Land and credits Cash for $115,000.

Land Improvements

Land improvements are structural additions with limited lives that are made to land, such as driveways, parking lots, fences, landscaping, and underground sprinklers. The cost of land improvements includes all expenditures necessary to make the improvements ready for their intended use. For example, the cost of a new company parking lot includes the amount paid for paving, fencing, and lighting. Thus, the company would debit the total of all of these costs to Land Improvements.

Land improvements have limited useful lives. Even when well-maintained, they will eventually need to be replaced. As a result, companies expense (depreciate) the cost of land improvements over their useful lives.

Buildings

Buildings are facilities used in operations, such as stores, offices, factories, warehouses, and airplane hangars. Companies charge to the Buildings account all necessary expenditures relating to the purchase or construction of a building. When a building is **purchased**, such costs include the purchase price, closing costs (attorney's fees, title insurance, etc.), and real estate broker's commission. Costs to make the building ready for its intended use consist of expenditures for remodeling rooms and offices and replacing or repairing the roof, floors, electrical wiring, and plumbing. When a new building is **constructed**, its cost consists of the contract price plus payments made by the owner for architects' fees, building permits, and excavation costs.

In addition, companies add certain interest costs to the cost of a building. Interest costs incurred to finance a construction project are included in the cost of the asset when a significant period of time is required to get the asset ready for use. In these circumstances, interest costs are considered as necessary as materials and labor. However, the inclusion of interest costs in the cost of a constructed building is **limited to interest costs incurred during the construction period**. When construction has been completed, subsequent interest payments on funds borrowed to finance the construction are recorded as increases (debits) to Interest Expense.

Equipment

Equipment includes assets used in operations, such as store check-out counters, office furniture, factory machinery, and delivery trucks. JetBlue Airways' equipment includes aircraft, in-flight entertainment systems, and trucks for ground operations. The cost of equipment consists of the cash purchase price, sales taxes, freight charges, and insurance during transit paid by the purchaser. It also includes expenditures required in assembling, installing, and testing the unit. However, companies treat as expenses the costs of motor vehicle licenses and accident insurance on company trucks and cars. Such items are **annual recurring expenditures and do not benefit future periods**. Two criteria apply in determining the cost of equipment: (1) the frequency of the cost—one time or recurring, and (2) the benefit period—the life of the asset or one year.

To illustrate, assume that Lenard Company purchases a delivery truck on January 1 at a cash price of $22,000. Related expenditures are sales taxes $1,320, painting and lettering $500, motor vehicle license $80, and a three-year accident insurance policy $1,600. The cost of the delivery truck is $23,820, computed as shown in Illustration 9-3.

ILLUSTRATION 9-3
Computation of cost of delivery truck

Delivery Truck	
Cash price	$ 22,000
Sales taxes	1,320
Painting and lettering	500
Cost of delivery truck	**$23,820**

Lenard treats the cost of a motor vehicle license as an expense and the cost of an insurance policy as a prepaid asset. Thus, the company records the purchase of the truck and related expenditures as follows.

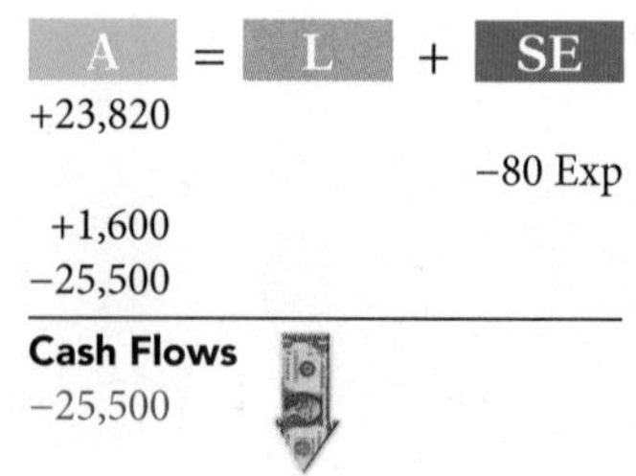

	Debit	Credit
Equipment	23,820	
License Expense	80	
Prepaid Insurance	1,600	
Cash		25,500
(To record purchase of delivery truck and related expenditures)		

For another example, assume Merten Company purchases factory machinery at a cash price of $50,000. Related expenditures are sales taxes $3,000, insurance during shipping $500, and installation and testing $1,000. The cost of the factory machinery is $54,500, computed as shown in Illustration 9-4.

ILLUSTRATION 9-4
Computation of cost of factory machinery

Factory Machinery	
Cash price	$ 50,000
Sales taxes	3,000
Insurance during shipping	500
Installation and testing	1,000
Cost of factory machinery	**$54,500**

Thus, Merten records the purchase and related expenditures as follows.

Equipment	54,500	
Cash		54,500
(To record purchase of factory machinery and related expenditures)		

A	=	L	+	SE
+54,500				
−54,500				

Cash Flows
−54,500

EXPENDITURES DURING USEFUL LIFE

During the useful life of a plant asset, a company may incur costs for ordinary repairs, additions, and improvements. **Ordinary repairs** are expenditures to maintain the operating efficiency and expected productive life of the unit. They usually are fairly small amounts that occur frequently throughout the service life. Examples are motor tune-ups and oil changes, the painting of buildings, and the replacing of worn-out gears on factory machinery. Ordinary repairs are debited to Maintenance and Repairs Expense as incurred.

In contrast, **additions and improvements** are costs incurred to **increase** the operating efficiency, productive capacity, or expected useful life of the plant asset. These expenditures are usually material in amount and occur infrequently during the period of ownership. Expenditures for additions and improvements increase the company's investment in productive facilities and are generally debited to the plant asset affected. Thus, they are **capital expenditures**. The accounting for capital expenditures varies depending on the nature of the expenditure.

Northwest Airlines at one time spent $120 million to spruce up 40 jets. The improvements were designed to extend the lives of the planes, meet stricter government noise limits, and save money. The capital expenditure was expected to extend the life of the jets by 10 to 15 years and save about $560 million compared to the cost of buying new planes. The jets were, on average, 24 years old.

ANATOMY OF A FRAUD

Bernie Ebbers was the founder and CEO of the phone company WorldCom. The company engaged in a series of increasingly large, debt-financed acquisitions of other companies. These acquisitions made the company grow quickly, which made the stock price increase dramatically. However, because the acquired companies all had different accounting systems, WorldCom's financial records were a mess. When WorldCom's performance started to flatten out, Bernie coerced WorldCom's accountants to engage in a number of fraudulent activities to make net income look better than it really was and thus prop up the stock price. One of these frauds involved treating $7 billion of line costs as capital expenditures. The line costs, which were rental fees paid to other phone companies to use their phone lines, had always been properly expensed in previous years. Capitalization delayed expense recognition to future periods and thus boosted current-period profits.

Total take: $7 billion

THE MISSING CONTROLS

Documentation procedures. The company's accounting system was a disorganized collection of non-integrated systems, which resulted from a series of corporate acquisitions. Top management took advantage of this disorganization to conceal its fraudulent activities.

Independent internal verification. A fraud of this size should have been detected by a routine comparison of the actual physical assets with the list of physical assets shown in the accounting records.

TO BUY OR LEASE?

In this chapter, we focus on purchased assets, but we want to expose you briefly to an alternative—leasing. A lease is a contractual agreement in which the owner of an asset (the **lessor**) allows another party (the **lessee**) to use the asset for a period of time at an agreed price. In many industries, leasing is quite common. For example, one-third of heavy-duty commercial trucks are leased.

Some advantages of leasing an asset versus purchasing it are:

1. **Reduced risk of obsolescence.** Frequently, lease terms allow the party using the asset (the lessee) to exchange the asset for a more modern one if it becomes outdated. This is much easier than trying to sell an obsolete asset.
2. **Little or no down payment.** To purchase an asset, most companies must borrow money, which usually requires a down payment of at least 20%. Leasing an asset requires little or no down payment.
3. **Shared tax advantages.** Startup companies typically earn little or no profit in their early years, and so they have little need for the tax deductions available from owning an asset. In a lease, the lessor gets the tax advantage because it owns the asset. It often will pass these tax savings on to the lessee in the form of lower lease payments.
4. **Assets and liabilities not reported.** Many companies prefer to keep assets and especially liabilities off their books. Reporting lower assets improves the return on assets (discussed later in this chapter). Reporting fewer liabilities makes the company look less risky. Certain types of leases, called **operating leases**, allow the lessee to account for the transaction as a rental, with neither an asset nor a liability recorded.

Airlines often choose to lease many of their airplanes in long-term lease agreements. In recent financial statements, JetBlue Airways stated that it leased 60 of its 169 planes under operating leases. Because operating leases are accounted for as rentals, these 60 planes were not presented on its balance sheet.

Under another type of lease, a **capital lease**, lessees show both the asset and the liability on the balance sheet. The lessee accounts for capital lease agreements in a way that is very similar to debt-financed purchases: The lessee shows the leased item as an asset on its balance sheet, and the obligation owed to the lessor as a liability. The lessee depreciates the leased asset in a manner similar to purchased assets. Only four of JetBlue's aircraft were held under capital leases. We discuss leasing further in Chapter 10.[1]

ACCOUNTING ACROSS THE ORGANIZATION

© Brian Raisbeck/iStockphoto

Many U.S. Firms Use Leases

Leasing is big business for U.S. companies. For example, in a recent year leasing accounted for about 33% of all business investment ($264 billion).

Who does the most leasing? Interestingly, major banks such as Continental Bank, J.P. Morgan Leasing, and US Bancorp Equipment Finance are the major lessors. Also, many companies have established separate leasing companies, such as Boeing Capital Corporation, Dell Financial Services, and John Deere Capital Corporation. As an example of the magnitude of leasing, leased planes account for nearly 40% of the U.S. fleet of commercial airlines. Lease Finance Corporation in Los Angeles owns more planes than any airline in the world.

Leasing is also becoming increasingly common in the hotel industry. Marriott, Hilton, and InterContinental are increasingly choosing to lease hotels that are owned by someone else.

Why might airline managers choose to lease rather than purchase their planes? (Go to WileyPLUS for this answer and additional questions.)

[1]The FASB is currently considering a new approach for accounting for leases.

DO IT! 1 Cost of Plant Assets

Assume that Drummond Corp. purchases a delivery truck for $15,000 cash plus sales taxes of $900 and delivery costs of $500. The buyer also pays $200 for painting and lettering, $600 for an annual insurance policy, and $80 for a motor vehicle license. Explain how the company should account for each of these costs.

Action Plan

✔ Identify expenditures made in order to get delivery equipment ready for its intended use.

✔ Expense operating costs incurred during the useful life of the equipment.

SOLUTION

The first four payments ($15,000 purchase price, $900 sales taxes, $500 delivery, and $200 painting and lettering) are expenditures necessary to make the truck ready for its intended use. Thus, the cost of the truck is $16,600. The payments for insurance and the license are operating expenses incurred annually during the useful life of the asset.

Related exercise material: **BE9-1, BE9-2, BE9-3,**  **9-1, E9-1, E9-2,** and **E9-3.**

LEARNING OBJECTIVE 2 Apply depreciation methods to plant assets.

As explained in Chapter 4, **depreciation is the process of allocating to expense the cost of a plant asset over its useful (service) life in a rational and systematic manner**. Such cost allocation is designed to properly match expenses with revenues (see Illustration 9-5).

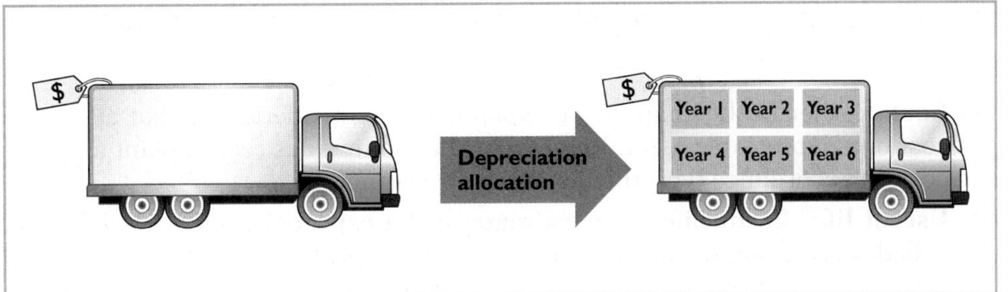

ILLUSTRATION 9-5
Depreciation as a cost allocation concept

Depreciation affects the balance sheet through accumulated depreciation, which companies report as a deduction from plant assets. It affects the income statement through depreciation expense.

It is important to understand that **depreciation is a cost allocation process, not an asset valuation process**. No attempt is made to measure the change in an asset's fair value during ownership. Thus, the **book value**—cost less accumulated depreciation—of a plant asset may differ significantly from its **fair value**. In fact, if an asset is fully depreciated, it can have zero book value but still have a significant fair value.

▼ HELPFUL HINT
Remember that depreciation is the process of *allocating cost* over the useful life of an asset. It is not a measure of value.

Depreciation applies to **three classes of plant assets**: land improvements, buildings, and equipment. Each of these classes is considered to be a **depreciable asset** because the usefulness to the company and the revenue-producing ability of each class decline over the asset's useful life. Depreciation **does not apply to land** because its usefulness and revenue-producing ability generally remain intact as long as the land is owned. In fact, in many cases, the usefulness of land increases over time because of the scarcity of good sites. Thus, **land is not a depreciable asset.**

▼ HELPFUL HINT
Land does not depreciate because it does not wear out.

During a depreciable asset's useful life, its revenue-producing ability declines because of wear and tear. A delivery truck that has been driven 100,000 miles will be less useful to a company than one driven only 800 miles.

ETHICS NOTE When a business is acquired, proper allocation of the purchase price to various asset classes is important since different depreciation treatment can materially affect income. For example, buildings are depreciated, but land is not.

A decline in revenue-producing ability may also occur because of obsolescence. **Obsolescence** is the process by which an asset becomes out of date before it physically wears out. The rerouting of major airlines from Chicago's Midway Airport to Chicago-O'Hare International Airport because Midway's runways were too short for giant jets is an example. Similarly, many companies replace their computers long before they originally planned to do so because technological improvements make their old hardware obsolete.

Recognizing depreciation for an asset does not result in the accumulation of cash for replacement of the asset. The balance in Accumulated Depreciation represents the total amount of the asset's cost that the company has charged to expense to date; **it is not a cash fund.**

FACTORS IN COMPUTING DEPRECIATION

Three factors affect the computation of depreciation, as shown in Illustration 9-6.

ILLUSTRATION 9-6
Three factors in computing depreciation

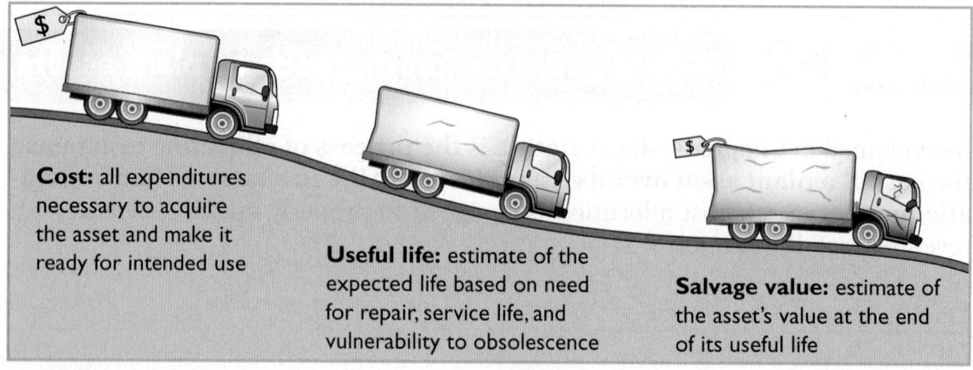

▼ HELPFUL HINT Depreciation expense is reported on the income statement. Accumulated depreciation is reported on the balance sheet as a deduction from plant assets.

1. **Cost.** Earlier in the chapter, we explained the considerations that affect the cost of a depreciable asset. Remember that companies record plant assets at cost, in accordance with the historical cost principle.
2. **Useful life.** Useful life is an estimate of the expected productive life, also called service life, of the asset for its owner. Useful life may be expressed in terms of time, units of activity (such as machine hours), or units of output. Useful life is an estimate. In making the estimate, management considers such factors as the intended use of the asset, repair and maintenance policies, and vulnerability of the asset to obsolescence. The company's past experience with similar assets is often helpful in deciding on expected useful life.
3. **Salvage value.** Salvage value is an estimate of the asset's value at the end of its useful life for its owner. Companies may base the value on the asset's worth as scrap or on its expected trade-in value. Like useful life, salvage value is an estimate. In making the estimate, management considers how it plans to dispose of the asset and its experience with similar assets.

DEPRECIATION METHODS

Although a number of methods exist, depreciation is generally computed using one of three methods:

1. Straight-line
2. Declining-balance
3. Units-of-activity

Like the alternative inventory methods discussed in Chapter 6, each of these depreciation methods is acceptable under generally accepted accounting principles.

Management selects the method it believes best measures an asset's contribution to revenue over its useful life. Once a company chooses a method, it should apply that method consistently over the useful life of the asset. Consistency enhances the ability to analyze financial statements over multiple years.

Our illustration of depreciation methods, both here and in the chapter appendix, is based on the following data relating to a small delivery truck purchased by Bill's Pizzas on January 1, 2017.

Cost	$13,000
Expected salvage value	$1,000
Estimated useful life (in years)	5
Estimated useful life (in miles)	100,000

Illustration 9-7 shows the distribution of the primary depreciation methods in a sample of the largest U.S. companies. Clearly, straight-line depreciation is the most widely used approach. In fact, because some companies use more than one method, **straight-line depreciation is used for some or all of the depreciation taken by more than 95% of U.S. companies**. For this reason, we illustrate procedures for straight-line depreciation and discuss the alternative depreciation approaches only at a conceptual level. This coverage introduces you to the basic idea of depreciation as an allocation concept without entangling you in too much procedural detail. (Also, note that many calculators are preprogrammed to perform the basic depreciation methods.) Details on the alternative approaches are presented in Appendix 9A (pages 449–451).

No matter what method is used, the total amount depreciated over the useful life of the asset is its depreciable cost. **Depreciable cost** is equal to the cost of the asset less its salvage value.

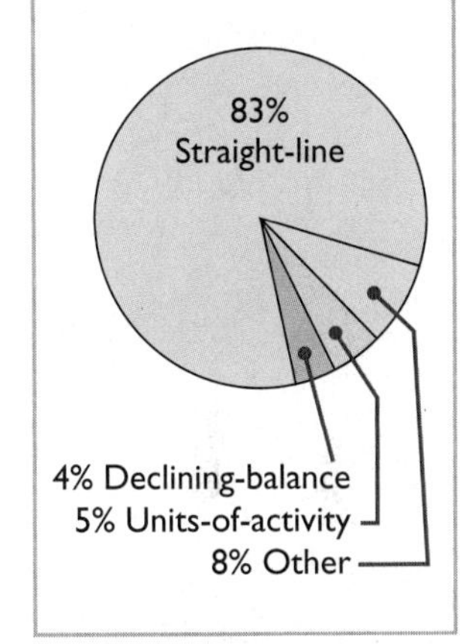

ILLUSTRATION 9-7
Use of depreciation methods in major U.S. companies

Straight-Line Method

Under the **straight-line method**, companies expense an equal amount of depreciation each year of the asset's useful life. Management must choose the useful life of an asset based on its own expectations and experience.

To compute the annual depreciation expense, we divide depreciable cost by the estimated useful life. As indicated above, depreciable cost represents the total amount subject to depreciation; it is calculated as the cost of the plant asset less its salvage value. Illustration 9-8 shows the computation of depreciation expense in the first year for Bill's Pizzas' delivery truck.

ILLUSTRATION 9-8
Formula for straight-line method

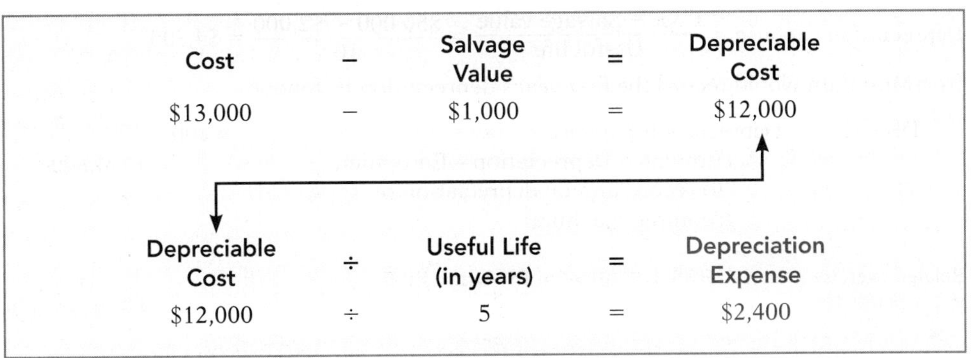

Alternatively, we can compute an annual **rate** at which the company depreciates the delivery truck. In this case, the rate is 20% (100% ÷ 5 years). When an annual rate is used under the straight-line method, the company applies the percentage rate to the depreciable cost of the asset, as shown in the **depreciation schedule** in Illustration 9-9 (page 432).

ILLUSTRATION 9-9
Straight-line depreciation schedule

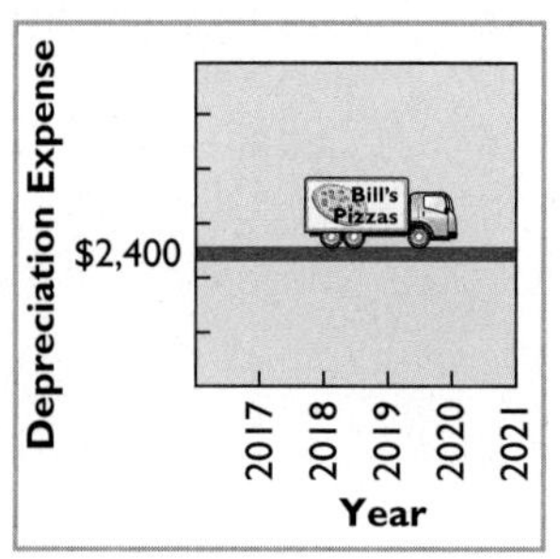

BILL'S PIZZAS

	Computation			Annual	End of Year	
Year	**Depreciable Cost**	×	**Depreciation Rate**	= **Depreciation Expense**	**Accumulated Depreciation**	**Book Value**
2017	$12,000		20%	$ 2,400	$ 2,400	$10,600*
2018	12,000		20	2,400	4,800	8,200
2019	12,000		20	2,400	7,200	5,800
2020	12,000		20	2,400	9,600	3,400
2021	12,000		20	2,400	12,000	1,000
			Total	$12,000		

*$13,000 − $2,400

Note that the depreciation expense of $2,400 is the same each year. The book value at the end of the useful life is equal to the estimated $1,000 salvage value.

What happens when an asset is purchased **during** the year, rather than on January 1 as in our example? In that case, it is necessary to **prorate the annual depreciation** for the portion of a year used. If Bill's Pizzas had purchased the delivery truck on April 1, 2017, the company would use the truck for 9 months in 2017. The depreciation for 2017 would be $1,800 ($12,000 × 20% × $\frac{9}{12}$ of a year).

As indicated earlier, the straight-line method predominates in practice. For example, such large companies as Campbell Soup, Marriott, and General Mills use the straight-line method. It is simple to apply, and it matches expenses with revenues appropriately when the use of the asset is reasonably uniform throughout the service life. The types of assets that give equal benefits over useful life generally are those for which daily use does not affect productivity. Examples are office furniture and fixtures, buildings, warehouses, and garages for motor vehicles.

DO IT! 2a Straight-Line Depreciation

On January 1, 2017, Iron Mountain Ski Corporation purchased a new snow-grooming machine for $50,000. The machine is estimated to have a 10-year life with a $2,000 salvage value. What journal entry would Iron Mountain Ski Corporation make at December 31, 2017, if it uses the straight-line method of depreciation?

Action Plan

- ✔ **Calculate depreciable cost (Cost − Salvage value).**
- ✔ **Divide the depreciable cost by the asset's estimated useful life.**

SOLUTION

$$\text{Depreciation expense} = \frac{\text{Cost} - \text{Salvage value}}{\text{Useful life}} = \frac{\$50{,}000 - \$2{,}000}{10} = \$4{,}800$$

Iron Mountain would record the first year's depreciation as follows.

Dec. 31	Depreciation Expense	4,800	
	Accumulated Depreciation—Equipment		4,800
	(To record annual depreciation on snow-grooming machine)		

Related exercise material: **BE9-4, DO IT! 9-2a, E9-4,** and **E9-5.**

Declining-Balance Method

The **declining-balance method** computes depreciation expense using a constant rate applied to a declining book value. This method is called an **accelerated-depreciation method** because it results in higher depreciation in the early years of an asset's life than does the straight-line approach. However, because the total amount of depreciation (the depreciable cost) taken over an asset's life is the same **no matter what approach** is used, the declining-balance method produces a decreasing annual depreciation expense over the asset's useful life. In early years, declining-balance depreciation expense will exceed straight-line. In later years, it will be less than straight-line. Managers might choose an accelerated approach if they think that an asset's utility will decline quickly.

Companies can apply the declining-balance approach at different rates, which result in varying speeds of depreciation. A common declining-balance rate is double the straight-line rate. Using that rate, the method is referred to as the **double-declining-balance method**.

If we apply the double-declining-balance method to Bill's Pizzas' delivery truck, assuming a five-year life, we get the pattern of depreciation shown in Illustration 9-10. **Illustration 9A-2 (page 450) presents the computations behind these numbers.** Again, note that total depreciation over the life of the truck is $12,000, the depreciable cost.

ILLUSTRATION 9-10
Declining-balance depreciation schedule

BILL'S PIZZAS

Year	Annual Depreciation Expense	End of Year: Accumulated Depreciation	End of Year: Book Value
2017	$ 5,200	$ 5,200	$7,800
2018	3,120	8,320	4,680
2019	1,872	10,192	2,808
2020	1,123	11,315	1,685
2021	685	12,000	1,000
Total	$12,000		

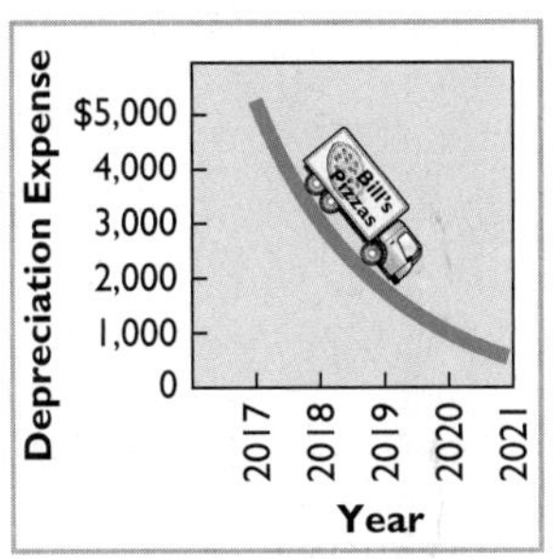

Units-of-Activity Method

As indicated earlier, useful life can be expressed in ways other than a time period. Under the **units-of-activity method**, useful life is expressed in terms of the total units of production or the use expected from the asset. The units-of-activity method is ideally suited to factory machinery: Companies can measure production in terms of units of output or in terms of machine hours used in operating the machinery. It is also possible to use the method for such items as delivery equipment (miles driven) and airplanes (hours in use). The units-of-activity method is generally not suitable for such assets as buildings or furniture because activity levels are difficult to measure for these assets.

Applying the units-of-activity method to the delivery truck owned by Bill's Pizzas, we first must know some basic information. Bill's expects to be able to drive the truck a total of 100,000 miles. Illustration 9-11 shows depreciation over the five-year life based on an assumed mileage pattern. **Illustration 9A-4 (page 451) presents the computations used to arrive at these results.**

ILLUSTRATION 9-11
Units-of-activity depreciation schedule

BILL'S PIZZAS

Year	Units of Activity (miles)	Annual Depreciation Expense	End of Year: Accumulated Depreciation	End of Year: Book Value
2017	15,000	$ 1,800	$ 1,800	$11,200
2018	30,000	3,600	5,400	7,600
2019	20,000	2,400	7,800	5,200
2020	25,000	3,000	10,800	2,200
2021	10,000	1,200	12,000	1,000
Total	100,000	$12,000		

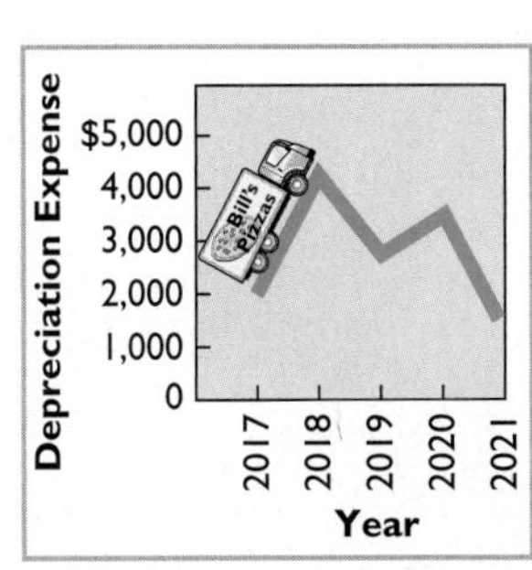

As the name implies, under units-of-activity depreciation, the amount of depreciation is proportional to the activity that took place during that period. For example, the delivery truck was driven twice as many miles in 2018 as in 2017, and depreciation was exactly twice as much in 2018 as it was in 2017.

Management's Choice: Comparison of Methods

Illustration 9-12 compares annual and total depreciation expense for Bill's Pizzas under the three methods.

ILLUSTRATION 9-12
Comparison of depreciation methods

Year	Straight-Line	Declining-Balance	Units-of-Activity
2017	$ 2,400	$ 5,200	$ 1,800
2018	2,400	3,120	3,600
2019	2,400	1,872	2,400
2020	2,400	1,123	3,000
2021	2,400	685	1,200
	$12,000	**$12,000**	**$12,000**

Annual depreciation expense varies considerably among the methods, but **total depreciation expense is the same ($12,000) for the five-year period**. Each method is acceptable in accounting because each recognizes the decline in service potential of the asset in a rational and systematic manner. Illustration 9-13 graphs the depreciation expense pattern under each method.

ILLUSTRATION 9-13
Patterns of depreciation

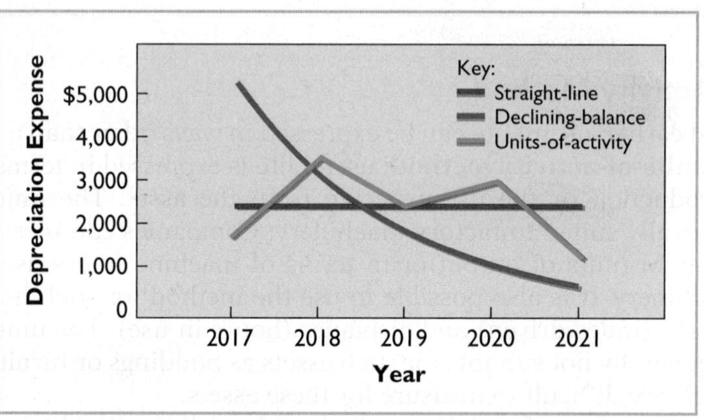

Depreciation and Income Taxes

▼ HELPFUL HINT
Depreciation per financial statements is usually different from depreciation per tax returns.

The Internal Revenue Service (IRS) allows corporate taxpayers to deduct depreciation expense when computing taxable income. However, the tax regulations of the IRS do not require the taxpayer to use the same depreciation method on the tax return that it uses in preparing financial statements.

Consequently, many large corporations use straight-line depreciation in their financial statements in order to maximize net income; at the same time, they use a special accelerated-depreciation method on their tax returns in order to minimize their income taxes. For tax purposes, taxpayers must use on their tax returns either the straight-line method or a special accelerated-depreciation method called the **Modified Accelerated Cost Recovery System** (MACRS).

Depreciation Disclosure in the Notes

Companies must disclose the choice of depreciation method in their financial statements or in related notes that accompany the statements. Illustration 9-14 shows excerpts from the "Property and equipment" notes from the financial statements of Southwest Airlines.

ILLUSTRATION 9-14
Disclosure of depreciation policies

Real World

SOUTHWEST AIRLINES
Notes to the Financial Statements

Property and equipment Depreciation is provided by the straight-line method to estimated residual values over periods ranging from 23 to 25 years for flight equipment and 5 to 30 years for ground property and equipment once the asset is placed in service. . . . Amortization of property under capital leases is on a straight-line basis over the lease term and is included in depreciation and amortization expense.

From this note, we learn that Southwest Airlines uses the straight-line method to depreciate its planes over periods of 23 to 25 years.

REVISING PERIODIC DEPRECIATION

Management should periodically review annual depreciation expense. If wear and tear or obsolescence indicates that annual depreciation is either inadequate or excessive, the company should change the depreciation expense amount.

When a change in an estimate is required, the company makes the change in **current and future years but not to prior periods**. Thus, when making the change, the company (1) does not change previously recorded depreciation expense, but (2) revises depreciation expense for current and future years. The rationale for this treatment is that continual restatement of prior periods would adversely affect users' confidence in financial statements.

To determine the new annual depreciation expense, the company first computes the asset's depreciable cost at the time of the revision. It then allocates the revised depreciable cost to the remaining useful life.

▼ **HELPFUL HINT**
Use a step-by-step approach: (1) determine new depreciable cost; (2) divide by remaining useful life.

To illustrate, assume that Bill's Pizzas decides at the end of 2020 (prior to the year-end adjusting entries) to extend the estimated useful life of the truck one year (a total life of six years) and increase its salvage value to $2,200. The company has used the straight-line method to depreciate the asset to date. Depreciation per year was $2,400 [($13,000 − $1,000) ÷ 5]. Accumulated depreciation after three years (2017–2019) is $7,200 ($2,400 × 3), and book value is $5,800 ($13,000 − $7,200). The new annual depreciation is $1,200, computed on December 31, 2020, as follows.

ILLUSTRATION 9-15
Revised depreciation computation

Book value, 1/1/20	$ 5,800	
Less: New salvage value	2,200	
Depreciable cost	$ 3,600	
Remaining useful life	3 years	(2020–2022)
Revised annual depreciation ($3,600 ÷ 3)	**$1,200**	

Bill's Pizzas does not make a special entry for the change in estimate. On December 31, 2020, during the preparation of adjusting entries, it records depreciation expense of $1,200 instead of the amount recorded in previous years.

Companies must disclose in the financial statements significant changes in estimates. Although a company may have a legitimate reason for changing an estimated life, financial statement users should be aware that some companies might change an estimate simply to achieve financial statement goals. For example, extending an asset's estimated life reduces depreciation expense and increases current period income.

In a recent year, AirTran Airways (now owned by Southwest Airlines) increased the estimated useful lives of some of its planes from 25 to 30 years and increased the estimated lives of related aircraft parts from 5 years to 30 years. It disclosed that the change in estimate decreased its net loss for the year by approximately $0.6 million, or about $0.01 per share. Whether these changes were appropriate depends on how reasonable it is to assume that planes will continue to be used for a long time. Our Feature Story suggests that although in the past many planes lasted a long time, it is also clear that because of high fuel costs, airlines are now scrapping many of their old, inefficient planes.

IMPAIRMENTS

As noted earlier, the book value of plant assets is rarely the same as the fair value. In instances where the value of a plant asset declines substantially, its fair value might fall materially below book value. This may happen because a machine has become obsolete, or the market for the product made by the machine has dried up or has become very competitive. A **permanent decline** in the fair value of an asset is referred to as an **impairment**. So as not to overstate the asset on the books, the company records a write-down, whereby the asset's cost is reduced to its new fair value during the year in which the decline in value occurs. Recently, Disney recorded a $200 million write-down on its action movie *John Carter*. Disney spent more than $300 million producing the film.

In the past, some companies **improperly** delayed recording losses on impairments until a year when it was "convenient" to do so—when the impact on the company's reported results was minimized. For example, in a year when a company has record profits, it can afford to write down some of its bad assets without hurting its reported results too much. As discussed in Chapter 4, the practice of timing the recognition of gains and losses to achieve certain income results is known as **earnings management**. Earnings management reduces earnings quality. To minimize earnings management, accounting standards now require immediate loss recognition on impaired assets.

Write-downs can create problems for users of financial statements. Critics of write-downs note that after a company writes down assets, its depreciation expense will be lower in all subsequent periods. Some companies improperly inflate asset write-downs in bad years, when they are going to report poor results anyway. (This practice is referred to as "taking a big bath.") Then in subsequent years, when the company recovers, its results will look even better because of lower depreciation expense.

DO IT! 2b Revised Depreciation

Chambers Corporation purchased a piece of equipment for $36,000. It estimated a 6-year life and $6,000 salvage value. Thus, straight-line depreciation was $5,000 per year [($36,000 − $6,000) ÷ 6]. At the end of year three (before the depreciation adjustment), it estimated the new total life to be 10 years and the new salvage value to be $2,000. Compute the revised depreciation.

Action Plan

✔ Calculate depreciable cost.

✔ Divide depreciable cost by new remaining life.

SOLUTION

Original depreciation expense = [($36,000 − $6,000) ÷ 6] = $5,000
Accumulated depreciation after 2 years = 2 × $5,000 = $10,000
Book value = $36,000 − $10,000 = $26,000

Book value after 2 years of depreciation	$26,000
Less: New salvage value	2,000
Depreciable cost	$24,000
Remaining useful life	8 years
Revised annual depreciation ($24,000 ÷ 8)	$ 3,000

Related exercise material: **BE9-6, DO IT! 9-2b,** and **E9-6.**

LEARNING OBJECTIVE 3 **Explain how to account for the disposal of plant assets.**

Companies dispose of plant assets that are no longer useful to them. Illustration 9-16 shows the three ways in which companies make plant asset disposals.

ILLUSTRATION 9-16
Methods of plant asset disposal

Whatever the disposal method, the company must determine the book value of the plant asset at the time of disposal in order to determine the gain or loss. Recall that the book value is the difference between the cost of the plant asset and the accumulated depreciation to date. If the disposal does not occur on the first day of the year, the company must record depreciation for the fraction of the year to the date of disposal. The company then eliminates the book value by reducing (debiting) Accumulated Depreciation for the total depreciation associated with that asset to the date of disposal and reducing (crediting) the asset account for the cost of the asset. A gain or loss on disposal may be needed to balance this entry, as discussed next.

SALE OF PLANT ASSETS

In a disposal by sale, the company compares the book value of the asset with the proceeds received from the sale. If the proceeds from the sale **exceed** the book value of the plant asset, a **gain on disposal** occurs. If the proceeds from the sale **are less than** the book value of the plant asset sold, a **loss on disposal** occurs.

Only by coincidence will the book value and the fair value of the asset be the same at the time the asset is sold. Gains and losses on sales of plant assets are therefore quite common. As an example, Delta Air Lines at one time reported a $94 million gain on the sale of five Boeing B-727-200 aircraft and five Lockheed L-1011-1 aircraft.

Gain on Sale

To illustrate a gain on sale of plant assets, assume that on July 1, 2017, Wright Company sells office furniture for $16,000 cash. The office furniture originally cost $60,000 and as of January 1, 2017, had accumulated depreciation of $41,000. Depreciation for the first six months of 2017 is $8,000. Wright records depreciation expense and updates accumulated depreciation to July 1 as follows.

July 1	Depreciation Expense	8,000	
	Accumulated Depreciation—Equipment		8,000
	(To record depreciation expense for the first 6 months of 2017)		

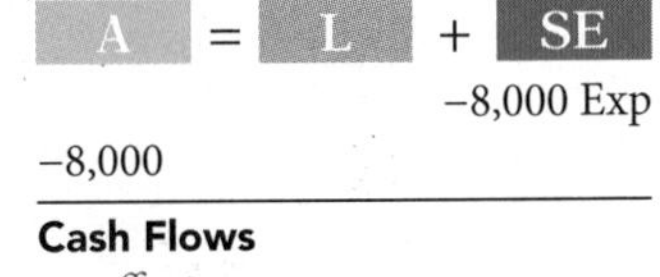

After the accumulated depreciation balance is updated, the company computes the gain or loss as the difference between the proceeds from sale and the book value at the date of disposal. Wright Company has a gain on disposal of $5,000, as computed in Illustration 9-17 (page 438).

ILLUSTRATION 9-17
Computation of gain on disposal

Cost of office furniture	$60,000
Less: Accumulated depreciation ($41,000 + $8,000)	49,000
Book value at date of disposal	11,000
Proceeds from sale	16,000
Gain on disposal of plant asset	**$ 5,000**

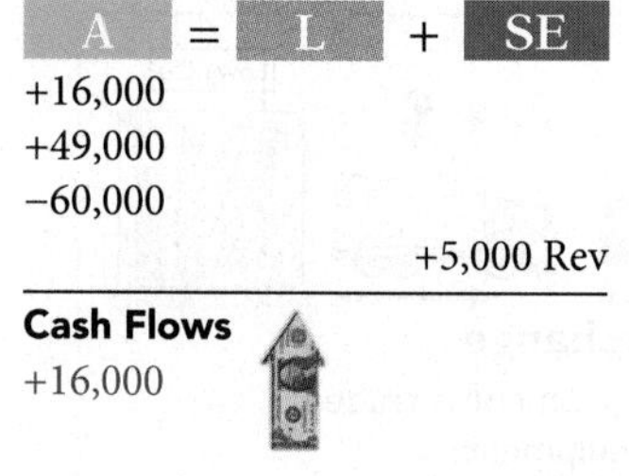

Wright records the sale and the gain on sale of the plant asset as follows.

July 1	Cash	16,000	
	Accumulated Depreciation—Equipment	49,000	
	Equipment		60,000
	Gain on Disposal of Plant Assets		5,000
	(To record sale of office furniture at a gain)		

Companies report a gain on disposal of plant assets in the "Other revenues and gains" section of the income statement. Recently, the shares of Sears Holdings Corporation rose 19% when the company announced its intention to sell 1,200 stores to raise cash.

Loss on Sale

Assume that instead of selling the office furniture for $16,000, Wright sells it for $9,000. In this case, Wright experiences a loss of $2,000, as computed in Illustration 9-18.

ILLUSTRATION 9-18
Computation of loss on disposal

Cost of office furniture	$60,000
Less: Accumulated depreciation	49,000
Book value at date of disposal	11,000
Proceeds from sale	9,000
Loss on disposal of plant asset	**$ 2,000**

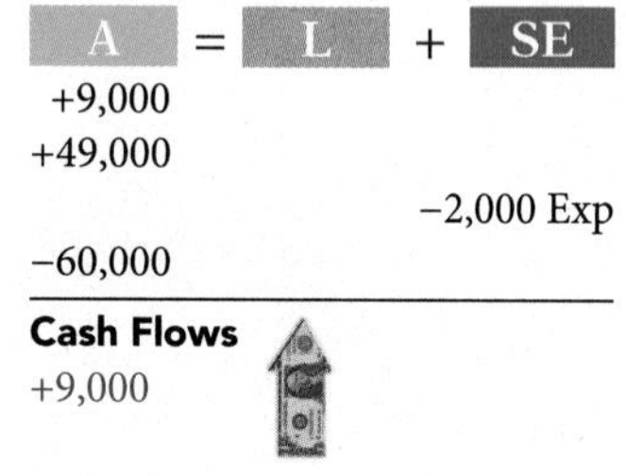

Wright records the sale and the loss on sale of the plant asset as follows.

July 1	Cash	9,000	
	Accumulated Depreciation—Equipment	49,000	
	Loss on Disposal of Plant Assets	2,000	
	Equipment		60,000
	(To record sale of office furniture at a loss)		

Companies report a loss on disposal of the plant asset in the "Other expenses and losses" section of the income statement.

RETIREMENT OF PLANT ASSETS

Companies simply retire, rather than sell, some assets at the end of their useful lives. For example, some productive assets used in manufacturing may have very specific uses, and they consequently have no ready market when the company no longer needs them. In such a case, the asset is simply retired.

Companies record retirement of an asset as a special case of a disposal where no cash is received. They decrease (debit) Accumulated Depreciation for the full amount of depreciation taken over the life of the asset and decrease (credit) the asset account for the original cost of the asset. The loss (a gain is not possible on a retirement) is equal to the asset's book value on the date of retirement.[2]

[2]More advanced courses discuss the accounting for exchanges, the third method of plant asset disposal.

DO IT! 3 Plant Asset Disposals

Overland Trucking has an old truck that cost $30,000 and has accumulated depreciation of $16,000. Assume two different situations:

1. The company sells the old truck for $17,000 cash.
2. The truck is worthless, so the company simply retires it.

What entry should Overland use to record each scenario?

SOLUTION

1. Sale of truck for cash:

Account	Debit	Credit
Cash	17,000	
Accumulated Depreciation—Equipment	16,000	
Equipment		30,000
Gain on Disposal of Plant Assets [$17,000 – ($30,000 – $16,000)]		3,000
(To record sale of truck at a gain)		

2. Retirement of truck:

Account	Debit	Credit
Accumulated Depreciation—Equipment	16,000	
Loss on Disposal of Plant Assets	14,000	
Equipment		30,000
(To record retirement of truck at a loss)		

Action Plan

✔ Compare the asset's book value and its fair value to determine whether a gain or loss has occurred.

✔ Make sure that both the Equipment account and Accumulated Depreciation—Equipment are reduced upon disposal.

Related exercise material: **BE9-7, BE9-8, DO IT! 9-3, E9-7, E9-8,** and **E9-9.**

LEARNING OBJECTIVE  Identify the basic issues related to reporting intangible assets.

Intangible assets are rights, privileges, and competitive advantages that result from ownership of long-lived assets that do not possess physical substance. Many companies' most valuable assets are intangible. Some widely known intangibles are Microsoft's patents, McDonald's franchises, the trade name iPod, and Nike's trademark "swoosh."

As you will learn in this section, financial statements report numerous intangibles. Yet, many other financially significant intangibles are not reported. To give an example, according to its financial statements in a recent year, Google had total stockholders' equity of $22.7 billion. But its market value—the total market price of all its shares on that same date—was roughly $178.5 billion. Thus, its actual market value was about $155.8 billion greater than the amount reported for stockholders' equity on the balance sheet. It is not uncommon for a company's reported book value to differ from its market value because balance sheets are reported at historical cost. But such an extreme difference seriously diminishes the usefulness of the balance sheet to decision-makers. In the case of Google, the difference is due to unrecorded intangibles. For many high-tech or so-called intellectual-property companies, most of their value is from intangibles, many of which are not reported under current accounting rules.

Intangibles may be evidenced by contracts, licenses, and other documents. Intangibles may arise from the following sources:

1. Government grants, such as patents, copyrights, licenses, trademarks, and trade names.
2. Acquisition of another business in which the purchase price includes a payment for goodwill.
3. Private monopolistic arrangements arising from contractual agreements, such as franchises and leases.

ACCOUNTING FOR INTANGIBLE ASSETS

Companies record intangible assets at cost. Cost is comprised of all expenditures necessary for the company to acquire the right, privilege, or competitive advantage. Intangibles are categorized as having either a limited life or an indefinite life. If an intangible has a **limited life**, the company allocates its cost over the asset's useful life using a process similar to depreciation. The process of allocating to expense the cost of intangibles is referred to as **amortization**. The cost of intangible assets with **indefinite lives should not be amortized.**

To record amortization of an intangible asset, a company increases (debits) Amortization Expense and decreases (credits) the specific intangible asset. (Alternatively, some companies choose to credit a contra account, such as Accumulated Amortization. *For homework, you should directly credit the specific intangible asset.*)

Intangible assets are typically amortized on a straight-line basis. For example, the legal life of a patent is 20 years. Companies **amortize the cost of a patent over its 20-year life or its useful life, whichever is shorter**. To illustrate the computation of patent amortization, assume that National Labs purchases a patent at a cost of \$60,000 on June 30. If National estimates the useful life of the patent to be eight years, the annual amortization expense is \$7,500 (\$60,000 ÷ 8) per year. National records \$3,750 (\$7,500 × $\frac{6}{12}$) of amortization for the six-month period ended December 31 as follows.

A	=	L	+	SE
				−3,750 Exp
−3,750				

Cash Flows
no effect

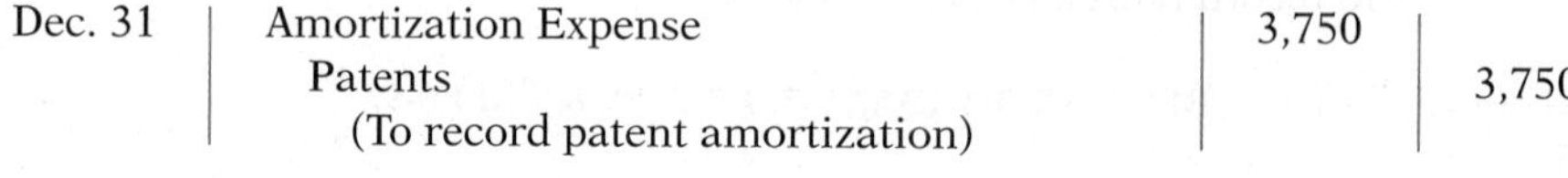

Dec. 31	Amortization Expense	3,750	
	Patents		3,750
	(To record patent amortization)		

When a company has significant intangibles, analysts should evaluate the reasonableness of the useful life estimates that the company discloses in the notes to its financial statements. In determining useful life, the company should consider obsolescence, inadequacy, and other factors. These may cause a patent or other intangible to become economically ineffective before the end of its legal life.

DECISION TOOLS

Evaluating a company's amortization of intangibles helps users determine if net income is overstated.

For example, suppose Intel obtained a patent on a new computer chip it had developed. The legal life of the patent is 20 years. From experience, however, we know that the useful life of a computer chip patent is rarely more than five years. Because new superior chips are developed so rapidly, existing chips become obsolete. Consequently, we would question the amortization expense of Intel if it amortized its patent on a computer chip for a life significantly longer than a five-year period. Amortizing an intangible over a period that is too long will understate amortization expense, overstate Intel's net income, and overstate its assets.

TYPES OF INTANGIBLE ASSETS

Patents

A **patent** is an exclusive right issued by the U.S. Patent Office that enables the recipient to manufacture, sell, or otherwise control an invention for a period of 20 years from the date of the grant. **The initial cost of a patent is the cash or cash equivalent price paid to acquire the patent.**

The saying "A patent is only as good as the money you're prepared to spend defending it" is very true. Most patents are subject to some type of litigation by competitors. A well-known example is the patent infringement suit brought by Amazon.com against Barnes & Noble.com regarding its online shopping software. If the owner incurs legal costs in successfully defending the patent in an infringement suit, such costs are considered necessary to establish the validity of the patent. Thus, **the owner adds those costs to the Patents account and amortizes them over the remaining life of the patent.**

Research and Development Costs

Research and development costs are expenditures that may lead to patents, copyrights, new processes, and new products. Many companies spend considerable sums of money on research and development (R&D) in an ongoing effort to develop new products or processes. For example, in a recent year Google spent over $9.8 billion on research and development. There are uncertainties in identifying the extent and timing of the future benefits of these expenditures. As a result, companies usually record research and development costs **as an expense when incurred**, whether the R&D is successful or not.

▼ **HELPFUL HINT**
Research and development costs are not intangible costs, but because these expenditures may lead to patents and copyrights, we discuss them in this section.

To illustrate, assume that Laser Scanner Company spent $3 million on research and development that resulted in two highly successful patents. It spent $20,000 on legal fees for the patents. It can include the legal fees in the cost of the patents but cannot include the R&D costs in the cost of the patents. Instead, Laser Scanner records the R&D costs as an expense when incurred.

Many disagree with this accounting approach. They argue that to expense these costs leads to understated assets and net income. Others argue that capitalizing these costs would lead to highly speculative assets on the balance sheet. Who is right is difficult to determine.

INTERNATIONAL NOTE
IFRS allows capitalization of some development costs. This may contribute to differences in R&D expenditures across nations.

Copyrights

The federal government grants **copyrights**, which give the owner the exclusive right to reproduce and sell an artistic or published work. Copyrights last for the life of the creator plus 70 years. The cost of the copyright consists of the **cost of acquiring and defending it**. The cost may be only the small fee paid to the U.S. Copyright Office, or it may amount to a great deal more if a copyright is acquired from another party. The useful life of a copyright generally is significantly shorter than its legal life.

Trademarks and Trade Names

A **trademark** or **trade name** is a word, phrase, jingle, or symbol that distinguishes or identifies a particular enterprise or product. Trade names like Wheaties, Monopoly, Sunkist, Kleenex, Coca-Cola, Big Mac, and Jeep create immediate product identification and generally enhance the sale of the product. The creator or original user may obtain the exclusive legal right to the trademark or trade name by registering it with the U.S. Patent Office. Such registration provides 20 years' protection and may be renewed indefinitely as long as the trademark or trade name is in use.

If a company purchases the trademark or trade name, the cost is the purchase price. If the company develops the trademark or trade name itself, the cost includes attorney's fees, registration fees, design costs, successful legal defense costs, and other expenditures directly related to securing it. Because trademarks and trade names have indefinite lives, they are not amortized.

ACCOUNTING ACROSS THE ORGANIZATION Google

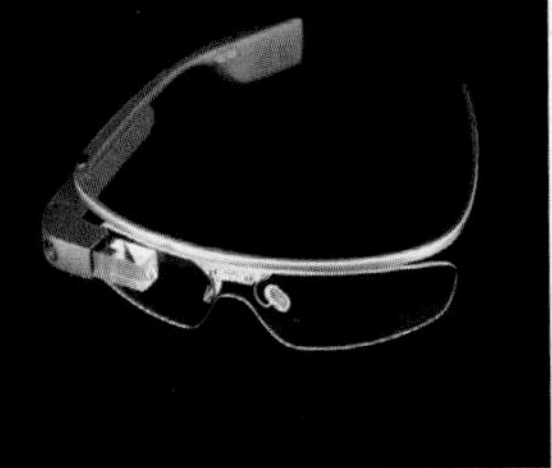

© Hattanas Kumchai/Shutterstock

We Want to Own Glass

Google, which has trademarked the term "Google Glass," now wants to trademark the term "Glass." Why? Because the simple word Glass has marketing advantages over the term Google Glass. It is easy to remember and is more universal. Regulators, however, are balking at Google's request. They say that the possible trademark is too similar to other existing or pending software trademarks that contain the word "glass." Also, regulators suggest that the term Glass is merely descriptive and therefore lacks trademark protection. For example, regulators note that a company that makes salsa could not trademark the term "Spicy Salsa."

BorderStylo LLC, which developed a Web-browser extension called Write on Glass, has filed a notice of opposition to Google's request. Google is fighting back and has sent the trademark examiner a 1,928-page application defense.

Source: Jacob Gershman, "Google Wants to Own 'Glass'," *Wall Street Journal* (April 4, 2014), p. B5.

If Google is successful in registering the term Glass, where will this trademark be reported on its financial statements? (Go to **WileyPLUS** for this answer and additional questions.)

Franchises

When you purchase a RAV4 from a Toyota dealer, fill up your tank at the corner Shell station, eat lunch at Subway, or make reservations at a Marriott hotel, you are dealing with franchises. A **franchise** is a contractual arrangement under which the franchisor grants the franchisee the right to sell certain products, to perform specific services, or to use certain trademarks or trade names, usually within a designated geographic area.

Another type of franchise is a license. Licenses granted by a governmental body permit a business to use public property in performing its services. Examples are the use of city streets for a bus line or taxi service; the use of public land for telephone, electric, and cable television lines; and the use of airwaves for radio or TV broadcasting. In a recent license agreement, Fox, CBS, and NBC agreed to pay $27.9 billion for the right to broadcast NFL football games over an eight-year period.

Franchises and licenses may be granted for a definite period of time, or the time period may be indefinite or perpetual. **When a company incurs costs in connection with the acquisition of the franchise or license, it should recognize an intangible asset.** Companies record as **operating expenses** annual payments made under a franchise agreement in the period in which they are incurred. In the case of a limited life, a company amortizes the cost of a franchise (or license) as operating expense over the useful life. If the life is indefinite or perpetual, the cost is not amortized.

Goodwill

Usually, the largest intangible asset that appears on a company's balance sheet is goodwill. **Goodwill** represents the value of all favorable attributes that relate to a company that are not attributable to any other specific asset. These include exceptional management, desirable location, good customer relations, skilled employees, high-quality products, fair pricing policies, and harmonious relations with labor unions. Goodwill is unique because unlike other assets such as investments, plant assets, and even other intangibles, which can be sold **individually** in the marketplace, goodwill can be identified only with the business **as a whole**.

If goodwill can be identified only with the business as a whole, how can it be determined? Certainly, many business enterprises have many of the factors cited above (exceptional management, desirable location, and so on). However, to determine the amount of goodwill in these situations would be difficult and very subjective. In other words, to recognize goodwill without an exchange transaction that puts a value on the goodwill would lead to subjective valuations that do not contribute to the reliability of financial statements. **Therefore, companies record goodwill only when there is an exchange transaction that involves the purchase of an entire business. When an entire business is purchased, goodwill is the excess of cost over the fair value of the net assets (assets less liabilities) acquired.**

In recording the purchase of a business, a company debits the identifiable acquired assets and credits liabilities at their fair values, credits cash for the purchase price, and records the difference as the cost of goodwill. Goodwill is not amortized because it is considered to have an indefinite life. However, it must be written down if a company determines the value of goodwill has been permanently impaired.

DO IT! ▶4 Classification Concepts

Match the statement with the term most directly associated with it.

Copyright	Amortization
Intangible assets	Franchise
Research and development costs	

1. ________ The allocation to expense of the cost of an intangible asset over the asset's useful life.

2. _______ Rights, privileges, and competitive advantages that result from the ownership of long-lived assets that do not possess physical substance.
3. _______ An exclusive right granted by the federal government to reproduce and sell an artistic or published work.
4. _______ A right to sell certain products or services or to use certain trademarks or trade names within a designated geographic area.
5. _______ Costs incurred by a company that often lead to patents or new products. These costs must be expensed as incurred.

SOLUTION

1. Amortization
2. Intangible assets
3. Copyright
4. Franchise
5. Research and development costs

Related exercise material: **BE9-9, DO IT! 9-4, E9-11, E9-12,** and **E9-13.**

Action Plan

✔ Know that the accounting for intangibles often depends on whether the item has a finite or indefinite life.

✔ Recognize the many similarities and differences between the accounting for plant assets and intangible assets.

LEARNING OBJECTIVE 5

Discuss how long-lived assets are reported and analyzed.

PRESENTATION

Usually, companies show plant assets in the financial statements under "Property, plant, and equipment," and they show intangibles separately under "Intangible assets." Illustration 9-19 shows a typical balance sheet presentation of long-lived assets, adapted from a recent The Coca-Cola Company balance sheet.

ILLUSTRATION 9-19
Presentation of property, plant, and equipment and intangible assets

Real World

THE COCA-COLA COMPANY Balance Sheet (partial) (in millions)	
Property, plant, and equipment	
Land	$ 972
Buildings and improvements	5,539
Machinery and equipment	18,225
Other	522
	25,258
Less: Accumulated depreciation	10,625
	14,633
Intangible assets	
Trademarks with indefinite lives	6,533
Goodwill	12,100
Bottlers' franchise rights with indefinite lives	6,689
Other intangible assets	1,050
	$26,372

When a plant asset is fully depreciated, the plant asset and related accumulated depreciation should continue to be reported on the balance sheet without further depreciation or adjustment until the asset is retired. Intangibles do not usually use a contra asset account like the contra asset account Accumulated Depreciation used for plant assets. Instead, companies record amortization of intangibles as a direct decrease (credit) to the asset account.

Either within the balance sheet or in the notes, companies should disclose the balances of the major classes of assets, such as land, buildings, and equipment, and of accumulated depreciation by major classes or in total. In addition, they should describe the depreciation and amortization methods used and disclose the amount of depreciation and amortization expense for the period.

PEOPLE, PLANET, AND PROFIT INSIGHT BHP Billiton

© Christian Uhrig/iStockphoto

Sustainability Report Please

Sustainability reports identify how the company is meeting its corporate social responsibilities. Many companies, both large and small, are now issuing these reports. For example, companies such as Disney, Best Buy, Microsoft, Ford, and ConocoPhilips issue these reports. Presented below is an adapted section of a recent BHP Billiton (a global mining, oil, and gas company) sustainability report on its environmental policies. These policies are to (1) take action to address the challenges of climate change, (2) set and achieve targets that reduce pollution, and (3) enhance biodiversity by assessing and considering ecological values and land-use aspects. Here is how BHP Billiton measures the success or failure of some of these policies:

Environment	Commentary	Target Date
We will maintain total greenhouse gas emissions below FY2006 levels.	FY2013 greenhouse gas emissions were lower than the FY2006 baseline.	30 June 2017
All operations to offset impacts to biodiversity and the related benefits derived from ecosystems.	Land and Biodiversity Management Plans were developed at all our operations.	Annual
We will finance the conservation and continuing management of areas of high biodiversity and ecosystem value.	Two projects of international conservation significance were established—the Five Rivers Conservation Project, in Australia, and the Valdivian Coastal Reserve Conservation Project, in Chile.	30 June 2017

In addition to the environment, BHP Billiton has sections in its sustainability report that discuss people, safety, health, and community.

Why do you believe companies issue sustainability reports? (Go to WileyPLUS for this answer and additional questions.)

ANALYSIS

The presentation of financial statement information about plant assets enables decision makers to analyze the company's use of its plant assets. We will use two measures to analyze plant assets: return on assets and asset turnover. We also show how profit margin relates to both.

Return on Assets

An overall measure of profitability is the **return on assets**. This ratio is computed by dividing net income by average total assets. (Average assets are commonly calculated by adding the beginning and ending values of assets and dividing by 2.) Return on assets indicates the amount of net income generated by each dollar of assets. Thus, the higher the return on assets, the more profitable the company.

DECISION TOOLS 

Return on assets helps users determine if a company is using its assets effectively.

Information is provided below related to JetBlue Airways.

	JetBlue (in millions)
Net income, 2014	$ 515
Total assets, 12/31/14	7,839
Total assets, 12/31/13	7,350
Net sales, 2014	5,817

Illustration 9-20 presents the 2014 and 2013 return on assets of JetBlue Airways, Southwest Airlines, and the industry average.

ILLUSTRATION 9-20
Return on assets for JetBlue and Southwest

$$\text{Return on Assets} = \frac{\text{Net Income}}{\text{Average Total Assets}}$$

JetBlue Airways ($ in millions)		Southwest Airlines	Industry Average
2014	2013	2014	2014
$\frac{\$515}{(\$7,839 + \$7,350)/2} = 6.8\%$	2.3%	5.7%	4.0%

JetBlue's return on assets was better than that of Southwest's and higher than the airline industry. At one time, the airline industry experienced financial difficulties as it attempted to cover high labor, fuel, and security costs while offering fares low enough to attract customers. Such difficulties were reflected in a low industry average for return on assets. In response, Southwest announced that it would not add additional planes beyond the 700 it already had until it met its investment-return targets. Instead, the company added seats to existing planes and replaced some smaller planes with larger ones.

ACCOUNTING ACROSS THE ORGANIZATION

© Walter G Arce/Cal Sport Media/ NewsCom

Marketing ROI as Profit Indicator

Marketing executives use the basic finance concept underlying return on assets to determine "marketing return on investment (ROI)." They calculate *marketing ROI* as the profit generated by a marketing initiative divided by the investment in that initiative.

It can be tricky to determine what to include in the "investment" amount and how to attribute profit to a particular marketing initiative. However, many firms feel that measuring marketing ROI is worth the effort because it allows managers to evaluate the relative effectiveness of various programs. In addition, it helps quantify the benefits that marketing provides to the organization. In periods of tight budgets, the marketing ROI number can provide particularly valuable evidence to help a marketing manager avoid budget cuts.

Source: James O. Mitchel, "Marketing ROI," *LIMRA's MarketFacts Quarterly* (Summer 2004), p. 15.

How does measuring marketing ROI support the overall efforts of the organization? (Go to **WileyPLUS** for this answer and additional questions.)

Asset Turnover

Asset turnover indicates how efficiently a company uses its assets to generate sales—that is, how many dollars of sales a company generates for each dollar invested in assets. It is calculated by dividing net sales by average total assets. When we compare two companies in the same industry, the one with the higher asset turnover is operating more efficiently. It is generating more sales per dollar invested in assets. Illustration 9-21 (page 446) presents the asset turnovers for JetBlue Airways and Southwest Airlines.

The asset turnover helps users determine how effectively a company is generating sales from its assets.

ILLUSTRATION 9-21
Asset turnovers for JetBlue and Southwest

$$\text{Asset Turnover} = \frac{\text{Net Sales}}{\text{Average Total Assets}}$$

JetBlue Airways ($ in millions)		Southwest Airlines	Industry Average
2014	2013	2014	2014
$\frac{\$5,817}{(\$7,839 + \$7,350)/2} = 0.77$ times	0.75 times	0.94 times	0.80 times

These asset turnover values tell us that for each dollar of assets, JetBlue generates sales of $0.77 and Southwest $0.94. Southwest is more successful in generating sales per dollar invested in assets. The average asset turnover for the airline industry is 0.80 times. In recent years, airlines have reduced both the number of planes used and routes flown to try to pack more customers on a plane. This would increase the asset turnover.

Asset turnovers vary considerably across industries. During a recent year, the average asset turnover for electric utility companies was 0.34. The grocery industry had an average asset turnover of 2.89. Asset turnover values, therefore, are only comparable within—not between—industries.

Profit Margin Revisited

In Chapter 5, you learned about **profit margin**. That ratio is calculated by dividing net income by net sales. It tells how effective a company is in turning its sales into income—that is, how much income each dollar of sales provides. Illustration 9-22 shows that return on assets can be computed as the product of profit margin and asset turnover.

ILLUSTRATION 9-22
Composition of return on assets

Profit Margin	×	Asset Turnover	=	Return on Assets
$\frac{\text{Net Income}}{\text{Net Sales}}$	×	$\frac{\text{Net Sales}}{\text{Average Total Assets}}$	=	$\frac{\text{Net Income}}{\text{Average Total Assets}}$

This relationship has very important strategic implications for management. From Illustration 9-22, we can see that if a company wants to increase its return on assets, it can do so in two ways: (1) by increasing the margin it generates from each dollar of goods that it sells (the profit margin), or (2) by increasing the volume of goods that it sells (the asset turnover). For example, most grocery stores have very low profit margins, often in the range of 1 or 2 cents for every dollar of goods sold. Grocery stores, therefore, focus on asset turnover: They rely on high turnover to increase their return on assets. Alternatively, a store selling luxury goods, such as expensive jewelry, does not generally have a high turnover. Consequently, a seller of luxury goods focuses on having a high profit margin. Recently, Apple decided to offer a less expensive version of its popular iPod. This new product would provide a lower margin but higher volume than Apple's more expensive version.

Let's evaluate the return on assets of JetBlue Airways for 2014 by evaluating its components—profit margin and asset turnover. See Illustration 9-23.

ILLUSTRATION 9-23
Components of rate of return for JetBlue and Southwest

	Profit Margin	×	Asset Turnover	=	Return on Assets
JetBlue Airways	8.8%	×	0.77	=	6.8%
Southwest Airlines	6.1%	×	0.94	=	5.7%

JetBlue's return on asset of 6.8% versus Southwest's 5.7% means that JetBlue generates 6.8 cents per each dollar invested in assets, while Southwest generates 5.7 cents. Illustration 9-23 reveals that although these two airlines have similar return on asset values, they achieve this return in a slightly different fashion. First, JetBlue's profit margin of 8.8% versus Southwest's 6.1% means that for every dollar of sales, JetBlue generates approximately 8.8 cents of net income, while Southwest generates approximately 6.1 cents. Second, JetBlue's asset turnover of 0.77 means that it generates 77 cents of sales per each dollar invested in assets, while Southwest generates 94 cents. Therefore, in 2014, Southwest was more effective at generating sales from its assets, while JetBlue was better at deriving profit from its sales.

KEEPING AN EYE ON CASH

Depreciation and amortization expense are among the biggest causes of differences between accrual-accounting net income and net cash provided by operating activities. Depreciation and amortization reduce net income, but they do not use up any cash. Therefore, to determine net cash provided by operating activities under a common approach referred to as the indirect method, companies add depreciation and amortization back to net income. For example, if a company reported net income of $175,000 during the year and had depreciation expense of $40,000, net cash provided by operating activities would be $215,000 (assuming no other accrual-accounting differences). The operating activities section of Coca-Cola's statement of cash flows reports the following adjustment for depreciation and amortization.

Real World

THE COCA-COLA COMPANY
Statement of Cash Flows (partial)
(in millions)

Cash flow from operating activities	
Net income	$7,124
Plus: Depreciation and amortization	1,976

The adjustment for depreciation and amortization was more than twice as big as any other adjustment required to convert net income to net cash provided by operating activities.

It is also interesting to examine the statement of cash flows to determine the amount of property, plant, and equipment a company purchased and the cash it received from property, plant, and equipment sold in a given year. For example, the investing activities section of Coca-Cola reports the following.

THE COCA-COLA COMPANY
Statement of Cash Flows (partial)
(in millions)

Cash flow from investing activities	
Acquisitions and investments	$(17,800)
Purchases of property, plant, and equipment	(2,406)
Proceeds from disposals of property, plant, and equipment	223
Other	(268)

As indicated, Coca-Cola made significant purchases and sales of property, plant, and equipment. The level of purchases suggests that Coca-Cola believes that it can earn a reasonable rate of return on these assets.

DO IT! 5 Asset Turnover

Paramour Company reported net income of $180,000, net sales of $420,000, and had total assets of $460,000 on January 1, 2017, and total assets on December 31, 2017, of $540,000. Determine Paramour's asset turnover for 2017.

Action Plan

✔ Recognize that the asset turnover analyzes the productivity of a company's assets.

✔ Know the formula Net sales ÷ Average total assets equals Asset turnover.

SOLUTION

The asset turnover for Paramour Company is computed as follows.

Net Sales	÷	Average Total Assets	=	Asset Turnover
$420,000	÷	$\frac{\$460,000 + \$540,000}{2}$	=	.84

Related exercise material: **BE9-10, DO IT! 9-5, E9-15, E9-16, and E9-17.**

USING DECISION TOOLS—DELTA AIR LINES

Delta Air Lines, Inc., headquartered in Atlanta, Georgia, is one of the largest airlines in the world. It serves 342 destinations in 61 countries.

INSTRUCTIONS

Review the excerpts from the company's 2014 annual report presented on page 449 and then answer the following questions.

1. What method does the company use to depreciate its aircraft? Over what period is the company depreciating these aircraft?
2. Compute the company's return on assets ratio, asset turnover ratio, and profit margin ratio for 2014 and 2013. Comment on your results.

(in millions)	2014	2013
Net income (loss)	$ 659	$10,540
Net sales	40,362	37,773
Beginning total assets	52,252	44,550
Ending total assets	54,121	52,252

DELTA AIR LINES, INC.
Notes to the Financial Statements (Partial)

Long-Lived Assets
The following table summarizes our property and equipment:

(in millions, except for estimated useful life)	Estimated Useful Life	December 31, 2014	December 31, 2013
Flight equipment	21–30 years	$24,313	$23,373
Ground property and equipment	3–40 years	5,198	4,596
Flight and ground equipment under capital leases	Shorter of lease term or estimated useful life	1,141	1,296
Advance payments for equipment		617	381
Less: accumulated depreciation and amortization[(1)]		(9,340)	(7,792)
Total property and equipment, net		$21,929	$21,854

[(1)]Includes accumulated amortization for flight and ground equipment under capital leases in the amount of $767 million and $657 million at December 31, 2014 and 2013, respectively.

We record property and equipment at cost and depreciate or amortize these assets on a straight-line basis to their estimated residual values over their estimated useful lives.

SOLUTION

1. The company depreciates property and equipment using the straight-line approach. It depreciates aircraft over a 21–30-year life.
2.

	2014	2013
Return on assets	$\frac{\$659}{(\$54{,}121 + \$52{,}252)/2} = 1.2\%$	$\frac{\$10{,}540}{(\$52{,}252 + \$44{,}550)/2} = 21.8\%$
Asset turnover	$\frac{\$40{,}362}{(\$54{,}121 + \$52{,}252)/2} = 0.76$ times	$\frac{\$37{,}773}{(\$52{,}252 + \$44{,}550)/2} = 0.78$ times
Profit margin	$\frac{\$659}{\$40{,}362} = 1.6\%$	$\frac{\$10{,}540}{\$37{,}773} = 27.9\%$

Delta's profit margin and return on assets decreased significantly from 2013 to 2014. (This huge drop occurred because the company had a massive, one-time tax benefit in 2013.) Its asset turnover decreased slightly.

LEARNING OBJECTIVE 

*6 APPENDIX 9A: Compute periodic depreciation using the declining-balance method and the units-of-activity method.

In this appendix, we show the calculations of the depreciation expense amounts that we used in the chapter for the declining-balance and units-of-activity methods.

DECLINING-BALANCE METHOD

The **declining-balance method** produces a decreasing annual depreciation expense over the useful life of the asset. The method is so named because the computation of periodic depreciation is based on a **declining book value** (cost less accumulated depreciation) of the asset. Annual depreciation expense is computed by multiplying the book value at the beginning of the year by the declining-balance depreciation rate. **The depreciation rate remains constant from year to year, but the book value to which the rate is applied declines each year.**

Book value for the first year is the cost of the asset because the balance in accumulated depreciation at the beginning of the asset's useful life is zero. In subsequent years, book value is the difference between cost and accumulated depreciation at the beginning of the year. **Unlike other depreciation methods, the declining-balance method ignores salvage value in determining the amount to which the declining-balance rate is applied.** Salvage value, however, does limit the total depreciation that can be taken. Depreciation stops when the asset's book value equals its expected salvage value.

Depreciation must be completed by the end of the asset's useful life. Therefore, in the last year of the asset's useful life, it is sometimes necessary to adjust the amount of depreciation expense so that the book value equals the expected salvage value. For example, note the adjustment to the final year in Illustration 9A-2.

▼ HELPFUL HINT
The straight-line rate is approximated as 1 ÷ Estimated life. In this case, it is 1 ÷ 5 = 20%.

As noted in the chapter, a common declining-balance rate is double the straight-line rate—the **double-declining-balance method.** If Bill's Pizzas uses the double-declining-balance method, the depreciation rate is 40% (2 × the straight-line rate of 20%). Illustration 9A-1 presents the formula and computation of depreciation for the first year on the delivery truck.

ILLUSTRATION 9A-1
Formula for declining-balance method

Book Value at Beginning of Year	×	Declining-Balance Rate	=	Depreciation Expense
$13,000	×	40%	=	$5,200

Illustration 9A-2 presents the depreciation schedule under this method.

ILLUSTRATION 9A-2
Double-declining-balance depreciation schedule

▼ HELPFUL HINT
Depreciation stops when the asset's book value equals its expected salvage value.

BILL'S PIZZAS

	Computation					End of Year	
Year	**Book Value Beginning of Year**	×	**Depreciation Rate**	=	**Annual Depreciation Expense**	**Accumulated Depreciation**	**Book Value**
2017	$13,000		40%		**$5,200**	$ 5,200	$7,800*
2018	7,800		40		**3,120**	8,320	4,680
2019	4,680		40		**1,872**	10,192	2,808
2020	2,808		40		**1,123**	11,315	1,685
2021	1,685		40		**685****	12,000	**1,000**

*$13,000 − $5,200
**Computation of $674 ($1,685 × 40%) is adjusted to $685 in order for book value to equal salvage value.

The delivery equipment is 69% depreciated ($8,320 ÷ $12,000) at the end of the second year. Under the straight-line method, it would be depreciated 40% ($4,800 ÷ $12,000) at that time. Because the declining-balance method produces higher depreciation expense in the early years than in the later years, it is considered an **accelerated-depreciation method.**

The declining-balance method is compatible with the expense recognition principle. It matches the higher depreciation expense in early years with the higher benefits received in these years. Conversely, it recognizes lower depreciation expense in later years when the asset's contribution to revenue is likely to be lower. Also, some assets lose their usefulness rapidly because of obsolescence. In these cases, the declining-balance method provides a more appropriate depreciation amount.

When an asset is purchased during the year, it is necessary to prorate the declining-balance depreciation in the first year on a time basis. For example, if Bill's Pizzas had purchased the delivery equipment on April 1, 2017, depreciation for 2017 would be $3,900 ($13,000 × 40% × $\frac{9}{12}$). The book value for computing depreciation in 2018 then becomes $9,100 ($13,000 − $3,900), and the 2018 depreciation is $3,640 ($9,100 × 40%).

UNITS-OF-ACTIVITY METHOD

ALTERNATIVE TERMINOLOGY
Another term often used is the *units-of-production method.*

Under the **units-of-activity method**, useful life is expressed in terms of the total units of production or use expected from the asset. The units-of-activity method is ideally suited to equipment whose activity can be measured in units of output, miles driven, or hours in use. The units-of-activity method is generally not suitable for assets for which depreciation is a function more of time than of use.

To use this method, a company estimates the total units of activity for the entire useful life and divides that amount into the depreciable cost to determine the depreciation cost per unit. It then multiplies the depreciation cost per unit by the units of activity during the year to find the annual depreciation for that year.

To illustrate, assume that Bill's Pizzas estimates it will drive its new delivery truck 15,000 miles in the first year. Illustration 9A-3 presents the formula and computation of depreciation expense in the first year.

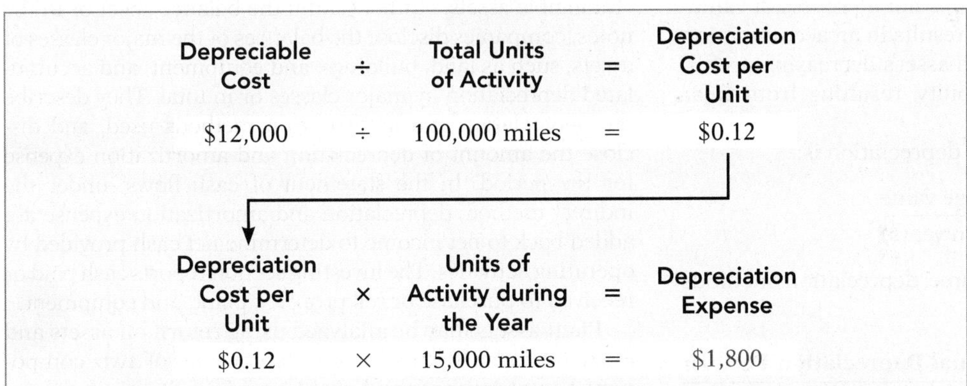

ILLUSTRATION 9A-3
Formula for units-of-activity method

Illustration 9A-4 shows the depreciation schedule, using assumed mileage data.

BILL'S PIZZAS

	Computation					Annual		End of Year	
Year	Units of Activity	×	Depreciation Cost/Unit	=	Annual Depreciation Expense		Accumulated Depreciation	Book Value
2017	15,000		$0.12		$1,800		$ 1,800	$11,200*
2018	30,000		0.12		3,600		5,400	7,600
2019	20,000		0.12		2,400		7,800	5,200
2020	25,000		0.12		3,000		10,800	2,200
2021	10,000		0.12		1,200		12,000	1,000

*$13,000 − $1,800

ILLUSTRATION 9A-4
Units-of-activity depreciation schedule

▼ **HELPFUL HINT**
Depreciation stops when the asset's book value equals its expected salvage value.

The units-of-activity method is not nearly as popular as the straight-line method, primarily because it is often difficult to make a reasonable estimate of total activity. However, this method is used by some very large companies, such as Standard Oil Company of California and Boise Cascade Corporation. When the productivity of the asset varies significantly from one period to another, the units-of-activity method results in the best matching of expenses with revenues.

This method is easy to apply when assets are purchased during the year. In such a case, companies use the productivity of the asset for the partial year in computing the depreciation.

REVIEW AND PRACTICE

LEARNING OBJECTIVES REVIEW

1 Explain the accounting for plant asset expenditures. The cost of plant assets includes all expenditures necessary to acquire the asset and make it ready for its intended use. Once cost is established, a company uses that amount as the basis of accounting for the plant asset over its useful life.

2 Apply depreciation methods to plant assets. Depreciation is the process of allocating to expense the cost of a plant asset over its useful (service) life in a rational and systematic manner. Depreciation is not a process of valuation, and it is not a process that results in an accumulation of cash. Depreciation reflects an asset's decreasing usefulness and revenue-producing ability, resulting from wear and tear and from obsolescence.

The formula for straight-line depreciation is:

$$\frac{\text{Cost} - \text{Salvage value}}{\text{Useful life (in years)}}$$

The expense patterns of the three depreciation methods are as follows.

Method	Annual Depreciation Pattern
Straight-line	Constant amount
Declining-balance	Decreasing amount
Units-of-activity	Varying amount

Companies make revisions of periodic depreciation in present and future periods, not retroactively.

3 Explain how to account for the disposal of plant assets. The procedure for accounting for the disposal of a plant asset through sale or retirement is (a) eliminate the book value of the plant asset at the date of disposal; (b) record cash proceeds, if any; and (c) account for the difference between the book value and the cash proceeds as a gain or a loss on disposal.

4 Identify the basic issues related to reporting intangible assets. Companies report intangible assets at their cost less any amounts amortized. If an intangible asset has a limited life, its cost should be allocated (amortized) over its useful life. Intangible assets with indefinite lives should not be amortized.

5 Discuss how long-lived assets are reported and analyzed. Companies usually show plant assets under "Property, plant, and equipment"; they show intangibles separately under "Intangible assets." Either within the balance sheet or in the notes, companies disclose the balances of the major classes of assets, such as land, buildings, and equipment, and accumulated depreciation by major classes or in total. They describe the depreciation and amortization methods used, and disclose the amount of depreciation and amortization expense for the period. In the statement of cash flows, under the indirect method, depreciation and amortization expense are added back to net income to determine net cash provided by operating activities. The investing section reports cash paid or received to purchase or sell property, plant, and equipment.

Plant assets may be analyzed using return on assets and asset turnover. Return on assets consists of two components: asset turnover and profit margin.

***6 Compute periodic depreciation using the declining-balance method and the units-of-activity method.** The depreciation expense calculation for each of these methods is:

Declining-balance:

$$\text{Book value at beginning of year} \times \text{Declining-balance rate} = \text{Depreciation expense}$$

Units-of-activity:

$$\text{Depreciable cost} \div \text{Total units of activity} = \text{Depreciation cost per unit}$$

$$\text{Depreciation cost per unit} \times \text{Units of activity during year} = \text{Depreciation expense}$$

DECISION TOOLS REVIEW

DECISION CHECKPOINTS	INFO NEEDED FOR DECISION	TOOL TO USE FOR DECISION	HOW TO EVALUATE RESULTS
Is the company's amortization of intangibles reasonable?	Estimated useful life of intangibles from notes to financial statements of this company and its competitors	If the company's estimated useful life significantly exceeds that of competitors or does not seem reasonable in light of the circumstances, the reason for the difference should be investigated.	Too high an estimated useful life will result in understating amortization expense and overstating net income.
Is the company using its assets effectively?	Net income and average total assets	$\text{Return on assets} = \frac{\text{Net income}}{\text{Average total assets}}$	Higher value suggests favorable efficiency (use of assets).
How effective is the company at generating sales from its assets?	Net sales and average total assets	$\text{Asset turnover} = \frac{\text{Net sales}}{\text{Average total assets}}$	Indicates the sales dollars generated per dollar of assets. A high value suggests the company is effective in using its resources to generate sales.

▶ GLOSSARY REVIEW

Accelerated-depreciation method A depreciation method that produces higher depreciation expense in the early years than the straight-line approach. (p. 432).

Additions and improvements Costs incurred to increase the operating efficiency, productive capacity, or expected useful life of a plant asset. (p. 427).

Amortization The process of allocating to expense the cost of an intangible asset. (p. 440).

Asset turnover Indicates how efficiently a company uses its assets to generate sales; calculated as net sales divided by average total assets. (p. 445).

Capital expenditures Expenditures that increase the company's investment in plant assets. (p. 424).

Capital lease A contractual agreement allowing one party (the lessee) to use another party's asset (the lessor); accounted for like a debt-financed purchase by the lessee. (p. 428).

Cash equivalent price An amount equal to the fair value of the asset given up or the fair value of the asset received, whichever is more clearly determinable. (p. 425).

Copyright An exclusive right granted by the federal government allowing the owner to reproduce and sell an artistic or published work. (p. 441).

Declining-balance method A depreciation method that applies a constant rate to the declining book value of the asset and produces a decreasing annual depreciation expense over the asset's useful life. (pp. 432, 449).

Depreciable cost The cost of a plant asset less its salvage value. (p. 431).

Depreciation The process of allocating to expense the cost of a plant asset over its useful life in a rational and systematic manner. (p. 429).

Franchise A contractual arrangement under which the franchisor grants the franchisee the right to sell certain products, to perform specific services, or to use certain trademarks or trade names, usually within a designated geographic area. (p. 442).

Goodwill The value of all favorable attributes that relate to a company that are not attributable to any other specific asset. (p. 442).

Impairment A permanent decline in the fair value of an asset. (p. 436).

Intangible assets Rights, privileges, and competitive advantages that result from the ownership of long-lived assets that do not possess physical substance. (p. 439).

Lessee A party that has made contractual arrangements to use another party's asset for a period at an agreed price. (p. 428).

Lessor A party that has agreed contractually to let another party use its asset for a period at an agreed price. (p. 428).

Operating lease A contractual agreement allowing one party (the lessee) to use the asset of another party (the lessor); accounted for as a rental by the lessee. (p. 428).

Ordinary repairs Expenditures to maintain the operating efficiency and expected productive life of the asset. (p. 427).

Patent An exclusive right issued by the U.S. Patent Office that enables the recipient to manufacture, sell, or otherwise control an invention for a period of 20 years from the date of the grant. (p. 440).

Plant assets Resources that have physical substance, are used in the operations of a business, and are not intended for sale to customers. (p. 424).

Research and development costs Expenditures that may lead to patents, copyrights, new processes, and new products; must be expensed as incurred. (p. 441).

Return on assets A profitability measure that indicates the amount of net income generated by each dollar of assets; computed as net income divided by average total assets. (p. 444).

Revenue expenditures Expenditures that are immediately charged against revenues as an expense. (p. 424).

Straight-line method A depreciation method in which companies expense an equal amount of depreciation for each year of the asset's useful life. (p. 431).

Trademark (trade name) A word, phrase, jingle, or symbol that distinguishes or identifies a particular enterprise or product. (p. 441).

Units-of-activity method A depreciation method in which useful life is expressed in terms of the total units of production or use expected from the asset. (pp. 433, 450).

▶ PRACTICE MULTIPLE-CHOICE QUESTIONS

(LO 1) 1. Corrieten Company purchased equipment and incurred these costs:

Cash price	$24,000
Sales taxes	1,200
Insurance during transit	200
Installation and testing	400
Total costs	$25,800

What amount should be recorded as the cost of the equipment?

(a) $24,000. (c) $25,400.
(b) $25,200. (d) $25,800.

2. Harrington Corporation recently leased a number of trucks from Andre Corporation. In inspecting the books of Harrington Corporation, you notice that the trucks have not been recorded as assets on its balance sheet. From this, you can conclude that Harrington is accounting for this transaction as a/an: (LO 1)

(a) operating lease. (c) purchase.
(b) capital lease. (d) None of the above.

(LO 1) 3. Additions to plant assets are:
(a) revenue expenditures.
(b) debited to the Repairs and Maintenance Expense account.
(c) debited to the Purchases account.
(d) capital expenditures.

(LO 2) 4. Depreciation is a process of:
(a) valuation. (c) cash accumulation.
(b) cost allocation. (d) appraisal.

(LO 2) 5. Cuso Company purchased equipment on January 1, 2016, at a total invoice cost of $400,000. The equipment has an estimated salvage value of $10,000 and an estimated useful life of 5 years. What is the amount of accumulated depreciation at December 31, 2017, if the straight-line method of depreciation is used?
(a) $80,000. (c) $78,000.
(b) $160,000. (d) $156,000.

(LO 2) 6. A company would minimize its depreciation expense in the first year of owning an asset if it used:
(a) a high estimated life, a high salvage value, and declining-balance depreciation.
(b) a low estimated life, a high salvage value, and straight-line depreciation.
(c) a high estimated life, a high salvage value, and straight-line depreciation.
(d) a low estimated life, a low salvage value, and declining-balance depreciation.

(LO 2) 7. When there is a change in estimated depreciation:
(a) previous depreciation should be corrected.
(b) current and future years' depreciation should be revised.
(c) only future years' depreciation should be revised.
(d) None of the above.

(LO 2) 8. Able Towing Company purchased a tow truck for $60,000 on January 1, 2017. It was originally depreciated on a straight-line basis over 10 years with an assumed salvage value of $12,000. On December 31, 2019, before adjusting entries had been made, the company decided to change the remaining estimated life to 4 years (including 2019) and the salvage value to $2,000. What was the depreciation expense for 2019?
(a) $6,000. (c) $15,000.
(b) $4,800. (d) $12,100.

(LO 3) 9. Bennie Razor Company has decided to sell one of its old manufacturing machines on June 30, 2017. The machine was purchased for $80,000 on January 1, 2013, and was depreciated on a straight-line basis for 10 years assuming no salvage value. If the machine was sold for $26,000, what was the amount of the gain or loss recorded at the time of the sale?
(a) $18,000 loss. (c) $22,000 gain.
(b) $54,000 loss. (d) $46,000 gain.

(LO 4) 10. Pierce Company incurred $150,000 of research and development costs in its laboratory to develop a new product. It spent $20,000 in legal fees for a patent granted on January 2, 2017. On July 31, 2017, Pierce paid $15,000 for legal fees in a successful defense of the patent. What is the total amount that should be debited to Patents through July 31, 2017?
(a) $150,000. (c) $185,000.
(b) $35,000. (d) $170,000.

11. Indicate which one of these statements is **true**. (LO 4)
(a) Since intangible assets lack physical substance, they need to be disclosed only in the notes to the financial statements.
(b) Goodwill should be reported as a contra account in the stockholders' equity section.
(c) Totals of major classes of assets can be shown in the balance sheet, with asset details disclosed in the notes to the financial statements.
(d) Intangible assets are typically combined with plant assets and inventory and then shown in the property, plant, and equipment section.

12. If a company reports goodwill as an intangible asset on its books, what is the one thing you know with certainty? (LO 4)
(a) The company is a valuable company worth investing in.
(b) The company has a well-established brand name.
(c) The company purchased another company.
(d) The goodwill will generate a lot of positive business for the company for many years to come.

13. Which of the following statements is **false**? (LO 4)
(a) If an intangible asset has a finite life, it should be amortized.
(b) The amortization period of an intangible asset can exceed 20 years.
(c) Goodwill is recorded only when a business is purchased.
(d) Research and development costs are expensed when incurred, except when the research and development expenditures result in a successful patent.

14. Which of the following measures provides an indication of how efficient a company is in employing its assets? (LO 5)
(a) Current ratio. (c) Debt to assets ratio.
(b) Profit margin. (d) Asset turnover.

15. Lake Coffee Company reported net sales of $180,000, net income of $54,000, beginning total assets of $200,000, and ending total assets of $300,000. What was the company's asset turnover? (LO 5)
(a) 0.90 (c) 0.72
(b) 0.20 (d) 1.39

*16. Kant Enterprises purchased a truck for $11,000 on January 1, 2016. The truck will have an estimated salvage value of $1,000 at the end of 5 years. If you use the units-of-activity method, the balance in accumulated depreciation at December 31, 2017, can be computed by the following formula: (LO 6)
(a) ($11,000 ÷ Total estimated activity) × Units of activity for 2017.
(b) ($10,000 ÷ Total estimated activity) × Units of activity for 2017.
(c) ($11,000 ÷ Total estimated activity) × Units of activity for 2016 and 2017.
(d) ($10,000 ÷ Total estimated activity) × Units of activity for 2016 and 2017.

*17. Jefferson Company purchased a piece of equipment on January 1, 2017. The equipment cost $60,000 and has an estimated life of 8 years and a salvage value of $8,000. What was the depreciation expense for the asset for 2018 under the double-declining-balance method? (LO 6)
(a) $6,500. (c) $15,000.
(b) $11,250. (d) $6,562.

SOLUTIONS

1. **(d)** All of the costs ($1,200 + $200 + $400) in addition to the cash price ($24,000) should be included in the cost of the equipment because they were necessary expenditures to acquire the asset and make it ready for its intended use. The other choices are therefore incorrect.
2. **(a)** Operating leases are accounted for as rentals and are not recorded on the balance sheet. The other choices are incorrect because (b) if the leased assets were accounted for as a capital lease or (c) if the assets were purchased, they would be reported on the balance sheet. Choice (d) is wrong as there is a correct answer.
3. **(d)** When an addition is made to plant assets, it is intended to increase productive capacity, increase the assets' useful life, or increase the efficiency of the assets. This is called a capital expenditure. The other choices are incorrect because (a) additions to plant assets are not revenue expenditures because the additions will have a long-term useful life whereas revenue expenditures are minor repairs and maintenance that do not prolong the life of the assets; (b) additions to plant assets are debited to Plant Assets, not Maintenance and Repairs Expense, because the Maintenance and Repairs Expense account is used to record expenditures not intended to increase the life of the assets; and (c) additions to plant assets are debited to Plant Assets, not Purchases, because the Purchases account is used to record assets intended for resale (inventory).
4. **(b)** Depreciation is a process of allocating the cost of an asset over its useful life, not a process of (a) valuation, (c) cash accumulation, or (d) appraisal.
5. **(d)** Accumulated depreciation will be the sum of 2 years of depreciation expense. Annual depreciation for this asset is ($400,000 − $10,000)/5 = $78,000. The sum of 2 years' depreciation is therefore $156,000 ($78,000 + $78,000), not (a) $80,000, (b) $160,000, or (c) $78,000.
6. **(c)** A high estimated life spreads the cost over a longer period of time, resulting in a smaller expense each year. The high salvage value limits the cost to be allocated. Straight-line depreciation yields a smaller depreciation charge in the first year than the declining-balance method. The other choices are therefore incorrect.
7. **(b)** When there is a change in estimated depreciation, the current and future years' depreciation computation should reflect the new estimates. The other choices are incorrect because (a) previous years' depreciation should not be adjusted when new estimates are made for depreciation, and (c) when there is a change in estimated depreciation, the current and future years' depreciation computation should reflect the new estimates. Choice (d) is wrong because there is a correct answer.
8. **(d)** First, calculate accumulated depreciation from January 1, 2017, through December 31, 2018, which is $9,600 [[($60,000 − $12,000)/10 years] × 2 years}. Next, calculate the revised depreciable cost, which is $48,400 ($60,000 − $9,600 − $2,000). Thus, the depreciation expense for 2019 is $12,100 ($48,400/4), not (a) $6,000, (b) $4,800, or (c) $15,000.
9. **(a)** First, the book value needs to be determined. The accumulated depreciation as of June 30, 2017, is $36,000 [($80,000/10) × 4.5 years]. Thus, the cost of the machine less accumulated depreciation equals $44,000 ($80,000 − $36,000). The loss recorded at the time of sale is $18,000 ($26,000 − $44,000), not (b) $54,000, (c) $22,000, or (d) $46,000.
10. **(b)** Because the $150,000 was spent developing the patent rather than buying it from another firm, it is debited to Research and Development Expense. Only the $35,000 spent on legal fees ($20,000 for granting patent and $15,000 for defense) can be debited to Patents, not (a) $150,000, (c) $185,000, or (d) $170,000.
11. **(c)** Reporting only totals of major classes of assets in the balance sheet is appropriate. Additional details can be shown in the notes to the financial statements. The other choices are false statements.
12. **(c)** In order to report goodwill, a company must have entered into an exchange transaction that involves the purchase of another business. Choices (a) the company is a valuable company worth investing in, (b) the company has a well-established brand name, and (d) the goodwill will generate a lot of positive business for the company for many years to come are not necessarily valid assumptions.
13. **(d)** Research and development (R&D) costs are expensed when incurred, regardless of whether the research and development expenditures result in a successful patent or not. The other choices are true statements.
14. **(d)** The asset turnover indicates how efficiently a company is employing its assets. The other choices are incorrect because (a) the current ratio is an indicator of liquidity and the company's ability to pay its obligations when they come due, (b) the profit margin is an indicator of how profitable a company is, and (c) the debt to assets ratio indicates the proportion of assets that are financed by debt rather than by equity.
15. **(c)** Asset turnover = Net sales ($180,000)/Average total assets [($200,000 + $300,000)/2] = 0.72 times, not (a) 0.90, (b) 0.20, or (d) 1.39 times.

*16. **(d)** The units-of-activity method takes salvage value into consideration; therefore, the depreciable cost is $10,000. This amount is divided by total estimated activity. The resulting number is multiplied by the units of activity used in 2016 and 2017 to compute the accumulated depreciation at the end of 2017, the second year of the asset's use. The other choices are therefore incorrect.

*17. **(b)** For the double-declining method, the depreciation rate would be 25% or (1/8 × 2). For 2017, annual depreciation expense is $15,000 ($60,000 book value × 25%); for 2018, annual depreciation expense is $11,250 [($60,000 − $15,000) × 25%], not (a) $6,500, (c) $15,000, or (d) $6,562.

PRACTICE EXERCISES

Compute revised annual depreciation.

(LO 2)

1. Will Smith, the new controller of Alexandria Company, has reviewed the expected useful lives and salvage values of selected depreciable assets at the beginning of 2017. Here are his findings:

Type of Asset	Date Acquired	Cost	Accumulated Depreciation, Jan. 1, 2017	Useful Life (in Years) Old	Useful Life (in Years) Proposed	Salvage Value Old	Salvage Value Proposed
Building	Jan. 1, 2009	$900,000	$172,000	40	50	$40,000	$47,600
Warehouse	Jan. 1, 2011	120,000	27,600	25	20	5,000	3,600

All assets are depreciated by the straight-line method. Alexandria Company uses a calendar year in preparing annual financial statements. After discussion, management has agreed to accept Will's proposed changes. (The "Proposed" useful life is total life, not remaining life.)

INSTRUCTIONS

(a) Compute the revised annual depreciation on each asset in 2017. (Show computations.)
(b) Prepare the entry (or entries) to record depreciation on the building in 2017.

SOLUTION

1. (a)

	Type of Asset: Building	Type of Asset: Warehouse
Book value, 1/1/17	$728,000	$92,400
Less: Salvage value	47,600	3,600
Depreciable cost (1)	$680,400	$88,800
Revised remaining useful life in years (2)	42*	14**
Revised annual depreciation (1) ÷ (2)	$16,200	$6,343

*(50 − 8); **(20 − 6)

(b) Dec. 31	Depreciation Expense	16,200	
	Accumulated Depreciation—Buildings		16,200

Prepare entries to set up appropriate accounts for different intangibles; amortize intangible assets.

(LO 4)

2. Lake Company, organized in 2017, has the following transactions related to intangible assets.

1/2/17	Purchased patent (8-year life)	$560,000
4/1/17	Goodwill purchased (indefinite life)	360,000
7/1/17	10-year franchise; expiration date 7/1/2027	440,000
9/1/17	Research and development costs	185,000

INSTRUCTIONS

Prepare the necessary entries to record these intangibles. All costs incurred were for cash. Make the adjusting entries as of December 31, 2017, recording any necessary amortization and reflecting all balances accurately as of that date.

SOLUTION

2. 1/2/17	Patents	560,000	
	Cash		560,000
4/1/17	Goodwill	360,000	
	Cash		360,000
	(Part of the entry to record purchase of another company)		
7/1/17	Franchises	440,000	
	Cash		440,000

9/1/17	Research and Development Expense	185,000	
	Cash		185,000
12/31/17	Amortization Expense		
	(\$560,000 ÷ 8) + [(\$440,000 ÷ 10) × 1/2]	92,000	
	Patents		70,000
	Franchises		22,000

Ending balances, 12/31/17:
Patents = \$490,000 (\$560,000 − \$70,000)
Goodwill = \$360,000
Franchises = \$418,000 (\$440,000 − \$22,000)
R&D expense = \$185,000

PRACTICE PROBLEMS

Compute depreciation under different methods.

(LO 2, 6)

1. DuPage Company purchases a factory machine at a cost of \$18,000 on January 1, 2017. DuPage expects the machine to have a salvage value of \$2,000 at the end of its 4-year useful life.

During its useful life, the machine is expected to be used 160,000 hours. Actual annual hourly use was 2017, 40,000; 2018, 60,000; 2019, 35,000; and 2020, 25,000.

INSTRUCTIONS

Prepare depreciation schedules for the following methods: (a) straight-line, (b) units-of-activity, and (c) declining-balance using double the straight-line rate. (Parts (b) and (c) are discussed in the chapter appendix.)

SOLUTION

1. (a) **Straight-Line Method**

	Computation					End of Year	
Year	Depreciable Cost*	×	Depreciation Rate	=	Annual Depreciation Expense	Accumulated Depreciation	Book Value
2017	\$16,000		25%		\$4,000	\$ 4,000	\$14,000**
2018	16,000		25%		4,000	8,000	10,000
2019	16,000		25%		4,000	12,000	6,000
2020	16,000		25%		4,000	16,000	2,000

*\$18,000 − \$2,000.
**\$18,000 − \$4,000.

(b) **Units-of-Activity Method**

	Computation					End of Year	
Year	Units of Activity	×	Depreciable Cost/Unit	=	Annual Depreciation Expense	Accumulated Depreciation	Book Value
2017	40,000		\$0.10*		\$4,000	\$ 4,000	\$14,000
2018	60,000		0.10		6,000	10,000	8,000
2019	35,000		0.10		3,500	13,500	4,500
2020	25,000		0.10		2,500	16,000	2,000

*(\$18,000 − \$2,000) ÷ 160,000.

(c) **Declining-Balance Method**

	Computation					End of Year	
Year	Book Value Beginning of Year	×	Depreciation Rate*	=	Annual Depreciation Expense	Accumulated Depreciation	Book Value
2017	\$18,000		50%		\$9,000	\$ 9,000	\$9,000
2018	9,000		50%		4,500	13,500	4,500
2019	4,500		50%		2,250	15,750	2,250
2020	2,250		50%		250**	16,000	2,000

*¼ × 2.
**Adjusted to \$250 because ending book value should not be less than expected salvage value.

Record disposal of plant asset.
(LO 3)

2. On January 1, 2014, Skyline Limousine Co. purchased a limousine at an acquisition cost of $28,000. Skyline depreciated the vehicle by the straight-line method using a 4-year service life and a $4,000 salvage value. The company's fiscal year ends on December 31.

INSTRUCTIONS

Prepare the journal entry or entries to record the disposal of the limousine, assuming that it was:
(a) Retired and scrapped with no salvage value on January 1, 2018.
(b) Sold for $5,000 on July 1, 2017.

SOLUTION

2. (a) Jan. 1, 2018	Accumulated Depreciation—Equipment	24,000*	
	Loss on Disposal of Plant Assets	4,000	
	Equipment		28,000
	(To record retirement of limousine)		

*[($28,000 – $4,000) ÷ 4] × 4

(b) July 1, 2017	Depreciation Expense	3,000*	
	Accumulated Depreciation—Equipment		3,000
	(To record depreciation to date of disposal)		

*[($28,000 – $4,000) ÷ 4] × $\frac{1}{2}$

	Cash	5,000	
	Accumulated Depreciation—Equipment	21,000*	
	Loss on Disposal of Plant Assets	2,000	
	Equipment		28,000
	(To record sale of limousine)		

*[($28,000 – $4,000) ÷ 4] × 3.5

WileyPLUS Brief Exercises, DO IT! Exercises, Exercises, Problems, and many additional resources are available for practice in WileyPLUS.

NOTE: All asterisked Questions, Exercises, and Problems relate to material in the appendix to the chapter.

QUESTIONS

1. Mrs. Harcross is uncertain about how the historical cost principle applies to plant assets. Explain the principle to Mrs. Harcross.
2. How is the cost for a plant asset measured in a cash transaction? In a noncash transaction?
3. Barrister Company acquires the land and building owned by Ansel Company. What types of costs may be incurred to make the asset ready for its intended use if Barrister Company wants to use only the land? If it wants to use both the land and the building?
4. Distinguish between ordinary repairs and capital expenditures during an asset's useful life.
5. Breton Inc. needs to upgrade its diagnostic equipment. At the time of purchase, Breton had expected the equipment to last 8 years. Unfortunately, it was obsolete after only 4 years. Nolan Rush, CFO of Breton Inc., is considering leasing new equipment rather than buying it. What are the potential benefits of leasing?
6. In a recent newspaper release, the president of Magnusson Company asserted that something has to be done about depreciation. The president said, "Depreciation does not come close to accumulating the cash needed to replace the asset at the end of its useful life." What is your response to the president?

7. Melanie is studying for the next accounting examination. She asks your help on two questions: (a) What is salvage value? (b) How is salvage value used in determining depreciable cost under the straight-line method? Answer Melanie's questions.
8. Contrast the straight-line method and the units-of-activity method in relation to (a) useful life and (b) the pattern of periodic depreciation over useful life.
9. Contrast the effects of the three depreciation methods on annual depreciation expense.
10. In the fourth year of an asset's 5-year useful life, the company decides that the asset will have a 6-year service life. How should the revision of depreciation be recorded? Why?
11. How is a gain or a loss on the sale of a plant asset computed?
12. Marsh Corporation owns a machine that is fully depreciated but is still being used. How should Marsh account for this asset and report it in the financial statements?
13. What does Apple use as the estimated useful life on its buildings? On its machinery and equipment? (*Hint:* You will need to find the notes to Apple's financial statements online. See the directions for finding the notes in Appendix A at the end of the textbook.)
14. What are the similarities and differences between depreciation and amortization?
15. During a recent management meeting, Bruce Dunn, director of marketing, proposed that the company begin capitalizing its marketing expenditures as goodwill. In his words, "Marketing expenditures create goodwill for the company which benefits the company for multiple periods. Therefore it doesn't make good sense to have to expense it as it is incurred. Besides, if we capitalize it as goodwill, we won't have to amortize it, and this will boost reported income." Discuss the merits of Bruce's proposal.
16. Warwick Company hires an accounting intern who says that intangible assets should always be amortized over their legal lives. Is the intern correct? Explain.
17. Goodwill has been defined as the value of all favorable attributes that relate to a business enterprise. What types of attributes could result in goodwill?
18. Kathy Malone, a business major, is working on a case problem for one of her classes. In this case problem, the company needs to raise cash to market a new product it developed. Doug Price, an engineering major, takes one look at the company's balance sheet and says, "This company has an awful lot of goodwill. Why don't you recommend that they sell some of it to raise cash?" How should Kathy respond to Doug?
19. Under what conditions is goodwill recorded? What is the proper accounting treatment for amortizing goodwill?
20. Often research and development costs provide companies with benefits that last a number of years. (For example, these costs can lead to the development of a patent that will increase the company's income for many years.) However, generally accepted accounting principles require that such costs be recorded as an expense when incurred. Why?
21. Suppose in 2017 that Campbell Soup Company reported average total assets of $6,265 million, net sales of $7,586 million, and net income of $736 million. What was Campbell Soup's return on assets?
22. Cassy Dominic, a marketing executive for Fresh Views Inc., has proposed expanding its product line of framed graphic art by producing a line of lower-quality products. These would require less processing by the company and would provide a lower profit margin. Mel Joss, the company's CFO, is concerned that this new product line would reduce the company's return on assets. Discuss the potential effect on return on assets that this product might have.
23. Give an example of an industry that would be characterized by (a) a high asset turnover and a low profit margin, and (b) a low asset turnover and a high profit margin.
24. Peyton Corporation and Rogers Corporation operate in the same industry. Peyton uses the straight-line method to account for depreciation, whereas Rogers uses an accelerated method. Explain what complications might arise in trying to compare the results of these two companies.
25. Mesa Corporation uses straight-line depreciation for financial reporting purposes but an accelerated method for tax purposes. Is it acceptable to use different methods for the two purposes? What is Mesa Corporation's motivation for doing this?
26. You are comparing two companies in the same industry. You have determined that Gore Corp. depreciates its plant assets over a 40-year life, whereas Ross Corp. depreciates its plant assets over a 20-year life. Discuss the implications this has for comparing the results of the two companies.
27. Explain how transactions related to plant assets and intangibles are reported in the statement of cash flows under the indirect method.

BRIEF EXERCISES

Determine the cost of land. (LO 1), AP

BE9-1 These expenditures were incurred by Dobbin Company in purchasing land: cash price $60,000, accrued taxes $5,000, attorney's fees $2,100, real estate broker's commission $3,300, and clearing and grading $3,500. What is the cost of the land?

Determine the cost of a truck. (LO 1), AP

BE9-2 Thoms Company incurs these expenditures in purchasing a truck: cash price $24,000, accident insurance (during use) $2,000, sales taxes $1,080, motor vehicle license $300, and painting and lettering $1,700. What is the cost of the truck?

Prepare entries for delivery truck costs.

(LO 1), AP

BE9-3 Krieg Company had the following two transactions related to its delivery truck.

1. Paid $38 for an oil change.
2. Paid $400 to install special shelving units, which increase the operating efficiency of the truck.

Prepare Krieg's journal entries to record these two transactions.

Compute straight-line depreciation.

(LO 2), AP

BE9-4 Gordon Chemicals Company acquires a delivery truck at a cost of $31,000 on January 1, 2017. The truck is expected to have a salvage value of $4,000 at the end of its 4-year useful life. Compute annual depreciation for the first and second years using the straight-line method.

Compute depreciation and evaluate treatment.

(LO 2), AN

BE9-5 Ivy Company purchased land and a building on January 1, 2017. Management's best estimate of the value of the land was $100,000 and of the building $250,000. However, management told the accounting department to record the land at $230,000 and the building at $120,000. The building is being depreciated on a straight-line basis over 20 years with no salvage value. Why do you suppose management requested this accounting treatment? Is it ethical?

Compute revised depreciation.

(LO 2), AP

BE9-6 On January 1, 2017, the Hermann Company ledger shows Equipment $36,000 and Accumulated Depreciation $13,600. The depreciation resulted from using the straight-line method with a useful life of 10 years and a salvage value of $2,000. On this date, the company concludes that the equipment has a remaining useful life of only 2 years with the same salvage value. Compute the revised annual depreciation.

Journalize entries for disposal of plant assets.

(LO 3), AP

BE9-7 Prepare journal entries to record these transactions. (a) Echo Company retires its delivery equipment, which cost $41,000. Accumulated depreciation is also $41,000 on this delivery equipment. No salvage value is received. (b) Assume the same information as in part (a), except that accumulated depreciation for the equipment is $37,200 instead of $41,000.

Journalize entries for sale of plant assets.

(LO 3), AP

BE9-8 Antone Company sells office equipment on July 31, 2017, for $21,000 cash. The office equipment originally cost $72,000 and as of January 1, 2017, had accumulated depreciation of $42,000. Depreciation for the first 7 months of 2017 is $4,600. Prepare the journal entries to (a) update depreciation to July 31, 2017, and (b) record the sale of the equipment.

Account for intangibles—patents.

(LO 4), AP

BE9-9 Abner Company purchases a patent for $156,000 on January 2, 2017. Its estimated useful life is 6 years.

(a) Prepare the journal entry to record amortization expense for the first year.
(b) Show how this patent is reported on the balance sheet at the end of the first year.

Compute return on assets and asset turnover.

(LO 5), AP

BE9-10 Suppose in its 2017 annual report that McDonald's Corporation reports beginning total assets of $28.46 billion, ending total assets of $30.22 billion, net sales of $22.74 billion, and net income of $4.55 billion.

(a) Compute McDonald's return on assets.
(b) Compute McDonald's asset turnover.

Classification of long-lived assets on balance sheet.

(LO 5), AP

BE9-11 Suppose Nike, Inc. reported the following plant assets and intangible assets for the year ended May 31, 2017 (in millions): other plant assets $965.8, land $221.6, patents and trademarks (at cost) $515.1, machinery and equipment $2,094.3, buildings $974.0, goodwill (at cost) $193.5, accumulated amortization $47.7, and accumulated depreciation $2,298.0. Prepare a partial balance sheet for Nike for these items.

Determine net cash provided by operating activities.

(LO 5), AP

BE9-12 Hunt Company reported net income of $157,000. It reported depreciation expense of $12,000 and accumulated depreciation of $47,000. Amortization expense was $8,000. Hunt purchased new equipment during the year for $50,000. Show how this information would be used to determine net cash provided by operating activities under the indirect method.

Compute declining-balance depreciation.

(LO 6), AP

***BE9-13** Depreciation information for Gordon Chemicals Company is given in BE9-4. Assuming the declining-balance depreciation rate is double the straight-line rate, compute annual depreciation for the first and second years under the declining-balance method.

***BE9-14** Kwik Taxi Service uses the units-of-activity method in computing depreciation on its taxicabs. Each cab is expected to be driven 150,000 miles. Taxi 10 cost $27,500 and is expected to have a salvage value of $500. Taxi 10 was driven 32,000 miles in 2016 and 33,000 miles in 2017. Compute the depreciation for each year.

Compute depreciation using units-of-activity method.

(LO 6), AP

DO IT! EXERCISES

DO IT! 9-1 Hummer Company purchased a delivery truck. The total cash payment was $30,020, including the following items.

Explain accounting for cost of plant assets

(LO 1), C

Negotiated purchase price	$24,000
Installation of special shelving	1,100
Painting and lettering	900
Motor vehicle license	180
Annual insurance policy	2,400
Sales tax	1,440
Total paid	$30,020

Explain how each of these costs would be accounted for.

DO IT! 9-2a On January 1, 2017, Salt Creek Country Club purchased a new riding mower for $15,000. The mower is expected to have a 10-year life with a $1,000 salvage value. What journal entry would Salt Creek make on December 31, 2017, if it uses straight-line depreciation?

Calculate depreciation expense and make journal entry.

(LO 2), AP

DO IT! 9-2b Fordon Corporation purchased a piece of equipment for $50,000. It estimated an 8-year life and $2,000 salvage value. At the end of year four (before the depreciation adjustment), it estimated the new total life to be 10 years and the new salvage value to be $4,000. Compute the revised depreciation.

Calculated revised depreciation

(LO 2), AP

DO IT! 9-3 Bylie Company has an old factory machine that cost $50,000. The machine has accumulated depreciation of $28,000. Bylie has decided to sell the machine.

Make journal entries to record plant asset disposal.

(LO 3), AP

(a) What entry would Bylie make to record the sale of the machine for $25,000 cash?
(b) What entry would Bylie make to record the sale of the machine for $15,000 cash?

DO IT! 9-4 Match the statement with the term most directly associated with it.

Match intangible assets with concepts.

(LO 4), C

Goodwill	Amortization
Intangible assets	Franchise
Research and development costs	

1. _______ Rights, privileges, and competitive advantages that result from the ownership of long-lived assets that do not possess physical substance.
2. _______ The allocation of the cost of an intangible asset to expense in a rational and systematic manner.
3. _______ A right to sell certain products or services, or use certain trademarks or trade names within a designated geographic area.
4. _______ Costs incurred by a company that often lead to patents or new products. These costs must be expensed as incurred.
5. _______ The excess of the cost of a company over the fair value of the net assets required.

DO IT! 9-5 For 2017, Sale Company reported beginning total assets of $300,000 and ending total assets of $340,000. Its net income for this period was $50,000, and its net sales were $400,000. Compute the company's asset turnover for 2017.

Calculate asset turnover.

(LO 5), AP

EXERCISES

E9-1 The following expenditures relating to plant assets were made by Glenn Company during the first 2 months of 2017.

Determine cost of plant acquisitions.

(LO 1), C

1. Paid $7,000 of accrued taxes at the time the plant site was acquired.
2. Paid $200 insurance to cover a possible accident loss on new factory machinery while the machinery was in transit.

3. Paid $850 sales taxes on a new delivery truck.
4. Paid $21,000 for parking lots and driveways on the new plant site.
5. Paid $250 to have the company name and slogan painted on the new delivery truck.
6. Paid $8,000 for installation of new factory machinery.
7. Paid $900 for a 1-year accident insurance policy on the new delivery truck.
8. Paid $75 motor vehicle license fee on the new truck.

Instructions

(a) Explain the application of the historical cost principle in determining the acquisition cost of plant assets.
(b) List the numbers of the transactions, and opposite each indicate the account title to which each expenditure should be debited.

Determine property, plant, and equipment costs.

(LO 1), C

E9-2 Adama Company incurred the following costs.

1. Sales tax on factory machinery purchased	$ 5,000
2. Painting of and lettering on truck immediately upon purchase	700
3. Installation and testing of factory machinery	2,000
4. Real estate broker's commission on land purchased	3,500
5. Insurance premium paid for first year's insurance on new truck	880
6. Cost of landscaping on property purchased	7,200
7. Cost of paving parking lot for new building constructed	17,900
8. Cost of clearing, draining, and filling land	13,300
9. Architect's fees on self-constructed building	10,000

Instructions

Indicate to which account Adama would debit each of the costs.

Determine acquisition costs of land.

(LO 1), AP

E9-3 On March 1, 2017, Boyd Company acquired real estate, on which it planned to construct a small office building, by paying $80,000 in cash. An old warehouse on the property was demolished at a cost of $8,200; the salvaged materials were sold for $1,700. Additional expenditures before construction began included $1,900 attorney's fee for work concerning the land purchase, $5,200 real estate broker's fee, $9,100 architect's fee, and $14,000 to put in driveways and a parking lot.

Instructions

(a) Determine the amount to be reported as the cost of the land.
(b) For each cost not used in part (a), indicate the account to be debited.

Understand depreciation concepts.

(LO 2), C

E9-4 Alysha Monet has prepared the following list of statements about depreciation.

1. Depreciation is a process of asset valuation, not cost allocation.
2. Depreciation provides for the proper matching of expenses with revenues.
3. The book value of a plant asset should approximate its fair value.
4. Depreciation applies to three classes of plant assets: land, buildings, and equipment.
5. Depreciation does not apply to a building because its usefulness and revenue-producing ability generally remain intact over time.
6. The revenue-producing ability of a depreciable asset will decline due to wear and tear and to obsolescence.
7. Recognizing depreciation on an asset results in an accumulation of cash for replacement of the asset.
8. The balance in accumulated depreciation represents the total cost that has been charged to expense since placing the asset in service.
9. Depreciation expense and accumulated depreciation are reported on the income statement.
10. Three factors affect the computation of depreciation: cost, useful life, and salvage value.

Instructions

Identify each statement as true or false. If false, indicate how to correct the statement.

Determine straight-line depreciation for partial period.

(LO 2), AP

E9-5 Gotham Company purchased a new machine on October 1, 2017, at a cost of $90,000. The company estimated that the machine has a salvage value of $8,000. The machine is expected to be used for 70,000 working hours during its 8-year life.

Instructions

Compute the depreciation expense under the straight-line method for 2017 and 2018, assuming a December 31 year-end.

E9-6 Victor Mineli, the new controller of Santorini Company, has reviewed the expected useful lives and salvage values of selected depreciable assets at the beginning of 2017. Here are his findings:

Compute revised annual depreciation.

(LO 2), AN

Type of Asset	Date Acquired	Cost	Accumulated Depreciation, Jan. 1, 2017	Useful Life (in years) Old	Useful Life (in years) Proposed	Salvage Value Old	Salvage Value Proposed
Building	Jan. 1, 2009	$700,000	$130,000	40	48	$50,000	$35,000
Warehouse	Jan. 1, 2012	120,000	23,000	25	20	5,000	3,600

All assets are depreciated by the straight-line method. Santorini Company uses a calendar year in preparing annual financial statements. After discussion, management has agreed to accept Victor's proposed changes. (The "Proposed" useful life is total life, not remaining life.)

Instructions

(a) Compute the revised annual depreciation on each asset in 2017. (Show computations.)
(b) Prepare the entry (or entries) to record depreciation on the building in 2017.

E9-7 Thieu Co. has delivery equipment that cost $50,000 and has been depreciated $24,000.

Journalize transactions related to disposals of plant assets.

(LO 3), AP

Instructions

Record entries for the disposal under the following assumptions.
(a) It was scrapped as having no value.
(b) It was sold for $37,000.
(c) It was sold for $20,000.

E9-8 Here are selected 2017 transactions of Akron Corporation.

Record disposal of equipment.

(LO 3), AP

Jan. 1	Retired a piece of machinery that was purchased on January 1, 2007. The machine cost $62,000 and had a useful life of 10 years with no salvage value.
June 30	Sold a computer that was purchased on January 1, 2015. The computer cost $36,000 and had a useful life of 3 years with no salvage value. The computer was sold for $5,000 cash.
Dec. 31	Sold a delivery truck for $9,000 cash. The truck cost $25,000 when it was purchased on January 1, 2014, and was depreciated based on a 5-year useful life with a $4,000 salvage value.

Instructions

Journalize all entries required on the above dates, including entries to update depreciation on assets disposed of, where applicable. Akron Corporation uses straight-line depreciation.

E9-9 Shown below are the T-accounts relating to equipment that was purchased for cash by a company on the first day of the current year. The equipment was depreciated on a straight-line basis with an estimated useful life of 10 years and a salvage value of $100. Part of the equipment was sold on the last day of the current year for cash proceeds.

Record equipment transactions and determine missing amounts.

(LO 1, 2, 3), AN

Cash

Debit	Credit
	Jan. 1 (a)
Dec. 31 450	

Equipment

Debit	Credit
Jan. 1 1,100	
	Dec. 31 440

Accumulated Depreciation—Equipment

Debit	Credit
	Dec. 31 100
Dec. 31 40	31 55

Depreciation Expense

Debit	Credit
Dec. 31 (b)	

Gain on Disposal of Plant Assets

Debit	Credit
	Dec. 31 (c)

Instructions

Prepare the journal entries to record the following and derive the missing amounts:
(a) Purchase of equipment on January 1. What was the cash paid?
(b) Depreciation recorded on December 31. What was the depreciation expense?
(c) Sale of part of the equipment on December 31. What was the gain on disposal?

E9-10 The following situations are independent of one another.

Apply accounting concepts.

(LO 1, 2, 3, 4), C

1. An accounting student recently employed by a small company doesn't understand why the company is only depreciating its buildings and equipment, but not its land. The student prepared journal entries to depreciate all the company's property, plant, and equipment for the current year-end.
2. The same student also thinks the company's amortization policy on its intangible assets is wrong. The company is currently amortizing its patents but not its goodwill.

As a result, the student added goodwill to her adjusting entry for amortization at the end of the current year. She told a fellow employee that she felt she had improved the consistency of the company's accounting policies by making these changes.

3. The same company has a building still in use that has a zero book value but a substantial fair value. The student felt that this practice didn't benefit the company's users—especially the bank—and wrote the building up to its fair value. After all, she reasoned, you can write down assets if fair values are lower. Writing them up if fair value is higher is yet another example of the improved consistency that she has brought to the company's accounting practices.

Instructions

Explain whether or not the accounting treatment in each of the above situations is in accordance with generally accepted accounting principles. Explain what accounting principle or assumption, if any, has been violated and what the appropriate accounting treatment should be.

Prepare adjusting entries for amortization.

(LO 4), AN

E9-11 These are selected 2017 transactions for Wyle Corporation:

Jan. 1	Purchased a copyright for $120,000. The copyright has a useful life of 6 years and a remaining legal life of 30 years.
Mar. 1	Purchased a patent with an estimated useful life of 4 years and a legal life of 20 years for $54,000.
Sept. 1	Purchased a small company and recorded goodwill of $150,000. Its useful life is indefinite.

Instructions

Prepare all adjusting entries at December 31 to record amortization required by the events.

Prepare entries to set up appropriate accounts for different intangibles; calculate amortization.

(LO 4), AN

E9-12 On January 1, 2017, Haley Company had a balance of $360,000 of goodwill on its balance sheet that resulted from the purchase of a small business in a prior year. The goodwill had an indefinite life. During 2017, the company had the following additional transactions.

Jan. 2	Purchased a patent (5-year life) $280,000.
July 1	Acquired a 9-year franchise; expiration date July 1, 2026, $540,000.
Sept. 1	Research and development costs $185,000.

Instructions

(a) Prepare the necessary entries to record the transactions related to intangibles. All costs incurred were for cash.
(b) Make the entries as of December 31, 2017, recording any necessary amortization.
(c) Indicate what the intangible asset account balances should be on December 31, 2017.

Discuss implications of amortization period.

(LO 4), C

E9-13 Alliance Atlantis Communications Inc. changed its accounting policy to amortize broadcast rights over the contracted exhibition period, which is based on the estimated useful life of the program. Previously, the company amortized broadcast rights over the lesser of 2 years or the contracted exhibition period.

Instructions

Write a short memo to your client explaining the implications this has for the analysis of Alliance Atlantis's results.

Answer questions on depreciation and intangibles.

(LO 2, 4), C

E9-14 The questions listed below are independent of one another.

Instructions

Provide a brief answer to each question.

(a) Why should a company depreciate its buildings?
(b) How can a company have a building that has a zero reported book value but substantial fair value?
(c) What are some examples of intangibles that you might find on your college campus?
(d) Give some examples of company or product trademarks or trade names. Are trade names and trademarks reported on a company's balance sheet?

Calculate asset turnover and return on assets.

(LO 5), AP

E9-15 Suppose during 2017 that Federal Express reported the following information (in millions): net sales of $35,497 and net income of $98. Its balance sheet also showed total assets at the beginning of the year of $25,633 and total assets at the end of the year of $24,244.

Instructions
Calculate the (a) asset turnover and (b) return on assets.

E9-16 Lymen International is considering a significant expansion to its product line. The sales force is excited about the opportunities that the new products will bring. The new products are a significant step up in quality above the company's current offerings, but offer a complementary fit to its existing product line. Fred Riddick, senior production department manager, is very excited about the high-tech new equipment that will have to be acquired to produce the new products. Barbara Dyson, the company's CFO, has provided the following projections based on results with and without the new products.

Calculate and interpret ratios.

(LO 5), AP

	Without New Products	With New Products
Sales revenue	$10,000,000	$16,000,000
Net income	$500,000	$960,000
Average total assets	$5,000,000	$12,000,000

Instructions
(a) Compute the company's return on assets, profit margin, and asset turnover, both with and without the new product line.
(b) Discuss the implications that your findings in part (a) have for the company's decision.

E9-17 Linley Company reports the following information (in millions) during a recent year: net sales, $11,408.5; net earnings, $264.8; total assets, ending, $4,312.6; and total assets, beginning, $4,254.3.

Calculate and interpret ratios.

(LO 5), AP

Instructions
(a) Calculate the (1) return on assets, (2) asset turnover, and (3) profit margin.
(b) Prove mathematically how the profit margin and asset turnover work together to explain return on assets, by showing the appropriate calculation.
(c) Linley Company owns Northgate (grocery), Linley Theaters, Oz Drugstores, and Ransome (heavy equipment), and manages commercial real estate, among other activities. Does this diversity of activities affect your ability to interpret the ratios you calculated in (a)? Explain.

E9-18 Mendez Corporation reported net income of $58,000. Depreciation expense for the year was $132,000. The company calculates depreciation expense using the straight-line method, with a useful life of 10 years. Top management would like to switch to a 15-year useful life because depreciation expense would be reduced to $88,000. The CEO says, "Increasing the useful life would increase net income and net cash provided by operating activities."

Determine net cash provided by operating activities.

(LO 5), AN

Instructions
Provide a comparative analysis showing net income and net cash provided by operating activities (ignoring other accrual adjustments) under the indirect method using a 10-year and a 15-year useful life. (Ignore income taxes.) Evaluate the CEO's suggestion.

***E9-19** Whippet Bus Lines uses the units-of-activity method in depreciating its buses. One bus was purchased on January 1, 2017, at a cost of $100,000. Over its 4-year useful life, the bus is expected to be driven 160,000 miles. Salvage value is expected to be $8,000.

Compute depreciation under units-of-activity method.

(LO 6), AP

Instructions
(a) Compute the depreciation cost per unit.
(b) Prepare a depreciation schedule assuming actual mileage was 2017, 40,000; 2018, 52,000; 2019, 41,000; and 2020, 27,000.

***E9-20** Basic information relating to a new machine purchased by Gotham Company is presented in E9-5.

Compute declining-balance and units-of-activity depreciation.

(LO 6), AP

Instructions
Using the facts presented in E9-5, compute depreciation using the following methods in the year indicated.
(a) Declining-balance using double the straight-line rate for 2017 and 2018.
(b) Units-of-activity for 2017, assuming machine usage was 480 hours. (Round depreciation per unit to the nearest cent.)

EXERCISES: SET B AND CHALLENGE EXERCISES

Visit the book's companion website, at **www.wiley.com/college/kimmel**, and choose the Student Companion site to access Exercises: Set B and Challenge Exercises.

PROBLEMS: SET A

Determine acquisition costs of land and building.
(LO 1), C

P9-1A Peete Company was organized on January 1. During the first year of operations, the following plant asset expenditures and receipts were recorded in random order.

	Debit
1. Excavation costs for new building	$ 23,000
2. Architect's fees on building plans	33,000
3. Full payment to building contractor	640,000
4. Cost of real estate purchased as a plant site (land $255,000 and building $25,000)	280,000
5. Cost of parking lots and driveways	29,000
6. Accrued real estate taxes paid at time of purchase of real estate	3,170
7. Installation cost of fences around property	6,800
8. Cost of demolishing building to make land suitable for construction of new building	31,000
9. Real estate taxes paid for the current year on land	6,400
	$1,052,370
	Credit
10. Proceeds from salvage of demolished building	$ 12,000

Instructions

Analyze the transactions using the following table column headings. Enter the number of each transaction in the Item column, and enter the amounts in the appropriate columns. For amounts in the Other Accounts column, also indicate the account title.

Land $302,170

Item	Land	Buildings	Other Accounts

Journalize equipment transactions related to purchase, sale, retirement, and depreciation.
(LO 2, 3, 5), AP

P9-2A At December 31, 2017, Arnold Corporation reported the following plant assets.

Land		$ 3,000,000
Buildings	$26,500,000	
Less: Accumulated depreciation—buildings	11,925,000	14,575,000
Equipment	40,000,000	
Less: Accumulated depreciation—equipment	5,000,000	35,000,000
Total plant assets		$52,575,000

During 2018, the following selected cash transactions occurred.

Apr. 1	Purchased land for $2,200,000.
May 1	Sold equipment that cost $600,000 when purchased on January 1, 2011. The equipment was sold for $170,000.
June 1	Sold land for $1,600,000. The land cost $1,000,000.
July 1	Purchased equipment for $1,100,000.
Dec. 31	Retired equipment that cost $700,000 when purchased on December 31, 2008. No salvage value was received.

Instructions

(a) Journalize the transactions. (*Hint:* You may wish to set up T-accounts, post beginning balances, and then post 2018 transactions.) Arnold uses straight-line depreciation for buildings and equipment. The buildings are estimated to have a 40-year useful life and no salvage value; the equipment is estimated to have a 10-year useful life and no salvage value. Update depreciation on assets disposed of at the time of sale or retirement.

(b) Record adjusting entries for depreciation for 2018.

(c) Tot. plant assets $50,037,500

(c) Prepare the plant assets section of Arnold's balance sheet at December 31, 2018.

P9-3A Pine Company had the following assets on January 1, 2017.

Journalize entries for disposal of plant assets.

(LO 3), AP

Item	Cost	Purchase Date	Useful Life (in years)	Salvage Value
Machinery	$71,000	Jan. 1, 2007	10	$ -0-
Forklift	30,000	Jan. 1, 2014	5	-0-
Truck	33,400	Jan. 1, 2012	8	3,000

During 2017, each of the assets was removed from service. The machinery was retired on January 1. The forklift was sold on June 30 for $12,000. The truck was discarded on December 31.

Instructions

Journalize all entries required on the above dates, including entries to update depreciation, where applicable, on disposed assets. The company uses straight-line depreciation. All depreciation was up to date as of December 31, 2016.

Loss on truck disposal $10,600

P9-4A At January 1, 2017, Youngstown Company reported the following property, plant, and equipment accounts:

Record property, plant, and equipment transactions; prepare partial balance sheet.

(LO 1, 2, 3, 5), AP

Accumulated depreciation—buildings	$ 62,200,000
Accumulated depreciation—equipment	54,000,000
Buildings	97,400,000
Equipment	150,000,000
Land	20,000,000

The company uses straight-line depreciation for buildings and equipment, its year-end is December 31, and it makes adjusting entries annually. The buildings are estimated to have a 40-year useful life and no salvage value; the equipment is estimated to have a 10-year useful life and no salvage value.

During 2017, the following selected transactions occurred:

Apr. 1	Purchased land for $4.4 million. Paid $1.1 million cash and issued a 3-year, 6% note payable for the balance. Interest on the note is payable annually each April 1.
May 1	Sold equipment for $300,000 cash. The equipment cost $2.8 million when originally purchased on January 1, 2009.
June 1	Sold land for $3.6 million. Received $900,000 cash and accepted a 3-year, 5% note for the balance. The land cost $1.4 million when purchased on June 1, 2011. Interest on the note is due annually each June 1.
July 1	Purchased equipment for $2.2 million cash.
Dec. 31	Retired equipment that cost $1 million when purchased on December 31, 2007. No proceeds were received.

Instructions

(a) Record the above transactions.
(b) Record any adjusting entries required at December 31.
(c) Prepare the property, plant, and equipment section of the company's statement of financial position at December 31.

Total PP&E $138,575,000

P9-5A The intangible assets section of Amato Corporation's balance sheet at December 31, 2017, is presented here.

Prepare entries to record transactions related to acquisition and amortization of intangibles; prepare the intangible assets section and note.

(LO 4, 5), AP

Patents ($60,000 cost less $6,000 amortization)	$54,000
Copyrights ($36,000 cost less $25,200 amortization)	10,800
Total	$64,800

The patent was acquired in January 2017 and has a useful life of 10 years. The copyright was acquired in January 2011 and also has a useful life of 10 years. The following cash transactions may have affected intangible assets during 2018.

Jan. 2	Paid $46,800 legal costs to successfully defend the patent against infringement by another company.
Jan.–June	Developed a new product, incurring $230,000 in research and development costs. A patent was granted for the product on July 1, and its useful life is equal to its legal life. Legal and other costs for the patent were $20,000.
Sept. 1	Paid $40,000 to a quarterback to appear in commercials advertising the company's products. The commercials will air in September and October.
Oct. 1	Acquired a copyright for $200,000. The copyright has a useful life and legal life of 50 years.

Instructions

(a) Prepare journal entries to record the transactions.

(b) Prepare journal entries to record the 2018 amortization expense for intangible assets.

(c) Tot. intangibles $315,300

(c) Prepare the intangible assets section of the balance sheet at December 31, 2018.

(d) Prepare the note to the financial statements on Amato Corporation's intangible assets as of December 31, 2018.

Prepare entries to correct errors in recording and amortizing intangible assets.

(LO 4), AP

P9-6A Due to rapid employee turnover in the accounting department, the following transactions involving intangible assets were improperly recorded by Inland Corporation.

1. Inland developed a new manufacturing process, incurring research and development costs of $160,000. The company also purchased a patent for $40,000. In early January, Inland capitalized $200,000 as the cost of the patents. Patent amortization expense of $10,000 was recorded based on a 20-year useful life.
2. On July 1, 2017, Inland purchased a small company and as a result recorded goodwill of $80,000. Inland recorded a half-year's amortization in 2017, based on a 20-year life ($2,000 amortization). The goodwill has an indefinite life.

Instructions

Prepare all journal entries necessary to correct any errors made during 2017. Assume the books have not yet been closed for 2017.

Calculate and comment on return on assets, profit margin, and asset turnover.

(LO 5), AN

P9-7A Blythe Corporation and Jacke Corporation, two companies of roughly the same size, are both involved in the manufacture of shoe-tracing devices. Each company depreciates its plant assets using the straight-line approach. An investigation of their financial statements reveals the information shown below.

	Blythe Corp.	**Jacke Corp.**
Net income	$ 240,000	$ 300,000
Sales revenue	1,150,000	1,200,000
Total assets (average)	3,200,000	3,000,000
Plant assets (average)	2,400,000	1,800,000
Intangible assets (goodwill)	300,000	0

Instructions

(a) For each company, calculate these values:
  (1) Return on assets.
  (2) Profit margin.
  (3) Asset turnover.

(b) Based on your calculations in part (a), comment on the relative effectiveness of the two companies in using their assets to generate sales. What factors complicate your ability to compare the two companies?

Compute depreciation under different methods.

(LO 2, 6), AP

***P9-8A** In recent years, Jayme Company has purchased three machines. Because of frequent employee turnover in the accounting department, a different accountant was in charge of selecting the depreciation method for each machine, and various methods have been used. Information concerning the machines is summarized in the table below.

Machine	Acquired	Cost	Salvage Value	Useful Life (in years)	Depreciation Method
1	Jan. 1, 2015	$96,000	$12,000	8	Straight-line
2	July 1, 2016	85,000	10,000	5	Declining-balance
3	Nov. 1, 2016	66,000	6,000	6	Units-of-activity

For the declining-balance method, Jayme Company uses the double-declining rate. For the units-of-activity method, total machine hours are expected to be 30,000. Actual hours of use in the first 3 years were 2016, 800; 2017, 4,500; and 2018, 6,000.

Instructions

(a) Machine 2 $60,520

(a) Compute the amount of accumulated depreciation on each machine at December 31, 2018.

(b) If machine 2 was purchased on April 1 instead of July 1, what would be the depreciation expense for this machine in 2016? In 2017?

Compute depreciation under different methods.

(LO 2, 6), AP

***P9-9A** Megan Corporation purchased machinery on January 1, 2017, at a cost of $250,000. The estimated useful life of the machinery is 4 years, with an estimated salvage value at the end of that period of $30,000. The company is considering different depreciation methods that could be used for financial reporting purposes.

Instructions

(a) Prepare separate depreciation schedules for the machinery using the straight-line method, and the declining-balance method using double the straight-line rate. (Round to the nearest dollar.)

(b) Which method would result in the higher reported 2017 income? In the highest total reported income over the 4-year period?

(c) Which method would result in the lower reported 2017 income? In the lowest total reported income over the 4-year period?

(a) Double-declining-balance expense 2019 $31,250

PROBLEMS: SET B AND SET C

Visit the book's companion website, at **www.wiley.com/college/kimmel**, and choose the Student Companion site to access Problems: Set B and Set C.

CONTINUING PROBLEM Cookie Creations

(*Note:* This is a continuation of the Cookie Creations problem from Chapters 1 through 8.)

© leungchopan/
Shutterstock

CC9 Part 1 Now that she is selling mixers and her customers can use credit cards to pay for them, Natalie is thinking of upgrading her website so that she can sell mixers online, to broaden her range of customers. She will need to know how to account for the costs of upgrading the site.

Part 2 Natalie is also thinking of buying a van that will be used only for business. Natalie is concerned about the impact of the van's cost on her income statement and balance sheet. She has come to you for advice on calculating the van's depreciation.

Go to the book's companion website, at **www.wiley.com/college/kimmel**, *to see the completion of this problem.*

COMPREHENSIVE ACCOUNTING CYCLE REVIEW

ACR9-1 Milo Corporation's unadjusted trial balance at December 1, 2017, is presented below.

	Debit	Credit
Cash	$ 22,000	
Accounts Receivable	36,800	
Notes Receivable	10,000	
Interest Receivable	–0–	
Inventory	36,200	
Prepaid Insurance	3,600	
Land	20,000	
Buildings	150,000	
Equipment	60,000	
Patent	9,000	
Allowance for Doubtful Accounts		$ 500
Accumulated Depreciation—Buildings		50,000
Accumulated Depreciation—Equipment		24,000
Accounts Payable		27,300
Salaries and Wages Payable		–0–
Notes Payable (due April 30, 2018)		11,000
Income Taxes Payable		–0–
Interest Payable		–0–
Notes Payable (due in 2023)		35,000
Common Stock		50,000
Retained Earnings		63,600
Dividends	12,000	
Sales Revenue		900,000

	Debit	Credit
Interest Revenue		–0–
Gain on Disposal of Plant Assets		–0–
Bad Debt Expense	–0–	
Cost of Goods Sold	630,000	
Depreciation Expense	–0–	
Income Tax Expense	–0–	
Insurance Expense	–0–	
Interest Expense	–0–	
Other Operating Expenses	61,800	
Amortization Expense	–0–	
Salaries and Wages Expense	110,000	
	$1,161,400	$1,161,400

The following transactions occurred during December.

Dec.	2	Purchased equipment for $16,000, plus sales taxes of $800 (paid in cash).
	2	Milo sold for $3,500 equipment which originally cost $5,000. Accumulated depreciation on this equipment at January 1, 2017, was $1,800; 2017 depreciation prior to the sale of equipment was $825.
	15	Milo sold for $5,000 on account inventory that cost $3,500.
	23	Salaries and wages of $6,600 were paid.

Adjustment data:

1. Milo estimates that uncollectible accounts receivable at year-end are $4,000.
2. The note receivable is a 1-year, 8% note dated April 1, 2017. No interest has been recorded.
3. The balance in prepaid insurance represents payment of a $3,600, 6-month premium on September 1, 2017.
4. The building is being depreciated using the straight-line method over 30 years. The salvage value is $30,000.
5. The equipment owned prior to this year is being depreciated using the straight-line method over 5 years. The salvage value is 10% of cost.
6. The equipment purchased on December 2, 2017, is being depreciated using the straight-line method over 5 years, with a salvage value of $1,800.
7. The patent was acquired on January 1, 2017, and has a useful life of 9 years from that date.
8. Unpaid salaries at December 31, 2017, total $2,200.
9. Both the short-term and long-term notes payable are dated January 1, 2017, and carry a 10% interest rate. All interest is payable in the next 12 months.
10. Income tax expense was $15,000. It was unpaid at December 31.

Instructions

(a) Prepare journal entries for the transactions listed above and adjusting entries.
(b) Prepare an adjusted trial balance at December 31, 2017.
(c) Prepare a 2017 income statement and a 2017 retained earnings statement.
(d) Prepare a December 31, 2017, balance sheet.

(b) Totals $1,205,775
(c) Net income $51,150
(d) Total assets $247,850

ACR9-2 Aberkonkie Corporation prepares quarterly financial statements. The post-closing trial balance at December 31, 2016, is presented below.

ABERKONKIE CORPORATION
Post-Closing Trial Balance
December 31, 2016

	Debit	Credit
Cash	$ 24,300	
Accounts Receivable	22,400	
Allowance for Doubtful Accounts		$ 1,200
Equipment	20,000	
Accumulated Depreciation—Equipment		15,000
Buildings	100,000	
Accumulated Depreciation—Buildings		15,000
Land	20,000	
Accounts Payable		12,370
Common Stock		90,000
Retained Earnings		53,130
	$186,700	$186,700

During the first quarter of 2017, the following transaction occurred:

1. On February 1, Aberkonkie collected fees of $12,000 in advance. The company will perform $1,000 of services each month from February 1, 2017, to January 31, 2018.
2. On February 1, Aberkonkie purchased computer equipment for $9,000 plus sales taxes of $600. $3,000 cash was paid with the rest on account. Check #455 was used.
3. On March 1, Aberkonkie acquired a patent with a 10-year life for $9,600 cash. Check #456 was used.
4. On March 28, Aberkonkie recorded the quarter's sales in a single entry. During this period, Aberkonkie had total sales of $140,000 (not including the sales referred to in item 1 above). All of the sales were on account.
5. On March 29, Aberkonkie collected $133,000 from customers on account.
6. On March 29, Aberkonkie paid $16,370 on accounts payable. Check #457 was used.
7. On March 29, Aberkonkie paid other operating expenses of $97,525. Check #458 was used.
8. On March 31, Aberkonkie wrote off a receivable of $200 for a customer who declared bankruptcy.
9. On March 31, Aberkonkie sold for $1,620 equipment that originally cost $11,000. It had an estimated life of 5 years and salvage of $1,000. Accumulated depreciation as of December 31, 2016, was $8,000 using the straight line method. (*Hint:* Record depreciation on the equipment sold, then record the sale.)

Bank reconciliation data and adjustment data:

1. The company reconciles its bank statement every quarter. Information from the December 31, 2016, bank reconciliation is:

Deposit in transit:	12/30/2016	$5,000
Outstanding checks	#440	3,444
	#452	333
	#453	865
	#454	5,845

The bank statement received for the quarter ended March 31, 2017, is as follows:

Beginning balance per bank	$ 29,787
Deposits: 1/2/2017, $5,000; 2/2/2017, $12,000; 3/30/2017, $133,000	150,000
Checks: #452, $333; #453, $865; #457, $16,370; #458, $97,525	(115,093)
Debit memo: Bank service charge (record as operating expense)	(100)
Ending bank balance	$ 64,594

2. Record revenue earned from item 1 above.
3. $26,000 of accounts receivable at March 31, 2017, are not past due yet. The bad debt percentage for these is 4%. The balance of accounts receivable are past due. The bad debt percentage for these is 23.75%. Record bad debt expense. (*Hint:* You will need to compute the balance in accounts receivable before calculating this.)
4. Depreciation is recorded on the equipment still owned at March 31, 2017. The new equipment purchased in February is being depreciated on a straight-line basis over 5 years and salvage value was estimated at $1,200. The old equipment still owned is being depreciated over a 10-year life using straight-line with no salvage value.
5. Depreciation is recorded on the building on a straight-line basis based on a 30-year life and a salvage value of $10,000.
6. Amortization is recorded on the patent.
7. The income tax rate is 30%. This amount will be paid when the tax return is due in April. (*Hint:* Prepare the income statement up to income before taxes and multiply by 30% to compute the amount.)

Instructions

(a) Record journal entries for transactions 1–9.
(b) Enter the December 31, 2016, balances in ledger accounts using T-accounts.
(c) Post the journal entries to the ledger accounts for items 1–9.
(d) Prepare an unadjusted trial balance at March 31.
(e) Prepare a bank reconciliation in good form.
(f) Journalize and post entries related to bank reconciliation and all adjusting entries.
(g) Prepare an adjusted trial balance.
(h) Prepare an income statement and a retained earnings statement for the quarter ended March 31, 2017, and a classified balance sheet at March 31, 2017.

(d) Trial balance total $320,730
(e) Adjusted balance per bank $44,325
(f) Total assets $196,590

EXPAND YOUR CRITICAL THINKING

Financial Reporting

FINANCIAL REPORTING PROBLEM: Apple Inc.

E **CT9-1** The financial statements of Apple Inc. are presented in Appendix A. Instructions for accessing and using the company's complete annual report, including the notes to the financial statements, are also provided in Appendix A.

Instructions

Answer the following questions.

(a) What were the total cost and book value of property, plant, and equipment at September 27, 2014?

(b) Using the notes to the financial statements, what method or methods of depreciation are used by Apple for financial reporting purposes?

(c) What was the amount of depreciation and amortization expense for each of the 3 years 2012–2014? (*Hint:* Use the statement of cash flows.)

(d) Using the statement of cash flows, what are the amounts of property, plant, and equipment purchased in 2014 and 2013?

(e) Using the notes to the financial statements, explain how Apple accounted for its intangible assets in 2014.

Financial Analysis

COMPARATIVE ANALYSIS PROBLEM: Columbia Sportswear Company vs. VF Corporation

E **CT9-2** The financial statements of Columbia Sportswear Company are presented in Appendix B. Financial statements of VF Corporation are presented in Appendix C. Instructions for accessing and using the companies' complete annual reports, including the notes to the financial statements, are also provided in Appendices B and C, respectively.

Instructions

(a) Based on the information in these financial statements and the accompanying notes and schedules, compute the following values for each company in 2014.

(1) Return on assets.

(2) Profit margin (use "Total Revenue").

(3) Asset turnover.

(b) What conclusions concerning the management of plant assets can be drawn from these data?

Financial Analysis

COMPARATIVE ANALYSIS PROBLEM: Amazon.com, Inc. vs. Wal-Mart Stores, Inc.

E **CT9-3** The financial statements of Amazon.com, Inc. are presented in Appendix D. Financial statements of Wal-Mart Stores, Inc. are presented in Appendix E. Instructions for accessing and using the companies' complete annual reports, including the notes to the financial statements, are also provided in Appendices D and E, respectively.

Instructions

(a) Based on the information in these financial statements and the accompanying notes and schedules, compute the following values for each company for the most recent fiscal year.

(1) Return on assets.

(2) Profit margin (use "Total Revenue").

(3) Asset turnover.

(b) What conclusions concerning the management of plant assets can be drawn from these data?

Financial Analysis

INTERPRETING FINANCIAL STATEMENTS

E **CT9-4** The March 29, 2012, edition of the *Wall Street Journal Online* contains an article by Miguel Bustillo entitled, "Best Buy Forced to Rethink Big Box." The article explains how the 1,100 giant stores, which enabled Best Buy to obtain its position as the largest retailer of electronics, are now reducing the company's profitability and even threatening its survival. The problem is that many customers go to Best Buy stores to see items but

then buy them for less from online retailers. As a result, Best Buy recently announced that it would close 50 stores and switch to smaller stores. However, some analysts think that these changes are not big enough.

Suppose the following data were extracted from the 2017 and 2012 annual reports of Best Buy. (All amounts are in millions.)

	2017	2016	2012	2011
Total assets at year-end	$17,849	$18,302	$11,864	$10,294
Net sales	50,272		30,848	
Net income	1,277		1,140	

Instructions
Using the data above, answer the following questions.

(a) How might the return on assets and asset turnover of Best Buy differ from an online retailer?
(b) Compute the profit margin, asset turnover, and return on assets for 2017 and 2012.
(c) Present the ratios calculated in part (b) in the equation format shown in Illustration 9-22 (page 446).
(d) Discuss the implications of the ratios calculated in parts (b) and (c).

REAL-WORLD FOCUS

CT9-5 ***Purpose:*** Use an annual report to identify a company's plant assets and the depreciation method used. AN

Address: **www.annualreports.com**

Steps
1. Select a particular company.
2. Search by company name.
3. Follow instructions below.

Instructions
Answer the following questions.

(a) What is the name of the company?
(b) What is the Internet address of the annual report?
(c) At fiscal year-end, what is the net amount of its plant assets?
(d) What is the accumulated depreciation?
(e) Which method of depreciation does the company use?

CT9-6 The November 16, 2011, edition of the *Wall Street Journal Online* contains an article by Maxwell Murphy entitled "The Big Number: 51." AN

Instructions
Read the article and answer the following questions.

(a) What do the 51 companies referred to in the title have in common? What implications does this have regarding the fair value of a company's assets?
(b) What significance does the common trait referred to in part (a) have for a company's goodwill?
(c) How does a company get to record goodwill on its books—that is, what must have occurred for goodwill to show up on a company's books?
(d) If these companies write down their goodwill, will this reduce their cash?

DECISION-MAKING ACROSS THE ORGANIZATION

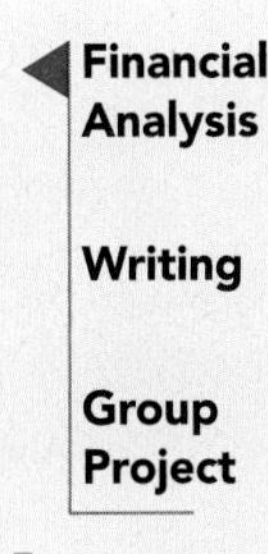

CT9-7 Brady Furniture Corp. is nationally recognized for making high-quality products. Management is concerned that it is not fully exploiting its brand power. Brady's production managers are also concerned because their plants are not operating at anywhere near full capacity. Management is currently considering a proposal to offer a new line of affordable furniture.

Those in favor of the proposal (including the vice president of production) believe that, by offering these new products, the company could attract a clientele that it is not currently servicing. Also, it could operate its plants at full capacity, thus taking better advantage of its assets. E

The vice president of marketing, however, believes that the lower-priced (and lower-margin) product would have a negative impact on the sales of existing products. The vice president believes that $10,000,000 of the sales of the new product will be from customers that would have purchased the more expensive product but switched to the lower-margin product because it was available. (This is often referred to as cannibalization of existing sales.) Top management feels, however, that even with cannibalization, the company's sales will increase and the company will be better off.

The following data are available.

(in thousands)	Current Results	Proposed Results without Cannibalization	Proposed Results with Cannibalization
Sales revenue	$45,000	$60,000	$50,000
Net income	$12,000	$13,500	$12,000
Average total assets	$100,000	$100,000	$100,000

Instructions

(a) Compute Brady's return on assets, profit margin, and asset turnover, both with and without the new product line.

(b) Discuss the implications that your findings in part (a) have for Brady's decision.

(c) Are there any other options that Brady should consider? What impact would each of these have on the above ratios?

COMMUNICATION ACTIVITY

E **CT9-8** The chapter presented some concerns regarding the current accounting standards for research and development expenditures.

Instructions

Assume that you are either (a) the president of a company that is very dependent on ongoing research and development, writing a memo to the FASB complaining about the current accounting standards regarding research and development, or (b) the FASB member defending the current standards regarding research and development. Your memo should address the following questions.

1. By requiring expensing of R&D, do you think companies will spend less on R&D? Why or why not? What are the possible implications for the competitiveness of U.S. companies?
2. If a company makes a commitment to spend money for R&D, it must believe it has future benefits. Shouldn't these costs therefore be capitalized just like the purchase of any long-lived asset that you believe will have future benefits?

ETHICS CASE

E **CT9-9** Clean Aire Anti-Pollution Company is suffering declining sales of its principal product, nonbiodegradable plastic cartons. The president, Wade Truman, instructs his controller, Kate Rollins, to lengthen asset lives to reduce depreciation expense. A processing line of automated plastic extruding equipment, purchased for $3.5 million in January 2017, was originally estimated to have a useful life of 8 years and a salvage value of $400,000. Depreciation has been recorded for 2 years on that basis. Wade wants the estimated life changed to 12 years total and the straight-line method continued. Kate is hesitant to make the change, believing it is unethical to increase net income in this manner. Wade says, "Hey, the life is only an estimate, and I've heard that our competition uses a 12-year life on their production equipment."

Instructions

(a) Who are the stakeholders in this situation?

(b) Is the proposed change in asset life unethical, or is it simply a good business practice by an astute president?

(c) What is the effect of Wade's proposed change on income before taxes in the year of change?

ALL ABOUT YOU

AN **CT9-10** A company's tradename is a very important asset to the company, as it creates immediate product identification. Companies invest substantial sums to ensure that their product is well-known to the consumer. Test your knowledge of who owns some famous brands and their impact on the financial statements.

Instructions

(a) Provide an answer to the four multiple-choice questions below.
   (1) Which company owns both Taco Bell and Pizza Hut?
      (a) McDonald's. (b) CKE. (c) Yum Brands. (d) Wendy's.
   (2) Dairy Queen belongs to:
      (a) Breyer. (b) Berkshire Hathaway. (c) GE. (d) The Coca-Cola Company.
   (3) Phillip Morris, the cigarette maker, is owned by:
      (a) Altria. (b) GE. (c) Boeing. (d) ExxonMobil.
   (4) AOL, a major Internet provider, belongs to:
      (a) Microsoft. (b) Cisco. (c) NBC. (d) Time Warner.

(b) How do you think the value of these brands is reported on the appropriate company's balance sheet?

FASB CODIFICATION ACTIVITY

CT9-11 If your school has a subscription to the FASB Codification, go to **http://aaahq.org/ascLogin.cfm** to log in and prepare responses to the following. AP

(a) What does it mean to capitalize an item?
(b) What is the definition provided for an intangible asset?
(c) Your great-uncle, who is a CPA, is impressed that you are taking an accounting class. Based on his experience, he believes that depreciation is something that companies do based on past practice, not on the basis of authoritative guidance. Provide the authoritative literature to support the practice of fixed-asset depreciation.

CONSIDERING PEOPLE, PLANET, AND PROFIT

CT9-12 The March 6, 2012, edition of the *Wall Street Journal Online* contains an article by David Kesmodel entitled "Air War: 'Winglet' Versus 'Sharklet'." This article demonstrates how a company focused on green technology has also been profitable. E

Instructions

Read the article and answer the following questions.

(a) Why did Airbus file a lawsuit against Aviation Partners?
(b) What are the percentage fuel savings provided by Aviation Partners' Winglets on Boeing jetliners? How much total jet fuel did Aviation Partners say that its Winglets have provided at the time the article was written?
(c) Describe the history of the relationship between Aviation Partners and Airbus, and the development of the Airbus Sharklet.
(d) What would be the likely accounting implications if Aviation Partners were to lose the lawsuit?

A Look at IFRS

LEARNING OBJECTIVE  7 **Compare the accounting for long-lived assets under GAAP and IFRS.**

IFRS follows most of the same principles as GAAP in the accounting for property, plant, and equipment. There are, however, some significant differences in the implementation. IFRS allows the use of revaluation of property, plant, and equipment, and it also requires the use of component depreciation. In addition, there are some significant differences in the accounting for both intangible assets and impairments.

KEY POINTS

The following are the key similarities and differences between GAAP and IFRS as related to the recording process for long-lived assets.

Similarities

- The definition for plant assets for both IFRS and GAAP is essentially the same.
- Both IFRS and GAAP follow the historical cost principle when accounting for property, plant, and equipment at date of acquisition. Cost consists of all expenditures necessary to acquire the asset and make it ready for its intended use.
- Under both IFRS and GAAP, interest costs incurred during construction are capitalized. Recently, IFRS converged to GAAP requirements in this area.
- The accounting for subsequent expenditures (such as ordinary repairs and additions) is essentially the same under IFRS and GAAP.
- IFRS also views depreciation as an allocation of cost over an asset's useful life. IFRS permits the same depreciation methods (e.g., straight-line, accelerated, and units-of-activity) as GAAP.
- Under both GAAP and IFRS, changes in the depreciation method used and changes in useful life are handled in current and future periods. Prior periods are not affected. GAAP recently conformed to international standards in the accounting for changes in depreciation methods.
- The accounting for plant asset disposals is essentially the same under IFRS and GAAP.
- The definition of intangible assets is essentially the same under IFRS and GAAP.
- The accounting for exchanges of nonmonetary assets has recently converged between IFRS and GAAP. GAAP now requires that gains on exchanges of nonmonetary assets be recognized if the exchange has commercial substance. This is the same framework used in IFRS.

Differences

- IFRS uses the term **residual value** rather than salvage value to refer to an owner's estimate of an asset's value at the end of its useful life for that owner.
- IFRS allows companies to revalue plant assets to fair value at the reporting date. Companies that choose to use the revaluation framework must follow revaluation procedures. If revaluation is used, it must be applied to all assets in a class of assets. Assets that are experiencing rapid price changes must be revalued on an annual basis, otherwise less frequent revaluation is acceptable.
- IFRS requires component depreciation. **Component depreciation** specifies that any significant parts of a depreciable asset that have different estimated useful lives should be separately depreciated. Component depreciation is allowed under GAAP but is seldom used.
- As in GAAP, under IFRS the costs associated with research and development are segregated into the two components. Costs in the research phase are always expensed under both IFRS and GAAP. Under IFRS, however, costs in the development phase are capitalized as Development Costs once technological feasibility is achieved.
- IFRS permits revaluation of intangible assets (except for goodwill). GAAP prohibits revaluation of intangible assets.

LOOKING TO THE FUTURE

The IASB and FASB have identified a project that would consider expanded recognition of internally generated intangible assets. IFRS permits more recognition of intangibles compared to GAAP.

IFRS Practice

IFRS SELF-TEST QUESTIONS

1. Which of the following statements is **correct**?
   (a) Both IFRS and GAAP permit revaluation of property, plant, and equipment and intangible assets (except for goodwill).
   (b) IFRS permits revaluation of property, plant, and equipment and intangible assets (except for goodwill).
   (c) Both IFRS and GAAP permit revaluation of property, plant, and equipment but not intangible assets.
   (d) GAAP permits revaluation of property, plant, and equipment but not intangible assets.
2. Research and development costs are:
   (a) expensed under GAAP.
   (b) expensed under IFRS.
   (c) expensed under both GAAP and IFRS.
   (d) None of the above.

IFRS EXERCISES

IFRS9-1 What is component depreciation, and when must it be used?

IFRS9-2 What is revaluation of plant assets? When should revaluation be applied?

IFRS9-3 Some product development expenditures are recorded as development expenses and others as development costs. Explain the difference between these accounts and how a company decides which classification is appropriate.

INTERNATIONAL FINANCIAL STATEMENT ANALYSIS: Louis Vuitton

IFRS9-4 The financial statements of Louis Vuitton are presented in Appendix F. Instructions for accessing and using the company's complete annual report, including the notes to its financial statements, are also provided in Appendix F.

Instructions
Use the company's annual report to answer the following questions.

(a) According to the notes to the financial statements, what method or methods does the company use to depreciate "property, plant, and equipment?" What useful lives does it use to depreciate property, plant, and equipment?
(b) Using the notes to the financial statements, explain how the company accounted for its intangible assets with indefinite lives.
(c) Using the notes to the financial statements, determine (1) the balance in Accumulated Amortization and Impairment for intangible assets (other than goodwill), and (2) the balance in Depreciation (and impairment) for property, plant, and equipment.

Answers to IFRS Self-Test Questions
1. b **2.** a

10

Reporting and Analyzing Liabilities

CHAPTER PREVIEW

The Feature Story suggests that General Motors (GM) and Ford accumulated tremendous amounts of debt in their pursuit of auto industry dominance. It is unlikely that they could have grown so large without this debt, but at times the debt threatened their very existence. Given this risk, why do companies borrow money? Why do they sometimes borrow short-term and other times long-term? Besides bank borrowings, what other kinds of debts do companies incur? In this chapter, we address these issues.

CHAPTER OUTLINE

LEARNING OBJECTIVES		PRACTICE
1 Explain how to account for current liabilities.	• What is a current liability? • Notes payable • Sales taxes payable • Unearned revenues • Current maturities of long-term debt • Payroll and payroll taxes payable	**DO IT!** 1 1a Current Liabilities 1b Wages and Payroll Taxes
2 Describe the major characteristics of bonds.	• Types of bonds • Issuing procedures • Determining the market price of bonds	**DO IT!** 2 Bond Terminology
3 Explain how to account for bond transactions.	• Issuing bonds at face value • Discount or premium on bonds • Issuing bonds at a discount • Issuing bonds at a premium • Redeeming bonds at maturity • Redeeming bonds before maturity	**DO IT!** 3 3a Bond Issuance 3b Bond Redemption
4 Discuss how liabilities are reported and analyzed.	• Presentation • Analysis	**DO IT!** 4 Analyzing Liabilities

Go to the ***REVIEW AND PRACTICE*** section at the end of the chapter for a targeted summary and exercises with solutions.

Visit **WileyPLUS** for additional tutorials and practice opportunities.

© Henrik Jonsson/iStockphoto

FEATURE STORY

And Then There Were Two

Debt can help a company acquire the things it needs to grow. But, it is often the very thing that can also kill a company. A brief history of Maxwell Car Company illustrates the role of debt in the U.S. auto industry. In 1920, Maxwell Car Company was on the brink of financial ruin. Because it was unable to pay its bills, its creditors stepped in and took over. They hired a former General Motors (GM) executive named Walter Chrysler to reorganize the company. By 1925, he had taken over the company and renamed it Chrysler. By 1933, Chrysler was booming, with sales surpassing even those of Ford.

But the next few decades saw Chrysler make a series of blunders. By 1980, with its creditors pounding at the gates, Chrysler was again on the brink of financial ruin.

At that point, Chrysler brought in a former Ford executive named Lee Iacocca to save the company. Iacocca argued that the United States could not afford to let Chrysler fail because of the loss of jobs. He convinced the federal government to grant loan guarantees—promises that if Chrysler failed to pay its creditors, the government would pay them. Iacocca then streamlined operations and brought out some profitable products. Chrysler repaid all of its government-guaranteed loans by 1983, seven years ahead of the scheduled final payment.

To compete in today's global vehicle market, you must be big—really big. So in 1998, Chrysler merged with German automaker Daimler-Benz to form DaimlerChrysler. For a time, this left just two U.S.-based auto manufacturers—GM and Ford. But in 2007, DaimlerChrysler sold 81% of Chrysler to Cerberus, an investment group, to provide much-needed cash infusions to the automaker. In 2009, Daimler turned over its remaining stake to Cerberus. Three days later, Chrysler filed for bankruptcy. But by 2010, it was beginning to show signs of a turnaround.

The car companies are giants. GM and Ford typically rank among the top five U.S. firms in total assets. But GM and Ford accumulated truckloads of debt on their way to getting big. Although debt made it possible to get so big, the Chrysler story, and GM's recent bankruptcy, make it clear that debt can also threaten a company's survival.

LEARNING OBJECTIVE ▶ 1 **Explain how to account for current liabilities.**

WHAT IS A CURRENT LIABILITY?

Liabilities are often defined as "creditors' claims on total assets" and as "existing debts and obligations." Companies must settle or pay these claims, debts, and obligations at some time in the future by transferring assets or services. The future date on which they are due or payable (the maturity date) is a significant feature of liabilities.

As explained in Chapter 2, a **current liability** is a debt that a company reasonably expects to pay (1) from existing current assets or through the creation of other current liabilities, and (2) within one year or the operating cycle, whichever is longer. Debts that do not meet both criteria are **long-term liabilities**.

Financial statement users want to know whether a company's obligations are current or long-term. A company that has more current liabilities than current assets often lacks liquidity, or short-term debt-paying ability. In addition, users want to know the types of liabilities a company has. If a company declares bankruptcy, a specific, predetermined order of payment to creditors exists. Thus, the amount and type of liabilities are of critical importance.

▼ **HELPFUL HINT**
In previous chapters, we explained the entries for accounts payable and the adjusting entries for some current liabilities.

The different types of current liabilities include notes payable, accounts payable, unearned revenues, and accrued liabilities such as taxes, salaries and wages, and interest. In the sections that follow, we discuss a few of the common types of current liabilities.

NOTES PAYABLE

Companies record obligations in the form of written notes as **notes payable**. They often use notes payable instead of accounts payable because notes payable provide written documentation of the obligation in case legal remedies are needed to collect the debt. Companies frequently issue notes payable to meet short-term financing needs. Notes payable usually require the borrower to pay interest.

Notes are issued for varying periods of time. **Those due for payment within one year of the balance sheet date are usually classified as current liabilities.**

To illustrate the accounting for notes payable, assume that on September 1, 2017, Cole Williams Co. signs a $100,000, 12%, four-month note maturing on January 1 with First National Bank. When a company issues an interest-bearing note, the amount of assets it receives generally equals the note's face value. Cole Williams Co. therefore will receive $100,000 cash and will make the following journal entry.

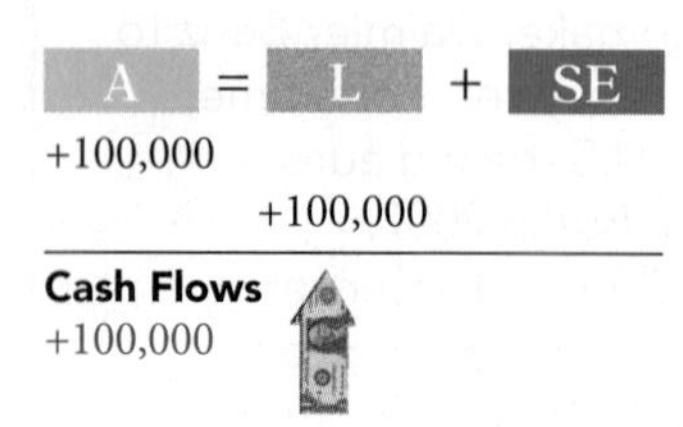

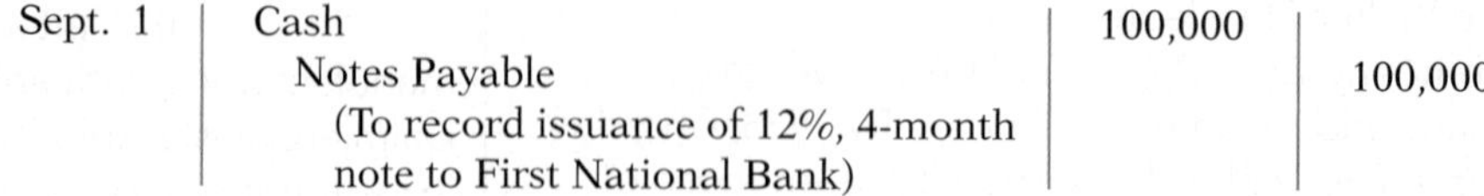

Sept. 1	Cash	100,000	
	Notes Payable		100,000
	(To record issuance of 12%, 4-month note to First National Bank)		

Interest accrues over the life of the note, and the issuer must periodically record that accrual. (You may find it helpful to review the discussion of interest computations that was provided in Chapter 8, page 388, with regard to notes receivable.) If Cole Williams Co. prepares financial statements annually, it makes an adjusting entry at December 31 to recognize four months of interest expense and interest payable of $4,000 ($100,000 × 12% × $\frac{4}{12}$):

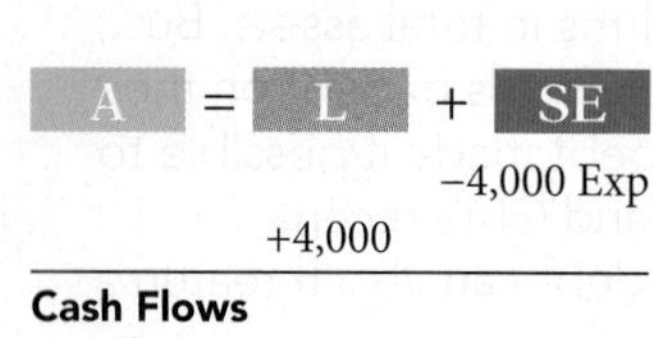

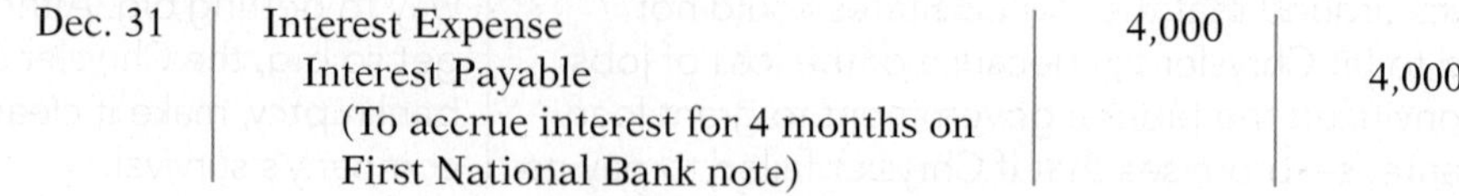

Dec. 31	Interest Expense	4,000	
	Interest Payable		4,000
	(To accrue interest for 4 months on First National Bank note)		

In the December 31 financial statements, the current liabilities section of the balance sheet will show notes payable $100,000 and interest payable $4,000. In addition, the company will report interest expense of $4,000 under "Other expenses and losses" in the income statement.

At maturity (January 1), Cole Williams Co. must pay the face value of the note ($100,000) plus $4,000 interest ($100,000 × 12% × $\frac{4}{12}$). It records payment of the note and accrued interest as follows.

Jan. 1	Notes Payable	100,000	
	Interest Payable	4,000	
	Cash		104,000
	(To record payment of First National Bank interest-bearing note and accrued interest at maturity)		

A	=	L	+	SE
		−100,000		
		−4,000		
−104,000				

Cash Flows
−104,000

Appendix 10C at the end of this chapter discusses the accounting for long-term installment notes payable.

SALES TAXES PAYABLE

Many of the products we purchase at retail stores are subject to sales taxes. Many states are now implementing sales taxes on purchases made on the Internet as well. Sales taxes are expressed as a percentage of the sales price. The selling company collects the tax from the customer when the sale occurs and periodically (usually monthly) remits the collections to the state's department of revenue. Collecting sales taxes is important. For example, the State of New York recently sued Sprint Corporation for $300 million for its alleged failure to collect sales taxes on phone calls.

Under most state laws, the selling company must enter separately on the cash register the amount of the sale and the amount of the sales tax collected. (Gasoline sales are a major exception.) The company then uses the cash register readings to credit Sales Revenue and Sales Taxes Payable. For example, if the March 25 cash register readings for Cooley Grocery show sales of $10,000 and sales taxes of $600 (sales tax rate of 6%), the journal entry is as follows.

▼ HELPFUL HINT
Check your sales receipts from local retailers to see whether the sales tax is computed separately.

Mar. 25	Cash	10,600	
	Sales Revenue		10,000
	Sales Taxes Payable		600
	(To record daily sales and sales taxes)		

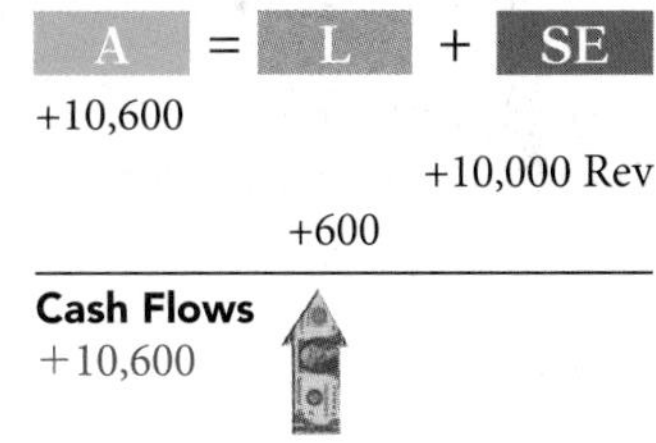

When the company remits the taxes to the taxing agency, it decreases (debits) Sales Taxes Payable and decreases (credits) Cash. The company does not report sales taxes as an expense. It simply forwards to the government the amount paid by the customer. Thus, Cooley Grocery serves only as a **collection agent** for the taxing authority.

Sometimes companies do not enter sales taxes separately on the cash register. To determine the amount of sales in such cases, divide total receipts by 100% plus the sales tax percentage. For example, assume that Cooley Grocery enters total receipts of $10,600. Because the amount received from the sale is equal to the sales price (100%) plus 6% of sales, or 1.06 times the sales total, we can compute sales as follows: $10,600 ÷ 1.06 = $10,000. Thus, we can find the sales tax amount of $600 by either (1) subtracting sales from total receipts ($10,600 − $10,000) or (2) multiplying sales by the sales tax rate ($10,000 × 6%).

UNEARNED REVENUES

A magazine publisher such as Sports Illustrated collects cash when customers place orders for magazine subscriptions. An airline company such as American Airlines often receives cash when it sells tickets for future flights. Season tickets for concerts, sporting events, and theatre programs are also paid for in advance.

How do companies account for unearned revenues that are received before goods are delivered or services are performed?

1. When the company receives an advance, it increases (debits) Cash and increases (credits) a current liability account identifying the source of the unearned revenue.
2. When the company recognizes revenue, it decreases (debits) the unearned revenue account and increases (credits) a revenue account.

To illustrate, assume that Superior University sells 10,000 season football tickets at $50 each for its five-game home schedule. The university makes the following entry for the sale of season tickets.

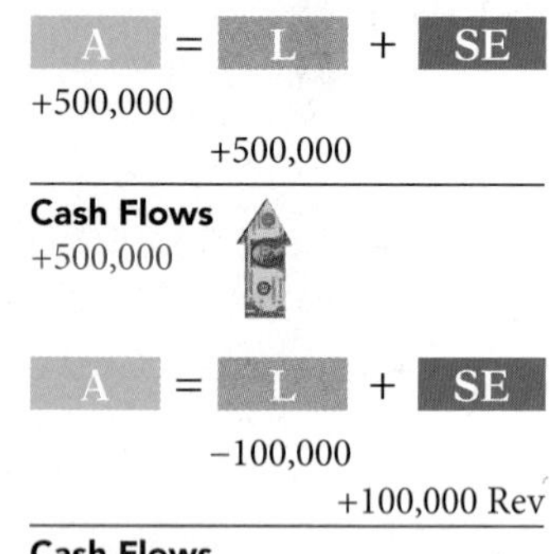

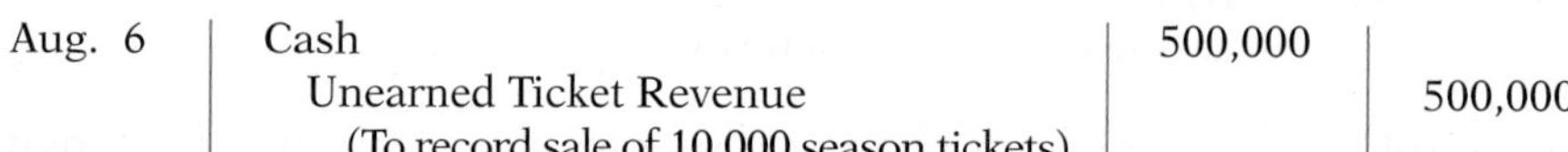

Aug. 6	Cash	500,000	
	Unearned Ticket Revenue		500,000
	(To record sale of 10,000 season tickets)		

As each game is completed, Superior records the recognition of $100,000 ($500,000 ÷ 5) of revenue with the following entry.

A = L + SE
−100,000 +100,000 Rev

Cash Flows
no effect

Sept. 7	Unearned Ticket Revenue	100,000	
	Ticket Revenue		100,000
	(To record football ticket revenues)		

The account Unearned Ticket Revenue represents unearned revenue, and Superior reports it as a current liability. As the school recognizes revenue, it reclassifies the amount from unearned revenue to Ticket Revenue. Unearned revenue is material for some companies. In the airline industry, tickets sold for future flights often represent almost 50% of total current liabilities. At United Air Lines, unearned ticket revenue is its largest current liability, recently amounting to more than $1 billion.

Illustration 10-1 shows specific unearned revenue and revenue accounts used in selected types of businesses.

ILLUSTRATION 10-1
Unearned revenue and revenue accounts

Type of Business	Account Title	
	Unearned Revenue	**Revenue**
Airline	Unearned Ticket Revenue	Ticket Revenue
Magazine publisher	Unearned Subscription Revenue	Subscription Revenue
Hotel	Unearned Rental Revenue	Rental Revenue

CURRENT MATURITIES OF LONG-TERM DEBT

Companies often have a portion of long-term debt that comes due in the current year. As an example, assume that Wendy Construction issues a five-year, interest-bearing $25,000 note on January 1, 2016. This note specifies that each January 1, starting January 1, 2017, Wendy should pay $5,000 of the note. When the company prepares financial statements on December 31, 2016, it should report $5,000 as a current liability and $20,000 as a long-term liability. (The $5,000 amount is the portion of the note that is due to be paid within the next 12 months.) Companies often identify current maturities of long-term debt on the balance sheet as **long-term debt due within one year**. In a recent year, General Motors had $724 million of such debt.

It is not necessary to prepare an adjusting entry to recognize the current maturity of long-term debt. At the balance sheet date, all obligations due within one year are classified as current, and all other obligations are long-term.

DO IT! ▶1a Current Liabilities

You and several classmates are studying for the next accounting examination. They ask you to answer the following questions.

1. If cash is borrowed on a $50,000, 6-month, 12% note on September 1, how much interest expense would be incurred by December 31?
2. The cash register total including sales taxes is $23,320, and the sales tax rate is 6%. What is the sales taxes payable?
3. If $15,000 is collected in advance on November 1 for 3 months' rent, what amount of rent revenue should be recognized by December 31?

Action Plan

✔ Use the interest formula: Face value of note × Annual interest rate × Time in terms of one year.

✔ Divide total receipts by 100% plus the tax rate to determine sales; then subtract sales from the total receipts.

✔ Determine what fraction of the total unearned rent should be recognized this year.

SOLUTION

1. $50,000 × 12% × 4/12 = $2,000
2. $23,320 ÷ 1.06 = $22,000; $23,320 − $22,000 = $1,320
3. $15,000 × 2/3 = $10,000

Related exercise material: **BE10-2, BE10-3, BE10-4, DO IT! 10-1a, E10-1, E10-2, E10-3, E10-4, E10-6,** and **E10-7.**

PAYROLL AND PAYROLL TAXES PAYABLE

Assume that Susan Alena works 40 hours this week for Pepitone Inc., earning a wage of $10 per hour. Will Susan receive a $400 check at the end of the week? Not likely. The reason: Pepitone is required to withhold amounts from her wages to pay various governmental authorities. For example, Pepitone will withhold amounts for Social Security taxes[1] and for federal and state income taxes. If these withholdings total $100, Susan will receive a check for only $300. Illustration 10-2 summarizes the types of payroll deductions that normally occur for most companies.

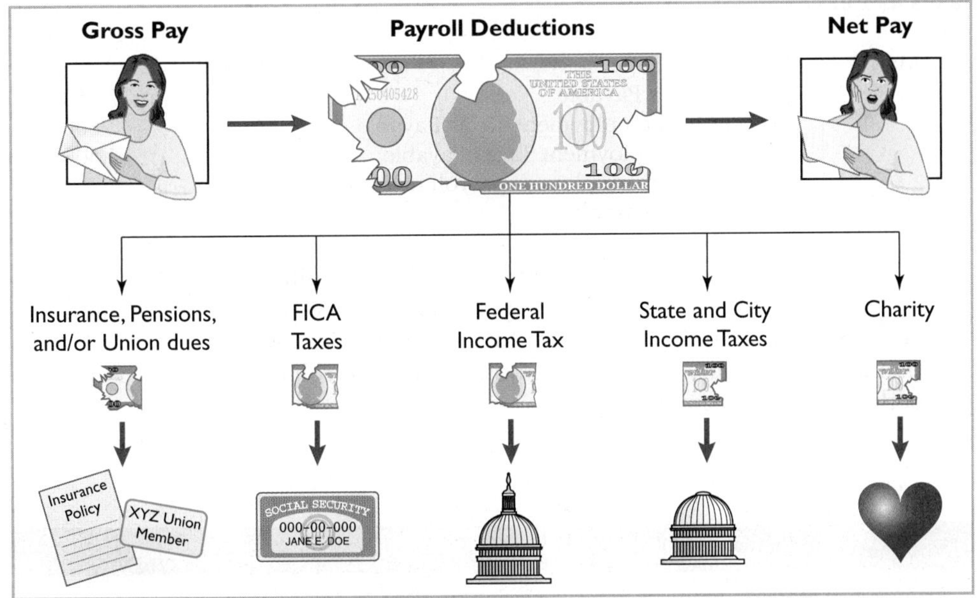

ILLUSTRATION 10-2
Payroll deductions

[1]Social Security taxes are commonly called FICA taxes. In 1937, Congress enacted the Federal Insurance Contribution Act (FICA). As can be seen in the journal entry and the payroll tax journal entry on the next page, the employee and employer must make equal contributions to Social Security. The Social Security rate in 2014 was 7.65%. *Our examples and homework use 7.65%.*

As a result of these deductions, companies withhold from employee paychecks amounts that must be paid to other parties. Pepitone therefore has incurred a liability to pay these third parties and must report this liability in its balance sheet.

As a second illustration, assume that Cargo Corporation records its payroll for the week of March 7 with the journal entry shown below.

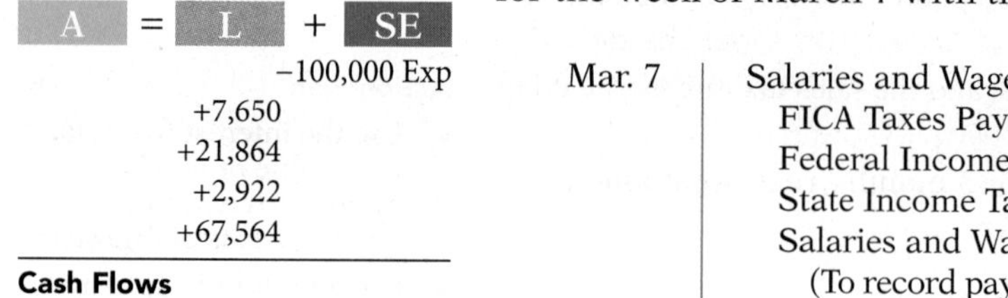

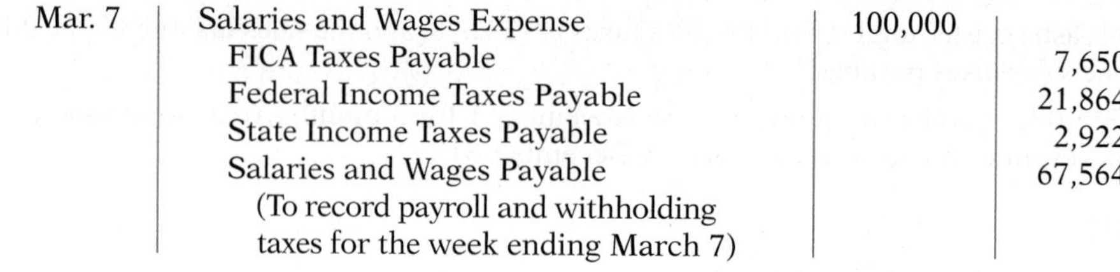

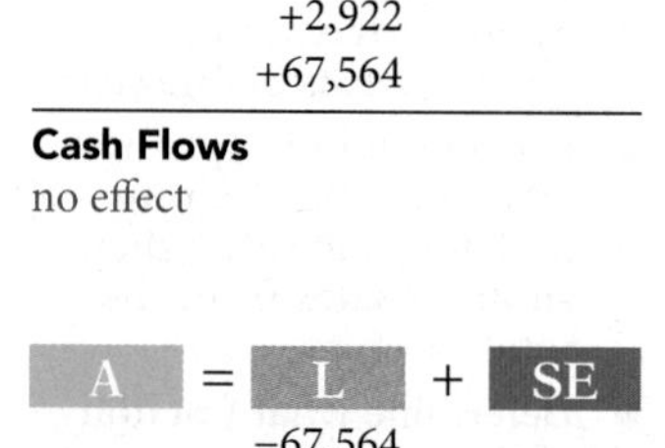

A	=	L	+	SE
				−100,000 Exp
		+7,650		
		+21,864		
		+2,922		
		+67,564		

Cash Flows
no effect

Mar. 7	Salaries and Wages Expense	100,000	
	FICA Taxes Payable		7,650
	Federal Income Taxes Payable		21,864
	State Income Taxes Payable		2,922
	Salaries and Wages Payable		67,564
	(To record payroll and withholding taxes for the week ending March 7)		

Cargo then records payment of this payroll on March 7 as follows.

A	=	L	+	SE
		−67,564		
−67,564				

Cash Flows
−67,564

Mar. 7	Salaries and Wages Payable	67,564	
	Cash		67,564
	(To record payment of the March 7 payroll)		

In this case, Cargo reports $100,000 in salaries and wages expense. In addition, it reports liabilities for the salaries and wages payable as well as liabilities to governmental agencies. Rather than pay the employees $100,000, Cargo instead must withhold the taxes and make the tax payments directly. In summary, Cargo is essentially serving as a tax collector.

In addition to the liabilities incurred as a result of withholdings, employers also incur a second type of payroll-related liability. With every payroll, the employer incurs liabilities to pay various **payroll taxes** levied upon the employer. These payroll taxes include the **employer's share** of Social Security (FICA) taxes and state and federal unemployment taxes. Based on Cargo's $100,000 payroll, the company would record the employer's expense and liability for these payroll taxes as follows.

A	=	L	+	SE
				−13,850 Exp
		+7,650		
		+800		
		+5,400		

Cash Flows
no effect

Mar. 7	Payroll Tax Expense	13,850	
	FICA Taxes Payable		7,650
	Federal Unemployment Taxes Payable		800
	State Unemployment Taxes Payable		5,400
	(To record employer's payroll taxes on March 7 payroll)		

Companies classify the payroll and payroll tax liability accounts as current liabilities because they must be paid to employees or remitted to taxing authorities periodically and in the near term. Taxing authorities impose substantial fines and penalties on employers if the withholding and payroll taxes are not computed correctly and paid on time.

ANATOMY OF A FRAUD

Art was a custodial supervisor for a large school district. The district was supposed to employ between 35 and 40 regular custodians, as well as 3 or 4 substitute custodians to fill in when regular custodians were absent. Instead, in addition to the regular custodians, Art "hired" 77 substitutes. In fact, almost none of these people worked for the district. Instead, Art submitted time cards for these people, collected their checks at the district office, and personally distributed the checks to the "employees." If a substitute's check was for $1,200, that person would cash the check, keep $200, and pay Art $1,000.

Total take: $150,000

THE MISSING CONTROLS

Human resource controls. Thorough background checks should be performed. No employees should begin work until they have been approved by the Board of Education and entered into the payroll system. No employees should be entered into the payroll system until they have been approved by a supervisor. All paychecks should be distributed directly to employees at the official school locations by designated employees or direct-deposited into approved employee bank accounts.

Independent internal verification. Budgets should be reviewed monthly to identify situations where actual costs significantly exceed budgeted amounts.

Source: Adapted from Wells, *Fraud Casebook* (2007), pp. 164–171.

DO IT! 1b Wages and Payroll Taxes

During the month of September, Lake Corporation's employees earned wages of $60,000. Withholdings related to these wages were $3,500 for Social Security (FICA), $6,500 for federal income tax, and $2,000 for state income tax. Costs incurred for unemployment taxes were $90 for federal and $150 for state.

Prepare the September 30 journal entries for (a) salaries and wages expense and salaries and wages payable, assuming that all September wages will be paid in October, and (b) the company's payroll tax expense.

SOLUTION

(a) To determine wages payable, reduce wages expense by the withholdings for FICA, federal income tax, and state income tax.

Date	Account	Debit	Credit
Sept. 30	Salaries and Wages Expense	60,000	
	FICA Taxes Payable		3,500
	Federal Income Taxes Payable		6,500
	State Income Taxes Payable		2,000
	Salaries and Wages Payable		48,000

(b) Payroll taxes would be for the company's share of FICA, as well as for federal and state unemployment tax.

Date	Account	Debit	Credit
Sept. 30	Payroll Tax Expense	3,740	
	FICA Taxes Payable		3,500
	Federal Unemployment Taxes Payable		90
	State Unemployment Taxes Payable		150

Action Plan

✔ Remember that wages earned are an expense to the company, but withholdings reduce the amount due to be paid to the employee.

✔ Payroll taxes are taxes the company incurs related to its employees.

Related exercise material: **BE10-5, BE10-6, DO IT! 10-1b,** and **E10-5.**

LEARNING OBJECTIVE 2 Describe the major characteristics of bonds.

Long-term liabilities are obligations that a company expects to pay more than one year in the future. In this section, we explain the accounting for the principal types of obligations reported in the long-term liabilities section of the balance sheet. These obligations often are in the form of bonds or long-term notes.

Bonds are a form of interest-bearing note payable issued by corporations, universities, and governmental agencies. Bonds, like common stock, are sold in small denominations (usually $1,000 or multiples of $1,000). As a result, bonds attract many investors. When a corporation issues bonds, it is borrowing money. The person who buys the bonds (the bondholder) is investing in bonds.

TYPES OF BONDS

Bonds may have different features. In the following sections, we describe some commonly issued types of bonds.

Convertible Bonds

Callable Bonds

Secured and Unsecured Bonds

Secured bonds have specific assets of the issuer pledged as collateral for the bonds. **Unsecured bonds** are issued against the general credit of the borrower. Large corporations with good credit ratings use unsecured bonds extensively. For example, at one time DuPont reported more than $2 billion of unsecured bonds outstanding.

Convertible and Callable Bonds

Bonds that can be converted into common stock at the bondholder's option are **convertible bonds**. Bonds that the issuing company can redeem (buy back) at a stated dollar amount prior to maturity are **callable bonds**. Convertible bonds have features that are attractive both to bondholders and to the issuer. The conversion feature often gives bondholders an opportunity to benefit if the market price of the common stock increases substantially. Furthermore, until conversion, the bondholder receives interest on the bond. For the issuer, the bonds sell at a higher price and pay a lower rate of interest than comparable debt securities that do not have a conversion option. Many corporations, such as USAir, United States Steel Corp., and General Motors Corporation, have issued convertible bonds.

ISSUING PROCEDURES

A **bond certificate** is issued to the investor to provide evidence of the investor's claim against the company. As Illustration 10-3 (page 487) shows, the bond certificate provides information such as the name of the company that issued the bonds, the face value of the bonds, the maturity date of the bonds, and the contractual interest rate. The **face value** is the amount of principal due at the maturity date. The **maturity date** is the date that the final payment is due to the investor from the issuing company. The **contractual interest rate** is the rate used to determine the amount of cash interest the issuer pays and the investor receives. Usually, the contractual rate is stated as an annual rate.

ALTERNATIVE TERMINOLOGY
The contractual rate is often referred to as the *stated rate*.

DETERMINING THE MARKET PRICE OF BONDS

Same dollars at different times are not equal.

If your company needed financing and wanted to attract investors to purchase its bonds, how would the market set the price for these bonds? To be more specific, assume that Coronet, Inc. issues a zero-interest (pays no interest) bond with a face value of $1,000,000 due in 20 years. For this bond, the only cash Coronet pays to bond investors is $1 million at the end of 20 years. Would investors pay $1 million for this bond? We hope not because $1 million received 20 years from now is not the same as $1 million received today.

The term **time value of money** is used to indicate the relationship between time and money—that a dollar received today is worth more than a dollar promised at some time in the future. If you had $1 million today, you would invest it and earn interest so that at the end of 20 years, your investment would be worth much more than $1 million. Thus, if someone is going to pay you $1 million 20 years from now, you would want to find its equivalent today, or its **present value**. In other words, you would want to determine the value today of the amount to be received in the future after taking into account current interest rates.

The current market price (present value) of a bond is therefore a function of three factors: (1) the dollar amounts to be received, (2) the length of time until the amounts are received, and (3) the market interest rate. The **market interest rate** is the rate investors demand for loaning funds.

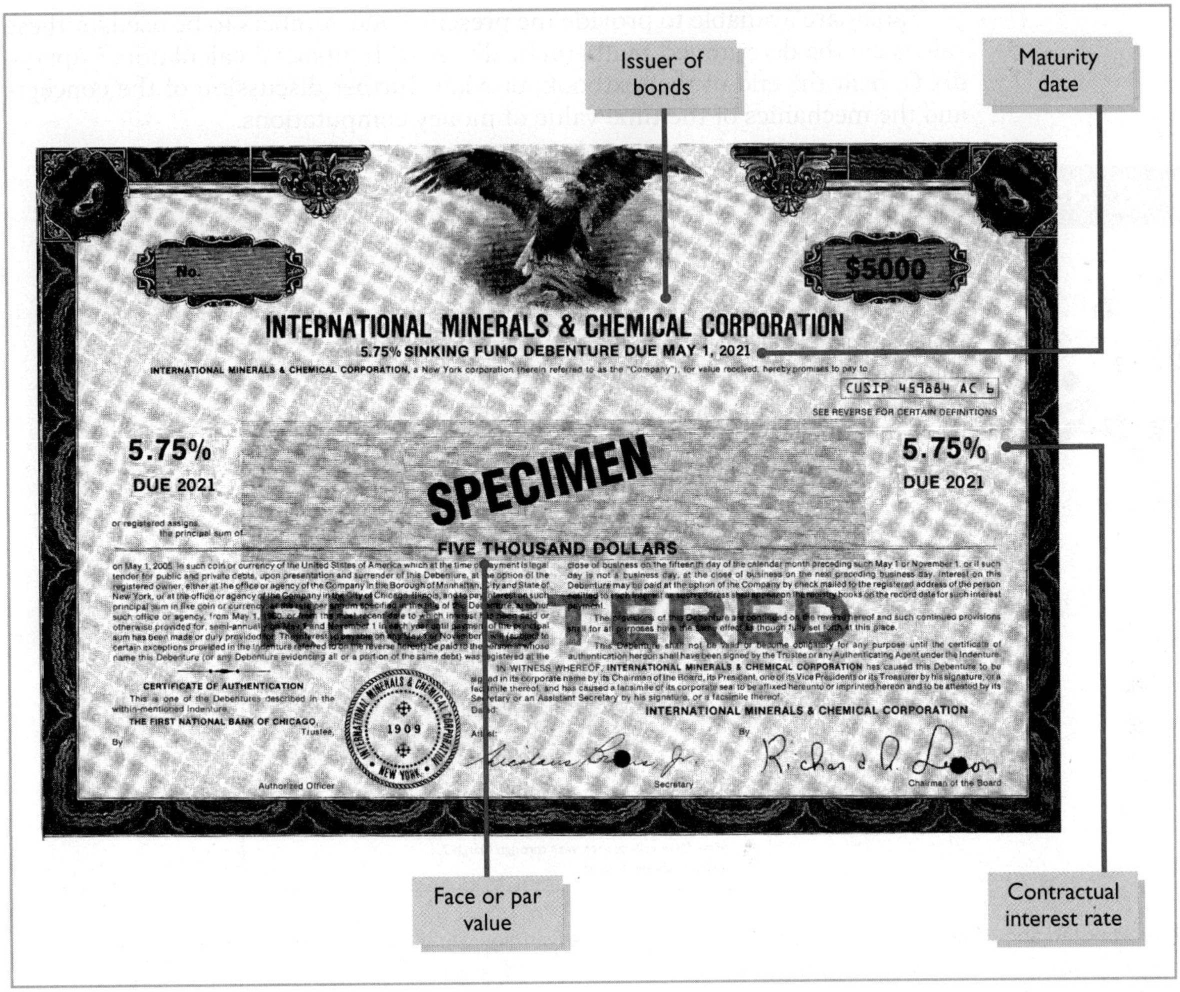

Issuer of bonds
Maturity date
$5000
INTERNATIONAL MINERALS & CHEMICAL CORPORATION
5.75% SINKING FUND DEBENTURE DUE MAY 1, 2021
5.75%
DUE 2021
5.75%
DUE 2021
SPECIMEN
FIVE THOUSAND DOLLARS
Face or par value
Contractual interest rate

ILLUSTRATION 10-3
Bond certificate

To illustrate, assume that Acropolis Company on January 1, 2017, issues \$100,000 of 9% bonds, due in five years, with interest payable annually at year-end. The purchaser of the bonds would receive the following two types of cash payments: (1) **principal** of \$100,000 to be paid at maturity, and (2) five \$9,000 **interest payments** (\$100,000 × 9%) over the term of the bonds. Illustration 10-4 shows a time diagram depicting both cash flows.

$100,000 Principal
$9,000
$9,000
$9,000
$9,000
$9,000 Interest
0
1
2
3
4
5
5-year period

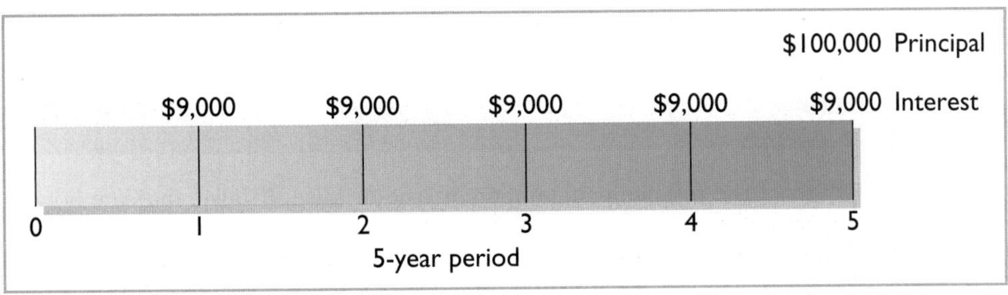

ILLUSTRATION 10-4
Time diagram depicting cash flows

The current market price of a bond is equal to the present value of all the future cash payments promised by the bond. Illustration 10-5 lists and totals the present values of these amounts, assuming the market rate of interest is 9%.

ILLUSTRATION 10-5
Computing the market price of bonds

Present value of \$100,000 received in 5 years	\$ 64,993
Present value of \$9,000 received annually for 5 years	35,007
Market price of bonds	**\$100,000**

Tables are available to provide the present value numbers to be used, or these values can be determined mathematically or with financial calculators.[2] Appendix G, near the end of the textbook, provides further discussion of the concepts and the mechanics of the time value of money computations.

INVESTOR INSIGHT

© alphaspirit/Shutterstock

Running Hot!

Recently, the market for bonds was running hot. For example, consider these two large deals: Apple Inc. sold $17 billion of debt, which at the time was the largest corporate bond ever sold. But shortly thereafter, it was beat by Verizon Communications Inc., which sold $49 billion of debt. The following chart highlights the increased issuance of bonds.

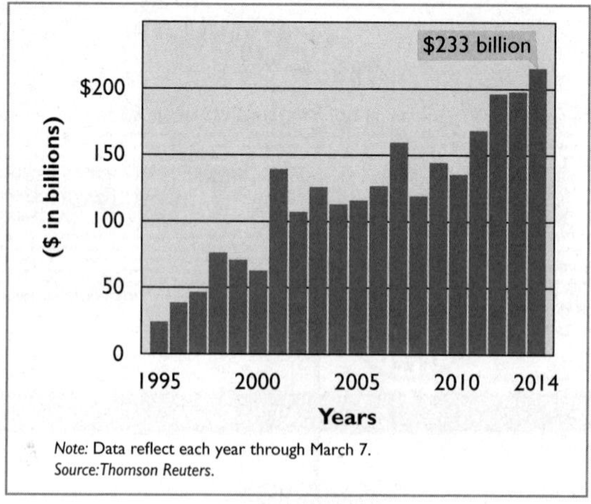

As one expert noted about these increases, "Companies are taking advantage of this lower-rate environment in the limited period of time it is going to be around." An interesting aspect of these bond issuances is that companies, like Philip Morris International, Medtronic, Inc., and Simon Properties, are even selling 30-year bonds. These bond issuers are benefitting from "a massive sentiment shift," says one bond expert. The belief that the economy will recover is making investors more comfortable holding longer-term bonds, as they search for investments that offer better returns than U.S. Treasury bonds.

Sources: Vipal Monga, "The Big Number," *Wall Street Journal* (March 20, 2012), p. B5; and Mike Cherney, "Renewed Embrace of Bonds Sparks Boom," *Wall Street Journal* (March 8–9, 2014), p. B5.

What are the advantages for companies of issuing 30-years bonds instead of 5-year bonds? (Go to WileyPLUS for this answer and additional questions.)

DO IT! 2 Bond Terminology

State whether each of the following statements is true or false. If false, indicate how to correct the statement.

_____ **1.** Secured bonds have specific assets of the issuer pledged as collateral.

_____ **2.** Callable bonds can be redeemed by the issuing company at a stated dollar amount prior to maturity.

_____ **3.** The contractual interest rate is the rate investors demand for loaning funds.

_____ **4.** The face value is the amount of principal the issuing company must pay at the maturity date.

_____ **5.** The market price of a bond is equal to its maturity value.

---

[2]For those knowledgeable in the use of present value tables, the computations in the example shown in Illustration 10-5 (page 487) are $100,000 × .64993 = $64,993 and $9,000 × 3.88965 = $35,007 (rounded).

SOLUTION

1. True. 2. True. 3. False. The contractual interest rate is used to determine the amount of cash interest the borrower pays. 4. True. 5. False. The market price of a bond is equal to the present value of all the future cash payments promised by the bond.

Action Plan

✔ **Review the types of bonds and the basic terms associated with bonds.**

Related exercise material: DO IT! **10-2.**

LEARNING OBJECTIVE ▶3 **Explain how to account for bond transactions.**

A corporation records bond transactions when it issues (sells) or redeems (buys back) bonds and when bondholders convert bonds into common stock. If bondholders sell their bond investments to other investors, the issuing corporation receives no further money on the transaction, **nor does the issuing corporation journalize the transaction** (although it does keep records of the names of bondholders in some cases).

Bonds may be issued at face value, below face value (discount), or above face value (premium). Bond prices for both new issues and existing bonds are quoted as **a percentage of the face value of the bond. Face value is usually $1,000.** Thus, a $1,000 bond with a quoted price of 97 means that the selling price of the bond is 97% of face value, or $970.

ISSUING BONDS AT FACE VALUE

To illustrate the accounting for bonds issued at face value, assume that Devor Corporation issues 100, five-year, 10%, $1,000 bonds dated January 1, 2017, at 100 (100% of face value). The entry to record the sale is as follows.

Jan. 1	Cash	100,000	
	Bonds Payable		100,000
	(To record sale of bonds at face value)		

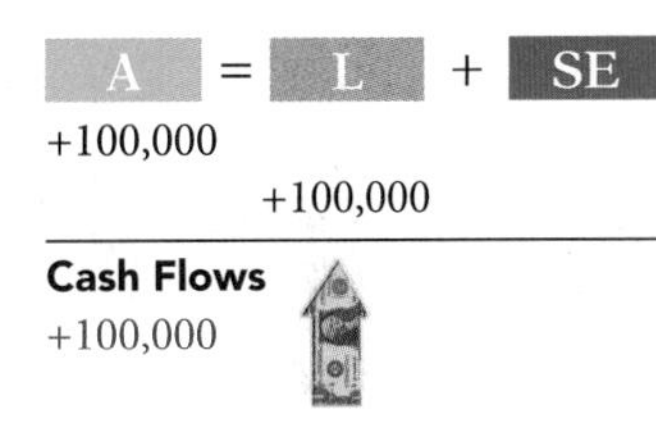

Devor reports bonds payable in the long-term liabilities section of the balance sheet because the maturity date is January 1, 2022 (more than one year away).

Over the term (life) of the bonds, companies make entries to record bond interest. Interest on bonds payable is computed in the same manner as interest on notes payable, as explained earlier. If we assume that interest is payable annually on January 1 on the bonds described above, Devor accrues interest of $10,000 ($\$100,000 \times 10\% \times \frac{12}{12}$) on December 31. At December 31, Devor recognizes the $10,000 of interest expense incurred with the following adjusting entry.

Dec. 31	Interest Expense	10,000	
	Interest Payable		10,000
	(To accrue bond interest)		

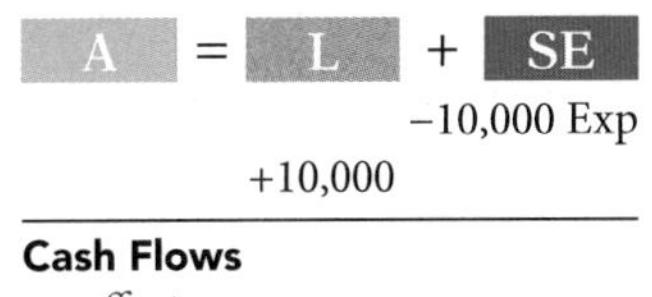

The company classifies **interest payable as a current liability** because it is scheduled for payment within the next year. When Devor pays the interest on January 1, 2018, it decreases (debits) Interest Payable and decreases (credits) Cash for $10,000. Devor records the payment on January 1 as follows.

Jan. 1	Interest Payable	10,000	
	Cash		10,000
	(To record payment of bond interest)		

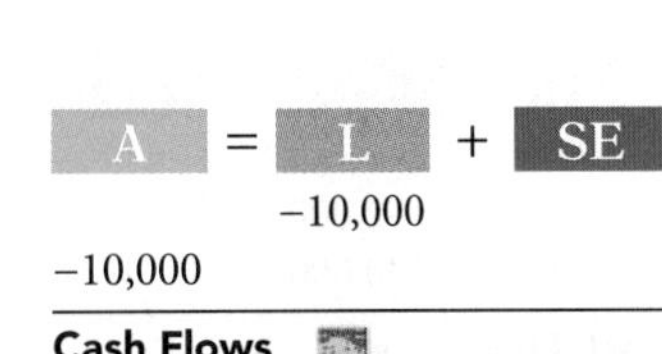

DISCOUNT OR PREMIUM ON BONDS

The previous example assumed that the contractual (stated) interest rate and the market (effective) interest rate paid on bonds were the same. Recall that the **contractual interest rate** is the rate applied to the face (par) value to arrive at the interest paid in a year. The **market interest rate** is the rate investors demand for loaning funds to the corporation. When the contractual interest rate and the market interest rate are the same, **bonds sell at face value**.

However, market interest rates change daily. The type of bond issued, the state of the economy, current industry conditions, and the company's individual performance all affect market interest rates. As a result, the contractual and market interest rates often differ. To make bonds salable when the two rates differ, bonds sell below or above face value.

To illustrate, suppose that a company issues 10% bonds at a time when other bonds of similar risk are paying 12%. Investors will not be interested in buying the 10% bonds, so their value will fall below their face value. When a bond is sold for less than its face value, the difference between the face value of a bond and its selling price is called a **discount**. As a result of the decline in the bonds' selling price, the actual interest rate incurred by the company increases to the level of the current market interest rate.

▼ **HELPFUL HINT**
Bond prices *vary inversely* with changes in the market interest rate. As market interest rates decline, bond prices increase. When a bond is issued, if the market interest rate is below the contractual rate, the bond price is higher than the face value.

Conversely, if the market rate of interest is **lower than** the contractual interest rate, investors will have to pay more than face value for the bonds. That is, if the market rate of interest is 8% but the contractual interest rate on the bonds is 10%, the price on the bonds will be bid up. When a bond is sold for more than its face value, the difference between the face value and its selling price is called a **premium**. Illustration 10-6 shows these relationships graphically.

ILLUSTRATION 10-6
Interest rates and bond prices

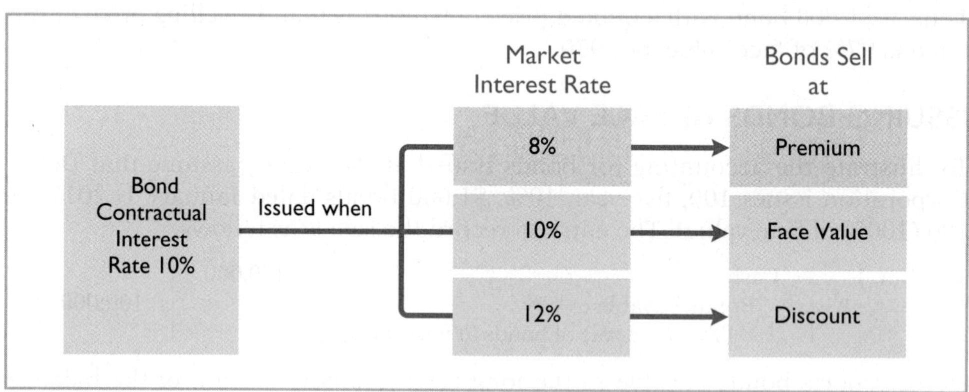

Issuance of bonds at an amount different from face value is quite common. By the time a company prints the bond certificates and markets the bonds, it will be a coincidence if the market rate and the contractual rate are the same. Thus, the issuance of bonds at a discount does not mean that the financial strength of the issuer is suspect. Conversely, the sale of bonds at a premium does not indicate that the financial strength of the issuer is exceptional.

▼ **HELPFUL HINT**
Some bonds are sold at a discount by design. "Zero-coupon" bonds, which pay no interest, sell at a deep discount to face value.

ISSUING BONDS AT A DISCOUNT

To illustrate the issuance of bonds at a discount, assume that on January 1, 2017, Candlestick Inc. sells $100,000, five-year, 10% bonds at 98 (98% of face value) with interest payable on January 1. The entry to record the issuance is as follows.

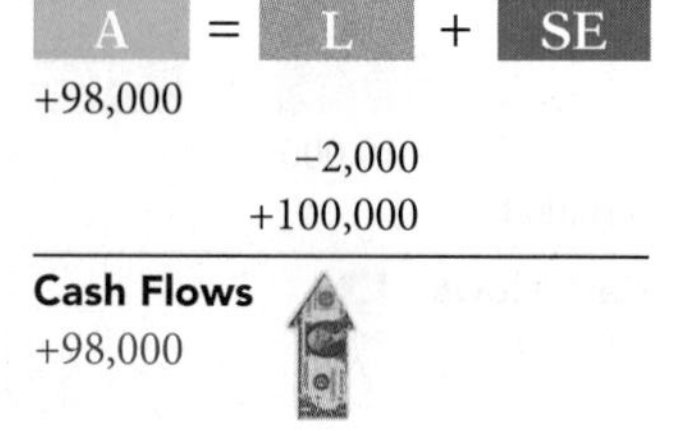

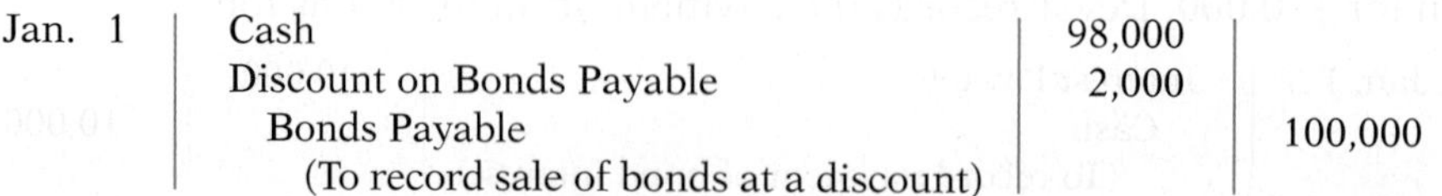

Jan. 1	Cash	98,000	
	Discount on Bonds Payable	2,000	
	Bonds Payable		100,000
	(To record sale of bonds at a discount)		

Although Discount on Bonds Payable has a debit balance, **it is not an asset**. Rather it is a **contra account**, which is **deducted from bonds payable** on the balance sheet as shown in Illustration 10-7. The $98,000 represents the **carrying (or book) value** of the bonds. On the date of issue, this amount equals the market price of the bonds.

CANDLESTICK INC. Balance Sheet (partial)		
Long-term liabilities		
Bonds payable	$100,000	
Less: Discount on bonds payable	**2,000**	$98,000

ILLUSTRATION 10-7
Statement presentation of discount on bonds payable

The issuance of bonds below face value causes the total cost of borrowing to differ from the bond interest paid. That is, the issuing corporation not only must pay the contractual interest rate over the term of the bonds but also must pay the face value (rather than the issuance price) at maturity. Therefore, the difference between the issuance price and the face value of the bonds—the discount—is an **additional cost of borrowing**. The company records this cost as **interest expense** over the life of the bonds. The total cost of borrowing $98,000 for Candlestick Inc. is $52,000, computed as shown in Illustration 10-8.

▼ HELPFUL HINT
The carrying value (book value) of bonds issued at a discount is determined by subtracting the balance of the discount account from the balance of the Bonds Payable account.

ILLUSTRATION 10-8
Computation of total cost of borrowing—bonds issued at discount

Bonds Issued at a Discount	
Annual interest payments	
($100,000 × 10% = $10,000; $10,000 × 5)	$50,000
Add: Bond discount ($100,000 − $98,000)	2,000
Total cost of borrowing	**$52,000**

Alternatively, we can compute the total cost of borrowing as shown in Illustration 10-9.

ILLUSTRATION 10-9
Alternative computation of total cost of borrowing—bonds issued at discount

Bonds Issued at a Discount	
Principal at maturity	$100,000
Annual interest payments ($10,000 × 5)	50,000
Cash to be paid to bondholders	150,000
Less: Cash received from bondholders	98,000
Total cost of borrowing	**$ 52,000**

To follow the expense recognition principle, companies allocate bond discount to expense in each period in which the bonds are outstanding. This is referred to as **amortizing the discount**. Amortization of the discount **increases** the amount of interest expense reported each period. That is, after the company amortizes the discount, the amount of interest expense it reports in a period will exceed the contractual amount. As shown in Illustration 10-8, for the bonds issued by Candlestick Inc., total interest expense will exceed the contractual interest by $2,000 over the life of the bonds.

As the discount is amortized, its balance declines. As a consequence, the carrying value of the bonds will increase, until at maturity the carrying value of the bonds equals their face amount. This is shown in Illustration 10-10. Appendices 10A and 10B at the end of this chapter discuss procedures for amortizing bond discount.

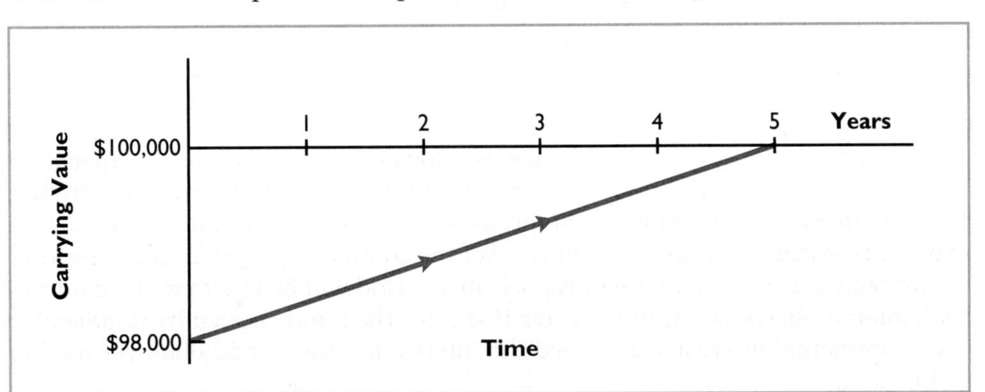

ILLUSTRATION 10-10
Amortization of bond discount

ISSUING BONDS AT A PREMIUM

We can illustrate the issuance of bonds at a premium by now assuming the Candlestick Inc. bonds described above sell at 102 (102% of face value) rather than at 98. The entry to record the sale is as follows.

A	=	L	+	SE
+102,000				
		+100,000		
		+2,000		

Cash Flows
+102,000

Jan. 1	Cash	102,000	
	Bonds Payable		100,000
	Premium on Bonds Payable		2,000
	(To record sale of bonds at a premium)		

Candlestick adds the premium on bonds payable **to the bonds payable** amount on the balance sheet, as shown in Illustration 10-11.

ILLUSTRATION 10-11
Statement presentation of bond premium

▼ HELPFUL HINT
Both a discount and a premium account are valuation accounts. A *valuation account* is one that is needed to value properly the item to which it relates.

CANDLESTICK INC. Balance Sheet (partial)		
Long-term liabilities		
Bonds payable	$100,000	
Add: Premium on bonds payable	**2,000**	**$102,000**

The sale of bonds above face value causes the total cost of borrowing to be **less than the bond interest paid** because the borrower is not required to pay the bond premium at the maturity date of the bonds. Thus, the premium is considered to be **a reduction in the cost of borrowing** that reduces bond interest expense over the life of the bonds. The total cost of borrowing $102,000 for Candlestick Inc. is $48,000, computed as in Illustration 10-12.

ILLUSTRATION 10-12
Computation of total cost of borrowing—bonds issued at a premium

Bonds Issued at a Premium	
Annual interest payments	
($100,000 × 10% = $10,000; $10,000 × 5)	$ 50,000
Less: Bond premium ($102,000 − $100,000)	2,000
Total cost of borrowing	**$48,000**

Alternatively, we can compute the cost of borrowing as shown in Illustration 10-13.

ILLUSTRATION 10-13
Alternative computation of total cost of borrowing—bonds issued at a premium

Bonds Issued at a Premium	
Principal at maturity	$100,000
Annual interest payments ($10,000 × 5)	50,000
Cash to be paid to bondholders	150,000
Less: Cash received from bondholders	102,000
Total cost of borrowing	**$ 48,000**

Similar to bond discount, companies allocate bond premium to expense in each period in which the bonds are outstanding. This is referred to as **amortizing the premium**. Amortization of the premium **decreases** the amount of interest expense reported each period. That is, after the company amortizes the premium, the amount of interest expense it reports in a period will be less than the contractual amount. As shown in Illustration 10-12, for the bonds issued by Candlestick Inc., contractual interest will exceed the interest expense by $2,000 over the life of the bonds.

As the premium is amortized, its balance declines. As a consequence, the carrying value of the bonds will decrease, until at maturity the carrying value of the bonds equals their face amount. This is shown in Illustration 10-14. Appendices 10A and 10B at the end of this chapter discuss procedures for amortizing bond premium.

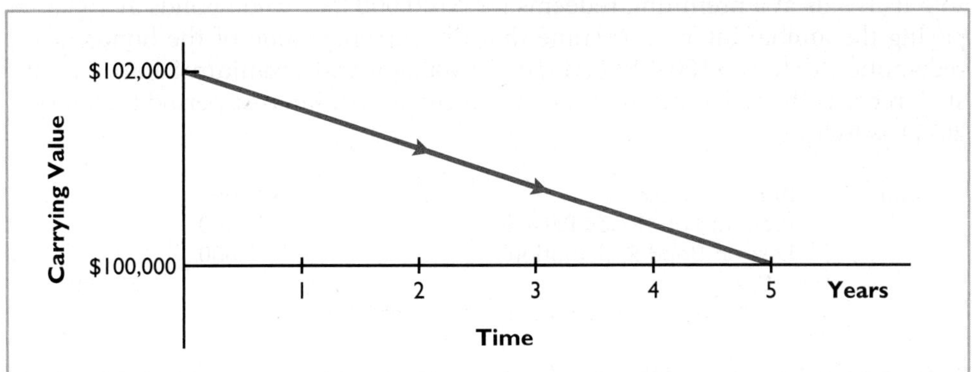

ILLUSTRATION 10-14
Amortization of bond premium

DO IT! 3a Bond Issuance

Giant Corporation issues $200,000 of bonds for $189,000. (a) Prepare the journal entry to record the issuance of the bonds, and (b) show how the bonds would be reported on the balance sheet at the date of issuance.

SOLUTION

(a)

Cash	189,000	
Discount on Bonds Payable	11,000	
Bonds Payable		200,000
(To record sale of bonds at a discount)		

(b)

Long-term liabilities		
Bonds payable	$200,000	
Less: Discount on bonds payable	11,000	$189,000

Action Plan

✔ Record cash received, bonds payable at face value, and the difference as a discount or premium.

✔ Report discount as a deduction from bonds payable and premium as an addition to bonds payable.

Related exercise material: **BE10-8, BE10-9, BE10-10, DO IT! 10-3a, E10-8, E10-9,** and **E10-10.**

REDEEMING BONDS AT MATURITY

Regardless of the issue price of bonds, the book value of the bonds at maturity will equal their face value. Assuming that the company pays and records separately the interest for the last interest period, Candlestick records the redemption of its bonds at maturity as follows.

Bonds Payable	100,000	
Cash		100,000
(To record redemption of bonds at maturity)		

A	=	L	+	SE
		−100,000		
−100,000				

Cash Flows
−100,000

REDEEMING BONDS BEFORE MATURITY

Bonds may be redeemed before maturity. A company may decide to redeem bonds before maturity in order to reduce interest cost and remove debt from its balance sheet. A company should redeem debt early only if it has sufficient cash resources.

When bonds are redeemed before maturity, it is necessary to (1) eliminate the carrying value of the bonds at the redemption date, (2) record the cash paid, and (3) recognize the gain or loss on redemption. The **carrying value** of the bonds is the face value of the bonds less unamortized bond discount or plus unamortized bond premium at the redemption date.

To illustrate, assume at the end of the fourth period, Candlestick Inc., having sold its bonds at a premium, redeems the $100,000 face value bonds at 103 after paying the annual interest. Assume that the carrying value of the bonds at the redemption date is $100,400 (principal $100,000 and premium $400). Candlestick records the redemption at the end of the fourth interest period (January 1, 2021) as follows.

A	=	L	+	SE
		−100,000		
		−400		
				−2,600 Exp
−103,000				

Cash Flows
−103,000

Jan. 1	Bonds Payable	100,000	
	Premium on Bonds Payable	400	
	Loss on Bond Redemption	2,600	
	Cash		103,000
	(To record redemption of bonds at 103)		

Note that the loss of $2,600 is the difference between the $103,000 cash paid and the $100,400 carrying value of the bonds.

PEOPLE, PLANET, AND PROFIT INSIGHT Unilever

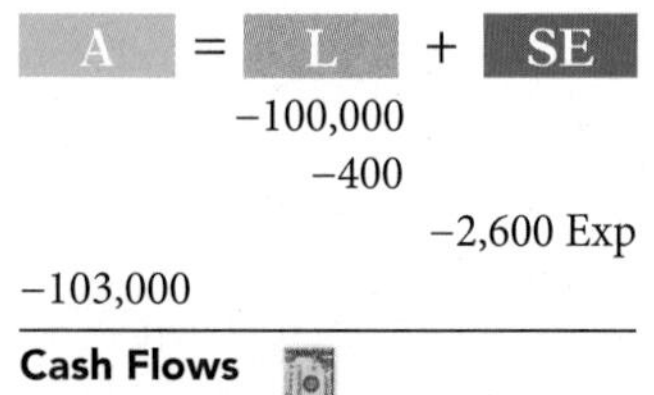
CarpathianPrince/Shutterstock

How About Some Green Bonds?

Unilever recently began producing popular frozen treats such as Magnums and Cornettos, funded by green bonds. Green bonds are debt used to fund activities such as renewable-energy projects. In Unilever's case, the proceeds from the sale of green bonds are used to clean up the company's manufacturing operations and cut waste (such as related to energy consumption).

The use of green bonds has taken off as companies now have guidelines as to how to disclose and report on these green-bond proceeds. These standardized disclosures provide transparency as to how these bonds are used and their effect on overall profitability.

Investors are taking a strong interest in these bonds. Investing companies are installing socially responsible investing teams and have started to integrate sustainability into their investment processes. The disclosures of how companies are using the bond proceeds help investors to make better financial decisions.

Source: Ben Edwards, "Green Bonds Catch On." *Wall Street Journal* (April 3, 2014), p. C5.

Why might standardized disclosure help investors to better understand how proceeds from the sale or issuance of bonds are used? (Go to WileyPLUS for this answer and additional questions.)

DO IT! 3b Bond Redemption

R & B Inc. issued $500,000, 10-year bonds at a discount. Prior to maturity, when the carrying value of the bonds is $496,000, the company redeems the bonds at 98. Prepare the entry to record the redemption of the bonds.

Action Plan

- ✔ Determine and eliminate the carrying value of the bonds.
- ✔ Record the cash paid.
- ✔ Compute and record the gain or loss (the difference between the first two items).

SOLUTION

There is a gain on redemption. The cash paid, $490,000 ($500,000 × 98%), is less than the carrying value of $496,000. The entry is:

Bonds Payable	500,000	
Cash		490,000
Discount on Bonds Payable		4,000
Gain on Bond Redemption		6,000
(To record redemption of bonds at 98)		

Related exercise material: **BE10-11, DO IT! 10-3b, E10-13, and E10-14.**

LEARNING OBJECTIVE **4** **Discuss how liabilities are reported and analyzed.**

PRESENTATION

Current liabilities are the first category under "Liabilities" on the balance sheet. Companies list each of the principal types of current liabilities separately within the category. Within the current liabilities section, companies often list notes payable first, followed by accounts payable.

Companies report long-term liabilities in a separate section of the balance sheet immediately following "Current liabilities." Illustration 10-15 shows an example.

ILLUSTRATION 10-15
Balance sheet presentation of liabilities

MARAIS COMPANY Balance Sheet (partial)		
Liabilities		
Current liabilities		
Notes payable	$ 250,000	
Accounts payable	125,000	
Current maturities of long-term debt	300,000	
Accrued liabilities	75,000	
Total current liabilities		$ 750,000
Long-term liabilities		
Bonds payable	1,000,000	
Less: Discount on bonds payable	80,000	920,000
Notes payable, secured by plant assets		540,000
Lease liability		500,000
Total long-term liabilities		1,960,000
Total liabilities		$2,710,000

Disclosure of debt is very important. Failures at Enron, WorldCom, and Global Crossing have made investors very concerned about companies' debt obligations. Summary data regarding debts may be presented in the balance sheet with detailed data (such as interest rates, maturity dates, conversion privileges, and assets pledged as collateral) shown in a supporting schedule in the notes. Companies should report current maturities of long-term debt as a current liability.

ETHICS NOTE

Some companies try to minimize the amount of debt reported on their balance sheets by not reporting certain types of commitments as liabilities. This subject is of intense interest in the financial community.

KEEPING AN EYE ON CASH

The balance sheet presents the balances of a company's debts at a point in time. The statement of cash flows also presents information about a company's debts. Information regarding cash inflows and outflows during the year that resulted from the principal portion of debt transactions appears in the "Financing activities" section of the statement of cash flows. Interest expense is reported in the "Operating activities" section even though it resulted from debt transactions.

The following statement of cash flows presents the cash flows from financing activities for General Motors Company. From this we learn that the company issued new debt of $31,373 million and repaid debt of $19,524 million.

Real World

GENERAL MOTORS COMPANY
Statement of Cash Flows (partial)
2014
(in millions)

Cash flows from financing activities	
Payments to purchase stock	$ (3,277)
Proceeds from issuance of debt	31,373
Payments of debt	(19,524)
Increase in short-term debt	391
Dividends paid	(3,165)
Other	(123)
Net cash provided by (used in) financing activities	$ 5,675

ANALYSIS

Careful examination of debt obligations helps you assess a company's ability to pay its current and long-term obligations. It also helps you determine whether a company can obtain debt financing in order to grow. We will use the following information from the financial statements of General Motors to illustrate the analysis of a company's liquidity and solvency.

ILLUSTRATION 10-16
Simplified balance sheets for General Motors

Real World

GENERAL MOTORS COMPANY
Balance Sheets
December 31, 2014 and 2013
(in millions)

Assets	**2014**	**2013**
Total current assets	$ 83,670	$ 81,501
Noncurrent assets	94,007	84,843
Total assets	$177,677	$166,344
Liabilities and Stockholders' Equity		
Total current liabilities	$ 65,701	$ 62,412
Noncurrent liabilities	75,952	60,758
Total liabilities	141,653	123,170
Total stockholders' equity	36,024	43,174
Total liabilities and stockholders' equity	$177,677	$166,344

Liquidity

Liquidity ratios measure the short-term ability of a company to pay its maturing obligations and to meet unexpected needs for cash. A commonly used measure of liquidity is the current ratio (presented in Chapter 2). The current ratio is calculated as current assets divided by current liabilities. Illustration 10-17 presents the current ratio for General Motors along with the industry average.

ILLUSTRATION 10-17
Current ratio

	General Motors ($ in millions)		Industry Average
Ratio	2014	2013	2014
Current Ratio	$\frac{\$83,670}{\$65,701} = 1.27:1$	$\frac{\$81,501}{\$62,412} = 1.31:1$	1.00:1

General Motors' current ratio declined from 1.31:1 to 1.27:1 from 2013 to 2014. Although General Motors' ratio declined, it still exceeds the industry average current ratio for manufacturers of autos and trucks of 1.00:1.

DECISION TOOLS 

Comparing available lines of credit to current liabilities as well as evaluating liquidity ratios helps users determine if a company can obtain short-term financing when necessary.

General Motors' current ratio, like the industry average, is quite low. Many companies today minimize their liquid assets (such as accounts receivable and inventory) in order to improve profitability measures, such as return on assets. This is particularly true of large companies such as Ford, General Motors, and Toyota. Companies that keep fewer liquid assets on hand must rely on other sources of liquidity. One such source is a **bank line of credit**. A line of credit is a prearranged agreement between a company and a lender that permits the company, should it be necessary, to borrow up to an agreed-upon amount. For example, a recent disclosure regarding debt in General Motors' annual report states that it has $12 billion of unused lines of credit.

Solvency

Solvency ratios measure the ability of a company to survive over a long period of time. The Feature Story in this chapter mentioned that, although there once were many U.S. automobile manufacturers, only three U.S.-based companies remain today. Many of the others went bankrupt. This highlights the fact that when making a long-term loan or purchasing a company's stock, you must give consideration to a company's solvency.

To reduce the risks associated with having a large amount of debt during an economic downturn, some U.S. automobile manufacturers took two precautionary steps while they enjoyed strong profits. First, they built up large balances of cash and cash equivalents to avoid a cash crisis. Second, they were reluctant to build new plants or hire new workers to meet their production needs. Instead, they asked workers to put in overtime, or they "outsourced" work to other companies. In this way, when the economic downturn occurred, they hoped to avoid having to make debt payments on idle production plants and to minimize layoffs. As a result, when the crisis first hit, Ford had cash of $29 billion, about double the amount of cash it would expect to use over a two-year period.

In Chapter 2, you learned that one measure of a company's solvency is the debt to assets ratio. This is calculated as total liabilities (debt) divided by total assets. This ratio indicates the extent to which a company's assets are financed with debt.

Another useful solvency measure is the **times interest earned**. It provides an indication of a company's ability to meet interest payments as they come due. It is computed by dividing the sum of net income, interest expense, and income tax expense by interest expense. It uses income before interest expense and taxes because this number best represents the amount available to pay interest.

Times interest earned helps users determine if a company can meet its obligations in the long term.

We can use the balance sheet information presented in Illustration 10-16 and the additional information below to calculate solvency ratios for General Motors.

($ in millions)	**2014**	**2013**
Net income	$4,018	$5,331
Interest expense	403	334
Income tax expense	228	2,127

The debt to assets ratios and times interest earned for General Motors and averages for the industry are shown in Illustration 10-18 (page 498).

$$\text{Debt to Assets Ratio} = \frac{\text{Total Liabilities}}{\text{Total Assets}}$$

$$\text{Times Interest Earned} = \frac{\text{Net Income + Interest Expense + Income Tax Expense}}{\text{Interest Expense}}$$

	General Motors ($ in millions)		Industry Average
Ratio	**2014**	**2013**	**2014**
Debt to Assets Ratio	$\frac{\$141,653}{\$177,677}$ = 80%	74%	62%
Times Interest Earned	$\frac{\$4,018 + \$403 + \$228}{\$403}$ = 11.5 times	23.3 times	3.2 times

ILLUSTRATION 10-18
Solvency ratios

General Motors' debt to assets ratio was 80%. The industry average for manufacturers of autos and trucks is 62%. Thus, General Motors is more reliant on debt financing than the average firm in the auto and truck industry. In part, General Motors' heavy reliance on debt is due to its substantial finance division.

General Motors' times interest earned decreased from 23.3 times in 2013 to 11.5 in 2014. This means that in 2014 General Motors had earnings before interest and taxes that were more than 11.5 times the amount needed to pay interest. The higher the multiple, the lower the likelihood that the company will default on interest payments. This suggests that while General Motors' ability to meet interest payments was high, the average company in the industry had a lower ability to meet interest payments in 2014.

INVESTOR INSIGHT

© Yenwen Lu/iStockphoto

Debt Masking

In the wake of the financial crisis, many financial institutions are wary of reporting too much debt on their financial statements, for fear that investors will consider them too risky. The Securities and Exchange Commission (SEC) is concerned that some companies engage in "debt masking" to make it appear that they use less debt than they actually do. These companies enter into transactions at the end of the accounting period that essentially remove debt from their books. Shortly after the end of the period, they reverse the transaction and the debt goes back on their books. The *Wall Street Journal* reported that 18 large banks "had consistently lowered one type of debt at the end of each of the past five quarters, reducing it on average by 42% from quarterly peaks."

Source: Tom McGinty, Kate Kelly, and Kara Scannell, "Debt 'Masking' Under Fire," *Wall Street Journal Online* (April 21, 2010).

What implications does debt masking have for an investor that is using the debt to assets ratio to evaluate a company's solvency? (Go to WileyPLUS for this answer and additional questions.)

Contingencies

DECISION TOOLS 

Understanding a company's contingent liabilities and significant off-balance-sheet financing helps users determine the potential impact on a company's financial position.

One reason a company's balance sheet might not fully reflect its potential obligations is due to contingencies. **Contingencies** are events with uncertain outcomes that may represent potential liabilities. A common type of contingency is lawsuits. Suppose, for example, that you were analyzing the financial statements of a cigarette manufacturer and did not consider the possible negative implications of existing unsettled lawsuits. Your analysis of the company's financial position would certainly be misleading. Other common types of contingencies are product warranties and environmental cleanup obligations. For example, in a recent year, Novartis AG began offering a money-back guarantee on its blood-pressure medications. This guarantee would necessitate an accrual for the estimated claims that will result from returns.

Accounting rules require that companies disclose contingencies in the notes. In some cases, they must accrue them as liabilities. For example, suppose that Waterbury Inc. is sued by a customer for $1 million due to an injury sustained by a defective product. If at the company's year-end the lawsuit had not yet been resolved, how should Waterbury account for this event? If the company can determine **a reasonable estimate** of the expected loss and if it is **probable** it will lose the suit, then the company should accrue for the loss. It records the loss by increasing (debiting) a loss account and increasing (crediting) a liability such as Lawsuit Liability. If **both** of these conditions are not met, then the company discloses the basic facts regarding this suit in the notes to its financial statements.

Leasing

A concern for analysts when they evaluate a company's liquidity and solvency is whether that company has properly recorded all of its obligations. The bankruptcy of Enron Corporation, one of the largest bankruptcies in U.S. history, demonstrated how much damage can result when a company does not properly record or disclose all of its debts. Many would say Enron was practicing off-balance-sheet financing. **Off-balance-sheet financing** is an intentional effort by a company to structure its financing arrangements so as to avoid showing liabilities on its balance sheet.

One common type of off-balance-sheet financing results from leasing. Most lessees do not like to report leases on their balance sheets because the lease increases the company's total liabilities. Recall from Chapter 9 that **operating leases** are treated like rentals—no asset or liabilities show on the books. **Capital leases** are treated like a debt-financed purchase—increasing both assets and liabilities. **As a result, many companies structure their lease agreements to avoid meeting the criteria of a capital lease.**[3]

Recall from Chapter 9 that many U.S. airlines lease a large portion of their planes without showing any debt related to them on their balance sheets. For example, the total increase in assets and liabilities that would result if Southwest Airlines recorded on the balance sheet its off-balance-sheet **"operating" leases** would be approximately $3.9 billion. Illustration 10-19 presents Southwest Airlines' debt to assets ratio for a recent year using the numbers presented in its balance sheet. It also shows the ratio after adjusting for the off-balance-sheet leases. After those adjustments, Southwest has a ratio of 72% versus 66% before. This means that of every dollar of assets, 72 cents was funded by debt. This would be of interest to analysts evaluating Southwest's solvency.

ETHICS NOTE
Accounting standard-setters are attempting to rewrite rules on lease accounting because of concerns that abuse of the current standards is reducing the usefulness of financial statements.

ILLUSTRATION 10-19
Debt to assets ratio adjusted for leases

	Using Numbers as Presented on Balance Sheet	Adjusted for Off-Balance-Sheet Leases
Debt to assets ratio	$\frac{\$13,425}{\$20,200} = 66\%$	$\frac{\$13,425 + \$3,866}{\$20,200 + \$3,866} = 72\%$

Critics of off-balance-sheet financing contend that many leases represent unavoidable obligations that meet the definition of a liability. Therefore, companies should report them as liabilities on the balance sheet. To reduce these concerns, companies are required to report their operating lease obligations for subsequent years in a note. This allows analysts and other financial statement users to adjust a company's financial statements by adding leased assets and lease liabilities if they feel that this treatment is more appropriate.

INTERNATIONAL NOTE
GAAP accounting for leases is more "rules-based" than IFRS. GAAP relies on precisely defined cut-offs to determine whether an item is treated as a capital or operating lease. This rules-based approach may enable companies to structure leases "around the rules." Creating a jointly prepared leasing standard is a top priority for the IASB and FASB.

[3]The FASB is currently considering a new approach to lease accounting. If adopted, this new approach would significantly change the accounting for leases.

INVESTOR INSIGHT

Paul Fleet/Alamy

"Covenant-Lite" Debt

In many corporate loans and bond issuances, the lending agreement specifies **debt covenants**. These covenants typically are specific financial measures, such as minimum levels of retained earnings, cash flows, times interest earned, or other measures that a company must maintain during the life of the loan. If the company violates a covenant, it is considered to have violated the loan agreement. The creditors can then demand immediate repayment, or they can renegotiate the loan's terms. Covenants protect lenders because they enable lenders to step in and try to get their money back before the borrower gets too deep into trouble.

During the 1990s, most traditional loans specified between three to six covenants or "triggers." In subsequent years, however, when there was lots of cash available, lenders began reducing or completely eliminating covenants from loan agreements in order to be more competitive with other lenders. Then, when the economy declined, these lenders lost big money when companies defaulted.

Sources: Cynthia Koons, "Risky Business: Growth of 'Covenant-Lite' Debt," *Wall Street Journal* (June 18, 2007), p. C2; and Katy Burne, "More Loans Come with Few Strings Attached," *Wall Street Journal* (June 12, 2014).

How can financial ratios such as those covered in this chapter provide protection for creditors? (Go to WileyPLUS for this answer and additional questions.)

DO IT! 4 Analyzing Liabilities

Trout Company provides you with the following balance sheet information as of December 31, 2017.

Current assets	$10,500	Current liabilities	$ 8,000
Long-term assets	24,200	Long-term liabilities	16,000
Total assets	$34,700	Stockholders' equity	10,700
		Total liabilities and stockholders' equity	$34,700

In addition, Trout reported net income for 2017 of $14,000, income tax expense of $2,800, and interest expense of $900.

INSTRUCTIONS

(a) Compute the current ratio and working capital for Trout for 2017.

(b) Assume that at the end of 2017, Trout used $2,000 cash to pay off $2,000 of accounts payable. How would the current ratio and working capital have changed?

(c) Compute the debt to assets ratio and the times interest earned for Trout for 2017.

Action Plan

✔ Use the formula for the current ratio: Current assets ÷ Current liabilities.

✔ Use the formula for working capital: Current assets − Current liabilities.

✔ Use the formula for the debt to assets ratio: Total liabilities ÷ Total assets.

SOLUTION

(a) Current ratio is 1.31:1 ($10,500/$8,000). Working capital is $2,500 ($10,500 − $8,000).

(b) Current ratio is 1.42:1 ($8,500/$6,000). Working capital is $2,500 ($8,500 − $6,000).

(c) Debt to assets ratio is 69.2% ($24,000/$34,700). Times interest earned is 19.67 times [($14,000 + $2,800 + $900)/$900].

Related exercise material: **BE10-14, BE10-15, DO IT! 10-4, E10-16, E10-17, and E10-18.**

USING DECISION TOOLS—FORD MOTOR COMPANY

Ford Motor Company has enjoyed some tremendous successes, including its popular Taurus and Explorer vehicles. Development of a new vehicle costs billions. A flop is financially devastating, and the financial effect is magnified if the company has large amounts of outstanding debt.

The following balance sheets provide financial information for Ford Motor Company as of December 31, 2014 and 2013.

FORD MOTOR COMPANY
Balance Sheets
December 31, 2014 and 2013
(in millions)

Assets	**2014**	**2013**
Current assets	$155,052	$151,569
Noncurrent assets	53,475	50,610
Total assets	$208,527	$202,179
Liabilities and Shareholders' Equity		
Current liabilities	$ 63,612	$ 60,417
Noncurrent liabilities	119,741	115,286
Total liabilities	183,353	175,703
Total shareholders' equity (deficit)	25,174	26,476
Total liabilities and shareholders' equity	$208,527	$202,179
Other Information		
Net income	$ 3,186	$ 7,175
Income tax expense (benefit)	1,156	(135)
Interest expense	797	829
Available lines of credit (Automotive Division)	12,200	

INSTRUCTIONS

1. Evaluate Ford's liquidity using appropriate ratios, and compare to those of General Motors and to industry averages presented in Illustration 10-17 (page 496).
2. Evaluate Ford's solvency using appropriate ratios, and compare to those of General Motors and to industry averages presented in Illustration 10-18 (page 498).
3. Comment on Ford's available lines of credit.

SOLUTION

1. Ford's liquidity can be measured using the current ratio:

	2014	2013
Current ratio	$\frac{\$155,052}{\$63,612} = 2.44:1$	$\frac{\$151,569}{\$60,417} = 2.51:1$

Ford's current ratio declined from 2013 to 2014. Ford's 2014 current ratio exceeds the industry average of 1.00:1 and General Motors'.

2. Ford's solvency can be measured with the debt to assets ratio and the times interest earned:

	2014	2013
Debt to assets ratio	$\frac{\$183,353}{\$208,527} = 88\%$	$\frac{\$175,703}{\$202,179} = 87\%$
Times interest earned	$\frac{\$3,186 + \$797 + \$1,156}{\$797} = 6.4 \text{ times}$	$\frac{\$7,175 + \$829 - \$135}{\$829} = 9.5 \text{ times}$

The debt to assets ratio suggests that Ford relies very heavily on debt financing. The ratio increased slightly from 2013 to 2014, indicating that the company's solvency declined slightly. Ford's reliance on debt, as measured by the debt to assets ratio, exceeds that of General Motors as well as the industry average.

The times interest earned is 6.4 times in 2014 and 9.5 times in 2013. This exceeds the industry average of 3.2 times. While not as high as that of General Motors, it is very strong.

3. Ford has available lines of credit of $12.2 billion. These financing sources significantly improve its liquidity and help reduce the concerns of its short-term creditors.

LEARNING OBJECTIVE *5

APPENDIX 10A: Apply the straight-line method of amortizing bond discount and bond premium.

AMORTIZING BOND DISCOUNT

To follow the expense recognition principle, companies allocate bond discount to expense in each period in which the bonds are outstanding. The **straight-line method of amortization** allocates the same amount to interest expense in each interest period. The calculation is presented in Illustration 10A-1.

ILLUSTRATION 10A-1
Formula for straight-line method of bond discount amortization

Bond Discount	÷	Number of Interest Periods	=	Bond Discount Amortization

In the Candlestick Inc. example (page 490), the company sold $100,000, five-year, 10% bonds on January 1, 2017, for $98,000. This resulted in a $2,000 bond discount ($100,000 − $98,000). The bond discount amortization is $400 ($2,000 ÷ 5) for each of the five amortization periods. Candlestick records the first accrual of bond interest and the amortization of bond discount on December 31 as follows.

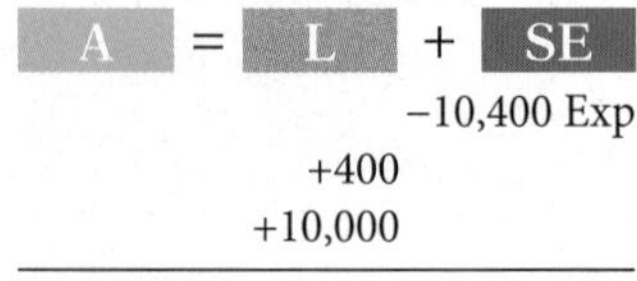

Dec. 31	Interest Expense	10,400	
	Discount on Bonds Payable		400
	Interest Payable		10,000
	(To record accrued bond interest and amortization of bond discount)		

ALTERNATIVE TERMINOLOGY
The amount in the Discount on Bonds Payable account is often referred to as *Unamortized Discount on Bonds Payable.*

Over the term of the bonds, the balance in Discount on Bonds Payable will decrease annually by the same amount until it has a zero balance at the maturity date of the bonds. Thus, the carrying value of the bonds at maturity will be equal to the face value of the bonds.

Preparing a bond discount amortization schedule, as shown in Illustration 10A-2, is useful to determine interest expense, discount amortization, and the carrying value of the bond. As indicated, the interest expense recorded each period is $10,400. Also note that the carrying value of the bond increases $400 each period until it reaches its face value of $100,000 at the end of period 5.

ILLUSTRATION 10A-2
Bond discount amortization schedule

Candlestick Inc.xls

CANDLESTICK INC.
Bond Discount Amortization Schedule
Straight-Line Method—Annual Interest Payments
$100,000 of 10%, 5-Year Bonds

Interest Periods	(A) Interest to Be Paid (10% × $100,000)	(B) Interest Expense to Be Recorded (A) + (C)	(C) Discount Amortization ($2,000 ÷ 5)	(D) Unamortized Discount (D) – (C)	(E) Bond Carrying Value ($100,000 – D)
Issue date				$2,000	$ 98,000
1	$10,000	$10,400	$ 400	1,600	98,400
2	10,000	10,400	400	1,200	98,800
3	10,000	10,400	400	800	99,200
4	10,000	10,400	400	400	99,600
5	10,000	10,400	400	0	100,000
	$50,000	$52,000	$2,000		

Column (A) remains constant because the face value of the bonds ($100,000) is multiplied by the annual contractual interest rate (10%) each period.
Column (B) is computed as the interest paid (Column A) plus the discount amortization (Column C).
Column (C) indicates the discount amortization each period.
Column (D) decreases each period by the same amount until it reaches zero at maturity.
Column (E) increases each period by the amount of discount amortization until it equals the face value at maturity.

AMORTIZING BOND PREMIUM

The amortization of bond premium parallels that of bond discount. Illustration 10A-3 presents the formula for determining bond premium amortization under the straight-line method.

Bond Premium	÷	Number of Interest Periods	=	Bond Premium Amortization

ILLUSTRATION 10A-3
Formula for straight-line method of bond premium amortization

Continuing our example, assume Candlestick Inc. sells the bonds described above for $102,000, rather than $98,000 (see page 492). This results in a bond premium of $2,000 ($102,000 – $100,000). The premium amortization for each interest period is $400 ($2,000 ÷ 5). Candlestick records the first accrual of interest on December 31 as follows.

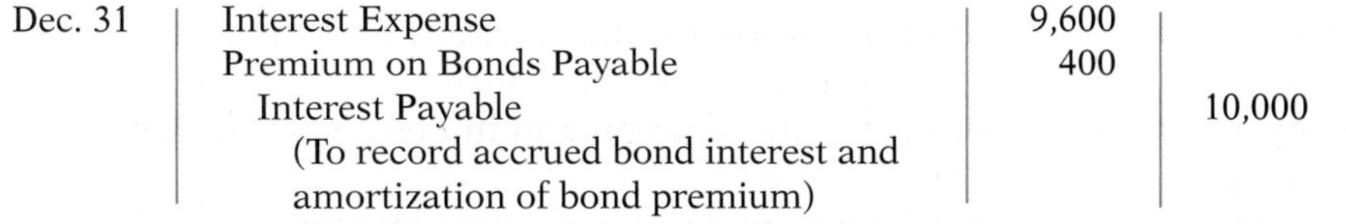

Dec. 31	Interest Expense	9,600	
	Premium on Bonds Payable	400	
	Interest Payable		10,000
	(To record accrued bond interest and amortization of bond premium)		

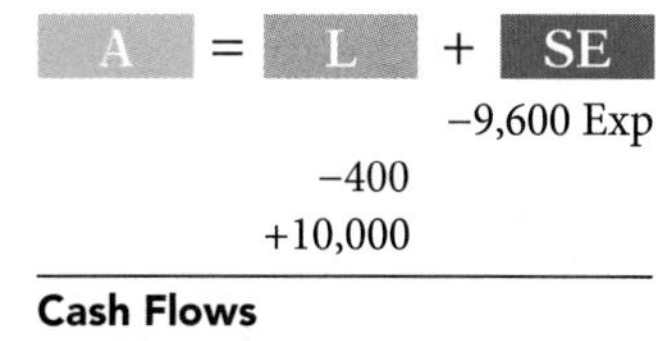

Over the term of the bonds, the balance in Premium on Bonds Payable will decrease annually by the same amount until it has a zero balance at maturity.

A bond premium amortization schedule, as shown in Illustration 10A-4 (page 504), is useful to determine interest expense, premium amortization, and the carrying value of the bond. As indicated, the interest expense Candlestick records each period is $9,600. Note that the carrying value of the bond decreases $400 each period until it reaches its face value of $100,000 at the end of period 5.

ILLUSTRATION 10A-4
Bond premium amortization schedule

Candlestick Inc.xls

CANDLESTICK INC.
Bond Premium Amortization Schedule
Straight-Line Method—Annual Interest Payments
$100,000 of 10%, 5-Year Bonds

Interest Periods	(A) Interest to Be Paid (10% × $100,000)	(B) Interest Expense to Be Recorded (A) – (C)	(C) Premium Amortization ($2,000 ÷ 5)	(D) Unamortized Premium (D) – (C)	(E) Bond Carrying Value ($100,000 + D)
Issue date				$2,000	$102,000
1	$ 10,000	$ 9,600	$ 400	1,600	101,600
2	10,000	9,600	400	1,200	101,200
3	10,000	9,600	400	800	100,800
4	10,000	9,600	400	400	100,400
5	10,000	9,600	400	0	100,000
	$50,000	$48,000	$2,000		

Column (A) remains constant because the face value of the bonds ($100,000) is multiplied by the annual contractual interest rate (10%) each period.
Column (B) is computed as the interest paid (Column A) less the premium amortization (Column C).
Column (C) indicates the premium amortization each period.
Column (D) decreases each period by the same amount until it reaches zero at maturity.
Column (E) decreases each period by the amount of premium amortization until it equals the face value at maturity.

LEARNING OBJECTIVE *6

APPENDIX 10B: Apply the effective-interest method of amortizing bond discount and bond premium.

To follow the expense recognition principle, companies allocate bond discount to expense in each period in which the bonds are outstanding. However, to completely comply with the expense recognition principle, interest expense as a percentage of carrying value should not change over the life of the bonds.

This percentage, referred to as the **effective-interest rate**, is established when the bonds are issued and remains constant in each interest period. Unlike the straight-line method, the effective-interest method of amortization accomplishes this result.

Under the **effective-interest method of amortization**, the amortization of bond discount or bond premium results in periodic interest expense equal to a constant percentage of the carrying value of the bonds. The effective-interest method results in **varying amounts** of amortization and interest expense per period but a **constant percentage rate**. In contrast, the straight-line method results in constant amounts of amortization and interest expense per period but a varying percentage rate.

Companies follow three steps under the effective-interest method:

1. Compute the **bond interest expense** by multiplying the carrying value of the bonds at the beginning of the interest period by the effective-interest rate.
2. Compute the **bond interest paid** (or accrued) by multiplying the face value of the bonds by the contractual interest rate.
3. Compute the **amortization amount** by determining the difference between the amounts computed in steps (1) and (2).

Illustration 10B-1 depicts these steps.

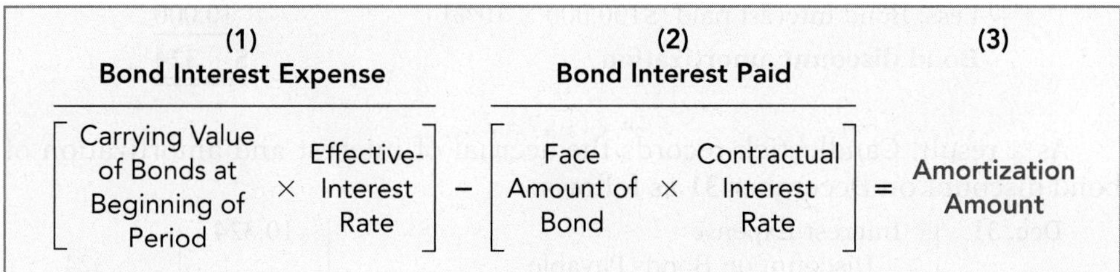

ILLUSTRATION 10B-1
Computation of amortization using effective-interest method

Both the straight-line and effective-interest methods of amortization result in the same total amount of interest expense over the term of the bonds. Furthermore, interest expense each interest period is generally comparable in amount. However, **when the amounts are materially different, generally accepted accounting principles (GAAP) require use of the effective-interest method.**

▼ HELPFUL HINT
Note that the amount of periodic interest expense increases over the life of the bonds when the effective-interest method is used for bonds issued at a discount. The reason is that a constant percentage is applied to an increasing bond carrying value to compute interest expense. The carrying value is increasing because of the amortization of the discount.

AMORTIZING BOND DISCOUNT

In the Candlestick Inc. example (page 490), the company sold $100,000, five-year, 10% bonds on January 1, 2017, for $98,000. This resulted in a $2,000 bond discount ($100,000 − $98,000). This discount results in an effective-interest rate of approximately 10.5348%. (The effective-interest rate can be computed using the techniques shown in Appendix G near the end of this textbook.)

Preparing a bond discount amortization schedule as shown in Illustration 10B-2 facilitates the recording of interest expense and the discount amortization. Note that interest expense as a percentage of carrying value remains constant at 10.5348%.

ILLUSTRATION 10B-2
Bond discount amortization schedule

Candlestick Inc.xls

CANDLESTICK INC.
Bond Discount Amortization Schedule
Effective-Interest Method—Annual Interest Payments
10% Bonds Issued at 10.5348%

Interest Periods	(A) Interest to Be Paid (10% × $100,000)	(B) Interest Expense to Be Recorded (10.5348% × Preceding Bond Carrying Value)		(C) Discount Amortization (B) − (A)	(D) Unamortized Discount (D) − (C)	(E) Bond Carrying Value ($100,000 − D)
Issue date					$2,000	$ 98,000
1	$10,000	$10,324	(10.5348% × $98,000)	$ 324	1,676	98,324
2	10,000	10,358	(10.5348% × $98,324)	358	1,318	98,682
3	10,000	10,396	(10.5348% × $98,682)	396	922	99,078
4	10,000	10,438	(10.5348% × $99,078)	438	484	99,516
5	10,000	10,484	(10.5348% × $99,516)	484	-0-	100,000
	$50,000	$52,000		$2,000		

Column (A) remains constant because the face value of the bonds ($100,000) is multiplied by the annual contractual interest rate (10%) each period.
Column (B) is computed as the preceding bond carrying value times the annual effective-interest rate (10.5348%).
Column (C) indicates the discount amortization each period.
Column (D) decreases each period until it reaches zero at maturity.
Column (E) increases each period until it equals face value at maturity.

For the first interest period, the computations of bond interest expense and the bond discount amortization are as follows.

ILLUSTRATION 10B-3
Computation of bond discount amortization

Bond interest expense ($98,000 × 10.5348%)	$10,324
Less: Bond interest paid ($100,000 × 10%)	10,000
Bond discount amortization	**$ 324**

As a result, Candlestick records the accrual of interest and amortization of bond discount on December 31 as follows.

A = L + SE
−10,324 Exp
+324
+10,000
Cash Flows
no effect

Dec. 31	Interest Expense	10,324	
	Discount on Bonds Payable		324
	Interest Payable		10,000
	(To record accrued interest and amortization of bond discount)		

For the second interest period, bond interest expense will be $10,358 ($98,324 × 10.5348%), and the discount amortization will be $358. At December 31, Candlestick makes the following adjusting entry.

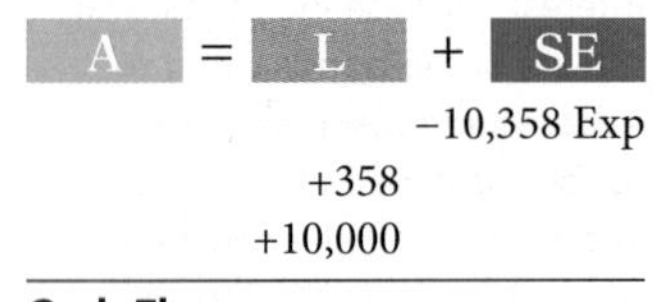

Cash Flows
no effect

Dec. 31	Interest Expense	10,358	
	Discount on Bonds Payable		358
	Interest Payable		10,000
	(To record accrued interest and amortization of bond discount)		

AMORTIZING BOND PREMIUM

Continuing our example, assume Candlestick Inc. sells the bonds described above for $102,000 rather than $98,000 (see page 492). This would result in a bond premium of $2,000 ($102,000 − $100,000). This premium results in an effective-interest rate of approximately 9.4794%. (The effective-interest rate can be computed using the techniques shown in Appendix G near the end of this textbook.) Illustration 10B-4 shows the bond premium amortization schedule.

ILLUSTRATION 10B-4
Bond premium amortization schedule

Candlestick Inc.xls

CANDLESTICK INC.
Bond Premium Amortization Schedule
Effective-Interest Method—Annual Interest Payments
10% Bonds Issued at 9.4794%

Interest Periods	(A) Interest to Be Paid (10% × $100,000)	(B) Interest Expense to Be Recorded (9.4794% × Preceding Bond Carrying Value)	(C) Premium Amortization (A) − (B)	(D) Unamortized Premium (D) − (C)	(E) Bond Carrying Value ($100,000 + D)
Issue date				$2,000	$102,000
1	$10,000	$ 9,669 (9.4794% × $102,000)	$ 331	1,669	101,669
2	10,000	9,638 (9.4794% × $101,669)	362	1,307	101,307
3	10,000	9,603 (9.4794% × $101,307)	397	910	100,910
4	10,000	9,566 (9.4794% × $100,910)	434	476	100,476
5	10,000	9,524* (9.4794% × $100,476)	476*	−0−	100,000
	$50,000	$48,000	$2,000		

Column (A) remains constant because the face value of the bonds ($100,000) is multiplied by the contractual interest rate (10%) each period.
Column (B) is computed as the carrying value of the bonds times the annual effective-interest rate (9.4794%).
Column (C) indicates the premium amortization each period.
Column (D) decreases each period until it reaches zero at maturity.
Column (E) decreases each period until it equals face value at maturity.

*Rounded to eliminate remaining discount resulting from rounding the effective rate.

For the first interest period, the computations of bond interest expense and the bond premium amortization are as follows.

Bond interest paid ($100,000 × 10%)	$10,000
Less: Bond interest expense ($102,000 × 9.4794%)	9,669
Bond premium amortization	$ 331

ILLUSTRATION 10B-5
Computation of bond premium amortization

The entry Candlestick makes on December 31 is as follows.

Dec. 31	Interest Expense	9,669	
	Premium on Bonds Payable	331	
	Interest Payable		10,000
	(To record accrued interest and amortization of bond premium)		

A	=	L	+	SE
				−9,669 Exp
		−331		
		+10,000		

Cash Flows
no effect

For the second interest period, interest expense will be $9,638, and the premium amortization will be $362. Note that the amount of periodic interest expense decreases over the life of the bond when companies apply the effective-interest method to bonds issued at a premium. The reason is that a constant percentage is applied to a decreasing bond carrying value to compute interest expense. The carrying value is decreasing because of the amortization of the premium.

LEARNING OBJECTIVE *7

APPENDIX 10C: Describe the accounting for long-term notes payable.

The use of notes payable in long-term debt financing is quite common. Long-term notes payable are similar to short-term interest-bearing notes payable except that the terms of the notes exceed one year. In periods of unstable interest rates, lenders may tie the interest rate on long-term notes to changes in the market rate for comparable loans. Examples are the 8.03% adjustable rate notes issued by General Motors and the floating-rate notes issued by American Express Company.

A long-term note may be secured by a document called a **mortgage** that pledges title to specific assets as security for a loan. Individuals widely use **mortgage notes payable** to purchase homes, as do many small and some large companies to acquire plant assets. For example, at one time approximately 18% of McDonald's long-term debt related to mortgage notes on land, buildings, and improvements.

Like other long-term notes payable, the mortgage loan terms may stipulate either a fixed or an adjustable interest rate. Typically, the terms require the borrower to make equal installment payments over the term of the loan. Each payment consists of (1) interest on the unpaid balance of the loan and (2) a reduction of loan principal. While the total amount paid remains constant, the interest decreases each period and the portion applied to the loan principal increases.

▼ HELPFUL HINT
Computer spreadsheet programs can create a schedule of installment loan payments. This allows you to put in the data for your own mortgage loan and get an illustration that really hits home.

Companies initially record mortgage notes payable at face value, and subsequently make entries for each installment payment. To illustrate, assume that Porter Technology Inc. issues a $500,000, 8%, 20-year mortgage note on December 31, 2017, to obtain needed financing for the construction of a new research laboratory. The terms provide for annual installment payments of $50,926 (not including real estate taxes and insurance). The installment payment schedule for the first four years is as follows.

ILLUSTRATION 10C-1
Mortgage installment payment schedule

Interest Period	(A) Cash Payment	(B) Interest Expense (D) × 8%	(C) Reduction of Principal (A) − (B)	(D) Principal Balance (D) − (C)
Issue date				$500,000
1	$50,926	$40,000	$10,926	489,074
2	50,926	39,126	11,800	477,274
3	50,926	38,182	12,744	464,530
4	50,926	37,162	13,764	450,766

Porter Technology records the mortgage loan on December 31, 2017, as follows.

A = L + SE
+500,000
+500,000
Cash Flows
+500,000

Dec. 31	Cash	500,000	
	Mortgage Payable		500,000
	(To record mortgage loan)		

On December 31, 2018, Porter records the first installment payment as follows.

A = L + SE
−40,000 Exp
−10,926
−50,926
Cash Flows
−50,926

Dec. 31	Interest Expense	40,000	
	Mortgage Payable	10,926	
	Cash		50,926
	(To record annual payment on mortgage)		

In the balance sheet, the company reports the reduction in principal for the next year as a current liability, and classifies the remaining unpaid principal balance as a long-term liability. At December 31, 2018, the total liability is $489,074. Of that amount, $11,800 is current and $477,274 ($489,074 − $11,800) is long-term.

REVIEW AND PRACTICE

LEARNING OBJECTIVES REVIEW

1 Explain how to account for current liabilities. A current liability is a debt that a company can reasonably expect to pay (a) from existing current assets or through the creation of other current liabilities and (b) within one year or the operating cycle, whichever is longer. The major types of current liabilities are notes payable, accounts payable, sales taxes payable, unearned revenues, and accrued liabilities such as taxes, salaries and wages, and interest payable.

When a note payable is interest-bearing, the amount of assets received upon the issuance of the note is generally equal to the face value of the note, and interest expense is accrued over the life of the note. At maturity, the amount paid is equal to the face value of the note plus accrued interest.

Companies record sales taxes payable at the time the related sales occur. The company serves as a collection agent for the taxing authority. Sales taxes are not an expense to the company. Companies hold employee withholding taxes and credit them to appropriate liability accounts, until they remit these taxes to the governmental taxing authorities. Unearned revenues are initially recorded in an unearned revenue account. As a company recognizes revenue, a transfer from unearned revenue to revenue occurs. Companies report the current maturities of long-term debt as a current liability in the balance sheet.

2 Describe the major characteristics of bonds. The following different types of bonds may be issued: secured and unsecured bonds, and convertible and callable bonds.

3 Explain how to account for bond transactions. When companies issue bonds, they debit Cash for the cash proceeds and credit Bonds Payable for the face value of the bonds. In addition, they use the accounts Premium on Bonds Payable and Discount on Bonds Payable to show the bond premium and bond discount, respectively. Bond discount and bond premium are amortized over the life of the bond, which increases or decreases interest expense, respectively.

When companies redeem bonds at maturity, they credit Cash and debit Bonds Payable for the face value of the bonds. When companies redeem bonds before maturity, they (a) eliminate the carrying value of the bonds at the redemption date, (b) record the cash paid, and (c) recognize the gain or loss on redemption.

4 Discuss how liabilities are reported and analyzed. Current liabilities appear first on the balance sheet, followed by long-term liabilities. Companies should report the nature and amount of each liability in the balance sheet or in schedules in the notes accompanying the statements. They report inflows and outflows of cash related to the principal portion of long-term debt in the financing section of the statement of cash flows.

The liquidity of a company may be analyzed by computing the current ratio. The long-run solvency of a company may be analyzed by computing the debt to assets ratio and the times interest earned. Other factors to consider are contingent liabilities and lease obligations.

***5 Apply the straight-line method of amortizing bond discount and bond premium.** The straight-line method of amortization results in a constant amount of amortization and interest expense per period.

***6 Apply the effective-interest method of amortizing bond discount and bond premium.** The effective-interest method results in varying amounts of amortization and interest expense per period but a constant percentage rate of interest. When the difference between the straight-line and effective-interest method is material, GAAP requires use of the effective-interest method.

***7 Describe the accounting for long-term notes payable.** Each payment consists of (1) interest on the unpaid balance of the loan, and (2) a reduction of loan principal. The interest decreases each period, while the portion applied to the loan principal increases each period.

DECISION TOOLS REVIEW

DECISION CHECKPOINTS	INFO NEEDED FOR DECISION	TOOL TO USE FOR DECISION	HOW TO EVALUATE RESULTS
Can the company obtain short-term financing when necessary?	Available lines of credit, from notes to the financial statements.	Compare available lines of credit to current liabilities. Also, evaluate liquidity ratios.	If liquidity ratios are low, then lines of credit should be high to compensate.
Can the company meet its obligations in the long term?	Interest expense and net income before interest and taxes	$\text{Times interest earned} = \dfrac{\text{Net income} + \text{Interest expense} + \text{Income tax expense}}{\text{Interest expense}}$	High ratio indicates ability to meet interest payments as scheduled.
Does the company have any contingent liabilities?	Knowledge of events with uncertain negative outcomes	Notes to financial statements and financial statements	If negative outcomes are possible, determine the probability, the amount of loss, and the potential impact on financial statements.
Does the company have significant off-balance-sheet financing, such as unrecorded lease obligations?	Information on unrecorded obligations, such as a schedule of minimum lease payments from the notes to the financial statements	Compare liquidity and solvency ratios with and without unrecorded obligations included	If ratios differ significantly after including unrecorded obligations, these obligations should not be ignored in analysis.

GLOSSARY REVIEW

Bond certificate A legal document that indicates the name of the issuer, the face value of the bonds, and other data such as the contractual interest rate and the maturity date of the bonds. (p. 486).

Bonds A form of interest-bearing notes payable issued by corporations, universities, and governmental agencies. (p. 485).

Callable bonds Bonds that the issuing company can redeem (buy back) at a stated dollar amount prior to maturity. (p. 486).

Capital lease A contractual agreement allowing one party (the lessee) to use the assets of another party (the lessor); accounted for like a debt-financed purchase by the lessee. (p. 499).

Contingencies Events with uncertain outcomes that may represent potential liabilities. (p. 498).

Contractual (stated) interest rate Rate used to determine the amount of interest the issuer pays and the investor receives. (p. 486).

Convertible bonds Bonds that can be converted into common stock at the bondholder's option. (p. 486).

Current liability A debt that a company reasonably expects to pay (1) from existing current assets or through the creation of other current liabilities, and (2) within one year or the operating cycle, whichever is longer. (p. 480).

Discount (on a bond) The difference between the face value of a bond and its selling price when a bond is sold for less than its face value. (p. 490).

***Effective-interest method of amortization** A method of amortizing bond discount or bond premium that results in periodic interest expense equal to a constant percentage of the carrying value of the bonds. (p. 504).

***Effective-interest rate** Rate established when bonds are issued that maintains a constant value for interest expense as a percentage of bond carrying value in each interest period. (p. 504).

Face value Amount of principal due at the maturity date of the bond. (p. 486).

Long-term liabilities Obligations that a company expects to pay more than one year in the future. (p. 485).

Market interest rate The rate investors demand for loaning funds to the corporation. (p. 486).

Maturity date The date on which the final payment on a bond is due from the bond issuer to the investor. (p. 486).

Mortgage note payable A long-term note secured by a mortgage that pledges title to specific assets as security for the loan. (p. 507).

Notes payable An obligation in the form of a written note. (p. 480).

Off-balance-sheet financing The intentional effort by a company to structure its financing arrangements so as to avoid showing liabilities on its balance sheet. (p. 499).

Operating lease A contractual agreement allowing one party (the lessee) to use the asset of another party (the lessor); accounted for as a rental. (p. 499).

Premium (on a bond) The difference between the selling price and the face value of a bond when a bond is sold for more than its face value. (p. 490).

Present value The value today of an amount to be received at some date in the future after taking into account current interest rates. (p. 486).

Secured bonds Bonds that have specific assets of the issuer pledged as collateral. (p. 486).

***Straight-line method of amortization** A method of amortizing bond discount or bond premium that allocates the same amount to interest expense in each interest period. (p. 502).

Times interest earned A measure of a company's solvency, calculated by dividing the sum of net income, interest expense, and income tax expense by interest expense. (p. 497).

Time value of money The relationship between time and money. A dollar received today is worth more than a dollar promised at some time in the future. (p. 486).

Unsecured bonds Bonds issued against the general credit of the borrower. (p. 486).

PRACTICE MULTIPLE-CHOICE QUESTIONS

(LO 1) 1. The time period for classifying a liability as current is one year or the operating cycle, whichever is:
(a) longer. (c) probable.
(b) shorter. (d) possible.

(LO 1) 2. To be classified as a current liability, a debt must be expected to be paid within:
(a) 1 year.
(b) the operating cycle.
(c) 2 years.
(d) (a) or (b), whichever is longer.

(LO 1) 3. Ottman Company borrows $88,500 on September 1, 2017, from Farley State Bank by signing an $88,500, 12%, 1-year note. What is the accrued interest at December 31, 2017?
(a) $2,655. (c) $4,425.
(b) $3,540. (d) $10,620.

(LO 1) 4. JD Company borrowed $70,000 on December 1 on a 6-month, 12% note. At December 31:
(a) neither the note payable nor the interest payable is a current liability.
(b) the note payable is a current liability but the interest payable is not.
(c) the interest payable is a current liability but the note payable is not.
(d) both the note payable and the interest payable are current liabilities.

(LO 1) 5. Alexis Company has total proceeds from sales of $4,515. If the proceeds include sales taxes of 5%, what is the amount to be credited to Sales Revenue?
(a) $4,000. (c) $4,289.25.
(b) $4,300. (d) The correct answer is not given.

6. When recording payroll: (LO 1)
(a) gross earnings are recorded as salaries and wages payable.
(b) net pay is recorded as salaries and wages expense.
(c) payroll deductions are recorded as liabilities.
(d) More than one of the above.

7. No Fault Insurance Company collected a premium of $18,000 for a 1-year insurance policy on April 1. What amount should No Fault report as a current liability for Unearned Insurance Premiums at December 31? (LO 1)
(a) $0. (c) $13,500.
(b) $4,500. (d) $18,000.

8. Employer payroll taxes do **not** include: (LO 1)
(a) federal unemployment taxes.
(b) state unemployment taxes.
(c) federal income taxes.
(d) FICA taxes.

9. What term is used for bonds that have specific assets pledged as collateral? (LO 2)
(a) Callable bonds. (c) Secured bonds.
(b) Convertible bonds. (d) Discount bonds.

10. The market interest rate: (LO 2)
(a) is the contractual interest rate used to determine the amount of cash interest paid by the borrower.

(b) is listed in the bond indenture.
(c) is the rate investors demand for loaning funds.
(d) More than one of the above is true.

(LO 3) 11. Laurel Inc. issues 10-year bonds with a maturity value of $200,000. If the bonds are issued at a premium, this indicates that:
(a) the contractual interest rate exceeds the market interest rate.
(b) the market interest rate exceeds the contractual interest rate.
(c) the contractual interest rate and the market interest rate are the same.
(d) no relationship exists between the two rates.

(LO 3) 12. On January 1, 2017, Kelly Corp. issues $200,000, 5-year, 7% bonds at face value. The entry to record the issuance of the bonds would include a:
(a) debit to Cash for $14,000.
(b) debit to Bonds Payable for $200,000.
(c) credit to Bonds Payable for $200,000.
(d) credit to Interest Expense of $14,000.

(LO 3) 13. Prescher Corporation issued bonds that pay interest every July 1 and January 1. The entry to accrue bond interest at December 31 includes a:
(a) debit to Interest Payable.
(b) credit to Cash.
(c) credit to Interest Expense.
(d) credit to Interest Payable.

(LO 3) 14. Goethe Corporation redeems its $100,000 face value bonds at 105 on January 1, following the payment of interest. The carrying value of the bonds at the redemption date is $103,745. The entry to record the redemption will include a:
(a) credit of $3,745 to Loss on Bond Redemption.
(b) debit of $3,745 to Premium on Bonds Payable.
(c) credit of $1,255 to Gain on Bond Redemption.
(d) debit of $5,000 to Premium on Bonds Payable.

(LO 4) 15. In a recent year, Derek Corporation had net income of $150,000, interest expense of $30,000, and income tax expense of $20,000. What was Derek Corporation's times interest earned for the year?
(a) 5.00. (c) 6.67.
(b) 4.00. (d) 7.50.

(LO 4) 16. Which of the following is **not** a measure of liquidity?
(a) Debt to assets ratio.
(b) Working capital.
(c) Current ratio.
(d) Current cash debt coverage.

(LO 5) *17. On January 1, Xiang Corporation issues $500,000, 5-year, 12% bonds at 96 with interest payable on January 1. The entry on December 31 to record accrued bond interest and the amortization of bond discount using the straight-line method will include a:
(a) debit to Interest Expense $57,600.
(b) debit to Interest Expense $60,000.
(c) credit to Discount on Bonds Payable $4,000.
(d) credit to Discount on Bonds Payable $2,000.

*18. For the bonds issued in Question 17, what is the carrying value of the bonds at the end of the third interest period? (LO 5)
(a) $492,000. (c) $472,000.
(b) $488,000. (d) $464,000.

*19. On January 1, Holly Ester Inc. issued $1,000,000, 10-year, 9% bonds for $938,554. The market rate of interest for these bonds is 10%. Interest is payable annually on December 31. Holly Ester uses the effective-interest method of amortizing bond discount. At the end of the first year, Holly Ester should report unamortized bond discount of: (LO 6)
(a) $54,900. (c) $51,610.
(b) $57,591. (d) $51,000.

*20. On January 1, Nicholas Corporation issued $1,000,000, 14%, 5-year bonds with interest payable on December 31. The bonds sold for $1,072,096. The market rate of interest for these bonds was 12%. On the first interest date, using the effective-interest method, the debit entry to Interest Expense is for: (LO 6)
(a) $120,000. (c) $128,652.
(b) $125,581. (d) $140,000.

*21. Sampson Corp. purchased a piece of equipment by issuing a $20,000, 6% installment note payable. Quarterly payments on the note are $1,165. What will be the reduction in the principal portion of the note payable that results from the first payment? (LO 7)
(a) $1,165. (c) $865.
(b) $300. (d) $1,200.

*22. Andrews Inc. issues a $497,000, 10% 3-year mortgage note on January 1. The note will be paid in three annual installments of $200,000, each payable at the end of the year. What is the amount of interest expense that should be recognized by Andrews Inc. in the second year? (LO 7)
(a) $16,567. (c) $34,670.
(b) $49,700. (d) $346,700.

*23. Howard Corporation issued a 20-year mortgage note payable on January 1, 2017. At December 31, 2017, the unpaid principal balance will be reported as: (LO 7)
(a) a current liability.
(b) a long-term liability.
(c) part current and part long-term liability.
(d) interest payable.

SOLUTIONS

1. **(a)** The time period for classifying a liability as current is one year or the operating cycle, whichever is longer, not (b) shorter, (c) probable, or (d) possible.
2. **(d)** To be classified as a current liability, a debt must be expected to be paid within 1 year or the operating cycle, whichever is longer. Choices (a) and (b) are both correct, but (d) is the better answer. Choice (c) is incorrect.
3. **(b)** Accrued interest at 12/31/17 is computed as the face value ($88,500) times the interest rate (12%) times the portion of the year the debt was outstanding (4 months out of 12), or $3,540 ($88,500 × 12% × $\frac{4}{12}$), not (a) $2,655, (c) $4,425, or (d) $10,620.
4. **(d)** A current liability is a debt the company reasonably expects to pay (1) from existing current assets or through the creation of other current liabilities, and (2) within the next year or the operating cycle, whichever is longer. Since both

the interest payable and the note payable are expected to be paid within one year, they both will be considered current liabilities. The other choices are therefore incorrect.

5. **(b)** Dividing the total proceeds ($4,515) by one plus the sales tax rate (1.05) will result in the amount of sales to be credited to the Sales Revenue account of $4,300 ($4,515 ÷ 1.05). The other choices are therefore incorrect.
6. **(c)** Payroll deductions are recorded as liabilities. The other choices are incorrect because (a) gross earnings are recorded as salaries and wages expense, and (b) net pay is recorded as salaries and wages payable. Choice (d) is wrong as there is only one correct answer.
7. **(b)** The monthly premium is $1,500 or $18,000 divided by 12. Because No Fault has recognized 9 months of insurance revenue (April 1–December 31), 3 months' insurance premium is still unearned. The amount that No Fault should report as Unearned Service Revenue is therefore $4,500 (3 months × $1,500), not (a) $0, (c) $13,500, or (d) $18,000.
8. **(c)** Federal income taxes are a payroll deduction, not an employer payroll tax. The employer is merely a collection agent. The other choices are all included in employer payroll taxes.
9. **(c)** Secured bonds are those that have specific assets of the issuer pledged as collateral. The other choices are incorrect because (a) callable bonds can be retired or paid off at the discretion of the issuer at a specified price prior to the maturity date, (b) convertible bonds can be converted into common stock at the discretion of the bondholder, and (d) discount bonds is not a term that is generally used when describing bonds.
10. **(c)** The market interest rate is the rate investors demand for loaning funds to the corporation. The other choices are incorrect because (a) the rate on the bond certificate is used to determine the interest payments, (b) the contract interest rate is listed in the bond indenture, and (d) there is only one correct answer.
11. **(a)** When bonds are issued at a premium, this indicates that the contractual interest rate is higher than the market interest rate. The other choices are incorrect because (b) when the market interest rate exceeds the contractual interest rate, bonds are sold at a discount; (c) when the contractual interest rate and the market interest rate are the same, bonds will be issued at par; and (d) the relationship between the market rate of interest and the contractual rate of interest determines whether bonds are issued at par, a discount, or a premium.
12. **(c)** The issuance entry for the bonds includes a debit to Cash for $200,000 and a credit to Bonds Payable for $200,000. The other choices are therefore incorrect.
13. **(d)** Since the interest has been accrued but not yet paid, it has to be recognized as an increase in expenses and liabilities. The entry would be a debit to Interest Expense and a credit to Interest Payable. The other choices are incorrect because (a) an interest accrual will increase, not decrease, Interest Payable; (b) interest accruals do not affect Cash; and (c) an interest accrual will increase, not decrease, Interest Expense.
14. **(b)** The entry to record the redemption of bonds will include a debit to Bonds Payable of $100,000, a debit to Premium on Bonds Payable of $3,745 ($103,745 − $100,000), a credit to Cash of $105,000 ($100,000 × 1.05) and a debit to Loss on Bond Redemption of $1,255 ($105,000 − $103,745). The other choices are therefore incorrect.
15. **(c)** Times interest earned = (Net income + Interest expense + Income tax expense) ÷ Interest expense = ($150,000 + $30,000 + $20,000) ÷ $30,000 = 6.67, not (a) 5.00, (b) 4.00, or (d) 7.50.
16. **(a)** Debt to assets ratio measures solvency, which is the ability of a company to survive over a long period of time. Choices (b) working capital, (c) current ratio, and (d) current cash debt coverage are all measures of liquidity.

*17. **(c)** [$500,000 − (96% × $500,000)] = $20,000; $20,000 ÷ 5 = $4,000 of discount to amortize annually. As a result, the entry would involve a credit to Discount on Bonds Payable $4,000. The other choices are therefore incorrect.

*18. **(a)** The carrying value of bonds increases by the amount of the periodic discount amortization. Discount amortization using the straight-line method is $4,000 each period. Total discount amortization for three periods is $12,000 ($4,000 × 3 periods) which is added to the initial carrying value ($480,000) to arrive at $492,000, the carrying value at the end of the third interest period, not (b) $488,000, (c) $486,000, or (d) $464,000.

*19. **(b)** The beginning balance of unamortized discount is $61,446 ($1,000,000 − $938,554). The discount amortization is $3,855, the difference between the cash interest payment of $90,000 ($1,000,000 × 9%) and the interest expense recorded of $93,855 ($938,554 × 10%). This discount amortization ($3,855) is then subtracted from the beginning balance of unamortized discount ($61,446), to arrive at a balance of $57,591 at the end of the first year, not (a) $54,900, (c) $51,610, or (d) $51,000.

*20. **(c)** The debit to Interest Expense = $1,072,096 (initial carrying value of bond) × 12% (market rate) = $128,652, not (a) $120,000, (b) $125,581, or (d) $140,000.

*21. **(c)** The reduction in the principle portion of the note payable that results from the first payment = $1,165 − ($200,000 × 0.015) = $865, not (a) $1,165, (b) $300, or (d) $1,200.

*22. **(c)** In the first year, Andrews will recognize $49,700 of interest expense ($497,000 × 10%). After the first payment is made, the amount remaining on the note will be $346,700 [$497,000 principal − ($200,000 payment − $49,700 interest)]. The remaining balance ($346,700) is multiplied by the interest rate (10%) to compute the interest expense to be recognized for the second year, $34,670 ($346,700 × 10%), not (a) $16,567, (b) $49,700, or (d) $346,700.

*23. **(c)** Howard Corporation reports the reduction in principal for the next year as a current liability, and it classifies the remaining unpaid principal balance as a long-term liability. The other choices are therefore incorrect.

PRACTICE EXERCISES

1. On June 1, JetSet Company borrows $150,000 from First Bank on a 6-month, $150,000, 8% note.

Prepare entries for interest-bearing notes.

(LO 1)

INSTRUCTIONS

(a) Prepare the entry on June 1.
(b) Prepare the adjusting entry on June 30.
(c) Prepare the entry at maturity (December 1), assuming monthly adjusting entries have been made through November 30.
(d) What was the total financing cost (interest expense)?

SOLUTION

		Debit	Credit
1. (a) June 1	Cash	150,000	
	Notes Payable		150,000
(b) June 30	Interest Expense	1,000	
	Interest Payable		
	($150,000 × 8% × 1/12)		1,000
(c) Dec. 1	Notes Payable	150,000	
	Interest Payable		
	($150,000 × 8% × 6/12)	6,000	
	Cash		156,000

(d) $6,000

2. Global Airlines Company issued $900,000 of 8%, 10-year bonds on January 1, 2017, at face value. Interest is payable annually on January 1.

Prepare entries for bonds issued at face value.

(LO 3)

INSTRUCTIONS

Prepare the journal entries to record the following events.

(a) The issuance of the bonds.
(b) The accrual of interest on December 31.
(c) The payment of interest on January 1, 2018.
(d) The redemption of bonds at maturity, assuming interest for the last interest period has been paid and recorded.

SOLUTION

2.

	Debit	Credit
January 1, 2017		
(a) Cash	900,000	
Bonds Payable		900,000
December 31, 2017		
(b) Interest Expense	72,000	
Interest Payable ($900,000 × 8%)		72,000
January 1, 2018		
(c) Interest Payable	72,000	
Cash		72,000
January 1, 2027		
(d) Bonds Payable	900,000	
Cash		900,000

***3.** Trawler Company borrowed $500,000 on December 31, 2017, by issuing a $500,000, 7% mortgage note payable. The terms call for annual installment payments of $80,000 on December 31. (This exercise is addressed in Appendix 10C.)

Prepare entries to record mortgage note and installment payments.

(LO 7)

INSTRUCTIONS

(a) Prepare the journal entries to record the mortgage loan and the first two installment payments.
(b) Indicate the amount of mortgage note payable to be reported as a current liability and as a long-term liability at December 31, 2018.

SOLUTION

3.

	December 31, 2017		
(a)	Cash	500,000	
	Mortgage Payable		500,000
	December 31, 2018		
	Interest Expense ($500,000 × 7%)	35,000	
	Mortgage Payable	45,000	
	Cash		80,000
	December 31, 2019		
	Interest Expense [($500,000 – $45,000) × 7%]	31,850	
	Mortgage Payable	48,150	
	Cash		80,000

(b) Current: $48,150
Long-term: $406,850 ($500,000 – $45,000 – $48,150)

▶ PRACTICE PROBLEM

Prepare entries to record issuance of bonds, interest accrual, and bond redemption.

(LO 3, 5)

Snyder Software Inc. successfully developed a new spreadsheet program. However, to produce and market the program, the company needed additional financing. On January 1, 2016, Snyder borrowed money as follows.

1. **Snyder issued $500,000, 11%, 10-year bonds. The bonds sold at face value and pay interest on January 1.**
2. **Snyder issued $1.0 million, 10%, 10-year bonds for $886,996. Interest is payable on January 1. Snyder uses the straight-line method of amortization.**

INSTRUCTIONS

(a) For the 11% bonds, prepare journal entries for the following items.
   (1) The issuance of the bonds on January 1, 2016.
   (2) Accrue interest expense on December 31, 2016.
   (3) The payment of interest on January 1, 2017.
(b) For the 10-year, 10% bonds:
   (1) Journalize the issuance of the bonds on January 1, 2016.
   (2) Prepare the entry for the redemption of the bonds at 101 on January 1, 2019, after paying the interest due on this date. The carrying value of the bonds at the redemption date was $920,897.

SOLUTION

(a) (1) 2016			
Jan. 1	Cash	500,000	
	Bonds Payable		500,000
	(To record issue of 11%, 10-year bonds at face value)		
(2) 2016			
Dec. 31	Interest Expense	55,000	
	Interest Payable		55,000
	(To record accrual of bond interest)		
(3) 2017			
Jan. 1	Interest Payable	55,000	
	Cash		55,000
	(To record payment of accrued interest)		
(b) (1) 2016			
Jan. 1	Cash	886,996	
	Discount on Bonds Payable	113,004	
	Bonds Payable		1,000,000
	(To record issuance of bonds at a discount)		

(2) 2019			
Jan. 1	Bonds Payable	1,000,000	
	Loss on Bond Redemption	89,103*	
	Discount on Bonds Payable		79,103
	Cash		1,010,000
	(To record redemption of bonds at 101)		
	*($1,010,000 − $920,897)		

WileyPLUS Brief Exercises, DO IT! Exercises, Exercises, Problems, and many additional resources are available for practice in WileyPLUS.

NOTE: All asterisked Questions, Exercises, and Problems relate to material in the appendices to the chapter.

QUESTIONS

1. Jenny Perez believes a current liability is a debt that can be expected to be paid in one year. Is Jenny correct? Explain.
2. Rayborn Company obtains $20,000 in cash by signing a 9%, 6-month, $20,000 note payable to First Bank on July 1. Rayborn's fiscal year ends on September 30. What information should be reported for the note payable in the annual financial statements?
3. (a) Your roommate says, "Sales taxes are reported as an expense in the income statement." Do you agree? Explain.
   (b) Leiana's Cafe has cash proceeds from sales of $8,550. This amount includes $550 of sales taxes. Give the entry to record the proceeds.
4. Carolina University sold 9,000 season football tickets at $100 each for its five-game home schedule. What entries should be made (a) when the tickets are sold and (b) after each game?
5. Identify three taxes commonly withheld by the employer from an employee's gross pay.
6. (a) Identify three taxes commonly paid by employers on employees' salaries and wages.
   (b) Where in the financial statements does the employer report taxes withheld from employees' pay?
7. Identify the liabilities classified by Apple as current.
8. (a) What are long-term liabilities? Give two examples.
   (b) What is a bond?
9. Contrast these types of bonds:
   (a) Secured and unsecured.
   (b) Convertible and callable.
10. Explain each of these important terms in issuing bonds:
    (a) Face value.
    (b) Contractual interest rate.
    (c) Bond certificate.
11. (a) What is a convertible bond?
    (b) Discuss the advantages of a convertible bond from the standpoint of the bondholders and of the issuing corporation.
12. Describe the two major obligations incurred by a company when bonds are issued.
13. Assume that Acorn Inc. sold bonds with a face value of $100,000 for $104,000. Was the market interest rate equal to, less than, or greater than the bonds' contractual interest rate? Explain.
14. Lee and Jay are discussing how the market price of a bond is determined. Lee believes that the market price of a bond is solely a function of the amount of the principal payment at the end of the term of a bond. Is he right? Discuss.
15. If a 6%, 10-year, $800,000 bond is issued at face value and interest is paid annually, what is the amount of the interest payment at the end of the first period?
16. If the Bonds Payable account has a balance of $700,000 and the Discount on Bonds Payable account has a balance of $36,000, what is the carrying value of the bonds?
17. Which accounts are debited and which are credited if a bond issue originally sold at a premium is redeemed before maturity at 97 immediately following the payment of interest?
18. Penny Lennon, the chief financial officer of Johnson Inc., is considering the options available to her for financing the company's new plant. Short-term interest rates right now are 6%, and long-term rates are 8%. The company's current ratio is 2.2:1. If she finances the new plant with short-term debt, the current ratio will fall to 1.5:1. Briefly discuss the issues that Penny should consider.
19. (a) In general, what are the requirements for the financial statement presentation of long-term liabilities?
    (b) What ratios may be computed to evaluate a company's liquidity and solvency?

20. Ernie Sams says that liquidity and solvency are the same thing. Is he correct? If not, how do they differ?

21. The management of Ingolls Corporation is concerned because survey data suggest that many potential customers do not buy vehicles due to quality concerns. It is considering taking the bold step of increasing the length of its warranty from the industry standard of 3 years up to an unprecedented 10 years in an effort to increase confidence in its quality. Discuss the business as well as accounting implications of this move.

22. Hank Mays needs a few new trucks for his business. He is considering buying the trucks but is concerned that the additional debt he will need to incur will make his liquidity and solvency ratios look bad. What options does he have other than purchasing the trucks, and how will these options affect his financial statements?

23. Anglo Corporation has a current ratio of 1.1. Jon has always been told that a corporation's current ratio should exceed 2.0. The company maintains that its ratio is low because it has a minimal amount of inventory on hand so as to reduce operating costs. Anglo also has significant available lines of credit. Is Jon still correct? What do some companies do to compensate for having fewer liquid assets?

24. What are the implications for analysis if a company has significant operating leases?

25. What criteria must be met before a contingency must be recorded as a liability? How should the contingency be disclosed if the criteria are not met?

*26. Explain the straight-line method of amortizing discount and premium on bonds payable.

*27. Robbins Corporation issues $200,000 of 6%, 5-year bonds on January 1, 2017, at 103. Assuming that the straight-line method is used to amortize the premium, what is the total amount of interest expense for 2017?

*28. Honore Draper is discussing the advantages of the effective-interest method of bond amortization with her accounting staff. What do you think Honore is saying?

*29. Dotsin Corporation issues $400,000 of 9%, 5-year bonds on January 1, 2017, at 104. If Dotsin uses the effective-interest method in amortizing the premium, will the annual interest expense increase or decrease over the life of the bonds? Explain.

*30. Your friend just received a car loan. It is a 7-year installment note. He does not understand the mechanics of how the loan works. Explain the important aspects of the installment note.

*31. Tim Rian, a friend of yours, has recently purchased a home for $125,000, paying $25,000 down and the remainder financed by a 6.5%, 20-year mortgage, payable at $745.57 per month. At the end of the first month, Tim receives a statement from the bank indicating that only $203.90 of principal was paid during the month. At this rate, he calculates that it will take over 40 years to pay off the mortgage. Is he right? Discuss.

BRIEF EXERCISES

Identify whether obligations are current liabilities.
(LO 1), C

BE10-1 Busch Company has these obligations at December 31: (a) a note payable for $100,000 due in 2 years, (b) a 10-year mortgage payable of $200,000 payable in ten $20,000 annual payments and (c) interest payable of $15,000 on the mortgage, and (d) accounts payable of $60,000. For each obligation, indicate whether it should be classified as a current liability, noncurrent liability, or both.

Prepare entries for an interest-bearing note payable.
(LO 1), AP

BE10-2 Hive Company borrows $90,000 on July 1 from the bank by signing a $90,000, 7%, 1-year note payable. Prepare the journal entries to record (a) the proceeds of the note and (b) accrued interest at December 31, assuming adjusting entries are made only at the end of the year.

Compute and record sales taxes payable.
(LO 1), AP

BE10-3 Greenspan Supply does not segregate sales and sales taxes at the time of sale. The register total for March 16 is $10,388. All sales are subject to a 6% sales tax. Compute sales taxes payable and make the entry to record sales taxes payable and sales.

Prepare entries for unearned revenues.
(LO 1), AP

BE10-4 Bramble University sells 3,500 season basketball tickets at $80 each for its 10-game home schedule. Give the entry to record (a) the sale of the season tickets and (b) the revenue recognized after playing the first home game.

Compute gross earnings and net pay.
(LO 1), AP

BE10-5 Betsy Strand's regular hourly wage rate is $16, and she receives an hourly rate of $24 for work in excess of 40 hours. During a January pay period, Betsy works 47 hours. Betsy's federal income tax withholding is $95, and she has no voluntary deductions. Compute Betsy Strand's gross earnings and net pay for the pay period. Assume that the FICA tax rate is 7.65%.

Record a payroll and the payment of wages.
(LO 1), AP

BE10-6 Data for Betsy Strand are presented in BE10-5. Prepare the employer's journal entries to record (a) Betsy's pay for the period and (b) the payment of Betsy's wages. Use January 15 for the end of the pay period and the payment date.

BE10-7 Data for Betsy Strand are presented in BE10-5. Prepare the employer's journal entry to record payroll taxes for the period. Ignore unemployment taxes.

Prepare entries for payroll taxes.
(LO 1), AP

BE10-8 Bridle Inc. issues $300,000, 10-year, 8% bonds at 98. Prepare the journal entry to record the sale of these bonds on March 1, 2017.

Prepare entries for issuance of bonds.
(LO 3), AP

BE10-9 Ravine Company issues $400,000, 20-year, 7% bonds at 101. Prepare the journal entry to record the sale of these bonds on June 1, 2017.

Prepare entries for issuance of bonds.
(LO 3), AP

BE10-10 Clooney Corporation issued 3,000 7%, 5-year, $1,000 bonds dated January 1, 2017, at face value. Interest is paid each January 1.
(a) Prepare the journal entry to record the sale of these bonds on January 1, 2017.
(b) Prepare the adjusting journal entry on December 31, 2017, to record interest expense.
(c) Prepare the journal entry on January 1, 2018, to record interest paid.

Prepare journal entries for bonds issued at face value.
(LO 3), AP

BE10-11 The balance sheet for Gelher Company reports the following information on July 1, 2017.

Prepare journal entry for redemption of bonds.
(LO 3), AP

GELHER COMPANY
Balance Sheet (partial)

Long-term liabilities		
Bonds payable	$2,000,000	
Less: Discount on bonds payable	45,000	$1,955,000

Gelher decides to redeem these bonds at 102 after paying annual interest. Prepare the journal entry to record the redemption on July 1, 2017.

BE10-12 Presented here are long-term liability items for Stevens Inc. at December 31, 2017. Prepare the long-term liabilities section of the balance sheet for Stevens Inc.

Prepare statement presentation of long-term liabilities.
(LO 4), AP

Bonds payable (due 2021)	$700,000
Notes payable (due 2019)	80,000
Discount on bonds payable	28,000

BE10-13 Presented here are liability items for O'Brian Inc. at December 31, 2017. Prepare the liabilities section of O'Brian's balance sheet.

Prepare liabilities section of balance sheet.
(LO 4), AP

Accounts payable	$157,000	FICA taxes payable	$ 7,800
Notes payable (due May 1, 2018)	20,000	Interest payable	40,000
		Notes payable (due 2019)	80,000
Bonds payable (due 2021)	900,000	Income taxes payable	3,500
Unearned rent revenue	240,000	Sales taxes payable	1,700
Discount on bonds payable	41,000		

BE10-14 Suppose the 2017 adidas financial statements contain the following selected data (in millions).

Analyze solvency.
(LO 4), AP

Current assets	$4,485	Interest expense	$169
Total assets	8,875	Income taxes	113
Current liabilities	2,836	Net income	245
Total liabilities	5,099		
Cash	775		

Compute the following values and provide a brief interpretation of each.
(a) Working capital.
(b) Current ratio.
(c) Debt to assets ratio.
(d) Times interest earned.

BE10-15 Suppose the Canadian National Railway Company's (CN) total assets in a recent year were $24,004 million and its total liabilities were $14,180 million. That year, CN reported operating lease commitments for its locomotives, freight cars, and equipment totaling $740 million. If these assets had been recorded as capital leases, assume that assets and liabilities would have risen by approximately $740 million.
(a) Calculate CN's debt to assets ratio, first using the figures reported, and then after increasing assets and liabilities for the unrecorded operating leases.
(b) Discuss the potential effect of these operating leases on your assessment of CN's solvency.

Analyze solvency.
(LO 4), AN

Prepare journal entries for bonds issued at a discount.

(LO 5), AP

***BE10-16** Alpine Company issues $2 million, 10-year, 7% bonds at 99, with interest payable on December 31. The straight-line method is used to amortize bond discount.
(a) Prepare the journal entry to record the sale of these bonds on January 1, 2017.
(b) Prepare the journal entry to record interest expense and bond discount amortization on December 31, 2017, assuming no previous accrual of interest.

Prepare journal entries for bonds issued at a premium.

(LO 5), AP

***BE10-17** Harvard Inc. issues $4 million, 5-year, 8% bonds at 102, with interest payable on January 1. The straight-line method is used to amortize bond premium.
(a) Prepare the journal entry to record the sale of these bonds on January 1, 2017.
(b) Prepare the journal entry to record interest expense and bond premium amortization on December 31, 2017, assuming no previous accrual of interest.

Use effective-interest method of bond amortization.

(LO 6), AP

***BE10-18** Presented below is the partial bond discount amortization schedule for Rohr Corp., which uses the effective-interest method of amortization.

Interest Periods	Interest to Be Paid	Interest Expense to Be Recorded	Discount Amortization	Unamortized Discount	Bond Carrying Value
Issue date				$38,609	$961,391
1	$45,000	$48,070	$3,070	35,539	964,461
2	45,000	48,223	3,223	32,316	967,684

Instructions

(a) Prepare the journal entry to record the payment of interest and the discount amortization at the end of period 1.
(b) Explain why interest expense is greater than interest paid.
(c) Explain why interest expense will increase each period.

Prepare entries for long-term notes payable.

(LO 7), AP

***BE10-19** Jenseng Inc. issues a $800,000, 10%, 10-year mortgage note on December 31, 2017, to obtain financing for a new building. The terms provide for annual installment payments of $130,196. Prepare the entry to record the mortgage loan on December 31, 2017, and the first installment payment on December 31, 2018.

DO IT! EXERCISES

Answer questions about current liabilities.

(LO 1), AP

DO IT! 10-1a You and several classmates are studying for the next accounting examination. They ask you to answer the following questions:

1. If cash is borrowed on a $60,000, 9-month, 10% note on August 1, how much interest expense would be incurred by December 31?
2. The cash register total including sales taxes is $42,000, and the sales tax rate is 5%. What is the sales taxes payable?
3. If $42,000 is collected in advance on November 1 for 6-month magazine subscriptions, what amount of subscription revenue should be recognized on December 31?

Prepare entries for payroll and payroll taxes.

(LO 1), AP

DO IT! 10-1b During the month of February, Hennesey Corporation's employees earned wages of $74,000. Withholdings related to these wages were $5,661 for Social Security (FICA), $7,100 for federal income tax, and $1,900 for state income tax. Costs incurred for unemployment taxes were $110 for federal and $160 for state.

Prepare the February 28 journal entries for (a) salaries and wages expense and salaries and wages payable assuming that all February wages will be paid in March and (b) the company's payroll tax expense.

Evaluate statements about bonds.

(LO 2), C

DO IT! 10-2 State whether each of the following statements is true or false.

_______ 1. Convertible bonds are also known as callable bonds.
_______ 2. The market rate is the rate investors demand for loaning funds.
_______ 3. Semiannual interest payments on bonds are equal to the face value times the stated rate times 6/12.
_______ 4. The present value of a bond is the value at which it should sell in the market.

Prepare journal entry for bond issuance and show balance sheet presentation.

(LO 3), AP

DO IT! 10-3a Smiley Corporation issues $300,000 of bonds for $315,000. (a) Prepare the journal entry to record the issuance of the bonds, and (b) show how the bonds would be reported on the balance sheet at the date of issuance.

DO IT! 10-3b Farmland Corporation issued $400,000 of 10-year bonds at a discount. Prior to maturity, when the carrying value of the bonds was $388,000, the company redeemed the bonds at 99. Prepare the entry to record the redemption of the bonds.

Prepare entry for bond redemption.

(LO 3), AP

DO IT! 10-4 Grouper Company provides you with the following balance sheet information as of December 31, 2017.

Analyze liabilities.

(LO 4), AN

Current assets	$11,500	Current liabilities	$12,000
Long-term assets	26,500	Long-term liabilities	14,000
Total assets	$38,000	Stockholders' equity	12,000
		Total liabilities and stockholders' equity	$38,000

In addition, Grouper reported net income for 2017 of $16,000, income tax expense of $3,200, and interest expense of $1,300.

(a) Compute the current ratio and working capital for Grouper for 2017.
(b) Assume that at the end of 2017, Grouper used $3,000 cash to pay off $3,000 of accounts payable. How would the current ratio and working capital have changed?
(c) Compute the debt to assets ratio and the times interest earned for Grouper for 2017.

EXERCISES

E10-1 Kelly Jones and Tami Crawford borrowed $15,000 on a 7-month, 8% note from Gem State Bank to open their business, JC's Coffee House. The money was borrowed on June 1, 2017, and the note matures January 1, 2018.

Prepare entries for interest-bearing notes.

(LO 1), AP

Instructions

(a) Prepare the entry to record the receipt of the funds from the loan.
(b) Prepare the entry to accrue the interest on June 30.
(c) Assuming adjusting entries are made at the end of each month, determine the balance in the Interest Payable account at December 31, 2017.
(d) Prepare the entry required on January 1, 2018, when the loan is paid back.

E10-2 On May 15, Wild Quest Clothiers borrowed some money on a 4-month note to provide cash during the slow season of the year. The interest rate on the note was 8%. At the time the note was due, the amount of interest owed was $480.

Prepare entries for interest-bearing notes.

(LO 1), AP

Instructions

(a) Determine the amount borrowed by Wild Quest.
(b) Independent of your answer in part (a), assume the amount borrowed was $18,500. What was the interest rate if the amount of interest owed was $555?
(c) Prepare the entry for the initial borrowing and the repayment for the facts in part (a).

E10-3 On June 1, Marchon Company Ltd. borrows $60,000 from Acme Bank on a 6-month, $60,000, 8% note. The note matures on December 1.

Prepare entries for interest-bearing notes.

(LO 1), AP

Instructions

(a) Prepare the entry on June 1.
(b) Prepare the adjusting entry on June 30.
(c) Prepare the entry at maturity (December 1), assuming monthly adjusting entries have been made through November 30.
(d) What was the total financing cost (interest expense)?

E10-4 In performing accounting services for small businesses, you encounter the following situations pertaining to cash sales.

Journalize sales and related taxes.

(LO 1), AP

1. Cerviq Company enters sales and sales taxes separately on its cash register. On April 10, the register totals are sales $22,000 and sales taxes $1,100.
2. Quartz Company does not segregate sales and sales taxes. Its register total for April 15 is $13,780, which includes a 6% sales tax.

Instructions

Prepare the entries to record the sales transactions and related taxes for (a) Cerviq Company and (b) Quartz Company.

Journalize payroll entries.

(LO 1), AP

E10-5 During the month of March, Munster Company's employees earned wages of $64,000. Withholdings related to these wages were $4,896 for Social Security (FICA), $7,500 for federal income tax, $3,100 for state income tax, and $400 for union dues. The company incurred no cost related to these earnings for federal unemployment tax but incurred $700 for state unemployment tax.

Instructions

(a) Prepare the necessary March 31 journal entry to record salaries and wages expense and salaries and wages payable. Assume that wages earned during March will be paid during April.
(b) Prepare the entry to record the company's payroll tax expense.

Journalize unearned revenue transactions.

(LO 1), AP

E10-6 Season tickets for the Dingos are priced at $320 and include 16 home games. An equal amount of revenue is recognized after each game is played. When the season began, the amount credited to Unearned Ticket Revenue was $1,728,000. By the end of October, $1,188,000 of the Unearned Ticket Revenue had been recognized as revenue.

Instructions

(a) How many season tickets did the Dingos sell?
(b) How many home games had the Dingos played by the end of October?
(c) Prepare the entry for the initial recording of the Unearned Ticket Revenue.
(d) Prepare the entry to recognize the revenue after the first home game had been played.

Journalize unearned subscription revenue.

(LO 1), AP

E10-7 Cassini Company Ltd. publishes a monthly sports magazine, *Fishing Preview*. Subscriptions to the magazine cost $28 per year. During November 2017, Cassini sells 6,300 subscriptions for cash, beginning with the December issue. Cassini prepares financial statements quarterly and recognizes subscription revenue at the end of the quarter. The company uses the accounts Unearned Subscription Revenue and Subscription Revenue. The company has a December 31 year-end.

Instructions

(a) Prepare the entry in November for the receipt of the subscriptions.
(b) Prepare the adjusting entry at December 31, 2017, to record subscription revenue in December 2017.
(c) Prepare the adjusting entry at March 31, 2018, to record subscription revenue in the first quarter of 2018.

Prepare journal entries for issuance of bonds and payment and accrual of interest.

(LO 3), AP

E10-8 On August 1, 2017, Gonzaga Corporation issued $600,000, 7%, 10-year bonds at face value. Interest is payable annually on August 1. Gonzaga's year-end is December 31.

Instructions

Prepare journal entries to record the following events.

(a) The issuance of the bonds.
(b) The accrual of interest on December 31, 2017.
(c) The payment of interest on August 1, 2018.

Prepare journal entries for issuance of bonds and payment and accrual of interest.

(LO 3), AP

E10-9 On January 1, Kirkland Company issued $300,000, 8%, 10-year bonds at face value. Interest is payable annually on January 1.

Instructions

Prepare journal entries to record the following events.

(a) The issuance of the bonds.
(b) The accrual of interest on December 31.
(c) The payment of interest on January 1.

Prepare entries for issuance of bonds, balance sheet presentation, and cause of deviations from face value.

(LO 3), AP

E10-10 Arroyo Company issued $600,000, 10-year, 6% bonds at 103.

Instructions

(a) Prepare the journal entry to record the sale of these bonds on January 1, 2017.
(b) Suppose the remaining Premium on Bonds Payable was $10,800 on December 31, 2020. Show the balance sheet presentation on this date.
(c) Explain why the bonds sold at a price above the face amount.

E10-11 Mobbe Company issued $500,000, 15-year, 7% bonds at 96.

Prepare entries for issuance of bonds, balance sheet presentation, and cause of deviations from face value.

(LO 3), AP

Instructions

(a) Prepare the journal entry to record the sale of these bonds on January 1, 2017.
(b) Suppose the remaining Discount on Bonds Payable was $12,000 on December 31, 2022. Show the balance sheet presentation on this date.
(c) Explain why the bonds sold at a price below the face amount.

E10-12 Assume that the following are independent situations recently reported in the *Wall Street Journal*.

Prepare entries for issue of bonds.

(LO 3), AN

1. General Electric (GE) 7% bonds, maturing January 28, 2018, were issued at 111.12.
2. Boeing 7% bonds, maturing September 24, 2032, were issued at 99.08.

Instructions

(a) Were GE and Boeing bonds issued at a premium or a discount?
(b) Explain how bonds, both paying the same contractual interest rate, could be issued at different prices.
(c) Prepare the journal entry to record the issue of each of these two bonds, assuming each company issued $800,000 of bonds in total.

E10-13 Kale Company issued $350,000 of 8%, 20-year bonds on January 1, 2017, at face value. Interest is payable annually on January 1.

Prepare journal entries to record issuance of bonds, payment of interest, and redemption at maturity.

(LO 3), AP

Instructions

Prepare the journal entries to record the following events.

(a) The issuance of the bonds.
(b) The accrual of interest on December 31, 2017.
(c) The payment of interest on January 1, 2018.
(d) The redemption of the bonds at maturity, assuming interest for the last interest period has been paid and recorded.

E10-14 The situations presented here are independent of each other.

Prepare journal entries for redemption of bonds.

(LO 3), AP

Instructions

For each situation, prepare the appropriate journal entry for the redemption of the bonds.

(a) Mikhail Corporation redeemed $140,000 face value, 9% bonds on April 30, 2017, at 101. The carrying value of the bonds at the redemption date was $126,500. The bonds pay annual interest, and the interest payment due on April 30, 2017, has been made and recorded.
(b) Oldman, Inc., redeemed $170,000 face value, 12.5% bonds on June 30, 2017, at 98. The carrying value of the bonds at the redemption date was $184,000. The bonds pay annual interest, and the interest payment due on June 30, 2017, has been made and recorded.

E10-15 Sanchez, Inc. reports the following liabilities (in thousands) on its December 31, 2017, balance sheet and notes to the financial statements.

Prepare liabilities section of balance sheet.

(LO 4), AP

Accounts payable	$4,263.9	Mortgage payable	$6,746.7
Accrued pension liability	1,115.2	Operating leases	1,641.7
Unearned rent revenue	1,058.1	Notes payable (due in 2020)	335.6
Bonds payable	1,961.2	Salaries and wages payable	858.1
Current portion of		Notes payable (due in 2018)	2,563.6
mortgage payable	1,992.2	Unused operating line of credit	3,337.6
Income taxes payable	265.2	Warranty liability—current	1,417.3

Instructions

(a) Identify which of the above liabilities are likely current and which are likely long-term. List any items that do not fit in either category. Explain the reasoning for your selection.
(b) Prepare the liabilities section of Sanchez's balance sheet as at December 31, 2017.

E10-16 Suppose McDonald's 2017 financial statements contain the following selected data (in millions).

Calculate liquidity and solvency ratios; discuss impact of unrecorded obligations on liquidity and solvency.

(LO 4), AP

Current assets	$ 3,416.3	Interest expense	$ 473.2
Total assets	30,224.9	Income taxes	1,936.0
Current liabilities	2,988.7	Net income	4,551.0
Total liabilities	16,191.0		

Instructions

(a) Compute the following values and provide a brief interpretation of each.
  (1) Working capital.
  (2) Current ratio.
  (3) Debt to assets ratio.
  (4) Times interest earned.

(b) Suppose the notes to McDonald's financial statements show that subsequent to 2017 the company will have future minimum lease payments under operating leases of $10,717.5 million. If these assets had been purchased with debt, assets and liabilities would rise by approximately $8,800 million. Recompute the debt to assets ratio after adjusting for this. Discuss your result.

Calculate current ratio before and after paying accounts payable.

(LO 4), AN

E10-17 Suppose 3M Company reported the following financial data for 2017 and 2016 (in millions).

3M COMPANY
Balance Sheet (partial)

	2017	2016
Current assets		
Cash and cash equivalents	$ 3,040	$1,849
Accounts receivable, net	3,250	3,195
Inventories	2,639	3,013
Other current assets	1,866	1,541
Total current assets	$10,795	$9,598
Current liabilities	$ 4,897	$5,839

Instructions

(a) Calculate the current ratio for 3M for 2017 and 2016.

(b) Suppose that at the end of 2017, 3M management used $300 million cash to pay off $300 million of accounts payable. How would its current ratio change?

Calculate current ratio before and after paying accounts payable.

(LO 4), AN

E10-18 Underwood Boutique reported the following financial data for 2017 and 2016.

UNDERWOOD BOUTIQUE
Balance Sheet (partial)
September 30 (in thousands)

	2017	2016
Current assets		
Cash and short-term deposits	$2,574	$1,021
Accounts receivable	2,147	1,575
Inventories	1,201	1,010
Other current assets	322	192
Total current assets	$6,244	$3,798
Current liabilities	$4,503	$2,619

Instructions

(a) Calculate the current ratio for Underwood Boutique for 2017 and 2016.

(b) Suppose that at the end of 2017, Underwood Boutique used $1.5 million cash to pay off $1.5 million of accounts payable. How would its current ratio change?

(c) At September 30, Underwood Boutique has an undrawn operating line of credit of $12.5 million. Would this affect any assessment that you might make of Underwood Boutique's short-term liquidity? Explain.

Discuss contingent liabilities.

(LO 4), C

E10-19 A large retailer was sued nearly 5,000 times in a recent year—about once every 2 hours every day of the year. It has been sued for everything imaginable—ranging from falls on icy parking lots to injuries sustained in shoppers' stampedes to a murder with a rifle purchased at one of its stores. The company reported the following in the notes to its financial statements:

The Company and its subsidiaries are involved from time to time in claims, proceedings, and litigation arising from the operation of its business. The Company does not believe that any such claim, proceeding, or litigation, either alone or in the aggregate, will have a material adverse effect on the Company's financial position or results of its operations.

Instructions

(a) Explain why the company does not have to record these contingent liabilities.
(b) Comment on any implications for analysis of the financial statements.

***E10-20** Sehr Company issued $500,000, 6%, 30-year bonds on January 1, 2017, at 103. Interest is payable annually on January 1. Sehr uses straight-line amortization for bond premium or discount.

Prepare journal entries to record issuance of bonds, payment of interest, amortization of premium using straight-line, and redemption at maturity.

(LO 3, 5), AP

Instructions

Prepare the journal entries to record the following events.
(a) The issuance of the bonds.
(b) The accrual of interest and the premium amortization on December 31, 2017.
(c) The payment of interest on January 1, 2018.
(d) The redemption of the bonds at maturity, assuming interest for the last interest period has been paid and recorded.

***E10-21** Motley Company issued $300,000, 8%, 15-year bonds on December 31, 2016, for $288,000. Interest is payable annually on December 31. Motley uses the straight-line method to amortize bond premium or discount.

Prepare journal entries to record issuance of bonds, payment of interest, amortization of discount using straight-line, and redemption at maturity.

(LO 3, 5), AP

Instructions

Prepare the journal entries to record the following events.
(a) The issuance of the bonds.
(b) The payment of interest and the discount amortization on December 31, 2017.
(c) The redemption of the bonds at maturity, assuming interest for the last interest period has been paid and recorded.

***E10-22** Woode Corporation issued $400,000, 7%, 20-year bonds on January 1, 2017, for $360,727. This price resulted in an effective-interest rate of 8% on the bonds. Interest is payable annually on January 1. Woode uses the effective-interest method to amortize bond premium or discount.

Prepare journal entries for issuance of bonds, payment of interest, and amortization of discount using effective-interest method.

(LO 3, 6), AP

Instructions

Prepare the journal entries to record (round to the nearest dollar):
(a) The issuance of the bonds.
(b) The accrual of interest and the discount amortization on December 31, 2017.
(c) The payment of interest on January 1, 2018.

***E10-23** Hernandez Company issued $380,000, 7%, 10-year bonds on January 1, 2017, for $407,968. This price resulted in an effective-interest rate of 6% on the bonds. Interest is payable annually on January 1. Hernandez uses the effective-interest method to amortize bond premium or discount.

Prepare journal entries for issuance of bonds, payment of interest, and amortization of premium using effective-interest method.

(LO 3, 6), AP

Instructions

Prepare the journal entries (rounded to the nearest dollar) to record:
(a) The issuance of the bonds.
(b) The accrual of interest and the premium amortization on December 31, 2017.
(c) The payment of interest on January 1, 2018.

***E10-24** Yancey Co. receives $300,000 when it issues a $300,000, 10%, mortgage note payable to finance the construction of a building at December 31, 2017. The terms provide for annual installment payments of $50,000 on December 31.

Prepare journal entries to record mortgage note and installment payments.

(LO 7), AP

Instructions

Prepare the journal entries to record the mortgage loan and the first two installment payments.

Determine balance sheet presentation of installment note payable.

(LO 7), AP

***E10-25** Waite Corporation issued a $50,000, 10%, 10-year installment note payable on January 1, 2017. Payments of $8,137 are made each January 1, beginning January 1, 2018.

Instructions

(a) What amounts should be reported under current liabilities related to the note on December 31, 2017?
(b) What should be reported under long-term liabilities?

EXERCISES: SET B AND CHALLENGE EXERCISES

Visit the book's companion website, at **www.wiley.com/college/kimmel**, and choose the Student Companion site to access Exercises: Set B and Challenge Exercises.

PROBLEMS: SET A

Prepare current liability entries, adjusting entries, and current liabilities section.

(LO 1, 4), AP

P10-1A On January 1, 2017, the ledger of Romada Company contained these liability accounts.

Accounts Payable	$42,500
Sales Taxes Payable	6,600
Unearned Service Revenue	19,000

During January, the following selected transactions occurred.

Jan.	1	Borrowed $18,000 in cash from Apex Bank on a 4-month, 5%, $18,000 note.
	5	Sold merchandise for cash totaling $6,254, which includes 6% sales taxes.
	12	Performed services for customers who had made advance payments of $10,000. (Credit Service Revenue.)
	14	Paid state treasurer's department for sales taxes collected in December 2016, $6,600.
	20	Sold 500 units of a new product on credit at $48 per unit, plus 6% sales tax.

During January, the company's employees earned wages of $70,000. Withholdings related to these wages were $5,355 for Social Security (FICA), $5,000 for federal income tax, and $1,500 for state income tax. The company owed no money related to these earnings for federal or state unemployment tax. Assume that wages earned during January will be paid during February. No entry had been recorded for wages or payroll tax expense as of January 31.

Instructions

(a) Journalize the January transactions.
(b) Journalize the adjusting entries at January 31 for the outstanding note payable and for salaries and wages expense and payroll tax expense.
(c) Prepare the current liabilities section of the balance sheet at January 31, 2017. Assume no change in Accounts Payable.

(c) Tot. current liabilities $146,724

Journalize and post note transactions; show balance sheet presentation.

(LO 1, 4), AP

P10-2A Ehler Corporation sells rock-climbing products and also operates an indoor climbing facility for climbing enthusiasts. During the last part of 2017, Ehler had the following transactions related to notes payable.

Sept. 1	Issued a $12,000 note to Pippen to purchase inventory. The 3-month note payable bears interest of 6% and is due December 1. (Ehler uses a perpetual inventory system.)
Sept. 30	Recorded accrued interest for the Pippen note.
Oct. 1	Issued a $16,500, 8%, 4-month note to Prime Bank to finance the purchase of a new climbing wall for advanced climbers. The note is due February 1.
Oct. 31	Recorded accrued interest for the Pippen note and the Prime Bank note.
Nov. 1	Issued a $26,000 note and paid $8,000 cash to purchase a vehicle to transport clients to nearby climbing sites as part of a new series of climbing classes. This note bears interest of 6% and matures in 12 months.
Nov. 30	Recorded accrued interest for the Pippen note, the Prime Bank note, and the vehicle note.
Dec. 1	Paid principal and interest on the Pippen note.
Dec. 31	Recorded accrued interest for the Prime Bank note and the vehicle note.

Instructions

(a) Prepare journal entries for the transactions noted above.
(b) Post the above entries to the Notes Payable, Interest Payable, and Interest Expense accounts. (Use T-accounts.)
(c) Show the balance sheet presentation of notes payable and interest payable at December 31.
(d) How much interest expense relating to notes payable did Ehler incur during the year?

(b) Interest Payable $590

P10-3A The following section is taken from Hardesty's balance sheet at December 31, 2016.

Prepare journal entries to record interest payments and redemption of bonds.

(LO 3), AP

Current liabilities	
Interest payable	$ 40,000
Long-term liabilities	
Bonds payable (8%, due January 1, 2020)	500,000

Interest is payable annually on January 1. The bonds are callable on any annual interest date.

Instructions

(a) Journalize the payment of the bond interest on January 1, 2017.
(b) Assume that on January 1, 2017, after paying interest, Hardesty calls bonds having a face value of $200,000. The call price is 103. Record the redemption of the bonds.
(c) Prepare the adjusting entry on December 31, 2017, to accrue the interest on the remaining bonds.

(b) Loss $6,000

P10-4A On October 1, 2016, Kristal Corp. issued $700,000, 5%, 10-year bonds at face value. The bonds were dated October 1, 2016, and pay interest annually on October 1. Financial statements are prepared annually on December 31.

Prepare journal entries to record issuance of bonds, interest, balance sheet presentation, and bond redemption.

(LO 3, 4), AP

Instructions

(a) Prepare the journal entry to record the issuance of the bonds.
(b) Prepare the adjusting entry to record the accrual of interest on December 31, 2016.
(c) Show the balance sheet presentation of bonds payable and bond interest payable on December 31, 2016.
(d) Prepare the journal entry to record the payment of interest on October 1, 2017.
(e) Prepare the adjusting entry to record the accrual of interest on December 31, 2017.
(f) Assume that on January 1, 2018, Kristal pays the accrued bond interest and calls the bonds. The call price is 104. Record the payment of interest and redemption of the bonds.

(f) Loss $28,000

P10-5A Malcolm Company sold $6,000,000, 7%, 15-year bonds on January 1, 2017. The bonds were dated January 1, 2017, and pay interest on December 31. The bonds were sold at 98.

Prepare journal entries to record issuance of bonds, show balance sheet presentation, and record bond redemption.

(LO 3, 4), AP

Instructions

(a) Prepare the journal entry to record the issuance of the bonds on January 1, 2017.
(b) At December 31, 2017, $8,000 of the bond discount had been amortized. Show the long-term liability balance sheet presentation of the bond liability at December 31, 2017.
(c) At January 1, 2019, when the carrying value of the bonds was $5,896,000, the company redeemed the bonds at 102. Record the redemption of the bonds assuming that interest for the year had already been paid.

(c) Loss $224,000

P10-6A Suppose you have been presented with selected information taken from the financial statements of Southwest Airlines Co., shown on the next page.

Calculate and comment on ratios.

(LO 4), AN

Instructions

(a) Calculate each of the following ratios for 2017 and 2016.
 (1) Current ratio.
 (2) Free cash flow.
 (3) Debt to assets ratio.
 (4) Times interest earned.
(b) Comment on the trend in ratios.
(c) Read the company's note on leases. If the operating leases had instead been accounted for like a purchase, assets and liabilities would increase by approximately $1,600 million. Recalculate the debt to assets ratio for 2017 in light of this information, and discuss the implications for analysis.

SOUTHWEST AIRLINES CO.
Balance Sheet (partial)
December 31
(in millions)

	2017	2016
Total current assets	$ 2,893	$ 4,443
Noncurrent assets	11,415	12,329
Total assets	$14,308	$16,772
Current liabilities	$ 2,806	$ 4,836
Long-term liabilities	6,549	4,995
Total liabilities	9,355	9,831
Shareholders' equity	4,953	6,941
Total liabilities and shareholders' equity	$14,308	$16,772

Other information:

	2017	2016
Net income (loss)	$ 178	$ 645
Income tax expense	100	413
Interest expense	130	119
Cash provided by operations	(1,521)	2,845
Capital expenditures	923	1,331
Cash dividends	13	14

Note 8. Leases
The majority of the Company's terminal operations space, as well as 82 aircraft, were under operating leases at December 31, 2017. Future minimum lease payments under noncancelable operating leases are as follows: 2018, $376,000; 2019, $324,000; 2020, $249,000; 2021, $208,000; 2022, $152,000; after 2023, $728,000.

Prepare journal entries to record interest payments, straight-line discount amortization, and redemption of bonds.
(LO 3, 5), AP

***P10-7A** The following information is taken from Lassen Corp.'s balance sheet at December 31, 2016.

Current liabilities		
Interest payable		$ 96,000
Long-term liabilities		
Bonds payable (4%, due January 1, 2027)	$2,400,000	
Less: Discount on bonds payable	24,000	2,376,000

Interest is payable annually on January 1. The bonds are callable on any annual interest date. Lassen uses straight-line amortization for any bond premium or discount. From December 31, 2016, the bonds will be outstanding for an additional 10 years (120 months).

Instructions
(Round all computations to the nearest dollar.)
(a) Journalize the payment of bond interest on January 1, 2017.
(b) Prepare the entry to amortize bond discount and to accrue the interest on December 31, 2017.
(c) Loss $11,600
(c) Assume on January 1, 2018, after paying interest, that Lassen Corp. calls bonds having a face value of $400,000. The call price is 102. Record the redemption of the bonds.
(d) Prepare the adjusting entry at December 31, 2018, to amortize bond discount and to accrue interest on the remaining bonds.

Prepare journal entries to record issuance of bonds, interest, and straight-line amortization, and balance sheet presentation.
(LO 3, 4, 5), AP

***P10-8A** Fong Corporation sold $2,000,000, 7%, 5-year bonds on January 1, 2017. The bonds were dated January 1, 2017, and pay interest on January 1. Fong Corporation uses the straight-line method to amortize bond premium or discount.

Instructions
(a) Prepare all the necessary journal entries to record the issuance of the bonds and bond interest expense for 2017, assuming that the bonds sold at 102.

(b) Prepare journal entries as in part (a) assuming that the bonds sold at 97.
(c) Show the balance sheet presentation for the bond issue at December 31, 2017, using (1) the 102 selling price, and then (2) the 97 selling price.

***P10-9A** Saylor Co. sold $3,000,000, 8%, 10-year bonds on January 1, 2017. The bonds were dated January 1, 2017, and pay interest on January 1. The company uses straight-line amortization on bond premiums and discounts. Financial statements are prepared annually.

Prepare journal entries to record issuance of bonds, interest, and straight-line amortization, and balance sheet presentation.

(LO 3, 4, 5), AP

Instructions

(a) Prepare the journal entries to record the issuance of the bonds assuming they sold at:
(1) 103.
(2) 98.
(b) Prepare amortization tables for both assumed sales for the first three interest payments.
(c) Prepare the journal entries to record interest expense for 2017 under both of the bond issuances assumed in part (a).
(d) Show the long-term liabilities balance sheet presentation for both of the bond issuances assumed in part (a) at December 31, 2017.

(c) (2) 12/31/17 Interest Expense $246,000

***P10-10A** On January 1, 2017, Lachte Corporation issued $1,800,000 face value, 5%, 10-year bonds at $1,667,518. This price resulted in an effective-interest rate of 6% on the bonds. Lachte uses the effective-interest method to amortize bond premium or discount. The bonds pay annual interest January 1.

Prepare journal entries to record issuance of bonds, payment of interest, and amortization of bond discount using effective-interest method.

(LO 3, 6), AP

Instructions

(Round all computations to the nearest dollar.)
(a) Prepare the journal entry to record the issuance of the bonds on January 1, 2017.
(b) Prepare an amortization table through December 31, 2019 (three interest periods) for this bond issue.
(c) Prepare the journal entry to record the accrual of interest and the amortization of the discount on December 31, 2017.
(d) Prepare the journal entry to record the payment of interest on January 1, 2018.
(e) Prepare the journal entry to record the accrual of interest and the amortization of the discount on December 31, 2018.

(c) Interest Expense $100,051

***P10-11A** On January 1, 2017, Opal Company issued $2,000,000 face value, 7%, 10-year bonds at $2,147,202. This price resulted in a 6% effective-interest rate on the bonds. Opal uses the effective-interest method to amortize bond premium or discount. The bonds pay annual interest on each January 1.

Prepare journal entries to record issuance of bonds, payment of interest, and effective-interest amortization, and balance sheet presentation.

(LO 3, 4, 6), AP

Instructions

(a) Prepare the journal entries to record the following transactions.
(1) The issuance of the bonds on January 1, 2017.
(2) Accrual of interest and amortization of the premium on December 31, 2017.
(3) The payment of interest on January 1, 2018.
(4) Accrual of interest and amortization of the premium on December 31, 2018.
(b) Show the proper long-term liabilities balance sheet presentation for the liability for bonds payable at December 31, 2018.
(c) Provide the answers to the following questions in narrative form.
(1) What amount of interest expense is reported for 2018?
(2) Would the bond interest expense reported in 2018 be the same as, greater than, or less than the amount that would be reported if the straight-line method of amortization were used?

(a) (4) Interest Expense $128,162

***P10-12A** Laverne purchased a new piece of equipment to be used in its new facility. The $370,000 piece of equipment was purchased with a $50,000 down payment and with cash received through the issuance of a $320,000, 8%, 5-year mortgage payable issued on January 1, 2017. The terms provide for annual installment payments of $80,146 on December 31.

Prepare installment payments schedule, journal entries, and balance sheet presentation for a mortgage note payable.

(LO 4, 7), AP

Instructions

(Round all computations to the nearest dollar.)
(a) Prepare an installment payments schedule for the first three payments of the notes payable.
(b) Prepare the journal entry related to the notes payable for December 31, 2017.

(c) Current portion $58,910

(c) Show the balance sheet presentation for this obligation for December 31, 2017. (*Hint:* Be sure to distinguish between the current and long-term portions of the note.)

Prepare journal entries to record payments for long-term note payable, and balance sheet presentation.

(LO 4, 7), AP

***P10-13A** Hetty Grey has just approached a venture capitalist for financing for her new business venture, the development of a local ski hill. On July 1, 2016, Hetty was loaned $150,000 at an annual interest rate of 7%. The loan is repayable over 5 years in annual installments of $36,584, principal and interest, due each June 30. The first payment is due June 30, 2017. Hetty uses the effective-interest method for amortizing debt. Her ski hill company's year-end will be June 30.

Instructions

(a) Prepare an amortization schedule for the 5 years, 2016–2021. (Round all calculations to the nearest dollar.)

(b) 6/30/17 Interest Expense $10,500

(b) Prepare all journal entries for Hetty Grey for the first 2 fiscal years ended June 30, 2017, and June 30, 2018. (Round all calculations to the nearest dollar.)

(c) Show the balance sheet presentation of the note payable as of June 30, 2018. (*Hint:* Be sure to distinguish between the current and long-term portions of the note.)

PROBLEMS: SET B AND SET C

Visit the book's companion website, at **www.wiley.com/college/kimmel**, and choose the Student Companion site to access Problems: Set B and Set C.

CONTINUING PROBLEM Cookie Creations

© leungchopan/ Shutterstock

(*Note:* This is a continuation of the Cookie Creations problem from Chapters 1 through 9.)

CC10 Recall that Cookie Creations borrowed $2,000 from Natalie's grandmother. Natalie now is thinking of repaying all amounts outstanding on that loan. She needs to know the amounts of interest payable and interest expense to make the correct journal entries for repayment of the loan.

Go to the book's companion website, at **www.wiley.com/college/kimmel**, *to see the completion of this problem.*

COMPREHENSIVE ACCOUNTING CYCLE REVIEW

ACR10 Aimes Corporation's balance sheet at December 31, 2016, is presented below.

AIMES CORPORATION
Balance Sheet
December 31, 2016

Cash	$ 30,000	Accounts payable	$ 13,750
Inventory	30,750	Interest payable	2,500
Prepaid insurance	5,600	Bonds payable	50,000
Equipment	38,000	Common stock	25,000
	$104,350	Retained earnings	13,100
			$104,350

During 2017, the following transactions occurred. Aimes uses a perpetual inventory system.

1. Aimes paid $2,500 interest on the bonds on January 1, 2017.
2. Aimes purchased $241,100 of inventory on account.
3. Aimes sold for $480,000 cash inventory which cost $265,000. Aimes also collected $28,800 sales taxes.
4. Aimes paid $230,000 on accounts payable.
5. Aimes paid $2,500 interest on the bonds on July 1, 2017.
6. The prepaid insurance ($5,600) expired on July 31.
7. On August 1, Aimes paid $10,200 for insurance coverage from August 1, 2017, through July 31, 2018.

8. Aimes paid $17,000 sales taxes to the state.
9. Paid other operating expenses, $91,000.
10. Redeemed the bonds on December 31, 2017, by paying $48,000 plus $2,500 interest.
11. Issued $90,000 of 8% bonds on December 31, 2017, at 103. The bonds pay interest every June 30 and December 31.

Adjustment data:

1. Recorded the insurance expired from item 7.
2. The equipment was acquired on December 31, 2016, and will be depreciated on a straight-line basis over 5 years with a $3,000 salvage value.
3. The income tax rate is 30%. (*Hint:* Prepare the income statement up to income before taxes and multiply by 30% to compute the amount.)

Instructions
(You may want to set up T-accounts to determine ending balances.)
(a) Prepare journal entries for the transactions listed above and adjusting entries.
(b) Prepare an adjusted trial balance at December 31, 2017. (b) Totals $687,695
(c) Prepare an income statement and a retained earnings statement for the year ending December 31, 2017, and a classified balance sheet as of December 31, 2017. (c) N.I. $72,905

EXPAND YOUR CRITICAL THINKING

FINANCIAL REPORTING PROBLEM: Apple Inc.

Financial Reporting

E

CT10-1 Refer to the financial statements of Apple Inc. in Appendix A.

Instructions
Answer the following questions.
(a) What were Apple's total current liabilities at September 27, 2014? What was the increase/decrease in Apple's total current liabilities from the prior year?
(b) How much were the accounts payable at September 27, 2014?
(c) What were the components of total current liabilities on September 27, 2014 (other than accounts payable already discussed above)?

COMPARATIVE ANALYSIS PROBLEM: Columbia Sportswear Company vs. VF Corporation

Financial Analysis

E

CT10-2 The financial statements of Columbia Sportswear Company are presented in Appendix B. Financial statements of VF Corporation are presented in Appendix C.

Instructions
(a) Based on the information contained in these financial statements, compute the current ratio for 2014 for each company. What conclusions concerning the companies' liquidity can be drawn from these ratios?
(b) Based on the information contained in these financial statements, compute the following 2014 ratios for each company.
(1) Debt to assets ratio.
(2) Times interest earned.
What conclusions about the companies' long-run solvency can be drawn from the ratios?

COMPARATIVE ANALYSIS PROBLEM: Amazon.com, Inc. vs. Wal-Mart Stores, Inc.

Financial Analysis

E

CT10-3 The financial statements of Amazon.com, Inc. are presented in Appendix D. Financial statements of Wal-Mart Stores, Inc. are presented in Appendix E.

Instructions
(a) Based on the information contained in these financial statements, compute the current ratio for the most recent fiscal year for each company. What conclusions concerning the companies' liquidity can be drawn from these ratios?

(b) Based on the information contained in these financial statements, compute the following ratios for each company's most recent fiscal year.
(1) Debt to assets ratio.
(2) Times interest earned.
What conclusions about the companies' long-run solvency can be drawn from the ratios?

Financial Analysis

INTERPRETING FINANCIAL STATEMENTS

E **CT10-4** Hechinger Co. and Home Depot are two home improvement retailers. Compared to Hechinger, founded in the early 1900s, Home Depot is a relative newcomer. But in recent years, while Home Depot was reporting large increases in net income, Hechinger was reporting increasingly large net losses. Finally, largely due to competition from Home Depot, Hechinger was forced to file for bankruptcy. Here are financial data for both companies (in millions).

	Hechinger	**Home Depot**
Cash	$ 21	$ 62
Receivables	0	469
Total current assets	1,153	4,933
Beginning total assets	1,668	11,229
Ending total assets	1,577	13,465
Beginning current liabilities	935	2,456
Ending current liabilities	938	2,857
Beginning total liabilities	1,392	4,015
Ending total liabilities	1,339	4,716
Interest expense	67	37
Income tax expense	3	1,040
Cash provided (used) by operations	(257)	1,917
Net income	(93)	1,614
Net sales	3,444	30,219

Instructions

Using the data provided, perform the following analysis.

(a) Calculate working capital and the current ratio for each company. Discuss their relative liquidity.
(b) Calculate the debt to assets ratio and times interest earned for each company. Discuss their relative solvency.
(c) Calculate the return on assets and profit margin for each company. Comment on their relative profitability.
(d) The notes to Home Depot's financial statements indicate that it leases many of its facilities using operating leases. If these assets had instead been purchased with debt, assets and liabilities would have increased by approximately $2,347 million. Calculate the company's debt to assets ratio employing this adjustment. Discuss the implications.

E **CT10-5** For many years, Borders Group and Barnes and Noble were the dominant booksellers in the United States. They experienced rapid growth, and in the process they forced many small, independent bookstores out of business. Recently, Borders filed for bankruptcy. It was the victim of its inability to change with the times. It did not develop a viable business plan for dealing with digital books and online sales. Below is financial information (in millions) for the two companies, taken from the annual reports of each company one year before Borders filed for bankruptcy.

	Borders	**Barnes and Noble**
Current assets	$ 978.7	$1,719.5
Total assets	1,415.6	3,705.7
Current liabilities	918.1	1,724.4
Total liabilities	1,257.3	2,802.3
Net income/(loss)	(109.4)	36.7
Interest expense	24.1	28.2
Tax expense/(income tax benefit)	(31.3)	8.4

Instructions

(a) Compute the current ratio for each company.
(b) Compute the debt to assets ratio and times interest earned for each company. (*Hint:* A tax benefit means that rather than pay taxes, the company was due a refund because of its losses. For ratio purposes, a tax benefit is treated the opposite of tax expense.)

(c) Discuss the relative liquidity and solvency of each company. Did the bankruptcy of Borders seem likely?

REAL-WORLD FOCUS

CT10-6 Bond or debt securities pay a stated rate of interest. This rate of interest is dependent on the risk associated with the investment. Also, bond prices change when the risks associated with those bonds change. Standard & Poor's provides ratings for companies that issue debt securities. E

***Address:* www.standardandpoors.com/ratings/definitions-and-faqs/en/us**

Instructions

Go to the website shown and answer the following questions.

(a) Explain the meaning of an "A" rating. Explain the meaning of a "C" rating.
(b) What types of things can cause a change in a company's credit rating?
(c) Explain the relationship between a company's credit rating and the merit of an investment in that company's bonds.

CT10-7 The September 1, 2009, edition of *CFO.com* contains an article by Marie Leone and Tim Reason entitled "Dirty Secrets." You can access this article at **www.cfo.com/article.cfm/14292477?f=singlepage**. E

Instructions

Read the article and answer the following questions.

(a) Summarize the accounting for contingent items that is provided in this textbook.
(b) The authors of the article suggest that many companies are basically accounting for contingencies on a cash basis. Is this consistent with the approach you described in part (a)?
(c) The article suggests that many companies report one set of liability estimates to insurers and a different (lower) set of numbers in their financial statements. How is this possible, and what are the implications for investors?
(d) How do international accounting standards differ in terms of the amounts reported in these types of situations?

DECISION-MAKING ACROSS THE ORGANIZATION

Financial Analysis

Writing

Group Project

CT10-8 On January 1, 2015, Picard Corporation issued $3,000,000, 5-year, 8% bonds at 97. The bonds pay interest annually on January 1. By January 1, 2017, the market rate of interest for bonds of risk similar to those of Picard Corporation had risen. As a result, the market price of these bonds was $2,500,000 on January 1, 2017—below their carrying value of $2,946,000.

Geoff Marquis, president of the company, suggests repurchasing all of these bonds in the open market at the $2,500,000 price. But to do so the company will have to issue $2,500,000 (face value) of new 10-year, 12% bonds at par. The president asks you, as controller, "What is the feasibility of my proposed repurchase plan?" E

Instructions

With the class divided into groups, answer the following.

(a) Prepare the journal entry to redeem the 5-year bonds on January 1, 2017. Prepare the journal entry to issue the new 10-year bonds.
(b) Prepare a short memo to the president in response to his request for advice. List the economic factors that you believe should be considered for his repurchase proposal.

COMMUNICATION ACTIVITY

CT10-9 Jerry Hogan, president of Norwest, Inc., is considering the issuance of bonds to finance an expansion of his business. He has asked you to do the following: (1) discuss the advantages of bonds over common stock financing, (2) indicate the types of bonds he might issue, and (3) explain the issuing procedures used in bond transactions. E

Instructions

Write a memorandum to the president, answering his request.

ETHICS CASES

CT10-10 The July 1998 issue of *Inc.* magazine includes an article by Jeffrey L. Seglin entitled "Would You Lie to Save Your Company?" It recounts the following true situation: E

"A Chief Executive Officer (CEO) of a $20-million company that repairs aircraft engines received notice from a number of its customers that engines that it had recently repaired had failed, and that the company's parts were to blame. The CEO had not yet determined whether his company's parts were, in fact, the cause of the problem. The Federal Aviation Administration (FAA) had been notified and was investigating the matter.

What complicated the situation was that the company was in the midst of its year-end audit. As part of the audit, the CEO was required to sign a letter saying that he was not aware of any significant outstanding circumstances that could negatively impact the company—in accounting terms, of any contingent liabilities. The auditor was not aware of the customer complaints or the FAA investigation.

The company relied heavily on short-term loans from eight banks. The CEO feared that if these lenders learned of the situation, they would pull their loans. The loss of these loans would force the company into bankruptcy, leaving hundreds of people without jobs. Prior to this problem, the company had a stellar performance record."

Instructions

Answer the following questions.

(a) Who are the stakeholders in this situation?

(b) What are the CEO's possible courses of action? What are the potential results of each course of action? (Take into account the two alternative outcomes: the FAA determines the company (1) was not at fault, and (2) was at fault.)

(c) What would you do, and why?

(d) Suppose the CEO decides to conceal the situation, and that during the next year the company is found to be at fault and is forced into bankruptcy. What losses are incurred by the stakeholders in this situation? Do you think the CEO should suffer legal consequences if he decides to conceal the situation?

E **CT10-11** During the summer of 2002, the financial press reported that Citigroup was being investigated for allegations that it had arranged transactions for Enron so as to intentionally misrepresent the nature of the transactions and consequently achieve favorable balance sheet treatment. Essentially, the deals were structured to make it appear that money was coming into Enron from trading activities, rather than from loans.

A July 23, 2002, *The New York Times* article by Richard Oppel and Kurt Eichenwald entitled "Citigroup Said to Mold Deal to Help Enron Skirt Rules" suggested that Citigroup intentionally kept certain parts of a secret oral agreement out of the written record for fear that it would change the accounting treatment. Critics contend that this had the effect of significantly understating Enron's liabilities, thus misleading investors and creditors. Citigroup maintains that, as a lender, it has no obligation to ensure that its clients account for transactions properly. The proper accounting, Citigroup insists, is the responsibility of the client and its auditor.

Instructions

Answer the following questions.

(a) Who are the stakeholders in this situation?

(b) Do you think that a lender, in general, in arranging so-called "structured financing" has a responsibility to ensure that its clients account for the financing in an appropriate fashion, or is this the responsibility of the client and its auditor?

(c) What effect did the fact that the written record did not disclose all characteristics of the transaction probably have on the auditor's ability to evaluate the accounting treatment of this transaction?

(d) *The New York Times* article noted that in one presentation made to sell this kind of deal to Enron and other energy companies, Citigroup stated that using such an arrangement "eliminates the need for capital markets disclosure, keeping structure mechanics private." Why might a company wish to conceal the terms of a financing arrangement from the capital markets (investors and creditors)? Is this appropriate? Do you think it is ethical for a lender to market deals in this way?

(e) Why was this deal more potentially harmful to shareholders than other off-balance-sheet transactions (for example, lease financing)?

ALL ABOUT YOU

E **CT10-12** For most U.S. families, medical costs are substantial and rising. But will medical costs be your most substantial expense over your lifetime? Not likely. Will it be housing or food? Again, not likely. The answer: Taxes are likely to be your biggest expense. On average, Americans work 74 days to afford their federal taxes. Companies, too, have large tax burdens. They look very hard at tax issues in deciding where to build their plants and where to locate their administrative headquarters.

Instructions

(a) Determine what your state income taxes are if your taxable income is $60,000 and you file as a single taxpayer in the state in which you live.

(b) Assume that you own a home worth $200,000 in your community and the tax rate is 2.1%. Compute the property taxes you would pay.

(c) Assume that the total gasoline bill for your automobile is $1,200 a year (300 gallons at $4 per gallon). What are the amounts of state and federal taxes that you pay on the $1,200?

(d) Assume that your purchases for the year total $9,000. Of this amount, $5,000 was for food and prescription drugs. What is the amount of sales tax you would pay on these purchases? (*Note:* Many states do not have a sales tax for food or prescription drug purchases. Does yours?)

(e) Determine what your Social Security taxes are if your income is $60,000.

(f) Determine what your federal income taxes are if your taxable income is $60,000 and you file as a single taxpayer.

(g) Determine your total taxes paid based on the above calculations, and determine the percentage of income that you would pay in taxes based on the following formula: Total taxes paid ÷ Total income.

FASB CODIFICATION ACTIVITY

CT10-13 If your school has a subscription to the FASB Codification, go to **http://aaahq.org/asclogin.cfm** to log in and prepare responses to the following. C

(a) What is the definition of current liabilities?

(b) What is the definition of long-term obligations?

(c) What guidance does the Codification provide for the disclosure of long-term obligations?

CONSIDERING PEOPLE, PLANET, AND PROFIT

CT10-14 The December 10, 2011, edition of *The Economist* contains an article entitled "Helping the Poor to Save: Small Wonder." This article discusses how many of the world's poorest people benefit from borrowing small amounts of money. E

Instructions

Read the article and answer the following questions. (The article can be accessed by doing an Internet search that includes the title of the article and magazine.)

(a) What monthly rate of interest do people pay on the loans they borrow from the microfinance organizations described in the article? What would these rates be on an annualized basis?

(b) The rates described in your answer to part (a) are very high. Explain how somebody can pay such high rates and yet still benefit from borrowing.

(c) Describe the structure of the typical village savings and loan organization.

A Look at IFRS

LEARNING OBJECTIVE 8 **Compare the accounting for liabilities under GAAP and IFRS.**

IFRS and GAAP have similar definitions of liabilities but have a different approach for recording certain liabilities.

KEY POINTS

Following are the key similarities and differences between GAAP and IFRS as related to accounting for liabilities.

Similarities

- The basic definition of a liability under GAAP and IFRS is very similar. In a more technical way, liabilities are defined by the IASB as a present obligation of the entity arising from past events, the settlement of which is expected to result in an outflow from the entity of resources embodying economic benefits.
- The accounting for current liabilities such as notes payable, unearned revenue, and payroll taxes payable are similar between GAAP and IFRS.
- IFRS requires that companies classify liabilities as current or noncurrent on the face of the statement of financial position (balance sheet), except in industries where a **presentation** based on liquidity would be considered to provide more useful information (such as financial institutions). When current liabilities (also called short-term liabilities) are presented, they are generally presented in order of liquidity.
- Under IFRS, liabilities are classified as current if they are expected to be paid within 12 months.
- Similar to GAAP, items are normally reported in order of liquidity. Companies sometimes show liabilities before assets. Also, they will sometimes show long-term liabilities before current liabilities.
- The basic calculation for bond valuation is the same under GAAP and IFRS. In addition, the accounting for bond liability transactions is essentially the same between GAAP and IFRS.
- IFRS requires use of the effective-interest method for amortization of bond discounts and premiums. GAAP also requires the effective-interest method, except that it allows use of the straight-line method where the difference is not material. Under IFRS, companies do not use a premium or discount account but instead show the bond at its net amount. For example, if a $100,000 bond was issued at 97, under IFRS a company would record:

Cash	97,000	
Bonds Payable		97,000

Differences

- The accounting for convertible bonds differs between IFRS and GAAP. Unlike GAAP, IFRS splits the proceeds from the convertible bond between an equity component and a debt component. The equity conversion rights are reported in equity.

  To illustrate, assume that Harris Corp. issues convertible 7% bonds with a face value of $1,000,000 and receives $1,000,000. Comparable bonds without a conversion feature would have required a 9% rate of interest. To determine how much of the proceeds would be allocated to debt and how much to equity, the promised payments of the bond obligation would be discounted at the market rate of 9%. Suppose that this results in a present value of $850,000. The entry to record the issuance would be:

Cash	1,000,000	
Bonds Payable		850,000
Share Premium—Conversion Equity		150,000

- Under IFRS, companies sometimes will net current liabilities against current assets to show working capital on the face of the statement of financial position.

LOOKING TO THE FUTURE

The FASB and IASB are currently involved in two projects, each of which has implications for the accounting for liabilities. One project is investigating approaches to differentiate between debt and equity instruments. The other project, the elements phase of the conceptual framework project, will evaluate the definitions of the fundamental building blocks of accounting. The results of these projects could change the classification of many debt and equity securities.

IFRS Practice

IFRS SELF-TEST QUESTIONS

1. Which of the following is **false**?
   (a) Under IFRS, current liabilities must always be presented before noncurrent liabilities.
   (b) Under IFRS, an item is a current liability if it will be paid within the next 12 months.
   (c) Under IFRS, current liabilities are sometimes netted against current assets on the statement of financial position.
   (d) Under IFRS, a liability is only recognized if it is a present obligation.

2. The accounting for bonds payable is:
   (a) essentially the same under IFRS and GAAP.
   (b) differs in that GAAP requires use of the straight-line method for amortization of bond premium and discount.
   (c) the same except that market prices may be different because the present value calculations are different between IFRS and GAAP.
   (d) not covered by IFRS.
3. Stevens Corporation issued 5% convertible bonds with a total face value of $3,000,000 for $3,000,000. If the bonds had not had a conversion feature, they would have sold for $2,600,000. Under IFRS, the entry to record the transaction would require a credit to:
   (a) Bonds Payable for $3,000,000.
   (b) Bonds Payable for $400,000.
   (c) Share Premium—Conversion Equity for $400,000.
   (d) Discount on Bonds Payable for $400,000.
4. Which of the following is **true** regarding accounting for amortization of bond discount and premium?
   (a) Both IFRS and GAAP must use the effective-interest method.
   (b) GAAP must use the effective-interest method, but IFRS may use either the effective-interest method or the straight-line method.
   (c) IFRS is required to use the effective-interest method.
   (d) GAAP is required to use the straight-line method.
5. The joint projects of the FASB and IASB could potentially:
   (a) change the definition of liabilities.
   (b) change the definition of equity.
   (c) change the definition of assets.
   (d) All of the above.

IFRS EXERCISES

IFRS10-1 Briefly describe some of the similarities and differences between GAAP and IFRS with respect to the accounting for liabilities.

IFRS10-2 Ratzlaff Company issues (in euros) €2 million, 10-year, 8% bonds at 97, with interest payable annually on January 1.

Instructions

(a) Prepare the journal entry to record the sale of these bonds on January 1, 2017.
(b) Assuming instead that the above bonds sold for 104, prepare the journal entry to record the sale of these bonds on January 1, 2017.

IFRS10-3 Archer Company issued (in pounds) £4,000,000 par value, 7% convertible bonds at 99 for cash. The net present value of the debt without the conversion feature is £3,800,000. Prepare the journal entry to record the issuance of the convertible bonds.

INTERNATIONAL FINANCIAL STATEMENT ANALYSIS: Louis Vuitton

IFRS10-4 The financial statements of Louis Vuitton are presented in Appendix F. Instructions for accessing and using the company's complete annual report, including the notes to its financial statements, are also provided in Appendix F.

Instructions

Use the company's annual report to answer the following questions.

(a) What were the total current liabilities for the company as of December 31, 2014? What portion of these current liabilities related to provisions?
(b) According to the notes to the financial statements, what is the composition of long-term gross borrowings?
(c) According to the accounting policy note to the financial statements, how are borrowings measured?
(d) Determine the amount of fixed-rate and adjustable-rate (floating) borrowings (gross) that the company reports.

Answers to IFRS Self-Test Questions

1. a **2.** a **3.** c **4.** c **5.** d

11

Reporting and Analyzing Stockholders' Equity

CHAPTER PREVIEW

Corporations like Facebook and Google have substantial resources at their disposal. In fact, the corporation is the dominant form of business organization in the United States in terms of sales, earnings, and number of employees. All of the 500 largest U.S. companies are corporations. In this chapter, we look at the essential features of a corporation and explain the accounting for a corporation's capital stock transactions.

CHAPTER OUTLINE

LEARNING OBJECTIVES		PRACTICE
1 Discuss the major characteristics of a corporation.	• Characteristics of a corporation • Forming a corporation • Stockholder rights • Stock issue considerations • Corporate capital	DO IT! 1 Corporate Organization
2 Explain how to account for the issuance of common and preferred stock, and the purchase of treasury stock.	• Accounting for common stock • Accounting for preferred stock • Treasury stock	DO IT! 2 2a Issuance of Stock 2b Treasury Stock
3 Explain how to account for cash dividends and describe the effect of stock dividends and stock splits.	• Cash dividends • Dividend preferences • Stock dividends • Stock splits	DO IT! 3 3a Preferred Stock Dividends 3b Stock Dividends; Stock Splits
4 Discuss how stockholders' equity is reported and analyzed.	• Retained earnings • Retained earnings restrictions • Balance sheet presentation of stockholders' equity • Analysis of stockholders' equity • Debt versus equity decision	DO IT! 4 4a Stockholders' Equity Section 4b Analyzing Stockholders' Equity

Go to the ***REVIEW AND PRACTICE*** section at the end of the chapter for a targeted summary and exercises with solutions.

Visit **WileyPLUS** for additional tutorials and practice opportunities.

Paul Sakuma/AP/Wide World Photos

FEATURE STORY

Oh Well, I Guess I'll Get Rich

Suppose you started one of the fastest-growing companies in the history of business. Now suppose that by "going public"—issuing stock of your company to outside investors who are foaming at the mouth for the chance to buy its shares—you would instantly become one of the richest people in the world. Would you hesitate?

That is exactly what Mark Zuckerberg, the founder of Facebook, did. Many people who start high-tech companies go public as soon as possible to cash in on their riches. But Zuckerberg was reluctant to do so. To understand why, you need to understand the advantages and disadvantages of being a public company.

The main motivation for issuing shares to the public is to raise money so you can grow your business. However, unlike a manufacturer or even an online retailer, Facebook doesn't need major physical resources, it doesn't have inventory, and it doesn't really need much money for marketing. But why not go public anyway, so the company would have some extra cash on hand—and so you personally get rich? As head of a closely held, nonpublic company, Zuckerberg was subject to far fewer regulations than a public company. Prior to going public, Zuckerberg could basically run the company however he wanted to.

For example, early in 2012, Facebook shocked the investment community by purchasing the photo-sharing service Instagram. The purchase was startling both for its speed (over a weekend) and price ($1 billion). Zuckerberg basically didn't seek anyone's approval. He thought it was a good idea, so he just did it. The structured decision-making process of a public company would make it very difficult for a public company to move that fast.

Speed is useful, but it is likely that Facebook will make even bigger acquisitions in the future. To survive among the likes of Microsoft, Google, and Apple, it needs lots of cash. To raise that amount of money, the company really needed to go public. So in 2012, Mark Zuckerberg reluctantly made Facebook a public company, thus becoming one of the richest people in the world.

LEARNING OBJECTIVE  1

Discuss the major characteristics of a corporation.

DECISION TOOLS 

Understanding the costs and benefits of different types of business organizations helps managers determine if incorporating is in the best interest of the company.

A corporation is created by law. As a legal entity, a **corporation** has most of the rights and privileges of a person. The major exceptions relate to privileges that can be exercised only by a living person, such as the right to vote or to hold public office. Similarly, a corporation is subject to the same duties and responsibilities as a person. For example, it must abide by the law and it must pay taxes.

We can classify corporations in a variety of ways. Two common classifications are **by purpose** and **by ownership**. A corporation may be organized for the purpose of making a profit (such as Facebook or General Motors), or it may be a nonprofit charitable, medical, or educational corporation (such as the Salvation Army or the American Cancer Society).

Classification by ownership differentiates publicly held and privately held corporations. A **publicly held corporation** may have thousands of stockholders, and its stock is traded on a national securities market such as the New York Stock Exchange. Examples are IBM, Caterpillar, and General Electric. In contrast, a **privately held corporation**, often referred to as a closely held corporation, usually has only a few stockholders and does not offer its stock for sale to the general public. Privately held companies are generally much smaller than publicly held companies although some notable exceptions exist. Before going public, Facebook was one example. Also, Cargill Inc., a private corporation that trades in grain and other commodities, is one of the largest companies in the United States. This chapter deals primarily with issues related to publicly held companies.

CHARACTERISTICS OF A CORPORATION

Many businesses start as partnerships or sole proprietorships but eventually convert to the corporate form. For example, Nike's founders formed their original organization as a partnership. In 1968, they reorganized the company as a corporation. A number of characteristics distinguish a corporation from sole proprietorships and partnerships. The most important of these characteristics are explained below.

Legal existence separate from owners

Separate Legal Existence

As an entity separate and distinct from its owners, the corporation acts under its own name rather than in the name of its stockholders. Facebook, for example, buys, owns, and sells property; borrows money; and enters into legally binding contracts in its own name. It may also sue or be sued. It pays taxes as a separate entity.

In a partnership, the acts of the owners (partners) bind the partnership. In contrast, the acts of corporate owners (stockholders) do not bind the corporation unless such owners are agents of the corporation. For example, if you own shares of Facebook stock, you do not have the right to purchase inventory for the company unless you are also designated as an agent of the corporation.

Limited liability of stockholders

Limited Liability of Stockholders

Since a corporation is a separate legal entity, creditors ordinarily have recourse only to corporate assets to satisfy their claims. The liability of stockholders is normally limited to their investment in the corporation. Creditors have no legal claim on the personal assets of the stockholders unless fraud has occurred. Thus, even in the event of bankruptcy of the corporation, stockholders' losses are generally limited to the amount of capital they have invested in the corporation.

Transferable Ownership Rights

Ownership of a corporation is held in shares of capital stock, which are transferable units. Stockholders may dispose of part or all of their interest in a corporation simply by selling their stock. The transfer of an ownership interest in a partnership requires the consent of each partner. In contrast, the transfer of stock is entirely at the discretion of the stockholder. It does not require the approval of either the corporation or other stockholders.

Transferable ownership rights

The transfer of ownership rights among stockholders normally has no effect on the operating activities of the corporation. Nor does it affect the corporation's assets, liabilities, and total stockholders' equity. The transfer of ownership rights is a transaction between individual owners. The company does not participate in the transfer of these ownership rights after the original sale of the capital stock.

Ability to Acquire Capital

It is relatively easy for a corporation to obtain capital through the issuance of stock. Buying stock in a corporation is often attractive to an investor because a stockholder has limited liability and shares of stock are readily transferable. Also, numerous individuals can become stockholders by investing small amounts of money.

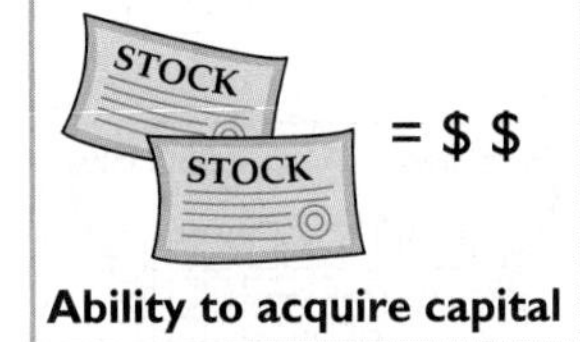

Ability to acquire capital

Continuous Life

The life of a corporation is stated in its charter. The life may be perpetual or it may be limited to a specific number of years. If it is limited, the company extends the period of existence through renewal of the charter. Since a corporation is a separate legal entity, its continuance as a going concern is not affected by the withdrawal, death, or incapacity of a stockholder, employee, or officer. As a result, a successful corporation can have a continuous and perpetual life.

Continuous life

Corporation Management

Although stockholders legally own the corporation, they manage it indirectly through a board of directors they elect. Mark Zuckerberg is the chairman of Facebook's board of directors. The board, in turn, formulates the operating policies for the company. The board also selects officers, such as a president and one or more vice presidents, to execute policy and to perform daily management functions. As a result of the Sarbanes-Oxley Act, the board is required to monitor management's actions closely. Many feel that the failures at Enron, WorldCom, and MF Global could have been avoided by more diligent boards.

Illustration 11-1 presents a typical organization chart showing the delegation of responsibility.

ILLUSTRATION 11-1
Corporation organization chart

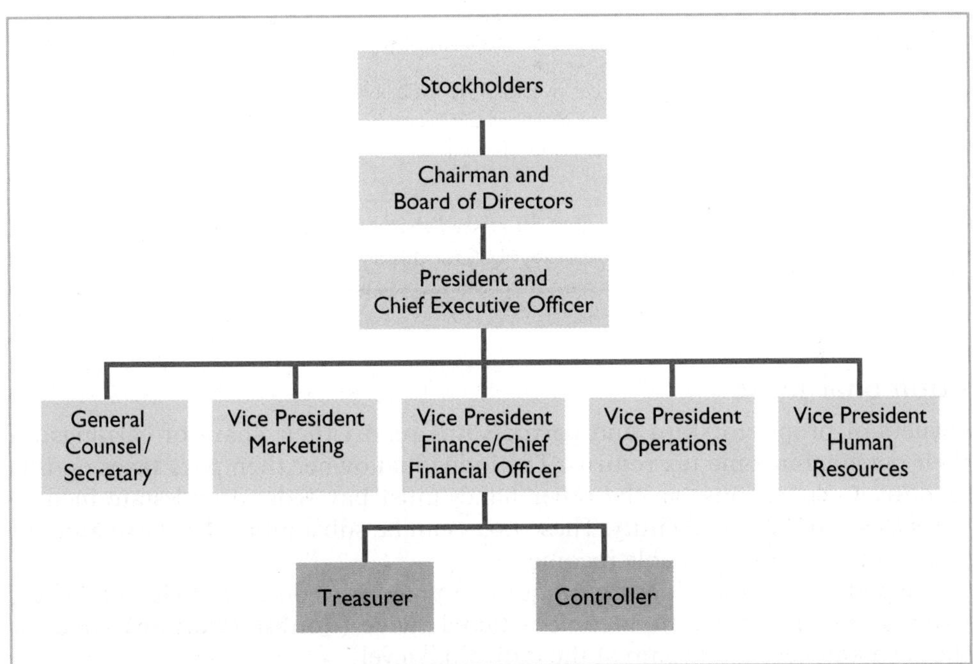

ETHICS NOTE
Managers who are not owners are often compensated based on the performance of the company. They thus may be tempted to exaggerate company performance by inflating income figures.

The chief executive officer (CEO) has overall responsibility for managing the business. As the organization chart shows, the CEO delegates responsibility to other officers. The chief accounting officer is the **controller**. The controller (1) maintains the accounting records, (2) ensures an adequate system of internal control, and (3) prepares financial statements, tax returns, and internal reports. The **treasurer** has custody of the corporation's funds and oversees the company's cash position.

The organizational structure of a corporation enables a company to hire professional managers to run the business. On the other hand, the separation of ownership and management often reduces an owner's ability to actively manage the company.

Government Regulations

Government regulations

A corporation is subject to numerous state and federal regulations. For example, state laws usually prescribe the requirements for issuing stock, the distributions of earnings permitted to stockholders, and acceptable methods for buying back and retiring stock. Federal securities laws govern the sale of capital stock to the general public. Also, publicly held corporations must disclose their financial affairs to the Securities and Exchange Commission (SEC) through quarterly and annual reports (Forms 10Q and 10K). The Sarbanes-Oxley Act increased the company's responsibility for the accuracy of these reports. In addition, when a corporate stock is listed and traded on organized securities exchanges, the corporation must comply with the reporting requirements of these exchanges.

PEOPLE, PLANET, AND PROFIT INSIGHT

© Robert Churchill/iStockphoto

The Impact of Corporate Social Responsibility

A survey conducted by Institutional Shareholder Services, a proxy advisory firm, shows that 83% of investors now believe environmental and social factors can significantly impact shareholder value over the long term. This belief is clearly visible in the rising level of support for shareholder proposals requesting action related to social and environmental issues.

The following table shows that the number of corporate social responsibility (CSR) related shareholder proposals rose from 150 in 2000 to 191 in 2010. Moreover, those proposals received average voting support of 18.4% of votes cast versus just 7.5% a decade earlier.

Trends in Shareholder Proposals on Corporate Responsibility

	2000	2005	2010
Number of proposals voted	150	155	191
Average voting support	7.5%	9.9%	18.4%
Percent proposals receiving >10% support	16.7%	31.2%	52.1%

Source: Investor Responsibility Research Center, Ernst & Young, *Seven Questions CEOs and Boards Should Ask About: "Triple Bottom Line" Reporting.*

Why are CSR-related shareholder proposals increasing? (Go to WileyPLUS for this answer and additional questions.)

Additional Taxes

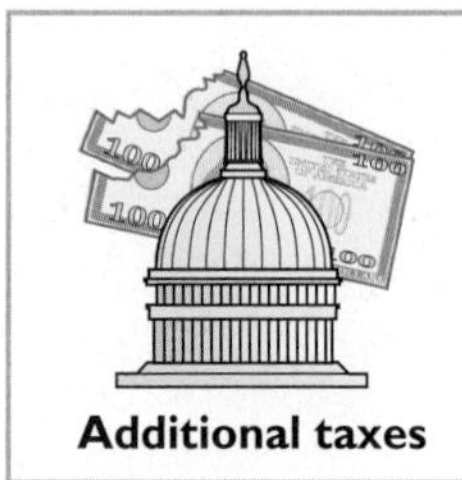
Additional taxes

Owners of proprietorships and partnerships report their share of earnings on their personal income tax returns. The individual owner then pays taxes on this amount. Corporations, on the other hand, must pay federal and state income taxes as a separate legal entity. These taxes can be substantial. They can amount to as much as 40% of taxable income.

In addition, stockholders are required to pay taxes on cash dividends. Thus, many argue that corporate income is **taxed twice (double taxation)**—once at the corporate level and again at the individual level.

Illustration 11-2 shows the advantages and disadvantages of a corporation compared to a sole proprietorship and partnership.

ILLUSTRATION 11-2
Advantages and disadvantages of a corporation

Advantages	Disadvantages
• Separate legal existence	• Corporation management—separation of ownership and management
• Limited liability of stockholders	• Government regulations
• Transferable ownership rights	• Additional taxes
• Ability to acquire capital	
• Continuous life	
• Corporation management—professional managers	

Other Forms of Business Organization

A variety of "hybrid" organizational forms—forms that combine different attributes of partnerships and corporations—now exist. For example, one type of corporate form, called an **S corporation**, allows for legal treatment as a corporation but tax treatment as a partnership—that is, no double taxation. Because of changes to the S corporation's rules, more small- and medium-sized businesses now may choose S corporation treatment. One of the primary criteria is that the company cannot have more than 100 shareholders. Other forms of organization include limited partnerships, limited liability partnerships (LLPs), and limited liability companies (LLCs).

FORMING A CORPORATION

A corporation is formed by grant of a state **charter**. The charter is a document that describes the name and purpose of the corporation, the types and number of shares of stock that are authorized to be issued, the names of the individuals that formed the company, and the number of shares that these individuals agreed to purchase. Regardless of the number of states in which a corporation has operating divisions, it is incorporated in only one state. It is to the company's advantage to incorporate in a state whose laws are favorable to the corporate form of business organization. For example, although Facebook has its headquarters in California, it is incorporated in Delaware. In fact, more and more corporations have been incorporating in states with rules that favor existing management. For example, Gulf Oil changed its state of incorporation to Delaware to thwart possible unfriendly takeovers. There, certain defensive tactics against takeovers can be approved by the board of directors alone, without a vote by shareholders.

Upon receipt of its charter from the state of incorporation, the corporation establishes **by-laws**. The by-laws establish the internal rules and procedures for conducting the affairs of the corporation. Corporations engaged in interstate commerce must also obtain a **license** from each state in which they do business. The license subjects the corporation's operating activities to the general corporation laws of the state.

STOCKHOLDER RIGHTS

When chartered, the corporation begins selling shares of stock. When a corporation has only one class of stock, it is identified as **common stock**. Each share of common stock gives the stockholder the ownership rights pictured in Illustration 11-3 (page 542). The articles of incorporation or the by-laws state the ownership rights of a share of stock.

Proof of stock ownership is evidenced by a printed or engraved form known as a **stock certificate**. As shown in Illustration 11-4 (page 542), the face of the certificate shows the name of the corporation, the stockholder's name, the class and special features of the stock, the number of shares owned, and the signatures of authorized corporate officials. Certificates are prenumbered to ensure proper control over their use; they may be issued for any quantity of shares.

ILLUSTRATION 11-3
Ownership rights of stockholders

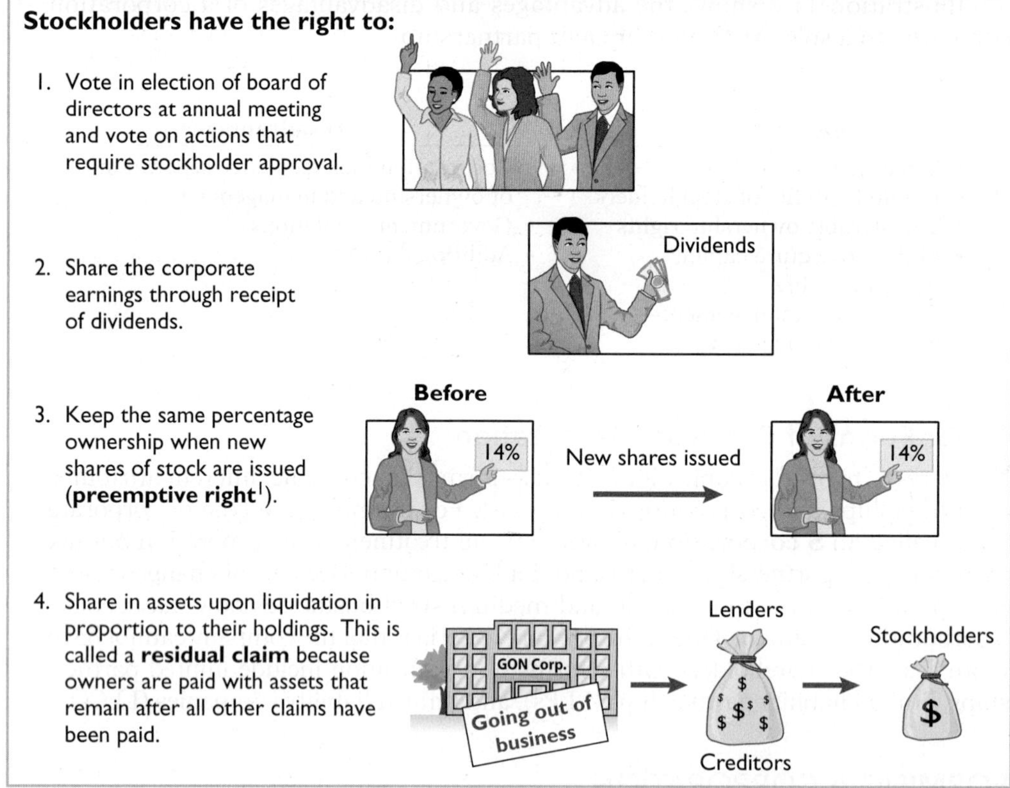

ILLUSTRATION 11-4
A stock certificate

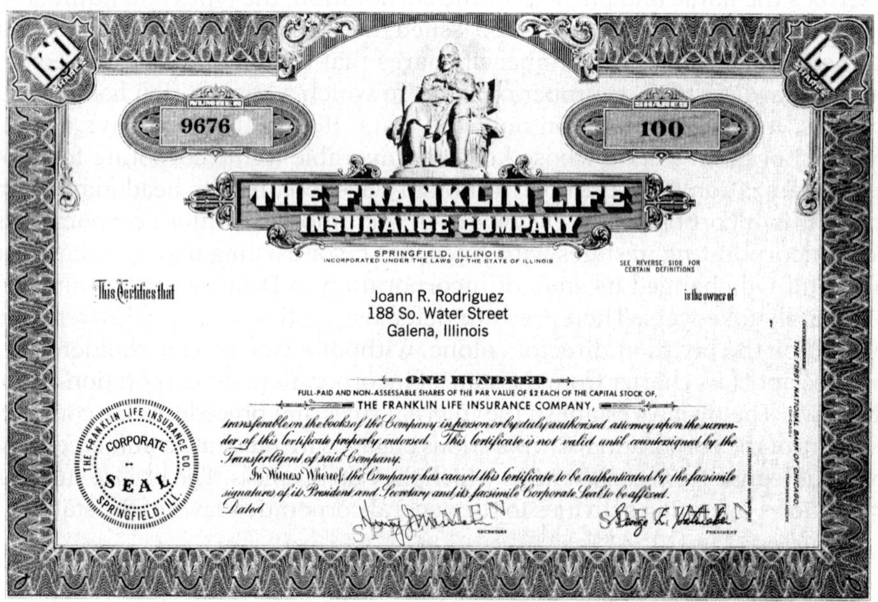

STOCK ISSUE CONSIDERATIONS

Although Facebook incorporated in 2004, it did not sell stock to the public until 2012. At that time, Facebook evidently decided it would benefit from the infusion of cash that a public sale of its shares would bring. When a corporation decides to issue stock, it must resolve a number of basic questions: How many shares

---

[1]A number of companies have eliminated the preemptive right because they believe it places an unnecessary and cumbersome demand on management. For example, IBM, by stockholder approval, has dropped its preemptive right for stockholders.

should it authorize for sale? How should it issue the stock? What value should it assign to the stock? We address these questions in the following sections.

Authorized Stock

Authorized stock is the amount of stock that a corporation is authorized to sell as indicated in its charter. If the corporation has sold all of its authorized stock, then it must obtain permission from the state to change its charter before it can issue additional shares.

The authorization of common stock does not result in a formal accounting entry. The reason is that the event has no immediate effect on either corporate assets or stockholders' equity. However, the corporation discloses in the stockholders' equity section of the balance sheet the number of shares authorized. Facebook, for example, has approximately 9 billion authorized shares.

Issuance of Stock

A corporation can issue common stock **directly** to investors. Alternatively, it can issue common stock **indirectly** through an investment banking firm that specializes in bringing securities to the attention of prospective investors. Direct issue is typical in closely held companies. Indirect issue is customary for a publicly held corporation.

New issues of stock may be offered for sale to the public through various organized U.S. or foreign securities exchanges. Five of the largest exchanges by value of shares traded are the New York Stock Exchange, Nasdaq stock market, London Stock Exchange, Tokyo Stock Exchange, and Euronext.

INTERNATIONAL NOTE
U.S. and U.K. corporations raise most of their capital through millions of outside shareholders and bondholders. In contrast, companies in Germany, France, and Japan acquire financing mostly from large banks or other financial institutions. Consequently, in the latter environment, shareholders are somewhat less important.

ANATOMY OF A FRAUD

The president, chief operating officer, and chief financial officer of SafeNet, a software encryption company, were each awarded employee stock options by the company's board of directors as part of their compensation package. Stock options enable an employee to buy a company's stock sometime in the future at the price that existed when the stock option was awarded. For example, suppose that you received stock options today, when the stock price of your company was $30. Three years later, if the stock price rose to $100, you could "exercise" your options and buy the stock for $30 per share, thereby making $70 per share. After being awarded their stock options, the three employees changed the award dates in the company's records to dates in the past, when the company's stock was trading at historical lows. For example, using the previous example, they would choose a past date when the stock was selling for $10 per share, rather than the $30 price on the actual award date. In our example, this would increase the profit from exercising the options to $90 per share.

Total take: $1.7 million

THE MISSING CONTROL

Independent internal verification. The company's board of directors should have ensured that the awards were properly administered. For example, the date on the minutes from the board meeting should be compared to the dates that were recorded for the awards. In addition, the dates should again be confirmed upon exercise.

Par and No-Par Value Stocks

Par value stock is capital stock that has been assigned a value per share in the corporate charter. Years ago, par value determined the **legal capital** that must be retained in the business for the protection of corporate creditors. That amount is not available for withdrawal by stockholders. Thus, in the past, most states required the corporation to sell its shares at par or above.

However, the usefulness of par value as a device to protect creditors was limited because par value was often immaterial relative to the value of the company's stock in the securities markets—even at the time of issue. For example,

Facebook's par value is $0.000006 per share, yet its market price recently was $84. Thus, par has no relationship with market price. In the vast majority of cases, it is an immaterial amount. As a consequence, today many states do not require a par value. Instead, they use other means to protect creditors.

No-par value stock is capital stock that has not been assigned a value in the corporate charter. No-par value stock is fairly common today. For example, Nike and Procter & Gamble both have no-par stock. In many states, the board of directors assigns a **stated value** to the no-par shares.

CORPORATE CAPITAL

Owners' equity is identified by various names: **stockholders' equity**, **shareholders' equity**, or **corporate capital**. The stockholders' equity section of a corporation's balance sheet consists of two parts: (1) paid-in (contributed) capital and (2) retained earnings (earned capital).

The distinction between **paid-in capital** and **retained earnings** is important from both a legal and a financial point of view. Legally, corporations can make distributions of earnings (declare dividends) out of retained earnings in all states. However, in many states they cannot declare dividends out of paid-in capital. Management, stockholders, and others often look to retained earnings for the continued existence and growth of the corporation.

Paid-in Capital

Paid-in capital is the total amount of cash and other assets paid in to the corporation by stockholders in exchange for capital stock. As noted earlier, when a corporation has only one class of stock, it is **common stock**.

Retained Earnings

Retained earnings is net income that a corporation retains in the business. Net income is recorded in Retained Earnings by a closing entry that debits Income Summary and credits Retained Earnings. Similarly, the Retained Earnings account is reduced by dividends (both cash dividends and stock dividends) by a closing entry that debits Retained Earnings and credits Dividends.

DO IT!  1 Corporate Organization

Indicate whether each of the following statements is true or false. If false, indicate how to correct the statement.

______ **1.** Similar to partners in a partnership, stockholders of a corporation have unlimited liability.

______ **2.** It is relatively easy for a corporation to obtain capital through the issuance of stock.

______ **3.** The separation of ownership and management is an advantage of the corporate form of business.

______ **4.** The journal entry to record the authorization of capital stock includes a credit to the appropriate capital stock account.

______ **5.** All states require a par value per share for capital stock.

Action Plan

✔ Review the characteristics of a corporation and understand which are advantages and which are disadvantages.

✔ Understand that corporations raise capital through the issuance of stock, which can be par or no-par.

SOLUTION

1. False. The liability of stockholders is normally limited to their investment in the corporation. 2. True. 3. False. The separation of ownership and management is a disadvantage of the corporate form of business. 4. False. The authorization of capital stock does not result in a formal accounting entry. 5. False. Many states do not require a par value.

Related exercise material: **BE11-1** and DO IT! **11-1.**

LEARNING OBJECTIVE 2 **Explain how to account for the issuance of common and preferred stock, and the purchase of treasury stock.**

ACCOUNTING FOR COMMON STOCK

Let's now look at how to account for new issues of common stock. The primary objectives in accounting for the issuance of common stock are (1) to identify the specific sources of paid-in capital and (2) to maintain the distinction between paid-in capital and retained earnings. As shown below, **the issuance of common stock affects only paid-in capital accounts.**

▼ **HELPFUL HINT**
Stock is sometimes issued in exchange for services (payment to attorneys or consultants, for example) or for noncash assets (land or buildings). The value recorded for the shares issued is determined by either the market price of the shares or the value of the good or service received, depending upon which amount the company can more readily determine.

Issuing Par Value Common Stock for Cash

As discussed earlier, par value does not indicate a stock's market price. The cash proceeds from issuing par value stock may be equal to, greater than, or less than par value. When a company records the issuance of common stock for cash, it credits the par value of the shares to Common Stock and records in a separate paid-in capital account the portion of the proceeds that is above or below par value.

To illustrate, assume that Hydro-Slide, Inc. issues 1,000 shares of $1 par value common stock at par for cash. The entry to record this transaction is as follows.

Cash	1,000	
Common Stock		1,000
(To record issuance of 1,000 shares of $1 par common stock at par)		

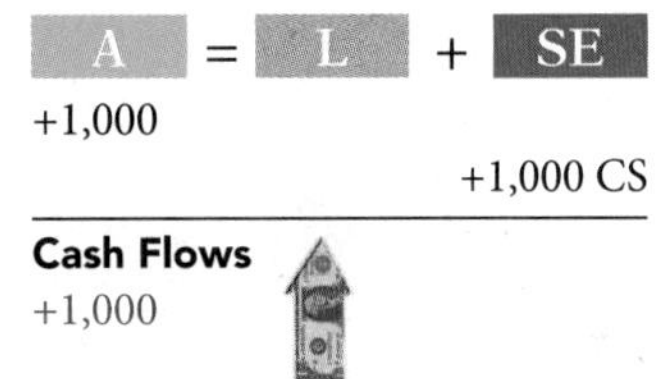

Now assume Hydro-Slide, Inc. issues an additional 1,000 shares of the $1 par value common stock for cash at $5 per share. The amount received above the par value, in this case $4 ($5 − $1), would be credited to Paid-in Capital in Excess of Par Value. The entry is as follows.

Cash	5,000	
Common Stock (1,000 × $1)		1,000
Paid-in Capital in Excess of Par Value		4,000
(To record issuance of 1,000 shares of common stock in excess of par)		

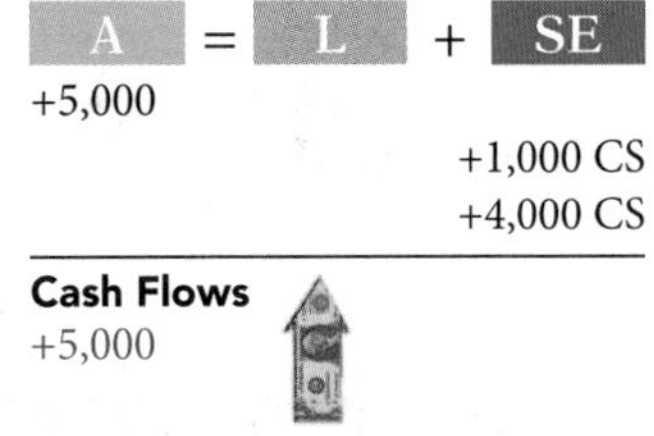

The total paid-in capital from these two transactions is $6,000. If Hydro-Slide, Inc. has retained earnings of $27,000, the stockholders' equity section of the balance sheet is as shown in Illustration 11-5.

HYDRO-SLIDE, INC.
Balance Sheet (partial)

Stockholders' equity	
Paid-in capital	
Common stock	$ 2,000
Paid-in capital in excess of par value	**4,000**
Total paid-in capital	6,000
Retained earnings	27,000
Total stockholders' equity	$33,000

ILLUSTRATION 11-5
Stockholders' equity—paid-in capital in excess of par value

Some companies issue no-par stock with a stated value. For accounting purposes, companies treat the stated value in the same way as the par value. For example, if in our Hydro-Slide example the stock was no-par stock with a stated value of $1, the entries would be the same as those presented for the par stock except the term "Par Value" would be replaced with "Stated Value." If a company issues no-par stock that does not have a stated value, then it credits to the Common Stock account the full amount received. In such a case, there is no need for the Paid-in Capital in Excess of Stated Value account.

ACCOUNTING FOR PREFERRED STOCK

To appeal to a larger segment of potential investors, a corporation may issue an additional class of stock, called preferred stock. **Preferred stock** has contractual provisions that give it preference or priority over common stock in certain areas. Typically, preferred stockholders have a priority in relation to (1) dividends and (2) assets in the event of liquidation. However, they sometimes do not have voting rights. Facebook had 543 million preferred shares held by investors at the end of 2011, prior to going public. Approximately 6% of U.S. companies have one or more classes of preferred stock.

Like common stock, companies issue preferred stock for cash or for noncash consideration. The entries for these transactions are similar to the entries for common stock. When a corporation has more than one class of stock, each paid-in capital account title should identify the stock to which it relates (e.g., Preferred Stock, Common Stock, Paid-in Capital in Excess of Par Value—Preferred Stock, and Paid-in Capital in Excess of Par Value—Common Stock).

Assume that Stine Corporation issues 10,000 shares of $10 par value preferred stock for $12 cash per share. The entry to record the issuance is as follows.

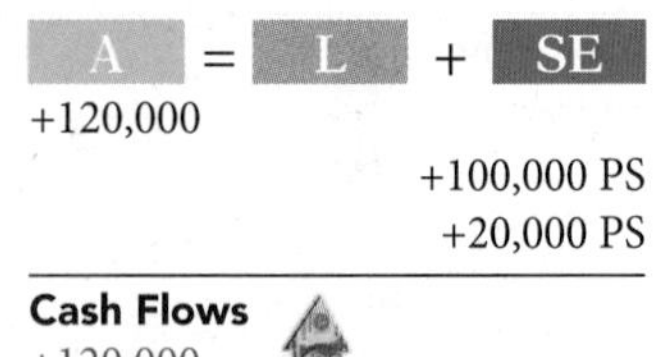

	Debit	Credit
Cash	120,000	
Preferred Stock		100,000
Paid-in Capital in Excess of Par Value—Preferred Stock		20,000
(To record issuance of 10,000 shares of $10 par value preferred stock)		

Preferred stock has either a par value or no-par value. In the stockholders' equity section of the balance sheet, companies show preferred stock first because of its dividend and liquidation preferences over common stock.

INVESTOR INSIGHT Facebook

Emmanuel Dunand/AFP/Getty Images

How to Read Stock Quotes

Organized exchanges trade the stock of publicly held companies at dollar prices per share established by the interaction between buyers and sellers. For each listed security, the financial press reports the high and low prices of the stock during the year, the total volume of stock traded on a given day, the high and low prices for the day, and the closing market price, with the net change for the day. Facebook is listed on the Nasdaq exchange. Here is a recent listing for Facebook:

	52 Weeks						
Stock	High	Low	Volume	High	Low	Close	Net Change
Facebook	86.07	54.66	54,156,600	85.59	83.11	84.63	.629

These numbers indicate the following. The high and low market prices for the last 52 weeks have been $86.07 and $54.66. The trading volume for the day was 54,156,600 shares. The high, low, and closing prices for that date were $85.59, $83.11, and $84.63, respectively. The net change for the day was a decrease of $0.629 per share.

For stocks traded on organized exchanges, how are the dollar prices per share established? What factors might influence the price of shares in the marketplace? (Go to WileyPLUS for this answer and additional questions.)

DO IT! ▶ 2a Issuance of Stock

Cayman Corporation begins operations on March 1 by issuing 100,000 shares of $1 par value common stock for cash at $12 per share. On March 28, Cayman issues 1,500 shares of $10 par value preferred stock for cash at $30 per share. Journalize the issuance of the common and preferred shares.

SOLUTION

Date	Account	Debit	Credit
Mar. 1	Cash	1,200,000	
	Common Stock (100,000 × $1)		100,000
	Paid-in Capital in Excess of Par Value—Common Stock		1,100,000
	(To record issuance of 100,000 shares at $12 per share)		
Mar. 28	Cash	45,000	
	Preferred Stock (1,500 × $10)		15,000
	Paid-in Capital in Excess of Par Value—Preferred Stock		30,000
	(To record issuance of 1,500 shares at $30 per share)		

Action Plan

- ✔ In issuing shares for cash, credit Common Stock for par value per share.
- ✔ Credit any additional proceeds in excess of par to a separate paid-in capital account.
- ✔ For the cash equivalent price, use either the fair value of what is given up or the fair value of what is received, whichever is more clearly determinable.

Related exercise material: **BE11-2, BE11-3, BE11-4, DO IT! 11-2a, E11-2,** and **E11-5.**

TREASURY STOCK

Treasury stock is a corporation's own stock that has been reacquired by the corporation and is being held for future use. A corporation may acquire treasury stock for various reasons:

1. To reissue the shares to officers and employees under bonus and stock compensation plans.
2. To increase trading of the company's stock in the securities market. Companies expect that buying their own stock will signal that management believes the stock is underpriced, which they hope will enhance its market price.
3. To have additional shares available for use in acquiring other companies.
4. To reduce the number of shares outstanding and thereby increase earnings per share.

A less frequent reason for purchasing treasury shares is to eliminate hostile shareholders by buying them out.

Many corporations have treasury stock. For example, in the United States approximately 65% of companies have treasury stock. During one quarter, companies in the Standard & Poor's 500-stock index spent a record of about $118 billion to buy treasury stock. In a recent year, Nike purchased more than 6 million treasury shares. At one point, stock repurchases were so substantial that a study by two Federal Reserve economists suggested that a sharp reduction in corporate purchases of treasury shares might result in a sharp drop in the value of the U.S. stock market.

Purchase of Treasury Stock

The purchase of treasury stock is generally accounted for by the **cost method**. This method derives its name from the fact that the Treasury Stock account is maintained at the cost of shares purchased. Under the cost method, **companies increase (debit) Treasury Stock by the price paid to reacquire the shares. Treasury Stock decreases by the same amount when the company later sells the shares.**

To illustrate, assume that on January 1, 2017, the stockholders' equity section for Mead, Inc. has 100,000 shares of $5 par value common stock outstanding (all issued at par value) and retained earnings of $200,000. Illustration 11-6 shows the stockholders' equity section of the balance sheet before purchase of treasury stock.

ILLUSTRATION 11-6
Stockholders' equity with no treasury stock

MEAD, INC. Balance Sheet (partial)	
Stockholders' equity	
Paid-in capital	
Common stock, $5 par value, 400,000 shares authorized, 100,000 shares issued and outstanding	$500,000
Retained earnings	200,000
Total stockholders' equity	$700,000

On February 1, 2017, Mead acquires 4,000 shares of its stock at $8 per share. The entry is as follows.

A	=	L	+	SE
				−32,000 TS
−32,000				

Cash Flows
−32,000

Feb. 1	Treasury Stock	32,000	
	Cash		32,000
	(To record purchase of 4,000 shares of treasury stock at $8 per share)		

The Treasury Stock account would increase by the cost of the shares purchased ($32,000). The original paid-in capital account, Common Stock, would not be affected because **the number of issued shares does not change**.

▼ HELPFUL HINT
Treasury Stock is a contra stockholders' equity account.

Companies show treasury stock as a deduction from total paid-in capital and retained earnings in the stockholders' equity section of the balance sheet. Illustration 11-7 shows this presentation for Mead, Inc. Thus, the acquisition of treasury stock reduces stockholders' equity.

ILLUSTRATION 11-7
Stockholders' equity with treasury stock

MEAD, INC. Balance Sheet (partial)	
Stockholders' equity	
Paid-in capital	
Common stock, $5 par value, 400,000 shares authorized, 100,000 shares issued and 96,000 shares outstanding	$500,000
Retained earnings	200,000
Total paid-in capital and retained earnings	700,000
Less: Treasury stock (4,000 shares)	**32,000**
Total stockholders' equity	$668,000

Company balance sheets disclose both the number of shares issued (100,000) and the number in the treasury (4,000). The difference is the number of shares of stock outstanding (96,000). The term **outstanding stock** means the number of shares of issued stock that are being held by stockholders.

ETHICS NOTE
The purchase of treasury stock reduces the cushion for creditors. To protect creditors, many states require that a portion of retained earnings equal to the cost of the treasury stock purchased be restricted from being paid as dividends.

In a bold (and some would say risky) move, Reebok at one time bought back nearly a third of its shares. This repurchase of shares dramatically reduced Reebok's available cash. In fact, the company borrowed significant funds to accomplish the repurchase. In a press release, management stated that it was repurchasing the shares because it believed that the stock was severely underpriced. The repurchase of so many shares was meant to signal management's belief in good future earnings.

Skeptics, however, suggested that Reebok's management repurchased the shares to make it less likely that the company would be acquired by another company (in which case Reebok's top managers would likely lose their jobs). Acquiring companies like to purchase companies with large cash reserves so they can pay off debt used in the acquisition. By depleting its cash through the purchase of treasury shares, Reebok became a less likely acquisition target.

DO IT! 2b Treasury Stock

Santa Anita Inc. purchases 3,000 shares of its $50 par value common stock for $180,000 cash on July 1. It expects to hold the shares in the treasury until resold. Journalize the treasury stock transaction.

SOLUTION

July 1	Treasury Stock	180,000	
	Cash		180,000
	(To record the purchase of 3,000 shares at $60 per share)		

Action Plan

✔ Record the purchase of treasury stock at cost.

✔ Report treasury stock as a deduction from stockholders' equity (contra account) at the bottom of the stockholders' equity section.

Related exercise material: **DO IT! 11-2b, E11-2, and E11-5.**

LEARNING OBJECTIVE 3 Explain how to account for cash dividends and describe the effect of stock dividends and stock splits.

As noted earlier, a **dividend is a distribution by a corporation to its stockholders on a pro rata** (proportional to ownership) **basis**. Pro rata means that if you own, say, 10% of the common shares, you will receive 10% of the dividend. Dividends can take four forms: cash, property, scrip (promissory note to pay cash), or stock. Cash dividends predominate in practice, although companies also declare stock dividends with some frequency.

Investors are very interested in a company's dividend practices. In the financial press, **dividends are generally reported quarterly as a dollar amount per share**. (Sometimes they are reported on an annual basis.) For example, the recent **quarterly** dividend rate was 24 cents per share for Nike, 22 cents per share for GE, and 25 cents per share for ConAgra Foods. Facebook does not pay dividends.

CASH DIVIDENDS

A **cash dividend** is a pro rata (proportional to ownership) distribution of cash to stockholders. Cash dividends are not paid on treasury shares. For a corporation to pay a cash dividend, it must have the following:

1. **Retained earnings.** Payment of dividends from retained earnings is legal in all states. In addition, loan agreements frequently constrain companies to pay dividends only from retained earnings. Many states prohibit payment of dividends from legal capital. However, payment of dividends from paid-in capital in excess of par value is legal in some states.
2. **Adequate cash.** Recently, Facebook had a balance in retained earnings of $6,099 million but a cash balance of only $4,315 million. If it had wanted to pay a dividend equal to its retained earnings, Facebook would have had to raise $1,784 million more in cash. It would have been unlikely to do this because it would not be able to pay this much in dividends in future years.

In addition, such a dividend would completely deplete Facebook's balance in retained earnings, so it would not be able to pay a dividend in the next year unless it had positive net income.

3. **Declared dividends.** The board of directors has full authority to determine the amount of income to distribute in the form of dividends. Dividends are not a liability until they are declared.

The amount and timing of a dividend are important issues for management to consider. The payment of a large cash dividend could lead to liquidity problems for the company. Conversely, a small dividend or a missed dividend may cause unhappiness among stockholders who expect to receive a reasonable cash payment from the company on a periodic basis. Many companies declare and pay cash dividends quarterly. On the other hand, a number of high-growth companies pay no dividends, preferring to conserve cash to finance future capital expenditures.

Investors monitor a company's dividend practices. For example, regular dividend boosts in the face of irregular earnings can be a warning signal. Companies with high dividends and rising debt may be borrowing money to pay shareholders. On the other hand, low dividends may not be a negative sign because it may mean the company is reinvesting in itself, which may result in high returns through increases in the stock price. Presumably, investors seeking regular dividends buy stock in companies that pay periodic dividends, and those seeking growth in the stock price (capital gains) buy stock in companies that retain their earnings rather than pay dividends.

Entries for Cash Dividends

Three dates are important in connection with dividends: (1) the declaration date, (2) the record date, and (3) the payment date. Companies make accounting entries on the declaration date and the payment date.

On the **declaration date**, the board of directors formally authorizes the cash dividend and announces it to stockholders. The declaration of a cash dividend **commits the corporation to a binding legal obligation**. Thus, the company must make an entry to recognize the increase in Cash Dividends and the increase in the liability Dividends Payable.

To illustrate, assume that on December 1, 2017, the directors of Media General declare a \$0.50 per share cash dividend on 100,000 shares of \$10 par value common stock. The dividend is \$50,000 (100,000 × \$0.50). The entry to record the declaration is as follows.

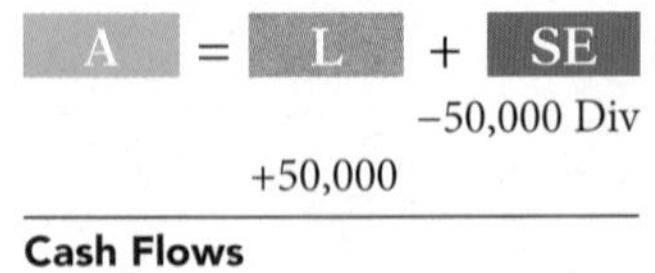

Declaration Date

Dec. 1	Cash Dividends	50,000	
	Dividends Payable		50,000
	(To record declaration of cash dividend)		

In Chapter 3, we used an account called Dividends to record a cash dividend. Here, we use the more specific title Cash Dividends to differentiate from other types of dividends, such as stock dividends. (*For homework problems, you should use the Cash Dividends account for recording dividend declarations*). Dividends Payable is a current liability. It will normally be paid within the next several months.

▼ **HELPFUL HINT**
The record date is important in determining the dividend to be paid to each stockholder.

At the **record date**, the company determines ownership of the outstanding shares for dividend purposes. The stockholders' records maintained by the corporation supply this information.

For Media General, the record date is December 22. No entry is required on the record date.

Record Date

Dec. 22	No entry necessary		

On the **payment date**, the company makes cash dividend payments to the stockholders on record as of December 22. It also records the payment of the dividend. If January 20 is the payment date for Media General, the entry on that date is as follows.

Payment Date

Jan. 20	Dividends Payable	50,000	
	Cash		50,000
	(To record payment of cash dividend)		

A	=	L	+	SE
		−50,000		
−50,000				

Cash Flows
−50,000

Note that payment of the dividend on the payment date reduces both current assets and current liabilities, but it has no effect on stockholders' equity. Cash Dividends is closed to Retained Earnings at the end of the accounting period. Thus, the cumulative effect of the **declaration and payment** of a cash dividend on a company's financial statements is to **decrease both stockholders' equity and total assets**.

ACCOUNTING ACROSS THE ORGANIZATION

Palto/iStockphoto

Up, Down, and ??

The decision whether to pay a dividend, and how much to pay, is a very important management decision. As the chart below shows, from 2002 to 2007, many companies substantially increased their dividends, and total dividends paid by U.S. companies hit record levels. One reason for the increase is that Congress lowered, from 39% to 15%, the tax rate paid by investors on dividends received, making dividends more attractive to investors.

Then the financial crisis of 2008 occurred. As a result, in 2009, 804 companies cut their dividends (see chart below), the highest level since Standard & Poor's started collecting data in 1995. In 2010, more companies started to increase their dividends. However, potential higher taxes on dividends coming in the future and the possibility of a low-growth economy may stall any significant increase.

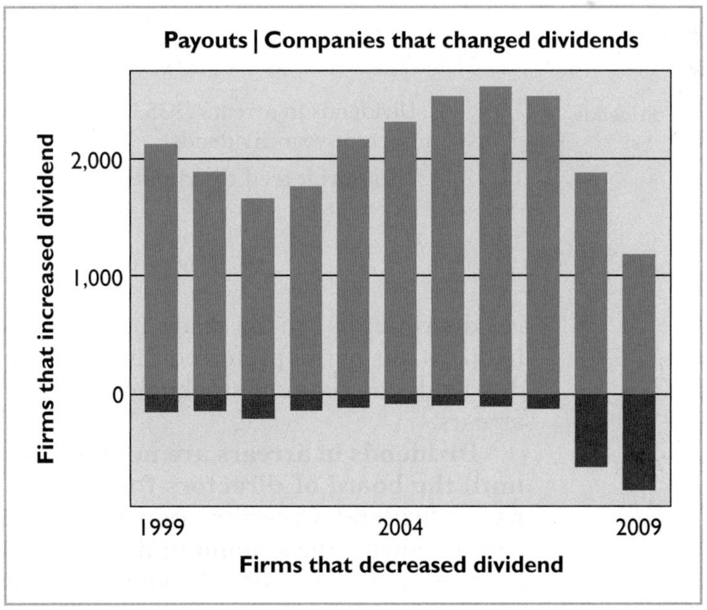

Source: Matt Phillips and Jay Miller, "Last Year's Dividend Slash Was $58 Billion," *Wall Street Journal* (January 8, 2010), p. C5.

What factors must management consider in deciding how large a dividend to pay? (Go to **WileyPLUS** for this answer and additional questions.)

DIVIDEND PREFERENCES

Preferred stockholders have the right to share in the distribution of corporate income before common stockholders. For example, if the dividend rate on preferred stock is $5 per share, common shareholders cannot receive any dividends in the current year until preferred stockholders have received $5 per share. The first claim to dividends does not, however, **guarantee** dividends. Dividends depend on many factors, such as adequate retained earnings and availability of cash.

For preferred stock, companies state the per share dividend amount as a percentage of the par value of the stock or as a specified amount. For example, EarthLink specifies a 3% dividend.

Most preferred stocks have a preference on corporate assets if the corporation fails. This feature provides security for the preferred stockholder. The preference to assets may be for the par value of the shares or for a specified liquidating value. For example, Commonwealth Edison issued preferred stock that entitled the holders to receive $31.80 per share, plus accrued and unpaid dividends, in the event of involuntary liquidation. The liquidation preference is used in litigation pertaining to bankruptcy lawsuits involving the respective claims of creditors and preferred stockholders.

Cumulative Dividend

Preferred stock contracts often contain a **cumulative dividend** feature. This feature stipulates that preferred stockholders must be paid both current-year dividends and any unpaid prior-year dividends before common stockholders are paid dividends. When preferred stock is cumulative, preferred dividends not declared that were supposed to be declared in a given period are called **dividends in arrears**.

To illustrate, assume that Scientific Leasing has 5,000 shares of 7%, $100 par value cumulative preferred stock outstanding. Each $100 share pays a $7 dividend (.07 × $100). The annual dividend is $35,000 (5,000 × $7 per share). If dividends are two years in arrears, preferred stockholders are entitled to receive in the current year the dividends as shown in Illustration 11-8.

ILLUSTRATION 11-8
Computation of total dividends to preferred stock

Dividends in arrears ($35,000 × 2)	$ 70,000
Current-year dividends	35,000
Total preferred dividends	**$105,000**

No distribution can be made to common stockholders until Scientific Leasing pays this entire preferred dividend. In other words, companies cannot pay dividends to common stockholders while any preferred stock dividend is in arrears.

Dividends in arrears are not considered a liability. No obligation exists until the board of directors formally "declares" that the corporation will pay a dividend. However, companies should disclose in the notes to the financial statements the amount of dividends in arrears. Doing so enables investors to assess the impact of this potential obligation on the corporation's financial position.

The investment community does not look favorably upon companies that are unable to meet their dividend obligations. As a financial officer noted in discussing one company's failure to pay its cumulative preferred dividend for a period of time, "Not meeting your obligations on something like that is a major black mark on your record."

DO IT! ▶ 3a Preferred Stock Dividends

MasterMind Corporation has 2,000 shares of 6%, $100 par value preferred stock outstanding at December 31, 2017. At December 31, 2017, the company declared a $60,000 cash dividend. Determine the dividend paid to preferred stockholders and common stockholders under each of the following scenarios.

1. The preferred stock is noncumulative, and the company has not missed any dividends in previous years.
2. The preferred stock is noncumulative, and the company did not pay a dividend in each of the two previous years.
3. The preferred stock is cumulative, and the company did not pay a dividend in each of the two previous years.

SOLUTION

1. The company has not missed past dividends and the preferred stock is noncumulative. Thus, the preferred stockholders are paid only this year's dividends. The dividend paid to preferred stockholders would be $12,000 (2,000 × .06 × $100). The dividend paid to common stockholders would be $48,000 ($60,000 − $12,000).
2. The preferred stock is noncumulative. Thus, past unpaid dividends do not have to be paid. The dividend paid to preferred stockholders would be $12,000 (2,000 × .06 × $100). The dividend paid to common stockholders would be $48,000 ($60,000 − $12,000).
3. The preferred stock is cumulative. Thus, dividends that have been missed (dividends in arrears) must be paid. The dividend paid to preferred stockholders would be $36,000 (3 × 2,000 × .06 × $100). Of the $36,000, $24,000 relates to dividends in arrears and $12,000 relates to the current dividend on preferred stock. The dividend paid to common stockholders would be $24,000 ($60,000 − $36,000).

Action Plan

✔ Determine dividends on preferred shares by multiplying the dividend rate times the par value of the stock times the number of preferred shares.

✔ Understand the cumulative feature: If preferred stock is cumulative, then any missed dividends (dividends in arrears) and the current year's dividend must be paid to preferred stockholders before dividends are paid to common stockholders.

Related exercise material: DO IT! **11-3a.**

STOCK DIVIDENDS

A **stock dividend** is a pro rata (proportional to ownership) distribution of the corporation's own stock to stockholders. Whereas a cash dividend is paid in cash, a stock dividend is paid in stock. **A stock dividend results in a decrease in retained earnings and an increase in paid-in capital.** Unlike a cash dividend, a stock dividend does not decrease total stockholders' equity or total assets.

Because a stock dividend does not result in a distribution of assets, some view it as nothing more than a publicity gesture. Stock dividends are often issued by companies that do not have adequate cash to issue a cash dividend. Such companies may not want to announce that they are not going to issue a cash dividend at their expected time. By issuing a stock dividend, they "save face" by giving the appearance of distributing a dividend. Note that since a stock dividend neither increases nor decreases the assets in the company, investors are not receiving anything they didn't already own. In a sense, it is like asking for two pieces of pie and having your host take one piece of pie and cut it into two smaller pieces. You are not better off, but you got your two pieces of pie.

To illustrate a stock dividend, assume that you have a 2% ownership interest in Cetus Inc.; you own 20 of its 1,000 shares of common stock. If Cetus declares a 10% stock dividend, it issues 100 shares (1,000 × 10%) of stock. You receive two shares (2% × 100), but your ownership interest remains at 2% (22 ÷ 1,100). **You now own more shares of stock, but your ownership interest has not changed.** Moreover, the company disburses no cash and assumes no liabilities.

What, then, are the purposes and benefits of a stock dividend? Corporations generally issue stock dividends for one of the following reasons:

1. To satisfy stockholders' dividend expectations without spending cash.
2. To increase the marketability of the stock by increasing the number of shares outstanding and thereby decreasing the market price per share. Decreasing the market price of the stock makes it easier for smaller investors to purchase the shares.
3. To emphasize that the company has permanently reinvested in the business a portion of stockholders' equity, which therefore is unavailable for cash dividends.

When the dividend is declared, the board of directors determines the size of the stock dividend and the value per share to use to record the transaction. In order to meet legal requirements, the per share amount must be at least equal to the par or stated value.

The accounting profession distinguishes between a **small stock dividend** (less than 20%–25% of the corporation's issued stock) and a **large stock dividend** (greater than 20%–25%). It recommends that the company use the **fair value per share** to record small stock dividends. The recommendation is based on the assumption that a small stock dividend will have little effect on the market price of the shares previously outstanding. Thus, many stockholders consider small stock dividends to be distributions of earnings equal to the fair value of the shares distributed. The accounting profession does not specify the value to use to record a large stock dividend. However, companies normally use **par or stated value per share**. Small stock dividends predominate in practice. In Appendix 11A at the end of the chapter, we illustrate the journal entries for small stock dividends.

Effects of Stock Dividends

▼ **HELPFUL HINT**
Because of its effects, a stock dividend is also referred to as *capitalizing retained earnings.*

How do stock dividends affect stockholders' equity? They **change the composition of stockholders' equity** because they result in a transfer of a portion of retained earnings to paid-in capital. However, **total stockholders' equity remains the same**. Stock dividends also have no effect on the par or stated value per share, but the number of shares outstanding increases.

Illustration 11-9 shows the effects that result when Medland Corp. declares a 10% stock dividend on its $10 par common stock when 50,000 shares were outstanding. The market price was $15 per share.

ILLUSTRATION 11-9
Stock dividend effects

	Before Dividend	Change	After Dividend
Stockholders' equity			
Paid-in capital			
Common stock, $10 par	$ 500,000	$ 50,000	$ 550,000
Paid-in capital in excess of par value	—	25,000	25,000
Total paid-in capital	500,000	+75,000	575,000
Retained earnings	300,000	−75,000	225,000
Total stockholders' equity	**$800,000**	$ 0	**$800,000**
Outstanding shares	**50,000**	+ 5,000	**55,000**
Par value per share	$ 10.00	$ 0	$ 10.00

In this example, total paid-in capital increased by $75,000 (50,000 shares × 10% × $15), and retained earnings decreased by the same amount. Note also that total stockholders' equity remains unchanged at $800,000. The number of shares increases by 5,000 (50,000 × 10%).

STOCK SPLITS

A **stock split**, like a stock dividend, involves the issuance of additional shares of stock to stockholders according to their percentage ownership. However, **a stock split results in a reduction in the par or stated value per share**. The purpose of a stock split is to increase the marketability of the stock by lowering its market price per share. This, in turn, makes it easier for the corporation to issue additional stock. After hitting a peak of 114 stock splits in 1986, the number of splits in the United States has fallen to about 30 per year. Google announced a 2-for-1 split recently when its stock was selling for $650 per share.

▼ **HELPFUL HINT**
A stock split changes the par value per share but does not affect any balances in stockholders' equity.

Like a stock dividend, a stock split increases the number of shares owned by a shareholder, but it does not change the percentage of the total company that the shareholder owns. The effects of a 4-for-1 split are shown in Illustration 11-10.

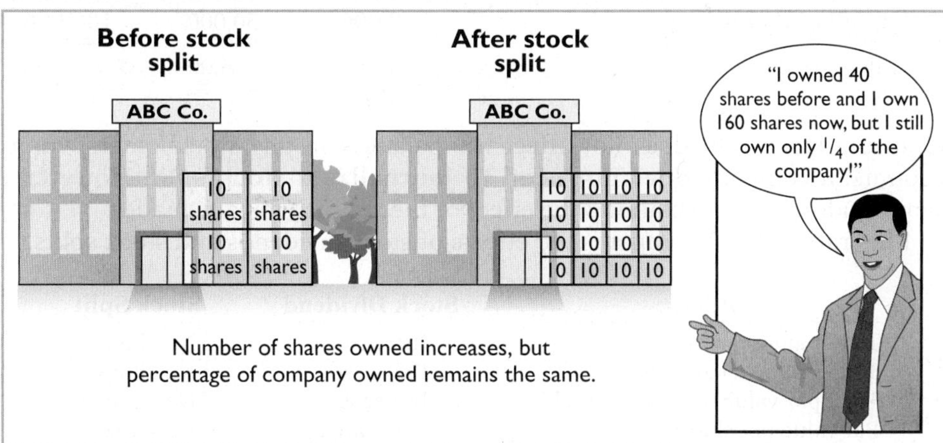

ILLUSTRATION 11-10
Effect of stock split for stockholders

The effect of a split on market price is generally **inversely proportional** to the size of the split. For example, after a recent 2-for-1 stock split, the market price of Nike's stock fell from $111 to approximately $55.

INVESTOR INSIGHT Berkshire Hathaway

Dietmar Klement/iStockphoto

A No-Split Philosophy

Warren Buffett's company, Berkshire Hathaway, has two classes of shares. Until recently, the company had never split either class of stock. As a result, the class A stock had a market price of $97,000 and the class B sold for about $3,200 per share. Because the price per share is so high, the stock does not trade as frequently as the stock of other companies. Buffett has always opposed stock splits because he feels that a lower stock price attracts short-term investors. He appears to be correct. For example, while more than 6 million shares of IBM are exchanged on the average day, only about 1,000 class A shares of Berkshire are traded. Despite Buffett's aversion to splits, in order to accomplish a recent acquisition, Berkshire decided to split its class B shares 50 to 1.

Source: Scott Patterson, "Berkshire Nears Smaller Baby B's," *Wall Street Journal Online* (January 19, 2010).

Why does Warren Buffett usually oppose stock splits? (Go to WileyPLUS for this answer and additional questions.)

In a stock split, the company increases the number of shares in the same proportion that it decreases the par or stated value per share. For example, in a 2-for-1 split, the company exchanges one share of $10 par value stock for two shares of $5 par value stock. **A stock split does not have any effect on paid-in capital, retained earnings, and total stockholders' equity.** However, the number of shares outstanding increases. The effects of a 2-for-1 stock split of Medland Corporation's common stock are shown in Illustration 11-11.

ILLUSTRATION 11-11
Stock split effects

	Before Stock Split	Change	After Stock Split
Stockholders' equity			
Paid-in capital			
Common stock			
(before: 50,000 $10 par shares; after: 100,000 $5 par shares)	$ 500,000		$ 500,000
Paid-in capital in excess of par value	0		0
Total paid-in capital	500,000	$ 0	500,000
Retained earnings	300,000	0	300,000
Total stockholders' equity	**$800,000**	$ 0	**$800,000**
Outstanding shares	**50,000**	+ 50,000	**100,000**
Par value per share	$ 10.00	−$ 5.00	$ 5.00

Because a stock split does not affect the balances in any stockholders' equity accounts, a company **does not need to journalize a stock split**. However, a memorandum entry explaining the effect of the split is typically made.

Illustration 11-12 compares the effects of stock dividends and stock splits.

ILLUSTRATION 11-12
Effects of stock splits and stock dividends differentiated

Item	Stock Dividend	Stock Split
Total paid-in capital	Increase	No change
Total retained earnings	Decrease	No change
Total par value (common stock)	Increase	No change
Par value per share	No change	Decrease
Shares outstanding	Increase	Increase
Total stockholders' equity	No change	No change

DO IT! 3b Stock Dividends; Stock Splits

Due to five years of record earnings at Sing CD Corporation, the market price of its 500,000 shares of $2 par value common stock tripled from $15 per share to $45. During this period, paid-in capital remained the same at $2,000,000. Retained earnings increased from $1,500,000 to $10,000,000. President Joan Elbert is considering either a 10% stock dividend or a 2-for-1 stock split. She asks you to show the before-and-after effects of each option on (a) retained earnings, (b) total stockholders' equity, and (c) par value per share.

Action Plan

- ✔ **Calculate the stock dividend's effect on retained earnings by multiplying the number of new shares times the market price of the stock (or par value for a large stock dividend).**
- ✔ **Recall that a stock dividend increases the number of shares without affecting total equity.**
- ✔ **Recall that a stock split only increases the number of shares outstanding and decreases the par value per share without affecting total equity.**

SOLUTION

The stock dividend amount is $2,250,000 [(500,000 × 10%) × $45]. The new balance in retained earnings is $7,750,000 ($10,000,000 − $2,250,000). The retained earnings balance after the stock split is the same as it was before the split: $10,000,000. The effects on the stockholders' equity accounts are as follows.

	Original Balances	After Dividend	After Split
Paid-in capital	$ 2,000,000	$ 4,250,000	$ 2,000,000
Retained earnings	10,000,000	7,750,000	10,000,000
Total stockholders' equity	$12,000,000	$12,000,000	$12,000,000
Shares outstanding	500,000	550,000	1,000,000
Par value per share	$ 2.00	$ 2.00	$ 1.00

Related exercise material: **BE11-6, BE11-7, DO IT! 11-3b, and E11-7.**

LEARNING OBJECTIVE 4 **Discuss how stockholders' equity is reported and analyzed.**

RETAINED EARNINGS

Retained earnings is net income that a company retains in the business. The balance in retained earnings is part of the stockholders' claim on the total assets of the corporation. It does not, however, represent a claim on any specific asset. Nor can the amount of retained earnings be associated with the balance of any asset account. For example, a $100,000 balance in retained earnings does not mean that there should be $100,000 in cash. The reason is that the company may have used the cash resulting from the excess of revenues over expenses to purchase buildings, equipment, and other assets. Illustration 11-13 shows recent amounts of retained earnings and cash in selected companies.

ILLUSTRATION 11-13
Retained earnings and cash balances

	(in millions)	
Company	**Retained Earnings**	**Cash**
Facebook	$ 3,159	$3,323
Google	61,262	8,989
Nike	5,695	3,337
Starbucks	4,130	2,576

When expenses exceed revenues, a **net loss** results. In contrast to net income, a net loss decreases retained earnings. In closing entries, a company debits a net loss to the Retained Earnings account. **It does not debit net losses to paid-in capital accounts.** To do so would destroy the distinction between paid-in and earned capital. If cumulative losses and dividends exceed cumulative income over a company's life, a debit balance in Retained Earnings results. A debit balance in Retained Earnings, such as that of Groupon, Inc. in a recent year, is a **deficit**. A company reports a deficit as a deduction in the stockholders' equity section of the balance sheet, as shown in Illustration 11-14.

ILLUSTRATION 11-14
Stockholders' equity with deficit

Real World

GROUPON, INC.
Balance Sheet (partial)
(in thousands)

Stockholders' equity		
Paid-in capital		
Common stock	$ 70	
Paid-in capital in excess of par value	1,885,301	
Total paid-in capital	1,885,371	
Accumulated deficit	**(921,960)**	
Total paid-in capital and retained earnings	963,411	
Less: Treasury stock	198,467	
Total stockholders' equity	$ 764,944	

RETAINED EARNINGS RESTRICTIONS

The balance in retained earnings is generally available for dividend declarations. Some companies state this fact. In some circumstances, however, there may be **retained earnings restrictions**. These make a portion of the balance currently unavailable for dividends. Restrictions result from one or more of these causes: legal, contractual, or voluntary.

Companies generally disclose retained earnings restrictions in the notes to the financial statements. For example, as shown in Illustration 11-15, Tektronix Inc., a manufacturer of electronic measurement devices, recently had total retained earnings of $774 million, but the unrestricted portion was only $223.8 million.

ILLUSTRATION 11-15
Disclosure of unrestricted retained earnings

TEKTRONIX INC.
Notes to the Financial Statements

Certain of the Company's debt agreements require compliance with debt covenants. The Company had unrestricted retained earnings of $223.8 million after meeting those requirements.

BALANCE SHEET PRESENTATION OF STOCKHOLDERS' EQUITY

In the stockholders' equity section of the balance sheet, companies report paid-in capital, retained earnings, accumulated other comprehensive income, and treasury stock. Within paid-in capital, two classifications are recognized:

1. **Capital stock**, which consists of preferred and common stock. Companies show preferred stock before common stock because of its preferential rights. They report information about the par value, shares authorized, shares issued, and shares outstanding for each class of stock.
2. **Additional paid-in capital**, which includes the excess of amounts paid in over par or stated value.

As discussed in Chapter 5, in some instances unrealized gains and losses are not included in net income. Instead, these excluded items, referred to as other comprehensive income items, are reported as part of a more inclusive earnings measure called comprehensive income. Examples of other comprehensive income items include certain adjustments to pension plan assets, types of foreign currency gains and losses, and some gains and losses on investments. The items reported as other comprehensive income are closed each year to the **Accumulated Other Comprehensive Income** account. Thus, this account includes the cumulative amount of all previous items reported as other comprehensive income. This account can have either a debit or credit balance depending on whether or not accumulated gains exceed accumulated losses over the years. If accumulated losses exceed gains, then the company reports accumulated other comprehensive loss.

Illustration 11-16 presents the stockholders' equity section of the balance sheet of Graber Inc. The company discloses a retained earnings restriction in the notes. The stockholders' equity section for Graber Inc. includes most of the accounts discussed in this chapter. The disclosures pertaining to Graber's common stock indicate that 400,000 shares are issued, 100,000 shares are unissued (500,000 authorized less 400,000 issued), and 390,000 shares are outstanding (400,000 issued less 10,000 shares in treasury).

ILLUSTRATION 11-16
Stockholders' equity section of balance sheet

GRABER INC.
Balance Sheet (partial)

Stockholders' equity		
Paid-in capital		
Capital stock		
9% preferred stock, $100 par value, cumulative, 10,000 shares authorized, 6,000 shares issued and outstanding		$ 600,000
Common stock, no par, $5 stated value, 500,000 shares authorized, 400,000 shares issued, and 390,000 outstanding		2,000,000
Total capital stock		2,600,000
Additional paid-in capital		
Paid-in capital in excess of par value—preferred stock	$ 30,000	
Paid-in capital in excess of stated value—common stock	1,050,000	
Total additional paid-in capital		1,080,000
Total paid-in capital		3,680,000
Retained earnings **(see Note R)**		1,050,000
Total paid-in capital and retained earnings		4,730,000
Accumulated other comprehensive income		110,000
Less: Treasury stock (10,000 common shares)		80,000
Total stockholders' equity		$4,760,000

Note R: Retained earnings is restricted for the cost of treasury stock, $80,000.

INTERNATIONAL NOTE
Like GAAP, under IFRS companies typically disclose separate categories of capital on the balance sheet. However, because of varying accounting treatments of certain transactions (such as treasury stock or asset revaluations), some categories used under IFRS vary from those under GAAP.

KEEPING AN EYE ON CASH

The balance sheet presents the balances of a company's stockholders' equity accounts at a point in time. Companies report in the financing activities section of the statement of cash flows information regarding cash inflows and outflows during the year that resulted from equity transactions. The excerpt below presents the cash flows from financing activities from the statement of cash flows of Sara Lee Corporation in a recent year. From this information, we learn that the company's purchases of treasury stock during the period far exceeded its issuances of new common stock, and its financing activities resulted in a net reduction in its cash balance.

Real World

SARA LEE CORPORATION
Statement of Cash Flows (partial)
(in millions)

Cash flows from financing activities	
Issuances of common stock	$ 38
Purchases of common stock	(686)
Payments of dividends	(374)
Borrowings of long-term debt	2,895
Repayments of long-term debt	(416)
Short-term (repayments) borrowings, net	(1,720)
Net cash used in financing activities	$ (263)

DO IT! 4a Stockholders' Equity Section

Jennifer Corporation has issued 300,000 shares of $3 par value common stock. It is authorized to issue 600,000 shares. The paid-in capital in excess of par value on the common stock is $380,000. The corporation has reacquired 15,000 shares at a cost of $50,000 and is currently holding those shares. It also had a cumulative other comprehensive loss of $82,000.

The corporation also has 4,000 shares issued and outstanding of 8%, $100 par value preferred stock. It is authorized to issue 10,000 shares. The paid-in capital in excess of par value on the preferred stock is $97,000. Retained earnings is $610,000.

Prepare the stockholders' equity section of the balance sheet.

Action Plan

- ✔ Present capital stock first; list preferred stock before common stock.
- ✔ Present additional paid-in capital after capital stock.
- ✔ Report retained earnings after capital stock and additional paid-in capital.
- ✔ Deduct treasury stock from total paid-in capital and retained earnings.

SOLUTION

JENNIFER CORPORATION
Balance Sheet (partial)

Stockholders' equity		
Paid-in capital		
Capital stock		
8% preferred stock, $100 par value, 10,000 shares authorized, 4,000 shares issued and outstanding	$ 400,000	
Common stock, $3 par value, 600,000 shares authorized, 300,000 shares issued, and 285,000 shares outstanding	900,000	
Total capital stock		$1,300,000
Additional paid-in capital		
Paid-in capital in excess of par value—preferred stock	97,000	
Paid-in capital in excess of par value—common stock	380,000	
Total additional paid-in capital		477,000
Total paid-in capital		1,777,000
Retained earnings		610,000
Total paid-in capital and retained earnings		2,387,000
Accumulated other comprehensive loss		82,000
Less: Treasury stock (15,000 common shares) (at cost)		50,000
Total stockholders' equity		$2,255,000

Related exercise material: **BE11-8, DO IT! 11-4a, E11-8, E11-9, and E11-10.**

ANALYSIS OF STOCKHOLDERS' EQUITY

Investors are interested in both a company's dividend record and its earnings performance. Although those two measures are often parallel, that is not always the case. Thus, investors should investigate each one separately.

Dividend Record

DECISION TOOLS

The payout ratio helps users determine the portion of a company's earnings that its pays out in dividends.

One way that companies reward stock investors for their investment is to pay them dividends. The **payout ratio** measures the percentage of earnings a company distributes in the form of cash dividends to common stockholders. It is computed by **dividing total cash dividends declared to common shareholders by net income**. Using the information shown below, the payout ratio for Nike in 2014 and 2013 is calculated in Illustration 11-17.

	2014	2013
Dividends (in millions)	$ 821	$ 727
Net income (in millions)	2,693	2,472

ILLUSTRATION 11-17
Nike's payout ratio

$$\text{Payout Ratio} = \frac{\text{Cash Dividends Declared on Common Stock}}{\text{Net Income}}$$

($ in millions)	2014	2013
Payout Ratio	$\frac{\$821}{\$2,693} = 30.5\%$	$\frac{\$727}{\$2,472} = 29.4\%$

Nike's payout ratio was relatively constant at approximately 30%. Companies attempt to set their dividend rate at a level that will be sustainable.

Companies that have high growth rates are characterized by low payout ratios because they reinvest most of their net income in the business. Thus, a low payout ratio is not necessarily bad news. Companies that believe they have many good opportunities for growth, such as Facebook, will reinvest those funds in the company rather than pay dividends. However, low dividend payments, or a cut in dividend payments, might signal that a company has liquidity or solvency problems and is trying to conserve cash by not paying dividends. Thus, investors and analysts should investigate the reason for low dividend payments.

Illustration 11-18 lists recent payout ratios of four well-known companies.

ILLUSTRATION 11-18
Payout ratios of companies

Company	Payout Ratio
Microsoft	24.5%
Kellogg	43.3%
Facebook	0%
Wal-Mart	49.0%

Earnings Performance

Another way to measure corporate performance is through profitability. A widely used ratio that measures profitability from the common stockholders' viewpoint is **return on common stockholders' equity (ROE)**. This ratio shows how many dollars of net income a company earned for each dollar of common stockholders' equity. It is computed by dividing net income available to common stockholders (Net income − Preferred dividends) by average common stockholders' equity. Common stockholders' equity is equal to total stockholders' equity minus any equity from preferred stock.

DECISION TOOLS 

Return on common stockholders' equity helps users determine a company's return on its common stockholders' investment.

Using the information on the previous page and the additional information presented below, Illustration 11-19 shows Nike's return on common stockholders' equity.

(in millions)	2014	2013	2012
Preferred dividends	$ -0-	$ -0-	$ -0-
Common stockholders' equity	10,824	11,081	10,319

ILLUSTRATION 11-19
Nike's return on common stockholders' equity

$$\text{Return on Common Stockholders' Equity} = \frac{\text{Net Income} - \text{Preferred Dividends}}{\text{Average Common Stockholders' Equity}}$$

($ in millions)	2014	2013
Return on Common Stockholders' Equity	$\frac{\$2,693 - \$0}{(\$10,824 + \$11,081)/2} = 24.6\%$	$\frac{\$2,472 - \$0}{(\$11,081 + \$10,319)/2} = 23.1\%$

From 2013 to 2014, Nike's return on common shareholders' equity increased. As a company grows larger, it becomes increasingly hard to sustain a high return. In Nike's case, since many believe the U.S. market for expensive sports shoes is saturated, it will need to grow either along new product lines, such as hiking shoes and golf equipment, or in new markets, such as Europe and Asia.

DEBT VERSUS EQUITY DECISION

When obtaining long-term capital, corporate managers must decide whether to issue bonds or to sell common stock. Bonds have three primary advantages relative to common stock, as shown in Illustration 11-20.

ILLUSTRATION 11-20
Advantages of bond financing over common stock

Bond Financing	Advantages
Ballot	1. **Stockholder control is not affected.** Bondholders do not have voting rights, so current owners (stockholders) retain full control of the company.
Tax Bill	2. **Tax savings result.** Bond interest is deductible for tax purposes; dividends on stock are not.
$ / STOCK	3. **Return on common stockholders' equity may be higher.** Although bond interest expense reduces net income, return on common stockholders' equity often is higher under bond financing because no additional shares of common stock are issued.

How does the debt versus equity decision affect the return on common stockholders' equity? Illustration 11-21 shows that the return on common stockholders' equity is affected by the return on assets and the amount of leverage a company uses—that is, by the company's reliance on debt (often measured by the debt to assets ratio). **If a company wants to increase its return on common stockholders' equity, it can either increase its return on assets or increase its reliance on debt financing.**

ILLUSTRATION 11-21
Components of the return on common stockholders' equity

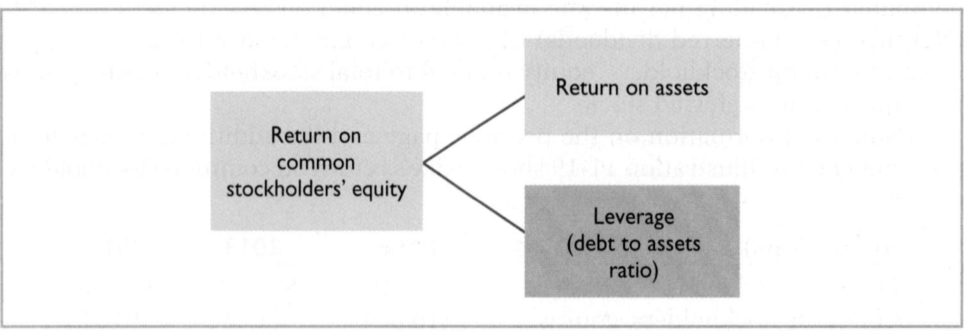

To illustrate the potential effect of debt financing on the return on common stockholders' equity, assume that Microsystems Inc. currently has 100,000 shares of common stock outstanding issued at $25 per share and no debt. It is considering two alternatives for raising an additional $5 million. Plan A involves issuing 200,000 shares of common stock at the current market price of $25 per share. Plan B involves issuing $5 million of 12% bonds at face value. Income before interest and taxes will be $1.5 million; income taxes are expected to be 30%. The alternative effects on the return on common stockholders' equity are shown in Illustration 11-22.

ILLUSTRATION 11-22
Effects on return on common stockholders' equity of issuing debt

	Plan A: Issue Stock	Plan B: Issue Bonds
Income before interest and taxes	$1,500,000	$1,500,000
Interest (12% × $5,000,000)	—	600,000
Income before income taxes	1,500,000	900,000
Income tax expense (30%)	450,000	270,000
Net income	$1,050,000	$ 630,000
Common stockholders' equity	$7,500,000	$2,500,000
Return on common stockholders' equity	14%	25.2%

Note that with long-term debt financing (bonds), net income is $420,000 ($1,050,000 − $630,000) less. However, the return on common stockholders' equity increases from 14% to 25.2% with the use of debt financing because net income is spread over a smaller amount of common stockholders' equity. **In general, as long as the return on assets rate exceeds the rate paid on debt, a company will increase the return on common stockholders' equity by the use of debt.**

After seeing this illustration, you might ask, why don't companies rely almost exclusively on debt financing rather than equity? Debt has one major disadvantage: **Debt reduces solvency. The company locks in fixed payments that it must make in good times and bad. The company must pay interest on a periodic basis and must pay the principal (face value) of the bonds at maturity.** A company with fluctuating earnings and a relatively weak cash position may experience great difficulty in meeting interest requirements in periods of low earnings. In the extreme, this can result in bankruptcy. With common stock financing, on the other hand, the company can decide to pay low (or no) dividends if earnings are low.

DO IT! 4b Analyzing Stockholders' Equity

On January 1, 2017, Siena Corporation purchased 2,000 shares of treasury stock. Other information regarding Siena Corporation is provided below.

	2017	2016
Net income	$110,000	$110,000
Dividends on preferred stock	$10,000	$10,000
Dividends on common stock	$1,600	$2,000
Common stockholders' equity, beginning of year	$400,000*	$500,000
Common stockholders' equity, end of year	$400,000	$500,000

*Adjusted for purchase of treasury stock.

Compute (a) return on common stockholders' equity for each year, and (b) discuss its change from 2016 to 2017.

Action Plan

✔ Determine return on common stockholders' equity by dividing net income available to common stockholders by average common stockholders' equity.

SOLUTION

(a)

	2017	2016
Return on common stockholders' equity	$\frac{(\$110{,}000 - \$10{,}000)}{(\$400{,}000 + \$400{,}000)/2} = 25\%$	$\frac{(\$110{,}000 - \$10{,}000)}{(\$500{,}000 + \$500{,}000)/2} = 20\%$

(b) Between 2016 and 2017, return on common stockholders' equity improved from 20% to 25%. While this would appear to be good news for the company's common stockholders, this increase should be carefully evaluated. It is important to note that net income did not change during this period. The increase in the ratio was due to the purchase of treasury shares, which reduced the denominator of the ratio. As the company repurchases its own shares, it becomes more reliant on debt and thus increases its risk.

Related exercise material: **BE11-10, DO IT! 11-4b, E11-11, E11-12, and E11-13.**

USING DECISION TOOLS—ADIDAS

adidas is one of Nike's competitors. In such a competitive and rapidly changing environment, one wrong step can spell financial disaster.

INSTRUCTIONS

The following facts are available from adidas's annual report. As a German company, adidas reports under International Financial Reporting Standards (IFRS). Using this information, evaluate its (1) payout ratio and (2) earnings per share and return on common stockholders' equity (ROE). (3) Compare the payout ratio and ROE with those for Nike for 2014 and 2013.

(in millions)	2014	2013	2012
Dividends declared	€314	€282	
Net income	€490	€787	
Preferred dividends	0	0	
Shares outstanding at end of year	204	209	209
Common stockholders' equity	€5,625	€5,489	€5,304

SOLUTION

1. A measure to evaluate a company's dividend record is the payout ratio. For adidas, this measure in 2014 and 2013 is calculated as shown below.

	2014	2013
Payout ratio	$\frac{€314}{€490} = 64.1\%$	$\frac{€282}{€787} = 35.8\%$

Nike's payout ratio was 30.5%. adidas's payout ratio dramatically increased from 2013 to 2014 and was significantly higher than Nike's ratio in 2014.

2. There are many measures of earnings performance. Some of those presented thus far in the textbook were earnings per share (page 53) and the return on common stockholders' equity (this chapter). These measures for adidas in 2014 and 2013 are calculated as shown here.

	2014	2013
Earnings per share	$\frac{€490 - 0}{(204 + 209)/2} = €2.37$	$\frac{€787 - 0}{(209 + 209)/2} = €3.77$
Return on common stockholders' equity	$\frac{€490 - 0}{(€5,625 + €5,489)/2} = 8.8\%$	$\frac{€787 - 0}{(€5,489 + €5,291)/2} = 14.6\%$

3. Nike's payout ratio was lower than that of adidas in both years. This means that adidas paid a higher percentage of its earnings as dividends. Nike had a higher return on shareholders' equity during this 2-year period.

LEARNING OBJECTIVE ▶ *5

APPENDIX 11A: Prepare entries for stock dividends.

To illustrate the accounting for stock dividends, assume that Medland Corporation has a balance of $300,000 in retained earnings and declares a 10% stock dividend on its 50,000 shares of $10 par value common stock. The current fair value of its stock is $15 per share. The number of shares to be issued is 5,000 (10% × 50,000), and the total amount to be debited to Stock Dividends is $75,000 (5,000 × $15). The entry to record this transaction at the declaration date is as follows.

Stock Dividends	75,000	
Common Stock Dividends Distributable		50,000
Paid-in Capital in Excess of Par Value		25,000
(To record declaration of 10% stock dividend)		

A	=	L	+	SE
				−75,000 Div
				+50,000 CS
				+25,000 CS

Cash Flows
no effect

At the declaration date, Medland increases (debits) Stock Dividends for the fair value of the stock issued, increases (credits) Common Stock Dividends Distributable for the par value of the dividend shares (5,000 × $10), and increases (credits) the excess over par (5,000 × $5) to an additional paid-in capital account.

Stock Dividends is closed to Retained Earnings at the end of the accounting period. Common Stock Dividends Distributable is a stockholders' equity account. It is not a liability because assets will not be used to pay the dividend. If Medland prepares a balance sheet before it issues the dividend shares, it reports the distributable account in paid-in capital as an addition to common stock issued, as shown in Illustration 11A-1.

▼ **HELPFUL HINT**
Note that the dividend account title is *distributable*, not *payable*.

ILLUSTRATION 11A-1
Statement presentation of common stock dividends distributable

MEDLAND CORPORATION
Balance Sheet (partial)

Paid-in capital	
Common stock	$500,000
Common stock dividends distributable	**50,000**
Paid-in capital in excess of par—common stock	25,000
Total paid-in capital	$575,000

When Medland issues the dividend shares, it decreases Common Stock Dividends Distributable and increases Common Stock as follows.

Common Stock Dividends Distributable	50,000	
Common Stock		50,000
(To record issuance of 5,000 shares in a stock dividend)		

A	=	L	+	SE
				−50,000 CS
				+50,000 CS

Cash Flows
no effect

REVIEW AND PRACTICE

▶ LEARNING OBJECTIVES REVIEW

1 Discuss the major characteristics of a corporation. The major characteristics of a corporation are separate legal existence, limited liability of stockholders, transferable ownership rights, ability to acquire capital, continuous life, corporation management, government regulations, and additional taxes.

2 Explain how to account for the issuance of common and preferred stock, and the purchase of treasury stock. When a company records issuance of common stock for cash, it credits the par value of the shares to Common Stock. It records in a separate paid-in capital account the portion of the proceeds that is above par value. When no-par common stock has a stated value, the entries are similar to those for par value stock. When no-par common stock does not have a stated value, the entire proceeds from the issue are credited to Common Stock.

Companies generally use the cost method in accounting for treasury stock. Under this approach, a company debits Treasury Stock at the price paid to reacquire the shares.

3 Explain how to account for cash dividends and describe the effect of stock dividends and stock splits. Companies make entries for dividends at the declaration date and the payment date. At the declaration date, the entries for a cash dividend are debit Cash Dividends and credit Dividends Payable.

Preferred stock has contractual provisions that give it priority over common stock in certain areas. Typically, preferred stockholders have a preference as to (1) dividends and (2) assets in the event of liquidation. However, they sometimes do not have voting rights.

The effects of stock dividends and splits are as follows. Small stock dividends transfer an amount equal to the fair value of the shares issued from retained earnings to the paid-in capital accounts. Stock splits reduce the par value per share of the common stock while increasing the number of shares so that the balance in the Common Stock account remains the same.

4 Discuss how stockholders' equity is reported and analyzed. Additions to retained earnings consist of net income. Deductions consist of net loss and cash and stock dividends. In some instances, portions of retained earnings are restricted, making that portion unavailable for the payment of dividends.

In the stockholders' equity section of the balance sheet, companies report paid-in capital and retained earnings and identify specific sources of paid-in capital. Within paid-in capital, companies show two classifications: capital stock and additional paid-in capital. If a corporation has treasury stock, it deducts the cost of treasury stock from total paid-in capital and retained earnings to determine total stockholders' equity.

A company's dividend record can be evaluated by looking at what percentage of net income it chooses to pay out in dividends, as measured by the payout ratio (dividends divided by net income). Earnings performance is measured with the return on common stockholders' equity (income available to common stockholders divided by average common stockholders' equity).

***5 Prepare entries for stock dividends.** To record the declaration of a small stock dividend (less than 20%), debit Stock Dividends for an amount equal to the fair value of the shares issued. Record a credit to a temporary stockholders' equity account—Common Stock Dividends Distributable—for the par value of the shares, and credit the balance to Paid-in Capital in Excess of Par Value. When the shares are issued, debit Common Stock Dividends Distributable and credit Common Stock.

DECISION TOOLS REVIEW

DECISION CHECKPOINTS	INFO NEEDED FOR DECISION	TOOL TO USE FOR DECISION	HOW TO EVALUATE RESULTS
Should the company incorporate?	Capital needs, growth expectations, type of business, tax status	Corporations have limited liability, better capital-raising ability, and professional managers. But they suffer from additional taxes, government regulations, and separation of ownership from management.	Must carefully weigh the costs and benefits in light of the particular circumstances.
What portion of its earnings does the company pay out in dividends?	Net income and total cash dividends on common stock	$\text{Payout ratio} = \dfrac{\text{Cash dividends declared on common stock}}{\text{Net income}}$	A low ratio may suggest that the company is retaining its earnings for investment in future growth.
What is the company's return on common stockholders' investment?	Earnings available to common stockholders and average common stockholders' equity	$\text{Return on common stockholders' equity} = \dfrac{\text{Net income} - \text{Preferred dividends}}{\text{Average common stockholders' equity}}$	A high measure suggests strong earnings performance from common stockholders' perspective.

GLOSSARY REVIEW

Accumulated Other Comprehensive Income This account includes the cumulative amount of all previous items reported as other comprehensive income. (p. 558).

Authorized stock The amount of stock that a corporation is authorized to sell as indicated in its charter. (p. 543).

Cash dividend A pro rata (proportional to ownership) distribution of cash to stockholders. (p. 549).

Charter A document that describes a corporation's name and purpose, types of stock and number of shares authorized, names of individuals involved in the formation, and number of shares each individual has agreed to purchase. (p. 541).

Corporation A company organized as a separate legal entity, with most of the rights and privileges of a person. (p. 538).

Cumulative dividend A feature of preferred stock entitling the stockholder to receive current and unpaid prior-year dividends before common stockholders receive any dividends. (p. 552).

Declaration date The date the board of directors formally authorizes the dividend and announces it to stockholders. (p. 550).

Deficit A debit balance in Retained Earnings. (p. 557).

Dividend A distribution by a corporation to its stockholders on a pro rata (proportional to ownership) basis. (p. 549).

Dividends in arrears Preferred dividends that were supposed to be declared but were not declared during a given period. (p. 552).

Legal capital The amount of capital that must be retained in the business for the protection of corporate creditors. (p. 543).

No-par value stock Capital stock that has not been assigned a value in the corporate charter. (p. 544).

Outstanding stock Capital stock that has been issued and is being held by stockholders. (p. 548).

Paid-in capital The amount stockholders paid in to the corporation in exchange for shares of ownership. (p. 544).

Par value stock Capital stock that has been assigned a value per share in the corporate charter. (p. 543).

Payment date The date cash dividend payments are made to stockholders. (p. 551).

Payout ratio A measure of the percentage of earnings a company distributes in the form of cash dividends to common stockholders. (p. 560).

Preferred stock Capital stock that has contractual preferences over common stock in certain areas. (p. 546).

Privately held corporation A corporation that has only a few stockholders and whose stock is not available for sale to the general public. (p. 538).

Publicly held corporation A corporation that may have thousands of stockholders and whose stock is traded on a national securities market. (p. 538).

Record date The date when the company determines ownership of outstanding shares for dividend purposes. (p. 550).

Retained earnings Net income that a company retains in the business. (p. 544).

Retained earnings restrictions Circumstances that make a portion of retained earnings currently unavailable for dividends. (p. 558).

Return on common stockholders' equity (ROE) A measure of profitability from the stockholders' point of view; computed by dividing net income minus preferred dividends by average common stockholders' equity. (p. 561).

Stated value The amount per share assigned by the board of directors to no-par stock. (p. 544).

Stock dividend A pro rata (proportional to ownership) distribution of the corporation's own stock to stockholders. (p. 553).

Stock split The issuance of additional shares of stock to stockholders accompanied by a reduction in the par or stated value per share. (p. 555).

Treasury stock A corporation's own stock that has been reacquired by the corporation and is being held for future use. (p. 547).

PRACTICE MULTIPLE-CHOICE QUESTIONS

(LO 1) **1.** Which of these is **not** a major advantage of a corporation?
(a) Separate legal existence.
(b) Continuous life.
(c) Government regulations.
(d) Transferable ownership rights.

(LO 1) **2.** A major **disadvantage** of a corporation is:
(a) limited liability of stockholders.
(b) additional taxes.
(c) transferable ownership rights.
(d) None of the above.

(LO 1) **3.** Which of these statements is **false**?
(a) Ownership of common stock gives the owner a voting right.
(b) The stockholders' equity section begins with paid-in capital.
(c) The authorization of capital stock does not result in a formal accounting entry.
(d) Legal capital is intended to protect stockholders.

(LO 2) **4.** ABC Corp. issues 1,000 shares of $10 par value common stock at $12 per share. When the transaction is recorded, credits are made to:
(a) Common Stock $10,000 and Paid-in Capital in Excess of Stated Value $2,000.
(b) Common Stock $12,000.
(c) Common Stock $10,000 and Paid-in Capital in Excess of Par Value $2,000.
(d) Common Stock $10,000 and Retained Earnings $2,000.

5. Treasury stock may be repurchased: (LO 2)
(a) to reissue the shares to officers and employees under bonus and stock compensation plans.
(b) to signal to the stock market that management believes the stock is underpriced.
(c) to have additional shares available for use in the acquisition of other companies.
(d) More than one of the above.

6. Preferred stock may have priority over common stock **except** in: (LO 3)
(a) dividend preference.
(b) preference to assets in the event of liquidation.
(c) cumulative dividends.
(d) voting.

(LO 3) 7. U-Bet Corporation has 10,000 shares of 8%, $100 par value, cumulative preferred stock outstanding at December 31, 2017. No dividends were declared in 2015 or 2016. If U-Bet wants to pay $375,000 of dividends in 2017, common stockholders will receive:
(a) $0. (c) $215,000.
(b) $295,000. (d) $135,000.

(LO 3) 8. Entries for cash dividends are required on the:
(a) declaration date and the record date.
(b) record date and the payment date.
(c) declaration date, record date, and payment date.
(d) declaration date and the payment date.

(LO 3) 9. Which of these statements about stock dividends is **true**?
(a) Stock dividends reduce a company's cash balance.
(b) A stock dividend has no effect on total stockholders' equity.
(c) A stock dividend decreases total stockholders' equity.
(d) A stock dividend ordinarily will increase total stockholders' equity.

(LO 3) 10. Zealot Inc. has retained earnings of $500,000 and total stockholders' equity of $2,000,000. It has 100,000 shares of $8 par value common stock outstanding, which is currently selling for $30 per share. If Zealot declares a 10% stock dividend on its common stock:
(a) net income will decrease by $80,000.
(b) retained earnings will decrease by $80,000 and total stockholders' equity will increase by $80,000.
(c) retained earnings will decrease by $300,000 and total stockholders' equity will increase by $300,000.
(d) retained earnings will decrease by $300,000 and total paid-in capital will increase by $300,000.

(LO 4) 11. In the stockholders' equity section of the balance sheet, common stock:
(a) is listed before preferred stock.
(b) is added to total capital stock.
(c) is part of paid-in capital.
(d) is part of additional paid-in capital.

12. In the stockholders' equity section, the cost of treasury stock is deducted from: (LO 4)
(a) total paid-in capital and retained earnings.
(b) retained earnings.
(c) total stockholders' equity.
(d) common stock in paid-in capital.

13. The return on common stockholders' equity is usually increased by all of the following, **except**: (LO 4)
(a) an increase in the return on assets ratio.
(b) an increase in the use of debt financing.
(c) an increase in the company's stock price.
(d) an increase in the company's net income.

14. Thomas is nearing retirement and would like to invest in a stock that will provide a good steady income. Thomas should choose a stock with a: (LO 4)
(a) high current ratio.
(b) high dividend payout.
(c) high earnings per share.
(d) high price-earnings ratio.

15. Jackson Inc. reported net income of $186,000 during 2017 and paid dividends of $26,000 on common stock. It also paid dividends on its 10,000 shares of 6%, $100 par value, noncumulative preferred stock. Common stockholders' equity was $1,200,000 on January 1, 2017, and $1,600,000 on December 31, 2017. The company's return on common stockholders' equity for 2017 is: (LO 4)
(a) 10.0%. (c) 7.1%.
(b) 9.0%. (d) 13.3%.

16. If everything else is held constant, earnings per share is increased by: (LO 4)
(a) the payment of a cash dividend to common shareholders.
(b) the payment of a cash dividend to preferred shareholders.
(c) the issuance of new shares of common stock.
(d) the purchase of treasury stock.

SOLUTIONS

1. **(c)** Government regulations are a disadvantage of a corporation. The other choices are advantages of a corporation.
2. **(b)** Additional taxes are a disadvantage of a corporation. The other choices are advantages of a corporation.
3. **(d)** Legal capital is intended to protect creditors, not stockholders. The other choices are true statements.
4. **(c)** Common Stock should be credited for $10,000 and Paid-in Capital in Excess of Par Value should be credited for $2,000. The stock is par value stock, not stated value stock, and this excess is contributed, not earned, capital. The other choices are therefore incorrect.
5. **(d)** Treasury stock may be repurchased to reissue the shares as part of bonus and stock compensation plans, to signal to the stock market that the stock is underpriced, and to have additional shares available for use in the acquisition of other companies. Choice (a), (b), (c) are all correct, but (d) is the best answer.
6. **(d)** Preferred stock usually does not have voting rights and therefore does not have priority over common stock on this issue. The other choices are true statements.
7. **(d)** The preferred stockholders will receive a total of $240,000 of dividends [dividends in arrears ($80,000 × 2 years) + current-year dividends ($80,000)]. If U-Bet wants to pay a total of $375,000 in 2017, then common stockholders will receive $135,000 ($375,000 − $240,000), not (a) $0, (b) $295,000, or (c) $215,000.
8. **(d)** Entries are required for dividends on the declaration date and the payment date, but not the record date. The other choices are therefore incorrect.
9. **(b)** A stock dividend moves amounts from retained earnings to paid-in capital and has no effect on stockholders' equity or cash. The other choices are therefore incorrect.

10. **(d)** A 10% stock dividend on the company's common stock will increase the number of shares issued by 10,000 (100,000 × 10%). At a market price of $30 per share, total paid-in capital will increase by $300,000 (10,000 shares × $30/share) and retained earnings will decrease by that same amount. The other choices are therefore incorrect.
11. **(c)** Common stock is part of paid-in capital. The other choices are incorrect because common stock (a) is listed after preferred stock, (b) is not added to total capital stock but is part of capital stock, and (d) is part of capital stock, not additional paid-in capital.
12. **(a)** The cost of treasury stock is deducted from total paid-in capital and retained earnings. The other choices are therefore incorrect.
13. **(c)** An increase in the company's stock price has no effect on the return on common stockholders' equity. The other choices are incorrect because (a) an increase in a firm's return on assets, (b) an increase in a firm's use of debt financing, and (c) an increase in a firm's net income will all increase the return on common stockholders' equity.
14. **(b)** Thomas should focus on a high dividend payout. The other choices are incorrect because a stock with a (a) high current ratio, (c) high earnings per share, or (d) high price-earnings ratio may or may not pay dividends on a consistent basis.
15. **(b)** Return on common stockholders' equity is net income available to common stockholders divided by average common stockholders' equity. Net income available to common stockholders is net income less preferred dividends = $126,000 [$186,000 − (10,000 × .06 × $100)]. The company's return on common stockholders' equity for the year is therefore 9.0% [$126,000/($1,200,000 + $1,600,000)/2)], not (a) 10.0%, (c) 7.1%, or (d) 13.3%.
16. **(d)** The purchase of treasury stock reduces the number of shares outstanding, which is the denominator of earnings per share (EPS). With a smaller denominator, EPS is larger. The other choices are incorrect because (a) the payment of a cash dividend to common stockholders does not affect the earnings or the number of outstanding shares, so EPS will stay the same; (b) the payment of a cash dividend to preferred stockholders will reduce the amount of earnings available to the common stockholders, thus reducing EPS; and (c) the issuance of new shares of common stock would not affect earnings but will increase the number of outstanding shares, thereby reducing EPS.

PRACTICE EXERCISES

1. Maci Co. had the following transactions during the current period.

Journalize issuance of common and preferred stock and purchase of treasury stock.

(LO 2)

June 12	Issued 60,000 shares of $5 par value common stock for cash of $370,000.
July 11	Issued 1,000 shares of $100 par value preferred stock for cash at $112 per share.
Nov. 28	Purchased 2,000 shares of treasury stock for $70,000.

INSTRUCTIONS

Journalize the transactions.

SOLUTION

1. June 12	Cash	370,000	
	Common Stock (60,000 × $5)		300,000
	Paid-in Capital in Excess of Par Value—Common Stock		70,000
July 11	Cash (1,000 × $112)	112,000	
	Preferred Stock (1,000 × $100)		100,000
	Paid-in Capital in Excess of Par Value—Preferred Stock (1,000 × $12)		12,000
Nov. 28	Treasury Stock	70,000	
	Cash		70,000

Journalize cash dividends; indicate statement presentation.

(LO 3, 4)

2. On January 1, Chong Corporation had 95,000 shares of no-par common stock issued and outstanding. The stock has a stated value of $5 per share. During the year, the following occurred.

Apr. 1	Issued 25,000 additional shares of common stock for $17 per share.
June 15	Declared a cash dividend of $1 per share to stockholders of record on June 30.
July 10	Paid the $1 cash dividend.
Dec. 1	Issued 2,000 additional shares of common stock for $19 per share.
15	Declared a cash dividend on outstanding shares of $1.20 per share to stockholders of record on December 31.

INSTRUCTIONS

(a) Prepare the entries, if any, on each of the three dividend dates.

(b) How are dividends and dividends payable reported in the financial statements prepared at December 31?

SOLUTION

2. (a) June 15	Cash Dividends (120,000 × $1)	120,000	
	Dividends Payable		120,000
July 10	Dividends Payable	120,000	
	Cash		120,000
Dec. 15	Cash Dividends (122,000 × $1.20)	146,400	
	Dividends Payable		146,400

(b) In the retained earnings statement, dividends of $266,400 will be deducted. In the balance sheet, Dividends Payable of $146,400 will be reported as a current liability.

PRACTICE PROBLEM

Journalize transactions and prepare stockholders' equity section.

(LO 2, 3, 4)

Rolman Corporation is authorized to issue 1,000,000 shares of $5 par value common stock. In its first year, the company has the following stock transactions.

Jan. 10	Issued 400,000 shares of stock at $8 per share.
Sept. 21	Purchased 10,000 shares of common stock for the treasury at $9 per share.
Dec. 24	Declared a cash dividend of 10 cents per share on common stock outstanding.

INSTRUCTIONS

(a) Journalize the transactions.

(b) Prepare the stockholders' equity section of the balance sheet, assuming the company had retained earnings of $150,600 at December 31 and an accumulated other comprehensive loss of $105,000.

SOLUTION

(a) Jan. 10	Cash	3,200,000	
	Common Stock		2,000,000
	Paid-in Capital in Excess of Par Value		1,200,000
	(To record issuance of 400,000 shares of $5 par value stock)		
Sept. 21	Treasury Stock	90,000	
	Cash		90,000
	(To record purchase of 10,000 shares of treasury stock at cost)		
Dec. 24	Cash Dividends	39,000	
	Dividends Payable		39,000
	(To record declaration of 10 cents per share cash dividend)		

(b)

ROLMAN CORPORATION Balance Sheet (partial)	
Stockholders' equity	
Paid-in capital	
Capital stock	
Common stock, $5 par value, 1,000,000 shares authorized, 400,000 shares issued, 390,000 outstanding	$2,000,000
Additional paid-in capital	
Paid-in capital in excess of par value—common stock	1,200,000
Total paid-in capital	3,200,000
Retained earnings	150,600
Total paid-in capital and retained earnings	3,350,600
Accumulated other comprehensive loss	105,000
Less: Treasury stock (10,000 shares)	90,000
Total stockholders' equity	$3,155,600

WileyPLUS Brief Exercises, DO IT! Exercises, Exercises, Problems, and many additional resources are available for practice in WileyPLUS.

NOTE: All asterisked Questions, Exercises, and Problems relate to material in the appendix to the chapter.

QUESTIONS

1. Joe, a student, asks your help in understanding some characteristics of a corporation. Explain each of these to Joe.
   (a) Separate legal existence.
   (b) Limited liability of stockholders.
   (c) Transferable ownership rights.
2. (a) Your friend G. C. Jones cannot understand how the characteristic of corporate management is both an advantage and a disadvantage. Clarify this problem for G. C.
   (b) Identify and explain two other disadvantages of a corporation.
3. Nona Jaymes believes a corporation must be incorporated in the state in which its headquarters office is located. Is Nona correct? Explain.
4. What are the basic ownership rights of common stockholders in the absence of restrictive provisions?
5. A corporation has been defined as an entity separate and distinct from its owners. In what ways is a corporation a separate legal entity?
6. What are the two principal components of stockholders' equity?
7. The corporate charter of Gage Corporation allows the issuance of a maximum of 100,000 shares of common stock. During its first 2 years of operation, Gage sold 70,000 shares to shareholders and reacquired 4,000 of these shares. After these transactions, how many shares are authorized, issued, and outstanding?
8. Which is the better investment—common stock with a par value of $5 per share or common stock with a par value of $20 per share?
9. For what reasons might a company like IBM repurchase some of its stock (treasury stock)?
10. Monet, Inc. purchases 1,000 shares of its own previously issued $5 par common stock for $11,000. Assuming the shares are held in the treasury, what effect does this transaction have on (a) net income, (b) total assets, (c) total paid-in capital, and (d) total stockholders' equity?
11. (a) What are the principal differences between common stock and preferred stock?
    (b) Preferred stock may be cumulative. Discuss this feature.
    (c) How are dividends in arrears presented in the financial statements?
12. Identify the events that result in credits and debits to retained earnings.
13. Indicate how each of these accounts should be classified in the stockholders' equity section of the balance sheet.
    (a) Common Stock.
    (b) Paid-in Capital in Excess of Par Value.

(c) Retained Earnings.
(d) Treasury Stock.
(e) Paid-in Capital in Excess of Stated Value.
(f) Preferred Stock.

14. What three conditions must be met before a cash dividend is paid?

15. Three dates associated with Petrie Company's cash dividend are May 1, May 15, and May 31. Discuss the significance of each date and give the entry at each date.

16. Contrast the effects of a cash dividend and a stock dividend on a corporation's balance sheet.

17. Doris Angel asks, "Since stock dividends don't change anything, why declare them?" What is your answer to Doris?

18. Jayne Corporation has 10,000 shares of $15 par value common stock outstanding when it announces a 3-for-1 split. Before the split, the stock had a market price of $120 per share. After the split, how many shares of stock will be outstanding, and what will be the approximate market price per share?

19. The board of directors is considering a stock split or a stock dividend. They understand that total stockholders' equity will remain the same under either action. However, they are not sure of the different effects of the two actions on other aspects of stockholders' equity. Explain the differences to the directors.

20. What was the total cost of Apple's treasury stock at September 27, 2014? What was the amount of the 2014 cash dividend? What was the size of the 2014 stock split?

21. (a) What is the purpose of a retained earnings restriction?
(b) Identify the possible causes of retained earnings restrictions.

22. Thom Inc.'s common stock has a par value of $1 and a current market price of $15. Explain why these amounts are different.

23. What is the formula for the payout ratio? What does it indicate?

24. Explain the circumstances under which debt financing will increase the return on common stockholders' equity.

25. Under what circumstances will the return on assets and the return on common stockholders' equity be equal?

26. Sauer Corp. has a return on assets of 12%. It plans to issue bonds at 8% and use the cash to repurchase stock. What effect will this have on its debt to assets ratio and on its return on common stockholders' equity?

BRIEF EXERCISES

Cite advantages and disadvantages of a corporation.
(LO 1), K

BE11-1 Hana Ascot is planning to start a business. Identify for Hana the advantages and disadvantages of the corporate form of business organization.

Journalize issuance of par value common stock.
(LO 2), AP

BE11-2 On May 10, Pilar Corporation issues 2,500 shares of $5 par value common stock for cash at $13 per share. Journalize the issuance of the stock.

Journalize issuance of no-par common stock.
(LO 2), AP

BE11-3 On June 1, Forrest Inc. issues 3,000 shares of no-par common stock at a cash price of $7 per share. Journalize the issuance of the shares.

Journalize issuance of preferred stock.
(LO 2), AP

BE11-4 Layes Inc. issues 8,000 shares of $100 par value preferred stock for cash at $106 per share. Journalize the issuance of the preferred stock.

Prepare entries for a cash dividend.
(LO 3), AP

BE11-5 Basse Corporation has 7,000 shares of common stock outstanding. It declares a $1 per share cash dividend on November 1 to stockholders of record on December 1. The dividend is paid on December 31. Prepare the entries on the appropriate dates to record the declaration and payment of the cash dividend.

Show before-and-after effects of a stock dividend.
(LO 3), AP

BE11-6 The stockholders' equity section of Mabry Corporation's balance sheet consists of common stock ($8 par) $1,000,000 and retained earnings $300,000. A 10% stock dividend (12,500 shares) is declared when the market price per share is $19. Show the before-and-after effects of the dividend on (a) the components of stockholders' equity and (b) the shares outstanding.

Compare impact of cash dividend, stock dividend, and stock split.
(LO 3), K

BE11-7 Indicate whether each of the following transactions would increase (+), decrease (−), or not affect (N/A) total assets, total liabilities, and total stockholders' equity.

Transaction	Assets	Liabilities	Stockholders' Equity
(a) Declared cash dividend.			
(b) Paid cash dividend declared in (a).			
(c) Declared stock dividend.			
(d) Distributed stock dividend declared in (c).			
(e) Split stock 3-for-1.			

Prepare a stockholders' equity section.
(LO 4), AP

BE11-8 Sudz Corporation has these accounts at December 31: Common Stock, $10 par, 5,000 shares issued, $50,000; Paid-in Capital in Excess of Par Value $22,000; Retained Earnings $42,000; and Treasury Stock, 500 shares, $11,000. Prepare the stockholders' equity section of the balance sheet.

Evaluate a company's dividend record.
(LO 4), C

BE11-9 Hans Miken, president of Miken Corporation, believes that it is a good practice for a company to maintain a constant payout of dividends relative to its earnings. Last year, net income was $600,000, and the corporation paid $120,000 in dividends. This year, due to some unusual circumstances, the corporation had income of $1,600,000. Hans expects next year's net income to be about $700,000. What was Miken Corporation's payout ratio last year? If it is to maintain the same payout ratio, what amount of dividends would it pay this year? Is this necessarily a good idea—that is, what are the pros and cons of maintaining a constant payout ratio in this scenario?

Calculate the return on stockholders' equity.
(LO 4), AP

BE11-10 SUPERVALU, one of the largest grocery retailers in the United States, is headquartered in Minneapolis. Suppose the following financial information (in millions) was taken from the company's 2017 annual report: net sales $44,597, net income $393, beginning stockholders' equity $2,581, and ending stockholders' equity $2,887. There were no dividends paid on preferred stock. Compute the return on common stockholders' equity. Provide a brief interpretation of your findings.

Compare bond financing to stock financing.
(LO 4), AP

BE11-11 Emron Inc. is considering these two alternatives to finance its construction of a new $2 million plant:

1. Issuance of 200,000 shares of common stock at the market price of $10 per share.
2. Issuance of $2 million, 6% bonds at face value.

Complete the table and indicate which alternative is preferable.

	Issue Stock	Issue Bonds
Income before interest and taxes	$1,500,000	$1,500,000
Interest expense from bonds		
Income before income taxes		
Income tax expense (30%)		
Net income	$	$
Outstanding shares		700,000
Earnings per share	$	$

Prepare entries for a stock dividend.
(LO 5), AP

***BE11-12** Stossel Corporation has 200,000 shares of $10 par value common stock outstanding. It declares a 12% stock dividend on December 1 when the market price per share is $17. The dividend shares are issued on December 31. Prepare the entries for the declaration and distribution of the stock dividend.

DO IT! EXERCISES

Analyze statements about corporate organization.
(LO 1), C

DO IT! 11-1 Indicate whether each of the following statements is true or false.

_____ 1. The corporation is an entity separate and distinct from its owners.
_____ 2. The liability of stockholders is normally limited to their investment in the corporation.
_____ 3. The relative lack of government regulation is an advantage of the corporate form of business.
_____ 4. There is no journal entry to record the authorization of capital stock.
_____ 5. No-par value stock is quite rare today.

Journalize issuance of stock.
(LO 2), AP

DO IT! 11-2a Beauty Island Corporation began operations on April 1 by issuing 55,000 shares of $5 par value common stock for cash at $13 per share. In addition, Beauty Island issued 1,000 shares of $1 par value preferred stock for $6 per share. Journalize the issuance of the common and preferred shares.

Journalize treasury stock transaction.
(LO 2), AP

DO IT! 11-2b Dinosso Corporation purchased 2,000 shares of its $10 par value common stock for $76,000 on August 1. It will hold these in the treasury until resold. Journalize the treasury stock transaction.

Determine dividends paid to preferred and common stockholders.

(LO 3), AP

DO IT! 11-3a Sparks Corporation has 3,000 shares of 8%, $100 par value preferred stock outstanding at December 31, 2017. At December 31, 2017, the company declared a $105,000 cash dividend. Determine the dividend paid to preferred stockholders and common stockholders under each of the following scenarios.

1. The preferred stock is noncumulative, and the company has not missed any dividends in previous years.
2. The preferred stock is noncumulative, and the company did not pay a dividend in each of the two previous years.
3. The preferred stock is cumulative, and the company did not pay a dividend in each of the two previous years.

Determine effects of stock dividend and stock split.

(LO 3), AP

DO IT! 11-3b Spears Company has had 4 years of record earnings. Due to this success, the market price of its 400,000 shares of $2 par value common stock has increased from $6 per share to $50. During this period, paid-in capital remained the same at $2,400,000. Retained earnings increased from $1,800,000 to $12,000,000. CEO Don Ames is considering either (1) a 15% stock dividend or (2) a 2-for-1 stock split. He asks you to show the before-and-after effects of each option on (a) retained earnings, (b) total stockholders' equity, and (c) par value per share.

Prepare stockholders' equity section.

(LO 4), AP

DO IT! 11-4a Hoyle Corporation has issued 100,000 shares of $5 par value common stock. It was authorized 500,000 shares. The paid-in capital in excess of par value on the common stock is $263,000. The corporation has reacquired 7,000 shares at a cost of $46,000 and is currently holding those shares. It also had accumulated other comprehensive income of $67,000.

The corporation also has 2,000 shares issued and outstanding of 9%, $100 par value preferred stock. It was authorized 10,000 shares. The paid-in capital in excess of par value on the preferred stock is $23,000. Retained earnings is $372,000. Prepare the stockholders' equity section of the balance sheet.

Compute return on stockholders' equity and discuss changes.

(LO 4), AP

DO IT! 11-4b On January 1, 2017, Vahsholtz Corporation purchased 5,000 shares of treasury stock. Other information regarding Vahsholtz Corporation is provided as follows.

	2017	2016
Net income	$110,000	$100,000
Dividends on preferred stock	$ 30,000	$ 30,000
Dividends on common stock	$ 25,000	$ 20,000
Weighted-average number of common shares outstanding	45,000	50,000
Common stockholders' equity beginning of year	$750,000	$600,000
Common stockholders' equity end of year	$830,000	$750,000

Compute (a) return on common stockholders' equity for each year, and (b) discuss the changes in each.

EXERCISES

Journalize issuance of common stock.

(LO 2), AP

E11-1 During its first year of operations, Mona Corporation had these transactions pertaining to its common stock.

Jan. 10	Issued 30,000 shares for cash at $5 per share.
July 1	Issued 60,000 shares for cash at $7 per share.

Instructions

(a) Journalize the transactions, assuming that the common stock has a par value of $5 per share.

(b) Journalize the transactions, assuming that the common stock is no-par with a stated value of $1 per share.

Journalize issuance of common stock and preferred stock and purchase of treasury stock.

(LO 2), AP

E11-2 Sagan Co. had these transactions during the current period.

June 12	Issued 80,000 shares of $1 par value common stock for cash of $300,000.
July 11	Issued 3,000 shares of $100 par value preferred stock for cash at $106 per share.
Nov. 28	Purchased 2,000 shares of treasury stock for $9,000.

Instructions
Prepare the journal entries for the Sagan Co. transactions.

E11-3 Penland Corporation is authorized to issue both preferred and common stock. The par value of the preferred is $50. During the first year of operations, the company had the following events and transactions pertaining to its preferred stock.

Journalize preferred stock transactions and indicate statement presentation.

(LO 2, 4), AP

Feb. 1 Issued 40,000 shares for cash at $51 per share.
July 1 Issued 60,000 shares for cash at $56 per share.

Instructions
(a) Journalize the transactions.
(b) Post to the stockholders' equity accounts. (Use T-accounts.)
(c) Discuss the statement presentation of the accounts.

E11-4 The stockholders' equity section of Lachlin Corporation's balance sheet at December 31 is presented here.

Answer questions about stockholders' equity section.

(LO 2, 4), C

LACHLIN CORPORATION
Balance Sheet (partial)

Stockholders' equity	
Paid-in capital	
Preferred stock, cumulative, 10,000 shares authorized, 6,000 shares issued and outstanding	$ 600,000
Common stock, no par, 750,000 shares authorized, 580,000 shares issued	2,900,000
Total paid-in capital	3,500,000
Retained earnings	1,158,000
Total paid-in capital and retained earnings	4,658,000
Less: Treasury stock (6,000 common shares)	32,000
Total stockholders' equity	$4,626,000

Instructions
From a review of the stockholders' equity section, answer the following questions.
(a) How many shares of common stock are outstanding?
(b) Assuming there is a stated value, what is the stated value of the common stock?
(c) What is the par value of the preferred stock?
(d) If the annual dividend on preferred stock is $36,000, what is the dividend rate on preferred stock?
(e) If dividends of $72,000 were in arrears on preferred stock, what would be the balance reported for retained earnings?

E11-5 Mesa Corporation recently hired a new accountant with extensive experience in accounting for partnerships. Because of the pressure of the new job, the accountant was unable to review what he had learned earlier about corporation accounting. During the first month, he made the following entries for the corporation's capital stock.

Prepare correct entries for capital stock transactions.

(LO 2), AN

Date	Account	Debit	Credit
May 2	Cash	104,000	
	Capital Stock		104,000
	(Issued 8,000 shares of $10 par value common stock at $13 per share)		
10	Cash	530,000	
	Capital Stock		530,000
	(Issued 10,000 shares of $20 par value preferred stock at $53 per share)		
15	Capital Stock	7,200	
	Cash		7,200
	(Purchased 600 shares of common stock for the treasury at $12 per share)		

Instructions
On the basis of the explanation for each entry, prepare the entries that should have been made for the capital stock transactions.

Journalize cash dividends and indicate statement presentation.

(LO 3), AP

E11-6 On January 1, Graves Corporation had 60,000 shares of no-par common stock issued and outstanding. The stock has a stated value of $4 per share. During the year, the following transactions occurred.

Apr. 1	Issued 9,000 additional shares of common stock for $11 per share.
June 15	Declared a cash dividend of $1.50 per share to stockholders of record on June 30.
July 10	Paid the $1.50 cash dividend.
Dec. 1	Issued 4,000 additional shares of common stock for $12 per share.
15	Declared a cash dividend on outstanding shares of $1.60 per share to stockholders of record on December 31.

Instructions

(a) Prepare the entries, if any, on each of the three dates that involved dividends.

(b) How are dividends and dividends payable reported in the financial statements prepared at December 31?

Compare effects of a stock dividend and a stock split.

(LO 3), AP

E11-7 On October 31, the stockholders' equity section of Manolo Company's balance sheet consists of common stock $648,000 and retained earnings $400,000. Manolo is considering the following two courses of action: (1) declaring a 5% stock dividend on the 81,000 $8 par value shares outstanding or (2) effecting a 2-for-1 stock split that will reduce par value to $4 per share. The current market price is $17 per share.

Instructions

Prepare a tabular summary of the effects of the alternative actions on the company's stockholders' equity and outstanding shares. Use these column headings: **Before Action, After Stock Dividend**, and **After Stock Split**.

Prepare a stockholders' equity section.

(LO 4), AP

E11-8 Wells Fargo & Company, headquartered in San Francisco, is one of the nation's largest financial institutions. Suppose it reported the following selected accounts (in millions) as of December 31, 2017.

Retained Earnings	$41,563
Preferred Stock	8,485
Common Stock—1\frac{2}{3}$ par value, authorized 6,000,000,000 shares; issued 5,245,971,422 shares	8,743
Treasury Stock—67,346,829 common shares	(2,450)
Paid-in Capital in Excess of Par Value—Common Stock	52,878
Accumulated Other Comprehensive Income	8,327

Instructions

Prepare the stockholders' equity section of the balance sheet for Wells Fargo as of December 31, 2017.

Prepare a stockholders' equity section.

(LO 4), AP

E11-9 The following stockholders' equity accounts, arranged alphabetically, are in the ledger of Ryder Corporation at December 31, 2017.

Common Stock ($2 stated value)	$1,600,000
Paid-in Capital in Excess of Par Value—Preferred Stock	45,000
Paid-in Capital in Excess of Stated Value—Common Stock	1,050,000
Preferred Stock (8%, $100 par, noncumulative)	600,000
Retained Earnings	1,334,000
Treasury Stock (12,000 common shares)	72,000

Instructions

Prepare the stockholders' equity section of the balance sheet at December 31, 2017.

Prepare a stockholders' equity section.

(LO 4), AP

E11-10 The following accounts appear in the ledger of Paisan Inc. after the books are closed at December 31, 2017.

Common Stock (no-par, $1 stated value, 400,000 shares authorized, 250,000 shares issued)	$ 250,000
Paid-in Capital in Excess of Stated Value—Common Stock	1,200,000
Preferred Stock ($50 par value, 8%, 40,000 shares authorized, 14,000 shares issued)	700,000
Retained Earnings	920,000
Treasury Stock (9,000 common shares)	64,000
Paid-in Capital in Excess of Par Value—Preferred Stock	24,000
Accumulated Other Comprehensive Loss	31,000

Instructions
Prepare the stockholders' equity section at December 31, assuming $100,000 of retained earnings is restricted for plant expansion. (Use Note R.)

E11-11 The following financial information is available for Flintlock Corporation.

Calculate ratios to evaluate dividend and earnings performance.

(LO 4), AP

(in millions)	2017	2016
Average common stockholders' equity	$2,532	$2,591
Dividends declared for common stockholders	298	611
Dividends declared for preferred stockholders	40	40
Net income	504	555

Instructions
Calculate the payout ratio and return on common stockholders' equity for 2017 and 2016. Comment on your findings.

E11-12 Suppose the following financial information is available for Walgreen Company.

Calculate ratios to evaluate dividend and earnings performance.

(LO 4), AP

(in millions)	2017	2016
Average common stockholders' equity	$13,622.5	$11,986.5
Dividends declared for common stockholders	471	394
Dividends declared for preferred stockholders	0	0
Net income	2,006	2,157

Instructions
Calculate the payout ratio and return on common stockholders' equity for 2017 and 2016. Comment on your findings.

E11-13 Kojak Corporation decided to issue common stock and used the $300,000 proceeds to redeem all of its outstanding bonds on January 1, 2017. The following information is available for the company for 2017 and 2016.

Calculate ratios to evaluate profitability and solvency.

(LO 4), AN

	2017	2016
Net income	$ 182,000	$ 150,000
Dividends declared for preferred stockholders	8,000	8,000
Average common stockholders' equity	1,000,000	700,000
Total assets	1,200,000	1,200,000
Current liabilities	100,000	100,000
Total liabilities	200,000	500,000

Instructions
(a) Compute the return on common stockholders' equity for both years.
(b) Explain how it is possible that net income increased but the return on common stockholders' equity decreased.
(c) Compute the debt to assets ratio for both years, and comment on the implications of this change in the company's solvency.

E11-14 Baja Airlines is considering these two alternatives for financing the purchase of a fleet of airplanes:

Compare issuance of stock financing to issuance of bond financing.

(LO 4), AN

1. Issue 50,000 shares of common stock at $40 per share. (Cash dividends have not been paid nor is the payment of any contemplated.)
2. Issue 12%, 10-year bonds at face value for $2,000,000.

It is estimated that the company will earn $800,000 before interest and taxes as a result of this purchase. The company has an estimated tax rate of 30% and has 90,000 shares of common stock outstanding prior to the new financing.

Instructions
Determine the effect on net income and earnings per share for (a) issuing stock and (b) issuing bonds. Assume the new shares or new bonds will be outstanding for the entire year.

E11-15 Cabo Company has $1,000,000 in assets and $1,000,000 in stockholders' equity, with 40,000 shares outstanding the entire year. It has a return on assets of 10%. During 2016, it had net income of $100,000. On January 1, 2017, it issued $400,000 in debt at 4% and immediately repurchased 20,000 shares for $400,000. Management expected that, had it not issued the debt, it would have had net income of $100,000 in 2017.

Compute ratios and interpret.

(LO 4), AN

Instructions

(a) Determine the company's net income and earnings per share for 2016 and 2017. (Ignore taxes in your computations.)
(b) Compute the company's return on common stockholders' equity for 2016 and 2017.
(c) Compute the company's debt to assets ratio for 2016 and 2017.
(d) Discuss the impact that the borrowing had on the company's profitability and solvency. Was it a good idea to borrow the money to buy the treasury stock?

Journalize stock dividends.
(LO 5), AP

***E11-16** On January 1, 2017, Lenne Corporation had $1,200,000 of common stock outstanding that was issued at par and retained earnings of $750,000. The company issued 30,000 shares of common stock at par on July 1 and earned net income of $400,000 for the year.

Instructions

Journalize the declaration of a 15% stock dividend on December 10, 2017, for the following two independent assumptions.
(a) Par value is $10 and market price is $15.
(b) Par value is $5 and market price is $8.

EXERCISES: SET B AND CHALLENGE EXERCISES

Visit the book's companion website, at **www.wiley.com/college/kimmel**, and choose the Student Companion site to access Exercises: Set B and Challenge Exercises.

PROBLEMS: SET A

Journalize stock transactions, post, and prepare paid-in capital section.
(LO 2, 4), AP

P11-1A Tidal Corporation was organized on January 1, 2017. It is authorized to issue 20,000 shares of 6%, $50 par value preferred stock and 500,000 shares of no-par common stock with a stated value of $1 per share. The following stock transactions were completed during the first year.

Jan. 10	Issued 70,000 shares of common stock for cash at $4 per share.
Mar. 1	Issued 12,000 shares of preferred stock for cash at $53 per share.
May 1	Issued 120,000 shares of common stock for cash at $6 per share.
Sept. 1	Issued 5,000 shares of common stock for cash at $5 per share.
Nov. 1	Issued 3,000 shares of preferred stock for cash at $56 per share.

Instructions

(a) Journalize the transactions.
(b) Post to the stockholders' equity accounts. (Use T-accounts.)
(c) Prepare the paid-in capital portion of the stockholders' equity section at December 31, 2017.

(c) Tot. paid-in capital $1,829,000

Journalize transactions, post, and prepare a stockholders' equity section; calculate ratios.
(LO 2, 3, 4), AP

P11-2A The stockholders' equity accounts of Cyrus Corporation on January 1, 2017, were as follows.

Preferred Stock (7%, $100 par noncumulative, 5,000 shares authorized)	$ 300,000
Common Stock ($4 stated value, 300,000 shares authorized)	1,000,000
Paid-in Capital in Excess of Par Value—Preferred Stock	15,000
Paid-in Capital in Excess of Stated Value—Common Stock	480,000
Retained Earnings	688,000
Treasury Stock (5,000 common shares)	40,000

During 2017, the corporation had the following transactions and events pertaining to its stockholders' equity.

Feb. 1	Issued 5,000 shares of common stock for $30,000.
Mar. 20	Purchased 1,000 additional shares of common treasury stock at $7 per share.
Oct. 1	Declared a 7% cash dividend on preferred stock, payable November 1.
Nov. 1	Paid the dividend declared on October 1.
Dec. 1	Declared a $0.50 per share cash dividend to common stockholders of record on December 15, payable December 31, 2017.
31	Determined that net income for the year was $280,000. Paid the dividend declared on December 1.

Instructions

(a) Journalize the transactions. (Include entries to close net income and dividends to Retained Earnings.)
(b) Enter the beginning balances in the accounts and post the journal entries to the stockholders' equity accounts. (Use T-accounts.)
(c) Prepare the stockholders' equity section of the balance sheet at December 31, 2017.
(d) Calculate the payout ratio, earnings per share, and return on common stockholders' equity. (*Note:* Use the common shares outstanding on January 1 and December 31 to determine the average shares outstanding.)

(c) Tot. paid-in capital $1,825,000

P11-3A On December 31, 2016, Jons Company had 1,300,000 shares of $5 par common stock issued and outstanding. At December 31, 2016, stockholders' equity had the amounts listed here.

Prepare a stockholders' equity section.

(LO 2, 3, 4), AP

Common Stock	$6,500,000
Additional Paid-in Capital	1,800,000
Retained Earnings	1,200,000

Transactions during 2017 and other information related to stockholders' equity accounts were as follows.

1. On January 10, 2017, issued at $107 per share 120,000 shares of $100 par value, 9% cumulative preferred stock.
2. On February 8, 2017, reacquired 15,000 shares of its common stock for $11 per share.
3. On May 9, 2017, declared the yearly cash dividend on preferred stock, payable June 10, 2017, to stockholders of record on May 31, 2017.
4. On June 8, 2017, declared a cash dividend of $1.20 per share on the common stock outstanding, payable on July 10, 2017, to stockholders of record on July 1, 2017.
5. Net income for the year was $3,600,000.

Instructions

Prepare the stockholders' equity section of Jons' balance sheet at December 31, 2017.

Tot. stockholders' equity $23,153,000

P11-4A The ledger of Waite Corporation at December 31, 2017, after the books have been closed, contains the following stockholders' equity accounts.

Reproduce Retained Earnings account, and prepare a stockholders' equity section.

(LO 3, 4), AP

Preferred Stock (10,000 shares issued)	$1,000,000
Common Stock (300,000 shares issued)	1,500,000
Paid-in Capital in Excess of Par Value—Preferred Stock	200,000
Paid-in Capital in Excess of Stated Value—Common Stock	1,600,000
Retained Earnings	2,860,000

A review of the accounting records reveals this information:

1. Preferred stock is 8%, $100 par value, noncumulative. Since January 1, 2016, 10,000 shares have been outstanding; 20,000 shares are authorized.
2. Common stock is no-par with a stated value of $5 per share; 600,000 shares are authorized.
3. The January 1, 2017, balance in Retained Earnings was $2,380,000.
4. On October 1, 60,000 shares of common stock were sold for cash at $9 per share.
5. A cash dividend of $400,000 was declared and properly allocated to preferred and common stock on November 1. No dividends were paid to preferred stockholders in 2016.
6. Net income for the year was $880,000.
7. On December 31, 2017, the directors authorized disclosure of a $160,000 restriction of retained earnings for plant expansion. (Use Note A.)

Instructions

(a) Reproduce the Retained Earnings account (T-account) for the year.
(b) Prepare the stockholders' equity section of the balance sheet at December 31.

(b) Tot. paid-in capital $4,300,000

P11-5A Layes Corporation has been authorized to issue 20,000 shares of $100 par value, 7%, noncumulative preferred stock and 1,000,000 shares of no-par common stock. The corporation assigned a $5 stated value to the common stock. At December 31, 2017, the ledger contained the following balances pertaining to stockholders' equity.

Prepare entries for stock transactions, and prepare a stockholders' equity section.

(LO 2, 4), AP

Preferred Stock	$ 150,000
Paid-in Capital in Excess of Par Value—Preferred Stock	20,000
Common Stock	2,000,000

Paid-in Capital in Excess of Stated Value—Common Stock	1,520,000
Treasury Stock (4,000 common shares)	36,000
Retained Earnings	82,000
Accumulated Other Comprehensive Income	51,000

The preferred stock was issued for $170,000 cash. All common stock issued was for cash. In November 4,000 shares of common stock were purchased for the treasury at a per share cost of $9. No dividends were declared in 2017.

Instructions

(a) Prepare the journal entries for the following.
(1) Issuance of preferred stock for cash.
(2) Issuance of common stock for cash.
(3) Purchase of common treasury stock for cash.

(b) Tot. stockholders' equity $3,787,000

(b) Prepare the stockholders' equity section of the balance sheet at December 31, 2017.

Prepare a stockholders' equity section.

(LO 2, 3, 4), AP

P11-6A On January 1, 2017, Kimbel Inc. had these stockholders' equity balances.

Common Stock, $1 par (2,000,000 shares authorized, 600,000 shares issued and outstanding)	$ 600,000
Paid-in Capital in Excess of Par Value	1,500,000
Retained Earnings	700,000
Accumulated Other Comprehensive Income	60,000

During 2017, the following transactions and events occurred.

1. Issued 50,000 shares of $1 par value common stock for $3 per share.
2. Issued 60,000 shares of common stock for cash at $4 per share.
3. Purchased 20,000 shares of common stock for the treasury at $3.80 per share.
4. Declared and paid a cash dividend of $207,000.
5. Earned net income of $410,000.
6. Had other comprehensive income of $17,000.

Tot. stockholders' equity $3,394,000

Instructions

Prepare the stockholders' equity section of the balance sheet at December 31, 2017.

Evaluate a company's profitability and solvency.

(LO 4), AP

P11-7A Spahn Company manufactures backpacks. During 2017, Spahn issued bonds at 10% interest and used the cash proceeds to purchase treasury stock. The following financial information is available for Spahn Company for the years 2017 and 2016.

	2017	**2016**
Sales revenue	$ 9,000,000	$ 9,000,000
Net income	2,240,000	2,500,000
Interest expense	500,000	140,000
Tax expense	670,000	750,000
Dividends paid on common stock	890,000	1,026,000
Dividends paid on preferred stock	300,000	300,000
Total assets (year-end)	14,500,000	16,875,000
Average total assets	15,687,500	17,763,000
Total liabilities (year-end)	6,000,000	3,000,000
Avg. total common stockholders' equity	9,400,000	14,100,000

Instructions

(a) Use the information above to calculate the following ratios for both years: (1) return on assets, (2) return on common stockholders' equity, (3) payout ratio, (4) debt to assets ratio, and (5) times interest earned.

(b) Referring to your findings in part (a), discuss the changes in the company's profitability from 2016 to 2017.

(c) Referring to your findings in part (a), discuss the changes in the company's solvency from 2016 to 2017.

(d) Based on your findings in (b), was the decision to issue debt to purchase common stock a wise one?

Prepare dividend entries, prepare a stockholders' equity section, and calculate ratios.

(LO 3, 4, 5), AP

***P11-8A** On January 1, 2017, Tacoma Corporation had these stockholders' equity accounts.

Common Stock ($10 par value, 70,000 shares issued and outstanding)	$700,000
Paid-in Capital in Excess of Par Value	500,000
Retained Earnings	620,000

During the year, the following transactions occurred.

Jan. 15	Declared a $0.50 cash dividend per share to stockholders of record on January 31, payable February 15.
Feb. 15	Paid the dividend declared in January.
Apr. 15	Declared a 10% stock dividend to stockholders of record on April 30, distributable May 15. On April 15, the market price of the stock was $14 per share.
May 15	Issued the shares for the stock dividend.
Dec. 1	Declared a $0.60 per share cash dividend to stockholders of record on December 15, payable January 10, 2018.
31	Determined that net income for the year was $400,000.

Instructions

(a) Journalize the transactions. (Include entries to close net income and dividends to Retained Earnings.)

(b) Enter the beginning balances and post the entries to the stockholders' equity T-accounts. (*Note:* Open additional stockholders' equity accounts as needed.)

(c) Prepare the stockholders' equity section of the balance sheet at December 31.

(d) Calculate the payout ratio and return on common stockholders' equity.

(c) Tot. stockholders' equity $2,138,800

PROBLEMS: SET B AND SET C

Visit the book's companion website, at **www.wiley.com/college/kimmel**, and choose the Student Companion site to access Problems: Set B and Set C.

CONTINUING PROBLEM Cookie Creations

(*Note:* This is a continuation of the Cookie Creations problem from Chapters 1 through 10.)

© leungchopan/Shutterstock

CC11 Part 1 Because Natalie has been so successful with Cookie Creations and her friend Curtis Lesperance has been just as successful with his coffee shop, they conclude that they could benefit from each other's business expertise. Curtis and Natalie next evaluate the different types of business organization. Because of the advantage of limited personal liability, they decide to form a corporation.

Natalie and Curtis are very excited about this new business venture. They come to you with information they have gathered about their companies and with a number of questions.

Part 2 After establishing their company's fiscal year to be October 31, Natalie and Curtis began operating Cookie & Coffee Creations Inc. on November 1, 2017. On that date, they issued both preferred and common stock. Natalie and Curtis now want to prepare financial information for the first year of operations.

Go to the book's companion website, at **www.wiley.com/college/kimmel**, *to find the completion of this problem.*

COMPREHENSIVE ACCOUNTING CYCLE REVIEW

Journalize transactions and prepare financial statements.

(LO 2, 3, 4), AP

ACR11-1 Hawkeye Corporation's balance sheet at December 31, 2016, is presented below.

HAWKEYE CORPORATION
Balance Sheet
December 31, 2016

Cash	$ 24,600	Accounts payable	$ 25,600
Accounts receivable	45,500	Common stock ($10 par)	80,000
Allowance for doubtful accounts	(1,500)	Retained earnings	127,400
Supplies	4,400		$233,000
Land	40,000		
Buildings	142,000		
Accumulated depreciation—buildings	(22,000)		
	$233,000		

During 2017, the following transactions occurred.

1. On January 1, 2017, Hawkeye issued 1,200 shares of $40 par, 7% preferred stock for $49,200.
2. On January 1, 2017, Hawkeye also issued 900 shares of the $10 par value common stock for $21,000.
3. Hawkeye performed services for $320,000 on account.
4. On April 1, 2017, Hawkeye collected fees of $36,000 in advance for services to be performed from April 1, 2017, to March 31, 2018.
5. Hawkeye collected $276,000 from customers on account.
6. Hawkeye bought $35,100 of supplies on account.
7. Hawkeye paid $32,200 on accounts payable.
8. Hawkeye reacquired 400 shares of its common stock on June 1, 2017, for $28 per share.
9. Paid other operating expenses of $188,200.
10. On December 31, 2017, Hawkeye declared the annual preferred stock dividend and a $1.20 per share dividend on the outstanding common stock, all payable on January 15, 2018.
11. An account receivable of $1,700 which originated in 2016 is written off as uncollectible.

Adjustment data:

1. A count of supplies indicates that $5,900 of supplies remain unused at year-end.
2. Recorded revenue from item 4 above.
3. The allowance for doubtful accounts should have a balance of $3,500 at year end.
4. Depreciation is recorded on the building on a straight-line basis based on a 30-year life and a salvage value of $10,000.
5. The income tax rate is 30%. (*Hint:* Prepare the income statement up to income before taxes and multiply by 30% to compute the amount.)

Instructions

(You may want to set up T-accounts to determine ending balances.)

(a) Prepare journal entries for the transactions listed above and adjusting entries.
(b) Prepare an adjusted trial balance at December 31, 2017.
(c) Prepare an income statement and a retained earnings statement for the year ending December 31, 2017, and a classified balance sheet as of December 31, 2017.

(b) Totals $740,690
(c) Net income $81,970
Tot. assets $421,000

Journalize transactions and prepare financial statements.

(LO 2, 3, 4), AP

ACR11-2 Karen Noonan opened Clean Sweep Inc. on February 1, 2017. During February, the following transactions were completed.

Feb. 1 Issued 5,000 shares of Clean Sweep common stock for $13,000. Each share has a $1.50 par.
1 Borrowed $8,000 on a 2-year, 6% note payable.
1 Paid $9,020 to purchase used floor and window cleaning equipment from a company going out of business ($4,820 was for the floor equipment and $4,200 for the window equipment).
1 Paid $220 for February Internet and phone services.
3 Purchased cleaning supplies for $980 on account.
4 Hired 4 employees. Each will be paid $480 per 5-day work week (Monday–Friday). Employees will begin working Monday, February 9.
5 Obtained insurance coverage for $9,840 per year. Coverage runs from February 1, 2017, through January 31, 2018. Karen paid $2,460 cash for the first quarter of coverage.
5 Discussions with the insurance agent indicated that providing outside window cleaning services would cost too much to insure. Karen sold the window cleaning equipment for $3,950 cash.
16 Billed customers $3,900 for cleaning services performed through February 13, 2017.
17 Received $540 from a customer for 4 weeks of cleaning services to begin February 21, 2017. (By paying in advance, this customer received 10% off the normal weekly fee of $150.)
18 Paid $300 on amount owed on cleaning supplies.
20 Paid $3 per share to buy 300 shares of Clean Sweep common stock from a shareholder who disagreed with management goals. The shares will be held as treasury shares.
23 Billed customers $4,300 for cleaning services performed through February 20.

24 Paid cash for employees' wages for 2 weeks (February 9–13 and 16–20).
25 Collected $2,500 cash from customers billed on February 16.
27 Paid $220 for Internet and phone services for March.
28 Declared and paid a cash dividend of $0.20 per share.

Instructions

(a) Journalize the February transactions. (You do not need to include an explanation for each journal entry.)
(b) Post to the ledger accounts (Use T-accounts.)
(c) Prepare a trial balance at February 28, 2017. (c) Totals $30,420
(d) Journalize the following adjustments. (Round all amounts to whole dollars.)
  (1) Services performed for customers through February 27, 2017, but unbilled and uncollected were $3,800.
  (2) Received notice that a customer who was billed $200 for services performed February 10 has filed for bankruptcy. Clean Sweep does not expect to collect any portion of this outstanding receivable.
  (3) Clean Sweep uses the allowance method to estimate bad debts. Clean Sweep estimates that 3% of its month-end receivables will not be collected.
  (4) Record 1 month of depreciation for the floor equipment. Use the straight-line method, an estimated life of 4 years, and $500 salvage value.
  (5) Record 1 month of insurance expense.
  (6) An inventory count shows $400 of supplies on hand at February 28.
  (7) One week of services were performed for the customer who paid in advance on February 17.
  (8) Accrue for wages owed through February 28, 2017.
  (9) Accrue for interest expense for 1 month.
  (10) Karen estimates a 20% income tax rate. (*Hint:* Prepare an income statement up to "income before taxes" to help with the income tax calculation.)
(e) Post adjusting entries to the T-accounts.
(f) Prepare an adjusted trial balance. (g) Net income $3,117 Tot. assets $26,101
(g) Prepare a **multiple-step income statement, a retained earnings statement,** and a **properly classified balance sheet** as of February 28, 2017.
(h) Journalize closing entries.

EXPAND YOUR CRITICAL THINKING

FINANCIAL REPORTING PROBLEM: Apple Inc.

Financial Reporting

CT11-1 The stockholders' equity section of Apple Inc.'s balance sheet is shown in the Consolidated Statement of Financial Position in Appendix A. Instructions for accessing and using the company's complete annual report, including the notes to its financial statements, are also provided in Appendix A. AP

Instructions

Answer the following questions.

(a) What is the par or stated value per share of Apple's common stock?
(b) What percentage of Apple's authorized common stock was issued at September 27, 2014? (Round to the nearest full percent.)
(c) How many shares of common stock were outstanding at September 28, 2013, and at September 27, 2014?
(d) Calculate the payout ratio, earnings per share, and return on common stockholders' equity for 2014.

COMPARATIVE ANALYSIS PROBLEM: Columbia Sportswear Company vs. VF Corporation

Financial Reporting

CT11-2 The financial statements of Columbia Sportswear Company are presented in Appendix B. Financial statements of VF Corporation are presented in Appendix C. AN

Instructions

(a) Based on the information in these financial statements, compute the 2014 return on common stockholders' equity, debt to assets ratio, and return on assets for each company.

(b) What conclusions concerning the companies' profitability can be drawn from these ratios? Which company relies more on debt to boost its return to common shareholders?

(c) Compute the payout ratio for each company. Which pays out a higher percentage of its earnings?

Financial Analysis

COMPARATIVE ANALYSIS PROBLEM: Amazon.com, Inc. vs. Wal-Mart Stores, Inc.

AN **CT11-3** The financial statements of Amazon.com, Inc. are presented in Appendix D. Financial statements of Wal-Mart Stores, Inc. are presented in Appendix E.

Instructions

(a) Based on the information in these financial statements, compute the 2014 return on common stockholders' equity, debt to assets ratio, and return on assets for each company.

(b) What conclusions concerning the companies' profitability can be drawn from these ratios? Which company relies more on debt to boost its return to common shareholders?

(c) Compute the payout ratio for each company. Which pays out a higher percentage of its earnings?

Financial Analysis

INTERPRETING FINANCIAL STATEMENTS

AN **CT11-4** Marriott Corporation split into two companies: Host Marriott Corporation and Marriott International. Host Marriott retained ownership of the corporation's vast hotel and other properties, while Marriott International, rather than owning hotels, managed them. The purpose of this split was to free Marriott International from the "baggage" associated with Host Marriott, thus allowing it to be more aggressive in its pursuit of growth. The following information (in millions) is provided for each corporation for their first full year operating as independent companies.

	Host Marriott	Marriott International
Sales revenue	$1,501	$8,415
Net income	(25)	200
Total assets	3,822	3,207
Total liabilities	3,112	2,440
Common stockholders' equity	710	767

Instructions

(a) The two companies were split by the issuance of shares of Marriott International to all shareholders of the previous combined company. Discuss the nature of this transaction.

(b) Calculate the debt to assets ratio for each company.

(c) Calculate the return on assets and return on common stockholders' equity for each company.

(d) The company's debtholders were fiercely opposed to the original plan to split the two companies because the original plan had Host Marriott absorbing the majority of the company's debt. They relented only when Marriott International agreed to absorb a larger share of the debt. Discuss the possible reasons the debtholders were opposed to the plan to split the company.

REAL-WORLD FOCUS

AN **CT11-5** ***Purpose:*** Use the stockholders' equity section of an annual report and identify the major components.

Address: **www.annualreports.com**

Steps

1. Select a particular company.
2. Search by company name.
3. Follow instructions below.

Instructions

Answer the following questions.

(a) What is the company's name?

(b) What classes of capital stock has the company issued?

(c) For each class of stock:
 (1) How many shares are authorized, issued, and/or outstanding?
 (2) What is the par value?
(d) What are the company's retained earnings?
(e) Has the company acquired treasury stock? How many shares?

DECISION-MAKING ACROSS THE ORGANIZATION

Financial Analysis

Writing

Group Project

CT11-6 During a recent period, the fast-food chain Wendy's International purchased many treasury shares. This caused the number of shares outstanding to fall from 124 million to 105 million. The following information was drawn from the company's financial statements (in millions).

E

	Information for the Year after Purchase of Treasury Stock	Information for the Year before Purchase of Treasury Stock
Net income	$ 193.6	$ 123.4
Total assets	2,076.0	1,837.9
Average total assets	2,016.9	1,889.8
Total common stockholders' equity	1,029.8	1,068.1
Average common stockholders' equity	1,078.0	1,126.2
Total liabilities	1,046.3	769.9
Average total liabilities	939.0	763.7
Interest expense	30.2	19.8
Income taxes	113.7	84.3
Cash provided by operations	305.2	233.8
Cash dividends paid on common stock	26.8	31.0
Preferred stock dividends	0	0
Average number of common shares outstanding	109.7	119.9

Instructions

Use the information provided to answer the following questions.

(a) Compute earnings per share, return on common stockholders' equity, and return on assets for both years. Discuss the change in the company's profitability over this period.
(b) Compute the dividend payout ratio. Also compute the average cash dividend paid per share of common stock (dividends paid divided by the average number of common shares outstanding). Discuss any change in these ratios during this period and the implications for the company's dividend policy.
(c) Compute the debt to assets ratio and times interest earned. Discuss the change in the company's solvency.
(d) Based on your findings in (a) and (c), discuss to what extent any change in the return on common stockholders' equity was the result of increased reliance on debt.
(e) Does it appear that the purchase of treasury stock and the shift toward more reliance on debt were wise strategic moves?

COMMUNICATION ACTIVITY

CT11-7 Earl Kent, your uncle, is an inventor who has decided to incorporate. Uncle Earl knows that you are an accounting major at U.N.O. In a recent letter to you, he ends with the question, "I'm filling out a state incorporation application. Can you tell me the difference among the following terms: (1) authorized stock, (2) issued stock, (3) outstanding stock, and (4) preferred stock?" C

Instructions

In a brief note, differentiate for Uncle Earl the four different stock terms. Write the letter to be friendly, yet professional.

ETHICS CASES

CT11-8 The R&D division of Pele Corp. has just developed a chemical for sterilizing the vicious Brazilian "killer bees" which are invading Mexico and the southern United States. The president of Pele is anxious to get the chemical on the market because Pele profits need a boost—and his job is in jeopardy because of decreasing sales and profits. Pele has E an opportunity to sell this chemical in Central American countries, where the laws are much more relaxed than in the United States.

The director of Pele's R&D division strongly recommends further research in the laboratory to test the side effects of this chemical on other insects, birds, animals, plants, and even humans. He cautions the president, "We could be sued from all sides if the chemical has tragic side effects that we didn't even test for in the lab." The president answers, "We can't wait an additional year for your lab tests. We can avoid losses from such lawsuits by establishing a separate wholly owned corporation to shield Pele Corp. from such lawsuits. We can't lose any more than our investment in the new corporation, and we'll invest just the patent covering this chemical. We'll reap the benefits if the chemical works and is safe, and avoid the losses from lawsuits if it's a disaster." The following week, Pele creates a new wholly owned corporation called Cabo Inc., sells the chemical patent to it for $10, and watches the spraying begin.

Instructions

(a) Who are the stakeholders in this situation?
(b) Are the president's motives and actions ethical?
(c) Can Pele shield itself against losses of Cabo Inc.?

AN **CT11-9** Cooper Corporation has paid 60 consecutive quarterly cash dividends (15 years). The last 6 months have been a real cash drain on the company, however, as profit margins have been greatly narrowed by increasing competition. With a cash balance sufficient to meet only day-to-day operating needs, the president, Sonny Boyd, has decided that a stock dividend instead of a cash dividend should be declared. He tells Cooper's financial vice president, Dana Marks, to issue a press release stating that the company is extending its consecutive dividend record with the issuance of a 5% stock dividend. "Write the press release convincing the stockholders that the stock dividend is just as good as a cash dividend," he orders. "Just watch our stock rise when we announce the stock dividend; it must be a good thing if that happens."

Instructions

(a) Who are the stakeholders in this situation?
(b) Is there anything unethical about president Boyd's intentions or actions?
(c) What is the effect of a stock dividend on a corporation's stockholders' equity accounts? Which would you rather receive as a stockholder—a cash dividend or a stock dividend? Why?

ALL ABOUT YOU

AN **CT11-10** In response to the Sarbanes-Oxley Act, many companies have implemented formal ethics codes. Many other organizations also have ethics codes.

Instructions

Obtain the ethics code from an organization that you belong to (e.g., student organization, business school, employer, or a volunteer organization). Evaluate the ethics code based on how clearly it identifies proper and improper behavior. Discuss its strengths, and how it might be improved.

FASB CODIFICATION ACTIVITY

C **CT11-11** If your school has a subscription to the FASB Codification, go to **http://aaahq.org/ascLogin.cfm** to log in and prepare responses to the following.

(a) What is the stock dividend?
(b) What is a stock split?
(c) At what percentage point does the issuance of additional shares qualify as a stock dividend, as opposed to a stock split?

CONSIDERING PEOPLE, PLANET, AND PROFIT

C **CT11-12** The January 19, 2012, edition of the *Wall Street Journal* contains an article by Angus Loten entitled "With New Law, Profits Take a Back Seat."

Instructions

Read the article and answer the following questions.

(a) Summarize the nature of the new law that is discussed in the article.
(b) What do some proponents of the law say is the "biggest value" of the law? How does the article say that this would have impacted Ben & Jerry's?

(c) What are some criticisms of the law?
(d) How does incorporation as a benefit corporation differ from B Corp certification?
(e) What are some of the companies that the article cites as either having adopted benefit corporation standing or are considering it?

A Look at IFRS

LEARNING OBJECTIVE 6 **Compare the accounting for stockholders' equity under GAAP and IFRS.**

The accounting for transactions related to stockholders' equity, such as issuance of shares and purchase of treasury stock, are similar under both IFRS and GAAP. Major differences relate to terminology used, introduction of items such as revaluation surplus, and presentation of stockholders' equity information.

KEY POINTS

Following are the key similarities and differences between GAAP and IFRS as related to stockholders' equity, dividends, retained earnings, and income reporting.

Similarities

- Aside from the terminology used, the accounting transactions for the issuance of shares and the purchase of treasury stock are similar.
- Like GAAP, IFRS does not allow a company to record gains or losses on purchases of its own shares.
- The accounting related to prior period adjustment is essentially the same under IFRS and GAAP.
- The income statement using IFRS is called the **statement of comprehensive income**. A statement of comprehensive income is presented in a one- or two-statement format. The single-statement approach includes all items of income and expense, as well as each component of other comprehensive income or loss by its individual characteristic. In the two-statement approach, a traditional income statement is prepared. It is then followed by a statement of comprehensive income, which starts with net income or loss and then adds other comprehensive income or loss items. Regardless of which approach is reported, income tax expense is required to be reported.
- The computations related to earnings per share are essentially the same under IFRS and GAAP.

Differences

- Under IFRS, the term **reserves** is used to describe all equity accounts other than those arising from contributed (paid-in) capital. This would include, for example, reserves related to retained earnings, asset revaluations, and fair value differences.
- Many countries have a different mix of investor groups than in the United States. For example, in Germany, financial institutions like banks are not only major creditors of corporations but often are the largest corporate stockholders as well. In the United States, Asia, and the United Kingdom, many companies rely on substantial investment from private investors.
- There are often terminology differences for equity accounts. The following summarizes some of the common differences in terminology.

GAAP	IFRS
Common stock	Share capital—ordinary
Stockholders	Shareholders
Par value	Nominal or face value
Authorized stock	Authorized share capital
Preferred stock	Share capital—preference
Paid-in capital	Issued/allocated share capital
Paid-in capital in excess of par—common stock	Share premium—ordinary
Paid-in capital in excess of par—preferred stock	Share premium—preference
Retained earnings	Retained earnings or Retained profits
Retained earnings deficit	Accumulated losses
Accumulated other comprehensive income	General reserve and other reserve accounts

As an example of how similar transactions use different terminology under IFRS, consider the accounting for the issuance of 1,000 shares of $1 par value common stock for $5 per share. Under IFRS, the entry is as follows.

Cash	5,000	
Share Capital—Ordinary		1,000
Share Premium—Ordinary		4,000

- A major difference between IFRS and GAAP relates to the account Revaluation Surplus. Revaluation surplus arises under IFRS because companies are permitted to revalue their property, plant, and equipment to fair value under certain circumstances. This account is part of general reserves under IFRS and is not considered contributed capital.
- IFRS often uses terms such as **retained profits** or **accumulated profit or loss** to describe retained earnings. The term retained earnings is also often used.
- Equity is given various descriptions under IFRS, such as shareholders' equity, owners' equity, capital and reserves, and shareholders' funds.

LOOKING TO THE FUTURE

The IASB and the FASB are currently working on a project related to financial statement presentation. An important part of this study is to determine whether certain line items, subtotals, and totals should be clearly defined and required to be displayed in the financial statements. For example, it is likely that the statement of stockholders' equity and its presentation will be examined closely.

Both the IASB and FASB are working toward convergence of any remaining differences related to earnings per share computations. This convergence will deal with highly technical changes beyond the scope of this textbook.

IFRS Practice

IFRS SELF-TEST QUESTIONS

1. Which of the following is **true**?
   (a) In the United States, the primary corporate stockholders are financial institutions.
   (b) Share capital means total assets under IFRS.
   (c) The IASB and FASB are presently studying how financial statement information should be presented.
   (d) The accounting for treasury stock differs extensively between GAAP and IFRS.
2. Under IFRS, the amount of capital received in excess of par value would be credited to:
   (a) Retained Earnings.
   (b) Contributed Capital.
   (c) Share Premium.
   (d) Par value is not used under IFRS.
3. Which of the following is **false**?
   (a) Under GAAP, companies cannot record gains on transactions involving their own shares.
   (b) Under IFRS, companies cannot record gains on transactions involving their own shares.
   (c) Under IFRS, the statement of stockholders' equity is a required statement.
   (d) Under IFRS, a company records a revaluation surplus when it experiences an increase in the price of its common stock.

4. Which of the following does **not** represent a pair of GAAP/IFRS-comparable terms?
   (a) Additional paid-in capital/Share premium.
   (b) Treasury stock/Repurchase reserve.
   (c) Common stock/Share capital.
   (d) Preferred stock/Preference shares.
5. The basic accounting for cash dividends and stock dividends:
   (a) is different under IFRS versus GAAP.
   (b) is the same under IFRS and GAAP.
   (c) differs only for the accounting for cash dividends between GAAP and IFRS.
   (d) differs only for the accounting for stock dividends between GAAP and IFRS.
6. Which item in **not** considered part of reserves?
   (a) Unrealized loss on available-for-sale investments.
   (b) Revaluation surplus.
   (c) Retained earnings.
   (d) Issued shares.
7. Under IFRS, a statement of comprehensive income must include:
   (a) accounts payable.
   (b) retained earnings.
   (c) income tax expense.
   (d) preference stock.
8. Which set of terms can be used to describe total stockholders' equity under IFRS?
   (a) Shareholders' equity, capital and reserves, other comprehensive income.
   (b) Capital and reserves, shareholders' equity, shareholders' funds.
   (c) Capital and reserves, retained earnings, shareholders' equity.
   (d) All of the answer choices are correct.
9. Earnings per share computations related to IFRS and GAAP:
   (a) are essentially similar.
   (b) result in an amount referred to as earnings per share.
   (c) must deduct preferred (preference) dividends when computing earnings per share.
   (d) All of the answer choices are correct.

IFRS EXERCISES

IFRS11-1 On May 10, Jaurez Corporation issues 1,000 shares of $10 par value ordinary shares for cash at $18 per share. Journalize the issuance of the shares.

IFRS11-2 Meenen Corporation has the following accounts at December 31, 2017 (in euros): Share Capital—Ordinary, €10 par, 5,000 shares issued, €50,000; Share Premium—Ordinary €10,000; Retained Earnings €45,000; and Treasury Shares—Ordinary, 500 shares, €11,000. Prepare the equity section of the statement of financial position (balance sheet).

IFRS11-3 Overton Co. had the following transactions during the current period.

Mar. 2	Issued 5,000 shares of $1 par value ordinary shares to attorneys in payment of a bill for $30,000 for services performed in helping the company to incorporate.
June 12	Issued 60,000 shares of $1 par value ordinary shares for cash of $375,000.
July 11	Issued 1,000 shares of $100 par value preference shares for cash at $110 per share.
Nov. 28	Purchased 2,000 treasury shares for $80,000.

Instructions
Journalize the above transactions.

INTERNATIONAL FINANCIAL REPORTING PROBLEM: Louis Vuitton

IFRS11-4 The financial statements of Louis Vuitton are presented in Appendix F. Instructions for accessing and using the company's complete annual report, including the notes to its financial statements, are also provided in Appendix F.

Instructions
Use the company's annual report to answer the following questions.

(a) Determine the following amounts at December 31, 2014: (1) total equity, (2) total revaluation reserve, and (3) number of treasury shares.
(b) Examine the equity section of the company's balance sheet. For each of the following, provide the comparable label that would be used under GAAP: (1) share capital, (2) share premium, and (3) net profit, group share.
(c) Did the company declare and pay any dividends for the year ended December 31, 2014?
(d) Compute the company's return on ordinary shareholders' equity for the year ended December 31, 2014.
(e) What was Louis Vuitton's earnings per share for the year ended December 31, 2014?

Answers to IFRS Self-Test Questions

1. c **2.** c **3.** d **4.** b **5.** b **6.** d **7.** c **8.** b **9.** d

12

Statement of Cash Flows

CHAPTER PREVIEW

The balance sheet, income statement, and retained earnings statement do not always show the whole picture of the financial condition of a company or institution. In fact, looking at the financial statements of some well-known companies, a thoughtful investor might ask questions like these: How did Eastman Kodak finance cash dividends of $649 million in a year in which it earned only $17 million? How could United Air Lines purchase new planes that cost $1.9 billion in a year in which it reported a net loss of over $2 billion? How did the companies that spent a combined fantastic $3.4 trillion on mergers and acquisitions in a recent year finance those deals? Answers to these and similar questions can be found in this chapter, which presents the statement of cash flows.

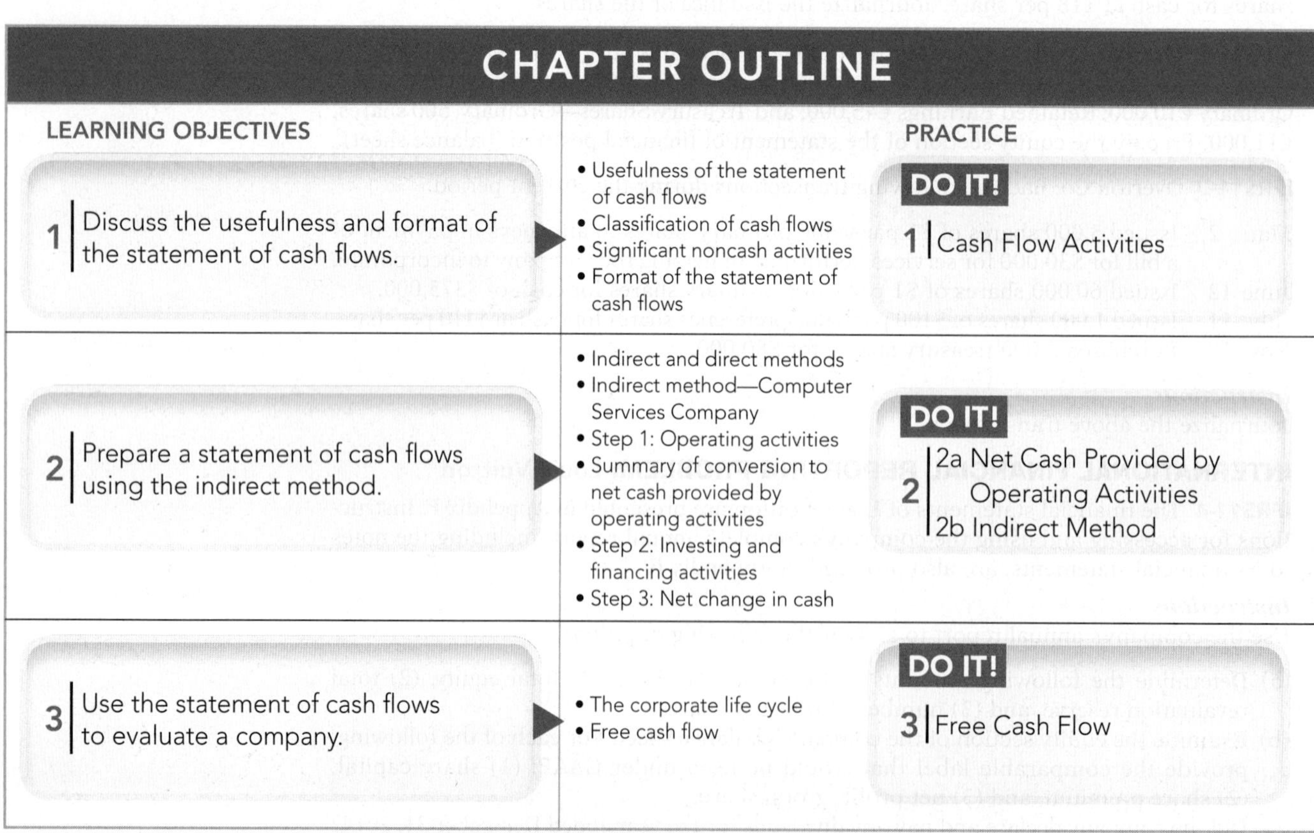

Go to the ***REVIEW AND PRACTICE*** section at the end of the chapter for a targeted summary and exercises with solutions.

Visit **WileyPLUS** for additional tutorials and practice opportunities.

TonyV3112/Shutterstock

FEATURE STORY

Got Cash?

Companies must be ready to respond to changes quickly in order to survive and thrive. This requires careful management of cash. One company that managed cash successfully in its early years was Microsoft. During those years, the company paid much of its payroll by giving employees stock options (rights to purchase company stock in the future at a given price) instead of cash. This conserved cash and turned more than a thousand of its employees into millionaires.

In recent years, Microsoft has had a different kind of cash problem. Now that it has reached a more "mature" stage in life, it generates so much cash—roughly $1 billion per month—that it cannot always figure out what to do with it. At one time, Microsoft had accumulated $60 billion.

The company said it was accumulating cash to invest in new opportunities, buy other companies, and pay off pending lawsuits. Microsoft's stockholders complained that holding all this cash was putting a drag on the company's profitability. Why? Because Microsoft had the cash invested in very low-yielding government securities. Stockholders felt that the company either should find new investment projects that would bring higher returns, or return some of the cash to stockholders.

Finally, Microsoft announced a plan to return cash to stockholders by paying a special one-time $32 billion dividend. This special dividend was so large that, according to the U.S. Commerce Department, it caused total personal income in the United States to rise by 3.7% in one month—the largest increase ever recorded by the agency. (It also made the holiday season brighter, especially for retailers in the Seattle area.) Microsoft also doubled its regular annual dividend to $3.50 per share. Further, it announced that it would spend another $30 billion buying treasury stock.

Apple has also encountered this cash "problem." Apple recently had nearly $100 billion in liquid assets (cash, cash equivalents, and investment securities). It was generating $37 billion of cash per year from its operating activities but spending only about $7 billion on plant assets and purchases of patents. In response to shareholder pressure, Apple announced that it would begin to pay a quarterly dividend of $2.65 per share and buy back up to $10 billion of its stock. Analysts noted that the dividend consumes only $10 billion of cash per year. This leaves Apple wallowing in cash. The rest of us should have such problems.

Source: "Business: An End to Growth? Microsoft's Cash Bonanza," *The Economist* (July 23, 2005), p. 61.

LEARNING OBJECTIVE 1

Discuss the usefulness and format of the statement of cash flows.

The balance sheet, income statement, and retained earnings statement provide only limited information about a company's cash flows (cash receipts and cash payments). For example, comparative balance sheets show the increase in property, plant, and equipment during the year. But, they do not show how the additions were financed or paid for. The income statement shows net income. But, it does not indicate the amount of cash generated by operating activities. The retained earnings statement shows cash dividends declared but not the cash dividends paid during the year. None of these statements presents a detailed summary of where cash came from and how it was used.

USEFULNESS OF THE STATEMENT OF CASH FLOWS

The **statement of cash flows** reports the cash receipts and cash payments from operating, investing, and financing activities during a period, in a format that reconciles the beginning and ending cash balances. The information in a statement of cash flows helps investors, creditors, and others assess the following.

1. **The entity's ability to generate future cash flows.** By examining relationships between items in the statement of cash flows, investors make predictions of the amounts, timing, and uncertainty of future cash flows better than they can from accrual-basis data.
2. **The entity's ability to pay dividends and meet obligations.** If a company does not have adequate cash, it cannot pay employees, settle debts, or pay dividends. Employees, creditors, and stockholders should be particularly interested in this statement because it alone shows the flows of cash in a business.
3. **The reasons for the difference between net income and net cash provided (used) by operating activities.** Net income provides information on the success or failure of a business enterprise. However, some financial statement users are critical of accrual-basis net income because it requires many estimates. As a result, users often challenge the reliability of the number. Such is not the case with cash. Many readers of the statement of cash flows want to know the reasons for the difference between net income and net cash provided by operating activities. Then they can assess for themselves the reliability of the income number.
4. **The cash investing and financing transactions during the period.** By examining a company's investing and financing transactions, a financial statement reader can better understand why assets and liabilities changed during the period.

ETHICS NOTE

Though we would discourage reliance on cash flows to the exclusion of accrual accounting, comparing net cash provided by operating activities to net income can reveal important information about the "quality" of reported net income. Such a comparison can reveal the extent to which net income provides a good measure of actual performance.

CLASSIFICATION OF CASH FLOWS

The statement of cash flows classifies cash receipts and cash payments as operating, investing, and financing activities. Transactions and other events characteristic of each kind of activity are as follows.

1. **Operating activities** include the cash effects of transactions that create revenues and expenses. They thus enter into the determination of net income.
2. **Investing activities** include (a) cash transactions that involve the purchase or disposal of investments and property, plant, and equipment, and (b) lending money and collecting the loans.
3. **Financing activities** include (a) obtaining cash from issuing debt and repaying the amounts borrowed, and (b) obtaining cash from stockholders, repurchasing shares, and paying dividends.

The operating activities category is the most important. It shows the cash provided by company operations. This source of cash is generally considered to be the best measure of a company's ability to generate sufficient cash to continue as a going concern.

Illustration 12-1 lists typical cash receipts and cash payments within each of the three classifications. **Study the list carefully.** It will be very useful in solving homework exercises and problems.

Types of Cash Inflows and Outflows

Operating activities—Income statement items
Cash inflows:
From sale of goods or services.
From interest received and dividends received.
Cash outflows:
To suppliers for inventory.
To employees for wages.
To government for taxes.
To lenders for interest.
To others for expenses.

Investing activities—Changes in investments and long-term assets
Cash inflows:
From sale of property, plant, and equipment.
From sale of investments in debt or equity securities of other entities.
From collection of principal on loans to other entities.
Cash outflows:
To purchase property, plant, and equipment.
To purchase investments in debt or equity securities of other entities.
To make loans to other entities.

Financing activities—Changes in long-term liabilities and stockholders' equity
Cash inflows:
From sale of common stock.
From issuance of debt (bonds and notes).
Cash outflows:
To stockholders as dividends.
To redeem long-term debt or reacquire capital stock (treasury stock).

ILLUSTRATION 12-1
Typical receipt and payment classifications

Operating activities

Investing activities

Financing activities

Note the following general guidelines:

1. Operating activities involve income statement items.
2. Investing activities involve cash flows resulting from changes in investments and long-term asset items.
3. Financing activities involve cash flows resulting from changes in long-term liability and stockholders' equity items.

Companies classify as operating activities some cash flows related to investing or financing activities. For example, receipts of investment revenue (interest and dividends) are classified as operating activities. So are payments of interest to lenders. Why are these considered operating activities? **Because companies report these items in the income statement, where results of operations are shown.**

SIGNIFICANT NONCASH ACTIVITIES

Not all of a company's significant activities involve cash. Examples of significant noncash activities are:

1. Direct issuance of common stock to purchase assets.
2. Conversion of bonds into common stock.
3. Direct issuance of debt to purchase assets.
4. Exchanges of plant assets.

INTERNATIONAL NOTE
The statement of cash flows is very similar under GAAP and IFRS. One difference is that, under IFRS, noncash investing and financing activities are not reported in the statement of cash flows but instead are reported in the notes to the financial statements.

▼ HELPFUL HINT
Do not include **noncash** investing and financing activities in the body of the statement of cash flows. Report this information in a separate schedule below the statement of cash flows.

Companies do not report in the body of the statement of cash flows significant financing and investing activities that do not affect cash. Instead, they report these activities in either a **separate schedule** at the bottom of the statement of cash flows or in a **separate note or supplementary schedule** to the financial statements. The reporting of these noncash activities in a separate schedule satisfies the **full disclosure principle**.

In solving homework assignments, you should present significant noncash investing and financing activities in a separate schedule at the bottom of the statement of cash flows. (See the last entry in Illustration 12-2 for an example.)

ACCOUNTING ACROSS THE ORGANIZATION **Target Corporation**

Darren McCollester/Getty Images, Inc.

Net *What?*

Net income is not the same as net cash provided by operating activities. Below are some results from recent annual reports (dollars in millions), including Target Corporation. Note how the numbers differ greatly across the list even though all these companies engage in retail merchandising.

Company	Net Income	Net Cash Provided by Operating Activities
Kohl's Corporation	$ 889	$ 1,884
Wal-Mart Stores, Inc.	16,669	25,591
J. C. Penney Company, Inc.	(1,388)	(1,814)
Costco Wholesale Corp.	20,391	3,437
Target Corporation	1,971	6,520

In general, why do differences exist between net income and net cash provided by operating activities? (Go to **WileyPLUS** for this answer and additional questions.)

FORMAT OF THE STATEMENT OF CASH FLOWS

The general format of the statement of cash flows presents the results of the three activities discussed previously—operating, investing, and financing—plus the significant noncash investing and financing activities. Illustration 12–2 shows a widely used form of the statement of cash flows.

ILLUSTRATION 12-2
Format of statement of cash flows

COMPANY NAME
Statement of Cash Flows
For the Period Covered

Cash flows from operating activities		
(List of individual items)	XX	
Net cash provided (used) by operating activities		XXX
Cash flows from investing activities		
(List of individual inflows and outflows)	XX	
Net cash provided (used) by investing activities		XXX
Cash flows from financing activities		
(List of individual inflows and outflows)	XX	
Net cash provided (used) by financing activities		XXX
Net increase (decrease) in cash		XXX
Cash at beginning of period		XXX
Cash at end of period		XXX
Noncash investing and financing activities		
(List of individual noncash transactions)		XXX

The cash flows from operating activities section always appears first, followed by the investing activities section and then the financing activities section. The sum of the operating, investing, and financing activities sections equals the net increase or decrease in cash for the period. This amount is added to the beginning cash balance to arrive at the ending cash balance—the same amount reported on the balance sheet.

DO IT!  Cash Flow Activities

During its first week, Duffy & Stevenson Company had these transactions.

1. Issued 100,000 shares of $5 par value common stock for $800,000 cash.
2. Borrowed $200,000 from Castle Bank, signing a 5-year note bearing 8% interest.
3. Purchased two semi-trailer trucks for $170,000 cash.
4. Paid employees $12,000 for salaries and wages.
5. Collected $20,000 cash for services performed.

Classify each of these transactions by type of cash flow activity. (*Hint:* Refer to Illustration 12-1.)

Action Plan

✔ Identify the three types of activities used to report all cash inflows and outflows.

✔ Report as operating activities the cash effects of transactions that create revenues and expenses and enter into the determination of net income.

✔ Report as investing activities transactions that (a) acquire and dispose of investments and productive long-lived assets and (b) lend money and collect loans.

✔ Report as financing activities transactions that (a) obtain cash from issuing debt and repay the amounts borrowed and (b) obtain cash from stockholders and pay them dividends.

SOLUTION

1. Financing activity
2. Financing activity
3. Investing activity
4. Operating activity
5. Operating activity

Related exercise material: **BE12-1, BE12-2, BE12-3, DO IT! 12-1, E12-1,** and **E12-2.**

LEARNING OBJECTIVE  Prepare a statement of cash flows using the indirect method.

Companies prepare the statement of cash flows differently from the three other basic financial statements. First, it is not prepared from an adjusted trial balance. It requires detailed information concerning the changes in account balances that occurred between two points in time. An adjusted trial balance will not provide the necessary data. Second, the statement of cash flows deals with cash receipts and payments. As a result, the company **adjusts** the effects of the use of accrual accounting **to determine cash flows**.

The information to prepare this statement usually comes from three sources:

- **Comparative balance sheets.** Information in the comparative balance sheets indicates the amount of the changes in asset, liability, and stockholders' equity accounts from the beginning to the end of the period.
- **Current income statement.** Information in this statement helps determine the amount of net cash provided or used by operating activities during the period.
- **Additional information.** Such information includes transaction data that are needed to determine how cash was provided or used during the period.

Preparing the statement of cash flows from these data sources involves three major steps, explained in Illustration 12-3.

ILLUSTRATION 12-3
Three major steps in preparing the statement of cash flows

STEP 1: Determine net cash provided/used by operating activities by converting net income from an accrual basis to a cash basis.

This step involves analyzing not only the current year's income statement but also comparative balance sheets and selected additional data.

STEP 2: Analyze changes in noncurrent asset and liability accounts and record as investing and financing activities, or disclose as noncash transactions.

This step involves analyzing comparative balance sheet data and selected additional information for their effects on cash.

STEP 3: Compare the net change in cash on the statement of cash flows with the change in the Cash account reported on the balance sheet to make sure the amounts agree.

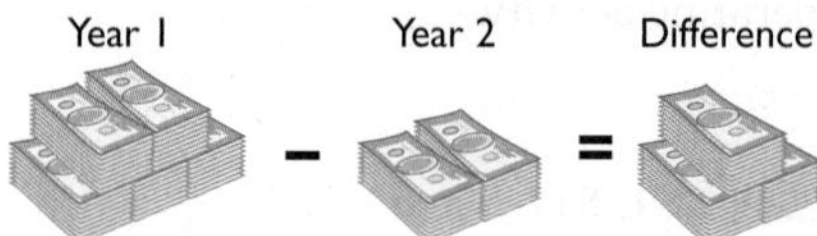

The difference between the beginning and ending cash balances can be easily computed from comparative balance sheets.

INDIRECT AND DIRECT METHODS

In order to perform Step 1, a company **must convert net income from an accrual basis to a cash basis**. This conversion may be done by either of two methods: (1) the indirect method or (2) the direct method. **Both methods arrive at the same total amount** for "Net cash provided by operating activities." They differ in **how** they arrive at the amount.

The **indirect method** adjusts net income for items that do not affect cash to determine net cash provided by operating activities. A great majority of companies (98%) use this method. Companies favor the indirect method for two reasons: (1) it is easier and less costly to prepare, and (2) it focuses on the differences between net income and net cash flow from operating activities.

The **direct method** shows operating cash receipts and payments. It is prepared by adjusting each item in the income statement from the accrual basis to the cash basis. The FASB has expressed a preference for the direct method but allows the use of either method.

The next section illustrates the more popular indirect method. Appendix 12A illustrates the direct method. Appendix 12B demonstrates an approach that employs T-accounts to prepare the statement of cash flows. Many students find the T-account approach provides a useful structure. We encourage you to give it a try as you walk through the Computer Services example.

INDIRECT METHOD—COMPUTER SERVICES COMPANY

To explain how to prepare a statement of cash flows using the indirect method, we use financial information from Computer Services Company. Illustration 12-4 presents Computer Services' current- and previous-year balance sheets, its current-year income statement, and related financial information.

ILLUSTRATION 12-4
Comparative balance sheets, income statement, and additional information for Computer Services Company

COMPUTER SERVICES COMPANY
Comparative Balance Sheets
December 31

Assets	**2017**	**2016**	**Change in Account Balance Increase/Decrease**
Current assets			
Cash	$ 55,000	$ 33,000	$ 22,000 Increase
Accounts receivable	20,000	30,000	10,000 Decrease
Inventory	15,000	10,000	5,000 Increase
Prepaid expenses	5,000	1,000	4,000 Increase
Property, plant, and equipment			
Land	130,000	20,000	110,000 Increase
Buildings	160,000	40,000	120,000 Increase
Accumulated depreciation—buildings	(11,000)	(5,000)	6,000 Increase
Equipment	27,000	10,000	17,000 Increase
Accumulated depreciation—equipment	(3,000)	(1,000)	2,000 Increase
Total assets	$398,000	$138,000	
Liabilities and Stockholders' Equity			
Current liabilities			
Accounts payable	$ 28,000	$ 12,000	$ 16,000 Increase
Income taxes payable	6,000	8,000	2,000 Decrease
Long-term liabilities			
Bonds payable	130,000	20,000	110,000 Increase
Stockholders' equity			
Common stock	70,000	50,000	20,000 Increase
Retained earnings	164,000	48,000	116,000 Increase
Total liabilities and stockholders' equity	$398,000	$138,000	

COMPUTER SERVICES COMPANY
Income Statement
For the Year Ended December 31, 2017

Sales revenue		$507,000
Cost of goods sold	$150,000	
Operating expenses (excluding depreciation)	111,000	
Depreciation expense	9,000	
Loss on disposal of plant assets	3,000	
Interest expense	42,000	315,000
Income before income tax		192,000
Income tax expense		47,000
Net income		$145,000

Additional information for 2017:

1. Depreciation expense was comprised of $6,000 for building and $3,000 for equipment.
2. The company sold equipment with a book value of $7,000 (cost $8,000, less accumulated depreciation $1,000) for $4,000 cash.
3. Issued $110,000 of long-term bonds in direct exchange for land.
4. A building costing $120,000 was purchased for cash. Equipment costing $25,000 was also purchased for cash.
5. Issued common stock for $20,000 cash.
6. The company declared and paid a $29,000 cash dividend.

We now apply the three steps to the information provided for Computer Services.

STEP 1: OPERATING ACTIVITIES

DETERMINE NET CASH PROVIDED/USED BY OPERATING ACTIVITIES BY CONVERTING NET INCOME FROM AN ACCRUAL BASIS TO A CASH BASIS

To determine net cash provided by operating activities under the indirect method, companies **adjust net income in numerous ways**. A useful starting point is to understand **why** net income must be converted to net cash provided by operating activities.

Under generally accepted accounting principles, most companies use the accrual basis of accounting. As you have learned, this basis requires that a company record revenue when the performance obligation is satisfied and record expenses when incurred. Revenues include credit sales for which the company has not yet collected cash. Expenses incurred include some items that it has not yet paid in cash. Thus, under the accrual basis of accounting, net income is not the same as net cash provided by operating activities.

Therefore, under the **indirect method**, companies must adjust net income to convert certain items to the cash basis. The indirect method (or reconciliation method) starts with net income and converts it to net cash provided by operating activities. Illustration 12-5 lists the three types of adjustments.

ILLUSTRATION 12-5
Three types of adjustments to convert net income to net cash provided by operating activities

Net Income +/−	Adjustments	=	Net Cash Provided/ Used by Operating Activities
	• **Add back noncash expenses,** such as depreciation expense and amortization expense. • **Deduct gains and add losses** that resulted from investing and financing activities. • **Analyze changes** to noncash current asset and current liability accounts.		

We explain the three types of adjustments in the next three sections.

▼ HELPFUL HINT
Depreciation is similar to any other expense in that it reduces net income. It differs in that it does not involve a current cash outflow. That is why it must be added back to net income to arrive at net cash provided by operating activities.

Depreciation Expense

Computer Services' income statement reports depreciation expense of $9,000. Although depreciation expense reduces net income, it does not reduce cash. In other words, depreciation expense is a noncash charge. The company must add it back to net income to arrive at net cash provided by operating activities. Computer Services reports depreciation expense as follows in the statement of cash flows.

ILLUSTRATION 12-6
Adjustment for depreciation

Cash flows from operating activities	
Net income	$145,000
Adjustments to reconcile net income to net cash provided by operating activities:	
Depreciation expense	**9,000**
Net cash provided by operating activities	$154,000

As the first adjustment to net income in the statement of cash flows, companies frequently list depreciation and similar noncash charges such as amortization of intangible assets and bad debt expense.

Loss on Disposal of Plant Assets

Illustration 12-1 states that cash received from the sale of plant assets is reported in the investing activities section. Because of this, **companies eliminate from net income all gains and losses resulting from investing activities, to arrive at net cash provided by operating activities.**

In our example, Computer Services' income statement reports a $3,000 loss on the disposal of plant assets (book value $7,000, less cash received from sale of equipment $4,000). The company's loss of $3,000 is eliminated in the operating activities section of the statement of cash flows. Illustration 12-7 shows that the $3,000 loss is eliminated by adding $3,000 back to net income to arrive at net cash provided by operating activities.

ILLUSTRATION 12-7
Adjustment for loss on disposal of plant assets

Cash flows from operating activities		
Net income		$145,000
Adjustments to reconcile net income to net cash provided by operating activities:		
Depreciation expense	$9,000	
Loss on disposal of plant assets	**3,000**	12,000
Net cash provided by operating activities		$157,000

If a gain on sale occurs, the company deducts the gain from net income in order to determine net cash provided by operating activities. **In the case of either a gain or a loss, companies report the actual amount of cash received from the sale, in this case $4,000, as a source of cash in the investing activities section of the statement of cash flows.**

Changes to Noncash Current Asset and Current Liability Accounts

A final step to reconcile net income to net cash provided by operating activities involves examining all changes in current asset and current liability accounts. The accrual-accounting process records revenues in the period in which the performance obligation is satisfied and expenses in the period incurred. For example, Accounts Receivable reflects amounts owed to the company for sales that have been made but for which cash collections have not yet been received. Prepaid Insurance reflects insurance that has been paid for but which has not yet expired and therefore has not been expensed. Similarly, Salaries and Wages Payable reflects salaries expense that has been incurred but has not been paid.

As a result, we need to adjust net income for these accruals and prepayments to determine net cash provided by operating activities. Thus, we must analyze the change in each current asset and current liability account to determine its impact on net income and cash.

CHANGES IN NONCASH CURRENT ASSETS. The adjustments required for changes in noncash current asset accounts are as follows. **Deduct from net income increases in current asset accounts, and add to net income decreases in current asset accounts, to arrive at net cash provided by operating activities.** We observe these relationships by analyzing the accounts of Computer Services.

DECREASE IN ACCOUNTS RECEIVABLE Computer Services' accounts receivable decreased by $10,000 (from $30,000 to $20,000) during the period. This means that cash receipts were $10,000 higher than sales revenue. The analysis of the Accounts Receivable account in Illustration 12-8 reveals this $10,000 difference. Computer Services had $507,000 in sales revenue (as reported on the income statement), but it collected $517,000 in cash.

ILLUSTRATION 12-8
Analysis of accounts receivable

Accounts Receivable

1/1/17	Balance	30,000	**Receipts from customers**	**517,000**
	Sales revenue	**507,000**		
12/31/17	Balance	20,000		

As shown in Illustration 12-9, to adjust net income to net cash provided by operating activities, the company adds to net income the decrease of $10,000 in accounts receivable.

ILLUSTRATION 12-9
Adjustments for changes in current asset accounts

Cash flows from operating activities		
Net income		$145,000
Adjustments to reconcile net income to net cash provided by operating activities:		
Depreciation expense	$ 9,000	
Loss on disposal of plant assets	3,000	
Decrease in accounts receivable	**10,000**	
Increase in inventory	**(5,000)**	
Increase in prepaid expenses	**(4,000)**	13,000
Net cash provided by operating activities		$158,000

When the Accounts Receivable balance increases, cash receipts are lower than revenue recorded under the accrual basis. Therefore, the company deducts from net income the amount of the increase in accounts receivable, to arrive at net cash provided by operating activities.

INCREASE IN INVENTORY Computer Services' inventory increased $5,000 (from $10,000 to $15,000) during the period. The change in the Inventory account reflects the difference between the amount of inventory purchased and the amount sold. For Computer Services, this means that the cost of merchandise purchased exceeded the cost of goods sold by $5,000. As a result, cost of goods sold does not reflect $5,000 of cash payments made for merchandise. The company deducts from net income this inventory increase of $5,000 during the period, to arrive at net cash provided by operating activities (see Illustration 12-9). If inventory decreases, the company adds to net income the amount of the change, to arrive at net cash provided by operating activities.

INCREASE IN PREPAID EXPENSES Computer Services' prepaid expenses increased during the period by $4,000. This means that cash paid for expenses is higher than expenses reported on an accrual basis. In other words, the company has made cash payments in the current period but will not charge expenses to income until future periods (as charges to the income statement). To adjust net income to net cash provided by operating activities, the company deducts from net income the $4,000 increase in prepaid expenses (see Illustration 12-9).

If prepaid expenses decrease, reported expenses are higher than the expenses paid. Therefore, the company adds to net income the decrease in prepaid expense, to arrive at net cash provided by operating activities.

CHANGES IN CURRENT LIABILITIES. The adjustments required for changes in current liability accounts are as follows. **Add to net income increases in current liability accounts, and deduct from net income decreases in current liability accounts, to arrive at net cash provided by operating activities.**

INCREASE IN ACCOUNTS PAYABLE For Computer Services, accounts payable increased by $16,000 (from $12,000 to $28,000) during the period. That means the company received $16,000 more in goods than it actually paid for. As shown in Illustration 12-10, to adjust net income to determine net cash provided by operating activities, the company adds to net income the $16,000 increase in the Accounts Payable account.

DECREASE IN INCOME TAXES PAYABLE When a company incurs income tax expense but has not yet paid its taxes, it records income taxes payable. A change in the Income Taxes Payable account reflects the difference between income tax expense incurred and income taxes actually paid. Computer Services' Income Taxes Payable account decreased by $2,000. That means the $47,000 of income tax expense reported on the income statement was $2,000 less than the amount of taxes paid during the period of $49,000. As shown in Illustration 12-10, to adjust net income to a cash basis, the company must reduce net income by $2,000.

ILLUSTRATION 12-10
Adjustments for changes in current liability accounts

Cash flows from operating activities		
Net income		$145,000
Adjustments to reconcile net income to net cash provided by operating activities:		
Depreciation expense	$ 9,000	
Loss on disposal of plant assets	3,000	
Decrease in accounts receivable	10,000	
Increase in inventory	(5,000)	
Increase in prepaid expenses	(4,000)	
Increase in accounts payable	**16,000**	
Decrease in income taxes payable	**(2,000)**	27,000
Net cash provided by operating activities		$172,000

Illustration 12-10 shows that after starting with net income of $145,000, the sum of all of the adjustments to net income was $27,000. This resulted in net cash provided by operating activities of $172,000.

SUMMARY OF CONVERSION TO NET CASH PROVIDED BY OPERATING ACTIVITIES—INDIRECT METHOD

As shown in the previous illustrations, the statement of cash flows prepared by the indirect method starts with net income. Items are then added or deducted to arrive at net cash provided by operating activities. The required adjustments are of three types:

1. Noncash charges such as depreciation and amortization.

2. Gains and losses from investing and financing transactions, such as the sale of plant assets.
3. Changes in noncash current asset and current liability accounts.

Illustration 12-11 provides a summary of these changes.

ILLUSTRATION 12-11
Adjustments required to convert net income to net cash provided by operating activities

		Adjustment Required to Convert Net Income to Net Cash Provided by Operating Activities
Noncash charges	Depreciation expense	Add
	Amortization expense	Add
Gains and losses	Loss on disposal of plant assets	Add
	Gain on disposal of plant assets	Deduct
Changes in current assets and current liabilities	Increase in current asset account	Deduct
	Decrease in current asset account	Add
	Increase in current liability account	Add
	Decrease in current liability account	Deduct

ANATOMY OF A FRAUD

For more than a decade, the top executives at the Italian dairy products company Parmalat engaged in multiple frauds that overstated cash and other assets by more than $1 billion while understating liabilities by between $8 and $12 billion. Much of the fraud involved creating fictitious sources and uses of cash. Some of these activities incorporated sophisticated financial transactions with subsidiaries created with the help of large international financial institutions. However, much of the fraud employed very basic, even sloppy, forgery of documents. For example, when outside auditors requested confirmation of bank accounts (such as a fake $4.8 billion account in the Cayman Islands), documents were created on scanners, with signatures that were cut and pasted from other documents. These were then passed through a fax machine numerous times to make them look real (if difficult to read). Similarly, fictitious bills were created in order to divert funds to other businesses owned by the Tanzi family (who controlled Parmalat).

Total take: Billions of dollars

THE MISSING CONTROL

Independent internal verification. Internal auditors at the company should have independently verified bank accounts and major transfers of cash to outside companies that were controlled by the Tanzi family.

DO IT! 2a Net Cash Provided by Operating Activities

Josh's PhotoPlus reported net income of $73,000 for 2017. Included in the income statement were depreciation expense of $7,000 and a gain on disposal of plant assets of $2,500. Josh's comparative balance sheets show the following balances.

	12/31/17	12/31/16
Accounts Receivable	$21,000	$17,000
Accounts Payable	2,200	6,000

Calculate net cash provided by operating activities for Josh's PhotoPlus.

SOLUTION

Cash flows from operating activities		
Net income		$73,000
Adjustments to reconcile net income to net cash provided by operating activities:		
Depreciation expense	$ 7,000	
Gain on disposal of plant assets	(2,500)	
Increase in accounts receivable	(4,000)	
Decrease in accounts payable	(3,800)	(3,300)
Net cash provided by operating activities		$69,700

Related exercise material: **BE12-4, BE12-5, BE12-6, DO IT! 12-2a, E12-3,** and **E12-4.**

Action Plan

✔ Add noncash charges such as depreciation back to net income to compute net cash provided by operating activities.

✔ Deduct gains and add back losses from the disposal of plant assets to compute net cash provided by operating activities.

✔ Use changes in noncash current asset and current liability accounts to compute net cash provided by operating activities.

STEP 2: INVESTING AND FINANCING ACTIVITIES

ANALYZE CHANGES IN NONCURRENT ASSET AND LIABILITY ACCOUNTS AND RECORD AS INVESTING AND FINANCING ACTIVITIES, OR DISCLOSE AS NONCASH TRANSACTIONS

INCREASE IN LAND As indicated from the change in the Land account and the additional information, Computer Services purchased land of $110,000 by directly exchanging bonds for land. The exchange of bonds payable for land has no effect on cash. But, it is a significant noncash investing and financing activity that merits disclosure in a separate schedule. (See Illustration 12–13, page 604.)

▼ HELPFUL HINT
The investing and financing activities are measured and reported the same under both the direct and indirect methods.

INCREASE IN BUILDINGS As the additional data indicate, Computer Services acquired an office building for $120,000 cash. This is a cash outflow reported in the investing activities section. (See Illustration 12–13.)

ETHICS NOTE
Because investors and management bonus contracts often focus on cash flow from operations, some managers have taken unethical actions to artificially increase cash flow from operations. For example, Dynegy restated its statement of cash flows because it had improperly included in operating activities $300 million that should have been reported as financing activities. This error increased cash from operating activities by 37%.

INCREASE IN EQUIPMENT The Equipment account increased $17,000. The additional information explains that this was a net increase that resulted from two transactions: (1) a purchase of equipment of $25,000, and (2) the sale for $4,000 of equipment costing $8,000. These transactions are both investing activities. The company should report each transaction separately. Thus, it reports the purchase of equipment as an outflow of cash for $25,000. It reports the sale as an inflow of cash for $4,000. The T-account below shows the reasons for the change in this account during the year.

ILLUSTRATION 12-12
Analysis of equipment

Equipment

1/1/17	Balance	10,000	Cost of equipment sold	8,000
	Purchase of equipment	**25,000**		
12/31/17	Balance	27,000		

The following entry shows the details of the equipment sale transaction.

Cash	4,000	
Accumulated Depreciation—Equipment	1,000	
Loss on Disposal of Plant Assets	3,000	
Equipment		8,000

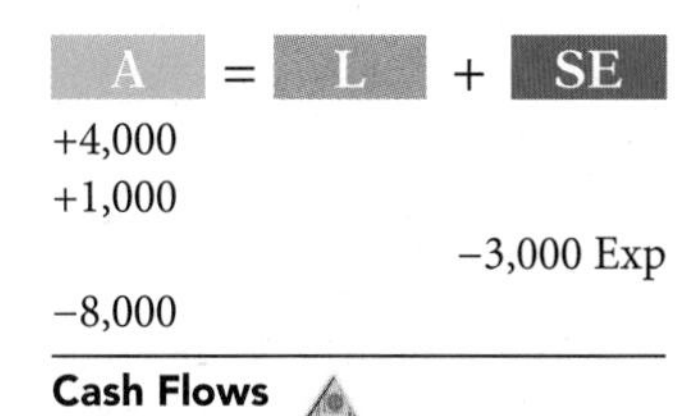

INCREASE IN BONDS PAYABLE The Bonds Payable account increased $110,000. As indicated in the additional information, the company acquired land by directly exchanging bonds for land. It reports this noncash transaction in a separate schedule at the bottom of the statement.

▼ **HELPFUL HINT**
When companies issue stocks or bonds for cash, the actual proceeds will appear in the statement of cash flows as a financing inflow (rather than the par value of the stocks or face value of bonds).

INCREASE IN COMMON STOCK The balance sheet reports an increase in Common Stock of $20,000. The additional information section notes that this increase resulted from the issuance of new shares of stock. This is a cash inflow reported in the financing activities section.

INCREASE IN RETAINED EARNINGS Retained earnings increased $116,000 during the year. This increase can be explained by two factors: (1) net income of $145,000 increased retained earnings, and (2) dividends of $29,000 decreased retained earnings. The company adjusts net income to net cash provided by operating activities in the operating activities section. Payment of the dividends (not the declaration) is a **cash outflow that the company reports as a financing activity**.

Statement of Cash Flows—2017

Using the previous information, we can now prepare a statement of cash flows for 2017 for Computer Services Company, as shown in Illustration 12-13.

ILLUSTRATION 12-13
Statement of cash flows, 2017—indirect method

COMPUTER SERVICES COMPANY Statement of Cash Flows—Indirect Method For the Year Ended December 31, 2017		
Cash flows from operating activities		
Net income		$ 145,000
Adjustments to reconcile net income to net cash provided by operating activities:		
Depreciation expense	$ 9,000	
Loss on disposal of plant assets	3,000	
Decrease in accounts receivable	10,000	
Increase in inventory	(5,000)	
Increase in prepaid expenses	(4,000)	
Increase in accounts payable	16,000	
Decrease in income taxes payable	(2,000)	27,000
Net cash provided by operating activities		172,000
Cash flows from investing activities		
Sale of equipment	4,000	
Purchase of building	(120,000)	
Purchase of equipment	(25,000)	
Net cash used by investing activities		(141,000)
Cash flows from financing activities		
Issuance of common stock	20,000	
Payment of cash dividends	(29,000)	
Net cash used by financing activities		(9,000)
Net increase in cash		22,000
Cash at beginning of period		33,000
Cash at end of period		$ 55,000
Noncash investing and financing activities		
Issuance of bonds payable to purchase land		$ 110,000

▼ **HELPFUL HINT**
Note that in the investing and financing activities sections, positive numbers indicate cash inflows (receipts), and negative numbers indicate cash outflows (payments).

STEP 3: NET CHANGE IN CASH

COMPARE THE NET CHANGE IN CASH ON THE STATEMENT OF CASH FLOWS WITH THE CHANGE IN THE CASH ACCOUNT REPORTED ON THE BALANCE SHEET TO MAKE SURE THE AMOUNTS AGREE

Illustration 12-13 indicates that the net change in cash during the period was an increase of $22,000. This agrees with the change in Cash account reported on the balance sheet in Illustration 12-4 (page 597).

ACCOUNTING ACROSS THE ORGANIZATION

© Soubrette/iStockphoto

Burning Through Our Cash

Box (cloud storage), Cyan (game creator), Fireeye (cyber security), and Mobile Iron (mobile security of data) are a few of the tech companies that recently have issued or are about to issue stock to the public. Investors now have to determine whether these tech companies have viable products and high chances for success.

An important consideration in evaluating a tech company is determining its financial flexibility—its ability to withstand adversity if an economic setback occurs. One way to measure financial flexibility is to assess a company's cash burn rate, which determines how long its cash will hold out if the company is expending more cash than it is receiving.

Fireeye, for example, burned cash in excess of $50 million in 2013. But the company also had over $150 million as a cash cushion, so it would take over 30 months before it runs out of cash. And even though Box has a much lower cash burn rate than Fireeye, it still has over a year's cushion. Compare that to the tech companies in 2000, when over one-quarter of them were on track to run out of cash within a year. And many did. Fortunately, the tech companies of today seem to be better equipped to withstand an economic setback.

Source: Shira Ovide, "Tech Firms' Cash Hoards Cool Fears of a Meltdown," *Wall Street Journal* (May 14, 2014).

What implications does a company's cash burn rate have for its survival? (See **WileyPLUS** for this answer and additional questions.)

DO IT! 2b Indirect Method

Use the following information to prepare a statement of cash flows using the indirect method.

REYNOLDS COMPANY
Comparative Balance Sheets
December 31

Assets	2017	2016	Change Increase/Decrease
Cash	$ 54,000	$ 37,000	$ 17,000 Increase
Accounts receivable	68,000	26,000	42,000 Increase
Inventory	54,000	-0-	54,000 Increase
Prepaid expenses	4,000	6,000	2,000 Decrease
Land	45,000	70,000	25,000 Decrease
Buildings	200,000	200,000	-0-
Accumulated depreciation—buildings	(21,000)	(11,000)	10,000 Increase
Equipment	193,000	68,000	125,000 Increase
Accumulated depreciation—equipment	(28,000)	(10,000)	18,000 Increase
Totals	$569,000	$386,000	
Liabilities and Stockholders' Equity			
Accounts payable	$ 23,000	$ 40,000	$ 17,000 Decrease
Accrued expenses payable	10,000	-0-	10,000 Increase
Bonds payable	110,000	150,000	40,000 Decrease
Common stock ($1 par)	220,000	60,000	160,000 Increase
Retained earnings	206,000	136,000	70,000 Increase
Totals	$569,000	$386,000	

REYNOLDS COMPANY
Income Statement
For the Year Ended December 31, 2017

Sales revenue		$890,000
Cost of goods sold	$465,000	
Operating expenses	221,000	
Interest expense	12,000	
Loss on disposal of equipment	2,000	700,000
Income before income taxes		190,000
Income tax expense		65,000
Net income		$125,000

Additional information:

1. Operating expenses include depreciation expense of $33,000.
2. Land was sold at its book value for cash.
3. Cash dividends of $55,000 were declared and paid in 2017.
4. Equipment with a cost of $166,000 was purchased for cash. Equipment with a cost of $41,000 and a book value of $36,000 was sold for $34,000 cash.
5. Bonds of $40,000 were redeemed at their face value for cash.
6. Common stock ($1 par) of $160,000 was issued for cash.

Action Plan

✔ Determine net cash provided/used by operating activities by adjusting net income for items that did not affect cash.

✔ Determine net cash provided/used by investing activities and financing activities.

✔ Determine the net increase/decrease in cash.

SOLUTION

REYNOLDS COMPANY
Statement of Cash Flows—Indirect Method
For the Year Ended December 31, 2017

Cash flows from operating activities		
Net income		$ 125,000
Adjustments to reconcile net income to net cash provided by operating activities:		
Depreciation expense	$ 33,000	
Loss on disposal of equipment	2,000	
Increase in accounts receivable	(42,000)	
Increase in inventory	(54,000)	
Decrease in prepaid expenses	2,000	
Decrease in accounts payable	(17,000)	
Increase in accrued expenses payable	10,000	(66,000)
Net cash provided by operating activities		59,000
Cash flows from investing activities		
Sale of land	25,000	
Sale of equipment	34,000	
Purchase of equipment	(166,000)	
Net cash used by investing activities		(107,000)
Cash flows from financing activities		
Redemption of bonds	(40,000)	
Sale of common stock	160,000	
Payment of dividends	(55,000)	
Net cash provided by financing activities		65,000
Net increase in cash		17,000
Cash at beginning of period		37,000
Cash at end of period		$ 54,000

Related exercise material: **BE12-4, BE12-5, BE12-6, BE12-7,** DO IT! **E12-2b, E12-5, E12-6,** and **E12-7.**

LEARNING OBJECTIVE 3 **Use the statement of cash flows to evaluate a company.**

Traditionally, investors and creditors used ratios based on accrual accounting. These days, cash-based ratios are gaining increased acceptance among analysts. In this section, we review the corporate life cycle and free cash flow.

THE CORPORATE LIFE CYCLE

All products go through a series of phases called the **product life cycle**. The phases (in order of their occurrence) are **introductory phase**, **growth phase**, **maturity phase**, and **decline phase**. The introductory phase occurs at the beginning of a company's life, when it purchases fixed assets and begins to produce and sell products. During the growth phase, the company strives to expand its production and sales. In the maturity phase, sales and production level off. During the decline phase, sales of the product decrease due to a weakening in consumer demand.

In the same way that products have life cycles, companies have life cycles as well. Companies generally have more than one product, and not all of a company's products are in the same phase of the product life cycle at the same time. This sometimes makes it difficult to classify a company's phase. Still, we can characterize a company as being in one of the four phases because the majority of its products are in a particular phase.

Illustration 12-14 shows that the phase a company is in affects its cash flows. In the **introductory phase**, we expect that the company will not generate positive cash from operations. That is, cash used in operations will exceed cash generated by operations in the introductory phase. Also, the company spends considerable amounts to purchase productive assets such as buildings and equipment. To support its asset purchases, the company issues stock or debt. Thus, during the introductory phase, we expect negative cash from operations, negative cash from investing, and positive cash from financing.

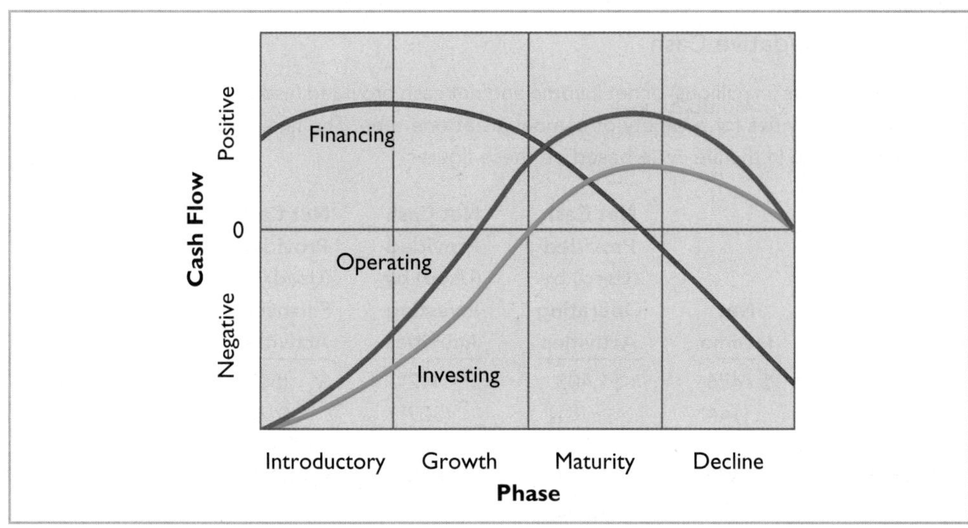

ILLUSTRATION 12-14
Impact of product life cycle on cash flows

During the **growth phase**, we expect to see the company start to generate small amounts of cash from operations. During this phase, net cash provided by operating activities on the statement of cash flows is less than net income. One reason net income exceeds cash flow from operations during this period is explained by the difference between the cash paid for inventory and the amount expensed as cost of goods sold. Since the company projects increasing sales, the size of inventory purchases increases. Thus, in the growth phase, the company expenses less inventory on an accrual basis than it purchases on a cash basis. Also, collections on accounts receivable lag behind sales, and accrual sales during a period exceed cash collections during that period. Cash needed for asset acquisitions will continue to exceed net cash provided by operating activities. The company makes up the deficiency by issuing new stock or debt. Thus, in the growth phase, the company continues to show negative cash from investing activities and positive cash from financing activities.

During the **maturity phase**, net cash provided by operating activities and net income are approximately the same. Cash generated from operations exceeds investing needs. Thus, in the maturity phase, the company starts to pay dividends, retire debt, or buy back stock.

Finally, during the **decline phase**, net cash provided by operating activities decreases. Cash from investing activities might actually become positive as the company sells off excess assets. Cash from financing activities may be negative as the company buys back stock and redeems debt.

Consider Microsoft. During its early years, it had significant product development costs and little revenue. Microsoft was lucky in that its agreement with IBM to provide the operating system for IBM PCs gave it an early steady source of cash to support growth. As noted in the Feature Story, Microsoft conserved cash by paying employees with stock options rather than cash. Today, Microsoft could be characterized as being in the maturity phase. It continues to spend considerable amounts on research and development and investment in new assets. In recent years, though, its net cash provided by operating activities has exceeded its net income. Also, cash from operations over this period exceeded cash used for investing, and common stock repurchased exceeded common stock issued. For Microsoft, as for any large company, the challenge is to maintain its growth. In the software industry, where products become obsolete very quickly, the challenge is particularly great.

INVESTOR INSIGHT

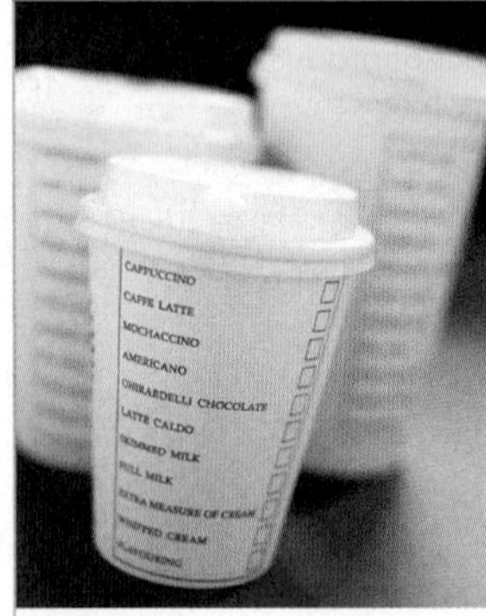

Neil Barclay/Retna

Operating with Negative Cash

Listed here are amounts (in millions) of net income and net cash provided (used) by operating, investing, and financing activities for a variety of companies at one time. The final column suggests each company's likely phase in the life cycle based on these figures.

Company	Net Income	Net Cash Provided (Used) by Operating Activities	Net Cash Provided (Used) by Investing Activities	Net Cash Provided (Used) by Financing Activities	Likely Phase in Life Cycle
Amazon.com	$ 476	$1,405	$ (42)	$ (50)	Early maturity
LDK Solar	(144)	(81)	(329)	462	Introductory/ early growth
United States Steel	879	1,745	(4,675)	(1,891)	Maturity
Kellogg	1,103	1,503	(601)	(788)	Early decline
Southwest Airlines	645	2,845	(1,529)	493	Maturity
Starbucks	673	1,331	(1,202)	(172)	Maturity

Why do companies have negative net cash provided by operating activities during the introductory phase? (Go to WileyPLUS for this answer and additional questions.)

FREE CASH FLOW

DECISION TOOLS

Free cash flows helps users determine the amount of cash the company generated to expand operations or pay dividends.

In the statement of cash flows, net cash provided by operating activities is intended to indicate the cash-generating capability of the company. Analysts have noted, however, that **cash provided by operating activities fails to take into account that a company must invest in new fixed assets** just to maintain its current level of operations. Companies also must at least **maintain dividends at current levels** to satisfy investors. As we discussed in Chapter 2, the measurement of free cash flow provides additional insight regarding a company's cash-generating ability. **Free cash flow** describes the net cash provided by operating activities after adjustment for capital expenditures and dividends.

Consider the following example. Suppose that MPC produced and sold 10,000 personal computers this year. It reported $100,000 cash provided by operating activities. In order to maintain production at 10,000 computers, MPC invested $15,000 in equipment. It chose to pay $5,000 in dividends. Its free cash flow was $80,000 ($100,000 − $15,000 − $5,000). The company could use this $80,000 either to purchase new assets, pay off debt, or pay an $80,000 dividend. In practice, free cash flow is often calculated with the formula in Illustration 12-15. Alternative definitions also exist.

ILLUSTRATION 12-15
Free cash flow

Free Cash Flow	=	Net Cash Provided by Operating Activities	−	Capital Expenditures	−	Cash Dividends

Illustration 12-16 provides basic information excerpted from the 2014 statement of cash flows of Apple (prior to the payment of its first dividends).

ILLUSTRATION 12-16
Apple's cash flow information ($ in millions)

Real World

APPLE INC.
Statement of Cash Flows Information (partial)
2014

Net cash provided by operating activities		$ 59,713
Cash flows from investing activities		
Additions to property and equipment and intangibles	$ (9,571)	
Purchases of investments	(217,128)	
Sales of investments	189,301	
Acquisitions of companies	(3,765)	
Maturities of investments	18,810	
Other	(226)	
Net cash used by investing activities		(22,579)
Cash paid for dividends		(11,126)

Apple's free cash flow is calculated as shown in Illustration 12-17 (in millions). Apple generated approximately $39 billion of free cash flow. This is a tremendous amount of cash generated in a single year. It is available for the acquisition of new assets, the buyback and retirement of stock or debt, or the payment of dividends.

ILLUSTRATION 12-17
Calculation of Apple's free cash flow ($ in millions)

Net cash provided by operating activities	$59,713
Less: Expenditures on property, plant, and equipment	9,571
Dividends paid	11,126
Free cash flow	$39,016

Also note that Apple's cash from operations of $59.7 billion exceeds its 2014 net income of $39.5 billion by $20.2 billion. This lends additional credibility to

Apple's income number as an indicator of potential future performance. If anything, Apple's net income might understate its actual performance.

KEEPING AN EYE ON CASH

Cash flow is closely monitored by analysts and investors for many reasons and in a variety of ways. One measure that is gaining increased attention is "price to cash flow." This is a variant of the price to earnings (P-E) ratio, which has been a staple of analysts for a long time. The difference is that rather than divide the company's stock price by its earnings per share (an accrual-accounting–based number), the price to cash flow ratio divides the company's stock price by its cash flow per share. A high measure suggests that the stock price is high relative to the company's ability to generate cash. A low measure indicates that the company's stock might be a bargain.

The following table provides values for some well-known companies in a recent year. While you should not use this measure as the sole factor in choosing a stock, it can serve as a useful screen by which to identify companies that merit further investigation.

Company	Price/Cash Flow	Price/EPS
Microsoft	55.6	62.5
Apple	11.1	12.5
Nike	19.1	24.8
Wal-Mart	9.0	15.7
Jet Blue	7.9	11.1

DO IT! 3 Free Cash Flow

Chicago Corporation issued the following statement of cash flows for 2017.

CHICAGO CORPORATION Statement of Cash Flows—Indirect Method For the Year Ended December 31, 2017		
Cash flows from operating activities		
Net income		$ 19,000
Adjustments to reconcile net income to net cash provided by operating activities:		
Depreciation expense	$ 8,100	
Loss on disposal of plant assets	1,300	
Decrease in accounts receivable	6,900	
Increase in inventory	(4,000)	
Decrease in accounts payable	(2,000)	10,300
Net cash provided by operating activities		29,300
Cash flows from investing activities		
Sale of investments	1,100	
Purchase of equipment	(19,000)	
Net cash used by investing activities		(17,900)
Cash flows from financing activities		
Issuance of stock	10,000	
Payment on long-term note payable	(5,000)	
Payment for dividends	(9,000)	
Net cash used by financing activities		(4,000)
Net increase in cash		7,400
Cash at beginning of year		10,000
Cash at end of year		$ 17,400

(a) Compute free cash flow for Chicago Corporation. (b) Explain why free cash flow often provides better information than "Net cash provided by operating activities."

SOLUTION

(a) Free cash flow = $29,300 − $19,000 − $9,000 = $1,300

(b) Net cash provided by operating activities fails to take into account that a company must invest in new plant assets just to maintain the current level of operation. Companies must also maintain dividends at current levels to satisfy investors. The measurement of free cash flow provides additional insight regarding a company's cash-generating ability.

Action Plan

✔ **Compute free cash flow as Net cash provided by operating activities − Capital expenditures − Cash dividends.**

Related exercise material: **BE12-9, BE12-10, BE12-11, BE12-12, DO IT! 12-3, E12-9,** and **E12-10.**

USING DECISION TOOLS—INTEL CORPORATION

Intel Corporation is the leading producer of computer chips for personal computers. Its primary competitor is AMD. Financial statement data for Intel are provided below.

INTEL CORPORATION
Statement of Cash Flows
For the Year Ended December 31, 2014 (in millions)

	2014
Net cash provided by operating activities	$ 20,418
Net cash used for investing activities	(9,905)
Net cash used for financing activities	(13,626)
Net increase (decrease) in cash and cash equivalents	$ (3,113)

Note. Cash spent on property, plant, and equipment in 2014 was $10,105. Cash paid for dividends was $4,409.

INSTRUCTIONS

Calculate free cash flow for Intel and compare it with that of AMD (−$193 million).

SOLUTION

Intel's free cash flow is $5,904 million ($20,418 − $10,105 − $4,409). AMD's is −$193 million. This gives Intel a huge advantage in the ability to move quickly to invest in new projects.

LEARNING OBJECTIVE *4

APPENDIX 12A: Prepare a statement of cash flows using the direct method.

To explain and illustrate the direct method, we will use the transactions of Computer Services Company for 2017 to prepare a statement of cash flows. Illustration 12A-1 (page 612) presents information related to 2017 for the company.

ILLUSTRATION 12A-1
Comparative balance sheets, income statement, and additional information for Computer Services Company

COMPUTER SERVICES COMPANY
Comparative Balance Sheets
December 31

Assets	2017	2016	Change in Account Balance Increase/Decrease
Current assets			
Cash	$ 55,000	$ 33,000	$ 22,000 Increase
Accounts receivable	20,000	30,000	10,000 Decrease
Inventory	15,000	10,000	5,000 Increase
Prepaid expenses	5,000	1,000	4,000 Increase
Property, plant, and equipment			
Land	130,000	20,000	110,000 Increase
Buildings	160,000	40,000	120,000 Increase
Accumulated depreciation—buildings	(11,000)	(5,000)	6,000 Increase
Equipment	27,000	10,000	17,000 Increase
Accumulated depreciation—equipment	(3,000)	(1,000)	2,000 Increase
Total assets	$398,000	$138,000	
Liabilities and Stockholders' Equity			
Current liabilities			
Accounts payable	$ 28,000	$ 12,000	$ 16,000 Increase
Income taxes payable	6,000	8,000	2,000 Decrease
Long-term liabilities			
Bonds payable	130,000	20,000	110,000 Increase
Stockholders' equity			
Common stock	70,000	50,000	20,000 Increase
Retained earnings	164,000	48,000	116,000 Increase
Total liabilities and stockholders' equity	$398,000	$138,000	

COMPUTER SERVICES COMPANY
Income Statement
For the Year Ended December 31, 2017

Sales revenue		$507,000
Cost of goods sold	$150,000	
Operating expenses (excluding depreciation)	111,000	
Depreciation expense	9,000	
Loss on disposal of plant assets	3,000	
Interest expense	42,000	315,000
Income before income tax		192,000
Income tax expense		47,000
Net income		$145,000

Additional information for 2017:

1. Depreciation expense was comprised of $6,000 for building and $3,000 for equipment.
2. The company sold equipment with a book value of $7,000 (cost $8,000, less accumulated depreciation $1,000) for $4,000 cash.
3. Issued $110,000 of long-term bonds in direct exchange for land.
4. A building costing $120,000 was purchased for cash. Equipment costing $25,000 was also purchased for cash.
5. Issued common stock for $20,000 cash.
6. The company declared and paid a $29,000 cash dividend.

To prepare a statement of cash flows under the direct approach, we will apply the three steps outlined in Illustration 12-3 (page 596).

STEP 1: OPERATING ACTIVITIES

DETERMINE NET CASH PROVIDED/USED BY OPERATING ACTIVITIES BY CONVERTING NET INCOME FROM AN ACCRUAL BASIS TO A CASH BASIS

Under the **direct method**, companies compute net cash provided by operating activities by **adjusting each item in the income statement** from the accrual basis to the cash basis. To simplify and condense the operating activities section, companies **report only major classes of operating cash receipts and cash payments**. For these major classes, the difference between cash receipts and cash payments is the net cash provided by operating activities. These relationships are as shown in Illustration 12A-2.

ILLUSTRATION 12A-2
Major classes of cash receipts and payments

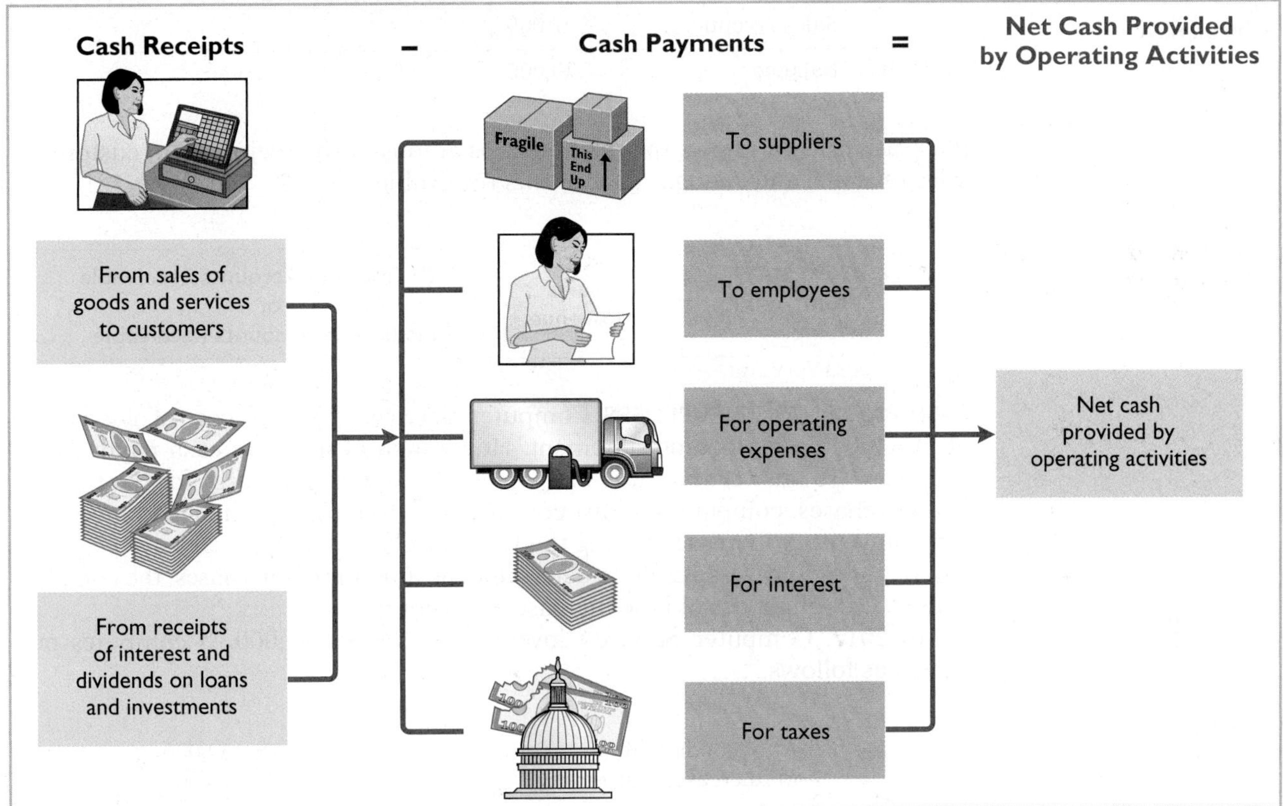

An efficient way to apply the direct method is to analyze the items reported in the income statement in the order in which they are listed. We then determine cash receipts and cash payments related to these revenues and expenses. The following pages present the adjustments required to prepare a statement of cash flows for Computer Services Company using the direct approach.

CASH RECEIPTS FROM CUSTOMERS The income statement for Computer Services reported sales revenue from customers of $507,000. How much of that was cash receipts? To answer that, companies need to consider the change in accounts receivable during the year. When accounts receivable increase during the year, revenues on an accrual basis are higher than cash receipts from customers. Operations led to revenues, but not all of these revenues resulted in cash receipts.

To determine the amount of cash receipts, the company deducts from sales revenue the increase in accounts receivable. On the other hand, there may be a decrease in accounts receivable. That would occur if cash receipts from customers exceeded sales revenue. In that case, the company adds to sales revenue the decrease in accounts receivable. For Computer Services, accounts receivable decreased $10,000. Thus, cash receipts from customers were $517,000, computed as shown in Illustration 12A-3.

ILLUSTRATION 12A-3
Computation of cash receipts from customers

Sales revenue	$ 507,000
Add: Decrease in accounts receivable	10,000
Cash receipts from customers	**$517,000**

Computer Services can also determine cash receipts from customers from an analysis of the Accounts Receivable account, as shown in Illustration 12A-4.

ILLUSTRATION 12A-4
Analysis of accounts receivable

Accounts Receivable

1/1/17	Balance	30,000	**Receipts from customers**	**517,000**
	Sales revenue	507,000		
12/31/17	Balance	20,000		

▼ HELPFUL HINT
The T-account shows that sales revenue plus decrease in accounts receivables equals cash receipts.

Illustration 12A-5 shows the relationships among cash receipts from customers, sales revenue, and changes in accounts receivable.

ILLUSTRATION 12A-5
Formula to compute cash receipts from customers—direct method

Cash Receipts from Customers	=	**Sales Revenue**	**+ Decrease in Accounts Receivable** **or** **− Increase in Accounts Receivable**

CASH PAYMENTS TO SUPPLIERS Computer Services reported cost of goods sold of $150,000 on its income statement. How much of that was cash payments to suppliers? To answer that, it is first necessary to find purchases for the year. To find purchases, companies adjust cost of goods sold for the change in inventory. When inventory increases during the year, purchases for the year have exceeded cost of goods sold. As a result, to determine the amount of purchases, the company adds to cost of goods sold the increase in inventory.

In 2017, Computer Services' inventory increased $5,000. It computes purchases as follows.

ILLUSTRATION 12A-6
Computation of purchases

Cost of goods sold	$ 150,000
Add: Increase in inventory	5,000
Purchases	**$155,000**

After computing purchases, a company can determine cash payments to suppliers. This is done by adjusting purchases for the change in accounts payable. When accounts payable increase during the year, purchases on an accrual basis are higher than they are on a cash basis. As a result, to determine cash payments to suppliers, a company deducts from purchases the increase in accounts payable. On the other hand, if cash payments to suppliers exceed purchases, there may be a decrease in accounts payable. In that case, a company adds to purchases the decrease in accounts payable. For Computer Services, cash payments to suppliers were $139,000, computed as follows.

ILLUSTRATION 12A-7
Computation of cash payments to suppliers

Purchases	$ 155,000
Deduct: Increase in accounts payable	16,000
Cash payments to suppliers	**$139,000**

Computer Services also can determine cash payments to suppliers from an analysis of the Accounts Payable account, as shown in Illustration 12A-8.

ILLUSTRATION 12A-8
Analysis of accounts payable

Accounts Payable			
Payments to suppliers	**139,000**	1/1/17 Balance	12,000
		Purchases	155,000
		12/31/17 Balance	28,000

▼ HELPFUL HINT
The T-account shows that purchases less increase in accounts payable equals payments to suppliers.

Illustration 12A-9 shows the relationships among cash payments to suppliers, cost of goods sold, changes in inventory, and changes in accounts payable.

ILLUSTRATION 12A-9
Formula to compute cash payments to suppliers—direct method

Cash Payments to Suppliers	=	Cost of Goods Sold	+ Increase in Inventory or − Decrease in Inventory	+ Decrease in Accounts Payable or − Increase in Accounts Payable

CASH PAYMENTS FOR OPERATING EXPENSES Computer Services reported on its income statement operating expenses of $111,000. How much of that amount was cash paid for operating expenses? To answer that, we need to adjust this amount for any changes in prepaid expenses and accrued expenses payable. For example, if prepaid expenses increased during the year, cash paid for operating expenses is higher than operating expenses reported on the income statement. To convert operating expenses to cash payments for operating expenses, a company adds the increase in prepaid expenses to operating expenses. On the other hand, if prepaid expenses decrease during the year, it deducts the decrease from operating expenses.

Companies must also adjust operating expenses for changes in accrued expenses payable. When accrued expenses payable increase during the year, operating expenses on an accrual basis are higher than they are in a cash basis. As a result, to determine cash payments for operating expenses, a company deducts from operating expenses an increase in accrued expenses payable. On the other hand, a company adds to operating expenses a decrease in accrued expenses payable because cash payments exceed operating expenses.

Computer Services' cash payments for operating expenses were $115,000, computed as follows.

ILLUSTRATION 12A-10
Computation of cash payments for operating expenses

Operating expenses	$ 111,000
Add: Increase in prepaid expenses	4,000
Cash payments for operating expenses	**$115,000**

Illustration 12A-11 shows the relationships among cash payments for operating expenses, changes in prepaid expenses, and changes in accrued expenses payable.

ILLUSTRATION 12A-11
Formula to compute cash payments for operating expenses—direct method

Cash Payments for Operating Expenses	=	Operating Expenses	+ Increase in Prepaid Expense or − Decrease in Prepaid Expense	+ Decrease in Accrued Expenses Payable or − Increase in Accrued Expenses Payable

DEPRECIATION EXPENSE AND LOSS ON DISPOSAL OF PLANT ASSETS Computer Services' depreciation expense in 2017 was $9,000. Depreciation expense is not shown on a statement of cash flows under the direct method because it is a noncash charge. If the amount for operating expenses includes depreciation expense, operating expenses must be reduced by the amount of depreciation to determine cash payments for operating expenses.

The loss on disposal of plant assets of $3,000 is also a noncash charge. The loss on disposal of plant assets reduces net income, but it does not reduce cash. Thus, the loss on disposal of plant assets is not shown on the statement of cash flows under the direct method.

Other charges to expense that do not require the use of cash, such as the amortization of intangible assets and bad debt expense, are treated in the same manner as depreciation.

CASH PAYMENTS FOR INTEREST Computer Services reported on the income statement interest expense of $42,000. Since the balance sheet did not include an accrual for interest payable for 2016 or 2017, the amount reported as expense is the same as the amount of interest paid.

CASH PAYMENTS FOR INCOME TAXES Computer Services reported income tax expense of $47,000 on the income statement. Income taxes payable, however, decreased $2,000. This decrease means that income taxes paid were more than income taxes reported in the income statement. Cash payments for income taxes were, therefore, $49,000 as shown below.

ILLUSTRATION 12A-12
Computation of cash payments for income taxes

Income tax expense	$ 47,000
Add: Decrease in income taxes payable	2,000
Cash payments for income taxes	**$49,000**

Illustration 12A-13 shows the relationships among cash payments for income taxes, income tax expense, and changes in income taxes payable.

ILLUSTRATION 12A-13
Formula to compute cash payments for income taxes—direct method

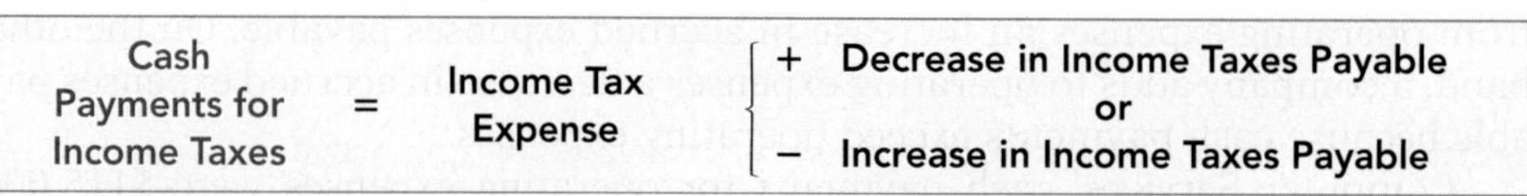

The operating activities section of the statement of cash flows of Computer Services is shown in Illustration 12A-14.

ILLUSTRATION 12A-14
Operating activities section of the statement of cash flows

Cash flows from operating activities		
Cash receipts from customers		$517,000
Less: Cash payments:		
To suppliers	$139,000	
For operating expenses	115,000	
For interest expense	42,000	
For income taxes	49,000	345,000
Net cash provided by operating activities		$172,000

When a company uses the direct method, it must also provide in a **separate schedule** (not shown here) the net cash flows from operating activities as computed under the indirect method.

STEP 2: INVESTING AND FINANCING ACTIVITIES

ANALYZE CHANGES IN NONCURRENT ASSET AND LIABILITY ACCOUNTS AND RECORD AS INVESTING AND FINANCING ACTIVITIES, OR DISCLOSE AS NONCASH TRANSACTIONS

INCREASE IN LAND As indicated from the change in the Land account and the additional information, Computer Services purchased land of $110,000 by directly exchanging bonds for land. The exchange of bonds payable for land has no effect on cash. But, it is a significant noncash investing and financing activity that merits disclosure in a separate schedule. (See Illustration 12A-16, page 618.)

▼ HELPFUL HINT
The investing and financing activities are measured and reported the same under both the direct and indirect methods.

INCREASE IN BUILDINGS As the additional data indicate, Computer Services acquired an office building for $120,000 cash. This is a cash outflow reported in the investing activities section. (See Illustration 12A-16, page 618.)

INCREASE IN EQUIPMENT The Equipment account increased $17,000. The additional information explains that this was a net increase that resulted from two transactions: (1) a purchase of equipment of $25,000, and (2) the sale for $4,000 of equipment costing $8,000. These transactions are investing activities. The company should report each transaction separately. The statement in Illustration 12A-16 reports the purchase of equipment as an outflow of cash for $25,000. It reports the sale as an inflow of cash for $4,000. The T-account below shows the reasons for the change in this account during the year.

ILLUSTRATION 12A-15
Analysis of equipment

Equipment

1/1/17	Balance	10,000	Cost of equipment sold	8,000
	Purchase of equipment	**25,000**		
12/31/17	Balance	27,000		

The following entry shows the details of the equipment sale transaction.

Cash	4,000	
Accumulated Depreciation—Equipment	1,000	
Loss on Disposal of Plant Assets	3,000	
Equipment		8,000

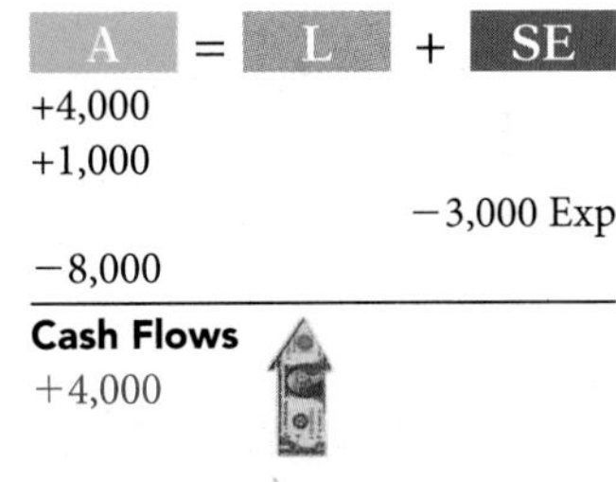

INCREASE IN BONDS PAYABLE The Bonds Payable account increased $110,000. As indicated in the additional information, the company acquired land by directly exchanging bonds for land. Illustration 12A-16 reports this noncash transaction in a separate schedule at the bottom of the statement.

INCREASE IN COMMON STOCK The balance sheet reports an increase in Common Stock of $20,000. The additional information section notes that this increase resulted from the issuance of new shares of stock. This is a cash inflow reported in the financing activities section in Illustration 12A-16 (page 618).

INCREASE IN RETAINED EARNINGS Retained earnings increased $116,000 during the year. This increase can be explained by two factors: (1) net income of $145,000 increased retained earnings, and (2) dividends of $29,000 decreased retained earnings. The company adjusts net income to net cash provided by operating activities in the operating activities section. **Payment** of the dividends (not the declaration) is a **cash outflow that the company reports as a financing activity in Illustration 12A-16.**

▼ HELPFUL HINT
When companies issue stocks or bonds for cash, the actual proceeds will appear in the statement of cash flows as a financing inflow (rather than the par value of the stocks or face value of bonds).

Statement of Cash Flows—2017

Illustration 12A-16 (page 618) shows the statement of cash flows for Computer Services Company.

ILLUSTRATION 12A-16
Statement of cash flows, 2017—direct method

COMPUTER SERVICES COMPANY Statement of Cash Flows—Direct Method For the Year Ended December 31, 2017		
Cash flows from operating activities		
Cash receipts from customers		$ 517,000
Less: Cash payments:		
To suppliers	$ 139,000	
For operating expenses	115,000	
For income taxes	49,000	
For interest expense	42,000	345,000
Net cash provided by operating activities		172,000
Cash flows from investing activities		
Sale of equipment	4,000	
Purchase of building	(120,000)	
Purchase of equipment	(25,000)	
Net cash used by investing activities		(141,000)
Cash flows from financing activities		
Issuance of common stock	20,000	
Payment of cash dividends	(29,000)	
Net cash used by financing activities		(9,000)
Net increase in cash		22,000
Cash at beginning of period		33,000
Cash at end of period		$ 55,000
Noncash investing and financing activities		
Issuance of bonds payable to purchase land		$ 110,000

STEP 3: NET CHANGE IN CASH

COMPARE THE NET CHANGE IN CASH ON THE STATEMENT OF CASH FLOWS WITH THE CHANGE IN THE CASH ACCOUNT REPORTED ON THE BALANCE SHEET TO MAKE SURE THE AMOUNTS AGREE

Illustration 12A-16 indicates that the net change in cash during the period was an increase of $22,000. This agrees with the change in balances in the Cash account reported on the balance sheets in Illustration 12A-1 (page 612).

LEARNING OBJECTIVE *5

APPENDIX 12B: Use the T-account approach to prepare a statement of cash flows.

Many people like to use T-accounts to provide structure to the preparation of a statement of cash flows. The use of T-accounts is based on the accounting equation that you learned in Chapter 1. The basic equation is:

Assets = Liabilities + Equity

Now, let's rewrite the left-hand side as:

Cash + Noncash Assets = Liabilities + Equity

Next, rewrite the equation by subtracting Noncash Assets from each side to isolate Cash on the left-hand side:

Cash = Liabilities + Equity − Noncash Assets

Finally, if we insert the Δ symbol (which means "change in"), we have:

Δ Cash = Δ Liabilities + Δ Equity − Δ Noncash Assets

What this means is that the change in cash is equal to the change in all of the other balance sheet accounts. Another way to think about this is that if we analyze the changes in all of the noncash balance sheet accounts, we will explain the change in the Cash account. This, of course, is exactly what we are trying to do with the statement of cash flows.

To implement this approach, first prepare a large Cash T-account with sections for operating, investing, and financing activities. Then, prepare smaller T-accounts for all of the other noncash balance sheet accounts. Insert the beginning and ending balances for each of these accounts. Once you have done this, then walk through the steps outlined in Illustration 12-3 (page 596). As you walk through the steps, enter debit and credit amounts into the affected accounts. When all of the changes in the T-accounts have been explained, you are done. To demonstrate, we will apply this approach to the example of Computer Services Company that is presented in the chapter. Each of the adjustments in Illustration 12B-1 is numbered so you can follow them through the T-accounts.

ILLUSTRATION 12B-1
T-account approach

Cash

	Debit	Credit	
Operating			
(1) Net income	145,000	5,000	Inventory (5)
(2) Depreciation expense	9,000	4,000	Prepaid expenses (6)
(3) Loss on equipment	3,000	2,000	Income taxes payable (8)
(4) Accounts receivable	10,000		
(7) Accounts payable	16,000		
Net cash provided by operating activities	172,000		
Investing			
(3) Sold equipment	4,000	120,000	Purchased building (10)
		25,000	Purchased equipment (11)
		141,000	Net cash used by investing activities
Financing			
(12) Issued common stock	20,000	29,000	Dividend paid (13)
		9,000	Net cash used by financing activities
	22,000		

Accounts Receivable

Debit	Credit
30,000	
	10,000 (4)
20,000	

Inventory

Debit	Credit
10,000	
(5) 5,000	
15,000	

Prepaid Expenses

Debit	Credit
1,000	
(6) 4,000	
5,000	

Land

Debit	Credit
20,000	
(9) 110,000	
130,000	

Buildings

Debit	Credit
40,000	
(10) 120,000	
160,000	

Accumulated Depreciation—Buildings

Debit	Credit
	5,000
	6,000 (2)
	11,000

Equipment

Debit	Credit
10,000	
(11) 25,000	8,000 (3)
27,000	

Accumulated Depreciation—Equipment

Debit	Credit
	1,000
(3) 1,000	3,000 (2)
	3,000

Accounts Payable

Debit	Credit
	12,000
	16,000 (7)
	28,000

Income Taxes Payable

Debit	Credit
	8,000
(8) 2,000	
	6,000

Bonds Payable

Debit	Credit
	20,000
	110,000 (9)
	130,000

Common Stock

Debit	Credit
	50,000
	20,000 (12)
	70,000

Retained Earnings

Debit	Credit
	48,000
	145,000 (1)
(13) 29,000	
	164,000

1. Post net income as a debit to the operating section of the Cash T-account and a credit to Retained Earnings. Make sure to label all adjustments to the Cash T-account. It also helps to number each adjustment so you can trace all of them if you make an error.

2. Post depreciation expense as a debit to the operating section of Cash and a credit to each of the appropriate accumulated depreciation accounts.
3. Post any gains or losses on the sale of property, plant, and equipment. To do this, it is best to first prepare the journal entry that was recorded at the time of the sale and then post each element of the journal entry. For example, for Computer Services the entry was:

Cash	4,000	
Accumulated Depreciation—Equipment	1,000	
Loss on Disposal of Plant Assets	3,000	
Equipment		8,000

The $4,000 cash entry is a source of cash in the investing section of the Cash account. Accumulated Depreciation—Equipment is debited for $1,000. The Loss on Disposal of Plant Assets is a debit to the operating section of the Cash T-account. Finally, Equipment is credited for $8,000.

4–8. Next, post each of the changes to the noncash current asset and current liability accounts. For example, to explain the $10,000 decline in Computer Services' accounts receivable, credit Accounts Receivable for $10,000 and debit the operating section of the Cash T-account for $10,000.

9. Analyze the changes in the noncurrent accounts. Land was purchased by issuing bonds payable. This requires a debit to Land for $110,000 and a credit to Bonds Payable for $110,000. Note that this is a significant noncash event that requires disclosure at the bottom of the statement of cash flows.
10. Buildings is debited for $120,000, and the investing section of the Cash T-account is credited for $120,000 as a use of cash from investing.
11. Equipment is debited for $25,000 and the investing section of the Cash T-account is credited for $25,000 as a use of cash from investing.
12. Common Stock is credited for $20,000 for the issuance of shares of stock, and the financing section of the Cash T-account is debited for $20,000.
13. Retained Earnings is debited to reflect the payment of the $29,000 dividend, and the financing section of the Cash T-account is credited to reflect the use of Cash.

At this point, all of the changes in the noncash accounts have been explained. All that remains is to subtotal each section of the Cash T-account and compare the total change in cash with the change shown on the balance sheet. Once this is done, the information in the Cash T-account can be used to prepare a statement of cash flows.

REVIEW AND PRACTICE

LEARNING OBJECTIVES REVIEW

1 Discuss the usefulness and format of the statement of cash flows. The statement of cash flows provides information about the cash receipts, cash payments, and net change in cash resulting from the operating, investing, and financing activities of a company during the period.

Operating activities include the cash effects of transactions that enter into the determination of net income. Investing activities involve cash flows resulting from changes in investments and long-term asset items. Financing activities involve cash flows resulting from changes in long-term liability and stockholders' equity items.

2 Prepare a statement of cash flows using the indirect method. The preparation of a statement of cash flows involves three major steps. (1) Determine net cash provided/used by operating activities by converting net income from an accrual basis to a cash basis. (2) Analyze changes in noncurrent asset and liability accounts and record as investing and financing activities, or disclose as noncash transactions. (3) Compare the net change in cash on the statement of cash flows with the change in the Cash account reported on the balance sheet to make sure the amounts agree.

3 Use the statement of cash flows to evaluate a company. During the introductory stage, net cash provided by operating activities and net cash provided by investing activities are negative, and net cash provided by financing activities is positive. During the growth stage, net cash provided by operating activities becomes positive but is still not sufficient to meet investing needs. During the maturity stage, net cash provided by operating activities exceeds investing needs, so the company begins to retire debt. During the decline stage, net cash provided by operating activities is reduced, net cash provided by investing activities becomes positive (from selling off assets), and net cash provided by financing activities becomes more negative.

Free cash flow indicates the amount of cash a company generated during the current year that is available for the payment of dividends or for expansion.

***4 Prepare a statement of cash flows using the direct method.** The preparation of the statement of cash flows involves three major steps. (1) Determine net cash provided/used by operating activities by converting net income from an accrual basis to a cash basis. (2) Analyze changes in noncurrent asset and liability accounts and record as investing and financing activities, or disclose as noncash transactions. (3) Compare the net change in cash on the statement of cash flows with the change in the Cash account reported on the balance sheet to make sure the amounts agree. The direct method reports cash receipts less cash payments to arrive at net cash provided by operating activities.

***5 Use the T-account approach to prepare a statement of cash flows.** To use T-accounts to prepare the statement of cash flows: (1) prepare a large Cash T-account with sections for operating, investing, and financing activities; (2) prepare smaller T-accounts for all other noncash accounts; (3) insert beginning and ending balances for all accounts; and (4) follows the steps in Illustration 12-3 (page 596), entering debit and credit amounts as needed.

DECISION TOOLS REVIEW

DECISION CHECKPOINTS	INFO NEEDED FOR DECISION	TOOL TO USE FOR DECISION	HOW TO EVALUATE RESULTS
How much cash did the company generate to either expand operations or pay dividends?	Net cash provided by operating activities, cash spent on fixed assets, and cash dividends	Free cash flow = Net cash provided by operating activities − Capital expenditures − Cash dividends	Significant free cash flow indicates greater potential to finance new investment and pay additional dividends.

▶ GLOSSARY REVIEW

Direct method A method of determining net cash provided by operating activities by adjusting each item in the income statement from the accrual basis to the cash basis. The direct method shows operating cash receipts and payments. (p. 596).

Financing activities Cash flow activities that include (a) obtaining cash from issuing debt and repaying the amounts borrowed and (b) obtaining cash from stockholders, repurchasing shares, and paying dividends. (p. 592).

Free cash flow Net cash provided by operating activities after adjusting for capital expenditures and cash dividends paid. (p. 609).

Indirect method A method of preparing a statement of cash flows in which net income is adjusted for items that do not affect cash, to determine net cash provided by operating activities. (p. 596).

Investing activities Cash flow activities that include (a) transactions that involve the purchase or disposal of investments and property, plant, and equipment using cash, and (b) lending money and collecting the loans. (p. 592).

Operating activities Cash flow activities that include the cash effects of transactions that create revenues and expenses and thus enter into the determination of net income. (p. 592).

Product life cycle A series of phases in a product's sales and cash flows over time. These phases, in order of occurrence, are introductory, growth, maturity, and decline. (p. 607).

Statement of cash flows A basic financial statement that provides information about the cash receipts and cash payments of an entity during a period, classified as operating, investing, and financing activities, in a format that reconciles the beginning and ending cash balances. (p. 592).

▶ PRACTICE MULTIPLE-CHOICE QUESTIONS

(LO 1) 1. Which of the following is **incorrect** about the statement of cash flows?
(a) It is a fourth basic financial statement.
(b) It provides information about cash receipts and cash payments of an entity during a period.
(c) It reconciles the ending cash account balance to the balance per the bank statement.
(d) It provides information about the operating, investing, and financing activities of the business.

(LO 1) **2.** Which of the following will **not** be reported in the statement of cash flows?
(a) The net change in stockholders' equity during the year.
(b) Cash payments for plant assets during the year.
(c) Cash receipts from sales of plant assets during the year.
(d) Sources of financing during the period.

(LO 1) **3.** The statement of cash flows classifies cash receipts and cash payments by these activities:
(a) operating and nonoperating.
(b) operating, investing, and financing.
(c) financing, operating, and nonoperating.
(d) investing, financing, and nonoperating.

(LO 1) **4.** Which is an example of a cash flow from an operating activity?
(a) Payment of cash to lenders for interest.
(b) Receipt of cash from the sale of common stock.
(c) Payment of cash dividends to the company's stockholders.
(d) None of the above.

(LO 1) **5.** Which is an example of a cash flow from an investing activity?
(a) Receipt of cash from the issuance of bonds payable.
(b) Payment of cash to repurchase outstanding common stock.
(c) Receipt of cash from the sale of equipment.
(d) Payment of cash to suppliers for inventory.

(LO 1) **6.** Cash dividends paid to stockholders are classified on the statement of cash flows as:
(a) operating activities.
(b) investing activities.
(c) a combination of (a) and (b).
(d) financing activities.

(LO 1) **7.** Which is an example of a cash flow from a financing activity?
(a) Receipt of cash from sale of land.
(b) Issuance of debt for cash.
(c) Purchase of equipment for cash.
(d) None of the above

(LO 1) **8.** Which of the following is **incorrect** about the statement of cash flows?
(a) The direct method may be used to report net cash provided by operating activities.
(b) The statement shows the net cash provided (used) for three categories of activity.
(c) The operating activities section is the last section of the statement.
(d) The indirect method may be used to report net cash provided by operating activities.

Use the indirect method to solve Questions 9 through 11.

(LO 2) **9.** Net income is $132,000, accounts payable increased $10,000 during the year, inventory decreased $6,000 during the year, and accounts receivable increased $12,000 during the year. Under the indirect method, what is net cash provided by operating activities?
(a) $102,000. (c) $124,000.
(b) $112,000. (d) $136,000.

(LO 2) **10.** Items that are added back to net income in determining net cash provided by operating activities under the indirect method do **not** include:
(a) depreciation expense.
(b) an increase in inventory.
(c) amortization expense.
(d) loss on disposal of equipment.

11. The following data are available for Bill Mack Corporation. (LO 2)

Net income	$200,000
Depreciation expense	40,000
Dividends paid	60,000
Gain on sale of land	10,000
Decrease in accounts receivable	20,000
Decrease in accounts payable	30,000

Net cash provided by operating activities is:
(a) $160,000. (c) $240,000.
(b) $220,000. (d) $280,000.

12. The following are data concerning cash received or paid from various transactions for Orange Peels Corporation. (LO 2)

Sale of land	$100,000
Sale of equipment	50,000
Issuance of common stock	70,000
Purchase of equipment	30,000
Payment of cash dividends	60,000

Net cash provided by investing activities is:
(a) $120,000. (c) $150,000.
(b) $130,000. (d) $190,000.

13. The following data are available for Retique! (LO 2)

Increase in accounts payable	$ 40,000
Increase in bonds payable	100,000
Sale of investment	50,000
Issuance of common stock	60,000
Payment of cash dividends	30,000

Net cash provided by financing activities is:
(a) $90,000. (c) $160,000.
(b) $130,000. (d) $170,000.

14. Free cash flow provides an indication of a company's ability to: (LO 3)
(a) manage inventory.
(b) generate cash to pay dividends.
(c) generate cash to invest in new capital expenditures.
(d) Both (b) and (c).

15. During the introductory phase of a company's life cycle, one would normally expect to see: (LO 3)
(a) negative cash from operations, negative cash from investing, and positive cash from financing.
(b) negative cash from operations, positive cash from investing, and positive cash from financing.
(c) positive cash from operations, negative cash from investing, and negative cash from financing.
(d) positive cash from operations, negative cash from investing, and positive cash from financing.

Use the direct method to solve Questions 16 and 17.

***16.** The beginning balance in accounts receivable is $44,000, the ending balance is $42,000, and sales during the period are $129,000. What are cash receipts from customers? (LO 4)
(a) $127,000. (c) $131,000.
(b) $129,000. (d) $141,000.

***17.** Which of the following items is reported on a statement of cash flows prepared by the direct method? (LO 4)
(a) Loss on disposal of building.
(b) Increase in accounts receivable.
(c) Depreciation expense.
(d) Cash payments to suppliers.

SOLUTIONS

1. **(c)** The statement of cash flows does not reconcile the ending cash balance to the balance per the bank statement. The other choices are true statements.
2. **(a)** The net change in stockholders' equity during the year is not reported in the statement of cash flows. The other choices are true statements.
3. **(b)** Operating, investing, and financing activities are the three classifications of cash receipts and cash payments used in the statement of cash flows. The other choices are therefore incorrect.
4. **(a)** Payment of cash to lenders for interest is an operating activity. The other choices are incorrect because (b) receipt of cash from the sale of common stock is a financing activity, (c) payment of cash dividends to the company's stockholders is a financing activity, and (d) there is a correct answer.
5. **(c)** Receipt of cash from the sale of equipment is an investing activity. The other choices are incorrect because (a) the receipt of cash from the issuance of bonds payable is a financing activity, (b) payment of cash to repurchase outstanding common stock is a financing activity, and (d) payment of cash to suppliers for inventory is an operating activity.
6. **(d)** Cash dividends paid to stockholders are classified as a financing activity, not (a) an operating activity, (b) an investing activity, or (c) a combination of (a) and (b).
7. **(b)** Issuance of debt for cash is a financing activity. The other choices are incorrect because (a) the receipt of cash for the sale of land is an investing activity, (c) the purchase of equipment for cash is an investing activity, and (d) there is a correct answer.
8. **(c)** The operating section of the statement of cash flows is the first, not the last, section of the statement. The other choices are true statements.
9. **(d)** Net cash provided by operating activities is computed by adjusting net income for the changes in the three current asset/current liability accounts listed. An increase in accounts payable ($10,000) and a decrease in inventory ($6,000) are added to net income ($132,000), while an increase in accounts receivable ($12,000) is subtracted from net income, or $132,000 + $10,000 + $6,000 − $12,000 = $136,000, not (a) $102,000, (b) $112,000, or (c) $124,000.
10. **(b)** An increase in inventory is subtracted, not added, to net income in determining net cash provided by operating activities. The other choices are incorrect because (a) depreciation expense, (c) amortization expense, and (d) loss on disposal of equipment are all added back to net income in determining net cash provided by operating activities.
11. **(b)** Net cash provided by operating activities is $220,000 (Net income $200,000 + Depreciation expense $40,000 − Gain on disposal of land $10,000 + Decrease in accounts receivable $20,000 − Decrease in accounts payable $30,000), not (a) $160,000, (c) $240,000, or (d) $280,000.
12. **(a)** Net cash provided by investing activities is $120,000 (Sale of land $100,000 + Sale of equipment $50,000 − Purchase of equipment $30,000), not (b) $130,000, (c) $150,000, or (d) $190,000. Issuance of common stock and payment of cash dividends are financing activities.
13. **(b)** Net cash provided by financing activities is $130,000 (Increase in bonds payable $100,000 + Issuance of common stock $60,000 − Payment of cash dividends $30,000), not (a) $90,000, (c) $160,000, or (d) $170,000. Increase in accounts payable is an operating activity, and sale of investment is an investing activity.
14. **(d)** Free cash flow provides an indication of a company's ability to generate cash to pay dividends and to invest in new capital expenditures. Choice (a) is incorrect because other measures besides free cash flow provide the best measure of a company's ability to manage inventory. Choices (b) and (c) are true statements, but (d) is the better answer.
15. **(a)** During the introductory phase of a company's life cycle, the company will most likely finance its operations and investing activities through borrowing or the issuance of stock. This means negative cash from operations and investing, and positive cash from financing. The other choices are incorrect because during the introductory phase of a company's life cycle, the company will most likely (b) purchase long-term assets which requires a cash outflow, (c) finance its operations and investing activities through borrowing or the issuance of stock which generates cash inflows from financing, and (d) use cash to fund operations until it establishes a customer base.

*16. **(c)** Cash receipts from customers amount to $131,000 ($129,000 + $2,000). The other choices are therefore incorrect.

*17. **(d)** Cash payments to suppliers are reported on a statement of cash flows prepared by the direct method. The other choices are incorrect because (a) loss on disposal of building, (b) increase in accounts receivable, and (c) depreciation expense are reported in the operating activities section of the statement of cash flows when the indirect, not direct, method is used.

PRACTICE EXERCISES

Prepare journal entries to determine effect on statement of cash flows.

(LO 2)

1. Furst Corporation had the following transactions.
   1. Paid salaries of $14,000.
   2. Issued 1,000 shares of $1 par value common stock for equipment worth $16,000.
   3. Sold equipment (cost $10,000, accumulated depreciation $6,000) for $3,000.

4. Sold land (cost $12,000) for $16,000.
5. Issued another 1,000 shares of $1 par value common stock for $18,000.
6. Recorded depreciation of $20,000.

INSTRUCTIONS

For each transaction above, (a) prepare the journal entry and (b) indicate how it would affect the statement of cash flows. Assume the indirect method.

SOLUTION

1\. 1. (a)

Account	Debit	Credit
Salaries and Wages Expense	14,000	
Cash		14,000

(b) Salaries and wages expense is not reported separately on the statement of cash flows. It is part of the computation of net income in the income statement and is included in the net income amount on the statement of cash flows.

2\. (a)

Account	Debit	Credit
Equipment	16,000	
Common Stock		1,000
Paid-in Capital in Excess of Par—Common Stock		15,000

(b) The issuance of common stock for equipment ($16,000) is reported as a noncash financing and investing activity at the bottom of the statement of cash flows.

3\. (a)

Account	Debit	Credit
Cash	3,000	
Loss on Disposal of Plant Assets	1,000	
Accumulated Depreciation—Equipment	6,000	
Equipment		10,000

(b) The cash receipt ($3,000) is reported in the investing section. The loss ($1,000) is added to net income in the operating section.

4\. (a)

Account	Debit	Credit
Cash	16,000	
Land		12,000
Gain on Disposal of Plant Assets		4,000

(b) The cash receipt ($16,000) is reported in the investing section. The gain ($4,000) is deducted from net income in the operating section.

5\. (a)

Account	Debit	Credit
Cash	18,000	
Common Stock		1,000
Paid-in Capital in Excess of Par—Common Stock		17,000

(b) The cash receipt ($18,000) is reported in the financing section.

6\. (a)

Account	Debit	Credit
Depreciation Expense	20,000	
Accumulated Depreciation—Equipment		20,000

(b) Depreciation expense ($20,000) is added to net income in the operating section.

Prepare statement of cash flows and compute free cash flow.
(LO 2, 3)

2. Strong Corporation's comparative balance sheets are presented below.

STRONG CORPORATION
Comparative Balance Sheets
December 31

	2017	2016
Cash	$ 28,200	$ 17,700
Accounts receivable	24,200	22,300
Investments	23,000	16,000
Equipment	60,000	70,000
Accumulated depreciation—equipment	(14,000)	(10,000)
Total	$ 121,400	$ 116,000
Accounts payable	$ 19,600	$ 11,100
Bonds payable	10,000	30,000
Common stock	60,000	45,000
Retained earnings	31,800	29,900
Total	$ 121,400	$ 116,000

Additional information:

1. Net income was $28,300. Dividends declared and paid were $26,400.
2. Equipment which cost $10,000 and had accumulated depreciation of $1,200 was sold for $4,300.
3. All other changes in noncurrent account balances had a direct effect on cash flows, except the change in accumulated depreciation.

INSTRUCTIONS

(a) Prepare a statement of cash flows for 2017 using the indirect method.

(b) Compute free cash flow.

SOLUTION

2. (a)

STRONG CORPORATION
Statement of Cash Flows
For the Year Ended December 31, 2017

Cash flows from operating activities		
Net income		$ 28,300
Adjustments to reconcile net income to net cash provided by operating activities:		
Depreciation expense	$ 5,200*	
Loss on sale of equipment	4,500**	
Increase in accounts payable	8,500	
Increase in accounts receivable	(1,900)	16,300
Net cash provided by operating activities		44,600
Cash flows from investing activities		
Sale of equipment	4,300	
Purchase of investments	(7,000)	
Net cash used by investing activities		(2,700)
Cash flows from financing activities		
Issuance of common stock	15,000	
Retirement of bonds	(20,000)	
Payment of dividends	(26,400)	
Net cash used by financing activities		(31,400)
Net increase in cash		10,500
Cash at beginning of period		17,700
Cash at end of period		$ 28,200

*[$14,000 – ($10,000 – $1,200)]; **[$4,300 – ($10,000 – $1,200)]

(b) $44,600 – $0 – $26,400 = $18,200

▶ PRACTICE PROBLEM

Prepare statement of cash flows using indirect and direct methods.

(LO 2, 4)

The income statement for Kosinski Manufacturing Company contains the following condensed information.

KOSINSKI MANUFACTURING COMPANY
Income Statement
For the Year Ended December 31, 2017

Sales revenue		$6,583,000
Cost of goods sold	$2,810,000	
Operating expenses, excluding depreciation	2,086,000	
Depreciation expense	880,000	
Loss on disposal of equipment	24,000	5,800,000
Income before income taxes		783,000
Income tax expense		353,000
Net income		$ 430,000

The $24,000 loss resulting from the sale of machinery resulted from selling equipment for $270,000 cash. Machinery was purchased at a cost of $750,000. The following balances are reported on Kosinski's comparative balance sheets at December 31.

	2017	2016
Cash	$672,000	$130,000
Accounts receivable	775,000	610,000
Inventory	834,000	867,000
Accounts payable	521,000	501,000

Income tax expense of $353,000 represents the amount paid in 2017. Dividends declared and paid in 2017 totaled $200,000.

INSTRUCTIONS

(a) Prepare the statement of cash flows using the indirect method.
*(b) Prepare the statement of cash flows using the direct method.

SOLUTION

(a)

KOSINSKI MANUFACTURING COMPANY
Statement of Cash Flows—Indirect Method
For the Year Ended December 31, 2017

Cash flows from operating activities		
Net income		$ 430,000
Adjustments to reconcile net income to net cash provided by operating activities:		
Depreciation expense	$ 880,000	
Loss on disposal of plant assets	24,000	
Increase in accounts receivable	(165,000)	
Decrease in inventory	33,000	
Increase in accounts payable	20,000	792,000
Net cash provided by operating activities		1,222,000
Cash flows from investing activities		
Sale of machinery	270,000	
Purchase of machinery	(750,000)	
Net cash used by investing activities		(480,000)
Cash flows from financing activities		
Payment of cash dividends	(200,000)	
Net cash used by financing activities		(200,000)
Net increase in cash		542,000
Cash at beginning of period		130,000
Cash at end of period		$ 672,000

*(b)

KOSINSKI MANUFACTURING COMPANY
Statement of Cash Flows—Direct Method
For the Year Ended December 31, 2017

Cash flows from operating activities		
Cash collections from customers		$6,418,000*
Cash payments:		
To suppliers	$2,757,000**	
For operating expenses	2,086,000	
For income taxes	353,000	5,196,000
Net cash provided by operating activities		1,222,000
Cash flows from investing activities		
Sale of machinery	270,000	
Purchase of machinery	(750,000)	
Net cash used by investing activities		(480,000)

Cash flows from financing activities		
Payment of cash dividends	(200,000)	
Net cash used by financing activities		(200,000)
Net increase in cash		542,000
Cash at beginning of period		130,000
Cash at end of period		$ 672,000

Direct-Method Computations:

*Computation of cash collections from customers:	
Sales revenue per the income statement	$ 6,583,000
Deduct: Increase in accounts receivable	(165,000)
Cash collections from customers	$ 6,418,000
**Computation of cash payments to suppliers	
Cost of goods sold per income statement	$ 2,810,000
Deduct: Decrease in inventories	(33,000)
Deduct: Increase in accounts payable	(20,000)
	$ 2,757,000

WileyPLUS Brief Exercises, DO IT! Exercises, Exercises, Problems, and many additional resources are available for practice in WileyPLUS.

NOTE: All asterisked Questions, Exercises, and Problems relate to material in the appendices to the chapter.

QUESTIONS

1. (a) What is a statement of cash flows?
   (b) Pat Marx maintains that the statement of cash flows is an optional financial statement. Do you agree? Explain.
2. What questions about cash are answered by the statement of cash flows?
3. Distinguish among the three activities reported in the statement of cash flows.
4. (a) What are the sources (inflows) of cash in a statement of cash flows?
   (b) What are the uses (outflows) of cash?
5. Why is it important to disclose certain noncash transactions? How should they be disclosed?
6. Helen Powell and Paul Tang were discussing the format of the statement of cash flows of Baumgarten Co. At the bottom of Baumgarten's statement of cash flows was a separate section entitled "Noncash investing and financing activities." Give three examples of significant noncash transactions that would be reported in this section.
7. Why is it necessary to use comparative balance sheets, a current income statement, and certain transaction data in preparing a statement of cash flows?
8. Contrast the advantages and disadvantages of the direct and indirect methods of preparing the statement of cash flows. Are both methods acceptable? Which method is preferred by the FASB? Which method is more popular?
9. When the total cash inflows exceed the total cash outflows in the statement of cash flows, how and where is this excess identified?
10. Describe the indirect method for determining net cash provided (used) by operating activities.
11. Why is it necessary to convert accrual-basis net income to cash-basis net income when preparing a statement of cash flows?
12. The president of Murquery Company is puzzled. During the last year, the company experienced a net loss of $800,000, yet its cash increased $300,000 during the same period of time. Explain to the president how this could occur.
13. Identify five items that are adjustments to convert net income to net cash provided by operating activities under the indirect method.
14. Why and how is depreciation expense reported in a statement of cash flows prepared using the indirect method?
15. Why is the statement of cash flows useful?
16. During 2017, Slivowitz Company exchanged $1,700,000 of its common stock for land. Indicate how the transaction would be reported on a statement of cash flows, if at all.
17. (a) What are the phases of the corporate life cycle?
    (b) What effect does each phase have on the amounts reported in a statement of cash flows?

18. Based on its statement of cash flows, in what stage of the product life cycle is Apple?

*19. Describe the direct method for determining net cash provided by operating activities.

*20. Give the formulas under the direct method for computing (a) cash receipts from customers and (b) cash payments to suppliers.

*21. Harbinger Inc. reported sales of $2 million for 2017. Accounts receivable decreased $150,000 and accounts payable increased $300,000. Compute cash receipts from customers, assuming that the receivable and payable transactions are related to operations.

*22. In the direct method, why is depreciation expense not reported in the cash flows from operating activities section?

BRIEF EXERCISES

Indicate statement presentation of selected transactions.

(LO 1), K

BE12-1 Each of these items must be considered in preparing a statement of cash flows for Irvin Co. for the year ended December 31, 2017. For each item, state how it should be shown in the statement of cash flows for 2017.

(a) Issued bonds for $200,000 cash.
(b) Purchased equipment for $180,000 cash.
(c) Sold land costing $20,000 for $20,000 cash.
(d) Declared and paid a $50,000 cash dividend.

Classify items by activities.

(LO 1), C

BE12-2 Classify each item as an operating, investing, or financing activity. Assume all items involve cash unless there is information to the contrary.

(a) Purchase of equipment.
(b) Sale of building.
(c) Redemption of bonds.
(d) Cash received from sale of goods.
(e) Payment of dividends.
(f) Issuance of capital stock.

Identify financing activity transactions.

(LO 1), AP

BE12-3 The following T-account is a summary of the Cash account of Alixon Company.

Cash (Summary Form)

Balance, Jan. 1	8,000		
Receipts from customers	364,000	Payments for goods	200,000
Dividends on stock investments	6,000	Payments for operating expenses	140,000
Proceeds from sale of equipment	36,000	Interest paid	10,000
Proceeds from issuance of		Taxes paid	8,000
bonds payable	300,000	Dividends paid	40,000
Balance, Dec. 31	316,000		

What amount of net cash provided (used) by financing activities should be reported in the statement of cash flows?

Compute net cash provided by operating activities—indirect method.

(LO 2), AP

BE12-4 Miguel, Inc. reported net income of $2.5 million in 2017. Depreciation for the year was $160,000, accounts receivable decreased $350,000, and accounts payable decreased $280,000. Compute net cash provided by operating activities using the indirect approach.

Compute net cash provided by operating activities—indirect method.

(LO 2), AP

BE12-5 The net income for Mongan Co. for 2017 was $280,000. For 2017, depreciation on plant assets was $70,000, and the company incurred a loss on disposal of plant assets of $28,000. Compute net cash provided by operating activities under the indirect method, assuming there were no other changes in the company's accounts.

Compute net cash provided by operating activities—indirect method.

(LO 2), AP

BE12-6 The comparative balance sheets for Gale Company show these changes in noncash current asset accounts: accounts receivable decreased $80,000, prepaid expenses increased $28,000, and inventories increased $40,000. Compute net cash provided by operating activities using the indirect method, assuming that net income is $186,000.

Determine cash received from sale of equipment.

(LO 2), AN

BE12-7 The T-accounts for Equipment and the related Accumulated Depreciation—Equipment for Goldstone Company at the end of 2017 are shown here.

Equipment

Beg. bal.	80,000	Disposals	22,000
Acquisitions	41,600		
End. bal.	99,600		

Accum. Depr.—Equipment

Disposals	5,100	Beg. bal.	44,500
		Depr. exp.	12,000
		End. bal.	51,400

In addition, Goldstone's income statement reported a loss on the disposal of plant assets of $3,500. What amount was reported on the statement of cash flows as "cash flow from sale of equipment"?

BE12-8

(a) Why is net cash provided by operating activities likely to be lower than reported net income during the growth phase?

(b) Why is net cash from investing activities often positive during the late maturity phase and during the decline phase?

Answer questions related to the phases of product life cycle.

(LO 3), C

BE12-9 Suppose during 2017 that Cypress Semiconductor Corporation reported net cash provided by operating activities of $89,303,000, cash used in investing of $43,126,000, and cash used in financing of $7,368,000. In addition, cash spent for fixed assets during the period was $25,823,000. No dividends were paid. Calculate free cash flow.

Calculate free cash flow.

(LO 3), AP

BE12-10 Sprouts Corporation reported net cash provided by operating activities of $412,000, net cash used by investing activities of $250,000, and net cash provided by financing activities of $70,000. In addition, cash spent for capital assets during the period was $200,000. No dividends were paid. Calculate free cash flow.

Calculate free cash flow.

(LO 3), AP

BE12-11 Suppose Canwest Global Communications Corp. reported net cash used by operating activities of $104,539,000 and sales revenue of $2,867,459,000 during 2017. Cash spent on plant asset additions during the year was $79,330,000. Calculate free cash flow.

Calculate free cash flow.

(LO 3), AP

BE12-12 The management of Uhuru Inc. is trying to decide whether it can increase its dividend. During the current year, it reported net income of $875,000. It had net cash provided by operating activities of $734,000, paid cash dividends of $92,000, and had capital expenditures of $310,000. Compute the company's free cash flow, and discuss whether an increase in the dividend appears warranted. What other factors should be considered?

Calculate and analyze free cash flow.

(LO 3), AN

***BE12-13** Suppose Columbia Sportswear Company had accounts receivable of $299,585,000 at January 1, 2017, and $226,548,000 at December 31, 2017. Assume sales revenue was $1,244,023,000 for the year 2017. What is the amount of cash receipts from customers in 2017?

Compute receipts from customers—direct method.

(LO 4), AP

***BE12-14** Hoffman Corporation reported income taxes of $370,000,000 on its 2017 income statement and income taxes payable of $277,000,000 at December 31, 2016, and $528,000,000 at December 31, 2017. What amount of cash payments were made for income taxes during 2017?

Compute cash payments for income taxes—direct method.

(LO 4), AP

***BE12-15** Pietr Corporation reports operating expenses of $90,000, excluding depreciation expense of $15,000, for 2017. During the year, prepaid expenses decreased $7,200 and accrued expenses payable increased $4,400. Compute the cash payments for operating expenses in 2017.

Compute cash payments for operating expenses—direct method.

(LO 4), AP

DO IT! EXERCISES

DO IT! 12-1 Moss Corporation had the following transactions.

1. Issued $160,000 of bonds payable.
2. Paid utilities expense.
3. Issued 500 shares of preferred stock for $45,000.
4. Sold land and a building for $250,000.
5. Loaned $30,000 to Dead End Corporation, receiving Dead End's 1-year, 12% note.

Classify each of these transactions by type of cash flow activity (operating, investing, or financing). (*Hint:* Refer to Illustration 12-1.)

Classify transactions by type of cash flow activity.

(LO 1), C

DO IT! 12-2a PK Photography reported net income of $100,000 for 2017. Included in the income statement were depreciation expense of $6,300, patent amortization expense of $4,000, and a gain on disposal of plant assets of $3,600. PK's comparative balance sheets show the following balances.

	12/31/17	12/31/16
Accounts receivable	$21,000	$27,000
Accounts payable	9,200	6,000

Calculate net cash provided by operating activities for PK Photography.

Calculate net cash from operating activities.

(LO 2), AP

Prepare statement of cash flows—indirect method.

(LO 2), AP

DO IT! 12-2b Alex Company reported the following information for 2017.

ALEX COMPANY
Comparative Balance Sheets
December 31

Assets	**2017**	**2016**	**Change Increase/Decrease**
Cash	$ 59,000	$ 36,000	$ 23,000 Increase
Accounts receivable	62,000	22,000	40,000 Increase
Inventory	44,000	–0–	44,000 Increase
Prepaid expenses	6,000	4,000	2,000 Increase
Land	55,000	70,000	15,000 Decrease
Buildings	200,000	200,000	–0–
Accumulated depreciation—buildings	(21,000)	(14,000)	7,000 Increase
Equipment	183,000	68,000	115,000 Increase
Accumulated depreciation—equipment	(28,000)	(10,000)	18,000 Increase
Totals	$560,000	$376,000	
Liabilities and Stockholders' Equity			
Accounts payable	$ 43,000	$ 40,000	$ 3,000 Increase
Accrued expenses payable	–0–	10,000	10,000 Decrease
Bonds payable	100,000	150,000	50,000 Decrease
Common stock ($1 par)	230,000	60,000	170,000 Increase
Retained earnings	187,000	116,000	71,000 Increase
Totals	$560,000	$376,000	

ALEX COMPANY
Income Statement
For the Year Ended December 31, 2017

Sales revenue		$941,000
Cost of goods sold	$475,000	
Operating expenses	231,000	
Interest expense	12,000	
Loss on disposal of equipment	2,000	720,000
Income before income taxes		221,000
Income tax expense		65,000
Net income		$156,000

Additional information:

1. Operating expenses include depreciation expense of $40,000.
2. Land was sold at its book value for cash.
3. Cash dividends of $85,000 were declared and paid in 2017.
4. Equipment with a cost of $166,000 was purchased for cash. Equipment with a cost of $51,000 and a book value of $36,000 was sold for $34,000 cash.
5. Bonds of $50,000 were redeemed at their face value for cash.
6. Common stock ($1 par) of $170,000 was issued for cash.

Use this information to prepare a statement of cash flows using the indirect method.

Compute and discuss free cash flow.

(LO 3), AP

DO IT! 12-3 Moskow Corporation issued the following statement of cash flows for 2017.

MOSKOW CORPORATION Statement of Cash Flows—Indirect Method For the Year Ended December 31, 2017		
Cash flows from operating activities		
Net income		$ 59,000
Adjustments to reconcile net income to net cash provided by operating activities:		
Depreciation expense	$ 9,100	
Decrease in accounts receivable	9,500	
Increase in inventory	(5,000)	
Decrease in accounts payable	(2,200)	
Loss on disposal of plant assets	3,300	14,700
Net cash provided by operating activities		73,700
Cash flows from investing activities		
Sale of investments	3,100	
Purchase of equipment	(24,200)	
Net cash used by investing activities		(21,100)
Cash flows from financing activities		
Issuance of stock	20,000	
Payment on long-term note payable	(10,000)	
Payment for dividends	(13,000)	
Net cash used by financing activities		(3,000)
Net increase in cash		49,600
Cash at beginning of year		13,000
Cash at end of year		$ 62,600

(a) Compute free cash flow for Moskow Corporation.
(b) Explain why free cash flow often provides better information than "Net cash provided by operating activities."

EXERCISES

Classify transactions by type of activity.

(LO 1), C

E12-1 Kiley Corporation had these transactions during 2017.
(a) Purchased a machine for $30,000, giving a long-term note in exchange.
(b) Issued $50,000 par value common stock for cash.
(c) Issued $200,000 par value common stock upon conversion of bonds having a face value of $200,000.
(d) Declared and paid a cash dividend of $13,000.
(e) Sold a long-term investment with a cost of $15,000 for $15,000 cash.
(f) Collected $16,000 from sale of goods.
(g) Paid $18,000 to suppliers.

Instructions

Analyze the transactions and indicate whether each transaction is an operating activity, investing activity, financing activity, or noncash investing and financing activity.

Classify transactions by type of activity.

(LO 1), C

E12-2 An analysis of comparative balance sheets, the current year's income statement, and the general ledger accounts of Hailey Corp. uncovered the following items. Assume all items involve cash unless there is information to the contrary.
(a) Payment of interest on notes payable.
(b) Exchange of land for patent.
(c) Sale of building at book value.
(d) Payment of dividends.
(e) Depreciation.
(f) Conversion of bonds into common stock.
(g) Receipt of interest on notes receivable.
(h) Issuance of capital stock.
(i) Amortization of patent.
(j) Issuance of bonds for land.
(k) Purchase of land.
(l) Receipt of dividends on investment in stock.
(m) Loss on disposal of plant assets.
(n) Retirement of bonds.

Instructions

Indicate how each item should be classified in the statement of cash flows (indirect method) using these four major classifications: operating activity (that is, the item would be listed among the adjustments to net income to determine net cash provided by operating activities under the indirect method), investing activity, financing activity, or significant noncash investing and financing activity.

Prepare the operating activities section—indirect method.

(LO 2), AP

E12-3 Sosa Company reported net income of $190,000 for 2017. Sosa also reported depreciation expense of $35,000 and a loss of $5,000 on the disposal of plant assets. The comparative balance sheets show an increase in accounts receivable of $15,000 for the year, a $17,000 increase in accounts payable, and a $4,000 increase in prepaid expenses.

Instructions

Prepare the operating activities section of the statement of cash flows for 2017. Use the indirect method.

Prepare the operating activities section—indirect method.

(LO 2), AP

E12-4 The current sections of Sunn Inc.'s balance sheets at December 31, 2016 and 2017, are presented here. Sunn's net income for 2017 was $153,000. Depreciation expense was $27,000.

	2017	2016
Current assets		
Cash	$105,000	$ 99,000
Accounts receivable	80,000	89,000
Inventory	168,000	172,000
Prepaid expenses	27,000	22,000
Total current assets	$380,000	$382,000
Current liabilities		
Accrued expenses payable	$ 15,000	$ 5,000
Accounts payable	85,000	92,000
Total current liabilities	$100,000	$ 97,000

Instructions

Prepare the net cash provided by operating activities section of the company's statement of cash flows for the year ended December 31, 2017, using the indirect method.

Prepare statement of cash flows—indirect method.

(LO 2), AP

E12-5 The following information is available for Stamos Corporation for the year ended December 31, 2017.

Beginning cash balance	$ 45,000
Accounts payable decrease	3,700
Depreciation expense	162,000
Accounts receivable increase	8,200
Inventory increase	11,000
Net income	284,100
Cash received for sale of land at book value	35,000
Cash dividends paid	12,000
Income taxes payable increase	4,700
Cash used to purchase building	289,000
Cash used to purchase treasury stock	26,000
Cash received from issuing bonds	200,000

Instructions

Prepare a statement of cash flows using the indirect method.

Prepare partial statement of cash flows—indirect method.

(LO 2), AN

E12-6 The following three accounts appear in the general ledger of Beiber Corp. during 2017.

Equipment

Date		Debit	Credit	Balance
Jan. 1	Balance			160,000
July 31	Purchase of equipment	70,000		230,000
Sept. 2	Cost of equipment constructed	53,000		283,000
Nov. 10	Cost of equipment sold		49,000	234,000

Accumulated Depreciation—Equipment

Date		Debit	Credit	Balance
Jan. 1	Balance			71,000
Nov. 10	Accumulated depreciation on equipment sold	16,000		55,000
Dec. 31	Depreciation for year		28,000	83,000

Retained Earnings

Date		Debit	Credit	Balance
Jan. 1	Balance			105,000
Aug. 23	Dividends (cash)	14,000		91,000
Dec. 31	Net income		72,000	163,000

Instructions

From the postings in the accounts, indicate how the information is reported on a statement of cash flows using the indirect method. The loss on disposal of plant assets was $8,000. (*Hint:* Cost of equipment constructed is reported in the investing activities section as a decrease in cash of $53,000.)

Prepare a statement of cash flows—indirect method.

(LO 2), AP

E12-7 The following are comparative balance sheets for Mitch Company.

MITCH COMPANY
Comparative Balance Sheets
December 31

Assets	**2017**	**2016**
Cash	$ 68,000	$ 22,000
Accounts receivable	88,000	76,000
Inventory	167,000	189,000
Land	80,000	100,000
Equipment	260,000	200,000
Accumulated depreciation—equipment	(66,000)	(32,000)
Total	$597,000	$555,000

Liabilities and Stockholders' Equity	**2017**	**2016**
Accounts payable	$ 39,000	$ 43,000
Bonds payable	150,000	200,000
Common stock ($1 par)	216,000	174,000
Retained earnings	192,000	138,000
Total	$597,000	$555,000

Additional information:

1. Net income for 2017 was $93,000.
2. Depreciation expense was $34,000.
3. Cash dividends of $39,000 were declared and paid.
4. Bonds payable amounting to $50,000 were redeemed for cash $50,000.
5. Common stock was issued for $42,000 cash.
6. No equipment was sold during 2017.
7. Land was sold for its book value.

Instructions

Prepare a statement of cash flows for 2017 using the indirect method.

Identify phases of product life cycle.

(LO 3), C

E12-8 The information in the table is from the statement of cash flows for a company at four different points in time (M, N, O, and P). Negative values are presented in parentheses.

	Point in Time			
	M	**N**	**O**	**P**
Net cash provided by operating activities	$ (60,000)	$ 30,000	$120,000	$(10,000)
Cash provided by investing activities	(100,000)	25,000	30,000	(40,000)
Cash provided by financing activities	70,000	(90,000)	(50,000)	120,000
Net income	(38,000)	10,000	100,000	(5,000)

Instructions

For each point in time, state whether the company is most likely in the introductory phase, growth phase, maturity phase, or decline phase. In each case, explain your choice.

Compare free cash flow of two companies.

(LO 3), AN

E12-9 Suppose the following is 2017 information for PepsiCo, Inc. and The Coca-Cola Company.

($ in millions)	**PepsiCo**	**Coca-Cola**
Net cash provided by operating activities	$ 6,796	$ 8,186
Average current liabilities	8,772	13,355
Net income	5,979	6,906
Sales revenue	43,232	30,990
Capital expenditures	2,128	1,993
Dividends paid	2,732	3,800

Instructions

Compute free cash flow for both companies and compare.

Compare free cash flow of two companies.

(LO 3), AN

E12-10 Information for two companies in the same industry, Merrill Corporation and Wingate Corporation, is presented here.

	Merrill Corporation	**Wingate Corporation**
Net cash provided by operating activities	$ 80,000	$100,000
Average current liabilities	50,000	100,000
Net income	200,000	200,000
Capital expenditures	40,000	70,000
Dividends paid	5,000	10,000

Instructions

Compute free cash flow for both companies and compare.

Compute cash provided by operating activities—direct method.

(LO 4), AP

***E12-11** Zimmer Company completed its first year of operations on December 31, 2017. Its initial income statement showed that Zimmer had sales revenue of $198,000 and operating expenses of $83,000. Accounts receivable and accounts payable at year-end were $60,000 and $23,000, respectively. Assume that accounts payable related to operating expenses. Ignore income taxes.

Instructions

Compute net cash provided by operating activity using the direct method.

Compute cash payments—direct method.

(LO 4), AP

***E12-12** Suppose the 2017 income statement for McDonald's Corporation shows cost of goods sold $5,178.0 million and operating expenses (including depreciation expense of $1,216.2 million) $10,725.7 million. The comparative balance sheets for the year show that inventory decreased $5.3 million, prepaid expenses increased $42.2 million, accounts payable (merchandise suppliers) increased $15.6 million, and accrued expenses payable increased $199.8 million.

Instructions

Using the direct method, compute (a) cash payments to suppliers and (b) cash payments for operating expenses.

Compute cash flow from operating activities—direct method.

(LO 4), AP

***E12-13** The 2017 accounting records of Megan Transport reveal these transactions and events.

Payment of interest	$ 10,000	Payment of salaries and wages	$ 53,000
Cash sales	48,000	Depreciation expense	16,000
Receipt of dividend revenue	18,000	Proceeds from sale of vehicles	812,000
Payment of income taxes	12,000	Purchase of equipment for cash	22,000
Net income	38,000	Loss on sale of vehicles	3,000
Payment for merchandise	97,000	Payment of dividends	14,000
Payment for land	74,000	Payment of operating expenses	28,000
Collection of accounts receivable	195,000		

Instructions

Prepare the cash flows from operating activities section using the direct method.

***E12-14** The following information is available for Balboa Corp. for 2017.

Prepare statement of cash flows—direct method.

(LO 4), AP

Cash used to purchase treasury stock	$ 48,100
Cash dividends paid	21,800
Cash paid for interest	22,400
Net income	464,300
Sales revenue	802,000
Cash paid for taxes	99,000
Cash received from customers	566,100
Cash received from sale of building (at book value)	197,600
Cash paid for operating expenses	77,000
Beginning cash balance	11,000
Cash paid for goods and services	279,100
Cash received from issuing common stock	355,000
Cash paid to redeem bonds at maturity	200,000
Cash paid to purchase equipment	113,200

Instructions

Prepare a statement of cash flows using the direct method.

***E12-15** The following information is taken from the 2017 general ledger of Preminger Company.

Calculate cash flows—direct method.

(LO 4), AN

Rent	Rent expense	$ 30,000
	Prepaid rent, January 1	5,900
	Prepaid rent, December 31	7,400
Salaries	Salaries and wages expense	$ 54,000
	Salaries and wages payable, January 1	2,000
	Salaries and wages payable, December 31	8,000
Sales	Sales revenue	$160,000
	Accounts receivable, January 1	16,000
	Accounts receivable, December 31	7,000

Instructions

In each case, compute the amount that should be reported in the operating activities section of the statement of cash flows under the direct method.

EXERCISES: SET B AND CHALLENGE EXERCISES

Visit the book's companion website, at **www.wiley.com/college/kimmel**, and choose the Student Companion site to access Exercises: Set B and Challenge Exercises.

PROBLEMS: SET A

P12-1A You are provided with the following information regarding events that occurred at Moore Corporation during 2017 or changes in account balances as of December 31, 2017.

Distinguish among operating, investing, and financing activities.

(LO 1, 2), AP

	(1) Statement of Cash Flow Section Affected	(2) If Operating, Did It Increase or Decrease Reported Cash from Operating Activities?
(a) Depreciation expense was $80,000.		
(b) Interest Payable account increased $5,000.		
(c) Received $26,000 from sale of plant assets.		
(d) Acquired land by issuing common stock to seller.		
(e) Paid $17,000 cash dividend to preferred stockholders.		
(f) Paid $4,000 cash dividend to common stockholders.		
(g) Accounts Receivable account decreased $10,000.		
(h) Inventory increased $2,000.		
(i) Received $100,000 from issuing bonds payable.		
(j) Acquired equipment for $16,000 cash.		

Instructions

Moore prepares its statement of cash flows using the indirect approach. Complete the first column of the table, indicating whether each item affects the operating activities section (O) (that is, the item would be listed among the adjustments to net income to determine net cash provided by operating activities under the indirect approach), investing activities section (I), financing activities section (F), or is a noncash (NC) transaction reported in a separate schedule. For those items classified as operating activities (O), indicate whether the item is added (A) or subtracted (S) from net income to determine net cash provided by operating activities.

Determine cash flow effects of changes in equity accounts.

(LO 2), AN

P12-2A The following account balances relate to the stockholders' equity accounts of Molder Corp. at year-end.

	2017	2016
Common stock, 10,500 and 10,000 shares, respectively, for 2017 and 2016	$160,800	$140,000
Preferred stock, 5,000 shares	125,000	125,000
Retained earnings	300,000	270,000

A small stock dividend was declared and issued in 2017. The market price of the shares was $8,800. Cash dividends were $20,000 in both 2017 and 2016. The common stock has no par or stated value.

Instructions

(a) Net income $58,800

(a) What was the amount of net income reported by Molder Corp. in 2017?
(b) Determine the amounts of any cash inflows or outflows related to the common stock and dividend accounts in 2017.
(c) Indicate where each of the cash inflows or outflows identified in (b) would be classified on the statement of cash flows.

Prepare the operating activities section—indirect method.

(LO 2), AP

P12-3A The income statement of Munsun Company is presented here.

MUNSUN COMPANY
Income Statement
For the Year Ended November 30, 2017

Sales revenue		$7,600,000
Cost of goods sold		
Beginning inventory	$1,900,000	
Purchases	4,400,000	
Goods available for sale	6,300,000	
Ending inventory	1,600,000	
Total cost of goods sold		4,700,000
Gross profit		2,900,000
Operating expenses		
Selling expenses	450,000	
Administrative expenses	700,000	1,150,000
Net income		$1,750,000

Additional information:

1. Accounts receivable decreased $380,000 during the year, and inventory decreased $300,000.
2. Prepaid expenses increased $150,000 during the year.
3. Accounts payable to suppliers of merchandise decreased $350,000 during the year.
4. Accrued expenses payable decreased $100,000 during the year.
5. Administrative expenses include depreciation expense of $110,000.

Instructions

Net cash provided $1,940,000

Prepare the operating activities section of the statement of cash flows for the year ended November 30, 2017, for Munsun Company, using the indirect method.

Prepare the operating activities section—direct method.

(LO 4), AP

Net cash provided—oper. act. $1,940,000

***P12-4A** Data for Munsun Company are presented in P12-3A.

Instructions

Prepare the operating activities section of the statement of cash flows using the direct method.

P12-5A Rewe Company's income statement contained the condensed information below.

Prepare the operating activities section—indirect method.

(LO 2), AP

REWE COMPANY
Income Statement
For the Year Ended December 31, 2017

Service revenue		$970,000
Operating expenses, excluding depreciation	$614,000	
Depreciation expense	55,000	
Loss on disposal of plant assets	16,000	685,000
Income before income taxes		285,000
Income tax expense		56,000
Net income		$229,000

Rewe's balance sheets contained the following comparative data at December 31.

	2017	2016
Accounts receivable	$70,000	$60,000
Accounts payable	41,000	32,000
Income taxes payable	13,000	7,000

Accounts payable pertain to operating expenses.

Instructions

Prepare the operating activities section of the statement of cash flows using the indirect method.

Net cash provided $305,000

***P12-6A** Data for Rewe Company are presented in P12-5A.

Prepare the operating activities section—direct method.

(LO 4), AP

Instructions

Prepare the operating activities section of the statement of cash flows using the direct method.

Net cash provided $305,000

P12-7A Presented below are the financial statements of Warner Company.

Prepare a statement of cash flows—indirect method, and compute free cash flow.

(LO 2, 3), AP

WARNER COMPANY
Comparative Balance Sheets
December 31

Assets	2017	2016
Cash	$ 35,000	$ 20,000
Accounts receivable	20,000	14,000
Inventory	28,000	20,000
Property, plant, and equipment	60,000	78,000
Accumulated depreciation	(32,000)	(24,000)
Total	$111,000	$108,000
Liabilities and Stockholders' Equity		
Accounts payable	$ 19,000	$ 15,000
Income taxes payable	7,000	8,000
Bonds payable	17,000	33,000
Common stock	18,000	14,000
Retained earnings	50,000	38,000
Total	$111,000	$108,000

WARNER COMPANY
Income Statement
For the Year Ended December 31, 2017

Sales revenue		$242,000
Cost of goods sold		175,000
Gross profit		67,000
Selling expenses	$18,000	
Administrative expenses	6,000	24,000
Income from operations		43,000
Interest expense		3,000
Income before income taxes		40,000
Income tax expense		8,000
Net income		$ 32,000

Additional data:

1. Depreciation expense was $17,500.
2. Dividends declared and paid were $20,000.
3. During the year equipment was sold for $8,500 cash. This equipment cost $18,000 originally and had accumulated depreciation of $9,500 at the time of sale.

(a) Net cash provided—oper. act. $38,500

Instructions

(a) Prepare a statement of cash flows using the indirect method.
(b) Compute free cash flow.

Prepare a statement of cash flows—direct method, and compute free cash flow.

(LO 3, 4), AP

(a) Net cash provided—oper. act. $38,500

***P12-8A** Data for Warner Company are presented in P12-7A. Further analysis reveals the following.

1. Accounts payable pertain to merchandise suppliers.
2. All operating expenses except for depreciation were paid in cash.
3. All depreciation expense is in the selling expense category.
4. All sales and purchases are on account.

Instructions

(a) Prepare a statement of cash flows for Warner Company using the direct method.
(b) Compute free cash flow.

Prepare a statement of cash flows—indirect method.

(LO 2), AP

P12-9A Condensed financial data of Granger Inc. follow.

GRANGER INC.
Comparative Balance Sheets
December 31

Assets	**2017**	**2016**
Cash	$ 80,800	$ 48,400
Accounts receivable	87,800	38,000
Inventory	112,500	102,850
Prepaid expenses	28,400	26,000
Long-term investments	138,000	109,000
Plant assets	285,000	242,500
Accumulated depreciation	(50,000)	(52,000)
Total	$682,500	$514,750
Liabilities and Stockholders' Equity		
Accounts payable	$102,000	$ 67,300
Accrued expenses payable	16,500	21,000
Bonds payable	110,000	146,000
Common stock	220,000	175,000
Retained earnings	234,000	105,450
Total	$682,500	$514,750

GRANGER INC.
Income Statement Data
For the Year Ended December 31, 2017

Sales revenue		$388,460
Less:		
Cost of goods sold	$135,460	
Operating expenses, excluding depreciation	12,410	
Depreciation expense	46,500	
Income tax expense	27,280	
Interest expense	4,730	
Loss on disposal of plant assets	7,500	233,880
Net income		$154,580

Additional information:

1. New plant assets costing $100,000 were purchased for cash during the year.
2. Old plant assets having an original cost of $57,500 and accumulated depreciation of $48,500 were sold for $1,500 cash.

3. Bonds payable matured and were paid off at face value for cash.
4. A cash dividend of $26,030 was declared and paid during the year.

Instructions

Prepare a statement of cash flows using the indirect method.

Net cash provided—oper. act. $176,930

***P12-10A** Data for Granger Inc. are presented in P12-9A. Further analysis reveals that accounts payable pertain to merchandise creditors.

Prepare a statement of cash flows—direct method.

(LO 4), AP

Instructions

Prepare a statement of cash flows for Granger Inc. using the direct method.

Net cash provided—oper. act. $176,930

P12-11A The comparative balance sheets for Spicer Company as of December 31 are presented below.

Prepare a statement of cash flows—indirect method.

(LO 2), AP

SPICER COMPANY
Comparative Balance Sheets
December 31

Assets	**2017**	**2016**
Cash	$ 68,000	$ 45,000
Accounts receivable	50,000	58,000
Inventory	151,450	142,000
Prepaid expenses	15,280	21,000
Land	145,000	130,000
Buildings	200,000	200,000
Accumulated depreciation—buildings	(60,000)	(40,000)
Equipment	225,000	155,000
Accumulated depreciation—equipment	(45,000)	(35,000)
Total	$749,730	$676,000
Liabilities and Stockholders' Equity		
Accounts payable	$ 44,730	$ 36,000
Bonds payable	300,000	300,000
Common stock, $1 par	200,000	160,000
Retained earnings	205,000	180,000
Total	$749,730	$676,000

Additional information:

1. Operating expenses include depreciation expense of $42,000.
2. Land was sold for cash at book value.
3. Cash dividends of $12,000 were paid.
4. Net income for 2017 was $37,000.
5. Equipment was purchased for $92,000 cash. In addition, equipment costing $22,000 with a book value of $10,000 was sold for $8,000 cash.
6. 40,000 shares of $1 par value common stock were issued in exchange for land with a fair value of $40,000.

Instructions

Prepare a statement of cash flows for the year ended December 31, 2017, using the indirect method.

Net cash provided—oper. act. $94,000

P12-12A You are provided with the following transactions that took place during the year.

Identify the impact of transactions on free cash flow.

(LO 3), C

Transactions	**Free Cash Flow ($125,000)**
(a) Recorded credit sales $2,500.	
(b) Collected $1,900 owed by customers.	
(c) Paid amount owed to suppliers $2,750.	
(d) Recorded sales returns of $500 and credited the customer's account.	
(e) Purchased new equipment $5,000; signed a long-term note payable for the cost of the equipment.	
(f) Purchased a patent and paid $65,000 cash for the asset.	

Instructions
For each transaction listed, indicate whether it will increase (I), decrease (D), or have no effect (NE) on free cash flow.

PROBLEMS: SET B AND SET C

Visit the book's companion website, at **www.wiley.com/college/kimmel**, and choose the Student Companion site to access Problems: Set B and Set C.

CONTINUING PROBLEM Cookie Creations

© leungchopan/ Shutterstock

(*Note:* This is a continuation of the Cookie Creations problem from Chapters 1 through 11.)

CC12 Natalie has prepared the balance sheet and income statement of Cookie & Coffee Creations Inc. and would like you to prepare the statement of cash flows.

Go to the book's companion website, at **www.wiley.com/college/kimmel**, *to find the completion of this problem.*

EXPAND YOUR CRITICAL THINKING

Financial Reporting

FINANCIAL REPORTING PROBLEM: Apple Inc.

CT12-1 The financial statements of Apple Inc. are presented in Appendix A.

E

Instructions
Answer the following questions.

(a) What was the amount of net cash provided by operating activities for the year ended September 27, 2014? For the year ended September 28, 2013?
(b) What was the amount of increase or decrease in cash and cash equivalents for the year ended September 27, 2014?
(c) Which method of computing net cash provided by operating activities does Apple use?
(d) From your analysis of the September 27, 2014, statement of cash flows, was the change in accounts receivable a decrease or an increase? Was the change in inventories a decrease or an increase? Was the change in accounts payable a decrease or an increase?
(e) What was the net cash used by investing activities for the year ended September 27, 2014?
(f) What was the amount of interest paid in the year ended September 27, 2014? What was the amount of income taxes paid for the same period?

Financial Analysis

COMPARATIVE ANALYSIS PROBLEM: Columbia Sportswear Company vs. VF Corporation

E **CT12-2** Columbia Sportswear Company's financial statements are presented in Appendix B. Financial statements of VF Corporation are presented in Appendix C.

Instructions
(a) Based on the information contained in these financial statements, compute free cash flow for each company.
(b) What conclusions concerning the management of cash can be drawn from these data?

COMPARATIVE ANALYSIS PROBLEM: Amazon.com, Inc. vs. Wal-Mart Stores, Inc.

Financial Analysis

CT12-3 Amazon.com, Inc.'s financial statements are presented in Appendix D. Financial statements of Wal-Mart Stores, Inc. are presented in Appendix E. E

Instructions

(a) Based on the information contained in these financial statements, compute free cash flow for each company.
(b) What conclusions concerning the management of cash can be drawn from these data?

REAL-WORLD FOCUS

CT12-4 ***Purpose:*** Use the Internet to view SEC filings. AN

Address: **biz.yahoo.com/i**

Steps

1. Enter a company's name.
2. Choose **Quote**. Answer questions (a) and (b).
3. Choose **Profile**; then choose **SEC**. Answer questions (c) and (d).

Instructions

Answer the following questions.

(a) What company did you select?
(b) What is its stock symbol? What is its selling price?
(c) What recent SEC filings are available for your viewing?
(d) Which filing is the most recent? What is the date?

CT12-5 The March 4, 2010, edition of the *Wall Street Journal Online* contains an article by Jeffrey McCracken and Tom McGinty entitled "With Fistfuls of Cash, Firms on Hunt." AP

Instructions

Read the article and answer the following questions.

(a) How much cash did the nonfinancial (that is, nonbank-like) firms in the Standard & Poor's 500 have at the end of 2009? How big an increase in cash did this represent over the prior year?
(b) What reasons are given in the article for why companies might not want to keep hoarding cash?
(c) What steps did Alcoa take to try to increase the company's cash? Were these efforts successful?
(d) Often, companies issue shares of stock to acquire other companies. This represents a significant noncash transaction. At the time the article was written, why were many companies using cash rather than stock to acquire other companies?
(e) In addition to acquisitions, what other steps can companies take to reduce their cash balances?

CT12-6 The November 23, 2011, edition of the *Wall Street Journal Online* contains an article by John Jannarone entitled "Backlash from Netflix Buybacks." AP

Instructions

Read the article and answer the following questions.

(a) What was the stock price for the shares of common stock issued by Netflix in the article? What was the price of the stock a few months previously?
(b) Why did Netflix issue new shares at a time when its stock price was so depressed relative to previous valuations for its stock?
(c) What previous actions had Netflix taken to reduce its cash balance?
(d) What does the article say is the lesson that growth companies should learn from the Netflix example?

Financial Analysis

Writing

Group Project

DECISION-MAKING ACROSS THE ORGANIZATION

E **CT12-7** Pete Kent and Maria Robles are examining the following statement of cash flows for Sullivan Company for the year ended January 31, 2017.

SULLIVAN COMPANY
Statement of Cash Flows
For the Year Ended January 31, 2017

Sources of cash	
From sales of merchandise	$385,000
From sale of capital stock	405,000
From sale of investment (purchased below)	80,000
From depreciation	55,000
From issuance of note for truck	20,000
From interest on investments	6,000
Total sources of cash	951,000
Uses of cash	
For purchase of fixtures and equipment	320,000
For merchandise purchased for resale	258,000
For operating expenses (including depreciation)	170,000
For purchase of investment	75,000
For purchase of truck by issuance of note	20,000
For purchase of treasury stock	10,000
For interest on note payable	3,000
Total uses of cash	856,000
Net increase in cash	$ 95,000

Pete claims that Sullivan's statement of cash flows is an excellent portrayal of a superb first year with cash increasing $95,000. Maria replies that it was not a superb first year. Rather, she says, the year was an operating failure, that the statement is presented incorrectly, and that $95,000 is not the actual increase in cash. The cash balance at the beginning of the year was $140,000.

Instructions

With the class divided into groups, answer the following.

(a) Using the data provided, prepare a statement of cash flows in proper form using the indirect method. The only noncash items in the income statement are depreciation and the gain from the sale of the investment.

(b) With whom do you agree, Pete or Maria? Explain your position.

COMMUNICATION ACTIVITY

E **CT12-8** Walt Jax, the owner-president of Computer Services Company, is unfamiliar with the statement of cash flows that you, as his accountant, prepared. He asks for further explanation.

Instructions

Write him a brief memo explaining the form and content of the statement of cash flows as shown in Illustration 12-13 (page 604).

ETHICS CASE

E **CT12-9** Pendleton Automotive Corp. is a medium-sized wholesaler of automotive parts. It has 10 stockholders who have been paid a total of $1 million in cash dividends for 8 consecutive years. The board's policy requires that, for this dividend to be declared, net cash provided by operating activities as reported in Pendleton Automotive's current year's statement of cash flows must exceed $1 million. President and CEO Hans Pfizer's job is secure so long as he produces annual operating cash flows to support the usual dividend.

At the end of the current year, controller Kurt Nolte presents president Hans Pfizer with some disappointing news. The net cash provided by operating activities is calculated by the indirect method to be only $970,000. The president says to Kurt, "We must get that amount above $1 million. Isn't there some way to increase operating cash flow by another $30,000?" Kurt answers, "These figures were prepared by my assistant. I'll go back to my office and see what I can do." The president replies, "I know you won't let me down, Kurt."

Upon close scrutiny of the statement of cash flows, Kurt concludes that he can get the operating cash flows above $1 million by reclassifying a $60,000, 2-year note payable listed in the financing activities section as "Proceeds from bank loan—$60,000." He will report the note instead as "Increase in payables—$60,000" and treat it as an adjustment of net income in the operating activities section. He returns to the president, saying, "You can tell the board to declare their usual dividend. Our net cash flow provided by operating activities is $1,030,000." "Good man, Kurt! I knew I could count on you," exults the president.

Instructions

(a) Who are the stakeholders in this situation?
(b) Was there anything unethical about the president's actions? Was there anything unethical about the controller's actions?
(c) Are the board members or anyone else likely to discover the misclassification?

ALL ABOUT YOU

CT12-10 In this chapter, you learned that companies prepare a statement of cash flows in order to keep track of their sources and uses of cash and to help them plan for their future cash needs. Planning for your own short- and long-term cash needs is every bit as important as it is for a company. E

Instructions

Read the article "Financial 'Uh-oh'? No Problem," at **www.fool.com/personal-finance/saving/financial-uh-oh-no-problem.aspx**, and answer the following questions.

(a) Describe the three factors that determine how much money you should set aside for short-term needs.
(b) How many months of living expenses does the article suggest to set aside?
(c) Estimate how much you should set aside based upon your current situation. Are you closer to Cliff's scenario or to Prudence's?

FASB CODIFICATION ACTIVITY

CT12-11 If your school has a subscription to the FASB Codification, go to **http://aaahq.org/ascLogin.cfm** to log in and prepare responses to the following. Use the Master Glossary to determine the proper definitions. AN

(a) What are cash equivalents?
(b) What are financing activities?
(c) What are investing activities?
(d) What are operating activities?
(e) What is the primary objective for the statement of cash flow? Is working capital the basis for meeting this objective?
(f) Do companies need to disclose information about investing and financing activities that do not affect cash receipts or cash payments? If so, how should such information be disclosed?

A Look at IFRS

LEARNING OBJECTIVE 6

Compare the procedures for the statement of cash flows under GAAP and IFRS.

As in GAAP, the statement of cash flows is a required statement for IFRS. In addition, the content and presentation of an IFRS statement of cash flows is similar to the one used for GAAP. However, the disclosure requirements related to the statement of cash flows are more extensive under GAAP. *IAS 7* ("Cash Flow Statements") provides the overall IFRS requirements for cash flow information.

RELEVANT FACTS

Following are the key similarities and differences between GAAP and IFRS as related to the statement of cash flows.

Similarities

- Companies preparing financial statements under IFRS must also prepare a statement of cash flows as an integral part of the financial statements.
- Both IFRS and GAAP require that the statement of cash flows should have three major sections—operating, investing, and financing activities—along with changes in cash and cash equivalents.
- Similar to GAAP, the statement of cash flows can be prepared using either the indirect or direct method under IFRS. In both U.S. and international settings, companies choose for the most part to use the indirect method for reporting net cash flows from operating activities.
- The definition of cash equivalents used in IFRS is similar to that used in GAAP. A major difference is that in certain situations, bank overdrafts are considered part of cash and cash equivalents under IFRS (which is not the case in GAAP). Under GAAP, bank overdrafts are classified as financing activities in the statement of cash flows and are reported as liabilities on the balance sheet.

Differences

- IFRS requires that noncash investing and financing activities be excluded from the statement of cash flows. Instead, these noncash activities should be reported elsewhere. This requirement is interpreted to mean that noncash investing and financing activities should be disclosed in the notes to the financial statements instead of in the financial statements. Under GAAP, companies may present this information on the face of the statement of cash flows.
- One area where there can be substantial differences between IFRS and GAAP relates to the classification of interest, dividends, and taxes. The following table indicates the differences between the two approaches.

Item	IFRS	GAAP
Interest paid	Operating or financing	Operating
Interest received	Operating or investing	Operating
Dividends paid	Operating or financing	Financing
Dividends received	Operating or investing	Operating
Taxes paid	Operating—unless specific identification with financing or investing activity	Operating

- Under IFRS, some companies present the operating section in a single line item, with a full reconciliation provided in the notes to the financial statements. This presentation is not seen under GAAP.

LOOKING TO THE FUTURE

Presently, the FASB and the IASB are involved in a joint project on the presentation and organization of information in the financial statements. One interesting approach, revealed in a published proposal from that project, is that in the future the income statement and balance sheet would adopt headings similar to those of the statement of cash flows. That is, the income statement and balance sheet would be broken into operating, investing, and financing sections.

IFRS PRACTICE

IFRS SELF-TEST QUESTIONS

1. Under IFRS, interest paid can be reported as:
   (a) only a financing activity.
   (b) a financing activity or an investing activity.
   (c) a financing activity or an operating activity.
   (d) only an operating activity.

2. IFRS requires that noncash items:
   (a) be reported in the section to which they relate, that is, a noncash investing activity would be reported in the investing section.

(b) be disclosed in the notes to the financial statements.
(c) do not need to be reported.
(d) be treated in a fashion similar to cash equivalents.

3. In the future, it appears likely that:
(a) the income statement and balance sheet will have headings of operating, investing, and financing activities, much like the statement of cash flows.
(b) cash and cash equivalents will be combined in a single line item.
(c) the IASB will not allow companies to use the direct approach to the statement of cash flows.
(d) None of the above.

4. Under IFRS:
(a) taxes are always treated as an operating activity.
(b) the income statement uses the headings operating, investing, and financing activities.
(c) dividends received can be either an operating or investing activity.
(d) dividends paid can be either an operating or investing activity.

5. Which of the following is **correct?**
(a) Under IFRS, the statement of cash flows is optional.
(b) IFRS requires use of the direct approach in preparing the statement of cash flows.
(c) The majority of companies following GAAP and the majority following IFRS employ the indirect approach to the statement of cash flows.
(d) Under IFRS, companies offset financing activities against investing activities.

IFRS EXERCISES

IFRS12-1 Discuss the differences that exist in the treatment of bank overdrafts under GAAP and IFRS.

IFRS12-2 Describe the treatment of each of the following items under IFRS versus GAAP.
(a) Interest paid.
(b) Interest received.
(c) Dividends paid.
(d) Dividends received.

INTERNATIONAL FINANCIAL REPORTING PROBLEM: Louis Vuitton

IFRS12-3 The financial statements of Louis Vuitton are presented in Appendix F. Instructions for accessing and using the company's complete annual report, including the notes to its financial statements, are also provided in Appendix F.

Instructions
Use the company's annual report to answer the following questions.

(a) In which section (operating, investing, or financing) does Louis Vuitton report interest paid (finance costs)?
(b) In which section (operating, investing, or financing) does Louis Vuitton report dividends received?
(c) If Louis Vuitton reported under GAAP rather than IFRS, how would its treatment of bank overdrafts differ?

Answers to IFRS Self-Test Questions
1. c **2.** b **3.** a **4.** c **5.** c

13

Financial Analysis: The Big Picture

CHAPTER PREVIEW

We can all learn an important lesson from Warren Buffett: Study companies carefully if you wish to invest. Do not get caught up in fads but instead find companies that are financially healthy. Using some of the basic decision tools presented in this textbook, you can perform a rudimentary analysis on any company and draw basic conclusions about its financial health. Although it would not be wise for you to bet your life savings on a company's stock relying solely on your current level of knowledge, we strongly encourage you to practice your new skills wherever possible. Only with practice will you improve your ability to interpret financial numbers.

Before we unleash you on the world of high finance, we present a few more important concepts and techniques as well as one more comprehensive review of corporate financial statements. We use all of the decision tools presented in this textbook to analyze a single company, with comparisons to a competitor and industry averages.

CHAPTER OUTLINE

LEARNING OBJECTIVES		PRACTICE
1 Apply the concepts of sustainable income and quality of earnings.	• Sustainable income • Quality of earnings	DO IT! 1 Unusual Items
2 Apply horizontal analysis and vertical analysis.	• Horizontal analysis • Vertical analysis	DO IT! 2 Horizontal Analysis
3 Analyze a company's performance using ratio analysis.	• Price-earnings ratio • Liquidity ratios • Solvency ratios • Profitability ratios	DO IT! 3 Ratio Analysis

Go to the ***REVIEW AND PRACTICE*** section at the end of the chapter for a targeted summary and exercises with solutions.

Visit **WileyPLUS** for additional tutorials and practice opportunities.

Daniel Acker/Bloomberg/Getty Images, Inc.

It Pays to Be Patient

A recent issue of *Forbes* magazine listed Warren Buffett as the second richest person in the world. His estimated wealth was $69 billion, give or take a few million. How much is $69 billion? If you invested $69 billion in an investment earning just 4%, you could spend $7.6 million per day—every day—forever.

So, how does Buffett spend his money? Basically, he doesn't! He still lives in the same house that he purchased in Omaha, Nebraska, in 1958 for $31,500. He still drives his own car (a Cadillac DTS). And, in case you were thinking that his kids are riding the road to Easy Street, think again. Buffett has committed to donate virtually all of his money to charity before he dies.

How did Buffett amass this wealth? Through careful investing. Buffett epitomizes a "value investor." He applies the basic techniques he learned in the 1950s from the great value investor Benjamin Graham. He looks for companies that have good long-term potential but are currently underpriced. He invests in companies that have low exposure to debt and that reinvest their earnings for future growth. He does not get caught up in fads or the latest trends.

For example, Buffett sat out on the dot-com mania in the 1990s. When other investors put lots of money into fledgling high-tech firms, Buffett didn't bite because he did not find dot-com companies that met his criteria. He didn't get to enjoy the stock price boom on the way up, but on the other hand, he didn't have to ride the price back down to Earth. When the dot-com bubble burst, everyone else was suffering from investment shock. Buffett swooped in and scooped up deals on companies that he had been following for years.

In 2012, the stock market had again reached near record highs. Buffett's returns had been significantly lagging the market. Only 26% of his investments at that time were in stock, and he was sitting on $38 billion in cash. One commentator noted that "if the past is any guide, just when Buffett seems to look most like a loser, the party is about to end."

If you think you want to follow Buffett's example and transform your humble nest egg into a mountain of cash, be warned. His techniques have been widely circulated and emulated, but never practiced with the same degree of success. You should probably start by honing your financial analysis skills. A good way for you to begin your career as a successful investor is to master the fundamentals of financial analysis discussed in this chapter.

Source: Jason Zweig, "Buffett Is Out of Step," *Wall Street Journal* (May 7, 2012).

LEARNING OBJECTIVE 1

Apply the concepts of sustainable income and quality of earnings.

SUSTAINABLE INCOME

The value of a company like Google is a function of the amount, timing, and uncertainty of its future cash flows. Google's current and past income statements are particularly useful in helping analysts predict these future cash flows. In using this approach, analysts must make sure that Google's past income numbers reflect its **sustainable income**, that is, do not include unusual (out-of-the-ordinary) revenues, expenses, gains, and losses. **Sustainable income** is, therefore, the most likely level of income to be obtained by a company in the future. Sustainable income differs from actual net income by the amount of unusual revenues, expenses, gains, and losses included in the current year's income. Analysts are interested in sustainable income because it helps them derive an estimate of future earnings without the "noise" of unusual items.

Fortunately, an income statement provides information on sustainable income by separating operating transactions from nonoperating transactions. This statement also highlights intermediate components of income such as income from operations, income before income taxes, and income from continuing operations. In addition, information on unusual items such as gains or losses on discontinued items and components of other comprehensive income are disclosed.

Illustration 13-1 presents a statement of comprehensive income for Cruz Company for the year 2017. A statement of comprehensive income includes not only net income but a broader measure of income called comprehensive income. (Recall that in Chapter 5 we instead presented comprehensive income in a separate statement called a comprehensive income statement. Both approaches are allowed under GAAP.) The two major unusual items in this statement are discontinued operations and other comprehensive income (highlighted in red). When estimating future cash flows, analysts must consider the implications of each of these components.

ILLUSTRATION 13-1
Statement of comprehensive income

CRUZ COMPANY Statement of Comprehensive Income For the year ended 2017	
Sales revenue	$900,000
Cost of goods sold	650,000
Gross profit	250,000
Operating expenses	100,000
Income from operations	150,000
Other revenues (expenses) and gains (losses)	20,000
Income before income taxes	170,000
Income tax expense	24,000
Income from continuing operations	146,000
Discontinued operations (net of tax)	**30,000**
Net income	176,000
Other comprehensive income items (net of tax)	**10,000**
Comprehensive income	$186,000

In looking at Illustration 13-1, note that Cruz Company's two major types of unusual items, discontinued operations and other comprehensive income, are reported net of tax. That is, Cruz first calculates income tax expense before income from continuing operations. Then, it calculates income tax expense related to the discontinued operations and other comprehensive income. The general concept is, "Let the tax follow the income or loss." We discuss discontinued operations and other comprehensive income in more detail next.

Discontinued Operations

DECISION TOOLS

The discontinued operations section alerts users to the sale of any of a company's major components of its business.

Discontinued operations refers to the disposal of a **significant component** of a business, such as the elimination of a major class of customers or an entire activity. For example, to downsize its operations, General Dynamics Corp. sold its missile business to Hughes Aircraft Co. for $450 million. In its statement of comprehensive income, General Dynamics reported the sale in a separate section entitled "Discontinued operations."

Following the disposal of a significant component, the company should report on its statement both income from continuing operations and income (or loss) from discontinued operations. **The income (loss) from discontinued operations consists of two parts: the income (loss) from operations** and **the gain (loss) on disposal of the component.**

To illustrate, assume that during 2017 Acro Energy Inc. has income before income taxes of $800,000. During 2017, Acro discontinued and sold its unprofitable chemical division. The loss in 2017 from chemical operations (net of $60,000 taxes) was $140,000. The loss on disposal of the chemical division (net of $30,000 taxes) was $70,000. Assuming a 30% tax rate on income, Illustration 13-2 shows Acro's statement of comprehensive income presentation.

ILLUSTRATION 13-2
Statement presentation of discontinued operations

ACRO ENERGY INC.
Statement of Comprehensive Income (partial)
For the Year Ended December 31, 2017

Income before income taxes		$800,000
Income tax expense		240,000
Income from continuing operations		560,000
Discontinued operations		
Loss from operation of chemical division, net of $60,000 income tax savings	**$140,000**	
Loss from disposal of chemical division, net of $30,000 income tax savings	**70,000**	**210,000**
Net income		$350,000

▼ HELPFUL HINT
Observe the dual disclosures: (1) the results of operation of the discontinued division must be eliminated from the results of continuing operations, and (2) the company must also report the disposal of the division.

Note that the statement uses the caption "Income from continuing operations" and adds a new section "Discontinued operations." **The new section reports both the operating loss and the loss on disposal net of applicable income taxes.** This presentation clearly indicates the separate effects of continuing operations and discontinued operations on net income.

INVESTOR INSIGHT

© Andrey Armyagov/iStockphoto

What Does "Non-Recurring" Really Mean?

Many companies incur restructuring charges as they attempt to reduce costs. They often label these items in the income statement as "non-recurring" charges, to suggest that they are isolated events, unlikely to occur in future periods. The question for analysts is, are these costs really one-time, "non-recurring events" or do they reflect problems that the company will be facing for many periods in the future? If they are one-time events, then they can be largely ignored when trying to predict future earnings.

But, some companies report "one-time" restructuring charges over and over again. For example, Procter & Gamble reported a restructuring charge in 12 consecutive quarters, and Motorola had "special" charges in 14 consecutive quarters. On the other hand, other companies have a restructuring charge only once in a 5- or 10-year period. There appears to be no substitute for careful analysis of the numbers that comprise net income.

If a company takes a large restructuring charge, what is the effect on the company's current income statement versus future ones? (Go to WileyPLUS for this answer and additional questions.)

Comprehensive Income

Most revenues, expenses, gains, and losses are included in net income. However, as discussed in earlier chapters, certain gains and losses that bypass net income are reported as part of a more inclusive earnings measure called comprehensive income. **Comprehensive income** is the sum of net income and other comprehensive income items.[1]

ILLUSTRATION OF COMPREHENSIVE INCOME Accounting standards require that companies adjust most investments in stocks and bonds up or down to their market price at the end of each accounting period. For example, assume that during 2017, its first year of operations, Stassi Corporation purchased IBM stock for $10,000 as an investment. At the end of 2017, Stassi was still holding the investment, but the stock's market price was now $8,000. In this case, Stassi is required to reduce the recorded value of its IBM investment by $2,000. The $2,000 difference is an unrealized loss.

Should Stassi include this $2,000 unrealized loss in net income? It depends on whether Stassi classifies the IBM stock as a trading security or an available-for-sale security. A **trading security** is bought and held primarily for sale in the near term to generate income on short-term price differences. Companies report unrealized losses on trading securities in the "Other expenses and losses" section of the income statement. The rationale: It is likely that the company will realize the unrealized loss (or an unrealized gain), so the company should report the loss (gain) as part of net income.

If Stassi did not purchase the investment for trading purposes, it is classified as available-for-sale. **Available-for-sale securities** are held with the intent of selling them sometime in the future. Companies do not include unrealized gains or losses on available-for-sale securities in net income. Instead, they report them as part of "Other comprehensive income." Other comprehensive income is not included in net income.

FORMAT As shown in Chapter 5, one format for reporting other comprehensive income is to report a separate comprehensive income statement. For example, assuming that Stassi Corporation has a net income of $300,000, the unrealized loss would be reported below net income as follows.

ILLUSTRATION 13-3
Lower portion of combined statement of income and comprehensive income

STASSI CORPORATION
Comprehensive Income Statement
For the Year Ended December 31, 2017

Net income	$300,000
Other comprehensive income	
Unrealized loss on available-for-sale securities	2,000
Comprehensive income	$298,000

As discussed in Chapter 11, companies report the cumulative amount of other comprehensive income from all years as a separate component of stockholders' equity. To illustrate, assume Stassi has common stock of $3,000,000, retained earnings of $300,000, and accumulated other comprehensive loss of $2,000. (To simplify, we are assuming that this is Stassi's first year of operations. Since it has only operated for one year, the cumulative amount of other comprehensive income is this year's loss of $2,000.) Illustration 13-4 shows the balance sheet presentation of the accumulated other comprehensive loss.

[1]The FASB'S Conceptual Framework describes comprehensive income as including all changes in stockholders' equity during a period except those changes resulting from investments by stockholders and distributions to stockholders.

ILLUSTRATION 13-4
Unrealized loss in stockholders' equity section

STASSI CORPORATION Balance Sheet (partial)	
Stockholders' equity	
Common stock	$3,000,000
Retained earnings	300,000
Total paid-in capital and retained earnings	3,300,000
Accumulated other comprehensive loss	**(2,000)**
Total stockholders' equity	$3,298,000

Note that the presentation of the accumulated other comprehensive loss is similar to the presentation of the cost of treasury stock in the stockholders' equity section. (An unrealized gain would be added in this section of the balance sheet.)

COMPLETE STATEMENT OF COMPREHENSIVE INCOME As seen in Illustration 13-1, as an alternative to preparing a separate comprehensive income statement, many companies report net income and other comprehensive income in a combined statement of comprehensive income. (*For your homework in this chapter, use this combined format.*) The statement of comprehensive income for Pace Corporation in Illustration 13-5 presents the types of items found on this statement, such as net sales, cost of goods sold, operating expenses, and income taxes. In addition, it shows how companies report discontinued operations and other comprehensive income (highlighted in red).

ILLUSTRATION 13-5
Complete statement of comprehensive income

PACE CORPORATION Statement of Comprehensive Income For the Year Ended December 31, 2017		
Net sales		$440,000
Cost of goods sold		260,000
Gross profit		180,000
Operating expenses		110,000
Income from operations		70,000
Other revenues and gains		5,600
Other expenses and losses		9,600
Income before income taxes		66,000
Income tax expense ($66,000 × 30%)		19,800
Income from continuing operations		46,200
Discontinued operations		
Loss from operation of plastics division, net of income tax savings $18,000 ($60,000 × 30%)	**$42,000**	
Gain on disposal of plastics division, net of $15,000 income taxes ($50,000 × 30%)	**35,000**	**7,000**
Net income		**39,200**
Other comprehensive income		
Unrealized gain on available-for-sale securities, net of income taxes ($15,000 × 30%)		**10,500**
Comprehensive income		**$ 49,700**

Changes in Accounting Principle

For ease of comparison, users of financial statements expect companies to prepare their statements on a basis **consistent** with the preceding period. A **change in accounting principle** occurs when the principle used in the current year is different from the one used in the preceding year. An example is a change in inventory costing methods (such as FIFO to average-cost). Accounting rules permit a change when management can show that the new principle is preferable to the old principle.

DECISION TOOLS 

Informing users of a change in accounting principle helps them determine the effect of this change on current and prior periods.

Companies report most changes in accounting principle retroactively.[2] That is, they report both the current period and previous periods using the new principle. As a result, the same principle applies in all periods. This treatment improves the ability to compare results across years.

INVESTOR INSIGHT United Parcel Service (UPS)

Larry MacDougal/AP/Wide World Photos

More Frequent Ups and Downs

In the past, U.S. companies used a method to account for their pension plans that smoothed out the gains and losses on their pension portfolios by spreading gains and losses over multiple years. Many felt that this approach was beneficial because it reduced the volatility of reported net income. However, recently some companies have opted to adopt a method that comes closer to recognizing gains and losses in the period in which they occur. Some of the companies that have adopted this approach are United Parcel Service (UPS), Honeywell International, IBM, AT&T, and Verizon Communications. The CFO at UPS said he favored the new approach because "events that occurred in prior years will no longer distort current-year results. It will result in better transparency by eliminating the noise of past plan performance." When UPS switched, it resulted in a charge of $827 million from the change in accounting principle.

Source: Bob Sechler and Doug Cameron, "UPS Alters Pension-Plan Accounting," *Wall Street Journal* (January 30, 2012).

When predicting future earnings, how should analysts treat the one-time charge that results from a switch to the different approach for accounting for pension plans? (Go to WileyPLUS for this answer and additional questions.)

QUALITY OF EARNINGS

The quality of a company's earnings is of extreme importance to analysts. A company that has a high **quality of earnings** provides full and transparent information that will not confuse or mislead users of the financial statements.

Recent accounting scandals suggest that some companies are spending too much time managing their income and not enough time managing their business. Here are some of the factors affecting quality of earnings.

Alternative Accounting Methods

Variations among companies in the application of generally accepted accounting principles may hamper comparability and reduce quality of earnings. For example, suppose one company uses the FIFO method of inventory costing, while another company in the same industry uses LIFO. If inventory is a significant asset to both companies, it is unlikely that their current ratios are comparable. For example, if General Motors Corporation used FIFO instead of LIFO for inventory valuation, its inventories in a recent year would have been 26% higher, which significantly affects the current ratio (and other ratios as well).

In addition to differences in inventory costing methods, differences also exist in reporting such items as depreciation and amortization. Although these differences in accounting methods might be detectable from reading the notes to the financial statements, adjusting the financial data to compensate for the different methods is often difficult, if not impossible.

Pro Forma Income

Companies whose stock is publicly traded are required to present their income statement following generally accepted accounting principles (GAAP). In recent

[2]An exception to the general rule is a change in depreciation methods. The effects of this change are reported in current and future periods. Discussion of this approach is left for more advanced courses.

years, many companies have been also reporting a second measure of income, called pro forma income. **Pro forma income** usually excludes items that the company thinks are unusual or non-recurring. For example, in a recent year, Cisco Systems (a high-tech company) reported a quarterly net loss under GAAP of $2.7 billion. Cisco reported pro forma income for the same quarter as a profit of $230 million. This large difference in profits between GAAP income numbers and pro forma income is not unusual. For example, during one nine-month period, the 100 largest companies on the Nasdaq stock exchange reported a total pro forma income of $19.1 billion but a total loss as measured by GAAP of $82.3 billion—a difference of about $100 billion!

To compute pro forma income, companies generally exclude any items they deem inappropriate for measuring their performance. Many analysts and investors are critical of the practice of using pro forma income because these numbers often make companies look better than they really are. As the financial press noted, pro forma numbers might be called "earnings before bad stuff." Companies, on the other hand, argue that pro forma numbers more clearly indicate sustainable income because they exclude unusual and non-recurring expenses. "Cisco's technique gives readers of financial statements a clear picture of Cisco's normal business activities," the company said in a statement issued in response to questions about its pro forma income accounting.

Recently, the SEC provided some guidance on how companies should present pro forma information. Stay tuned: Everyone seems to agree that pro forma numbers can be useful if they provide insights into determining a company's sustainable income. However, many companies have abused the flexibility that pro forma numbers allow and have used the measure as a way to put their companies in a more favorable light.

Improper Recognition

Because some managers feel pressure from Wall Street to continually increase earnings, they manipulate earnings numbers to meet these expectations. The most common abuse is the improper recognition of revenue. One practice that some companies use is called **channel stuffing**. Offering deep discounts, companies encourage customers to buy early (stuff the channel) rather than later. This boosts earnings in the current period, but it often leads to a disaster in subsequent periods because customers have no need for additional goods. To illustrate, Bristol-Myers Squibb at one time indicated that it used sales incentives to encourage wholesalers to buy more drugs than they needed. As a result, the company had to issue revised financial statements showing corrected revenues and income.

Another practice is the improper capitalization of operating expenses. WorldCom capitalized over $7 billion of operating expenses in order to report positive net income. In other situations, companies fail to report all their liabilities. Enron promised to make payments on certain contracts if financial difficulty developed, but these guarantees were not reported as liabilities. In addition, disclosure was so lacking in transparency that it was impossible to understand what was happening at the company.

DO IT!  1 Unusual Items

In its proposed 2017 income statement, AIR Corporation reports income before income taxes $400,000, unrealized gain on available-for-sale securities $100,000, income taxes $120,000 (not including unusual items), loss from operation of discontinued flower division $50,000, and loss on disposal of discontinued flower division $90,000. The income tax rate is 30%. Prepare a correct statement of comprehensive income, beginning with "Income before income taxes."

Action Plan

✔ Show discontinued operations and other comprehensive income net of tax.

SOLUTION

AIR CORPORATION
Statement of Comprehensive Income (partial)
For the Year Ended December 31, 2017

Income before income taxes		$400,000
Income tax expense		120,000
Income from continuing operations		280,000
Discontinued operations		
Loss from operation of flower division, net of $15,000 income tax savings	$35,000	
Loss on disposal of flower division, net of $27,000 income tax savings	63,000	98,000
Net income		182,000
Other comprehensive income		
Unrealized gain on available-for-sale securities, net of $30,000 income taxes		70,000
Comprehensive income		$252,000

Related exercise material: **BE13-1, BE13-2, DO IT! 13-1, E13-1, and E13-2.**

LEARNING OBJECTIVE 2

Apply horizontal analysis and vertical analysis.

As indicated, in assessing the financial performance of a company, investors are interested in the core or sustainable earnings of a company. In addition, investors are interested in making comparisons from period to period. Throughout this textbook, we have relied on three types of comparisons to improve the decision-usefulness of financial information:

1. **Intracompany basis.** Comparisons within a company are often useful to detect changes in financial relationships and significant trends. For example, a comparison of Kellogg's current year's cash amount with the prior year's cash amount shows either an increase or a decrease. Likewise, a comparison of Kellogg's year-end cash amount with the amount of its total assets at year-end shows the proportion of total assets in the form of cash.
2. **Intercompany basis.** Comparisons with other companies provide insight into a company's competitive position. For example, investors can compare Kellogg's total sales for the year with the total sales of its competitors in the breakfast cereal area, such as General Mills.
3. **Industry averages.** Comparisons with industry averages provide information about a company's relative position within the industry. For example, financial statement readers can compare Kellogg's financial data with the averages for its industry compiled by financial rating organizations such as Dun & Bradstreet, Moody's, and Standard & Poor's, or with information provided on the Internet by organizations such as Yahoo! on its financial site.

INTERNATIONAL NOTE

As more countries adopt IFRS, the ability of analysts to compare companies from different countries should improve. However, IFRSs are open to widely varying interpretations. In addition, some countries adopt IFRS "with modifications." As a consequence, most cross-country comparisons are still not as transparent as within-country comparisons.

We use three basic tools in financial statement analysis to highlight the significance of financial statement data:

1. Horizontal analysis
2. Vertical analysis
3. Ratio analysis

In previous chapters, we relied primarily on ratio analysis, supplemented with some basic horizontal and vertical analysis. In the remainder of this section, we introduce more formal forms of horizontal and vertical analysis. In the next section, we review ratio analysis in some detail.

HORIZONTAL ANALYSIS

DECISION TOOLS

Horizontal analysis helps users compare a company's financial position and operating results with those of the previous period.

Horizontal analysis, also known as trend analysis, is a technique for evaluating a series of financial statement data over a period of time. Its purpose is to determine the increase or decrease that has taken place, expressed as either an amount or a percentage. For example, here are recent net sales figures (in thousands) of Chicago Cereal Company:

2014	2013	2012	2011	2010
$11,776	$10,907	$10,177	$9,614	$8,812

If we assume that 2010 is the base year, we can measure all percentage increases or decreases relative to this base-period amount with the formula shown in Illustration 13-6.

ILLUSTRATION 13-6
Horizontal analysis—computation of changes since base period

$$\text{Change Since Base Period} = \frac{\text{Current-Year Amount} - \text{Base-Year Amount}}{\text{Base-Year Amount}}$$

For example, we can determine that net sales for Chicago Cereal increased approximately 9.1% [($9,614 − $8,812) ÷ $8,812] from 2010 to 2011. Similarly, we can also determine that net sales increased by 33.6% [($11,776 − $8,812) ÷ $8,812] from 2010 to 2014.

Alternatively, we can express current-year sales as a percentage of the base period. To do so, we would divide the current-year amount by the base-year amount, as shown in Illustration 13-7.

ILLUSTRATION 13-7
Horizontal analysis—computation of current year in relation to base year

$$\text{Current Results in Relation to Base Period} = \frac{\text{Current-Year Amount}}{\text{Base-Year Amount}}$$

Current-period sales expressed as a percentage of the base period for each of the five years, using 2010 as the base period, are shown in Illustration 13-8.

ILLUSTRATION 13-8
Horizontal analysis of net sales

CHICAGO CEREAL COMPANY
Net Sales (in thousands)
Base Period 2010

2014	2013	2012	2011	2010
$11,776	$10,907	$10,177	$9,614	$8,812
133.6%	123.8%	115.5%	109.1%	100%

The large increase in net sales during 2011 would raise questions regarding possible reasons for such a significant change. Chicago Cereal's 2011 notes to the financial statements explain that the company completed an acquisition of Elf Foods Company during 2011. This major acquisition would help explain the increase in sales highlighted by horizontal analysis.

To further illustrate horizontal analysis, we use the financial statements of Chicago Cereal Company. Its two-year condensed balance sheets for 2014 and 2013, showing dollar and percentage changes, are presented in Illustration 13-9 (page 656).

ILLUSTRATION 13-9
Horizontal analysis of balance sheets

▼ HELPFUL HINT
When using horizontal analysis, be sure to examine both dollar amount changes and percentage changes. It is not necessarily bad if a company's earnings are growing at a declining rate. The amount of increase may be the same as or more than the base year, but the percentage change may be less because the base is greater each year.

CHICAGO CEREAL COMPANY
Condensed Balance Sheets
December 31 (in thousands)

			Increase (Decrease) during 2014	
Assets	**2014**	**2013**	**Amount**	**Percent**
Current assets	$ 2,717	$ 2,427	$ 290	11.9
Property assets (net)	2,990	2,816	174	6.2
Other assets	5,690	5,471	219	4.0
Total assets	$11,397	$10,714	$683	6.4
Liabilities and Stockholders' Equity				
Current liabilities	$ 4,044	$ 4,020	$ 24	0.6
Long-term liabilities	4,827	4,625	202	4.4
Total liabilities	8,871	8,645	226	2.6
Stockholders' equity				
Common stock	493	397	96	24.2
Retained earnings	3,390	2,584	806	31.2
Treasury stock (cost)	(1,357)	(912)	(445)	48.8
Total stockholders' equity	2,526	2,069	457	22.1
Total liabilities and stockholders' equity	$11,397	$10,714	$ 683	6.4

The comparative balance sheets show that a number of changes occurred in Chicago Cereal's financial position from 2013 to 2014. In the assets section, current assets increased $290,000, or 11.9% ($290 ÷ $2,427), and property assets (net) increased $174,000, or 6.2%. Other assets increased $219,000, or 4.0%. In the liabilities section, current liabilities increased $24,000, or 0.6%, while long-term liabilities increased $202,000, or 4.4%. In the stockholders' equity section, we find that retained earnings increased $806,000, or 31.2%.

Illustration 13-10 presents two-year comparative income statements of Chicago Cereal Company for 2014 and 2013, showing dollar and percentage changes.

ILLUSTRATION 13-10
Horizontal analysis of income statements

▼ HELPFUL HINT
Note that, in a horizontal analysis, while the amount column is additive (the total is $99,000), the percentage column is not additive (9.9% is not a total).

CHICAGO CEREAL COMPANY
Condensed Income Statements
For the Years Ended December 31 (in thousands)

			Increase (Decrease) during 2014	
	2014	**2013**	**Amount**	**Percent**
Net sales	$11,776	$10,907	$869	8.0
Cost of goods sold	6,597	6,082	515	8.5
Gross profit	5,179	4,825	354	7.3
Selling and administrative expenses	3,311	3,059	252	8.2
Income from operations	1,868	1,766	102	5.8
Interest expense	319	307	12	3.9
Other income (expense), net	(2)	13	(15)	(115.4)
Income before income taxes	1,547	1,472	75	5.1
Income tax expense	444	468	(24)	(5.1)
Net income	$ 1,103	$ 1,004	$ 99	9.9

Horizontal analysis of the income statements shows the following changes. Net sales increased $869,000, or 8.0% ($869 ÷ $10,907). Cost of goods sold increased $515,000, or 8.5% ($515 ÷ $6,082). Selling and administrative expenses increased $252,000, or 8.2% ($252 ÷ $3,059). Overall, gross profit increased 7.3% and net income increased 9.9%. The increase in net income can be attributed to the increase in net sales and a decrease in income tax expense.

The measurement of changes from period to period in percentages is relatively straightforward and quite useful. However, complications can result in making the computations. If an item has no value in a base year or preceding year and a value in the next year, no percentage change can be computed. Likewise, no percentage change can be computed if a negative amount appears in the base or preceding period and a positive amount exists the following year.

VERTICAL ANALYSIS

Vertical analysis, also called common-size analysis, is a technique for evaluating financial statement data that expresses each item in a financial statement as a **percentage of a base amount**. For example, on a balance sheet we might express current assets as 22% of total assets (total assets being the base amount). Or, on an income statement we might express selling expenses as 16% of net sales (net sales being the base amount).

DECISION TOOLS

Vertical analysis helps users compare relationships between financial statement items with those of last year or of competitors.

Presented in Illustration 13-11 are the comparative balance sheets of Chicago Cereal for 2014 and 2013, analyzed vertically. The base for the asset items is **total assets**, and the base for the liability and stockholders' equity items is **total liabilities and stockholders' equity**.

ILLUSTRATION 13-11
Vertical analysis of balance sheets

CHICAGO CEREAL COMPANY
Condensed Balance Sheets
December 31 (in thousands)

	2014		2013	
Assets	**Amount**	**Percent***	**Amount**	**Percent***
Current assets	$ 2,717	23.8	$ 2,427	22.6
Property assets (net)	2,990	26.2	2,816	26.3
Other assets	5,690	50.0	5,471	51.1
Total assets	$11,397	100.0	$10,714	100.0
Liabilities and Stockholders' Equity				
Current liabilities	$ 4,044	35.5	$ 4,020	37.5
Long-term liabilities	4,827	42.4	4,625	43.2
Total liabilities	8,871	77.9	8,645	80.7
Stockholders' equity				
Common stock	493	4.3	397	3.7
Retained earnings	3,390	29.7	2,584	24.1
Treasury stock (cost)	(1,357)	(11.9)	(912)	(8.5)
Total stockholders' equity	2,526	22.1	2,069	19.3
Total liabilities and stockholders' equity	$11,397	100.0	$10,714	100.0

*Numbers have been rounded to total 100%.

In addition to showing the relative size of each category on the balance sheets, vertical analysis can show the percentage change in the individual asset, liability, and stockholders' equity items. In this case, current assets increased $290,000 from 2013 to 2014, and they increased from 22.6% to 23.8% of total assets. Property assets (net) decreased from 26.3% to 26.2% of total assets. Other assets decreased from 51.1% to 50.0% of total assets. Also, retained earnings increased by $806,000 from 2013 to 2014, and total stockholders' equity increased from 19.3% to 22.1% of total liabilities and stockholders' equity. This switch to a higher percentage of equity financing has two causes. First, while total liabilities increased by $226,000, the percentage of liabilities declined from 80.7% to 77.9% of total liabilities and stockholders' equity. Second, retained earnings increased by $806,000, from 24.1% to 29.7% of total liabilities and stockholders' equity. Thus, the company shifted toward equity financing by relying less on debt and by increasing the amount of retained earnings.

Vertical analysis of the comparative income statements of Chicago Cereal, shown in Illustration 13-12, reveals that cost of goods sold **as a percentage of net sales** increased from 55.8% to 56.0%, and selling and administrative expenses increased from 28.0% to 28.1%. Net income as a percentage of net sales increased from 9.1% to 9.4%. Chicago Cereal's increase in net income as a percentage of sales is due primarily to the decrease in interest expense and income tax expense as a percentage of sales.

ILLUSTRATION 13-12
Vertical analysis of income statements

CHICAGO CEREAL COMPANY
Condensed Income Statements
For the Years Ended December 31 (in thousands)

	2014		2013	
	Amount	**Percent***	**Amount**	**Percent***
Net sales	$11,776	100.0	$10,907	100.0
Cost of goods sold	6,597	56.0	6,082	55.8
Gross profit	5,179	44.0	4,825	44.2
Selling and administrative expenses	3,311	28.1	3,059	28.0
Income from operations	1,868	15.9	1,766	16.2
Interest expense	319	2.7	307	2.8
Other income (expense), net	(2)	.0	13	.0
Income before income taxes	1,547	13.2	1,472	13.4
Income tax expense	444	3.8	468	4.3
Net income	$ 1,103	9.4	$ 1,004	9.1

*Numbers have been rounded to total 100%.

Vertical analysis also enables you to compare companies of different sizes. For example, one of Chicago Cereal's competitors is General Mills. General Mills' sales are 1,000 times larger than those of Chicago Cereal. Vertical analysis enables us to meaningfully compare the condensed income statements of Chicago Cereal and General Mills, as shown in Illustration 13-13.

ILLUSTRATION 13-13
Intercompany comparison by vertical analysis

CONDENSED INCOME STATEMENTS
For the Years Ended December 31, 2014 (Chicago Cereal), and May 25, 2014 (General Mills)

	Chicago Cereal (in thousands)		General Mills, Inc. (in millions)	
	Amount	**Percent***	**Amount**	**Percent***
Net sales	$11,776	100.0	$17,910	100.0
Cost of goods sold	6,597	56.0	11,540	64.4
Gross profit	5,179	44.0	6,370	35.6
Selling and administrative expenses	3,311	28.1	3,474	19.4
Non-recurring charges and (gains)	0	—	(62)	(0.3)
Income from operations	1,868	15.9	2,958	16.5
Other expenses and revenues (including income taxes)	765	6.5	1,134	6.3
Net income	$ 1,103	9.4	$ 1,824	10.2

*Numbers have been rounded to total 100%.

Although Chicago Cereal's net sales are much less than those of General Mills, vertical analysis eliminates the impact of this size difference for our analysis. Chicago Cereal has a higher gross profit percentage 44.0%, compared to 35.6% for General Mills. But, Chicago Cereal's selling and administrative expenses are 28.1% of net sales, while those of General Mills are 19.4% of net sales. Looking at net income, we see that General Mills' percentage is higher. Chicago Cereal's net income as a percentage of net sales is 9.4%, compared to 10.2% for General Mills.

ANATOMY OF A FRAUD

This final *Anatomy of a Fraud* box demonstrates that sometimes relationships between numbers can be used to detect fraud. Financial ratios that appear abnormal or statistical abnormalities in the numbers themselves can reveal fraud. For example, the fact that WorldCom's line costs, as a percentage of either total expenses or revenues, differed very significantly from its competitors should have alerted people to the possibility of fraud. Or, consider the case of a bank manager, who cooperated with a group of his friends to defraud the bank's credit card department. The manager's friends would apply for credit cards and then run up balances of slightly less than $5,000. The bank had a policy of allowing bank personnel to write-off balances of less than $5,000 without seeking supervisor approval. The fraud was detected by applying statistical analysis based on Benford's Law. Benford's Law states that in a random collection of numbers, the frequency of lower digits (e.g., 1, 2, or 3) should be much higher than higher digits (e.g., 7, 8, or 9). In this case, bank auditors analyzed the first two digits of amounts written off. There was a spike at 48 and 49, which was not consistent with what would be expected if the numbers were random.

Total take: Thousands of dollars

THE MISSING CONTROL

Independent internal verification. While it might be efficient to allow employees to write off accounts below a certain level, it is important that these write-offs be reviewed and verified periodically. Such a review would likely call attention to an employee with large amounts of write-offs, or in this case, write-offs that were frequently very close to the approval threshold.

Source: Mark J. Nigrini, "I've Got Your Number," *Journal of Accountancy Online* (May 1999).

DO IT! 2 Horizontal Analysis

Summary financial information for Rosepatch Company is as follows.

	December 31, 2017	December 31, 2016
Current assets	$234,000	$180,000
Plant assets (net)	756,000	420,000
Total assets	$990,000	$600,000

Compute the amount and percentage changes in 2017 using horizontal analysis, assuming 2016 is the base year.

SOLUTION

	Increase in 2017	
	Amount	Percent
Current assets	$ 54,000	30% [($234,000 − $180,000) ÷ $180,000]
Plant assets (net)	336,000	80% [($756,000 − $420,000) ÷ $420,000]
Total assets	$390,000	65% [($990,000 − $600,000) ÷ $600,000]

Action Plan

✔ Find the percentage change by dividing the amount of the increase by the 2016 amount (base year).

Related exercise material: **BE13-4, BE13-6, BE13-7, BE13-9, DO IT! 13-2, E13-3, E13-5,** and **E13-6.**

LEARNING OBJECTIVE 3

Analyze a company's performance using ratio analysis.

In previous chapters, we presented many ratios used for evaluating the financial health and performance of a company. Here, we introduce one more ratio, the price-earnings ratio, and then we provide a summary listing of all ratios presented in the textbook. (Page references to prior discussions are provided if you feel you need to review any individual ratios.) Appendix 13A provides an example of a comprehensive financial analysis employing these ratios.

PRICE-EARNINGS RATIO

Earnings per share is net income available to common stockholders divided by the average number of common shares outstanding. The market price of a company's stock changes based on investors' expectations about a company's future earnings per share. To compare market prices and earnings across firms, investors calculate the **price-earnings (P-E) ratio**. The P-E ratio divides the market price of a share of common stock by earnings per share.

ILLUSTRATION 13-14
Formula for price-earnings (P-E) ratio

$$\text{Price-Earnings (P-E) Ratio} = \frac{\text{Market Price per Share}}{\text{Earnings per Share}}$$

The P-E ratio reflects investors' assessment of a company's future earnings. The ratio of price to earnings will be higher if investors think that earnings will increase substantially in the future and therefore are willing to pay more per share of stock. A low price-earnings ratio often signifies that investors think the company's future earnings will not be strong. In addition, sometimes a low P-E ratio reflects the market's belief that a company has poor-quality earnings.

To illustrate, assume that two identical companies each have earnings per share of $5. Suppose one of the companies manipulated its accounting numbers to achieve the $5 figure. If investors perceive that firm has lower-quality earnings, this perception will be reflected in a lower stock price and, consequently, a lower P-E.

Illustration 13-15 shows earnings per share and P-E ratios for five companies for a recent year.

ILLUSTRATION 13-15
Earnings per share and P-E ratios of various companies

Company	Earnings per Share	Price-Earnings Ratio
Southwest Airlines	$ 1.65	19.5
Google	29.80	27.0
Apple	6.49	15.6
Skechers USA	2.74	34.0
Nike	3.05	28.7

LIQUIDITY RATIOS

Liquidity ratios (Illustration 13-16) measure the short-term ability of the company to pay its maturing obligations and to meet unexpected needs for cash. Short-term creditors such as bankers and suppliers are particularly interested in assessing liquidity.

ILLUSTRATION 13-16
Summary of liquidity ratios

Liquidity Ratios		
Working capital	Current assets − Current liabilities	p. 54
Current ratio	$\frac{\text{Current assets}}{\text{Current liabilities}}$	p. 54
Inventory turnover	$\frac{\text{Cost of goods sold}}{\text{Average inventory}}$	p. 283
Days in inventory	$\frac{\text{365 days}}{\text{Inventory turnover}}$	p. 283
Accounts receivable turnover	$\frac{\text{Net credit sales}}{\text{Average net accounts receivable}}$	p. 395
Average collection period	$\frac{\text{365 days}}{\text{Accounts receivable turnover}}$	p. 395

INVESTOR INSIGHT

Nova Stock/SuperStock

How to Manage the Current Ratio

The apparent simplicity of the current ratio can have real-world limitations because adding equal amounts to both the numerator and the denominator causes the ratio to decrease.

Assume, for example, that a company has $2,000,000 of current assets and $1,000,000 of current liabilities. Its current ratio is 2:1. If it purchases $1,000,000 of inventory on account, it will have $3,000,000 of current assets and $2,000,000 of current liabilities. Its current ratio decreases to 1.5:1. If, instead, the company pays off $500,000 of its current liabilities, it will have $1,500,000 of current assets and $500,000 of current liabilities. Its current ratio increases to 3:1. Thus, any trend analysis should be done with care because the ratio is susceptible to quick changes and is easily influenced by management.

How might management influence a company's current ratio? (Go to WileyPLUS for this answer and additional questions.)

SOLVENCY RATIOS

Solvency ratios (Illustration 13-17) measure the ability of the company to survive over a long period of time. Long-term creditors and stockholders are interested in a company's long-run solvency, particularly its ability to pay interest as it comes due and to repay the balance of debt at its maturity.

ILLUSTRATION 13-17
Summary of solvency ratios

Solvency Ratios		
Debt to assets ratio	$\frac{\text{Total liabilities}}{\text{Total assets}}$	p. 56
Times interest earned	$\frac{\text{Net income + Interest expense + Income tax expense}}{\text{Interest expense}}$	p. 497
Free cash flow	Net cash provided by operating activities − Capital expenditures − Cash dividends	p. 57

PROFITABILITY RATIOS

Profitability ratios (Illustration 13-18 on page 662) measure the income or operating success of a company for a given period of time. A company's income, or lack of it, affects its ability to obtain debt and equity financing, its liquidity position, and its ability to grow. As a consequence, creditors and investors alike are interested in evaluating profitability. Profitability is frequently used as the ultimate test of management's operating effectiveness.

ILLUSTRATION 13-18
Summary of profitability ratios

Profitability Ratios		
Earnings per share	$\frac{\text{Net income} - \text{Preferred dividends}}{\text{Weighted-average common shares outstanding}}$	p. 53
Price-earnings ratio	$\frac{\text{Market price per share}}{\text{Earnings per share}}$	p. 660
Gross profit rate	$\frac{\text{Gross profit}}{\text{Net sales}}$	p. 234
Profit margin	$\frac{\text{Net income}}{\text{Net sales}}$	p. 235
Return on assets	$\frac{\text{Net income}}{\text{Average total assets}}$	p. 444
Asset turnover	$\frac{\text{Net sales}}{\text{Average total assets}}$	p. 446
Payout ratio	$\frac{\text{Cash dividends declared on common stock}}{\text{Net income}}$	p. 560
Return on common stockholders' equity	$\frac{\text{Net income} - \text{Preferred dividends}}{\text{Average common stockholders' equity}}$	p. 561

INVESTOR INSIGHT

© Ferran Traite Soler/iStockphoto

High Ratings Can Bring Low Returns

Moody's, Standard & Poor's, and Fitch are three big firms that perform financial analysis on publicly traded companies and then publish ratings of the companies' creditworthiness. Investors and lenders rely heavily on these ratings in making investment and lending decisions. Some people feel that the collapse of the financial markets was worsened by inadequate research reports and ratings provided by the financial rating agencies. Critics contend that the rating agencies were reluctant to give large companies low ratings because they feared that by offending them they would lose out on business opportunities. For example, the rating agencies gave many so-called mortgage-backed securities ratings that suggested that they were low risk. Later, many of these very securities became completely worthless. Steps have been taken to reduce the conflicts of interest that lead to these faulty ratings.

Source: Aaron Lucchetti and Judith Burns, "Moody's CEO Warned Profit Push Posed a Risk to Quality of Ratings," *Wall Street Journal Online* (October 23, 2008).

Why are credit rating agencies important to the financial markets? (Go to WileyPLUS for this answer and additional questions.)

DO IT! 3 Ratio Analysis

The condensed financial statements of John Cully Company, for the years ended June 30, 2017 and 2016, are presented on the next page.

JOHN CULLY COMPANY
Balance Sheets
June 30

	(in thousands)	
Assets	**2017**	**2016**
Current assets		
Cash and cash equivalents	$ 553.3	$ 611.6
Accounts receivable (net)	776.6	664.9
Inventory	768.3	653.5
Prepaid expenses and other current assets	204.4	269.2
Total current assets	2,302.6	2,199.2
Investments	12.3	12.6
Property, plant, and equipment (net)	694.2	647.0
Intangibles and other assets	876.7	849.3
Total assets	$3,885.8	$3,708.1
Liabilities and Stockholders' Equity		
Current liabilities	$1,497.7	$1,322.0
Long-term liabilities	679.5	637.1
Stockholders' equity—common	1,708.6	1,749.0
Total liabilities and stockholders' equity	$3,885.8	$3,708.1

JOHN CULLY COMPANY
Income Statements
For the Year Ended June 30

	(in thousands)	
	2017	**2016**
Sales revenue	$6,336.3	$5,790.4
Costs and expenses		
Cost of goods sold	1,617.4	1,476.3
Selling and administrative expenses	4,007.6	3,679.0
Interest expense	13.9	27.1
Total costs and expenses	5,638.9	5,182.4
Income before income taxes	697.4	608.0
Income tax expense	291.3	232.6
Net income	$ 406.1	$ 375.4

Compute the following ratios for 2017 and 2016.

(a) Current ratio.

(b) Inventory turnover. (Inventory on 6/30/15 was $599.0.)

(c) Profit margin.

(d) Return on assets. (Assets on 6/30/15 were $3,349.9.)

(e) Return on common stockholders' equity. (Stockholders' equity on 6/30/15 was $1,795.9.)

(f) Debt to assets ratio.

(g) Times interest earned.

Action Plan

✔ Remember that the current ratio includes all current assets.

✔ Use average balances for turnover ratios like inventory, accounts receivable, and return on assets.

SOLUTION

	2017	2016
(a) Current ratio:		
$2,302.6 ÷ $1,497.7 =	1.5:1	
$2,199.2 ÷ $1,322.0 =		1.7:1
(b) Inventory turnover:		
$1,617.4 ÷ [($768.3 + $653.5) ÷ 2] =	2.3 times	
$1,476.3 ÷ [($653.5 + $599.0) ÷ 2] =		2.4 times
(c) Profit margin:		
$406.1 ÷ $6,336.3 =	6.4%	
$375.4 ÷ $5,790.4 =		6.5%
(d) Return on assets:		
$406.1 ÷ [($3,885.8 + $3,708.1) ÷ 2] =	10.7%	
$375.4 ÷ [($3,708.1 + $3,349.9) ÷ 2] =		10.6%
(e) Return on common stockholders' equity:		
($406.1 − $0) ÷ [($1,708.6 + $1,749.0) ÷ 2] =	23.5%	
($375.4 − $0) ÷ [($1,749.0 + $1,795.9) ÷ 2] =		21.2%
(f) Debt to assets ratio:		
($1,497.7 + $679.5) ÷ $3,885.8 =	56.0%	
($1,322.0 + $637.1) ÷ $3,708.1 =		52.8%
(g) Times interest earned:		
($406.1 + $13.9 + $291.3) ÷ $13.9 =	51.2 times	
($375.4 + $27.1 + $232.6) ÷ $27.1 =		23.4 times

Related exercise material: **BE13-10, BE13-11, BE13-12, BE13-13, BE13-14, BE13-15, DO IT! 13-3, E13-7, E13-8, E13-9, E13-10, E13-11, E13-12,** and **E13-13.**

USING DECISION TOOLS—KELLOGG COMPANY

In analyzing a company, you should always investigate an extended period of time in order to determine whether the condition and performance of the company are changing. The condensed financial statements of Kellogg Company for 2014 and 2013 are presented here.

KELLOGG COMPANY, INC.
Balance Sheets
January 3, 2015, and December 28, 2013
(in millions)

Assets	**2014**	**2013**
Current assets		
Cash	$ 443	$ 273
Accounts receivable (net)	1,276	1,423
Inventories	1,279	1,248
Other current assets	342	323
Total current assets	3,340	3,267
Property (net)	3,769	3,856
Other assets	8,044	8,351
Total assets	$15,153	$15,474
Liabilities and Stockholders' Equity		
Current liabilities	$ 4,364	$ 3,835
Long-term liabilities	7,938	8,032
Stockholders' equity—common	2,851	3,607
Total liabilities and stockholders' equity	$15,153	$15,474

KELLOGG COMPANY, INC.
Condensed Income Statements
For the Years Ended January 3, 2015, and December 28, 2013
(in millions)

	2014	2013
Net sales	$14,580	$14,792
Cost of goods sold	9,517	8,689
Gross profit	5,063	6,103
Selling and administrative expenses	4,039	3,266
Income from operations	1,024	2,837
Interest expense	209	235
Other (income) expense, net	(3)	3
Income before income taxes	818	2,599
Income tax expense	186	792
Net income	$ 632	$ 1,807

INSTRUCTIONS

Compute the following ratios for Kellogg for 2014 and discuss your findings (2013 values are provided for comparison).

1. Liquidity:
   (a) Current ratio (2013: .85:1).
   (b) Inventory turnover (2013: 6.7 times).
2. Solvency:
   (a) Debt to assets ratio (2013: 77%).
   (b) Times interest earned (2013: 12.1 times).
3. Profitability:
   (a) Return on assets (2013: 11.8%).
   (b) Profit margin (2013: 12.2%).
   (c) Return on common stockholders' equity (2013: 60%).

SOLUTION

1. Liquidity
   (a) Current ratio:

$$2014: \frac{\$3,340}{\$4,364} = .77:1 \qquad 2013: \ .85:1$$

   (b) Inventory turnover:

$$2014: \frac{\$9,517}{(\$1,279 + \$1,248)/2} = 7.5 \text{ times} \qquad 2013: \ 6.7 \text{ times}$$

We see that between 2013 and 2014, the current ratio declined, which suggests a decline in liquidity. The inventory turnover increased, which suggests an improvement in liquidity.

2. Solvency
   (a) Debt to assets ratio:

$$2014: \frac{\$4,364 + \$7,938}{\$15,153} = 81\% \qquad 2013: \ 77\%$$

   (b) Times interest earned:

$$2014: \frac{\$632 + \$209 + \$186}{\$209} = 4.9 \text{ times} \qquad 2013: \ 12.1 \text{ times}$$

Kellogg's solvency as measured by the debt to assets ratio decreased in 2014, and its times interest earned declined as well.

3. Profitability

(a) Return on assets:

2014: $\frac{\$632}{(\$15{,}153 + \$15{,}474)/2} = 4.1\%$ 2013: 11.8%

(b) Profit margin:

2014: $\frac{\$632}{\$14{,}580} = 4.3\%$ 2013: 12.2%

(c) Return on common stockholders' equity:

2014: $\frac{\$632}{(\$2{,}851 + \$3{,}607)/2} = 20\%$ 2013: 60%

Kellogg's return on assets declined. Its profit margin and return on stockholders' equity also declined. The company experienced a sharp drop in net income.

LEARNING OBJECTIVE

*4 APPENDIX 13A: Evaluate a company comprehensively using ratio analysis.

In previous chapters, we presented many ratios used for evaluating the financial health and performance of a company. In this appendix, we provide a comprehensive review of those ratios and discuss some important relationships among them. Since earlier chapters demonstrated the calculation of each of these ratios, in this appendix we instead focus on their interpretation. Page references to prior discussions point you to any individual ratios you feel you need to review.

We used the financial information in Illustrations 13A-1 through 13A-4 to calculate Chicago Cereal Company's 2014 ratios. You can use these data to review the computations.

ILLUSTRATION 13A-1
Chicago Cereal Company's balance sheets

CHICAGO CEREAL COMPANY
Balance Sheets
December 31 (in thousands)

Assets	**2014**	**2013**
Current assets		
Cash	$ 524	$ 411
Accounts receivable	1,026	945
Inventory	924	824
Prepaid expenses and other current assets	243	247
Total current assets	2,717	2,427
Property assets (net)	2,990	2,816
Intangibles and other assets	5,690	5,471
Total assets	$11,397	$10,714
Liabilities and Stockholders' Equity		
Current liabilities	$ 4,044	$ 4,020
Long-term liabilities	4,827	4,625
Stockholders' equity—common	2,526	2,069
Total liabilities and stockholders' equity	$11,397	$10,714

ILLUSTRATION 13A-2
Chicago Cereal Company's income statements

CHICAGO CEREAL COMPANY
Condensed Income Statements
For the Years Ended December 31 (in thousands)

	2014	2013
Net sales	$11,776	$10,907
Cost of goods sold	6,597	6,082
Gross profit	5,179	4,825
Selling and administrative expenses	3,311	3,059
Income from operations	1,868	1,766
Interest expense	319	307
Other income (expense), net	(2)	13
Income before income taxes	1,547	1,472
Income tax expense	444	468
Net income	$ 1,103	$ 1,004

ILLUSTRATION 13A-3
Chicago Cereal Company's statements of cash flows

CHICAGO CEREAL COMPANY
Condensed Statements of Cash Flows
For the Years Ended December 31 (in thousands)

	2014	2013
Cash flows from operating activities		
Cash receipts from operating activities	$11,695	$10,841
Cash payments for operating activities	10,192	9,431
Net cash provided by operating activities	1,503	1,410
Cash flows from investing activities		
Purchases of property, plant, and equipment	(472)	(453)
Other investing activities	(129)	8
Net cash used in investing activities	(601)	(445)
Cash flows from financing activities		
Issuance of common stock	163	218
Issuance of debt	2,179	721
Reductions of debt	(2,011)	(650)
Payment of dividends	(475)	(450)
Repurchase of common stock and other items	(645)	(612)
Net cash provided (used) by financing activities	(789)	(773)
Increase (decrease) in cash and cash equivalents	113	192
Cash and cash equivalents at beginning of year	411	219
Cash and cash equivalents at end of year	$ 524	$ 411

ILLUSTRATION 13A-4
Additional information for Chicago Cereal Company

Additional information:

	2014	2013
Average number of shares (thousands)	418.7	418.5
Stock price at year-end	$52.92	$50.06

As indicated in the chapter, we can classify ratios into three types for analysis of the primary financial statements:

1. **Liquidity ratios.** Measures of the short-term ability of the company to pay its maturing obligations and to meet unexpected needs for cash.
2. **Solvency ratios.** Measures of the ability of the company to survive over a long period of time.
3. **Profitability ratios.** Measures of the income or operating success of a company for a given period of time.

As a tool of analysis, ratios can provide clues to underlying conditions that may not be apparent from an inspection of the individual components of a particular ratio. But, a single ratio by itself is not very meaningful. Accordingly, in this discussion we use the following three comparisons.

1. **Intracompany comparisons** covering two years for Chicago Cereal (using comparative financial information from Illustrations 13A-1 through 13A-4).
2. **Intercompany comparisons** using General Mills as one of Chicago Cereal's competitors.
3. **Industry average comparisons** based on MSN.com median ratios for manufacturers of flour and other grain mill products and comparisons with other sources. For some of the ratios that we use, industry comparisons are not available (denoted "na").

LIQUIDITY RATIOS

Liquidity ratios measure the short-term ability of the company to pay its maturing obligations and to meet unexpected needs for cash. Short-term creditors such as bankers and suppliers are particularly interested in assessing liquidity. The measures used to determine the company's short-term debt-paying ability are the current ratio, the accounts receivable turnover, the average collection period, the inventory turnover, and days in inventory.

1. **Current ratio.** The **current ratio** expresses the relationship of current assets to current liabilities, computed by dividing current assets by current liabilities. It is widely used for evaluating a company's liquidity and short-term debt-paying ability. The 2014 and 2013 current ratios for Chicago Cereal and comparative data are shown in Illustration 13A-5.

ILLUSTRATION 13A-5
Current ratio

Ratio	Formula	Indicates	Chicago Cereal 2014	Chicago Cereal 2013	General Mills 2014	Industry 2014	Page in Textbook
Current ratio	$\frac{\text{Current assets}}{\text{Current liabilities}}$	Short-term debt-paying ability	.67	.60	.67	1.06	54

What do the measures tell us? Chicago Cereal's 2013 current ratio of .67 means that for every dollar of current liabilities, it has $0.67 of current assets. We sometimes state such ratios as .67:1 to reinforce this interpretation. Its current ratio—and therefore its liquidity—increased significantly in 2014. It is well below the industry average but the same as that of General Mills.

2. **Accounts receivable turnover.** Analysts can measure liquidity by how quickly a company converts certain assets to cash. Low values of the previous ratios can sometimes be compensated for if some of the company's current assets are highly liquid.

   How liquid, for example, are the receivables? The ratio used to assess the liquidity of the receivables is the **accounts receivable turnover**, which measures the number of times, on average, a company collects receivables during the period. The accounts receivable turnover is computed by dividing net credit sales (net sales less cash sales) by average net accounts receivable during the year. The accounts receivable turnover for Chicago Cereal is shown in Illustration 13A-6.

ILLUSTRATION 13A-6
Accounts receivable turnover

Ratio	Formula	Indicates	Chicago Cereal 2014	Chicago Cereal 2013	General Mills 2014	Industry 2014	Page in Textbook
Accounts receivable turnover	$\frac{\text{Net credit sales}}{\text{Average net accounts receivable}}$	Liquidity of receivables	11.9	12.0	12.2	11.2	395

In computing the rate, we assumed that all Chicago Cereal's sales are credit sales. Its accounts receivable turnover declined slightly in 2014. The turnover of 11.9 times is higher than the industry average of 11.2 times, and slightly lower than General Mills' turnover of 12.2 times.

3. **Average collection period.** A popular variant of the accounts receivable turnover converts it into an **average collection period** in days. This is done by dividing the accounts receivable turnover into 365 days. The average collection period for Chicago Cereal is shown in Illustration 13A-7.

ILLUSTRATION 13A-7
Average collection period

Ratio	Formula	Indicates	Chicago Cereal 2014	Chicago Cereal 2013	General Mills 2014	Industry 2014	Page in Textbook
Average collection period	365 days / Accounts receivable turnover	Liquidity of receivables and collection success	30.7	30.4	29.9	32.6	395

Chicago Cereal's 2014 accounts receivable turnover of 11.9 times is divided into 365 days to obtain approximately 31 days. This means that the average collection period for receivables is about 31 days. Its average collection period is slightly longer than that of General Mills and shorter than that of the industry.

Analysts frequently use the average collection period to assess the effectiveness of a company's credit and collection policies. The general rule is that the collection period should not greatly exceed the credit term period (i.e., the time allowed for payment).

4. **Inventory turnover.** The **inventory turnover** measures the number of times average inventory was sold during the period. Its purpose is to measure the liquidity of the inventory. A high measure indicates that inventory is being sold and replenished frequently. The inventory turnover is computed by dividing the cost of goods sold by the average inventory during the period. Unless seasonal factors are significant, average inventory can be computed from the beginning and ending inventory balances. Chicago Cereal's inventory turnover is shown in Illustration 13A-8.

ILLUSTRATION 13A-8
Inventory turnover

Ratio	Formula	Indicates	Chicago Cereal 2014	Chicago Cereal 2013	General Mills 2014	Industry 2014	Page in Textbook
Inventory turnover	Cost of goods sold / Average inventory	Liquidity of inventory	7.5	7.9	7.4	6.7	283

Chicago Cereal's inventory turnover decreased slightly in 2014. The turnover of 7.5 times is higher than the industry average of 6.7 times and similar to that of General Mills. Generally, the faster the inventory turnover, the less cash is tied up in inventory and the less the chance of inventory becoming obsolete. Of course, a downside of high inventory turnover is that it sometimes results in lost sales because if a company keeps less inventory on hand, it is more likely to run out of inventory when it is needed.

5. **Days in inventory.** A variant of the inventory turnover is the **days in inventory**, which measures the average number of days inventory is held. The days in inventory for Chicago Cereal is shown in Illustration 13A-9 (page 670).

Ratio	Formula	Indicates	Chicago Cereal 2014	Chicago Cereal 2013	General Mills 2014	Industry 2014	Page in Textbook
Days in inventory	365 days / Inventory turnover	Liquidity of inventory and inventory management	48.7	46.2	49.3	54.5	283

ILLUSTRATION 13A-9
Days in inventory

Chicago Cereal's 2014 inventory turnover of 7.5 divided into 365 is approximately 49 days. An average selling time of 49 days is faster than the industry average and similar to that of General Mills. Some of this difference might be explained by differences in product lines across the two companies, although in many ways the types of products of these two companies are quite similar.

Inventory turnovers vary considerably among industries. For example, grocery store chains have a turnover of 10 times and an average selling period of 37 days. In contrast, jewelry stores have an average turnover of 1.3 times and an average selling period of 281 days. Within a company, there may even be significant differences in inventory turnover among different types of products. Thus, in a grocery store the turnover of perishable items such as produce, meats, and dairy products is faster than the turnover of soaps and detergents.

To conclude, nearly all of these liquidity measures suggest that Chicago Cereal's liquidity changed little during 2014. Its liquidity appears acceptable when compared to the industry as a whole and when compared to General Mills.

SOLVENCY RATIOS

Solvency ratios measure the ability of the company to survive over a long period of time. Long-term creditors and stockholders are interested in a company's long-run solvency, particularly its ability to pay interest as it comes due and to repay the face value of debt at maturity. The debt to assets ratio and times interest earned provide information about debt-paying ability. In addition, free cash flow provides information about the company's solvency and its ability to pay additional dividends or invest in new projects.

6. **Debt to assets ratio.** The **debt to assets ratio** measures the percentage of total financing provided by creditors. It is computed by dividing total liabilities (both current and long-term debt) by total assets. This ratio indicates the degree of financial leveraging. It also provides some indication of the company's ability to withstand losses without impairing the interests of its creditors. The higher the percentage of debt to assets, the greater the risk that the company may be unable to meet its maturing obligations. Thus, from the creditors' point of view, a low ratio of debt to assets is desirable. Chicago Cereal's debt to assets ratio is shown in Illustration 13A-10.

ILLUSTRATION 13A-10
Debt to assets ratio

Ratio	Formula	Indicates	Chicago Cereal 2014	Chicago Cereal 2013	General Mills 2014	Industry 2014	Page in Textbook
Debt to assets ratio	Total liabilities / Total assets	Percentage of total assets provided by creditors	78%	81%	55%	55%	56

Chicago Cereal's 2014 ratio of 78% means that creditors have provided financing sufficient to cover 78% of the company's total assets. Alternatively, it says that it would have to liquidate 78% of its assets at their book value in order to pay off all of its debts. Its ratio is above the industry average of 55%, as well as that of General Mills. This suggests that it is less solvent than the industry average and General Mills. Chicago Cereal's solvency improved slightly during the year.

The adequacy of this ratio is often judged in light of the company's earnings. Generally, companies with relatively stable earnings, such as public utilities, have higher debt to assets ratios than cyclical companies with widely fluctuating earnings, such as many high-tech companies.

Another ratio with a similar meaning is the **debt to equity ratio**. It shows the relative use of borrowed funds (total liabilities) compared with resources invested by the owners. Because this ratio can be computed in several ways, be careful when making comparisons with it. Debt may be defined to include only the noncurrent portion of liabilities, and intangible assets may be excluded from stockholders' equity (which would equal tangible net worth). If debt and assets are defined as above (all liabilities and all assets), then when the debt to assets ratio equals 50%, the debt to equity ratio is 1:1.

7. **Times interest earned.** The **times interest earned** (also called interest coverage) indicates the company's ability to meet interest payments as they come due. It is computed by dividing the sum of net income, interest expense, and income tax expense by interest expense. Note that this ratio uses income before interest expense and income taxes because this amount represents what is available to cover interest. Chicago Cereal's times interest earned is shown in Illustration 13A-11.

ILLUSTRATION 13A-11
Times interest earned

Ratio	Formula	Indicates	Chicago Cereal 2014	Chicago Cereal 2013	General Mills 2014	Industry 2014	Page in Textbook
Times interest earned	(Net Income + Interest expense + Income tax expense) / Interest expense	Ability to meet interest payments as they come due	5.8	5.8	9.9	5.5	497

For Chicago Cereal, the 2014 interest coverage was 5.8, which indicates that income before interest and taxes was 5.8 times the amount needed for interest expense. This is less than the rate for General Mills, but it slightly exceeds the rate for the industry. The debt to assets ratio decreased for Chicago Cereal during 2014, and its times interest earned held constant.

8. **Free cash flow.** One indication of a company's solvency, as well as of its ability to pay dividends or expand operations, is the amount of excess cash it generated after investing in capital expenditures and paying dividends. This amount is referred to as **free cash flow**. For example, if you generate $100,000 of net cash provided by operating activities but you spend $30,000 on capital expenditures and pay $10,000 in dividends, you have $60,000 ($100,000 − $30,000 − $10,000) to use either to expand operations, pay additional dividends, or pay down debt. Chicago Cereal's free cash flow is shown in Illustration 13A-12.

ILLUSTRATION 13A-12
Free cash flow

Ratio	Formula	Indicates	Chicago Cereal 2014	Chicago Cereal 2013	General Mills 2014	Industry 2014	Page in Textbook
Free cash flow	Net cash provided by operating activities − Capital expenditures − Cash dividends	Cash available for paying dividends or expanding operations	$556 (in thousands)	$507	$895 (in millions)	na	57

Chicago Cereal's free cash flow increased slightly from 2013 to 2014. During both years, the net cash provided by operating activities was more than enough to allow it to acquire additional productive assets and maintain dividend payments. It could have used the remaining cash to reduce debt if necessary. Given that Chicago Cereal is much smaller than General Mills, we would expect its free cash flow to be substantially smaller, which it is.

PROFITABILITY RATIOS

Profitability ratios measure the income or operating success of a company for a given period of time. A company's income, or the lack of it, affects its ability to obtain debt and equity financing, its liquidity position, and its ability to grow. As a consequence, creditors and investors alike are interested in evaluating profitability. Analysts frequently use profitability as the ultimate test of management's operating effectiveness.

Throughout this textbook, we have introduced numerous measures of profitability. The relationships among measures of profitability are very important. Understanding them can help management determine where to focus its efforts to improve profitability. Illustration 13A-13 diagrams these relationships. Our discussion of Chicago Cereal's profitability is structured around this diagram.

ILLUSTRATION 13A-13
Relationships among profitability measures

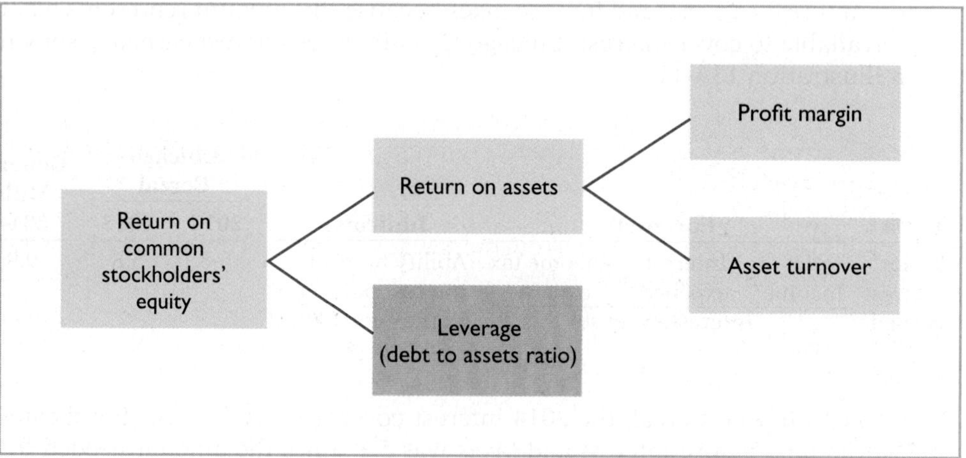

9. **Return on common stockholders' equity (ROE).** A widely used measure of profitability from the common stockholder's viewpoint is the **return on common stockholders' equity (ROE)**. This ratio shows how many dollars of net income the company earned for each dollar invested by the owners. It is computed by dividing net income minus any preferred dividends—that is, income available to common stockholders—by average common stockholders' equity. The return on common stockholders' equity for Chicago Cereal is shown in Illustration 13A-14.

ILLUSTRATION 13A-14
Return on common stockholders' equity

Ratio	Formula	Indicates	Chicago Cereal 2014	Chicago Cereal 2013	General Mills 2014	Industry 2014	Page in Textbook
Return on common stockholders' equity	$\frac{\text{Net Income} - \text{Preferred dividends}}{\text{Average common stockholders' equity}}$	Profitability of common stockholders' investment	48%	46%	25%	19%	561

Chicago Cereal's 2014 return on common stockholders' equity is unusually high at 48%. The industry average is 19% and General Mills' return is 25%. In the subsequent sections, we investigate the causes of this high return.

10. **Return on assets.** The return on common stockholders' equity is affected by two factors: the **return on assets** and the degree of leverage. The return on assets measures the overall profitability of assets in terms of the income earned on each dollar invested in assets. It is computed by dividing net income by average total assets. Chicago Cereal's return on assets is shown in Illustration 13A-15.

ILLUSTRATION 13A-15
Return on assets

Ratio	Formula	Indicates	Chicago Cereal 2014	Chicago Cereal 2013	General Mills 2014	Industry 2014	Page in Textbook
Return on assets	Net income / Average total assets	Overall profitability of assets	10.0%	9.4%	6.2%	5.3%	444

Chicago Cereal had a 10.0% return on assets in 2014. This rate is significantly higher than that of General Mills and the industry average.

Note that its rate of return on common stockholders' equity (48%) is substantially higher than its rate of return on assets (10%). The reason is that it has made effective use of **leverage**. **Leveraging** or **trading on the equity** at a gain means that the company has borrowed money at a lower rate of interest than the rate of return it earns on the assets it purchased with the borrowed funds. Leverage enables management to use money supplied by nonowners to increase the return to owners.

A comparison of the rate of return on assets with the rate of interest paid for borrowed money indicates the profitability of trading on the equity. If you borrow money at 8% and your rate of return on assets is 11%, you are trading on the equity at a gain. Note, however, that trading on the equity is a two-way street. For example, if you borrow money at 11% and earn only 8% on it, you are trading on the equity at a loss.

Chicago Cereal earns more on its borrowed funds than it has to pay in interest. Thus, the return to stockholders exceeds the return on assets because of the positive benefit of leverage. Recall from our earlier discussion that Chicago Cereal's percentage of debt financing, as measured by the ratio of debt to assets (or debt to equity), was higher than General Mills' and the industry average. It appears that Chicago Cereal's high return on common stockholders' equity is due in part to its use of leverage.

11. **Profit margin.** The return on assets is affected by two factors, the first of which is the profit margin. The **profit margin**, or rate of return on sales, is a measure of the percentage of each dollar of sales that results in net income. It is computed by dividing net income by net sales for the period. Chicago Cereal's profit margin is shown in Illustration 13A-16.

ILLUSTRATION 13A-16
Profit margin

Ratio	Formula	Indicates	Chicago Cereal 2014	Chicago Cereal 2013	General Mills 2014	Industry 2014	Page in Textbook
Profit margin	Net income / Net sales	Net income generated by each dollar of sales	9.4%	9.2%	8.2%	6.1%	235

Chicago Cereal experienced a slight increase in its profit margin from 2013 to 2014 of 9.2% to 9.4%. Its profit margin was higher than the industry average and that of General Mills.

High-volume (high inventory turnover) businesses such as grocery stores and pharmacy chains generally have low profit margins. Low-volume businesses such as jewelry stores and airplane manufacturers have high profit margins.

12. **Asset turnover.** The other factor that affects the return on assets is the asset turnover. The **asset turnover** measures how efficiently a company uses its assets to generate sales. It is determined by dividing net sales by average total assets for the period. The resulting number shows the dollars of sales produced by each dollar invested in assets. Illustration 13A-17 shows the asset turnover for Chicago Cereal.

ILLUSTRATION 13A-17
Asset turnover

Ratio	Formula	Indicates	Chicago Cereal 2014	Chicago Cereal 2013	General Mills 2014	Industry 2014	Page in Textbook
Asset turnover	$\frac{\text{Net sales}}{\text{Average total assets}}$	How efficiently assets are used to generate sales	1.07	1.02	.76	.87	446

The asset turnover shows that in 2014, Chicago Cereal generated sales of $1.07 for each dollar it had invested in assets. The ratio rose from 2013 to 2014. Its asset turnover is above the industry average and that of General Mills.

Asset turnovers vary considerably among industries. The average asset turnover for utility companies is .45, for example, while the grocery store industry has an average asset turnover of 3.49.

In summary, Chicago Cereal's return on assets increased from 9.4% in 2013 to 10.0% in 2014. Underlying this increase was an increased profitability on each dollar of sales (as measured by the profit margin) and a rise in the sales-generating efficiency of its assets (as measured by the asset turnover). We can analyze the combined effects of profit margin and asset turnover on return on assets for Chicago Cereal as shown in Illustration 13A-18.

ILLUSTRATION 13A-18
Composition of return on assets

Ratios:	Profit Margin	×	Asset Turnover	=	Return on Assets
	$\frac{\text{Net Income}}{\text{Net Sales}}$	×	$\frac{\text{Net Sales}}{\text{Average Total Assets}}$	=	$\frac{\text{Net Income}}{\text{Average Total Assets}}$
Chicago Cereal					
2014	9.4%	×	1.07 times	=	10.1%*
2013	9.2%	×	1.02 times	=	9.4%

*Difference from value in Illustration 13A-15 due to rounding.

13. **Gross profit rate.** One factor that strongly influences the profit margin is the gross profit rate. The **gross profit rate** is determined by dividing gross profit (net sales less cost of goods sold) by net sales. This rate indicates a company's ability to maintain an adequate selling price above its cost of goods sold.

As an industry becomes more competitive, this ratio declines. For example, in the early years of the personal computer industry, gross profit rates were quite high. Today, because of increased competition and a belief that most brands of personal computers are similar in quality, gross profit rates have become thin. Analysts should closely monitor gross profit rates over time. Illustration 13A-19 shows Chicago Cereal's gross profit rate.

Ratio	Formula	Indicates	Chicago Cereal 2014	Chicago Cereal 2013	General Mills 2014	Industry 2014	Page in Textbook
Gross profit rate	$\frac{\text{Gross profit}}{\text{Net sales}}$	Margin between selling price and cost of goods sold	44%	44%	34%	30%	234

ILLUSTRATION 13A-19
Gross profit rate

Chicago Cereal's gross profit rate remained constant from 2013 to 2014.

14. **Earnings per share (EPS).** Stockholders usually think in terms of the number of shares they own or plan to buy or sell. Expressing net income earned on a per share basis provides a useful perspective for determining profitability. **Earnings per share** is a measure of the net income earned on each share of common stock. It is computed by dividing net income by the average number of common shares outstanding during the year.

    The terms "net income per share" or "earnings per share" refer to the amount of net income applicable to each share of **common stock**. Therefore, when we compute earnings per share, if there are preferred dividends declared for the period, we must deduct them from net income to arrive at income available to the common stockholders. Chicago Cereal's earnings per share is shown in Illustration 13A-20.

ILLUSTRATION 13A-20
Earnings per share

Ratio	Formula	Indicates	Chicago Cereal 2014	Chicago Cereal 2013	General Mills 2014	Industry 2014	Page in Textbook
Earnings per share (EPS)	$\frac{\text{Net income} - \text{Preferred dividends}}{\text{Weighted-average common shares outstanding}}$	Net income earned on each share of common stock	\$2.63	\$2.40	\$2.90	na	53

Note that no industry average is presented in Illustration 13A-20. Industry data for earnings per share are not reported, and in fact the Chicago Cereal and General Mills ratios should not be compared. Such comparisons are not meaningful because of the wide variations in the number of shares of outstanding stock among companies. Chicago Cereal's earnings per share increased 23 cents per share in 2014. This represents a 9.6% increase from the 2013 EPS of \$2.40.

15. **Price-earnings ratio.** The **price-earnings ratio** is an oft-quoted statistic that measures the ratio of the market price of each share of common stock to the earnings per share. The price-earnings (P-E) ratio reflects investors' assessments of a company's future earnings. It is computed by dividing the market price per share of the stock by earnings per share. Chicago Cereal's price-earnings ratio is shown in Illustration 13A-21.

ILLUSTRATION 13A-21
Price-earnings ratio

Ratio	Formula	Indicates	Chicago Cereal 2014	Chicago Cereal 2013	General Mills 2014	Industry 2014	Page in Textbook
Price-earnings ratio	$\frac{\text{Market price per share}}{\text{Earnings per share}}$	Relationship between market price per share and earnings per share	20.1	20.9	24.3	35.8	660

At the end of 2014 and 2013, the market price of Chicago Cereal's stock was \$52.92 and \$50.06, respectively.

In 2014, each share of Chicago Cereal's stock sold for 20.1 times the amount that was earned on each share. Chicago Cereal's price-earnings ratio is lower than General Mills' ratio of 24.3 and lower than the industry average of 35.8 times. Its lower P-E ratio suggests that the market is less optimistic about Chicago Cereal than about General Mills. However, it might also signal that Chicago Cereal's stock is underpriced.

16. Payout ratio. The **payout ratio** measures the percentage of earnings distributed in the form of cash dividends. It is computed by dividing cash dividends declared on common stock by net income. Companies that have high growth rates are characterized by low payout ratios because they reinvest most of their net income in the business. The payout ratio for Chicago Cereal is shown in Illustration 13A-22.

ILLUSTRATION 13A-22
Payout ratio

Ratio	Formula	Indicates	Chicago Cereal 2014	Chicago Cereal 2013	General Mills 2014	Industry 2014	Page in Textbook
Payout ratio	$\frac{\text{Cash dividends declared on common stock}}{\text{Net income}}$	Percentage of earnings distributed in the form of cash dividends	43%	45%	54%	37%	560

The 2014 and 2013 payout ratios for Chicago Cereal are slightly lower than that of General Mills (54%) but higher than the industry average (37%).

Management has some control over the amount of dividends paid each year, and companies are generally reluctant to reduce a dividend below the amount paid in a previous year. Therefore, the payout ratio will actually increase if a company's net income declines but the company keeps its total dividend payment the same. Of course, unless the company returns to its previous level of profitability, maintaining this higher dividend payout ratio is probably not possible over the long run.

Before drawing any conclusions regarding Chicago Cereal's dividend payout ratio, we should calculate this ratio over a longer period of time to evaluate any trends and also try to find out whether management's philosophy regarding dividends has changed recently. The "Selected Financial Data" section of Chicago Cereal's Management Discussion and Analysis shows that over a 5-year period, earnings per share rose 45%, while dividends per share grew only 19%.

In terms of the types of financial information available and the ratios used by various industries, what can be practically covered in this textbook gives you only the "Titanic approach." That is, you are seeing only the tip of the iceberg compared to the vast databases and types of ratio analysis that are available on computers. The availability of information is not a problem. The real trick is to be discriminating enough to perform relevant analysis and select pertinent comparative data.

REVIEW AND PRACTICE

▶ LEARNING OBJECTIVES REVIEW

1 Apply the concepts of sustainable income and quality of earnings. Sustainable income analysis is useful in evaluating a company's performance. Sustainable income is the most likely level of income to be obtained by the company in the future. Discontinued operations and other comprehensive income are presented on the statement of comprehensive income to highlight their unusual nature. Items below income from continuing operations must be presented net of tax.

A high quality of earnings provides full and transparent information that will not confuse or mislead users of the financial statements. Issues related to quality of earnings are (1) alternative accounting methods, (2) pro forma income, and (3) improper recognition.

2 Apply horizontal analysis and vertical analysis. Horizontal analysis is a technique for evaluating a series of data over a period of time to determine the increase or decrease that has taken place, expressed as either an amount or a percentage.

Vertical analysis is a technique that expresses each item in a financial statement as a percentage of a relevant total or a base amount

3 Analyze a company's performance using ratio analysis. The price-earnings (P-E) ratio reflects investors' assessment of a company's future earnings potential. Financial ratios are provided in Illustration 13-16 (liquidity), Illustration 13-17 (solvency), and Illustration 13-18 (profitability).

***4 Evaluate a company comprehensively using ratio analysis.** To evaluate a company, ratios (liquidity, solvency, and profitability) provide clues to underlying conditions, but intracompany, intercompany, and industry average comparisons are also needed.

DECISION TOOLS REVIEW

DECISION CHECKPOINTS	INFO NEEDED FOR DECISION	TOOL TO USE FOR DECISION	HOW TO EVALUATE RESULTS
Has the company sold any major components of its business?	Discontinued operations section of income statement	Anything reported in this section indicates that the company has discontinued a major component of its business.	If a major component has been discontinued, its results during the current period should not be included in estimates of future net income.
Has the company changed any of its accounting principles?	Effect of change in accounting principle on current and prior periods	Management indicates that the new principle is preferable to the old principle.	Examine current and prior years' reported income, using new-principle basis to assess trends for estimating future income.
How do the company's financial position and operating results compare with those of the previous period?	Income statement and balance sheet	Comparative financial statements should be prepared over at least two years, with the first year reported being the base year. Changes in each line item relative to the base year should be presented both by amount and by percentage. This is called **horizontal analysis.**	Significant changes should be investigated to determine the reason for the change.
How do the relationships between items in this year's financial statements compare with those of last year or those of competitors?	Income statement and balance sheet	Each line item on the income statement should be presented as a percentage of net sales, and each line item on the balance sheet should be presented as a percentage of total assets or total liabilities and stockholders' equity. These percentages should be investigated for differences either across years in the same company or in the same year across different companies. This is called **vertical analysis.**	Any significant differences either across years or between companies should be investigated to determine the cause.

GLOSSARY REVIEW

***Accounts receivable turnover** A measure of the liquidity of receivables; computed as net credit sales divided by average net accounts receivable. (p. 668).

***Asset turnover** A measure of how efficiently a company uses its assets to generate sales; computed as net sales divided by average total assets. (p. 674).

Available-for-sale securities Securities that are held with the intent of selling them sometime in the future. (p. 650).

***Average collection period** The average number of days that receivables are outstanding; calculated as accounts receivable turnover divided into 365 days. (p. 669).

Change in accounting principle Use of an accounting principle in the current year different from the one used in the preceding year. (p. 651).

Comprehensive income The sum of net income and other comprehensive income items. (p. 650).

***Current ratio** A measure used to evaluate a company's liquidity and short-term debt-paying ability; calculated as current assets divided by current liabilities. (p. 668).

***Days in inventory** A measure of the average number of days inventory is held; computed as inventory turnover divided into 365 days. (p. 669).

***Debt to assets ratio** A measure of the percentage of total financing provided by creditors; computed as total liabilities divided by total assets. (p. 670).

Discontinued operations The disposal of a significant component of a business. (p. 649).

***Earnings per share** The net income earned by each share of common stock; computed as net income less preferred dividends divided by the weighted-average common shares outstanding. (p. 675).

***Free cash flow** A measure of solvency. Cash remaining from operating activities after adjusting for capital expenditures and dividends paid. (p. 671).

***Gross profit rate** Gross profit expressed as a percentage of sales; computed as gross profit divided by net sales. (p. 674).

Horizontal analysis A technique for evaluating a series of financial statement data over a period of time to determine the increase (decrease) that has taken place, expressed as either an amount or a percentage. (p. 655).

***Inventory turnover** A measure of the liquidity of inventory. Measures the number of times average inventory was sold during the period; computed as cost of goods sold divided by average inventory. (p. 669).

***Leveraging** Borrowing money at a lower rate of interest than can be earned by using the borrowed money; also referred to as *trading on the equity*. (p. 673).

Liquidity ratios Measures of the short-term ability of the company to pay its maturing obligations and to meet unexpected needs for cash. (p. 660).

***Payout ratio** A measure of the percentage of earnings distributed in the form of cash dividends; calculated as cash dividends declared on common stock divided by net income. (p. 676).

Price-earnings (P-E) ratio A comparison of the market price of each share of common stock to the earnings per share; computed as the market price of the stock divided by earnings per share. (pp. 660, 675).

Profitability ratios Measures of the income or operating success of a company for a given period of time. (p. 661).

***Profit margin** A measure of the net income generated by each dollar of sales; computed as net income divided by net sales. (p. 673).

Pro forma income A measure of income that usually excludes items that a company thinks are unusual or nonrecurring. (p. 653).

Quality of earnings Indicates the level of full and transparent information that is provided to users of the financial statements. (p. 652).

***Return on assets** A profitability measure that indicates the amount of net income generated by each dollar of assets; calculated as net income divided by average total assets. (p. 673).

***Return on common stockholders' equity (ROE)** A measure of the dollars of net income earned for each dollar invested by the owners; computed as income available to common stockholders divided by average common stockholders' equity. (p. 672).

Solvency ratios Measures of the ability of a company to survive over a long period of time, particularly to pay interest as it comes due and to repay the balance of debt at its maturity. (p. 661).

Sustainable income The most likely level of income to be obtained by a company in the future. (p. 648).

***Times interest earned** A measure of a company's solvency and ability to meet interest payments as they come due; calculated as the sum of net income, interest expense, and income tax expense divided by interest expense. (p. 671).

***Trading on the equity** *See leveraging*. (p. 673).

Trading securities Securities bought and held primarily for sale in the near term to generate income on short-term price differences. (p. 650).

Vertical analysis A technique for evaluating financial statement data that expresses each item in a financial statement as a percentage of a base amount. (p. 657).

PRACTICE MULTIPLE-CHOICE QUESTIONS

All of the Practice Multiple-Choice Questions in this chapter employ decision tools.

(LO 1) 1. In reporting discontinued operations, the income statement should show in a special section:
(a) gains on the disposal of the discontinued component.
(b) losses on the disposal of the discontinued component.
(c) Neither (a) nor (b).
(d) Both (a) and (b).

2. Cool Stools Corporation has income before taxes of $400,000 and a loss on discontinued operations of $100,000. If the income tax rate is 25% on all items, the statement of comprehensive income should show income from continuing operations and discontinued operations, respectively, of (LO 1)
(a) $325,000 and $100,000.
(b) $325,000 and $75,000.
(c) $300,000 and $100,000.
(d) $300,000 and $75,000.

(LO 1) 3. Which of the following would be considered an "Other comprehensive income" item?
(a) Gain on disposal of discontinued operations.
(b) Unrealized loss on available-for-sale securities.
(c) Loss related to flood.
(d) Net income.

(LO 1) 4. Which situation below might indicate a company has a low quality of earnings?
(a) The same accounting principles are used each year.
(b) Revenue is recognized when the performance obligation is satisfied.
(c) Maintenance costs are capitalized and then depreciated.
(d) The company's P-E ratio is high relative to competitors.

(LO 2) 5. In horizontal analysis, each item is expressed as a percentage of the:
(a) net income amount.
(b) stockholders' equity amount.
(c) total assets amount.
(d) base-year amount.

(LO 2) 6. Adams Corporation reported net sales of $300,000, $330,000, and $360,000 in the years 2015, 2016, and 2017, respectively. If 2015 is the base year, what percentage do 2017 sales represent of the base?
(a) 77%. (c) 120%.
(b) 108%. (d) 130%.

(LO 2) 7. The following schedule is a display of what type of analysis?

	Amount	Percent
Current assets	$200,000	25%
Property, plant, and equipment	600,000	75%
Total assets	$800,000	

(a) Horizontal analysis. (c) Vertical analysis.
(b) Differential analysis. (d) Ratio analysis.

(LO 2) 8. In vertical analysis, the base amount for depreciation expense is generally:
(a) net sales.
(b) depreciation expense in a previous year.
(c) gross profit.
(d) fixed assets.

(LO 3) 9. Which measure is an evaluation of a company's ability to pay current liabilities?
(a) Accounts receivable turnover.
(b) Current ratio.
(c) Both (a) and (b).
(d) None of the above.

10. Which measure is useful in evaluating the efficiency in managing inventories? (LO 3)
(a) Inventory turnover.
(b) Days in inventory.
(c) Both (a) and (b).
(d) None of the above.

11. Which of these is **not** a liquidity ratio? (LO 3)
(a) Current ratio.
(b) Asset turnover.
(c) Inventory turnover.
(d) Accounts receivable turnover.

12. Plano Corporation reported net income $24,000, net sales $400,000, and average assets $600,000 for 2017. What is the 2017 profit margin? (LO 3)
(a) 6%. (c) 40%.
(b) 12%. (d) 200%.

Use the following financial statement information as of the end of each year to answer Questions 13–17.

	2017	2016
Inventory	$ 54,000	$ 48,000
Current assets	81,000	106,000
Total assets	382,000	326,000
Current liabilities	27,000	36,000
Total liabilities	102,000	88,000
Common stockholders' equity	240,000	198,000
Net sales	784,000	697,000
Cost of goods sold	306,000	277,000
Net income	134,000	90,000
Income tax expense	22,000	18,000
Interest expense	12,000	12,000
Dividends paid to preferred stockholders	4,000	4,000
Dividends paid to common stockholders	15,000	10,000

13. Compute the days in inventory for 2017. (LO 3)
(a) 64.4 days. (c) 6 days.
(b) 60.8 days. (d) 24 days.

14. Compute the current ratio for 2017. (LO 3)
(a) 1.26:1. (c) 0.80:1.
(b) 3.0:1. (d) 3.75:1.

15. Compute the profit margin for 2017. (LO 3)
(a) 17.1%. (c) 37.9%.
(b) 18.1%. (d) 5.9%.

16. Compute the return on common stockholders' equity for 2017. (LO 3)
(a) 54.2%. (c) 61.2%.
(b) 52.5%. (d) 59.4%.

17. Compute the times interest earned for 2017. (LO 3)
(a) 11.2 times. (c) 14.0 times.
(b) 65.3 times. (d) 13.0 times.

SOLUTIONS

1. **(d)** Gains and losses from the operations of a discontinued segment and gains and losses on the disposal of the discontinued segment are shown in a separate section immediately after continuing operations in the income statement. Choices (a) and (b) are correct, but (d) is the better answer. Choice (c) is wrong as there is a correct answer.

2. **(d)** Income tax expense = 25% × $400,000 = $100,000; therefore, income from continuing operations = $400,000 − $100,000 = $300,000. The loss on discontinued operations is shown net of tax, $100,000 × 75% = $75,000. The other choices are therefore incorrect.

3. **(b)** Unrealized gains and losses on available-for-sale securities are part of other comprehensive income. The other choices are incorrect because (a) a gain on the disposal of discontinued operations is reported as an unusual item, (c) loss related to a flood is reported among other expenses and losses, and (d) net income is a separate line item.

4. **(c)** Capitalizing and then depreciating maintenance costs suggests that a company is trying to avoid expensing certain costs by deferring them to future accounting periods to increase current-period income. The other choices are incorrect because (a) using the same accounting principles each year and (b) recognizing revenue when the performance obligation is satisfied is in accordance with GAAP. Choice (d) is incorrect because a high P-E ratio does not suggest that a firm has low quality of earnings.
5. **(d)** Horizontal analysis converts each succeeding year's balance to a percentage of the base year amount, not (a) net income amount, (b) stockholders' equity amount, or (c) total assets amount.
6. **(c)** The trend percentage for 2017 is 120% ($360,000/$300,000), not (a) 77%, (b) 108%, or (d) 130%.
7. **(c)** The data in the schedule is a display of vertical analysis because the individual asset items are expressed as a percentage of total assets. The other choices are therefore incorrect. Horizontal analysis is a technique for evaluating a series of data over a period of time.
8. **(a)** In vertical analysis, net sales is used as the base amount for income statement items, not (b) depreciation expense in a previous year, (c) gross profit, or (d) fixed assets.
9. **(c)** Both the accounts receivable turnover and the current ratio measure a firm's ability to pay current liabilities. Choices (a) and (b) are correct but (c) is the better answer. Choice (d) is incorrect because there is a correct answer.
10. **(c)** Both inventory turnover and days in inventory measure a firm's efficiency in managing inventories. Choices (a) and (b) are correct but (c) is the better answer. Choice (d) is incorrect because there is a correct answer.
11. **(b)** Asset turnover is a measure of profitability. The other choices are incorrect because the (a) current ratio, (c) inventory turnover, and (d) accounts receivable turnover are all measures of a firm's liquidity.
12. **(a)** Profit margin = Net income ($24,000) ÷ Net sales ($400,000) = 6%, not (b) 12%, (c) 40%, or (d) 200%.
13. **(b)** Inventory turnover = Cost of goods sold/Average inventory [$306,000/[($54,000 + $48,000)/2]] = 6 times. Thus, days in inventory = 60.8 (365/6), not (a) 64.4, (c) 6, or (d) 24 days.
14. **(b)** Current ratio = Current assets/Current liabilities ($81,000/$27,000) = 3.0:1, not (a) 1.26:1, (c) 0.80:1, or (d) 3.75:1.
15. **(a)** Profit margin = Net income/Net sales ($134,000/$784,000) =17.1%, not (b) 18.1%, (c) 37.9%, or (d) 5.9%.
16. **(d)** Return on common stockholders' equity = Net income ($134,000) − Dividends to preferred stockholders ($4,000)/ Average common stockholders' equity [($240,000 + $198,000)/2] = 59.4%, not (a) 54.2%, (b) 52.5%, or (c) 61.2%.
17. **(c)** Times interest earned = Net income + Interest expense + Income tax expense divided by Interest expense [($134,000 + $12,000 + $22,000)/$12,000] = 14.0 times, not (a) 11.2, (b) 65.3, or (d) 13.0 times.

PRACTICE EXERCISES

Prepare horizontal and vertical analysis.

(LO 2)

1. The comparative condensed balance sheets of Roadway Corporation are presented below.

ROADWAY CORPORATION
Condensed Balance Sheets
December 31

	2017	2016
Assets		
Current assets	$ 76,000	$ 80,000
Property, plant, and equipment (net)	99,000	90,000
Intangibles	25,000	40,000
Total assets	$200,000	$210,000
Liabilities and Stockholders' Equity		
Current liabilities	$ 40,800	$ 48,000
Long-term liabilities	143,000	150,000
Stockholders' equity	16,200	12,000
Total liabilities and stockholders' equity	$200,000	$210,000

INSTRUCTIONS

(a) Prepare a horizontal analysis of the balance sheet data for Roadway Corporation using 2016 as a base.
(b) Prepare a vertical analysis of the balance sheet data for Roadway Corporation in columnar form for 2017.

SOLUTION

1. (a)

ROADWAY CORPORATION
Condensed Balance Sheets
December 31

	2017	2016	Increase (Decrease)	Percent Change from 2016
Assets				
Current assets	$ 76,000	$ 80,000	$ (4,000)	(5.0%)
Property, plant, and equipment (net)	99,000	90,000	9,000	10.0%
Intangibles	25,000	40,000	(15,000)	(37.5%)
Total assets	$200,000	$210,000	$(10,000)	(4.8%)
Liabilities and Stockholders' Equity				
Current liabilities	$ 40,800	$ 48,000	$ (7,200)	(15.0%)
Long-term liabilities	143,000	150,000	(7,000)	(4.7%)
Stockholders' equity	16,200	12,000	4,200	35.0%
Total liabilities and stockholders' equity	$200,000	$210,000	$(10,000)	(4.8%)

(b)

ROADWAY CORPORATION
Condensed Balance Sheet
December 31, 2017

	Amount	Percent
Assets		
Current assets	$ 76,000	38.0%
Property, plant, and equipment (net)	99,000	49.5%
Intangibles	25,000	12.5%
Total assets	$200,000	100.0%
Liabilities and Stockholders' Equity		
Current liabilities	$ 40,800	20.4%
Long-term liabilities	143,000	71.5%
Stockholders' equity	16,200	8.1%
Total liabilities and stockholders' equity	$200,000	100.0%

2. Rondo Corporation's comparative balance sheets are presented below.

Compute ratios.

(LO 3)

RONDO CORPORATION
Balance Sheets
December 31

	2017	2016
Cash	$ 5,300	$ 3,700
Accounts receivable	21,200	23,400
Inventory	9,000	7,000
Land	20,000	26,000
Buildings	70,000	70,000
Accumulated depreciation—buildings	(15,000)	(10,000)
Total	$110,500	$120,100
Accounts payable	$ 10,370	$ 31,100
Common stock	75,000	69,000
Retained earnings	25,130	20,000
Total	$110,500	$120,100

Rondo's 2017 income statement included net sales of $120,000, cost of goods sold of $70,000, and net income of $14,000.

INSTRUCTIONS

Compute the following ratios for 2017.

(a) Current ratio.
(b) Accounts receivable turnover.
(c) Inventory turnover.
(d) Profit margin.
(e) Asset turnover.
(f) Return on assets.
(g) Return on common stockholders' equity.
(h) Debt to assets ratio.

SOLUTION

2. (a) ($5,300 + $21,200 + $9,000)/$10,370 = 3.42
   (b) $120,000/[($21,200 + $23,400)/2] = 5.38
   (c) $70,000/[($9,000 + $7,000)/2] = 8.8
   (d) $14,000/$120,000 = 11.7%
   (e) $120,000/[($110,500 + $120,100)/2] = 1.04
   (f) $14,000/[($110,500 + $120,100)/2] = 12.1%
   (g) $14,000/[($100,130 + $89,000)/2] = 14.8%
   (h) $10,370/$110,500 = 9.4%

PRACTICE PROBLEM

Prepare a statement of comprehensive income.

(LO 1)

The events and transactions of Dever Corporation for the year ending December 31, 2017, resulted in the following data.

Cost of goods sold	$2,600,000
Net sales	4,400,000
Other expenses and losses	9,600
Other revenues and gains	5,600
Selling and administrative expenses	1,100,000
Income from operations of plastics division	70,000
Gain from disposal of plastics division	500,000
Unrealized loss on available-for-sale securities	60,000

Analysis reveals the following:

1. All items are before the applicable income tax rate of 30%.
2. The plastics division was sold on July 1.
3. All operating data for the plastics division have been segregated.

INSTRUCTIONS

Prepare a statement of comprehensive income for the year.

SOLUTION

DEVER CORPORATION Statement of Comprehensive Income For the Year Ended December 31, 2017	
Net sales	$4,400,000
Cost of goods sold	2,600,000
Gross profit	1,800,000
Selling and administrative expenses	1,100,000
Income from operations	700,000
Other revenues and gains	5,600
Other expenses and losses	9,600
Income before income taxes	696,000
Income tax expense ($696,000 × 30%)	208,800
Income from continuing operations	487,200

Discontinued operations		
Income from operation of plastics division, net of $21,000 income taxes ($70,000 × 30%)	49,000	
Gain from disposal of plastics division, net of $150,000 income taxes ($500,000 × 30%)	350,000	399,000
Net income		886,200
Unrealized loss on available-for-sale securities, net of $18,000 income tax savings ($60,000 × 30%)		42,000
Comprehensive income		$844,200

WileyPLUS Brief Exercises, DO IT! Exercises, Exercises, Problems, and many additional resources are available for practice in WileyPLUS.

NOTE: All asterisked Questions, Exercises, and Problems relate to material in the appendix to the chapter.

QUESTIONS

All of the Questions in this chapter employ decision tools.

1. Explain sustainable income. What relationship does this concept have to the treatment of discontinued operations on the income statement?

2. Hogan Inc. reported 2016 earnings per share of $3.26 and had no discontinued operations. In 2017, earnings per share on income from continuing operations was $2.99, and earnings per share on net income was $3.49. Do you consider this trend to be favorable? Why or why not?

3. Moosier Inc. has been in operation for 3 years and uses the FIFO method of pricing inventory. During the fourth year, Moosier changes to the average-cost method for all its inventory. How will Moosier report this change?

4. What amount did Apple report as "Other comprehensive earnings" in its consolidated statement of comprehensive income ending September 27, 2014? By what percentage did Apple's "Comprehensive income" differ from its "Net income"?

5. Identify and explain factors that affect quality of earnings.

6. Explain how the choice of one of the following accounting methods over the other raises or lowers a company's net income during a period of continuing inflation.
   (a) Use of FIFO instead of LIFO for inventory costing.
   (b) Use of a 6-year life for machinery instead of a 9-year life.
   (c) Use of straight-line depreciation instead of declining-balance depreciation.

7. Two popular methods of financial statement analysis are horizontal analysis and vertical analysis. Explain the difference between these two methods.

8. (a) If Erin Company had net income of $300,000 in 2016 and it experienced a 24.5% increase in net income for 2017, what is its net income for 2017?
   (b) If 6 cents of every dollar of Erin's revenue is net income in 2016, what is the dollar amount of 2016 revenue?

9. (a) Gina Jaimes believes that the analysis of financial statements is directed at two characteristics of a company: liquidity and profitability. Is Gina correct? Explain.
   (b) Are short-term creditors, long-term creditors, and stockholders interested in primarily the same characteristics of a company? Explain.

10. (a) Distinguish among the following bases of comparison: intracompany, intercompany, and industry averages.
    (b) Give the principal value of using each of the three bases of comparison.

11. Name the major ratios useful in assessing (a) liquidity and (b) solvency.

12. Vern Thoms is puzzled. His company had a profit margin of 10% in 2017. He feels that this is an indication that the company is doing well. Tina Amos, his accountant, says that more information is needed to determine the company's financial well-being. Who is correct? Why?

13. What does each type of ratio measure?
    (a) Liquidity ratios.
    (b) Solvency ratios.
    (c) Profitability ratios.

14. What is the difference between the current ratio and working capital?

15. Handi Mart, a retail store, has an accounts receivable turnover of 4.5 times. The industry average is 12.5 times. Does Handi Mart have a collection problem with its receivables?

16. Which ratios should be used to help answer each of these questions?
    (a) How efficient is a company in using its assets to produce sales?
    (b) How near to sale is the inventory on hand?
    (c) How many dollars of net income were earned for each dollar invested by the owners?
    (d) How able is a company to meet interest charges as they fall due?

17. At year-end, the price-earnings ratio of General Motors was 11.3, and the price-earnings ratio of Microsoft was 28.14. Which company did the stock market favor? Explain.

18. What is the formula for computing the payout ratio? Do you expect this ratio to be high or low for a growth company?

19. Holding all other factors constant, indicate whether each of the following changes generally signals good or bad news about a company.
    (a) Increase in profit margin.
    (b) Decrease in inventory turnover.
    (c) Increase in current ratio.
    (d) Decrease in earnings per share.
    (e) Increase in price-earnings ratio.
    (f) Increase in debt to assets ratio.
    (g) Decrease in times interest earned.

20. The return on assets for Ayala Corporation is 7.6%. During the same year, Ayala's return on common stockholders' equity is 12.8%. What is the explanation for the difference in the two rates?

21. Which two ratios do you think should be of greatest interest in each of the following cases?
    (a) A pension fund considering the purchase of 20-year bonds.
    (b) A bank contemplating a short-term loan.
    (c) A common stockholder.

22. Keanu Inc. has net income of $200,000, average shares of common stock outstanding of 40,000, and preferred dividends for the period of $20,000. What is Keanu's earnings per share of common stock? Fred Tyme, the president of Keanu, believes that the computed EPS of the company is high. Comment.

BRIEF EXERCISES

All of the Brief Exercises in this chapter employ decision tools.

Prepare a discontinued operations section of an income statement. (LO 1), AP

BE13-1 On June 30, Flores Corporation discontinued its operations in Mexico. On September 1, Flores disposed of the Mexico facility at a pretax loss of $640,000. The applicable tax rate is 25%. Show the discontinued operations section of Flores's statement of comprehensive income.

Prepare statement of comprehensive income including unusual items. (LO 1), AP

BE13-2 An inexperienced accountant for Silva Corporation showed the following in the income statement: income before income taxes $450,000 and unrealized gain on available-for-sale securities (before taxes) $70,000. The unrealized gain on available-for-sale securities and income before income taxes are both subject to a 25% tax rate. Prepare a correct statement of comprehensive income.

Indicate how a change in accounting principle is reported. (LO 1), C

BE13-3 On January 1, 2017, Bryce Inc. changed from the LIFO method of inventory pricing to the FIFO method. Explain how this change in accounting principle should be treated in the company's financial statements.

Prepare horizontal analysis. (LO 2), AP

BE13-4 Using these data from the comparative balance sheet of Rollaird Company, perform horizontal analysis.

	December 31, 2017	December 31, 2016
Accounts receivable	$ 460,000	$ 400,000
Inventory	780,000	650,000
Total assets	3,164,000	2,800,000

Prepare vertical analysis. (LO 2), AP

BE13-5 Using the data presented in BE13-4 for Rollaird Company, perform vertical analysis.

Calculate percentage of change. (LO 2), AP

BE13-6 Net income was $500,000 in 2015, $485,000 in 2016, and $518,400 in 2017. What is the percentage of change from (a) 2015 to 2016, and (b) from 2016 to 2017? Is the change an increase or a decrease?

Calculate net income. (LO 2), AP

BE13-7 If Coho Company had net income of $382,800 in 2017 and it experienced a 16% increase in net income over 2016, what was its 2016 net income?

Analyze change in net income. (LO 2), AP

BE13-8 Vertical analysis (common-size) percentages for Palau Company's sales revenue, cost of goods sold, and expenses are listed here.

Vertical Analysis	2017	2016	2015
Sales revenue	100.0%	100.0%	100.0%
Cost of goods sold	60.5	62.9	64.8
Expenses	26.0	26.6	27.5

Did Palau's net income as a percent of sales increase, decrease, or remain unchanged over the 3-year period? Provide numerical support for your answer.

BE13-9 Horizontal analysis (trend analysis) percentages for Phoenix Company's sales revenue, cost of goods sold, and expenses are listed here.

Analyze change in net income.

(LO 2), AP

Horizontal Analysis	2017	2016	2015
Sales revenue	96.2%	104.8%	100.0%
Cost of goods sold	101.0	98.0	100.0
Expenses	105.6	95.4	100.0

Explain whether Phoenix's net income increased, decreased, or remained unchanged over the 3-year period.

BE13-10 Suppose these selected condensed data are taken from recent balance sheets of Bob Evans Farms (in thousands).

Calculate current ratio.

(LO 3), AP

	2017	2016
Cash	$ 13,606	$ 7,669
Accounts receivable	23,045	19,951
Inventory	31,087	31,345
Other current assets	12,522	11,909
Total current assets	$ 80,260	$ 70,874
Total current liabilities	$245,805	$326,203

Compute the current ratio for each year and comment on your results.

BE13-11 The following data are taken from the financial statements of Colby Company.

Evaluate collection of accounts receivable.

(LO 3), AN

	2017	2016
Accounts receivable (net), end of year	$ 550,000	$ 540,000
Net sales on account	4,300,000	4,000,000
Terms for all sales are 1/10, n/45		

Compute for each year (a) the accounts receivable turnover and (b) the average collection period. What conclusions about the management of accounts receivable can be drawn from these data? At the end of 2015, accounts receivable was $520,000.

BE13-12 The following data were taken from the income statements of Mydorf Company.

Evaluate management of inventory.

(LO 3), AN

	2017	2016
Sales revenue	$6,420,000	$6,240,000
Beginning inventory	960,000	840,000
Purchases	4,840,000	4,661,000
Ending inventory	1,020,000	960,000

Compute for each year (a) the inventory turnover and (b) days in inventory. What conclusions concerning the management of the inventory can be drawn from these data?

BE13-13 Staples, Inc. is one of the largest suppliers of office products in the United States. Suppose it had net income of $738.7 million and sales of $24,275.5 million in 2017. Its total assets were $13,073.1 million at the beginning of the year and $13,717.3 million at the end of the year. What is Staples, Inc.'s (a) asset turnover and (b) profit margin? (Round to two decimals.) Provide a brief interpretation of your results.

Calculate profitability ratios.

(LO 3), AN

Calculate profitability ratios.
(LO 3), AN

BE13-14 Hollie Company has stockholders' equity of $400,000 and net income of $72,000. It has a payout ratio of 18% and a return on assets of 20%. How much did Hollie pay in cash dividends, and what were its average total assets?

Calculate and analyze free cash flow.
(LO 3), AN

BE13-15 Selected data taken from a recent year's financial statements of trading card company Topps Company, Inc. are as follows (in millions).

Net sales	$326.7
Current liabilities, beginning of year	41.1
Current liabilities, end of year	62.4
Net cash provided by operating activities	10.4
Total liabilities, beginning of year	65.2
Total liabilities, end of year	73.2
Capital expenditures	3.7
Cash dividends	6.2

Compute the free cash flow. Provide a brief interpretation of your results.

DO IT! EXERCISES

Prepare statement of comprehensive income including unusual items.
(LO 1), AP

DO IT! 13-1 In its proposed 2017 income statement, Hrabik Corporation reports income before income taxes $500,000, income taxes $100,000 (not including unusual items), loss on operation of discontinued music division $60,000, gain on disposal of discontinued music division $40,000, and unrealized loss on available-for-sale securities $150,000. The income tax rate is 20%. Prepare a correct statement of comprehensive income, beginning with income before income taxes.

Prepare horizontal analysis.
(LO 2), AP

DO IT! 13-2 Summary financial information for Gandaulf Company is as follows.

	Dec. 31, 2017	Dec. 31, 2016
Current assets	$ 200,000	$ 220,000
Plant assets	1,040,000	780,000
Total assets	$1,240,000	$1,000,000

Compute the amount and percentage changes in 2017 using horizontal analysis, assuming 2016 is the base year.

Compute ratios.
(LO 3), AP

DO IT! 13-3 The condensed financial statements of Murawski Company for the years 2016 and 2017 are presented as follows. (Amounts in thousands.)

MURAWSKI COMPANY
Balance Sheets
December 31

	2017	2016
Current assets		
Cash and cash equivalents	$ 330	$ 360
Accounts receivable (net)	470	400
Inventory	460	390
Prepaid expenses	120	160
Total current assets	1,380	1,310
Investments	10	10
Property, plant, and equipment	420	380
Intangibles and other assets	530	510
Total assets	$2,340	$2,210
Current liabilities	$ 900	$ 790
Long-term liabilities	410	380
Stockholders' equity—common	1,030	1,040
Total liabilities and stockholders' equity	$2,340	$2,210

MURAWSKI COMPANY
Income Statements
For the Years Ended December 31

	2017	2016
Sales revenue	$3,800	$3,460
Costs and expenses		
Cost of goods sold	955	890
Selling & administrative expenses	2,400	2,330
Interest expense	25	20
Total costs and expenses	3,380	3,240
Income before income taxes	420	220
Income tax expense	126	66
Net income	$ 294	$ 154

Compute the following ratios for 2017 and 2016.

(a) Current ratio.
(b) Inventory turnover. (Inventory on 12/31/15 was $340.)
(c) Profit margin.
(d) Return on assets. (Assets on 12/31/15 were $1,900.)
(e) Return on common stockholders' equity. (Stockholders' equity on 12/31/15 was $900.)
(f) Debt to assets ratio.
(g) Times interest earned.

EXERCISES

Prepare a correct statement of comprehensive income.

(LO 1), AP

E13-1 For its fiscal year ending October 31, 2017, Haas Corporation reports the following partial data shown below.

Income before income taxes	$540,000
Income tax expense (20% × $420,000)	84,000
Income from continuing operations	456,000
Loss on discontinued operations	120,000
Net income	$336,000

The loss on discontinued operations was comprised of a $50,000 loss from operations and a $70,000 loss from disposal. The income tax rate is 20% on all items.

Instructions

(a) Prepare a correct statement of comprehensive income beginning with income before income taxes.
(b) Explain in memo form why the income statement data are misleading.

Prepare statement of comprehensive income.

(LO 1), AP

E13-2 Trayer Corporation has income from continuing operations of $290,000 for the year ended December 31, 2017. It also has the following items (before considering income taxes).

1. An unrealized loss of $80,000 on available-for-sale securities.
2. A gain of $30,000 on the discontinuance of a division (comprised of a $10,000 loss from operations and a $40,000 gain on disposal).
3. A correction of an error in last year's financial statements that resulted in a $20,000 understatement of 2016 net income.

Assume all items are subject to income taxes at a 20% tax rate.

Instructions

Prepare a statement of comprehensive income, beginning with income from continuing operations.

Prepare horizontal analysis.
(LO 2), AP

E13-3 Here is financial information for Glitter Inc.

	December 31, 2017	December 31, 2016
Current assets	$106,000	$ 90,000
Plant assets (net)	400,000	350,000
Current liabilities	99,000	65,000
Long-term liabilities	122,000	90,000
Common stock, $1 par	130,000	115,000
Retained earnings	155,000	170,000

Instructions

Prepare a schedule showing a horizontal analysis for 2017, using 2016 as the base year.

Prepare vertical analysis.
(LO 2), AP

E13-4 Operating data for Joshua Corporation are presented below.

	2017	2016
Sales revenue	$800,000	$600,000
Cost of goods sold	520,000	408,000
Selling expenses	120,000	72,000
Administrative expenses	60,000	48,000
Income tax expense	30,000	24,000
Net income	70,000	48,000

Instructions

Prepare a schedule showing a vertical analysis for 2017 and 2016.

Prepare horizontal and vertical analyses.
(LO 2), AP

E13-5 Suppose the comparative balance sheets of Nike, Inc. are presented here.

NIKE, INC.
Comparative Balance Sheets
May 31
($ in millions)

Assets	**2017**	**2016**
Current assets	$ 9,734	$ 8,839
Property, plant, and equipment (net)	1,958	1,891
Other assets	1,558	1,713
Total assets	$13,250	$12,443
Liabilities and Stockholders' Equity		
Current liabilities	$ 3,277	$ 3,322
Long-term liabilities	1,280	1,296
Stockholders' equity	8,693	7,825
Total liabilities and stockholders' equity	$13,250	$12,443

Instructions

(a) Prepare a horizontal analysis of the balance sheet data for Nike, using 2016 as a base. (Show the amount of increase or decrease as well.)
(b) Prepare a vertical analysis of the balance sheet data for Nike for 2017.

Prepare horizontal and vertical analyses.
(LO 2), AP

E13-6 Here are the comparative income statements of Delaney Corporation.

DELANEY CORPORATION
Comparative Income Statements
For the Years Ended December 31

	2017	2016
Net sales	$598,000	$500,000
Cost of goods sold	477,000	420,000
Gross profit	121,000	80,000
Operating expenses	80,000	44,000
Net income	$ 41,000	$ 36,000

Instructions

(a) Prepare a horizontal analysis of the income statement data for Delaney Corporation, using 2016 as a base. (Show the amounts of increase or decrease.)

(b) Prepare a vertical analysis of the income statement data for Delaney Corporation for both years.

E13-7 Nordstrom, Inc. operates department stores in numerous states. Suppose selected financial statement data (in millions) for 2017 are presented below.

Compute liquidity ratios.

(LO 3), AP

	End of Year	Beginning of Year
Cash and cash equivalents	$ 795	$ 72
Accounts receivable (net)	2,035	1,942
Inventory	898	900
Other current assets	326	303
Total current assets	$4,054	$3,217
Total current liabilities	$2,014	$1,601

For the year, net credit sales were $8,258 million, cost of goods sold was $5,328 million, and net cash provided by operating activities was $1,251 million.

Instructions

Compute the current ratio, accounts receivable turnover, average collection period, inventory turnover, and days in inventory at the end of the current year.

E13-8 Gwynn Incorporated had the following transactions involving current assets and current liabilities during February 2017.

Perform current ratio analysis.

(LO 3), AP

Feb.	3	Collected accounts receivable of $15,000.
	7	Purchased equipment for $23,000 cash.
	11	Paid $3,000 for a 1-year insurance policy.
	14	Paid accounts payable of $12,000.
	18	Declared cash dividends, $4,000.

Additional information:

As of February 1, 2017, current assets were $120,000 and current liabilities were $40,000.

Instructions

Compute the current ratio as of the beginning of the month and after each transaction.

E13-9 Lendell Company has these comparative balance sheet data:

Compute selected ratios.

(LO 3), AP

LENDELL COMPANY
Balance Sheets
December 31

	2017	2016
Cash	$ 15,000	$ 30,000
Accounts receivable (net)	70,000	60,000
Inventory	60,000	50,000
Plant assets (net)	200,000	180,000
	$345,000	$320,000
Accounts payable	$ 50,000	$ 60,000
Mortgage payable (15%)	100,000	100,000
Common stock, $10 par	140,000	120,000
Retained earnings	55,000	40,000
	$345,000	$320,000

Additional information for 2017:

1. Net income was $25,000.
2. Sales on account were $375,000. Sales returns and allowances amounted to $25,000.
3. Cost of goods sold was $198,000.
4. Net cash provided by operating activities was $48,000.
5. Capital expenditures were $25,000, and cash dividends were $10,000.

Instructions

Compute the following ratios at December 31, 2017.

(a) Current ratio.
(b) Accounts receivable turnover.
(c) Average collection period.
(d) Inventory turnover.
(e) Days in inventory.
(f) Free cash flow.

Compute selected ratios.

(LO 3), AP

E13-10 Suppose selected comparative statement data for the giant bookseller Barnes & Noble are presented here. All balance sheet data are as of the end of the fiscal year (in millions).

	2017	2016
Net sales	$5,121.8	$5,286.7
Cost of goods sold	3,540.6	3,679.8
Net income	75.9	135.8
Accounts receivable	81.0	107.1
Inventory	1,203.5	1,358.2
Total assets	2,993.9	3,249.8
Total common stockholders' equity	921.6	1,074.7

Instructions

Compute the following ratios for 2017.

(a) Profit margin.
(b) Asset turnover.
(c) Return on assets.
(d) Return on common stockholders' equity.
(e) Gross profit rate.

Compute selected ratios.

(LO 3), AP

E13-11 Here is the income statement for Myers, Inc.

MYERS, INC.
Income Statement
For the Year Ended December 31, 2017

Sales revenue	$400,000
Cost of goods sold	230,000
Gross profit	170,000
Expenses (including $16,000 interest and $24,000 income taxes)	98,000
Net income	$ 72,000

Additional information:

1. Common stock outstanding January 1, 2017, was 32,000 shares, and 40,000 shares were outstanding at December 31, 2017.
2. The market price of Myers stock was $14 in 2017.
3. Cash dividends of $21,000 were paid, $5,000 of which were to preferred stockholders.

Instructions

Compute the following measures for 2017.

(a) Earnings per share.
(b) Price-earnings ratio.
(c) Payout ratio.
(d) Times interest earned.

Compute amounts from ratios.

(LO 3), AP

E13-12 Panza Corporation experienced a fire on December 31, 2017, in which its financial records were partially destroyed. It has been able to salvage some of the records and has ascertained the following balances.

	December 31, 2017	December 31, 2016
Cash	$ 30,000	$ 10,000
Accounts receivable (net)	72,500	126,000
Inventory	200,000	180,000
Accounts payable	50,000	90,000
Notes payable	30,000	60,000
Common stock, $100 par	400,000	400,000
Retained earnings	113,500	101,000

Additional information:

1. The inventory turnover is 3.8 times.
2. The return on common stockholders' equity is 22%. The company had no additional paid-in capital.
3. The accounts receivable turnover is 11.2 times.
4. The return on assets is 18%.
5. Total assets at December 31, 2016, were $605,000.

Instructions

Compute the following for Panza Corporation.

(a) Cost of goods sold for 2017.
(b) Net credit sales for 2017.
(c) Net income for 2017.
(d) Total assets at December 31, 2017.

E13-13 The condensed financial statements of Ness Company for the years 2016 and 2017 are presented below.

Compute ratios.

(LO 3), AP

NESS COMPANY
Balance Sheets
December 31 (in thousands)

	2017	**2016**
Current assets		
Cash and cash equivalents	$ 330	$ 360
Accounts receivable (net)	470	400
Inventory	460	390
Prepaid expenses	130	160
Total current assets	1,390	1,310
Property, plant, and equipment (net)	410	380
Investments	10	10
Intangibles and other assets	530	510
Total assets	$2,340	$2,210
Current liabilities	$ 820	$ 790
Long-term liabilities	480	380
Stockholders' equity—common	1,040	1,040
Total liabilities and stockholders' equity	$2,340	$2,210

NESS COMPANY
Income Statements
For the Year Ended December 31 (in thousands)

	2017	**2016**
Sales revenue	$3,800	$3,460
Costs and expenses		
Cost of goods sold	970	890
Selling & administrative expenses	2,400	2,330
Interest expense	10	20
Total costs and expenses	3,380	3,240
Income before income taxes	420	220
Income tax expense	168	88
Net income	$ 252	$ 132

Compute the following ratios for 2017 and 2016.

(a) Current ratio.
(b) Inventory turnover. (Inventory on December 31, 2015, was $340.)
(c) Profit margin.
(d) Return on assets. (Assets on December 31, 2015, were $1,900.)
(e) Return on common stockholders' equity. (Equity on December 31, 2015, was $900.)
(f) Debt to assets ratio.
(g) Times interest earned.

EXERCISES: SET B AND CHALLENGE EXERCISES

Visit the book's companion website, at **www.wiley.com/college/kimmel**, and choose the Student Companion site to access Exercises: Set B and Challenge Exercises.

PROBLEMS: SET A

All of the Problems in this chapter employ decision tools.

Prepare vertical analysis and comment on profitability.

(LO 2, 3), AN

P13-1A Here are comparative statement data for Duke Company and Lord Company, two competitors. All balance sheet data are as of December 31, 2017, and December 31, 2016.

	Duke Company		Lord Company	
	2017	**2016**	**2017**	**2016**
Net sales	$1,849,000		$546,000	
Cost of goods sold	1,063,200		289,000	
Operating expenses	240,000		82,000	
Interest expense	6,800		3,600	
Income tax expense	62,000		28,000	
Current assets	325,975	$312,410	83,336	$ 79,467
Plant assets (net)	526,800	500,000	139,728	125,812
Current liabilities	66,325	75,815	35,348	30,281
Long-term liabilities	113,990	90,000	29,620	25,000
Common stock, $10 par	500,000	500,000	120,000	120,000
Retained earnings	172,460	146,595	38,096	29,998

Instructions

(a) Prepare a vertical analysis of the 2017 income statement data for Duke Company and Lord Company.

(b) Comment on the relative profitability of the companies by computing the 2017 return on assets and the return on common stockholders' equity for both companies.

Compute ratios from balance sheets and income statements.

(LO 3), AP

P13-2A The comparative statements of Wahlberg Company are presented here.

WAHLBERG COMPANY
Income Statements
For the Years Ended December 31

	2017	2016
Net sales	$1,890,540	$1,750,500
Cost of goods sold	1,058,540	1,006,000
Gross profit	832,000	744,500
Selling and administrative expenses	500,000	479,000
Income from operations	332,000	265,500
Other expenses and losses		
Interest expense	22,000	20,000
Income before income taxes	310,000	245,500
Income tax expense	92,000	73,000
Net income	$ 218,000	$ 172,500

WAHLBERG COMPANY
Balance Sheets
December 31

Assets	2017	2016
Current assets		
Cash	$ 60,100	$ 64,200
Debt investments (short-term)	74,000	50,000
Accounts receivable	117,800	102,800
Inventory	126,000	115,500
Total current assets	377,900	332,500
Plant assets (net)	649,000	520,300
Total assets	$1,026,900	$852,800

Liabilities and Stockholders' Equity	2017	2016
Current liabilities		
Accounts payable	$ 160,000	$145,400
Income taxes payable	43,500	42,000
Total current liabilities	203,500	187,400
Bonds payable	220,000	200,000
Total liabilities	423,500	387,400
Stockholders' equity		
Common stock ($5 par)	290,000	300,000
Retained earnings	313,400	165,400
Total stockholders' equity	603,400	465,400
Total liabilities and stockholders' equity	$1,026,900	$852,800

All sales were on account. Net cash provided by operating activities for 2017 was $220,000. Capital expenditures were $136,000, and cash dividends were $70,000.

Instructions

Compute the following ratios for 2017.

(a) Earnings per share.
(b) Return on common stockholders' equity.
(c) Return on assets.
(d) Current ratio.
(e) Accounts receivable turnover.
(f) Average collection period.
(g) Inventory turnover.
(h) Days in inventory.
(i) Times interest earned.
(j) Asset turnover.
(k) Debt to assets ratio.
(l) Free cash flow.

Perform ratio analysis, and discuss changes in financial position and operating results.

(LO 3), AN

P13-3A Condensed balance sheet and income statement data for Jergan Corporation are presented here.

JERGAN CORPORATION
Balance Sheets
December 31

	2017	2016	2015
Cash	$ 30,000	$ 20,000	$ 18,000
Accounts receivable (net)	50,000	45,000	48,000
Other current assets	90,000	95,000	64,000
Investments	55,000	70,000	45,000
Plant and equipment (net)	500,000	370,000	358,000
	$725,000	$600,000	$533,000
Current liabilities	$ 85,000	$ 80,000	$ 70,000
Long-term debt	145,000	85,000	50,000
Common stock, $10 par	320,000	310,000	300,000
Retained earnings	175,000	125,000	113,000
	$725,000	$600,000	$533,000

JERGAN CORPORATION
Income Statements
For the Years Ended December 31

	2017	2016
Sales revenue	$740,000	$600,000
Less: Sales returns and allowances	40,000	30,000
Net sales	700,000	570,000
Cost of goods sold	425,000	350,000
Gross profit	275,000	220,000
Operating expenses (including income taxes)	180,000	150,000
Net income	$ 95,000	$ 70,000

Additional information:

1. The market price of Jergan's common stock was $7.00, $7.50, and $8.50 for 2015, 2016, and 2017, respectively.
2. You must compute dividends paid. All dividends were paid in cash.

Instructions

(a) Compute the following ratios for 2016 and 2017.

(1) Profit margin.
(2) Gross profit rate.
(3) Asset turnover.
(4) Earnings per share.
(5) Price-earnings ratio.
(6) Payout ratio.
(7) Debt to assets ratio.

(b) Based on the ratios calculated, discuss briefly the improvement or lack thereof in the financial position and operating results from 2016 to 2017 of Jergan Corporation.

Compute ratios; comment on overall liquidity and profitability.

(LO 3), AN

P13-4A The following financial information is for Priscoll Company.

PRISCOLL COMPANY
Balance Sheets
December 31

Assets	2017	2016
Cash	$ 70,000	$ 65,000
Debt investments (short-term)	55,000	40,000
Accounts receivable	104,000	90,000
Inventory	230,000	165,000
Prepaid expenses	25,000	23,000
Land	130,000	130,000
Building and equipment (net)	260,000	185,000
Total assets	$874,000	$698,000
Liabilities and Stockholders' Equity		
Notes payable	$170,000	$120,000
Accounts payable	65,000	52,000
Accrued liabilities	40,000	40,000
Bonds payable, due 2020	250,000	170,000
Common stock, $10 par	200,000	200,000
Retained earnings	149,000	116,000
Total liabilities and stockholders' equity	$874,000	$698,000

PRISCOLL COMPANY
Income Statements
For the Years Ended December 31

	2017	2016
Sales revenue	$882,000	$790,000
Cost of goods sold	640,000	575,000
Gross profit	242,000	215,000
Operating expenses	190,000	167,000
Net income	$ 52,000	$ 48,000

Additional information:

1. Inventory at the beginning of 2016 was $115,000.
2. Accounts receivable (net) at the beginning of 2016 were $86,000.
3. Total assets at the beginning of 2016 were $660,000.
4. No common stock transactions occurred during 2016 or 2017.
5. All sales were on account.

Instructions

(a) Indicate, by using ratios, the change in liquidity and profitability of Priscoll Company from 2016 to 2017. (*Note:* Not all profitability ratios can be computed nor can cash-basis ratios be computed.)

(b) The following are three independent situations and a ratio that may be affected. For each situation, compute the affected ratio (1) as of December 31, 2017, and (2) as of December 31, 2018, after giving effect to the situation. Net income for 2018 was $54,000. Total assets on December 31, 2018, were $900,000.

Situation	Ratio
1. 18,000 shares of common stock were sold at par on July 1, 2018.	Return on common stockholders' equity
2. All of the notes payable were paid in 2018.	Debt to assets ratio
3. The market price of common stock was $9 and $12 on December 31, 2017 and 2018, respectively.	Price-earnings ratio

Compute selected ratios, and compare liquidity, profitability, and solvency for two companies.

(LO 3), AN

P13-5A Suppose selected financial data of Target and Wal-Mart for 2017 are presented here (in millions).

	Target Corporation	Wal-Mart Stores, Inc.
	Income Statement Data for Year	
Net sales	$65,357	$408,214
Cost of goods sold	45,583	304,657
Selling and administrative expenses	15,101	79,607
Interest expense	707	2,065
Other income (expense)	(94)	(411)
Income tax expense	1,384	7,139
Net income	$ 2,488	$ 14,335
	Balance Sheet Data (End of Year)	
Current assets	$18,424	$ 48,331
Noncurrent assets	26,109	122,375
Total assets	$44,533	$170,706
Current liabilities	$11,327	$ 55,561
Long-term debt	17,859	44,089
Total stockholders' equity	15,347	71,056
Total liabilities and stockholders' equity	$44,533	$170,706
	Beginning-of-Year Balances	
Total assets	$44,106	$163,429
Total stockholders' equity	13,712	65,682
Current liabilities	10,512	55,390
Total liabilities	30,394	97,747
	Other Data	
Average net accounts receivable	$ 7,525	$ 4,025
Average inventory	6,942	33,836
Net cash provided by operating activities	5,881	26,249
Capital expenditures	1,729	12,184
Dividends	496	4,217

Instructions

(a) For each company, compute the following ratios.

(1) Current ratio.
(2) Accounts receivable turnover.
(3) Average collection period.
(4) Inventory turnover.
(5) Days in inventory.
(6) Profit margin.
(7) Asset turnover.
(8) Return on assets.
(9) Return on common stockholders' equity.
(10) Debt to assets ratio.
(11) Times interest earned.
(12) Free cash flow.

(b) Compare the liquidity, solvency, and profitability of the two companies.

▶ PROBLEMS: SET B AND SET C

Visit the book's companion website, at **www.wiley.com/college/kimmel**, and choose the Student Companion site to access Problems: Set B and Set C.

▶ CONTINUING PROBLEM Cookie Creations

© leungchopan/ Shutterstock

(*Note:* This is a continuation of the Cookie Creations problem from Chapters 1 through 12.)

CC13 Natalie and Curtis have comparative balance sheets and income statements for Cookie & Coffee Creations Inc. They have been told that they can use these financial statements to prepare horizontal and vertical analyses, to calculate financial ratios, to analyze how their business is doing, and to make some decisions they have been considering.

Go to the book's companion website, at **www.wiley.com/college/kimmel**, *to find the completion of this problem.*

EXPAND YOUR CRITICAL THINKING

Financial Reporting

FINANCIAL REPORTING PROBLEM: Apple Inc.

AN

CT13-1 Your parents are considering investing in Apple Inc. common stock. They ask you, as an accounting expert, to make an analysis of the company for them. Financial statements of Apple are presented in Appendix A. Instructions for accessing and using the company's complete annual report, including the notes to its financial statements, are also provided in Appendix A.

Instructions

(a) Make a 5-year trend analysis, using 2010 as the base year, of (1) net sales and (2) net income. Comment on the significance of the trend results.

(b) Compute for 2014 and 2013 the (1) debt to assets ratio and (2) times interest earned. (See Note 3 for interest expense.) How would you evaluate Apple's long-term solvency?

(c) Compute for 2014 and 2013 the (1) profit margin, (2) asset turnover, (3) return on assets, and (4) return on common stockholders' equity. How would you evaluate Apple's profitability? Total assets at September 29, 2012, were $176,064 million and total stockholders' equity at September 29, 2012, was $118,210 million.

(d) What information outside the annual report may also be useful to your parents in making a decision about Apple?

Financial Analysis

COMPARATIVE ANALYSIS PROBLEM: Columbia Sportswear Company vs. VF Corporation

AN

CT13-2 The financial statements of Columbia Sportswear Company are presented in Appendix B. Financial statements of VF Corporation are presented in Appendix C.

Instructions

(a) Based on the information in the financial statements, determine each of the following for each company:
   (1) The percentage increase (i) in net sales and (ii) in net income from 2013 to 2014.
   (2) The percentage increase (i) in total assets and (ii) in total stockholders' equity from 2013 to 2014.
   (3) The basic earnings per share for 2014.

(b) What conclusions concerning the two companies can be drawn from these data?

Financial Analysis

COMPARATIVE ANALYSIS PROBLEM: Amazon.com, Inc. vs. Wal-Mart Stores, Inc.

AN

CT13-3 The financial statements of Amazon.com, Inc. are presented in Appendix D. Financial statements of Wal-Mart Stores, Inc. are presented in Appendix E.

Instructions

(a) Based on the information in the financial statements, determine each of the following for each company:
   (1) The percentage increase (i) in net sales and (ii) in net income from 2013 to 2014.
   (2) The percentage increase (i) in total assets and (ii) in total stockholders' equity from 2013 to 2014.
   (3) The basic earnings per share for 2014.

(b) What conclusions concerning the two companies can be drawn from these data?

INTERPRETING FINANCIAL STATEMENTS

Financial Analysis

CT13-4 The Coca-Cola Company and PepsiCo, Inc. provide refreshments to every corner of the world. Suppose selected data from recent consolidated financial statements for The Coca-Cola Company and for PepsiCo, Inc. are presented here (in millions). AN

	Coca-Cola	PepsiCo
Total current assets	$17,551	$12,571
Total current liabilities	13,721	8,756
Net sales	30,990	43,232
Cost of goods sold	11,088	20,099
Net income	6,824	5,946
Average (net) accounts receivable for the year	3,424	4,654
Average inventories for the year	2,271	2,570
Average total assets	44,595	37,921
Average common stockholders' equity	22,636	14,556
Average current liabilities	13,355	8,772
Average total liabilities	21,960	23,466
Total assets	48,671	39,848
Total liabilities	23,872	23,044
Income taxes	2,040	2,100
Interest expense	355	397
Net cash provided by operating activities	8,186	6,796
Capital expenditures	1,993	2,128
Cash dividends	3,800	2,732

Instructions

(a) Compute the following liquidity ratios for Coca-Cola and for PepsiCo and comment on the relative liquidity of the two competitors.
(1) Current ratio.
(2) Accounts receivable turnover.
(3) Average collection period.
(4) Inventory turnover.
(5) Days in inventory.

(b) Compute the following solvency ratios for the two companies and comment on the relative solvency of the two competitors.
(1) Debt to assets ratio.
(2) Times interest earned.
(3) Free cash flow.

(c) Compute the following profitability ratios for the two companies and comment on the relative profitability of the two competitors.
(1) Profit margin.
(2) Asset turnover.
(3) Return on assets.
(4) Return on common stockholders' equity.

REAL-WORLD FOCUS

CT13-5 ***Purpose:*** To employ comparative data and industry data to evaluate a company's performance and financial position. E

Address: **http://www.msn.com/en-us/money**, or go to **www.wiley.com/college/kimmel**

Steps

(1) Identify two competing companies.
(2) Go to the above address.
(3) Type in the first company's stock symbol or name. (Use "symbol look-up.")
(4) Under the "Fundamentals" heading, use the Growth, Profitability, Financial health, Price ratios, and Management effectiveness tabs to answer parts (a), (b), and (c) below.

Instructions

(a) Evaluate the company's liquidity relative to the industry averages and to the competitor that you chose.
(b) Evaluate the company's solvency relative to the industry averages and to the competitor that you chose.
(c) Evaluate the company's profitability relative to the industry averages and to the competitor that you chose.

E **CT13-6** The April 25, 2012, edition of the *Wall Street Journal* contains an article by Spencer Jakab entitled "Amazon's Valuation Is Hard to Justify."

Instructions

Read the article and answer the following questions.

(a) Explain what is meant by the statement that "On a split-adjusted basis, today's share price is the equivalent of $1,166."

(b) The article says that Amazon.com nearly doubled its capital spending on items such as fulfillment centers (sophisticated warehouses where it finds, packages, and ships goods to customers). Discuss the implications that this spending would have on the company's return on assets in the short-term and in the long-term.

(c) How does Amazon's P-E ratio compare to that of Apple, Netflix, and Wal-Mart? What does this suggest about investors' expectations about Amazon's future earnings?

(d) What factor does the article cite as a possible hurdle that might reduce Amazon's ability to raise its operating margin back to previous levels?

Financial Analysis

Writing

Group Project

DECISION-MAKING ACROSS THE ORGANIZATION

E **CT13-7** You are a loan officer for White Sands Bank of Taos. Paul Jason, president of P. Jason Corporation, has just left your office. He is interested in an 8-year loan to expand the company's operations. The borrowed funds would be used to purchase new equipment. As evidence of the company's debt-worthiness, Jason provided you with the following facts.

	2017	2016
Current ratio	3.1	2.1
Asset turnover	2.8	2.2
Net income	Up 32%	Down 8%
Earnings per share	$3.30	$2.50

Jason is a very insistent (some would say pushy) man. When you told him that you would need additional information before making your decision, he acted offended and said, "What more could you possibly want to know?" You responded that, at a minimum, you would need complete, audited financial statements.

Instructions

With the class divided into groups, answer the following.

(a) Explain why you would want the financial statements to be audited.

(b) Discuss the implications of the ratios provided for the lending decision you are to make. That is, does the information paint a favorable picture? Are these ratios relevant to the decision?

(c) List three other ratios that you would want to calculate for this company, and explain why you would use each.

COMMUNICATION ACTIVITY

E **CT13-8** Larry Dundee is the chief executive officer of Palmer Electronics. Dundee is an expert engineer but a novice in accounting. Dundee asks you, as an accounting student, to explain (a) the bases for comparison in analyzing Palmer's financial statements and (b) the limitations, if any, in financial statement analysis.

Instructions

Write a memo to Larry Dundee that explains the basis for comparison and the factors affecting quality of earnings.

ETHICS CASE

E **CT13-9** René Kelly, president of RL Industries, wishes to issue a press release to bolster her company's image and maybe even its stock price, which has been gradually falling. As controller, you have been asked to provide a list of 20 financial ratios and other operating statistics for RL Industries' first-quarter financials and operations.

Two days after you provide the data requested, Erin Lourdes, the public relations director of RL, asks you to prove the accuracy of the financial and operating data contained in the press release written by the president and edited by Erin. In the news release, the president highlights the sales increase of 25% over last year's first quarter and the positive change in the current ratio from 1.5:1 last year to 3:1 this year. She also emphasizes that production was up 50% over the prior year's first quarter.

You note that the release contains only positive or improved ratios and none of the negative or deteriorated ratios. For instance, no mention is made that the debt to assets ratio has increased from 35% to 55%, that inventories are up 89%, and that although the current ratio improved, the accounts receivable turnover fell from 12 to 9. Nor is there any mention that the reported profit for the quarter would have been a loss had not the estimated lives of RL plant and machinery been increased by 30%. Erin emphasized, "The Pres wants this release by early this afternoon."

Instructions

(a) Who are the stakeholders in this situation?
(b) Is there anything unethical in the president's actions?
(c) Should you as controller remain silent? Does Erin have any responsibility?

ALL ABOUT YOU

CT13-10 In this chapter, you learned how to use many tools for performing a financial analysis of a company. When making personal investments, however, it is most likely that you won't be buying stocks and bonds in individual companies. Instead, when most people want to invest in stock, they buy mutual funds. By investing in a mutual fund, you reduce your risk because the fund diversifies by buying the stock of a variety of different companies, bonds, and other investments, depending on the stated goals of the fund. E

Before you invest in a fund, you will need to decide what type of fund you want. For example, do you want a fund that has the potential of high growth (but also high risk), or are you looking for lower risk and a steady stream of income? Do you want a fund that invests only in U.S. companies, or do you want one that invests globally? Many resources are available to help you with these types of decisions.

Instructions

Go to **http://web.archive.org/web/20050210200843/http://www.cnb1.com/invallocmdl.htm** and complete the investment allocation questionnaire. Add up your total points to determine the type of investment fund that would be appropriate for you.

FASB CODIFICATION ACTIVITY

CT13-11 If your school has a subscription to the FASB Codification, go to **http://aaahq.org/ascLogin.cfm** to log in and prepare responses to the following. Use the Master Glossary for determining the proper definitions. AP

(a) Discontinued operations.
(b) Comprehensive income.

A Look at IFRS

LEARNING OBJECTIVE 5 **Compare financial statement analysis and income statement presentation under GAAP and IFRS.**

The tools of financial statement analysis are the same throughout the world. Techniques such as vertical and horizontal analysis, for example, are tools used by analysts regardless of whether GAAP- or IFRS-related financial statements are being evaluated. In addition, the ratios provided in the textbook are the same ones that are used internationally.

The beginning of this chapter relates to the income statement. As in GAAP, the income statement is a required statement under IFRS. In addition, the content and presentation of an IFRS income statement is similar to the one used for GAAP. *IAS 1* (revised), "Presentation of Financial Statements," provides general guidelines for the reporting of income statement information. In general, the differences in the presentation of financial statement information are relatively minor.

RELEVANT FACTS

Following are the key similarities between GAAP and IFRS as related to financial statement analysis and income statement presentation. There are no significant differences between the two standards.

- The tools of financial statement analysis covered in this chapter are universal and therefore no significant differences exist in the analysis methods used.
- The basic objectives of the income statement are the same under both GAAP and IFRS. As indicated in the textbook, a very important objective is to ensure that users of the income statement can evaluate the sustainable income of the company. Thus, both the IASB and the FASB are interested in distinguishing normal levels of income from unusual items in order to better predict a company's future profitability.
- The basic accounting for discontinued operations is the same under IFRS and GAAP.
- The accounting for changes in accounting principles and changes in accounting estimates are the same for both GAAP and IFRS.
- Both GAAP and IFRS follow the same approach in reporting comprehensive income.

LOOKING TO THE FUTURE

The FASB and the IASB are working on a project that would rework the structure of financial statements. Recently, the IASB decided to require a statement of comprehensive income, similar to what was required under GAAP. In addition, another part of this project addresses the issue of how to classify various items in the income statement. A main goal of this new approach is to provide information that better represents how businesses are run. In addition, the approach draws attention away from one number—net income.

IFRS Practice

IFRS SELF-TEST QUESTIONS

1. The basic tools of financial analysis are the same under both GAAP and IFRS **except** that:
   (a) horizontal analysis cannot be done because the format of the statements is sometimes different.
   (b) analysis is different because vertical analysis cannot be done under IFRS.
   (c) the current ratio cannot be computed because current liabilities are often reported before current assets in IFRS statements of position.
   (d) None of the above.
2. Presentation of comprehensive income must be reported under IFRS in:
   (a) the statement of stockholders' equity.
   (b) the income statement ending with net income.
   (c) the notes to the financial statements.
   (d) a statement of comprehensive income.
3. In preparing its income statement for 2017, Parmalane assembles the following information.

Sales revenue	$500,000
Cost of goods sold	300,000
Operating expenses	40,000
Loss on discontinued operations	20,000

   Ignoring income taxes, what is Parmalane's income from continuing operations for 2017 under IFRS?
   (a) $260,000.
   (b) $250,000.
   (c) $240,000.
   (d) $160,000.

INTERNATIONAL FINANCIAL REPORTING PROBLEM: Louis Vuitton

IFRS13-1 The financial statements of Louis Vuitton are presented in Appendix F. Instructions for accessing and using the company's complete annual report, including the notes to its financial statements, are also provided in Appendix F.

Instructions

Use the company's **2014 annual report** to answer the following questions.

(a) What was the company's profit margin for 2014? Has it increased or decreased from 2013?
(b) What was the company's operating profit for 2014?
(c) The company reported comprehensive income of €3,267 billion in 2014. What are the other comprehensive gains and losses recorded in 2014?

Answers to IFRS Self-Test Questions

1. d **2.** d **3.** d

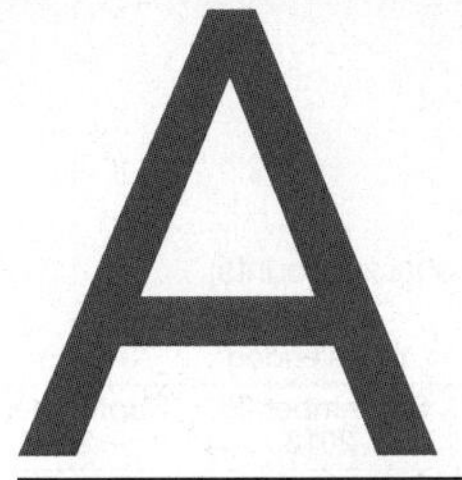

Specimen Financial Statements: Apple Inc.

Once each year, a corporation communicates to its stockholders and other interested parties by issuing a complete set of audited financial statements. The **annual report**, as this communication is called, summarizes the financial results of the company's operations for the year and its plans for the future. Many annual reports are attractive, multicolored, glossy public relations pieces, containing pictures of corporate officers and directors as well as photos and descriptions of new products and new buildings. Yet the basic function of every annual report is to report financial information, almost all of which is a product of the corporation's accounting system.

The content and organization of corporate annual reports have become fairly standardized. Excluding the public relations part of the report (pictures, products, etc.), the following are the traditional financial portions of the annual report:

- Financial Highlights
- Letter to the Stockholders
- Management's Discussion and Analysis
- Financial Statements
- Notes to the Financial Statements
- Management's Responsibility for Financial Reporting
- Management's Report on Internal Control over Financial Reporting
- Report of Independent Registered Public Accounting Firm
- Selected Financial Data

The official SEC filing of the annual report is called a **Form 10-K**, which often omits the public relations pieces found in most standard annual reports. On the following pages, we present Apple Inc.'s financial statements taken from the company's 2014 Form 10-K. To access Apple's Form 10-K, including notes to the financial statements, follow these steps:

1. Go to **http://investor.apple.com**.
2. Select the Financial Information tab.
3. Select the 10-K annual report dated September 29, 2014.
4. The Notes to Consolidated Financial Statements begin on page 50.

CONSOLIDATED STATEMENTS OF OPERATIONS

(In millions, except number of shares which are reflected in thousands and per share amounts)

	Years ended		
	September 27, 2014	September 28, 2013	September 29, 2012
Net sales	$ 182,795	$ 170,910	$ 156,508
Cost of sales	112,258	106,606	87,846
Gross margin	70,537	64,304	68,662
Operating expenses:			
Research and development	6,041	4,475	3,381
Selling, general and administrative	11,993	10,830	10,040
Total operating expenses	18,034	15,305	13,421
Operating income	52,503	48,999	55,241
Other income/(expense), net	980	1,156	522
Income before provision for income taxes	53,483	50,155	55,763
Provision for income taxes	13,973	13,118	14,030
Net income	$ 39,510	$ 37,037	$ 41,733
Earnings per share:			
Basic	$ 6.49	$ 5.72	$ 6.38
Diluted	$ 6.45	$ 5.68	$ 6.31
Shares used in computing earnings per share:			
Basic	6,085,572	6,477,320	6,543,726
Diluted	6,122,663	6,521,634	6,617,483
Cash dividends declared per common share	$ 1.82	$ 1.64	$ 0.38

See accompanying Notes to Consolidated Financial Statements.

CONSOLIDATED STATEMENTS OF COMPREHENSIVE INCOME

(In millions)

	Years ended		
	September 27, 2014	September 28, 2013	September 29, 2012
Net income	$ 39,510	$ 37,037	$ 41,733
Other comprehensive income/(loss):			
Change in foreign currency translation, net of tax effects of $50, $35 and $13, respectively	(137)	(112)	(15)
Change in unrecognized gains/losses on derivative instruments:			
Change in fair value of derivatives, net of tax benefit/(expense) of $(297), $(351) and $73, respectively	1,390	522	(131)
Adjustment for net losses/(gains) realized and included in net income, net of tax expense/(benefit) of $(36), $255 and $220, respectively	149	(458)	(399)
Total change in unrecognized gains/losses on derivative instruments, net of tax	1,539	64	(530)
Change in unrealized gains/losses on marketable securities:			
Change in fair value of marketable securities, net of tax benefit/(expense) of $(153), $458 and $(421), respectively	285	(791)	715
Adjustment for net losses/(gains) realized and included in net income, net of tax expense/(benefit) of $71, $82 and $68, respectively	(134)	(131)	(114)
Total change in unrealized gains/losses on marketable securities, net of tax	151	(922)	601
Total other comprehensive income/(loss)	1,553	(970)	56
Total comprehensive income	$ 41,063	$ 36,067	$ 41,789

See accompanying Notes to Consolidated Financial Statements.

CONSOLIDATED BALANCE SHEETS

(In millions, except number of shares which are reflected in thousands and par value)

	September 27, 2014	September 28, 2013
ASSETS:		
Current assets:		
Cash and cash equivalents	$ 13,844	$ 14,259
Short-term marketable securities	11,233	26,287
Accounts receivable, less allowances of $86 and $99, respectively	17,460	13,102
Inventories	2,111	1,764
Deferred tax assets	4,318	3,453
Vendor non-trade receivables	9,759	7,539
Other current assets	9,806	6,882
Total current assets	68,531	73,286
Long-term marketable securities	130,162	106,215
Property, plant and equipment, net	20,624	16,597
Goodwill	4,616	1,577
Acquired intangible assets, net	4,142	4,179
Other assets	3,764	5,146
Total assets	$ 231,839	$ 207,000
LIABILITIES AND SHAREHOLDERS' EQUITY:		
Current liabilities:		
Accounts payable	$ 30,196	$ 22,367
Accrued expenses	18,453	13,856
Deferred revenue	8,491	7,435
Commercial paper	6,308	0
Total current liabilities	63,448	43,658
Deferred revenue – non-current	3,031	2,625
Long-term debt	28,987	16,960
Other non-current liabilities	24,826	20,208
Total liabilities	120,292	83,451
Commitments and contingencies		
Shareholders' equity:		
Common stock and additional paid-in capital, $0.00001 par value; 12,600,000 shares authorized; 5,866,161 and 6,294,494 shares issued and outstanding, respectively	23,313	19,764
Retained earnings	87,152	104,256
Accumulated other comprehensive income/(loss)	1,082	(471)
Total shareholders' equity	111,547	123,549
Total liabilities and shareholders' equity	$ 231,839	$ 207,000

See accompanying Notes to Consolidated Financial Statements.

CONSOLIDATED STATEMENTS OF SHAREHOLDERS' EQUITY

(In millions, except number of shares which are reflected in thousands)

	Common Stock and Additional Paid-In Capital		Retained Earnings	Accumulated Other Comprehensive Income/(Loss)	Total Shareholders' Equity
	Shares	Amount			
Balances as of September 24, 2011	6,504,937	$ 13,331	$ 62,841	$ 443	$ 76,615
Net income	0	0	41,733	0	41,733
Other comprehensive income/(loss)	0	0	0	56	56
Dividends and dividend equivalents declared	0	0	(2,523)	0	(2,523)
Share-based compensation	0	1,740	0	0	1,740
Common stock issued, net of shares withheld for employee taxes	69,521	200	(762)	0	(562)
Tax benefit from equity awards, including transfer pricing adjustments	0	1,151	0	0	1,151
Balances as of September 29, 2012	6,574,458	16,422	101,289	499	118,210
Net income	0	0	37,037	0	37,037
Other comprehensive income/(loss)	0	0	0	(970)	(970)
Dividends and dividend equivalents declared	0	0	(10,676)	0	(10,676)
Repurchase of common stock	(328,837)	0	(22,950)	0	(22,950)
Share-based compensation	0	2,253	0	0	2,253
Common stock issued, net of shares withheld for employee taxes	48,873	(143)	(444)	0	(587)
Tax benefit from equity awards, including transfer pricing adjustments	0	1,232	0	0	1,232
Balances as of September 28, 2013	6,294,494	19,764	104,256	(471)	123,549
Net income	0	0	39,510	0	39,510
Other comprehensive income/(loss)	0	0	0	1,553	1,553
Dividends and dividend equivalents declared	0	0	(11,215)	0	(11,215)
Repurchase of common stock	(488,677)	0	(45,000)	0	(45,000)
Share-based compensation	0	2,863	0	0	2,863
Common stock issued, net of shares withheld for employee taxes	60,344	(49)	(399)	0	(448)
Tax benefit from equity awards, including transfer pricing adjustments	0	735	0	0	735
Balances as of September 27, 2014	5,866,161	$ 23,313	$ 87,152	$ 1,082	$111,547

See accompanying Notes to Consolidated Financial Statements.

CONSOLIDATED STATEMENTS OF CASH FLOWS
(In millions)

	Years ended		
	September 27, 2014	September 28, 2013	September 29, 2012
Cash and cash equivalents, beginning of the year	$ 14,259	$ 10,746	$ 9,815
Operating activities:			
Net income	39,510	37,037	41,733
Adjustments to reconcile net income to cash generated by operating activities:			
Depreciation and amortization	7,946	6,757	3,277
Share-based compensation expense	2,863	2,253	1,740
Deferred income tax expense	2,347	1,141	4,405
Changes in operating assets and liabilities:			
Accounts receivable, net	(4,232)	(2,172)	(5,551)
Inventories	(76)	(973)	(15)
Vendor non-trade receivables	(2,220)	223	(1,414)
Other current and non-current assets	167	1,080	(3,162)
Accounts payable	5,938	2,340	4,467
Deferred revenue	1,460	1,459	2,824
Other current and non-current liabilities	6,010	4,521	2,552
Cash generated by operating activities	59,713	53,666	50,856
Investing activities:			
Purchases of marketable securities	(217,128)	(148,489)	(151,232)
Proceeds from maturities of marketable securities	18,810	20,317	13,035
Proceeds from sales of marketable securities	189,301	104,130	99,770
Payments made in connection with business acquisitions, net	(3,765)	(496)	(350)
Payments for acquisition of property, plant and equipment	(9,571)	(8,165)	(8,295)
Payments for acquisition of intangible assets	(242)	(911)	(1,107)
Other	16	(160)	(48)
Cash used in investing activities	(22,579)	(33,774)	(48,227)
Financing activities:			
Proceeds from issuance of common stock	730	530	665
Excess tax benefits from equity awards	739	701	1,351
Taxes paid related to net share settlement of equity awards	(1,158)	(1,082)	(1,226)
Dividends and dividend equivalents paid	(11,126)	(10,564)	(2,488)
Repurchase of common stock	(45,000)	(22,860)	0
Proceeds from issuance of long-term debt, net	11,960	16,896	0
Proceeds from issuance of commercial paper, net	6,306	0	0
Cash used in financing activities	(37,549)	(16,379)	(1,698)
Increase/(decrease) in cash and cash equivalents	(415)	3,513	931
Cash and cash equivalents, end of the year	$ 13,844	$ 14,259	$ 10,746
Supplemental cash flow disclosure:			
Cash paid for income taxes, net	$ 10,026	$ 9,128	$ 7,682
Cash paid for interest	$ 339	$ 0	$ 0

See accompanying Notes to Consolidated Financial Statements.

B

Specimen Financial Statements: Columbia Sportswear Company

Columbia Sportswear Company is a leader in outdoor sportswear. The following are Columbia's financial statements as presented in its 2014 annual report. To access Columbia's complete annual report, including notes to the financial statements, follow these steps:

1. Go to **www.columbia.com**.
2. Select Financial Information and then Annual Reports under the Investor Relations tab near the bottom of the page.
3. Select the 2014 Annual Report.
4. The Notes to Consolidated Financial Statements begin on page 50.

COLUMBIA SPORTSWEAR COMPANY

CONSOLIDATED STATEMENTS OF OPERATIONS
(In thousands, except per share amounts)

	Year Ended December 31,		
	2014	2013	2012
Net sales	$ 2,100,590	$ 1,684,996	$ 1,669,563
Cost of sales	1,145,639	941,341	953,169
Gross profit	954,951	743,655	716,394
Selling, general and administrative expenses	763,063	625,656	596,635
Net licensing income	6,956	13,795	13,769
Income from operations	198,844	131,794	133,528
Interest income, net	1,004	503	379
Interest expense on note payable to related party (Note 22)	(1,053)	—	—
Other non-operating expense	(274)	(871)	—
Income before income tax	198,521	131,426	133,907
Income tax expense (Note 11)	(56,662)	(37,823)	(34,048)
Net income	141,859	93,603	99,859
Net income (loss) attributable to non-controlling interest	4,686	(738)	—
Net income attributable to Columbia Sportswear Company	$ 137,173	$ 94,341	$ 99,859
Earnings per share attributable to Columbia Sportswear Company (Note 17):			
Basic	$ 1.97	$ 1.37	$ 1.48
Diluted	1.94	1.36	1.46
Weighted average shares outstanding (Note 17):			
Basic	69,807	68,756	67,680
Diluted	70,681	69,434	68,264

See accompanying notes to consolidated financial statements

COLUMBIA SPORTSWEAR COMPANY

CONSOLIDATED BALANCE SHEETS
(In thousands)

	December 31, 2014	December 31, 2013
ASSETS		
Current Assets:		
Cash and cash equivalents	$ 413,558	$ 437,489
Short-term investments	27,267	91,755
Accounts receivable, net (Note 6)	344,390	306,878
Inventories	384,650	329,228
Deferred income taxes (Note 11)	57,001	52,041
Prepaid expenses and other current assets	39,175	33,081
Total current assets	1,266,041	1,250,472
Property, plant, and equipment, net (Note 7)	291,563	279,373
Intangible assets, net (Notes 3, 8)	143,731	36,288
Goodwill (Notes 3, 8)	68,594	14,438
Other non-current assets	22,280	25,017
Total assets	$ 1,792,209	$ 1,605,588
LIABILITIES AND EQUITY		
Current Liabilities:		
Accounts payable	$ 214,275	$ 173,557
Accrued liabilities (Note 10)	144,288	120,397
Income taxes payable (Note 11)	14,388	7,251
Deferred income taxes (Note 11)	169	49
Total current liabilities	373,120	301,254
Note payable to related party (Note 22)	15,728	—
Other long-term liabilities (Notes 12, 13)	35,435	29,527
Income taxes payable (Note 11)	9,388	13,984
Deferred income taxes (Note 11)	3,304	7,959
Total liabilities	436,975	352,724
Commitments and contingencies (Note 14)		
Shareholders' Equity:		
Preferred stock; 10,000 shares authorized; none issued and outstanding	—	—
Common stock (no par value); 250,000 shares authorized; 69,828 and 69,190 issued and outstanding (Note 15)	72,700	52,325
Retained earnings	1,255,070	1,157,733
Accumulated other comprehensive income (Note 18)	15,833	35,360
Total Columbia Sportswear Company shareholders' equity	1,343,603	1,245,418
Non-controlling interest (Note 5)	11,631	7,446
Total equity	1,355,234	1,252,864
Total liabilities and equity	$ 1,792,209	$ 1,605,588

See accompanying notes to consolidated financial statements

COLUMBIA SPORTSWEAR COMPANY

CONSOLIDATED STATEMENTS OF COMPREHENSIVE INCOME
(In thousands)

	Year Ended December 31, 2014	2013	2012
Net income	$ 141,859	$ 93,603	$ 99,859
Other comprehensive loss:			
Unrealized holding gains (losses) on available-for-sale securities (net of tax (expense) benefit of ($5), ($2), and $4, respectively)	10	3	(7)
Unrealized gains (losses) on derivative transactions (net of tax (expense) benefit of ($1,507), $9 and ($171), respectively)	7,751	(1,261)	(4,745)
Foreign currency translation adjustments (net of tax benefit (expense) of $1,023, ($191) and ($59), respectively)	(27,789)	(9,861)	4,518
Other comprehensive loss	(20,028)	(11,119)	(234)
Comprehensive income	121,831	82,484	99,625
Comprehensive income (loss) attributable to non-controlling interest	4,185	(554)	—
Comprehensive income attributable to Columbia Sportswear Company	$ 117,646	$ 83,038	$ 99,625

See accompanying notes to consolidated financial statements

COLUMBIA SPORTSWEAR COMPANY

CONSOLIDATED STATEMENTS OF CASH FLOWS
(In thousands)

	Year Ended December 31,		
	2014	2013	2012
Cash flows from operating activities:			
Net income	$ 141,859	$ 93,603	$ 99,859
Adjustments to reconcile net income to net cash provided by operating activities:			
Depreciation and amortization	54,017	40,871	40,892
Loss on disposal or impairment of property, plant, and equipment	481	9,344	1,582
Deferred income taxes	(6,978)	8,818	7,140
Stock-based compensation	11,120	8,878	7,833
Excess tax benefit from employee stock plans	(4,927)	(1,532)	(1,016)
Changes in operating assets and liabilities:			
Accounts receivable	(31,478)	27,442	18,166
Inventories	(62,086)	34,089	2,951
Prepaid expenses and other current assets	(4,869)	5,166	(2,025)
Other assets	4,291	(4,215)	(1,259)
Accounts payable	41,941	31,711	(12,330)
Accrued liabilities	35,051	12,210	(5,199)
Income taxes payable	1,166	5,534	(11,052)
Other liabilities	6,195	2,356	3,126
Net cash provided by operating activities	185,783	274,275	148,668
Cash flows from investing activities:			
Acquisition of business, net of cash acquired	(188,467)	—	—
Purchases of short-term investments	(48,243)	(125,390)	(83,969)
Sales of short-term investments	112,895	78,636	42,319
Capital expenditures	(60,283)	(69,443)	(50,491)
Proceeds from sale of property, plant, and equipment	71	111	7,099
Net cash used in investing activities	(184,027)	(116,086)	(85,042)
Cash flows from financing activities:			
Proceeds from credit facilities	52,356	69,136	100,654
Repayments on credit facilities	(52,205)	(69,292)	(100,498)
Proceeds from issuance of common stock under employee stock plans	22,277	19,537	14,600
Tax payments related to restricted stock unit issuances	(3,141)	(2,291)	(1,486)
Excess tax benefit from employee stock plans	4,927	1,532	1,016
Repurchase of common stock	(15,000)	—	(206)
Proceeds from note payable to related party	16,072	—	—
Capital contribution from non-controlling interest	—	8,000	—
Cash dividends paid	(39,836)	(31,298)	(29,780)
Net cash used in financing activities	(14,550)	(4,676)	(15,700)
Net effect of exchange rate changes on cash	(11,137)	(6,805)	1,821
Net increase (decrease) in cash and cash equivalents	(23,931)	146,708	49,747
Cash and cash equivalents, beginning of year	437,489	290,781	241,034
Cash and cash equivalents, end of year	$ 413,558	$ 437,489	$ 290,781

Supplemental disclosures of cash flow information:			
Cash paid during the year for income taxes	$ 53,958	$ 22,771	$ 43,696
Supplemental disclosures of non-cash investing activities:			
Capital expenditures incurred but not yet paid	7,196	5,195	5,313

See accompanying notes to consolidated financial statements

COLUMBIA SPORTSWEAR COMPANY

CONSOLIDATED STATEMENTS OF EQUITY
(In thousands)

	Columbia Sportswear Company Shareholders' Equity					
	Common Stock					
	Shares Outstanding	Amount	Retained Earnings	Accumulated Other Comprehensive Income	Non-Controlling Interest	Total
BALANCE, JANUARY 1, 2012	67,276	$ 3,037	$ 1,024,611	$ 46,897	$ —	$ 1,074,545
Net income	—	—	99,859	—	—	99,859
Other comprehensive income (loss):						
Unrealized holding losses on available-for-sale securities, net	—	—	—	(7)	—	(7)
Unrealized holding losses on derivative transactions, net	—	—	—	(4,745)	—	(4,745)
Foreign currency translation adjustment, net	—	—	—	4,518	—	4,518
Cash dividends ($0.44 per share)	—	—	(29,780)	—	—	(29,780)
Issuance of common stock under employee stock plans, net	882	13,114	—	—	—	13,114
Tax adjustment from stock plans	—	1,036	—	—	—	1,036
Stock-based compensation expense	—	7,833	—	—	—	7,833
Repurchase of common stock	(8)	(206)	—	—	—	(206)
BALANCE, DECEMBER 31, 2012	68,150	24,814	1,094,690	46,663	—	1,166,167
Net income (loss)	—	—	94,341	—	(738)	93,603
Other comprehensive income (loss):						
Unrealized holding gains on available-for-sale securities, net	—	—	—	3	—	3
Unrealized holding losses on derivative transactions, net	—	—	—	(1,261)	—	(1,261)
Foreign currency translation adjustment, net	—	—	—	(10,045)	184	(9,861)
Cash dividends ($0.46 per share)	—	—	(31,298)	—	—	(31,298)
Issuance of common stock under employee stock plans, net	1,040	17,246	—	—	—	17,246
Capital contribution from non-controlling interest	—	—	—	—	8,000	8,000
Tax adjustment from stock plans	—	1,387	—	—	—	1,387
Stock-based compensation expense	—	8,878	—	—	—	8,878
BALANCE, DECEMBER 31, 2013	69,190	52,325	1,157,733	35,360	7,446	1,252,864
Net income	—	—	137,173	—	4,686	141,859
Other comprehensive income (loss):						
Unrealized holding gains on available-for-sale securities, net	—	—	—	10	—	10
Unrealized holding gains on derivative transactions, net	—	—	—	7,751	—	7,751
Foreign currency translation adjustment, net	—	—	—	(27,288)	(501)	(27,789)
Cash dividends ($0.57 per share)	—	—	(39,836)	—	—	(39,836)
Issuance of common stock under employee stock plans, net	1,059	19,136	—	—	—	19,136
Tax adjustment from stock plans	—	5,119	—	—	—	5,119
Stock-based compensation expense	—	11,120	—	—	—	11,120
Repurchase of common stock	(421)	(15,000)	—	—	—	(15,000)
BALANCE, DECEMBER 31, 2014	69,828	$ 72,700	$ 1,255,070	$ 15,833	$ 11,631	$ 1,355,234

See accompanying notes to consolidated financial statements

Specimen Financial Statements: VF Corporation

VF Corporation is a leader in outdoor sportswear. The following are VF's financial statements as presented in its 2014 annual report. To access VF's complete annual report, including notes to the financial statements, follow these steps:

1. Go to **www.vfc.com**.
2. Select the Investor Relations link and then select Financial Reports.
3. Select the 2014 Annual Report on Form 10-K.
4. The Notes to Consolidated Financial Statements begin on page F-10.

VF CORPORATION

Consolidated Balance Sheets

	December 2014	December 2013
	In thousands, except share amounts	
ASSETS		
Current assets		
Cash and equivalents	$ 971,895	$ 776,403
Accounts receivable, less allowance for doubtful accounts of $26,694 in 2014 and $45,350 in 2013	1,276,224	1,360,443
Inventories	1,482,804	1,399,062
Deferred income taxes	154,285	169,321
Other current assets	300,646	177,753
Total current assets	4,185,854	3,882,982
Property, plant and equipment	942,181	932,792
Intangible assets	2,433,552	2,960,201
Goodwill	1,824,956	2,021,750
Other assets	593,597	517,718
Total assets	$ 9,980,140	$ 10,315,443
LIABILITIES AND STOCKHOLDERS' EQUITY		
Current liabilities		
Short-term borrowings	$ 21,822	$ 18,810
Current portion of long-term debt	3,975	5,167
Accounts payable	690,842	638,732
Accrued liabilities	903,602	905,292
Total current liabilities	1,620,241	1,568,001
Long-term debt	1,423,581	1,426,829
Other liabilities	1,305,436	1,243,575
Commitments and contingencies		
Stockholders' equity		
Preferred Stock, par value $1; shares authorized, 25,000,000; no shares outstanding in 2014 and 2013	—	—
Common Stock, stated value $0.25; shares authorized, 1,200,000,000; 432,859,891 shares outstanding in 2014 and 440,310,370 in 2013	108,215	110,078
Additional paid-in capital	2,993,186	2,746,590
Accumulated other comprehensive income (loss)	(702,272)	(211,720)
Retained earnings	3,231,753	3,432,090
Total stockholders' equity	5,630,882	6,077,038
Total liabilities and stockholders' equity	$ 9,980,140	$ 10,315,443

See notes to consolidated financial statements.

VF CORPORATION

Consolidated Statements of Income

	Year Ended December 2014	2013	2012
	In thousands, except per share amounts		
Net sales	$ 12,154,784	$ 11,302,350	$ 10,766,020
Royalty income	127,377	117,298	113,835
Total revenues	12,282,161	11,419,648	10,879,855
Costs and operating expenses			
Cost of goods sold	6,288,190	5,931,469	5,817,880
Selling, general and administrative expenses	4,159,885	3,841,032	3,596,708
Impairment of goodwill and intangible assets	396,362	—	—
	10,844,437	9,772,501	9,414,588
Operating income	1,437,724	1,647,147	1,465,267
Interest income	6,911	4,141	3,353
Interest expense	(86,725)	(84,773)	(93,605)
Other income (expense), net	(5,544)	(4,025)	46,860
Income before income taxes	1,352,366	1,562,490	1,421,875
Income taxes	304,861	352,371	335,737
Net income	1,047,505	1,210,119	1,086,138
Net income attributable to noncontrolling interests	—	—	(139)
Net income attributable to VF Corporation common stockholders	$ 1,047,505	$ 1,210,119	$ 1,085,999
Earnings per common share attributable to VF Corporation common stockholders			
Basic	$ 2.42	$ 2.76	$ 2.47
Diluted	2.38	2.71	2.43
Cash dividends per common share	$ 1.1075	$ 0.9150	$ 0.7575

See notes to consolidated financial statements.

VF CORPORATION

Consolidated Statements of Comprehensive Income

	Year Ended December 2014	2013	2012
	In thousands		
Net income	$1,047,505	$1,210,119	$1,086,138
Other comprehensive income (loss)			
Foreign currency translation			
Gains (losses) arising during year	(469,663)	109,463	37,648
Less income tax effect	6,075	1,252	9,443
Defined benefit pension plans			
Current year actuarial gains (losses) and plan amendments	(203,234)	146,746	(173,959)
Amortization of net deferred actuarial losses	37,518	85,356	69,744
Amortization of deferred prior service costs	5,445	1,270	3,357
Less income tax effect	60,588	(90,285)	37,013
Derivative financial instruments			
Gains (losses) arising during year	88,387	(8,133)	(9,555)
Less income tax effect	(34,736)	3,196	3,976
Reclassification to net income for (gains) losses realized	32,111	(12,169)	(15,883)
Less income tax effect	(12,619)	4,782	6,199
Marketable securities			
Gains (losses) arising during year	(698)	1,239	(401)
Less income tax effect	274	(542)	—
Other comprehensive income (loss)	(490,552)	242,175	(32,418)
Comprehensive income including noncontrolling interests	556,953	1,452,294	1,053,720
Comprehensive (income) loss attributable to noncontrolling interests	—	—	(139)
Comprehensive income attributable to VF Corporation	$ 556,953	$1,452,294	$1,053,581

See notes to consolidated financial statements.

VF CORPORATION

Consolidated Statements of Cash Flows

	Year Ended December		
	2014	2013	2012
	In thousands		
Operating activities			
Net income	$ 1,047,505	$1,210,119	$1,086,138
Adjustments to reconcile net income to cash provided by operating activities:			
Impairment of goodwill and intangible assets	396,362	—	—
Depreciation	172,443	157,810	148,969
Amortization of intangible assets	42,061	45,787	47,929
Other amortization	60,379	49,676	41,058
Stock-based compensation	104,313	87,118	92,814
Provision for doubtful accounts	(2,198)	15,756	19,264
Pension expense less than contributions	(9,864)	(28,102)	(20,198)
Deferred income taxes	(78,064)	(12,370)	(20,797)
Gain on sale of businesses	—	—	(44,485)
Other, net	4,112	14,306	(40,931)
Changes in operating assets and liabilities, net of purchases and sales of businesses:			
Accounts receivable	854	(155,053)	(111,571)
Inventories	(130,540)	(47,240)	87,620
Accounts payable	69,807	75,073	(74,294)
Income taxes	(44,144)	16,628	26,213
Accrued liabilities	41,989	84,472	(35,912)
Other assets and liabilities	22,614	(7,939)	73,183
Cash provided by operating activities	1,697,629	1,506,041	1,275,000
Investing activities			
Capital expenditures	(234,077)	(271,153)	(251,940)
Business acquisitions, net of cash acquired	—	—	(1,750)
Proceeds from sale of businesses	—	—	72,519
Software purchases	(67,943)	(53,989)	(30,890)
Other, net	(27,235)	(25,131)	(8,230)
Cash used by investing activities	(329,255)	(350,273)	(220,291)
Financing activities			
Net increase (decrease) in short-term borrowings	4,761	9,032	(269,010)
Payments on long-term debt	(4,760)	(404,872)	(2,776)
Purchases of treasury stock	(727,795)	(282,024)	(307,282)
Cash dividends paid	(478,933)	(402,136)	(333,229)
Proceeds from issuance of Common Stock, net of shares withheld for taxes	34,869	48,029	62,770
Tax benefits of stock-based compensation	64,437	48,140	47,213
Other, net	—	—	(201)
Cash used by financing activities	(1,107,421)	(983,831)	(802,515)
Effect of foreign currency rate changes on cash and equivalents	(65,461)	7,005	4,039
Net change in cash and equivalents	195,492	178,942	256,233
Cash and equivalents — beginning of year	776,403	597,461	341,228
Cash and equivalents — end of year	$ 971,895	$ 776,403	$ 597,461

See notes to consolidated financial statements.

VF CORPORATION

Consolidated Statements of Stockholders' Equity

	VF Corporation Stockholders					
	Common Stock		Additional Paid-in Capital	Accumulated Other Comprehensive Income (Loss)	Retained Earnings	Non-controlling Interests
	Shares	Amounts				
	In thousands, except share amounts					
Balance, December 2011	442,227,924	$110,557	$2,316,107	$ (421,477)	$2,520,804	$ (816)
Net income	—	—	—	—	1,085,999	139
Dividends on Common Stock	—	—	—	—	(333,229)	—
Purchase of treasury stock	(8,072,920)	(2,018)	—	—	(297,692)	—
Stock-based compensation, net	6,663,932	1,666	211,761	—	(34,435)	—
Disposition of noncontrolling interests	—	—	—	—	—	677
Foreign currency translation	—	—	—	47,091	—	—
Defined benefit pension plans	—	—	—	(63,845)	—	—
Derivative financial instruments	—	—	—	(15,263)	—	—
Marketable securities	—	—	—	(401)	—	—
Balance, December 2012	440,818,936	$110,205	$2,527,868	$ (453,895)	$2,941,447	$ —
Net income	—	—	—	—	1,210,119	—
Dividends on Common Stock	—	—	—	—	(402,136)	—
Purchase of treasury stock	(6,849,160)	(1,712)	—	—	(280,408)	—
Stock-based compensation, net	6,340,594	1,585	218,722	—	(36,932)	—
Foreign currency translation	—	—	—	110,715	—	—
Defined benefit pension plans	—	—	—	143,087	—	—
Derivative financial instruments	—	—	—	(12,324)	—	—
Marketable securities	—	—	—	697	—	—
Balance, December 2013	440,310,370	$110,078	$2,746,590	$ (211,720)	$3,432,090	$ —
Net income	—	—	—	—	1,047,505	—
Dividends on Common Stock	—	—	—	—	(478,933)	—
Purchase of treasury stock	(12,037,000)	(3,009)	—	—	(724,786)	—
Stock-based compensation, net	4,586,521	1,146	246,596	—	(44,123)	—
Foreign currency translation	—	—	—	(463,588)	—	—
Defined benefit pension plans	—	—	—	(99,683)	—	—
Derivative financial instruments	—	—	—	73,143	—	—
Marketable securities	—	—	—	(424)	—	—
Balance, December 2014	432,859,891	$108,215	$2,993,186	$ (702,272)	$3,231,753	$ —

See notes to consolidated financial statements.

Specimen Financial Statements: Amazon.com, Inc.

Amazon.com, Inc. is the world's largest online retailer. It also produces consumer electronics—notably the Kindle e-book reader and the Kindle Fire Tablet computer—and is a major provider of cloud computing services. The following are Amazon's financial statements as presented in the company's 2014 annual report. To access Amazon's complete annual report, including notes to the financial statements, follow these steps:

1. Go to **www.amazon.com**.
2. Select the Investor Relations link at the bottom of the page and then select the 2014 Annual Report under Annual Reports and Proxies.
3. The Notes to Consolidated Financial Statements begin on page 43.

AMAZON.COM, INC.
CONSOLIDATED STATEMENTS OF CASH FLOWS
(in millions)

	Year Ended December 31,		
	2014	2013	2012
CASH AND CASH EQUIVALENTS, BEGINNING OF PERIOD	$ 8,658	$ 8,084	$ 5,269
OPERATING ACTIVITIES:			
Net income (loss)	(241)	274	(39)
Adjustments to reconcile net income (loss) to net cash from operating activities:			
Depreciation of property and equipment, including internal-use software and website development, and other amortization	4,746	3,253	2,159
Stock-based compensation	1,497	1,134	833
Other operating expense (income), net	129	114	154
Losses (gains) on sales of marketable securities, net	(3)	1	(9)
Other expense (income), net	62	166	253
Deferred income taxes	(316)	(156)	(265)
Excess tax benefits from stock-based compensation	(6)	(78)	(429)
Changes in operating assets and liabilities:			
Inventories	(1,193)	(1,410)	(999)
Accounts receivable, net and other	(1,039)	(846)	(861)
Accounts payable	1,759	1,888	2,070
Accrued expenses and other	706	736	1,038
Additions to unearned revenue	4,433	2,691	1,796
Amortization of previously unearned revenue	(3,692)	(2,292)	(1,521)
Net cash provided by (used in) operating activities	6,842	5,475	4,180
INVESTING ACTIVITIES:			
Purchases of property and equipment, including internal-use software and website development	(4,893)	(3,444)	(3,785)
Acquisitions, net of cash acquired, and other	(979)	(312)	(745)
Sales and maturities of marketable securities and other investments	3,349	2,306	4,237
Purchases of marketable securities and other investments	(2,542)	(2,826)	(3,302)
Net cash provided by (used in) investing activities	(5,065)	(4,276)	(3,595)
FINANCING ACTIVITIES:			
Excess tax benefits from stock-based compensation	6	78	429
Common stock repurchased	—	—	(960)
Proceeds from long-term debt and other	6,359	394	3,378
Repayments of long-term debt	(513)	(231)	(82)
Principal repayments of capital lease obligations	(1,285)	(775)	(486)
Principal repayments of finance lease obligations	(135)	(5)	(20)
Net cash provided by (used in) financing activities	4,432	(539)	2,259
Foreign-currency effect on cash and cash equivalents	(310)	(86)	(29)
Net increase (decrease) in cash and cash equivalents	5,899	574	2,815
CASH AND CASH EQUIVALENTS, END OF PERIOD	$ 14,557	$ 8,658	$ 8,084
SUPPLEMENTAL CASH FLOW INFORMATION:			
Cash paid for interest on long-term debt	$ 91	$ 97	$ 31
Cash paid for income taxes (net of refunds)	177	169	112
Property and equipment acquired under capital leases	4,008	1,867	802
Property and equipment acquired under build-to-suit leases	920	877	29

See accompanying notes to consolidated financial statements.

AMAZON.COM, INC.
CONSOLIDATED STATEMENTS OF OPERATIONS
(in millions, except per share data)

	Year Ended December 31,		
	2014	2013	2012
Net product sales	$ 70,080	$ 60,903	$ 51,733
Net service sales	18,908	13,549	9,360
Total net sales	88,988	74,452	61,093
Operating expenses (1):			
Cost of sales	62,752	54,181	45,971
Fulfillment	10,766	8,585	6,419
Marketing	4,332	3,133	2,408
Technology and content	9,275	6,565	4,564
General and administrative	1,552	1,129	896
Other operating expense (income), net	133	114	159
Total operating expenses	88,810	73,707	60,417
Income from operations	178	745	676
Interest income	39	38	40
Interest expense	(210)	(141)	(92)
Other income (expense), net	(118)	(136)	(80)
Total non-operating income (expense)	(289)	(239)	(132)
Income (loss) before income taxes	(111)	506	544
Provision for income taxes	(167)	(161)	(428)
Equity-method investment activity, net of tax	37	(71)	(155)
Net income (loss)	$ (241)	$ 274	$ (39)
Basic earnings per share	$ (0.52)	$ 0.60	$ (0.09)
Diluted earnings per share	$ (0.52)	$ 0.59	$ (0.09)
Weighted average shares used in computation of earnings per share:			
Basic	462	457	453
Diluted	462	465	453

(1) Includes stock-based compensation as follows:			
Fulfillment	$ 375	$ 294	$ 212
Marketing	125	88	61
Technology and content	804	603	434
General and administrative	193	149	126

See accompanying notes to consolidated financial statements.

AMAZON.COM, INC.
CONSOLIDATED STATEMENTS OF COMPREHENSIVE INCOME
(in millions)

	Year Ended December 31,		
	2014	2013	2012
Net income (loss)	$ (241)	$ 274	$ (39)
Other comprehensive income (loss):			
Foreign currency translation adjustments, net of tax of $(3), $(20), and $(30)	(325)	63	76
Net change in unrealized gains on available-for-sale securities:			
Unrealized gains (losses), net of tax of $1, $3, and $(3)	2	(10)	8
Reclassification adjustment for losses (gains) included in "Other income (expense), net," net of tax of $(1), $(1), and $3	(3)	1	(7)
Net unrealized gains (losses) on available-for-sale securities	(1)	(9)	1
Total other comprehensive income (loss)	(326)	54	77
Comprehensive income (loss)	$ (567)	$ 328	$ 38

See accompanying notes to consolidated financial statements.

AMAZON.COM, INC.

CONSOLIDATED BALANCE SHEETS
(in millions, except per share data)

	December 31, 2014	December 31, 2013
ASSETS		
Current assets:		
Cash and cash equivalents	$ 14,557	$ 8,658
Marketable securities	2,859	3,789
Inventories	8,299	7,411
Accounts receivable, net and other	5,612	4,767
Total current assets	31,327	24,625
Property and equipment, net	16,967	10,949
Goodwill	3,319	2,655
Other assets	2,892	1,930
Total assets	$ 54,505	$ 40,159
LIABILITIES AND STOCKHOLDERS' EQUITY		
Current liabilities:		
Accounts payable	$ 16,459	$ 15,133
Accrued expenses and other	9,807	6,688
Unearned revenue	1,823	1,159
Total current liabilities	28,089	22,980
Long-term debt	8,265	3,191
Other long-term liabilities	7,410	4,242
Commitments and contingencies (Note 8)		
Stockholders' equity:		
Preferred stock, $0.01 par value:		
Authorized shares — 500		
Issued and outstanding shares — none	—	—
Common stock, $0.01 par value:		
Authorized shares — 5,000		
Issued shares — 488 and 483		
Outstanding shares — 465 and 459	5	5
Treasury stock, at cost	(1,837)	(1,837)
Additional paid-in capital	11,135	9,573
Accumulated other comprehensive loss	(511)	(185)
Retained earnings	1,949	2,190
Total stockholders' equity	10,741	9,746
Total liabilities and stockholders' equity	$ 54,505	$ 40,159

See accompanying notes to consolidated financial statements.

AMAZON.COM, INC.

CONSOLIDATED STATEMENTS OF STOCKHOLDERS' EQUITY
(in millions)

	Common Stock Shares	Common Stock Amount	Treasury Stock	Additional Paid-In Capital	Accumulated Other Comprehensive Income (Loss)	Retained Earnings	Total Stockholders' Equity
Balance as of January 1, 2012	455	$ 5	$ (877)	$ 6,990	$ (316)	$ 1,955	$ 7,757
Net loss	—	—	—	—	—	(39)	(39)
Other comprehensive income	—	—	—	—	77	—	77
Exercise of common stock options	4	—	—	8	—	—	8
Repurchase of common stock	(5)	—	(960)	—	—	—	(960)
Excess tax benefits from stock-based compensation	—	—	—	429	—	—	429
Stock-based compensation and issuance of employee benefit plan stock	—	—	—	854	—	—	854
Issuance of common stock for acquisition activity	—	—	—	66	—	—	66
Balance as of December 31, 2012	454	5	(1,837)	8,347	(239)	1,916	8,192
Net income	—	—	—	—	—	274	274
Other comprehensive income	—	—	—	—	54	—	54
Exercise of common stock options	5	—	—	4	—	—	4
Repurchase of common stock	—	—	—	—	—	—	—
Excess tax benefits from stock-based compensation	—	—	—	73	—	—	73
Stock-based compensation and issuance of employee benefit plan stock	—	—	—	1,149	—	—	1,149
Balance as of December 31, 2013	459	5	(1,837)	9,573	(185)	2,190	9,746
Net loss	—	—	—	—	—	(241)	(241)
Other comprehensive loss	—	—	—	—	(326)	—	(326)
Exercise of common stock options	6	—	—	2	—	—	2
Excess tax benefits from stock-based compensation	—	—	—	6	—	—	6
Stock-based compensation and issuance of employee benefit plan stock	—	—	—	1,510	—	—	1,510
Issuance of common stock for acquisition activity	—	—	—	44	—	—	44
Balance as of December 31, 2014	465	$ 5	$ (1,837)	$ 11,135	$ (511)	$ 1,949	$ 10,741

See accompanying notes to consolidated financial statements.

Specimen Financial Statements: Wal-Mart Stores, Inc.

The following are Wal-Mart Stores, Inc.'s financial statements as presented in the company's 2015 annual report. To access Wal-Mart's complete annual report, including notes to the financial statements, follow these steps:

1. Go to **http://corporate.walmart.com**.
2. Select Financial Information and then Annual Reports & Proxies under the Investors tab.
3. Select the 2015 Annual Report (Wal-Mart's fiscal year ends January 31).
4. The Notes to Consolidated Financial Statements begin on page 40.

Wal-Mart Stores, Inc.
Consolidated Statements of Income

	Fiscal Years Ended January 31,		
(Amounts in millions, except per share data)	**2015**	**2014**	**2013**
Revenues:			
Net sales	$ 482,229	$ 473,076	$ 465,604
Membership and other income	3,422	3,218	3,047
Total revenues	485,651	476,294	468,651
Costs and expenses:			
Cost of sales	365,086	358,069	352,297
Operating, selling, general and administrative expenses	93,418	91,353	88,629
Operating income	27,147	26,872	27,725
Interest:			
Debt	2,161	2,072	1,977
Capital leases	300	263	272
Interest income	(113)	(119)	(186)
Interest, net	2,348	2,216	2,063
Income from continuing operations before income taxes	24,799	24,656	25,662
Provision for income taxes:			
Current	8,504	8,619	7,976
Deferred	(519)	(514)	(18)
Total provision for income taxes	7,985	8,105	7,958
Income from continuing operations	16,814	16,551	17,704
Income from discontinued operations, net of income taxes	285	144	52
Consolidated net income	17,099	16,695	17,756
Less consolidated net income attributable to noncontrolling interest	(736)	(673)	(757)
Consolidated net income attributable to Walmart	$ 16,363	$ 16,022	$ 16,999
Basic net income per common share:			
Basic income per common share from continuing operations attributable to Walmart	$ 5.01	$ 4.87	$ 5.03
Basic income per common share from discontinued operations attributable to Walmart	0.06	0.03	0.01
Basic net income per common share attributable to Walmart	$ 5.07	$ 4.90	$ 5.04
Diluted net income per common share:			
Diluted income per common share from continuing operations attributable to Walmart	$ 4.99	$ 4.85	$ 5.01
Diluted income per common share from discontinued operations attributable to Walmart	0.06	0.03	0.01
Diluted net income per common share attributable to Walmart	$ 5.05	$ 4.88	$ 5.02
Weighted-average common shares outstanding:			
Basic	3,230	3,269	3,374
Diluted	3,243	3,283	3,389
Dividends declared per common share	$ 1.92	$ 1.88	$ 1.59

See accompanying notes.

Wal-Mart Stores, Inc.
Consolidated Statements of Comprehensive Income

	Fiscal Years Ended January 31,		
(Amounts in millions)	2015	2014	2013
Consolidated net income	$ 17,099	$ 16,695	$ 17,756
Less consolidated net income attributable to nonredeemable noncontrolling interest	(736)	(606)	(684)
Less consolidated net income attributable to redeemable noncontrolling interest	—	(67)	(73)
Consolidated net income attributable to Walmart	16,363	16,022	16,999
Other comprehensive income (loss), net of income taxes			
Currency translation and other	(4,179)	(3,146)	1,042
Derivative instruments	(470)	207	136
Minimum pension liability	(69)	153	(166)
Other comprehensive income (loss), net of income taxes	(4,718)	(2,786)	1,012
Less other comprehensive income (loss) attributable to nonredeemable noncontrolling interest	546	311	(138)
Less other comprehensive income (loss) attributable to redeemable noncontrolling interest	—	66	(51)
Other comprehensive income (loss) attributable to Walmart	(4,172)	(2,409)	823
Comprehensive income, net of income taxes	12,381	13,909	18,768
Less comprehensive income (loss) attributable to nonredeemable noncontrolling interest	(190)	(295)	(822)
Less comprehensive income (loss) attributable to redeemable noncontrolling interest	—	(1)	(124)
Comprehensive income attributable to Walmart	$ 12,191	$ 13,613	$ 17,822

See accompanying notes.

Wal-Mart Stores, Inc.
Consolidated Balance Sheets

(Amounts in millions)	As of January 31, 2015	2014
ASSETS		
Current assets:		
Cash and cash equivalents	$ 9,135	$ 7,281
Receivables, net	6,778	6,677
Inventories	45,141	44,858
Prepaid expenses and other	2,224	1,909
Current assets of discontinued operations	—	460
Total current assets	63,278	61,185
Property and equipment:		
Property and equipment	177,395	173,089
Less accumulated depreciation	(63,115)	(57,725)
Property and equipment, net	114,280	115,364
Property under capital leases:		
Property under capital leases	5,239	5,589
Less accumulated amortization	(2,864)	(3,046)
Property under capital leases, net	2,375	2,543
Goodwill	18,102	19,510
Other assets and deferred charges	5,671	6,149
Total assets	$ 203,706	$ 204,751
LIABILITIES, REDEEMABLE NONCONTROLLING INTEREST, AND EQUITY		
Current liabilities:		
Short-term borrowings	$ 1,592	$ 7,670
Accounts payable	38,410	37,415
Accrued liabilities	19,152	18,793
Accrued income taxes	1,021	966
Long-term debt due within one year	4,810	4,103
Obligations under capital leases due within one year	287	309
Current liabilities of discontinued operations	—	89
Total current liabilities	65,272	69,345
Long-term debt	41,086	41,771
Long-term obligations under capital leases	2,606	2,788
Deferred income taxes and other	8,805	8,017
Redeemable noncontrolling interest	—	1,491
Commitments and contingencies		
Equity:		
Common stock	323	323
Capital in excess of par value	2,462	2,362
Retained earnings	85,777	76,566
Accumulated other comprehensive income (loss)	(7,168)	(2,996)
Total Walmart shareholders' equity	81,394	76,255
Nonredeemable noncontrolling interest	4,543	5,084
Total equity	85,937	81,339
Total liabilities, redeemable noncontrolling interest, and equity	$ 203,706	$ 204,751

See accompanying notes.

Wal-Mart Stores, Inc.
Consolidated Statement of Shareholders' Equity and Redeemable Noncontrolling Interest

(Amounts in millions)	Common Stock Shares	Common Stock Amount	Capital in Excess of Par Value	Retained Earnings	Accumulated Other Comprehensive Income (Loss)	Total Walmart Shareholders' Equity	Nonredeemable Noncontrolling Interest	Total Equity	Redeemable Noncontrolling Interest
Balances as of February 1, 2012	3,418	$ 342	$ 3,692	$ 68,691	$ (1,410)	$ 71,315	$ 4,446	$ 75,761	$ 404
Consolidated net income	—	—	—	16,999	—	16,999	684	17,683	73
Other comprehensive income, net of income taxes	—	—	—	—	823	823	138	961	51
Cash dividends declared ($1.59 per share)	—	—	—	(5,361)	—	(5,361)	—	(5,361)	—
Purchase of Company stock	(115)	(11)	(357)	(7,341)	—	(7,709)	—	(7,709)	—
Nonredeemable noncontrolling interest of acquired entity	—	—	—	—	—	—	469	469	—
Other	11	1	285	(10)	—	276	(342)	(66)	(9)
Balances as of January 31, 2013	3,314	332	3,620	72,978	(587)	76,343	5,395	81,738	519
Consolidated net income	—	—	—	16,022	—	16,022	595	16,617	78
Other comprehensive loss, net of income taxes	—	—	—	—	(2,409)	(2,409)	(311)	(2,720)	(66)
Cash dividends declared ($1.88 per share)	—	—	—	(6,139)	—	(6,139)	—	(6,139)	—
Purchase of Company stock	(87)	(9)	(294)	(6,254)	—	(6,557)	—	(6,557)	—
Redemption value adjustment of redeemable noncontrolling interest	—	—	(1,019)	—	—	(1,019)	—	(1,019)	1,019
Other	6	—	55	(41)	—	14	(595)	(581)	(59)
Balances as of January 31, 2014	3,233	323	2,362	76,566	(2,996)	76,255	5,084	81,339	1,491
Consolidated net income	—	—	—	16,363	—	16,363	736	17,099	—
Other comprehensive income, net of income taxes	—	—	—	—	(4,172)	(4,172)	(546)	(4,718)	—
Cash dividends declared ($1.92 per share)	—	—	—	(6,185)	—	(6,185)	—	(6,185)	—
Purchase of Company stock	(13)	(1)	(29)	(950)	—	(980)	—	(980)	—
Purchase of redeemable noncontrolling interest	—	—	—	—	—	—	—	—	(1,491)
Other	8	1	129	(17)	—	113	(731)	(618)	—
Balances as of January 31, 2015	3,228	$ 323	$ 2,462	$ 85,777	$ (7,168)	$ 81,394	$ 4,543	$ 85,937	$ —

See accompanying notes.

Wal-Mart Stores, Inc.
Consolidated Statements of Cash Flows

(Amounts in millions)	Fiscal Years Ended January 31, 2015	2014	2013
Cash flows from operating activities:			
Consolidated net income	$ 17,099	$ 16,695	$ 17,756
Income from discontinued operations, net of income taxes	(285)	(144)	(52)
Income from continuing operations	16,814	16,551	17,704
Adjustments to reconcile income from continuing operations to net cash provided by operating activities:			
Depreciation and amortization	9,173	8,870	8,478
Deferred income taxes	(503)	(279)	(133)
Other operating activities	785	938	602
Changes in certain assets and liabilities, net of effects of acquisitions:			
Receivables, net	(569)	(566)	(614)
Inventories	(1,229)	(1,667)	(2,759)
Accounts payable	2,678	531	1,061
Accrued liabilities	1,249	103	271
Accrued income taxes	166	(1,224)	981
Net cash provided by operating activities	28,564	23,257	25,591
Cash flows from investing activities:			
Payments for property and equipment	(12,174)	(13,115)	(12,898)
Proceeds from the disposal of property and equipment	570	727	532
Proceeds from the disposal of certain operations	671	—	—
Other investing activities	(192)	(138)	(271)
Net cash used in investing activities	(11,125)	(12,526)	(12,637)
Cash flows from financing activities:			
Net change in short-term borrowings	(6,288)	911	2,754
Proceeds from issuance of long-term debt	5,174	7,072	211
Payments of long-term debt	(3,904)	(4,968)	(1,478)
Dividends paid	(6,185)	(6,139)	(5,361)
Purchase of Company stock	(1,015)	(6,683)	(7,600)
Dividends paid to noncontrolling interest	(600)	(426)	(282)
Purchase of noncontrolling interest	(1,844)	(296)	(132)
Other financing activities	(409)	(260)	(58)
Net cash used in financing activities	(15,071)	(10,789)	(11,946)
Effect of exchange rates on cash and cash equivalents	(514)	(442)	223
Net increase (decrease) in cash and cash equivalents	1,854	(500)	1,231
Cash and cash equivalents at beginning of year	7,281	7,781	6,550
Cash and cash equivalents at end of year	$ 9,135	$ 7,281	$ 7,781
Supplemental disclosure of cash flow information:			
Income taxes paid	8,169	8,641	7,304
Interest paid	2,433	2,362	2,262

See accompanying notes.

F

Specimen Financial Statements: Louis Vuitton

Louis Vuitton is a French company and is one of the leading international fashion houses in the world. Louis Vuitton has been named the world's most valuable luxury brand. Note that its financial statements are IFRS-based and are presented in euros (€). To access the company's complete financial statements, follow these steps:

1. Go to **www.lvmh.com/investor-relations**.
2. Select All publications, then the Reports tab, and then 2014 Consolidated financial statements.
3. Note that the comments (notes) to the financial statements begin on page 7.

CONSOLIDATED INCOME STATEMENT

(EUR millions, except for earnings per share)	Notes	2014	2013[1]	2012[1]
Revenue	23-24	30,638	29,016	27,970
Cost of sales		(10,801)	(9,997)	(9,863)
Gross margin		**19,837**	**19,019**	**18,107**
Marketing and selling expenses		(11,744)	(10,767)	(10,013)
General and administrative expenses		(2,373)	(2,212)	(2,151)
Income (loss) from joint ventures and associates	7	(5)	(23)	(19)
Profit from recurring operations	23-24	**5,715**	**6,017**	**5,924**
Other operating income and expenses	25	(284)	(119)	(182)
Operating profit		**5,431**	**5,898**	**5,742**
Cost of net financial debt		(115)	(101)	(138)
Other financial income and expenses		3,062	(97)	126
Net financial income (expense)	26	**2,947**	**(198)**	**(12)**
Income taxes	27	(2,273)	(1,753)	(1,821)
Net profit before minority interests		**6,105**	**3,947**	**3,909**
Minority interests	17	(457)	(511)	(484)
Net profit, Group share		**5,648**	**3,436**	**3,425**
Basic Group share of net earnings per share *(EUR)*	28	**11.27**	**6.87**	**6.86**
Number of shares on which the calculation is based		501,309,369	500,283,414	499,133,643
Diluted Group share of net earnings per share *(EUR)*	28	**11.21**	**6.83**	**6.82**
Number of shares on which the calculation is based		503,861,733	503,217,497	502,229,952

(1) The financial statements as of December 31, 2013 and 2012 have been restated to reflect the retrospective application as of January 1, 2012 of IFRS 11 Joint Arrangements. See Note 1.2.

CONSOLIDATED STATEMENT OF COMPREHENSIVE GAINS AND LOSSES

(EUR millions)	2014	2013[1]	2012[1]
Net profit before minority interests	**6,105**	**3,947**	**3,909**
Translation adjustments	534	(346)	(99)
Tax impact	104	(48)	(18)
	638	**(394)**	**(117)**
Change in value of available for sale financial assets	494	963	(27)
Amounts transferred to income statement	(3,326)	(16)	(14)
Tax impact	184	(35)	(6)
	(2,648)	**912**	**(47)**
Change in value of hedges of future foreign currency cash flows	(30)	304	182
Amounts transferred to income statement	(163)	(265)	13
Tax impact	57	(17)	(50)
	(136)	**22**	**145**
Gains and losses recognized in equity, transferable to income statement	**(2,146)**	**540**	**(19)**
Change in value of vineyard land	(17)	369	85
Amounts transferred to consolidated reserves	(10)	-	-
Tax impact	9	(127)	(28)
	(18)	**242**	**57**
Employee benefit commitments: change in value resulting from actuarial gains and losses	(161)	80	(101)
Tax impact	52	(22)	29
	(109)	**58**	**(72)**
Gains and losses recognized in equity, not transferable to income statement	**(127)**	**300**	**(15)**
Comprehensive income	**3,832**	**4,787**	**3,875**
Minority interests	(565)	(532)	(469)
Comprehensive income, Group share	**3,267**	**4,255**	**3,406**

(1) The financial statements as of December 31, 2013 and 2012 have been restated to reflect the retrospective application as of January 1, 2012 of IFRS 11 Joint Arrangements. See Note 1.2.

CONSOLIDATED BALANCE SHEET

ASSETS *(EUR millions)*	Notes	2014	2013[1][2]	2012[1]
Brands and other intangible fixed assets	3	13,031	12,596	11,322
Goodwill	4	8,810	9,058	7,709
Property, plant and equipment	6	10,387	9,621	8,694
Investments in joint ventures and associates	7	519	480	483
Non-current available for sale financial assets	8	580	7,080	6,004
Other non-current assets	9	489	457	519
Deferred tax	27	1,436	913	952
Non-current assets		**35,252**	**40,205**	**35,683**
Inventories and work in progress	10	9,475	8,492	7,994
Trade accounts receivable	11	2,274	2,174	1,972
Income taxes		354	223	201
Other current assets	12	1,916	1,856	1,813
Cash and cash equivalents	14	4,091	3,226	2,187
Current assets		**18,110**	**15,971**	**14,167**
Total assets		**53,362**	**56,176**	**49,850**

LIABILITIES AND EQUITY *(EUR millions)*	Notes	2014	2013[1][2]	2012[1]
Share capital	15.1	152	152	152
Share premium account	15.1	2,655	3,849	3,848
Treasury shares and LVMH-share settled derivatives	15.2	(374)	(451)	(414)
Cumulative translation adjustment	15.4	492	(8)	342
Revaluation reserves		1,019	3,900	2,731
Other reserves		12,171	16,001	14,340
Net profit, Group share		5,648	3,436	3,425
Equity, Group share		21,763	26,879	24,424
Minority interests	17	1,240	1,028	1,084
Total equity		**23,003**	**27,907**	**25,508**
Long-term borrowings	18	5,054	4,149	3,825
Non-current provisions	19	2,291	1,797	1,772
Deferred tax	27	4,392	4,280	3,884
Other non-current liabilities	20	6,447	6,404	5,456
Non-current liabilities		**18,184**	**16,630**	**14,937**
Short-term borrowings	18	4,189	4,674	2,950
Trade accounts payable		3,606	3,297	3,118
Income taxes		549	357	442
Current provisions	19	332	324	335
Other current liabilities	21	3,499	2,987	2,560
Current liabilities		**12,175**	**11,639**	**9,405**
Total liabilities and equity		**53,362**	**56,176**	**49,850**

(1) The financial statements as of December 31, 2013 and 2012 have been restated to reflect the retrospective application as of January 1, 2012 of IFRS 11 Joint Arrangements. See Note 1.2.

(2) The consolidated balance sheet as of December 31, 2013 has been restated to reflect the finalized purchase price allocation for Loro Piana. See Note 2.

CONSOLIDATED STATEMENT OF CHANGES IN EQUITY

(EUR millions)	Number of shares	Share capital	Share premium account	Treasury shares and LVMH-share settled derivatives	Cumulative translation adjustment	Revaluation reserves				Net profit and other reserves	Total equity		
						Available for sale financial assets	Hedges of future foreign currency cash flows	Vineyard land	Employee benefit commitments		Group share	Minority interests	Total
Notes		15.1		15.2	15.4							17	
As of December 31, 2011	**507,815,624**	**152**	**3,801**	**(485)**	**431**	**1,990**	**(15)**	**714**	**(28)**	**15,811**	**22,371**	**1,055**	**23,426**
Gains and losses recognized in equity					(89)	(47)	133	44	(60)	-	(19)	(15)	(34)
Net profit										3,425	3,425	484	3,909
Comprehensive income		**-**	**-**	**-**	**(89)**	**(47)**	**133**	**44**	**(60)**	**3,425**	**3,406**	**469**	**3,875**
Stock option plan and similar expenses										50	50	3	53
(Acquisition)/disposal of treasury shares and LVMH-share settled derivatives				24						(12)	12	-	12
Exercise of LVMH share subscription options	1,344,975		94								94	-	94
Retirement of LVMH shares	(997,250)		(47)	47							-	-	-
Capital increase in subsidiaries											-	8	8
Interim and final dividends paid										(1,447)	(1,447)	(317)	(1,764)
Changes in control of consolidated entities										(12)	(12)	(11)	(23)
Acquisition and disposal of minority interests' shares										(40)	(40)	(25)	(65)
Purchase commitments for minority interests' shares										(10)	(10)	(98)	(108)
As of December 31, 2012	**508,163,349**	**152**	**3,848**	**(414)**	**342**	**1,943**	**118**	**758**	**(88)**	**17,765**	**24,424**	**1,084**	**25,508**
Gains and losses recognized in equity					(350)	912	18	188	51	-	819	21	840
Net profit										3,436	3,436	511	3,947
Comprehensive income		**-**	**-**	**-**	**(350)**	**912**	**18**	**188**	**51**	**3,436**	**4,255**	**532**	**4,787**
Stock option plan and similar expenses										31	31	3	34
(Acquisition)/disposal of treasury shares and LVMH-share settled derivatives				(103)						(7)	(110)	-	(110)
Exercise of LVMH share subscription options	1,025,418		67								67	-	67
Retirement of LVMH shares	(1,395,106)		(66)	66							-	-	-
Capital increase in subsidiaries											-	8	8
Interim and final dividends paid										(1,500)	(1,500)	(228)	(1,728)
Acquisition of a controlling interest in Loro Piana[1]											-	235	235
Changes in control of consolidated entities										1	1	(1)	-
Acquisition and disposal of minority interests' shares										(73)	(73)	(76)	(149)
Purchase commitments for minority interests' shares[1]										(216)	(216)	(529)	(745)
As of December 31, 2013	**507,793,661**	**152**	**3,849**	**(451)**	**(8)**	**2,855**	**136**	**946**	**(37)**	**19,437**	**26,879**	**1,028**	**27,907**
Gains and losses recognized in equity					500	(2,648)	(122)	(15)	(96)	-	(2,381)	108	(2,273)
Net profit										5,648	5,648	457	6,105
Comprehensive income		**-**	**-**	**-**	**500**	**(2,648)**	**(122)**	**(15)**	**(96)**	**5,648**	**3,267**	**565**	**3,832**
Stock option plan and similar expenses										37	37	2	39
(Acquisition)/disposal of treasury shares and LVMH-share settled derivatives				27						(17)	10	-	10
Exercise of LVMH share subscription options	980,323		59								59	-	59
Retirement of LVMH shares	(1,062,271)		(50)	50							-	-	-
Capital increase in subsidiaries											-	3	3
Interim and final dividends paid										(1,579)	(1,579)	(328)	(1,907)
Distribution in kind of Hermès shares. See Note 8.			(1,203)							(5,652)	(6,855)	-	(6,855)
Changes in control of consolidated entities										(5)	(5)	11	6
Acquisition and disposal of minority interests' shares										(2)	(2)	32	30
Purchase commitments for minority interests' shares										(48)	(48)	(73)	(121)
As of December 31, 2014	**507,711,713**	**152**	**2,655**	**(374)**	**492**	**207**	**14**	**931**	**(133)**	**17,819**	**21,763**	**1,240**	**23,003**

(1) The consolidated balance sheet as of December 31, 2013 has been restated to reflect the finalized purchase price allocation for Loro Piana. See Note 2.

CONSOLIDATED CASH FLOW STATEMENT

(EUR millions)	Notes	2014	2013[1]	2012[1]
I. OPERATING ACTIVITIES AND OPERATING INVESTMENTS				
Operating profit		5,431	5,898	5,742
Income/(loss) and dividends from joint ventures and associates[a]	7	26	49	37
Net increase in depreciation, amortization and provisions		1,895	1,435	1,289
Other computed expenses		(188)	(29)	(59)
Other adjustments		(84)	(76)	(52)
Cash from operations before changes in working capital		**7,080**	**7,277**	**6,957**
Cost of net financial debt: interest paid		(116)	(111)	(152)
Income taxes paid[a]		(1,639)	(1,832)	(1,880)
Net cash from operating activities before changes in working capital		**5,325**	**5,334**	**4,925**
Change in working capital	14.1	(718)	(620)	(810)
Net cash from operating activities		**4,607**	**4,714**	**4,115**
Operating investments	14.2	(1,775)	(1,657)	(1,694)
Net cash from operating activities and operating investments (free cash flow)		**2,832**	**3,057**	**2,421**
II. FINANCIAL INVESTMENTS				
Purchase of non-current available for sale financial assets	8	(57)	(197)	(131)
Proceeds from sale of non-current available for sale financial assets	8	160	38	36
Dividends received[a]	8	69	71	179
Income tax related to financial investments[a]		(237)	(11)	(21)
Impact of purchase and sale of consolidated investments	2.4	(167)	(2,161)	(59)
Net cash from (used in) financial investments		**(232)**	**(2,260)**	**4**
III. TRANSACTIONS RELATING TO EQUITY				
Capital increases of LVMH SE	15.1	59	66	95
Capital increases of subsidiaries subscribed by minority interests	17	3	7	8
Acquisition and disposals of treasury shares and LVMH-share settled derivatives	15.2	1	(113)	5
Interim and final dividends paid by LVMH SE	15.3	(1,619)[b]	(1,501)	(1,447)
Income taxes paid related to interim and final dividends paid[a]		(79)	(137)	(73)
Interim and final dividends paid to minority interests in consolidated subsidiaries	17	(336)	(220)	(314)
Purchase and proceeds from sale of minority interests	2.4	10	(150)	(206)
Net cash from (used in) transactions relating to equity		**(1,961)**	**(2,048)**	**(1,932)**
Change in cash before financing activities		**639**	**(1,251)**	**493**
IV. FINANCING ACTIVITIES				
Proceeds from borrowings		2,407	3,095	1,028
Repayment of borrowings		(2,100)	(1,057)	(1,494)
Purchase and proceeds from sale of current available for sale financial assets	13	(106)	101	(67)
Net cash from (used in) financing activities		**201**	**2,139**	**(533)**
V. EFFECT OF EXCHANGE RATE CHANGES		27	47	(43)
NET INCREASE (DECREASE) IN CASH AND CASH EQUIVALENTS (I+II+III+IV+V)		**867**	**935**	**(83)**
CASH AND CASH EQUIVALENTS AT BEGINNING OF PERIOD	14	**2,916**	**1,981**	**2,064**
CASH AND CASH EQUIVALENTS AT END OF PERIOD	14	**3,783**	**2,916**	**1,981**
TOTAL INCOME TAXES PAID		**(1,955)**	**(1,980)**	**(1,974)**
Transactions included in the table above, generating no change in cash:				
- acquisition of assets by means of finance leases		5	7	5

(a) Restated to reflect the amended presentation of dividends received and income tax paid starting in 2014. See Note 1.4.

(b) The distribution in kind of Hermès shares had no impact on cash, apart from related income tax effects. See Note 8.

(1) The financial statements as of December 31, 2013 and 2012 have been restated to reflect the retrospective application as of January 1, 2012 of IFRS 11 Joint Arrangements. See Note 1.2.

Time Value of Money

APPENDIX PREVIEW

Would you rather receive $1,000 today or a year from now? You should prefer to receive the $1,000 today because you can invest the $1,000 and then earn interest on it. As a result, you will have more than $1,000 a year from now. What this example illustrates is the concept of the **time value of money**. Everyone prefers to receive money today rather than in the future because of the interest factor.

APPENDIX OUTLINE

LEARNING OBJECTIVES	
1 Compute interest and future values.	• Nature of interest • Future value of a single amount • Future value of an annuity
2 Compute present values.	• Present value variables • Present value of a single amount • Present value of an annuity • Time periods and discounting • Present value of a long-term note or bond
3 Use a financial calculator to solve time value of money problems.	• Present value of a single sum • Present value of an annuity • Useful financial calculator applications

LEARNING OBJECTIVE 1 **Compute interest and future values.**

NATURE OF INTEREST

Interest is payment for the use of another person's money. It is the difference between the amount borrowed or invested (called the **principal**) and the amount repaid or collected. The amount of interest to be paid or collected is usually stated as a rate over a specific period of time. The rate of interest is generally stated as an annual rate.

The amount of interest involved in any financing transaction is based on three elements:

1. **Principal (p):** The original amount borrowed or invested.
2. **Interest Rate (i):** An annual percentage of the principal.
3. **Time (n):** The number of periods that the principal is borrowed or invested.

Simple Interest

Simple interest is computed on the principal amount only. It is the return on the principal for one period. Simple interest is usually expressed as shown in Illustration G-1.

ILLUSTRATION G-1
Interest computation

$$\text{Interest} = \underset{p}{\text{Principal}} \times \underset{i}{\text{Rate}} \times \underset{n}{\text{Time}}$$

For example, if you borrowed $5,000 for 2 years at a simple interest rate of 12% annually, you would pay $1,200 in total interest, computed as follows.

$$\begin{aligned} \text{Interest} &= p \times i \times n \\ &= \$5{,}000 \times .12 \times 2 \\ &= \$1{,}200 \end{aligned}$$

Compound Interest

Compound interest is computed on principal **and** on any interest earned that has not been paid or withdrawn. It is the return on (or growth of) the principal for two or more time periods. Compounding computes interest not only on the principal but also on the interest earned to date on that principal, assuming the interest is left on deposit.

To illustrate the difference between simple and compound interest, assume that you deposit $1,000 in Bank Two, where it will earn simple interest of 9% per year, and you deposit another $1,000 in Citizens Bank, where it will earn compound interest of 9% per year compounded annually. Also assume that in both cases you will not withdraw any cash until three years from the date of deposit. Illustration G-2 shows the computation of interest to be received and the accumulated year-end balances.

ILLUSTRATION G-2
Simple versus compound interest

Bank Two

Simple Interest Calculation	Simple Interest	Accumulated Year-End Balance
Year 1 $1,000.00 × 9%	$ 90.00	$1,090.00
Year 2 $1,000.00 × 9%	90.00	$1,180.00
Year 3 $1,000.00 × 9%	90.00	$1,270.00
	$ 270.00	

Citizens Bank

Compound Interest Calculation	Compound Interest	Accumulated Year-End Balance
Year 1 $1,000.00 × 9%	$ 90.00	$1,090.00
Year 2 $1,090.00 × 9%	98.10	$1,188.10
Year 3 $1,188.10 × 9%	106.93	$1,295.03
	$ 295.03	

$25.03 Difference

Note in Illustration G-2 that simple interest uses the initial principal of $1,000 to compute the interest in all three years. Compound interest uses the accumulated balance (principal plus interest to date) at each year-end to compute interest in the succeeding year—which explains why your compound interest account is larger.

Obviously, if you had a choice between investing your money at simple interest or at compound interest, you would choose compound interest, all other things—

especially risk—being equal. In the example, compounding provides \$25.03 of additional interest income. For practical purposes, compounding assumes that unpaid interest earned becomes a part of the principal, and the accumulated balance at the end of each year becomes the new principal on which interest is earned during the next year.

Illustration G-2 indicates that you should invest your money at the bank that compounds interest. Most business situations use compound interest. Simple interest is generally applicable only to short-term situations of one year or less.

FUTURE VALUE OF A SINGLE AMOUNT

The **future value of a single amount** is the value at a future date of a given amount invested, assuming compound interest. For example, in Illustration G-2, \$1,295.03 is the future value of the \$1,000 investment earning 9% for three years. The \$1,295.03 is determined more easily by using the following formula.

ILLUSTRATION G-3
Formula for future value

$$FV = p \times (1 + i)^n$$

where:

FV = future value of a single amount
p = principal (or present value; the value today)
i = interest rate for one period
n = number of periods

The \$1,295.03 is computed as follows.

$$\begin{aligned} FV &= p \times (1 + i)^n \\ &= \$1{,}000 \times (1 + .09)^3 \\ &= \$1{,}000 \times 1.29503 \\ &= \$1{,}295.03 \end{aligned}$$

The 1.29503 is computed by multiplying (1.09 × 1.09 × 1.09), where 1.09 is 1 plus the interest rate of 9%. Thus, 1.29503 represents the 9% rate compounded for three years. The amounts in this example can be depicted in the time diagram shown in Illustration G-4.

ILLUSTRATION G-4
Time diagram

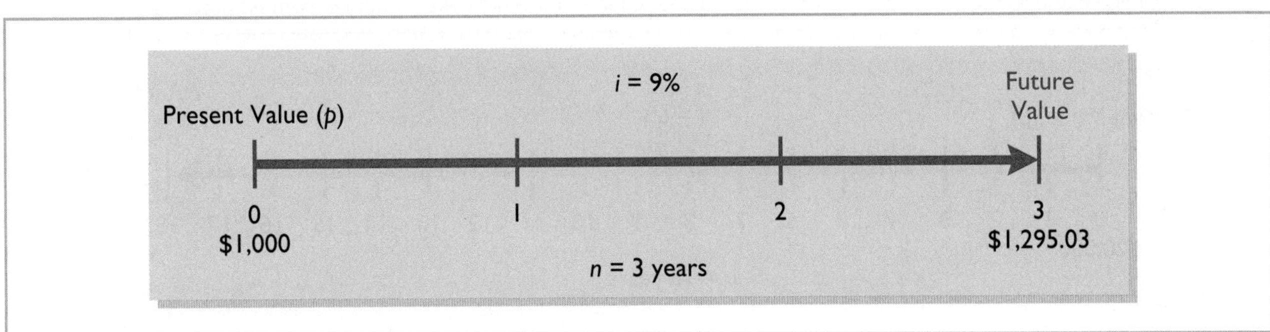

Another method used to compute the future value of a single amount involves a compound interest table. This table shows the future value of 1 for n periods. Table 1 (page G-4) is such a table.

In Table 1, n is the number of compounding periods, the percentages are the periodic interest rates, and the 5-digit decimal numbers in the respective columns are the future value of 1 factors. To use Table 1, you multiply the principal amount by the future value factor for the specified number of periods and interest rate. For example, the future value factor for two periods at 9% is 1.18810. Multiplying this factor by \$1,000 equals \$1,188.10—which is the accumulated balance at the end of year 2 in the Citizens Bank example in Illustration G-2. The

TABLE 1 Future Value of 1

(*n*) Periods	4%	5%	6%	7%	8%	9%	10%	11%	12%	15%
0	1.00000	1.00000	1.00000	1.00000	1.00000	1.00000	1.00000	1.00000	1.00000	1.00000
1	1.04000	1.05000	1.06000	1.07000	1.08000	1.09000	1.10000	1.11000	1.12000	1.15000
2	1.08160	1.10250	1.12360	1.14490	1.16640	1.18810	1.21000	1.23210	1.25440	1.32250
3	1.12486	1.15763	1.19102	1.22504	1.25971	1.29503	1.33100	1.36763	1.40493	1.52088
4	1.16986	1.21551	1.26248	1.31080	1.36049	1.41158	1.46410	1.51807	1.57352	1.74901
5	1.21665	1.27628	1.33823	1.40255	1.46933	1.53862	1.61051	1.68506	1.76234	2.01136
6	1.26532	1.34010	1.41852	1.50073	1.58687	1.67710	1.77156	1.87041	1.97382	2.31306
7	1.31593	1.40710	1.50363	1.60578	1.71382	1.82804	1.94872	2.07616	2.21068	2.66002
8	1.36857	1.47746	1.59385	1.71819	1.85093	1.99256	2.14359	2.30454	2.47596	3.05902
9	1.42331	1.55133	1.68948	1.83846	1.99900	2.17189	2.35795	2.55803	2.77308	3.51788
10	1.48024	1.62889	1.79085	1.96715	2.15892	2.36736	2.59374	2.83942	3.10585	4.04556
11	1.53945	1.71034	1.89830	2.10485	2.33164	2.58043	2.85312	3.15176	3.47855	4.65239
12	1.60103	1.79586	2.01220	2.25219	2.51817	2.81267	3.13843	3.49845	3.89598	5.35025
13	1.66507	1.88565	2.13293	2.40985	2.71962	3.06581	3.45227	3.88328	4.36349	6.15279
14	1.73168	1.97993	2.26090	2.57853	2.93719	3.34173	3.79750	4.31044	4.88711	7.07571
15	1.80094	2.07893	2.39656	2.75903	3.17217	3.64248	4.17725	4.78459	5.47357	8.13706
16	1.87298	2.18287	2.54035	2.95216	3.42594	3.97031	4.59497	5.31089	6.13039	9.35762
17	1.94790	2.29202	2.69277	3.15882	3.70002	4.32763	5.05447	5.89509	6.86604	10.76126
18	2.02582	2.40662	2.85434	3.37993	3.99602	4.71712	5.55992	6.54355	7.68997	12.37545
19	2.10685	2.52695	3.02560	3.61653	4.31570	5.14166	6.11591	7.26334	8.61276	14.23177
20	2.19112	2.65330	3.20714	3.86968	4.66096	5.60441	6.72750	8.06231	9.64629	16.36654

$1,295.03 accumulated balance at the end of the third year is calculated from Table 1 by multiplying the future value factor for three periods (1.29503) by the $1,000.

The demonstration problem in Illustration G-5 shows how to use Table 1.

ILLUSTRATION G-5
Demonstration problem—Using Table 1 for *FV* of 1

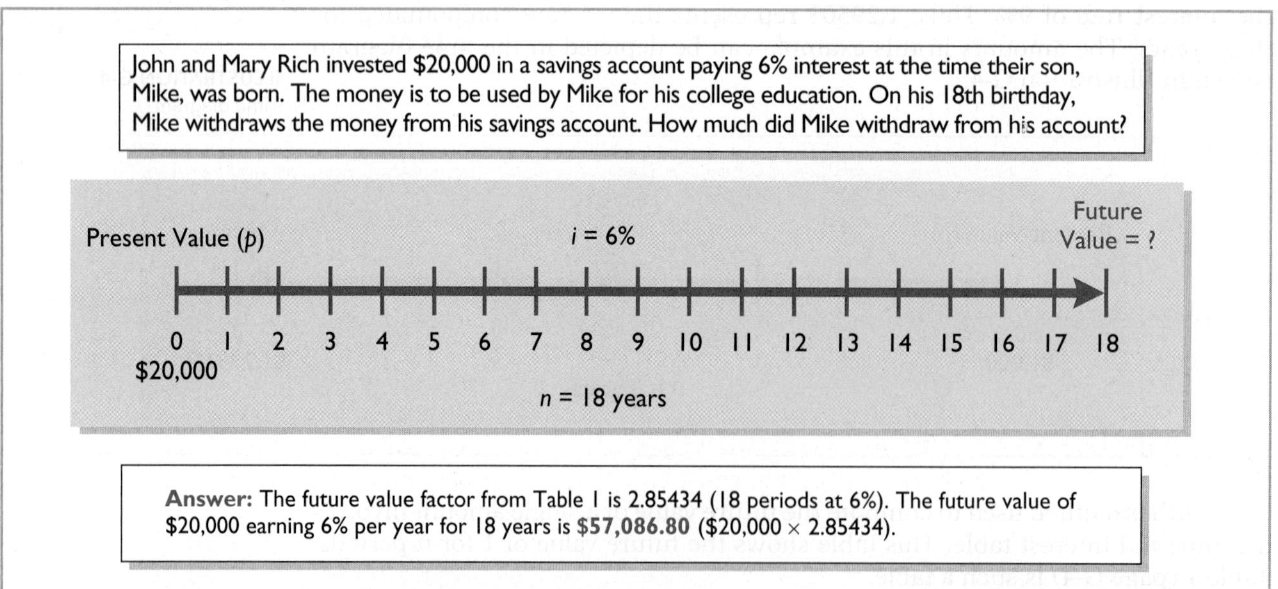

FUTURE VALUE OF AN ANNUITY

The preceding discussion involved the accumulation of only a single principal sum. Individuals and businesses frequently encounter situations in which a

series of equal dollar amounts are to be paid or received at evenly spaced time intervals (periodically), such as loans or lease (rental) contracts. A series of payments or receipts of equal dollar amounts is referred to as an **annuity**.

The **future value of an annuity** is the sum of all the payments (receipts) plus the accumulated compound interest on them. In computing the future value of an annuity, it is necessary to know (1) the interest rate, (2) the number of payments (receipts), and (3) the amount of the periodic payments (receipts).

To illustrate the computation of the future value of an annuity, assume that you invest $2,000 at the end of each year for three years at 5% interest compounded annually. This situation is depicted in the time diagram in Illustration G-6.

ILLUSTRATION G-6
Time diagram for a three-year annuity

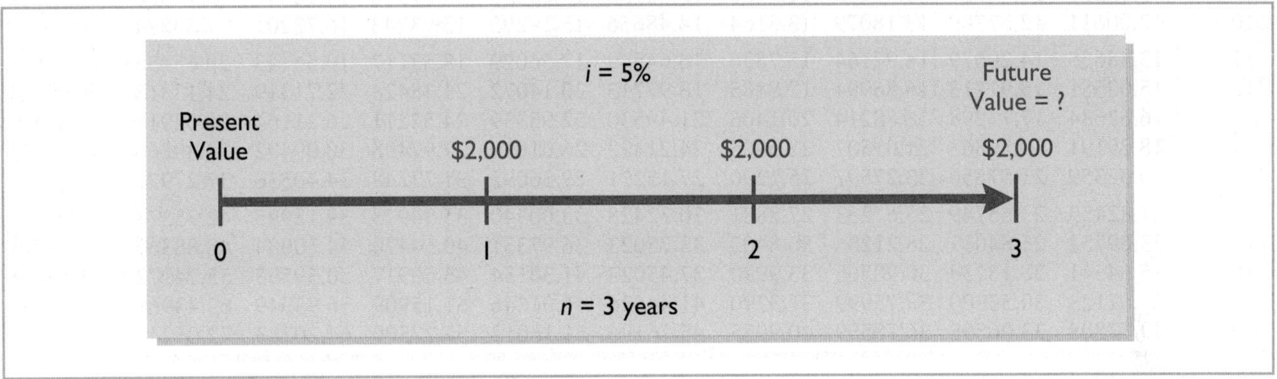

The $2,000 invested at the end of year 1 will earn interest for two years (years 2 and 3), and the $2,000 invested at the end of year 2 will earn interest for one year (year 3). However, the last $2,000 investment (made at the end of year 3) will not earn any interest. Using the future value factors from Table 1, the future value of these periodic payments is computed as shown in Illustration G-7.

ILLUSTRATION G-7
Future value of periodic payment computation

Invested at End of Year	Number of Compounding Periods	Amount Invested	×	Future Value of 1 Factor at 5%	=	Future Value
1	2	$2,000		1.10250		$2,205
2	1	2,000		1.05000		2,100
3	0	2,000		1.00000		2,000
				3.15250		**$6,305**

The first $2,000 investment is multiplied by the future value factor for two periods (1.1025) because two years' interest will accumulate on it (in years 2 and 3). The second $2,000 investment will earn only one year's interest (in year 3) and therefore is multiplied by the future value factor for one year (1.0500). The final $2,000 investment is made at the end of the third year and will not earn any interest. Thus, $n = 0$ and the future value factor is 1.00000. Consequently, the future value of the last $2,000 invested is only $2,000 since it does not accumulate any interest.

Calculating the future value of each individual cash flow is required when the periodic payments or receipts are not equal in each period. However, when the periodic payments (receipts) are **the same in each period**, the future value can be computed by using a future value of an annuity of 1 table. Table 2 (page G-6) is such a table.

Table 2 shows the future value of 1 to be received periodically for a given number of payments. It assumes that each payment is made at the **end** of each period. We can see from Table 2 that the future value of an annuity of 1 factor for

TABLE 2 Future Value of an Annuity of 1

(*n*) Payments	4%	5%	6%	7%	8%	9%	10%	11%	12%	15%
1	1.00000	1.00000	1.00000	1.0000	1.00000	1.00000	1.00000	1.00000	1.00000	1.00000
2	2.04000	2.05000	2.06000	2.0700	2.08000	2.09000	2.10000	2.11000	2.12000	2.15000
3	3.12160	3.15250	3.18360	3.2149	3.24640	3.27810	3.31000	3.34210	3.37440	3.47250
4	4.24646	4.31013	4.37462	4.4399	4.50611	4.57313	4.64100	4.70973	4.77933	4.99338
5	5.41632	5.52563	5.63709	5.7507	5.86660	5.98471	6.10510	6.22780	6.35285	6.74238
6	6.63298	6.80191	6.97532	7.1533	7.33592	7.52334	7.71561	7.91286	8.11519	8.75374
7	7.89829	8.14201	8.39384	8.6540	8.92280	9.20044	9.48717	9.78327	10.08901	11.06680
8	9.21423	9.54911	9.89747	10.2598	10.63663	11.02847	11.43589	11.85943	12.29969	13.72682
9	10.58280	11.02656	11.49132	11.9780	12.48756	13.02104	13.57948	14.16397	14.77566	16.78584
10	12.00611	12.57789	13.18079	13.8164	14.48656	15.19293	15.93743	16.72201	17.54874	20.30372
11	13.48635	14.20679	14.97164	15.7836	16.64549	17.56029	18.53117	19.56143	20.65458	24.34928
12	15.02581	15.91713	16.86994	17.8885	18.97713	20.14072	21.38428	22.71319	24.13313	29.00167
13	16.62684	17.71298	18.88214	20.1406	21.49530	22.95339	24.52271	26.21164	28.02911	34.35192
14	18.29191	19.59863	21.01507	22.5505	24.21492	26.01919	27.97498	30.09492	32.39260	40.50471
15	20.02359	21.57856	23.27597	25.1290	27.15211	29.36092	31.77248	34.40536	37.27972	47.58041
16	21.82453	23.65749	25.67253	27.8881	30.32428	33.00340	35.94973	39.18995	42.75328	55.71747
17	23.69751	25.84037	28.21288	30.8402	33.75023	36.97351	40.54470	44.50084	48.88367	65.07509
18	25.64541	28.13238	30.90565	33.9990	37.45024	41.30134	45.59917	50.39593	55.74972	75.83636
19	27.67123	30.53900	33.75999	37.3790	41.44626	46.01846	51.15909	56.93949	63.43968	88.21181
20	29.77808	33.06595	36.78559	40.9955	45.76196	51.16012	57.27500	64.20283	72.05244	102.44358

three payments at 5% is 3.15250. The future value factor is the total of the three individual future value factors as shown in Illustration G-7. Multiplying this amount by the annual investment of $2,000 produces a future value of $6,305.

The demonstration problem in Illustration G-8 shows how to use Table 2.

ILLUSTRATION G-8
Demonstration problem—Using Table 2 for *FV* of an annuity of 1

John and Char Lewis's daughter, Debra, has just started high school. They decide to start a college fund for her and will invest $2,500 in a savings account at the end of each year she is in high school (4 payments total). The account will earn 6% interest compounded annually. How much will be in the college fund at the time Debra graduates from high school?

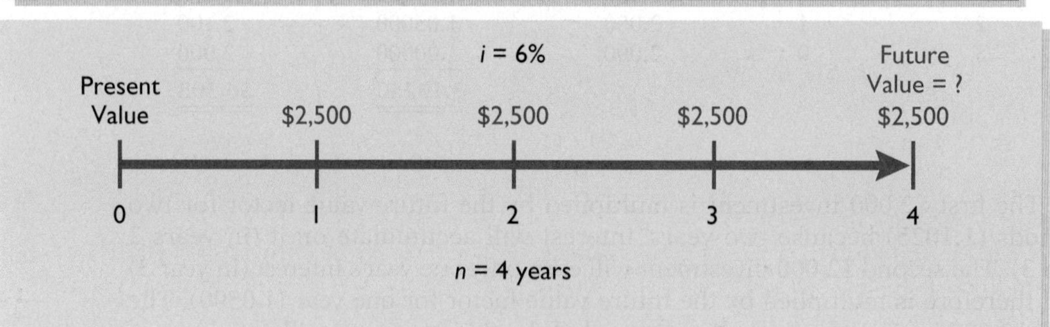

Answer: The future value factor from Table 2 is 4.37462 (4 payments at 6%). The future value of $2,500 invested each year for 4 years at 6% interest is **$10,936.55** ($2,500 × 4.37462).

Note that we can apply the same concepts in situations where the future value and interest rate are known, but the payment must be calculated. Suppose, for example, that in Illustration G-8 that the amount that Debra needs to accumulate in her college fund by the end of four years is $10,936.55. If Debra earns 6% on her four annual payments, we can solve for the amount of the annuity payments by dividing $10,936.55 by the future value factor of 4.37462 to determine the payment amount of $2,500.

LEARNING OBJECTIVE **2** **Compute present values.**

PRESENT VALUE VARIABLES

The **present value** is the value now of a given amount to be paid or received in the future, assuming compound interest. The present value, like the future value, is based on three variables: (1) the dollar amount to be received (future amount), (2) the length of time until the amount is received (number of periods), and (3) the interest rate (the discount rate). The process of determining the present value is referred to as **discounting the future amount.**

Present value computations are used in measuring many items. For example, the present value of principal and interest payments is used to determine the market price of a bond. Determining the amount to be reported for notes payable and lease liabilities also involves present value computations. In addition, capital budgeting and other investment proposals are evaluated using present value computations. Finally, all rate of return and internal rate of return computations involve present value techniques.

PRESENT VALUE OF A SINGLE AMOUNT

To illustrate present value, assume that you want to invest a sum of money today that will provide $1,000 at the end of one year. What amount would you need to invest today to have $1,000 one year from now? If you want a 10% rate of return, the investment or present value is $909.09 ($1,000 ÷ 1.10). The formula for calculating present value is shown in Illustration G-9.

$$\text{Present Value } (PV) = \text{Future Value } (FV) \div (1 + i)^n$$

ILLUSTRATION G-9
Formula for present value

The computation of $1,000 discounted at 10% for one year is as follows.

$$\begin{aligned} PV &= FV \div (1 + i)^n \\ &= \$1{,}000 \div (1 + .10)^1 \\ &= \$1{,}000 \div 1.10 \\ &= \$909.09 \end{aligned}$$

The future amount ($1,000), the discount rate (10%), and the number of periods (1) are known. The variables in this situation are depicted in the time diagram in Illustration G-10.

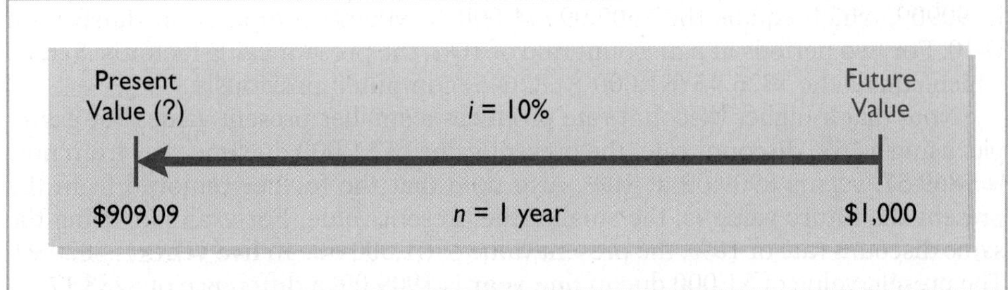

ILLUSTRATION G-10
Finding present value if discounted for one period

If the single amount of $1,000 is to be received **in two years** and discounted at 10% [$PV = \$1,000 \div (1 + .10)^2$], its present value is $826.45 [($1,000 ÷ 1.21), depicted in Illustration G-11.

ILLUSTRATION G-11
Finding present value if discounted for two periods

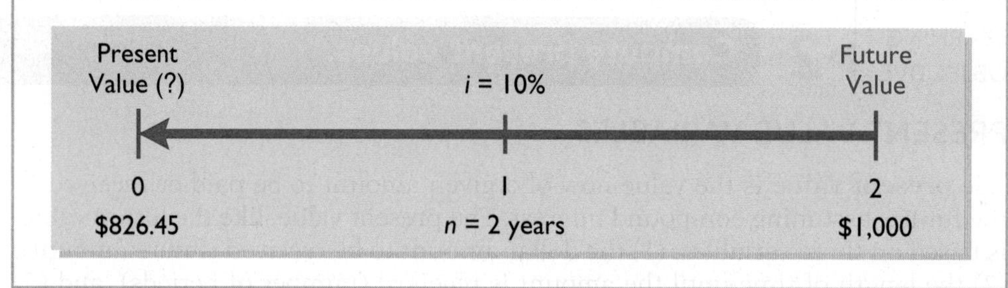

The present value of 1 may also be determined through tables that show the present value of 1 for n periods. In Table 3 (see below), n is the number of discounting periods involved. The percentages are the periodic interest rates or discount rates, and the 5-digit decimal numbers in the respective columns are the present value of 1 factors.

When using Table 3, the future value is multiplied by the present value factor specified at the intersection of the number of periods and the discount rate.

TABLE 3 Present Value of 1

(*n*) Periods	4%	5%	6%	7%	8%	9%	10%	11%	12%	15%
1	.96154	.95238	.94340	.93458	.92593	.91743	.90909	.90090	.89286	.86957
2	.92456	.90703	.89000	.87344	.85734	.84168	.82645	.81162	.79719	.75614
3	.88900	.86384	.83962	.81630	.79383	.77218	.75132	.73119	.71178	.65752
4	.85480	.82270	.79209	.76290	.73503	.70843	.68301	.65873	.63552	.57175
5	.82193	.78353	.74726	.71299	.68058	.64993	.62092	.59345	.56743	.49718
6	.79031	.74622	.70496	.66634	.63017	.59627	.56447	.53464	.50663	.43233
7	.75992	.71068	.66506	.62275	.58349	.54703	.51316	.48166	.45235	.37594
8	.73069	.67684	.62741	.58201	.54027	.50187	.46651	.43393	.40388	.32690
9	.70259	.64461	.59190	.54393	.50025	.46043	.42410	.39092	.36061	.28426
10	.67556	.61391	.55839	.50835	.46319	.42241	.38554	.35218	.32197	.24719
11	.64958	.58468	.52679	.47509	.42888	.38753	.35049	.31728	.28748	.21494
12	.62460	.55684	.49697	.44401	.39711	.35554	.31863	.28584	.25668	.18691
13	.60057	.53032	.46884	.41496	.36770	.32618	.28966	.25751	.22917	.16253
14	.57748	.50507	.44230	.38782	.34046	.29925	.26333	.23199	.20462	.14133
15	.55526	.48102	.41727	.36245	.31524	.27454	.23939	.20900	.18270	.12289
16	.53391	.45811	.39365	.33873	.29189	.25187	.21763	.18829	.16312	.10687
17	.51337	.43630	.37136	.31657	.27027	.23107	.19785	.16963	.14564	.09293
18	.49363	.41552	.35034	.29586	.25025	.21199	.17986	.15282	.13004	.08081
19	.47464	.39573	.33051	.27615	.23171	.19449	.16351	.13768	.11611	.07027
20	.45639	.37689	.31180	.25842	.21455	.17843	.14864	.12403	.10367	.06110

For example, the present value factor for one period at a discount rate of 10% is .90909, which equals the $909.09 ($1,000 × .90909) computed in Illustration G-10. For two periods at a discount rate of 10%, the present value factor is .82645, which equals the $826.45 ($1,000 × .82645) computed previously.

Note that a higher discount rate produces a smaller present value. For example, using a 15% discount rate, the present value of $1,000 due one year from now is $869.57, versus $909.09 at 10%. Also note that the further removed from the present the future value is, the smaller the present value. For example, using the same discount rate of 10%, the present value of $1,000 due in **five years** is $620.92. The present value of $1,000 due in **one year** is $909.09, a difference of $288.17.

The following two demonstration problems (Illustrations G-12 and G-13) illustrate how to use Table 3.

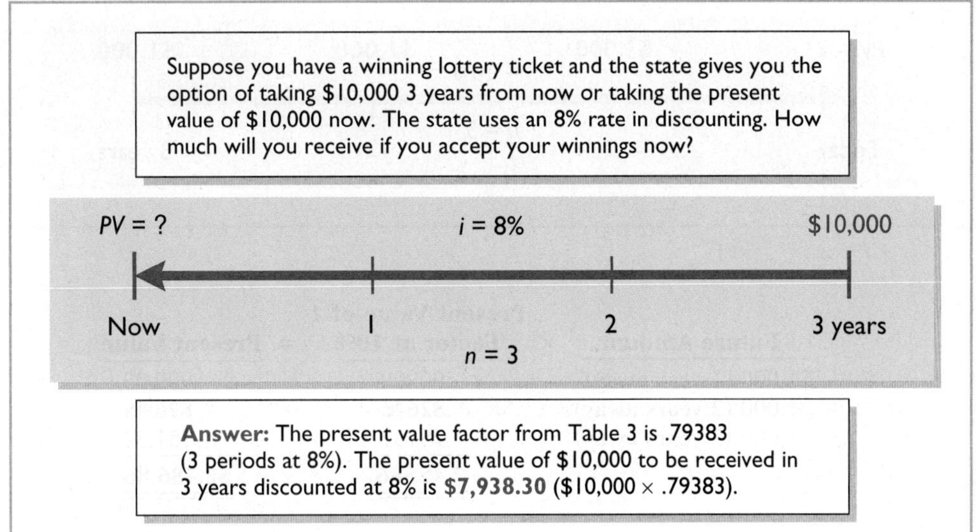

ILLUSTRATION G-12
Demonstration problem—Using Table 3 for *PV* of 1

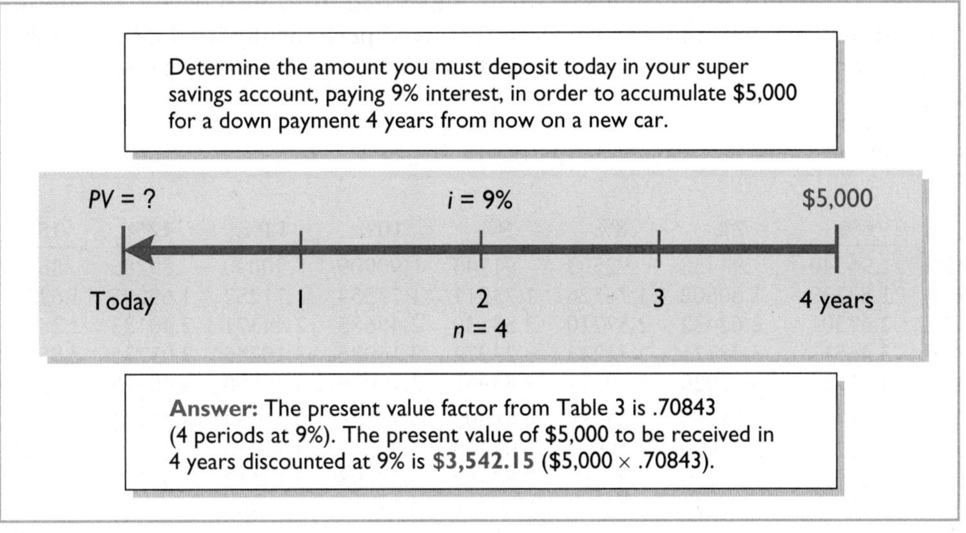

ILLUSTRATION G-13
Demonstration problem—Using Table 3 for *PV* of 1

PRESENT VALUE OF AN ANNUITY

The preceding discussion involved the discounting of only a single future amount. Businesses and individuals frequently engage in transactions in which a series of equal dollar amounts are to be received or paid at evenly spaced time intervals (periodically). Examples of a series of periodic receipts or payments are loan agreements, installment sales, mortgage notes, lease (rental) contracts, and pension obligations. As discussed earlier, these periodic receipts or payments are **annuities**.

The **present value of an annuity** is the value now of a series of future receipts or payments, discounted assuming compound interest. In computing the present value of an annuity, it is necessary to know (1) the discount rate, (2) the number of payments (receipts), and (3) the amount of the periodic receipts or payments. To illustrate the computation of the present value of an annuity, assume that you will receive $1,000 cash annually for three years at a time when the discount rate is 10%. This situation is depicted in the time diagram in Illustration G-14. Illustration G-15 shows the computation of its present value in this situation.

ILLUSTRATION G-14
Time diagram for a three-year annuity

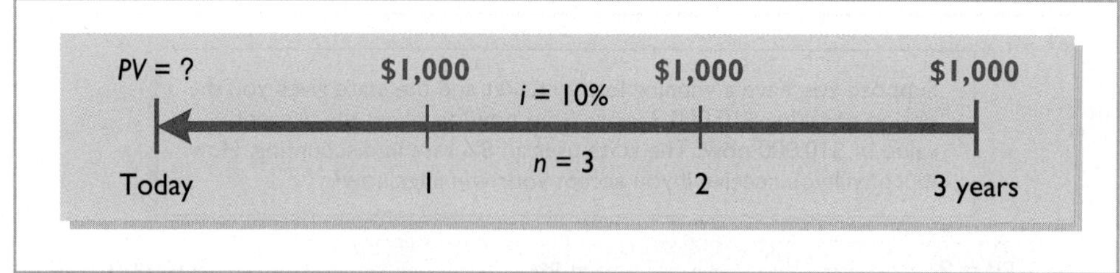

ILLUSTRATION G-15
Present value of a series of future amounts computation

Future Amount	×	Present Value of 1 Factor at 10%	=	Present Value
$1,000 (1 year away)		.90909		$ 909.09
1,000 (2 years away)		.82645		826.45
1,000 (3 years away)		.75132		751.32
		2.48686		$2,486.86

This method of calculation is required when the periodic cash flows are not uniform in each period. However, when the future receipts are the same in each period, an annuity table can be used. As illustrated in Table 4 below, an annuity table shows the present value of 1 to be received periodically for a given number of payments. It assumes that each payment is made at the end of each period.

TABLE 4 Present Value of an Annuity of 1

(n) Payments	4%	5%	6%	7%	8%	9%	10%	11%	12%	15%
1	.96154	.95238	.94340	.93458	.92593	.91743	.90909	.90090	.89286	.86957
2	1.88609	1.85941	1.83339	1.80802	1.78326	1.75911	1.73554	1.71252	1.69005	1.62571
3	2.77509	2.72325	2.67301	2.62432	2.57710	2.53130	2.48685	2.44371	2.40183	2.28323
4	3.62990	3.54595	3.46511	3.38721	3.31213	3.23972	3.16986	3.10245	3.03735	2.85498
5	4.45182	4.32948	4.21236	4.10020	3.99271	3.88965	3.79079	3.69590	3.60478	3.35216
6	5.24214	5.07569	4.91732	4.76654	4.62288	4.48592	4.35526	4.23054	4.11141	3.78448
7	6.00205	5.78637	5.58238	5.38929	5.20637	5.03295	4.86842	4.71220	4.56376	4.16042
8	6.73274	6.46321	6.20979	5.97130	5.74664	5.53482	5.33493	5.14612	4.96764	4.48732
9	7.43533	7.10782	6.80169	6.51523	6.24689	5.99525	5.75902	5.53705	5.32825	4.77158
10	8.11090	7.72173	7.36009	7.02358	6.71008	6.41766	6.14457	5.88923	5.65022	5.01877
11	8.76048	8.30641	7.88687	7.49867	7.13896	6.80519	6.49506	6.20652	5.93770	5.23371
12	9.38507	8.86325	8.38384	7.94269	7.53608	7.16073	6.81369	6.49236	6.19437	5.42062
13	9.98565	9.39357	8.85268	8.35765	7.90378	7.48690	7.10336	6.74987	6.42355	5.58315
14	10.56312	9.89864	9.29498	8.74547	8.24424	7.78615	7.36669	6.98187	6.62817	5.72448
15	11.11839	10.37966	9.71225	9.10791	8.55948	8.06069	7.60608	7.19087	6.81086	5.84737
16	11.65230	10.83777	10.10590	9.44665	8.85137	8.31256	7.82371	7.37916	6.97399	5.95424
17	12.16567	11.27407	10.47726	9.76322	9.12164	8.54363	8.02155	7.54879	7.11963	6.04716
18	12.65930	11.68959	10.82760	10.05909	9.37189	8.75563	8.20141	7.70162	7.24967	6.12797
19	13.13394	12.08532	11.15812	10.33560	9.60360	8.95012	8.36492	7.83929	7.36578	6.19823
20	13.59033	12.46221	11.46992	10.59401	9.81815	9.12855	8.51356	7.96333	7.46944	6.25933

Table 4 shows that the present value of an annuity of 1 factor for three payments at 10% is 2.48685.[1] This present value factor is the total of the three

[1]The difference of .00001 between 2.48686 and 2.48685 is due to rounding.

individual present value factors, as shown in Illustration G-15. Applying this amount to the annual cash flow of $1,000 produces a present value of $2,486.85.

The following demonstration problem (Illustration G-16) illustrates how to use Table 4.

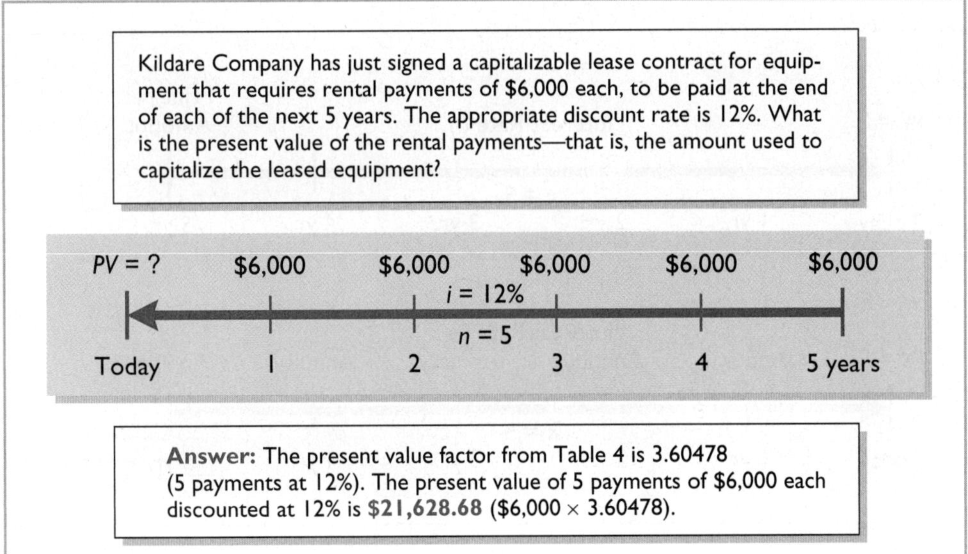

ILLUSTRATION G-16
Demonstration problem—Using Table 4 for *PV* of an annuity of 1

Note that the same concepts apply in situations when the price and interest rate are known, but the payment must be calculated. Suppose, for example, that in Illustration G-16 that the price of the lease contract is $21,628.68 and that Kildare Company wants to finance the lease contract by making five annual lease payments when the annual rate of interest is 12%. In this case, rather than solving for the present value, we need to solve for the amount of the annual payment. To do this, we divide the price (the present value) of $21,628.68 by the present value factor of 3.60478 to arrive at an annual payment of $6,000.

TIME PERIODS AND DISCOUNTING

In the preceding calculations, the discounting was done on an annual basis using an annual interest rate. Discounting may also be done over shorter periods of time such as monthly, quarterly, or semiannually.

When the time frame is less than one year, it is necessary to convert the annual interest rate to the applicable time frame. Assume, for example, that the investor in Illustration G-14 received $500 **semiannually** for three years instead of $1,000 annually. In this case, the number of periods becomes six (3 × 2), the discount rate is 5% (10% ÷ 2), the present value factor from Table 4 is 5.07569 (6 periods at 5%), and the present value of the future cash flows is $2,537.85 (5.07569 × $500). This amount is slightly higher than the $2,486.86 computed in Illustration G-15 because interest is computed twice during the same year. That is, during the second half of the year, interest is earned on the first half-year's interest.

PRESENT VALUE OF A LONG-TERM NOTE OR BOND

The present value (or market price) of a long-term note or bond is a function of three variables: (1) the payment amounts, (2) the length of time until the amounts are paid, and (3) the discount rate. Our example uses a five-year bond issue.

The first variable (dollars to be paid) is made up of two elements: (1) a series of interest payments (an annuity) and (2) the principal amount (a single sum). To compute the present value of the bond, both the interest payments and the principal amount must be discounted—two different computations. The time diagrams for a bond due in five years are shown in Illustration G-17.

ILLUSTRATION G-17
Time diagrams for the present value of a bond

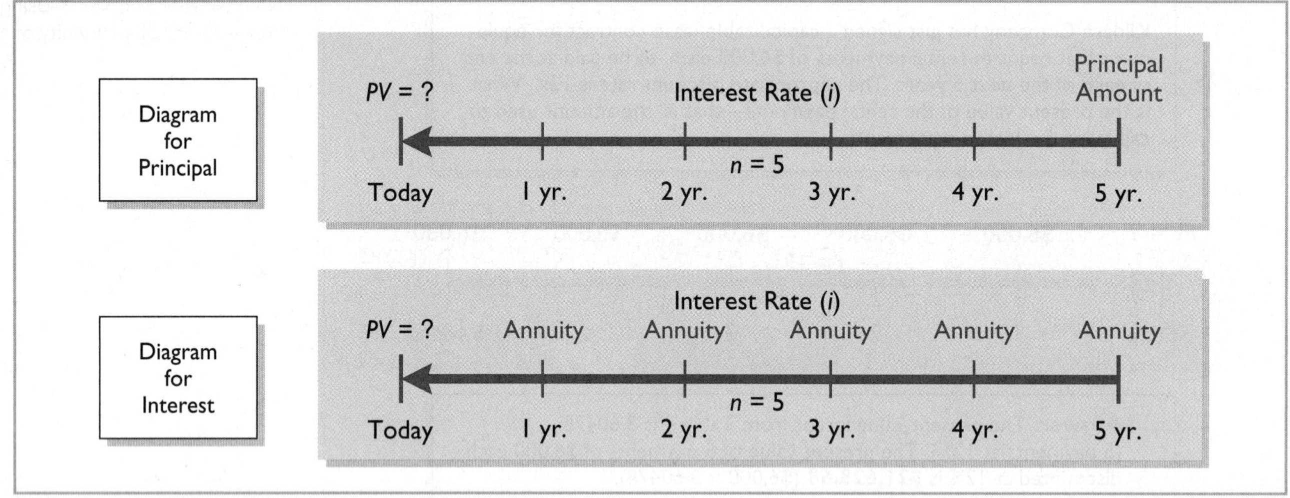

When the investor's market interest rate is equal to the bond's contractual interest rate, the present value of the bonds will equal the face value of the bonds. To illustrate, assume a bond issue of 10%, five-year bonds with a face value of $100,000 with interest payable **semiannually** on January 1 and July 1. If the discount rate is the same as the contractual rate, the bonds will sell at face value. In this case, the investor will receive (1) $100,000 at maturity and (2) a series of ten $5,000 interest payments [($100,000 × 10%) ÷ 2] over the term of the bonds. The length of time is expressed in terms of interest periods—in this case—10, and the discount rate per interest period, 5%. The following time diagram (Illustration G-18) depicts the variables involved in this discounting situation.

ILLUSTRATION G-18
Time diagram for present value of a 10%, five-year bond paying interest semiannually

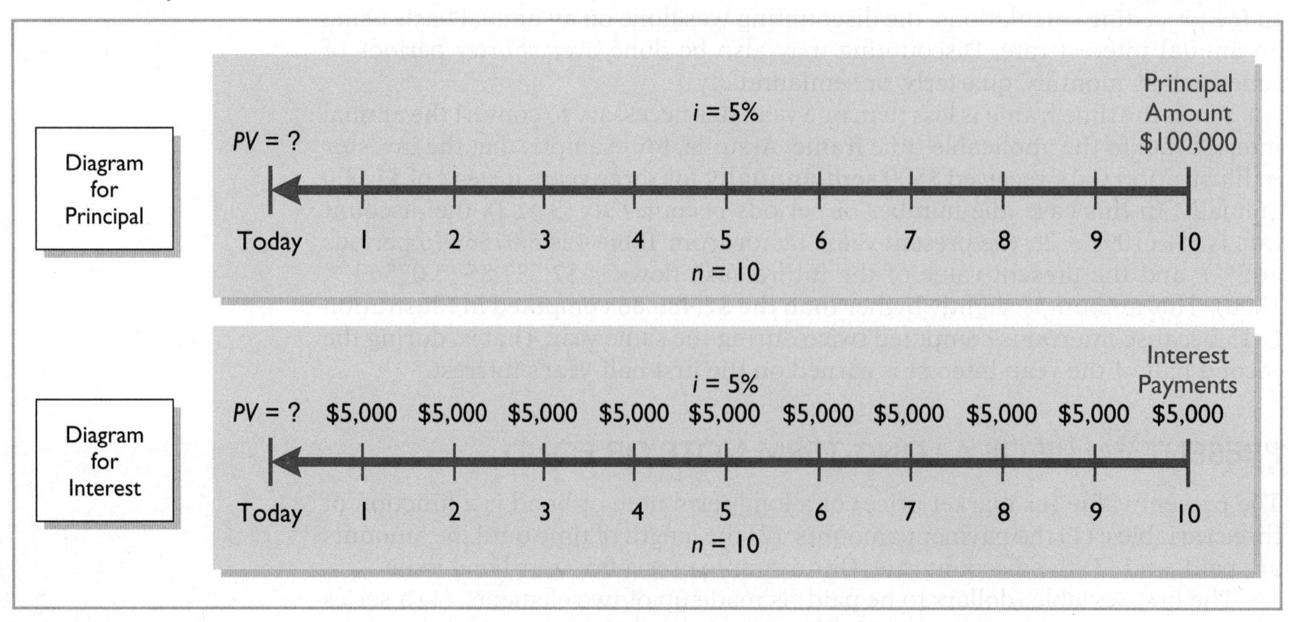

Illustration G-19 shows the computation of the present value of these bonds.

ILLUSTRATION G-19
Present value of principal and interest—face value

10% Contractual Rate—10% Discount Rate	
Present value of principal to be received at maturity	
$100,000 × *PV* of 1 due in 10 periods at 5%	
$100,000 × .61391 (Table 3)	$ 61,391
Present value of interest to be received periodically over the term of the bonds	
$5,000 × *PV* of 1 due periodically for 10 periods at 5%	
$5,000 × 7.72173 (Table 4)	38,609*
Present value of bonds	**$100,000**

*Rounded

Now assume that the investor's required rate of return is 12%, not 10%. The future amounts are again $100,000 and $5,000, respectively, but now a discount rate of 6% (12% ÷ 2) must be used. The present value of the bonds is $92,639, as computed in Illustration G-20.

ILLUSTRATION G-20
Present value of principal and interest—discount

10% Contractual Rate—12% Discount Rate	
Present value of principal to be received at maturity	
$100,000 × .55839 (Table 3)	$ 55,839
Present value of interest to be received periodically over the term of the bonds	
$5,000 × 7.36009 (Table 4)	36,800
Present value of bonds	**$92,639**

Conversely, if the discount rate is 8% and the contractual rate is 10%, the present value of the bonds is $108,111, computed as shown in Illustration G-21.

ILLUSTRATION G-21
Present value of principal and interest—premium

10% Contractual Rate—8% Discount Rate	
Present value of principal to be received at maturity	
$100,000 × .67556 (Table 3)	$ 67,556
Present value of interest to be received periodically over the term of the bonds	
$5,000 × 8.11090 (Table 4)	40,555
Present value of bonds	**$108,111**

The above discussion relied on present value tables in solving present value problems. Calculators may also be used to compute present values without the use of these tables. Many calculators, especially financial calculators, have present value (*PV*) functions that allow you to calculate present values by merely inputting the proper amount, discount rate, periods, and pressing the PV key. We discuss the use of financial calculators in the next section.

LEARNING OBJECTIVE 3 Use a financial calculator to solve time value of money problems.

Business professionals, once they have mastered the underlying time value of money concepts, often use a financial calculator to solve these types of problems. To use financial calculators, you enter the time value of money variables into the calculator. Illustration G-22 shows the five most common keys used to solve time value of money problems.[2]

ILLUSTRATION G-22
Financial calculator keys

where:

N = number of periods
I = interest rate per period (some calculators use I/YR or i)
PV = present value (occurs at the beginning of the first period)
PMT = payment (all payments are equal, and none are skipped)
FV = future value (occurs at the end of the last period)

In solving time value of money problems in this appendix, you will generally be given three of four variables and will have to solve for the remaining variable. The fifth key (the key not used) is given a value of zero to ensure that this variable is not used in the computation.

PRESENT VALUE OF A SINGLE SUM

To illustrate how to solve a present value problem using a financial calculator, assume that you want to know the present value of $84,253 to be received in five years, discounted at 11% compounded annually. Illustration G-23 depicts this problem.

ILLUSTRATION G-23
Calculator solution for present value of a single sum

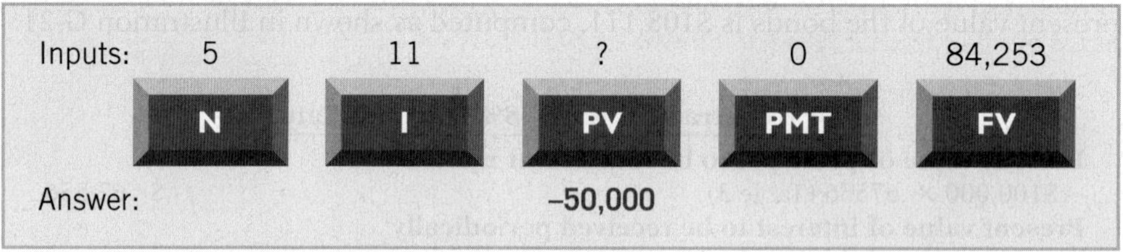

Illustration G-23 shows you the information (inputs) to enter into the calculator: N = 5, I = 11, PMT = 0, and FV = 84,253. You then press PV for the answer: −$50,000. As indicated, the PMT key was given a value of zero because a series of payments did not occur in this problem.

Plus and Minus

The use of plus and minus signs in time value of money problems with a financial calculator can be confusing. Most financial calculators are programmed so that the positive and negative cash flows in any problem offset each other. In the present value problem above, we identified the $84,253 future value initial investment as a positive (inflow); the answer −$50,000 was shown as a negative amount, reflecting a cash outflow. If the 84,253 were entered as a negative, then the final answer would have been reported as a positive 50,000.

Hopefully, the sign convention will not cause confusion. If you understand what is required in a problem, you should be able to interpret a positive or negative amount in determining the solution to a problem.

---

[2]On many calculators, these keys are actual buttons on the face of the calculator; on others, they appear on the display after the user accesses a present value menu.

Compounding Periods

In the previous problem, we assumed that compounding occurs once a year. Some financial calculators have a default setting, which assumes that compounding occurs 12 times a year. You must determine what default period has been programmed into your calculator and change it as necessary to arrive at the proper compounding period.

Rounding

Most financial calculators store and calculate using 12 decimal places. As a result, because compound interest tables generally have factors only up to five decimal places, a slight difference in the final answer can result. In most time value of money problems in this textbook, the final answer will not include more than two decimal places.

PRESENT VALUE OF AN ANNUITY

To illustrate how to solve a present value of an annuity problem using a financial calculator, assume that you are asked to determine the present value of rental receipts of $6,000 each to be received at the end of each of the next five years, when discounted at 12%, as pictured in Illustration G-24.

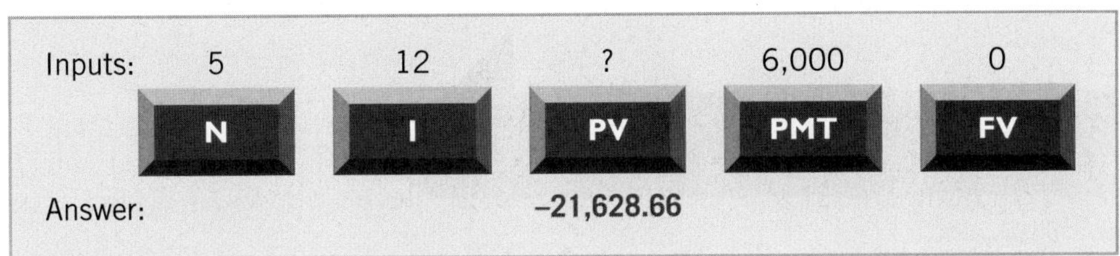

ILLUSTRATION G-24
Calculator solution for present value of an annuity

In this case, you enter N = 5, I = 12, PMT = 6,000, FV = 0, and then press PV to arrive at the answer of −$21,628.66.

USEFUL APPLICATIONS OF THE FINANCIAL CALCULATOR

With a financial calculator, you can solve for any interest rate or for any number of periods in a time value of money problem. Here are some examples of these applications.

Auto Loan

Assume you are financing the purchase of a used car with a three-year loan. The loan has a 9.5% stated annual interest rate, compounded monthly. The price of the car is $6,000, and you want to determine the monthly payments, assuming that the payments start one month after the purchase. This problem is pictured in Illustration G-25.

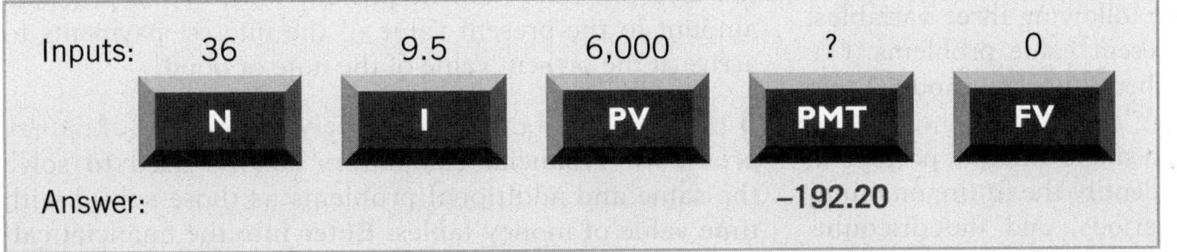

ILLUSTRATION G-25
Calculator solution for auto loan payments

To solve this problem, you enter N = 36 (12 × 3), I = 9.5, PV = 6,000, FV = 0, and then press PMT. You will find that the monthly payments will be $192.20. Note that the payment key is usually programmed for 12 payments per year. Thus, you must change the default (compounding period) if the payments are other than monthly.

Mortgage Loan Amount

Say you are evaluating financing options for a loan on a house (a mortgage). You decide that the maximum mortgage payment you can afford is $700 per month. The annual interest rate is 8.4%. If you get a mortgage that requires you to make monthly payments over a 15-year period, what is the maximum home loan you can afford? Illustration G-26 depicts this problem.

ILLUSTRATION G-26
Calculator solution for mortgage amount

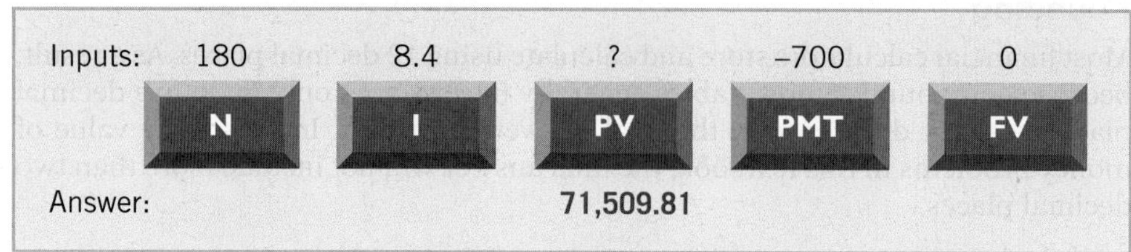

You enter N = 180 (12 × 15 years), I = 8.4, PMT = −700, FV = 0, and press PV. With the payments-per-year key set at 12, you find a present value of $71,509.81—the maximum home loan you can afford, given that you want to keep your mortgage payments at $700. Note that by changing any of the variables, you can quickly conduct "what-if" analyses for different situations.

REVIEW

▶ LEARNING OBJECTIVES REVIEW

1 Compute interest and future values. Simple interest is computed on the principal only, while compound interest is computed on the principal and any interest earned that has not been withdrawn.

To solve for future value of a single amount, prepare a time diagram of the problem. Identify the principal amount, the number of compounding periods, and the interest rate. Using the future value of 1 table, multiply the principal amount by the future value factor specified at the intersection of the number of periods and the interest rate.

To solve for future value of an annuity, prepare a time diagram of the problem. Identify the amount of the periodic payments (receipts), the number of payments (receipts), and the interest rate. Using the future value of an annuity of 1 table, multiply the amount of the payments by the future value factor specified at the intersection of the number of periods and the interest rate.

2 Compute present value. The following three variables are fundamental to solving present value problems: (1) the future amount, (2) the number of periods, and (3) the interest rate (the discount rate).

To solve for present value of a single amount, prepare a time diagram of the problem. Identify the future amount, the number of discounting periods, and the discount (interest) rate. Using the present value of a single amount table, multiply the future amount by the present value factor specified at the intersection of the number of periods and the discount rate.

To solve for present value of an annuity, prepare a time diagram of the problem. Identify the amount of future periodic receipts or payments (annuities), the number of payments (receipts), and the discount (interest) rate. Using the present value of an annuity of 1 table, multiply the amount of the annuity by the present value factor specified at the intersection of the number of payments and the interest rate.

To compute the present value of notes and bonds, determine the present value of the principal amount and the present value of the interest payments. Multiply the principal amount (a single future amount) by the present value factor (from the present value of 1 table) intersecting at the number of periods (number of interest payments) and the discount rate. To determine the present value of the series of interest payments, multiply the amount of the interest payment by the present value factor (from the present value of an annuity of 1 table) intersecting at the number of periods (number of interest payments) and the discount rate. Add the present value of the principal amount to the present value of the interest payments to arrive at the present value of the note or bond.

3 Use a financial calculator to solve time value of money problems. Financial calculators can be used to solve the same and additional problems as those solved with time value of money tables. Enter into the financial calculator the amounts for all of the known elements of a time value of money problem (periods, interest rate, payments, future or present value), and it solves for the unknown element. Particularly useful situations involve interest rates and compounding periods not presented in the tables.

▶ GLOSSARY REVIEW

Annuity A series of equal dollar amounts to be paid or received at evenly spaced time intervals (periodically). (p. G-5).

Compound interest The interest computed on the principal and any interest earned that has not been paid or withdrawn. (p. G-2).

Discounting the future amount(s) The process of determining present value. (p. G-7).

Future value of an annuity The sum of all the payments (receipts) plus the accumulated compound interest on them. (p. G-5).

Future value of a single amount The value at a future date of a given amount invested, assuming compound interest. (p. G-3).

Interest Payment for the use of another person's money. (p. G-1).

Present value The value now of a given amount to be paid or received in the future, assuming compound interest. (p. G-7).

Present value of an annuity The value now of a series of future receipts or payments, discounted assuming compound interest. (p. G-9).

Principal The amount borrowed or invested. (p. G-1).

Simple interest The interest computed on the principal only. (p. G-2).

▶ BRIEF EXERCISES

(Use tables to solve exercises BEG-1 to BEG-23.)

BEG-1 Jozy Altidore invested $6,000 at 5% annual interest, and left the money invested without withdrawing any of the interest for 12 years. At the end of the 12 years, Jozy withdrew the accumulated amount of money. (a) What amount did Jozy withdraw, assuming the investment earns simple interest? (b) What amount did Jozy withdraw, assuming the investment earns interest compounded annually?

Compute the future value of a single amount.

(LO 1), AP

BEG-2 For each of the following cases, indicate (a) what interest rate columns and (b) what number of periods you would refer to in looking up the future value factor.

Use future value tables.

(LO 1), C

(1) In Table 1 (future value of 1):

	Annual Rate	Number of Years Invested	Compounded
Case A	5%	3	Annually
Case B	12%	4	Semiannually

(2) In Table 2 (future value of an annuity of 1):

	Annual Rate	Number of Years Invested	Compounded
Case A	3%	8	Annually
Case B	8%	6	Semiannually

BEG-3 Liam Company signed a lease for an office building for a period of 12 years. Under the lease agreement, a security deposit of $9,600 is made. The deposit will be returned at the expiration of the lease with interest compounded at 4% per year. What amount will Liam receive at the time the lease expires?

Compute the future value of a single amount.

(LO 1), AP

Compute the future value of an annuity.

(LO 1), AP

BEG-4 Bates Company issued $1,000,000, 10-year bonds and agreed to make annual sinking fund deposits of $78,000. The deposits are made at the end of each year into an account paying 6% annual interest. What amount will be in the sinking fund at the end of 10 years?

Compute the future value of a single amount and of an annuity.

(LO 1), AP

BEG-5 Andrew and Emma Garfield invested $8,000 in a savings account paying 5% annual interest when their daughter, Angela, was born. They also deposited $1,000 on each of her birthdays until she was 18 (including her 18th birthday). How much was in the savings account on her 18th birthday (after the last deposit)?

Compute the future value of a single amount.

(LO 1), AP

BEG-6 Hugh Curtin borrowed $35,000 on July 1, 2017. This amount plus accrued interest at 8% compounded annually is to be repaid on July 1, 2022. How much will Hugh have to repay on July 1, 2022?

Compute the annuity payment amount of a known future value.

(LO 1), AP

BEG-7 Sara has just graduated from college. She has determined that to purchase a home in 8 years she needs to accumulate $20,000 for a down payment. If Sara can earn 6% per year on her savings, what is the amount of the annual annuity payment that Sara must make at the end of each year for 8 years?

Use present value tables.

(LO 2), C

BEG-8 For each of the following cases, indicate (a) what interest rate columns and (b) what number of periods you would refer to in looking up the discount rate.

(1) In Table 3 (present value of 1):

	Annual Rate	Number of Years Involved	Discounts per Year
Case A	12%	7	Annually
Case B	8%	11	Annually
Case C	10%	8	Semiannually

(2) In Table 4 (present value of an annuity of 1):

	Annual Rate	Number of Years Involved	Number of Payments Involved	Frequency of Payments
Case A	10%	20	20	Annually
Case B	10%	7	7	Annually
Case C	6%	5	10	Semiannually

Determine present values.

(LO 2), AP

BEG-9 (a) What is the present value of $25,000 due 9 periods from now, discounted at 10%?
(b) What is the present value of $25,000 to be received at the end of each of 6 periods, discounted at 9%?

Compute the present value of a single amount investment.

(LO 2), AP

BEG-10 Messi Company is considering an investment that will return a lump sum of $900,000 6 years from now. What amount should Messi Company pay for this investment to earn an 8% return?

Compute the present value of a single amount investment.

(LO 2), AP

BEG-11 Lloyd Company earns 6% on an investment that will return $450,000 8 years from now. What is the amount Lloyd should invest now to earn this rate of return?

Compute the present value of an annuity investment.

(LO 2), AP

BEG-12 Robben Company is considering investing in an annuity contract that will return $40,000 annually at the end of each year for 15 years. What amount should Robben Company pay for this investment if it earns an 8% return?

Compute the present value of an annual investment.

(LO 2), AP

BEG-13 Kaehler Enterprises earns 5% on an investment that pays back $80,000 at the end of each of the next 6 years. What is the amount Kaehler Enterprises invested to earn the 5% rate of return?

Compute the present value of bonds.

(LO 2), AP

BEG-14 Dempsey Railroad Co. is about to issue $400,000 of 10-year bonds paying an 11% interest rate, with interest payable semiannually. The discount rate for such securities is 10%. How much can Dempsey expect to receive for the sale of these bonds?

Compute the present value of bonds.

(LO 2), AP

BEG-15 Assume the same information as BEG-14 except that the discount rate is 12% instead of 10%. In this case, how much can Dempsey expect to receive from the sale of these bonds?

BEG-16 Neymar Taco Company receives a $75,000, 6-year note bearing interest of 4% (paid annually) from a customer at a time when the discount rate is 6%. What is the present value of the note received by Neymar?

Compute the present value of a note.

(LO 2), AP

BEG-17 Gleason Enterprises issued 6%, 8-year, $2,500,000 par value bonds that pay interest semiannually on October 1 and April 1. The bonds are dated April 1, 2017, and are issued on that date. The discount rate of interest for such bonds on April 1, 2017, is 8%. What cash proceeds did Gleason receive from issuance of the bonds?

Compute the present value of bonds.

(LO 2), AP

BEG-18 Frazier Company issues a 10%, 5-year mortgage note on January 1, 2017, to obtain financing for new equipment. Land is used as collateral for the note. The terms provide for semiannual installment payments of $48,850. What are the cash proceeds received from the issuance of the note?

Compute the present value of a note.

(LO 2), AP

BEG-19 If Colleen Mooney invests $4,765.50 now and she will receive $12,000 at the end of 12 years, what annual rate of interest will Colleen earn on her investment? (*Hint:* Use Table 3.)

Compute the interest rate on a single amount.

(LO 2), AP

BEG-20 Tim Howard has been offered the opportunity of investing $36,125 now. The investment will earn 11% per year and at the end of that time will return Tim $75,000. How many years must Tim wait to receive $75,000? (*Hint:* Use Table 3.)

Compute the number of periods of a single amount.

(LO 2), AP

BEG-21 Joanne Quick made an investment of $10,271.38. From this investment, she will receive $1,200 annually for the next 15 years starting one year from now. What rate of interest will Joanne's investment be earning for her? (*Hint:* Use Table 4.)

Compute the interest rate on an annuity.

(LO 2), AP

BEG-22 Kevin Morales invests $7,793.83 now for a series of $1,300 annual returns beginning one year from now. Kevin will earn a return of 9% on the initial investment. How many annual payments of $1,300 will Kevin receive? (*Hint:* Use Table 4.)

Compute the number of periods of an annuity.

(LO 2), AP

BEG-23 Sophie Corp. purchased a new blending machine for $3,150.15. It paid $500 down and financed the remaining $2,650.15. It is required to pay 10 annual payments at the end of each year at an annual rate of interest of 11%. What is the amount of the annual payment?

Compute the annuity payment amount of a known present value.

(LO 2), AP

BEG-24 Carly Simon wishes to invest $18,000 on July 1, 2017, and have it accumulate to $50,000 by July 1, 2027. Use a financial calculator to determine at what exact annual rate of interest Carly must invest the $18,000.

Determine interest rate.

(LO 3), AP

BEG-25 On July 17, 2016, Keith Urban borrowed $42,000 from his grandfather to open a clothing store. Starting July 17, 2017, Keith has to make 10 equal annual payments of $6,500 each to repay the loan. Use a financial calculator to determine what interest rate Keith is paying.

Determine interest rate.

(LO 3), AP

BEG-26 As the purchaser of a new house, Carrie Underwood has signed a mortgage note to pay the Nashville National Bank and Trust Co. $8,400 every 6 months for 20 years, at the end of which time she will own the house. At the date the mortgage is signed, the purchase price was $198,000 and Underwood made a down payment of $20,000. The first payment will be made 6 months after the date the mortgage is signed. Using a financial calculator, compute the exact rate of interest earned on the mortgage by the bank.

Determine interest rate.

(LO 3), AP

BEG-27 Using a financial calculator, solve for the unknowns in each of the following situations.

(a) On June 1, 2016, Jennifer Lawrence purchases lakefront property from her neighbor, Josh Hutcherson, and agrees to pay the purchase price in seven payments of $16,000 each, the first payment to be payable June 1, 2017. (Assume that interest compounded at an annual rate of 7.35% is implicit in the payments.) What is the purchase price of the property?

Various time value of money situations.

(LO 3), AP

(b) On January 1, 2016, Gerrard Corporation purchased 200 of the $1,000 face value, 8% coupon, 10-year bonds of Sterling Inc. The bonds mature on January 1, 2026, and pay interest annually beginning January 1, 2017. Gerrard purchased the bonds to yield 10.65%. How much did Gerrard pay for the bonds?

Various time value of money situations.

(LO 3), AP

BEG-28 Using a financial calculator, provide a solution to each of the following situations.

(a) Lynn Anglin owes a debt of $42,000 from the purchase of her new sport utility vehicle. The debt bears annual interest of 7.8% compounded monthly. Lynn wishes to pay the debt and interest in equal monthly payments over 8 years, beginning one month hence. What equal monthly payments will pay off the debt and interest?

(b) On January 1, 2017, Roger Molony offers to buy Dave Feeney's used snowmobile for $8,000, payable in five equal annual installments, which are to include 7.25% interest on the unpaid balance and a portion of the principal. If the first payment is to be made on December 31, 2017, how much will each payment be?

Reporting and Analyzing Investments

APPENDIX PREVIEW

Some companies believe in aggressive growth through investing in the stock of existing companies. Besides purchasing stock, companies also purchase other securities such as bonds issued by corporations or by governments. Companies can make investments for a short or long period of time, as a passive investment, or with the intent to control another company. As you will see in this appendix, the way in which a company accounts for its investments is determined by a number of factors.

APPENDIX OUTLINE

LEARNING OBJECTIVES	
1 Explain how to account for debt investments.	• Why corporations invest • Accounting for debt investments
2 Explain how to account for stock investments.	• Holdings of less than 20% • Holdings between 20% and 50% • Holdings of more than 50%
3 Discuss how debt and stock investments are reported in the financial statements.	• Categories of securities • Balance sheet presentation • Presentation of realized and unrealized gain or loss • Statement of cash flows presentation

LEARNING OBJECTIVE  1 **Explain how to account for debt investments.**

WHY CORPORATIONS INVEST

Corporations purchase investments in debt or equity securities generally for one of three reasons. First, a corporation may **have excess cash** that it does not need for the immediate purchase of operating assets. For example, many companies experience seasonal fluctuations in sales. A Cape Cod marina has more sales in the spring and summer than in the fall and winter. The reverse is true for an Aspen ski shop. Thus, at the end of an operating cycle, many companies may have cash on hand that is temporarily idle until the start of another operating cycle. These companies may invest the excess funds to earn—through interest and dividends—a greater return than they would get by just holding the funds in the bank. Illustration H-1 shows the role that such temporary investments play in the operating cycle.

ILLUSTRATION H-1
Temporary investments and the operating cycle

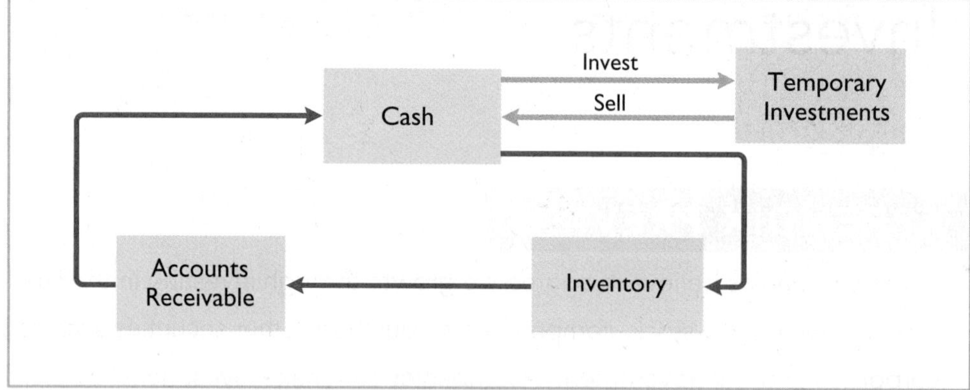

A second reason some companies such as banks purchase investments is to generate **earnings from investment income**. Although banks make most of their earnings by lending money, they also generate earnings by investing in primarily debt securities. Banks purchase investment securities because loan demand varies both seasonally and with changes in the economic climate. Thus, when loan demand is low, a bank must find other uses for its cash.

Some companies attempt to generate investment income through speculative investments. That is, they are speculating that the investment will increase in value and thus result in positive returns. Therefore, they invest mostly in the common stock of other corporations.

Third, companies also invest for **strategic reasons**. A company may purchase a noncontrolling interest in another company in a related industry in which it wishes to establish a presence. Or, a company can exercise some influence over one of its customers or suppliers by purchasing a significant, but not controlling, interest in that company. Another option is for a corporation to purchase a controlling interest in another company in order to enter a new industry without incurring the costs and risks associated with starting from scratch.

In summary, businesses invest in other companies for the reasons shown in Illustration H-2.

ILLUSTRATION H-2
Why corporations invest

Reason	Typical Investment
To house excess cash until needed	Low-risk, highly liquid, short-term securities such as government-issued securities
To generate earnings	Banks and financial institutions often purchase debt securities, while mutual funds and index funds purchase both debt and stock securities
To meet strategic goals	Stocks of companies in a related industry or in an unrelated industry that the company wishes to enter

ACCOUNTING FOR DEBT INVESTMENTS

Debt investments are investments in government and corporation bonds. In accounting for debt investments, companies must make entries to record (1) the acquisition, (2) the interest revenue, and (3) the sale.

Recording Acquisition of Bonds

At acquisition, debt investments are recorded at cost. Cost includes all expenditures necessary to acquire these investments, such as the price paid plus brokerage fees (commissions), if any.

For example, assume that Kuhl Corporation acquires 50 Doan Inc. 8%, 10-year, $1,000 bonds on January 1, 2017, at a cost of $50,000. Kuhl records the investment as:

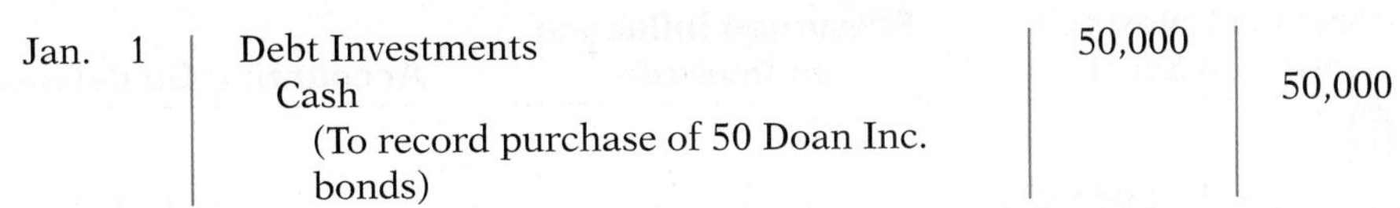

Jan. 1	Debt Investments	50,000	
	Cash		50,000
	(To record purchase of 50 Doan Inc. bonds)		

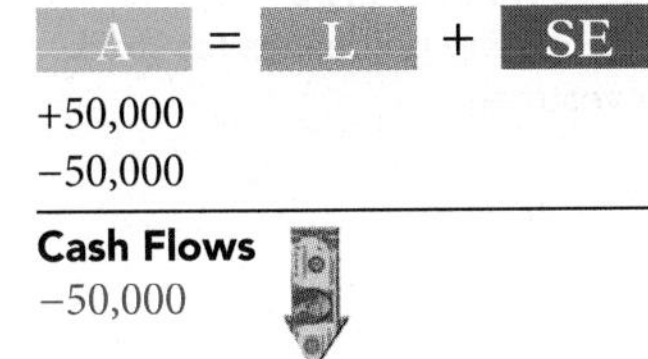

Recording Bond Interest

The Doan Inc. bonds pay interest of $4,000 annually on January 1 ($50,000 × 8%). If Kuhl Corporation's fiscal year ends on December 31, it accrues the interest of $4,000 earned since January 1. The adjusting entry is:

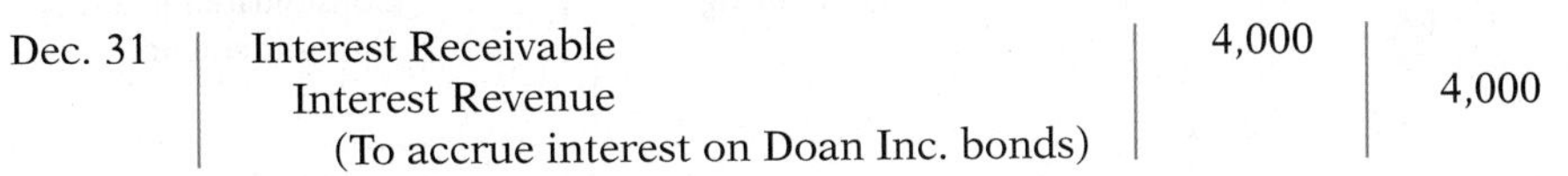

Dec. 31	Interest Receivable	4,000	
	Interest Revenue		4,000
	(To accrue interest on Doan Inc. bonds)		

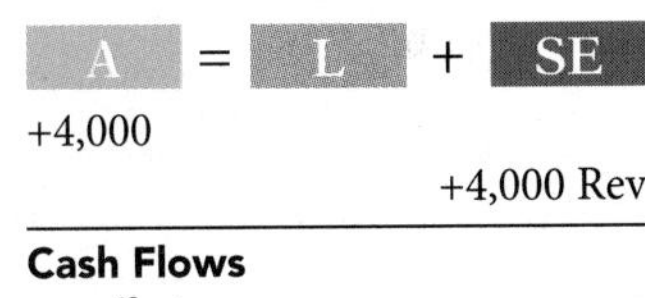

Kuhl reports Interest Receivable as a current asset in the balance sheet. It reports Interest Revenue under "Other revenues and gains" in the income statement.

Kuhl records receipt of the interest on January 1 as follows.

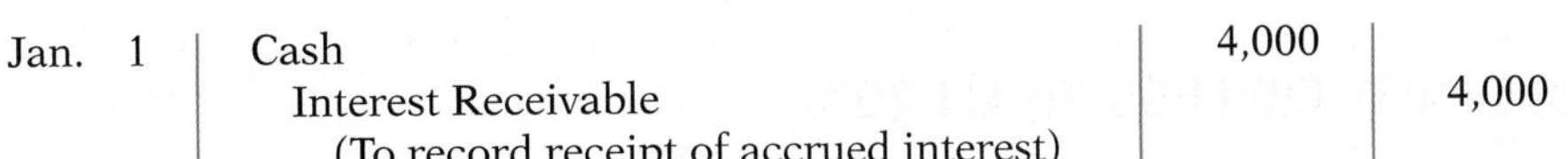

Jan. 1	Cash	4,000	
	Interest Receivable		4,000
	(To record receipt of accrued interest)		

A = L + SE
+4,000
−4,000
Cash Flows
+4,000

A credit to Interest Revenue at this time would be incorrect. Why? Because the company earned and accrued the interest revenue in the preceding accounting period.

Recording Sale of Bonds

When Kuhl Corporation sells the bond investments, it credits the investment account for the cost of the bonds. The company records as a gain or loss any difference between the net proceeds from the sale (sales price less brokerage fees) and the cost of the bonds.

Assume, for example, that Kuhl receives net proceeds of $54,000 on the sale of the Doan Inc. bonds on January 1, 2018, after receiving the interest due. Since the securities cost $50,000, Kuhl has realized a gain of $4,000. It records the sale as follows.

▼ HELPFUL HINT
The accounting for short-term debt investments and long-term debt investments is similar. Any exceptions are discussed in more advanced courses.

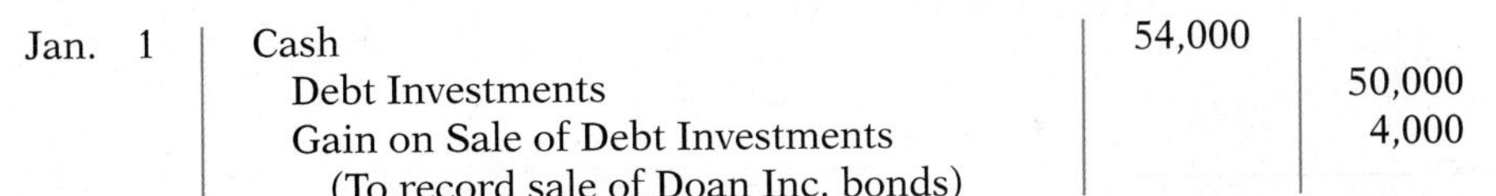

Jan. 1	Cash	54,000	
	Debt Investments		50,000
	Gain on Sale of Debt Investments		4,000
	(To record sale of Doan Inc. bonds)		

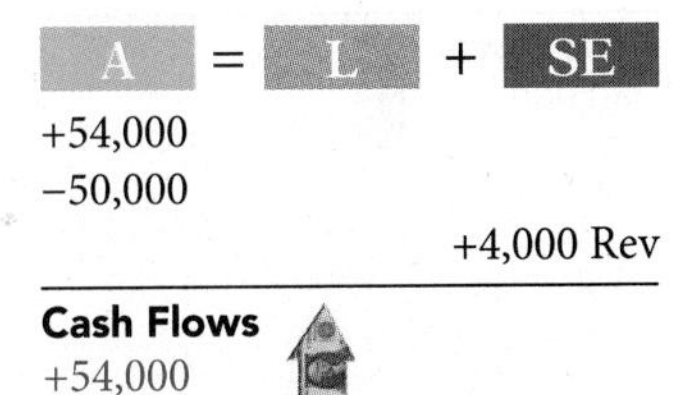

Kuhl reports the gain on the sale of debt investments under "Other revenues and gains" in the income statement and reports losses under "Other expenses and losses."

LEARNING OBJECTIVE 2

Explain how to account for stock investments.

Stock investments are investments in the capital stock of corporations. When a company holds stock (and/or debt) of several different corporations, the group of securities is an **investment portfolio**.

The accounting for investments in common stock depends on the extent of the investor's influence over the operating and financial affairs of the issuing corporation (the **investee**). Illustration H-3 shows the general guidelines.

ILLUSTRATION H-3
Accounting guidelines for stock investments

Investor's Ownership Interest in Investee's Common Stock	Presumed Influence on Investee	Accounting Guidelines
Less than 20%	Insignificant	Cost method
Between 20% and 50%	Significant	Equity method
More than 50%	Controlling	Consolidated financial statements

Companies are required to use judgment instead of blindly following the guidelines.[1] We explain and illustrate the application of each guideline next.

HOLDINGS OF LESS THAN 20%

In the accounting for stock investments of less than 20%, companies use the cost method. Under the **cost method**, companies record the investment at cost and recognize revenue only when cash dividends are received.

Recording Acquisition of Stock

At acquisition, stock investments are recorded at cost. Cost includes all expenditures necessary to acquire these investments, such as the price paid plus brokerage fees (commissions), if any.

Assume, for example, that on July 1, 2017, Sanchez Corporation acquires 1,000 shares (10% ownership) of Beal Corporation common stock at $40 per share. The entry for the purchase is:

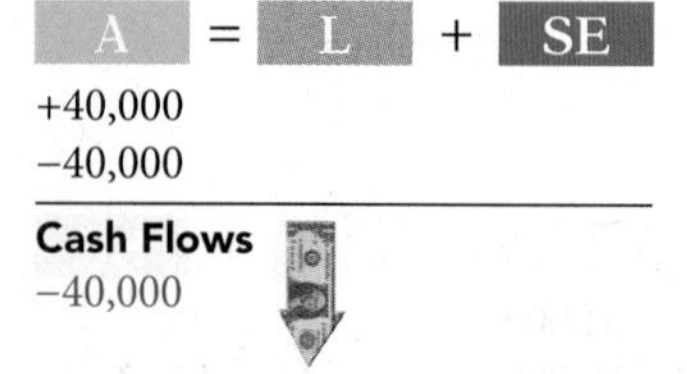

July 1	Stock Investments	40,000	
	Cash		40,000
	(To record purchase of 1,000 shares of Beal common stock)		

[1]Among the factors that companies should consider in determining an investor's influence are whether (1) the investor has representation on the investee's board of directors, (2) the investor participates in the investee's policy-making process, (3) there are material transactions between the investor and the investee, and (4) the common stock held by other stockholders is concentrated or dispersed.

Recording Dividends

During the time the company holds the stock, it makes entries for any cash dividends received. Thus, if Sanchez Corporation receives a $2 per share dividend on December 31, the entry is:

Dec. 31	Cash (1,000 × $2)	2,000	
	Dividend Revenue		2,000
	(To record receipt of a cash dividend)		

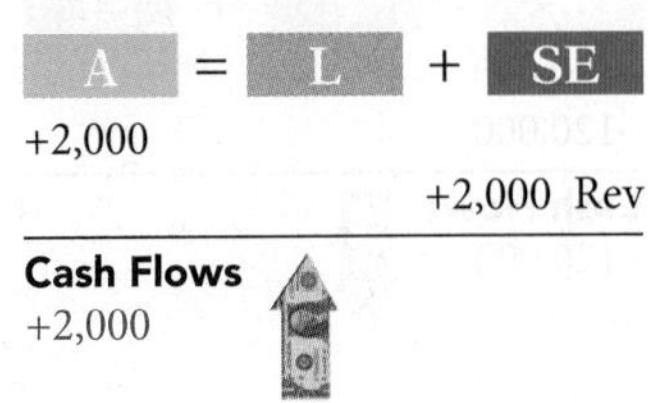

Sanchez reports Dividend Revenue under "Other revenues and gains" in the income statement.

Recording Sale of Stock

When a company sells a stock investment, it recognizes the difference between the net proceeds from the sale (sales price less brokerage fees) and the cost of the stock as a gain or a loss.

Assume, for instance, that Sanchez Corporation receives net proceeds of $39,500 on the sale of its Beal Corporation stock on February 10, 2018. Because the stock cost $40,000, Sanchez has incurred a loss of $500. It records the sale as:

Feb. 10	Cash	39,500	
	Loss on Sale of Stock Investments	500	
	Stock Investments		40,000
	(To record sale of Beal common stock)		

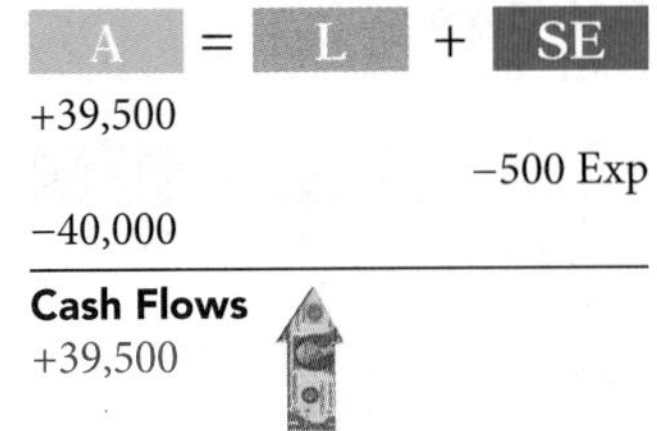

Sanchez reports the loss account under "Other expenses and losses" in the income statement and shows a gain on sale under "Other revenues and gains."

HOLDINGS BETWEEN 20% AND 50%

When an investor company owns only a small portion of the shares of stock of another company, the investor cannot exercise control over the investee. But when an investor owns between 20% and 50% of the common stock of a corporation, it is presumed that the investor has significant influence over the financial and operating activities of the investee. The investor probably has a representative on the investee's board of directors. Through that representative, the investor begins to exercise some control over the investee—and the investee company in some sense becomes part of the investor company.

For example, even prior to purchasing all of Turner Broadcasting, Time Warner owned 20% of Turner. Because it exercised significant control over major decisions made by Turner, Time Warner used an approach called the equity method. Under the **equity method, the investor records its share of the net income of the investee in the year when it is earned**. An alternative might be to delay recognizing the investor's share of net income until a cash dividend is declared. But that approach would ignore the fact that the investor and investee are, in some sense, one company, making the investor better off by the investee's earned income.

Under the **equity method**, the company initially records the investment in common stock at cost. After that, it adjusts the investment account **annually** to show the investor's equity in the investee. Each year, the investor does the following. (1) It increases (debits) the investment account and increases (credits) revenue for its share of the investee's net income.[2] (2) The investor also decreases (credits) the investment account for the amount of dividends received. The investment account is reduced for dividends received because payment of a dividend decreases the net assets of the investee.

[2]Conversely, the investor increases (debits) a loss account and decreases (credits) the investment account for its share of the investee's net loss.

Recording Acquisition of Stock

Assume that Milar Corporation acquires 30% of the common stock of Beck Company for $120,000 on January 1, 2017. The entry to record this transaction is:

A = L + SE
+120,000
−120,000
Cash Flows
−120,000

Jan. 1	Stock Investments	120,000	
	Cash		120,000
	(To record purchase of Beck common stock)		

Recording Revenue and Dividends

For 2017, Beck reports net income of $100,000. It declares and pays a $40,000 cash dividend. Milar must record (1) its share of Beck's income, $30,000 (30% × $100,000), and (2) the reduction in the investment account for the dividends received, $12,000 (30% × $40,000). The entries are:

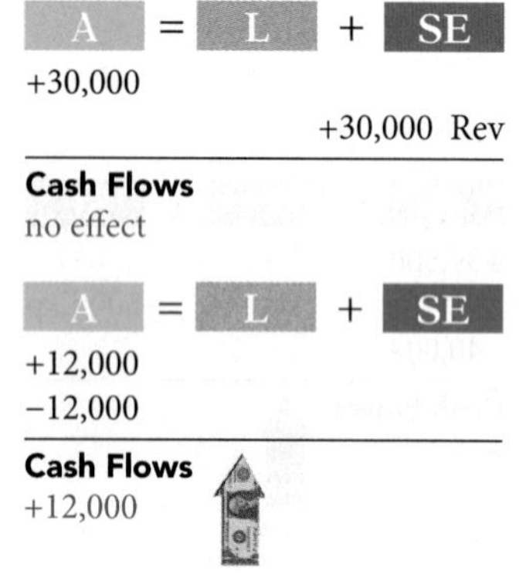

(1)

Dec. 31	Stock Investments	30,000	
	Revenue from Stock Investments		30,000
	(To record 30% equity in Beck's 2017 net income)		

(2)

Dec. 31	Cash	12,000	
	Stock Investments		12,000
	(To record dividends received)		

After Milar posts the transactions for the year, the investment and revenue accounts are as shown in Illustration H-4.

ILLUSTRATION H-4
Investment and revenue accounts after posting

Stock Investments

Jan. 1	120,000	Dec. 31	**12,000**
Dec. 31	**30,000**		
Dec. 31	Bal. 138,000		

Revenue from Stock Investments

		Dec. 31	**30,000**

During the year, the investment account increased by $18,000. This $18,000 is explained as follows: (1) Milar records a $30,000 increase in revenue from its stock investment in Beck, and (2) Milar records a $12,000 decrease due to dividends received from its stock investment in Beck.

Note that the difference between reported revenue under the cost method and reported revenue under the equity method can be significant. For example, Milar would report only $12,000 of dividend revenue (30% × $40,000) if it used the cost method.

HOLDINGS OF MORE THAN 50%

A company that owns more than 50% of the common stock of another entity is known as the **parent company**. The entity whose stock is owned by the parent company is called the **subsidiary (affiliated) company**. Because of its stock ownership, the parent company has a **controlling interest** in the subsidiary company.

When a company owns more than 50% of the common stock of another company, it usually prepares **consolidated financial statements**. Consolidated financial statements present the assets and liabilities controlled by the parent company. They also present the total revenues and expenses of the subsidiary companies. Companies prepare consolidated statements **in addition to** the financial statements for the individual parent and subsidiary companies.

As noted earlier, prior to acquiring all of Turner Broadcasting, Time Warner accounted for its investment in Turner using the equity method. Time Warner's net investment in Turner was reported in a single line item—Other investments. After the merger, Time Warner instead consolidated Turner's results with its own. Under this approach, Time Warner included the individual assets and liabilities of Turner with its own assets. That is, Turner's plant and equipment were added to Time Warner's plant and equipment, its receivables were added to Time Warner's receivables, and so on. A similar sort of consolidation went on when AOL merged with Time Warner.

▼ HELPFUL HINT
If the parent (A) has three wholly owned subsidiaries (B, C, and D), there are four separate legal entities but only one economic entity from the viewpoint of the shareholders of the parent company.

Consolidated statements are useful to the stockholders, board of directors, and management of the parent company. Consolidated statements indicate to creditors, prospective investors, and regulatory agencies the magnitude and scope of operations of the companies under common control. For example, regulators and the courts undoubtedly used the consolidated statements of AT&T to determine whether a breakup of the company was in the public interest. Illustration H-5 lists three companies that prepare consolidated statements and some of the companies they have owned.

PepsiCo	Cendant	The Walt Disney Company
Frito-Lay	Howard Johnson	Capital Cities/ABC, Inc.
Tropicana	Ramada Inn	Disneyland, Disney World
Quaker Oats	Century 21	Mighty Ducks
Pepsi-Cola	Coldwell Banker	Anaheim Angels
Gatorade	Avis	ESPN

ILLUSTRATION H-5
Examples of consolidated companies and their subsidiaries

LEARNING OBJECTIVE 

Discuss how debt and stock investments are reported in the financial statements.

The value of debt and stock investments may fluctuate greatly during the time they are held. For example, in a 12-month period, the stock of Time Warner hit a high of 58½ and a low of 9. In light of such price fluctuations, how should companies value investments at the balance sheet date? Valuation could be at cost, at fair value, or at the lower-of-cost-or-market value.

Many people argue that fair value offers the best approach because it represents the expected cash realizable value of securities. **Fair value** is the amount for which a security could be sold in a normal market. Others counter that unless a security is going to be sold soon, the fair value is not relevant because the price of the security will likely change again.

CATEGORIES OF SECURITIES

For purposes of valuation and reporting at a financial statement date, debt and stock investments are classified into three categories of securities[3]:

1. **Trading securities** are bought and held primarily for sale in the near term to generate income on short-term price differences.
2. **Available-for-sale securities** are held with the intent of selling them sometime in the future.
3. **Held-to-maturity securities** are debt securities that the investor has the intent and ability to hold to maturity.[4]

INTERNATIONAL NOTE
A recent U.S. accounting standard gives companies the "option" of applying fair value accounting, rather than historical cost, to certain types of assets and liabilities. This makes U.S. accounting closer to international standards.

[3]The FASB is currently considering a new approach to reporting investment securities. If adopted, the new approach could significantly change the reporting of investments.

[4]This category is provided for completeness. The accounting and valuation issues related to held-to-maturity securities are discussed in more advanced accounting courses.

Illustration H-6 shows the valuation guidelines for these securities. **These guidelines apply to all debt securities and to those stock investments in which the holdings are less than 20%.**

ILLUSTRATION H-6
Valuation guidelines for securities

Trading Securities

Trading securities are held with the intention of selling them in a short period of time (generally less than three months and sometimes less than a full day). **Trading** means frequent buying and selling. As indicated in Illustration H-6, companies adjust trading securities to fair value at the end of each period (an approach referred to as **mark-to-market** accounting). They report changes from cost **as part of net income**. The changes are reported as **unrealized gains or losses** because the securities have not been sold. The unrealized gain or loss is the difference between the **total cost** of trading securities and their **total fair value**. Companies classify trading securities as a current asset.

As an example, Illustration H-7 shows the costs and fair values for investments classified as trading securities for Pace Corporation on December 31, 2017. Pace has an unrealized gain of $7,000 because total fair value ($147,000) is $7,000 greater than total cost ($140,000).

ILLUSTRATION H-7
Valuation of trading securities

Trading Securities, December 31, 2017

Investments	Cost	Fair Value	Unrealized Gain (Loss)
Yorkville Company bonds	$ 50,000	$ 48,000	$(2,000)
Kodak Company stock	90,000	99,000	9,000
Total	$140,000	$147,000	$ 7,000

▼ **HELPFUL HINT**
Companies report an unrealized gain or loss in the income statement because of the likelihood that the securities will be sold at fair value since they are a short-term investment.

The fact that trading securities are a short-term investment increases the likelihood that Pace will sell them at fair value for a gain. Pace records fair value and the unrealized gain through an adjusting entry at the time it prepares financial statements. In this entry, the company uses a valuation allowance account, Fair Value Adjustment—Trading, to record the difference between the total cost and the total fair value of the securities. The adjusting entry for Pace is:

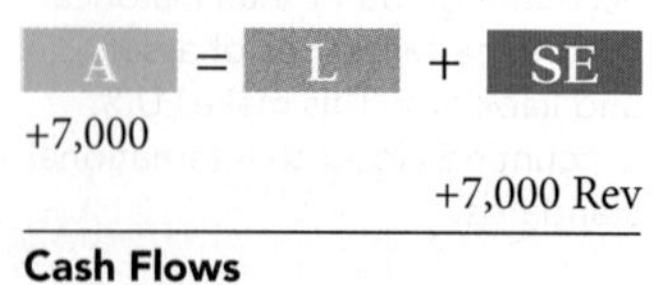

Cash Flows
no effect

Dec. 31	Fair Value Adjustment—Trading	7,000	
	Unrealized Gain—Income		7,000
	(To record unrealized gain on trading securities)		

The use of the Fair Value Adjustment—Trading account enables the company to maintain a record of the investment cost. Actual cost is needed to determine the gain or loss realized when the securities are sold. The company adds the debit balance (or subtracts a credit balance) of the Fair Value Adjustment—Trading account to the cost of the investments to arrive at a fair value for the trading securities.

The fair value of the securities is the amount companies report on the balance sheet. They report the unrealized gain on the income statement under "Other revenues and gains." The term **income** in the account title indicates that the gain affects net income.

If the total cost of the trading securities is greater than total fair value, an unrealized loss has occurred. In such a case, the adjusting entry is a debit to Unrealized Loss—Income and a credit to Fair Value Adjustment—Trading. Companies report the unrealized loss under "Other expenses and losses" in the income statement.

The fair value adjustment account is carried forward into future accounting periods. No entries are made to this account during the period. At the end of each reporting period, a company adjusts the balance in the account to the difference between cost and fair value at that time. It closes the Unrealized Gain—Income account or Unrealized Loss—Income account at the end of the reporting period.

Available-for-Sale Securities

As indicated earlier, available-for-sale securities are held with the intent of selling them sometime in the future. If the intent is to sell the securities within the next year or operating cycle, a company classifies the securities as current assets in the balance sheet. Otherwise, it classifies them as long-term assets in the investments section of the balance sheet.

Companies also report available-for-sale securities at fair value. The procedure for determining fair value and unrealized gain or loss for these securities is the same as that for trading securities. To illustrate, assume that Elbert Corporation has two securities that are classified as available-for-sale. Illustration H-8 provides information on the cost, fair value, and amount of the unrealized gain or loss on December 31, 2017. There is an unrealized loss of $9,537 because total cost ($293,537) is $9,537 more than total fair value ($284,000).

ILLUSTRATION H-8
Valuation of available-for-sale securities

Available-for-Sale Securities, December 31, 2017

Investments	Cost	Fair Value	Unrealized Gain (Loss)
Campbell Soup Corporation 8% bonds	$ 93,537	$103,600	$10,063
Hershey Foods stock	200,000	180,400	(19,600)
Total	$293,537	$284,000	$ (9,537)

Both the adjusting entry and the reporting of the unrealized loss from Elbert's available-for-sale securities differ from those illustrated for trading securities. The differences result because these securities are not going to be sold in the near term. Thus, prior to actual sale it is much more likely that changes in fair value may reverse the unrealized loss. Therefore, Elbert does not report an unrealized loss in the income statement. Instead, the company reports it as an item of other comprehensive income in the comprehensive income statement, as discussed in Chapter 5. In the adjusting entry, Elbert identifies the fair value adjustment account with available-for-sale securities, and identifies the unrealized gain or loss account with stockholders' equity. The adjusting entry for Elbert to record the unrealized loss of $9,537 is:

▼ HELPFUL HINT
The entry is the same regardless of whether the securities are considered short-term or long-term.

Dec. 31	Unrealized Gain or Loss—Equity	9,537	
	Fair Value Adjustment—Available-for-Sale		9,537
	(To record unrealized loss on available-for-sale securities)		

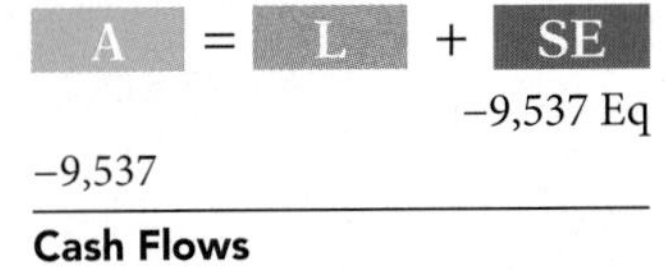

Cash Flows
no effect

If total fair value exceeds total cost, Elbert would record the adjusting entry as an increase (debit) to Fair Value Adjustment—Available-for-Sale and a credit to Unrealized Gain or Loss—Equity.

Elbert's unrealized loss of $9,537 would appear in the comprehensive income statement as shown in Illustration H-9.

ILLUSTRATION H-9
Comprehensive income statement

ELBERT CORPORATION Comprehensive Income Statement For the Year Ended December 31, 2017	
Net income	$118,000
Other comprehensive income	
Unrealized loss on available-for-sale securities	(9,537)
Comprehensive income	$108,463

ETHICS NOTE Recently, the SEC accused investment bank Morgan Stanley of overstating the value of certain bond investments by $75 million. The SEC stated that, in applying fair value accounting, Morgan Stanley used its own more optimistic assumptions rather than relying on external pricing sources.

For available-for-sale securities, the company carries forward the Unrealized Gain or Loss—Equity account to future periods. At each future balance sheet date, the account is adjusted with the fair value adjustment account to show the difference between cost and fair value at that time.

BALANCE SHEET PRESENTATION

In the balance sheet presentation, companies must classify investments as either short-term or long-term.

Short-Term Investments

Short-term investments (also called **marketable securities**) are securities held by a company that are (1) **readily marketable** and (2) **intended to be converted into cash** within the next year or operating cycle, whichever is longer. Investments that do not meet **both criteria** are classified as **long-term investments**.

▼ HELPFUL HINT Trading securities are always classified as short-term. Available-for-sale securities can be either short-term or long-term.

READILY MARKETABLE **An investment is readily marketable when it can be sold easily whenever the need for cash arises.** Short-term paper[5] meets this criterion because a company can readily sell it to other investors. Stocks and bonds traded on organized securities markets, such as the New York Stock Exchange, are readily marketable because they can be bought and sold daily. In contrast, there may be only a limited market for the securities issued by small corporations and no market for the securities of a privately held company.

INTENT TO CONVERT **Intent to convert means that management intends to sell the investment within the next year or operating cycle, whichever is longer.** Generally, this criterion is satisfied when the investment is considered a resource that the company will use whenever the need for cash arises. For example, a ski resort may invest idle cash during the summer months with the intent to sell the securities to buy supplies and equipment shortly before the next winter season. This investment is considered short-term even if lack of snow cancels the next ski season and eliminates the need to convert the securities into cash as intended.

Because of their high liquidity, companies list short-term investments immediately below Cash in the current assets section of the balance sheet. Short-term investments are reported at fair value. For example, Weber Corporation would report its trading securities as shown in Illustration H-10.

[5]Short-term paper includes (1) certificates of deposits (CDs) issued by banks, (2) money market certificates issued by banks and savings and loan associations, (3) Treasury bills issued by the U.S. government, and (4) commercial paper issued by corporations with good credit ratings.

ILLUSTRATION H-10
Balance sheet presentation of short-term investments

WEBER CORPORATION Balance Sheet (partial)	
Current assets	
Cash	$21,000
Short-term investments, at fair value	**60,000**

Long-Term Investments

Companies generally report long-term investments in a separate section of the balance sheet immediately below "Current assets," as shown in Illustration H-11. Long-term investments in available-for-sale securities are reported at fair value. Investments in common stock accounted for under the equity method are reported at equity.

ILLUSTRATION H-11
Balance sheet presentation of long-term investments

WEBER CORPORATION Balance Sheet (partial)		
Investments		
Bond sinking fund	$100,000	
Investments in stock of less than 20% owned companies, at fair value	**50,000**	
Investment in stock of 20%–50% owned company, at equity	**150,000**	
Total investments		$300,000

PRESENTATION OF REALIZED AND UNREALIZED GAIN OR LOSS

Companies must present in the financial statements gains and losses on investments, whether realized or unrealized. In the income statement, companies report gains and losses, as well as interest and dividend revenue, in the nonoperating activities section under the categories listed in Illustration H-12.

ILLUSTRATION H-12
Nonoperating items related to investments

Other Revenue and Gains	**Other Expenses and Losses**
Interest Revenue	Loss on Sale of Investments
Dividend Revenue	Unrealized Loss—Income
Gain on Sale of Investments	
Unrealized Gain—Income	

As discussed in Chapter 11, companies report the cumulative amount of other comprehensive income items from the current and previous years as a separate component of stockholders' equity. To illustrate, assume that Muzzillo Inc. has common stock of $3,000,000, retained earnings of $1,500,000, and an accumulated other comprehensive loss of $100,000. Illustration H-13 shows the financial statement presentation of the accumulated other comprehensive loss.

ILLUSTRATION H-13
Unrealized loss in stockholders' equity section

MUZZILLO INC. Balance Sheet (partial)	
Stockholders' equity	
Common stock	$3,000,000
Retained earnings	1,500,000
Total paid-in capital and retained earnings	4,500,000
Accumulated other comprehensive loss	**(100,000)**
Total stockholders' equity	$4,400,000

Note that the presentation of the accumulated other comprehensive loss is similar to the presentation of the cost of treasury stock in the stockholders' equity section. (It decreases stockholders' equity.) Accumulated other comprehensive income would be added in this section.

Companies must report, as part of a more inclusive measure called **comprehensive income**, items such as unrealized gains and losses on available-for-sale securities, which affect stockholders' equity but are not included in the calculation of net income. Comprehensive income is discussed more fully in Chapter 13.

STATEMENT OF CASH FLOWS PRESENTATION

As shown previously in Illustrations H-10, H-11, and H-13, the balance sheet presents a company's investment accounts at a point in time. The "Investing activities" section of the statement of cash flows reports information on the cash inflows and outflows during the period that resulted from investment transactions.

Illustration H-14 presents the cash flows from investing activities from a recent statement of cash flows of The Walt Disney Company. From this information, we learn that Disney received $1,530 million from the sale or redemption of investments during the year.

ILLUSTRATION H-14
Statement of cash flows presentation of investment activities

Real World

THE WALT DISNEY COMPANY
Statement of Cash Flows (partial)
(in millions)

Investing Activities	
Investments in parks, resorts and other property	$(1,566)
Acquisitions	(588)
Dispositions	
Proceeds from sale of investments	**1,530**
Other	6
Cash used by investing activities	$ (618)

REVIEW

▶ LEARNING OBJECTIVES REVIEW

1 Explain how to account for debt investments. Corporations invest for three common reasons: (a) they have excess cash, (b) they view investment income as a significant revenue source, and (c) they have strategic goals such as gaining control of a competitor or supplier or moving into a new line of business.

Entries for investments in debt securities are required when companies purchase bonds, receive or accrue interest, and sell bonds.

2 Explain how to account for stock investments. Entries for investments in common stock are required when companies purchase stock, receive dividends, and sell stock. When ownership is less than 20%, the cost method is used—the investment is recorded at cost. When ownership is between 20% and 50%, the equity method should be used—the investor records its share of the net income of the investee in the year it is earned. When ownership is more than 50%, consolidated financial statements should be prepared.

When a company owns more than 50% of the common stock of another company, consolidated financial statements are usually prepared. These statements are especially useful to the stockholders, board of directors, and management of the parent company.

3 Discuss how debt and stock investments are reported in the financial statements. Investments in debt and stock securities are classified as trading, available-for-sale, or held-to-maturity for valuation and reporting purposes. Trading securities are reported as current assets at fair value, with changes from cost reported in net income. Available-for-sale securities are also reported at fair value, with the changes from cost reported as items of other comprehensive income. Available-for-sale securities are classified as short-term or long-term depending on their expected realization.

Short-term investments are securities held by a company that are readily marketable and intended to be converted to cash within the next year or operating cycle, whichever is longer. Investments that do not meet both criteria are classified as long-term investments.

▶ GLOSSARY REVIEW

Available-for-sale securities Securities that are held with the intent of selling them sometime in the future. (p. H-7).

Consolidated financial statements Financial statements that present the assets and liabilities controlled by the parent company and the total revenues and expenses of the subsidiary companies. (p. H-6).

Controlling interest Ownership of more than 50% of the common stock of another entity. (p. H-6).

Cost method An accounting method in which the investment in common stock is recorded at cost and revenue is recognized only when cash dividends are received. (p. H-4).

Debt investments Investments in government and corporation bonds. (p. H-3).

Equity method An accounting method in which the investment in common stock is initially recorded at cost, and the investment account is then adjusted annually to show the investor's equity in the investee. (p. H-5).

Fair value Amount for which a security could be sold in a normal market. (p. H-7).

Held-to-maturity securities Debt securities that the investor has the intent and ability to hold to maturity. (p. H-7).

Long-term investments Investments that are not readily marketable or that management does not intend to convert into cash within the next year or operating cycle, whichever is longer. (p. H-10).

Mark-to-market A method of accounting for certain investments that requires that they be adjusted to their fair value at the end of each period. (p. H-8).

Parent company A company that owns more than 50% of the common stock of another entity. (p. H-6).

Short-term investments (marketable securities) Investments that are readily marketable and intended to be converted into cash within the next year or operating cycle, whichever is longer. (p. H-10).

Stock investments Investments in the capital stock of corporations. (p. H-4).

Subsidiary (affiliated) company A company in which more than 50% of its stock is owned by another company. (p. H-6).

Trading securities Securities bought and held primarily for sale in the near term to generate income on short-term price differences. (p. H-7).

▶ QUESTIONS

1. What are the reasons that companies invest in securities?
2. (a) What is the cost of an investment in bonds?
   (b) When is interest on bonds recorded?
3. Geena Jaymes is confused about losses and gains on the sale of debt investments. Explain these issues to Geena:
   (a) How the gain or loss is computed.
   (b) The statement presentation of gains and losses.
4. Heliy Company sells bonds that cost $40,000 for $45,000, including $1,000 of accrued interest. In recording the sale, Heliy books a $5,000 gain. Is this correct? Explain.
5. What is the cost of an investment in stock?
6. To acquire Gaines Corporation stock, Palmer Co. pays $61,500 in cash. What entry should be made for this investment, assuming the stock is readily marketable?
7. (a) When should a long-term investment in common stock be accounted for by the equity method?
   (b) When is revenue recognized under the equity method?
8. Stetson Corporation uses the equity method to account for its ownership of 30% of the common stock of Pike Packing. During 2017, Pike reported a net income of $80,000 and declares and pays cash dividends of $10,000. What recognition should Stetson Corporation give to these events?
9. What constitutes "significant influence" when an investor's financial interest is less than 50%?
10. Distinguish between the cost and equity methods of accounting for investments in stocks.
11. What are consolidated financial statements?
12. What are the valuation guidelines for trading and available-for-sale investments at a balance sheet date?

13. Pat Ernst is the controller of J-Products, Inc. At December 31, the end of its first year of operations, the company's investments in trading securities cost $74,000 and have a fair value of $70,000. Indicate how Pat would report these data in the financial statements prepared on December 31.

14. Using the data in Question 13, how would Pat report the data if the investments were long-term and the securities were classified as available-for-sale?

15. Boise Company's investments in available-for-sale securities at December 31 show total cost of $202,000 and total fair value of $210,000. Prepare the adjusting entry.

16. Using the data in Question 15, prepare the adjusting entry, assuming the securities are classified as trading securities.

17. Where is Accumulated Other Comprehensive Loss reported on the balance sheet?

18. Bargain Wholesale Supply owns stock in Cyrus Corporation, which it intends to hold indefinitely because of some negative tax consequences if sold. Should the investment in Cyrus be classified as a short-term investment? Why?

BRIEF EXERCISES

Journalize entries for debt investments.
(LO 1), AP

BEH-1 Craig Corporation purchased debt investments for $40,800 on January 1, 2017. On July 1, 2017, Craig received cash interest of $1,660. Journalize the purchase and the receipt of interest. Assume no interest has been accrued.

Journalize entries for stock investments.
(LO 2), AP

BEH-2 On August 1, Snow Company buys 1,000 shares of BCN common stock for $35,600 cash. On December 1, the stock investments are sold for $38,000 in cash. Journalize the purchase and sale of the common stock.

Journalize transactions under the equity method.
(LO 2), AP

BEH-3 Tote Company owns 25% of Toppe Company. For the current year, Toppe reports net income of $150,000 and declares and pays a $60,000 cash dividend. Record Tote's equity in Toppe's net income and the receipt of dividends from Toppe.

Prepare adjusting entry using fair value.
(LO 3), AP

BEH-4 Cost and fair value data for the trading securities of Lecler Company at December 31, 2017, are $62,000 and $59,600, respectively. Prepare the adjusting entry to record the securities at fair value.

Indicate statement presentation using fair value.
(LO 3), AN

BEH-5 For the data presented in BEH-4, show the financial statement presentation of the trading securities and related accounts.

Prepare adjusting entry using fair value.
(LO 3), AP

BEH-6 In its first year of operations, Machin Corporation purchased available-for-sale stock securities costing $72,000 as a long-term investment. At December 31, 2017, the fair value of the securities is $69,000. Prepare the adjusting entry to record the securities at fair value.

Indicate statement presentation using fair value.
(LO 3), AN

BEH-7 For the data presented in BEH-6, show the financial statement presentation of the securities and related accounts. Assume the securities are noncurrent.

Prepare investments section of balance sheet.
(LO 3), AP

BEH-8 Perth Corporation has these long-term investments: common stock of Vejas Co. (10% ownership) held as available-for-sale securities, cost $108,000, fair value $112,000; common stock of Penn Inc. (30% ownership), cost $210,000, equity $230,000; and a bond sinking fund of $150,000. Prepare the investments section of the balance sheet.

EXERCISES

Journalize debt investment transactions, and accrue interest.
(LO 1), AP

EH-1 Chopin Corporation had these transactions pertaining to debt investments:

Jan.	1	Purchased 90 10%, $1,000 Martine Co. bonds for $90,000 cash. Interest is payable semiannually on July 1 and January 1.
July	1	Received semiannual interest on Martine Co. bonds.
July	1	Sold 30 Martine Co. bonds for $32,000.

Instructions

(a) Journalize the transactions.
(b) Prepare the adjusting entry for the accrual of interest at December 31.

EH-2 Soylent Company had these transactions pertaining to stock investments:

Journalize stock investment transactions, and explain income statement presentation.

(LO 2, 3), AN

Feb. 1	Purchased 1,200 shares of BJ common stock (2% of outstanding shares) for $8,400.
July 1	Received cash dividends of $2 per share on BJ common stock.
Sept. 1	Sold 500 shares of BJ common stock for $5,400.
Dec. 1	Received cash dividends of $1 per share on BJ common stock.

Instructions

(a) Journalize the transactions.
(b) Explain how dividend revenue and the gain (loss) on sale should be reported in the income statement.

EH-3 Cooper Inc. had these transactions pertaining to investments in common stock:

Journalize transactions for investments in stock.

(LO 2), AP

Jan. 1	Purchased 1,200 shares of Gate Corporation common stock (5% of outstanding shares) for $59,200 cash.
July 1	Received a cash dividend of $7 per share.
Dec. 1	Sold 900 shares of Gate Corporation common stock for $47,200 cash.
31	Received a cash dividend of $7 per share.

Instructions

Journalize the transactions.

EH-4 On January 1, Lyon Corporation purchased a 25% equity investment in Shane Corporation for $150,000. At December 31, Shane declared and paid a $80,000 cash dividend and reported net income of $380,000.

Journalize and post transactions under the equity method.

(LO 2), AP

Instructions

(a) Journalize the transactions.
(b) Determine the amount to be reported as an investment in Shane stock at December 31.

EH-5 These are two independent situations:

Journalize entries under cost and equity methods.

(LO 2), AP

1. Sosey Cosmetics acquired 12% of the 300,000 shares of common stock of Elite Fashion at a total cost of $14 per share on March 18, 2017. On June 30, Elite declared and paid a $75,000 dividend. On December 31, Elite reported net income of $244,000 for the year. At December 31, the market price of Elite Fashion was $16 per share. The stock is classified as available-for-sale.
2. Williams Inc. obtained significant influence over Kasey Corporation by buying 25% of Kasey's 30,000 outstanding shares of common stock at a total cost of $11 per share on January 1, 2017. On June 15, Kasey declared and paid a cash dividend of $35,000. On December 31, Kasey reported a net income of $120,000 for the year.

Instructions

Prepare all the necessary journal entries for 2017 for (a) Sosey Cosmetics and (b) Williams Inc.

EH-6 At December 31, 2017, the trading securities for Gwynn, Inc. are as follows.

Prepare adjusting entry to record fair value, and indicate statement presentation.

(LO 3), AP

Security	Cost	Fair Value
A	$18,100	$16,000
B	12,500	14,800
C	23,000	18,000
Total	$53,600	$48,800

Instructions

(a) Prepare the adjusting entry at December 31, 2017, to report the securities at fair value.
(b) Show the balance sheet and income statement presentation at December 31, 2017, after adjustment to fair value.

EH-7 Data for investments in stock classified as trading securities are presented in EH-6. Assume instead that the investments are classified as available-for-sale securities with the same cost and fair value data. The securities are considered to be a long-term investment.

Prepare adjusting entry to record fair value, and indicate statement presentation.

(LO 3), AN

Instructions

(a) Prepare the adjusting entry at December 31, 2017, to report the securities at fair value.
(b) Show the statement presentation at December 31, 2017, after adjustment to fair value.
(c) Pam Jenks, a member of the board of directors, does not understand the reporting of the unrealized gains or losses on trading securities and available-for-sale securities. Write a letter to Ms. Jenks explaining the reporting and the purposes it serves.

Prepare adjusting entries for fair value, and indicate statement presentation for two classes of securities.

(LO 3), AN

EH-8 Weston Company has these data at December 31, 2017, the end of its first year of operations.

Securities	Cost	Fair Value
Trading	$110,000	$122,000
Available-for-sale	100,000	96,000

The available-for-sale securities are held as a long-term investment.

Instructions

(a) Prepare the adjusting entries to report each class of securities at fair value.
(b) Indicate the statement presentation of each class of securities and the related unrealized gain (loss) accounts.

PROBLEMS

Journalize debt investment transactions.

(LO 1), AN

PH-1 Penn Farms is a grower of hybrid seed corn for Bend Genetics Corporation. It has had two exceptionally good years and has elected to invest its excess funds in bonds. The following selected transactions relate to bonds acquired as an investment by Penn Farms, whose fiscal year ends on December 31.

2017

Jan. 1	Purchased at par $600,000 of Dover Corporation 10-year, 7% bonds dated January 1, 2017, directly from the issuing corporation.
July 1	Received the semiannual interest on the Dover bonds.
Dec. 31	Accrual of interest at year-end on the Dover bonds.

Assume that all intervening transactions and adjustments have been properly recorded and the number of bonds owned has not changed from December 31, 2017, to December 31, 2019.

2020

Jan. 1	Received the semiannual interest on the Dover bonds.
Jan. 1	Sold $300,000 of Dover bonds at 110.
July 1	Received the semiannual interest on the Dover bonds.
Dec. 31	Accrual of interest at year-end on the Dover bonds.

Instructions

Journalize the listed transactions for the years 2017 and 2020.

Journalize investment transactions, prepare adjusting entry, and show financial statement presentation.

(LO 1, 2, 3), AN

GLS

PH-2 In January 2017, the management of Northern Company concludes that it has sufficient cash to purchase some short-term investments in debt and stock securities. During the year, the following transactions occurred.

Feb. 1	Purchased 1,200 shares of LAF common stock for $51,600.
Mar. 1	Purchased 500 shares of NCL common stock for $18,500.
Apr. 1	Purchased 70 $1,000, 8% TRC bonds for $70,000. Interest is payable semi-annually on April 1 and October 1.
July 1	Received a cash dividend of $0.80 per share on the LAF common stock.
Aug. 1	Sold 200 shares of LAF common stock at $42 per share.
Sept. 1	Received $2 per share cash dividend on the NCL common stock.
Oct. 1	Received the semiannual interest on the TRC bonds.
Oct. 1	Sold the TRC bonds for $75,700.

At December 31, the fair values of the LAF and NCL common stocks were $39 and $30 per share, respectively.

Instructions

(a) Journalize the transactions and post to the accounts Debt Investments and Stock Investments. (Use the T-account form.)
(b) Prepare the adjusting entry at December 31, 2017, to report the investments at fair value. All securities are considered to be trading securities.
(c) Show the balance sheet presentation of investment securities at December 31, 2017.
(d) Identify the income statement accounts and give the statement classification of each account.

Journalize transactions, prepare adjusting entry for stock investments, and show balance sheet presentation.

(LO 2, 3), AN

PH-3 On December 31, 2016, the end of its first year of operations, Botani Associates owned the following securities that are held as long-term investments.

Common Stock	Shares	Cost
C Co.	1,000	$48,000
D Co.	5,000	36,000
E Co.	1,200	24,000

On this date, the total fair value of the securities was equal to its cost. The securities are not held for influence or control over the investees. In 2017, the following transactions occurred.

July 1	Received $2.00 per share semiannual cash dividend on D Co. common stock.
Aug. 1	Received $0.50 per share cash dividend on C Co. common stock.
Sept. 1	Sold 1,000 shares of D Co. common stock for cash at $9 per share.
Oct. 1	Sold 300 shares of C Co. common stock for cash at $53 per share.
Nov. 1	Received $1 per share cash dividend on E Co. common stock.
Dec. 15	Received $0.50 per share cash dividend on C Co. common stock.
31	Received $2.20 per share semiannual cash dividend on D Co. common stock.

At December 31, the fair values per share of the common stocks were C Co. $47, D Co. $7, and E Co. $24.

Instructions

(a) Journalize the 2017 transactions and post to the account Stock Investments. (Use the T-account form.)
(b) Prepare the adjusting entry at December 31, 2017, to show the securities at fair value. The stock should be classified as available-for-sale securities.
(c) Show the balance sheet presentation of the investments and the unrealized gain (loss) at December 31, 2017. At this date, Botani Associates has common stock $2,000,000 and retained earnings $1,200,000.

Prepare entries under cost and equity methods, and prepare memorandum.

(LO 2), AN

PH-4 Wellman Company acquired 30% of the outstanding common stock of Grinwold Inc. on January 1, 2017, by paying $1,800,000 for 60,000 shares. Grinwold declared and paid a $0.50 per share cash dividend on June 30 and again on December 31, 2017. Grinwold reported net income of $800,000 for the year.

Instructions

(a) Prepare the journal entries for Wellman Company for 2017, assuming Wellman cannot exercise significant influence over Grinwold. (Use the cost method.)
(b) Prepare the journal entries for Wellman Company for 2017, assuming Wellman can exercise significant influence over Grinwold. (Use the equity method.)
(c) The board of directors of Wellman Company is confused about the differences between the cost and equity methods. Prepare a memorandum for the board that explains each method and shows in tabular form the account balances under each method at December 31, 2017.

Journalize stock transactions, and show balance sheet presentation.

(LO 2, 3), AN

PH-5 Here is Kalvin Company's portfolio of long-term available-for-sale securities at December 31, 2016, the end of its first year of operations.

	Cost
1,400 shares of Batone Inc. common stock	$73,500
1,200 shares of Mendez Corporation common stock	84,000
800 shares of P. Tillman Corporation preferred stock	33,600

On December 31, the total cost of the portfolio equaled the total fair value. Kalvin had the following transactions related to the securities during 2017.

Jan.	20	Sold 1,400 shares of Batone Inc. common stock at $55 per share.
	28	Purchased 400 shares of $10 par value common stock of P. Wahl Corporation at $78 per share.
	30	Received a cash dividend of $1.25 per share on Mendez Corporation common stock.
Feb.	8	Received cash dividends of $0.40 per share on P. Tillman Corporation preferred stock.
	18	Sold all 800 shares of P. Tillman preferred stock at $35 per share.
July	30	Received a cash dividend of $1.10 per share on Mendez Corporation common stock.
Sept.	6	Purchased an additional 600 shares of the $10 par value common stock of P. Wahl Corporation at $82 per share.
Dec.	1	Received a cash dividend of $1.50 per share on P. Wahl Corporation common stock.

At December 31, 2017, the fair values of the securities were:

Mendez Corporation common stock	$65 per share
P. Wahl Corporation common stock	$77 per share

Kalvin uses separate account titles for each investment, such as Investment in Mendez Corporation Common Stock.

Instructions

(a) Prepare journal entries to record the transactions.
(b) Post to the investment accounts. (Use separate T-accounts for each investment.)
(c) Prepare the adjusting entry at December 31, 2017, to report the portfolio at fair value.
(d) Show the balance sheet presentation at December 31, 2017.

Prepare a balance sheet.
(LO 3), AP

PH-6 The following data, presented in alphabetical order, are taken from the records of Manfreid Corporation.

Accounts payable	$ 150,000
Accounts receivable	90,000
Accumulated depreciation—buildings	180,000
Accumulated depreciation—equipment	52,000
Allowance for doubtful accounts	6,000
Bonds payable (10%, due 2028)	350,000
Buildings	900,000
Cash	63,000
Common stock ($5 par value; 500,000 shares authorized, 240,000 shares issued)	1,200,000
Debt investments	400,000
Discount on bonds payable	20,000
Dividends payable	50,000
Equipment	275,000
Goodwill	190,000
Income taxes payable	70,000
Inventory	170,000
Land	410,000
Notes payable (due 2018)	70,000
Paid-in capital in excess of par value	464,000
Prepaid insurance	16,000
Retained earnings	310,000
Stock investments (Horton Inc. stock, 30% ownership, at equity)	240,000
Stock investments (short-term, at fair value)	128,000

Instructions

Prepare a balance sheet at December 31, 2017.

COMPANY INDEX

SUBJECT INDEX

M

RAPID REVIEW
Chapter Content

ACCOUNTING CONCEPTS (Chapters 2–4)

Fundamental Qualities	Enhancing Qualities	Assumptions	Principles	Constraint
Relevance Faithful representation	Comparability Consistency Verifiability Timeliness Understandability	Monetary unit Economic entity Periodicity Going concern Accrual basis	Historical cost Fair value Full disclosure Revenue recognition Expense recognition	Materiality

BASIC ACCOUNTING EQUATION (Chapter 3)

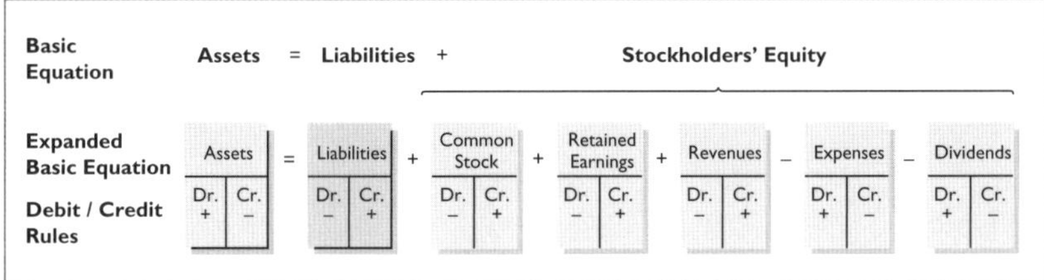

INVENTORY (Chapters 5 and 6)

Ownership

Freight Terms	Ownership of goods on public carrier resides with:
FOB Shipping point	Buyer
FOB Destination	Seller

ADJUSTING ENTRIES (Chapter 4)

	Type	Adjusting Entry	
Deferrals	1. Prepaid expenses 2. Unearned revenues	Dr. Expenses Dr. Liabilities	Cr. Assets Cr. Revenues
Accruals	1. Accrued revenues 2. Accrued expenses	Dr. Assets Dr. Expenses	Cr. Revenues Cr. Liabilities

Note: Each adjusting entry will affect one or more income statement accounts and one or more balance sheet accounts.

Interest Computation

Interest = Face value of note × Annual interest rate × Time in terms of one year

CLOSING ENTRIES (Chapter 4)

Purpose

1. Update the Retained Earnings account in the ledger by transferring net income (loss) and dividends to retained earnings.
2. Prepare the temporary accounts (revenue, expense, dividends) for the next period's postings by reducing their balances to zero.

ACCOUNTING CYCLE (Chapter 4)

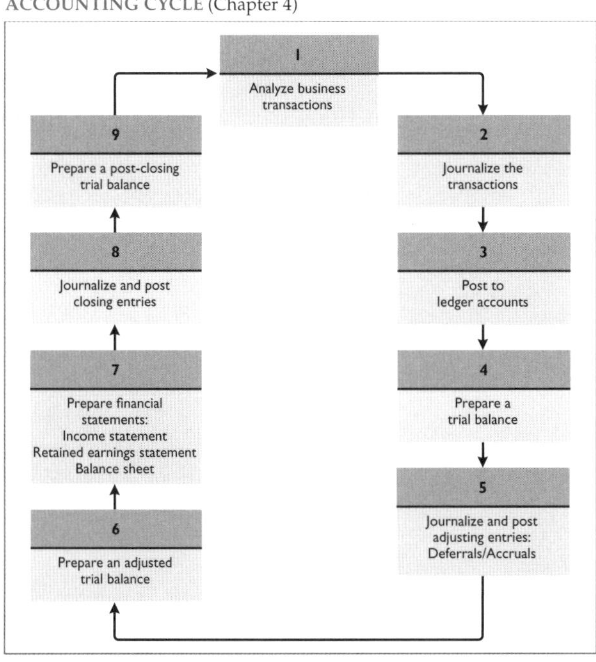

Perpetual vs. Periodic Journal Entries

Event	Perpetual	Periodic
Purchase of goods	Inventory Cash (A/P)	Purchases Cash (A/P)
Freight (shipping point)	Inventory Cash	Freight-In Cash
Return of purchased goods	Cash (or A/P) Inventory	Cash (or A/P) Purchase Returns and Allowances
Sale of goods	Cash (or A/R) Sales Revenue Cost of Goods Sold Inventory	Cash (or A/R) Sales Revenue No entry
Return of sold goods	Sales Returns and Allowances Accounts Receivable Inventory Cost of Goods Sold	Sales Returns and Allowances Accounts Receivable No entry
End of period	No entry	Closing or adjusting entry required

FRAUD, INTERNAL CONTROL, AND CASH (Chapter 7)

Principles of Internal Control

Establishment of responsibility
Segregation of duties
Documentation procedures
Physical controls
Independent internal verification
Human resource controls

The Fraud Triangle

Opportunity

Financial pressure — Rationalization

Bank Reconciliation

Bank	Books
Balance per bank statement Add: Deposits in transit Deduct: Outstanding checks Adjusted cash balance	Balance per books Add: Unrecorded credit memoranda from bank statement Deduct: Unrecorded debit memoranda from bank statement Adjusted cash balance

Note: 1. Errors should be offset (added or deducted) on the side that made the error.
2. Adjusting journal entries should only be made for items affecting books.

STOP AND CHECK: Does the adjusted cash balance in the Cash account equal the reconciled balance?

RAPID REVIEW
Chapter Content

RECEIVABLES (Chapter 8)

Two Methods to Account for Uncollectible Accounts

Direct write-off method	Record bad debt expense when the company determines a particular account to be uncollectible.
Allowance method	At the end of each period, estimate the amount of uncollectible receivables. Debit Bad Debt Expense and credit Allowance for Doubtful Accounts in an amount that results in a balance in the allowance account equal to the estimate of uncollectibles. As specific accounts become uncollectible, debit Allowance for Doubtful Accounts and credit Accounts Receivable.

Steps to Manage Accounts Receivable

1. Determine to whom to extend credit.
2. Establish a payment period.
3. Monitor collections.
4. Evaluate the receivables balance.
5. Accelerate cash receipts from receivables when necessary.

PLANT ASSETS (Chapter 9)

Computation of Annual Depreciation Expense

Straight-line	$\frac{\text{Cost} - \text{Salvage value}}{\text{Useful life (in years)}}$
***Declining-balance**	Book value at beginning of year × Declining balance rate* *Declining-balance rate = 1 ÷ Useful life (in years)
***Units-of-activity**	$\frac{\text{Cost} - \text{Salvage value}}{\text{Useful life (in units)}} \times$ Units of activity during year

Note: If depreciation is calculated for partial periods, the straight-line and declining-balance methods must be adjusted for the relevant proportion of the year. Multiply the annual depreciation expense by the number of months expired in the year divided by 12 months.

BONDS (Chapter 10)

Premium	Market interest rate < Contractual interest rate
Face Value	Market interest rate = Contractual interest rate
Discount	Market interest rate > Contractual interest rate

Computation of Annual Bond Interest Expense

Interest expense = Interest paid (payable) + Amortization of discount (OR − Amortization of premium)

***Straight-line amortization**	$\frac{\text{Bond discount (premium)}}{\text{Number of interest periods}}$	
***Effective-interest amortization (preferred method)**	Bond interest expense	Bond interest paid
	Carrying value of bonds at beginning of period × Effective-interest rate	Face amount of bonds × Contractual interest rate

STOCKHOLDERS' EQUITY (Chapter 11)

No-Par Value vs. Par Value Stock Journal Entries

No-Par Value	Par Value
Cash Common Stock	Cash Common Stock (par value) Paid-in Capital in Excess of Par Value

Comparison of Dividend Effects

	Cash	Common Stock	Retained Earnings
Cash dividend	↓	No effect	↓
Stock dividend	No effect	↑	↓
Stock split	No effect	No effect	No effect

*Items with asterisk are covered in appendix.

STATEMENT OF CASH FLOWS (Chapter 12)

Cash flows from operating activities (**indirect method**)

Net income		
Add: Amortization and depreciation	$ X	
Losses on disposals of assets	X	
Decreases in current assets	X	
Increases in current liabilities	X	
Deduct: Increases in current assets	(X)	
Decreases in current liabilities	(X)	
Gains on disposals of assets	(X)	
Net cash provided (used) by operating activities		$ X

Cash flows from operating activities (**direct method**)

Cash receipts		
(Examples: from sales of goods and services to customers, from receipts of interest and dividends)	$ X	
Cash payments		
(Examples: to suppliers, for operating expenses, for interest, for taxes)	(X)	
Net cash provided (used) by operating activities		$ X

FINANCIAL STATEMENT ANALYSIS (Chapter 13)

Discontinued operations	Income statement (presented separately after "Income from continuing operations")
Extraordinary items	Income statement (presented separately after "Discontinued operations")
Changes in accounting principle	In most instances, use the new method in current period and restate previous years' results using new method. For changes in depreciation and amortization methods, use the new method in the current period, but do not restate previous periods.

Income Statement and Comprehensive Income

Sales	$ XX
Cost of goods sold	XX
Gross profit	XX
Operating expenses	XX
Income from operations	XX
Other revenues (expenses) and gains (losses)	XX
Income before income taxes	XX
Income tax expense	XX
Income before irregular items	XX
Irregular items (net of tax)	**XX**
Net income	**XX**
Other comprehensive income items (net of tax)	**XX**
Comprehensive income	**$ XX**

INVESTMENTS (Appendix H)

Comparison of Long-Term Bond Investment and Liability Journal Entries

Event	Investor	Investee
Purchase / issue of bonds	Debt Investments Cash	Cash Bonds Payable
Interest receipt / payment	Cash Interest Revenue	Interest Expense Cash

Comparison of Cost and Equity Methods of Accounting for Long-Term Stock Investments

Event	Cost	Equity
Acquisition	Stock Investments Cash	Stock Investments Cash
Investee reports earnings	No entry	Stock Investments Investment Revenue
Investee pays dividends	Cash Dividend Revenue	Cash Stock Investments

RAPID REVIEW
Financial Statements

Order of Preparation	Date
1. Income statement	For the period ended
2. Retained earnings statement	For the period ended
3. Balance sheet	As of the end of the period
4. Statement of cash flows	For the period ended

Income Statement (perpetual inventory system)

Name of Company
Income Statement
For the Period Ended

Sales revenues		
Sales	$ X	
Less: Sales returns and allowances	X	
Sales discounts	X	
Net sales		$ X
Cost of goods sold		X
Gross profit		X
Operating expenses		
(Examples: store salaries, advertising, delivery, rent, depreciation, utilities, insurance)		X
Income from operations		X
Other revenues and gains		
(Examples: interest, gains)	X	
Other expenses and losses		
(Examples: interest, losses)	X	X
Income before income taxes		X
Income tax expense		X
Net income		$ X

Income Statement (periodic inventory system)

Name of Company
Income Statement
For the Period Ended

Sales revenues			
Sales		$ X	
Less: Sales returns and allowances		X	
Sales discounts		X	
Net sales			$ X
Cost of goods sold			
Beginning inventory		X	
Purchases	$ X		
Less: Purchase returns and allowances	X		
Net purchases	X		
Add: Freight in	X		
Cost of goods purchased		X	
Cost of goods available for sale		X	
Less: Ending inventory		X	
Cost of goods sold			X
Gross profit			X
Operating expenses			
(Examples: store salaries, advertising, delivery, rent, depreciation, utilities, insurance)			X
Income from operations			X
Other revenues and gains			
(Examples: interest, gains)		X	
Other expenses and losses			
(Examples: interest, losses)		X	X
Income before income taxes			X
Income tax expense			X
Net income			$ X

Name of Company
Comprehensive Income Statement
For the Period Ended

Net income	$XX
Other comprehensive income	XX
Comprehensive income	$XX

Retained Earnings Statement

Name of Company
Retained Earnings Statement
For the Period Ended

Retained earnings, beginning of period	$ X
Add: Net income (or deduct net loss)	X
	X
Deduct: Dividends	X
Retained earnings, end of period	$ X

STOP AND CHECK: Net income (loss) presented on the retained earnings statement must equal the net income (loss) presented on the income statement.

Balance Sheet

Name of Company
Balance Sheet
As of the End of the Period

Assets

Current assets			
(Examples: cash, short-term investments, accounts receivable, inventory, prepaids)			$ X
Long-term investments			
(Examples: investments in bonds, investments in stocks)			X
Property, plant, and equipment			
Land		$ X	
Buildings and equipment	$ X		
Less: Accumulated depreciation	X	X	X
Intangible assets			X
Total assets			$ X

Liabilities and Stockholders' Equity

Liabilities	
Current liabilities	
(Examples: notes payable, accounts payable, accruals, unearned revenues, current portion of notes payable)	$ X
Long-term liabilities	
(Examples: notes payable, bonds payable)	X
Total liabilities	X
Stockholders' equity	
Common stock	X
Retained earnings	X
Total liabilities and stockholders' equity	$ X

STOP AND CHECK: Total assets on the balance sheet must equal total liabilities plus stockholders' equity; and, ending retained earnings on the balance sheet must equal ending retained earnings on the retained earnings statement.

Statement of Cash Flows

Name of Company
Statement of Cash Flows
For the Period Ended

Cash flows from operating activities	
Note: May be prepared using the direct or indirect method	
Net cash provided (used) by operating activities	$ X
Cash flows from investing activities	
(Examples: purchase / sale of long-term assets)	
Net cash provided (used) by investing activities	X
Cash flows from financing activities	
(Examples: issue / repayment of long-term liabilities, issue of stock, payment of dividends)	
Net cash provided (used) by financing activities	X
Net increase (decrease) in cash	X
Cash, beginning of the period	X
Cash, end of the period	$ X

STOP AND CHECK: Cash, end of the period, on the statement of cash flows must equal cash presented on the balance sheet.

RAPID REVIEW

Tools for Analysis

Liquidity

Ratio	Formula	Page
Working capital	Current assets − Current liabilities	p. 54
Current ratio	$\frac{\text{Current assets}}{\text{Current liabilities}}$	p. 54
Inventory turnover	$\frac{\text{Cost of goods sold}}{\text{Average inventory}}$	p. 283
Days in inventory	$\frac{\text{365 days}}{\text{Inventory turnover}}$	p. 283
Accounts receivable turnover	$\frac{\text{Net credit sales}}{\text{Average net accounts receivable}}$	p. 395
Average collection period	$\frac{\text{365 days}}{\text{Accounts receivable turnover}}$	p. 395

Solvency

Ratio	Formula	Page
Debt to assets ratio	$\frac{\text{Total liabilities}}{\text{Total assets}}$	p. 56
Times interest earned	$\frac{\text{Net income + Interest expense + Income tax expense}}{\text{Interest expense}}$	p. 497
Free cash flow	Net cash provided by operating activities − Capital expenditures − Cash dividends	p. 57

Profitability

Ratio	Formula	Page
Earnings per share	$\frac{\text{Net income − Preferred dividends}}{\text{Weighted-average common shares outstanding}}$	p. 53
Price-earnings ratio	$\frac{\text{Market price per share}}{\text{Earnings per share}}$	p. 660
Gross profit rate	$\frac{\text{Gross profit}}{\text{Net sales}}$	p. 234
Profit margin	$\frac{\text{Net income}}{\text{Net sales}}$	p. 235
Return on assets	$\frac{\text{Net income}}{\text{Average total assets}}$	p. 444
Asset turnover	$\frac{\text{Net sales}}{\text{Average total assets}}$	p. 446
Payout ratio	$\frac{\text{Cash dividends declared on common stock}}{\text{Net income}}$	p. 560
Return on common stockholders' equity	$\frac{\text{Net income − Preferred dividends}}{\text{Average common stockholders' equity}}$	p. 561